1999 EDITION

Panorama of European Business, 1999

Data 1988-1998

.... Immediate access to harmonized statistical data

Eurostat Data Shops:

A personalised data retrieval service

In order to provide the greatest possible number of people with access to high-quality statistical information, Eurostat has developed an extensive network of Data Shops ([1]).

Data Shops provide a wide range of **tailor-made services**:

★ immediate information searches undertaken by a team of experts in European statistics;

★ rapid and personalised response that takes account of the specified search requirements and intended use;

★ a choice of data carrier depending on the type of information required.

Information can be requested by phone, mail, fax or e-mail.

([1]) See list of Eurostat Data Shops at the end of the publication.

Internet:

Essentials on Community statistical news

★ Euro indicators: more than 100 indicators on the euro-zone; harmonized, comparable, and free of charge;

★ About Eurostat: what it does and how it works;

★ Products and databases: a detailed description of what Eurostat has to offer;

★ Indicators on the European Union: convergence criteria; euro yield curve and further main indicators on the European Union at your disposal;

★ Press releases: direct access to all Eurostat press releases.

For further information, visit us on the Internet at: http://europa.eu.int/comm/eurostat/

"The chapters with economic analysis are under the responsibility of DG Enterprises"

A great deal of additional information on the European Union is available on the Internet.
It can be accessed through the Europa server (http://europa.eu.int).

Cataloguing data can be found at the end of this publication.

Luxembourg: Office for Official Publications of the European Communities, 2000

ISBN 92-828-7638-1

Printed in Belgium

PRINTED ON WHITE CHLORINE-FREE PAPER

EUROSTAT

L-2920 Luxembourg — Tel. (352) 43 01-1 — Telex COMEUR LU 3423
Rue de la Loi 200, B-1049 Bruxelles — Tel. (32-2) 299 11 11

Eurostat is the Statistical Office of the European Communities. Its task is to provide the European Union with statistics at a European level, that allow comparisons to be made between countries and regions. Eurostat consolidates and harmonizes the data collected by the Member States.

To ensure that the vast quantity of accessible data is made widely available, and to help each user make proper use of the information, Eurostat has set up a publications and services programme.

This programme makes a clear distinction between general and specialist users and particular collections have been developed for these different groups. The collections *Press releases*, *Statistics in focus*, *Panorama of the European Union*, *Key indicators* and *Catalogues* are aimed at general users. They give immediate key information through analyses, tables, graphs and maps.

The collections *Methods and nomenclatures, Detailed tables* and *Studies and research* suit the needs of the specialist who is prepared to spend more time analysing and using very detailed information and tables.

All Eurostat products are disseminated through the Data Shop network or the sales agents of the Office for Official Publications of the European Communities. Data Shops are available in 12 of the 15 Member States as well as in Switzerland, Norway and the United States. They provide a wide range of services from simple database extracts to tailor-made investigations. The information is provided on paper and/or in electronic form via e-mail, on diskette or CD-ROM.

As part of the new programme Eurostat has developed its website. It includes a broad range of on-line information on Eurostat products and services, newsletters, catalogues, on-line publications as well as indicators on the euro-zone.

Yves Franchet
Director-General

Entrepreneurship is the key to the future prosperity of the European Union and its citizens. Entrepreneurial talent and the willingness to accept risk are the lifeblood of an innovative, knowledge-driven economy. Yet as this panorama shows, the opportunities created by new technology, structural changes in economic activities and globalisation are not being exploited to the full. Europe still suffers from a lack of entrepreneurial spirit, and the pace of adjustment is too slow.

The Panorama of European Business has a new format and accompanies the new enterprise policy of the European Commission for a dialogue with the business community. The Panorama is now more concise and covers all economic activities and in particular service-related activities, which should embody new entrepreneurial spirit. Its predecessor, the Panorama of EU Industry, was very much focussed on industrial sector descriptions. This volume provides an overview on structural changes in all economic activities demonstrating the trend toward higher quality, knowledge and service requirements. Panorama indicates in which directions markets shift and reflects competitiveness in view of Europe's main trade partner the United States and Japan. The Panorama of European Business also indicates the internal market volume in specific segments, a prerequisite for investment decisions and for entrepreneurial orientation.

Monitoring Europe's economic performance reveals a need for action to foster entrepreneurship, and open up markets to budding entrepreneurs. Fostering entrepreneurial drive kick-starts competitive innovation, and opening up markets gives entrepreneurs the returns they need to sustain it. This is the creative dynamic that lifts economies out of stagnation, through competitive innovation, to become world-beaters. Societies that promote entrepreneurship as a viable and rewarding vocation, and open up their markets to entrepreneurs, reap the benefits in new jobs, economic growth, and the prosperity that is vital to social progress.

Fostering entrepreneurial drive means building a new entrepreneurial paradigm into European culture. National educational and training systems should place more emphasis on entrepreneurship as a high-value, high-status vocation. Schools, universities and research institutes should provide would-be entrepreneurs with skills and motivation. Local support services need to be networked to give entrepreneurs and SMEs "one-stop shops" for all the advice they need, and every employee should be helped and encouraged to act like an entrepreneur.

Opening up markets to entrepreneurs means cutting red tape, promoting innovation, improving intellectual property protection, improving the availability of venture capital and harnessing the power of electronic commerce.

As the Union shifts gear from industrial economy to service-based information society, the Commission's Enterprise Directorate General is working to create a business climate in which all European enterprises can fully realise their potential. The Panorama of European business provides a comprehensive information on the wide variety of economic activities in the Union to which European enterprise policy is intended to respond in order to enhance competitiveness, stimulate economic growth and create jobs.

Erkki Liikanen
Member of the European Commission

The introduction of the euro on 1 January 1999 has been a major achievement. Meticulous preparation ensured a very smooth changeover to the new single currency and the sound economic policy framework established in the run-up to EMU is beginning to yield results.

On the basis of sound economic fundamentals, an appropriate and credible policy mix and a brightening external environment the euro-area economy should accelerate further and reach growth rates above 3% over the next years. Net job creation is expected to be above 1%, meaning 1.5 million new jobs each year. The inflation rate is expected to stay close to historically low levels despite an almost three fold increase in oil prices over the last two years. All in all, we expect a steady recovery in the euro-area economy, with equally steady gains in employment.

As the macroeconomic policy framework is beginning to yield results the Union is, like every other region, facing a paradigm shift driven by globalisation and the new knowledge based economy. This has an impact on every facet of life and requires a transformation of Europe's economy and society. The challenges are enormous: from changing the skills needed for work through education and training, to introducing more dynamism and entrepreneurship to the European economy, to ensuring that the new knowledge based society is inclusive for all citizens.

European business practice, particularly at an international level, must therefore adapt to these changes in order to maintain and increase performance, competitiveness and market shares. Product markets are relatively well integrated within the euro area, thanks in particular to the implementation of the Internal Market legislation. However, there remains room for improvements as there are a number of underperforming sectors. The more the EU's product market are integrated, the more the euro will contribute to price transparency and competition.

This new edition of the Panorama of European Business monitors developments in European industry at both EU and national level. It analyses the structure and evolution of European businesses, their business conduct and the production factors used are covered for a broad range of economic activities. Given the increasing importance of the services sectors in the new global economy the Panorama has now extended and improved the level of information on the service economy.

The information on Structural Business Statistics is for the first time compiled from harmonised statistical information in line with Council Regulation 58/97. This primary source of information is supplemented with data from other Eurostat sources such as social statistics, external trade statistics, National Accounts, etc. Information provided by various EU business associations has also been used, and their input highlights the close co-operation between these associations and Eurostat in the production of European business statistics. As in the past the new Panorama establishes new standards of quality and reflects the performance of the European Statistical System with regard to business-related information.

Pedro Solbes
Member of the European Commission

The new Enterprise Directorate General and Eurostat jointly present the new Panorama of European Business - the first edition to encompass all economic activities in Europe at a consistent statistical level (NACE Rev. 1 3-digit level). This volume is the successor to the Panorama of EU Industry, a prize-winning reference survey of European industry that has long served Europe as the US Industrial Outlook serves our main global trading partner.

Although widely respected, the old Panorama had outgrown the format of a manageable book and even CD ROMs could no longer handle the overwhelming flow of information. The former Industry Directorate-General responded by radically overhauling Panorama's content and changing its publication strategy.

Firstly, the sector-specific reviews of various economic activities have been refocused on enterprise policy aims, by linking them with an analysis of structural economic trends. This analysis is also in line with the Enterprise Directorate-General's annual competitiveness report.

Secondly, the former concentration on manufacturing industry is being better balanced with economic activities in the service sector. As the quality of national statistics improves, so the focus on services will be sharpened, but already, substantial progress has been made.

Thirdly, the consistency of the statistical data, and hence their quality, has been improved thanks to Eurostat. The Commission continues to co-operate with economic and professional associations on data collection and verification, and appreciates their input of expertise.

Finally, this edition of Panorama of European Business may be supplemented with more detailed sector-specific monographs as and when required.

The Enterprise DG is convinced that this new Panorama meets the demands of a very diverse user community. Panorama is an authoritative reference work that sets the standard for other, privately-produced, products providing sector-specific economic data. We and our colleagues from Eurostat are proud to present the new edition to the public, and would welcome an suggestions as to how to improve Panorama further.

Magnus Lemmel
Director-General of the European Commission

1999 EDITION

Panorama of European Business, 1999

Data 1988-1998

Panorama of European Business
This publication is a joint project of Eurostat and the Enterprise DG. It has been managed by unit D2 of Eurostat, responsible for structural business statistics. The opinions expressed are those of the individual authors alone and do not necessarily reflect the position of the European Commission.

Head of unit:
Bernard Langevin
Eurostat D2

Co-ordinators:
Emmanuel Raulin / August Götzfried
Eurostat D2
Statistical Office of the
European Communities
Bâtiment Joseph Bech
Rue Alphonse Weicker, 5
L-2721 Luxembourg
emmanuel.raulin@cec.eu.int
august.goetzfried@cec.eu.int

Werner Wobbe
Enterprise DG
Commission of the European
Communities
Rue de la Loi, 200
B-1049 Bruxelles
werner.wobbe@cec.eu.int

Production:
data processing, statistical analysis, economic analysis, design and desktop publishing
Informa sàrl
Giovanni Albertone, Simon Allen, Laurence Bastin, Iain Christopher, Stephen Evans, Sabine Joham, Andrew Redpath, Markus Voget, Daniel Waterschoot
informa@informa.lu

Translation:
translation service of the European Commission, Luxembourg

Published by:
Office for Official Publications
of the European Communities,
Luxembourg 2000

Enquiries regarding the purchase of data should be addressed to:
Eurostat Datashop
Rue Alphonse Weicker, 4
L-2721 Luxembourg
tel: (352) 43 35 22 51
fax: (352) 43 35 22 221
dslux@eurostat.datashop.lu

A great deal of additional information on the European Union is available on the Internet. It can be accessed through the Europa server at http://europa.eu.int

Panorama highlights

Introduction

This is the first edition of the Panorama of European Business. The publication follows on from the Panorama of European Industry, which appeared seven times during the late eighties and nineties. Panorama became a much respected reference document during this time.

Following a review conducted by DG III of the European Commission (responsible for industry, information technology and telecommunications) a new-look Panorama has been produced this year by Eurostat and the Enterprise DG. The main aims of the publication remain the same, however there has been a distinct change in the format.

The publication is focused on providing a standard set of information for all industrial and service activities within the European Union. The analysis provided this year concentrates on the 3-digit level of the NACE Rev. 1 classification of economic activities. There are a number of reasons behind this change of policy regarding the dissemination of the Panorama family of products. It became clear that the majority of users who were interested in detailed information (at the 4-digit level of the NACE Rev. 1 classification) wished to access the underlying data, as they already had an in-depth knowledge of the industry they were studying.

To meet these needs there has been a considerable expansion in the data content of the professional CD-ROM product, containing a wide variety of sources (including information received from European trade associations). The CD-ROM interface for Panorama has therefore been improved allowing users the opportunity to find the information that they are looking for in a quick and efficient manner, through the use of a dedicated navigational system.

For generalists, the paper and standard CD-ROM editions contain broad overviews of European industrial and service activities. A smaller sub-set of the data is provided on the standard CD-ROM, including the main indicators and trade association data.

The paper publication has been reduced to around 500 pages, with the same basic structure as before. Each chapter begins with an overview of the industry or service covered. It is followed by a breakdown of the activity, supplemented by trade association data. There follows a standard set of tables with data for EU totals and individual Member States. Each 3-digit NACE Rev. 1 activity has the same information presented as key indicators at the end of the commentary (subject to data availability).

GUIDE TO THE PUBLICATION

Panorama of European Business provides a comprehensive picture of industry and services within the European Union. It is intended for all those requiring an update of the present situation in industrial and service activities throughout the EU.

The data provided in Panorama traces the major developments in production, employment, trade and structural change across the EU. The information is often supplemented at a detailed level by information that originates from European professional trade associations.

The publication is divided into three main areas of analysis, studying the competitiveness of European industry, industrial activities and service activities. Due to the nature of the European system for data collection, services' statistics do not allow a time-series analysis to be presented for the moment. This is the underlying reason behind splitting industrial and service activities. As such, the data presented for industry is considerably different to that found for services, both in the coverage of countries, variables and years (as industry data collection systems have been in existence in most Member States for considerably longer). This results in time-series being presented for industrial activities from 1988 to 1998, whilst services' chapters are largely based on 1996 as a single reference period. Within the two main sections (industry and services) every effort has been made to present comparable information across activities. For services chapters (due to the lack of official data sources) more emphasis has been placed on publishing data collected from trade associations. Industrial trade association data is also provided within the database component of the CD-ROM.

The ordering of industrial and services chapters is largely based on the NACE Rev. 1 classification system. More detailed information on the definition of activities is available within the NACE Rev. 1 classification of economic activities, published by Eurostat (NACE Rev. 1, ISBN 92-826-8767-8). This publication is available from the usual outlets for Commission products. NACE Rev. 1 is subdivided into hierarchical Sections (1-digit codes), Divisions (2-digit codes), Groups (3-digit codes) and Classes (4-digit codes). NACE Rev. 1 is an activity based classification, users should be aware that if an enterprise is active in industries X, Y and Z, with value added of 33%, 33% and 34%, all the data provided are assigned to activity Z (in other words, secondary activities are taken into account in the main activity).

Within this publication every effort has been made to label the text and accompanying tables and figures with specific NACE Rev. 1 labels. This however only occurs in the case of official data sources being presented. For non-official sources there is no NACE Rev. 1 label in the title of either tables or figures. Users are advised not to make direct comparisons between official and non-official sources. Most chapters are also headed by appropriate NACE Rev. 1 codes, however, some do not have a code indicated as the activity is not found within the classification. For this reason each chapter begins with a preliminary section explaining the sectoral coverage of the chapter, indicating the extent to which this deviates from NACE Rev. 1. CD-ROM users will find the NACE Rev. 1 classification provided in the info component.

GUIDE TO THE STATISTICS

Time frame

The data provided in the form of tables, figures and text was extracted from Eurostat databases during April 1999. Time series for industrial activities generally run from 1988 to 1998. Gaps in the data were filled (wherever possible) by estimates. At present the estimation procedures are only used for manufacturing activities (i.e. NACE Rev. 1 Section D). The majority of data presented for services comes from reference year 1996. The industry and services' reviews were written during the second and third quarters of 1999.

Statistical data

Two main sources of data are used in this publication, official data provided by the Member States to Eurostat, as well as specific information provided by European professional trade associations. Data sources are indicated for each statistical table and figure. Furthermore, the data coverage of each table and figure is provided within the respective titles.

For industrial activities the key indicators presented include production-related indicators, covering production, producer prices, value added and the number of persons employed. There is in addition information on market-related indicators, including apparent consumption (production - exports + imports), exports, imports, the trade balance (net exports), the export ratio (exports / production), the import penetration ratio (imports / apparent consumption) and the cover ratio (exports / imports). Finally a labour-related indicators table gives information on personnel costs, social charges, labour productivity (value added / persons employed) and wage adjusted labour productivity (value added / personnel costs), adjusted to take account of self-proprietors and family workers by multiplying by the ratio of employees to persons employed.

Every effort has been made to include data for all 15 Member States. Figures for Germany are on a post-unification basis, unless otherwise stated. Data for the USA are derived from the Federal Administration, whilst Japanese data come from MITI. To compare the EU data with that of the other two Triad members, Eurostat use tables correlating NACE Rev. 1 with the US SIC and NAICS classifications and the Japanese JSIC classification.

Production and employment

Time-series data for production and employment come from annual enquiries conducted by the Member States relating to industrial activities. Figures are generally available at the 3-digit NACE Rev. 1 level. The production data exclude VAT, and the employment data relate to persons employed, excluding home workers. The definitions are standardised, and so the figures are comparable across industries and countries.

The statistical data in Panorama should be regarded with some caution, particularly for the more recent years where data have often been estimated. Eurostat have in particular made estimates for the EU-15 aggregate. Gaps in Eurostat's data for production and employment sent by the Member States have, where possible, been filled using estimation techniques. Estimates are derived from short-term indicators such as indices of production, producer prices and employment. Data for 1998 are based on monthly indicators for that year.

Whilst the industry data that is presented generally covers enterprises with 20 or more persons employed (from 1988 to 1998), services data cover all enterprises (for a single reference year, 1996). This is not to say that the Member States do not provide industrial data to Eurostat covering enterprises of all sizes. However, in order to present a time-series it is necessary that the 20 or more persons employed series is preferred. Otherwise, the basis for the collection of the data is the same, with data collected under the Council Regulation (EC, EURATOM) No. 58/97 of December 1996 concerning structural business statistics.

For the series with 20 or more persons employed, estimates are not supplied to Eurostat by Member States for the firms not covered, and hence the time-series data for industrial activities under-reports employment and production. Derived statistics calculated from production and trade statistics will also be affected; apparent consumption will be understated, and import penetration ratios and export ratios are likely to be overstated.

Producer price indices have been used to deflate production and value added data. In the cases where the corresponding NACE Rev. 1 3-digit index has not been available, the NACE Rev. 1 2-digit index has been used. Constant price data and price indices have been re-based to 1988=100 to aid the user in studying the trend of the series in question.

Foreign trade data

The trade data are reported in terms of EU trade flows with the rest of the world for the EU-15 aggregate, whilst for the individual Member States total trade flows are used (i.e. including trade with the other Member States). All trade figures are given in current ECU terms. Trade data is available through until 1998, no estimates are made (although it is possible that revisions will occur to the data). The trade data are processed by summing together product statistics (using a conversion table from the CN product classification to NACE Rev. 1) to create industrial activity series.

Please note that the EU export specialisation ratio is calculated as the share of extra-EU exports compared to the sum of exports for each Member State compared to the same ratio for total manufacturing. Hence, if greater than 100%, the industry is orientated to third country markets, if less than 100% the industry is orientated to the internal market.

Exchange rates

All data are reported in ECU, with national currencies converted using average exchange rates prevailing for the year in question. With the large fluctuations seen in currency markets, the reader should consider such effects on ECU values (especially at an individual country level).

Non-availability

Data given as "0" in tables are true zeros. Data presented as ":" are not available. In graphics, data that are not available are left blank (i.e. no shading) and have an asterisk next to the label. If shading exists (for example, in a bar graph) then the value is close (or equal) to zero. Earlier years have been used in graphics wherever possible to complete the data provided, although these data are not footnoted.

Trends in the European economy

Whilst the main aim of Panorama is to provide sectoral analysis of industrial and service activities, it is useful to begin by looking at the relative importance of these two branches in the European economy. Using National Accounts data we can trace the development of both value added and employment in the European Union.

Figure 1.1 shows the important gains made by service sectors of the economy in the last three decades. Indeed, when looking at the share of total value added that is accounted for by the market services and non-market services, we find they are the only two branches of the European economy to report an expansion in their shares (relative to the other branches). Market services accounted for the vast majority of growth in the European economy (their share rising by over 14.0 percentage points). Non-market services saw their share rise by 3.2 percentage points. Manufacturing activities lost more than 10.0 percentage points in the total European economy during the period 1970-1997.

Turning to look at the breakdown of employment in the European Union, a similar picture to that of value added was seen. Services again gained a large share of the total number of persons occupied during the period studied. Indeed, services accounted for almost 68% of the total number of occupied persons in the EU in 1997. Gains of more than 15.0 percentage points were recorded in market services, whilst for non-market services the share in the total number of persons occupied rose by 6.0 percentage points. As with value added, manufacturing saw its share of total employment fall by more than 10.0 percentage points.

Figure 1.1 (% of total)

Trends in value added in the EU (1)

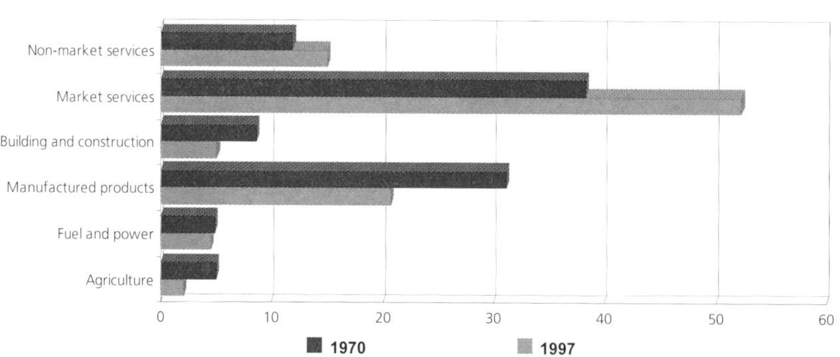

(1) Estimates.

Source: Eurostat (National Accounts)

Figure 1.2 (% of total)

Trends in employment in the EU (1)

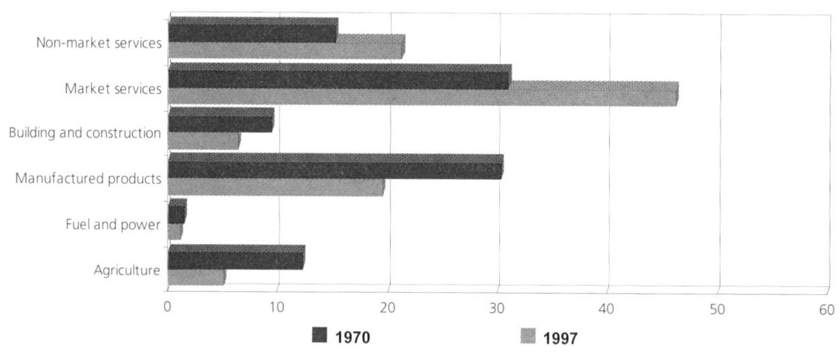

(1) Estimates.

Source: Eurostat (National Accounts)

The structural shift in the European economy from industry (and more specifically from manufacturing) towards services (and in particular market services) is a trend that has been witnessed in the USA (at a faster rate than in Europe) and in Japan (at a somewhat slower rate). European policy has increasingly tried to target the service sector of the economy, as this area appears to offer the key to growth in terms of both wealth creation and employment. The remarkable development of service activities in the last three decades in the Triad can largely be attributed to the shift in the structure of the economies, with manufacturing enterprises increasingly outsourcing non-core activities to independent service providers. This has led to rapid growth in activities such as accounting, advertising, cleaning or security. The sector has also benefited from strong internal growth, thanks to ever-increasing demand, mainly in response to the growing complexity of the business process and the introduction of new technologies.

Industry highlights

Given that data availability is much better for industrial activities, the majority of the chapters in Panorama are dedicated to this area of the economy. This highlights section will look at the industrial economy of the European Union at the 2-digit level of the NACE Rev. 1 classification. It aims to give readers an idea of the size of different activities and the rate of growth of each activity over a ten-year period.

With the process of globalisation, it is becoming increasingly difficult to determine the performance of individual Member States. The data presented in Panorama do not take account of the ownership of the enterprises in question, in other words a Japanese implant in one of the Member States is classified as belonging to the Member State in question for all economic and social variables. Panorama presents a limited amount of data on foreign direct investment, which comes from balance of payments sources.

There are a number of different indicators we can look at when trying to measure the largest activities in the European Union. If we take current price production value as the first measure we see that the largest activity in the EU is that of food products and beverages (which attained nearly 500 billion ECU of output in 1995). Behind the food and drink industry was chemicals and motor vehicles (at some distance), followed by machinery and equipment in fourth place. The second to fourth placed industries all reported output between 300 and 400 billion ECU.

In terms of value added the same four activities occupied the top four places in the ranking, however they were in a different order. Chemicals and machinery and equipment generated the highest levels of value added. Food products and beverages were the only other activity to report more than 100 billion ECU of value added (falling two places in the ranking when compared to the top ten based on production values). Looking further down the ranking of value added, the same top ten activities were found to be present for both value added and production. Indeed, there was very little change in the order they appeared either, with no further industry moving by more than one place in the ranking (other than machinery and equipment and food products and beverages).

(million ECU) — Table 1.1

Ten largest manufacturing activities in the EU in terms of production value, 1995 (1)

NACE Rev. 1		
15	**Food products and beverages**	494,665
24	**Chemicals**	369,054
34	**Motor vehicles**	333,658
29	**Machinery and equipment**	314,752
28	**Fabricated metal products**	194,619
27	**Basic metals**	186,040
31	**Electrical machinery**	143,977
22	**Publishing, printing and reproduction of recorded media**	136,485
25	**Rubber and plastics**	131,877
26	**Other non-metallic mineral products**	121,894

(1) Excluding NACE Rev. 1 16, 21, 23, 32 and 37.

Source: Eurostat (SBS)

(million ECU) — Table 1.2

Ten largest manufacturing activities in the EU in terms of value added, 1995 (1)

NACE Rev. 1		
24	**Chemicals**	126,644
29	**Machinery and equipment**	115,882
15	**Food products and beverages**	111,646
34	**Motor vehicles**	91,341
28	**Fabricated metal products**	76,211
31	**Electrical machinery**	54,674
27	**Basic metals**	53,813
22	**Publishing, printing and reproduction of recorded media**	53,039
26	**Other non-metallic mineral products**	49,488
25	**Rubber and plastics**	48,639

(1) Excluding NACE Rev. 1 16, 21, 23, 32 and 37.

Source: Eurostat (SBS)

(thousands) — Table 1.3

Ten largest manufacturing activities in the EU in terms of persons employed, 1995 (1)

NACE Rev. 1		
29	**Machinery and equipment**	2,631
15	**Food products and beverages**	2,596
28	**Fabricated metal products**	2,020
34	**Motor vehicles**	1,797
24	**Chemicals**	1,699
31	**Electrical machinery**	1,232
22	**Publishing, printing and reproduction of recorded media**	1,187
25	**Rubber and plastics**	1,150
26	**Other non-metallic mineral products**	1,090
17	**Textiles**	1,011

(1) Excluding NACE Rev. 1 16, 21, 23, 32 and 37.

Source: Eurostat (SBS)

As a final measure of activity size we will look at the ranking of NACE Rev. 1 Divisions in terms of the number of persons employed. We find that machinery and equipment rises to first place in the ranking, with more than 2.6 million persons employed. Two other activities were able to report more than 2 million persons employed within the EU, they were food products and beverages and fabricated metal products (only fifth in the ranking by production and value added). The fourth to tenth largest manufacturing activities in the EU all employed between one and two million persons. It is possible to note labour-intensive industries rising in the ranking. For example, textiles appeared for the first time in the top ten of any ranking. Chemicals, on the other hand, moved down to fifth place in the ranking by the number of persons employed, after having been in first place in terms of value added, suggesting that labour productivity in this activity was considerably higher than in many other manufacturing activities in Europe.

Turning attention to the fastest growing manufacturing industries in Europe we find a somewhat different picture. The fastest growing activity was rubber and plastics (a medium-sized industry in terms of output). Motor vehicles and publishing were next in the ranking, they also had growth rates in excess of 6% per annum. Please note however that the data given do not take account of the changes in prices over the period considered, which may vary to a large degree between industries.

The slowest growth was found in traditional manufacturing activities that were in decline, as well as in labour-intensive activities, where competition from third countries with cheaper labour input has resulted in the re-location of EU production facilities. Coke, refined petroleum and nuclear fuel was the slowest growing industry during the eighties and nineties, as local stocks of coal were exhausted and rationalisation and privatisation programmes led to increased imports (especially from Eastern Europe). In addition, where coal mines stayed open there was a switch in production, with far greater reliance on machinery and capital equipment than on labour. Other activities with low levels of growth included textiles, basic metals and leather products, where imports from third countries with cheaper labour took many European markets.

Table 1.4 (% growth of production per annum)

Five fastest growing manufacturing activities in the EU, 1985-1995 (1)

NACE Rev. 1		
25	**Rubber and plastics**	6.9
34	**Motor vehicles**	6.5
22	**Publishing, printing and reproduction of recorded media**	6.5
28	**Fabricated metal products**	5.8
36	**Manufacture of furniture; manufacturing n.e.c.**	5.5

(1) Excluding NACE Rev. 1 32.

Source: Eurostat (SBS)

Table 1.5 (% growth of production per annum)

Five slowest growing manufacturing activities in the EU, 1985-1995 (1)

NACE Rev. 1		
23	**Coke, refined petroleum and nuclear fuel**	0.5
17	**Textiles**	1.6
27	**Basic metals**	1.6
19	**Leather products**	1.8
35	**Other transport equipment**	2.9

(1) Excluding NACE Rev. 1 32.

Source: Eurostat (SBS)

Table 1.6 (million ECU)

Five largest manufacturing trade surpluses in the EU, 1998 (1)

NACE Rev. 1		
29	**Machinery and equipment**	65,458
24	**Chemicals**	37,652
34	**Motor vehicles**	34,671
35	**Other transport equipment**	9,534
28	**Fabricated metal products**	8,575

(1) Excluding NACE Rev. 1 20 and 37; earlier years had to be used for NACE Rev. 1 34 and 35.

Source: Eurostat (SBS)

With markets for manufactures becoming increasingly global, export performance took on added significance for European producers. Generally speaking Europe tries to specialise in high value added products for export, whilst imports tend to be basic materials, that are cheaper in price. Nevertheless, as we will see, many consumer goods' markets have a high degree of trade. The five largest trade surpluses recorded in the EU were in fairly mature industries, as opposed to dynamic industries (machinery and equipment, chemicals, transport equipment and fabricated metal products).

On the other hand, when studying the five largest trade deficits there was a mixed pattern to the type of activity. Basic industries, such as clothing and basic metals were found in the top five with deficits of 15 and 22 billion ECU respectively. Some of the other activities were high-technology products that have become consumer goods produced in mass during the last two decades, for example, office equipment and computers (where a deficit of 31 billion ECU was recorded) or radio, television and communication equipment.

The export ratio measures the percentage of domestic production that is destined for third country markets. This ratio, given as a percentage, allows us to see which industries are orientated towards export markets. However, it is important to note that many products cannot be traded (especially outside of the EU) due to their nature, such as perishable goods, products with a high price-weight ratio or goods that can be easily damaged when transported. The five most export-orientated activities in the EU were all fairly small activities in terms of output (with the exception of machinery and equipment). Other transport equipment and medical, precision and optical instruments, watches and clocks can be considered as fairly high value added activities. The EU exported 46.6% and 37.3% of its production in these two activities, whilst just under a third of machinery and equipment output was exported.

The least export-orientated manufacturing activities were publishing, food products and beverages and wood products. All three of these NACE Rev. 1 Divisions exported less than 10% of their output to countries outside of the EU.

Import penetration into the European Union was very evenly spread between a number of different activities. The five manufacturing activities at the top of the ranking reported that between 35.1% and 37.0% of their consumption was satisfied by imports from third countries. The manufacturing industries covered were a mixture of high technology industries and labour-intensive industries, including office machinery and computers; medical, precision and optical instruments, watches and clocks; radio, television and communication equipment; as well as wearing apparel, dressing and dyeing of fur.

Imports entering the EU accounted for less than 10% of consumption in all five of the least import-intensive industries. Only just over 2% of European demand was satisfied by foreign imports in the publishing industry. It was also no surprise to find that the EU was almost self-sufficient with respect to other non-metallic minerals and food products, as both of these activities relied to a large degree on regional supply (due to high transportation costs). It was perhaps more surprising to find that motor vehicles were in fifth position, with only 7.6% of the EU's consumption satisfied by production in third countries. However, the high level of foreign direct investment in this industry has led to many production facilities being set-up by competitors from outside the EU, in order to have production facilities within the Single Market, rather than face import tariffs and quotas.

(million ECU) Table 1.7

Five largest manufacturing trade deficits in the EU, 1998 (1)

NACE Rev. 1		
30	**Office machinery and computers**	-30,901
18	**Wearing apparel; dressing and dyeing of fur**	-22,034
27	**Basic metals**	-15,115
32	**Radio, television and communication equipment**	-3,332
36	**Furniture; other manufacturing n.e.c.**	-3,081

(1) Excluding NACE Rev. 1 20 and 37; earlier years had to be used for NACE Rev. 1 34 and 35.

Source: Eurostat (SBS)

(%) Table 1.8

Five most export-orientated manufacturing activities in the EU, 1998 (1)

NACE Rev. 1		
35	**Other transport equipment**	46.6
33	**Medical, precision and optical instruments, watches and clocks**	37.3
29	**Machinery and equipment**	32.2
19	**Leather products**	31.6
32	**Radio, television and communication equipment**	28.3

(1) Excluding NACE Rev. 1 37; earlier years had to be used for some activities.

Source: Eurostat (SBS)

(%) Table 1.9

Five least export-orientated manufacturing activities in the EU, 1998 (1)

NACE Rev. 1		
22	**Publishing, printing and reproduction of recorded media**	4.3
15	**Food products and beverages**	7.4
20	**Wood products**	8.2
21	**Pulp, paper and paper products**	10.2
28	**Fabricated metal products**	10.4

(1) Excluding NACE Rev. 1 37; earlier years had to be used for some activities.

Source: Eurostat (SBS)

(%) Table 1.10

Five most import-intensive manufacturing activities in the EU, 1998 (1)

NACE Rev. 1		
18	**Wearing apparel; dressing and dyeing of fur**	37.0
35	**Other transport equipment**	36.9
30	**Office machinery and computers**	36.8
33	**Medical, precision and optical instruments, watches and clocks**	36.3
32	**Radio, television and communication equipment**	35.1

(1) Excluding NACE Rev. 1 37; earlier years had to be used for some activities.

Source: Eurostat (SBS)

(%) Table 1.11

Five least import-intensive manufacturing activities in the EU, 1998 (1)

NACE Rev. 1		
22	**Publishing, printing and reproduction of recorded media**	2.1
26	**Other non-metallic mineral products**	5.4
15	**Food products and beverages**	5.6
28	**Fabricated metal products**	6.7
34	**Motor vehicles**	7.6

(1) Excluding NACE Rev. 1 20 and 37; earlier years had to be used for some activities.

Source: Eurostat (SBS)

Services highlights

Data collected under the SBS Regulation does not presently allow for European totals to be created across service activities. It is therefore necessary to turn to National Accounts data in an attempt to look at the importance of services in the European economy.

We have already seen that services account for the majority of the European economy in terms of both wealth created and number of occupied persons. Table 1.12 gives more details of the breakdown of market services within the European Union. Other market services (largely composed of business services) accounted for by far the largest share of value added in this branch of the economy (almost 50%), followed by distributive trades and financial services. Transport services, Horeca and communication services were far less important in terms of the wealth they created for the European economy. Very similar patterns were observed in the other two Triad economies, with other business services somewhat more important in the United States and Horeca in Japan.

Using current price data we may note that through the majority of the Member States there was rapid growth in similar areas of the service economy, namely communication services, other business services, Horeca, and to a lesser degree, financial services.

Market services have been one of the main areas of growth for jobs in the past three decades in the European Union. Whilst more traditional areas of the economy (agriculture, energy and industry) have all seen their employment shares fall, the number of persons employed in services has continued to grow (as both a share and in real terms). One of the key areas that distinguish services from other areas of the economy is that labour is generally their main input. Human resources, their development and renewal are key elements for the success of the European labour market. Fundamental to this is training and the use of technology, as well as increased education for all members of the European workforce.

Table 1.12 (billion ECU)

Structure of services' value added in the Triad, 1997

	EU-15 (1)	EUR-11 (1)	USA (2)	Japan
Market services, of which	3,485	2,488	3,299	2,060
Communication services	4.5%	4.4%	4.9%	2.4%
Distributive trades	24.7%	25.0%	26.0%	24.0%
Financial services	10.6%	10.1%	9.2%	6.5%
Horeca	5.6%	5.5%	5.6%	12.5%
Other market services	46.5%	47.5%	48.2%	45.1%
Transport services	8.1%	7.5%	6.3%	9.5%
Non-market services	1,002	736	1,113	297
Total economy	6,660	4,836	6,024	3,781

(1) Earlier years had to be used for some countries for the breakdown of market services.
(2) 1996.

Source: Eurostat (National Accounts)

Table 1.13 (annual average growth of value added, %)

Ranking of the fastest growing market services, 1980-1996 (1)

	First	Second	Third
B	Other market services	Horeca	Communication services
DK	Communication services	Horeca	Other market services
D	Other market services	Financial services	Communication services
EL	:	:	:
E	Horeca	Communication services	Other market services
F	Other market services	Horeca	Communication services
IRL	Communication services	Other market services	Financial services
I	Communication services	Other market services	Horeca
L	Communication services	Other market services	Financial services
NL	Communication services	Horeca	Distributive trades
A	Other market services	Financial services	Communication services
P	Other market services	Communication services	Horeca
FIN	Other market services	Communication services	Financial services
S	Other market services	Horeca	Communication services
UK	Financial services	Horeca	Other market services

(1) Earlier years had to be used for some countries instead of 1996.

Source: Eurostat (National Accounts)

Table 1.14 (units)

Ranking of the most important market services by number of persons employed, 1996 (1)

	First	Second	Third
B	Other market services	Distributive trades	Transport services
DK	Distributive trades	Other market services	Transport services
D	Other market services	Distributive trades	Horeca
EL	Distributive trades	Other market services	Horeca
E	Other market services	Distributive trades	Horeca
F	Other market services	Distributive trades	Transport services
IRL	Distributive trades	Other market services	Horeca
I	Distributive trades	Other market services	Transport services
L	Other market services	Distributive trades	Financial services
NL	Distributive trades	Other market services	Transport services
A	Distributive trades	Other market services	Horeca
P	Distributive trades	Other market services	Horeca
FIN	Distributive trades	Other market services	Transport services
S	Other market services	Distributive trades	Transport services
UK	Other market services	Distributive trades	Horeca

(1) Earlier years had to be used for some countries; for Ireland and the United Kingdom number of wage and salary earners.

Source: Eurostat (National Accounts)

Distributive trades were the largest employer in the majority of the Member States in the EU when studying market services in 1996[1]. Other market services employed the highest number of persons in the remaining seven Member States. The third most important employer in the market services' branch of the European economy was either transport services or Horeca, except in Luxembourg, where more persons were employed in the financial services' branch of the economy.

1) Please note that the data provided does not take account of the number of hours worked by each ocupied person. Hence, the figures are likely to be over-stated in activities such as distributive trades, where a large share of the workforce are working on a part-time basis, in the evenings or at weekends.

Employment was concentrated mainly within the two largest market services of distributive trades and other market services. Whilst other market services reported one of the highest rates of growth of any branch of the economy for creating new jobs, the same was not true for distributive trades, where a moderate rate of growth was recorded over the last thirty years. Nevertheless, it is important to note that many services (such as distributive trades) offer a high degree of flexibility in the jobs that are created, allowing employees to balance their private and professional lives, through part-time work or evening work. These types of jobs are particularly relevant for women, the young and the elderly, who often find it difficult to balance these commitments when searching for employment.

Structure and performance of European industry

OUTLINE

The purpose of this report[1] is to identify strengths and weaknesses in competitive performance by looking at the current patterns and changes in the structure of European manufacturing industries.

Following a similar pattern to that set for the economy as a whole, European manufacturing matched, between 1989 and 1996, both the USA and Japan in terms of nominal growth in value added, but performed worse in terms of employment. In recent years growth was higher in the USA, but output dropped in Japan.

With the share of the manufacturing sector in total GDP amounting to 20.6%, the EU is positioned between Japan (24.7%) and the USA (18.0%).

Overall performance of manufacturing industry
The overall performance of the manufacturing industry can be summarised as follows:
1. Given the lags of European manufacturing in terms of aggregate labour productivity, modest growth performance and rapidly declining employment, the sectoral analysis indicates neither over specialisation in low productivity industries nor a lack of technological competence and manufacturing skills.
2. Compared to the USA, structural differences arise primarily from poor performance in creating lead-time in fast moving markets, where competitive advantage is based on intangible investment in research and marketing. Since first mover advantages create substantial benefits in terms of growth and employment, the USA seems to have a greater ability to benefit from the particularly high growth dynamics in these industries.

1) This report was provided by Karl Aiginger, Steve Davies, Michael Peneder (project leader) and Michael Pfaffermayr for the Competitiveness Report of Directorate General III of the European Commission 1998 and updated by WIFO for the production of this book. Assistance from Dagmar Guttmann, Traude Novak and Eva Sokoll is acknowledged.

External balances are not a constraint

Global competition: as a natural consequence of faster growth in other areas, notably in the dynamic Asian countries, the total market share of the EU, Japan and the USA has declined. However, their overall trade balance is positive and increasing. This implies that the global integration of world markets and the increasing competition with low wage economies may have reduced employment opportunities in specific industries, but not contributed directly to the overall decline in European manufacturing employment.

Favourable external balances: external balances are currently not constraining European performance. The EU enjoys larger world market shares for its manufacturing exports than Japan or the USA in 1997 (EU: 42.6%, Japan: 23.6%, USA: 33.7%). The EU's trade balance for manufacturing goods is positive and increasing.

European quality mark up: the European trade surplus is generated by a quality premium in the sense that exports are more highly valued than imports. This quality premium arises primarily from trade with countries other than Japan and the USA, e.g. in Central and Eastern Europe. As a consequence of Japanese specialisation in the export of goods from high unit value industries, the unit value of European imports from Japan is twice as large as that of exports to Japan. Comparing bilateral trade flows with the USA, the number of industries in which Europe has higher or lower export unit values is roughly equal.

Productivity

Gaps in labour productivity: labour productivity of European manufacturing is significantly lower than that of Japan and the USA. The exact magnitude at the industry level is blurred by measurement problems, which stem in part from the interface between manufacturing and industry services. Differences in industrial structure do not affect the European productivity gap in manufacturing.

Modest catching up in productivity: labour productivity in the EU is rising slightly faster than in the USA. Given the large initial gap, catching up is progressing slowly and it stopped in the most recent years due to higher demand in the USA. In the period investigated, about one third of European productivity growth was due to structural change towards industries with higher productivity. This trend was supported by the simultaneous decline in employment shares in low productivity industries, e.g. in the clothing sector, as well as by growing shares of high productivity industries, such as pharmaceuticals. Although productivity growth is, for the most part, still affected by general factors that apply equally across industries, catching up relative to the USA would not have been possible without structural change. The larger increase in value added in the USA between 1997 and 1998 will probably lead to a temporary halt to Europe playing catch up with respect to productivity in the USA.

Patterns of specialisation

Technological competence and skills: the EU proves its considerable technological competence and skills in mainstream manufacturing and the research-intensive industries outside the information technologies. The EU is most competitive in the sectors of machinery, vehicles and chemicals, which together create a trade surplus larger than the overall surplus of the EU.

Lags in fast moving, dynamic markets: European manufacturing compares poorly in the fastest moving markets, characterised either by recent technological upturns, as is the case of ICT-related research-intensive industries, or by easily changing consumer tastes. Compared to the USA, the low shares in total value added of research and advertising intensive industries reveals shortcomings in innovation and marketing strategies in these most dynamic markets.

European restructuring by multinational activity: European manufacturing is characterised by a significant increase in intra-EU multinational investment. This type of investment provides an important impetus for the ongoing restructuring of European manufacturing, especially for industries relying largely on intangible firm-specific assets like innovation and marketing.

Diffusion of best practice: a high degree of disparity within the EU was found to exist for example with regard to labour productivity. This underlines the importance of policies directed at the diffusion of best practices within the EU both in business and in policy.

1. COMPETITIVENESS AND SECTORAL DEVELOPMENT: BUILDING THE LINKS

The purpose of this report is to identify strengths and weaknesses in competitive performance by looking at the current patterns and changes in the structure of European manufacturing. The analysis is based upon the assumption that competitiveness, structural development and standard of living are strongly interlinked phenomena. Within this context, the term "structural" refers exclusively to the distribution of production across sectors and industries[2].

After presenting evidence of the differences in the specialisation patterns within the EU, the subsequent sections:
(a) investigate the impact of structural development on growth and employment potential;
(b) provide basic referential data on European competitive performance relative to Japan and the USA, and;
(c) try to identify underlying forces and broad patterns in the strategic behaviour of firms by applying a new industry typology.

The results will be interpreted in the context of economic predictions on structure and specialisation in a high wage economy.

2) Throughout the analysis higher aggregated levels corresponding to NACE Rev. 1 2-digits will be referred to as "sectors", while the term "industry" will be used for lower aggregations corresponding to NACE Rev. 1 3-digits.

Structure of the analysis

The report is organised as follows:

1. Competitiveness and structural development: building the links: the introductory section describes international specialisation patterns in industrial production. Theories on growth, international trade and investment as well as industrial organisation are screened for relevant hypotheses. In this way, a broad analytical framework for structural analysis can be developed.

2. Sectoral growth, employment and productivity: the focus of section 2 is on internal performance - i.e. the sectoral contributions to growth in income, employment and consumption. After summarising the major trends and growth patterns at the sectoral level, the relationship between economic growth and employment at the industry level is tested. This reveals significant differences between the EU, Japan and the USA. These differences extend to the sources of growth in labour productivity: shifts in the sectoral composition of output appear to have a substantial impact in Europe and Japan, but not in the USA.

3. Competitive performance of European industries: section 3 examines the EU's position in the global marketplace, with particular emphasis on international market shares and trade balances. Comparisons with Japan and the USA provide benchmarks for evaluating relative strengths and weaknesses. The specific nature of trade data allows a distinction to be made between competition based purely on prices and competition based primarily on quality and product differentiation. For example, the data reveal that the EU enjoys a considerable quality premium in its trade relationship.

4. Underlying forces of structural development: to improve the economic relevance of sectoral analysis, a new typology of industries is created, based on typical factor input combinations and using statistical cluster techniques (section 4). The analysis illustrates that the EU is locked into rather traditional industries, characterised by high levels of labour input and physical capital. The EU is lagging behind the USA in the fastest moving markets, in which competition is characterised by investment in intangible assets, such as marketing and innovation.

5. Global investment, multinational firms and the structure of European industry: in addition to growing trade, foreign direct investment and multinational activity are the primary driving forces of global economic integration (section 5). At the same time, casual evidence based on observations in large multinational firms suggests a tendency towards reducing diversification and a return to core businesses. Drawing on a unique data set, section 5 examines these trends in more detail. A pronounced increase in intra-EU multinational activity is identified but the tendency to revert to the core business turns out to be weaker than expected. Furthermore, foreign direct investments are found to be driven mainly by the objectives of market access and exploitation of knowledge-based assets.

6. Competitive strengths and weaknesses of European manufacturing - summary and conclusions: this report presents a range of perspectives on and approaches to the analysis of structural development and competitive performance. The final summary attempts to draw a number of distinct lines of argument together and to give a short and concise assessment of the major strengths and weaknesses of European industry. The general policy implications are sketched and support an overall emphasis on horizontal measures fostering productivity and growth, rather than on sectoral targeting.

1.1 The international division of labour

Reflecting the Ricardian notion of comparative advantage, absolute advantages across all industries are neither achievable nor desirable for an economy. In each location, certain industries must be more efficient than others in the use of productive resources. The international division of labour and foreign trade then creates mutual benefits from the distinct patterns of industrial specialisation. On this basis, a broad description of the international division of labour is provided as a general background.

The global division of labour: EU, Japan and USA

The specialisation patterns of the EU, Japan and the USA exhibit a high degree of similarity at the more aggregate sectoral levels but reveal considerable differences when further disaggregated into individual industries. This is in line with trade theory, which predicts that developed nations will eventually switch from specialisation governed by exogenous endowments to specialisation governed by differentiated firm strategies, enabling first mover advantages and the formation of industrial clusters.

With the notable exception of radio, TV and communication equipment, where in 1997 shares in the EU (4%) lagged considerably behind those in the USA (9%) and in Japan (8%), the distribution of shares in total value added measured at the sectoral level is relatively even (see Table 1.1).

However, a higher degree of differentiation in the composition of output emerges when individual industries are examined. Relative specialisation in production is measured by the ratio of a specific industry's value added in the share of a particular country's total manufacturing relative to the same ratio for the EU, Japan and the USA taken together (see Figure 1.1). The following examples demonstrate the diversity that typically emerges within sectors.

In the electronics sector, the EU has the greatest degree of specialisation relative to Japan and the USA. Japan shows a clear profile of specialisation in electronic consumer goods, for example audio-visual apparatus, watches and clocks, as well as electronic components. The USA has its greatest strength in advanced technologies, such as medical equipment, precision instruments and optical instruments.

Table 1.1 (%)

Sectoral shares in manufacturing of value added, 1997

	EU-15	Japan	USA	Total
Food products and beverages	10.7	10.9	10.2	10.5
Tobacco products	0.7	0.3	1.4	1.0
Textiles	2.8	2.4	2.0	2.3
Wearing apparel; dressing and dyeing of fur	1.5	1.1	1.6	1.5
Tanning and dressing of leather	0.8	0.4	0.2	0.5
Wood, products of wood and cork	1.6	1.7	1.7	1.7
Pulp, paper and paper products	3.1	2.9	3.8	3.4
Publishing, printing and reproduction	5.3	5.9	7.2	6.3
Coke, refined petroleum and nuclear fuel	1.7	1.0	1.7	1.5
Chemical and chemical products	11.9	10.4	12.3	11.7
Rubber and plastic products	4.4	4.8	4.0	4.3
Other non-metallic mineral products	4.4	4.3	2.6	3.6
Basic metals	4.8	4.9	3.4	4.2
Fabricated metal products	7.1	7.1	5.4	6.3
Machinery and equipment n.e.c.	11.0	11.4	8.9	10.2
Office machinery and computers	1.6	2.5	2.7	2.3
Electrical machinery and apparatus n.e.c.	5.3	4.7	3.4	4.3
Radio, TV and communication equipment	3.5	8.1	8.9	7.0
Medical, precision and optical instruments, watches	2.6	2.0	4.6	3.4
Motor vehicles, trailers and semi-trailers	9.4	8.7	6.6	7.9
Other transport equipment	3.0	2.0	4.3	3.4
Furniture; manufacturing n.e.c.	2.8	2.4	3.0	2.8

Source: Eurostat (SBS), WIFO calculations

Figure 1.1

Industries with top shares in value added relative to the total of EU-Japan-USA, 1995

USA	EU	Japan
Aircraft & spacecraft	Ceramic tiles & flags	Motorcycles & bicycles
Grain mill products	Construction materials	Fish & fish products
Medical equipment	Leather clothes	Processing of stone
Sports goods	Recorded media	Musical instruments
Electronic components	Steam generators	Knitted fabrics
Precision instruments	Footwear	Audio-visual apparatus
Agro-chemical products	Dressing of leather	Watches & clocks
Tobacco products	Textile fibres	Other wood & cork products
Optical instruments	Railway vehicles	Domestic appliances
Bodies for motor vehicles	Knitted and crocheted articles	Parts for motor vehicles
Weapons and ammunition	Insulated wire and cable	Electrical equipment
Made-up textile articles	Articles of fur	Structural metal products
Other mineral products	Cement, lime and plaster	Electronic components
Pulp, paper & paperboard.	Luggage, handbags, etc.	Accumulators & batteries
Cutlery, tools & hardware	Motor vehicles	Finishing of textiles

Source: Eurostat (SBS), WIFO calculations

Figure 1.2

Specialisation within the EU, 1996 (1)

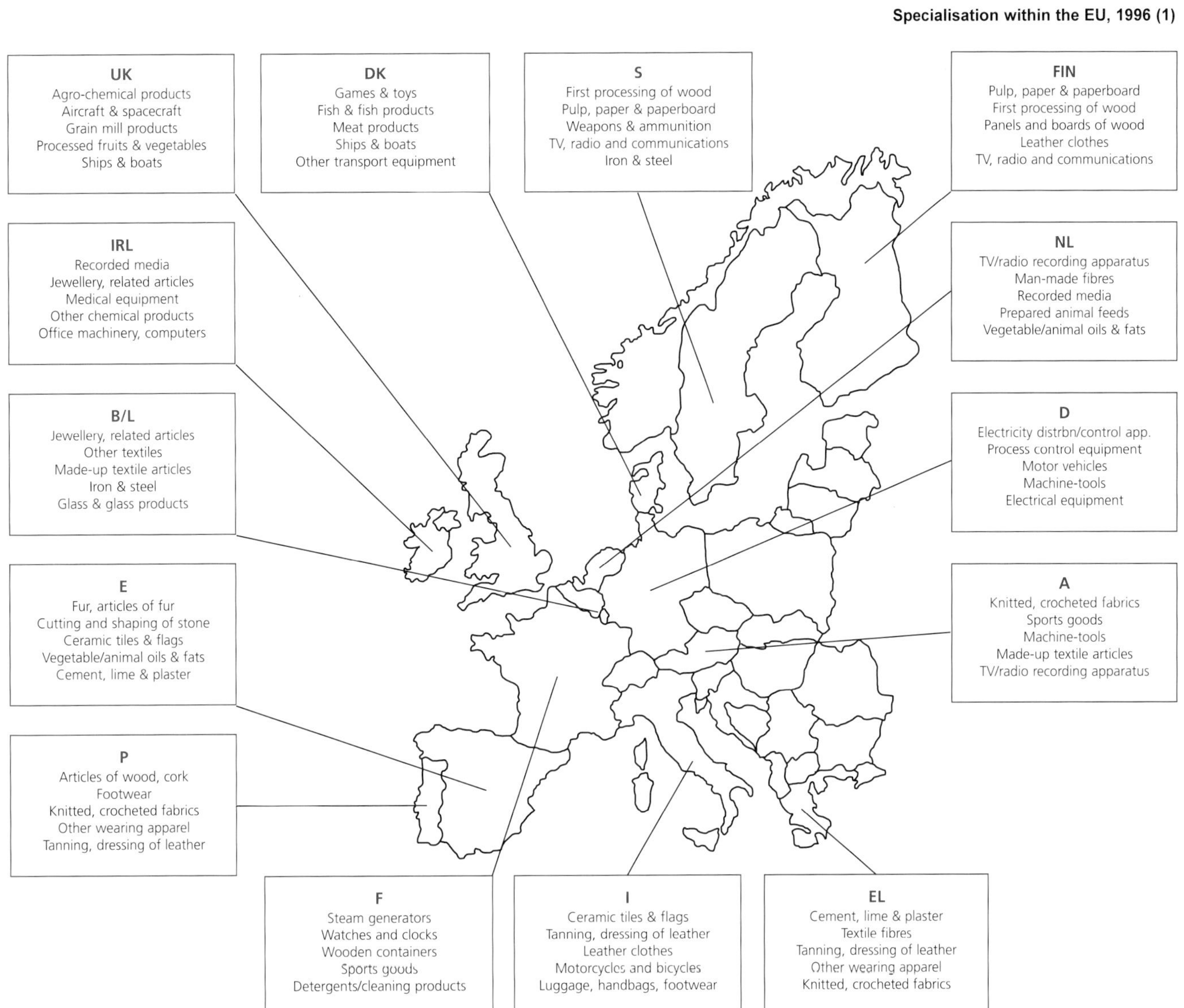

(1) Industries are ranked according to their shares in manufacturing value added relative to the total of the EU.

Source: Eurostat (SBS), WIFO calculations

With regard to transportation vehicles, the EU is most specialised in the manufacture of railway and motor vehicles. Compared to the total of the three economic areas, Japan has its highest shares of value added in motorcycles and bicycles, as well as in motor vehicle parts. The USA is most specialised in aircraft and spacecraft.

Within textiles and clothing, the EU is most specialised in textile fibres and the processing of leather and fur, while Japan specialises in the finishing of textiles and in knitted and crocheted fabrics. The USA appears to be markedly specialised only in textile articles.

Specialisation within the EU

Most of the following analysis will treat Europe as one single economic area. It is, nevertheless, worthwhile considering the broad patterns of specialisation across the Member States as these show some interesting features. Listing the top 5 industries with the highest shares in value added relative to the EU total reveals some pronounced country specific advantages and particular success stories of industrial locations within the EU (see Figure 1.2). For example, in interpreting the patterns, different endowments of natural resources can easily be recognised as the underlying causes of the high share of sawmilling, planing and impregnation of wood, pulp and paper in Sweden and Finland, articles of wood and cork in Portugal, and fish products in Denmark. In addition, the high relative shares of apparel, luggage, handbags and footwear, tanning and articles of fur, and similar products in Portugal, Spain, Italy and Greece indicate comparative advantages with regard to labour costs. On the other hand, specific demand conditions can account for the specialisation in the manufacture of ships and boats in Denmark and the United Kingdom.

Besides these examples, the specialisation patterns observed strongly indicate the existence of location-specific pools of technological knowledge and marketing skills, and, accordingly, of cluster dynamics, generated and magnified by the interplay of historical circumstances, entrepreneurial achievements and locational advantages[3]. Particular examples include the high share of food processing and games and toys in Denmark; agro-chemical products, food processing, and aircraft and spacecraft in the United Kingdom; power generation or typical marketing industries, such as sports goods, detergents, cleaning agents and perfumes in France; communication technologies in both Sweden and Finland; consumer electronics in the Netherlands; and various types of electrical and mechanical machinery in Germany. Finally, Ireland is a special case, since its top 5 industries (with the highest relative shares in value added) strongly reflect the "youth" of such products as office machinery and recorded media, the production of which was recently located there through an inflow of foreign direct investment.

3) Peneder, M., "Creating a Coherent Design for Cluster Analysis and Related Policies", in OECD, Boosting Innovations, The Cluster Approach, Paris, 1999.

1.2 Competitive performance and industrial structure

Specialisation and differentiated patterns of industrial production reflect what economic theory suggests will appear, given open markets and free trade on the one hand, and an uneven distribution of comparative advantage or economies of scale on the other.

Beyond these descriptive observations, two key questions lie at the heart of the analysis. Firstly, do the observable specialisation patterns provide clues as to the underlying strengths and weaknesses of economic performance, such as the ability to innovate and adapt to fast changing environments? Secondly, do they make a difference in terms of long term prospects for growth, employment and general welfare in an economy? In other words, does it matter that the EU is particularly specialised in industries such as mineral products or textiles and clothing whereas the USA is specialised in air- and spacecraft or medical equipment, and Japan in a number of electronic industries?

These questions are inherently related to the notion of competitiveness. The term competitiveness essentially deals with the performance of individual firms, while at the level of aggregate economies, the broader concept of competitive performance is more appropriate. The clear target is to optimise the overall standard of living, consistent with sustainable development. This is what is meant by an economy's "ability to produce goods and services that meet the test of international markets while our citizens enjoy a standard of living that is both rising and sustainable"[4].

4) Tyson, L., "Who's bashing whom? Trade conflict in high-technology industries", Institute for International Economics, Washington D.C., 1993. A similar definition is provided in Aiginger, K., "A framework for evaluating the dynamic competitiveness of countries", Structural Change and Economic Dynamics, No 9, 1998, pp. 159-188.

As the preceding figures illustrate, distinct economic areas differ with regard to the sectoral distribution of production. Moreover, industries themselves may also differ with regard to their potential contributions to the achievement of a society's desired macroeconomic goals. Industries may exhibit different prospects for overall growth in demand, income, employment and productivity, for example. They may also differ with regard to their ability to generate positive externalities to other industries via flows of tacit knowledge, common pools of specific labour and vertical supply relationships. Finally, their exposure to pure price competition and the global pressure on factor incomes and wage levels in particular may differ according to distinct degrees of homogeneity in product markets.

The combination of (i) differences in the sectoral composition of output, and (ii) differences across industries in their potential contribution to economic welfare builds the link between sectoral analysis on the one hand and competitive performance on the other. It is also the motivation for the kind of structural analysis carried out here. Empirical observations across industries help to map the major sources of strength and weakness across European manufacturing industries. They also help to demonstrate that the economy is an interlocking system in which policy must be customised according to specific needs, reflecting current structures as well as desired directions of future development.

1.3 Factors determining industrial structure

Economic theory currently does not provide a uniform framework for assessing which kind of industrial structure is most suitable for generating sustainable high incomes and employment. However, for the purpose of the analysis, three broad analytical criteria are identified. In short, industrial structures are presumed to be beneficial to overall economic performance the more they:
a) support the accumulation of knowledge and create positive externalities;
b) correspond to the distribution of comparative advantage and dynamic economies of scale, and;
c) allow for product differentiation and investment in firm specific assets like innovation and marketing.

Spill-overs and the accumulation of knowledge

Growth theory investigates which factors determine the growth path of nations and why growth rates differ. Although aggregate models are by definition not designed to provide predictions for structural developments, many underlying assumptions have found their way into sectoral analysis and shaped the way of thinking about factors of growth and structural change.

A particularly important aspect in the context of this report concerns the accumulation of knowledge and the extent of positive externalities[5]. In the absence of continuous technological progress, the mere accumulation of physical capital is assumed to exhibit diminishing returns. This generates the pessimistic prediction that the mere investment of physical capital in mature economies eventually causes per capita growth to cease. However, this is not the case when inputs are invested in knowledge, since no general assumption of diminishing returns applies to knowledge creation. On the contrary, the specific characteristics of knowledge accumulation and accordingly of moves upward on the learning curve even suggest increasing returns, allowing endogenous, sustainable growth in per capita income. In addition, knowledge usually is not perfectly appropriable and non-rival in its use. Thus, being close to public goods, knowledge spillovers to other producers work against the general tendency of diminishing returns in physical capital as well.

5) Aghion, P., Howitt, P., "Endogenous Growth Theory", MIT Press, Cambridge, MA, 1998.

The main implication for structural analysis is that industries investing more in knowledge creation can also be expected to contribute more than others to the overall prospects for sustainable growth in the economy. From this perspective, the share of technically sophisticated industries can be monitored as an important indicator of economic growth potential. However, no clear prediction on the growth enhancing effects of the creation of knowledge spillovers emerges, since the acceleration of knowledge diffusion also reduces the incentives to invest in R&D.

Comparative advantages and dynamic economies of scale

Trade theory explains the causes and the direction of trade, forecasting how countries specialise under equilibrium conditions. Equilibrium implies that all factors are fully utilised, trade balances are zero and product prices are equalised. The most fundamental prediction for the analysis of structural development is that the specialisation pattern in trade follows the distribution of comparative cost advantages. This is determined by differences in available technologies (Ricardo) or by the endowment with general (Heckscher-Ohlin) and sector specific (Ricardo-Viner) production factors.

However, traditional trade theory can only explain inter-industry trade between differently endowed or productive economic areas. A large proportion of international trade flows originates from sources other than comparative advantage, especially those between similar trading partners. This intra-industry trade also shapes industrial structures.

In markets characterised by product differentiation, each country limits itself to the production and export of a limited number of varieties or certain quality segments. Within these segments, firms are able to produce at sufficiently high volumes and exploit internal and external economies of scale. In a dynamic perspective, economies of scale additionally generate self-reinforcing feedback mechanisms, path dependency and - like a "river that digs its own bed deeper"[6] - first mover advantages come into existence. Lead-time then enables fast moving firms to top the learning curve and reinforce the productivity advantage. Cluster effects based on external economies of scale within a certain location then broaden and foster such specialisation.

6) Krugman, P., "Rethinking International Trade", MIT Press, Cambridge, MA, 1991.

The most direct implication for structural analysis would be the ineffectiveness of policy interventions, designed in negligence of the actual distribution of comparative advantages and inherited specialisation based on dynamic economies of scale.

Product differentiation

Industrial organisation describes the optimising behaviour of firms, taking into account strategic interactions within specific markets. Equilibrium is assumed insofar as demand equals supply, and a firm's decision proves optimal given the available information about the actions of other firms. Research in this area focuses mainly on the performance of firms and of markets (prices are related to marginal costs). Many factors are important: the variables to be set (available strategies), the mode of conduct, the time horizon of strategic interaction, the information structure and specific institutional settings like the severity of anti-trust legislation.

Perhaps the most fundamental distinction in models of industrial organisation concerns the degree of product differentiation: in homogenous markets, competition drives down profits and prices to a uniform level, and production shifts to the competitor with the lowest unit costs. In contrast, heterogeneous markets allow firms to create the surplus necessary for covering the fixed costs of investments in e.g. innovation, vertical product differentiation, marketing and design. Firms in high wage countries can continue to survive by upgrading quality and introducing new process and product innovations. In such an environment, firms are able to supply products, which are less sensitive to prices, and thereby create a basis for maintaining high factor incomes.

The degree of product differentiation in a market does not necessarily arise from a "natural" exogenously predetermined magnitude. In the first place, profit maximising firms locate themselves in the most profitable market niches and try to differentiate their products as much as possible from their competitors. Secondly, as Sutton (1991)[7] has pointed out, in advertising- and research-intensive industries, such investments are best interpreted as an endogenous variable within the strategic interaction of firms. In these industries, investment in response to newly entering firms shapes the structure of markets. In a particular market, endogenous sunk costs determine the amount of fixed capital expenditures spent on research and advertising and thus define the height of the entry barriers in a particular market.

Beyond the strict model focusing on the explanation of market structure, the inherent dynamic economies of scale in these industries suggest that the firm specific advantages thus created can foster and deepen industrial specialisation patterns over time.

Firm specific assets and multinational enterprises

Multinational investment is a key driving force in the international relocation of production and thus an important determinant of European industrial structure. In addition to location specific comparative advantages, multinational investment is motivated by the exploitation of firm specific assets. Individual enterprises develop their competitive strengths by accumulating technological and organisational knowledge, or by brand creation and reputation. Often, they are able to exploit these assets more efficiently within their organisation, rather than through arms length trade, such as selling licences or franchise agreements. For successful firms, constraints on growth in the home market additionally create important push factors for the expansion of activities into foreign markets. Firm specific assets generate multi-plant economies of scale, which tend to make such investments more profitable than in single plant firms. It can therefore be expected that MNEs not only shape industrial structure by relocating production, but also generate additional productivity advantages as firms grow and endogenously invest in these firm specific assets.

7) Sutton, J., "Sunk Costs and Market Structure", MIT Press, Cambridge, MA, 1991. Sutton shows that in markets with exogenous sunk costs (entry costs or costs defined by minimum efficient scale) increasing the market size leads to fragmentation, in markets in which goodwill, advertising or research and development are important, the number of firms will not increase with market size.

The relationship between exports and FDI is a significant determinant of the contribution of foreign direct investment to employment, structural development and growth. Based on the proximity/plant size trade-off, a substitution-type relationship implies the delocation of production. A complementary relationship on the other hand strengthens the performance of industries and may even create new jobs in both the home and the host countries. The general pattern is expected to differ according to industry characteristics, form (vertical vs. horizontal FDI) and motives (cost efficiency, market access, strategy) for FDI. Firms also invest abroad for strategic reasons and engage in merger and acquisition activities. Although no additional production capacity is created, the impact on market structure and intensity of competition may be significant.

Finally, multinational activity is also motivated by specialisation within the organisation of firms. Within their own organisations, multinationals increasingly spread production stages across countries, according to the comparative advantages of the host countries. This new division of labour within multinational firms intensifies the competition among locations for the most attractive parts in the value-added chain.

The common theme

The overall focus of the analysis is on structural development and competitive performance, i.e. the relative strengths and weaknesses of European manufacturing across industries. Obviously, the selected economic theories mentioned above are not intended to form the basis for strict econometric testing of particular hypotheses. Instead, they provide the broad analytical framework, which shapes the different perspectives, angles of perception and deliberate choices in the analysis that follows.

Drawing together some major threads of and insights from economic theory on growth, trade, international investment and industrial organisations, an important distinction between the different sources of competitive advantage and structural development emerges. On the one hand, the sectoral distribution of industrial production is shaped by current or historic differences in "natural" advantages, in the sense of exogenously given factors. On the other hand, advantages may be "strategic" in the sense of being endogenously raised by targeted investment.

"Strategic" advantages deserve special attention, since such forms of purposeful investment are sensitive to public policy. In the subsequent sections, therefore, the structural analysis is intended to raise awareness of two different poles in the spectrum of policy instruments. Policy can either emphasise low costs and low factor prices or concentrate on the capability to produce at the higher ends of a differentiated bandwidth of perceived quality. While both aspects must be pursued simultaneously, the option that ultimately receives greatest emphasis can be decisive in determining the dynamic prospects of an economy.

(annual average growth, %)

Table 2.1

Sectoral growth 1989 to 1997

	EU-15			Japan			USA			Total		
	Market demand	Value added	Empl.	Market demand	Value added	Empl.	Market demand	Value added	Empl.	Market demand	Value added	Empl.
Food & beverages	3.4	3.4	-0.1	3.0	4.0	0.9	3.1	4.5	0.5	3.2	4.0	0.3
Tobacco	4.2	4.8	-3.2	1.9	6.2	-4.5	4.2	4.3	-4.3	3.7	4.5	-3.6
Textiles	0.3	0.2	-3.9	-2.7	-2.4	-4.4	2.2	2.2	-0.4	0.2	0.3	-2.9
Clothing	2.9	-0.5	-2.9	0.6	-2.2	-4.6	3.1	1.2	-3.7	2.6	0.0	-3.5
Leather products	1.0	0.1	-3.3	1.6	-1.3	-3.9	2.6	-2.7	-5.8	1.6	-0.9	-3.8
Wood & products	2.5	2.2	-0.7	2.0	1.3	-1.9	5.8	4.8	1.1	3.7	3.1	-0.2
Pulp, paper & products	2.3	1.5	-2.0	1.0	1.9	-0.8	1.7	1.9	-0.2	1.8	1.8	-1.1
Publishing & printing	5.1	3.6	0.6	2.7	2.9	0.0	3.6	4.0	0.3	3.9	3.7	0.3
Refined petroleum	5.9	2.2	-0.6	3.4	5.8	-0.6	1.8	3.9	-1.3	3.9	3.5	-0.9
Chemicals	3.1	3.1	-1.4	1.0	2.0	-0.3	4.3	4.5	-0.3	3.2	3.6	-0.9
Rubber & plastic products	4.3	3.8	-0.1	6.4	2.5	0.1	4.5	5.4	2.0	5.0	4.1	0.7
Non-metalic mineral products	1.9	1.6	-1.9	0.7	0.8	-1.4	3.1	3.5	-0.2	1.9	2.0	-1.4
Basic metals	-0.1	-0.2	-4.4	-2.9	-2.1	-2.5	2.0	2.8	-0.9	-0.2	0.3	-3.0
Fabricated metal	3.6	3.3	-0.4	1.8	2.5	-0.3	3.7	4.3	0.6	3.2	3.5	0.0
Machinery, other fab. metal	2.3	2.7	-1.5	0.4	1.1	-1.0	4.4	4.6	0.5	2.5	3.0	-0.8
Office machinery	3.2	-1.5	-3.5	2.6	-1.8	-1.4	11.1	5.5	-2.0	6.3	1.7	-2.3
Electrical machinery	2.9	2.2	-2.5	-1.0	1.0	-2.5	5.1	5.0	-0.7	2.5	2.8	-2.0
Radio, TV & communication	3.6	4.7	-1.1	2.3	2.1	-1.7	11.7	14.5	0.9	6.4	8.4	-0.7
Precision instruments	2.4	2.4	-2.5	-0.9	-0.8	-2.7	2.7	2.9	-1.9	2.0	2.2	-2.3
Motor vehicles	4.1	3.3	-0.6	1.4	2.2	-0.1	4.4	4.4	1.4	3.6	3.4	0.0
Other transport	1.4	2.4	-2.5	0.9	3.2	-0.3	1.3	0.7	-5.2	1.3	1.4	-3.7
Other manufacturing	3.9	2.6	-0.3	0.7	0.3	-2.4	5.4	4.3	0.4	3.9	2.9	-0.3
Total manufacturing	3.1	2.5	-1.4	1.4	1.5	-1.2	4.2	4.5	-0.3	3.1	3.2	-1.0

Source: Eurostat (SBS), WIFO calculations

2. SECTORAL GROWTH, EMPLOYMENT AND PRODUCTIVITY

The empirical assessment of structural development has been split into the two dimensions of internal and external performance. While the latter deals directly with external exchange relationships via trade or foreign direct investment (both are investigated in subsequent sections), internal performance is understood as the ability of an economic area to achieve the macroeconomic goals of growth in income, employment and consumption. Certainly, both dimensions are interlinked, since external relationships also contribute to income and employment.

This section is organised as follows: first of all, the size of manufacturing and the major trends in demand, industrial production and employment are investigated at the sectoral level. Secondly, panel regression tests the relationship between economic growth and employment at the industry level, with respect to significant differences between the EU, Japan and the USA. Finally, decomposition techniques are used to investigate the impact of structural change on labour productivity.

2.1 Overall trends

In general, the analysis focuses on differences in size and dynamics across industries within manufacturing. However, a few remarks on the development of total manufacturing are provided in order to put the results into a broader perspective.

Manufacturing produces about one fifth of European gross domestic product. Over time, the share decreases slightly, mainly as a result of two occurrences: first of all, higher productivity leads to lower prices, notably in high tech areas such as new information and communication technologies. Secondly, as the degree of outsourcing increases, manufacturing becomes the source of booming industry-related services. Business services are among the few areas in which employment is increasing over time. Many of these jobs are inherently related to innovation, marketing, product differentiation and restructuring in manufacturing.

The share of manufacturing value added in GDP is larger in Europe (20.6%) than in the USA (18.0%), but lower than in Japan (24.7%)[8]. Comparing absolute size, the USA has the largest industrial sector, producing 41.5% of the common manufacturing value added, while the EU follows in second place with 32.8%, and Japan supplies slightly more than one quarter.

Taking the EU, Japan and the USA together, demand for manufacturing grew by an average of 3.1% p.a. between 1989 and 1997 (see Table 2.1). The two most rapidly growing sectors are both related to information and communication technologies, namely radio, TV and communication equipment and office machinery. Demand has also grown rapidly in rubber and plastic products, motor vehicles, and publishing and printing. Food and beverages and chemicals contributed substantially to overall demand growth in absolute terms. Lower growth rates were experienced in clothing, leather products, and precision instruments. The demand for products from the textile and basic metals sectors was either stagnant or in absolute decline.

8) Figures from OECD (National Accounts, Vol. II, 1997, p. 67). Data for the EU and Japan are for 1995, those for the USA for 1994.

Figure 2.1 (million ECU)

Average annual change in apparent consumption, 1989-1997

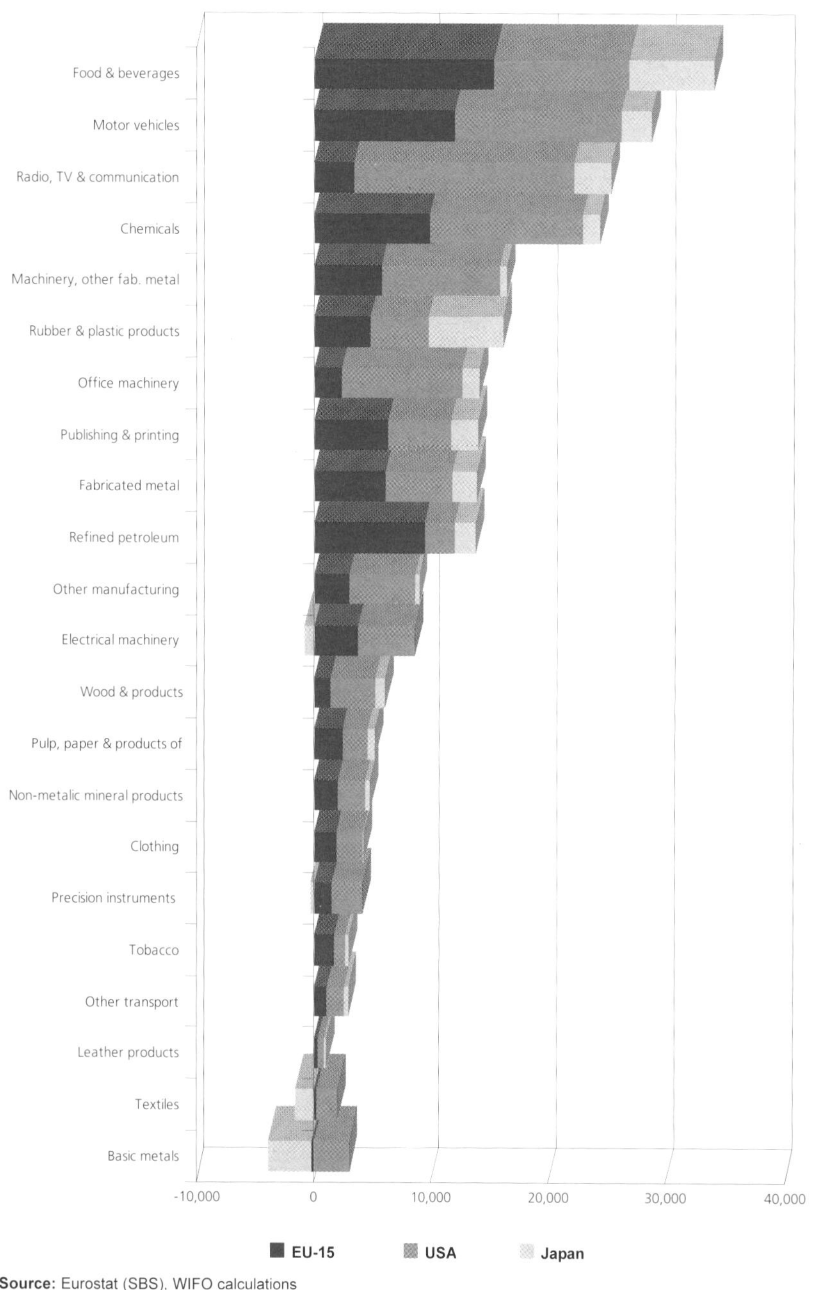

Source: Eurostat (SBS), WIFO calculations

Comparing the dynamics of apparent consumption, the most significant differences are in office machinery, where the USA (11.1%) exhibits particularly strong and rising demand for information technology, outperforming Japan (2.6%) and the EU (3.2%). At the same time, the American market shows the lowest growth in apparent consumption in other transport (1.3%), as well as refined petroleum (1.8%). With regard to the basic metals industry, the fastest decline in demand was in Japan (-2.9%).

The dominant trends in demand are also mirrored by the patterns of growth in value added since 1989, although the global distribution of competitive advantage leads to more marked differences between the three economic areas.

Overall value added increased by 2.5% p.a. in the EU. Growth was higher in the USA and lower in Japan. The fastest growing sector in Europe was tobacco, rubber and plastics followed in third place. Radio, TV and communication equipment was the only "high tech" sector within Europe's five fastest growing industries.

The European food industry is an illustrative example of how the introduction of new product variations, marketing, and the focus on specific tastes and needs can change the dynamics and structure of a rather mature market. In the process, the food industry has also contradicted Engel's famous law, which predicts a decreasing share of food consumption in high-income countries. Experiencing the fifth highest growth in value added among EU sectors, growth was lower than in the USA and one percentage point higher than growth in total manufacturing. Consequently, the share of value added and the share in consumption increased between 1989 and 1997. The fact that growth was highest in the heterogeneous subgroup "other products" indicates the positive effect of product differentiation and innovation, since this category typically includes new and upcoming articles (among these are ready-to-eat foods, frozen foods, low calorie foods and foods for special diets). This heterogeneous subgroup created 15,033 additional jobs, contributing to an industry total of 922,824 in 1997. Of all individual industries, the food industry therefore provides the second highest number of jobs. Together with meat products, which added 26,804 new jobs, these two industries were amongst only 12 in Europe, in which employment did not decline.

Petroleum, tobacco, plastic products, communication equipment, and other transport (particularly shipping) are high-growth industries in both Japan and Europe. Radio, TV and communication equipment and office machinery are the two fastest growing industries in the USA.

With regard to employment, the overall pattern again reflects developments in value added. However, in most sectors productivity growth is higher than growth of output, resulting in decreasing employment. The USA outperformed the EU, as well as Japan: between 1989 and 1997, employment grew in nine out of 22 sectors. Growth was also evident in three Japanese sectors, but only one sector in the EU achieved growth in employment.

In absolute terms, the EU lost most jobs in basic metals, textiles, and machinery. At the industry level, pharmaceuticals and medical equipment were able to increase employment slightly, both benefiting from the general trend of rising expenditures on health and medical care.

Industries producing textiles, clothing, machinery and electrical machinery were the biggest job cutters in Japan. In the USA, major losses in employment were registered in the manufacture of other transport, clothing as well as medical, precision and optical instruments, while net gains in employment were achieved in radio, TV and communication, plastic products, motor vehicles, food processing and machinery.

The case of the USA and its competitive strength in the field of new ICTs illustrates the potentially powerful leverage exerted on aggregate employment when the combination of high growth in demand and competitive advantage successfully match each other. The manufacture of radio, TV and communication equipment exhibited the highest rate of annual growth in demand throughout the 1990s. While growth was very high and value added rose accordingly, the USA was the only country with a sufficiently strong competitive position to enable benefits in terms of job creation. The overall share of American ICT industries in the common value added was 42%, which was significantly larger than the European (23%) and Japanese (35%) shares. Following successful restructuring during the early 1990s, about 97,000 new manufacturing jobs were created in the USA between 1993 and 1996 alone. In 1996, this amounted to a net gain in employment relative to 1989, of 63,000 jobs. In contrast, during the years following 1993, both the EU and Japan experienced job cuts to the magnitude of 16,000 and 62,000 persons, respectively.

Demand conditions exert decisive influences, for example by supporting economies of scale and thereby creating dynamic first mover advantages. Similar to Japan, but in contrast to the EU, growth in the USA was driven by domestic demand, not by trade. This demand surge in the USA was presumably due to early liberalisation, product innovation and efficient service providers, but also reflects the highly absorbent capacity of end-users. According to a recent report by the European Information Technology Observatory, Europe lags considerably with regard to its investment in information and communication technology. In 1996, the EU invested 2.26% of gross domestic product in information technology hardware. In contrast, the equivalent figures are 2.51% for Japan and an impressive 4.08% for the USA[9].

(million ECU) Figure 2.2

Average annual change in value added, 1989-1997

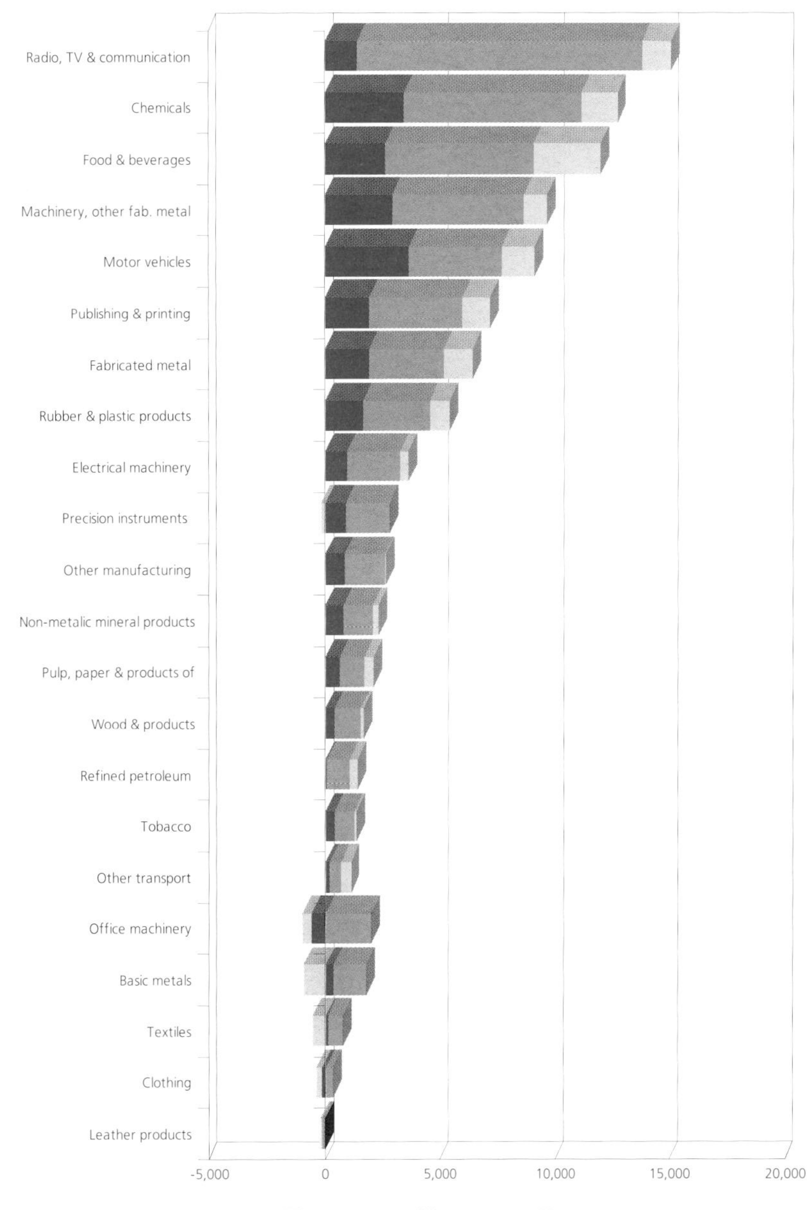

Source: Eurostat (SBS), WIFO calculations

9) Figures from EITO (European Information Technology Observatory) 1998, Frankfurt/Main, 1998, p. 371.

Figure 2.3 (units)

Average annual change in persons employed, 1989-1997

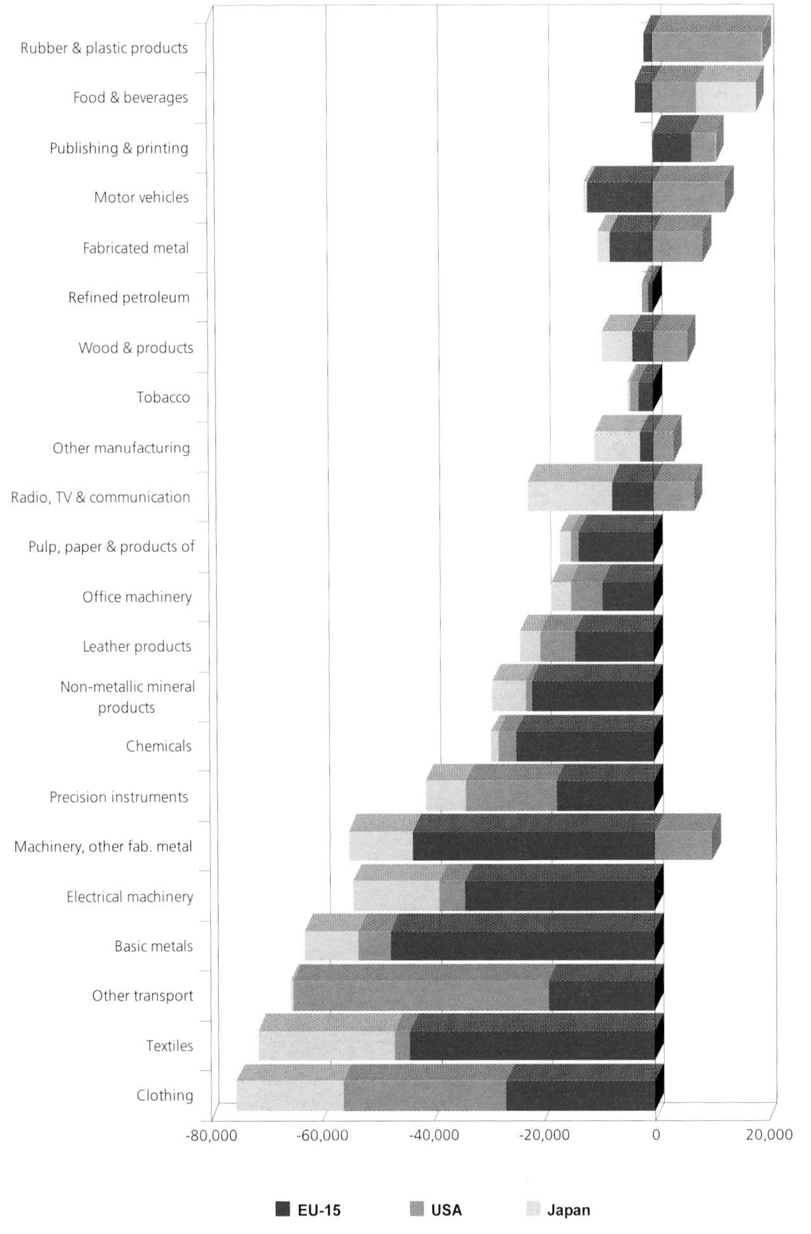

Source: Eurostat (SBS), WIFO calculations

2.2 Growth and the creation of jobs

The relationship between growth in value added and the development of jobs across industries is still strong. The correlation is significant for each area. However, in recent years growth has not been strong enough to stabilise or even increase manufacturing employment.

Between 1989 and 1997, productivity measured at current prices increased fastest in Europe (4.7%), followed by Japan (3.8%) and the USA (3.0%). Overall employment in manufacturing declined by 0.3% in the USA, 1.2% in Japan and 1.4% in Europe. During the same period, only one sector was strong enough to increase employment in the EU.

The fundamental ambiguity between the macroeconomic goals of high income and employment on the one hand, and high productivity as an important measure of competitiveness on the other, deserves special attention. Since labour productivity is defined as the ratio of value added to employment, its rise can be based on an increase in value added and/or on a decline in employment. As the data illustrate, the high rates of productivity growth observed in the manufacturing sector actually result from the simultaneous interplay of both effects. For the EU, Japan and the USA combined, between 1989 and 1997, employment decreased in all but three of the 22 sectors, although at the same time all but one experienced increases in total value added.

It is tempting to question whether economic growth is still positively linked to changes in employment, or whether any changes in the technological or economic regime may have disrupted that relationship. The scatter diagram in Figure 2.4 shows that the correlation between growth in value added and changes in employment is still impressively strong. The correlation coefficient ranges between 0.669 for Japan, 0.711 for the USA and 0.750 for the EU, with all three being significant at the 0.01 level. In other words, roughly 50% of the total variation in average annual changes in employment are related to average annual growth in value added. Although in most manufacturing industries growth may not suffice to create new jobs, it nevertheless remains the essential prerequisite for the maintenance of employment.

A closer inspection of Figure 2.4 indicates another interesting story behind the data. Although the correlation between employment and growth is similar in all three areas, the USA seems to perform particularly well in the field of job creation. Many USA industries are located in the upper tail of the scatter distribution, whereas many European industries fall near the lower bound.

Okun's law summarises the empirical relationship between employment growth and output growth, indicating the amount of output growth which is necessary to stabilise employment. Okun's law is usually applied in the context of macroeconomic analysis. Making use of the available disaggregated data, a panel regression is applied to investigate the analogous relationship at the level of a typical manufacturing industry. The estimations are not based on a strict economic model, but rather aim only at evaluating the stylised empirical relationship. Nevertheless, two striking results emerge.

Firstly, in the EU, the labour intensity of employment growth as measured by the elasticity with respect to growth in real value added is 0.37. This parameter is highly significant and implies that 1% growth in value added, ceteris paribus, (i.e. without any changes in labour productivity) generates 0.37% growth in employment. Relative to the EU, output growth in the USA is significantly more labour intensive (0.48), whereas for Japan no significant difference relative to the EU can be found. No easy explanation of this finding is available, but the data seem to suggest that relative factor prices favour employment growth more in the USA than in the EU and Japan.

Secondly, for a typical manufacturing industry, intercepts are significantly less negative in the USA and Japan relative to the EU. This reflects mainly differences in the growth of labour productivity, implying for the typical European industry a process of catching up on American and Japanese levels.

(%) Figure 2.4

Growth and employment across industries, 1989-1996

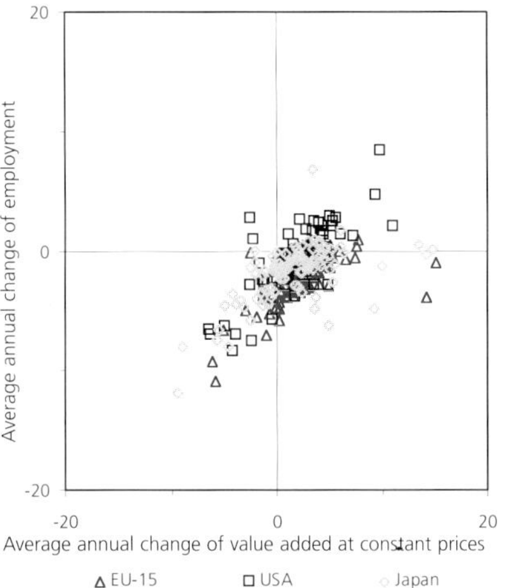

Source: Eurostat (SBS), WIFO calculations

As a consequence of both - higher productivity growth and lower labour intensity of growth in value added - output growth in the EU has to be significantly higher to stabilise employment. According to the estimations of the model, this requires approximately 7.3% growth in the value added of European manufacturing, compared to 4.4% in Japan and 3.3% in the USA. Figure 2.5 illustrates this point by plotting the relationship between employment growth and output growth as estimated by the panel regression for a typical industry.

Detailed technical information on the data, the results of the estimation, as well as an extension of the basic specifications to include a differentiation across industry types are provided in section 4.

The empirical observation of catching up in labour productivity without significantly higher growth in output adds an important perspective on Europe's unemployment problem. It implies that on average, European manufacturing loses more jobs per year than Japan or the USA. This loss increases the pressure to create new jobs in the service sector. Furthermore, the evidence suggests that European industries are more eager to rationalise production and substitute capital for labour. This hypothesis should, however, be more deeply investigated in further research.

(%) Figure 2.5

Okun's law at the industry level

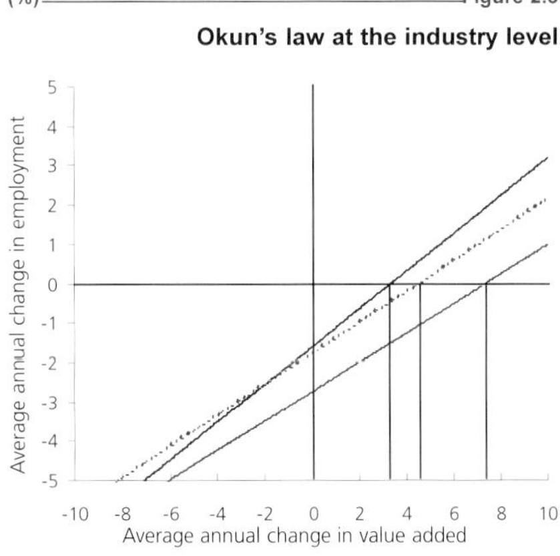

EU-15 USA Japan

Source: Eurostat (SBS), WIFO calculations

2.3 Sectoral development and productivity

Relative to the USA, European manufacturing is catching up in productivity, although productivity levels are still much higher in the USA than in Europe. The following section will analyse to what extent structural developments contribute to aggregate growth in labour productivity.

Productivity is a particularly important measure of competitiveness. When calculated as the ratio of factor inputs to the value of economic output, its attractiveness arises from the fact that it simultaneously reflects two important dimensions of economic performance. The first is the efficiency of production and thus the technological and organisational knowledge employed and the second is the willingness to pay for that output, thus reflecting quality as perceived by consumers and dependent on product development, design and marketing skills. Nevertheless the empirical assessment of productivity exhibits some shortcomings, which require that it be analysed as a complement to and not in place of other indicators such as market shares in foreign trade or flows in foreign direct investment. The first reason is that there is a lack of a reliable database on factor inputs other than labour, hence the analysis is usually restricted to labour productivity. The second concern deals with underlying assumptions on market structure: although the value of output is systematically distorted by the type of competitive process dominating the market place, any direct comparison between countries inevitably neglects differences in the market structures of distinct economic areas. In addition, it must be remembered that productivity growth is highly variable when measured over short periods of time because of its sensitivity to the business cycle. During periods of high growth in value added, for example at the beginning of an upward movement, high rates of productivity growth are typical concomitants.

Keeping in mind the limitations mentioned above, two questions will be addressed in the following analysis: whether and to what extent does the sectoral composition of manufacturing output affect (i) differences in overall productivity between countries, or (ii) changes in total productivity over time?

Decomposition techniques, as recently demonstrated by Davies-Lyons (1991, 1996)[10] and Dollar-Wolff (1995)[11], offer a particularly instructive approach. The basic idea is to compare actual productivity levels of total manufacturing in individual countries with a hypothetical benchmark of aggregate productivity under the assumption of uniform or at least constant size for all industries. Eliminating structural effects, this benchmark isolates the general trends, which apply equally across industries. Contrasting this benchmark to actual labour productivity allows the inference of information about the impact of the structural component.

Structural effects on productivity differentials

The impact of sectoral composition on existing gaps in productivity levels between the individual Member States of the EU, as well as between the EU, Japan and the USA, is identified via the application of a decomposition analysis developed by Davies-Lyons (1991).

10) Davies, S., Lyons, B., "Characterising relative performance: the productivity advantage of foreign owned firms in the United Kingdom", Oxford Economic Papers, No 43, 1991, pp. 584-595. Davies, S., Lyons, B., et al., "Industrial Organisation in the European Union", Structure, Strategy, and the Competitive Mechanism, Oxford University Press, Oxford, 1996.

11) Dollar, D., Wolff, E.N., "Competitiveness, Convergence, and International Specialisation", MIT Press, Cambridge, MA, 1993.

Looking at the distinct effects of locational and structural components on differences in productivity levels relative to Japan and the USA in 1995 (see Box 2.1), the EU does not appear to suffer from structural deficits in the sense of being less specialised in high productivity industries. The difference in aggregate labour productivity[12] is entirely due to general locational components, irrespective of the sectoral composition of production (see Table 2.2). The purely locational component, reflecting differences in productivity and assuming uniform distribution of industries of equal size across the EU, Japan and the USA, would even be higher. This implies that the structural component alone would even speak somewhat in favour of European productivity.

Comparing the locational and structural components of the gaps in labour productivity between individual Member States of the EU illustrates that sectoral composition may nevertheless matter. The impact of the structural component differs across Member States. It is strongest in Ireland, Finland, Sweden, and the Netherlands, and also exerts a positive influence in France and to a lesser extent in Germany[13]. In all of these countries, the sectoral composition of production favours a higher level of labour productivity relative to the EU. The current patterns of sectoral specialisation have a slightly negative effect on relative productivity performance in Greece, Denmark, the United Kingdom, and Italy, whereas in Spain and Portugal the impact of the structural component is substantial.

12) Both Japan and the USA achieved considerably higher labour productivity in manufacturing measured at current prices than the EU total. Yet the absolute size of this gap must be interpreted with care. The comparison of absolute levels of labour productivity suffers from severe shortcomings stemming e.g. from exchange rate regimes, the influence of PPPs, as well as the lack of information on actual working hours per employee.

13) For both Germany and France, the structural component is more pronounced when measured at the sectoral level.

Structural effects on productivity dynamics

Complementing the comparison of labour productivity levels between countries, similar decomposition techniques (see for example Dollar-Wolff, 1995) can be used to investigate the impact of shifts in the sectoral composition of employment on productivity growth in individual countries. This time, the actual development of labour productivity in the manufacturing sector of a country will be contrasted to a benchmark of presumed productivity growth, assuming each industry's share in total employment remained constant (in other words, as if there were no shifts in the sectoral composition of total employment). This sub-component represents aggregate growth in labour productivity within industries. The difference between the two index numbers is taken to represent the structural effect, i.e. the contribution of shifts in industrial specialisation to aggregate productivity growth in the manufacturing sector.

There are many sources of influence on aggregate productivity growth. Structural transition from low- to high-productivity sectors, is only one of them. Other underlying sources, which can apply either uniformly or differentially across sectors, are the accumulation of physical and human capital, technological progress, or the exploitation of economies of scale.

Table 2.2 (EU-15=100)

Decomposition of productivity differentials (1)

	NACE Rev. 1 3-digits			NACE Rev. 1 2-digits		
	Total productivity gap	Locational component	Structural component	Total productivity gap	Locational component	Structural component
DK	1.21	1.24	0.98	1.17	0.99	1.18
D	1.15	1.09	1.05	1.12	0.92	1.21
EL	0.44	0.45	0.99	0.42	0.39	1.08
E	0.75	0.84	0.89	0.72	0.71	1.02
F	1.08	1.08	1.01	1.06	0.85	1.25
IRL	1.54	1.25	1.23	1.49	1.45	1.03
I	1.13	1.20	0.94	1.12	1.56	0.72
NL	1.27	1.17	1.08	1.25	1.04	1.21
P	0.34	0.47	0.72	0.34	0.80	0.43
FIN	1.32	1.20	1.10	1.26	1.01	1.25
S	1.26	1.16	1.08	1.21	1.05	1.14
UK	0.82	0.86	0.95	0.80	0.80	0.99
USA	1.63	1.71	0.95	1.61	1.54	1.03
Japan	1.98	2.26	0.88	1.96	2.07	0.96

(1) Total productivity gap = locational component x structural component; labour productivity calculated at current prices.

Source: Eurostat (SBS), WIFO calculations

(1993=100) Table 2.3

Decomposition of productivity growth (1)

		1993	1994	1995	1996
EU-15	Total	100.0	108.2	113.5	115.2
	Structural effect	100.0	102.5	103.2	104.9
	Within industries	100.0	105.7	110.2	110.3
DK	Total	100.0	103.7	104.7	:
	Structural effect	100.0	96.4	93.1	:
	Within industries	100.0	107.2	111.6	:
D	Total	100.0	109.0	115.8	119.4
	Structural effect	100.0	106.4	109.4	113.5
	Within industries	100.0	102.6	106.4	105.9
EL	Total	100.0	105.5	113.8	:
	Structural effect	100.0	102.9	105.7	:
	Within industries	100.0	102.6	108.1	:
E	Total	100.0	107.8	115.9	115.8
	Structural effect	100.0	101.2	102.7	102.3
	Within industries	100.0	106.5	113.2	113.5
F	Total	100.0	107.5	109.4	112.2
	Structural effect	100.0	100.4	100.1	101.3
	Within industries	100.0	107.1	109.3	110.9
IRL	Total	100.0	105.8	107.6	107.7
	Structural effect	100.0	97.0	90.8	85.0
	Within industries	100.0	108.8	116.8	122.6
I	Total	100.0	116.3	124.6	124.3
	Structural effect	100.0	101.2	104.4	106.0
	Within industries	100.0	115.1	120.2	118.3
NL	Total	100.0	109.6	111.9	115.4
	Structural effect	100.0	96.9	90.4	84.0
	Within industries	100.0	112.7	121.5	131.5
A	Total	100.0	107.9	124.1	127.5
	Structural effect	100.0	100.8	101.9	106.3
	Within industries	100.0	107.1	122.3	121.2
P	Total	100.0	103.3	113.5	123.3
	Structural effect	100.0	99.9	104.7	110.3
	Within industries	100.0	103.3	108.7	113.0
FIN	Total	100.0	107.7	110.6	:
	Structural effect	100.0	99.5	93.8	:
	Within industries	100.0	108.2	116.9	:
S	Total	100.0	111.5	118.2	120.4
	Structural effect	100.0	97.5	92.8	91.7
	Within industries	100.0	113.9	125.4	128.7
UK	Total	100.0	106.3	104.3	105.3
	Structural effect	100.0	100.7	97.6	97.2
	Within industries	100.0	105.6	106.6	108.1
USA	Total	100.0	105.0	107.1	110.4
	Structural effect	100.0	99.2	97.9	98.8
	Within industries	100.0	105.9	109.2	111.6
Japan	Total	100.0	104.6	110.7	119.1
	Structural effect	100.0	104.4	106.7	109.9
	Within industries	100.0	100.2	103.9	109.2

(1) 1993 has been chosen as the basis in order to exclude the influence of changes in the statistical classification scheme to NACE Rev. 1.

Source: Eurostat (SBS), WIFO calculations

Within industry, productivity growth comprises all the distinct sources that work equally across industries and apply to the economy as a whole. This measure points primarily towards differences in general framework conditions, such as the incentive effects of particular government regulations on business practices. In contrast, the structural effect simply measures the impact of shifts in employment from low- to high-productivity industries. A positive contribution of structural effects on aggregate productivity growth implies either that industries with low levels of productivity reduced or industries with high levels of productivity expanded their shares in total employment. If the contribution is negative, the interpretation is simply reversed analogously.

The observation period is very short and every interpretation should therefore be cautious. What can again be seen is that within the EU, the sign of the structural effects differs significantly across Member

Box 2.1:

Decomposition of productivity differentials

Following a decomposition technique developed by Davies-Lyons (1991), the ratios of aggregate index numbers are decomposed into two components reflecting relative differences (i) in the distribution of industries and (ii) in performance within individual industries. Multiplication of the two components again gives the true value of the aggregate index.

For the current research, this method is applied to aggregate gaps in labour productivity between pairs of countries or different economic areas. Calculations are restricted to first-tier decomposition, omitting further decomposition of the resulting two components, which are considerably more complex.

The formula for decomposition emerges after rearranging the correlation coefficient (r) between the two variables a and b. The total productivity gap (R) can then be expressed as dependent of the respective arithmetic means of labour productivity (avp_a, avp_b), the correlation coefficients between employment shares and labour productivity ($r^{e,p}_a$, $r^{e,p}_b$), and the coefficients of variation (vc^e_a, vc^e_b; vc^p_a, vc^p_a): $R = T \times S = (avp_a/avp_b) \times (1+ r^{e,p}_a\, vc^e_a\, vc^p_a)/(1+ r^{e,p}_b\, vc^e_b\, vc^p_b)$.

The general within industries component T is the ratio of the unweighted means of labour productivity in locations A and B, respectively. The structural component S reveals the impact of differences between A and B on the distribution of industries with lower or higher productivity. The total productivity gap R is the product of both effects.

To give a hypothetical example, if R = T x S = 150.00 = 130.00 x 115.38, then these numbers reveal the following three facts:
i) Total labour productivity in location A is 50% higher than in location B.
ii) If in both locations employment were identically and uniformly distributed across industries, the aggregate differential would fall to 30%.
iii) Even if average productivity across industries were identical in both locations, the larger shares of high productivity industries in location A would be capable of generating a productivity lead of approximately 15% on their own.

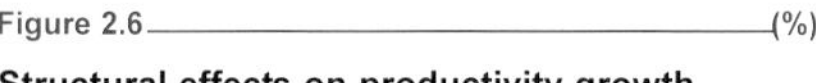

Figure 2.6 (%)

Structural effects on productivity growth

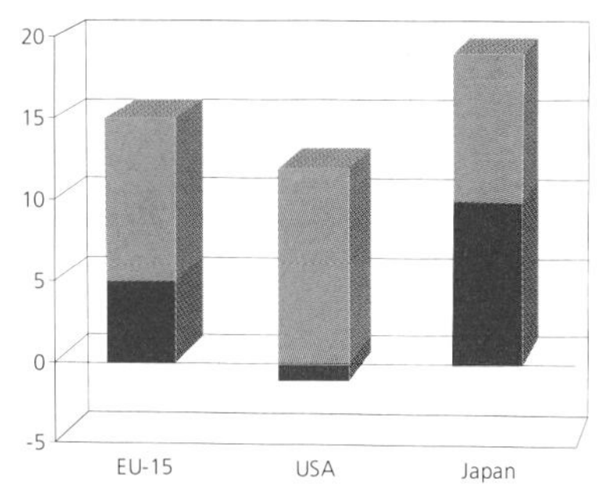

■ **Structural effects** ■ **Within industries**

Source: Eurostat (SBS), WIFO calculations

States (see Table 2.3). Between 1993 and 1996, total labour productivity profited from structural shifts to higher productivity industries in Germany, Italy, Portugal, Austria, and Greece. At the same time, the United Kingdom, France and Spain remained largely unaffected. However, in the Netherlands, Ireland, Finland and Sweden the negative impact of shifts in the sectoral composition indicated either that industries with low levels of productivity expanded faster or that high productivity sectors lost a significant amount of jobs.

Aggregate productivity in the EU as a whole has profited from structural change. This also applies to Japan, while productivity growth in American manufacturing remained unaffected by shifts in sectoral composition. Structural change currently accounts for one third of productivity growth in the EU and for one half in Japan (see Figure 2.6). Between 1993 and 1996, labour productivity increased fastest in Japan, followed by the EU and the USA. Without structural shifts, the order would have been reversed, although differences in productivity growth within industries are rather small. The striking feature is that the observable differences in aggregate productivity growth across the three economic areas were due to structural change.

This structural change towards higher productivity industries was caused by the simultaneous decline in the employment shares of low productivity industries (for example in the clothing sector) and growth in the shares of high productivity industries, such as pharmaceuticals.

Summary and conclusions

Summing up these findings on structural change and productivity, two important policy implications emerge. Firstly, structural change currently enhances aggregate productivity growth in the EU by about one third. However, the European productivity disadvantage relative to the USA does not stem from a structural component in the sense of less specialisation in high productivity industries. Thus, the sectoral analysis supports horizontal policy measures to improve the general economic environment for European business. The challenge is to raise both productivity and growth. In contrast, there is no indication of a general structural weakness influencing aggregate productivity, which would call for vertical targeting of individual industries.

Secondly, the data reveal enormous differences within the EU, both in the levels and in the growth dynamics of labour productivity. Technically, there is huge potential for countries such as Portugal, Greece or Spain to catch up. Such an upward convergence within the EU would automatically reduce the overall gap relative to Japan and the USA. Expanding the diffusion of best business and policy practices within the EU is therefore an important policy target.

3. COMPETITIVE PERFORMANCE OF EUROPEAN INDUSTRIES IN WORLD MARKETS

In this section, stylised facts will be used to illustrate how European industries have performed on world markets compared to their counterparts in Japan and the USA, and how their performance has changed over time. The analysis focuses on external performance, taking into account the results on internal performance from the preceding section. Specifically, the analysis investigates the EU's strategy for coping with the competition of low wage countries by shifting to higher quality and more sophisticated segments in markets with differentiated products.

Competitiveness has been defined as the ability of an economy to increase its standard of living and to create employment, while maintaining a sustainable external balance. Internal and external performance are strongly linked: in open economies, growth in output and the creation of jobs requires industries to be competitive on an international scale. Otherwise, imports would increase, thereby dampening the prospects for job creation in domestic firms. High and increasing productivity is therefore the precondition for exports and domestic production.

There are at least three reasons for a specific focus on external performance. Firstly, trade balances and international market shares are very sensitive indicators of changes in competitive position. Compared to domestic production, which is often distorted by local demand conditions, trade data provide relatively early signals of shifts in the balance of competitive strengths and weaknesses. Secondly, the external analysis profits from the fact that trade statistics are less blurred by national conventions and accounting systems, and are available at a very disaggregated level. Finally, trade statistics permit concentration on the qualitative element of competitiveness, revealing for example whether low prices or high quality determines the competitive edge, or whether a country is specialising in the high or low quality segment of a market. Additionally, economic theories differ to some extent in their forecasts on specialisation and performance.

3.1 Market shares and trade balances

Favourable European trade performance

The overall assessment of external trade performance for the EU appears rather favourable: European manufacturing exports are greater than those of Japan and the USA, even when intra-European trade is excluded. The trade balance is positive and increasing.

Europe has within the Triad the largest export share (42.6% in 1997), it has declined slightly since 1989. The Japanese share drops from 27.4% to 23.6%, the USA increased its share by 5 points to 33.7%. In absolute numbers, the EU increased its trade surplus from ECU 12 billion in 1989 to ECU 169 billion in 1997, while Japan's surplus fell below the EU level (ECU 138 billion) and the USA accrued a deficit of ECU 171 billion.

Table 3.1

Trade in total manufacturing (1)

	Market shares (%)		Trade balance (billion ECU)		Annual growth (%)	
	1989	1997	1989	1997	Exports	Imports
EU-15	43.9	42.6	11.8	169.1	6.6	5.4
Japan	27.4	23.6	122.3	138.3	4.9	7.7
USA	28.7	33.7	-125.9	-171.1	9.0	7.5

(1) Export shares are defined as a percentage of Triad exports.

Source: Eurostat (Comext), WIFO calculations

Europe's highest export market shares appear in sectors with medium technical sophistication. Three metal-based sectors (other transport, machinery, and fabricated metal) are complemented by mineral products and the chemical sector in the top five, ranked according to market shares in 1996 (see Table 3.2). The machinery, transport and metal sector includes 8 of the 10 industries with the highest gains in market shares. The large increases achieved by aircraft and spacecraft and TV and radio transmitters as well as by steam generators and weapons and ammunitions hint at some EU inroads in technically more sophisticated industries. As far as the trade balance is concerned, machinery plus motor vehicles together create a surplus of ECU 100 billion, and the chemical industry adds another ECU 32 billion.

The USA quickly goes multinational

By far the greatest market share held by the USA is in the tobacco industry, followed by other transport equipment (for example aircraft and spacecraft). The USA also enjoys a strong position in printing, paper products and precision instruments. Disaggregation to industry level reveals a two-tiered picture: some of the leading industries are resource based, partly linked to the food sector (tobacco, mill products, meat), while others are primarily technology based (aircraft and spacecraft, medical equipment, precision instruments). The largest gains in market shares have been achieved in the vehicles industry (without decreasing the absolute deficit of ECU 46 billion), in metal products and rubber and plastics. In all of these sectors, gains were made at the expense of Japan and not of Europe. In nine of the ten sectors in which the USA gained large market shares, Japan's share was reduced.

The data indicate that the USA does not attempt to exploit comparative advantages to the same extent as Europe or Japan via the trade of products. The three largest contributors to the trade balance at the sectoral level add up to only ECU 38 billion for the USA, ECU 132 billion for Europe and ECU 122 billion for Japan (see Figure 3.1). At the industry level, the same tendency holds: no large surpluses are accrued, and existing ones tend to evaporate, rather than accumulate over time. One probable explanation is that USA firms exploit advantages earlier via direct investment abroad, while European and Japanese firms prefer to exploit competitive advantages (longer) through trade. This may partly be due to a stronger emphasis in the USA on firm specific advantages (for example by innovation and marketing) in contrast to the general comparative advantages of a particular location (for example factor prices, market access or available skills). This question will be further investigated in the following section. In any case, going multinational rapidly implies limits on the

Table 3.2

Top performing sectors and industries according to their market share (1)

Market share in the Triad total 1996	1996 (%)	Increase in Triad market share	Change 1989/96 (%)	1996 (%)
EU-15 top 3 sectors		EU-15 top 3 sectors		
Other transport equipment	49.1	Other transport equipment	14.5	49.1
Machinery and equipment n. e. c.	45.5	Motor vehicles, trailers and semi-trailers	5.9	29.8
Other non-metallic mineral products	43.4	Coke, refined petroleum and nuclear fuel	4.4	19.0
EU-15 top 5 industries		EU-15 top 5 industries		
Steam generators	111.3	Steam generators	47.2	111.3
Ceramic tiles and flags	95.4	Weapons and ammunition	38.0	55.0
Dairy products; ice cream	89.6	Ships and boats	32.0	67.1
Beverages	73.6	Aircraft and spacecraft	16.0	53.0
Tanks, reservoirs, central heating radiators, boilers	71.2	TV, radio transmitters, apparatus for line telephony	10.5	34.4
Japan top 3 sectors		Japan top 3 sectors		
Motor vehicles, trailers and semi-trailers	31.1	Other transport equipment	4.3	17.7
Machinery and equipment n. e. c.	22.2	Coke, refined petroleum and nuclear fuel	1.7	2.5
Radio, TV and communication equipment	21.6	Tobacco products	0.4	3.3
Japan top 5 industries		Japan top 5 industries		
Ships and boats	73.4	Ships and boats	33.1	73.4
Motorcycles and bicycles	46.9	Cement, lime and plaster	3.8	18.3
Accumulators, primary cells, primary batteries	33.0	Parts and accessories for motor vehicles	3.1	31.3
Optical instruments, photographic equipment	31.9	Refined petroleum products	2.1	2.3
Motor vehicles	31.6	Bricks, tiles and construction products	1.2	5.3
USA top 3 sectors		USA top 3 sectors		
Tobacco products	71.2	Motor vehicles, trailers and semi-trailers	4.2	22.5
Other transport equipment	43.0	Fabricated metal products	3.4	18.9
Publishing, printing, reproduction	35.6	Rubber and plastic products	2.8	21.4
USA top 5 industries		USA top 5 industries		
Weapons and ammunition	144.5	Weapons and ammunition	9.7	144.4
Tobacco products	71.2	Meat products	7.9	32.9
Aircraft and spacecraft	58.0	Parts, accessories for motor vehicles	7.4	40.1
Grain mill products and starches	44.4	TV, radio transmitters, apparatus for line telephony	6.2	23.1
Medical equipment	41.7	Other fabricated metal products	6.1	19.4

(1) Market share defined as exports as a percentage of total Triad imports; they do not add up due to divergent methods of reporting.

Source: Eurostat (Compet), WIFO calculations

(billion ECU) Figure 3.1

The top sectors with the largest trade surplus

EU-15

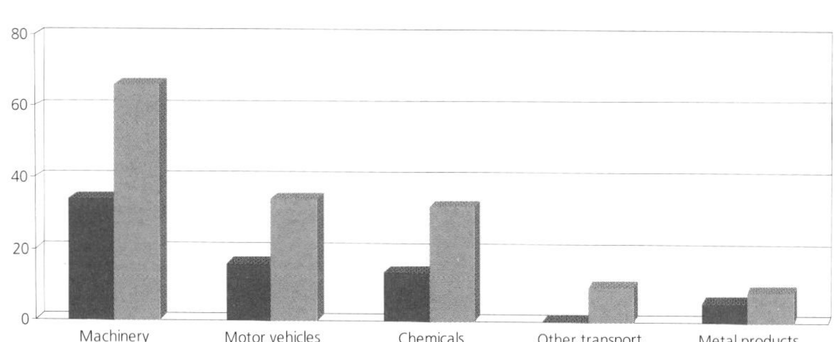

USA

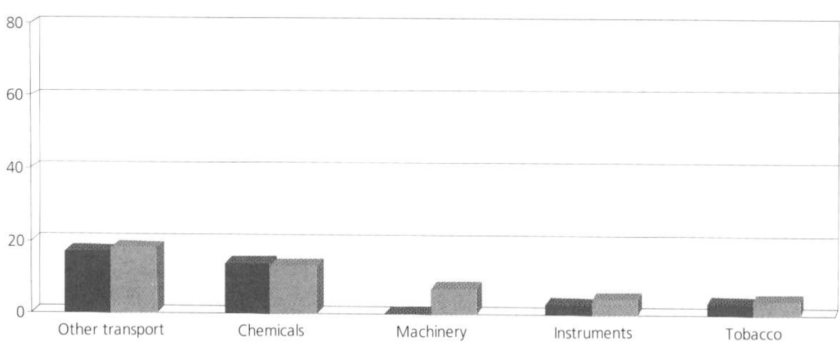

Japan

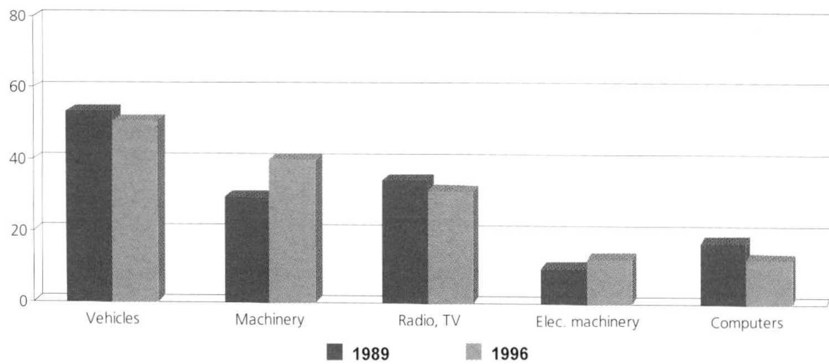

■ 1989 ■ 1996

Source: Eurostat (Compet), WIFO calculations

Box 3.1:
The data

The SBS database provided by EUROSTAT is used for internal performance. This database provides consistent data for value added, employment, as well as other main indicators for EU countries, Japan and the USA. Data are fairly complete from 1989 to 1997/1998. In some 3-digit industries, estimates for missing data primarily up to 1993 and for 1997 are provided. Nominal value added at factor costs has been selected as the main activity indicator.

The analysis of external performance is based on the COMEXT database, which consists of exports and imports for EU, Japan and the USA. Additionally, information on qualitative performance is based on the COMEXT database, which provides disaggregated data for up to 6-digit product groups and allows for more detailed information on the EU trade structure. Trade data from COMEXT are linked to the NACE Rev. 1 industry classification by a correspondence table.

Throughout the study, 2-digit data are referred to as sectors and 3-digit data as industries (officially, EUROSTAT labels them "Divisions" and "Groups").

Table 3.3 (%)

Concentration of exports, 1996

	EU-15	USA	Japan
Share of 4 largest sectors			
Exports	47.6	46.6	60.3
Imports	39.4	41.6	34.0
Share of 10 largest industries			
Exports	42.4	51.0	62.2
Imports	32.1	42.0	39.5
Trade surplus of 4 largest sectors (million ECU)	141,409	42,756	134,393
10 industries with largest disadvantage			
Standard deviation of RCA across industries (1)	0.557	1.002	1.825
Import/export relation (RCA)	-1.576	-2.225	-5.395
Imports/value added (%)	177.9	276.1	89.9
Exports/value added (%)	66.1	26.3	0.8
Trade deficit (billion ECU)	-49.3	-35.8	-26.6

(1) RCA: revealed comparative advantage ln ((Xi/Mi)/(X/M)).

Source: Eurostat (Compet), WIFO calculations

Figure 3.2

Abandoning markets with comparative disadvantages (ten industries with the lowest RCA values)

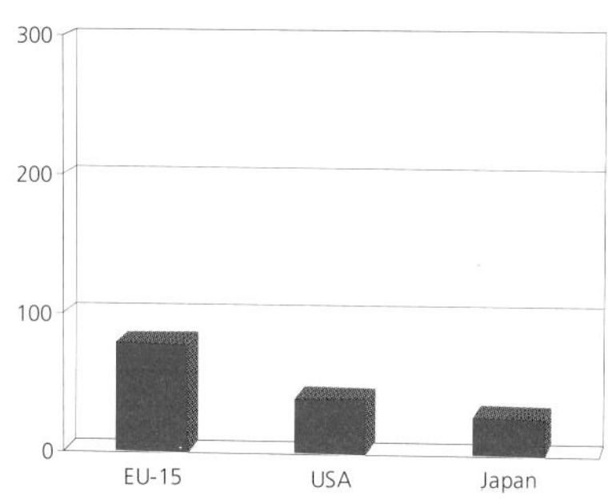

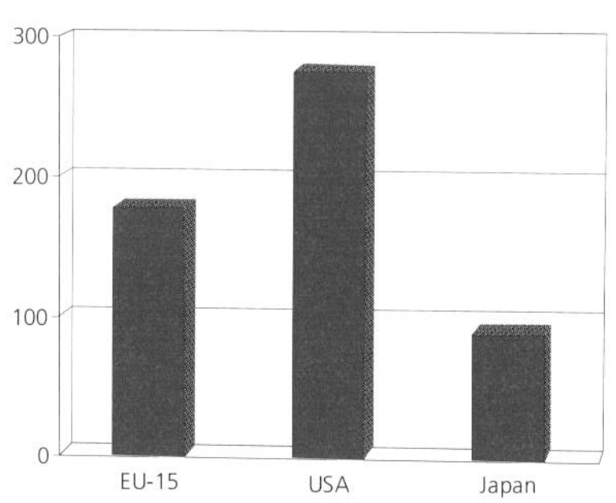

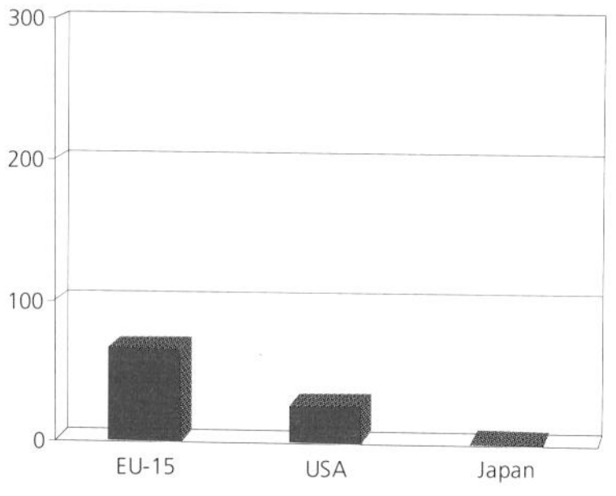

Source: Eurostat (Compet, SBS), WIFO calculations

extent of trade surpluses in sectors with firm specific assets. Income in production and for blue-collar workers is reduced, whereas income from capital and financial assets increases.

Japan focuses on comparative advantages

Japanese exports are heavily concentrated, notably in engineering skills. Indeed, all sectors in which Japan has high market shares are skill-intensive industries. Motor vehicles and machinery lead the sector ranking, radio, TV and communication equipment, electrical machinery, precision instruments and other transport equipment follow. At industry level, all but one of the top ten are engineering industries encompassing ships and boats, motorcycles and motor vehicles, as well as accumulators and optical instruments. The top 4 sectors cover 60% of overall Japanese exports, compared with 48% in Europe and 47% in the USA (see Table 3.3). Switching to the industry level, 62% of Japanese exports stem from the 10 largest exporting industries, again compared to 51% in the USA and only 42% in Europe. With respect to imports, there is no significant difference in these quasi-concentration rates across the three areas, which indicates that specialisation and not differences in demand are the driving force.

The high negative specialisation ratios exhibited by Japan as soon as comparative disadvantages are revealed in any particular industry are unrivalled. The average of the industries with the greatest de-specialisation (measured by the lowest ten RCA values) is -5.4 in Japan, compared to -1.6 in Europe and -2.2 in the USA (see Figure 3.2). Exports as a share of value added in these industries is 66% in Europe, 26% in the USA, but only 1% in Japan. This indicates that Japan gives up exports completely, while in Europe and in the USA some firms continue supplying in niches. However, imports do not rise so much in Japan, amounting to ECU 27 billion (ECU 78 billion in the EU and ECU 40 billion in the USA). The relation between imports and domestic value added is 178% in Europe, 276% in the USA, and only 90% in Japan. This implies that production for the home market continues to a certain extent, indicating either consumer preferences for domestic varieties or some sort of import barrier.

The extremely favourable starting point in 1989 explains why in Japan almost no sector has been able to expand its share in the world market. Increases in individual industries were moderate; some of them were in construction materials and in the chemical sector and only two in sophisticated industries. In the ten industries in which Japan gained market shares, the USA was confronted with losses in eight, Europe in seven.

3.2 Competition in quality

Rationale and measurement

The more an economy is able to produce goods which are appreciated for their quality and for fulfilling specific needs, the larger the potential for further increases in living standards, and the smaller the overall exposure to low cost producers. A high wage area facing new competitors has to differentiate products and shift into higher priced segments or into less price sensitive industries.

The unit values of exports and imports will be compared to reveal whether the EU successfully specialises in higher valued market segments. Further disaggregation indicates for which exports the price or the quality defines the prime competitive edge. Finally, industries are classified according to their respective price elasticities and the importance of quality competition. Producing higher quality and increasing productivity may be alternative or complementary strategies. Both strategies imply creating more value for a given quantity. Productivity is usually thought of as the relation of a physical output to a measure of labour input (labour productivity) or to a weighted input of several quantitatively measured inputs (total factor productivity). One way to measure quality is to estimate the value created for the consumer by the consumption of one unit of a good. Thus productivity stresses the relation between a physical output and a physical input, while quality emphasises value per output. An increase in value added per employee, however, is a measure that should ideally include changes in values as well as productivity increases, in the sense defined above. It is interesting to see which component prevails: that of physical output to physical inputs or that of shifting to higher valued goods.

Quality premium in total trade

The export unit value of European manufacturing is 40% higher than that of imports (see Table 3.4). Roughly half of this "quality mark up" in European trade comes from specialisation in high unit value industries, and roughly half from higher unit values within the same industries. If exports had the same (quantitative) composition as imports, the unit values would still be 20% higher than that of aggregate imports. This "within industry" premium of higher unit values in exports than imports applies to 18 sectors out of 22, and 71 industries out of 95.

Box 3.2:
Unit values and their use

The unit value is defined as nominal value divided into physical volume. Increasing unit values may either be due to rising demand or rising costs. But unit values also reflect changes in quality, shifts to higher product segments and to more specific value enhancing features. Therefore, unit value is often applied as an indicator in attempts to measure quality and vertical product differentiation.

However, its use has been limited by the fact that high quality and high costs caused by less efficient techniques are difficult to disentangle. Aiginger (1997)[a] shows that the unit value is near to a productivity measure, if the product is homogenous and the number of workers needed to produce one unit of output is relatively constant. But the unit value approaches a pure price or consumer valuation if the product or service is differentiated and the value is related to the input unit (counselling fee per hour, construction fee per square meter or cost per kilo of cement).

The hierarchy of unit values across industries also reflects the number of stages in processing. In some cases, it is of limited value, since there are industries in which the unit values are intrinsically higher than in others, while neither high tech, nor skilled labour, nor physical capital is involved. This holds for example for textile and apparel industries in which the unit values are high, since the weight in tons is low. The same holds for precious metals, where supply is scarce relative to demand. Therefore, jewellery, leather, furs, footwear and apparel are among the top industries as far as the absolute unit value is concerned, without indicating for example the use of skilled labour or research. High tech or high skill industries - like aircraft and spacecraft, watches and clocks, TV and radio transmitters and instruments - are also among the industries with the highest export unit values. In all these industries, unit values are much higher for processed goods and those made with large inputs of research and human capital, than for semi-finished goods, structural metals etc. At the bottom of a list ranking industries according to their unit values are industries at the early stages of processing, producing inputs for other industries, such as cement, bricks, coke oven products, petroleum, sawmilling, or planing and impregnation of wood. At sectoral level, the ranking of unit values fits reasonably well into the notion of competition in product quality: the four sectors at the top of absolute unit values in the EU are four technically sophisticated industries: precision instruments, office machinery, TV and communication equipment and other transport equipment. The four sectors with the lowest export unit values are basic goods industries (refined petroleum, construction materials, basic metals, pulp and paper).

Additionally, it has been shown that at national level, countries with higher incomes tend to export goods with high unit values and import those with low unit values.

Comparing the hierarchy of industries according to both unit values and labour productivity reveals similarities and differences between the two concepts. The main coincidence lies in the high tech industries mentioned above, which enjoy high unit values and high labour productivity. Among the exceptions is the evaluation of medical instruments and other transport as industries with low labour productivity but high unit values. The second difference lies in the evaluation of capital- and energy-intensive basic goods industries. Petroleum, paper and basic metals are highly ranked by labour productivity, but have low unit values. The third group consists of textiles and clothing industries, which have low labour productivity but intrinsically high unit values.

[a] Aiginger, K., "The use of unit values to discriminate between price and quality competition", Cambridge Journal of Economics, Vol. 21, 1997, pp. 571-592.

Table 3.4

Quality premium of EU exports over imports, 1996 (1)

	Exports (billion ECU)	Imports (billion ECU)	Export unit value (ECU/kg)	Import unit value (ECU/kg)	Relative unit value	Higher export unit value of EU	
						Number of sectors	Number of industries
Total trade of EU	575.6	452.0	2.070	1.492	1.387	17	71
EU trade vs. USA	104.1	96.2	2.736	2.616	1.046	11	49
EU trade vs. Japan	33.3	51.4	6.177	12.245	0.504	11	42
EU trade vs. "Other Countries"	438.3	304.4	1.869	1.162	1.609	20	77
EU trade vs. DYNAS	85.4	91.5	3.246	3.820	0.850	17	70

(1) Relative unit value = unit value exports/unit value imports (=quality premium); DYNAS: Thailand, Indonesia, Malaysia, Singapore, Philippines, China, South-Korea, Taiwan, Hong Kong, also included in "other countries"; total number of sectors n=22; total number of industries n=95.

Source: Eurostat (Comext), WIFO calculations

The industries in which Europe has higher unit values in exports than in imports can be broadly split into two groups. Firstly, industries in which the EU is a net importer and low cost countries have positive specialisation. Consequently, the export unit values are much higher for the EU, since it concentrates only on the highest valued market segments. This group comprises leather clothes, textile weaving, as well as sports goods and furniture.

Secondly, technically sophisticated industries with differentiated products, in which Europe faces tough competition from suppliers in Japan and the USA. In most of these industries, the unit values of exports are higher than of imports, but due to competition within industrialised countries, the ratio is lower than in the industries mentioned above. Examples are audio-visual apparatus, office machinery, and optical instruments.

Unit values of European exports are lower than for imports in 24 industries. The largest are non-ferrous metals, sawmilling, certain industries in the food sector, and also some electrical industries. Basic metals is the only sector in which import unit values are significantly higher. In the industries labelled other transport, a large negative margin between the export unit value and the import unit value declined considerably.

Quality premium in trade with Japan and the USA

Unit values are not available for Japanese and USA exports, since some industries do not report quantities consistent with European data. The following analysis is therefore restricted to bilateral trade flows, taking the EU as the reporting country.

European trade with the USA is approximately balanced. European exports to the USA are 7% higher than imports and the unit value of European exports is 5% higher than that of the imports from the USA. These margins apply relatively evenly across industries and sectors. Significantly higher unit values, which are to the advantage of the EU, are given for the food sector, in which European exports exceed imports by 57% and cover higher priced segments within 7 out of 9 industries. Similar specialisation is revealed in the leather industries and in wood processing. Within the larger industries, the unit value is 46% higher in the vehicles industry. It is somewhat higher in the chemical sector and lower in the machinery sector. In several sophisticated industries, such as office machinery, electronic components and special purpose machinery, the EU exports goods at a lower unit value to the USA than it imports. Pharmaceuticals, aircraft and spacecraft are examples in which Europe has higher unit values.

European exports to Japan cover only 65% of imports. The total trade deficit in manufacturing can be explained by the lower unit values of European exports. While the unit value of European imports is 12.2 ECU/kg, its exports are priced at only 6.2 ECU/kg. This significant effect does not stem from differences within industries - the numbers of sectors and industries with higher and lower unit values are roughly equal - but rather from Japan's concentration on higher valued goods (engineering and electronic industries), while the exports of labour and resource intensive industries are largely abandoned. In the vehicle industry, European exports are valued 70% higher in bilateral trade. In office machinery, the European unit value of exports is nearly four times higher than that of imports. Similar relations are evident in the apparel industry and TV and radio equipment. In resource based industries, Japan's trade is balanced, but focuses on higher priced segments.

Surplus and quality versus other areas

Europe's trade surplus stems from trade with countries outside the EU-Japan-USA-area: exports of ECU 440 billion compared with imports of only ECU 300 billion. The unit values for other countries are lower than those for total trade, the export unit value is 1.9 ECU/kg and the import value is only 1.2 ECU/kg. The quality premium amounts to 60%, and reflects differences both in endowments and in vertical product differentiation. Large differences are exhibited within the "other countries". While the unit values of exports in the EU's trade with Central and Eastern European transition countries are much higher than for imports, they are slightly lower in trade with dynamic Asian economies. As with trade with Japan, this stems mainly from the high specialisation of the dynamic Asian countries in the engineering and electronic industries. However, there is a difference between Japan and the other dynamic Asian countries insofar as the latter produce at lower prices (two thirds of the exports from these countries are lower valued than European exports). This pattern reflects the strategic focus of domestic as well as multinational enterprises (partly Japanese and European) on labour intensive production processes within technically sophisticated and dynamically growing industries. This strategy permits the dynamic Asian countries to benefit simultaneously from a powerful combination of general locational advantages (low wages) on the one hand, and firm specific advantages (based on technological knowledge) on the other.

The major findings may be summarised as follows: the total European trade surplus originates in a general quality mark up and this quality mark up stems from trade with countries other than Japan and the USA.

Competition within the industrialised countries is an important benchmark, specifically for the high valued segment of the market, which may provide a valuable early indication of future developments in quality competition. But in quantitative terms, the largest part of total European trade flows stems from the exchange of goods with countries other than Japan and the USA. To give a few examples: of the total exports from the EU, only 18% go to the USA and 6% to Japan. 10.1% of the EU's exports go to the Central and Eastern European transition economies and 14.5% to the dynamic Asian countries. Their respective shares as a source of the EU's imports are 8.2% and 16.9%. Two western European countries, which are not members of the Union (Switzerland and Norway), account for a larger part of the EU's total trade than Japan. However, these figures should not downplay the importance of the competitive performance between the EU, Japan and the USA, especially since all of them also compete for export shares in other markets.

Four segments of competition according to quality and price

Information regarding relative prices and physical quantities traded is used to reveal whether the EU trades more in industries with a high price elasticity or in industries in which competition in quality dominates. Other things being equal, demand is negatively related to price. Consequently, this implies that if an economy is able to sell products at higher unit values and, nevertheless, enjoys an export surplus, there is a supply of higher quality within the same industry. In the following analysis, this rationale is used to assess the quality position of the EU and to rank industries according to their respective price elasticities.

1. Successful quality competition: in 36 industries, the EU is a net exporter in quantity, despite higher unit values. This segment contains mainly technically demanding engineering industries. The largest surplus occurs in other special purpose machinery and in motor vehicles; considerable surpluses also occur in pharmaceuticals, machinery for producing mechanical power as well as air- and spacecraft. The total surplus generated in this market segment is ECU 161 billion. 51% of total European exports originate in this segment. The common surplus is larger than in total trade.

(billion ECU) Figure 3.3

Trade balance by quality segments, 1996

EU vs. world

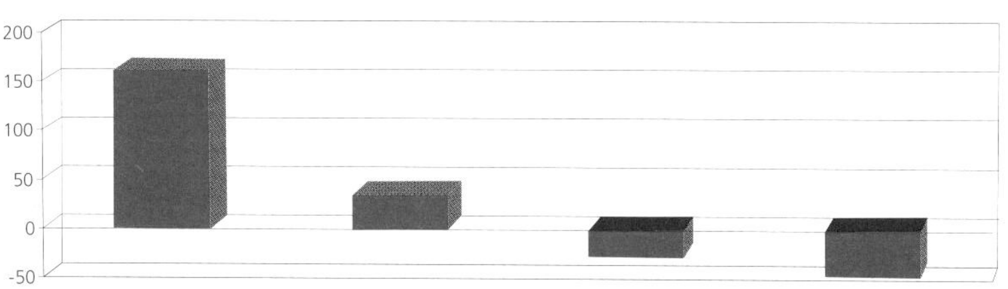

EU vs. USA

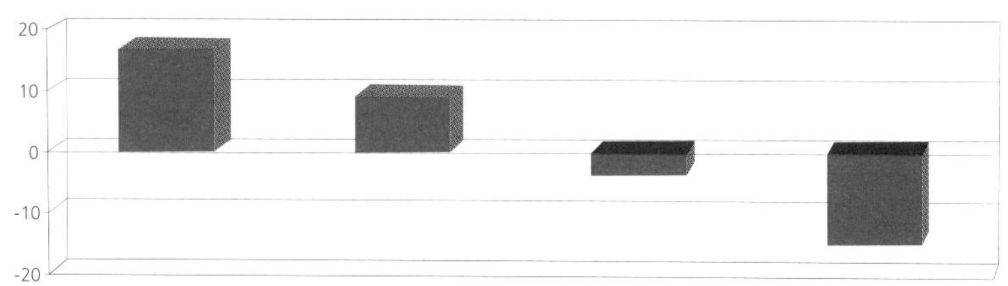

EU vs. Japan

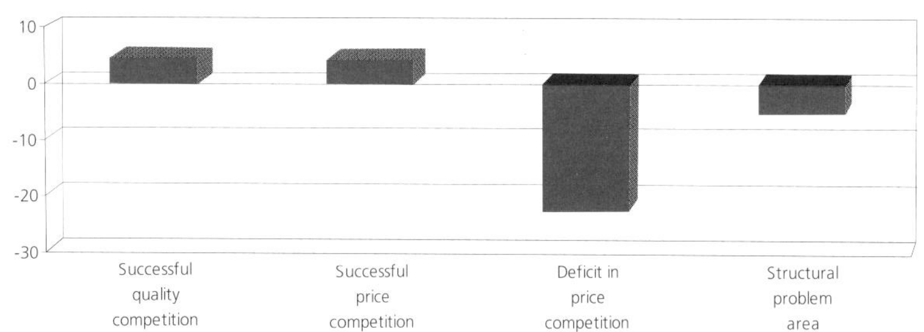

Source: Eurostat (Comext), WIFO calculations

(billion ECU) Table 3.5

Trade balance in different market segments, 1996

EU vs.	**Successful quality competition** Quantity surplus, higher export price	**Successful price competition** Quantity surplus, lower export price	**Deficit in price competition** Quantity deficit higher export price	**Structural problem area** Quantity deficit Lower export price
World	*36 industries, e.g.* Motor vehicles Machinery Air-, spacecraft	*17 industries, e.g.* Other chemical products	*35 industries, e.g.* Basic chemicals Petroleum products	*7 industries, e.g.* Electronic components Wearing apparel Non-ferrous metals
USA	*14 industries, e.g.* Vehicles Beverages	*35 industries, e.g.* Special machinery	*35 industries, e.g.* Air-, spacecraft Basic chemicals	*11 industries, e.g.* Computer
Japan	*17 industries, e.g.* Apparel Luggage, bags Textile weaving	*40 industries, e.g.* Basic chemicals Beverages Meat	*25 industries, e.g.* Motor vehicles Pharmaceuticals Computers	*13 industries, e.g.* Special machinery Machinery Optical instruments

Source: Eurostat (Comext), WIFO calculations

Box 3.3:
Measuring price elasticities according to the Cambridge E3ME model[a]

Measuring the response of demand to price changes is a topic which is as important as it is complex. If demand changes dramatically in reaction to even minor price changes, goods are labelled as price elastic and firms use price as their main instrument to gain a competitive advantage. Costs become the crucial constraint for management since low costs are needed to undercut prices and no firm can produce at higher than average cost price in the long run.

If the product is horizontally or vertically differentiated, different specifications, locations, qualities become important and price elasticity is reduced. Specifically high wage countries have to shift to industries in which they either have a technological advantage or produce superior quality. We used unit values and the resulting quantity response to discriminate between segments in which prices and quality are the decisive determinant of success.

An alternative approach is to measure the price responsiveness with time series on prices and quantities. This approach yields a quantitative measure of the price elasticity, if the data sets are reliable and if the data include information about all the other determinants of supply and those of demand. If these are available an economic model can be estimated, which provides information about the price elasticity. If the model is sufficiently disaggregated, the price elasticity of imports and exports for different sectors and specific regions can be estimated.

The econometric model of Cambridge Econometrics includes 13 sectors within manufacturing, which roughly coincide with the NACE '70 classification. Exports and imports are available for all EU countries with the exception of Sweden, so that a regional breakdown is possible allowing estimated elasticities for trade flows to differ across more or less developed areas. Demand is assumed to depend on technology and price and the relation is log-linear, giving elasticities which can be easily interpreted.

Limits of the analysis using trade equations alone come from the fact that partial analysis is used, that price and output data may not reflect pure changes in quantities and prices properly and that there may be omitted variables and structural breaks in the time series. Techniques available in econometrics are applied to minimise the danger of mis-specification and errors in data.

The study shows that:

· all price elasticities are relatively low, the largest export elasticities amount to 0.6, meaning that a 1% change in prices results in a 0.6% change of quantity. Average elasticities are around 0.4.

· import price elasticities tend to be higher than export price elasticities. This fits with the finding that EU exports are sold to a larger extent on markets in which quality is more important, but imports are of lower quality-type goods and are therefore to a higher degree price dependent.

· export price elasticities are lower for the North than for the South, for the core than for the periphery and for members of the euro-zone than for the non-members. Import elasticities on the other hand are approximately equal across the regions. As regards individual countries, import elasticities are relatively high for Greece and the United Kingdom, implying a greater threat of competition from low cost countries.

· at industry level, the computer industry and transport equipment are price elastic while chemicals and plastics are not. While the latter finding is in line with the information from the qualitative method using unit values, the assessment for office machinery and transport is not in line with the findings by the calculation of price elasticities. This hints at the possibility that in heterogeneous industries with rapid technological change, the influence of prices and quality is particularly difficult to disentangle and econometrics and methods to detect vertical product differentiation are complementary.

[a] The study was commissioned by WIFO and performed by Cambridge Econometrics: Gardiner, B., "Analysis of EU trade-price elasticities by sector and country", Cambridge, 1998.

2. Structural problem area: another segment, in which prices and net quantities have the same sign, is labelled "structural problem area", since the EU exhibits both a deficit in trade and lower unit values. This segment contains only 7 industries. Other apparel is creating the largest deficit, followed by basic precious and non-ferrous metals. Electronic components, fish and fish products, sawmilling, planing and impregnation of wood, man-made fibres and the processing of nuclear fuel are the other industries in which unit values are high, but quantities exported are smaller than those imported. Imports are worth ECU 83 billion (18% of total imports), and the trade deficit amounts to ECU 46 billion.

3. Gap in price competitiveness: the EU suffers a trade deficit in terms of physical quantities in 35 industries, while its unit values are higher in exports than in imports. Basic chemicals, petroleum products, pulp and paper, textile weaving and furniture belong to this segment. The single largest deficit occurs in the office machinery and computer industry, where the EU has a deficit in the low and medium ranged quality segments. The EU exports only in the higher valued niches of the market. As a consequence, the unit value of exports is 50% above that of imports, although in physical quantities exports are low. The total group of industries in which unit values are higher in European exports than in imports, but the quantities sold are lower, comprises imports of ECU 174 billion. Taken together, the overall trade deficit only amounts to ECU 27 billion.

4. Successful price competition: in this group, the EU has lower prices (in terms of the ratio of unit values in export to imports) and simultaneously enjoys a trade surplus when measured in physical quantities. This segment comprises 17 rather small industries, ranging from other chemicals or machine tools to detergents. The exports of all industries together generate ECU 98 billion or 17% of total exports. The trade surplus is ECU 35 billion, which is considerably below the ECU 161 billion in the segment of successful quality competition.

To sum up the results in a nutshell: the industries in which total EU trade is revealed to be price elastic on the one hand, and those in which it depends more on quality on the other, are approximately equal. In 52 industries, relative prices have the opposite sign to the physical quantities traded and can be labelled as the price elastic segment. In 43 industries they have the same sign, revealing a considerable degree of quality competition. Total trade flow is larger in the quality dominated group (exports: ECU 330 billion; imports: ECU 215 billion), where the European trade surplus is generated. In the particularly price elastic industries, exports of ECU 245 billion were only slightly above imports of ECU 237 billion in 1996.

This disaggregation reveals a rather favourable story on European external performance: the EU enjoys a trade surplus. This is largely generated by industries in which it enjoys a quantity surplus despite higher unit values, providing a rather clear indication that superior quality is the most important instrument for creating a competitive advantage. Lower prices generate a small additional surplus. A gap in price competitiveness occurs in several industries, but does not result in a large trade deficit. The structural problem area is very low.

Bilateral trade with Japan and the USA
European trade with Japan is dominated by cost advantages in Japan: in 40 industries, unit values are lower, and quantities exported are higher, generating a Japanese trade surplus of ECU 22 billion. There are also 25 industries in which Europe produces cheaper goods, but the resulting surplus is low. The same applies to the 17 industries with successful quality competition (some of them in the textiles sector). Taken with the earlier results on the high degree of specialisation in Japanese exports, the following picture emerges: Japan concentrates on high unit value industries, and uses rather low prices (or placement in the middle quality segments) to gain large surpluses in trade. However, imports remain low even when price advantages are missing or Europe offers superior quality as measured by unit values.

Bilateral trade with the USA indicates that price competition is neither creating the large surpluses, nor is it the source of major sectoral deficits. Europe has a gap in price competitiveness in 35 industries, resulting in a total deficit of only ECU 3.5 billion. Revealed price advantage in another 35 industries provides a surplus of ECU 9 billion. Larger trade imbalances in particular industries result from specialisation and non-price determinants. The segment in which Europe provides higher quality and enjoys a surplus in quantities comprises 14 industries resulting in a surplus of ECU 17 billion. Motor vehicles and beverages are the main industries in this segment. The segment in which European goods have lower unit values, but in which the trade balance is nevertheless negative, contributes a deficit of ECU 15 billion. Office machinery and computers are the major source. The overall results indicate that technological advantages and successful placement in quality segments tend to be more important determinants of trade between the USA and the EU than prices and costs.

Quality as a general industry characteristic
So far, exports from the EU to the world, and then the bilateral flows in trade with Japan and the USA, have been classified according to the relation between prices and net quantities. The four segments classified as modes of competition, allow industries to be classified according to their trade balance (flows).

In this following section, the positive or negative signs revealed by the trade flows of many countries are used to classify industries as typically price elastic or quality dependent. The larger the number of opposite signs in all observed trade relations is, the greater the price elasticity should be. The higher the number of identical signs in trade flows (higher prices coinciding with higher quantities and vice versa), the higher the probability of quality as a dominant determinant of performance. This ranking of the revealed importance of quality as an industry characteristic complements the more direct quantitative estimation of price elasticities (see Box 3.3)[14].

This exercise can be performed in many variations, of which three have been chosen. For all three, the shares of bilateral trade flows in which relative prices and net quantities had the opposite sign (price elastic flows) and in which they had the same sign (non-price elastic flows) were calculated. Finally, the industries were ranked according to the number of identical signs, obtaining, in this way, an indicator of the importance of non-price elements.

14) The method was developed in Aiginger, K., "The use of unit values to discriminate between price and quality competition", Cambridge Journal of Economics, Vol. 21, 1997, pp. 571-592.

Quality indicator 1: using the EU as the reporting country, the flows vis-à-vis individual countries for all 6-digit industries (n * k flows, if n is the number of trading partners and k the number of 6-digits within an industry) were calculated. This indicator mirrors the assumption that the EU is one entity and supplies different geographical and product markets (double differentiation).

Quality indicator 2: using the individual Member States as reporters and total exports in each of the other 6-digit industries provides a second indicator. This indicator assumes that each country is one entity that exports to one geographical market (all partners), but in different product markets (r * k, with r as the number of EU countries) (product differentiation).

Quality indicator 3: using the individual Member States as reporters and all other countries as different markets, but confining the analysis to the 3-digit level, provides a third indicator. This indicator assumes that each country is an entity exporting to different geographical markets, but without product heterogeneity within the industry (geographical differentiation).

Many more possible choices exist, and none of them is an exact replica of the industrial organisation model with firms supplying well-defined markets in geographical as well as product space. However, each of the chosen indicators contributes some valuable information about specific market characteristics. Together with other indicators of product differentiation and expenditures on advertising, they help us to understand the structure of markets and the respective importance of prices versus quality as determinants of the competitive process.

The ranking according to relative shares of positive signs in the quality indicators 1, 2 and 3 has been used to sort industries into three distinct groups, namely quality competition, medium price elastic industries and highly price elastic industries (allocating one third of the industries to each group). Overall, the rankings produced rather similar results.

Table 3.6 (%)

Shares in the world market according to revealed quality competition (1)

		EU-15		USA		Japan	
		1989	1996	1989	1996	1989	1996
Quality indicator 1	High	32.78	33.62	22.93	20.77	24.36	16.93
	Medium	23.34	24.06	18.44	19.07	10.67	10.01
	Low	21.88	19.03	17.73	14.99	22.71	16.09
Quality indicator 2	High	30.06	31.84	23.31	21.33	24.14	17.20
	Medium	23.48	22.66	19.51	18.49	16.81	13.79
	Low	28.21	25.18	12.77	12.76	11.52	8.95
Quality indicator 3	High	30.92	30.34	19.44	18.51	24.68	16.34
	Medium	24.71	24.54	24.18	21.41	19.32	15.69
	Low	23.21	23.22	17.56	16.48	10.84	9.74

(1) Variables are ranked in declining order of the criteria: high, one third of industries with highest ranks; medium, one third of industries with medium ranks; low, one third of industries with lowest ranks; quality indicator = number of identical signs in unit value and quantity;
Q1: EU vs. countries, 6-digit level; Q2: country vs. world, 6-digit level; Q3: country vs. country, 3-digit level;
market share is defined as exports as a percentage of world imports.

Source: Eurostat (Comext, SBS), WIFO calculations

The EU has its highest market shares in industries characterised by quality competition according to all indicators (see Table 3.6). The market shares of the price elastic industries are especially low for quality indicator 1. Under the assumption that each Member State is one individual entity, it is revealed that several European countries compete as well in price elastic industries. USA market shares are above average in medium price elastic goods, while Japan has a split between industries with high emphasis on quality and those with high price elasticity.

3.3 Further disaggregations

Inter- vs. intra-industry trade
Rising economic development is expected to shift the predominant sources of industrial specialisation from inter-industry trade based on general factor endowments (for example in labour, physical capital or natural resources) to more differentiated intra-industry trade based on knowledge appropriation, marketing or other firm specific entrepreneurial skills.

Inter-industry trade amounts to 43%, intra-industry trade to 57% of the EU's trade with the world. This implies that, at the level of product groups, more than half of trade occurs within the same industry. Breaking down intra-industry trade further into the predominant mode of differentiation[15], 75% appears to be vertically differentiated, while only one quarter is categorised as horizontally differentiated. Within the vertically differentiated industries, the EU lies primarily in the higher valued market segments (34% of total trade is in the higher valued segment, 13% in the lower).

In line with trade theory, more technically sophisticated industries are well represented among the industries with high intra-industry trade. Four of the ten industries with the greatest shares are engineering industries; the largest are aircraft and spacecraft, precision instruments and medical equipment. Interestingly, horizontal differentiation dominates in each of these industries, against the general trend. Furthermore, within the vertically segmented markets, the EU is also present in the lower priced segments. The cement industry and basic chemicals are among the industries with large shares in intra-industry trade. Both are low growth and high energy-intensive industries, and cross border trade may occur.

Among the industries with low intra-industry trade, food and beverages are well represented; steam generators is the only engineering industry in which vertical product differentiation dominates, but even here the level is low in absolute terms. In comparison with Japan and the USA, the EU concentrates its exports in industries with relatively low shares of intra-industry trade. Applying the same split of industries (based on EU trade data), the USA and Japan have larger market shares in industries with high intra-industry trade and high degrees of product differentiation.

Europe is not specialised in industries that typically have high intra-industry trade. Its market share is 28.1% in this group and 29.6% in those industries in which inter-industry trade dominates (see Table 3.7). Japan has slightly higher shares in the first group, the USA has much higher market shares in the industries in which data show high intra-industry trade.

Product differentiation
In homogenous markets, all products are sold at a unique price. However, each statistical unit (specifically those on a 3-digit industry level) comprises a large number of products, some homogenous, some of them differentiated. The variance of unit values of exports summarises the variation of prices for the same product group, as well as the variation, which arises from mixing different products in one industry. In the following, three different measures of heterogeneity are calculated: the standard deviation of the export unit value across EU countries (SD1); across the 6-digit industries for EU exports (SD2); and finally the standard deviation over countries and products (SD3). The three indicators reflect different assumptions regarding the relevant markets. The first concept assumes implicitly that each European country is one economic unit, serving different regional markets. The second assumes that the EU is one firm serving different product markets, while the third implies separated products and geographical markets. The resulting indicators are positively correlated, but are far from identical.

The first indicator stresses differences in price across regions. Jewellery and nuclear fuel have large standard deviations, according to all calculations, which across regions are less than their mean, while those across products are ten times larger. Other high standard deviations across markets occur in the electronic components industry, and for audio-visual apparatus. In the pharmaceuticals, aircraft and spacecraft, ships and boats, precision instruments and optical instruments industries, standard deviation across products is much higher than across markets. In the petroleum products, pulp and paper, iron and steel, bricks, and mineral products industries, all standard deviations are very low, even compared to the low unit values in these industries. Splitting exports according to product differentiation (SD3 in Table 3.6) shows that Europe and Japan enjoy the highest market shares in industries with medium product differentiation, while the USA is specialised in industries with high product differentiation.

15) It has become a convention to use the criteria that the unit values of exports and imports do not differ by more than 15% to indicate horizontal product differentiation, whereas larger differences reveal vertical product differentiation.

Performance in globalised industries

By ranking industries according to their exposure to international competition (calculated by the ratio of imports plus exports to Triad apparent consumption) the following results emerge. Office machinery, watches, and medical equipment belong to the highest globalised industries, with ratios over 75%, whereas beverages and cement are examples of low levels of global competition, with ratios of less than 25%. In contrast to Japan and the USA, the EU is characterised by high shares in world markets in industries with low globalisation. In the USA, market shares are more evenly distributed, while Japanese manufacturing is concentrated intensely in highly and moderately globalised industries, with market shares three times those of industries with low levels of globalisation.

Market growth, wage levels and productivity

When market growth is defined as the annual growth of apparent consumption in the three areas EU-Japan-USA, Japan and the USA enjoy their largest shares in the world market in high growth industries, the EU in low growth industries. Europe, as well as Japan, enjoys the largest surplus in medium growth industries, where the USA has its largest deficit. Taken together, the EU, Japan, and the USA are specialised in high growth industries, where annual growth of value added amounts to 4.3% and employment is relatively stable.

The EU enjoys its highest market share and largest trade surplus in medium wage industries. In high wage industries, the EU increased its share and has generated a considerable trade surplus. In contrast, the market shares in low wage industries are decreasing and the trade balance is marginally negative. The USA, as well as Japan, has much smaller market shares and larger trade deficits in the low wage industries. The USA market share is decreasing in the high wage industries, and is stable in low wage industries.

A final disaggregation according to productivity levels reveals that the EU increased slightly its specialisation in high productivity industries and has achieved a high and increasing trade surplus. The level of specialisation of the USA in this segment decreased, resulting in a larger trade deficit. Japan has the lowest market share in the low productivity segment and a trade deficit.

(%) Table 3.7

Shares in world market according to market characteristics (1)

		EU		USA		Japan	
		1989	**1996**	**1989**	**1996**	**1989**	**1996**
Globalisation	High	25.3	24.7	22.6	16.4	20.5	18.1
	Medium	26.9	28.1	17.7	14.1	19.0	19.3
	Low	36.2	36.5	4.4	4.4	21.3	21.4
Market growth	High	26.0	25.2	23.7	17.1	23.7	20.9
	Medium	27.7	27.5	20.8	14.2	17.2	16.9
	Low	27.1	28.5	11.7	10.8	20.9	18.6
Productivity	High	29.6	31.2	21.8	16.4	23.8	21.4
	Medium	26.9	24.9	22.2	17.6	20.3	20.5
	Low	21.2	20.4	8.1	5.2	8.9	8.3
Wage level	High	28.9	30.6	21.0	16.9	24.1	22.4
	Medium	28.1	25.2	22.9	17.5	20.1	18.7
	Low	21.4	20.0	9.7	4.7	8.9	8.9
***Intra* industry trade**	High	29.0	28.1	18.2	14.8	25.7	21.9
	Medium	24.8	24.0	21.6	15.2	19.0	17.7
	Low	27.0	28.6	17.9	13.1	15.0	15.5
Product differentiation	High	22.9	23.1	19.1	14.8	23.3	19.8
	Medium	31.7	32.0	24.1	17.1	17.6	18.6
	Low	28.9	28.1	8.4	6.2	16.2	15.3

(1) Industries are ranked in declining order: high, medium, low (one third with highest, medium and lowest ranks);
globalisation: (imports + exports)/apparent consumption in the Triad (extra-EU trade only);
market growth: growth of apparent consumption in the Triad; productivity, wage level: value added resp. wages per worker in the EU;
intra-industry trade: share of intra industry trade (EU-world); product differentiation: standard deviation across markets and products of EU export unit values.

Source: Eurostat (Comext, SBS), WIFO calculations

3.4 Summary

Overall, the analysis of unit values in trade proves to be a valuable complement to the measurement of productivity. Unit values highlight the role of quality within industries and downgrade distortions in the measurement of labour productivity. This applies for example with regard to capital intensive industries, where high productivity is usually measured because of data restrictions with regard to only one input factor.

The EU specialises in more traditional industries, supplying high quality goods based on skilled and well-trained people. In many industries, the EU is a net exporter, despite higher prices.

Three sectors - machinery, motor vehicles, and chemicals - contribute more than proportionally to the large and increasing trade surplus, but inroads are also being made in more traditional industries like food, or in high tech industries, such as aircraft and spacecraft and radio, TV and communication equipment. Europe creates its trade surplus by trading with countries other than Japan and the USA, where it enjoys a quality premium of about 60%.

The deficit in trade with Japan stems from the concentration of Japanese exports in products that exhibit high unit values. Japan has abandoned exports in low productivity industries, but maintains a large share of the domestic market. Japan keeps a large part of its competitive advantage through lower prices, but in high value industries.

Trade with the USA is balanced both in value and in quantity. The USA seems to exploit competitive advantages to a lesser degree by trade, but shifts production earlier to other locations via foreign direct investment. Europe's trade with the USA does not rely on lower prices, but on mutual specialisation and competitive advantages in specific segments.

Taken as one single entity, the EU enjoys its highest market shares in industries characterised by quality competition. However, individual Member States still hold large market shares in price elastic industries.

4. UNDERLYING FORCES OF STRUCTURAL DEVELOPMENT

The two preceding sections explored the structural features of internal and external performance. In this section, both dimensions will be re-examined with a special focus on analytical criteria considered relevant to the strategic options of firms in the creation of specific competitive advantages. The particular purpose of this section is to apply a new and comprehensive typology of manufacturing industries based upon their typical patterns of factor input combinations and strategic investment.

The economic rationale for the new typology is based upon the recent emphasis on irreversible investments or so called "sunk costs" as a means of increasing differentiation and thereby moving away from pure cost competition. Sunk costs can either be exogenously determined by technology (involving investment in physical capital) or endogenously by the strategic decisions of firms to invest in intangible assets such as technological expertise or the creation of brands and goodwill[16]. The purpose of irreversible investment for example in advertising and research is to raise perceived quality and thus enhance the consumer's willingness to pay for a particular product, thereby also reducing its substitutability.

The new typology categorises industries according to the traditional factor intensities of labour and capital and additionally takes into account the inputs spent on research and development as well as advertising. By the means of statistical cluster techniques applied to USA input data, a complete and mutually exclusive classification covering all manufacturing industries was created. Analytically, the novel feature of this typology is the particular choice of variables, i.e. the combination of the traditional factors of labour and capital inputs, largely reflecting exogenously given technology, to the endogenous strategic investment in advertising and innovation. Technically, the use of statistical cluster analysis provides a number of advantages relative to traditional cut-off procedures, since it represents a statistical technique specifically designed for this purpose.

4.1 Firm's strategies

Discriminating industries according to the broad strategic options available to firms for creating competitive advantages, a new typology categorises them according to the traditional factor intensities of labour and capital, as well as the inputs spent on research and advertising. A residual fifth category, labelled mainstream, uses factor inputs in similar proportions to total manufacturing (see Box 4.1).

16) Sutton, J., "Sunk Costs and Market Structure", MIT Press, Cambridge, MA, 1991.

In principle, objections could be raised to the classification into the four chosen dimensions. Industries always exhibit combinations of some or all these variables. In particular, the combination of high expenditures on research as well as advertising came to prominence in a similar typology by Davies-Lyons (1996)[17]. One rationale is that advertising is often modelled as a complementary activity to research and development in order to provide consumers with information when a new product is introduced to the market. This story applies easily to industries such as pharmaceuticals and optical instruments, which fall under the heading of research intensive industries as well as to detergents, games and toys or publishing, which are classified here as advertising intensive industries.

Nevertheless, the reliance on two or more distinct inputs is not unique to advertising and research but also applies equally well to the other factor inputs. For example research intensive industries repeatedly go along with high capital investment. Many of the advertising intensive industries simultaneously rely strongly on labour inputs. Actually, the cluster algorithm showed the latter two combinations of industries to be closer than advertising and research intensive industries are. Finally, no pronounced combination of input factors emerged in the clustering process, supporting the view that each input variable spans a linearly independent dimension of its own. The following section briefly characterises the types of industries.

Labour intensive industries

One quarter of manufacturing industries have been labelled as particularly labour intensive. Their share in total employment of the EU, Japan and the USA amounts to 22.1%, contrasted by a much lower share in total value added of 14.6% (see Table 4.1). Only 10.2% of the common manufacturing exports originate in this group, compared to 15.6% of total imports. Typical examples include textiles and clothing, construction materials, wood-, and metal processing.

17) Davies, S., Lyons, B., et al., "Industrial Organisation in the European Union", Structure, Strategy, and the Competitive Mechanism, Oxford University Press, Oxford, 1996.

Production techniques typically show low degrees of complexity and can rather easily be adopted in locations less endowed with manufacturing skills. Low wage countries may therefore enjoy substantial comparative advantages based on labour costs. The modest technological and organisational requirements limit the opportunities for individual enterprises to create specific competitive advantages. In economic areas characterised by high wages, substitution of labour is the logical consequence. Increasing degrees of mechanisation are typical for example in industries such as textiles, wood and metal processing.

A second means of restructuring, which is particularly important in, for example, the clothing industries, is outward processing. While parts of production migrate into low wage areas, corporate control and higher valued activities can be maintained in the home location.

Finally, suppliers of construction material, for example, build specific advantages around local user-supplier relationships, benefiting from high transportation costs, which arise from the high physical weight of their products relative to economic value.

Capital intensive industries

In this subgroup only 9.9% of total manufacturing employment in the three economic areas produces 13.4% of its value added. Economies of scale support specialisation and enhance trade flows, such that this group accounts for about 17% of both total exports and imports. Typical examples are pulp and paper, refined petroleum, basic chemicals and iron and steel.

These capital-intensive industries produce basic intermediate goods, which are supplied to other downstream industries. Products are typically highly homogeneous and of a commodity-like nature. Dependent on the demand of downstream manufacturing, these industries are highly exposed to fluctuations in the business cycle. As a consequence of large scale and the substantial element of sunk investment in physical capital, fluctuations in commodity prices and profits are further aggravated by sticky capacities.

Box 4.1:

Factor inputs and strategic investment: the WIFO taxonomy (Peneder, 1999)[a]

The new WIFO classification groups individual industries according to their typical combinations of factor inputs, in order to reveal information about differences across industries with regard to the dominant modes of creating competitive advantage in specific marketplaces. In particular, the typology is directed towards distinction between (i) exogenously given competitive advantages based on factor endowments and (ii) endogenously created advantages based on strategic investment in intangible assets such as marketing and innovation. The new classification is based on Eurostat's revised NACE Rev. 1 classification at the 3-digit level. For more details see Peneder (1999).

Data and the choice of variables

The clustering process is based on the following four variables, which are designed to span four orthogonal dimensions of how to spend available units of productive inputs:

- wages and salaries
- physical capital
- advertising
- research and development.

Ratios to total value added have been calculated for wages and physical capital. Expenditures on advertising and R&D are represented by their ratios to total sales. The latter are derived directly from balance sheet data. All four variables have been used in their standardised form, i.e. transformed by calculating the difference to the mean divided by the standard deviation of the variables. Data sources are SBS (labour and capital inputs) and COMPUSTAT (advertising and R&D). Since all four dimensions of input data were available only for the USA, the clustering process is exclusively based on USA-data. Correlations between the four variables are low or non-existent.

Statistical clustering

Cluster analysis classifies individual observations, depending on their relative similarity or nearness to an array of different variables. The basic idea is one of dividing a specific data profile into segments by creating maximum homogeneity within and maximum distance between groups. For the current analysis one hundred NACE Rev. 1 3-digit manufacturing industries are taken as observations, while the four factor inputs given above determined the discriminating variables.

A two step procedure was applied. In the first step, a non-hierarchical optimisation cluster technique, based on the iterative minimisation of within group dispersion, was used to provide a more aggregate picture of typical input combinations. For the necessary choice of a predetermined number of clusters, the following self-binding rule of thumb was used: "choose the lowest number g that maximises the quantity of individual clusters which include more than 5% of the observed cases." (Peneder, 1995, p. 297)[b]. The outcome was g = 32 clusters, of which 9 comprise more than 5% of total observations.

In a second step, the 32 clusters from the first partition were taken as individual observations on which a hierarchical clustering algorithm was applied. This implies that no predefined number of clusters is required. Relative distances are measured, specifically focusing on similarities in patterns instead of size. In the following iterative process, clusters are formed according to the average linkage between groups, which aggregates the distances of all single pairs between an observation outside and each observation inside the cluster.

The final solution of the hierarchical clustering algorithm groups all observations into four categories, each one related to particularly high values in one of the four dimensions. After applying several variations on both (i) the measures for distance/similarity and (ii) the clustering algorithm itself, no successful alternative partition to this solution emerged. Finally, a number of industries which had no particularly pronounced reliance on any of the input variables were placed in a residual category called "mainstream" manufacturing. This more or less represents the input combination of a "typical" 3-digit manufacturing industry.

The taxonomy

Precisely 100 NACE Rev. 1 3-digit manufacturing industries have been completely categorised under the following five mutually exclusive groupings of mainstream manufacturing, particularly labour-, capital-, advertising- and research intensive industries.

Like any broad classification, this new typology must be interpreted with care, since industries within these five categories are still heterogeneous and exhibit combinations of some or all these variables.

[a] Peneder, M., "Intangible Investment and Human Resources. The new WIFO Taxonomy of Manufacturing Industry", WIFO Working Papers No. 114, Vienna, 1999.

[b] Peneder, M., "Cluster Techniques as a Method to Analyse Industrial Competitiveness", IAER-International Advances in Economic Research, Vol. I, No 3, August 1995, pp. 295-303.

Table 4.1 (%)

Shares in Triad manufacturing, 1996

	Value added	Employment	Exports	Imports
Labour intensive	14.6	22.1	10.2	15.6
Capital intensive	13.4	9.9	16.9	17.5
Advertising intensive	22.2	22.1	10.0	14.1
Research intensive	25.3	18.6	38.8	37.0
Mainstream manufacturing	24.5	27.3	24.1	15.8
Total manufacturing	100.0	100.0	100.0	100.0

Source: Eurostat (SBS, Compet), WIFO calculations

Lacking opportunities for product differentiation, strategic options for individual firms most commonly include (i) a continuous process of re-engineering and cost cutting, (ii) forward integration into related business activities or (iii) participation in joint ventures, mergers and take-overs, to create economies of scale and enhance strategic positions as a major player in the market place.

Mainstream manufacturing

Mainstream manufacturing is a residual category of 25 industries, in which input combinations did not show a pronounced reliance on any particular factor. This group accounts for about one quarter of manufacturing value added, employment and exports, but for only 15.8% of imports, when the EU, Japan and the USA are taken together. Typical examples are paper articles, plastic products, electronic equipment, motorcycles and machinery.

Although in the typical mainstream manufacturing industry production is more complex than in simple labour intensive industries, the processes involved are usually based on traditional technological regimes, mostly founded in electro-mechanical engineering.

A typical example is the machinery sector, which falls almost entirely into this group. Firm specific advantages are primarily based on bespoke developments for specific customer needs. The importance of complementary services such as planning, maintenance and training is increasing. A technically skilled workforce and the innovative upgrading of traditional technology with applications of, for example, new ICTs is essential. Close ties to downstream industries are of great importance. Thus, together with the demand for skilled labour, geographic proximity and cluster formation contribute to specific locational advantages.

Advertising intensive industries

This group comprises 23 industries, which together account for about 22% of total employment and value added in the three areas. This is in sharp contrast to the low shares in trade, where only 10.0% of total exports and 14.1% of total imports are generated. The low share of traded goods indicates the high importance of both local production on the one hand, and multinational investment on the other.

The most typical example is the food sector, which belongs entirely to this category. In addition, detergents and perfumes, as well as sports goods, musical instruments and games and toys, largely associated with leisure time and entertainment, fall into this category of fast moving consumer markets. Industries are often dualistic, with high quality brands on the one hand, and lower-priced, unbranded products on the other.

Strikingly characteristic of many of these industries are the easy shifts in consumer tastes. New products and temporary fashions often induce changes in preferences. Brand creation is a strategic means of differentiating products and thus reducing their substitutability. This leads to a reduction in a firm's exposure to pure cost competition. In addition, advertising stabilises the preferences of consumers.

One particular strategy is to build up integrated product lines under common brands, generating economies of scope between related products from the sharing of advertising outlays. Thus, successful brand names provide specific advantages to firms and consequently support growth strategies based on diversification as well as multinational activity.

Besides the aspect of differentiation, strategic interdependence between producers and distributors is one of the most important competitive challenges, increasingly requiring professional distribution management. Rising concentration in distribution channels is being experienced in many of these areas. The creation of brands and their support through continuous advertising is one way of reducing the producer's dependence on the retail sector. This is particularly applicable to large, primarily multinational enterprises, which are able to raise the necessary financial resources. In contrast, for small and medium-sized "no name" producers, or even for firms successfully marketing local brands, the strategic disadvantage tends to encourage joint ventures, mergers and takeovers, as efforts to counterbalance high concentration rates in the distribution networks.

Research intensive industries

This grouping comprises 14 industries, which together account for 25.3% of total value added and 18.6% of total employment in the three areas. Reflecting high economies of scale, product differentiation and specialisation, research intensive goods are more highly traded than any other category. Their share in total exports and imports amounts to an outstanding 38.8% and 37.0%, respectively. Industries typically belong to one of three distinct technology fields: (i) chemicals and biotechnology; (ii) information and communication and (iii) transportation vehicles.

The nature of technological competition is highly complex and R&D efforts are a particularly risky sort of investment. Even when inventions are successfully managed in terms of technology, economic benefits are uncertain, due to their extreme dependence upon the speed and timeliness of their introduction to the market. Compensating for the higher risks, the possibility to top vertically differentiated markets induces investment in R&D through the bright prospects for higher profits. Similar to brand creation, successful innovation is a strong motivation for multinational investment.

A wide range of market failures surrounds the production and dissemination of knowledge. Probably the most serious problem concerns appropriability, since the knowledge created by innovators is exposed to imitation and diffusion by its competitors. Basically, "a public good like knowledge remains in circulation no matter how many people consume it, and this undermines any attempt to create an artificial market" (Geroski, 1995, p.92)[18]. The consequences threaten to undermine the proper incentives to invest in R&D.

With regard to specific strategic challenges, two major themes arise: firstly, the management of knowledge creation is a highly demanding organisational task, requiring a balance between efficient and speedy processes, while simultaneously providing room for the creative interplay of unexpected ideas. Secondly, the management of knowledge appropriation involves a number of instruments, including legal protection through patents or secrecy. Given imperfect knowledge foreclosure, it is essential that the strategy strives for lead-time and generates benefits from cumulative learning processes. For this purpose, the successful marketing of new products is an important complement to R&D.

4.2 Contributions to overall economic performance

In the preceding section, some major qualitative characteristics of the new industry groupings were singled out according to different strategic options for the creation of firm specific advantages. This section offers a quantitative investigation of apparent differences in terms of productivity, wage levels, unit values and growth across industry types.

Productivity and wages

The productivity of any single input factor strongly depends on the amount of complementary inputs to production. Thus, for example, high amounts of physical capital, installed to support pure labour in production, necessarily implies higher value added per employee. The same rationale extends to other (intangible) inputs as well. The underlying hypothesis therefore states that labour productivity is higher in industries where pure labour is complemented by other inputs such as physical capital, research, advertising or skills.

18) Geroski, P., "Markets for technology: knowledge, innovation and appropriability", in Stoneman, P. (ed.), Handbook of the economics of innovation and technological change, Basil Blackwell, Oxford, 1995.

(thousand ECU per head) — Figure 4.1

Average labour productivity in Triad manufacturing, 1996

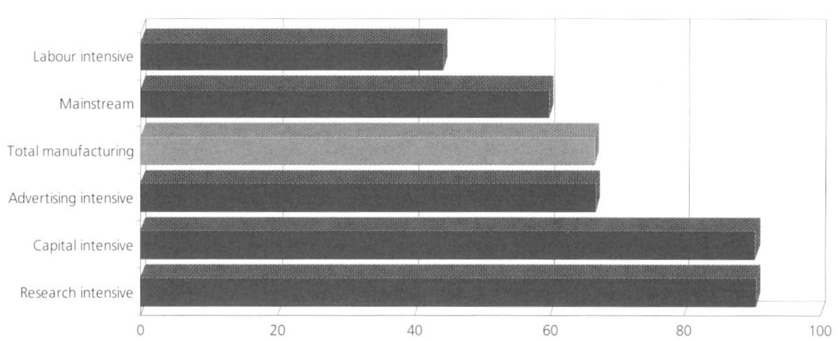

Source: Eurostat (SBS), WIFO calculations

(thousand ECU per head) — Figure 4.2

Average wages and salaries in Triad manufacturing, 1996

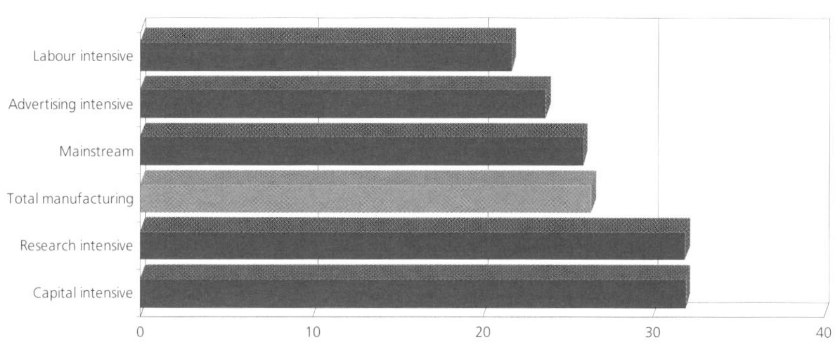

Source: Eurostat (SBS), WIFO calculations

Based on a cumulative ranking of the EU, Japan and the USA according to the level of labour productivity, research- and capital intensive industries emerge highest, followed by advertising intensive industries (see Figure 4.1). In all of them, the value of pure labour is augmented by the respective complementary inputs. Reflecting the high skills of trained workers, labour productivity in mainstream manufacturing is still higher than in labour intensive industries.

Wage levels are assumed to correspond with labour productivity. With the exception of advertising industries, where the overall wage level is lower than in the mainstream manufacturing industries, the same ranking applies as above (see Figure 4.2).

Unit values and vertical differentiation

As with productivity (measured in nominal terms), unit values reflect the valuation of goods and services by consumers and are therefore directly linked to the potential for quality competition and vertical differentiation. Again as with productivity, unit values are not a pure and undistorted measure. The more processing stages are involved, the more value is added relative to the pure volume of the initial physical material inputs. Therefore, the number of processing stages involved in production blurs the interpretation.

Figure 4.3 (ECU/kg)

Unit values in EU trade, 1996

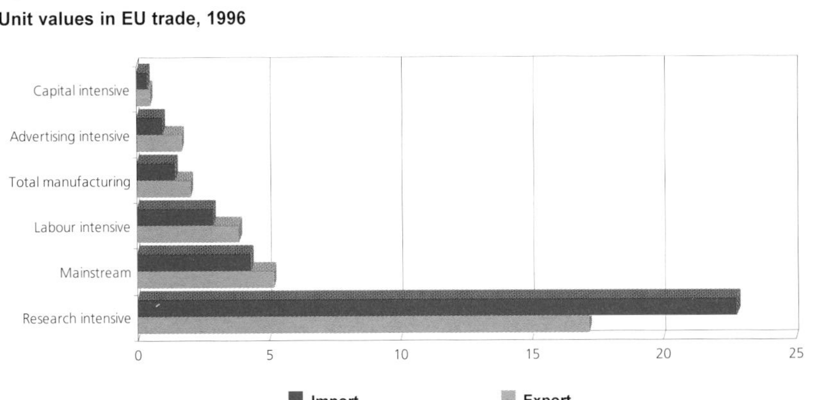

Source: Eurostat (Compet), WIFO calculations

Figure 4.4

Standard deviation of unit values in EU trade, 1996

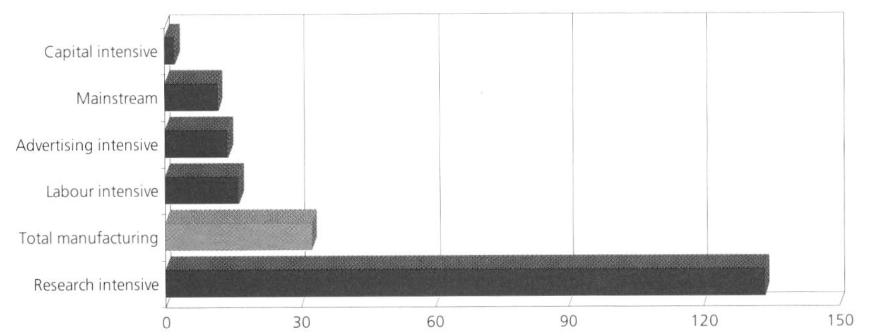

Source: Eurostat (Compet), WIFO calculations

Figure 4.5 (%)

Share of total trade to production for Triad maufacturing, 1996

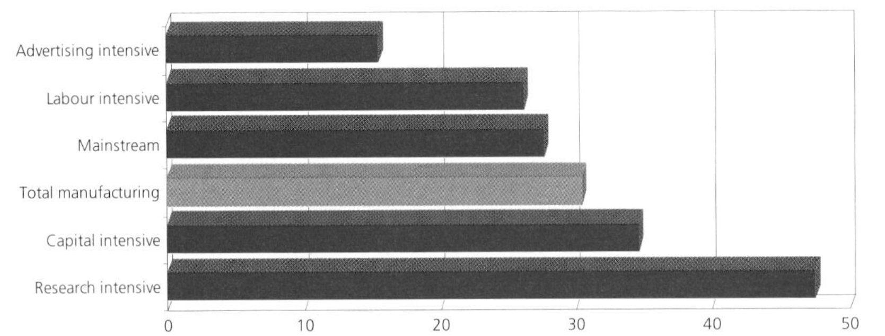

Source: Eurostat (SBS), WIFO calculations

Looking at aggregated unit values across the five industry types in European trade, exports and imports are ranked identically (see Figure 4.3). Thanks to ample opportunities for vertical differentiation, research intensive industries show by far the highest unit values. Mainstream manufacturing with its large share in the skill-dependent and development-oriented machinery sector comes in second, followed by labour, advertising and finally capital intensive industries. The latter clearly reflects an early stage in the production chain and its accordingly high weight of raw materials.

Since advertising entered the analysis precisely because of its presumed ability to raise perceived quality, the low ranking of advertising intensive industries may come as a surprise. Although mostly directed towards final consumers, the explanation is in part analogous to the case of capital intensive industries, due to lacking depth in the value added chain and the relatively high importance of initial material inputs, for example in the food sector. Another explanation is linked to the presumed horizontal nature of product differentiation within this group of advertising industries.

The puzzling feature is that individual consumers may experience a sort of vertical differentiation, since advertising tends to raise consumer willingness to pay via perceived quality. Nevertheless, the same does not apply to aggregate markets, in which different consumers have distinct valuations for the differentiated attributes. Thus, at the industry level, competing brands within this group are best interpreted as varieties, for which quality is not strictly comparable on a single vertical scale and therefore goods are horizontally differentiated. Finally, average unit values may be dampened by the dualistic nature of advertising intensive industries, where high quality brands often coexist with low priced unbranded products.

A number of different methods can be used to measure the degree of vertical product differentiation. Comparing standard deviations of unit values in European trade, vertical differentiation is almost entirely absorbed by the group of research intensive industries, for which the dispersion of unit values is consistently high and far above the four other groupings (see Figure 4.4). This result also corresponds to the calculations of Grubel-Lloyd indices applied at the 6-digit level, which measure the extent of differentiated intra-industry trade versus inter-industry trade.

Growth, employment, productivity

Turning to the dynamic characteristics across industry types, growth in market demand for the total of the EU, Japan and the USA shows some substantial variations. In particular, demand for capital intensive industries lags behind total manufacturing (see Figure 4.6). As a consequence of low demand, capital intensive industries also experience the lowest growth in value added and the highest decreases in employment.

Despite average growth in market demand, growth in the value added of labour intensive industries lags behind total manufacturing because of increasing competition from low wage economies (see Figure 4.7). Since growth in productivity matches total manufacturing (see Figure 4.8), employment is decreasing faster (see Figure 4.9).

For the advertising industries, both growth in market demand and growth in labour productivity largely correspond to total manufacturing. Nevertheless, the decrease in employment is the lowest of all five industry types, as a result of benefits from the high, above average growth in value added. Partly reflecting specific local demand conditions, partly reflecting the great importance of multinational production, the ratio of total trade to production is again the lowest across all types of industry.

In research intensive industries, market demand moves ahead faster than in any other category and growth in value added is second only to that in the advertising intensive industries. Also exhibiting the highest rates of productivity growth and the greatest exposure to international trade, employment nevertheless decreased at a faster rate than in total manufacturing.

(%) Figure 4.6

Annual growth of market demand for Triad manufacturing, 1989 to 1996

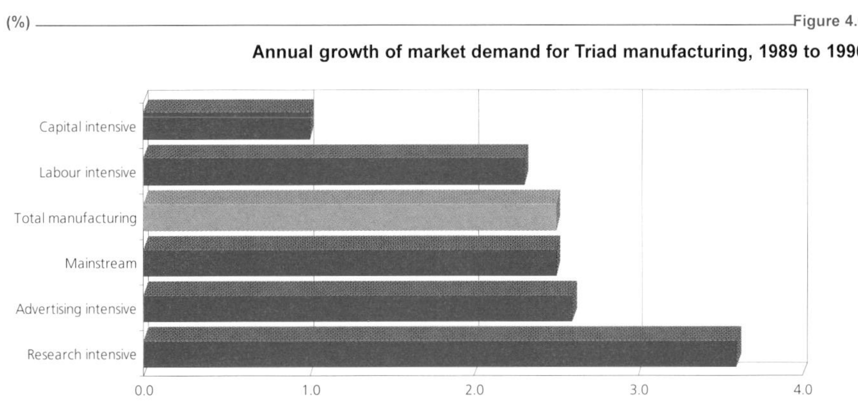

Source: Eurostat (SBS), WIFO calculations

(%) Figure 4.7

Annual growth of value added for Triad manufacturing, 1989 to 1996

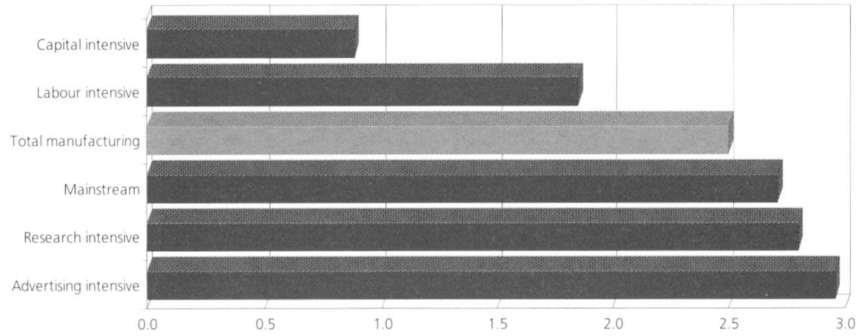

Source: Eurostat (SBS), WIFO calculations

(%) Figure 4.8

Annual growth of productivity for Triad manufacturing, 1989 to 1996

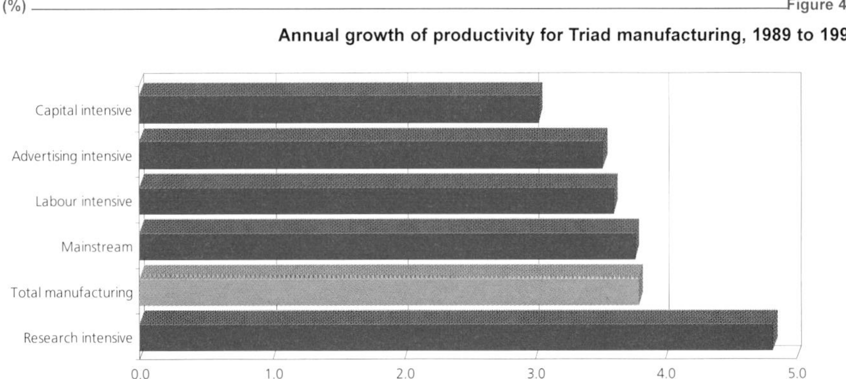

Source: Eurostat (SBS), WIFO calculations

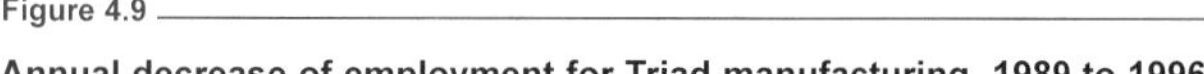

Figure 4.9 (%)

Annual decrease of employment for Triad manufacturing, 1989 to 1996

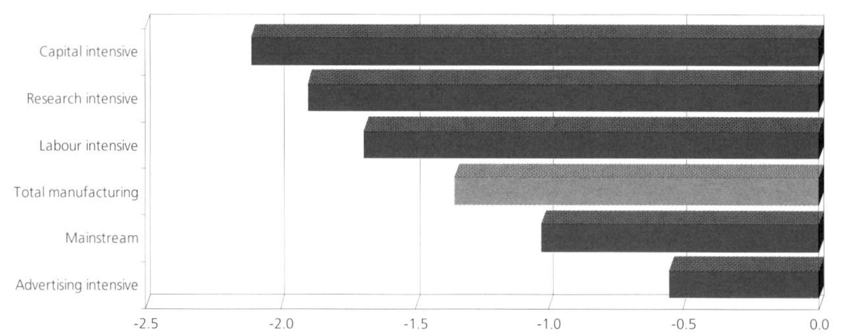

Source: Eurostat (SBS), WIFO calculations

To sum up, the following broad generalisations can be made across the five types of industry:

1. Lacking alternative options for creating competitive advantages, labour intensive industries, which produce tradable goods, are highly exposed to foreign competition on low labour costs. Despite paying the lowest wages per employee, prospects for growth in production are therefore modest.
2. Capital intensive industries can afford to pay high wages because of high labour productivity. However, they are most exposed to stagnating demand and, accordingly, to large job losses across all three major economic areas.
3. Exhibiting average growth dynamics, the high wages paid to skilled labour enables mainstream manufacturing to make attractive contributions to overall income creation.
4. In the fast-moving consumer markets made up of advertising intensive industries, the overall economic impact has been characterised by high growth dynamics paired with outstandingly low decreases in employment during the past years.
5. Finally, research intensive industries present themselves as most attractive, because of their high levels of productivity, wages and growth dynamics. In addition they are assumed to produce the most positive external effects in terms of knowledge spill-over to other industries and in terms of demand for sophisticated industry services.

4.3 Okun's law by type of industry

With respect to the analysis of the relationship between employment growth and output growth in section 2, the new typology is integrated into the panel regression on Okun's law. As before, the estimated specifications are not based on a strict economic model, but rather aim only at exploring the stylised empirical relationship concerning the amount of output growth, which is necessary for stabilising employment.

The assessment of internal performance in section 2 has already revealed some substantial differences in the employment intensity of value added growth between the EU, Japan and the USA (Specification I in Table 4.2). At this stage, however, the investigation can be carried one step further by introducing the differentiation across industry types into the panel regression (Specification II and III). Technical details are given in Box 4.2.

The new question under consideration is, whether or not the observed differences in the employment intensity of value added growth apply equally to all industry types. The panel regression reveals significant differences in the employment stabilising rates of output growth between the three economic areas according to the type of industry (see Table 4.2). Relative to a typical European industry, growth of output needed to stabilise employment is particularly low in the USA for mainstream manufacturing, labour- and capital intensive industries. In Japan, capital- and advertising intensive industries exhibit a significantly lower employment stabilising rate of output growth. The most striking result is that research intensive industries exhibit no significant differences across the three economic areas.

Box 4.2:

Okun's law in a panel regression

The relationship between employment growth and output growth is investigated in a panel of industries by regressing employment growth on growth in real value added. Fixed industry and time effects control for unobserved variables which are constant over time or over industries. The panel consists of 3-digit industries in the EU, Japan, and the USA from the SBS database provided by EUROSTAT. The estimation of fixed effect regressions produces within-group estimates. Therefore, the estimated parameter for value added growth refers to a typical industry (which emerges after correction for industry and time means). The estimated intercepts as well as the dummies for the three economic areas reflect different trends in labour productivity and/or in the capital/labour ratio. Time effects capture evenly the impact of the business cycle, to which all industries are exposed. The estimation results are summarised in Table 4.2 below.

With regard to outliers, the estimation takes a careful and restrictive approach. It includes only industries in the panel for which observations have proved valid in all three areas. Four dummies are used to control for outlying values. Additionally, ten obvious outliers have been removed. Although the panel is prone to extreme values, the estimation results are remarkably robust.

Three distinct specifications are estimated: Specification I represents the standard fixed effects model, with value added growth as well as dummies for the EU, Japan and the USA as independent variables. Specification II adds dummies for industry groups in Japan and the USA. Specification III replaces the fixed industry effects with the industry groups. The formulation of the econometric model uses the EU as a baseline, so that all coefficients referring to Japan and the USA have to be interpreted as the difference to the EU. Note that specifications II and III differ only in their definitions of the baseline: the typical EU industry is the baseline in the former, whereas the respective industry group is used as the basis for comparison in the latter case.

Table 4.2

Estimation results of the employment growth - output growth relationship

	Specification I ß	Specification I t	Specification II ß	Specification II t	Specification III ß	Specification III t
Growth in value added						
Base=EU	0.37	14.42**)	0.37	14.20**)	0.39	16.86**)
USA	0.11	2.94**)	0.10	2.78**)	0.12	3.87**)
Japan	0.02	0.52	0.03	0.69	0.00	0.13
Intercept - base = EU (average of industry effects)						
Intercept - USA	1.12	5.44**)	-	-	-	-
Mainstream industries	-	-	1.87	5.50**)	1.75	4.31**)
Labour intensive	-	-	1.32	3.22**)	1.26	3.39**)
Capital intensive	-	-	1.45	2.58**)	1.37	2.36**)
Advertising	-	-	0.18	0.48	0.26	0.63
R&D intensive	-	-	0.46	0.68	0.44	0.60
Intercept - Japan	0.99	5.34**)	-	-	-	-
Mainstream industries	-	-	0.84	2.55**)	0.87	2.16 *)
Labour intensive	-	-	0.41	1.20	0.43	1.15
Capital intensive	-	-	1.86	3.12**)	1.88	2.24**)
Advertising	-	-	1.56	4.61**)	1.72	4.10**)
R&D intensive	-	-	0.42	0.64	0.47	0.64
N=66, NT=1371						
R^2	0.57		0.58		0.53	
Standard error of the estimate	2.98		2.96		3.07	
Likelihood ratio tests for:[a]						
Fixed industry effects	167.48 (65)**)		173.72 (65)**)			
Fixed group effects					6.75 (5)	
Interactions: industry-type*US			44.48 (5)**)		44.47 (5)**)	
Interactions: industry-type*JP			33.40 (5)**)		34.00 (5)**)	
Fixed time effects	103.25 (6)**)		103.18 (6)**)		103.18 (6)**)	

Note: Time dummies and four dummies for particular high or low productivity shocks are not reported.
Estimates are corrected for heteroscedasticity.
a) degrees of freedom in paranthesis
**) significant at 1%; *) significant at 5%

Source: Eurostat (SBS), WIFO calculations

(%) Table 4.3

Average annual growth in labour productivity, 1989 to 1996

	EU	USA	Japan	Triad
Labour intensive	4.1	2.6	4.2	3.6
Capital intensive	3.1	1.7	3.0	3.0
Advertising intensive	4.9	2.5	3.1	3.5
Research intensive	5.0	5.0	4.1	4.8
Mainstream manufacturing	4.7	2.4	3.9	3.8
Total manufacturing	4.7	3.0	3.8	3.8

Source: Eurostat (SBS), WIFO calculations

This outcome is also reflected in the aggregated growth rates of labour productivity (see Table 4.3). In line with the process of catching up, growth in labour productivity has been higher in the EU than in the USA in all but the research-intensive industries. In contrast to the other four industry types, the USA managed to increase productivity at the same rate as the EU and even faster than Japan.

The general implication of this finding is not immediately clear. However, this result illustrates that catching up in labour productivity is not a mechanical certainty, irrespective of the particular industry characteristics. The fact that the USA has maintained its considerable lead in research-intensive industries indicates that this phenomenon is linked to the particulars of creating and appropriating technological knowledge. One thought-provoking interpretation might be that despite rapidly changing environments in dynamic markets, leads can be maintained over time and actually support the steady increase of sustainable competitive advantages. This suggests an increase in the obstacles to catching up, the more complex production technologies are. Certainly, further research into the general patterns, directions and speed of catching up processes across industries is needed, in order to draw more firm and robust conclusions on this observation.

Table 4.4 (%)

Competitive performance by type of industry (1)

	Share in world market						Value added shares in the Triad					
	EU		USA		Japan		EU		USA		Japan	
	1989	1996	1989	1996	1989	1996	1989	1996	1989	1996	1989	1996
Labour intensive	28.0	25.6	10.4	9.8	11.5	9.4	35.0	35.4	36.7	36.5	28.3	28.1
Capital intensive	21.7	22.7	19.3	19.3	11.5	11.7	34.9	31.8	37.1	38.6	28.0	29.6
Advertising intensive	28.6	26.3	16.4	15.4	5.8	3.6	30.1	32.1	47.1	45.2	22.8	22.7
Research intensive	22.8	24.3	25.7	22.1	31.7	20.5	29.7	29.8	46.3	46.9	24.0	23.2
Mainstream manufacturing	40.0	37.4	21.3	21.0	23.1	17.6	34.0	34.1	38.3	38.4	27.6	27.6
Total manufacturing	27.0	26.9	20.2	18.8	19.2	14.5	32.5	32.9	41.9	41.6	25.7	25.6

(1) Market share: defined as exports as a percentage of world imports.

Source: Eurostat (SBS, Compet), WIFO calculations

4.4 Competitive performance

The purpose of the new typology is to compare performance across the three major economic areas by reference to analytical benchmarks of the underlying forces of the competitive market process. Accordingly, the strategic options available to enterprises for strengthening specific advantages are highlighted. In order to provide a comprehensive assessment of the relative strengths and weaknesses, both the relative shares of industry types in total production, as well as the export shares of each economic area in world imports, will be examined.

With regard to overall shares in the world market, as well as in domestic production, the EU is strongest in mainstream industries (see Table 4.4), partly focusing on skill intensive sub-segments. In labour intensive industries, Europe consistently holds above average shares in value added, but below average shares in export markets. Capital and advertising intensive industries hold average shares in value added.

In the case of Japan, shares in domestic value added and world trade do not easily match. The former are much more evenly distributed, whereas the market shares of Japan's exports in world imports are highest in research intensive industries, followed by other mainstream technologies. In both cases, between 1989 and 1996, competition from emerging economies outside these three areas caused a sharp decline in market shares. Japan kept a low profile as an exporter of products from labour intensive and above all from advertising intensive industries.

In contrast to the EU, the USA is characterised by a strong - albeit in trade figures slightly eroding - position in research intensive industries, and low shares in labour intensive industries. Shares in capital intensive and other mainstream industries are broadly in line with the overall size of the economy. Advertising intensive industries exhibit high shares in domestic production, but low shares in foreign trade, indicating the particular importance of multinational activities, presumably substituting exports with foreign direct investment.

Focusing on research intensive industries, the EU has maintained its strong position within the research-intensive branches of the chemicals sector, particularly in the fast-growing pharmaceuticals industry (see Table 4.5). At the same time, the EU gained market shares in both value added and world trade in innovative industries related to transport. In air and spacecraft, the EU considerably narrowed the gap in foreign trade, and also caught up in value added relative to the USA. In contrast, within the automobile industry, the EU won shares mainly at the expense of Japan. The EU also defended its strong position in the manufacturing of electrical machinery and control apparatus.

Partly reflecting stronger demand on world markets than on domestic markets, the EU's trade balance for the group of research intensive industries turned from a deficit of ECU 12 billion in 1989 to a surplus of ECU 27 billion in 1996. This was mainly due to improving balances in motor vehicles, pharmaceuticals and other chemicals, as well as in telecommunication equipment. The only research-intensive industries in which the trade balance deteriorated were office machinery and electronic components. The share of research-intensive industries in value added remained constant.

Isolating those industries related to the information and communication technologies, the other "non-ICT" research-intensive industries show quite a favourable performance in the EU. Production in this sub-segment is growing faster in Europe than in either the USA or Japan, and trade is creating a higher surplus than in Japan, while the USA is suffering a deficit. European shares in exports are growing, and shares in value added correspond to the average of total manufacturing.

On the other hand, this split pins down the actual area of concern, namely information and communication technologies (ICTs), such as office machinery, electronic components, audio-visual apparatus, and sophisticated applications in medical equipment and precision instruments. All of these have remained either American or Japanese strongholds. It is only in the manufacturing of telecommunication equipment that the EU has shown some strength. However, in that field American leadership benefits largely from the added stimulus of rapid growth in domestic demand.

(%) Table 4.5

Competitive performance in research intensive industries (1)

	Share in world market						Value added shares in the Triad					
	EU		USA		Japan		EU		USA		Japan	
	1989	1996	1989	1996	1989	1996	1989	1996	1989	1996	1989	1996
Agro-chemical products	74.1	67.2	51.8	31.7	12.5	5.9	27.1	30.3	59.9	57.8	13.0	11.9
Pharmaceuticals	56.5	56.1	21.8	17.4	7.1	5.4	29.7	31.3	41.1	42.8	29.2	25.9
Other chemicals	29.9	32.2	26.8	30.0	24.3	22.2	29.4	29.9	52.2	48.5	18.4	21.5
Office machinery	11.5	10.4	29.0	20.0	29.3	17.7	27.3	21.8	40.7	49.9	32.1	28.2
Electricity apparatus	35.9	37.3	22.3	21.0	31.1	25.7	47.9	45.8	28.9	28.8	23.2	25.3
Electronic components	8.8	8.9	22.8	17.4	31.9	24.3	8.9	8.6	42.7	55.4	48.4	36.0
Telecom equipment	23.9	34.4	16.8	23.1	54.1	19.4	34.7	28.9	46.3	40.4	19.0	30.7
Audio visual apparatus	7.7	10.5	9.8	10.1	42.0	17.1	30.7	27.3	7.3	7.1	62.0	65.6
Medical equipment	38.4	36.1	41.7	41.7	19.6	12.8	20.8	24.0	65.8	66.8	13.4	9.2
Precision instruments	32.8	30.5	36.2	33.2	18.7	18.5	21.6	26.2	65.2	58.8	13.1	15.0
Optical instruments	20.7	18.9	16.7	13.2	46.3	31.9	17.1	23.6	56.3	55.7	26.6	20.7
Motor vehicles	24.4	30.9	12.9	15.8	45.9	31.5	44.2	47.6	36.4	37.5	19.4	14.9
Air- and spacecraft	37.1	53.0	68.9	58.0	1.2	2.0	21.3	26.5	76.3	69.6	2.3	3.8

(1) Market share: defined as exports as a percentage of world imports; they do not add up due to divergent methods of reporting.

Source: Eurostat (SBS, Compet), WIFO calculations

Sectoral structures within the EU exhibit a high degree of disparity (see Table 4.6). Labour intensive industries are most prominent in the exports of Portugal, Greece and Italy. Capital intensive industries account for particularly high shares in Finland and Sweden, Belgium/Luxembourg, the Netherlands and Greece. Of all EU Member States, Italy has the highest share in mainstream manufacturing, followed by Austria, Germany and Denmark. Advertising industries contribute most to total manufacturing exports in Denmark, Greece, the Netherlands and Ireland. Research intensive industries exhibit the highest shares in Ireland, the United Kingdom, France, and to a lesser extent Sweden and Germany. However, as the data only reveal the share of research-intensive products, but not the share of a country's own innovative effort, interpretation should be guarded. For example in the case of Ireland, the importance of large and recent inflows of multinational investment is particularly striking, whereas for example the more modest share in Germany may be more closely associated with new research effort.

(%) Table 4.6

Share in manufacturing exports, 1996

	Labour intensive	Capital intensive	Advertising intensive	Research intensive	Mainstream manufacturing
B	12.17	26.43	13.81	27.81	19.77
DK	14.78	9.64	30.07	18.36	27.16
D	9.77	19.11	9.64	33.60	27.88
EL	23.82	29.30	28.59	4.92	13.36
E	10.96	21.50	17.29	31.96	18.29
F	8.66	17.06	17.13	36.88	20.28
IRL	3.99	13.98	21.76	51.61	8.66
I	20.18	13.89	15.58	16.14	34.21
NL	6.15	24.87	22.34	30.09	16.55
A	16.13	18.43	11.70	22.76	30.98
P	30.23	13.17	17.01	22.56	17.03
FIN	15.01	35.90	5.33	20.34	23.42
S	11.49	25.91	5.34	33.98	23.28
UK	8.73	16.08	12.08	42.17	20.93

Source: Eurostat (Comext), WIFO calculations

4.5 Summary

To sum up, the analysis of underlying forces of competitive performance has produced the following broad picture of the EU's structural strengths and weaknesses.

Relative to Japan and the USA, industrial production in the EU exhibits the highest degree of specialisation in more traditional industries, which are still based to a large extent on labour inputs and physical capital. The EU proves its considerable technological competence and skills in mainstream manufacturing and the research-intensive industries outside the ICT sector.

Nevertheless, performance is poor compared to that of the USA and Japan in the fastest moving markets, characterised either by recent technological upturns, as in the case of ICTs, or by easily shifting consumer tastes in the advertising industries. The data suggest that the EU has missed opportunities to benefit more from the high growth dynamics of these industries, particularly when compared with the USA.

5. GLOBAL INVESTMENT AND MULTINATIONAL FIRMS

In the preceding section, the underlying forces of structural development were investigated with a strong focus on competitive advantages generated by investments in innovation and marketing. It is precisely the exploitation of these firm-specific advantages, which is commonly viewed as a major motivation for multinational activity. Alongside increasing trade volumes, multinational activity is apparently the main driving force of the globalisation process, with far-reaching influences on both the performance and structure of the economy.

Following an introductory discussion of theoretical perspectives in section 5.1, this section looks at two aspects of multinational enterprises (MNEs) in the European context. In section 5.2, a novel data set is used to describe the changing structure of European manufacturing industry between 1987 and 1993 and the role of MNEs therein. This is a micro database containing detailed information on turnover, market shares and diversification across industries, as well as on the multinationality, of the EU's leading manufacturing firms. The database is used here mainly to explore the structural implications of intra-EU multinationality. Subsequently in section 5.3, statistics on foreign direct investment (FDI) are explored at a more aggregate level. This section investigates the interrelationship between extra-EU multinationality and trade performance from 1989 to 1995. It compares the 5 largest EU Member States with Japan and the USA, using both descriptive statistics and an econometric model.

5.1 Determinants and structural impact of multinational activity

At the level of individual enterprises, the exploitation of firm specific assets (knowledge-based or derived from special organisational know-how, brands or reputation) is the most common explanation of multinational activity. In addition, constraints on growth in the firm's primary/home market often provide important push factors. The decision to set up plants abroad and become multinational is also influenced by tariff and non-tariff impediments, as well as transport costs which may render exportation a sub-optimal means of servicing foreign markets. In broad terms, this reflects proximity advantages such as easier market access and the supply of additional services, more efficient distribution systems, transportation costs, tariffs and non-tariff barriers to trade. On the other hand, economies of scale at plant level tend to favour exporting over multinational activities.

However, whilst the proximity/plant size trade-off is often the driving force behind the export versus foreign production decision, it does not capture the whole story. Many firms invest abroad for strategic reasons. In particular, mergers and acquisitions based on strategic motives now form an important part of FDI. Another important aspect of multinational activity lies in the specialisation within the organisation of firms. Increasingly, parts of the production process are being spread across countries within the organisation of multinational enterprises, according to the comparative advantages of home and host countries. In particular for firms located in high wage economies, this is an important strategy for remaining competitive in world markets.

The costs and benefits of multinational activity in the European context depend crucially on its motivation and on industry characteristics, as well as its impact on structural development. On the one hand, by supplementing trade, FDI might create stronger links between economies. Intra-EU FDI, in particular, may foster the European integration process. Moreover, to the extent that FDI facilitates the exploitation of comparative advantage, this should increase specialisation within the EU, resulting in pronounced structural effects on employment, productivity and growth. On the other hand, high costs, over-regulation and insufficient dynamism in the European economy might lead investors to set up plants at more favourable locations, using FDI as a substitute for exports and choosing to supply the European market with imports.

Perhaps more importantly, the growing importance of MNEs within individual markets may sometimes be a cause of concern in competition policy: the very specific assets which give the MNEs their cutting edge may also result in a dampening of competition - both between incumbents and from potential entrants. If so, the expected benefits from the expansion of the European market may be constrained by the increased market shares of the leading firms, who are able to exploit market power, both at the aggregate European level and (where applicable) in national markets.

5.2 The multinationality of Europe's leading manufacturers[19]

Using a unique database of leading manufacturers within the EU, this section assesses the extent of and trends in (1987-1993) multinational activity, diversification and concentration in the EU (see Box 5.1). For each of nearly 100 disaggregated 3-digit industries, the 5 largest EU-producers were identified. The market shares within the EU of all such firms were estimated, as well as their production across industries and across each of the Member States. The resulting database amounts to a three dimensional matrix, in which firms' EU turnovers are disaggregated across industries, and then, within industries, across the Member States. This provides a rich source of information on the structure of individual markets, and the market shares, multinationality and diversification of individual firms. The database is available for two years, 1987 and 1993, and the sample includes about 300 firms and 96 industries in both years. During 1987 and 1993, these firms accounted for roughly one third of the entire turnover of the manufacturing sector in the EU. However, it should be remembered that the data are confined exclusively to manufacturing within the EU.

Box 5.1:
The leading manufacturers in the EU

This database is based on three criteria. First it includes all firms which can be defined as "leading" EU manufacturers, in the sense that, measured by the scale of their turnover produced within the EU, they are amongst the largest 5 firms in at least one 3-digit manufacturing industry. Secondly, for all firms satisfying the first criterion, data were collected on their turnover in all the industries in which they operate (not only those industries in which they are "leaders" in the above sense). Thirdly, all such estimates were compiled for both the EU as an aggregate and for all individual Member States in which the firm operates. It should be noted that (i) some firms will have non-EU parents, (ii) estimates are confined only to manufacturing operations in the EU.

The sources of the data are mainly company reports, supplemented by business directories, financial databases etc. Throughout, size is measured by the value of turnover produced in the EU. A detailed statement of the underlying data methodology can be found in Davies-Lyons, et al. (1996).

Table 5.1

Countries of origin of the EU's leading firms and their intra-EU multinationality (1)

Country	Number of firms	1987 Total sales (billion ECU)	1987 % outside home country	1993 Total sales (billion ECU)	1993 % outside home country
D	64	214.0	11.5	276.5	13.9
UK	52	113.3	20.9	110.1	29.2
F	48	136.5	20.7	161.4	31.3
I	47	72.1	12.1	87.0	22.8
NL	9	39.7	51.9	45.6	59.5
Other Member States	22	16.9	20.0	25.2	25.0
Non-EU firms	53	98.4	100.0	141.6	100.0
EU	294	689.8	29.9	846.4	37.3

(1) Two anglo/dutch firms (Unilever and Royal Dutch Shell) and the anglo/french firm (GEC/Alsthom) have been allocated 50:50 to the United Kingdom, the Netherlands and France respectively.

Source: Davies-Rondi-Sembenellli, 1998

Intra-EU multinationality

Two thirds of these firms originate from the four largest Member States, and over 50 of the others are subsidiaries of non-EU (mainly the USA) MNEs (see Table 5.1). The latter statistic is testament to the significance of inward FDI from outside the EU, and the former establishes the dominant roles of Germany, France, the United Kingdom and Italy (although, the Netherlands is also an important source of a few very large firms). In 1987, these firms produced nearly 30% of their EU turnover outside of their home countries. Moreover, between 1987 and 1993 there was a pronounced increase in this intra-EU multinationality (outside home country shares rose from 30% to 37%).

This trend of increasing intra-EU multinationality can be found in all the major Member States. From Table 5.2, it can be seen that Germany, France, the United Kingdom, Italy and Spain (in that order) are the major host countries, whilst France, Germany, the United Kingdom, the Netherlands and Italy are the major sources. Non-EU based multinationals continue to account for nearly half of the inward production in manufacturing.

Multinational operations are highest in differentiated product industries, but they have also grown across the board. This underlines the importance of firm-specific assets as the main characteristic of multinational firms.

Industries most sensitive to the Single European Market have experienced some of the major increases. This confirms that the establishment of the Single European Market has led not only to an expansion of intra-EU trade volumes, but also that firms have responded by setting-up additional plants in other Member States. This is not in line with the hypothesis that multinationality is influenced by a proximity to the market/plant size trade off (since, as non-tariff barriers to trade have diminished, one might have expected that more firms would switch to exports).

The main reason for this increase in intra-EU multinational activity would appear to lie in corporate strategy. Firms expand production in foreign Member States for strategic reasons, for example as a response to the potential entry of new exporting firms. Multinational enterprises based outside the EU invested directly to circumvent barriers to trade and/or to participate in the further integration of the large European market. In this case trade is likely to be substituted, creating new jobs within the EU[20].

19) The results in this section are taken from a recently completed and updated 1993 "EU-market share matrix", produced by Rondi and Sembenelli (of CERIS-CNR, Turin) and Davies. The authors gratefully acknowledge their debt to Rondi and Sembenelli, and thank them for their permission to draw on this matrix so soon after the completion of their own data collection work. A more comprehensive discussion of the matrix, and what it reveals about the structure of EU manufacturing is to be found in Davies, S.W., Rondi, L., Sembenelli, A., "Industrial Organisation in EU Manufacturing: Dynamics, 1987-93" (as a University of East Anglia Discussion Paper, 1998). An earlier version of the matrix was produced for the late 1980s, reported in Davies, S., Lyons, B., et al., "Industrial Organisation in the European Union", Structure, Strategy, and the Competitive Mechanism, Oxford University Press, Oxford, 1996.

20) Belderbos, R., Sleuwaegen, L., "Tariff Jumping DFI and Export Substitution: Japanese Electronics Firms in Europe", International Journal of Industrial Organisation, Vol. XVI, No 5, 1998, pp. 601-638.

Table 5.2 (%)

Aggregate inward and outward flows of MNEs (1)

Country	Inward: Production by firms originating from outside — 1993 share of EU total	Inward: 1987/1993 growth (%)	Outward: Production in other Member States — 1993 share of EU total	Outward: 1987/1993 growth (%)
B	7.2	22.0	2.0	102.6
F	17.2	57.3	16.0	78.8
D	27.3	58.0	12.2	56.8
I	11.2	60.9	6.3	127.3
NL	5.7	78.1	8.4	28.7
E	10.2	46.2	:	:
UK	17.1	48.3	10.2	36.0
Other Member States	3.9	58.8	0.2	:
Non-EU states	:	:	44.8	45.2
EU	100.0	53.1	100.0	53.1

(1) Two anglo/dutch firms (Unilever and Royal Dutch Shell) and the anglo/french firm (GEC/Alsthom) have been allocated 50:50 to the United Kingdom, the Netherlands and France respectively.

Source: Davies-Rondi-Sembenellli, 1998

The Top 100

Comparing the joint turnover of the top 100 firms in this database between 1987 and 1993, it does not appear that this increase in intra-EU multinationality has led to an increased aggregate concentration in European manufacturing as a whole. In fact, the share of the top 100 has remained more or less constant, falling marginally (by roughly 30%).

This has occurred despite an increase in the index of multinationality for these firms from 2.4 to 2.87 (i.e. about 20%, see Table 5.3). The other row in the table shows part of the reason why this has not led to increased aggregate concentration: whilst these very large firms have increased their multinationality, they have also tended to decrease their diversification across industries.

Table 5.3

Concentration, diversification and multinationality of the top 100 firms in EU manufacturing (1)

Aggregate concentration	1987	1993
Share of top 100 firms (%)	29.60	28.60
Diversification index	4.34	3.95
Intra EU multinationality index	2.40	2.87

(1) These indices indicate in how many countries and in how many markets a firm is typically working. Increasing entropy indices of diversification and multinationality reflect both an increasing number of industries and countries in which the firms operate, and/or growing scales of operations. The index is calculated as number equivalent of the mean entropy index, which shows how many equally sized firms would be required to produce this concentration. The entropy index is defined as: $-\sum_{i=1}^{n} s_i \ln s$, where s_i measures the country or industry share. The figures shown are the arithmetic averages for the top 100.

Source: Davies-Rondi-Sembenellli, 1998

Notwithstanding this return to core activities, it is clear that the top 100 firms remain very large in terms of their aggregate sales, and that they are very often the leaders in many individual markets (see Table 5.4). In the typical industry 2 or 3 of the 5 market leaders come from within the top 100 firms. Indeed, in 57 of the 96 industries, the largest firm is from the top 100.

Market concentration

This leads to the key anti-trust question: has the increased multinationality of Europe's very largest manufacturers resulted in increasing concentration (and potentially market power) within individual markets? In fact, market concentration also appears to have remained more or less constant on average: in the typical industry, the top 5 firms account for 25.7% of the market (see Table 5.5). This is a one-percentage point increase compared to 1987, but this difference is not statistically significant. This is not to say, however, there are not distinct differences between types of industry - in both the level of, and changes in, concentration. "No change on average" conceals a multitude of significant differences and changes between individual firms and industries. In particular, concentration has tended to arise in two broad types of industry: (i) where advertising is prominent, and (ii) where the EU anticipated major structural effects of the Single European Market Programme. The latter suggests that there has been an impact resulting from the establishment of the Single Market, where major welfare effects - besides lower prices from increased competition - were expected from the removal of market imperfections and consequent exploitation of scale economies. The former - increasing concentration in advertising industries - can be interpreted in terms of Sutton's endogenous sunk cost explanation of market structure (see Box 5.2). In these industries, concentration does not decrease as market size increases because incumbent firms invest heavily in advertising, with a resulting increase in the height of entry barriers for potential entrants.

Diversification

Returning to the top 100 firms, nearly all are significantly diversified across manufacturing industries: the average entropy index is about 4 (see Table 5.3). This is a "numbers equivalent index", which indicates that, on average, these firms spread their turnover across markets with a distribution which is arithmetically equivalent to operating on equal scales in four different industries. Since this index tends to weigh small-scale operations only very marginally, a numerical equivalent of 4 is indicative of widespread diversification - often across up to more than 10 markets.

Nevertheless, it is the case that this diversification declined between 1987 and 1993 - albeit not drastically. Perhaps this is to be expected, bearing in mind the widespread anecdotal evidence in recent years of a "return to core business", but it still raises an intriguing question. According to the intangible specific asset story, both R&D and advertising expenditures often form the basis of firms' competitive advantages. In many cases, these are not transferable via arm's-length trade and are best exploited by internalisation within the firm. This should apply to both diversification and multinationality, yet we have observed that, during this period, the former has tended to decrease, whilst the latter has increased strongly. Undoubtedly, this divergence deserves further analysis.

Table 5.4

The prominence of top 100 firms in individual markets, 1993

	1993
Number of top 100 firms in the top 5 in the average industry	2.6
Probability that a top 100 firm will be ranked no. x in a given 3 digit industry:	
no.1	0.6
no.2	0.6
no.3	0.6
no.4	0.5
no.5	0.4

Source: Davies-Rondi-Sembenellli, 1998

Box 5.2:

Multinational activity - theoretical perspectives

Starting with the work of Dunning (1994)[a] on ownership advantages, locational advantages and internationalisation, economic modelling provides two strands on the role of firm-specific assets in the relationship between multinationality and trade.

General equilibrium models

First, there is a small body of literature using general equilibrium models (e.g. Brainard, 1993, Markusen-Venables, 1995 and 1996)[b]. In the Helpman-Krugman model[c], firms expand vertically by setting up plants in low wage countries and by producing skill-intensive intermediates as well as headquarter services at the MNE's home in high wage countries. Since these models do not take transportation costs - or more general proximity advantages - into consideration, they are only able to explain one-way FDI according to a north-south type pattern. More recent approaches have introduced transportation costs, interpreted in the broad sense of advantages from proximity to the market. They can explain the widely found two-way pattern of multinational activity and trade between similarly endowed countries, depending on the trade-off between proximity advantages on the one hand and economies of scale at the enterprise and plant level on the other. The key propositions of these models are that (i) MNE activity is more intensive the more similar countries are, (ii) high trade costs tend to favour FDI over exporting - and discourage it if plant economies of scale are important and (iii) exports and MNE activity may grow complementarily over time (Pfaffermayr, 1997)[d]. Moreover, Markusen-Venables (1996), conclude that (iv) convergence in income levels between the major trading blocks (EU, USA and Japan) may be one cause of growth in multinational activities. Their model furthermore suggests that convergence in country size may not be associated with growing volumes of intra-industry trade as some of this trade is displaced by multinationals. (v) In this model the world, as a whole, benefits from multinationals, but the gains accrue disproportionately to countries which would have had more national firms in the absence of multinationals. There may also be a welfare loss for a country which would have had a large share of world industry in the absence of multinationals.

Industrial organisation

The second strand is the industrial organisation literature, which takes a partial equilibrium approach, but still remains within a model structure embodying a trade off between proximity advantages and economies of scale (e.g. Horstmann-Markusen, 1992)[e]. It illustrates the commitment value of FDI in the corporate strategies of multinational firms, and, furthermore, shows that setting-up plants abroad, instead of exporting, is significantly related to market structure (causation goes in both directions). In many cases, multinational activity is motivated by first mover advantages and market access, but not necessarily by cost motives. Multinational enterprises are expected to be most active in what have become known as endogenous sunk-cost industries[f]. These industries are characterised by large and escalating expenditures on advertising as well as research and development (the scales of which are endogenously determined in the oligopoly game). These endogenous sunk costs are precisely those employed to exploit the firm specific assets usually associated with MNEs.

[a] Dunning, J.H., "Multinational Enterprises and the Global Economy", Addison-Wesley, Wokingham, 1994.

[b] See Brainard, S.L., "A Simple Theory of Multinational Corporations with a Trade-off between Proximity and Concentration", NBER-Working paper, No 4269, 1993, Markusen, J.R., Venables, A.J., "Multinational Firms and the New Trade Theory", NBER-Working Paper, No 5036, 1995, Markusen, J.R., Venables, A.J., "The Theory of Endowment, Intra-Industry and Multinational Trade", Centre for Economic Policy Research, Discussion Paper, No 5036, February 1995.

[c] Helpman, E., Krugman, P., "Market Structure and Foreign Trade", MIT - Press, Cambridge, MA, 1985.

[d] Pfaffermayr, M., "Multinational firms, trade and growth: a simple model with a trade off between proximity to the market and plant set-up costs under international trade in assets", WIFO Working Paper, No. 90, 1997.

[e] Horstmann, I.J., Markusen, J.R., "Endogenous Market Structures in International Trade (natura facit saltum)", Journal of International Economics, No 32, 1992, pp. 109-129.

[f] Sutton, J., "Sunk Costs and Market Structure", MIT Press, Cambridge, MA, 1991.

(%) Table 5.5

Change in concentration by industry type

	Mean C5		
	1987	1993	1987/93 (% change)
All manufacturing	24.5	25.7	1.2
By sensitivity to SEM			
high	29.0	32.4	3.4
medium	24.1	23.9	-0.2
low	23.5	25.0	1.5
By type of product			
homogeneous	16.5	18.0	1.5
Differentiated			
by advertising only	22.1	25.1	3.0
by R&D only	34.2	33.6	-0.6
by both advertising and R&D	40.4	41.5	1.1

Source: Davies-Rondi-Sembenellli, 1998

5.3 FDI and trade

Due to data constraints, this section must take a more aggregated, sectoral approach. It first describes the structure and trends of outward and inward FDI[21] of the five major EU-Member States, and contrasts them with the FDI-activities of Japan and the USA, in order to identify particular areas of European competitive strength. It then tests the common determinants of trade and investment in a panel regression, in order to identify whether they are primarily complements or substitutes.

The capacity to attract foreign direct investment benefits the EU in creating new jobs, in taking advantage of the transfer of knowledge and technology and in this way assists the ongoing structural change in European industry. On the other hand, the outward investments of European firms may foster their competitive positions and improve or initiate their access to foreign markets. In as much as outward investment is based on a cost minimising strategy to relocate to low cost countries, it may also indicate lacking European attractiveness as a location of production.

FDI can take a variety of forms, including greenfield investments as well as mergers and acquisitions of existing firms. Here, the stock of FDI is measured as the book value of tangible and intangible assets held by multinational firms in foreign countries[22].

From a conceptual point of view, the distinction between horizontal and vertical investments is particularly important (although, the data provide no information in this respect). Horizontal investments are presumably determined by the proximity/plant size trade-off as well as cost considerations, whereas vertical investments either secure supply of intermediates and materials or are market orientated to provide additional services locally. Vertical investments do not lead to a de-location of production, but may be viewed as a necessary means of increasing export performance. Horizontal foreign direct investment may relocate production, and thereby reduce employment opportunities depending on the height of trade barriers (and more generally the costs of lacking proximity to the markets), economies of scale in production and the importance of knowledge-based firm-specific assets.

21) The study uses FDI-data provided by the OECD and Eurostat (OECD, 1996, Eurostat, 1996) at a sectoral level. Although the disaggregation is not detailed enough from an industrial economics perspective, it is the most comprehensive source covering inward as well as outward flows and stocks of FDI for most OECD-countries. It is possible to construct a common database with structural indicators at the same level of aggregation for the 1980s and 1990s.
22) This is only an imperfect measure of multinational activity as it is heavily affected by differences in valuation and accounting standards, but, unfortunately, data on better measures are unavailable for these purposes.

Table 5.6 (%)

Flows of FDI: share of total FDI, 1996

	Outflows to			Inflows from		
	EU-5	USA	Japan	EU-5	USA	Japan
F	62.7	24.0	0.3	62.4	23.0	2.5
NL	55.0	12.5	4.1	53.5	16.4	7.9
D	62.2	16.6	0.5	49.8	16.2	4.9
I	82.1	8.7	0.0	69.7	7.9	2.0
UK	34.1	47.1	0.5	19.1	84.0	0.0
EU-5	56.6	23.6	0.9	49.9	32.6	3.2

Source: Eurostat, OECD, WIFO calculations

Patterns of FDI and trade

Despite these limitations, FDI-data do reveal some clear trends concerning the development of FDI and trade[23]. First, in the EU5 FDI is mainly within the EU: Table 5.6 shows, that in 1995, 56.6% of the FDI outflows from the EU5 countries were directed to other members of the EU. This figure is even higher without the United Kingdom, which invests heavily in the USA. The inflows to the EU5 show a similar pattern, with 49.9% originating from EU15 countries. Again the United Kingdom, with its strong ties to the USA, is an exception.

Secondly, time series evidence on the relation between outward FDI-flows and GDP indicates that American firms started multinationalisation earlier than the EU and Japan. In the seventies (1970-1983) the average outward FDI to GDP ratio of the EU, Japan and the USA members[24] amounted to 0.5% in the USA, 0.3% in the EU, and 0.1% in Japan (see Figure 5.1 and Table 5.7).

23) For the estimations below, a consistent data set for the five largest EU-countries, Japan, and the USA was established. As shown in the previous section, these five Member States account for the overwhelming majority of leading EU manufacturing MNEs.
24) Data on aggregate FDI flows are available for the EU countries.

Table 5.7 (%)

Outward FDI as a share of GDP (1)

Average	EU	USA	Japan
1970-83	0.03	0.05	0.01
1984-91	1.02	0.47	1.00
1992-96	1.21	1.05	0.42

(1) FDI-flows of EU include intra EU-FDI.

Source: Eurostat, OECD, WIFO calculations

In the second half of the 1980s, multinationality accelerated significantly in the European Member States, as well as in Japan, while the USA exhibited less dynamic growth and fell behind. During the 1993-recession, FDI-outward flows from Japan decreased significantly, but less so in the EU. The USA experienced a steady increase during this period, so that now the USA and the EU hold comparable positions.

Thirdly, in total manufacturing, the volume of FDI (now measured as inward and outward stock of FDI relative to production) and especially the volume of trade (measured as exports and imports relative to production) is considerably higher in the EU5 than in Japan and the USA (see Figure 5.2 and Figure 5.3). In 1995, the volume of FDI amounted to 19.0% in the EU5, compared to 13.1% in the USA and only 5.1% in Japan. For the volume of trade (including intra-EU trade), the corresponding figures are 73.3% for the EU5, 32.4% for the USA and 20.1% for Japan.

(%) Figure 5.1

Flows of total outward FDI in relation to GDP, 1970-1996

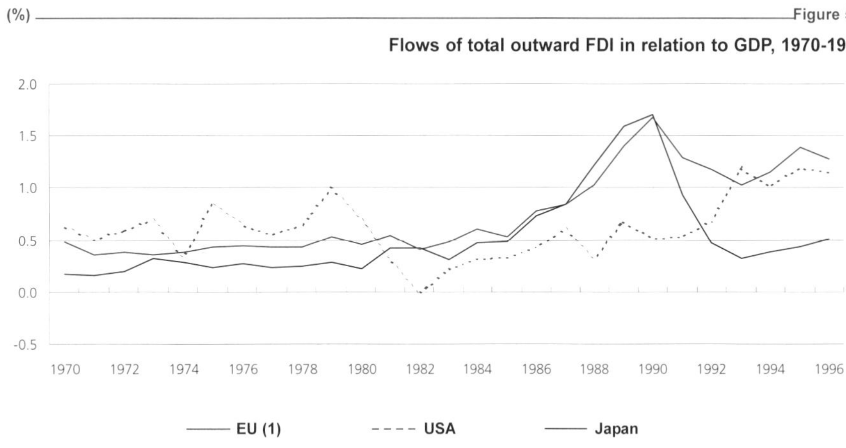

(1) EU includes intra-EU FDI.

Source: IMF

(%) Figure 5.2

Volume of trade as a share in manufacturing production

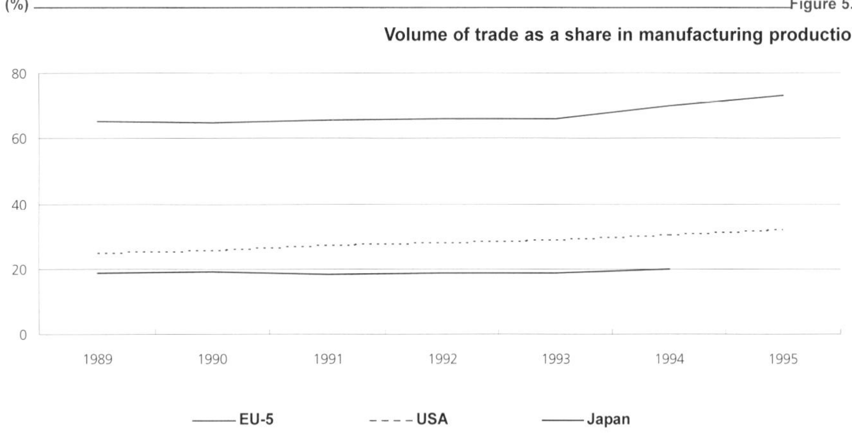

Source: Eurostat, OECD, WIFO calculations

(%) Figure 5.3

Volume of FDI as a share in manufacturing production

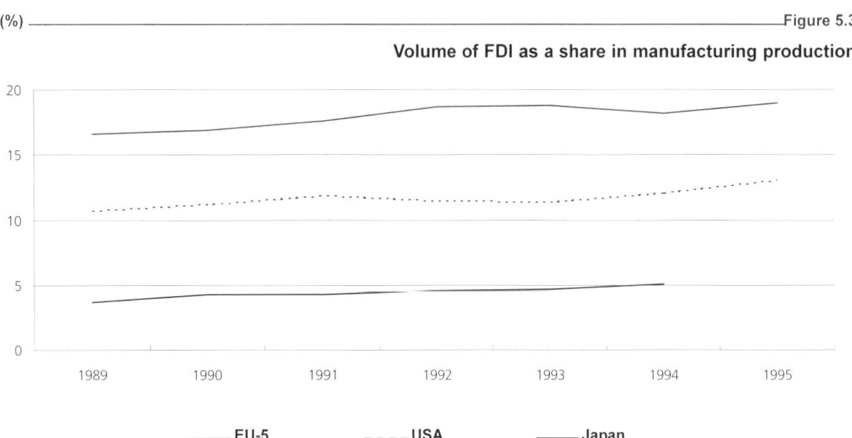

Source: Eurostat, OECD, WIFO calculations

Figure 5.4 (1989=100)

FDI vs. trade in EU-5 manufacturing: balance

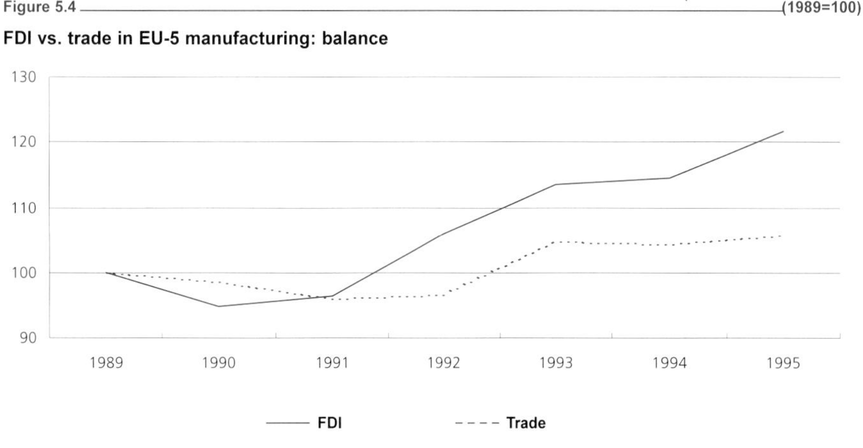

Source: Eurostat, OECD, WIFO calculations

Figure 5.5 (1989=100)

FDI vs. trade in US manufacturing: balance

130
120
110
100
90
1989 1990 1991 1992 1993 1994 1995

FDI ---- Trade

Source: Eurostat, OECD, WIFO calculations

Figure 5.6 (1989=100)

FDI vs. trade in EU-5 manufacturing: volume as a share in production

120
110
100
90
1989 1990 1991 1992 1993 1994 1995

FDI ---- Trade

Source: Eurostat, OECD, WIFO calculations

This pattern reflects proximity advantages of European countries in trade and FDI and - to a lesser extent - differences in country size. Furthermore, it underlines the important role of FDI in the European integration process. In the EU5, the outward stock outweighs inward FDI. The former increased steadily during the most recent years, whilst the latter peaked in 1992, when non-EU MNEs invested in the EU in order to take advantage of the Single European Market. The evidence suggests that the European integration process goes hand in hand with an increase in intra-EU FDI, but has not led to significant "tariff jumping" from outside since the peak in 1992. This can also be seen in figures on FDI flows, which can be decomposed into an intra- and extra-EU component (European Economy, 1996, p. 89).

Fourthly, in the period up to 1995, a pronounced increase in the volume of trade relative to production can be observed in the EU5 (8.0% points) and the USA (7.5% points), whereas Japan's increase amounted to just to 1.3 percentage points. In the EU5, most of the increase took place in 1994 and 1995, perhaps as a late consequence of the Single European Market programme. Between 1989 and 1995, the volume of FDI in relation to production grew by 2.4 percentage points in Japan, 2.4 percentage points in the EU5 and 2.3 percentage points in the USA. In all three areas, this growth in the FDI volume mainly came from increased outward FDI.

For the EU5 and the USA, a simultaneous increase in the FDI balance (outward stock over inward stock) and the trade balance (exports over imports) was observed, suggesting a complementary relationship between trade and FDI (see Figure 5.4 and Figure 5.5).

There are several reasons to expect complementarity between FDI and trade; most prominent are the large share of vertical investments, market access as a motive for FDI and the exploitation of knowledge-based firm-specific assets (see Figure 5.6 and Figure 5.7).

In Japan inward investment is negligible in size, reflecting restrictive policies in the past and domestic barriers against foreign direct investment. Outward FDI dominates by far. The FDI balance, however, does not seem to develop complementarily (see Figure 5.8 and Figure 5.9).

Figure 5.7

FDI vs. trade in US manufacturing: volume as a share in production

Source: Eurostat, OECD, WIFO calculations

Figure 5.8

FDI vs. trade in Japanese manufacturing: volume as a share in production

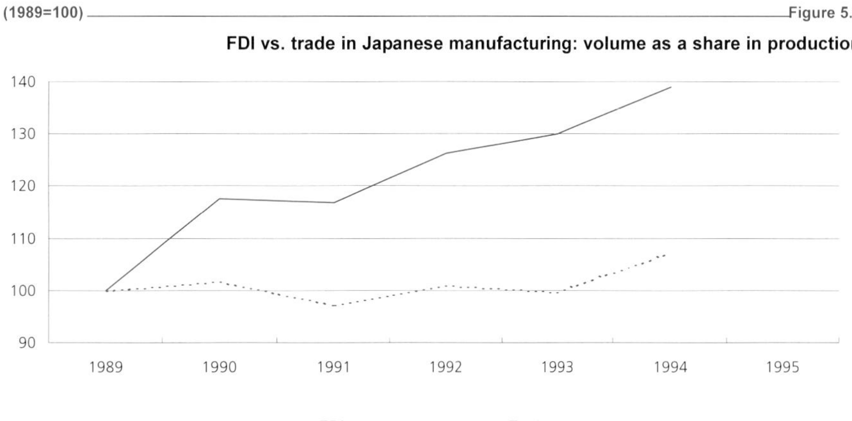

Source: Eurostat, OECD, WIFO calculations

Figure 5.9

FDI vs. trade in Japanese manufacturing: balance

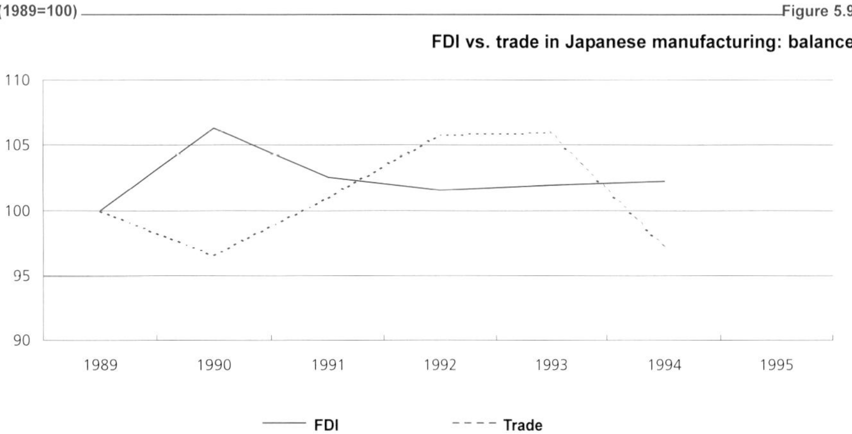

Source: Eurostat, OECD, WIFO calculations

Table 5.8 (%)

FDI and trade ratios at sectoral level, 1994

	Cover ratio		Volume as % of production			
	FDI	Trade	FDI	Inward FDI	Outward FDI	Trade
EU-5 (1)						
Food products	169.1	99.0	20.2	7.5	12.7	42.1
Textiles, wood activities	127.1	63.5	71.3	31.4	39.9	92.7
Metal and mechanical products	141.6	138.2	10.9	4.5	6.4	73.9
Petroleum, chemical. rubber, plastics	185.7	129.3	45.9	16.1	29.8	81.9
Information & communication equipment	108.8	81.5	58.3	27.9	30.4	165.8
Vehicles, transport equipment	131.2	109.3	11.6	5.0	6.6	78.7
Total manufacturing	157.8	108.6	18.2	7.1	11.2	69.9
USA						
Food products	138.5	131.8	11.5	4.8	6.7	9.5
Textiles, wood activities	85.6	52.9	20.1	10.9	9.3	18.0
Metal and mechanical products	152.2	95.1	11.3	4.5	6.8	30.6
Petroleum, chemical. rubber, plastics	108.6	127.3	30.7	14.7	16.0	22.9
Information & communication equipment	98.5	72.0	18.4	9.3	9.1	87.6
Vehicles, transport equipment	560.5	76.1	7.2	1.1	6.1	43.0
Total manufacturing	117.3	79.1	12.1	5.6	6.5	30.8
Japan						
Food products	1,311.0	5.0	2.5	0.2	2.4	11.0
Metal and mechanical products	261.1	295.9	5.9	1.6	4.3	17.4
Total manufacturing	685.4	194.8	5.1	0.6	4.4	20.1

(1) EU-5: France, the Netherlands, Germany, Italy and the United Kingdom. For the Netherlands and Italy, some industries are missing. Cover ratio: ratio of stock of FDI over inward stock of FDI, exports over imports. Volumes: inward plus outward FDI stock in relation to production, exports plus imports to production. Data for 1994 are used since they were most comprehensive in their coverage.

Source: Eurostat, OECD, WIFO calculations

Turning to the broad sectors within manufacturing, a complicated pattern of trade and FDI emerges: Table 5.8 reports on the cross-section of industries in EU5, Japan and the USA for 1994 - the year with the most comprehensive data coverage. This shows that in the EU5 and the USA, the inward and outward FDI shares in production tend to match each other, suggesting that FDI is mainly intra-industry and between similarly endowed countries.

Furthermore, there is a positive correlation between trade and FDI, both between volumes and between balances. In the EU5, outward investment is higher than inward investment in all 6 sectors, with the highest balance in petroleum and chemical products, food products, metals and mechanical products. The American balance in FDI is particularly high in the vehicles and other transport equipment industry, metals and mechanical products and food products. Measured as shares in production, the EU5 FDI volume is highest in textiles and wood processing, office machinery, the petroleum industry and chemical products. In the USA the highest FDI volumes are in petroleum and chemical products, textiles, wood processing and office machinery.

The relationship between FDI and trade has been estimated in a panel regression combining data on FDI as well as on industry structures (see Table 5.9 and Box 5.3). Summing up the major results, significant complementarity is detected in outward activities with respect to R&D intensity, openness, average capital intensity and average firm size. However, there are also some indications of a substitutional relationship with regard to unit labour costs.

Inward activities show a substitutional relationship with respect to average firm size and an insignificant relationship with respect to unit labour costs. With respect to the proximity/plants size trade-off, there is significant substitutability. This must be interpreted with care, however, due to a possible endogeneity bias.

Box 5.3:

An econometric investigation of the FDI-trade relationship

Since trade and FDI are endogenously determined by common factors, these two forms of market penetration are defined as complements/substitutes with reference to variations in any exogenous variable, if they move in the same/opposite direction in the case of an exogenous change (Pfaffermayr, 1997)[a].

The vector of explanatory variables draws on the theory of FDI and trade described earlier. The share of R&D in sales and average firm size are used as rough measures of firm-specific assets. Average firm size, defined as industry output divided by the number of enterprises, also gives information on economies of scale at the enterprise level. It is positively correlated with R&D intensity. Both form proxies for knowledge-based ownership advantages. Furthermore, capital intensity (average investment relative to production) and trade openness (exports + imports relative to production) are intended to capture the proximity/size trade-off. In order to represent unit labour costs, cost differences and specialisation are included.

Data and variables

Stocks of inward and outward foreign direct investment are only available at a highly aggregated industry level (EUROSTAT, OECD; 1997). FDI-data are matched with data on trade and industry structure. A consistent data set is available for the EU5 (France, the Netherlands, Germany, Italy, the United Kingdom), Japan and the USA. For the Netherlands, Italy and Japan some industries are missing. Thus, consistent data on 6 industries and 7 countries over the period 1989 to 1995 - in an unbalanced three-way panel - form the basis for the analysis of trade and FDI in this section. Since no information on stocks of intra-EU FDI is available, effects of the European integration process and the Single Market programme can only be measured indirectly.

Econometric estimation and results

For purposes of econometric estimation, a three-way panel, with fixed country, industry and time effects is used. This gives an indication of the determinants of both FDI and trade.

Besides the explanatory variables mentioned above, the additional inclusion of industry fixed effects implies that the estimated parameters have to be interpreted as effects of within industry variation of the exogenous variables. The variation across countries, industries and over time is captured by the corresponding dummies as fixed effects. The estimated results should be interpreted as referring to the "typical industry".

The estimated results are largely in line with theoretical expectations: consistent with the proximity/plant size trade-off hypothesis, trade openness, as a proxy for barriers to trade, reduces both the volume of inward and outward FDI. In the export and import equations, it is significantly positive, but some bias may remain due to endogeneity.

Both R&D intensity and average firm size are significantly positive determinants of outward FDI and exports. Inward FDI is likewise positively determined by R&D intensity, however average firm size is a negative determinant. Turning to the volume of imports, both variables have a negative impact.

Combined with the findings on average investment intensity, the results suggest that outward activities are mainly based on knowledge-specific assets and are more prominent in less capital intensive industries, whereas inward activities are more concentrated in capital intensive, but not R&D intensive industries.

The insignificance of unit labour costs as determinants of inward FDI suggests that cost considerations do not form an important motive for investment in these countries and that market orientated FDI may dominate. Outward FDI is positively related to unit labour costs at the 10% level, supporting the cost motive to some extent. In contrast, both exports and imports are heavily affected by unit labour costs exhibiting the expected signs.

There are also some interesting differences across countries and industries. Compared to the USA, outward FDI, inward FDI and export volume are all significantly higher in the EU countries, whereas import volume is lower. For outward FDI, the highest country effects are exhibited by the Netherlands, the United Kingdom and Italy. The most export orientated countries are Germany, the Netherlands, the United Kingdom and France. Inward investment shows the highest country effects for the Netherlands, the United Kingdom, France, and the USA. The Netherlands and Germany exhibit the highest country effects in the import equation. There is also a pronounced pattern of industry effects in textiles and wood processing, exhibiting high levels in both inward and outward FDI, especially in the EU5, despite their low R&D intensity.

The evolution of trade and FDI over time is captured by time effects. However, these are only significant in the outward FDI-equation, indicating an upward trend, notably during the most recent years. In contrast, the trade equations reveal no exogenous trend.

[a] Pfaffermayr, M., "Multinational firms, trade and growth: a simple model with a trade off between proximity to the market and plant set-up costs under international trade in assets", WIFO Working Paper, No. 90, 1997.

Table 5.9

FDI and trade as shares in production, 1989-1995

Independent Variable	FDI-out		Exports		FDI-in		Imports	
	ß	t	ß	t	ß	t	ß	t
Log R&D intensity	0.4	3.8**)	0.1	2.7**)	-0.3	-2.7**)	-0.1	-3.2**)
Log average capital intensity	-0.7	-2.7**)	-0.2	-2.8**)	0.7	3.0**)	0.2	2.4**)
Log average firm size	0.9	8.6**)	0.2	8.6**)	0.4	2.4**)	-0.3	-9.5**)
Log unit labour costs	0.4	1.6 *)	-0.6	-8.9**)	-0.2	-0.8	0.5	7.5**)
Log openness	-0.5	-4.2**)	0.9	22.1**)	-1.0	-8.3**)	1.1	27.7**)
EU-integration dummy	-0.1	-0.5	0.1	1.6 *)	0.1	1.0	0.0	0.1
Constant	-5.4	-9.6**)	-2.7	-12.9**)	-8.4	-12.3**)	1.3	5.9**)
France	1.1	5.7**)	0.1	2.3**)	1.2	7.7**)	-0.2	-2.9**)
Netherlands	2.9	10.1**)	0.3	3.7**)	3.3	12.5**)	-0.5	-4.7**)
Germany	0.5	1.9 *)	0.4	5.5**)	0.6	3.1**)	-0.4	-5.9**)
Italy	1.3	5.3**)	0.0	0.0	0.7	4.0**)	-0.1	-1.8**)
UK	1.7	7.5**)	0.1	1.9 *)	2.0	13.7**)	-0.2	-3.0**)
Japan	0.7	2.7**)	-1.5	-17.3**)	-1.8	-4.7**)	0.0	-0.3
Textiles, wood activities	2.0	10.0**)	0.5	7.2**)	2.5	10.5**)	-0.5	-7.0**)
Petroleum, chemical. rubber, plastics	0.7	2.2**)	0.3	2.7**)	2.2	8.7**)	-0.2	-1.9 *)
Metals and mechanical products	0.5	2.5**)	0.7	8.4**)	1.8	7.6**)	-0.6	-7.6**)
Information & communication equipment	0.3	0.7**)	0.0	-0.1	3.5	9.1**)	0.1	0.7
Vehicles, transport equipment	-1.5	-4.5**)	0.0	-0.4	0.8	2.6**)	0.1	1.2
1990	0.1	0.8	0.0	-0.2	0.1	0.7	0.0	0.4**)
1991	0.1	1.3	0.0	0.9	0.2	2.5**)	0.0	-0.5
1992	0.2	2.3**)	0.0	1.0	0.2	1.4	0.0	-0.7
1993	0.3	1.9 *)	0.0	0.5	0.1	0.8	-0.1	-1.4
1994	0.3	2.0**)	0.0	0.6	0.2	1.5	-0.1	-1.6
1995	0.3	2.3**)	0.0	0.1	0.2	1.6	0.0	-1.0
R^2	0.88		0.99		0.92		0.98	
standard error of the estimate	0.38		0.11		0.36		0.11	
Heteroscedasticity	81.24 (29)		35.02 (25)		65.44 (28)		33.28 (24)	
RESET	0.71		1.93*)		-5.94**)		0.08	
Normal residuals (Jarque-Bera)	6.95**)		4.37		6.29**)		4.47	

Note: Outlier dummies are skipped. Standard errors are corrected for heteroscedasticity.
*) significant at 10%
**) significant at 5%

Source: Eurostat, OECD, WIFO calculations

5.4 Summary

This section provides a number of insights into the extent and impact of multinational activities, both extra- and intra-EU. The analysis of FDI statistics demonstrates the importance of knowledge-based assets as an important common determinant of outward FDI and trade. Furthermore, FDI seems to be motivated by market access and to a lesser extent by cost considerations. In the main, FDI and trade appear to be complementary.

The analysis of firm and industry structure confirms the magnitude of the increase in intra-EU multinationality, and suggests that this is now an integral feature in the corporate structure of most large firms. Whilst it appears to have had only a minor impact, on average, on aggregate and market concentration, in some markets concentration has increased noticeably over this period. If, as seems increasingly likely, multinationality is stimulated by strategic motivation, there does exist at least potential for an anti-trust dimension in some cases.

6. THE COMPETITIVE STRENGTHS AND WEAKNESSES OF EUROPEAN MANUFACTURING: SUMMARY AND CONCLUSIONS

This report has explored many basic facts of specialisation, structural development and competitive performance at industry level. The overall objective has been to screen the data for direct and indirect information about the competitive strengths and weaknesses of European manufacturing. The term competitiveness has been defined as the ability to raise standards of living and employment, while maintaining a sustainable environment and sustainable external balances.

Industry structure and competitive performance

The most important messages can be summarised as follows:

· *Intermediate specialisation of production in manufacturing industries:* with the share of the manufacturing sector in total GDP amounting to 20.6%, the EU is positioned between Japan (24.7%) and the USA (18.0%). This difference in the broad patterns of specialisation is consistent with the deficit in the trade of manufacturing goods for the USA and analogously explains the aggregate trade surpluses of the manufacturing sector enjoyed in Japan and the EU

· *Global competition:* as a natural consequence of faster growth in other areas, notably in the dynamic Asian countries, the total market share of the EU, Japan and the USA has declined. However, their overall trade balance is positive and increasing. This implies that the global integration of world markets and the increasing competition of low wage economies may have reduced employment opportunities in specific industries, but has not contributed to the overall decline in European manufacturing employment.

· *Favourable external balances:* external balances are currently not constraining European performance. The EU enjoys larger market shares for its manufacturing exports than Japan or the USA. Despite increasing competition from emerging economies, European market shares remained stable between 1989 and 1997. In contrast, Japanese exports lost market shares, and the USA increased their share by five points. The EU's trade balance for manufacturing goods is positive and increasing.

· *European quality mark-up:* the European trade surplus is generated by a quality premium in the sense that exports are more highly valued than imports. This quality premium arises primarily from trade with countries other than Japan and the USA, e.g. in Central and Eastern Europe. As a consequence of Japanese specialisation in the export of goods from high unit value industries, the unit value of European imports from Japan is twice as large as that of exports to Japan. Comparing bilateral trade flows with the USA, the number of industries in which Europe has higher or lower export unit values is roughly equal.

· *Gaps in labour productivity:* labour productivity of European manufacturing is significantly lower than that of Japan and the USA. The exact magnitude at the industry level is blurred by measurement problems, which stem in part from the interface between manufacturing and industry services. For the aggregate economy, European GDP per capita in 1997 was 14% lower than in Japan and 33% below the American level. Differences in industrial structure do not affect the European productivity gap in manufacturing, which would basically remain unaffected, if all industries were of uniform size in all the three areas.

· *Modest catching up in productivity:* labour productivity in the EU was rising faster up to the mid-eighties than in the USA. Given the large initial gap, catching up is, however, progressing slowly, in recent years (1997, 1998) it has come to a stop due to slow growth in the EU. In past years, about one third of European productivity growth was due to structural change towards industries with higher productivity. This trend was supported by the simultaneous decline in employment shares in low productivity industries, e.g. in the clothing sector, as well as by growing shares of high productivity industries, such as pharmaceuticals. Although productivity growth is, for the most part, still affected by general factors that apply equally across industries, catching up relative to the USA would not have been possible without structural change.

· *Growth and employment:* job creation and growth are positively related across industries in all three economic areas, but growth in manufacturing has not been high enough to stabilise employment. Between 1989 and 1996, European manufacturing matched in the long run both Japan and the USA in terms of nominal growth in value added, but performed worse in terms of employment. Econometric estimates show that the level of output growth necessary to stabilise employment is significantly lower in the USA than in the EU, which is mainly a reflection of differences in productivity growth. However, the evidence additionally suggests that European industries are more eager to rationalise production and substitute labour for capital, indicating that relative factor prices favour employment growth more in the USA than in the EU.

· *Structural pressures on employment:* relative to Japan and the USA, European manufacturing is still more specialised in labour- and capital intensive industries. Lacking alternative opportunities to create competitive advantages through product differentiation and investment in intangible assets, these industries are highly exposed to continuous cost cutting and rationalisation with a resulting substitution of labour. Thus, besides the general trends in productivity and growth, the specific industrial structure adds to the overall downward pressure on European employment.

· *Lags in fast-moving markets despite technological competence and skills:* the EU proves its considerable technological competence and skills in mainstream manufacturing and the research-intensive industries outside of the information technologies. The EU is most competitive in the machinery, vehicles, and chemicals sectors, which together create a trade surplus larger than the overall surplus of the EU. However, in comparison to the USA, the low shares in total value added reveal weaknesses in innovation and marketing strategies in the most dynamic markets. European manufacturing compares poorly in the fastest moving markets, characterised either by recent technological upturns, as in the case of ICT-related research intensive industries or by easily changing consumer tastes in advertising industries.

· *European restructuring by multinational activity:* European manufacturing is characterised by a significant increase in intra-EU multinational investment. Fostering the integration process and reducing regional disparities, this provides an important impetus for the ongoing restructuring of European manufacturing. This applies especially to industries relying largely on intangible firm-specific assets like innovation and marketing.

Given the lags of European manufacturing in terms of aggregate labour productivity, modest growth performance and rapidly declining employment, the sectoral analysis neither indicates overspecialisation in low productivity industries, nor a lack of technological competence and manufacturing skills. Compared to the USA, structural differences arise primarily from poor performance in creating lead-time in the fast-moving markets, where competitive advantage is based on intangible investment in research and marketing[25]. Since first mover advantages create substantial benefits in terms of growth and employment, the USA seems to have a greater ability to benefit from the particularly high growth dynamics of these industries.

25) See also Peneder, M., Miles, I., Tomlinson, M., "Intangible Investments, Industrial Sectors and Competitiveness", Report to the European Commission, DG III, A5, 1999.

Economic policy

Four policy issues arising from the empirical findings deserve special attention:

1. Sectoral analysis does not imply any vertical targeting of individual industries by subsidies or strategic trade arrangements: in particular, two arguments support horizontal as opposed to vertical policies. (i) The policy of "picking winners" generates opportunity costs relative to private market-based solutions and is subject to informational asymmetries with resulting agency problems. (ii) In addition, the analysis revealed that lower European labour productivity does not stem from structural weaknesses in the sense of being less specialised in high productivity industries than the USA.

2. Continuous upgrading of European industry: unit labour costs in the EU are higher than in the USA, and - by a much wider margin - higher than in developing and transition countries. Low wage economies may successfully compete on price and focus on homogenous, mature products. The EU needs to invest continuously in quality and to shift to new products at earlier stages of the product cycle. Economic policy in the EU has to promote, therefore, innovation, adaptability and the upgrading of human capital.

3. Elimination of institutional barriers: weaknesses were identified in some dynamic markets characterised by product differentiation, marketing and innovation. The fast moving environment of these markets requires flexibility in entrepreneurial response. A prime policy target therefore is the elimination of institutional barriers to the creative and flexible management of change. Such rigidities are to be found in financial, labour and product markets, in particular in basic services, as well as in the highly disparate nature of European innovation systems.

4. European convergence and the diffusion of best practice: a high degree of disparity within the EU was found to exist for example with regard to specialisation patterns and labour productivity. An upward convergence in performance within the EU could provide a major impetus to the reduction of weaknesses observed relative to Japan and the USA. This underlines the importance of policies directed at the diffusion of best practices within the EU both in business and policy.

Energy

Industry description and main indicators

The activities covered in this chapter of Panorama are those classified under the Sub-section CA of NACE Rev. 1 (mining and quarrying of energy producing materials), Sub-section DF (the manufacture of coke, refined petroleum products and nuclear fuel) and Section E (electricity, gas and water supply).

The energy sector plays a significant role in the European economy. According to National Accounts compiled by Eurostat, the 1.7 million persons employed in the energy branch of the EU generated a value added worth 305 billion ECU in 1997, which represented some 4.5% of GDP. In addition to its economic weight, the energy sector is also for obvious reasons a strategic one, at the base of most economic activity. Energy production, distribution and use have indeed a great impact on the economic, physical and social environment. Energy can affect competitiveness of businesses and standards of living of households, but also raises questions on matters, such as environmental issues and sustainable development, which are not addressed within this publication.

A distinction is sometimes made between different types of energy consumption. Primary energy consumption refers to the sum of all energies either used by consumers or used as an input to the production of other energy forms, for example the input of fuels such as coal, natural gas and heavy fuel oil that may be required for the production of electricity. On the other hand, reference is often made to "gross inland energy consumption", which is the key aggregate in the energetic balance sheet. This term refers to the quantity of energy necessary to satisfy inland consumption of the geographical entity under consideration, and corresponds to the sum of consumption, distribution and transformation losses. As regards "final energy available for consumption", this term refers to the sum of all energy used by consumers, including electricity produced from other fuels, generally excluding transformation and distribution losses.

The activities covered in this chapter include:

- 10.1: mining and agglomeration of hard coal;
- 10.2: mining and agglomeration of lignite;
- 10.3: extraction and agglomeration of peat;
- 11.1: extraction of crude petroleum and natural gas;
- 11.2: service activities incidental to oil and gas extraction, excluding surveying;
- 12: mining of uranium and thorium ores;
- 23.1: manufacture of coke oven products;
- 23.2: manufacture of refined petroleum products;
- 23.3: processing of nuclear fuel;
- 40.1: production and distribution of electricity;
- 40.2: manufacture of gas; distribution of gaseous fuels through mains;
- 40.3: steam and hot water supply;
- 41: collection, purification and distribution of water.

Recent trends

Gross inland energy consumption of the EU was worth about 1.4 billion TOE[1] in 1997, a level 6.4% higher than in 1990. This corresponded to an average growth rate of just under 1% per annum. Due to colder weather conditions, energy demand increased strongly in 1995 and 1996, by over 2%, after a period of constant demand between 1990 and 1994. In 1997 energy consumption declined by 1%.

Energy intensity, defined as gross inland energy consumption per unit of GDP, has witnessed a strong decline[2] over the past decade in the EU and was in 1997 more than 8 percentage points lower than in 1988 (see figure 1.1). These gains can be explained by the maturity of EU energy markets, where growth has been primarily in sectors with low energy intensity (e.g. service activities), whilst energy intensive industry has tended to decline in relative importance. In addition, energy gains can also result from industries investing in more energy-efficient capital.

Oil accounted for about 42% of the gross inland energy consumption of the EU in 1997, a share that has hardly changed over the past decade. Absolute consumption showed an average annual increase of slightly more than 1% since 1988, to reach 588 million TOE in 1997. Natural gas experienced much stronger growth, averaging 4.3% over the same period, to attain 302 million TOE in 1997. Gas consumption was equivalent to 21.5% of gross energy consumption in 1997, up from 16% in 1988. Solid fuels, in contrast, demonstrated a continuous decrease and saw their share in gross consumption plunge to under 16% in 1997, down from 24% in 1988. New electric power plants have increasingly tended to be fuelled by natural gas in the 1990s, both for environmental and economic reasons. Natural gas-fired plants achieve lower airborne emissions than coal-fired plants, while combined-cycle gas turbine power plants have higher efficiency rates and shorter construction times than coal-fired power plants. The other sources of energy, including nuclear and renewable ones, increased their share of the energy mix from 18% in 1987 to 21% in 1997, of which 5.8% could be attributed to renewable sources.

As regards final consumption of energy, the mix has also evolved over the decade. Natural gas and nuclear electricity substantially increased their share at the expense of solid fuels and, to some extent, oil. The latest figures for 1997 show that oil represented more than 46% of final energy consumption ahead of natural gas with 23% (up from 20% in 1988) and electricity with 19% (up from 17.5%). Coal and other solid fuels accounted for only 5% of final consumption, a share that was halved when compared to 1988.

The principal sectors of final energy demand are industry, transport, households and the tertiary sector. All main end-use sectors have shown growth in energy consumption since 1993, but the structure has somewhat changed. Whilst the share of the household and the tertiary sector has remained stable at around 40% of the total, that of industry declined to 28% in 1997, or 262 million TOE, down from 32% in 1988. In contrast, the transport sector

1) TOE: tonne of oil equivalent, or 107 kilocalories, or 41.86 GJ.
2) From a qualitative point of view, a lowering of energy intensity is considered as an improvement, meaning that less energy was required to produce the same amount of domestic product.

Figure 1.1 (1988=100)
Energy intensity of EU

120
110
100
90
1988 1989 1990 1991 1992 1993 1994 1995 1996 1997
Energy intensity
Gross domestic product (constant prices)
Gross inland energy consumption

Source: Eurostat (Sirene)

Figure 1.2
Gross inland energy consumption by fuel in the EU, 1997

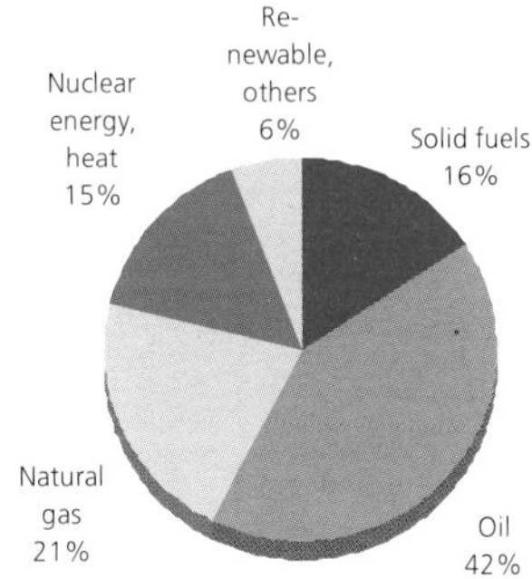

Source: Eurostat (Sirene)

Figure 1.3
Final energy consumption by fuel in the EU, 1997

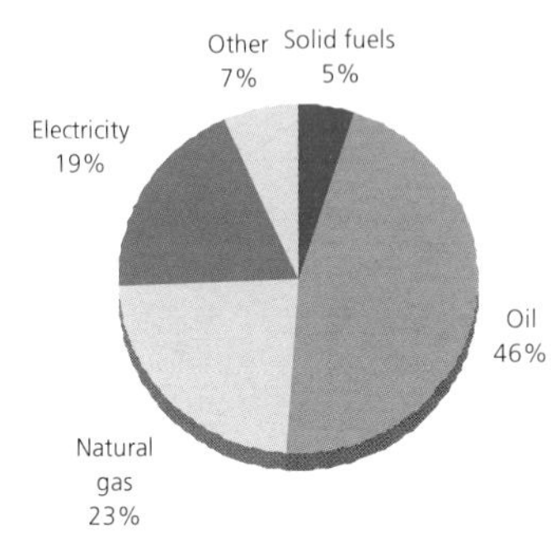

Source: Eurostat (Sirene)

Figure 1.4
Final energy consumption by user in the EU, 1997

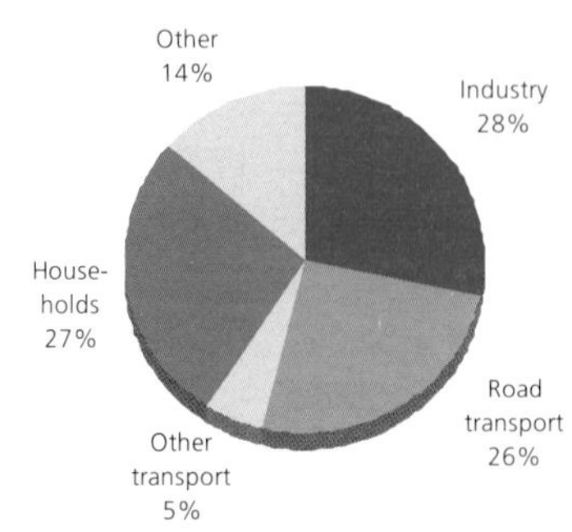

Source: Eurostat (Sirene)

has increased its share, in line with the increase in personal mobility allied with rising living standards, and increased freight transport by truck with the development of intra-EU trade (see chapter on road transport services). The transport sector has now overtaken industry to become the second most important final use for energy at 31% of final energy consumption, or 289 million TOE in 1997.

Energy consumption by households and the tertiary sector is dominated by heating applications, that can be fuelled either by electricity, natural gas or petroleum. Other applications include cooking and the provision of hot water, lighting and appliances. Energy demand growth is principally due to increased appliance penetration and usage, which was only partly offset by technological improvements improving energy efficiency.

There are many different uses for energy in industry, from space heating and lighting, steam-raising in industrial boilers, drying and many specific process applications. In the latter category, there is a shift towards electricity use as many new industrial processes are exclusively powered by electricity. The other fuels compete for more traditional steam-raising, heating and process uses, with natural gas gaining market share at the expense of coal and oil. Transport is dominated by oil, since, as yet, no alternative fuels have made a significant penetration of this market. Consumer choice is thus focused almost exclusively on gasoline and diesel fuels refined from oil. In the long term, alternative fuelled vehicles, using electricity or liquified natural gas are likely to become more available, but are not excepted to be seen making significant inroads into the dominant position held by oil.

(million TOE) Figure 1.5

Evolution of final energy consumption in the EU by user

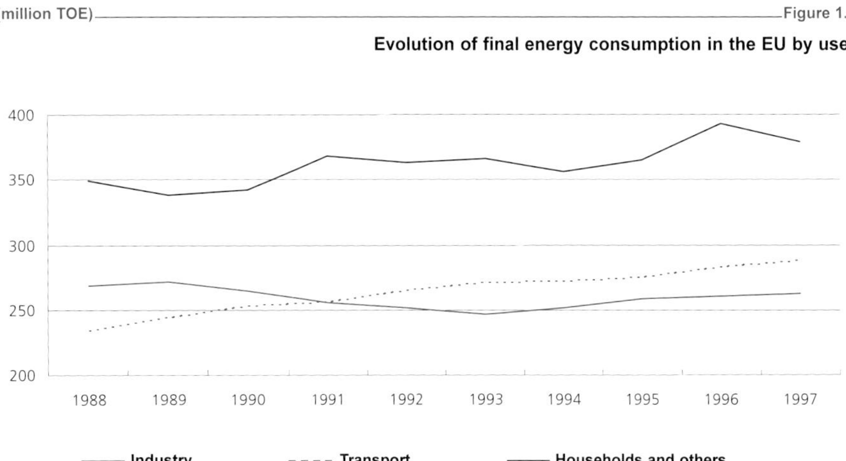

Source: Eurostat (Sirene)

(million TOE) Figure 1.6

Evolution of gross inland consumption in the EU by fuel

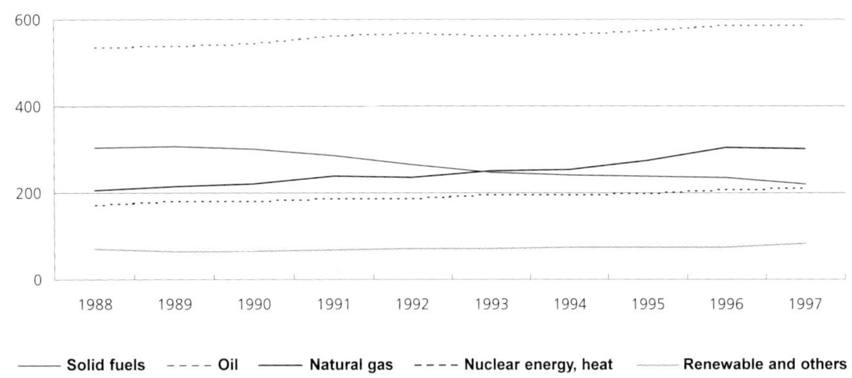

Source: Eurostat (Sirene)

(ECU/hour) Figure 1.7

Labour costs by Member State, 1996

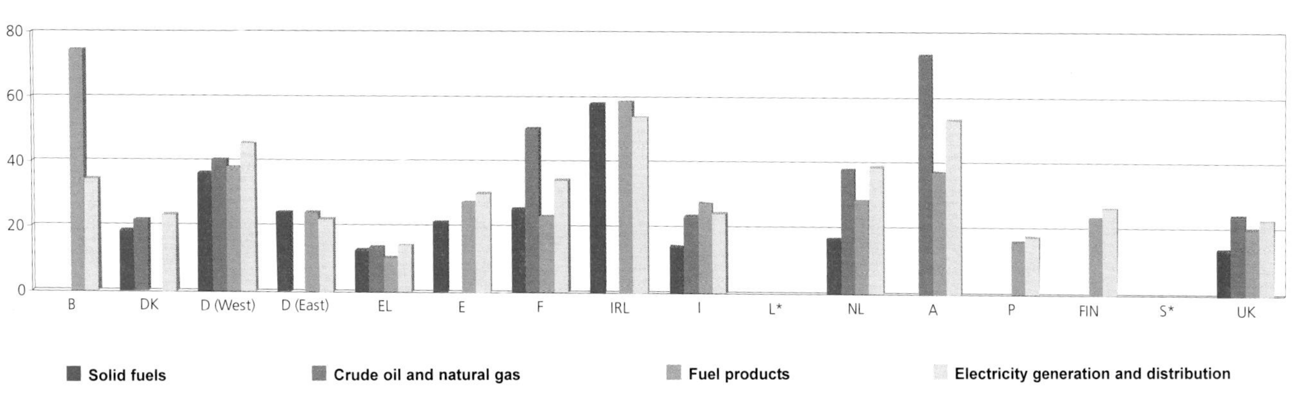

Source: Eurostat (LCS)

International comparison

The level of gross inland energy consumption represented in 1997 just over 15% of the world total, making the EU one of the most important energy markets in the world after North America (27%) and Asia (22%). Asia is the fastest growing area of energy demand in the world, including the relatively mature energy market of Japan, but also the high-growth economies of China, India and the south-eastern Asia. The EU is a significant net importer of energy. Net imports were over 800 million TOE in 1993, or 73% of gross inland energy consumption.

Imports of oil, natural gas and coal have all risen over the past ten years as rising demand has outstripped production growth. The Middle East and Norway have been the principal sources of crude oil imports, Algeria, Norway and the former USSR are the most important natural gas suppliers from outside the EU, whilst coal imports are dominated by supplies from the USA, Australia and South Africa.

Figure 1.8

Gross inland energy consumption by world region, 1996

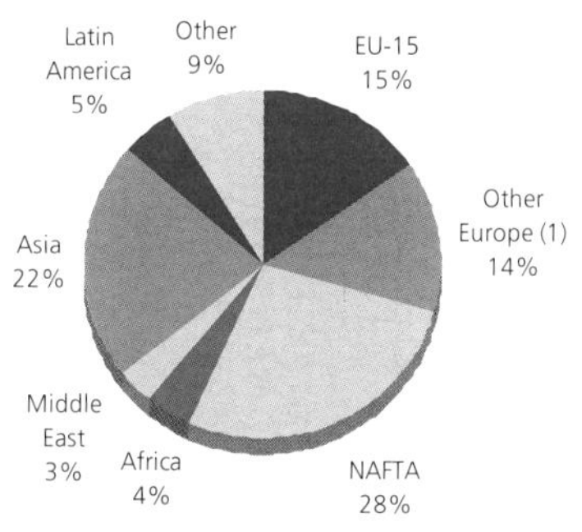

(1) Including EFTA, Central and Eastern European Countries, the CIS and Baltic States.

Source: Eurostat, DG XVII

Solid fuels (NACE Rev. 1 10 and 23.1)

This section covers the extraction, as well as the associated washing, grading and ranking processes, of all types of coal, including hard coal (NACE Rev. 1 Group 10.1), lignite (Group 10.2) and peat (Group 10.3). It also covers the manufacture of coke oven products (Group 23.1). Hard coal represents almost 70% of total solid fuel consumption on an energy equivalent basis in the EU. Lignite and peat have a much lower energy content than hard coal, and are primarily used in applications close to the site of production.

Solid fuels are used less and less to satisfy energy demand in the EU. Gross inland consumption has fallen by an average of 3.5% per annum between 1988 and 1997 to reach 222 million TOE, down from 305 million TOE. On the supply side, production of hard coal in the EU has witnessed a constant decline since the mid-1980s, largely as a result of cut-backs in production capacity or the termination of coal production in several Member States. As of 1997, only Germany, Spain, France and the United Kingdom still had active coal mining industries. Solid fuel production in the EU countries fell by an average of 6.5% per annum between 1988 and 1997, a decline of 45% to just over 125 million TOE. This has partly been offset by a rise in the level of net imports, that progressed on average by 3% per annum, to reach 97 million TOE in 1997.

Several factors can be put forward to explain this evolution. Firstly, there has been a growing gap between extraction costs in the EU and those from lower-cost countries, stemming both from lower labour costs and geological constraints. Indeed, EU production tends to be from deep mines whereas an increasing proportion of high-quality production comes from countries where low-cost surface mining is possible. In addition, hard coal was further hit in 1986 by the fall in the price of hydrocarbons, with which coal competes in power generation, its main market. In addition, the end in 1991 of a 1975 Community restriction on the use of natural gas for electricity generation resulted in a shift towards gas-fired power stations, which had the advantages of faster construction times, lower capital costs, and higher efficiency rates than coal-fired generating units.

The power generation market is clearly the most important market for solid fuels as it accounted for 68% of gross inland consumption in 1997. A further 24% was accounted for as inputs of patent fuel and briquetting plants, coke-ovens or blast-furnaces. After taking into account all transformation inputs, outputs, and losses as well as own consumption of the energy branch, there were some 50 million TOE of solid fuels available for final energy consumption in the EU in 1997, practically half the quantity of ten years before and 23% of total gross inland consumption. Most of this was used by energy-intensive intermediate goods' industries, where plants are typically large-scale, such as iron and steel (53% of final energy consumption in 1997), or chemicals (6%). Households accounted for 16% of final energy consumption of solid fuels, a drop of 10 percentage points compared to 1988.

Figure 1.9 (million TOE)

Solid fuels evolution of main indicators

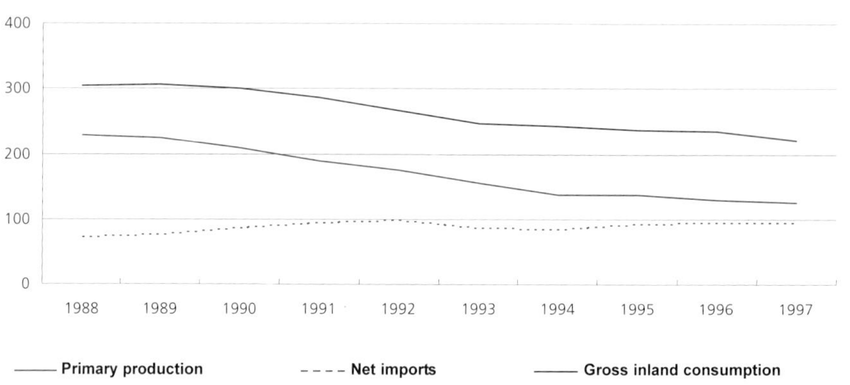

Source: Eurostat (Sirene)

(%) Figure 1.10

Breakdown of final energy consumption of solid fuels in the EU

Source: Eurostat (Sirene)

One reason for the growing concentration of demand for coal in just a few sectors is the high cost of combustion equipment and the greater difficulty of transportation compared with liquid or gaseous fuels. Coal is therefore only an attractive option when economies of scale can be achieved, and where the cost of transportation can be limited, such as in the power station market. In small-scale markets, such as commercial and domestic boilers, coal has difficulty competing with gas and heating oil. In addition, more stringent environmental regulations regarding airborne emissions and the disposal of combustion waste have also tended to reduce the coal market as large industries were the main ones able to afford the investments needed to abate the environmental impact of coal combustion.

Foreign trade

Solid fuels production accounted for about one quarter of the world's energy production, a ratio that has remained stable since the beginning of the 1980s. The largest producer in 1996 was Asia, accounting for 40% of the total, up from 22% in the early 1980s, followed by North America, with 26%. Increased production in these two regions compensated for the slowdown witnessed in Europe (in its geographical understanding) due to the restructuring of the coal sector. In 1996, the two biggest producers were China (686 million TOE) and the United States (547 million TOE), followed by India (140 million TOE), Australia (130 million TOE) and Russia (107 million TOE).

The EU is one of the main importers of solid fuels from international markets. Indigenous production accounted for just over 56% of gross consumption in 1997, with the remainder being covered by net imports (44%, up from around 24% in 1988).

(% of TOE) Figure 1.11

Production of solid fuels by world region, 1996

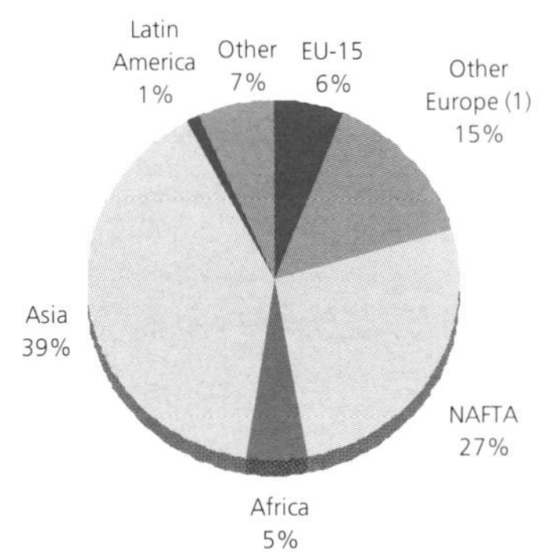

(1) Including EFTA, Central and Eastern European Countries, the CIS and Baltic States.

Source: Eurostat, DG XVII

Figure 1.12

Solid fuels (NACE Rev. 1 10 and 23.1) Origin of EU imports, 1998

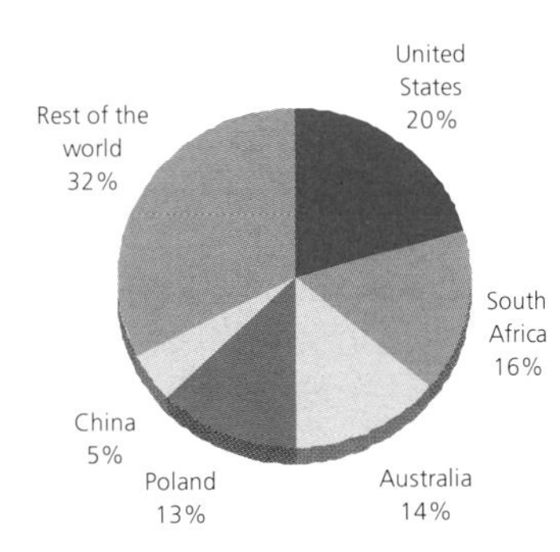

Source: Eurostat (Comext)

Figure 1.13

Solid fuels (NACE Rev. 1 10 and 23.1) Destination of EU exports, 1998

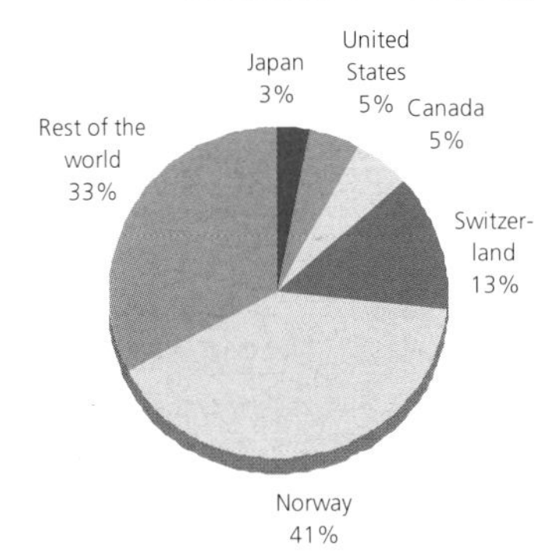

Source: Eurostat (Comext)

Figure 1.14 (million TOE)

Natural gas: evolution of main indicators

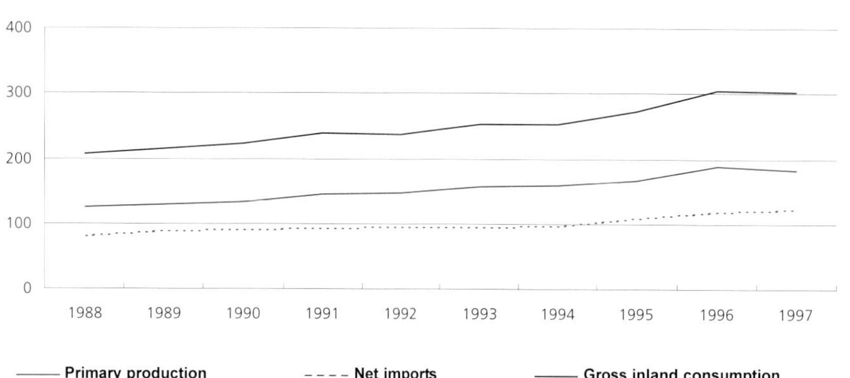

Source: Eurostat (Sirene)

Figure 1.15 (million TOE)

Oil: evolution of main indicators

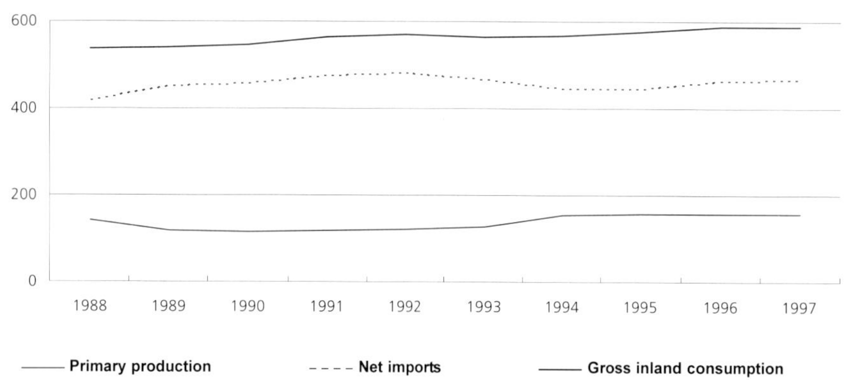

Source: Eurostat (Sirene)

Figure 1.16 (%)

Breakdown of final energy consumption of natural gas in the EU

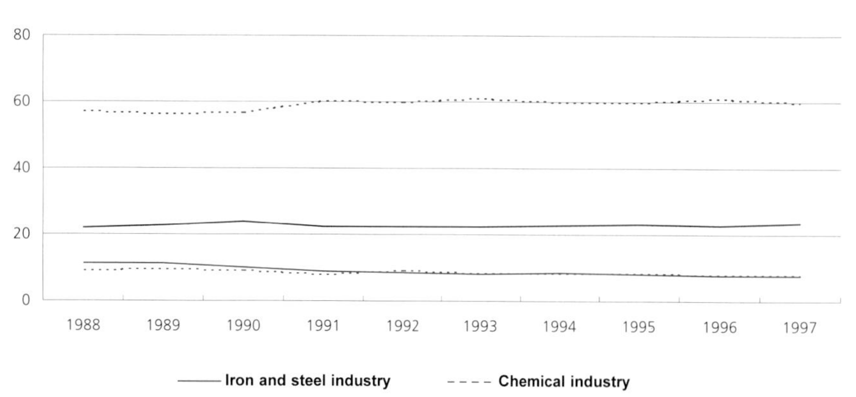

Source: Eurostat (Sirene)

Crude oil and natural gas (NACE Rev. 1 11 and 23.2)

The activities covered in this section can be subdivided into two main groups. On the one hand there is the extraction and production of crude oil and natural gas, and on the other the manufacture of products derived from oil. This split is mirrored in the activity classification definitions. NACE Rev. 1 Division 11 covers the extraction side, and comprises four main activities: exploration for crude oil and natural gas; production of crude oil, condensates and other liquids resulting from gas processing operations; production of natural gas; service activities in support of oil and gas exploration and production (excluding surveying). NACE Rev. 1 Division 23.2 is defined as the manufacture of refined petroleum products. The main final products of this process include liquified petroleum gases (LPG), naphtha, motor gasoline, aviation fuels, kerosene, gas-oil (diesel fuel and heating oil), residual fuel oils and lubricants.

Production of oil and gas in the EU increased steadily up until the middle of the 1980s, stimulated by rising oil prices following the oil price shocks of the 1970s. However, the 1986 oil price collapse reduced the attractiveness of upstream investment and set output on a downward trend. By 1989, oil and gas production had fallen to pre-1983 levels at under 250 million TOE. Since then, hydrocarbons output has increased to 340 million TOE in 1997, with both oil and gas production on a rising trend.

EU oil output experienced strong growth in the first half of the 1990s, after suffering a severe contraction in the late 1980s. It stabilised at around 160 million TOE between 1994 and 1997, a level 35% higher than in 1990. The increase was largely owed to a build-up in Britain's North Sea crude oil production. As for natural gas, production grew by an average of 4% per annum between 1989 and 1997, to over 180 million TOE, despite a 3.4% decline in 1997. It is interesting to note that natural gas output has been greater than oil output since 1989. The two principal natural gas producers are the Netherlands and the United Kingdom, each with around 37% of EU production.

(%) Table 1.1

Crude oil and natural gas (NACE Rev. 1 11)
Composition of the labour force, 1997

	Females	Part-time	Highly-educated
D	:	:	33.8
E	:	:	54.9
F	:	:	45.7
IRL	22.6	:	48.3
I	17.7	:	17.3
NL	:	:	45.2
UK	15.9	:	41.0

Source: Eurostat (LFS)

(%) Table 1.2

Fuel products (NACE Rev. 1 23)
Composition of the labour force, 1997

	Females	Part-time	Highly-educated
B	:	:	39.8
D	31.0	:	18.9
E	20.5	:	44.9
F	23.2	:	35.7
IRL	22.4	3.9	36.9
I	18.3	:	14.4
NL	:	:	34.5
UK	17.7	:	40.6

Source: Eurostat (LFS)

(years) Table 1.3

Proven reserves relative to production

	1996	1998
United Kingdom	4.5	5.3
Norge	7.3	9.1
USA	8.0	7.9
Kuwait	122.8	126.5
United Arab Emirates	114.1	110.1
Saudi Arabia	83.1	79.3
Iran	65.5	68.9
Libya	58.2	57.3
Venezuela	54.2	56.4
Mexico	41.5	32.0
Brunei	22.7	23.0
Former Soviet Union	22.1	21.7
Angola	21.0	20.5
China	20.7	20.4
Algeria	20.9	20.3
Nigeria	26.8	20.3
Gabon	10.1	18.4
India	22.7	16.0
Oman	15.8	15.9
Malaysia	17.2	15.7
Qatar	23.2	15.5
Brazil	14.2	15.2
Ecuador	14.4	14.3
Egypt	11.7	11.9
Colombia	14.7	11.3
Indonesia	9.1	9.3
Australia	7.9	8.5
Argentina	7.5	8.3
Canada	7.3	6.9
World	41.2	40.3

Source: CPDP

(%) Figure 1.17

Breakdown of final energy consumption of oil in the EU

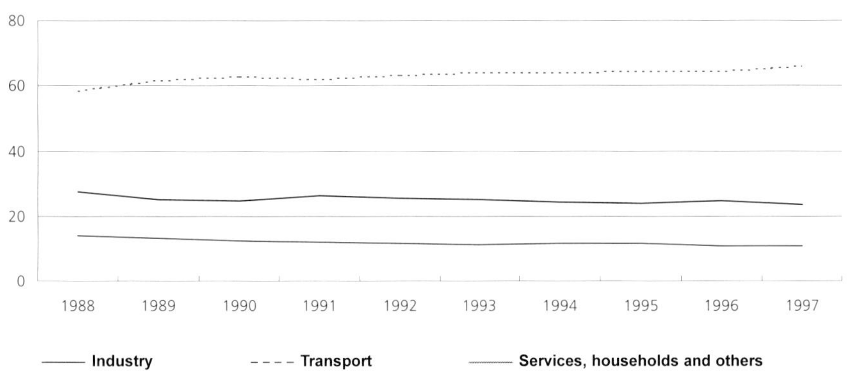

Source: Eurostat (Sirene)

(%) Figure 1.18

Net share of energy use by transformation activities

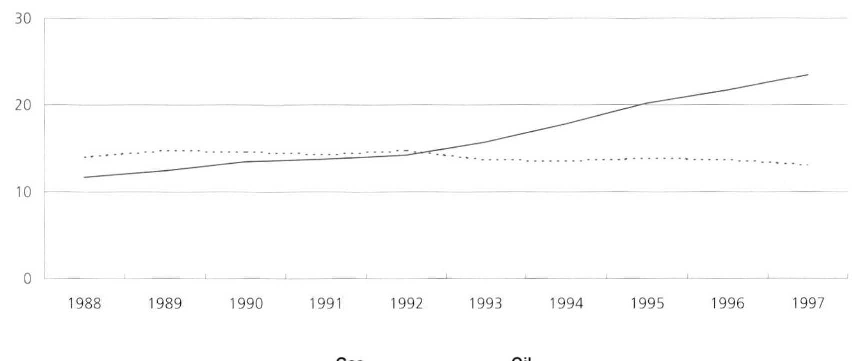

Source: Eurostat (Sirene)

Turning to the demand side, EU gross inland consumption of oil and gas reached 890 million TOE in 1997, a slight decrease of 0.2% compared to 1996. Oil represented the largest share of consumption, with close to 590 million TOE, whilst natural gas accounted for just over 300 million TOE. Oil consumption has been growing at a slower pace than natural gas. Gross inland consumption of oil progressed by 1% per annum on average between 1988 and 1997, whilst gas consumption grew at a rate twice as high.

The ratio between final energy available for consumption and gross inland consumption allows for an estimation of the share of energy that is absorbed by transformation processes, mainly by thermal power stations and refineries. In the case of hydrocarbons, it was equal to 17% in 1997, up from 12% in 1988. This rise can be almost exclusively attributed to the increasing use of natural gas power stations, whose share in gross inland consumption soared from 15% in 1988 to 23% in 1997. In the case of oil, only 7% of gross consumption is used for power generation, a share that has remained constant since the mid-1980s.

After taking into account all transformation input and output, as well as transformation and distribution losses and own consumption by the energy sector, around 741 million TOE of hydrocarbon were available for final consumption in the EU in 1997, of which 231 million TOE were gas and 510 million TOE were oil. The transport sector was the key market for petroleum and derived products, accounting for two-thirds of final energy consumption of oil. It was also the only market to report a growing trend (see figure 1.17), and should stay that way as long as ready substitutes are not available on a large-scale. Services activities and households accounted for one-quarter of oil consumption but as much 60% of natural gas final consumption.

Foreign trade

Oil was in 1996 still the most important fuel with 37% of the total energy production in the world. Natural gas, that met about a fifth of world energetic needs displayed considerable growth. The 11 Member States of OPEC[3] remained the major oil producers, accounting as a whole for 40% of world production, down from 46% in 1980, and 54% in 1973. Since 1990, the share of Western Europe has sharply increased, to reach 9% in 1996, half of which was accounted for by the EU. As for natural gas, the EU accounted for a tenth of 1996 world production, which was dominated by North America (32%) and the CIS (30%).

Despite rising oil output the EU is still heavily dependent on oil imports, with net imports covering as much as 80% of gross inland consumption in 1997, down from 85% in 1990 thanks to increasing North Sea output since 1994. Extra-EU imports of crude oil into the EU stood at 470 million TOE in 1997, less than 1% higher than the year before, but 3% lower than their peak of 1992. The Middle East is by far the most important supplier of crude oil to the EU, together with African countries (mainly Nigeria, Libya and Algeria) and Norway.

Turning to natural gas, the share of EU gross inland consumption met by indigenous production fell steadily over the 1980s to a low point of 58% in 1990. As larger quantities of gas have been brought on stream, EU natural gas self-sufficiency rose to 62% in the mid-1990s, only to fall back at 59% in 1997. Natural gas net imports of the EU rose by 4.8% to 124 million TOE in 1997, a level one-third higher than in 1990. The greatest proportion of imports came from the CIS, Algeria and Norway.

3) OPEC is the organisation of oil producing and exporting countries: Algeria, Libya, Nigeria, Indonesia, Iran, Iraq, Kuwait, Qatar, Saudi Arabia, the United Arab Emirates and Venezuela.

Figure 1.19 (% of TOE)

Oil production by world region, 1996

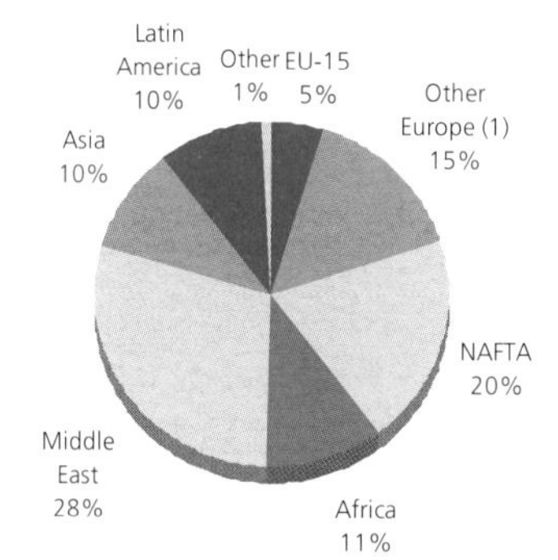

(1) Including EFTA, Central and Eastern European Countries, the CIS and Baltic States.

Source: Eurostat, DG XVII

Figure 1.20 (% of TOE)

Natural gas production by world region, 1996

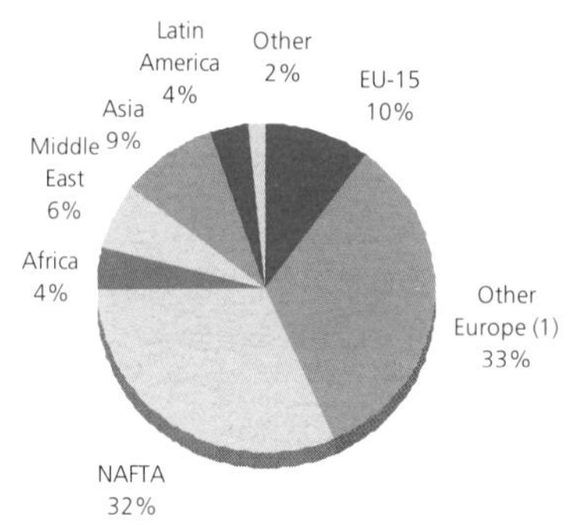

(1) Including EFTA, Central and Eastern European Countries, the CIS and Baltic States.

Source: Eurostat, DG XVII

Figure 1.21

Crude oil and natural gas (NACE Rev. 1 11 and 23.2) Origin of EU imports, 1998

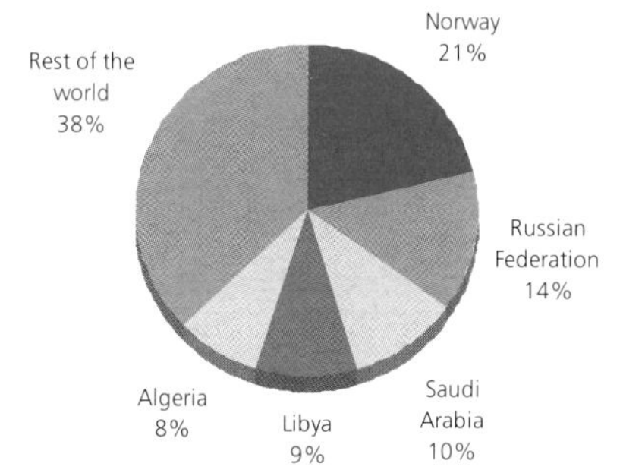

Source: Eurostat (Comext)

Figure 1.22

Crude oil and natural gas (NACE Rev. 1 11 and 23.2) Destination of EU exports, 1998

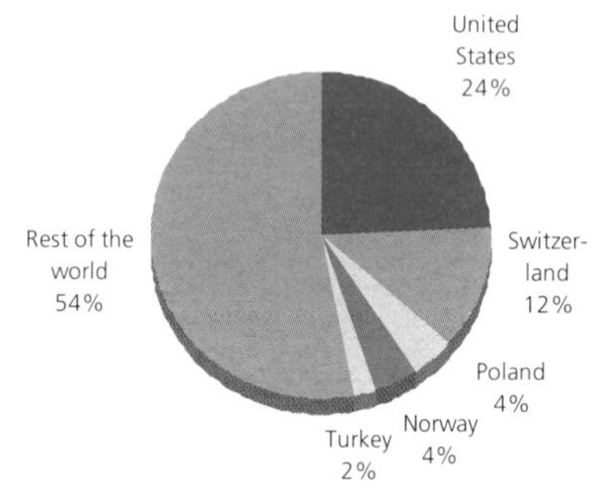

Source: Eurostat (Comext)

Nuclear fuels (NACE Rev. 1 12 and 23.3)

Production of nuclear fuels is covered by NACE Rev. 1 Division 12, which includes the mining of uranium and thorium ores, and thus relates specifically to the supply of raw materials; and by NACE Rev. 1 Division 23.3 which includes the processing of nuclear fuels, involving the production of enriched uranium, of fuel elements for nuclear reactors, of radioactive elements for industrial or medical use and the treatment of nuclear waste.

Companies active in the field of nuclear fuel include both dedicated nuclear companies and those providing a wide range of engineering services. The most important nuclear fuel companies in the EU include ABB-Atom AB in Sweden, which is a private company, BNFL in the United Kingdom, which is state-owned, and COGEMA, which is owned by the French State and the private oil company Total. Other companies are ENUSA, a 60% privately held Spanish company and, in Germany, Siemens (also privately held).

Capacity in uranium production within the EU has been on a downward trend since the early 1990s. Most of the cuts in production capacity have taken place in France, which more than halved its uranium output between 1992 and 1995. Germany has also cut back its output in response to high production costs. EU production decreased from 1,050 tU in 1997 to 800 tU in 1998 and this trend was excepted to continue, as ENUSA announced the closure of its mine in Spain, and uranium mining in France was expected to be terminated in the near to medium future.

The Euratom supply agency estimate average reactor needs for natural uranium until 2008 in the EU at about 21.6 thousand tonnes/year, and average net requirements at about 19.2 thousand tU/year. Relative to 1997 the reactor requirements are hence expected to remain stable but the net requirements to decrease slightly (net requirements = reactor needs - planned uranium/plutonium recycling +/- stock changes).

Uranium enrichment, which accounts for about one-quarter of the cost of the nuclear fuel cycle, is the process that increases the content of U235 (fissile uranium) in the fuel from 0.7% to between 2% and 5%. Most modern reactors require enriched uranium fuel. There are two commercial processes used for uranium enrichment, firstly gas diffusion and secondly centrifugal separation. Gas diffusion is a widely used technology, but is more energy intensive. Production in the EU is in the hands of two groups, Eurodif (F), using gas diffusion technology, and Urenco (UK, NL, D), using gas centrifuge technology. Several new technologies for enriching uranium using lasers to separate the U235 atoms from the other uranium atoms are undergoing research and development. These technologies are called MLIS and AVLIS (Molecular Laser Isotopic Separation and Atomic Vapour Laser Isotopic Separation). AVLIS has been selected by Cogema, USEC (in the USA) and in Japan, but there are currently no plans to build a new enrichment plant until after 2000. MLIS is a chemical laser separation process which has been under investigation in a number of countries and a demonstration plant may be built in South Africa.

International markets for fuel elements are not developed. Fuel assemblies have to comply with certain specific criteria (technology, local regulation etc.), so most EU countries with established nuclear programs have a fuel fabrication plant and are hence self-sufficient in fuel element fabrication. Demand for different types of fuel elements stems from the different types of nuclear reactors. The main reactor designs currently in large-scale use in Europe are:

- PWR (Pressurised Water Reactor), the most common reactor type which uses enriched uranium or mixed oxide fuel (MOX);
- BWR (Boiling Water Reactor), which uses enriched uranium fuel or MOX fuel;
- AGR (Advanced Gas-cooled Reactor), which requires enriched uranium fuel;
- GCR/MAGNOX (Gas Cooled Reactor) requiring natural uranium fuel;
- FR (Fast Reactor), using plutonium fuel that is separated from spent fuel from other reactor types.

The largest producer of fuel elements for light water reactors (LWR) within the EU is FBFC, a subsidiary of the French companies Framatome and COGEMA, with plants in Belgium and France. Other EU producers include ABB Atom AB (S), Siemens (D), ENUSA (E), and BNFL (UK). BNFL produces fuel assemblies for both LWR and GCR. The production capacity of fuel elements has been relatively stable, and is expected to remain so. However, there is a small but expanding market for the fabrication of plutonium into MOX fuel. Companies in Belgium, France and the United Kingdom are all providing this additional service for customers who choose to reprocess and recycle their spent fuel.

After the fuel is burned in the reactor for a specified period of time, it is removed and placed in temporary storage. Then, depending upon which option has been chosen, the waste will either be reprocessed or sent to a facility for storage and then burial. In some countries both options are possible. According to a recent OECD study, fuel reprocessing and waste management represent about 25% of the total fuel cost. In direct disposal, the spent fuel is stored temporarily, to be eventually buried encapsulated in stainless steel containers in a deep geological facility. For those countries which have selected reprocessing, the fuel is placed in a canister and transported to a special facility for reprocessing. The spent fuel is processed in order to separate the uranium and plutonium, and the remaining material (about 3% of the total) is vitrified and then sent to a waste facility.

Table 1.4

Forecasts of uranium and separative work requirements in the EU

	1999	2000	2001	2002	2003	2004	2005	2006	2007	2008	Average 1999-2008
Uranium (tU)											
Reactor needs	21,300	21,200	21,500	21,800	21,300	22,100	21,600	21,700	21,600	21,600	21,600
Net requirements	18,100	18,300	18,400	19,000	19,000	20,000	19,500	20,000	19,800	19,800	19,200
Separative Work (tSW)											
Reactor needs	12,000	11,700	12,000	12,200	11,900	12,400	12,200	12,200	12,400	12,300	12,100
Net requirements	11,100	10,900	11,200	11,200	10,900	11,600	11,300	11,300	11,400	11,300	11,200

Source: Euratom Supply Agency

Foreign trade

The EU is largely dependent upon imports to satisfy its demand in nuclear fuel. The EU produced in 1998 only 6% of its annual uranium requirements, the rest being imported. The largest suppliers from outside the EU were Niger and Russia, both representing some 25%. Other major suppliers included South Africa, Australia and Canada.

Table 1.5 (tonnes)

Production of uranium in the world

	1993	1994	1995	1996	1997
World	33,237	31,611	32,254	36,195	:
Canada	9,155	9,647	10,473	11,706	:
Australia	2,256	2,208	3,712	4,975	:
Niger	2,914	2,975	2,974	3,321	3,400
Namibia	1,679	1,895	2,016	2,447	3,000
Russia	2,697	2,541	2,160	2,605	2,800
USA	1,180	1,289	2,324	2,431	:
Uzbekistan	2,600	2,015	1,644	1,459	2,050
Kazakhstan	2,700	2,240	1,630	1,210	1,500
South Africa	1,699	1,671	1,421	1,436	1,450
Ukraine	1,000	1,000	1,000	1,000	1,000
France	1,730	1,053	1,016	930	761
Czech Republic	950	541	600	604	609
China (1)	780	480	500	560	600
Gabon	556	650	652	568	587
España	184	256	255	255	255
India (1)	148	155	155	250	250
Hungary	380	413	210	200	200
Argentina	126	80	65	28	40
Deutschland	116	47	35	39	30
Brazil	24	106	106	0	0
Bulgaria	100	70	0	0	0
Belgique/België (2)	34	40	25	28	0

(1) Estimates.
(2) Production from imported phosphates.

Source: NEA

Figure 1.23

Breakdown of net electricity capacity in the EU, 1997

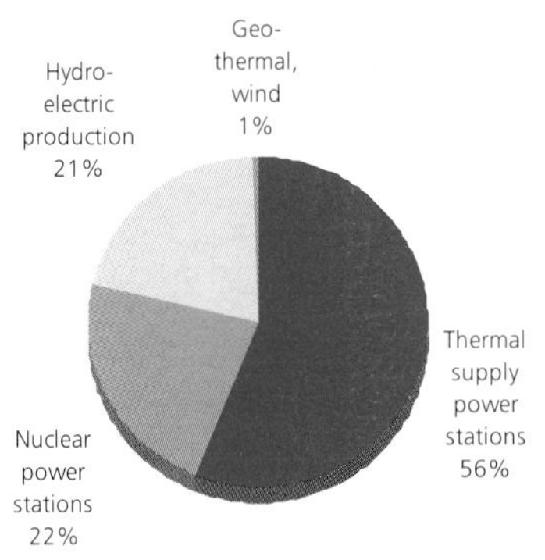

Hydro-electric production 21%

Geo-thermal, wind 1%

Thermal supply power stations 56%

Nuclear power stations 22%

Source: Eurostat (Sirene)

Figure 1.24

Net production mix of electricity in the EU, 1997

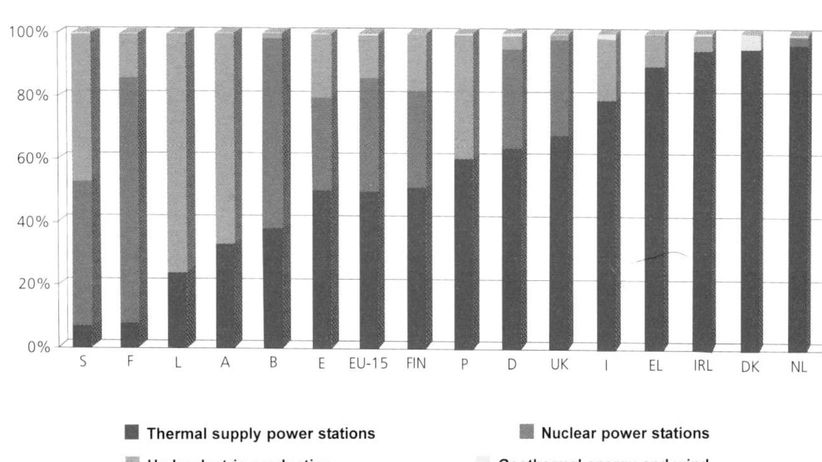

Source: Eurostat (Sirene)

Electricity generation and distribution (NACE Rev. 1 40.1)

This section covers the activities of electricity production, transmission and distribution as defined by NACE Rev.1 40.1, which includes the generation of electricity by all means, including thermal, nuclear, hydroelectric, gas turbine, diesel and renewable energies, and the transmission, distribution and supply of electricity.

Electricity is used in all almost every sphere of human activity in developed countries, and its consumption is hence very closely correlated with economic activity. Improvements in the energy efficiency of electric equipment, which would tend to slow demand growth, are often offset by the penetration of new equipment and applications using electricity. As a consequence, electricity consumption in the EU has grown at a relatively fast rate in recent decades. Due to the economic slowdown of 1992-93, slower growth was recorded at the start of the 1990s, but since 1994 electricity demand grew again at levels close to the long-term average of 2.7%.

Electricity steadily increased its penetration of total final energy consumption over the 1980s, rising from less than 15% in the early 1980s to reach 19% by 1997. The share of electricity in final energy consumption varies substantially between countries, reflecting the structure of industry, the level of automation in industry, the use of electricity for space heating, the level of appliance ownership in the domestic sector, and the availability of natural gas to compete with electricity for space-heating, water-heating and cooking in households and the services sector. The Benelux countries, for example, have low shares of electricity in the final energy mix (see figure 1.25) mainly because of the maturity of their natural gas supply systems.

In the EU, the vast majority of electricity is provided for by conventional thermal power stations that accounted for 56% of net electricity capacity in 1997. Nuclear power stations and hydroelectric production represented about a fifth each, the rest being generated by sources such as geothermal energy or wind. In terms of production, differences across the EU in the mix of electricity sources are spectacular, reflecting access to the various primary energy sources, and differing responses to policy needs to ensure security and diversity of energy supply. In 1997, conventional thermal power stations supplied less than a tenth of electricity production in Sweden

(%)

Figure 1.25

Share of electricity in final energy consumption, 1997

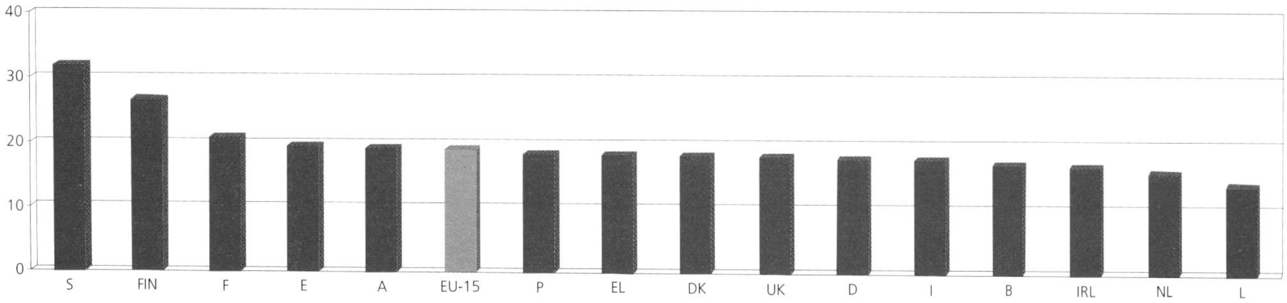

40
30
20
10
0
S FIN F E A EU-15 P EL DK UK D I B IRL NL L

Source: Eurostat (Sirene)

Figure 1.26 (%)

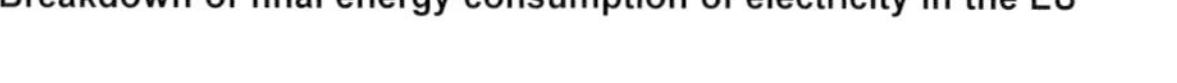

Breakdown of final energy consumption of electricity in the EU

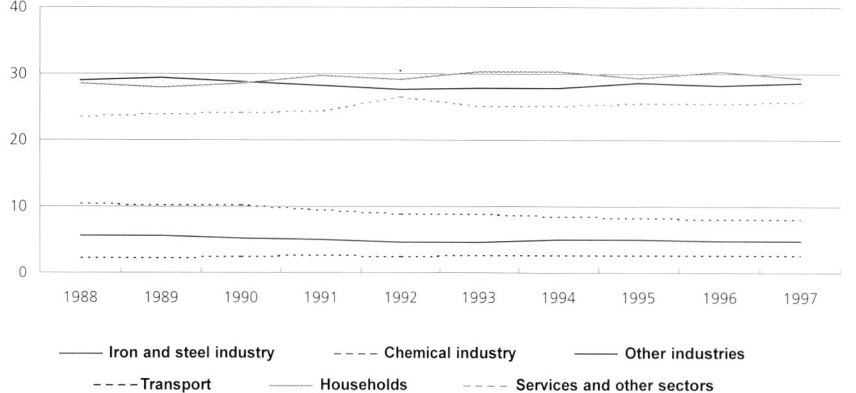

Source: Eurostat (Sirene)

Table 1.6 (%)

Electricity, gas, steam and hot water supply (NACE Rev. 1 40)

Composition of the labour force, 1997

	Females	Part-time	Highly-educated
EU-15	17.2	:	:
B	11.8	:	34.0
DK	19.9	:	27.5
D	22.3	5.1	30.4
EL	19.9	:	19.5
E	9.3	:	42.8
F	22.4	6.7	26.0
IRL	14.5	4.6	26.4
I	12.3	:	6.3
L	:	:	:
NL	15.4	19.1	27.8
A	10.5	:	:
P	14.3	:	12.8
FIN	30.9	:	37.4
S	18.6	:	24.4
UK	24.3	5.7	36.3

Source: Eurostat (LFS)

and France, but 95% or more in Ireland, Denmark or the Netherlands. Similarly, nuclear power accounted for 78% of electricity production in France, but only 30% in Finland and the United Kingdom, and no production in seven Member States. Hydroelectric sources accounted for a large share of net electricity consumption in Luxembourg (76%) and Austria (67%), as well as Portugal (40%) and Spain (20%). As for the other sources, the only significant inroad was recorded in Denmark, where wind power accounted for 4.6% of net production in 1997.

Turning to the demand side, electricity has an important role in all end-use energy demand sectors except transport, where it represents a very small component of final energy consumption (3%), almost exclusively stemming from rail transport. The energy needs of road, marine and air transport are overwhelmingly supplied by petroleum products, and there is little prospect of widespread introduction of electric-powered vehicles in the short to medium-term. Thus, most electricity consumption is concentrated within industry (42%) and the household and service sectors (55%). Electricity demand growth has been faster in recent years in the residential and commercial sectors than in industry. Increased levels of appliance ownership, together with the development of new electricity-specific applications, such as personal computing, advanced communications technologies and automated building management systems are the main reasons for this trend.

Figure 1.27 (%)

Net electricity imports as a share of national net production, 1997 (1)

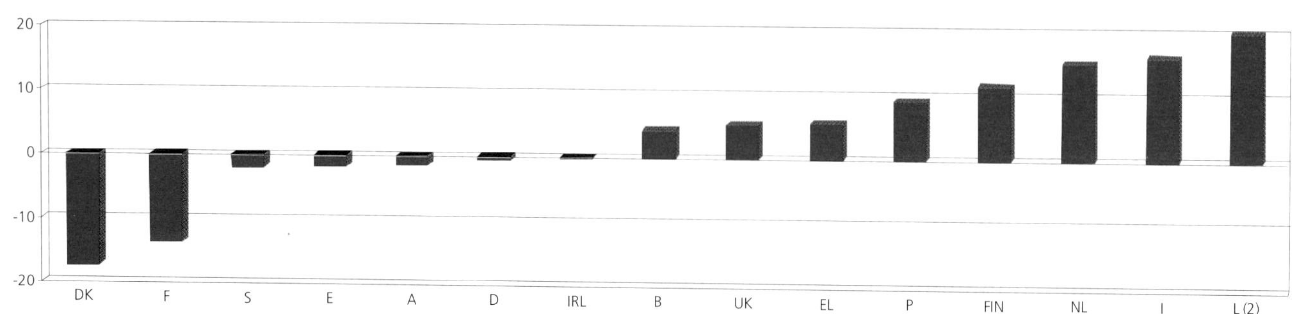

(1) A negative sign indicates net exports.
(2) Luxembourg = 417.2.

Source: UNIPEDE

Foreign trade

Europe is one of the world's most mature markets for electricity, together with North America and Japan. All these regions are characterised by relatively stable levels of electricity intensity of GDP, and development of capacity in line with, or ahead of, demand trends. This contrasts with developing countries, particularly in Asia, where economic growth and electricity demand growth have moved at a faster pace than the ability of utilities to add new generation capacity.

Trade with countries outside the EU is still very limited owing to the lack of interconnections between countries. Only Switzerland and Norway currently exchange significant amounts of electricity with the EU. Switzerland has, for many years, traded electricity with other European countries. Opportunities for electricity trade with Central and Eastern European countries have historically been limited by the lack of grid interconnection, but this is being changed since the network was linked up with Germany in 1995. Poland, the Czech Republic, Slovakia and Hungary (already inter-linked in the Centrel grid) are also now linked up with the European UCPTE grid.

The UCPTE grid is a co-operative organisation of the electricity authorities in Austria, Belgium, France, Germany, Italy, Luxembourg, Netherlands, Switzerland, Greece, Portugal, Spain and former Yugoslavia. It co-ordinates electricity transfers between countries which have been negotiated on a bi-lateral basis between national utilities. A similar organisation in the Nordic countries, known as NORDEL, co-ordinates electric power exchanges between Denmark, Norway, Sweden and Finland.

It has been the intention of the European Commission since the beginning of the 1990s to stimulate greater competition in electricity markets by measures to develop an Internal Energy Market. The cornerstone of this structure is the opening up of access to transmission grids for consumers and distributors, who are thus able to choose suppliers on an economic basis, irrespective of national boundaries. Such a system should lead to an important increase in electricity trade among EU Member States.

Figure 1.28

Electricity generation and distribution (NACE Rev. 1 40.1) Origin of EU imports, 1998

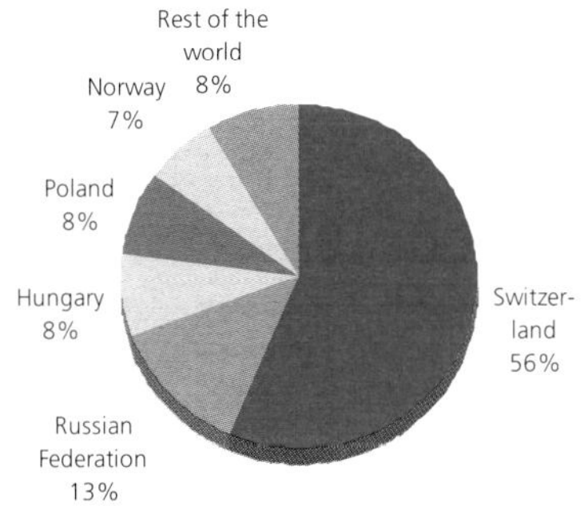

Source: Eurostat (Comext)

Figure 1.29

Electricity generation and distribution (NACE Rev. 1 40.1) Destination of EU exports, 1998

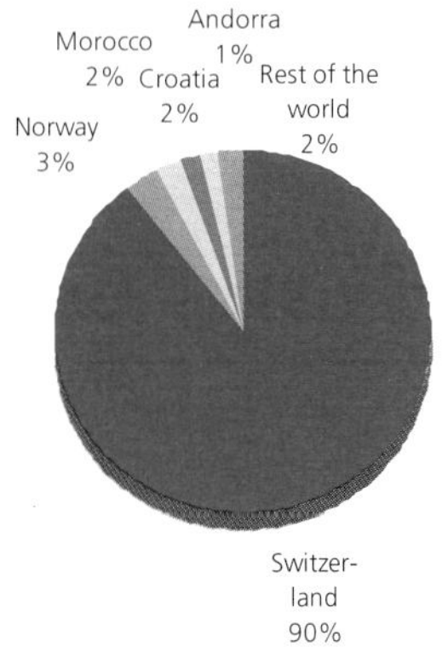

Source: Eurostat (Comext)

Water supply and distribution (NACE Rev. 1 41)

The water supply sector covered in this section is defined within the NACE Rev. 1 classification as the collection, purification and distribution of water, including the desalting of sea water, but excluding irrigation systems operation for agricultural purposes and treatment of waste water solely in order to prevent pollution.

In the European Union, the supply of drinking water is provided by private companies as well as public companies and municipalities. Some Member States have chosen to delegate the management of all or part of their water supply and waste water treatment services to private or public organisations which take responsibility, on a contractual basis and using methods agreed upon by both parties, for all or part of the infrastructure and the services.

Because water is essentially a local product, differences in price can be significant across the EU, but also inside the same country. Several reasons can be put forward to explain these disparities, such as geographical or geological conditions, the quality of the water resource, the number and size of production and water treatment units required, population density and demand conditions. Moreover, water prices may or may not cover all of the costs of the service provided. In some Member States, water prices incorporate not only the costs of the service, including the protection of resources, or the investment requirements imposed on water services, but also various taxes (such as taxes on water abstraction) and charges for waste water treatment. In France, for example, up to a fifth of the average price per cubic metre can be accounted for by taxes, and 30% by the treatment of polluted waste water, so only half of the price paid stems from water abstraction, treatment and distribution. Across the EU, Denmark and Germany appear to have the highest prices in the European Union, whereas prices are generally lower in the southern countries of the European Union (i.e. Portugal, Spain, Italy and Greece).

There is however a general trend to increase the price of water services, particularly in the waste water treatment segment, that can be mainly explained by investments being made to modernise installations and improve processes in order to meet ever increasing quality requirements, but also due to investments for aquifer protection, water treatment, maintenance of networks and modernisation of distribution (automation, remote metering where applied, leakage detection).

Figure 1.30 (litres per inhabitant per day)

Estimated per capita water consumption in selected Member States

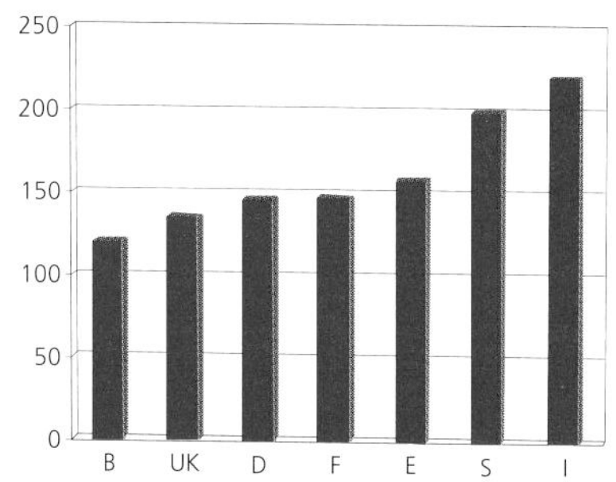

Source: Trade press

Factors influencing drinking water demand are demographic evolution, consumer habits (varying in the Member States), climate, price structures, as well as the number/types of sanitary installations and industrial developments. Thermal power stations are very important clients of water companies, and can account for up to half the water consumption, as is the case in France. The rest is almost equally distributed between industry, agriculture and households. As regards the latter, it is estimated that about 60% of daily household water consumption is accounted for by personal hygiene and sanitary treatment, one fifth to dishes and clothes washing, and less than a tenth to food and drink.

There is a clear tendency in some of the Member States to give preference to abstraction from surface water sources because groundwater sources are insufficient and their protection is becoming more and more difficult with less certain results. In other countries, groundwater abstraction is increasing to ensure sufficient resources.

In all Member States raw water abstraction for the production of drinking water is a key priority and must be carried out in accordance with conditions ensuring adequate protection of the environment and economic use of water resources, with measures taken to encourage water conservation, including leakage control.

Table 1.7 (%)

Water supply and distribution (NACE Rev. 1 41)
Composition of the labour force, 1997

	Females	Part-time	Highly-educated
EU-15	:	:	:
B	:	:	31.2
DK	:	:	:
D	20.3	8.1	21.5
EL	:	:	:
E	14.2	:	28.3
F	27.8	:	23.6
IRL	10.2	5.6	21.4
I	17.6	:	:
L	:	:	:
NL	:	:	32.8
A	:	:	:
P	:	:	:
FIN	:	:	:
S	:	:	:
UK	21.2	5.9	36.6

Source: Eurostat (LFS)

Foreign trade

Water is essentially a national, regional or even local product. It is usually not transported over very long distances because of bacteriological and cost considerations.

A number of water suppliers nevertheless export their know-how in the framework of international co-operation agreements (e.g. technical assistance or training); water suppliers can also delegate some of their activities to foreign partners, and sometimes they purchase foreign materials and products to carry out their services.

Some public or private entities have been developing operations, service provisions and co-operation and training programmes with other countries (for example, the Netherlands in Indonesia and Germany in Eastern Europe). The French company Lyonnaise des Eaux and the Spanish company Aguas de Barcelona have for example agreed to lead an ECU 750 million consortium aimed at securing water distribution and purification in the Santa Fe Province of Argentina for a period of 30 years.

Professional associations representing the industries within this chapter

CPDP
Comité Professionnel du Pétrole
B.P. 282
F-92505 Rueil Malmaison
tel: (33) 1 47 16 94 60
fax: (33) 1 47 08 10 57

EURELECTRIC / UNIPEDE
International Union of Producers and Distributors of Electrical Energy
66/2, boulevard de l'Impératrice
B-1000 Bruxelles
tel: (32) 2 515 10 00
fax: (32) 2 46 94 45 45
e-mail: unipede@unipede.org

(thousand TOE) — Table 1.8

Interior flows of solid fuels, 1997

	EU-15	B	DK	D	EL	E	F	IRL	I	L	NL	A (1)	P	FIN	S	UK
Primary production	**125,106**	**0**	**0**	**70,637**	**8,073**	**9,867**	**3,894**	**739**	**26**	**0**	**0**	**265**	**0**	**2,664**	**261**	**28,681**
Recovery	1,147	180	0	0	0	22	195	0	0	0	0	0	0	0	0	749
Variation of stocks	-944	87	-1,346	1,231	-20	1,529	807	173	555	0	-1,280	200	-132	-31	-264	-2,453
Net imports	96,513	8,095	8,003	14,856	763	7,045	9,679	1,955	10,637	312	10,385	3,103	3,623	4,648	2,477	10,934
Gross inland consumption	**221,822**	**8,362**	**6,656**	**86,723**	**8,817**	**18,464**	**14,576**	**2,867**	**11,218**	**312**	**9,105**	**3,567**	**3,491**	**7,281**	**2,473**	**37,912**
Transformation input	204,778	6,994	6,295	81,535	8,043	18,364	11,511	2,193	10,743	70	8,835	3,105	3,238	6,230	2,239	35,382
-conventional thermal power stations	*150,016*	*3,120*	*6,292*	*64,104*	*8,019*	*15,170*	*4,958*	*2,074*	*4,513*	*0*	*5,158*	*1,215*	*2,867*	*4,800*	*601*	*27,123*
Transformation output	33,624	2,495	0	11,402	47	1,989	3,979	143	3,735	0	2,059	1,066	235	598	790	5,085
Consumption of the energy branch	539	7	0	233	0	7	182	0	39	0	0	45	0	0	0	26
Available for final consumption	**50,129**	**3,855**	**361**	**16,357**	**821**	**2,083**	**6,862**	**817**	**4,170**	**242**	**2,329**	**1,483**	**488**	**1,649**	**1,024**	**7,590**
Final non-energy consumption	**1,595**	**171**	**0**	**274**	**0**	**188**	**115**	**0**	**355**	**0**	**180**	**15**	**4**	**0**	**20**	**273**
Chemical industry	1,087	171	0	72	0	188	115	0	182	0	82	0	4	0	0	273
Others	508	0	0	202	0	0	0	0	173	0	98	15	0	0	20	0
Final energy consumption	**45,901**	**3,706**	**370**	**13,396**	**964**	**1,851**	**7,039**	**865**	**3,871**	**237**	**1,556**	**1,440**	**487**	**1,045**	**1,043**	**8,033**
Industry	37,176	3,376	335	10,637	909	1,625	5,916	89	3,745	234	1,524	1,010	487	1,018	1,040	5,231
-iron and steel industry	*24,357*	*2,930*	*0*	*5,948*	*0*	*1,182*	*4,519*	*0*	*3,159*	*151*	*1,393*	*689*	*125*	*534*	*679*	*3,048*
-non ferrous metals industry	*859*	*29*	*207*	*129*	*153*	*65*	*0*	*0*	*84*	*0*	*0*	*0*	*0*	*5*	*38*	*148*
-chemical industry	*2,563*	*37*	*12*	*1,392*	*16*	*74*	*352*	*0*	*10*	*0*	*46*	*44*	*10*	*17*	*7*	*545*
-non-metallic mineral products	*5,746*	*266*	*24*	*2,205*	*726*	*240*	*271*	*47*	*371*	*83*	*51*	*197*	*352*	*123*	*185*	*603*
-ore extraction industry	*124*	*0*	*33*	*16*	*0*	*0*	*0*	*0*	*0*	*0*	*0*	*2*	*0*	*0*	*73*	*0*
-food, drink and tobacco industry	*722*	*41*	*59*	*280*	*10*	*14*	*39*	*24*	*0*	*0*	*28*	*0*	*0*	*0*	*16*	*212*
-textile, leather and clothing industry	*132*	*5*	*0*	*49*	*0*	*0*	*2*	*18*	*14*	*0*	*0*	*0*	*0*	*0*	*0*	*44*
-paper and printing industry	*969*	*36*	*0*	*462*	*0*	*6*	*220*	*0*	*0*	*0*	*0*	*79*	*0*	*0*	*24*	*143*
-engineering and other metals	*269*	*11*	*0*	*58*	*4*	*40*	*0*	*0*	*61*	*0*	*0*	*0*	*0*	*0*	*13*	*81*
-other industries	*925*	*17*	*0*	*92*	*0*	*0*	*357*	*0*	*3*	*0*	*0*	*0*	*0*	*339*	*0*	*117*
-adjustment	*510*	*4*	*1*	*6*	*0*	*3*	*155*	*0*	*43*	*0*	*6*	*-2*	*0*	*0*	*5*	*288*
Transport	14	0	0	5	1	0	0	0	0	0	0	9	0	0	0	0
-railways	*14*	*0*	*0*	*5*	*1*	*0*	*0*	*0*	*0*	*0*	*0*	*9*	*0*	*0*	*0*	*0*
Households, etc.	8,710	330	35	2,753	54	226	1,124	776	126	2	32	421	0	27	3	2,802
-households	*7,642*	*330*	*4*	*2,228*	*46*	*216*	*1,124*	*765*	*126*	*2*	*6*	*421*	*0*	*27*	*0*	*2,347*
-agriculture	*39*	*0*	*30*	*0*	*8*	*0*	*0*	*0*	*0*	*0*	*0*	*0*	*0*	*0*	*1*	*0*
-others	*1,029*	*0*	*1*	*525*	*0*	*11*	*0*	*11*	*0*	*0*	*26*	*0*	*0*	*0*	*1*	*455*
Statistical divergence	2,634	-22	-9	2,688	-142	43	-292	-48	-56	5	593	29	-3	604	-40	-716

(1) Most data are provisional.

Source: Eurostat (Sirene)

(million ECU) — Table 1.9

Solid fuels (NACE Rev. 1 10)

Market related indicators, 1998

	B/L	DK	D	EL	E	F	IRL	I	NL	A	P	FIN	S	UK
Apparent consumption (1)	:	:	7,749	:	1,890	1,678	159	813	:	:	199	473	231	5,201
Exports	123	11	187	5	2	10	39	1	177	3	0	11	10	78
Imports	592	23	883	46	549	695	125	738	818	214	185	184	142	990
Trade balance	-469	-12	-696	-41	-547	-686	-87	-737	-641	-210	-185	-173	-132	-912
Export ratio (%) (1)	:	:	4.7	:	0.0	5.9	525.6	:	:	:	0.5	2.8	11.8	1.7
Import penetration ratio (%) (1)	:	:	9.7	:	25.8	42.7	115.7	100.2	:	:	99.1	48.5	67.7	19.5
Cover ratio (%)	20.8	47.5	21.2	10.8	0.4	1.4	30.9	0.2	21.7	1.5	0.0	5.7	7.2	7.9

(1) IRL (1990); UK (1992); F (1993); I, P (1995); D, E, FIN, S (1996).

Source: Eurostat (SBS)

Table 1.10 (thousand TOE)

Evolution of interior flows of solid fuels, EU-15

	1988	1989	1990	1991	1992	1993	1994	1995	1996	1997
Primary production	**228,834**	**225,728**	**208,219**	**188,121**	**175,011**	**154,746**	**136,769**	**136,607**	**130,041**	**125,106**
Recovery	1,801	1,580	1,656	1,965	1,047	1,040	728	1,416	1,255	1,147
Variation of stocks	1,586	1,274	3,028	107	-8,086	4,667	18,822	5,342	8,276	-944
Net imports	73,142	77,471	88,248	96,077	98,639	86,606	86,341	94,408	95,222	96,513
Gross inland consumption	**305,363**	**306,052**	**301,152**	**286,270**	**266,611**	**247,059**	**242,660**	**237,773**	**234,795**	**221,822**
Transformation input	286,124	289,077	282,779	266,412	248,156	227,742	223,475	220,497	215,921	204,778
-conventional thermal power stations	*173,749*	*178,264*	*182,318*	*184,349*	*176,132*	*163,185*	*162,824*	*161,820*	*160,862*	*150,016*
Transformation output	75,127	73,091	66,028	52,734	45,077	40,017	37,495	34,714	34,275	33,624
Consumption of the energy branch	1,121	1,054	952	1,222	863	753	768	493	521	539
Available for final consumption	**93,246**	**89,012**	**83,448**	**71,370**	**62,669**	**58,580**	**55,914**	**51,498**	**52,627**	**50,129**
Final non-energy consumption	**3,625**	**3,783**	**3,401**	**2,890**	**2,913**	**2,474**	**2,756**	**1,737**	**1,599**	**1,595**
Chemical industry	1,947	1,992	1,971	1,915	1,932	1,719	1,729	1,166	1,093	1,087
Others	1,679	1,791	1,430	975	981	755	1,027	571	506	508
Final energy consumption	**89,177**	**85,408**	**80,089**	**68,902**	**61,270**	**54,982**	**51,912**	**49,073**	**46,691**	**45,901**
Industry	57,606	57,015	53,451	47,684	45,173	40,143	40,152	39,230	36,718	37,176
-iron and steel industry	*26,191*	*26,253*	*25,626*	*24,460*	*22,701*	*21,391*	*23,738*	*24,711*	*23,158*	*24,357*
-non ferrous metals industry	*1,246*	*1,389*	*1,167*	*865*	*1,011*	*944*	*868*	*730*	*694*	*859*
-chemical industry	*7,690*	*7,335*	*6,277*	*4,387*	*3,899*	*3,341*	*3,253*	*2,724*	*2,555*	*2,563*
-non-metallic mineral products	*10,900*	*10,564*	*10,312*	*9,993*	*9,622*	*8,083*	*7,657*	*6,907*	*6,432*	*5,746*
-ore extraction industry	*659*	*645*	*506*	*219*	*225*	*144*	*91*	*158*	*92*	*124*
-food, drink and tobacco industry	*2,659*	*2,628*	*2,238*	*1,701*	*1,561*	*1,412*	*1,294*	*987*	*835*	*722*
-textile, leather and clothing industry	*1,035*	*1,012*	*857*	*615*	*536*	*388*	*341*	*260*	*181*	*132*
-paper and printing industry	*1,725*	*1,538*	*1,512*	*1,340*	*1,445*	*1,350*	*1,322*	*1,394*	*989*	*969*
-engineering and other metals	*3,341*	*3,207*	*2,584*	*1,774*	*1,443*	*1,041*	*796*	*501*	*380*	*269*
-other industries	*2,087*	*1,863*	*2,055*	*1,439*	*2,281*	*1,843*	*686*	*536*	*1,157*	*925*
-adjustment	*73*	*582*	*316*	*892*	*449*	*205*	*107*	*322*	*244*	*510*
Transport	43	36	32	24	21	14	12	14	15	14
-railways	*43*	*36*	*32*	*24*	*21*	*14*	*12*	*14*	*15*	*14*
Households, etc.	31,528	28,357	26,606	21,193	16,076	14,826	11,749	9,828	9,958	8,710
-households	*23,499*	*20,427*	*19,751*	*18,789*	*12,667*	*12,089*	*10,148*	*8,086*	*8,294*	*7,642*
-agriculture	*129*	*112*	*100*	*108*	*128*	*119*	*117*	*114*	*103*	*39*
-others	*7,900*	*7,817*	*6,755*	*2,296*	*3,281*	*2,618*	*1,484*	*1,628*	*1,562*	*1,029*
Statistical divergence	443	-179	-42	-422	-1,514	1,123	1,245	687	4,337	2,634

Source: Eurostat (Sirene)

Table 1.11 (million ECU)

Solid fuel products (NACE Rev. 1 23.1)

Market related indicators, 1998

	B/L	DK	D	EL	E	F	IRL	I	NL	A	P	FIN	S	UK
Apparent consumption (1)	92	5	:	2	43	194	1	:	:	67	:	43	28	166
Exports (2)	62	0	25	0	43	60	0	22	64	1	7	3	7	31
Imports	105	5	364	2	27	179	1	57	34	56	2	46	36	69
Trade balance (2)	-43	-5	-339	-4	17	-118	-1	-36	30	-55	5	-43	-29	-37
Export ratio (%) (3)	:	:	:	:	45.0	80.0	:	:	:	:	:	32,091.4	:	15.3
Import penetration ratio (%) (1)	165.4	100.0	:	105.6	70.5	92.2	100.3	:	:	100.3	:	107.5	131.4	31.2
Cover ratio (%) (2)	59.2	0.0	7.0	0.0	162.6	33.7	7.6	37.8	189.7	1.5	310.7	7.0	19.1	45.5

(1) B/L, UK (1993); E (1994); EL, A (1995); DK, IRL, S (1996). (2) DK (1996); EL (1997). (3) UK (1993); E (1994).

Source: Eurostat (SBS)

(thousand TOE) Table 1.12

Interior flows of crude oil and petroleum products, 1997

	EU-15	B	DK	D	EL	E	F	IRL	I	L	NL	A (1)	P	FIN	S	UK
Primary production	**158,016**	**0**	**11,590**	**2,836**	**466**	**369**	**2,417**	**0**	**6,002**	**0**	**2,960**	**977**	**0**	**0**	**0**	**130,400**
Recovery	266	0	0	200	0	0	66	0	0	0	0	0	0	0	0	0
Variations of stocks	312	116	269	648	-393	-509	-787	-107	758	8	-48	37	-100	230	54	137
Net imports	469,287	27,409	-395	135,534	18,104	61,909	88,665	6,693	88,282	1,913	36,462	10,695	14,464	10,169	17,013	-47,631
Marine bunkers	40,108	5,062	1,481	2,146	3,119	5,669	2,917	150	2,385	0	12,091	0	492	403	1,300	2,893
Gross inland consumption	**587,774**	**22,464**	**9,983**	**137,072**	**15,059**	**56,100**	**87,444**	**6,436**	**92,657**	**1,921**	**27,284**	**11,708**	**13,871**	**9,996**	**15,767**	**80,013**
Transformation input	707,554	35,951	10,489	116,676	22,791	60,123	93,415	3,724	121,518	0	81,677	10,919	14,664	12,442	22,725	100,442
-conventional thermal power stations	*38,459*	*201*	*1,633*	*1,318*	*1,964*	*2,717*	*1,167*	*790*	*23,261*	*0*	*735*	*582*	*1,444*	*284*	*608*	*1,755*
-refineries	*666,703*	*35,750*	*8,801*	*114,226*	*20,806*	*57,333*	*92,168*	*2,934*	*98,252*	*0*	*80,942*	*10,157*	*13,168*	*11,934*	*21,731*	*98,502*
Transformation output	661,854	35,512	8,896	112,405	20,715	56,816	91,920	2,902	97,308	0	80,403	10,160	13,074	11,863	21,459	98,423
Exchanges, transfers, returns	5,214	1,154	-15	197	62	-380	92	0	4,083	0	-284	0	-21	40	-30	316
Consumption of the energy branch	37,072	1,739	399	6,723	899	4,138	5,486	87	4,590	0	3,921	439	603	561	427	7,059
Available for final consumption	**510,215**	**21,439**	**7,976**	**126,275**	**12,145**	**48,275**	**80,555**	**5,527**	**67,939**	**1,921**	**21,805**	**10,510**	**11,657**	**8,896**	**14,045**	**71,251**
Final non-energy consumption	**85,149**	**4,175**	**433**	**21,545**	**391**	**6,278**	**15,443**	**334**	**12,865**	**14**	**5,872**	**1,343**	**2,069**	**1,206**	**2,326**	**10,854**
Chemical industry	57,898	3,488	0	16,475	51	3,714	11,450	0	9,475	2	3,744	0	1,203	463	1,193	6,640
Others	27,251	687	433	5,070	339	2,564	3,993	334	3,390	12	2,127	1,343	866	743	1,133	4,215
Final energy consumption	**430,072**	**17,327**	**7,384**	**105,317**	**12,058**	**41,341**	**70,108**	**5,340**	**54,421**	**1,908**	**15,858**	**8,874**	**9,233**	**7,265**	**12,261**	**61,375**
Industry	45,641	1,595	718	7,168	2,127	6,952	6,693	722	6,489	98	1,066	764	2,358	819	1,781	6,289
-iron and steel industry	*3,386*	*40*	*7*	*1,425*	*26*	*460*	*142*	*2*	*100*	*40*	*5*	*115*	*44*	*118*	*312*	*550*
-non ferrous metals industry	*1,434*	*44*	*0*	*155*	*190*	*112*	*548*	*246*	*12*	*0*	*0*	*16*	*17*	*20*	*27*	*47*
-chemical industry	*7,485*	*368*	*52*	*270*	*201*	*1,906*	*624*	*49*	*2,191*	*8*	*801*	*53*	*385*	*125*	*58*	*395*
-non-metallic mineral products	*8,511*	*153*	*130*	*1,234*	*443*	*2,355*	*741*	*25*	*2,143*	*0*	*48*	*194*	*582*	*81*	*142*	*240*
-ore extraction industry	*864*	*0*	*28*	*115*	*95*	*103*	*51*	*20*	*13*	*0*	*30*	*8*	*3*	*36*	*55*	*307*
-food, drink and tobacco industry	*4,827*	*237*	*194*	*1,025*	*251*	*771*	*738*	*148*	*321*	*5*	*25*	*79*	*292*	*105*	*193*	*443*
-textile, leather and clothing industry	*1,512*	*24*	*8*	*188*	*134*	*180*	*171*	*27*	*280*	*0*	*1*	*52*	*289*	*28*	*38*	*94*
-paper and printing industry	*2,604*	*36*	*11*	*408*	*91*	*267*	*310*	*10*	*324*	*0*	*3*	*100*	*335*	*53*	*536*	*118*
-engineering and other metals	*3,335*	*47*	*73*	*1,125*	*7*	*352*	*236*	*50*	*549*	*0*	*21*	*67*	*46*	*73*	*212*	*478*
-other industries	*10,343*	*641*	*214*	*1,222*	*637*	*436*	*2,090*	*48*	*544*	*25*	*131*	*62*	*364*	*181*	*198*	*3,550*
-adjustment	*1,339*	*6*	*1*	*-1*	*51*	*11*	*1,043*	*97*	*14*	*20*	*0*	*19*	*2*	*0*	*11*	*66*
Transport	283,442	9,080	4,727	62,236	6,711	27,696	45,911	2,920	37,728	1,460	13,354	5,979	5,227	4,198	7,435	48,779
-railways	*2,715*	*61*	*94*	*677*	*42*	*404*	*418*	*87*	*194*	*5*	*0*	*101*	*54*	*55*	*35*	*488*
-road transport	*238,168*	*7,285*	*3,654*	*54,734*	*4,918*	*21,942*	*39,600*	*2,365*	*34,366*	*1,204*	*9,663*	*5,369*	*4,526*	*3,602*	*6,424*	*38,516*
-air transport	*36,044*	*1,342*	*818*	*6,423*	*1,187*	*3,649*	*5,154*	*434*	*2,720*	*251*	*3,003*	*508*	*604*	*463*	*876*	*8,611*
-inland navigation	*6,515*	*393*	*161*	*402*	*563*	*1,701*	*739*	*34*	*448*	*0*	*687*	*0*	*44*	*78*	*99*	*1,164*
Households, etc.	100,989	6,651	1,939	35,914	3,221	6,693	17,504	1,698	10,204	350	1,438	2,131	1,647	2,248	3,045	6,307
-households	*64,419*	*4,195*	*1,126*	*22,455*	*2,141*	*3,825*	*14,516*	*680*	*6,297*	*321*	*93*	*2,124*	*740*	*1,365*	*1,385*	*3,158*
-fisheries	*0*	*0*	*0*	*0*	*0*	*0*	*0*	*0*	*0*	*0*	*0*	*0*	*0*	*0*	*0*	*0*
-agriculture	*13,928*	*1,041*	*639*	*1,647*	*835*	*1,703*	*2,688*	*261*	*2,680*	*14*	*275*	*0*	*481*	*516*	*390*	*760*
-others	*22,643*	*1,416*	*175*	*11,812*	*245*	*1,165*	*300*	*757*	*1,227*	*16*	*1,071*	*7*	*426*	*367*	*1,270*	*2,390*
Statistical divergence	-5,005	-63	158	-588	-304	656	-4,996	-147	653	-1	75	292	355	424	-542	-978

(1) Most data are provisional.

Source: Eurostat (Sirene)

Table 1.13 (thousand TOE)

Evolution of interior flows of crude oil and petroleum products, EU-15

	1988	1989	1990	1991	1992	1993	1994	1995	1996	1997
Primary production	**143,478**	**119,850**	**116,798**	**118,075**	**121,315**	**126,993**	**156,242**	**159,341**	**158,870**	**158,016**
Recovery	67	155	166	200	182	176	175	313	310	266
Variations of stocks	4,001	-1,574	1,397	2,363	547	4,538	-1,302	4,367	-791	312
Net imports	420,652	453,430	460,856	476,288	483,762	467,564	446,342	446,732	465,270	469,287
Marine bunkers	31,852	31,840	34,166	33,893	34,177	35,082	33,746	34,714	36,834	40,108
Gross inland consumption	**536,345**	**540,020**	**545,051**	**563,033**	**571,630**	**564,190**	**567,711**	**576,039**	**586,824**	**587,774**
Transformation input	620,106	630,077	639,232	651,691	671,435	674,128	681,562	680,878	697,651	707,554
-conventional thermal power stations	*36,686*	*42,201*	*42,559*	*44,275*	*46,114*	*42,204*	*40,390*	*43,650*	*41,701*	*38,459*
-refineries	*580,065*	*584,922*	*593,671*	*603,763*	*621,992*	*628,729*	*638,229*	*635,197*	*653,808*	*666,703*
Transformation output	575,636	581,189	589,768	600,820	618,642	625,898	634,445	631,238	649,481	661,854
Exchanges, transfers, returns	1,201	1,408	1,568	1,953	2,392	6,005	6,677	6,151	5,364	5,214
Consumption of the energy branch	31,782	32,232	32,320	32,394	34,172	35,346	36,591	36,819	38,317	37,072
Available for final consumption	**461,293**	**460,308**	**464,835**	**481,720**	**487,057**	**486,619**	**490,679**	**495,731**	**505,702**	**510,215**
Final non-energy consumption	**68,609**	**68,223**	**69,315**	**73,328**	**76,977**	**72,525**	**78,390**	**81,146**	**80,032**	**85,149**
Chemical industry	42,801	42,215	44,089	46,403	50,496	47,409	51,282	55,991	55,533	57,898
Others	25,808	26,008	25,226	26,925	26,482	25,115	27,108	25,154	24,499	27,251
Final energy consumption	**394,749**	**390,494**	**396,805**	**408,321**	**412,819**	**417,296**	**416,348**	**419,590**	**431,510**	**430,072**
Industry	55,528	51,953	48,885	48,287	47,727	46,602	48,878	48,669	46,187	45,641
-iron and steel industry	*4,247*	*4,398*	*3,730*	*3,597*	*3,479*	*3,628*	*3,828*	*3,787*	*3,345*	*3,386*
-non ferrous metals industry	*1,703*	*1,413*	*1,965*	*1,397*	*1,347*	*1,316*	*1,324*	*1,241*	*1,266*	*1,434*
-chemical industry	*11,943*	*11,302*	*10,338*	*9,957*	*10,049*	*9,042*	*9,902*	*9,279*	*7,370*	*7,485*
-non-metallic mineral products	*9,408*	*9,625*	*9,605*	*9,355*	*9,007*	*8,534*	*8,644*	*8,403*	*8,276*	*8,511*
-ore extraction industry	*823*	*769*	*759*	*750*	*803*	*755*	*762*	*928*	*890*	*864*
-food, drink and tobacco industry	*6,562*	*6,047*	*5,968*	*6,165*	*6,082*	*5,780*	*5,865*	*5,655*	*5,293*	*4,827*
-textile, leather and clothing industry	*2,549*	*2,412*	*2,291*	*2,102*	*1,889*	*1,829*	*2,002*	*1,642*	*1,598*	*1,512*
-paper and printing industry	*3,252*	*3,112*	*2,938*	*2,916*	*2,701*	*2,549*	*2,852*	*2,827*	*2,746*	*2,604*
-engineering and other metals	*5,621*	*4,727*	*4,474*	*4,643*	*4,321*	*3,859*	*3,752*	*3,439*	*3,630*	*3,335*
-other industries	*8,974*	*7,715*	*7,273*	*7,853*	*8,184*	*8,307*	*8,830*	*10,230*	*10,554*	*10,343*
-adjustment	*446*	*432*	*-457*	*-447*	*-134*	*1,002*	*1,117*	*1,238*	*1,219*	*1,339*
Transport	230,846	241,072	249,603	252,649	260,789	266,476	267,283	270,716	278,150	283,442
-railways	*3,144*	*3,006*	*2,852*	*2,821*	*2,829*	*2,836*	*2,674*	*2,732*	*2,722*	*2,715*
-road transport	*197,261*	*205,176*	*212,260*	*215,108*	*222,024*	*226,690*	*226,337*	*228,753*	*234,198*	*238,168*
-air transport	*25,435*	*26,815*	*27,808*	*27,877*	*28,796*	*30,049*	*31,303*	*32,545*	*34,368*	*36,044*
-inland navigation	*5,005*	*6,076*	*6,683*	*6,843*	*7,140*	*6,901*	*6,969*	*6,686*	*6,862*	*6,515*
Households, etc.	108,375	97,469	98,318	107,384	104,303	104,218	100,187	100,205	107,173	100,989
-households	*68,922*	*67,444*	*64,242*	*70,235*	*66,904*	*66,376*	*62,698*	*63,331*	*68,118*	*64,419*
-fisheries	*1,278*	*496*	*372*	*135*	*0*	*0*	*0*	*0*	*0*	*0*
-agriculture	*13,064*	*12,138*	*12,155*	*13,257*	*13,341*	*13,188*	*13,470*	*13,716*	*14,196*	*13,928*
-others	*25,111*	*17,391*	*21,549*	*23,757*	*24,058*	*24,654*	*24,019*	*23,158*	*24,860*	*22,643*
Statistical divergence	-2,065	1,591	-1,285	71	-2,740	-3,202	-4,059	-5,005	-5,840	-5,005

Source: Eurostat (Sirene)

(thousand TOE) — Table 1.14

Interior flows of gas, 1997

	EU-15	B	DK	D (1)	EL (1)	E	F	IRL	I	L	NL	A (1)	P	FIN	S	UK
Primary production	**182,167**	**0**	**6,958**	**15,943**	**45**	**163**	**2,127**	**1,906**	**15,780**	**0**	**60,591**	**1,216**	**0**	**0**	**0**	**77,439**
Variations of stocks	-4,556	-16	-316	-3,098	-3	-395	-138	0	-270	0	-12	195	-13	0	0	-491
Net imports	124,255	11,280	-2,781	58,249	129	11,540	29,350	865	31,976	626	-25,247	5,129	99	2,907	719	-588
Gross inland consumption	**301,866**	**11,265**	**3,862**	**71,094**	**171**	**11,308**	**31,339**	**2,772**	**47,486**	**626**	**35,333**	**6,539**	**87**	**2,907**	**719**	**76,360**
Transformation input	74,963	2,971	1,558	16,488	87	3,022	1,502	1,388	12,515	74	10,878	2,875	94	1,852	473	19,188
-conventional thermal power stations	*69,862*	*2,971*	*1,453*	*12,202*	*87*	*3,012*	*1,502*	*1,388*	*12,515*	*74*	*10,878*	*2,376*	*76*	*1,714*	*426*	*19,188*
Transformation output	19,717	1,379	0	6,227	14	992	2,594	0	2,190	70	1,438	649	178	545	584	2,858
Exchanges, transfers, returns	78	0	46	0	0	0	32	0	0	0	0	0	0	0	0	0
Consumption of the energy branch	13,210	319	464	2,257	25	340	808	0	956	0	1,655	531	29	0	95	5,730
Distribution losses	2,584	0	4	717	2	246	163	47	213	6	0	112	9	0	59	1,006
Available for final consumption	**230,904**	**9,354**	**1,882**	**57,859**	**70**	**8,692**	**31,493**	**1,337**	**35,992**	**617**	**24,238**	**3,670**	**133**	**1,600**	**675**	**53,294**
Final non-energy consumption	**10,964**	**724**	**0**	**1,935**	**40**	**533**	**2,352**	**466**	**963**	**0**	**2,687**	**304**	**0**	**32**	**0**	**929**
Chemical industry	10,964	724	0	1,935	40	533	2,352	466	963	0	2,687	304	0	32	0	929
Final energy consumption	**215,868**	**8,717**	**1,844**	**52,481**	**45**	**7,921**	**29,425**	**871**	**35,031**	**617**	**21,927**	**3,835**	**133**	**1,560**	**654**	**50,809**
Industry	86,431	4,059	872	21,252	36	6,322	12,252	379	15,626	416	6,371	1,757	71	1,496	501	15,020
-iron and steel industry	*17,145*	*1,089*	*48*	*5,011*	*0*	*902*	*1,796*	*17*	*2,271*	*181*	*802*	*723*	*33*	*578*	*231*	*3,462*
-non ferrous metals industry	*2,161*	*103*	*0*	*792*	*0*	*115*	*359*	*0*	*327*	*0*	*96*	*0*	*0*	*0*	*8*	*360*
-chemical industry	*18,054*	*1,143*	*78*	*4,984*	*0*	*1,171*	*1,737*	*126*	*2,763*	*0*	*2,324*	*182*	*0*	*31*	*56*	*3,458*
-non-metallic mineral products	*11,941*	*417*	*105*	*2,793*	*0*	*1,495*	*1,612*	*45*	*3,268*	*0*	*632*	*266*	*33*	*109*	*22*	*1,145*
-ore extraction industry	*492*	*0*	*9*	*113*	*0*	*90*	*149*	*12*	*40*	*0*	*15*	*61*	*0*	*0*	*3*	*0*
-food, drink and tobacco industry	*10,474*	*196*	*368*	*1,842*	*1*	*594*	*2,096*	*145*	*1,611*	*0*	*1,239*	*165*	*0*	*33*	*93*	*2,092*
-textile, leather and clothing industry	*3,403*	*63*	*30*	*445*	*1*	*573*	*411*	*0*	*1,154*	*0*	*156*	*45*	*0*	*0*	*3*	*522*
-paper and printing industry	*8,035*	*90*	*67*	*1,795*	*1*	*817*	*1,294*	*0*	*1,462*	*0*	*390*	*190*	*0*	*724*	*47*	*1,160*
-engineering and other metals	*9,244*	*156*	*108*	*2,660*	*0*	*509*	*1,537*	*0*	*1,948*	*0*	*530*	*70*	*4*	*0*	*26*	*1,696*
-other industries	*5,419*	*801*	*60*	*815*	*0*	*57*	*1,259*	*34*	*781*	*235*	*189*	*26*	*2*	*22*	*12*	*1,126*
-adjustment	*62*	*0*	*0*	*0*	*33*	*0*	*0*	*0*	*0*	*0*	*0*	*29*	*0*	*0*	*0*	*0*
Transport	303	0	0	0	0	0	0	0	278	0	0	25	0	0	0	0
-road transport	*303*	*0*	*0*	*0*	*0*	*0*	*0*	*0*	*278*	*0*	*0*	*25*	*0*	*0*	*0*	*0*
Households, etc.	129,135	4,658	972	31,229	8	1,598	17,173	492	19,127	201	15,556	2,052	62	63	153	35,789
-households	*93,605*	*3,196*	*668*	*22,820*	*0*	*1,161*	*8,869*	*285*	*19,010*	*201*	*8,467*	*2,052*	*43*	*19*	*75*	*26,739*
-agriculture	*4,225*	*0*	*96*	*246*	*0*	*27*	*211*	*0*	*118*	*0*	*3,402*	*0*	*0*	*15*	*0*	*112*
-others	*31,305*	*1,463*	*209*	*8,163*	*8*	*410*	*8,094*	*206*	*0*	*0*	*3,686*	*0*	*19*	*30*	*78*	*8,938*
Statistical divergence	4,072	-88	38	3,443	-14	238	-284	0	-2	0	-376	-469	0	9	21	1,556

(1) Most data are provisional.

Source: Eurostat (Sirene)

Table 1.15 (thousand TOE)

Evolution of interior flows of gas, EU-15

	1988	1989	1990	1991	1992	1993	1994	1995	1996	1997
Primary production	**124,723**	**129,085**	**132,871**	**145,680**	**146,838**	**157,894**	**159,737**	**166,597**	**188,632**	**182,167**
Variations of stocks	-566	-2,301	-3,112	-322	-4,946	-609	-3,448	-1,872	-1,953	-4,556
Net imports	82,364	88,867	92,293	94,335	95,221	94,945	97,345	108,626	118,458	124,255
Gross inland consumption	**206,521**	**215,651**	**222,052**	**239,693**	**237,113**	**252,230**	**253,635**	**273,351**	**305,137**	**301,866**
Transformation input	37,163	40,447	41,865	42,076	41,735	47,172	51,746	61,223	69,362	74,963
-conventional thermal power stations	*31,344*	*34,908*	*36,530*	*36,708*	*36,839*	*42,462*	*46,843*	*55,170*	*64,156*	*69,862*
Transformation output	27,648	28,198	26,283	23,698	21,680	20,598	20,036	20,033	19,653	19,717
Exchanges, transfers, returns	40	46	39	17	73	26	31	40	40	78
Consumption of the energy branch	12,105	12,074	11,628	11,536	10,930	11,252	11,574	12,467	13,280	13,210
Distribution losses	2,061	2,517	2,877	3,126	2,665	1,497	1,583	1,635	3,090	2,584
Available for final consumption	**182,881**	**188,856**	**192,005**	**206,670**	**203,536**	**212,933**	**208,797**	**218,099**	**239,098**	**230,904**
Final non-energy consumption	**13,191**	**13,354**	**12,487**	**11,925**	**9,821**	**10,307**	**11,254**	**11,417**	**10,419**	**10,964**
Chemical industry	13,191	13,354	12,487	11,925	9,821	10,307	11,254	11,417	10,419	10,964
Final energy consumption	**169,644**	**175,559**	**178,233**	**193,559**	**193,108**	**198,393**	**195,423**	**205,745**	**227,713**	**215,868**
Industry	72,234	76,580	77,160	76,435	77,248	77,302	78,106	82,008	88,238	86,431
-iron and steel industry	*19,021*	*19,704*	*18,014*	*17,176*	*16,344*	*16,088*	*16,964*	*17,083*	*17,470*	*17,145*
-non ferrous metals industry	*1,743*	*1,867*	*1,839*	*1,836*	*1,816*	*1,784*	*1,791*	*1,931*	*2,035*	*2,161*
-chemical industry	*15,739*	*17,016*	*16,795*	*15,749*	*18,000*	*17,132*	*17,016*	*17,620*	*18,674*	*18,054*
-non-metallic mineral products	*10,021*	*10,722*	*10,771*	*10,495*	*10,500*	*10,711*	*10,754*	*11,574*	*12,329*	*11,941*
-ore extraction industry	*480*	*520*	*535*	*653*	*546*	*554*	*530*	*621*	*675*	*492*
-food, drink and tobacco industry	*7,007*	*7,575*	*7,614*	*8,235*	*8,538*	*8,740*	*8,929*	*9,598*	*10,533*	*10,474*
-textile, leather and clothing industry	*2,129*	*2,305*	*2,526*	*2,849*	*2,807*	*3,042*	*2,919*	*3,304*	*3,489*	*3,403*
-paper and printing industry	*4,169*	*4,669*	*5,267*	*5,596*	*5,803*	*6,316*	*6,765*	*6,960*	*7,547*	*8,035*
-engineering and other metals	*7,638*	*7,923*	*7,978*	*9,196*	*8,847*	*8,669*	*8,060*	*9,073*	*8,727*	*9,244*
-other industries	*4,335*	*4,296*	*5,636*	*4,661*	*4,043*	*4,239*	*4,320*	*4,231*	*6,733*	*5,419*
-adjustment	*-49*	*-17*	*184*	*-11*	*4*	*28*	*57*	*13*	*26*	*62*
Transport	223	212	208	213	236	239	250	267	289	303
-road transport	*223*	*212*	*208*	*213*	*236*	*239*	*250*	*267*	*289*	*303*
Households, etc.	97,187	98,767	100,865	116,911	115,624	120,852	117,067	123,470	139,187	129,135
-households	*67,690*	*74,148*	*76,039*	*84,126*	*83,305*	*87,232*	*84,319*	*88,664*	*100,897*	*93,605*
-agriculture	*2,858*	*3,034*	*3,508*	*4,023*	*4,048*	*4,295*	*3,945*	*4,385*	*4,205*	*4,225*
-others	*26,640*	*21,584*	*21,318*	*28,762*	*28,271*	*29,326*	*28,803*	*30,420*	*34,084*	*31,305*
Statistical divergence	47	-57	1,285	1,185	607	4,233	2,121	937	966	4,072

Source: Eurostat (Sirene)

(million ECU) Table 1.16

Crude petroleum and natural gas (NACE Rev. 1 11)

Market related indicators, 1998

	B/L	DK	D	EL	E	F	IRL	I	NL	A	P	FIN	S	UK
Apparent consumption (1)	:	:	20,674	1,015	5,262	12,054	295	12,906	:	:	:	1,237	2,478	:
Exports (2)	1	654	13	72	3	106	0	14	2,902	10	0	0	0	6,538
Imports	4,022	444	15,412	1,323	5,756	10,640	408	7,211	5,640	1,228	1,129	1,274	1,612	3,322
Trade balance (2)	-4,022	210	-15,399	-1,250	-5,754	-10,534	-288	-7,197	-2,738	-1,218	-1,129	-1,274	-1,612	3,216
Export ratio (%) (3)	:	:	7.2	68.1	1.3	0.2	:	0.6	:	:	:	:	:	:
Import penetration ratio (%) (1)	:	:	92.2	98.7	98.6	82.6	100.0	54.0	:	:	:	100.0	100.0	:
Cover ratio (%) (2)	0.0	147.3	0.1	5.5	0.0	1.0	0.0	0.2	51.5	0.8	0.0	0.0	0.0	196.8

(1) IRL (1990); E (1994); EL, I (1995); D, F, FIN, S (1996). (2) IRL (1996). (3) E (1994); EL, I (1995); D, F (1996).

(million ECU) Table 1.17

Manufacture of refined petroleum products (NACE Rev. 1 23.2)

Market related indicators in the EU

	1988	1989	1990	1991	1992	1993	1994	1995	1996	1997	1998
Apparent consumption	:	:	:	:	:	:	:	163,001	:	:	:
Exports	6,112	8,232	8,087	9,850	9,053	10,209	10,886	8,713	11,459	12,308	9,269
Imports	8,456	8,891	10,924	11,078	10,054	8,966	8,858	9,659	9,334	9,624	6,296
Trade balance	-2,344	-659	-2,837	-1,229	-1,001	1,243	2,028	-946	2,124	2,684	2,974
Export ratio (%)	:	:	:	:	:	:	:	5.4	:	:	:
Import penetration ratio (%)	:	:	:	:	:	:	:	5.9	:	:	:
Cover ratio (%)	72.3	92.6	74.0	88.9	90.0	113.9	122.9	90.2	122.8	127.9	147.2

(million ECU) Table 1.18

Manufacture of refined petroleum products (NACE Rev. 1 23.2)

Market related indicators, 1998

	B/L	DK	D	EL	E	F	IRL	I	NL	A	P	FIN	S	UK
Apparent consumption (1)	:	221	:	1,901	8,307	35,700	:	39,029	:	3,392	:	1,822	1,864	51,433
Exports	3,371	323	2,543	568	1,870	2,624	104	2,321	5,447	230	299	689	1,040	3,284
Imports	2,568	561	5,245	282	1,110	2,981	412	2,605	2,106	682	432	415	813	1,931
Trade balance	804	-238	-2,703	286	759	-357	-307	-283	3,341	-451	-133	274	227	1,353
Export ratio (%) (1)	:	1,808.1	:	26.0	20.6	7.4	:	6.0	:	5.3	:	28.9	49.7	6.2
Import penetration ratio (%) (1)	:	341.2	:	14.8	13.4	8.4	:	6.7	:	14.8	:	22.4	43.6	3.8
Cover ratio (%)	131.3	57.5	48.5	201.5	168.4	88.0	25.4	89.1	258.7	33.8	69.3	166.0	127.9	170.1

(1) A (1994); FIN (1995); DK (1997).

Source: Eurostat (SBS)

Table 1.19 (thousand TOE)

Interior flows of electricity, 1997

	EU-15	B	DK	D	EL	E	F	IRL	I	L	NL	A	P	FIN	S	UK
Net imports	**669**	**281**	**-624**	**-202**	**197**	**-264**	**-5,623**	**-1**	**3,339**	**446**	**1,086**	**-66**	**249**	**658**	**-233**	**1,425**
Gross inland consumption	**669**	**281**	**-624**	**-202**	**197**	**-264**	**-5,623**	**-1**	**3,339**	**446**	**1,086**	**-66**	**249**	**658**	**-233**	**1,425**
Transformation output	180,564	6,673	3,640	45,369	3,386	12,934	37,464	1,631	17,609	28	7,403	1,682	1,803	4,894	6,895	29,154
-conventional thermal power stations	*106,626*	*2,597*	*3,640*	*30,723*	*3,386*	*8,180*	*3,458*	*1,631*	*17,609*	*28*	*7,196*	*1,682*	*1,803*	*3,097*	*882*	*20,715*
-nuclear power stations	*73,938*	*4,076*	*0*	*14,646*	*0*	*4,755*	*34,005*	*0*	*0*	*0*	*207*	*0*	*0*	*1,797*	*6,013*	*8,439*
Exchanges, transfers, returns	26,067	27	168	1,750	337	3,037	5,399	63	3,587	7	49	3,094	1,130	1,054	5,952	412
Consumption of the energy branch	18,105	484	271	5,334	439	1,059	4,233	114	1,703	31	519	236	161	338	982	2,201
Distribution losses	12,533	322	176	1,882	329	1,436	2,467	143	1,524	14	321	274	280	218	948	2,200
Available for final consumption	**176,662**	**6,175**	**2,738**	**39,701**	**3,153**	**13,212**	**30,539**	**1,435**	**21,309**	**436**	**7,697**	**4,200**	**2,741**	**6,050**	**10,684**	**26,591**
Final energy consumption	**176,658**	**6,175**	**2,738**	**39,701**	**3,153**	**13,204**	**30,539**	**1,435**	**21,309**	**441**	**7,697**	**4,200**	**2,741**	**6,050**	**10,684**	**26,591**
Industry	73,954	3,132	853	17,738	1,058	5,606	10,980	569	10,621	272	3,326	1,593	1,225	3,394	4,580	9,006
-iron and steel industry	*8,772*	*542*	*60*	*2,072*	*72*	*908*	*1,353*	*24*	*1,588*	*145*	*200*	*227*	*61*	*202*	*427*	*890*
-non ferrous metals industry	*5,156*	*162*	*0*	*1,480*	*284*	*723*	*741*	*26*	*464*	*0*	*423*	*0*	*9*	*160*	*230*	*454*
-chemical industry	*14,605*	*1,060*	*107*	*4,595*	*100*	*804*	*2,188*	*76*	*1,744*	*23*	*1,047*	*213*	*206*	*370*	*442*	*1,631*
-non-metallic mineral products	*5,409*	*213*	*56*	*1,280*	*167*	*606*	*755*	*47*	*1,040*	*27*	*135*	*135*	*170*	*62*	*94*	*624*
-ore extraction industry	*908*	*32*	*0*	*177*	*25*	*127*	*83*	*23*	*95*	*1*	*22*	*34*	*32*	*43*	*213*	*0*
-food, drink and tobacco industry	*6,901*	*314*	*204*	*1,166*	*87*	*550*	*1,450*	*138*	*876*	*6*	*541*	*120*	*112*	*127*	*215*	*994*
-textile, leather and clothing industry	*2,972*	*161*	*18*	*375*	*84*	*289*	*334*	*30*	*954*	*24*	*54*	*54*	*221*	*23*	*29*	*321*
-paper and printing industry	*9,748*	*205*	*61*	*1,692*	*39*	*416*	*1,017*	*13*	*782*	*0*	*306*	*355*	*158*	*2,055*	*1,804*	*847*
-engineering and other metals	*10,531*	*250*	*171*	*2,178*	*57*	*632*	*2,029*	*75*	*1,905*	*47*	*365*	*231*	*110*	*181*	*585*	*1,716*
-other industries	*8,942*	*193*	*168*	*2,723*	*143*	*551*	*1,030*	*118*	*1,173*	*0*	*233*	*224*	*146*	*171*	*541*	*1,528*
-adjustment	*9*	*0*	*8*	*0*	*0*	*0*	*0*	*0*	*0*	*0*	*0*	*0*	*0*	*0*	*0*	*0*
Transport	4,875	108	25	1,450	14	302	934	2	664	7	135	246	29	43	250	667
-railways	*4,875*	*108*	*25*	*1,450*	*14*	*302*	*934*	*2*	*664*	*7*	*135*	*246*	*29*	*43*	*250*	*667*
Households, etc.	97,829	2,936	1,860	20,513	2,080	7,296	18,625	864	10,024	163	4,236	2,360	1,487	2,613	5,854	16,917
-households	*52,112*	*1,972*	*912*	*11,248*	*1,058*	*3,481*	*10,239*	*458*	*5,031*	*66*	*1,754*	*1,113*	*755*	*1,498*	*3,547*	*8,982*
-agriculture	*2,993*	*0*	*144*	*662*	*196*	*375*	*234*	*0*	*374*	*7*	*279*	*138*	*48*	*71*	*137*	*327*
-others	*42,725*	*964*	*804*	*8,604*	*826*	*3,440*	*8,151*	*407*	*4,619*	*90*	*2,202*	*1,110*	*685*	*1,045*	*2,170*	*7,609*
Statistical divergence	3	0	0	0	0	9	0	0	0	-6	0	0	0	0	0	0

Source: Eurostat (Sirene)

(thousand TOE) — Table 1.20

Evolution of interior flows of electricity, EU-15

	1988	1989	1990	1991	1992	1993	1994	1995	1996	1997
Net imports	**2,086**	**2,297**	**2,333**	**1,218**	**1,616**	**1,881**	**1,552**	**1,496**	**-136**	**669**
Gross inland consumption	**2,086**	**2,297**	**2,333**	**1,218**	**1,616**	**1,881**	**1,552**	**1,496**	**-136**	**669**
Transformation output	150,336	159,580	161,617	165,963	165,109	165,114	167,283	173,214	180,213	180,564
-conventional thermal power stations	*91,693*	*97,380*	*99,692*	*101,702*	*99,767*	*96,817*	*99,187*	*103,544*	*107,023*	*106,626*
-nuclear power stations	*58,643*	*62,200*	*61,925*	*64,261*	*65,342*	*68,296*	*68,096*	*69,670*	*73,190*	*73,938*
Exchanges, transfers, returns	26,790	21,664	22,342	23,175	24,708	25,066	25,834	25,296	25,226	26,067
Consumption of the energy branch	17,764	17,595	17,982	18,341	18,226	17,714	17,373	18,016	18,305	18,105
Distribution losses	11,535	11,365	11,583	12,012	11,624	11,866	12,380	12,623	13,147	12,533
Available for final consumption	**149,913**	**154,582**	**156,727**	**160,004**	**161,583**	**162,481**	**164,916**	**169,368**	**173,851**	**176,662**
Final energy consumption	**148,986**	**153,761**	**155,972**	**158,810**	**163,740**	**161,053**	**163,631**	**169,368**	**173,849**	**176,658**
Industry	67,287	69,584	69,287	68,142	67,815	66,935	67,983	71,356	71,734	73,954
-iron and steel industry	*8,459*	*8,596*	*8,209*	*8,160*	*7,914*	*7,802*	*8,352*	*8,586*	*8,458*	*8,772*
-non ferrous metals industry	*5,814*	*5,839*	*5,819*	*5,634*	*5,450*	*5,108*	*4,792*	*4,979*	*5,093*	*5,156*
-chemical industry	*15,584*	*15,908*	*16,059*	*15,283*	*14,799*	*14,436*	*14,080*	*14,165*	*14,178*	*14,605*
-non-metallic mineral products	*4,936*	*5,208*	*5,002*	*4,947*	*4,998*	*4,862*	*5,100*	*5,316*	*5,421*	*5,409*
-ore extraction industry	*1,076*	*907*	*1,136*	*1,110*	*1,053*	*964*	*779*	*933*	*925*	*908*
-food, drink and tobacco industry	*5,241*	*5,507*	*5,793*	*5,965*	*6,120*	*6,231*	*6,217*	*6,570*	*6,737*	*6,901*
-textile, leather and clothing industry	*2,899*	*3,078*	*3,003*	*2,964*	*2,929*	*2,808*	*2,936*	*2,871*	*2,857*	*2,972*
-paper and printing industry	*7,411*	*7,678*	*7,867*	*7,869*	*7,948*	*8,191*	*8,495*	*9,253*	*9,173*	*9,748*
-engineering and other metals	*10,663*	*11,229*	*11,434*	*11,148*	*11,123*	*10,652*	*10,949*	*9,902*	*10,137*	*10,531*
-other industries	*5,202*	*5,633*	*4,921*	*5,060*	*5,473*	*5,880*	*6,269*	*8,767*	*8,742*	*8,942*
-adjustment	*0*	*0*	*45*	*3*	*7*	*2*	*14*	*14*	*15*	*9*
Transport	3,626	3,697	4,004	4,237	4,283	4,469	4,609	4,691	4,831	4,875
-railways	*3,626*	*3,697*	*4,004*	*4,237*	*4,283*	*4,469*	*4,609*	*4,691*	*4,831*	*4,875*
Households, etc.	78,073	80,480	82,680	86,431	91,642	89,649	91,039	93,320	97,284	97,829
-households	*42,614*	*43,274*	*44,618*	*47,291*	*47,952*	*49,032*	*49,554*	*50,046*	*52,662*	*52,112*
-agriculture	*2,544*	*2,593*	*2,696*	*2,822*	*2,804*	*2,822*	*2,860*	*2,960*	*3,006*	*2,993*
-others	*32,916*	*34,614*	*35,366*	*36,318*	*40,885*	*37,795*	*38,625*	*40,314*	*41,617*	*42,725*
Statistical divergence	927	821	755	1,194	-2,156	1,428	1,285	0	1	3

Source: Eurostat (Sirene)

(million ECU) — Table 1.21

Electricity, gas, steam and hot water supply (NACE Rev. 1 40)
Market related indicators, 1998

	B/L	DK	D	EL	E	F	IRL	I	NL	A	P	FIN	S	UK
Apparent consumption (1)	:	6,999	112,566	:	17,726	41,205	1,932	37,199	3,185	9,562	5,590	4,712	:	48,835
Exports (2)	150	148	531	1	34	2,724	1	0	13	166	0	10	0	6
Imports	296	58	534	53	90	320	2	0	198	129	5	197	0	513
Trade balance (2)	-146	90	-4	-13	-56	2,404	-2	0	-186	36	-51	-187	0	-507
Export ratio (%) (1)	:	1.2	0.5	:	0.3	6.6	0.2	0.0	0.3	2.7	0.0	3.1	:	0.0
Import penetration ratio (%) (1)	:	0.8	0.6	:	0.9	0.4	0.0	0.0	3.0	1.4	0.2	4.0	:	1.1
Cover ratio (%) (2)	50.6	253.9	99.3	7.3	37.6	850.9	26.6	5.9	6.4	128.0	0.0	5.2	56.4	1.2

(1) NL (1989); UK (1993); DK, I, A, P (1995); D, E, F, IRL, FIN (1996). (2) EL (1992); P (1997).

Source: Eurostat (SBS)

Table 1.22 — (million ECU)

Processing of nuclear fuel (NACE Rev. 1 23.3)

Market related indicators, 1998

	B/L	DK	D	EL	E	F	IRL	I	NL	A	P	FIN	S	UK
Apparent consumption (1)	888	4	:	5	:	4,727	2	:	-119	14	:	39	271	1,599
Exports	45	0	230	0	40	869	0	10	204	0	0	3	53	433
Imports	490	6	495	3	127	901	1	35	71	9	2	52	186	319
Trade balance	-444	-6	-265	-3	-88	-33	-1	-25	134	-9	-2	-48	-134	113
Export ratio (%) (1)	10.3	:	:	:	:	18.5	:	:	:	:	:	:	38.3	31.6
Import penetration ratio (%) (1)	55.2	104.9	:	100.0	:	19.1	112.9	:	-99.6	120.1	:	106.6	68.8	25.0
Cover ratio (%)	9.3	2.0	46.4	0.1	31.0	96.4	33.8	28.4	288.8	4.3	0.0	6.1	28.2	135.5

(1) NL (1992); EL, UK (1993); A, FIN (1995); DK, IRL (1996).

Source: Eurostat (SBS)

Table 1.23 — (thousand TOE)

Interior flows of other energy sources, 1997

	EU-15	B	DK	D	EL	E	F	IRL	I	L	NL	A	P	FIN	S	UK
Nuclear energy																
Primary production	**212,615**	**11,958**	**0**	**41,114**	**0**	**13,511**	**98,766**	**0**	**0**	**0**	**591**	**0**	**0**	**5,390**	**18,038**	**23,248**
Transformation input	212,615	11,958	0	41,114	0	13,511	98,766	0	0	0	591	0	0	5,390	18,038	23,248
-nuclear power stations	*212,615*	*11,958*	*0*	*41,114*	*0*	*13,511*	*98,766*	*0*	*0*	*0*	*591*	*0*	*0*	*5,390*	*18,038*	*23,248*
Available for final consumption	0	0	0	0	0	0	0	0	0	0	0	0	0	0	0	0
Statistical divergence	0	0	0	0	0	0	0	0	0	0	0	0	0	0	0	0
Derived heat (1)																
Transformation output	23,521	294	2,960	9,950	0	69	0	0	0	13	2,068	1,046	67	3,002	4,050	0
-conventional thermal power stations	*17,257*	*294*	*2,313*	*7,101*	*0*	*69*	*0*	*0*	*0*	*13*	*2,068*	*732*	*67*	*2,394*	*2,206*	*0*
Consumption of the energy branch	244	0	0	232	0	0	0	0	0	0	0	12	0	0	0	0
Distribution losses	2,534	23	566	982	0	0	0	0	0	0	311	90	0	249	312	0
Available for final consumption	20,743	270	2,394	8,737	0	69	0	0	0	13	1,757	944	67	2,753	3,738	0
Final energy consumption	20,446	270	2,269	8,737	0	69	0	0	0	13	1,757	825	67	2,699	3,738	0
Industry	4,191	241	139	1,672	0	69	0	0	0	10	836	158	67	625	374	0
-iron and steel industry	*16*	*11*	*0*	*5*	*0*	*0*	*0*	*0*	*0*	*0*	*0*	*0*	*0*	*0*	*0*	*0*
-chemical industry	*643*	*89*	*0*	*475*	*0*	*12*	*0*	*0*	*0*	*0*	*0*	*21*	*46*	*0*	*0*	*0*
-non-metallic mineral products	*53*	*0*	*0*	*53*	*0*	*0*	*0*	*0*	*0*	*0*	*0*	*0*	*0*	*0*	*0*	*0*
-food, drink and tobacco industry	*154*	*0*	*0*	*134*	*0*	*0*	*0*	*0*	*0*	*0*	*0*	*11*	*10*	*0*	*0*	*0*
-textile, leather and clothing industry	*60*	*0*	*0*	*49*	*0*	*0*	*0*	*0*	*0*	*0*	*0*	*0*	*11*	*0*	*0*	*0*
-paper and printing industry	*127*	*0*	*0*	*92*	*0*	*0*	*0*	*0*	*0*	*0*	*0*	*35*	*0*	*0*	*0*	*0*
-engineering and other metals	*549*	*0*	*0*	*518*	*0*	*0*	*0*	*0*	*0*	*0*	*0*	*31*	*0*	*0*	*0*	*0*
-other industries	*852*	*141*	*0*	*282*	*0*	*0*	*0*	*0*	*0*	*0*	*0*	*56*	*0*	*0*	*374*	*0*
-adjustment	*1,737*	*0*	*139*	*64*	*0*	*57*	*0*	*0*	*0*	*10*	*836*	*4*	*1*	*625*	*0*	*0*
Households, etc.	16,255	30	2,130	7,065	0	0	0	0	0	3	921	668	0	2,075	3,364	0
-households	*9,637*	*15*	*1,465*	*4,081*	*0*	*0*	*0*	*0*	*0*	*3*	*176*	*596*	*0*	*1,286*	*2,014*	*0*
-agriculture	*45*	*0*	*45*	*0*	*0*	*0*	*0*	*0*	*0*	*0*	*0*	*0*	*0*	*0*	*0*	*0*
-others	*6,573*	*15*	*619*	*2,984*	*0*	*0*	*0*	*0*	*0*	*0*	*745*	*72*	*0*	*788*	*1,350*	*0*
Statistical divergence	297	0	125	0	0	0	0	0	0	0	0	119	0	54	0	0
Renewable energies																
Primary production	81,458	653	1,717	7,734	1,364	6,928	16,020	225	12,928	47	1,492	6,602	3,597	6,680	13,415	2,057
Transformation input	14,307	367	991	1,767	0	595	1,159	22	2,726	24	1,047	772	198	1,519	2,272	847
-conventional thermal power stations	*12,262*	*367*	*501*	*1,317*	*0*	*595*	*1,140*	*22*	*2,719*	*24*	*1,047*	*639*	*198*	*1,373*	*1,472*	*847*
Exchanges, transfers, returns	-26,070	-27	-168	-1,753	-337	-3,037	-5,399	-63	-3,587	-7	-49	-3,094	-1,130	-1,054	-5,952	-412
Consumption of the energy branch	0	0	0	0	0	0	0	0	0	0	0	0	0	0	0	0
Distribution losses	0	0	0	0	0	0	0	0	0	0	0	0	0	0	0	0
Available for final consumption	41,081	258	558	4,213	1,027	3,296	9,462	141	6,614	16	396	2,736	2,269	4,107	5,191	798
Final energy consumption	41,077	258	558	4,214	1,027	3,293	9,462	139	6,614	15	396	2,736	2,269	4,107	5,191	798
Industry	14,998	88	115	461	209	1,270	1,897	98	977	0	70	867	1,102	3,033	4,224	586
Households, etc.	26,078	170	443	3,753	818	2,023	7,565	42	5,637	15	325	1,869	1,166	1,074	966	212
-households	*24,800*	*170*	*336*	*3,720*	*816*	*2,023*	*7,565*	*42*	*5,465*	*15*	*323*	*916*	*1,160*	*1,074*	*966*	*209*
-agriculture	*1,012*	*0*	*59*	*0*	*0*	*0*	*0*	*0*	*0*	*0*	*0*	*953*	*0*	*0*	*0*	*0*
-others	*267*	*0*	*49*	*32*	*2*	*0*	*0*	*0*	*172*	*0*	*2*	*0*	*6*	*0*	*0*	*3*
Statistical divergence	4	0	0	0	0	3	0	1	0	0	0	0	0	0	0	0

(1) Most data are provisional.

Source: Eurostat (Sirene)

(thousand TOE) Table 1.24

Evolution of energy flows of other energy sources, EU-15

	1988	1989	1990	1991	1992	1993	1994	1995	1996	1997
Nuclear energy										
Primary production	**173,332**	**182,429**	**181,439**	**187,021**	**188,267**	**197,558**	**197,271**	**201,239**	**208,864**	**212,615**
Transformation input	173,227	182,328	181,351	187,021	188,267	197,558	197,271	201,239	208,864	212,615
-nuclear power stations	*173,227*	*182,328*	*181,351*	*187,021*	*188,267*	*197,558*	*197,271*	*201,239*	*208,864*	*212,615*
Available for final consumption	105	101	88	0	0	0	0	0	0	0
Statistical divergence	105	101	88	0	0	0	0	0	0	0
Derived heat										
Transformation output	18,713	17,839	18,840	18,914	17,985	19,968	20,421	21,885	23,725	23,521
-conventional thermal power stations	*4,776*	*4,005*	*4,884*	*5,736*	*5,524*	*6,071*	*6,949*	*15,184*	*17,010*	*17,257*
Consumption of the energy branch	493	438	376	225	237	256	218	232	244	244
Distribution losses	1,654	1,169	1,867	1,993	1,914	2,177	2,102	2,441	2,542	2,534
Available for final consumption	**16,567**	**16,232**	**16,598**	**16,696**	**15,834**	**17,535**	**18,101**	**19,212**	**20,939**	**20,743**
Final energy consumption	**16,517**	**16,186**	**16,601**	**16,657**	**15,798**	**17,524**	**18,004**	**19,089**	**20,692**	**20,446**
Industry	3,749	3,648	3,750	3,179	2,371	2,521	2,583	3,091	4,078	4,191
-iron and steel industry	*116*	*135*	*101*	*70*	*70*	*59*	*59*	*12*	*13*	*16*
-chemical industry	*844*	*860*	*837*	*663*	*640*	*649*	*631*	*625*	*692*	*643*
-non-metallic mineral products	*229*	*195*	*89*	*64*	*44*	*43*	*50*	*53*	*53*	*53*
-food, drink and tobacco industry	*251*	*247*	*332*	*267*	*147*	*143*	*152*	*148*	*150*	*154*
-textile, leather and clothing industry	*125*	*132*	*75*	*55*	*36*	*39*	*44*	*53*	*56*	*60*
-paper and printing industry	*44*	*56*	*95*	*87*	*78*	*91*	*119*	*128*	*127*	*127*
-engineering and other metals	*722*	*711*	*934*	*911*	*717*	*677*	*671*	*555*	*549*	*549*
-other industries	*450*	*411*	*359*	*381*	*385*	*520*	*544*	*745*	*832*	*852*
-adjustment	*968*	*900*	*927*	*681*	*255*	*301*	*312*	*772*	*1,606*	*1,737*
Households, etc.	12,768	12,538	12,851	13,477	13,426	15,003	15,422	15,998	16,614	16,255
-households	*6,729*	*6,470*	*6,710*	*7,816*	*7,745*	*9,821*	*10,095*	*9,787*	*10,028*	*9,637*
-agriculture	*45*	*0*	*0*	*45*	*45*	*45*	*45*	*45*	*40*	*45*
-others	*5,994*	*6,068*	*6,141*	*5,617*	*5,637*	*5,138*	*5,282*	*6,167*	*6,546*	*6,573*
Statistical divergence	50	46	-3	39	37	10	97	124	247	297
Renewable energies										
Primary production	**68,057**	**63,656**	**61,915**	**67,035**	**68,868**	**70,803**	**71,591**	**72,484**	**75,341**	**81,458**
Transformation input	7,868	8,200	8,289	8,510	9,918	10,885	11,147	11,629	13,305	14,307
-conventional thermal power stations	*7,462*	*7,743*	*7,838*	*8,016*	*9,305*	*10,130*	*10,219*	*10,639*	*11,173*	*12,262*
Exchanges, transfers, returns	-26,798	-21,664	-22,341	-23,177	-24,720	-25,085	-25,834	-25,296	-25,230	-26,070
Consumption of the energy branch	0	0	0	0	0	0	0	0	0	0
Distribution losses	0	1	0	0	0	0	0	1	0	0
Available for final consumption	**33,392**	**33,792**	**31,285**	**35,348**	**34,229**	**34,833**	**34,609**	**35,558**	**36,806**	**41,081**
Final energy consumption	**33,414**	**33,792**	**33,671**	**35,346**	**34,228**	**34,759**	**34,607**	**35,953**	**36,572**	**41,077**
Industry	12,124	12,668	12,362	12,441	11,851	12,808	13,803	14,071	13,917	14,998
Households, etc.	21,290	21,123	21,308	22,905	22,377	21,951	20,804	21,883	22,656	26,078
-households	*20,275*	*19,925*	*20,093*	*21,647*	*21,082*	*20,840*	*19,763*	*20,724*	*21,411*	*24,800*
-agriculture	*1,003*	*1,016*	*1,032*	*1,080*	*1,098*	*920*	*849*	*954*	*987*	*1,012*
-others	*12*	*182*	*182*	*178*	*197*	*191*	*192*	*205*	*258*	*267*
Statistical divergence	-23	0	-2,386	2	2	74	2	-395	234	4

Source: Eurostat (Sirene)

Table 1.25

Structural indicators of the energy market, 1997

		EU-15	B	DK	D	EL	E	F	IRL	I	L	NL	A	P	FIN	S	UK
Coal	Number of active firms	158	0	:	17	:	114	4	0	:	:	:	:	0	:	:	23
Oil	Refinery capacity (thousand tonnes)	639,400	35,700	9,000	108,100	19,100	62,000	93,200	3,200	102,400	:	59,500	10,000	14,400	11,900	20,100	90,800
Natural gas	Length of distribution network (km)	:	46,480	17,536	335,500	:	27,022	177,842	6,752	197,100	1,080	:	:	:	2,000	310	421,000
Electricity	Installed net capacity (MW)	555,366	14,693	11,778	112,963	9,574	48,199	112,687	4,297	70,250	1,275	20,091	17,859	9,461	15,697	34,044	72,498

Source: Eurostat (Sirene)

Non-energy mining and quarrying

The activities covered in this chapter include:

13.1: mining of metal ores;
13.2: mining of non-ferrous metal ores, except uranium and thorium ores;
14.1: quarrying of stone;
14.2: quarrying of sand and clay;
14.3: mining of chemical and fertiliser minerals;
14.4: production of salt;
14.5: other mining and quarrying n.e.c.

Industry description

The mining industry has a long tradition in most Member States, often laying the foundations for industrialisation. However, during the past two decades, mining in European countries has generally been in decline. New mineral resources have been discovered within the European Union, however, European mining enterprises now quarry to a large degree outside the European continent (by doing so, they maintain an important role in world markets). Europe has remained one of the main processing regions of the world and exerts an influence on world demand for raw materials.

This chapter covers mining of all solid non-energy minerals (excluding coal and uranium ore): iron and non-ferrous ores (NACE Rev. 1 13), construction raw materials such as sand and clay, chemical and physical industrial minerals (NACE Rev. 1 14). The products of non-energy mining and quarrying are used in the manufacture of metals and metal products, chemicals, engineering and construction.

Europe does not possess to any large degree reserves of metal ores. Its metal processing industries rely on non-European sources for raw materials. Within the EU, the main metal ore deposits are found in Sweden, with lesser deposits in Spain, Austria and Finland. The Swedish production value of metal ores amounted to almost 1,300 million ECU in 1996, easily the highest figure in Europe. Sweden was the main producer within the activity of mining iron ore (41.9% of the EU total or 543 million ECU). In comparison, Spain (the second largest metal ores industry, when ranked by production value), had activity of only 122.7 million ECU. In Ireland an important industry has developed around the mining of lead and zinc in the past three decades. Metal ore deposits are also found in France, Portugal and Greece, whilst metal mining in the other Member States is of low or no significance.

Figure 2.1 (1988=100)

Non-energy mining and quarrying (NACE Rev. 1 13 and 14)

Production, employment and value added compared to EU total manufacturing

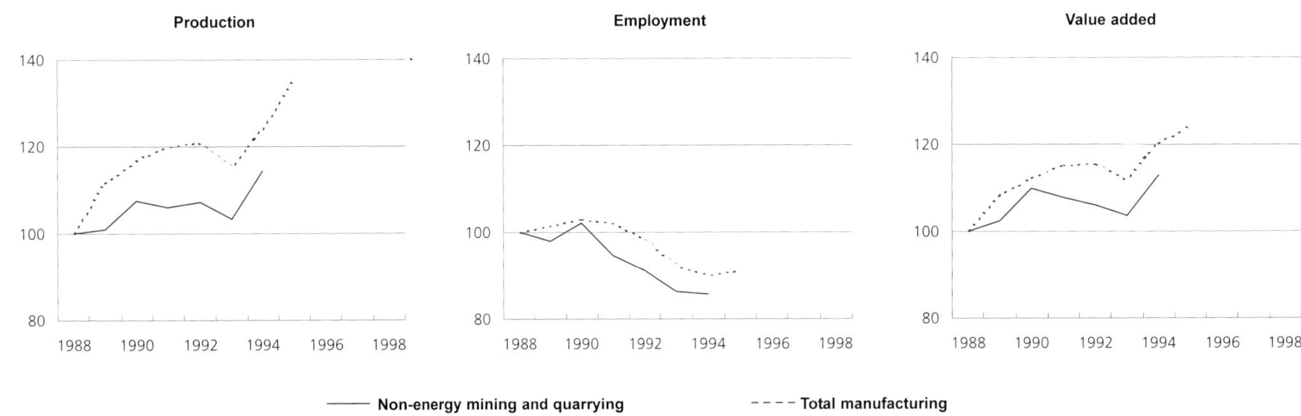

Source: Eurostat (SBS)

Minerals are extracted throughout Europe but the deposits are largely small in terms of world reserves. There are however about two thirds of the world's reserves of mercury within the EU, mainly in Spain. Spanish production of mercury was equal to one million tonnes in 1998, 38.5% of world production. Europe has the second largest reserves in the world of fluorite and large deposits of potash are found in Germany, the United Kingdom and Spain (estimates suggest that there are over 750 million tonnes that could be economically exploited). Finally, there are some kaolin and ball clay reserves in the United Kingdom.

During recent years, there was growing importance in relative terms for the mining of minerals. On the one hand, many metal ore mining facilities were closed down, whilst there was an expansion of activity in the area of non-metal extraction. In all reporting countries, production value for the mining of minerals was higher than the corresponding figure for metal ores (except in Sweden, where the mining of metal ores accounted for 83.0% of the total in 1996).

The extraction and primary transformation of metals and minerals (into ore and concentrates) is a highly automated process. In 1996 the average number of persons employed to produce one million ECU of output varied considerably between the reporting countries. In Sweden and in Belgium non-energy mining and quarrying employed on average 4.6 and 5.1 persons per one million ECU of production value. In Finland and in Germany there were 6.5 and 7.6 persons, whilst in Spain the figure was as high as 11.1 persons.

Recent trends

European non-energy mining and quarrying enterprises have been faced with deposits of low-grade ore, high labour costs, falling world prices and increased competition from producers outside of the EU. This has led to the closure of many mines within Europe and a change of focus towards mining units situated abroad.

The figures for employment show a downward trend in the evolution of this particular activity. This may be largely attributed to the on-going mechanisation process that has occurred within the mining activity. Taking the period 1990 to 1996 the number of persons employed in the EU decreased in all Member States by between 1% and 5% per annum. The exception was Germany where in the mining of minerals the number of persons employed increased by 1.2% per annum.

Labour productivity within non-energy mining increased (when measured as value added per person employed). This increase was due to rationalisation within the industry. However, the rising trend of labour productivity was halted in a number of Member States, for example in France a decrease of 3.4 thousand ECU per head was recorded in 1996. High labour productivity was registered in Belgium and Denmark (76.8 and 76.1 thousand ECU), as well as Sweden (69.6 thousand ECU).

Hourly labour costs per head were higher in the mining of metal ores than the mining of minerals. As an example of these differentials we can take the case of Spain, where metal mining enterprises faced labour costs for each employee of 17.8 ECU per hour in 1996, whilst non-metallic minerals' enterprises faced average costs of only 13.3 ECU per hour. Indeed, the United Kingdom was the only country to report lower costs in the mining of metal ores industry (9.0 ECU compared to 12.6 ECU). Non-metallic mining labour costs increased in all of the countries for which data was available for the period 1992 to 1995 (growth ranging between 6.2% per annum in Belgium and 0.7% per annum in the United Kingdom).

(%) Table 2.1

Non-energy mining and quarrying (NACE Rev. 1 13 and 14) Composition of the labour force, 1997

	Females	Part-time	Highly-educated
EU-15	:	:	:
B	:	:	:
DK	:	:	:
D	11.6	:	12.4
EL	:	:	:
E	:	:	10.5
F	13.9	:	:
IRL	8.3	:	10.7
I	10.5	:	:
L	:	:	:
NL	9.8	14.2	:
A	:	:	:
P	:	:	:
FIN	:	:	:
S	:	:	:
UK	17.4	:	14.8

Source: Eurostat (LFS)

(ECU/hour) Figure 2.2

Non-energy mining and quarrying (NACE Rev. 1 13 and 14) Labour costs by Member State, 1996

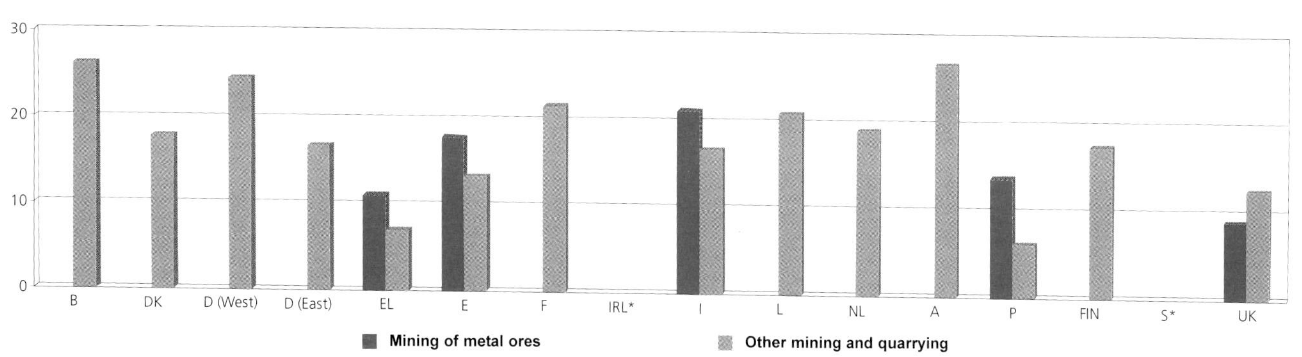

Source: Eurostat (LCS)

Figure 2.3 (million ECU)

Non-energy mining and quarrying (NACE Rev. 1 13 and 14)

Foreign net direct investment

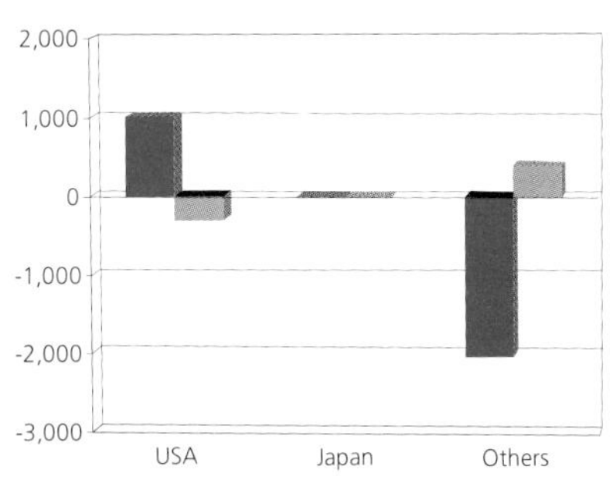

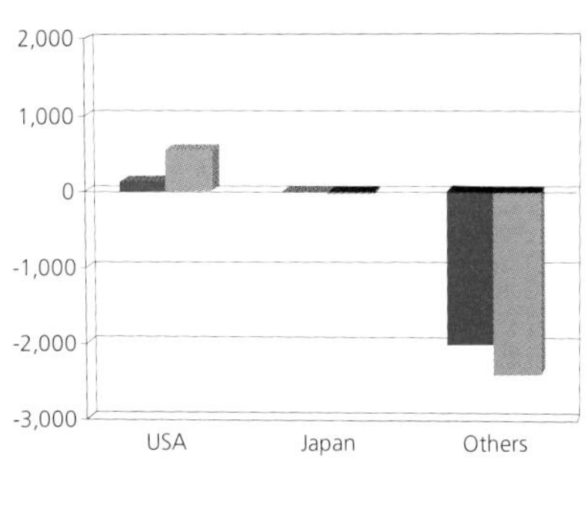

1988 1998

Source: Eurostat (BOP)

Foreign trade

Whilst the production value of the EU was equal to approximately 17 billion ECU in 1996, demand was far higher. As a result, the European trade balance was negative. This was also the case in the other two countries that form the Triad: however, the EU trade deficit was seven times that observed in the USA. Japan reported a trade deficit that was almost the same size as that of the EU, equivalent to some 90.9% of the European figure.

In 1998 only three Member States reported a trade surplus (using world trade flows) in non-energy mining: Sweden, Portugal and Greece. The latter two countries saw their positive balance decreasing in recent years. Swedish industry also saw its trade balance reduced during the nineties.

Sweden did however report the highest export ratio within the European Union. As regards imports from third countries penetrating the Swedish market, they increased by 7.4% in value terms between 1990 and 1996. This led to an increase of 2.1 percentage points in the import penetration ratio.

Figure 2.4

Non-energy mining and quarrying (NACE Rev. 1 13 and 14)

Destination of EU exports, 1998

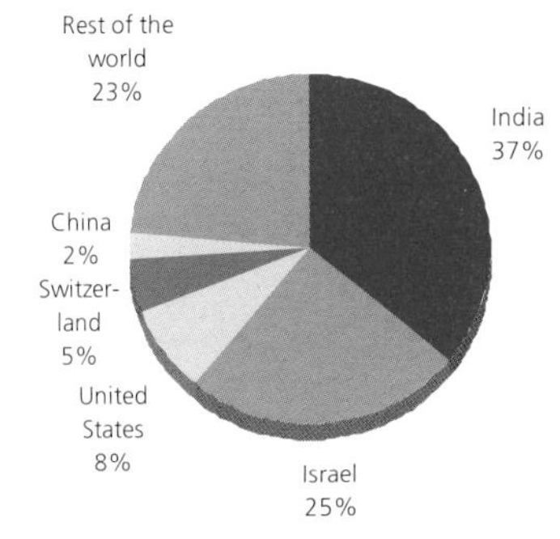

Source: Eurostat (Comext)

Figure 2.5

Non-energy mining and quarrying NACE Rev. 1 13 and 14)

Origin of EU imports, 1998

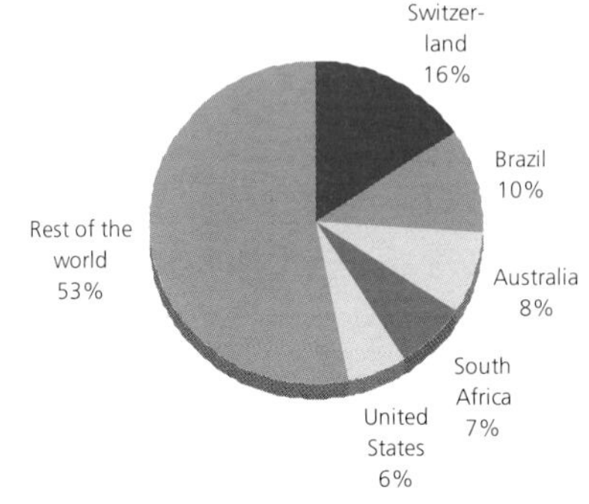

Source: Eurostat (Comext)

Iron ore (NACE Rev. 1 13.1)

Iron is the fourth most common chemical element found in the crust of the Earth and the basic material used in the iron and steel industry. Thus, this commodity plays an important role in the economic development of many countries. Nevertheless, the iron and steel industry has faced a declining trend in recent years, largely due to competition from other substitute materials, as well as declining prices.

By means of international comparison we find that the iron ore processing industry in the USA was much less dependent on imports than either of the other two Triad economies. The USA imported iron ore to the value of 564.5 million ECU in 1997.

Sweden is the largest producer within the European Union. Nevertheless, the role of Sweden as an international player is limited with output accounting for less than a tenth of the output of China, which has the largest iron ore mining industry in the world. Brazil was the second largest producer, with production value some eight times the value of that found in Sweden.

On the supply side of iron ore mining, we can observe a high degree of concentration in the industry. In Sweden and Austria there was only one enterprise engaged in the iron ore industry, whilst in France there were just two enterprises. Spanish industrial structure took a somewhat different pattern, as there were 13 enterprises recorded in 1996. The ownership of enterprises within the EU often involved some role for national government. For example, 38.8% of the Austrian enterprise VOEST-ALPINE Stahl AG was still owned by the government in 1998 (through a holding company, ÖIAG). The Luxembourg government owned 29.8% of ARBED, and the Swedish government maintained a 100% share of LKAB in 1998.

The production value of mining of iron ore within the EU was in decline in the majority of Member States. For example, in Spain there was a decline of 28.5% in 1996 and in France output fell by as much as 70.7% (during the four-year period 1992 to 1996). This trend has seen a large number of iron mines close during the last decade. However, declining output was interrupted in 1995 when the enlargement of the EU to fifteen Member States took place. The extraction of iron ore in Sweden (and to a lesser extent Austria and Finland) increased the output of the EU significantly. This improvement was notable not just on the basis of an increase in volume terms, but also because the quality of iron ore produced in Sweden was above the average European level. Swedish iron ore is of particularly high grade and has an iron content of some 60%. In 1996, Swedish mines extracted iron ore to the value of some 543 million ECU. At the beginning of the nineties there was still extraction of iron ore in Germany, Portugal and Finland. However, during the mid-nineties these countries have seen the industry cease to exist on their national territory.

The number of persons employed reflected the same evolution as production, with a downward trend at a rapid pace. During the period 1992 to 1996, employment fell by 38.7% in Spain and by as much as 63.3% in France.

Figure 2.6

Iron ore (NACE Rev. 1 13.1)
Destination of EU exports, 1998

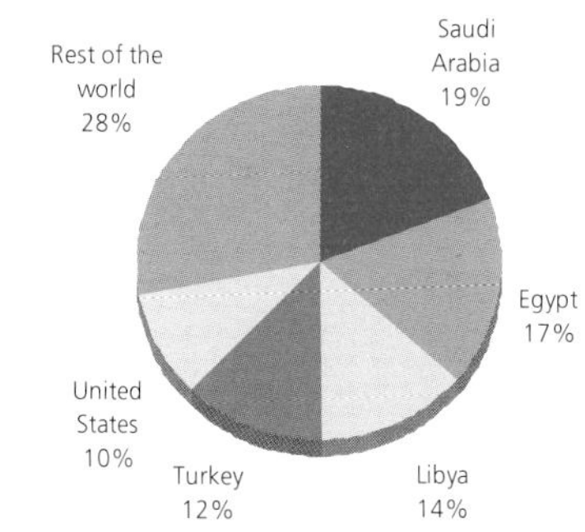

Source: Eurostat (Comext)

Figure 2.7

Iron ore (NACE Rev. 1 13.1)
Origin of EU imports, 1998

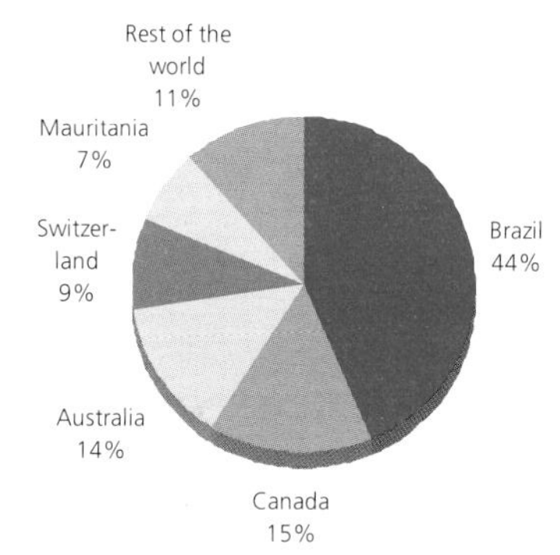

Source: Eurostat (Comext)

Non-ferrous metal ores (NACE Rev. 1 13.2)

This activity includes mining and the preparation of various non-ferrous metal ores such as copper, bauxite or lead, as well as precious metals. In the EU a larger number of Member States were involved in the extraction of non-ferrous metals than in the iron ore industry (although there was no activity in Germany or Denmark).

Western Europe remained one of the main producers of copper, lead, and zinc in 1998[1]. Sweden was the largest producer of non-ferrous metals within the Union, with production value of 753 million ECU (some 27.9% higher than Swedish production of iron ore). Sweden was the largest producer of lead and silver and one of the largest of copper and zinc within the Union. Ireland became an important producer of lead and zinc from the 1960's onwards. Sweden and Ireland accounted for about 75% of the EU's lead production (Sweden contributing around 50% of the total). Lead is used in many downstream industries, such as the manufacture of car batteries, chemicals, sheets, cable sheathing and gasoline additives. Nevertheless, some traditional markets have been lost due to substitute products that have been adopted due to environmental concerns.

The main producers of copper within the EU are Portugal and Sweden. Nevertheless, their aggregated production was less than a tenth of that seen in Chile, the world's leading producer (ahead of the United States, the second most important producer in the world). Copper is used within the construction industry, the manufacture of electrical and electronic goods and in the transport equipment industry.

Zinc is used within similar downstream industries as copper. The majority of activity concerning the mining of zinc within the EU was found in Ireland, Spain and Sweden. The output of the EU was equivalent to around 3.5% of world production. China (the largest global producer) accounted for only 7% of total world production (1995).

1) US Geological Survey (USGS).

The structure of the bauxite industry (used in the production of aluminium) was somewhat different within the EU. Rather than be highly concentrated in a small number of mines, there were many mines in Greece, the leading EU producer. Nevertheless, Greece produced only a small share of global bauxite production. A similar picture was seen in the nickel industry, with Greece again reporting the largest number of mines and the highest level of output in the EU. Once more, production value was only a small share of global production (1.1% of world output in 1998). The two largest producers of nickel in the world were Russia and Canada, together they accounted for 41.8% of world output.
The steel industry is the main downstream activity that purchases manganese and demand is closely linked to that for steel. Extraction in the EU was marginal in 1998, with a few small enterprises operating in Greece, Italy and Austria. European extraction of tungsten accounted for 6.9% of world production in1998, largely through mines in Portugal and Austria.

Besides mercury (where Spanish mining accounted for 38.5% of world production in 1998), silver is the only other precious metal that is extracted to a large degree in Europe. All European silver production is a by-product of lead, zinc and copper mining. The main deposits are found in the Nordic and Iberian countries, with Swedish mines accounting for about 50% of European output. Mining of gold and platinum within the EU contributed about 1% of the total extracted globally.

Demand for non-ferrous metal ores was at least three times higher than production within the EU. In 1996, Sweden and Finland consumed nearly as much non-ferrous metal ores as Germany and France together (96.9%). Whilst Germany had to import all its demand for non-ferrous metals, Sweden reported a small trade surplus. In Portugal there was also a trade surplus, although this was rapidly being reduced, down by 59% between 1990 and 1998. Besides Greece, all other Member States reported higher demand for non-ferrous metal ores than their domestic production.

Due to the comparatively small size of this industry within Europe, it was not surprising to find that the structure of the number of enterprises in the non-ferrous metal ores industry was highly concentrated in Ireland and Sweden, with one and four enterprises respectively. In Spain there were some 22 mining enterprises, with average production of 4.6 million ECU each in 1996. The same figure in Sweden revealed that average production value per enterprise was equal to 188.2 million ECU.

Figure 2.8

Non-ferrous metal ores (NACE Rev. 1 13.2)
Destination of EU exports, 1998

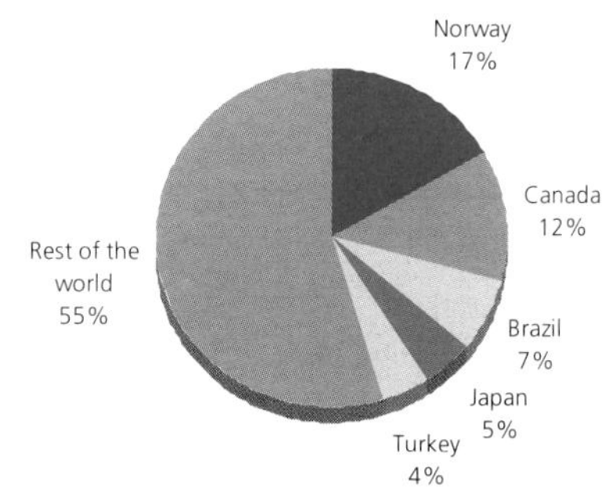

Source: Eurostat (Comext)

Figure 2.9

Non-ferrous metal ores (NACE Rev. 1 13.2)
Origin of EU imports, 1998

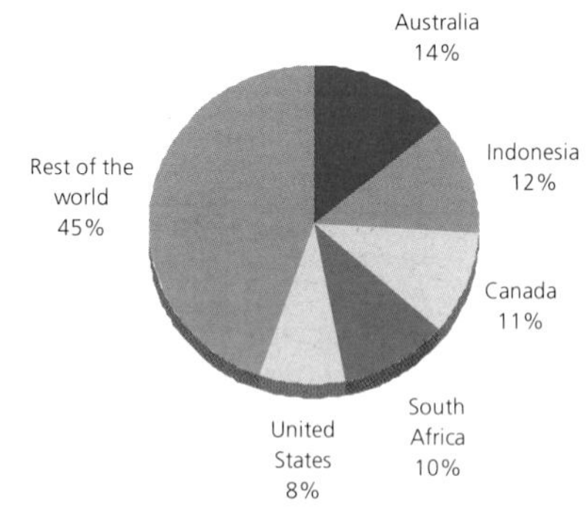

Source: Eurostat (Comext)

Other mining and quarrying (NACE Rev. 1 14)

Other mining and quarrying made up the majority of the production value of non-energy mining and quarrying, with a 100% share in Germany and Denmark and 97.4% of activity in France. The only country where the mining of metal ores was more important was Sweden.

As with the whole of non-energy mining, the other mining and quarrying industry faced falling production and value added trends in the nineties. Even though mining enterprises in other mining and quarrying reported a less dramatic situation than in the mining of metal ores, they also faced strong competition from outside the EU, where lower labour costs and considerable natural deposits made extraction more economically viable.

Production of construction raw materials includes the quarrying of stone, sand and clay. Quarrying in this industry is largely tied to the performance of the construction industry. Some products, such as limestone and dolomite are also used in the manufacture of glass and ceramics, in the metal processing industry, or the manufacture of paper, plastics or paints. Quarrying for clay was usually the most important activity within construction raw materials, accounting for 80.4% of the industry in the United Kingdom, 76.8% in Sweden and 66.1% in Germany - all 1996. Spain was the largest producing country for the quarrying of stone in Europe, with production value of 501 million ECU. Crushed rock, sand and gravel are three ingredients used in concrete and bituminous mixes such as asphalt. In addition, these materials are used in the construction of buildings and civil engineering. Most of the markets for crushed rock, sand and gravel are regional and therefore trade across borders is weak.

In Germany the production of lime was the third largest in the world equal to 8 million tonnes in 1998. There was also a high level of production in Italy and France (3.5 and 2.8 million tonnes respectively). Gypsum, mainly used as plaster in construction and decorating was mined to a large degree in Spain and France (7.4 and 5.0 million tonnes respectively).

(thousand tonnes) Table 2.2

Consumption of bitumen by the road construction industry

	1997	1996	1996/97 (%)
EU-15	13,440	12,840	4.7
B	220	180	22.2
DK	180	180	0.0
D	2,680	2,580	3.9
EL	370	350	5.7
E	1,320	1,230	7.3
F	2,900	2,650	9.4
IRL	210	200	5.0
I	1,950	1,700	14.7
NL	330	340	-2.9
A	320	320	0.0
P	580	360	61.1
FIN	250	300	-16.7
S	320	350	-8.6
UK	1,810	2,100	-13.8

Source: EAPA (European Asphalt Pavement Association)

Another important activity covered by data in this section is the production of asphalt and bitumen. In 1997 there were nearly four thousand asphalt production plants in the EU, with 790 located in Germany, 650 in Italy and 407 in France. In addition, there were 535 mobile plants within the EU with the largest numbers in Portugal and Spain (120 each). Most of the production sites suitable for warm recycling of asphalt were found in Germany (700), whilst in France there were only five sites (figures from EAPA, European Asphalt Pavement Association). The European asphalt industry produced 277.7 million tonnes of hot asphalt in 1997, some 1.9% more than a year before. Road construction consumed 13.4 million tonnes of bitumen in 1997 (an increase of 4.7% compared to 1996). The USA was the largest producer of asphalt in the world, with output some 80% above the European level. American consumption was twice as high as that seen within the Union (26.7 million tonnes), whilst in Japan consumption was only 3.6 million tonnes.

The mining of chemical and fertiliser minerals in the EU includes phosphates, sulphur and potash. The EU is one of the main producers of potash. In 1998 Germany was the third largest world producer, with output of 3.6 million tonnes, following Canada and Russia. Mining of sulphur was equal to 1.1 million tonnes in Germany and France and 750 thousand tonnes in Spain. These three countries together accounted for 5.5% of world production, hence the EU had to import the majority of the phosphates it consumed. Indeed, in 1998 there was a trade deficit throughout the EU (except in Germany). In the USA and Japan there was also a negative trade balance.

The market for salt is dependent on climatic conditions (which affects the production of sea salt harvested in the Mediterranean basin or the demand for road salt). At the same time there are efforts being made to minimise road salt consumption without reducing the level of road security. Demand for salt was also reduced as the manufacture of paper changed its bleaching method to avoid the use of chlorine. European salt producers also face competition in terms of price with respect to low-grade salt from outside Europe. The most important downstream industry for salt was the chemical industry (43.5%), followed by use on roads for de-icing (25.5%) and food grade salt (11.5%). The residual (19.5%) was distributed amongst many other manufacturing areas, such as textiles, leather and metal processing. Due to high transportation costs (relative to its value), salt is not traded to a large degree.

In 1997 the five largest producers of the EU accounted for 18.4% of world production, nearly as much as the USA. The USA was the largest salt producer in the world (20.6% of world production).

In 1997 salt production in the EU was equal to some 35.4 million tonnes, down by 4.2% when compared to data for 1996 (figures from ESPA, European Salt Producers' Association). The share of rock salt in total production went down by 6.7 percentage points in 1997, whilst the share of sea salt went up by 1.6 percentage points, returning to the levels of the early nineties. The last year that any growth in output took place in the EU salt industry was in 1994 (when production rose by 3.4%), due to cyclical demand for road salt. In 1997, sales of crystallised salt were down by 12.0%, again largely due to the demand for road salt (down by 35.6%). This was partly due to a running down of stocks, which had built up the year before.

Figure 2.11

Other mining and quarrying (NACE Rev. 1 14)
Destination of EU exports, 1998

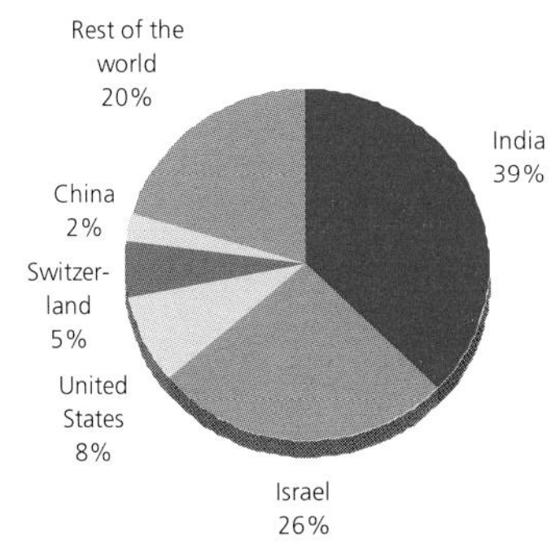

Source: Eurostat (Comext)

Figure 2.10

Consumption of salt by use, 1997

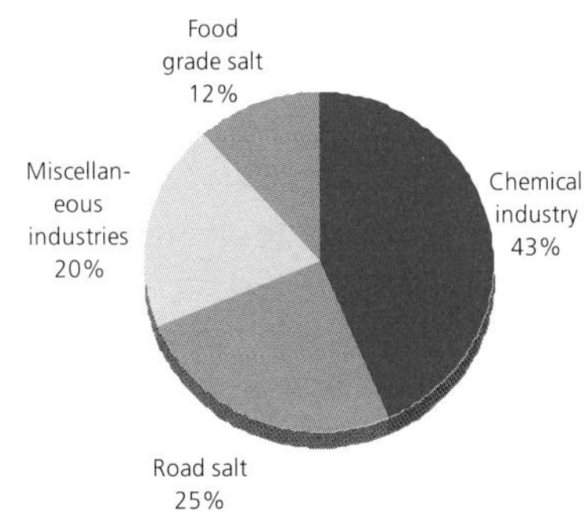

Source: ESPA (European Salt Producers' Association)

Figure 2.12

Other mining and quarrying (NACE Rev. 1 14)
Origin of EU imports, 1998

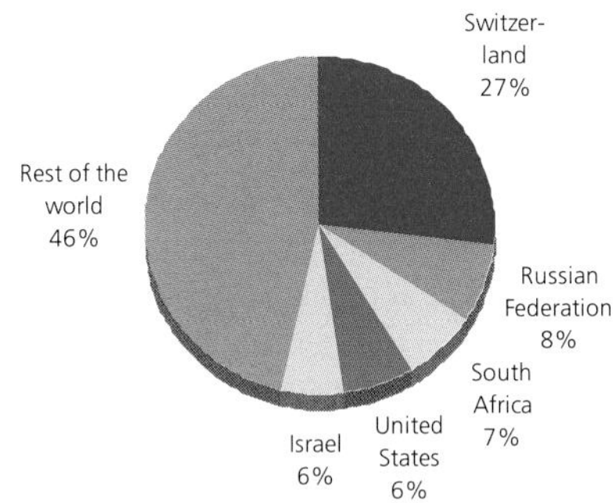

Source: Eurostat (Comext)

Professional associations representing the industries within this Chapter

ESPA
European Salt Producers'
Association
17, rue Daru
F-75008 Paris
tel: (33) 1 47 66 52 90
fax: (33) 1 47 66 52 66
e-mail:
bmoinier@eu-salt.com

(million ECU) — Table 2.3

Mining of iron ores (NACE Rev. 1 13.1)

Production related indicators, 1996

	B	DK	D	EL	E	F	IRL	I (1)	L	NL	A	P	FIN	S	UK
Production value	:	0	0	:	22	18	0	0	:	:	:	:	0	543	:
Value added	:	0	0	:	7	9	0	0	:	:	:	:	0	220	:
Number of persons employed (units)	:	0	0	:	473	244	0	0	:	:	:	:	0	2,710	:

(1) 1995.

(million ECU) — Table 2.4

Mining of iron ores (NACE Rev. 1 13.1)

Market related indicators, 1998

	B/L	DK	D	EL	E	F	IRL	I	NL	A	P	FIN	S	UK
Apparent consumption (1)	:	:	950	:	153	360	0	372	:	:	:	62	167	:
Exports (2)	1	0	1	1	1	2	0	0	505	0	0	0	472	0
Imports	338	1	1,249	0	199	417	0	415	586	186	15	111	5	469
Trade balance (2)	-337	-1	-1,249	1	-198	-414	0	-415	-81	-186	-16	-111	467	-469
Export ratio (%) (3)	:	:	:	:	35.8	69.1	:	:	:	:	:	:	70.8	:
Import penetration ratio (%) (1)	:	:	100.2	:	90.9	98.4	-19.4	100.0	:	:	:	100.0	4.9	:
Cover ratio (%) (2)	0.3	4.7	0.0	740.8	0.6	0.6	1.6	0.0	86.1	0.0	0.0	0.0	10,078.2	0.0

(1) I, FIN (1995); D, E, F, IRL, S (1996). (2) EL (1994); P (1995). (3) EL, F, S (1996).

Table 2.5

Mining of iron ores (NACE Rev. 1 13.1)

Labour related indicators, 1996

	EU-15	B	DK	D	EL	E	F	IRL	I (1)	L	NL	A	P	FIN	S	UK
Personnel costs (million ECU)	:	:	0	0	:	12	11	0	0	:	:	:	:	0	113	:
Personnel costs/employee (thousand ECU)	:	:	:	:	:	24.6	43.4	:	:	:	:	:	:	:	41.6	:
Social charges/personnel costs (%)	:	:	:	:	:	23.5	38.9	:	:	:	:	:	:	:	:	:
Labour productivity (thousand ECU/head)	:	:	:	:	:	15.8	37.3	:	:	:	:	:	:	:	81.1	:
Wage adjusted labour productivity (%)	:	:	:	:	:	64.4	86.0	:	:	:	:	:	:	:	195.0	:

(1) 1995.

Source: Eurostat (SBS)

Table 2.6 (million ECU)

Mining of non-ferrous metal ores, except uranium and thorium ores (NACE Rev. 1 13.2)

Production related indicators, 1996

	B	DK	D	EL (1)	E	F	IRL	I (1)	L	NL	A (1)	P (1)	FIN	S	UK
Production value	0	0	0	88	101	66	:	32	:	:	0	218	81	753	:
Value added	0	0	0	51	21	24	:	8	:	:	0	:	23	175	:
Number of persons employed (units)	0	0	0	2,421	1,195	675	:	520	:	:	0	1,301	541	2,965	:

(1) 1995.

Table 2.7 (million ECU)

Mining of non-ferrous metal ores, except uranium and thorium ores (NACE Rev. 1 13.2)

Market related indicators in the EU

	1988	1989	1990	1991	1992	1993	1994	1995	1996	1997	1998
Apparent consumption	:	:	:	:	:	:	:	:	:	:	:
Exports	41	50	38	22	28	29	21	42	33	22	47
Imports	752	1,664	402	:	:	:	:	310	:	:	672
Trade balance	-712	-1,614	-364	:	:	:	:	-268	:	:	-625
Export ratio (%)	:	:	:	:	:	:	:	:	:	:	:
Import penetration ratio (%)	:	:	:	:	:	:	:	:	:	:	:
Cover ratio (%)	5.4	3.0	9.5	:	:	:	:	13.7	:	:	7.1

Table 2.8 (million ECU)

Mining of non-ferrous metal ores, except uranium and thorium ores (NACE Rev. 1 13.2)

Market related indicators, 1998

	B/L	DK	D	EL	E	F	IRL	I	NL	A	P	FIN	S	UK
Apparent consumption (1)	:	1	808	65	759	446	:	304	:	59	8	478	737	:
Exports	314	0	36	18	50	17	73	22	73	0	106	17	125	24
Imports	469	1	838	4	734	426	99	335	268	47	4	434	65	393
Trade balance	-155	-1	-802	14	-684	-409	-26	-313	-195	-47	102	-417	60	-369
Export ratio (%)	:	:	:	29.8	49.6	23.6	:	49.6	:	:	97.8	19.5	17.2	:
Import penetration ratio (%) (2)	:	111.8	103.7	4.3	93.3	88.6	:	94.7	:	101.4	40.0	86.4	15.4	:
Cover ratio (%) (1)	67.0	11.7	4.3	412.9	6.8	4.1	73.6	6.5	27.2	0.7	2,571.6	3.9	193.0	6.2

(1) EL, I, A, P (1995); DK, D, E, F, FIN, S (1996). (2) EL, I, P (1995); E, F, FIN, S (1996).

Table 2.9

Mining of non-ferrous metal ores, except uranium and thorium ores (NACE Rev. 1 13.2)

Labour related indicators, 1996

	EU-15	B	DK	D	EL (1)	E	F	IRL	I (1)	L	NL	A (1)	P (1)	FIN	S	UK
Personnel costs (million ECU)	:	0	0	0	53	31	20	:	14	:	:	0	30	24	119	:
Personnel costs/employee (thousand ECU)	:	:	:	:	21.7	26.6	28.9	:	27.6	:	:	:	:	43.8	40.2	:
Social charges/personnel costs (%)	:	:	:	:	21.9	22.0	30.6	:	33.1	:	:	:	:	25.4	:	:
Labour productivity (thousand ECU/head)	:	:	:	:	21.0	17.2	36.0	:	15.6	:	:	:	:	42.2	59.2	:
Wage adjusted labour productivity (%)	:	:	:	:	96.7	64.7	124.4	:	56.4	:	:	:	:	96.4	147.4	:

(1) 1995.

Source: Eurostat (SBS)

(million ECU) Table 2.10

Quarrying of stone (NACE Rev. 1 14.1)
Production related indicators in the EU

	1988	1989	1990	1991	1992	1993	1994	1995	1996	1997	1998
Production value	:	:	:	:	:	3,065	2,972	:	:	:	:
Producer price index (1995=100)	:	:	:	:	:	:	:	:	:	:	:
Value added	:	:	:	:	:	1,373	1,374	:	:	:	:
Number of persons employed (thousands)	:	:	:	:	:	40.7	37.3	:	:	:	:

(million ECU) Table 2.11

Quarrying of stone (NACE Rev. 1 14.1)
Production related indicators, 1996

	B	DK	D	EL (1)	E	F	IRL	I (1)	L	NL	A (2)	P	FIN	S	UK
Production value	244	:	200	36	500	477	:	392	:	:	113	:	42	59	323
Value added	96	:	91	21	214	178	:	175	:	:	62	:	19	24	154
Number of persons employed (units)	1,749	:	1,357	910	6,918	3,896	:	4,572	:	:	1,101	:	369	375	3,347

(1) 1995. (2) 1994.

(million ECU) Table 2.12

Quarrying of stone (NACE Rev. 1 14.1)
Market related indicators in the EU

	1988	1989	1990	1991	1992	1993	1994	1995	1996	1997	1998
Apparent consumption	:	:	:	:	:	2,940	2,840	:	:	:	:
Exports	109	194	174	169	186	205	238	217	279	399	342
Imports	223	96	70	101	307	80	106	180	506	579	570
Trade balance	-114	98	104	68	-120	125	132	37	-228	-180	-229
Export ratio (%)	:	:	:	:	:	6.7	8.0	:	:	:	:
Import penetration ratio (%)	:	:	:	:	:	2.7	3.7	:	:	:	:
Cover ratio (%)	48.9	201.6	249.5	166.8	60.7	255.1	224.9	120.6	55.0	69.0	59.9

(million ECU) Table 2.13

Quarrying of stone (NACE Rev. 1 14.1)
Market related indicators, 1998

	B/L	DK	D	EL	E	F	IRL	I	NL	A	P	FIN	S	UK
Apparent consumption (1)	:	:	292	19	471	487	:	556	:	117	:	40	37	356
Exports	87	16	26	20	208	73	2	207	17	8	51	30	37	27
Imports	84	20	126	10	108	103	9	407	101	13	13	31	22	89
Trade balance	3	-4	-101	10	100	-30	-6	-200	-84	-5	38	-1	15	-62
Export ratio (%) (1)	:	:	14.5	58.6	24.2	15.6	:	49.6	:	6.4	:	75.0	68.3	7.3
Import penetration ratio (%) (1)	:	:	41.4	23.7	19.4	17.3	:	64.5	:	9.4	:	73.6	50.5	15.7
Cover ratio (%)	103.2	78.3	20.4	196.0	193.2	70.8	28.8	50.8	16.4	59.8	407.1	97.2	166.7	30.2

(1) A (1994); EL, I (1995); D, E, F, FIN, S, UK (1996).

Table 2.14

Quarrying of stone (NACE Rev. 1 14.1)
Labour related indicators, 1996

	EU-15 (1)	B	DK	D	EL (2)	E	F	IRL	I (2)	L	NL	A (1)	P	FIN	S	UK
Personnel costs (million ECU)	826	62	:	49	12	118	134	:	121	:	:	40	:	10	14	73
Personnel costs/employee (thousand ECU)	:	35.8	:	36.7	14.9	18.3	34.3	:	26.4	:	:	36.1	:	30.7	37.0	21.9
Social charges/personnel costs (%) (3)	:	29.2	:	20.6	22.5	24.1	30.9	:	33.0	:	:	21.9	:	23.6	27.1	13.5
Labour productivity (thousand ECU/head)	36.8	54.9	:	67.4	22.7	30.9	45.6	:	38.3	:	:	56.4	:	51.1	63.8	46.1
Wage adjusted labour productivity (%)	:	153.5	:	183.5	153.2	169.0	132.9	:	145.2	:	:	156.3	:	166.5	172.5	210.0

(1) 1994. (2) 1995. (3) S (1994).

Source: Eurostat (SBS, EBT)

Table 2.15 (million ECU)

Quarrying of sand and clay (NACE Rev. 1 14.2)

Production related indicators in the EU

	1988	1989	1990	1991	1992	1993	1994	1995	1996	1997	1998
Production value	:	:	:	:	:	9,998	11,349	:	:	:	:
Producer price index (1995=100)	:	:	:	:	:	:	:	:	:	:	:
Value added	:	:	:	:	:	4,050	4,478	:	:	:	:
Number of persons employed (thousands)	:	:	:	:	:	80.6	83.1	:	:	:	:

Table 2.16 (million ECU)

Quarrying of sand and clay (NACE Rev. 1 14.2)

Production related indicators, 1996

	B	DK	D	EL (1)	E	F	IRL	I (1)	L	NL	A (1)	P	FIN	S	UK
Production value	613	34	3,218	97	730	2,279	:	436	:	173	185	:	217	203	2,554
Value added	249	14	1,473	49	277	808	:	202	:	76	97	:	77	80	1,131
Number of persons employed (units)	2,736	262	23,786	1,254	7,583	15,055	:	3,459	:	:	1,278	:	1,378	1,113	21,074

(1) 1995.

Table 2.17 (million ECU)

Quarrying of sand and clay (NACE Rev. 1 14.2)

Market related indicators in the EU

	1988	1989	1990	1991	1992	1993	1994	1995	1996	1997	1998
Apparent consumption	:	:	:	:	:	10,001	11,183	:	:	:	:
Exports	181	171	186	186	185	203	224	237	232	261	271
Imports	144	175	178	217	235	206	59	396	425	502	340
Trade balance	37	-4	9	-31	-50	-3	165	-159	-193	-241	-68
Export ratio (%)	:	:	:	:	:	2.0	2.0	:	:	:	:
Import penetration ratio (%)	:	:	:	:	:	2.1	0.5	:	:	:	:
Cover ratio (%)	125.8	98.0	104.9	85.7	78.6	98.4	382.3	59.8	54.6	52.0	79.8

Table 2.18 (million ECU)

Quarrying of sand and clay (NACE Rev. 1 14.2)

Market related indicators, 1998

	B/L	DK	D	EL	E	F	IRL	I	NL	A	P	FIN	S	UK
Apparent consumption (1)	:	47	3,312	101	752	2,190	:	656	358	173	:	354	262	2,213
Exports	223	21	363	4	38	246	6	75	108	76	3	9	32	478
Imports	219	55	442	12	78	174	18	305	291	58	19	177	98	103
Trade balance	4	-34	-79	-8	-40	72	-12	-230	-183	19	-17	-169	-66	376
Export ratio (%) (1)	:	77.1	10.9	5.4	4.8	10.8	:	13.8	72.1	39.5	:	1.4	18.3	16.5
Import penetration ratio (%) (1)	:	83.4	13.4	9.1	7.6	7.2	:	42.7	86.5	35.6	:	39.4	36.6	3.6
Cover ratio (%)	101.9	38.4	82.2	32.1	48.9	141.7	32.3	24.6	37.2	132.5	14.9	5.0	32.9	465.2

(1) EL, I, A (1995); DK, D, E, F, NL, FIN, S, UK (1996).

Table 2.19

Quarrying of sand and clay (NACE Rev. 1 14.2)

Labour related indicators, 1996

	EU-15 (1)	B	DK	D	EL (2)	E	F	IRL	I (2)	L	NL	A (2)	P	FIN	S	UK
Personnel costs (million ECU)	2,409	117	9	907	21	143	502	:	102	:	29	51	:	41	39	472
Personnel costs/employee (thousand ECU)	:	43.2	32.7	38.6	17.3	20.1	33.4	:	29.6	:	:	40.0	:	32.1	35.3	22.4
Social charges/personnel costs (%) (3)	:	28.4	3.8	20.5	22.4	22.3	31.5	:	31.0	:	19.8	24.0	:	24.4	29.3	13.6
Labour productivity (thousand ECU/head)	53.9	91.2	55.3	61.9	39.1	36.5	53.7	:	58.5	:	:	75.6	:	55.9	72.0	53.7
Wage adjusted labour productivity (%)	:	211.1	169.3	160.4	225.7	182.1	160.9	:	197.6	:	:	189.1	:	174.3	204.2	239.8

(1) 1994. (2) 1995. (3) S (1995).

Source: Eurostat (SBS, EBT)

(million ECU) Table 2.20

Mining of chemical and fertiliser minerals (NACE Rev. 1 14.3)
Production related indicators in the EU

	1988	1989	1990	1991	1992	1993	1994	1995	1996	1997	1998
Production value	:	:	:	:	:	1,231	1,541	:	:	:	:
Producer price index (1995=100)	:	:	:	:	:	:	:	:	:	:	:
Value added	:	:	:	:	:	528	671	:	:	:	:
Number of persons employed (thousands)	:	:	:	:	:	15.6	16.4	:	:	:	:

(million ECU) Table 2.21

Mining of chemical and fertiliser minerals (NACE Rev. 1 14.3)
Production related indicators, 1996

	B (1)	DK	D	EL	E	F	IRL	I (2)	L	NL	A	P (3)	FIN	S	UK
Production value	0	0	1,050	:	177	163	0	24	0	:	:	3	0	0	190
Value added	:	0	429	:	73	60	0	9	0	:	:	:	0	0	88
Number of persons employed (units)	0	0	9,162	:	1,687	2,690	0	159	0	:	:	470	0	0	1,531

(1) 1994. (2) 1995. (3) 1993.

(million ECU) Table 2.22

Mining of chemical and fertiliser minerals (NACE Rev. 1 14.3)
Market related indicators in the EU

	1988	1989	1990	1991	1992	1993	1994	1995	1996	1997	1998
Apparent consumption	:	:	:	:	:	1,229	:	:	:	:	:
Exports	68	101	79	75	68	69	62	89	90	125	119
Imports	319	469	93	324	166	67	:	114	75	:	80
Trade balance	-251	-368	-14	-248	-97	2	:	-25	15	:	39
Export ratio (%)	:	:	:	:	:	5.6	4.0	:	:	:	:
Import penetration ratio (%)	:	:	:	:	:	5.4	:	:	:	:	:
Cover ratio (%)	21.2	21.6	85.1	23.3	41.2	102.9	:	78.2	119.3	:	148.9

(million ECU) Table 2.23

Mining of chemical and fertiliser minerals (NACE Rev. 1 14.3)
Market related indicators, 1998

	B/L	DK	D	EL	E	F	IRL	I	NL	A	P	FIN	S	UK
Apparent consumption (1)	:	4	996	:	204	280	2	90	:	:	14	8	17	208
Exports	44	0	180	2	82	23	0	32	70	8	1	11	3	26
Imports	146	7	136	32	135	153	5	88	126	30	15	11	34	49
Trade balance	-102	-7	44	-30	-53	-129	-5	-57	-57	-22	-14	0	-31	-23
Export ratio (%) (2)	:	:	16.3	:	49.2	20.3	:	80.9	:	:	0.7	39.6	:	13.4
Import penetration ratio (%) (1)	:	127.2	11.7	:	55.9	53.6	100.1	95.0	:	:	78.7	135.4	108.5	21.0
Cover ratio (%)	30.2	6.0	132.4	5.4	60.5	15.2	0.8	35.6	55.1	26.2	3.9	95.8	9.3	53.8

(1) P (1993); I (1995); DK, D, E, F, IRL, FIN, S, UK (1996). (2) FIN (1991); P (1993); I (1995); D, E, F, UK (1996).

Table 2.24

Mining of chemical and fertiliser minerals (NACE Rev. 1 14.3)
Labour related indicators, 1996

	EU-15 (1)	B	DK	D	EL	E	F	IRL	I (2)	L	NL	A	P (3)	FIN	S	UK
Personnel costs (million ECU)	605	:	0	388	:	49	134	0	4	0	:	:	6	0	0	46
Personnel costs/employee (thousand ECU)	:	:	:	42.4	:	29.3	49.8	:	27.6	:	:	:	:	:	:	30.4
Social charges/personnel costs (%)	:	:	:	25.0	:	24.4	40.2	:	36.2	:	:	:	:	:	:	11.3
Labour productivity (thousand ECU/head)	40.8	:	:	46.8	:	43.4	22.5	:	54.2	:	:	:	:	:	:	57.3
Wage adjusted labour productivity (%)	:	:	:	110.5	:	148.0	45.1	:	196.2	:	:	:	:	:	:	188.6

(1) 1994. (2) 1995. (3) 1993.

Source: Eurostat (SBS, EBT)

Table 2.25 (million ECU)

Production of salt (NACE Rev. 1 14.4)

Production related indicators in the EU

	1988	1989	1990	1991	1992	1993	1994	1995	1996	1997	1998
Production value	:	:	:	:	:	935	913	:	:	:	:
Producer price index (1995=100)	:	:	89.2	93.4	96.7	97.9	99.6	100.0	98.3	97.1	95.3
Value added	:	:	:	:	:	413	389	:	:	:	:
Number of persons employed (thousands)	:	:	:	:	:	8.5	7.6	:	:	:	:

Table 2.26 (million ECU)

Production of salt (NACE Rev. 1 14.4)

Production related indicators, 1996

	B	DK	D	EL (1)	E	F	IRL	I (1)	L	NL (1)	A	P (1)	FIN	S	UK (2)
Production value	0	:	301	20	79	197	0	98	0	0	:	7	0	0	116
Value added	0	:	121	8	34	106	0	25	0	0	:	:	0	0	61
Number of persons employed (units)	0	:	1,904	416	721	1,589	0	754	0	:	:	300	0	0	754

(1) 1995. (2) 1994.

Table 2.27 (million ECU)

Production of salt (NACE Rev. 1 14.4)

Market related indicators in the EU

	1988	1989	1990	1991	1992	1993	1994	1995	1996	1997	1998
Apparent consumption	:	:	:	:	:	910	:	:	:	:	:
Exports	10	25	16	29	28	27	28	30	34	37	35
Imports	:	:	:	:	:	2	:	:	:	:	6
Trade balance	:	:	:	:	:	25	:	:	:	:	30
Export ratio (%)	:	:	:	:	:	2.9	3.0	:	:	:	:
Import penetration ratio (%)	:	:	:	:	:	0.2	:	:	:	:	:
Cover ratio (%)	:	:	:	:	:	1,489.6	:	:	:	:	629.0

Table 2.28 (million ECU)

Production of salt (NACE Rev. 1 14.4)

Market related indicators, 1998

	B/L	DK	D	EL	E	F	IRL	I	NL	A	P	FIN	S	UK
Apparent consumption (1)	:	:	259	22	60	186	8	114	-90	:	10	14	42	105
Exports	3	12	81	2	19	39	0	10	65	9	1	0	1	25
Imports	53	12	63	5	4	37	8	31	13	6	4	15	39	17
Trade balance	-49	0	18	-3	15	3	-7	-21	52	3	-3	-15	-38	8
Export ratio (%) (2)	:	:	33.2	7.1	28.8	22.3	:	6.6	:	:	7.1	:	:	20.8
Import penetration ratio (%) (1)	:	:	22.2	14.7	6.3	17.9	100.8	20.0	-19.1	:	34.3	104.1	104.3	12.7
Cover ratio (%)	6.4	99.0	128.7	34.7	485.4	106.8	1.0	31.2	497.8	140.3	24.3	3.3	3.0	145.4

(1) UK (1994); EL, I, NL, P (1995); D, E, F, IRL, FIN, S (1996). (2) UK (1994); EL, I, P (1995); D, E, F (1996).

Table 2.29

Production of salt (NACE Rev. 1 14.4)

Labour related indicators, 1996

	EU-15 (1)	B	DK	D	EL (2)	E	F	IRL	I (2)	L	NL (2)	A	P (2)	FIN	S	UK (1)
Personnel costs (million ECU)	243	0	:	95	6	18	66	0	20	0	0	:	2	0	0	24
Personnel costs/employee (thousand ECU)	:	:	:	49.8	13.7	25.7	41.3	:	26.4	:	:	:	:	:	:	31.6
Social charges/personnel costs (%)	:	:	:	23.9	21.3	23.7	33.3	:	29.6	:	:	:	:	:	:	13.8
Labour productivity (thousand ECU/head)	51.1	:	:	63.6	18.7	47.6	66.6	:	32.7	:	:	:	:	:	:	81.1
Wage adjusted labour productivity (%)	:	:	:	127.7	136.5	185.1	161.4	:	123.9	:	:	:	:	:	:	256.8

(1) 1994. (2) 1995.

Source: Eurostat (SBS, EBT)

(million ECU) Table 2.30

Other mining and quarrying (NACE Rev. 1 14.5)
Production related indicators in the EU

	1988	1989	1990	1991	1992	1993	1994	1995	1996	1997	1998
Production value	:	:	:	:	:	690	844	:	:	:	:
Producer price index (1995=100)	:	:	:	:	:	:	:	:	:	:	:
Value added	:	:	:	:	:	325	364	:	:	:	:
Number of persons employed (thousands)	:	:	:	:	:	6.4	6.5	:	:	:	:

(million ECU) Table 2.31

Other mining and quarrying (NACE Rev. 1 14.5)
Production related indicators, 1996

	B (1)	DK	D	EL (2)	E	F	IRL	I (2)	L	NL (1)	A	P	FIN	S	UK
Production value	24	:	97	81	146	115	:	251	0	100	:	:	156	3	:
Value added	:	:	40	37	56	45	:	99	0	30	:	:	58	1	:
Number of persons employed (units)	87	:	594	1,011	929	764	:	2,140	0	:	:	:	928	28	:

(1) 1994. (2) 1995.

(million ECU) Table 2.32

Other mining and quarrying (NACE Rev. 1 14.5)
Market related indicators in the EU

	1988	1989	1990	1991	1992	1993	1994	1995	1996	1997	1998
Apparent consumption	:	:	:	:	:	1,667	1,673	:	:	:	:
Exports	3,926	4,681	3,911	3,878	3,844	4,953	5,377	5,617	6,212	6,944	5,733
Imports	4,835	5,404	4,927	4,663	4,657	5,930	6,205	6,552	6,589	7,660	6,975
Trade balance	-909	-723	-1,015	-785	-813	-977	-829	-935	-378	-716	-1,242
Export ratio (%)	:	:	:	:	:	717.8	636.8	:	:	:	:
Import penetration ratio (%)	:	:	:	:	:	355.7	370.9	:	:	:	:
Cover ratio (%)	81.2	86.6	79.4	83.2	82.5	83.5	86.6	85.7	94.3	90.7	82.2

(million ECU) Table 2.33

Other mining and quarrying (NACE Rev. 1 14.5)
Market related indicators, 1998

	B/L	DK	D	EL	E	F	IRL	I	NL	A	P	FIN	S	UK
Apparent consumption (1)	:	:	304	19	169	136	:	290	113	:	:	158	13	:
Exports	4,666	18	91	65	46	84	2	57	82	60	12	32	12	3,152
Imports	4,947	58	274	5	79	102	12	156	102	77	55	7	28	3,873
Trade balance	-281	-39	-183	60	-33	-18	-10	-98	-20	-18	-44	25	-16	-722
Export ratio (%) (1)	:	:	87.7	85.5	29.1	68.1	:	23.6	55.4	:	:	2.4	404.9	:
Import penetration ratio (%) (1)	:	:	96.1	37.1	38.6	73.1	:	33.8	60.4	:	:	3.9	165.8	:
Cover ratio (%)	94.3	31.6	33.3	1,227.0	57.8	82.5	16.9	36.9	80.6	77.3	21.3	453.4	41.8	81.4

(1) NL (1994); EL, I (1995); D, E, F, FIN, S (1996).

Table 2.34

Other mining and quarrying (NACE Rev. 1 14.5)
Labour related indicators, 1996

	EU-15 (1)	B	DK	D	EL (2)	E	F	IRL	I (2)	L	NL (1)	A	P	FIN	S	UK
Personnel costs (million ECU)	183	:	:	23	22	22	32	:	62	0	13	:	:	28	1	:
Personnel costs/employee (thousand ECU)	:	:	:	38.4	21.9	23.9	41.4	:	28.7	:	:	:	:	30.6	37.0	:
Social charges/personnel costs (%)	:	:	:	23.7	23.5	22.3	34.0	:	33.2	:	14.4	:	:	23.6	:	:
Labour productivity (thousand ECU/head)	56.2	:	:	67.6	36.4	59.8	59.5	:	46.2	:	:	:	:	62.9	42.2	:
Wage adjusted labour productivity (%)	:	:	:	176.1	166.4	250.5	143.4	:	160.7	:	:	:	:	205.6	113.9	:

(1) 1994. (2) 1995.

Source: Eurostat (SBS, EBT)

Food, drink and tobacco

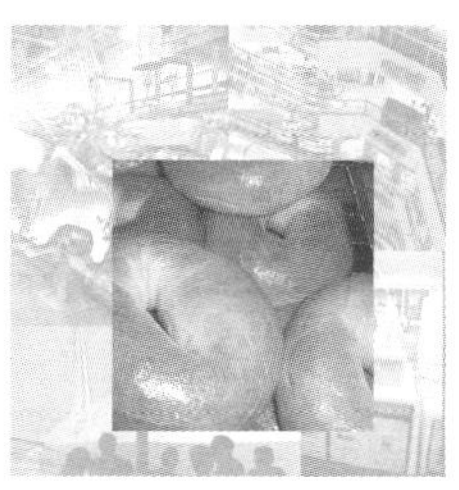

Industry description

This chapter of the Panorama is dedicated to all economic activities relating to food, drink and tobacco processing industries, covered by Divisions 15 (manufacture of food products and beverages) and 16 (manufacture of tobacco products) of the NACE Rev. 1 classification. The output of the industry consists of either products for final consumption or intermediate products used for further processing. Structural statistics compiled by Eurostat suggest that production value of this sector was worth almost 600 billion ECU, about 15% of total manufacturing output, just ahead of the transport equipment industry. An international comparison of the industry reveals the EU as the world's largest producer of food, drink and tobacco products, with output values of 460 billion ECU in the USA and 260 billion ECU in Japan.

Amongst the food and drinks industry, the largest share was accounted for by the composite group defined by NACE Rev. 1 Group 15.8 (the manufacture of bread and pastry, biscuits, sugar, chocolate, noodles, tea and coffee, condiments, food preparations and other miscellaneous food). The production value of these activities exceeded 125 billion ECU in 1998, or 22% of the total for the food, drink and tobacco industry, ahead of the manufacture of meat products (NACE Rev. 1 15.1) with 100 billion ECU, or 17% of the total. The beverages industry and the dairy products industry came next, both with output of some 90 billion ECU, or 15% of the total. The tobacco industry represented less than a tenth of the sector. The activities with the lowest output were the manufacture of grain mill and starch products (20 billion ECU) and the fish processing and preserving industry (10 billion ECU).

(%) Figure 3.1

Food, drink and tobacco
(NACE Rev. 1 15 and 16)
Share of EU value added in total manufacturing

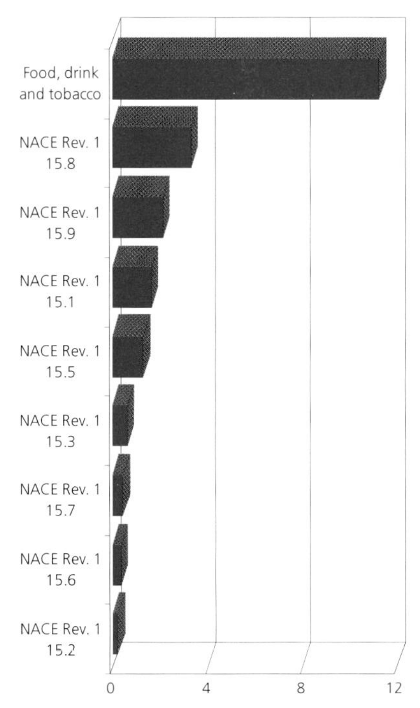

Source: Eurostat (SBS)

The activities covered in this chapter include:

- 15.1: production, processing and preserving of meat and meat products;
- 15.2: processing and preserving of fish and fish products;
- 15.3: processing and preserving of fruit and vegetables;
- 15.4: manufacture of vegetable and animal oils and fats;
- 15.5: manufacture of dairy products;
- 15.6: manufacture of grain mill products, starches and starch products;
- 15.7: manufacture of prepared animal feeds;
- 15.8: manufacture of other food products;
- 15.9: manufacture of beverages;
- 16: manufacture of tobacco products.

Figure 3.2 (1988=100)

Food, drink and tobacco (NACE Rev. 1 15 and 16)

Production, employment and value added compared to EU total manufacturing

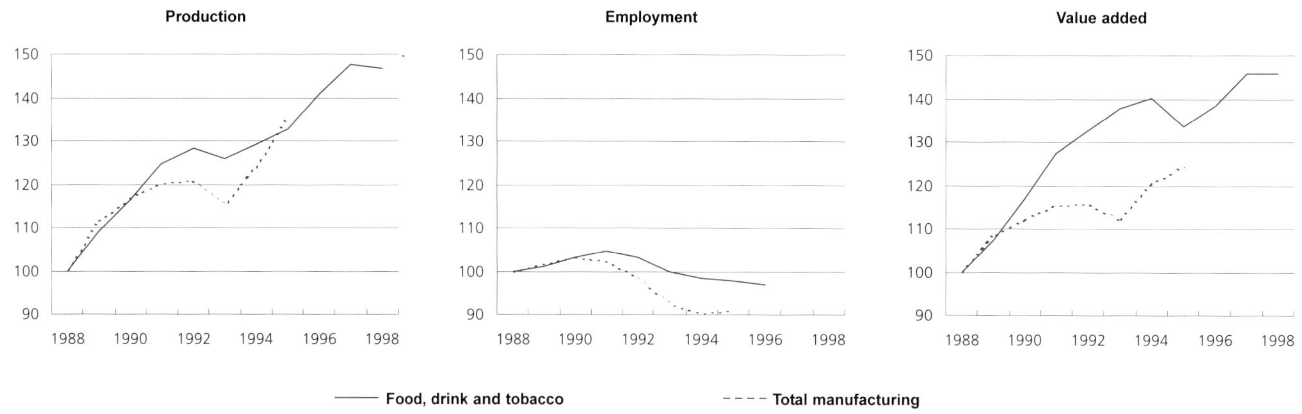

Source: Eurostat (SBS)

Four countries displayed a significant specialisation in food, drink and tobacco activities: Ireland and Denmark, where the share of this industry in national manufacturing output was more than twice the EU average (specialisation ratio greater than 200%), Greece (172%) and the Netherlands (163%). In contrast, Germany and Italy displayed production specialisation ratios below 75%.

Figure 3.3

Food, drink and tobacco (NACE Rev. 1 15 and 16)

International comparison of main indicators in current prices

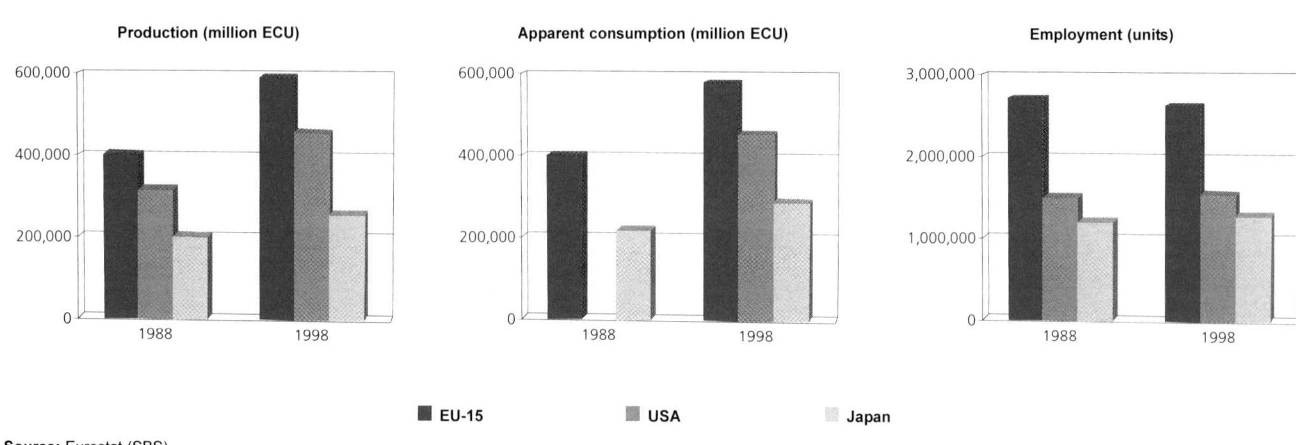

Source: Eurostat (SBS)

(ECU/hour) Figure 3.4

Food, drink and tobacco (NACE Rev. 1 15 and 16)
Labour costs by Member State, 1996

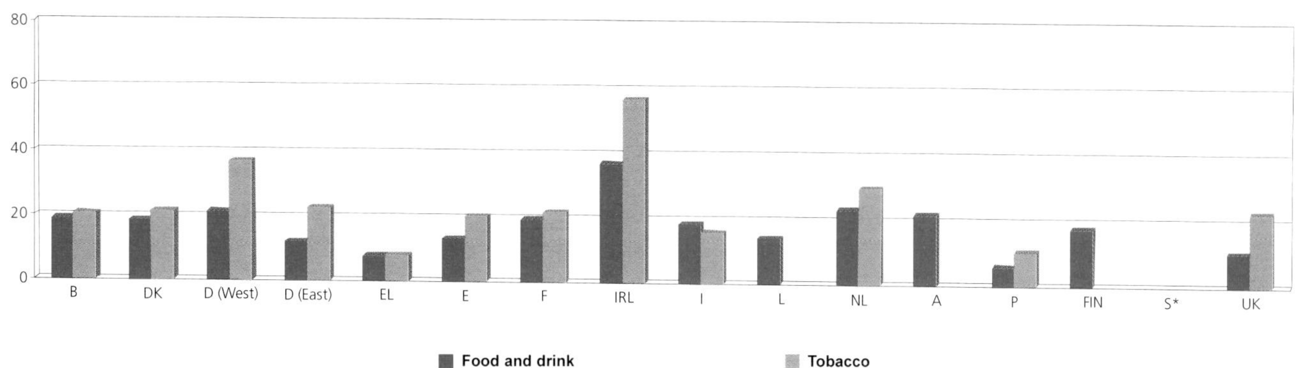

Source: Eurostat (LCS)

Recent trends

The European food, drink and tobacco sector can be considered as a mature industry, and was hence characterised by modest growth rates. This was reflected in the evolution of domestic demand, which stood at 560 billion ECU in 1998, showing no change on the figures for 1997. Since the beginning of the decade the industry faced demand growth of 2.7% per annum on average, a rate just below that of manufacturing as a whole (2.8%). Growth rates varied significantly across the industry, depending on the type of activity considered. For example, amongst food products, apparent consumption of processed or preserved fruits and vegetables (NACE Rev. 1 15.3) grew on average by over 3% per annum, whilst it progressed by only 0.4% for animal feed (NACE Rev. 1 15.7). These specific trends will be analysed in more detail within the different sections of this chapter.

Demand for food and drink is by nature not elastic. Consumer spending on food and drink represented a steadily decreasing share of European household budgets that could be estimated at about 12% in 1997, down from 18% in 1980 and 21% in 1970.

As a consequence, the trends affecting the industry are characterised more by an evolution of consumption patterns rather than an increase of consumption itself. Amongst the major social factors affecting consumer purchases is the evolution of the European population, which is continuing to age, whilst the average size of households shrinks. The increased activity rate of women at work and the rising number of single-persons or single-parent households has led to a redistribution of food and drink towards "out-of-home" consumption at the expense of "at-home" consumption, as exemplified by the success of fast-food outlets. This change in consumption patterns has also been seen in the market for high value-added products such as ready-made dishes (whose success was further aided by the introduction of microwave ovens). Other notable social trends affecting the industry include the desire for refined food and for foreign and exotic products; a trend towards dietary products; more diversity in the choice of food; and finally, the increasing importance of vegetarian, fresh and organic food. The variety of trends mentioned above has led to greater fragmentation of demand and, correspondingly, to a higher number of market segments devoted to products that place a particular emphasis on safety, healthiness, environmental concern, animal welfare, convenience, variety, etc.

(%) Table 3.1

Food, drink and tobacco
(NACE Rev. 1 15 and 16)
Composition of the labour force, 1997

	Females	Part-time	Highly-educated
EU-15	36.7	:	:
B	27.9	3.9	16.0
DK	41.1	:	:
D	47.4	17.6	14.2
EL	32.8	:	9.4
E	32.1	3.0	11.2
F	38.6	6.4	8.8
IRL	27.6	3.5	17.1
I	33.7	2.9	:
L	27.4	:	:
NL	33.5	16.8	11.3
A	29.4	:	:
P	39.2	:	3.5
FIN	53.1	:	:
S	40.4	:	:
UK	31.8	2.1	11.4

Source: Eurostat (LFS)

Figure 3.5 (million ECU)

Food, drink and tobacco (NACE Rev. 1 15 and 16)

Foreign net direct investment (1)

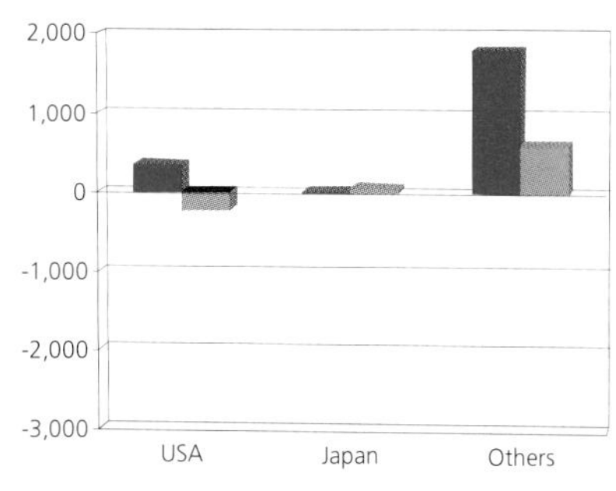

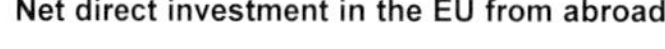

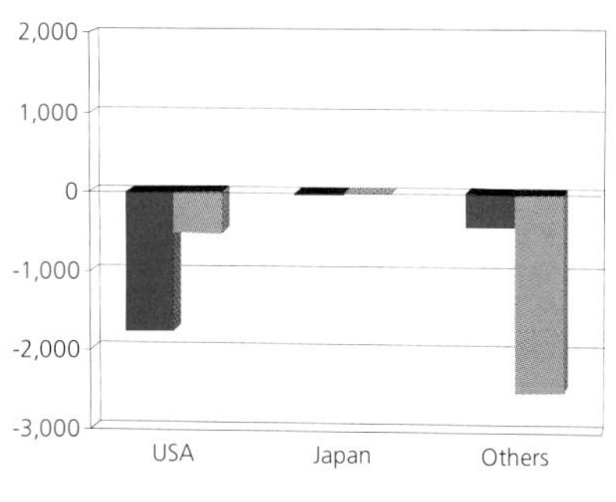

(1) NACE Rev. 1 15 excluding 15.9.

Source: Eurostat (BOP)

Employment in the food and drinks industry has followed a growing trend, rising about 1.3% per annum between the mid-1980s and the mid-1990s, to reach some 2.6 million persons in 1995 (the last year for which official figures for the EU as a whole are available). More recent figures (for 1998) allow us to estimate employment at a comparable level. In the tobacco industry, however, the picture is somewhat different as heavy job losses were suffered over the past decade.

Men constitute the largest share of persons employed in the sector, accounting for 63% of the labour force for food and drink and 65% of the labour force for tobacco products in 1997. The highest presence of women was recorded in Germany and Finland, at around 45% of the total number of persons employed. The share of women was at its lowest in Spain, Ireland and Luxembourg, where practically three-quarters of the employed were men.

The share of persons employed working part-time was relatively high in food and drinks manufacturing, at 12%. It was closer to the average of manufacturing activities in the tobacco industry, at just 5%; the countries that made the largest use of part-time work included the Netherlands and Denmark, where one-quarter and one-fifth of the workforce were employed on a part-time basis.

Foreign trade

Extra-EU exports of food and drink products practically doubled between 1988 and 1998 to reach 41 billion ECU. Imports progressed much more slowly over the same period, resulting in the trade balance growing rapidly from almost zero in 1988 to a 12 billion ECU surplus in 1997 (before falling somewhat in 1998 to 8.5 billion ECU). In the meantime, the USA displayed a trade balance that oscillated (with a deficit in most years), whilst Japan recorded a very large deficit of 28 billion ECU in 1997 (up from 17 billion ECU in 1988).

Inside the EU, three of the largest Member States recorded significant structural trade deficits in food products: Italy (3 billion ECU in 1998), Germany (4 billion ECU) and the United Kingdom (7 billion ECU). The Netherlands, France and Denmark, on the other hand, were all large net exporters (with surpluses of between 9 and 4 billion ECU respectively in 1998). These observations were confirmed by looking at export specialisation: Denmark (325%) and the Netherlands (178%) ranked in 1998 amongst the most specialised countries, along with Greece (262%). However, Italy, Germany and the United Kingdom were all well below the average, whilst the least specialised country was Sweden (30%).

Figure 3.6

Food, drink and tobacco
(NACE Rev. 1 15 and 16)
Destination of EU exports, 1998

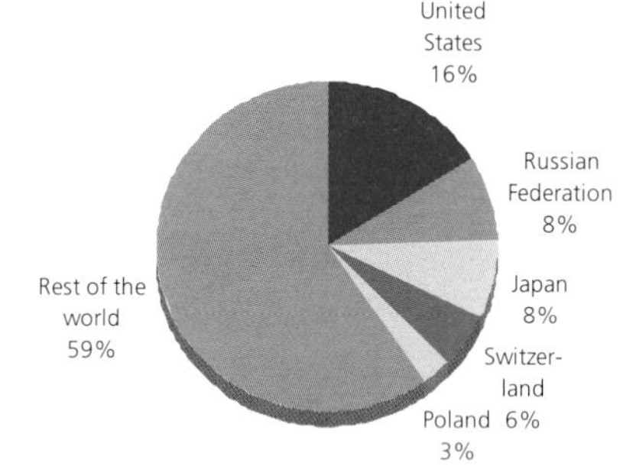

Source: Eurostat (Comext)

Figure 3.7

Food, drink and tobacco
(NACE Rev. 1 15 and 16)
Origin of EU imports, 1998

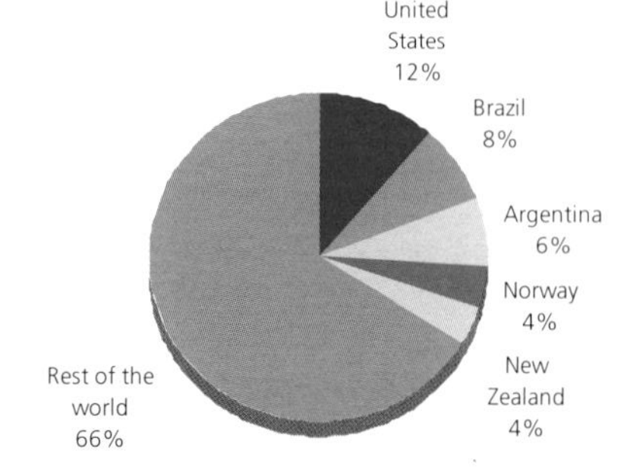

Source: Eurostat (Comext)

Meat (NACE Rev. 1 15.1)

The animal slaughtering and meat processing industry includes all processing stages which follow animal rearing activities right up to final consumption. The industry includes the activities of slaughtering, processing, and the storage of beef, veal, pork, sheep and goat meat, and poultry as defined by the NACE Rev. 1 classification. Also included is the intermediate processing of products like the manufacturing of plasma and related activities and the melting of animal fats. Final products include cuts of meat, cured and processed meat, as well as chilled, frozen and canned meats.

Meat accounted for approximately 28% of EU household expenditure on food products (excluding drinks) in 1997, making it the largest single category. This figure was particularly high in France, Belgium, Luxembourg and Denmark, at 30% or more, whilst the lowest figures were found in Greece, Finland and Sweden (around 20%).

Total meat production reached 37 million tonnes in 1997, of which only a fraction was exported (2.7 million tonnes). The largest meat producers within the EU were France (7.5 million tonnes in 1998) and Germany (6.4 million tonnes in 1998). Pork meat had the highest production (16 million tonnes), representing not far from half of all meat produced in the EU in 1997. Since 1996 poultry has been the second largest sector in the EU (8.5 million tonnes in 1997), ahead of beef (7 million tonnes). Smaller production levels were recorded for offal (2.2 million tonnes), sheep meat (1.1 million tonnes), and horse meat (48 thousand tonnes). Irish meat production was particularly specialised in beef, Danish production in pork, Greek production in sheep and goats, and the United Kingdom in poultry.

Figure 3.8

Meat (NACE Rev. 1 15.1)

Production and employment in the Triad

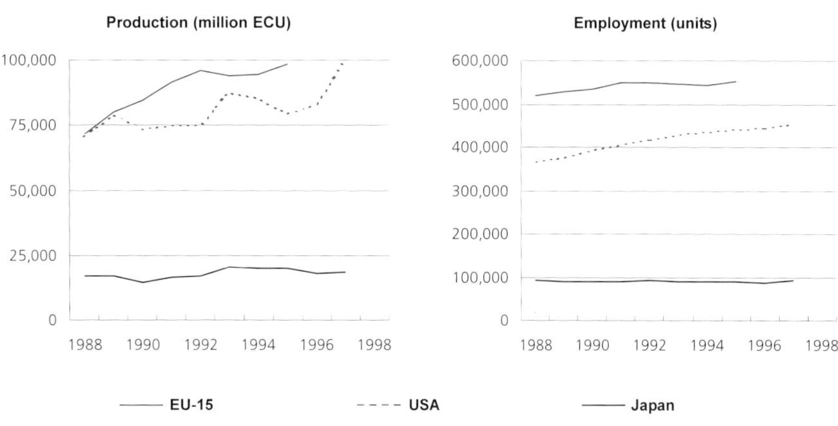

Source: Eurostat (SBS)

(%)

Figure 3.9

Meat (NACE Rev. 1 15.1)

Production and export specialisation by Member State, 1998

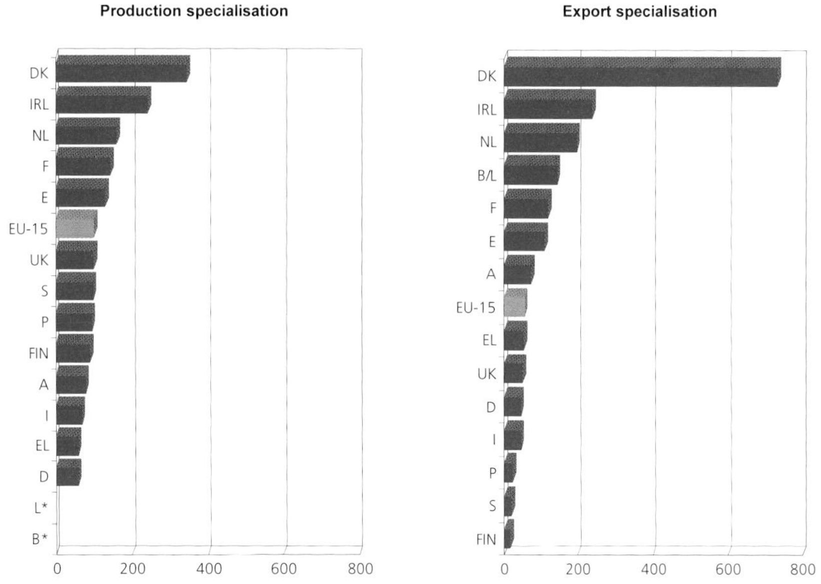

Source: Eurostat (SBS)

Professional associations representing the industries within this chapter

CIMCEE	EDMMA	ETC	EUROGLACES	EUROMALT	UEITP
Committee of the Mustard Industry of the EU 30, avenue de Roodebeek B-1030 Bruxelles tel: (32) 2 743 87 30 fax: (32) 2 736 81 75	European Dessert Mixes Manufacturers Association 30, avenue de Roodebeek B-1030 Bruxelles tel: (32) 2 743 87 30 fax: (32) 2 736 81 75	European Tea Committee 18, rue de la Pépinière F-75008 Paris tel: (33) 1 53 42 13 38 fax: (33) 1 53 42 13 39	Association of the ice cream industry of the EEC 18, rue de la Pépinière F-75008 Paris tel: (33) 1 53 42 13 38 fax: (33) 1 53 42 13 39	Working Committee of the Malting Industry of the EU 9, avenue des Gaulois B-1040 Bruxelles tel: (32) 2 736 53 54 fax: (32) 2 732 34 27 e-mail: euromalt@ecco.be	European Association of Potato Processing Industry Von-der-Heydt Straße 9 D-53177 Bonn tel: (49) 228 35 40 25 fax: (49) 228 36 18 89

Table 3.2 (%)

Production specialisation by kind of meat, 1998

	Cattle	Pigs	Sheep and goats	Equidae	Poultry	Offal	Other meat
B/L	78	132	7	124	80	89	46
DK	36	180	3	36	39	68	6
D	105	133	23	55	52	86	55
EL (1)	47	59	766	0	135	150	30
E	55	124	169	121	80	117	128
F	117	71	64	99	134	110	167
IRL (1)	234	48	217	68	47	182	28
I (1)	110	78	47	275	125	95	233
NL (1)	89	117	27	57	106	69	13
A (1)	124	127	30	74	54	60	27
P (1)	60	89	110	99	147	125	126
FIN	121	116	11	86	73	62	88
S	108	127	19	223	61	59	102
UK	81	64	319	11	164	114	12

(1) 1997.

Source: Eurostat (ZPA)

Figure 3.10

Breakdown of meat production in the EU, 1997

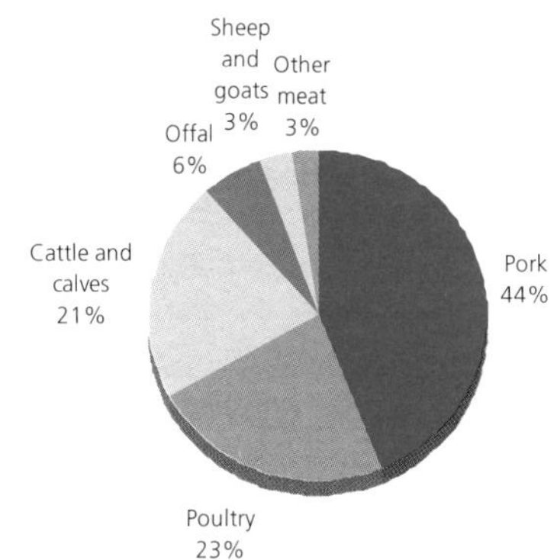

Source: Eurostat (ZPA)

In value terms, total production value of the meat industry reached 100 billion ECU in 1998, a decline of 4% compared to 1997. Over the longer term, output progressed by an average rate of 2.7% per annum (from 1988 to 1998). Apparent consumption broadly followed the same trend to reach 98 billion ECU in 1998. Eurostat figures indicate that each European citizen consumed on average some 92 kilos of meat in 1998: the Spanish (123 kg), the French (109 kg) and the Irish (108 kg) were clearly above average, whilst meat was less popular in Sweden (71 kg) and Finland (69 kg).

One of the most important trends that affected meat demand over the last decade has been the ascent of poultry meat at the expense of red meats. Poultry demand has increased on the one hand due to its lower price compared with red meats, and on the other because of the convenience of processed poultry products and its favourable image (less fat and healthier). Within some European markets, there is increasing demand for certified-label products guaranteeing the type of farming (such as slaughtering techniques, the type of feed, life spans, the percentage of various feeds used, etc). These trends are likely to be further fuelled by concerns raised by recent health scandals, whereby it became apparent that the quality of animal feed was not always as it should have been. Meat consumption was seriously affected by the outbreak of "mad cow" disease, which came to light after scientists linked BSE with a fatal human brain disease (Creutzfeld-Jacobs syndrome). Whilst the beef sector was clearly the most harmed, the whole meat sector felt the effects of changing consumption patterns, with substitution effects not strong enough to fully compensate for the decline in beef consumption.

Figure 3.11 (%)

Share of meat products in household food consumption, 1997 (1)

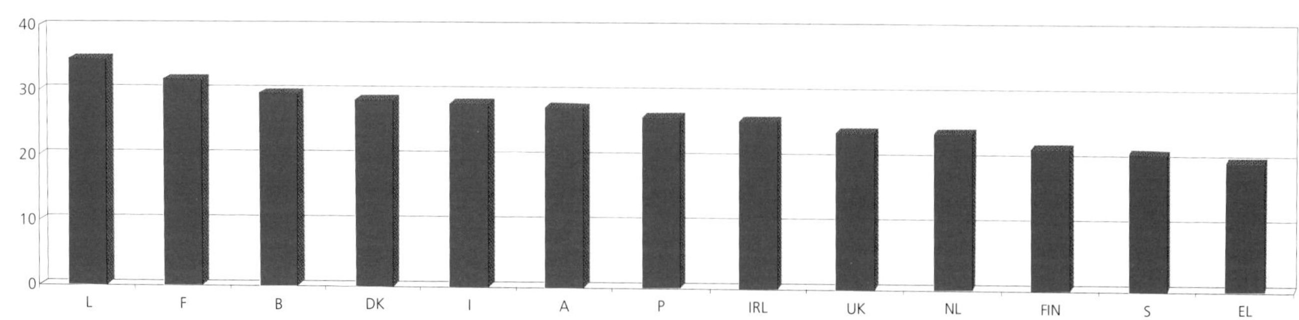

(1) Earlier years had to be used for some countries.

Source: Eurostat (National Accounts)

The meat sector comprises a number of large companies, as well as numerous small and medium-sized enterprises. The industry structure is fragmented although the EU's new agricultural policy and the level of concentration achieved by distribution networks has given rise to increased concentration in the sector. The major enterprises at a European level belong to highly diversified multinational groups such as Unilever (UK/NL) and Nestlé (CH). Other large enterprises for which meat is the core business include Südfleisch (D), Nordfleisch (D), Socopa (F), Arcadie (F), Vital Sogesviandes (F), Moksel (D) and Cremonini (I).

EU employment in the meat sector could be estimated at around 540 thousand persons in 1998, down from 550 thousand in 1995. The reduction in employment levels can be explained mainly by the reorganisation of cattle slaughtering plants, which has taken place mainly in the southern Member States.

Internationally, the EU has been the largest meat producer within the Triad. EU production value was worth 104 billion ECU in 1997, 4 billion ECU more than in the USA (99.6 billion ECU) and more than more than five times the level reached in Japan (18.4 billion ECU). International trade, however, is not very developed, as the EU exported less than 5% of its production in 1998. The EU's trade balance with the rest of the world was practically in equilibrium, with surpluses or deficits of a few hundred million ECU in recent years.

Intra-EU trade was much more developed, with the sum of non-domestic deliveries of meat products representing more than one fifth of production in 1998. The most export-specialised country was Denmark, where the share of meat exports in total manufacturing exports was more than seven times the European average (export specialisation ratio of 734%). Ireland (238%) and the Netherlands (198%) also displayed high export specialisation, in contrast with Portugal (24%), Sweden (20%) or Finland (17%).

Figure 3.12

Meat (NACE Rev. 1 15.1)

Destination of EU exports, 1998

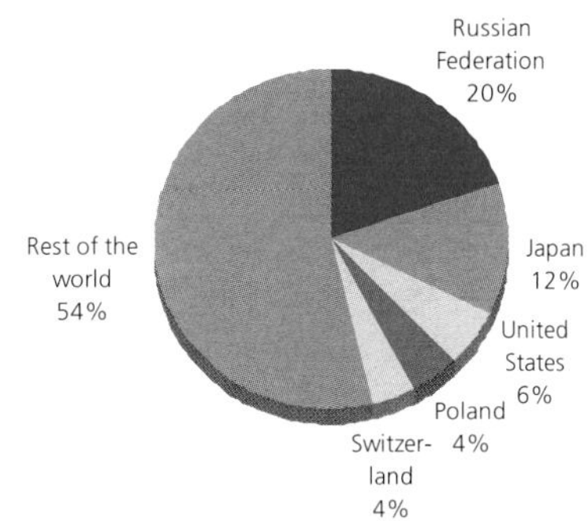

Source: Eurostat (Comext)

Figure 3.13

Meat (NACE Rev. 1 15.1)

Origin of EU imports, 1998

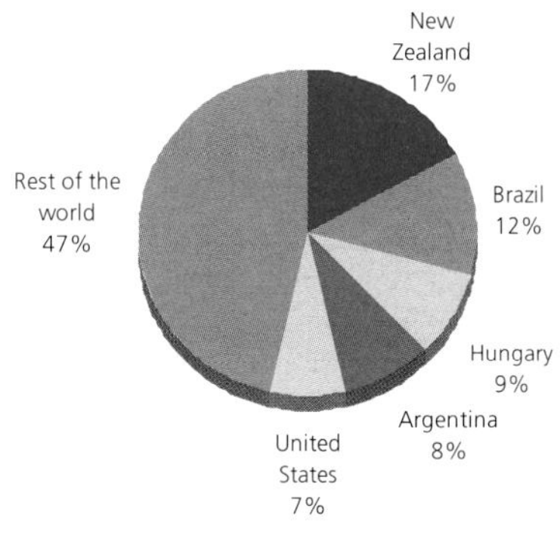

Source: Eurostat (Comext)

Professional associations representing the industries within this chapter

AIPCEE
Association des Industries du Poisson de l'UE
30, avenue de Roodebeek
B-1030 Bruxelles
tel: (32) 2 743 87 30
fax: (32) 2 743 81 75

CBMC
Trade Confederation of the Brewing Industry in the European Union
181, chaussées de la Hulpe
Boîte 20
B-1170 Bruxelles
tel: (32) 2 672 23 92
fax: (32) 2 660 94 02
e-mail: infos@cbmc.org

CECCM
Confederation of European Community Cigarette Manufacturers
125, avenue Louise
B-1050 Bruxelles
tel: (32) 2 541 00 41
fax: (32) 2 541 00 45

CEFS
European Committee of Sugar Industry
182, avenue de Tervueren
B-1150 Bruxelles
tel: (32) 2 762 07 60
fax: (32) 2 771 00 26
e-mail: cefs@euronet.be

OEITFL
Association of European Fruit and Vegetable Processing Industries
30, avenue de Roodebeek
B-1030 Bruxelles
tel: (32) 2 743 87 30
fax: (32) 2 736 81 75
e-mail:
ereco@bipeeurope.fr

UNAFPA
Union of Organisations of Manufacturers of Pasta Products in the EEC
c/o UNIPI
Via Po 102
I-00198 Roma
tel: (39) 06 85 43 291
fax: (39) 06 84 15 132
e-mail: unipi@foodarea.it

Fish (NACE Rev. 1 15.2)

The activities covered in this section are defined as the preparation and preservation of fish, crustaceans and molluscs and production of fish, crustacean and mollusc products, including prepared fish dishes. The output of this industry can be divided into five major categories:

- frozen fish (excluding whole fish), e.g. frozen fish fillets, which are partly processed items using basic raw seafood material which can be either further processed into prepared dishes or sold to consumers in that form;
- dried, salted and smoked fish, e.g. smoked salmon, salted cod, consumed without any further industrial processing;
- prepared or preserved fish, e.g. cans of tuna, prepared dishes, surimi, which are basically value-added ready to eat items;
- aquatic invertebrates, frozen dried or salted e.g. cuttlefish fillets, frozen mussels, which can be either further processed into prepared dishes or sold to consumers in that form;
- crustaceans, molluscs and other aquatic invertebrates, prepared or preserved e.g. cans of crab, shellfish salads, which are ready-to-eat items.

Production value of the fish processing and preserving sector could be estimated at over 11.6 billion ECU in 1998[1], a progression of 4% when compared to 1997. France was the largest producer of fish products with almost 2 billion ECU of output in 1998, ahead of Spain (1.9 billion ECU), Germany and the United Kingdom (1.7 billion ECU each). However, Denmark boasted the highest specialisation ratio, as the weight of its fish processing industry relative to the whole of manufacturing was almost eight times higher than the EU average (772%) in 1998. Other relatively specialised countries included Portugal (289%) and Spain (249%). Overall, EU production grew by an average of just over 2% per annum between 1988 and 1998, although annual growth rates were equal to just 0.6% since 1990. These relatively low rates hide much larger short-term variations, with output increasing by as much of 10.5% in 1988 and 1989, or declining by 9.2% in 1995.

1) Excluding Luxembourg and Austria.

Figure 3.14

Fish (NACE Rev. 1 15.2)

Production and employment in the Triad

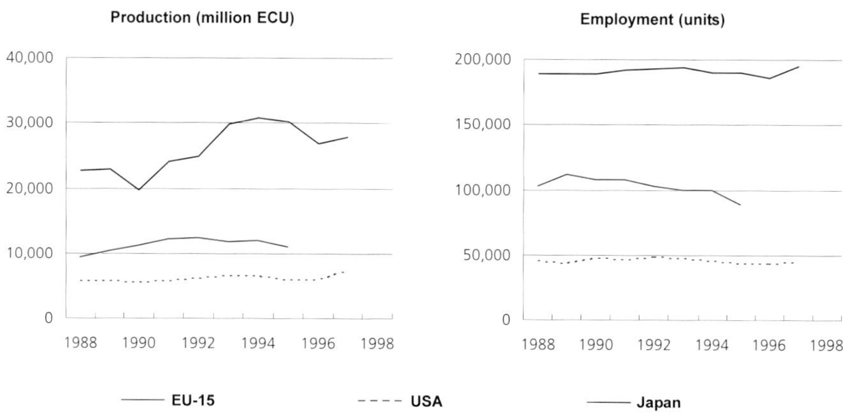

Source: Eurostat (SBS)

Figure 3.15 (%)

Fish (NACE Rev. 1 15.2)

Production and export specialisation by Member State, 1998

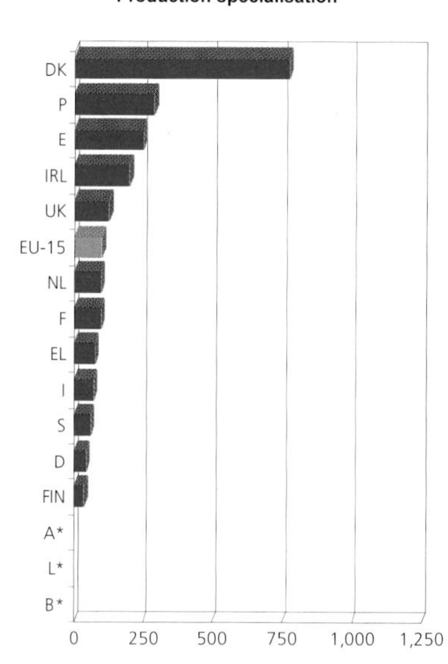

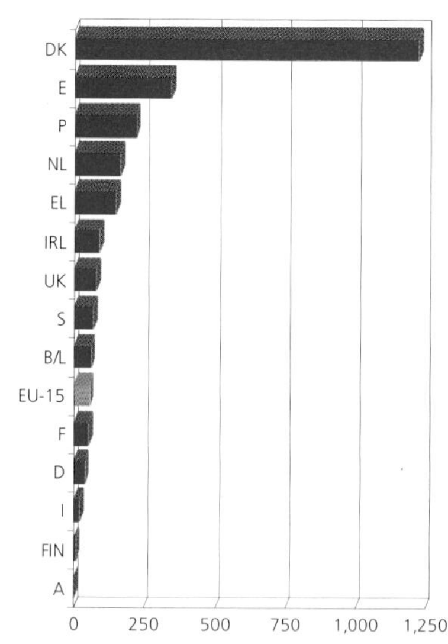

Source: Eurostat (SBS)

(thousand tonnes) Table 3.3

Production of fishery commodities, 1997

	Crustaceans & molluscs fresh, chilled or frozen	Crustaceans & molluscs products & preparations	Fish products & preparations	Fish dried, salted or smoked	Fish fresh, chilled or frozen	Meals, solubles, etc.	Oils & fats
B	6.6	2.4	11.3	3.3	8.3	0.5	:
DK	5.0	25.5	88.2	29.4	133.2	395.3	131.1
D	4.0	1.5	168.9	18.6	282.1	14.5	5.0
EL	2.5	2.2	2.8	10.8	4.4	0.6	:
E	164.5	87.7	262.7	33.1	318.6	93.3	17.3
F	0.7	0.8	82.1	12.3	176.6	21.3	4.1
IRL	7.1	3.8	4.1	6.3	150.0	21.8	6.3
I	3.9	2.4	98.1	14.2	11.0	2.8	:
NL	:	9.7	22.1	29.4	358.2	:	:
A	:	:	:	0.5	:	:	:
P	0.4	0.4	48.3	:	16.2	5.1	0.4
FIN	:	:	0.9	9.4	42.0	10.0	:
S	0.1	2.1	23.2	2.0	15.1	17.5	5.4
UK	18.6	:	19.7	29.8	231.4	51.0	8.8
USA	275.4	61.3	372.4	24.8	1,019.1	394.0	128.5
Japan	571.6	67.1	1,454.4	855.1	2,459.2	405.2	52.8

Source: FAO

On the consumer side, fish products accounted for approximately 6% of total food (excluding drinks and tobacco) consumption in the EU[2]. Portugal was the country where the share was highest (at 15%). Belgium (8%) and Italy (7%) followed, whilst Ireland (3%) and Austria (2%) were at the other end of the ranking.

Apparent consumption figures show that demand for fish products was almost two-thirds higher than EU production (almost 20 billion ECU in 1998), and growing at a much faster rate (2.8% per annum since 1990). One fundamental factor behind this growth in demand is the fact that fish products are increasingly seen by consumers as a healthy alternative to meat (albeit a more expensive one). In addition, the development of the market for ready-to-eat meals has also contributed to a boost demand for processed seafood. These trends are accentuated by changing social factors: such as the growing number of working women, more fragmented meal times, and the growing number of single-person or single-parent households.

2) Excluding Germany and Spain.

(%) Figure 3.16

Share of fish products in household food consumption, 1997 (1)

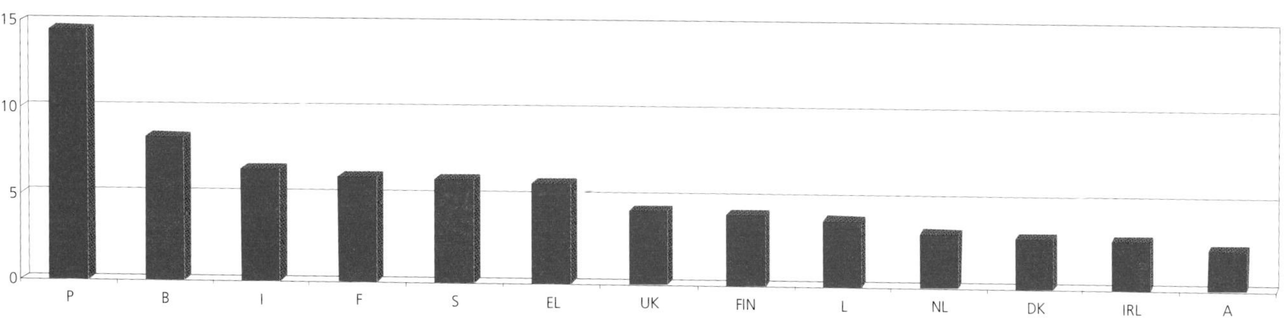

(1) Earlier years had to be used for some countries.

Source: Eurostat (National Accounts)

Figure 3.17 (thousand tonnes)

Annual marine fish catches in the Triad

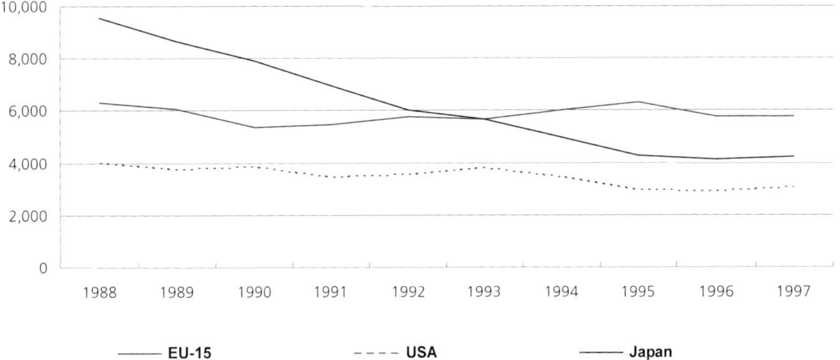

Source: Eurostat (FISH)

As far as employment is concerned, Eurostat data estimate that some 84 thousand persons were employed in the European fish processing industry in 1998, down from 88 thousand in 1995. This was mainly a result of the difficulties faced by small firms and industrial strategy to realise economies of scale through mergers and take-overs by larger firms.

The EU imports large quantities of fish products in order to satisfy its internal demand. Its own production is largely insufficient to meet consumption, and only few EU fishery landings are used by the fish processing industry because they are too costly and most landings are directed towards the fresh market. The two major imported items are aquatic invertebrates, which are either frozen, dried or salted (mainly shrimps, approximately one third of total extra-EU imports) as well as frozen fish. These products are basically semi-processed items which are then further processed into higher value-added items. Extra-EU exports are dominated by prepared and preserved fish, and by semi-processed materials imported from third countries and re-exported after repackaging under a European brand label.

The trade deficit is structural and the situation is not expected to improve in the future. The EU fishery sector suffers from severe resource depletion and extra-EU countries are increasingly able to supply processed seafood products to the EU at attractive prices and with a guaranteed supply.

The main suppliers of processed products are Iceland and Norway (mostly frozen fillets of white fish, such as cod, haddock, and saithe, as well as salted or smoked fish, such as smoked salmon). They are followed by countries like Thailand, Morocco and USA for which the seafood canning industry is important. In addition, countries like Argentina and many Asian countries supply large quantities of processed fish and shellfish (especially cultured shrimps).

Figure 3.18

Fish (NACE Rev. 1 15.2)

Destination of EU exports, 1998

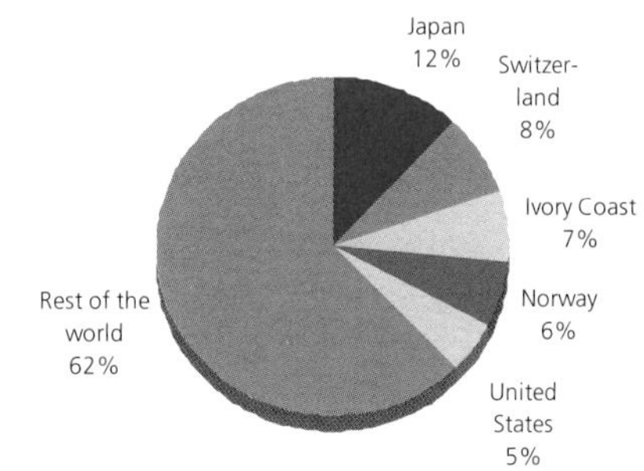

Source: Eurostat (Comext)

Figure 3.19

Fish (NACE Rev. 1 15.2)

Origin of EU imports, 1998

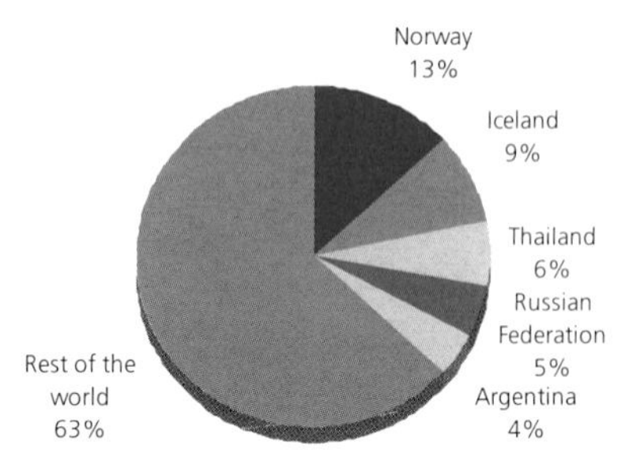

Source: Eurostat (Comext)

Fruit and vegetables (NACE Rev. 1 15.3)

This sector includes all activities relating to the processing of fruit and vegetables and their preservation. The main product categories are tomato and other vegetable preserves, jams and marmalades, pickled vegetables, fruit juices and nectars. Frozen vegetables and fruits are not classified here, they are included within the sub-chapter on deep-frozen foods.

Overall, the fruit and vegetable processing and preserving industry recorded production value in excess of 31.2 million ECU in 1998. Modest growth of 0.8% was reported compared to 1997[3], after two years of rapid expansion (5.4% in 1997 and 6.9% in 1996). The United Kingdom recorded the highest output in the EU (5.9 billion ECU in 1998), supplanting Germany (5.3 billion ECU) in 1997 as the leading EU producer. The Netherlands recorded output of 2 billion ECU and ranked amongst the most specialised countries in this activity, with a share in manufacturing activity almost twice as high as the EU average (180%). However, Greece recorded the highest production specialisation ratio (439%).

France was the leading European producer of canned vegetables in 1997 with 1.3 billion tins, followed by the Netherlands (with 0.5 billion tins), Spain, Italy and the United Kingdom with some 270 million tins each. In the case of canned fruits, production was concentrated in the Mediterranean countries. Spain produced 420 million tins in 1997, followed by Greece (245 million tins), France and Italy (234 million tins each). Finally, in the jam, marmalade and jelly sector, production was concentrated mainly in two countries: Germany (212 million tins) and France (156 million tins).

3) Excluding Luxembourg.

Figure 3.20

Fruit and vegetables (NACE Rev. 1 15.3)
Production and employment in the Triad

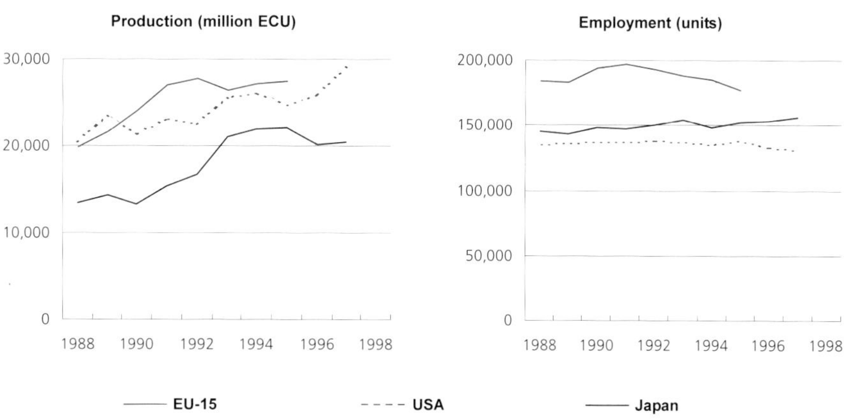

Source: Eurostat (SBS)

Growth of the fruit and vegetable processing and preserving sector during the 1990s has been higher than the average for food and drink, reaching 4.6% per annum between 1988 and 1998. During this period, production growth was accompanied by an almost continuous decline in employment levels (-1.4% per annum for the period 1990 to 1998). There were some 173 thousand persons employed in the sector in 1998, about twenty thousand jobs less than in 1990. The sector is distinguished by a strong seasonal demand for labour.

Average growth in apparent consumption equalled 4.2% per annum between 1995 and 1998, with market value equal to 33 billion ECU. This was a marked improvement compared to the first half of the decade, which was marked by stagnant demand. Canned vegetables and preserved fruits face competition from fresh products and frozen products. Generally speaking raw materials of somewhat lower quality go into canning processes compared to those which are sold fresh or deep-frozen: consequently, these products fall into the low or medium-price bracket and do not produce large returns for manufacturers.

(million of 850 ml tins) Figure 3.21

Production of preserved and processed fruits and vegetables, 1997

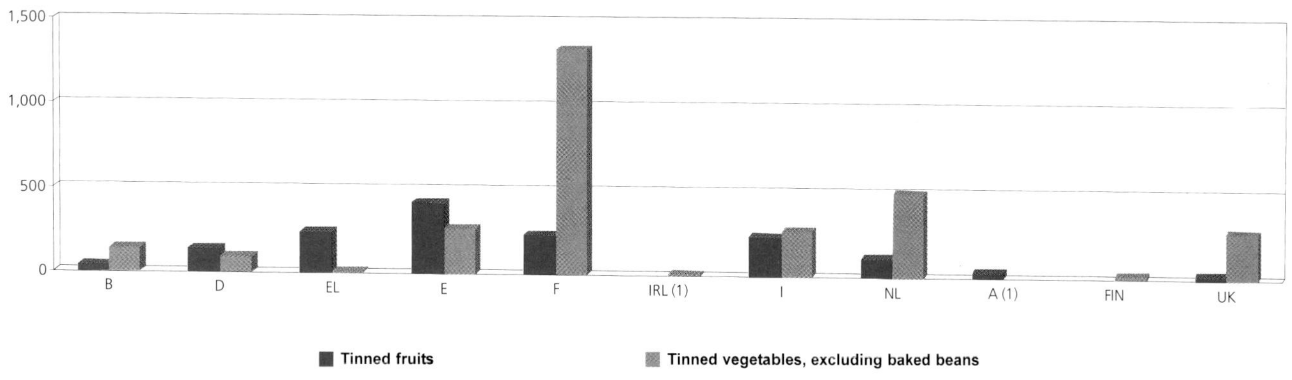

(1) 1995.

Source: OEITFL

Table 3.4 (thousand tonnes)

Consumption of raw potatoes used for processing, 1997

	Pre-fried, frozen/chilled products	Dehydrated products	Snacks	Other products	Total
B	:	:	:	:	1,119
D	568	886	331	281	2,066
F	584	293	170	97	1,145
I	75	20	87	:	182
NL	2,336	391	127	20	2,874
S	:	:	80	:	200
UK	1,112	96	718	:	1,926

Source: UEITP

In the jam and marmalade sector, consumption is tied to breakfast and between-meal snacks, and the biggest growth rates have benefited products with a strong "natural" image. Consumption of jam and marmalade is particularly concentrated in northern Europe: the highest per capita consumption is found in Sweden and Finland (5.7 kg per capita per year), followed by Denmark (2.4 kg) and Norway (2.3 kg). Italy has the lowest per capita consumption (just 0.5 kg).

The fruit juice and nectars segment has enjoyed steady market expansion during the past decade. This is particularly true with regard to products made from 100% fruit juice. The main reason for this success is to be found in the "healthy" image of fruit juices that has been propagated by marketing specialists over recent years (despite the fact that there has been little or no product innovation). Germany, with 50 litres per head is the biggest consumer of fruit juices, followed by the Netherlands (22 litres) and the United Kingdom (19 litres).

Figure 3.22 (%)

Share of fruit and vegetables in household food consumption, 1997 (1)

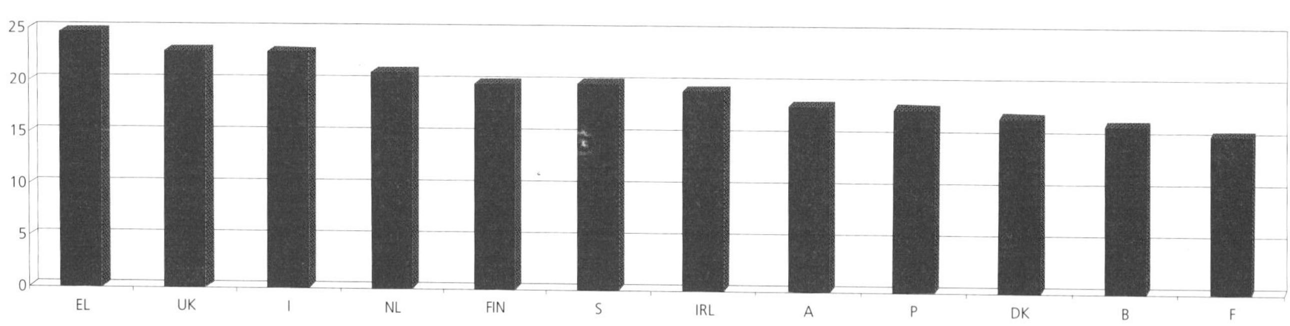

(1) Earlier years had to be used for some countries.

Source: Eurostat (National Accounts)

(%) Figure 3.23

Fruit and vegetables (NACE Rev. 1 15.3)
Production and export specialisation by Member State, 1998

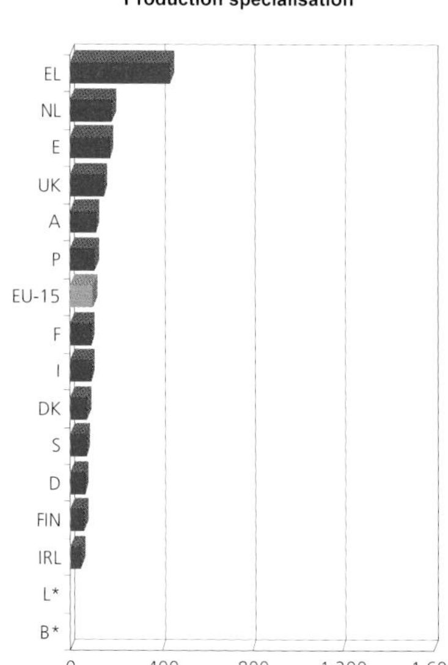

Source: Eurostat (SBS)

Figure 3.24

Fruit and vegetables (NACE Rev. 1 15.3)
Destination of EU exports, 1998

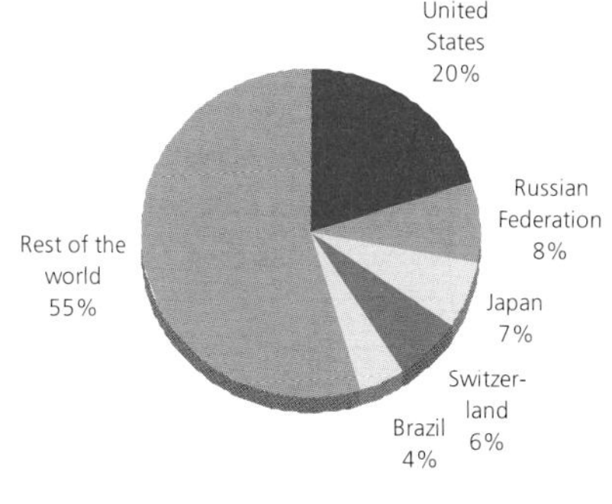

Source: Eurostat (Comext)

Figure 3.25

Fruit and vegetables (NACE Rev. 1 15.3)
Origin of EU imports, 1998

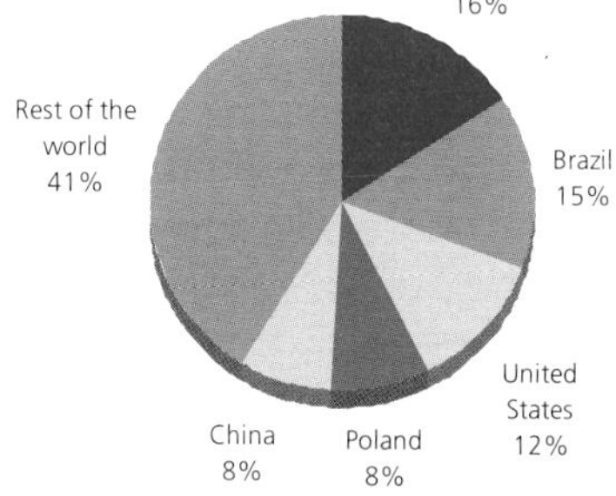

Source: Eurostat (Comext)

Internationally speaking, the EU was the world's largest producer (31 billion ECU in 1998, excluding Luxembourg) of processed fruit and vegetables ahead of the USA (29 billion ECU in 1997) and Japan with 20 billion ECU (again 1997). During the course of the decade, both the USA and Japan enjoyed strong production growth, which exceeded 4.1% per annum on average between 1988 and 1997 in the USA and 4.7% in Japan (over the same period).

The USA remained the largest exporter of processed fruit and vegetables (2.6 billion ECU in 1997), followed by the EU with 2.1 billion ECU[4] and Japan with only 44 million ECU. Within the EU, Greece was by far the most specialised country in exporting processed fruit and vegetable products. Other export-specialised countries included Spain and the Netherlands. However, the majority of countries were not able to satisfy their domestic demand, and the trade balance of the EU with the rest of the world was characterised by a structural deficit, which could be estimated on the basis on existing data as exceeding 2 billion ECU.

4) Excluding Ireland and Finland.

Professional associations representing the industries within this chapter

AFCASOLE
European Soluble Coffee Manufacturers Association
18, rue de la Pépinière
F-75008 Paris
tel: (33) 1 53 42 13 38
fax: (33) 1 53 42 13 39

CPIV
Permanent International Vinegar Committee
Reuterstraße 151
D-53113 Bonn
tel: (49) 228 21 20 17
fax: (49) 228 22 94 60

EURA
European Renderers Association
Heer Bokelweg 157b
PO Box 202
NL-3000 AE Rotterdam
tel: (31) 10 467 31 88
fax: (31) 10 467 87 61

FEFAC
European Compound Feed Manufacturers Federation
223, rue de la Loi, boîte 3
B-1040 Bruxelles
tel: (32) 2 285 00 50
fax: (32) 2 230 57 22
e-mail: mlibeau.fefac@compuserve.com

IMACE
International Federation of Margarine Associations
168, avenue de Tervueren
Boîte 12
B-1150 Bruxelles
tel: (32) 2 772 33 53
fax: (32) 2 771 47 53
e-mail: imace.ifma@pophost.eunet.be

UASUE
European Grain Mill Association
c/o Italmopa
Via dei Crociferi 44
I-00187 Roma
tel: (39) 06 678 54 09
fax: (39) 06 678 30 54
e-mail: italmopa@foodarea.it

Oils and fats (NACE Rev. 1 15.4)

This section addresses the production and processing of oils and fats, as used for inputs in the manufacturing process of other industrial sectors and as end products for direct consumption. Demand for oil and fats originates from their importance as inputs in the manufacturing process of many other sectors (paints, inks, textile dyeing, lubricants and plastic materials), as well as from their direct use for human and animal consumption. Human consumption is directed above all towards olive oil, vegetable oils, margarine and low-fat content products, whilst seeds, oils, fats, cakes and meals, are used as animal feed.

The production of the oil and fats sector was estimated at 26 billion ECU in 1998, up from 22 billion ECU in 1996. Growth could be almost exclusively attributed to Spain, whose production rose by 3.4 billion ECU over the same period, the highest output in the EU (at 8.5 billion ECU), almost double the production value of Germany (4.6 billion ECU).

Fediol, the EC seed crushers' and oil processors' federation, estimate that the industry processed some 29.5 million tonnes of oilseed in 1997, up 6.7% when compared to the preceding year[5]. Output rose by 6.2% for cakes and meals to 20.4 million tonnes and by 7.2% for crude oil and fats to 8.5 million tonnes. Looking in more detail at production by Member State, we find that Europe's largest producer in 1997 was Germany (27% of the oilseeds processed), ahead of the Netherlands (17%) and France (14%).

5) It should be noted that olives, maize germs, grape and tomato pips are excluded from these figures.

Table 3.5 (thousand tonnes)

Industrial production of oil products, 1997

	Oilseeds processed (1)	Crude oil & fats produced (1)	Cakes & meals produced (2)
B	2,061	585	1,406
DK	418	135	273
D	7,928	2,488	5,376
EL	815	149	607
E	4,002	1,003	2,775
F	2,883	1,118	1,795
I	2,166	535	1,642
NL	4,887	1,125	3,661
A	173	70	94
P	1,050	255	780
FIN	313	85	220
S	243	98	140
UK	2,544	893	1,614
Total	29,483	8,539	20,383

(1) Excluding olives, maize germs, grape and tomato pips.
(2) Excluding olives.

Source: Fediol

Figure 3.26

Oils and fats (NACE Rev. 1 15.4)
Production and employment in the Triad

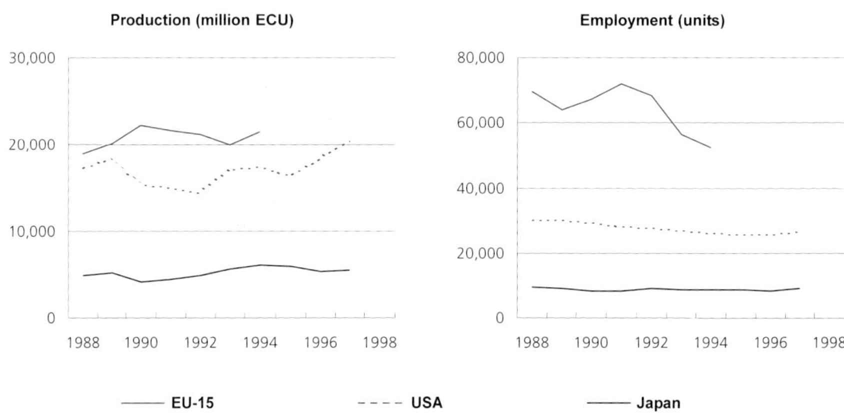

Source: Eurostat (SBS)

Figure 3.27 (%)

Oils and fats (NACE Rev. 1 15.4)
Production and export specialisation by Member State, 1998

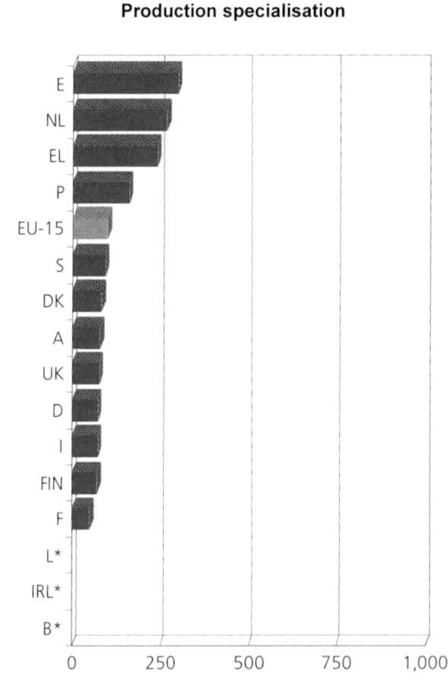

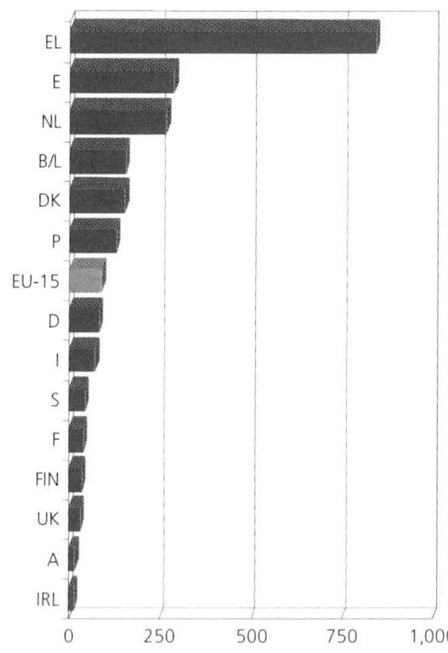

Source: Eurostat (SBS)

The EU has to import products from the rest of the world to satisfy its domestic consumption for vegetable and marine oils, as well as for fats used in cakes and meals. This was particularly true in the case of cakes and meals, where apparent consumption was equal to 37 million tonnes in 1997 (almost double production, 20 million tonnes). Soya cakes, which accounted for nearly 60% of oil cake consumption, were the main reason for import dependency, as the EU imported almost half of its domestic consumption. Amongst the different categories of oil and fat products, the EU was self-sufficient in liquid oils and linseed oil.

(thousand tonnes) Table 3.6

Vegetable and marine oils and fats in the EU, 1997

	Production	Imports	Exports	Apparent consumption	Self-sufficiency ratio (%)
Liquid oils	8,277	279	2,008	6,548	126
Lauric oils	67	1,042	64	1,045	6
Linseed oil	185	2	49	138	134
Castor oil	10	106	:	116	9
Palm oil	:	2,021	77	1,944	:
Vegetable oils and fats total	8,539	3,450	2,198	9,791	87
Marine oil	158	263	63	358	44
Total (1)	8,697	3,713	2,261	10,149	86

(1) Excluding olives, maize germs, grape and tomato pips.

Source: Fediol

(thousand tonnes) Table 3.7

Olive oil production and consumption, 1997

	Production	Consumption	Self-sufficiency ratio (%)
EL	470	199	236
E	1,024	475	215
F	2	44	5
I	421	637	66
P	49	59	84

Source: Fedolive

(thousand tonnes) Table 3.8

Margarine and blends in the EU, 1997

	Production	Imports	Exports	Apparent consumption	Self-sufficiency ratio (%)	Per capita margarine consumption (kg)
B	264.3	90.5	233.7	121.1	218.2	11.5
DK	117.1	0.5	32.2	85.4	137.2	16.7
D	805.7	23.7	257.3	572.1	140.8	7.0
EL	37.3	14.9	2.3	49.9	74.7	4.8
E	86.8	14.1	12.2	88.7	97.9	2.2
F	162.6	112.7	35.0	216.0	75.3	3.7
IRL	14.3	1.4	3.7	12.1	118.4	3.5
I	85.8	21.2	10.9	96.0	89.3	1.7
NL	329.9	24.5	198.8	155.6	212.1	10.0
A	45.5	4.0	7.2	42.3	107.4	5.2
P	44.7	0.2	2.6	42.3	105.7	4.3
FIN	77.0	22.6	58.0	57.1	134.9	11.1
S	183.0	10.3	121.0	135.4	135.2	15.3
UK	460.9	27.9	14.7	474.1	97.2	8.1

Source: IMACE, IFMA

The EU is by far the world's largest producer of olive oil. According to the Food and Agriculture Organisation of the United Nations (FAO), EU olive oil accounted for more than three-quarters (76%) of the world's production in 1997 (Spain, Italy, Greece, Portugal and France). Fedolive estimate that Spain was the EU's largest producer in 1997, with over 1 million tonnes of output, more than twice the production of Greece (0.5 million tonnes) or Italy (0.4 million tonnes). The production of Portugal and France was marginal. Outside of the EU, production was concentrated in the Mediterranean area, especially Tunisia (9% of world production), Syria (5%) and Morocco (3%).

Germany accounted for about 30% of the EU's production of margarine and spreadable fats in 1997, followed by the United Kingdom (17%), the Netherlands (12%) and Belgium (10%). EU production was almost three times the level of the second world producer, the USA, whose production reached 1 million tonnes in 1997.

Turning to the production of animal oils and fats, the European Renderers' Association (EURA) estimate that EU production reached 4.3 million tonnes in 1997, of which two-thirds (2.9 million tonnes) was attributed to meal and one-third (1.4 million tonnes) to animal fats. Production is concentrated in a few countries, with Germany and France accounting for 40% of the EU total, followed by Italy (14%), Spain (13%) and the Netherlands (9%). The breakdown of production was concentrated within a few products (85% of animal fat production was attributed to inedible mixed fats, whilst the same proportion of animal meal was accounted for by meat and bone meal).

At the beginning of the 1980s demand for fats and oils for industrial use represented less than one third of direct human consumption levels. Industry demand has grown substantially over the last few years, and represented over 40% of overall demand by the mid-nineties. The main use of these products is in the production of cosmetics (soaps, perfumes and detergents), pharmaceuticals and chemicals (paints, inks, textile dyes, lubricants and plastics). Particularly important is the demand for oilseed, with some 95% of oilseed used within industrial processing. A large share of the demand for seeds, oils, fats, cakes and meals comes from the livestock breeding sector. The human consumption of vegetable oil has undergone strong growth throughout the EU in recent years. In the food sector, the most consumed products remain groundnut oil and sunflower oil. The consumption of olive oil is above all concentrated within those countries which are the largest producers (Italy, Spain, Greece, Portugal and France), but is gaining popularity in the rest of the EU. Margarine consumption is traditionally concentrated in northern European countries, with the highest consumption in Denmark (17 kg per capita), Sweden (15 kg), Belgium (11.5 kg), Finland (11kg) and the Netherlands (10 kg).

Figure 3.28 (thousand tonnes)

Production of animal fats and meals, 1997

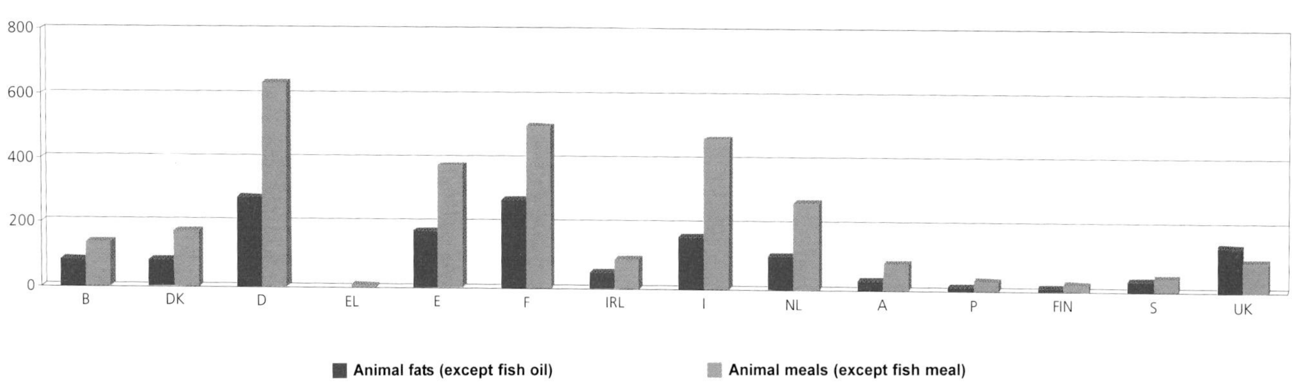

Source: EURA

Figure 3.29 (%)

Share of oils and fats in food consumption of households, 1997 (1)

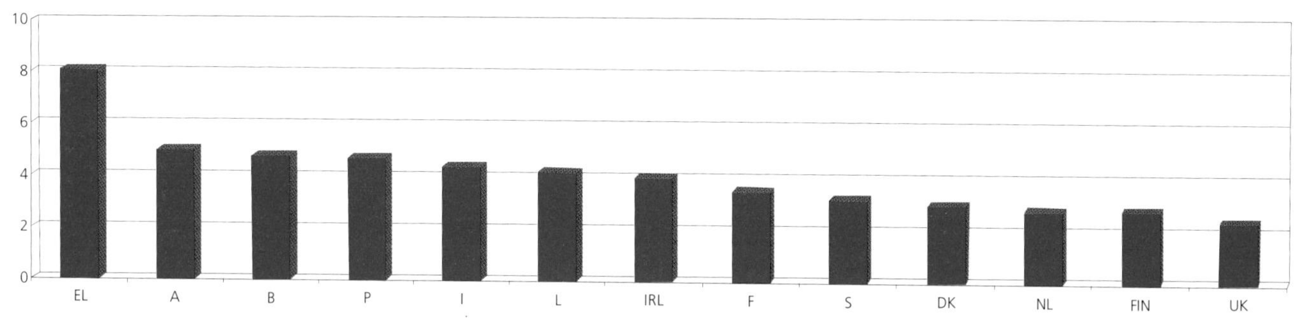

(1) Earlier years had to be used for some countries.

Source: Eurostat (National Accounts)

At an international level, the EU is the Triad's largest producer of oils and fats (estimated at 26 billion ECU in 1998), ahead of the USA (20.5 billion ECU in 1997) and Japan (5.5 billion ECU in 1997). America was strongly export oriented. The intensity of trade in oilseed was explained by two factors: the relatively low price of transporting bulk raw materials and the fact that processing plants were generally located away from production. The EU remained a net importer of oils and fats, despite the increase in production recorded in the second half of the 1980s. Particularly important in this sense was soya, which accounted for the largest share of the EU's imports. Less important, although still in deficit, was the deficit of rape and sunflowers. On the other hand, the EU can boast a high degree of self-sufficiency in vegetable oil.

Figure 3.30

Oils and fats (NACE Rev. 1 15.4)
Destination of EU exports, 1998

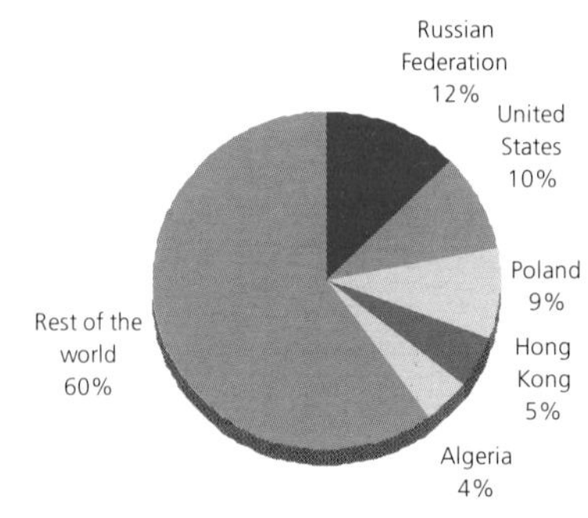

Source: Eurostat (Comext)

Figure 3.31

Oils and fats (NACE Rev. 1 15.4)
Origin of EU imports, 1998

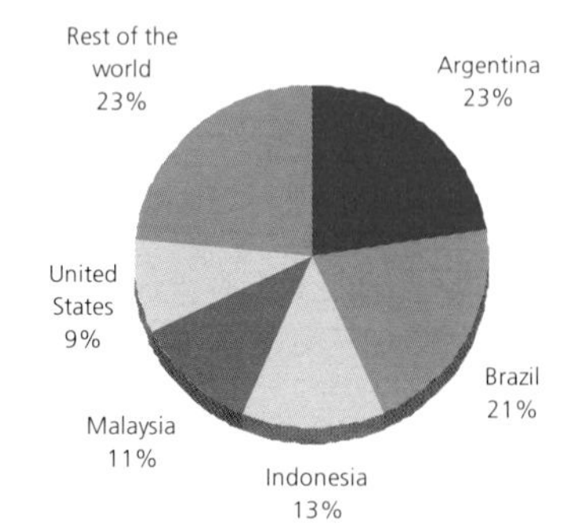

Source: Eurostat (Comext)

Dairy products (NACE Rev. 1 15.5)

Dairy products include liquid milk, butter, yoghurt and cheese, milk powder, whey and casein, as well as ice cream. In the EU this sector employed nearly 300 thousand persons and recorded a production value of over 85 billion ECU in 1998. Dairy products accounted for over 2% of total manufacturing in the EU, although their share has decreased somewhat in recent years. The main markets for dairy products were private households (around 75% of sales), restaurants, hotels and bakeries. The structure of demand for dairy products is largely determined by culture and cooking traditions. For example, the consumption of butter has been traditionally higher in northern Europe than in the Mediterranean countries.

In 1998 milk producers delivered 113.2 million tonnes of cow milk to dairies in the EU. Within the Member States the largest fluctuations were observed in Portugal and Austria (where deliveries increased by 8.6% and 6.2% between 1995 and 1998) and Ireland (where a decline of 4.0% was recorded). Dairy farmers reduced their livestock by 5.1% to 21.1 million cows during this period. In 1998, 6.2% of all European dairy cows grazed on Irish pastures. Indeed, with output equivalent to 3.5 billion ECU of production value in 1998, the Irish dairy industry accounted for around 4% of the European total. Denmark reported similar degrees of production specialisation, with the share of dairies in manufacturing output two and a half times higher than the European average. France had the highest total output, some 18.7 billion ECU in 1998.

(kg/capita) Table 3.9

Consumption of dairy products, 1997

	Cheese	Butter	Liquid milk
B/L	16.5	6.3	94.1
DK	16.4	2.0	136.0
D	20.3	7.1	87.7
EL	24.2	0.9	:
E	8.5	1.0	119.0
F	23.4	8.3	94.6
IRL	8.3	3.5	178.0
I	18.7	2.1	85.9
NL	16.4	3.5	127.7
A	16.0	4.6	99.5
P	7.0	1.6	:
FIN	16.4	5.8	188.0
S	16.3	1.7	150.8
UK	9.5	3.1	118.8

Source: ZMP

Figure 3.32

Dairy products (NACE Rev. 1 15.5)
Production and employment in the Triad

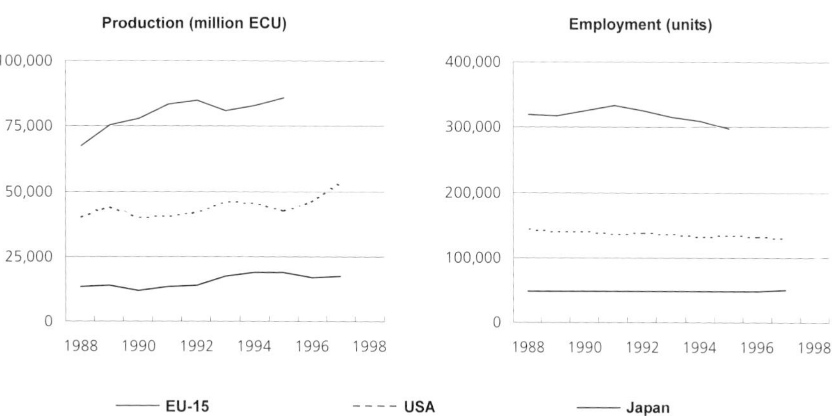

Source: Eurostat (SBS)

(%) Figure 3.33

Dairy products (NACE Rev. 1 15.5)
Production and export specialisation by Member State, 1998

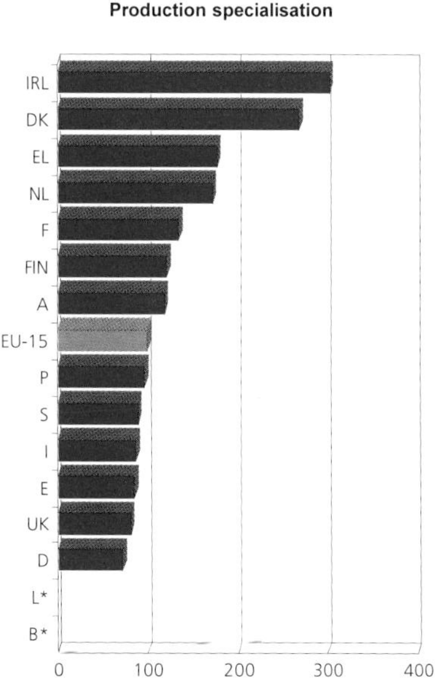

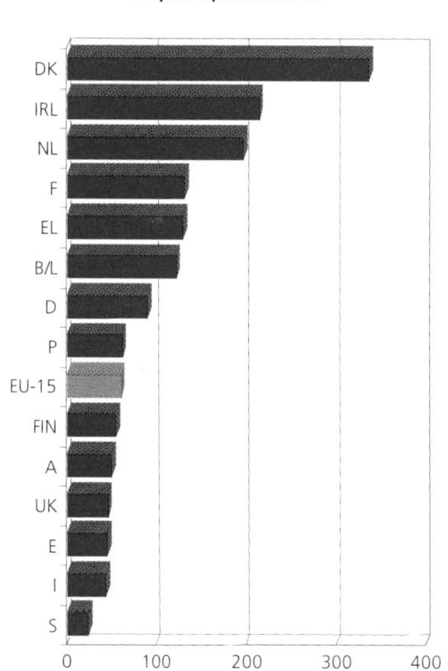

Source: Eurostat (SBS)

Figure 3.34 (litres/capita)

Ice cream consumption in the EU

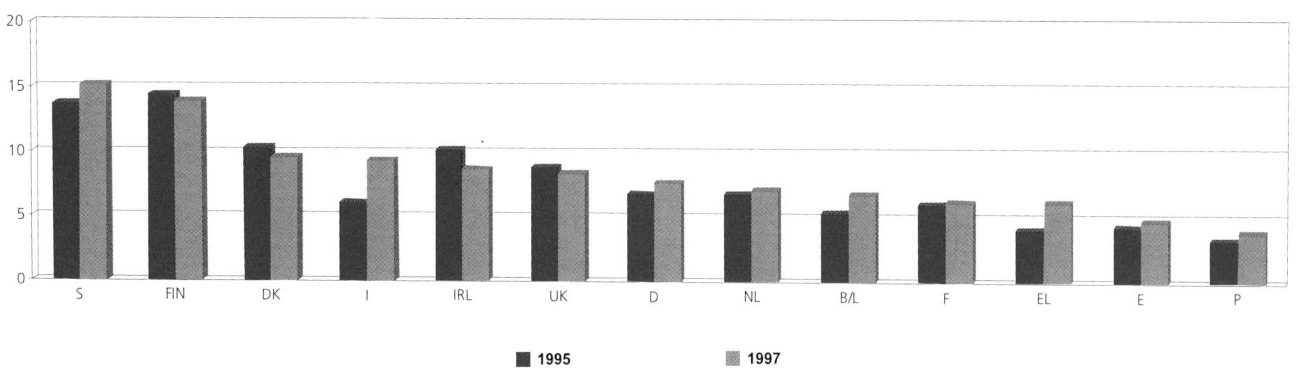

Source: EUROGLACES

Production of dairy products evolved moderately between 1990 and 1998 with growth rates ranging from -2.9% per annum in Finland to +2.3% per annum in the United Kingdom and +4.1% per annum in the Netherlands. The market was generally saturated and product differentiation is the only means of developing new markets. Manufacturers introduced new product lines such as snacks and health-based products, developing existing products with nutritional additives (for example, adapted to children's diets).

There was constant pressure to reduce production costs in the dairy industry, especially with respect to labour costs. During the course of the nineties employment figures fell in most countries, for example, in France by 2.0% per annum (between 1990 and 1998). The structure of supply was increasingly dominated by large dairy producers, who concentrated on developing their distribution networks (a process encouraged by the extended bargaining power of supermarket chains within the retail sector). In Germany the number of dairy producers decreased by 13% to 165 enterprises in 1998. International competition increased in the course of the nineties, especially from New Zealand, Australia and Argentina. The dairy industry is in part controlled by a quota system, which limits the delivery of milk in the EU (as part of the Common Agricultural Policy). A further challenge that will need to be met by EU producers is the enlargement of the EU, which is likely to lead to increased competition.

The European[6] ice cream market was equal to 2.7 billion litres in 1997 (in terms of sales). The largest market was Germany with 620.2 million litres, followed by Italy with 534.8 million litres of ice cream. The Nordic Member States recorded the highest per head consumption. Production was split between large industrials (in the Nordic countries) and small-scale local producers (especially in Italy, 35% of the domestic market in 1997).

For the whole dairy industry, Denmark reported the highest export specialisation, followed by Ireland and the Netherlands. Danish dairies exported 41.7% of their production in 1998. There was a fairly high level of intra-Community trade, for example in Germany 81.9% of exports were directed to the fellow European Member States.

6) Excluding Austria.

Figure 3.35

Dairy products (NACE Rev. 1 15.5)

Destination of EU exports, 1998

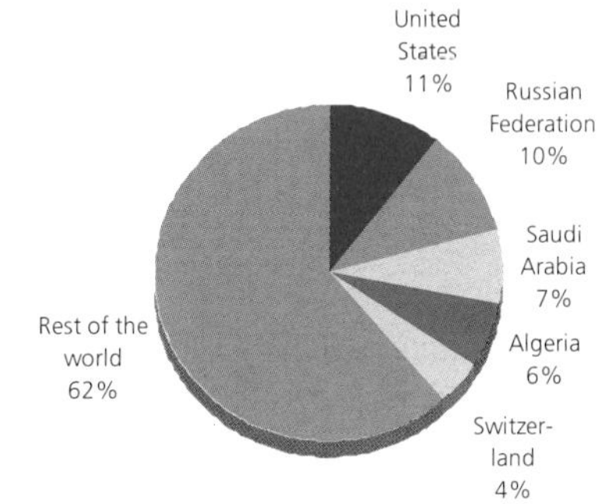

Source: Eurostat (Comext)

Figure 3.36

Dairy products (NACE Rev. 1 15.5)

Origin of EU imports, 1998

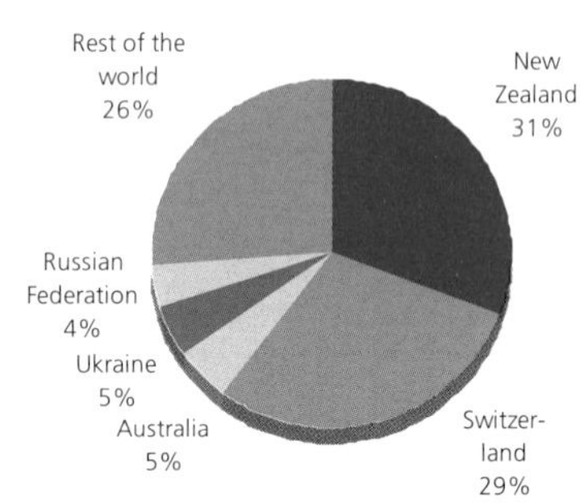

Source: Eurostat (Comext)

Beverages (NACE Rev. 1 15.9)

Beverages accounted for more than 2% of total manufacturing in the EU in terms of production value in 1998. The largest sector was found in the United Kingdom (with 22.2 billion ECU of production value), followed by Germany (19.0 billion ECU). Within the smaller Member States Greece and Ireland reported a high production specialisation.

The production of beverages did not follow a uniform evolution in the EU. Whilst production increased in the United Kingdom and France by 2.0% and 1.8% per annum between 1990 and 1998, output in Spain was reduced by 3.4% per annum. Even larger decreases were recorded in Sweden and Finland (which may have been partly due to policies to reduce the consumption of alcoholic beverages). During the nineties, beverage producers automated production processes in response to stiff competition.

Ireland exported 26.6% of its output in 1998, whilst almost 20% of the United Kingdom's production went to third countries. In France, 58.9% of home production was destined for export markets, whilst imports accounted for 21.5% of domestic consumption in 1998.

Figure 3.37
Beverages (NACE Rev. 1 15.9)
Production and employment in the Triad

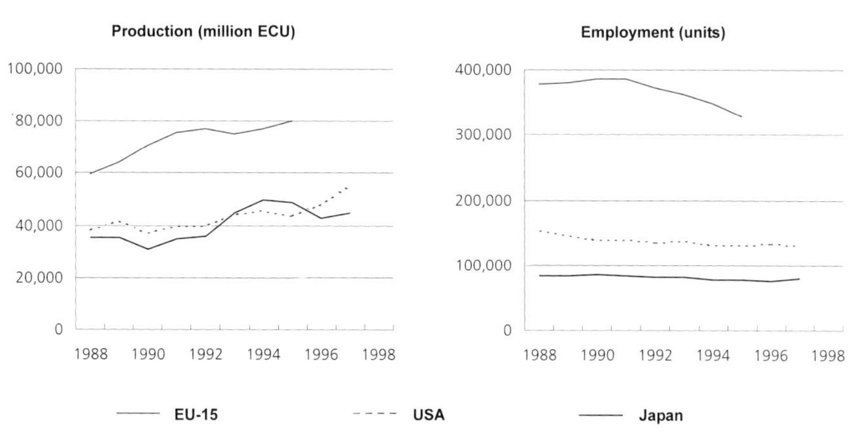

Source: Eurostat (SBS)

Figure 3.39
Beverages (NACE Rev. 1 15.9)
Destination of EU exports, 1998

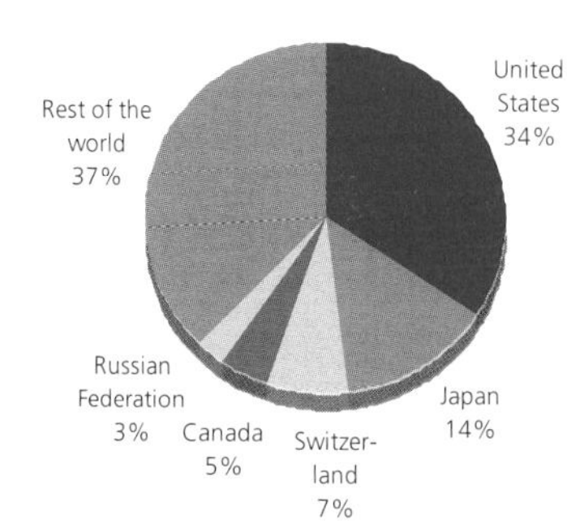

Source: Eurostat (Comext)

(%) Figure 3.38
Beverages (NACE Rev. 1 15.9)
Production and export specialisation by Member State, 1998

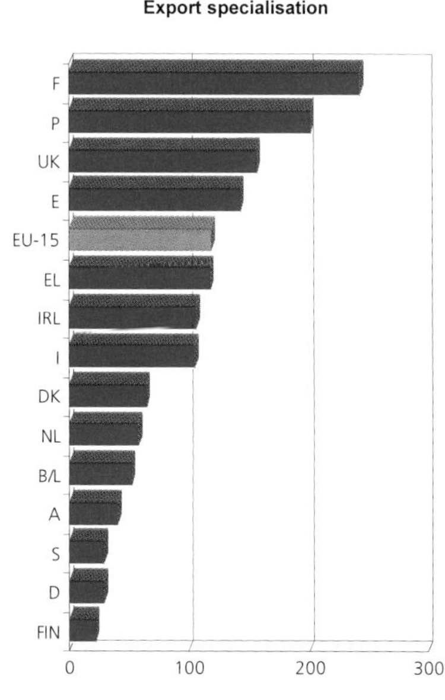

Source: Eurostat (SBS)

Figure 3.40
Beverages (NACE Rev. 1 15.9)
Origin of EU imports, 1998

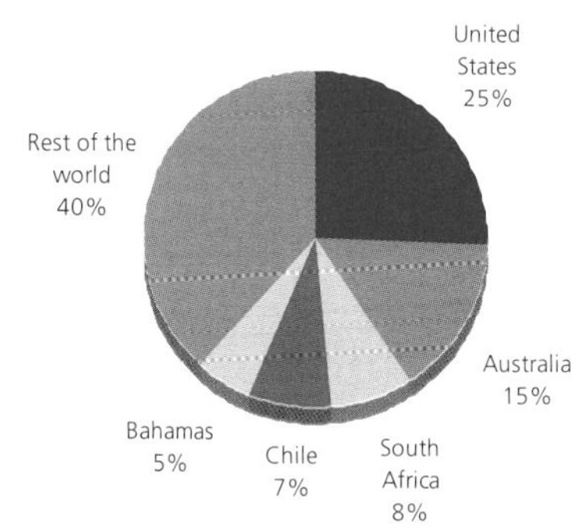

Source: Eurostat (Comext)

Alcohol (NACE Rev. 1 15.91 and 15.92)

There are two main markets for alcohol production: firstly, human consumption and secondly industrial use (cosmetics and pharmaceuticals). Human consumption of alcohol was on a downward trend induced by healthier life-styles and by higher taxes on alcohol products. In many European countries there was discussion concerning whether or not to restrict the advertisement of alcohol products.

Sales of whisky were on an upward trend, whilst sales of cognac were decreasing. Distillers of the latter product struggled because of changes in consumer taste, whilst several Scottish malt distilleries were strongly marketed as brand images. There has been a marked level of consolidation in the alcohol and spirits industry over the past ten years, which continued in 1999, when Remy Cointreau (F) concluded a joint-venture with Highland Distillers (UK) and Jim Beam Brands (USA) to combine distribution outside the USA. In June 1999, Pernod Ricard (F) made a takeover bid for Allied Domecq (UK).

The alcohol and spirits industry was an important tax source for European governments. With the Single Market the duty free sale of spirits stopped for intra-EU travel on July 1st 1999.

Wine (NACE Rev. 1 15.93 and 15.94)

The main factors that determine the structure of the wine industry are climate and soil type, which differs greatly amongst the regions of the EU. Small and medium-sized vineyards dominated European wine growing until recently, often in the form of co-operative producers. An increasing number of wine growers have noted that many consumers are now prepared to pay for higher quality wines, with higher disposable incomes.

European wine production[7] accounted for 61.3% of the world's production or 15.8 million tonnes in 1998, with France, Italy and Spain producing 13.8 million tonnes together. Even though production overseas was generally much lower (for example, 2.0 million tonnes in the USA and 741.5 thousand tonnes in Australia), European producers faced increasing competition from "new world" wines. Overseas production was dominated by large wine producers, expanding the number of varieties and areas under cultivation. In Australia the area cultivated grew by five thousand hectares per annum during the nineties.

7) Data on wine production from FAO.

Brewing (NACE Rev. 1 15.96)

The European brewing industry produced 315.9 million hectolitres of beer in 1997 or 25% of world output. The industry consumed 4.8 million tonnes of malt and other cereal products, 40 thousand tonnes of hops, 160 thousand tonnes of fine cane sugar and 50 thousand tonnes of fruit (used in specialist beers) per year. Capacity of malt production in Europe[8] expanded by 8.9% to 7.5 million tonnes between 1994 and 1997, whilst the number of malting enterprises decreased by 15.8% to 139 units.

Table 3.10

The malting industry in the EU, 1997

	Number of enterprises (units)	Production capacity (thousand tonnes)
D	73	2,090
UK	18	1,669
F	6	1,293
B	7	795
NL	3	296
DK	3	231
IRL	3	170
I	2	47

Source: EUROMALT

During the nineties European beer production remained more or less unchanged, with EU consumption showing a downward trend. Germany brewed more than one third of all European beer in 1997, some 11.5 billion litres, followed by the United Kingdom with 5.9 billion litres. Nevertheless, the largest brewing groups were situated outside Germany, with Heineken (NL) the largest. Five brewing groups carried out more than half of all the brewing in western Europe. The beer industry faced strong price competition, which was caused by overcapacity (reaching 30% in Germany the late nineties), as well as the oligopolistic market structure and the strong bargaining power of retail trade outlets. In addition, the sector had to deal with declining beer consumption in the EU; decreasing by 1.0 billion litres a year on average in the nineties to 29.6 billion litres by 1997. The most rapid reductions were recorded in Belgium and Germany (down by 7.8% and 5.6%), whilst Ireland recorded an increase of 24.7% (1991-1997).

8) EU-15 excluding Greece, Luxembourg and Portugal.

(litres/capita) — Table 3.11

Beer consumption in Europe

	1990	1997
D	142.7	131.1
IRL	123.9	123.7
DK	127.2	116.7
L	116.8	115.0
A	121.3	113.3
UK	113.2	103.6
B	121.6	101.0
NL	90.0	86.4
FIN	84.2	81.1
EU-15	80.7	79.2
E	71.9	67.1
P	69.3	63.6
S	60.1	61.7
CH	70.7	59.5
NO	52.3	52.9
EL	41.0	39.0
F	41.5	37.0
I	23.0	25.4

Source: CBMC

The restructuring of the European market led to increased merger activity, as well as many closures. In many Member States supply is highly concentrated, for example output of BRAU AG (4.2 million hectolitres) accounted for 45% of the Austrian market (in 1998). In Germany a regional brewing structure exists (with 1,269 breweries in 1997). Industry sources expect the reduction of plants to continue. One area where market expansion is expected is the Central European Countries (CECs). Many international brewery groups have foreseen this development and purchased breweries or established plants in neighbouring countries. In 1997 consumption of beer in the CECs increased by 6% to 114 million hectolitres (or 27 litres per head).

Mineral waters and soft drinks (NACE Rev. 1 15.98)

The European soft drinks industry (excluding mineral waters) produced over 27 billion litres in 1997. Consumption per head varied widely between 35.6 litres in France and 99.9 litres in Ireland in 1997. Germany was the only country where consumption decreased during the period studied to reach 81.1 litres per head.

(litres/capita) — Table 3.12

European consumption of soft drinks

	1990	1997
IRL	67.9	99.9
B	80.2	90.8
DK	56.9	87.0
UK	73.0	86.1
E	73.1	85.7
NL	76.1	83.8
A	77.5	82.4
D	82.6	81.1
S	55.2	65.8
EL	55.1	62.4
FIN	41.7	51.1
I	46.9	47.2
P	33.8	42.9
F	30.4	35.6

Source: UNESDA

Soft drinks were to a large extent sugar sweetened carbonated drinks. The consumption of different flavours varied considerably across the Member States, although colas dominated each market (with between 37% in Portugal and 62% in Belgium, 1997). Nevertheless, the industry developed new products, particularly low calorie and sports drinks (the former accounted for 13% of the soft drinks market in 1997), and designed a wide range of new products. The sector adapted to consumer demand for lighter packaging and decreased its reliance on glass as a packaging material (20% in 1997). The soft drinks industry was dominated by large, international enterprises, which delivered to local markets on a franchise/distribution basis.

The consumption of soft drinks increased by more than 40% in Europe between 1987 and 1997, whilst the corresponding growth rates for bottled water were 50%. By means of comparison the share of milk in total packaged beverages fell by 16% during the same period.

In the EU[9] the production of mineral water increased by 4.3% to 25.8 billion litres in 1997. The largest producers were Italy and Germany (both with 7.5 billion litres in 1997). Consumption per head increased throughout Europe, ranging from 14.0 litres in Ireland to 133.0 litres in Italy (for 1997). Consumers continued to move towards flat mineral water.

(million litres) — Table 3.13

Production of mineral waters, 1997

	Flat mineral water	Sparkling mineral water	Total
B	734	315	1,049
D	:	7,515	7,515
E	2,352	124	2,476
F	4,266	1,274	5,540
IRL	31	16	47
I	4,675	2,865	7,540
NL	63	38	101
A	:	574	574
P	325	91	416
UK	365	196	561

Source: UNESEM

In the mineral water industry competition caused a decline in prices and turnover. Rationalisation led to restructuring in logistics and a reduction in employment levels. In the soft drinks market mergers were frequent: Coca-Cola (USA) grew through acquisitions, however, its high market share and powerful distribution network led to regulatory concern with respect to the take-over of Orangina (F) and the soft drinks business of Cadbury Schweppes (UK). In the former case, French competition authorities demanded the exclusion of the Orangina distribution network for restaurants and hotels (for ten years), whilst in the latter European competition authorities required the planned sale to be scaled down.

9) Excluding Denmark, Finland, Greece, Luxembourg and Sweden.

Tobacco (NACE Rev. 1 16)

European smokers consumed 593.8 billion cigarettes in 1997, a decrease of 1.0% or 6.0 billion cigarettes when compared to data for 1995. The number of smokers in the EU decreased by 3.8% to 91.7 million persons (1995 to 1997). The share of smokers in the population varied across the Member States, from 13.6% of the population in Sweden to 30.2% in Denmark. In the Mediterranean Member States smokers tended to consume more cigarettes per day than in other countries; the highest ratio was found in Portugal with 31.4 cigarettes per day.

Table 3.14

Consumption of cigarettes in the EU, 1997

	Number of smokers (millions)	Share of total population (%)	Daily consumption per smoker (units)
P	1.4	14.1	31.4
A	1.6	19.8	23.3
EL	3.7	34.7	22.4
E	10.5	26.7	22.1
IRL	0.8	21.7	20.5
I	12.4	21.5	20.0
D	20.5	25.0	18.8
EU-15	91.7	24.5	17.8
B	2.7	25.4	17.0
FIN	0.8	15.5	16.2
F	15.0	25.5	15.2
DK	1.6	30.2	14.1
UK	15.0	25.4	14.0
S	1.2	13.6	13.7
NL	4.5	28.8	10.1

Source: CECCM

The European tobacco industry produced 771.9 billion cigarettes and cigars and 75.4 thousand tonnes of pipe and hand rolling tobacco in 1997. The only upward tendency was recorded for pipe tobacco, which increased by 26.8% as compared to data for 1995. Cigarette output declined by 2.0% over the same period.

Figure 3.41

Tobacco (NACE Rev. 1 16)

Production and employment in the Triad

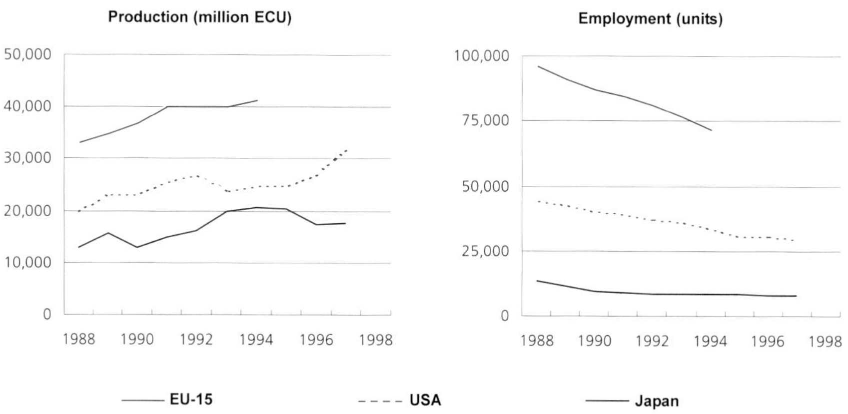

Source: Eurostat (SBS)

Figure 3.42 (%)

Tobacco (NACE Rev. 1 16)

Production and export specialisation by Member State, 1998

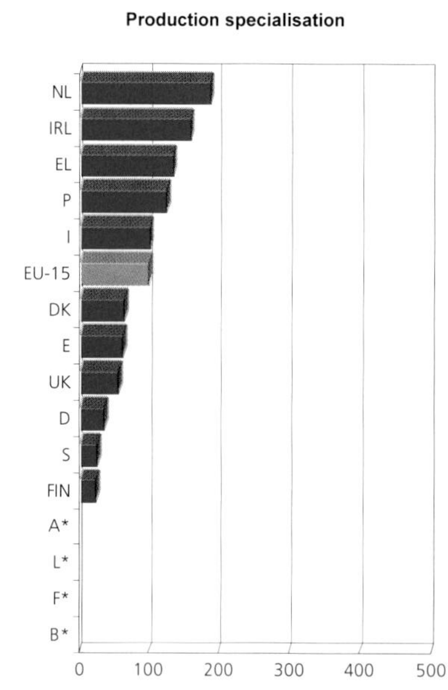

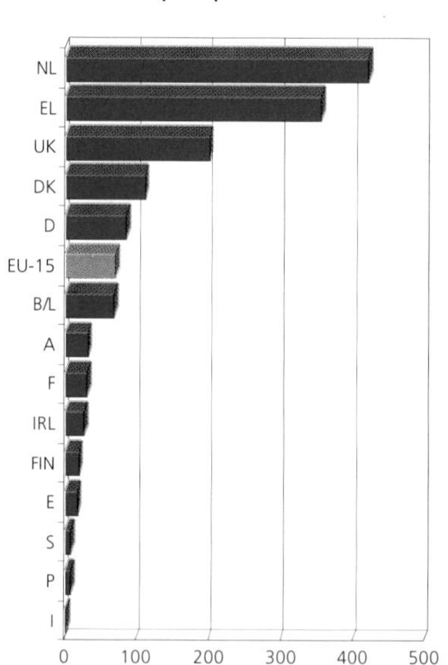

Source: Eurostat (SBS)

Manufacturers of tobacco continued to automate production processes, despite the already capital-intensive nature of the industry. Between 1988 and 1998 the production value per person employed increased in the United Kingdom from 609 thousand ECU to 2.4 million ECU. Reductions in employment were observed throughout Europe, ranging from 5.5% per annum in Finland to 0.9% per annum in Greece and Spain (between 1988 and 1998).

Tobacco products bore excise taxes besides value added tax (VAT). The receipts from excise and VAT on all tobacco products were on an upward trend and reached some 60.0 billion ECU in 1997. The share of tax receipts in total central government tax revenues ranged from 1.88% in Sweden to 5.8% in Denmark in 1997.

In addition to declining demand, the tobacco industry faced the threat of expensive legal actions for compensation, particularly in the USA, which led to falling quotations on stock markets. In November 1998 a deal was concluded between the tobacco industry and several US states, whereby the states will refrain from actions for compensation in exchange for excise tax of about 35 cents per pack, as well as some marketing restrictions.

In the EU a ban on advertisements on tobacco products was adopted by the European Parliament and the Council in July 1998 (with a transition period until autumn 2006 before advertisements on tobacco will be totally banned). With increased health consciousness, tobacco enterprises felt pressure to diversify their product ranges. At the same time, manufacturers focused their strategies on developing international markets (especially in the developing world).

International comparison showed that the largest tobacco industry was found in the EU (41.5 billion ECU in 1994). The USA reported production value equivalent to 32.0 billion ECU and Japan some 17.7 billion ECU in 1997. Between 1993 and 1997 output in the USA grew, whilst the Japanese sector felt the effects of recession, tobacco production decreasing by 2.8% per annum. A few large players dominated the industry in the USA, with Philip Morris as the largest tobacco manufacturer in the world.

Figure 3.43

Tobacco (NACE Rev. 1 16)
Destination of EU exports, 1998

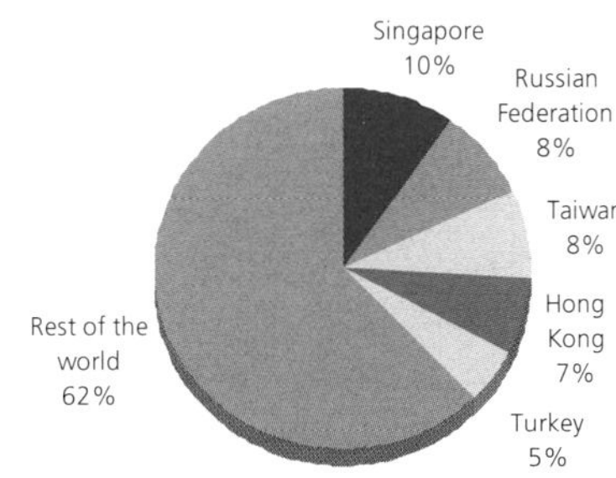

Source: Eurostat (Comext)

Figure 3.44

Tobacco (NACE Rev. 1 16)
Origin of EU imports, 1998

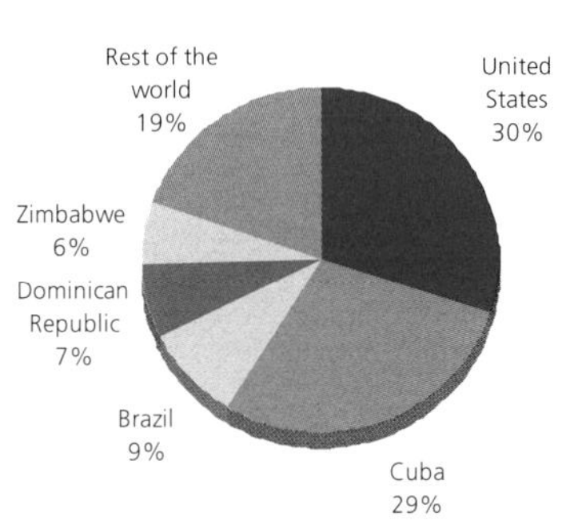

Source: Eurostat (Comext)

Other food products (NACE Rev. 1 15.6 to 15.8)

The other food products industry includes grain milling, sugar products, biscuits and confectionery, pasta, seasonings, tea and coffee, as well as prepared animal feed. The production value of the industry was equal to 170.6 billion ECU or 33.9% of the total output of the EU's food and beverage industry, employing 1.1 million persons in 1996.

Figure 3.45

Other food products (NACE Rev. 1 15.6 to 15.8)
Production and employment in the Triad

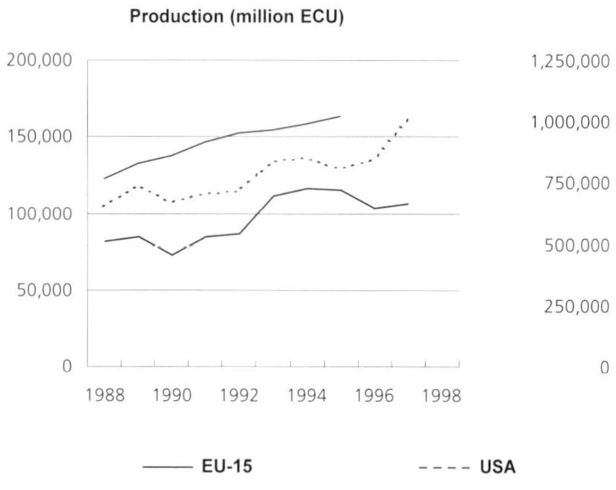

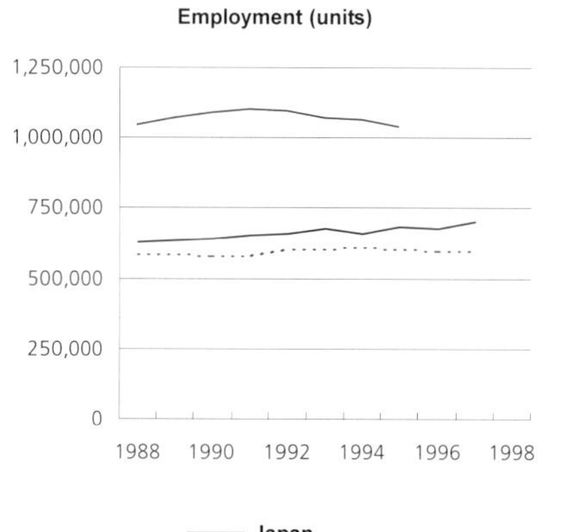

EU-15 ---- USA —— Japan

Source: Eurostat (SBS)

Figure 3.46 (%)

Other food products (NACE Rev. 1 15.6 to 15.8)
Production and export specialisation by Member State, 1998

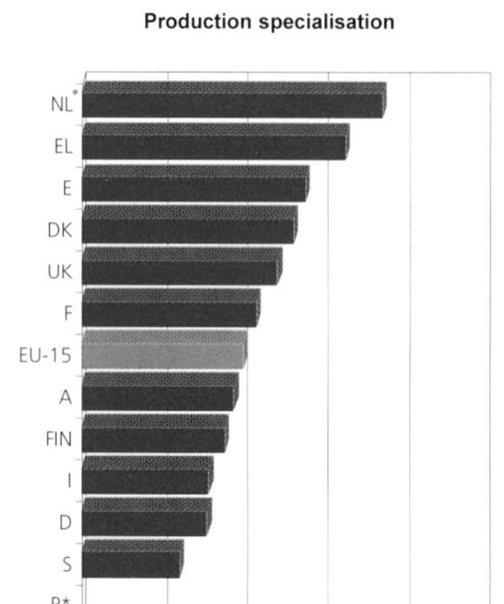

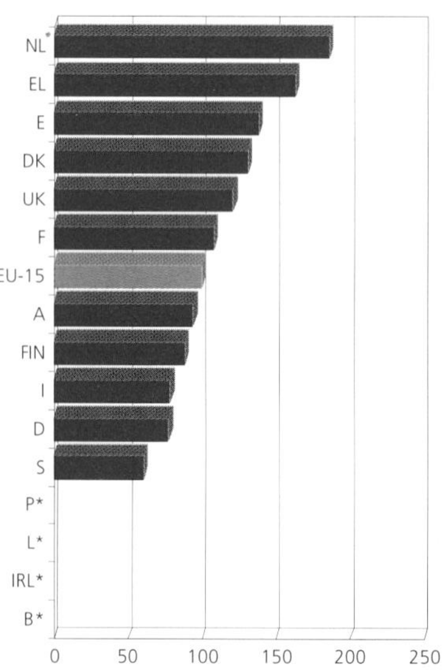

Source: Eurostat (SBS)

Figure 3.47

Other food products (NACE Rev. 1 15.6 to 15.8)
Destination of EU exports, 1998

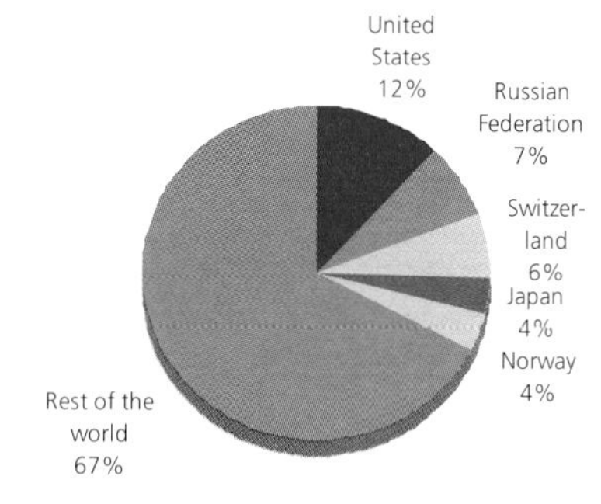

Source: Eurostat (Comext)

Figure 3.48

Other food products (NACE Rev. 1 15.6 to 15.8)
Origin of EU imports, 1998

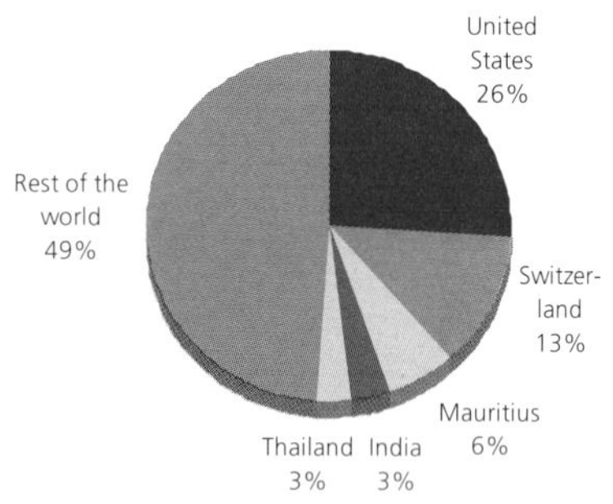

Source: Eurostat (Comext)

Grain milling (NACE Rev. 1 15.6)

Grain milling products include bran, rice, flour and mixes for bread, confectionery and biscuits, which are produced through the milling of cereals and processing of seeds and grains. The performance of the industry is closely linked to agricultural policy. The major downstream industries include pasta, bread and confectionery industries.

Bakeries were by far the largest consumer of grain milling products in the EU, with shares ranging from 60.0% in Finland to 85.5% in Belgium in 1997. Biscuit and rusk manufacturers were responsible for around 15% of grain milling consumption (highest in France with 23.9%). The consumption of grain milling products by households was generally low, for example, less than 2% in Belgium and the Netherlands. This was not the case in the Nordic Member States (such as Finland 26.0%) or Austria (15%). The declining share of household flour reflected changes in cooking habits and the increased consumption of ready-made dishes.

(%) Table 3.15

Consumption of grain mill products in the EU, 1997

	Bakeries	Biscuits and rusk manufacturers	Households	Other users
DK (1)	88.0	:	12.0	0.0
B	85.5	9.0	1.5	4.0
P	80.0	5.0	7.0	8.0
E	79.3	16.2	1.6	2.9
I (2)	74.0	26.0	:	:
D	71.0	15.0	7.0	7.0
A	67.0	16.0	15.0	2.0
F	66.3	23.9	4.7	5.0
NL	64.3	21.8	0.1	13.8
UK	63.7	14.6	4.2	17.5
FIN	60.0	5.0	26.0	9.0

(1) Biscuits and rusks manufacturers are included in bakeries.
(2) Households and other users are included in biscuits and rusk manufacturers.

Source: GAM

In the EU[10] grain milling production was equal to 27.3 million tonnes in 1997. There was a large grain milling industry in France and Italy with 5.2 and 4.9 million tonnes respectively. Portugal and the Netherlands reported relatively high specialisation, with shares of European output equal to 2.7% and 5.3% respectively in 1997. The number of mills was reduced during the course of the nineties, falling by almost 2.5 thousand units between 1994 and 1997 in the EU[11]. The average size of each plant varied between 4.9 thousand tonnes in Austria and 58.7 thousand tonnes in the United Kingdom. Processing was usually established near raw material sources or near downstream industries, to reduce transportation and distribution costs.

Prepared animal feed (NACE Rev. 1 15.7)

The manufacture of prepared animal feed includes products for feeding and breeding livestock as well as products for domestic animals. In the EU[12] production of compound animal feed in volume terms reached 120.1 million tonnes in 1997, an increase of 1.4% per annum since 1990. Turnover increased by 1.1% per annum (between 1990 and 1996) to reach 28.0 billion ECU.

France reported production volumes of 23.2 million tonnes in 1997, some 19.3% of the European total. Second in the ranking was Germany (with 18.8 million tonnes), followed by the Netherlands and Spain (16 and 15.3 million tonnes respectively). Product innovation and diversification were key elements to success, with diversification into the areas of veterinary consultancy and financing.

10) Excluding Finland, Greece, Ireland and Sweden.
11) Excluding Greece, Ireland and Sweden.
12) Excluding Greece and Luxembourg.

(%) Table 3.16

Compound animal feed in the EU by market segment in volume terms, 1997 (1)

Cattle	27.5
Pigs	35.2
Poultry	28.9
Milk replacers	1.3
Other compound feed	7.1

(1) Excluding Greece and Luxembourg.

Source: FEFAC

Biscuits, cocoa and sugar confectionery (NACE Rev. 1 15.82 and 15.84)

In the EU biscuits, preserved pastry goods and cakes as well as cocoa, chocolate and sugar confectionery (such as chewing gum, pastilles or nougats) saw their production volume equal 10.1 million tonnes in 1997. When compared to data for 1991, output increased by 1.6 million tonnes (or 19.1%). The largest share of production was recorded in the United Kingdom (2.8 million tonnes or 27.8%) in 1997, followed by Germany (with 2.1 million tonnes or 20.9%). Within the smaller Member States the Netherlands, Belgium and Denmark reported a comparatively large biscuit and confectionery industry.

(%) Table 3.17

Production of biscuits, cocoa and confectionery in the EU in volume terms, 1997

Biscuits	35.4
Other baked goods	21.1
Chocolate confectionery	22.5
Other chocolate products	4.7
Sugar confectionery	16.2

Source: CAOBISCO

The production of biscuits and confectionery was highly concentrated; with a few multinationals providing a varied range of products. Smaller producers concentrated on domestic markets and were often co-packers for larger companies. Often they lost a great deal of their independence (other than in craft markets). When smaller producers were responsible for well-established local brands they were often potential candidates for acquisitions.

European demand for biscuits and confectionery was equal to 9.2 million tonnes in 1997, growth of 12.6% since 1991. Changing eating habits supported the sale of more sweet snacks, however, the market conditions and high levels of competition meant that continuous product innovation and advertising was required. Biscuits and confectionery are to a large extent bought on impulse, with promotional campaigns and packaging often considerably increasing the attractiveness of a particular product. Within the EU consumer tastes varied, even though there was a tendency towards more uniform consumption patterns (per capita consumption of biscuits and other baked goods was 32.1kg in the United Kingdom, whilst in Austria only 1.9kg in 1997).

Sugar (NACE Rev. 1 15.83)

The sugar industry provides saccharose, syrup and sugar surrogates using sugar cane, sugar beet, maple and palm as inputs. Main downstream industries include other food sectors, chemicals and pharmaceuticals. The food processing industry uses sugar for tinned food, beverages, syrups, confectionery and bakery products (amongst others). Industrial human consumption accounted for around two-thirds of total consumption (ranging between 72.8% in Sweden and 36.3% in Greece). Direct human consumption varied between 40.1% in Italy and 19.3% in Germany.

In 1997 the EU sugar industry produced 17.6 million tonnes of white sugar, which was 6.6% more than in 1996. The French sugar industry was responsible for 4.7 million tonnes or 26.9% of the European total, followed by Germany with 4.0 million tonnes.

Refining of sugar beet was seasonal, concentrated in the period after harvesting (from August to November). Production and yield of sugar beet was highly influenced by weather conditions, with a significant influence on raw material costs. European agricultural policy fixed quotas to avoid the over-production of sugar beet. Average yields from beet were equal to 8.0 tonnes per hectare in 1997.

Table 3.18 (1987=100)

Production of white sugar

	1987	1988	1989	1990	1991	1992	1993	1994	1995	1996	1997
EU-15	100.0	106.4	110.4	121.3	111.6	121.6	123.3	110.6	113.8	120.6	126.6
D	100.0	101.2	112.5	157.5	143.1	148.0	158.8	133.7	139.4	153.1	147.0
F	100.0	110.9	108.8	119.4	111.3	119.1	119.1	110.0	115.1	114.5	129.4
UK	100.0	106.6	103.3	100.9	99.2	120.1	117.2	102.9	99.2	120.0	129.5
I	100.0	86.1	100.6	84.9	87.8	108.8	82.6	86.8	86.8	83.6	101.3

Source: CEFS

Pasta (NACE Rev. 1 15.85)

Consumption of pasta in the EU[13] was equal to 3.0 million tonnes in 1997. Consumption has grown at a moderate pace in the EU since 1990. Consumption per head varied widely between 8.7kg in Greece and 2.5kg in the United Kingdom, with one exception, Italy (where 27.2kg per capita of pasta were consumed on average each year). There were 149 enterprises operating in Italy in 1997.

Table 3.19 (%)

European production of pasta in volume terms, 1998 (1)

I	72.5
F	10.8
E	7.1
D	4.9
EL	2.9
P	1.4
A	0.5

(1) As a share of UASUE membership.

Source: UASUE

Italy was responsible for the main share of production with 3.2 million tonnes of output in volume terms in 1998 (well ahead of France with 468 thousand tonnes). Growth in production was mainly stimulated by product development (such as ready-made dishes).

13) Excluding Austria, Denmark, Finland and Ireland.

Tea and coffee (NACE Rev. 1 15.86)

The tea and coffee industry faced saturated demand. In 1997 coffee consumption in the EU varied between 11.2kg per head in Sweden and 3.5kg in Portugal. In several Member States consumption decreased during the course of the nineties, for example in Germany, falling from 7.5kg in 1993 to 6.7kg in 1997.

In Germany sales of instant coffee products, introduced in the middle of the eighties, increased to 15.8 thousand tonnes by 1997. The Netherlands reported remarkable growth within the market for instant coffee products, rising 19% in 1997. In Italy decaffeinated and soluble coffee gained market share.

The production chain of coffee and tea was increasingly integrated, such as "just-in-time logistics", which required relationships to be developed between the grower and the processor. Furthermore, "efficient consumer response" was part of the production process, with information on consumer behaviour and buying patterns exchanged between retailers, distributors and manufacturers.

Mustard and vinegar (NACE Rev. 1 15.87)

NACE Rev. 1 15.87 includes the manufacture of condiments and seasonings, such as mustard. Production of mustard in volume terms was equal to 168.3 thousand tonnes in 1997[14], an increase of 12.3% compared to 1994. Consumption per capita was very low in the southern Member States, for example in Italy (0.02kg), whilst in France it was as high as 1.1kg per head in 1997.

(thousand tonnes) Table 3.21

Consumption of soluble coffee

	1990	1997
UK	45.2	45.1
F	16.5	23.0
D	12.5	13.0
E	9.6	9.4
I	1.8	2.2

Source: AFCASOLE

(1993=100) Table 3.20

Imports of green coffee and tea into the EU in volume terms

	1993	1994	1995	1996	1997
Green coffee	100.0	97.6	91.4	102.1	102.1
Tea	100.0	94.6	88.7	100.5	99.4

Source: ECF, ETC

(1988=100) Table 3.22

Production of mustard

	1988	1989	1990	1991	1992	1993	1994	1995	1996	1997
B	100.0	121.7	134.8	115.2	110.9	60.9	34.8	34.8	50.2	41.5
D	100.0	102.8	116.3	135.4	141.4	146.7	146.2	144.8	145.1	157.4
E	100.0	108.3	91.7	100.0	108.3	108.3	108.3	116.7	114.7	167.6
F	100.0	103.6	103.8	105.1	97.9	100.3	105.3	114.5	102.8	123.4
I	100.0	100.0	100.0	100.0	122.2	144.4	133.3	133.3	138.3	136.9
UK	100.0	100.0	25.8	28.9	27.0	28.3	27.7	29.6	29.6	29.6

Source: CIMCEE

EU production of fermented vinegar was equal to almost 568 million litres in 1997[15]. Producers had to adapt to modern distribution channels that were largely controlled by the retail market. This led to the number of vinegar enterprises being substantially reduced. Vinegar consumption was highest in Austria (the only country to report per capita consumption above 2 litres), whilst lowest in Finland (0.5 litres per head).

(litres/capita) Table 3.23

Consumption of fermented vinegar, 1997

A	2.4
B	1.9
F	1.9
D	1.8
E	1.3
DK	1.1
P	0.8
FIN	0.5

Source: CPIV

14) CIMCEE membership (Austria, Belgium, Germany, Spain, France, Italy and the United Kingdom).
15) Excluding Greece, Ireland, Luxembourg and Sweden.

Professional associations representing the industries within this chapter

CAOBISCO
Association of the Chocolate, Confectionery, Biscuit industries of the EU
1, rue Defacqz, boîte 7
B-1050 Bruxelles
tel: (32) 2 539 18 00
fax: (32) 2 539 15 75
e-mail: caobisco@caobisco.be

CIDE
European Deshydrators Association
45, rue de Richelieu
F-75001 Paris
tel: (33) 1 42 61 72 94
fax: (33) 1 49 27 02 73
e-mail: cide@wanadoo.fr

ECF
European Coffee Federation
21, boulevard Roi Baudouin
Boîte 7
B-1000 Bruxelles
tel: (32) 2 203 51 41
fax: (32) 2 203 32 44

EDA
European Dairy Association
14, rue Montoyer
B-1000 Bruxelles
tel: (32) 2 549 50 40
fax: (32) 2 549 50 49
e-mail: eda@arcadis.be

FAIBP
European soups and broths manufacturers
Reuterstraße 151
D-53113 Bonn
tel: (49) 228 21 20 17
fax: (49 228 22 94 60

FAFPAS
Fédération des Associations de Fabricants de Produits Alimentaires Surgelés de l'UE
30, avenue de Roodebeek
B-1030 Bruxelles
tel: (32) 2 743 87 30
fax: (32) 2 736 81 75

FEDIOL
EC Seed Crushers' and Oil Processors' Federation
168, avenue de Tervueren
Boîte 12
B-1150 Bruxelles
tel: (32) 2 771 53 30
fax: (32) 2 771 38 17
e-mail: fediol@pophost.eunet.be

FEDOLIVE
European Federation of Olive Oil producers
c/o Assitol
Piazza di Campitelli, 3
I-00186 Roma
tel: (39) 06 69 94 00 58
fax: (39) 06 69 94 01 18
e-mail: Assitol@foodarea.it

GISEM / UNESEM
European Union Mineral Water producers
76 Serrano
E-28006 Madrid
tel: (34) 91 57 58 226
fax: (34) 91 57 81 816

IMA / GAM
International Milling Association
9, avenue des Gaulois
B-1040 Bruxelles
tel: (32) 2 736 53 54
fax: (32) 2 732 34 27
e-mail: gam@ecco.be

UEPA
European Alcohol Producers Association
192, avenue de Tervueren
Boîte 3
B-1150 Bruxelles
tel: (32) 2 772 98 30
fax: (32) 2 772 98 30

UNESDA / CISDA
Union of EU Soft Drinks Associations
35, boulevard Louis Schmidt
Boîte 14
B-1040 Bruxelles
tel: (32) 2 735 37 49
fax: (32) 2 732 51 02
e-mail: mail@unesda-cisda.org

Table 3.24 (million ECU)

Production, processing and preserving of meat and meat products (NACE Rev. 1 15.1)

Production related indicators in the EU

	1988	1989	1990	1991	1992	1993	1994	1995	1996	1997	1998
Production value	71,650	80,106	84,617	91,657	96,029	93,830	94,607	98,567	:	:	:
Producer price index (1995=100)	:	:	99.9	98.7	102.1	100.7	99.9	100.0	:	:	:
Value added	12,885	13,823	15,029	16,354	16,761	17,348	17,079	17,492	:	:	:
Number of persons employed (thousands)	520.6	528.2	534.1	548.9	549.0	545.4	544.4	551.4	:	:	:

Table 3.25 (million ECU)

Production, processing and preserving of meat and meat products (NACE Rev. 1 15.1)

Production related indicators, 1998

	B	DK	D	EL	E	F	IRL	I	L	NL	A	P	FIN	S	UK
Production value (1)	4,611	4,836	17,735	328	9,626	22,075	2,865	9,817	71	6,551	1,610	1,423	1,596	2,768	13,379
Value added (2)	676	1,078	3,409	64	1,598	3,770	446	1,402	14	887	373	:	435	528	3,375
Number of persons employed (units) (3)	17,618	21,511	96,093	3,560	62,943	119,285	12,931	35,700	438	23,766	10,622	14,211	10,724	14,429	93,944

(1) L (1995); (2) L (1995). (3) L (1995); NL (1992).

Table 3.26 (million ECU)

Production, processing and preserving of meat and meat products (NACE Rev. 1 15.1)

Market related indicators in the EU

	1988	1989	1990	1991	1992	1993	1994	1995	1996	1997	1998
Apparent consumption	72,362	80,688	85,174	91,516	96,198	93,449	94,405	98,272	:	:	:
Exports	3,172	3,674	3,407	3,811	3,806	4,179	4,729	4,672	5,028	5,492	4,796
Imports	3,884	4,256	3,964	3,669	3,975	3,798	4,527	4,377	4,474	5,029	4,629
Trade balance	-712	-582	-557	141	-169	381	202	295	554	464	167
Export ratio (%)	4.4	4.6	4.0	4.2	4.0	4.5	5.0	4.7	:	:	:
Import penetration ratio (%)	5.4	5.3	4.7	4.0	4.1	4.1	4.8	4.5	:	:	:
Cover ratio (%)	81.7	86.3	86.0	103.9	95.7	110.0	104.5	106.7	112.4	109.2	103.6

Table 3.27 (million ECU)

Production, processing and preserving of meat and meat products (NACE Rev. 1 15.1)

Market related indicators, 1998

	B/L	DK	D	EL	E	F	IRL	I	NL	A	P	FIN	S	UK
Apparent consumption	:	1,970	19,912	987	9,453	21,245	1,646	12,921	3,979	1,594	1,773	1,635	2,933	15,304
Exports	2,649	3,376	2,528	52	1,145	3,978	1,428	1,152	3,839	427	57	77	166	1,383
Imports	1,177	511	4,706	711	972	3,148	209	4,256	1,267	410	407	116	331	3,308
Trade balance	1,472	2,865	-2,178	-659	173	830	1,219	-3,104	2,572	16	-350	-39	-165	-1,925
Export ratio (%)	:	69.8	14.3	15.8	11.9	18.0	49.8	11.7	58.6	26.5	4.0	4.8	6.0	10.3
Import penetration ratio (%)	:	25.9	23.6	72.1	10.3	14.8	12.7	32.9	31.8	25.8	23.0	7.1	11.3	21.6
Cover ratio (%)	225.1	660.7	53.7	7.3	117.8	126.4	682.7	27.1	303.0	104.0	14.1	66.4	50.1	41.8

Table 3.28

Production, processing and preserving of meat and meat products (NACE Rev. 1 15.1)

Labour related indicators, 1998

	EU-15	B	DK	D	EL	E	F	IRL	I	L	NL	A	P	FIN	S	UK
Personnel costs (million ECU) (1)	12,498	538	708	2,441	45	1,036	3,000	234	1,017	12	571	279	114	294	439	2,033
Personnel costs/employee (thousand ECU) (2)	24.6	33.8	34.4	26.1	13.9	18.1	25.6	17.9	26.0	26.4	:	27.6	:	28.3	31.9	17.6
Social charges/personnel costs (%) (3)	20.7	30.7	2.9	16.7	24.7	22.1	29.1	13.0	33.4	12.2	15.1	23.5	:	22.4	28.8	10.1
Labour productivity (thousand ECU/head) (4)	31.7	38.4	50.1	35.5	18.1	25.4	31.6	34.5	39.3	30.9	33.7	35.1	:	40.5	36.6	35.9
Wage adjusted labour productivity (%) (5)	129.0	137.6	143.7	127.6	120.4	154.1	125.2	187.6	146.2	116.8	:	131.5	:	140.9	116.6	174.4

(1) EU-15, L (1995). (2) EU-15, EL, I, L, A (1995); B, DK, D, E, F, IRL, FIN, S, UK (1996). (3) EU-15, L, S (1995). (4) NL (1992); EU-15, L (1995).
(5) EU-15, EL, I, L, A (1995); B, DK, D, E, F, IRL, NL, P, S, UK (1996).

Source: Eurostat (SBS, EBT)

(million ECU) Table 3.29

Processing and preserving of fish and fish products (NACE Rev. 1 15.2)
Production related indicators in the EU

	1988	1989	1990	1991	1992	1993	1994	1995	1996	1997	1998
Production value	9,434	10,422	11,054	12,098	12,410	11,736	12,009	10,903	:	:	:
Producer price index (1995=100)	:	:	:	:	:	:	:	:	:	:	:
Value added	2,323	2,621	2,643	2,871	2,900	2,866	2,692	2,420	:	:	:
Number of persons employed (thousands)	102.3	111.0	107.2	107.4	102.1	99.6	99.2	88.2	:	:	:

(million ECU) Table 3.30

Processing and preserving of fish and fish products (NACE Rev. 1 15.2)
Production related indicators, 1998

	B	DK	D	EL	E	F	IRL	I	L (1)	NL (2)	A	P (3)	FIN	S	UK
Production value	374	1,196	1,736	56	1,890	1,944	369	1,185	0	427	:	418	95	242	1,696
Value added	60	257	437	11	421	430	104	261	0	91	:	:	26	58	440
Number of persons employed (units)	1,366	6,276	10,582	785	20,948	11,866	3,194	4,793	0	3,201	:	6,012	564	1,422	12,842

(1) 1996. (2) 1992. (3) 1997.

(million ECU) Table 3.31

Processing and preserving of fish and fish products (NACE Rev. 1 15.2)
Market related indicators in the EU

	1988	1989	1990	1991	1992	1993	1994	1995	1996	1997	1998
Apparent consumption	10,933	14,504	13,735	14,369	15,770	13,703	14,718	12,944	:	:	:
Exports	1,000	1,068	1,006	1,103	1,029	1,071	1,280	1,356	1,426	1,578	1,531
Imports	2,499	5,150	3,688	3,374	4,389	3,038	3,989	3,397	6,215	7,725	6,680
Trade balance	-1,499	-4,082	-2,682	-2,271	-3,360	-1,967	-2,709	-2,041	-4,789	-6,147	-5,148
Export ratio (%)	10.6	10.2	9.1	9.1	8.3	9.1	10.7	12.4	:	:	:
Import penetration ratio (%)	22.9	35.5	26.8	23.5	27.8	22.2	27.1	26.2	:	:	:
Cover ratio (%)	40.0	20.7	27.3	32.7	23.5	35.3	32.1	39.9	22.9	20.4	22.9

(million ECU) Table 3.32

Processing and preserving of fish and fish products (NACE Rev. 1 15.2)
Market related indicators, 1998

	B/L	DK	D	EL	E	F	IRL	I	NL	A	P	FIN	S	UK
Apparent consumption (1)	:	391	2,920	218	3,164	3,634	263	2,942	281	:	833	179	413	2,901
Exports	351	1,759	722	45	1,120	559	168	179	1,004	4	166	13	189	683
Imports	695	953	1,906	207	2,394	2,249	62	1,937	858	114	705	97	360	1,888
Trade balance	-344	805	-1,184	-161	-1,274	-1,690	106	-1,757	147	-110	-540	-84	-171	-1,205
Export ratio (%) (1)	:	147.0	41.6	80.7	59.3	28.8	45.6	15.1	235.1	:	44.7	14.1	78.1	40.3
Import penetration ratio (%) (1)	:	243.9	65.3	95.0	75.7	61.9	23.7	65.8	305.5	:	72.3	54.5	87.2	65.1
Cover ratio (%)	50.5	184.5	37.9	22.0	46.8	24.9	268.9	9.3	117.1	3.3	23.5	13.7	52.4	36.2

(1) P (1997).

Table 3.33

Processing and preserving of fish and fish products (NACE Rev. 1 15.2)
Labour related indicators, 1998

	EU-15	B	DK	D	EL	E	F	IRL	I	L	NL	A	P	FIN	S	UK
Personnel costs (million ECU) (1)	1,692	36	161	315	7	284	301	49	127	0	62	:	42	12	43	243
Personnel costs/employee (thousand ECU) (2)	21.7	27.1	27.6	29.8	9.5	14.3	25.8	15.4	24.1	:	:	:	:	23.0	31.9	15.3
Social charges/personnel costs (%) (3)	18.7	24.6	3.5	18.3	23.3	22.7	27.8	13.7	36.2	:	9.7	:	:	21.0	28.6	9.7
Labour productivity (thousand ECU/head) (4)	27.4	44.0	41.0	41.3	13.6	20.1	36.3	32.5	54.5	:	32.2	:	:	46.1	40.8	34.3
Wage adjusted labour productivity (%) (2)	126.5	137.4	148.6	121.9	106.3	160.3	126.7	192.8	188.5	:	:	:	:	142.9	130.1	155.0

(1) EU-15 (1995); L (1996). (2) EU-15, EL, I (1995); B, DK, D, E, F, IRL, FIN, S, UK (1996). (3) EU-15, S (1995). (4) NL (1992); EU-15 (1995).

Source: Eurostat (SBS, EBT)

Table 3.34 (million ECU)

Processing and preserving of fruit and vegetables (NACE Rev. 1 15.3)
Production related indicators in the EU

	1988	1989	1990	1991	1992	1993	1994	1995	1996	1997	1998
Production value	19,921	21,595	24,003	26,992	27,721	26,351	27,199	27,476	:	:	:
Producer price index (1995=100)	:	:	:	:	:	:	:	:	:	:	:
Value added	4,807	5,291	5,657	6,464	6,779	6,625	7,040	6,795	:	:	:
Number of persons employed (thousands)	184.0	183.2	194.5	196.9	193.2	188.5	185.2	177.3	:	:	:

Table 3.35 (million ECU)

Processing and preserving of fruit and vegetables (NACE Rev. 1 15.3)
Production related indicators, 1998

	B	DK	D	EL	E	F	IRL	I	L	NL	A	P	FIN	S	UK
Production value	1,394	356	5,347	814	4,699	4,114	184	4,134	:	2,078	715	525	277	628	5,946
Value added	267	88	1,219	120	1,105	825	69	910	:	494	188	:	70	180	2,010
Number of persons employed (units) (1)	6,191	1,832	26,135	7,232	30,779	21,974	1,637	23,309	:	8,150	2,646	4,057	1,875	3,311	34,391

(1) NL (1996).

Table 3.36 (million ECU)

Processing and preserving of fruit and vegetables (NACE Rev. 1 15.3)
Market related indicators in the EU

	1988	1989	1990	1991	1992	1993	1994	1995	1996	1997	1998
Apparent consumption	21,804	23,409	26,278	29,359	30,092	28,238	29,301	29,654	:	:	:
Exports	1,085	1,319	1,202	1,259	1,282	1,463	1,810	1,787	1,944	2,081	2,236
Imports	2,968	3,133	3,476	3,626	3,653	3,349	3,912	3,966	4,269	4,218	4,230
Trade balance	-1,883	-1,814	-2,274	-2,367	-2,371	-1,887	-2,102	-2,178	-2,325	-2,137	-1,994
Export ratio (%)	5.4	6.1	5.0	4.7	4.6	5.6	6.7	6.5	:	:	:
Import penetration ratio (%)	13.6	13.4	13.2	12.4	12.1	11.9	13.4	13.4	:	:	:
Cover ratio (%)	36.5	42.1	34.6	34.7	35.1	43.7	46.3	45.1	45.5	49.3	52.9

Table 3.37 (million ECU)

Processing and preserving of fruit and vegetables (NACE Rev. 1 15.3)
Market related indicators, 1998

	B/L	DK	D	EL	E	F	IRL	I	NL	A	P	FIN	S	UK
Apparent consumption	:	482	7,352	260	3,917	4,994	174	3,480	1,554	773	548	392	916	7,716
Exports	1,656	178	1,195	695	1,260	1,146	201	1,608	1,795	245	129	39	72	351
Imports	1,111	304	3,201	141	478	2,026	191	954	1,270	303	152	155	359	2,122
Trade balance	545	-126	-2,005	554	782	-880	10	654	524	-58	-23	-116	-288	-1,770
Export ratio (%)	:	50.1	22.4	85.4	26.8	27.9	109.3	38.9	86.4	34.2	24.6	14.2	11.5	5.9
Import penetration ratio (%)	:	63.1	43.5	54.3	12.2	40.6	109.9	27.4	81.7	39.2	27.8	39.5	39.3	27.5
Cover ratio (%)	149.0	58.6	37.3	492.8	263.7	56.6	105.2	168.6	141.3	80.9	85.1	25.3	20.0	16.6

Table 3.38

Processing and preserving of fruit and vegetables (NACE Rev. 1 15.3)
Labour related indicators, 1998

	EU-15	B	DK	D	EL	E	F	IRL	I	L	NL	A	P	FIN	S	UK
Personnel costs (million ECU) (1)	3,936	186	53	768	79	462	621	35	584	:	271	90	45	50	115	918
Personnel costs/employee (thousand ECU) (2)	24.0	30.3	30.4	29.9	11.9	15.8	28.7	21.2	22.9	:	:	34.1	:	28.4	36.3	21.6
Social charges/personnel costs (%) (3)	20.4	25.8	3.9	17.1	22.8	22.4	29.3	14.6	31.1	:	14.7	23.2	:	21.3	30.6	9.9
Labour productivity (thousand ECU/head) (4)	38.3	43.2	48.0	46.7	16.5	35.9	37.5	42.4	39.1	:	51.7	70.9	:	37.6	54.3	58.4
Wage adjusted labour productivity (%) (2)	159.7	168.4	153.4	155.6	106.8	179.9	127.0	188.7	161.5	:	:	184.9	:	156.2	152.0	221.6

(1) EU-15 (1995). (2) EU-15, EL, I, A (1995); B, DK, D, E, F, IRL, FIN, S, UK (1996). (3) EU-15, S (1995). (4) NL (1992); EU-15 (1995).

Source: Eurostat (SBS, EBT)

(million ECU) Table 3.39

Manufacture of vegetable and animal oils and fats (NACE Rev. 1 15.4)
Production related indicators in the EU

	1988	1989	1990	1991	1992	1993	1994	1995	1996	1997	1998
Production value	18,940	20,187	22,240	21,626	21,195	20,057	21,484	:	21,997	:	:
Producer price index (1995=100)	:	:	:	:	:	:	:	:	:	:	:
Value added	3,326	2,954	3,762	3,323	3,785	3,056	2,830	:	2,485	:	:
Number of persons employed (thousands)	69.5	63.9	67.4	72.0	68.5	56.5	52.7	:	43.1	:	:

(million ECU) Table 3.40

Manufacture of vegetable and animal oils and fats (NACE Rev. 1 15.4)
Production related indicators, 1998

	B	DK	D	EL	E	F	IRL	I	L	NL	A	P	FIN	S	UK
Production value (1)	1,636	251	4,602	304	8,572	1,503	:	1,703	0	2,781	418	563	238	578	2,611
Value added (1)	98	37	643	57	707	222	:	191	0	389	90	:	51	135	183
Number of persons employed (units) (1) (2)	1,354	718	7,219	1,466	14,690	4,010	:	3,386	0	3,923	1,331	3,326	727	1,618	2,651

(1) DK, A (1994); F (1995); L (1996). (2) NL (1992).

(million ECU) Table 3.41

Manufacture of vegetable and animal oils and fats (NACE Rev. 1 15.4)
Market related indicators in the EU (million ECU)

	1988	1989	1990	1991	1992	1993	1994	1995	1996	1997	1998
Apparent consumption	19,766	21,701	22,687	22,313	21,815	21,377	22,907	:	23,531	:	:
Exports	1,176	1,406	1,373	1,306	1,547	1,341	1,776	2,315	1,977	2,750	2,910
Imports	2,003	2,920	1,820	1,993	2,167	2,660	3,199	2,789	3,512	2,596	4,194
Trade balance	-827	-1,514	-447	-687	-620	-1,319	-1,423	-475	-1,534	154	-1,284
Export ratio (%)	6.2	7.0	6.2	6.0	7.3	6.7	8.3	:	9.0	:	:
Import penetration ratio (%)	10.1	13.5	8.0	8.9	9.9	12.4	14.0	:	14.9	:	:
Cover ratio (%)	58.7	48.2	75.4	65.5	71.4	50.4	55.5	83.0	56.3	105.9	69.4

(million ECU) Table 3.42

Manufacture of vegetable and animal oils and fats (NACE Rev. 1 15.4)
Market related indicators, 1998

	B/L	DK	D	EL	E	F	IRL	I	NL	A	P	FIN	S	UK
Apparent consumption (1)	:	603	4,298	100	8,077	2,448	:	2,629	2,222	588	691	260	654	3,415
Exports	1,063	265	1,766	309	1,141	507	35	697	1,947	40	119	64	145	336
Imports	928	610	1,462	105	646	1,806	235	1,623	1,389	211	246	86	221	1,140
Trade balance	136	-345	304	204	495	-1,298	-200	-926	558	-171	-127	-22	-76	-804
Export ratio (%) (1)	:	65.1	38.4	101.7	13.3	32.9	:	40.9	70.0	2.4	21.2	26.8	25.1	12.9
Import penetration ratio (%) (1)	:	85.4	34.0	105.1	8.0	58.8	:	61.7	62.5	30.6	35.7	33.1	33.8	33.4
Cover ratio (%)	114.6	43.4	120.8	293.5	176.5	28.1	15.0	42.9	140.2	19.2	48.4	74.0	65.7	29.5

(1) DK, A (1994); F (1995).

Table 3.43

Manufacture of vegetable and animal oils and fats (NACE Rev. 1 15.4)
Labour related indicators, 1998

	EU-15	B	DK	D	EL	E	F	IRL	I	L	NL	A	P	FIN	S	UK
Personnel costs (million ECU) (1)	1,451	63	26	359	31	237	167	:	108	0	140	79	33	26	61	88
Personnel costs/employee (thousand ECU) (2)	:	47.0	:	47.9	23.2	21.0	41.7	:	29.2	:	:	59.1	:	37.5	39.7	26.8
Social charges/personnel costs (%) (3)	:	27.6	8.9	23.2	22.1	19.3	30.9	:	36.2	:	16.7	20.0	:	23.2	28.0	12.0
Labour productivity (thousand ECU/head) (4)	57.6	72.5	52.1	89.1	38.6	48.1	55.3	:	56.5	:	71.4	67.7	:	70.3	83.2	69.0
Wage adjusted labour productivity (%) (5)	:	163.1	:	144.9	162.7	201.0	132.5	:	189.3	:	:	114.6	:	198.9	213.1	209.0

(1) DK, A (1994); F (1995); EU-15, L (1996). (2) A (1994); EL, F, I (1995); B, D, E, FIN, S, UK (1996). (3) D, A, S (1994). (4) NL (1992); DK, A (1994); F (1995); EU-15 (1996).
(5) A (1994); EL, F, I (1995); B, D, E, FIN, S, UK (1996).

Source: Eurostat (SBS, EBT)

Table 3.44 (million ECU)

Manufacture of dairy products (NACE Rev. 1 15.5)

Production related indicators in the EU

	1988	1989	1990	1991	1992	1993	1994	1995	1996	1997	1998
Production value	67,402	74,896	77,732	83,286	84,775	80,384	82,828	85,607	:	:	:
Producer price index (1995=100)	:	:	94.7	92.4	94.5	96.4	97.6	100.0	:	:	:
Value added	11,061	11,969	12,476	14,106	14,246	13,875	13,965	13,912	:	:	:
Number of persons employed (thousands)	319.3	317.0	323.8	331.7	323.5	313.7	308.1	297.1	:	:	:

Table 3.45 (million ECU)

Manufacture of dairy products (NACE Rev. 1 15.5)

Production related indicators, 1998

	B	DK	D	EL	E	F	IRL	I	L	NL	A	P	FIN	S	UK
Production value	2,630	3,118	17,140	844	5,068	18,702	3,459	11,331	:	5,995	2,170	1,243	1,919	2,564	9,582
Value added	343	448	2,472	165	1,046	2,549	590	2,082	:	837	207	:	316	513	1,996
Number of persons employed (units) (1)	7,463	10,378	45,224	6,025	29,119	62,035	11,432	39,855	:	16,856	5,736	9,589	6,070	9,289	35,880

(1) NL (1992).

Table 3.46 (million ECU)

Manufacture of dairy products (NACE Rev. 1 15.5)

Market related indicators in the EU

	1988	1989	1990	1991	1992	1993	1994	1995	1996	1997	1998
Apparent consumption	64,691	71,600	75,135	80,527	81,524	77,102	79,838	82,087	:	:	:
Exports	3,346	3,893	3,302	3,402	3,910	4,008	3,752	4,363	4,248	4,510	4,419
Imports	635	598	705	644	659	726	762	843	825	900	920
Trade balance	2,711	3,295	2,597	2,759	3,251	3,281	2,991	3,520	3,423	3,611	3,500
Export ratio (%)	5.0	5.2	4.2	4.1	4.6	5.0	4.5	5.1	:	:	:
Import penetration ratio (%)	1.0	0.8	0.9	0.8	0.8	0.9	1.0	1.0	:	:	:
Cover ratio (%)	527.3	651.1	468.2	528.7	593.4	551.7	492.7	517.5	514.8	501.4	480.4

Table 3.47 (million ECU)

Manufacture of dairy products (NACE Rev. 1 15.5)

Market related indicators, 1998

	B/L	DK	D	EL	E	F	IRL	I	NL	A	P	FIN	S	UK
Apparent consumption	:	2,037	15,765	1,191	5,485	16,958	2,585	12,918	4,391	2,165	1,256	1,812	2,573	10,191
Exports	1,895	1,301	4,242	107	391	3,724	1,081	938	3,211	242	127	214	165	1,044
Imports	1,927	220	2,867	453	808	1,980	207	2,525	1,607	237	139	107	173	1,652
Trade balance	-32	1,081	1,375	-346	-417	1,744	874	-1,587	1,604	5	-13	106	-9	-608
Export ratio (%)	:	41.7	24.7	12.6	7.7	19.9	31.2	8.3	53.6	11.1	10.2	11.1	6.4	10.9
Import penetration ratio (%)	:	10.8	18.2	38.0	14.7	11.7	8.0	19.5	36.6	10.9	11.1	5.9	6.7	16.2
Cover ratio (%)	98.3	591.7	148.0	23.6	48.4	188.1	522.2	37.2	199.8	102.0	91.0	199.0	95.1	63.2

Table 3.48

Manufacture of dairy products (NACE Rev. 1 15.5)

Labour related indicators, 1998

	EU-15	B	DK	D	EL	E	F	IRL	I	L	NL	A	P	FIN	S	UK
Personnel costs (million ECU) (1)	8,756	249	335	1,681	97	682	1,934	321	1,333	:	578	233	99	178	285	994
Personnel costs/employee (thousand ECU) (2)	32.4	35.6	33.7	37.6	17.6	24.4	31.7	27.6	30.5	:	:	42.2	:	30.1	32.2	22.4
Social charges/personnel costs (%) (3)	23.0	28.1	3.4	18.2	23.0	22.1	29.3	14.8	33.4	:	22.8	23.2	:	20.2	30.5	10.9
Labour productivity (thousand ECU/head) (4)	46.8	45.9	43.2	54.7	27.5	35.9	41.1	51.7	52.2	:	52.5	36.1	:	52.0	55.3	55.6
Wage adjusted labour productivity (%) (2)	144.4	133.0	164.4	144.2	144.2	182.9	127.4	206.5	161.5	:	:	82.6	:	159.6	174.4	208.8

(1) EU-15 (1995). (2) EU-15, EL, I, A (1995); B, DK, D, E, F, IRL, FIN, S, UK (1996). (3) EU-15, S (1995). (4) NL (1992); EU-15 (1995).

Source: Eurostat (SBS, EBT)

(million ECU) Table 3.49

Manufacture of grain mill products, starches and starch products (NACE Rev. 1 15.6)
Production related indicators in the EU

	1988	1989	1990	1991	1992	1993	1994	1995	1996	1997	1998
Production value	15,957	16,729	16,536	18,034	18,147	18,031	17,441	18,264	:	:	:
Producer price index (1995=100)	:	:	98.0	97.2	99.1	101.1	100.2	100.0	100.9	100.9	99.8
Value added	3,137	3,401	3,490	3,715	3,704	3,758	3,721	3,997	:	:	:
Number of persons employed (thousands)	72.5	69.5	67.0	68.5	64.2	62.9	61.2	55.4	:	:	:

(million ECU) Table 3.50

Manufacture of grain mill products, starches and starch products (NACE Rev. 1 15.6)
Production related indicators, 1998

	B	DK	D	EL	E	F	IRL	I	L	NL	A	P	FIN	S	UK
Production value (1)	1,304	283	2,924	367	1,769	3,681	148	2,443	:	1,394	216	:	280	288	4,147
Value added (2)	231	66	615	46	342	803	28	451	:	367	57	:	60	63	1,069
Number of persons employed (units) (3)	2,900	835	9,980	1,646	10,043	11,951	473	5,497	:	4,591	1,236	:	967	873	11,393

(1) IRL (1990). (2) IRL (1993). (3) IRL (1993); NL (1992).

(million ECU) Table 3.51

Manufacture of grain mill products, starches and starch products (NACE Rev. 1 15.6)
Market related indicators in the EU

	1988	1989	1990	1991	1992	1993	1994	1995	1996	1997	1998
Apparent consumption	15,896	16,244	16,059	17,618	17,471	17,206	16,788	17,247	:	:	:
Exports	1,011	1,365	1,345	1,450	1,642	1,658	1,686	1,756	1,657	2,031	1,874
Imports	950	879	868	1,034	966	834	1,033	739	711	735	762
Trade balance	61	486	477	416	676	824	653	1,017	946	1,296	1,112
Export ratio (%)	6.3	8.2	8.1	8.0	9.0	9.2	9.7	9.6	:	:	:
Import penetration ratio (%)	6.0	5.4	5.4	5.9	5.5	4.8	6.2	4.3	:	:	:
Cover ratio (%)	106.5	155.2	154.9	140.2	170.0	198.8	163.2	237.7	233.1	276.2	246.0

(million ECU) Table 3.52

Manufacture of grain mill products, starches and starch products (NACE Rev. 1 15.6)
Market related indicators, 1998

	B/L	DK	D	EL	E	F	IRL	I	NL	A	P	FIN	S	UK
Apparent consumption (1)	:	351	2,871	423	1,676	3,456	324	2,073	1,045	295	:	384	462	4,136
Exports	593	122	885	30	354	1,019	32	703	789	53	18	56	37	711
Imports	511	189	832	87	262	793	181	333	439	132	98	160	211	700
Trade balance	81	-67	53	-57	93	226	-148	370	349	-79	-79	-104	-174	11
Export ratio (%) (1)	:	43.0	30.3	8.3	20.0	27.7	5.8	28.8	56.6	24.6	:	20.0	12.8	17.1
Import penetration ratio (%) (1)	:	53.9	29.0	20.6	15.6	22.9	56.8	16.1	42.0	44.7	:	41.6	45.7	16.9
Cover ratio (%)	115.9	64.5	106.3	34.8	135.5	128.5	17.8	211.0	179.5	40.4	18.8	35.0	17.5	101.6

(1) IRL (1990).

Table 3.53

Manufacture of grain mill products, starches and starch products (NACE Rev. 1 15.6)
Labour related indicators, 1998

	EU-15	B	DK	D	EL	E	F	IRL	I	L	NL	A	P	FIN	S	UK
Personnel costs (million ECU) (1)	1,941	144	35	365	27	210	454	19	179	:	147	51	:	31	31	418
Personnel costs/employee (thousand ECU) (2)	35.7	52.9	43.5	39.3	17.9	21.7	38.6	:	29.8	:	:	42.3	:	34.0	37.6	29.6
Social charges/personnel costs (%) (3)	23.0	27.9	6.7	19.1	23.7	21.6	31.0	:	35.1	:	14.8	23.1	:	22.6	29.2	12.1
Labour productivity (thousand ECU/head) (4)	72.2	79.6	79.1	61.6	27.9	34.0	67.2	59.9	82.0	:	75.5	46.1	:	61.7	71.7	93.8
Wage adjusted labour productivity (%) (2)	202.5	183.3	176.2	157.6	140.6	221.4	174.9	:	222.0	:	:	101.3	:	184.0	193.7	266.6

(1) EU-15 (1995); IRL (1990). (2) EU-15, EL, I, A (1995); B, DK, D, E, F, FIN, S, UK (1996). (3) EU-15, S (1995). (4) EU-15 (1995); IRL (1993); NL (1992).

Source: Eurostat (SBS, EBT)

Table 3.54 (million ECU)

Manufacture of prepared animal feeds (NACE Rev. 1 15.7)

Production related indicators in the EU

	1988	1989	1990	1991	1992	1993	1994	1995	1996	1997	1998
Production value	27,938	30,398	29,639	30,502	30,522	30,952	31,127	32,112	:	:	:
Producer price index (1995=100)	:	:	99.6	98.6	99.1	100.2	100.3	100.0	:	:	:
Value added	4,309	4,692	4,755	4,819	4,959	4,862	5,025	4,763	:	:	:
Number of persons employed (thousands)	95.9	96.2	97.3	97.3	95.9	93.0	91.4	91.2	:	:	:

Table 3.55 (million ECU)

Manufacture of prepared animal feeds (NACE Rev. 1 15.7)

Production related indicators, 1998

	B	DK	D	EL	E	F	IRL	I	L	NL	A	P	FIN	S	UK
Production value (1)	2,128	322	3,979	162	4,460	6,136	547	2,976	0	3,763	520	1,003	484	206	4,726
Value added (2)	217	82	823	14	542	780	110	433	0	529	95	:	87	20	1,039
Number of persons employed (units) (3)	4,022	1,254	11,425	945	11,342	16,900	1,598	6,555	0	9,822	1,888	4,470	1,411	343	15,613

(1) A (1994). (2) L (1996); A (1994). (3) L (1996); NL (1992); A (1994).

Table 3.56 (million ECU)

Manufacture of prepared animal feeds (NACE Rev. 1 15.7)

Market related indicators in the EU

	1988	1989	1990	1991	1992	1993	1994	1995	1996	1997	1998
Apparent consumption	27,567	29,965	29,254	30,129	29,912	30,297	30,419	31,434	:	:	:
Exports	377	464	472	554	659	763	802	894	951	971	1,091
Imports	6	31	87	182	49	108	94	216	189	403	112
Trade balance	371	433	385	373	611	655	708	678	762	568	979
Export ratio (%)	1.3	1.5	1.6	1.8	2.2	2.5	2.6	2.8	:	:	:
Import penetration ratio (%)	0.0	0.1	0.3	0.6	0.2	0.4	0.3	0.7	:	:	:
Cover ratio (%)	6,162.3	1,480.1	540.9	305.2	1,358.5	705.0	857.0	414.1	503.3	240.9	969.9

Table 3.57 (million ECU)

Manufacture of prepared animal feeds (NACE Rev. 1 15.7)

Market related indicators, 1998

	B/L	DK	D	EL	E	F	IRL	I	NL	A	P	FIN	S	UK
Apparent consumption (1)	:	114	4,089	253	4,576	5,492	590	3,314	3,279	506	1,135	520	294	4,714
Exports	449	317	618	4	129	1,006	69	133	848	76	8	18	12	437
Imports	455	108	727	95	246	362	111	471	364	70	140	54	100	424
Trade balance	-5	209	-109	-91	-117	645	-43	-339	484	6	-132	-36	-88	13
Export ratio (%) (1)	:	98.2	15.5	2.4	2.9	16.4	12.6	4.5	22.5	8.6	0.8	3.6	5.8	9.2
Import penetration ratio (%) (1)	:	95.0	17.8	37.6	5.4	6.6	18.9	14.2	11.1	6.0	12.3	10.4	34.1	9.0
Cover ratio (%)	98.8	293.7	85.0	4.0	52.4	278.3	61.7	28.2	233.1	108.5	5.7	32.7	12.0	103.0

(1) A (1994).

Table 3.58

Manufacture of prepared animal feeds (NACE Rev. 1 15.7)

Labour related indicators, 1998

	EU-15	B	DK	D	EL	E	F	IRL	I	L	NL	A	P	FIN	S	UK
Personnel costs (million ECU) (1)	2,801	152	46	502	14	205	642	39	224	0	298	65	51	51	12	503
Personnel costs/employee (thousand ECU) (2)	36.5	40.2	38.7	45.1	16.0	21.2	38.7	24.1	31.3	:	:	34.4	:	37.5	36.3	26.1
Social charges/personnel costs (%) (3)	22.4	27.5	3.4	18.6	23.3	21.8	30.2	15.7	35.9	:	18.0	22.7	:	22.4	28.2	13.7
Labour productivity (thousand ECU/head) (4)	52.2	53.9	65.5	72.0	14.4	47.8	46.1	68.8	66.1	:	54.2	50.1	:	61.9	57.3	66.6
Wage adjusted labour productivity (%) (2)	142.9	154.8	164.3	160.7	92.5	218.7	125.4	272.9	174.1	:	:	145.8	:	164.1	160.6	214.6

(1) A (1994); EU-15 (1995); L (1996). (2) A (1994); EU-15, EL, I (1995); B, DK, D, E, F, IRL, FIN, S, UK (1996). (3) A, S (1994); EU-15 (1995). (4) NL (1992); EU-15 (1995).

Source: Eurostat (SBS, EBT)

(million ECU) Table 3.59

Manufacture of other food products (NACE Rev. 1 15.8)
Production related indicators in the EU

	1988	1989	1990	1991	1992	1993	1994	1995	1996	1997	1998
Production value	79,376	86,202	91,863	98,497	104,568	106,035	110,734	113,462	:	:	:
Producer price index (1995=100)	:	:	89.7	89.1	91.5	93.9	96.8	100.0	100.1	97.1	95.5
Value added	24,080	25,937	28,740	31,438	33,357	34,471	35,652	35,166	:	:	:
Number of persons employed (thousands)	883.8	907.8	929.4	940.2	943.4	920.8	917.8	896.2	:	:	:

(million ECU) Table 3.60

Manufacture of other food products (NACE Rev. 1 15.8)
Production related indicators, 1998

	B	DK	D	EL	E	F	IRL	I	L	NL	A	P	FIN	S	UK
Production value	6,963	3,034	31,668	1,098	10,622	20,903	:	14,028	120	7,729	2,628	:	2,035	2,358	22,920
Value added (1)	1,832	1,014	9,711	302	3,791	5,207	594	3,694	60	2,386	1,057	:	752	806	8,680
Number of persons employed (units) (2)	51,339	16,106	236,468	12,178	149,818	109,645	11,316	65,714	2,210	40,166	22,119	:	16,808	16,553	177,648

(1) IRL (1990). (2) IRL (1990); NL (1992).

(million ECU) Table 3.61

Manufacture of other food products (NACE Rev. 1 15.8)
Market related indicators in the EU

	1988	1989	1990	1991	1992	1993	1994	1995	1996	1997	1998
Apparent consumption	77,008	83,027	88,215	95,179	100,926	101,507	105,108	107,039	:	:	:
Exports	4,823	5,586	6,115	5,970	6,432	7,450	8,847	9,686	9,904	10,918	10,685
Imports	2,455	2,411	2,467	2,652	2,791	2,921	3,221	3,263	3,536	3,520	3,682
Trade balance	2,367	3,176	3,648	3,318	3,642	4,528	5,626	6,423	6,368	7,398	7,003
Export ratio (%)	6.1	6.5	6.7	6.1	6.2	7.0	8.0	8.5	:	:	:
Import penetration ratio (%)	3.2	2.9	2.8	2.8	2.8	2.9	3.1	3.0	:	:	:
Cover ratio (%)	196.4	231.7	247.9	225.1	230.5	255.0	274.7	296.8	280.1	310.1	290.2

(million ECU) Table 3.62

Manufacture of other food products (NACE Rev. 1 15.8)
Market related indicators, 1998

	B/L	DK	D	EL	E	F	IRL	I	NL	A	P	FIN	S	UK
Apparent consumption	:	2,531	30,728	1,341	10,782	19,257	:	12,353	6,027	2,770	:	2,192	2,588	24,138
Exports	3,319	1,160	5,185	136	1,312	5,433	1,564	3,063	2,989	516	168	213	485	2,878
Imports	2,310	656	4,245	379	1,472	3,787	565	1,388	1,288	658	470	370	715	4,096
Trade balance	1,009	504	940	-243	-160	1,646	1,000	1,674	1,702	-142	-302	-157	-230	-1,218
Export ratio (%)	:	38.2	16.4	12.4	12.4	26.0	:	21.8	38.7	19.6	:	10.5	20.6	12.6
Import penetration ratio (%)	:	25.9	13.8	28.3	13.7	19.7	:	11.2	21.4	23.8	:	16.9	27.6	17.0
Cover ratio (%)	143.7	176.8	122.1	35.9	89.1	143.5	277.0	220.6	232.2	78.5	35.8	57.6	67.8	70.3

Table 3.63

Manufacture of other food products (NACE Rev. 1 15.8)
Labour related indicators, 1998

	EU-15	B	DK	D	EL	E	F	IRL	I	L	NL	A	P	FIN	S	UK
Personnel costs (million ECU) (1)	21,560	1,120	594	6,505	175	2,164	3,458	209	2,119	40	1,329	664	:	438	530	3,953
Personnel costs/employee (thousand ECU) (2)	26.1	26.8	38.6	27.9	15.8	17.2	32.1	:	29.4	19.9	:	29.9	:	27.5	33.6	19.8
Social charges/personnel costs (%) (3)	21.1	26.6	5.3	18.1	23.1	22.1	29.0	:	34.7	13.7	17.6	22.6	:	21.8	29.2	11.1
Labour productivity (thousand ECU/head) (4)	39.2	35.7	62.9	41.1	24.8	25.3	47.5	52.5	56.2	27.0	44.8	47.8	:	44.8	48.7	48.9
Wage adjusted labour productivity (%) (2)	150.5	139.0	153.0	144.2	127.4	141.7	148.7	:	173.4	131.9	:	143.6	:	154.7	147.4	210.5

(1) IRL (1990); EU-15 (1995). (2) EU-15, EL, I, A (1995); B, DK, D, E, F, IRL, FIN, S, UK (1996). (3) EU-15, L, S (1995). (4) IRL (1990); NL (1992); EU-15 (1995).

Source: Eurostat (SBS, EBT)

Table 3.64 (million ECU)

Manufacture of beverages (NACE Rev. 1 15.9)

Production related indicators in the EU

	1988	1989	1990	1991	1992	1993	1994	1995	1996	1997	1998
Production value	58,986	63,892	70,370	75,019	76,447	74,702	76,767	79,816	:	:	:
Producer price index (1995=100)	:	:	87.1	88.1	91.7	94.4	96.7	100.0	100.1	97.1	95.5
Value added	18,471	19,526	21,226	22,260	22,943	22,889	22,747	22,550	:	:	:
Number of persons employed (thousands)	376.3	377.2	384.3	384.6	371.0	361.2	346.1	326.8	:	:	:

Table 3.65 (million ECU)

Manufacture of beverages (NACE Rev. 1 15.9)

Production related indicators, 1998

	B	DK	D	EL	E	F	IRL	I	L	NL	A	P	FIN	S	UK
Production value (1)	3,189	1,157	18,952	1,263	10,184	14,014	2,430	9,719	217	3,153	2,041	2,237	802	1,290	22,152
Value added (1)	849	392	5,114	326	3,003	3,806	992	1,844	68	1,068	675	:	279	404	5,324
Number of persons employed (units) (2)	10,353	5,661	74,907	7,110	38,892	42,197	4,656	30,318	1,000	11,426	9,941	14,926	3,686	6,475	52,127

(1) L (1995). (2) NL (1992); L (1995).

Table 3.66 (million ECU)

Manufacture of beverages (NACE Rev. 1 15.9)

Market related indicators in the EU

	1988	1989	1990	1991	1992	1993	1994	1995	1996	1997	1998
Apparent consumption	54,056	58,116	64,511	69,069	70,317	68,063	69,361	72,300	:	:	:
Exports	5,506	6,488	6,745	6,922	7,257	7,834	8,700	8,804	9,370	10,604	10,163
Imports	576	712	885	973	1,126	1,195	1,293	1,288	1,632	2,013	2,226
Trade balance	4,930	5,776	5,859	5,950	6,130	6,639	7,407	7,516	7,738	8,591	7,937
Export ratio (%)	9.3	10.2	9.6	9.2	9.5	10.5	11.3	11.0	:	:	:
Import penetration ratio (%)	1.1	1.2	1.4	1.4	1.6	1.8	1.9	1.8	:	:	:
Cover ratio (%)	956.2	911.6	761.8	711.7	644.3	655.7	672.8	683.7	574.1	526.8	456.6

Table 3.67 (million ECU)

Manufacture of beverages (NACE Rev. 1 15.9)

Market related indicators, 1998

	B/L	DK	D	EL	E	F	IRL	I	NL	A	P	FIN	S	UK
Apparent consumption	:	1,339	20,204	1,391	9,597	7,333	2,127	7,782	2,847	1,990	1,991	862	1,465	21,760
Exports	963	302	1,630	117	1,524	8,261	647	2,740	1,144	234	498	104	250	4,347
Imports	1,379	485	2,882	245	937	1,579	344	804	838	183	252	165	424	3,955
Trade balance	-416	-183	-1,252	-128	587	6,682	303	1,937	306	51	245	-61	-175	392
Export ratio (%)	:	26.1	8.6	9.3	15.0	58.9	26.6	28.2	36.3	11.4	22.2	13.0	19.4	19.6
Import penetration ratio (%)	:	36.2	14.3	17.6	9.8	21.5	16.2	10.3	29.4	9.2	12.7	19.2	29.0	18.2
Cover ratio (%)	69.9	62.3	56.6	47.7	162.7	523.0	188.0	341.0	136.5	127.8	197.3	63.2	58.9	109.9

Table 3.68

Manufacture of beverages (NACE Rev. 1 15.9)

Labour related indicators, 1998

	EU-15	B	DK	D	EL	E	F	IRL	I	L	NL	A	P	FIN	S	UK
Personnel costs (million ECU) (1)	11,336	401	216	3,165	144	1,044	1,807	195	1,113	32	515	412	188	129	231	1,887
Personnel costs/employee (thousand ECU) (2)	38.2	45.3	40.2	42.3	22.2	28.5	43.5	41.3	33.5	32.2	:	42.3	:	36.1	37.4	29.3
Social charges/personnel costs (%) (3)	22.3	30.6	7.2	15.3	24.5	20.1	30.1	23.1	34.7	14.0	19.6	23.1	:	24.9	29.2	14.0
Labour productivity (thousand ECU/head) (4)	69.0	82.0	69.3	68.3	45.9	77.2	90.2	213.1	60.8	68.2	83.4	67.9	:	75.6	62.4	102.1
Wage adjusted labour productivity (%) (2)	180.4	171.5	175.7	156.8	159.8	217.2	189.7	435.8	184.1	212.1	:	157.6	:	182.2	169.4	293.6

(1) EU-15, L (1995). (2) EU-15, EL, I, L, A (1995); B, DK, D, E, F, IRL, FIN, S, UK (1996). (3) EU-15, L, S (1995). (4) EU-15, L, NL (1995).

Source: Eurostat (SBS, EBT)

(million ECU) Table 3.69

Manufacture of tobacco products (NACE Rev. 1 16)
Production related indicators in the EU

	1988	1989	1990	1991	1992	1993	1994	1995	1996	1997	1998
Production value	33,320	35,061	37,067	40,407	40,187	40,288	41,455	:	:	:	:
Producer price index (1995=100)	:	:	:	:	:	:	:	:	:	:	:
Value added	4,404	5,045	5,191	6,778	7,311	11,599	12,483	:	:	:	:
Number of persons employed (thousands)	96.4	91.5	87.4	85.2	81.4	77.0	72.3	:	:	:	:

(million ECU) Table 3.70

Manufacture of tobacco products (NACE Rev. 1 16)
Production related indicators, 1998

	B	DK	D	EL	E	F	IRL	I	L	NL	A	P	FIN	S	UK
Production value (1)	1,847	377	13,750	473	2,231	:	928	6,965	:	3,780	:	1,064	110	300	21,695
Value added (1)	236	190	1,473	124	568	:	201	806	:	1,411	:	:	35	176	2,376
Number of persons employed (units) (2)	2,795	1,415	12,584	2,980	11,966	:	1,131	16,204	:	5,937	:	1,329	699	930	9,142

(1) DK (1994). (2) NL (1992); DK (1994).

(million ECU) Table 3.71

Manufacture of tobacco products (NACE Rev. 1 16)
Market related indicators in the EU

	1988	1989	1990	1991	1992	1993	1994	1995	1996	1997	1998
Apparent consumption	32,720	34,388	36,266	39,211	38,850	38,934	40,604	:	:	:	:
Exports	626	699	829	1,231	1,374	1,395	898	782	1,096	1,841	1,748
Imports	25	26	28	35	36	41	47	40	95	44	158
Trade balance	601	673	800	1,196	1,338	1,354	851	742	1,001	1,797	1,591
Export ratio (%)	1.9	2.0	2.2	3.0	3.4	3.5	2.2	:	:	:	:
Import penetration ratio (%)	0.1	0.1	0.1	0.1	0.1	0.1	0.1	:	:	:	:
Cover ratio (%)	2,502.7	2,722.3	2,919.4	3,504.6	3,815.5	3,375.5	1,906.6	1,960.4	1,156.9	4,138.3	1,108.4

(million ECU) Table 3.72

Manufacture of tobacco products (NACE Rev. 1 16)
Market related indicators, 1998

	B/L	DK	D	EL	E	F	IRL	I	NL	A	P	FIN	S	UK
Apparent consumption (1)	:	279	13,044	512	2,514	:	921	7,975	1,818	:	1,097	115	345	20,377
Exports	356	146	1,336	98	53	303	46	13	2,316	53	6	26	21	1,550
Imports	352	19	631	137	336	1,454	40	1,023	354	33	39	31	67	232
Trade balance	4	126	706	-39	-283	-1,151	6	-1,010	1,961	20	-34	-5	-45	1,318
Export ratio (%) (1)	:	30.2	9.7	20.6	2.4	:	5.0	0.2	61.3	:	0.5	24.1	7.1	7.1
Import penetration ratio (%) (1)	:	5.8	4.8	26.7	13.4	:	4.4	12.8	19.5	:	3.6	27.2	19.3	1.1
Cover ratio (%)	101.2	758.9	211.9	71.4	15.8	20.8	115.1	1.3	653.6	160.2	14.3	84.9	32.0	668.1

(1) DK (1994).

Table 3.73

Manufacture of tobacco products (NACE Rev. 1 16)
Labour related indicators, 1998

	EU-15	B	DK	D	EL	E	F	IRL	I	L	NL	A	P	FIN	S	UK
Personnel costs (million ECU) (1)	2,578	113	43	690	60	359	:	38	349	:	275	:	31	23	38	478
Personnel costs/employee (thousand ECU) (2)	:	40.2	:	55.3	21.9	31.3	:	37.5	19.7	:	:	:	:	34.1	43.0	42.7
Social charges/personnel costs (%) (3)	:	29.4	6.8	24.7	24.6	21.8	:	17.8	8.1	:	16.8	:	:	20.8	27.5	13.2
Labour productivity (thousand ECU/head) (4)	172.7	84.3	134.4	117.1	41.6	47.5	:	177.8	49.8	:	127.8	:	:	49.4	189.6	259.9
Wage adjusted labour productivity (%) (2)	:	189.7	:	186.5	142.0	156.6	:	419.2	215.1	:	:	:	:	135.3	519.1	507.2

(1) EU-15, DK (1994). (2) EL, I (1995); B, D, E, IRL, FIN, S, UK (1996). (3) DK, S (1994). (4) NL (1992); EU-15, DK (1994).

Source: Eurostat (SBS, EBT)

Textiles, clothing, leather and footwear

Industrial description

The textile, clothing, leather and footwear industry includes both the production of raw materials and consumer goods. Many raw materials after a first processing stage are then subject to further transformation, resulting in end-products for consumers, such as wearing apparel, bags or footwear, as well as made-up furnishings or carpets. Around 80% of the output of the industry is sold to end-consumers, largely via retail trade outlets. The manufacture of textiles, clothing, leather and footwear is therefore to a great extent dependent on the structure of consumer expenditure and hence to the business cycle and consumer confidence.

Within the EU, the share of clothing and footwear in total consumer expenditure varied from 4.5% in Finland to 10.5% in Greece. By means of comparison, the share of expenditure on food, beverages and tobacco ranged from 14.1% in the Netherlands to 27.0% in Portugal (all figures for 1997). Household expenditure on clothing and footwear has been reduced relative to other expenditure from 1990 onwards. In France and Italy the reduction was equal to 1.3 percentage points to 5.2% and 8.7% of total expenditure during the period 1990 to 1997. The only two countries that did not follow this trend were Greece and Ireland.

(%) Figure 4.1

Textiles, clothing, leather and footwear (NACE Rev. 1 17 to 19)

Share of EU value added in total manufacturing

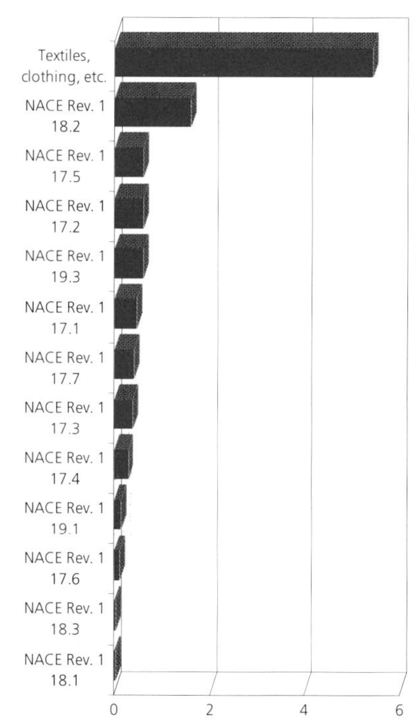

Source: Eurostat (SBS)

The activities covered in this chapter include:

- 17.1: preparation and spinning of textile fibres;
- 17.2: textile weaving;
- 17.3: finishing of textiles;
- 17.4: manufacture of made-up textiles, except apparel;
- 17.5: manufacture of other textiles;
- 17.6: manufacture of knitted and crocheted fabrics;
- 17.7: manufacture of knitted and crocheted articles;
- 18.1: manufacture of leather clothes;
- 18.2: manufacture of other wearing apparel and accessories;
- 18.3: dressing and dyeing of fur; manufacture of articles of fur;
- 19.1: tanning and dressing of leather;
- 19.2: manufacture of luggage, handbags and the like, saddlery and harness;
- 19.3: manufacture of footwear.

Figure 4.2 (ECU)

Consumer spending per head on textiles and clothing, 1997

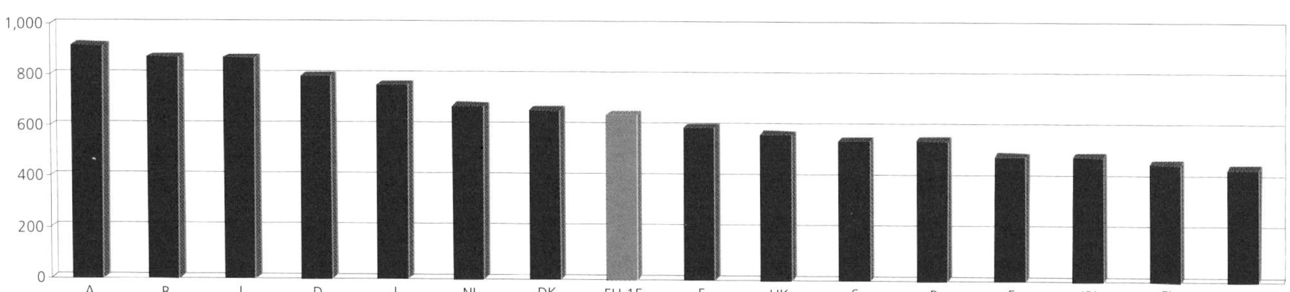

Source: OETH

The downward trend in the share of clothing and footwear in total consumer expenditure may be partly explained as the result of falling relative prices. The main reasons for this included increased competition within the retail trade sector, as well as a growing level of imports from low-cost countries.

In 1988 textiles, clothing, leather and footwear contributed around 6.5% of total manufacturing output in the EU, a share that diminished to around 5% by the end of the nineties, in terms of both production value and value added. The reduction in activity was observed for both the manufacture of raw materials (such as fibres and leather), as well as of for final consumer products.

The manufacture of textiles, clothing, leather and footwear was concentrated in the Mediterranean Member States, where half of the production value of the EU was generated in 1998. Within the Member States, Italy reported the largest industry, contributing one third of total EU output. In comparison, Germany was responsible for just 15% of the European total. Portugal reported the highest production specialisation ratio amongst the Member States, with output of textiles, clothing, leather and footwear contributing 3.5 times more to the production value of total manufacturing than the European average.

The nature of the manufacturing process changed during the course of the eighties, with a marked reduction in the output of textiles, clothing, leather and footwear in the EU. Global competition and production across borders by foreign affiliates changed completely the organisation of the industry, with knowledge being spread to third countries in the fields of production, marketing and logistics. European manufacturers were under constant pressure to increase their competitiveness, not only by reducing costs, but also through introducing innovations in fabric technology, placing a greater emphasis on design and brands, as well as searching for strategic alliances (particularly in distribution) and for new distribution channels (for example, electronic commerce).

Figure 4.3 (1988=100)

Textiles, clothing, leather and footwear (NACE Rev. 1 17 to 19)

Production, employment and value added compared to EU total manufacturing

Source: Eurostat (SBS)

Figure 4.4

Textiles, clothing, leather and footwear (NACE Rev. 1 17 to 19)

International comparison of main indicators in current prices

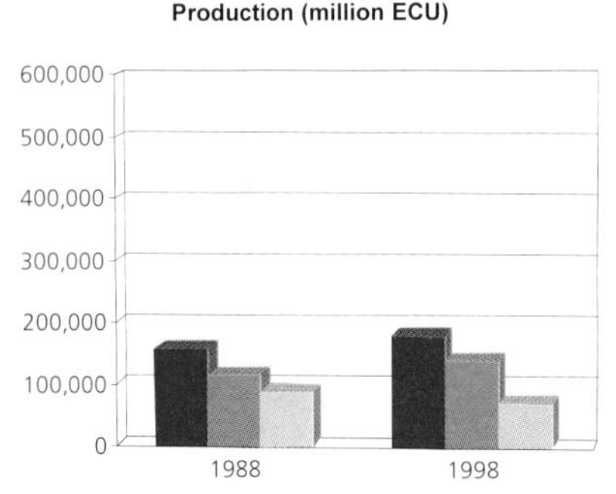

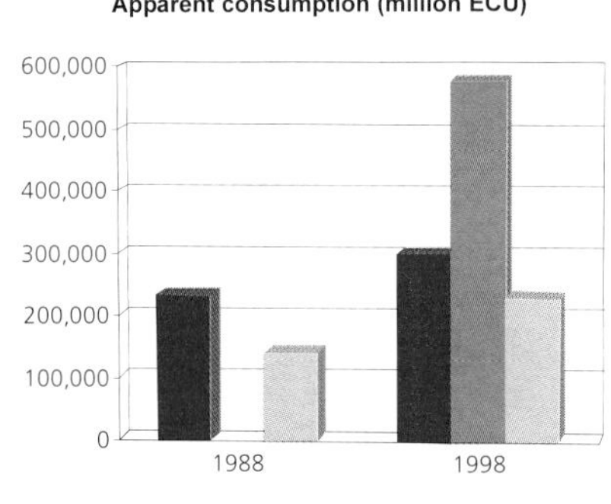

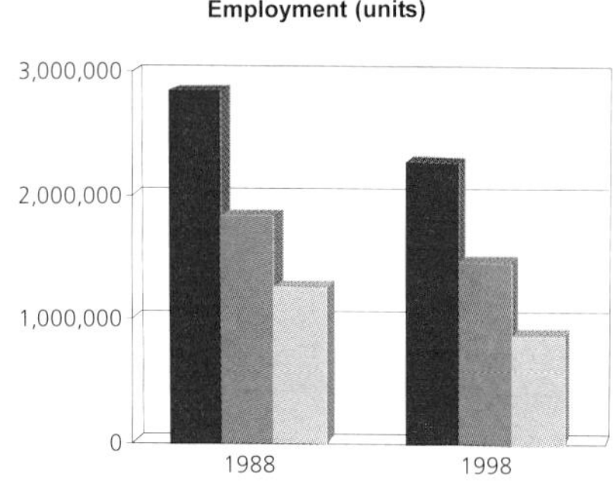

EU-15 USA Japan

Source: Eurostat (SBS)

The manufacture of textiles, clothing, leather and footwear was dominated by small and medium-sized enterprises. Spanish and Portuguese enterprises reported average production values below one million ECU, whereas in Italy and the United Kingdom the average enterprise generated about six million ECU of production value. The largest enterprises in the EU were found in Germany and Austria, equivalent to about 12 million ECU of production value per enterprise.

Smaller enterprises were well placed to serve niche markets and to react flexibly to changing fashion cycles. However, they suffered generally in the competitive environment, due to the fact that they were less active in the fields of research and development and new technologies. Larger enterprises had an advantage in serving clients abroad and in providing dedicated customer services. In addition, small manufacturers were placed under increasing pressure as the bargaining power of large retailers and wholesalers rose with the continued increase of concentration levels in the distributive trades.

The other main area where competition has increased in the last couple of decades is from low-wage cost countries. Low-price products from third countries (in particular south-east Asia and Eastern Europe) gained market share at a rapid pace. This was mainly a result of the fact that many parts of the industry require a high labour content as an input to the production process. Other activities such as the spinning, weaving and knitting of textiles or the cutting of clothing have become highly automated. Between 1988 and 1998 European manufacturers reduced the share of labour in the production process. One measure of labour intensity that we may use is the number of persons required to produce one million ECU of production value. In Italy this ratio fell by almost 4 persons per million ECU of output to 7.9 persons during the period 1988 and 1998. In Germany the number of persons required to produce one million ECU of output was almost halved to 8.3 persons. Within the Member States the ratio varied widely, from an average of almost 36 persons in Portugal to 6.9 persons employed in Denmark. However, labour costs varied significantly, for example, in Portugal employers paid average labour costs of 4.2 ECU per hour in the activity of leather and leather products, whilst their German[1] counterparts faced labour costs as high as 18.5 ECU per hour (1996).

1) Excluding the new Länder.

The differences in labour costs led in part to the relocation of the industry. European manufacturers were shifting production facilities of basic materials to low-wage countries, increasing their levels of outward processing (for example, activities such as the processing of fibres or fabrics, skins or leather). After sub-contractors or foreign affiliates have carried out the labour-intensive processing stage then the goods are often re-imported for further processing.

Suppliers in the EU sub-contracted to Eastern Europe or North African countries, but also on an intra-Community basis, for example to Portugal and Greece. As many sub-contractors were small enterprises and they were often specialised in this type of industrial relationship they were often heavily dependent on the lead contractor.

Figure 4.5 (ECU/hour)

Textiles, clothing, leather and footwear (NACE Rev. 1 17 to 19)

Labour costs by Member State, 1996

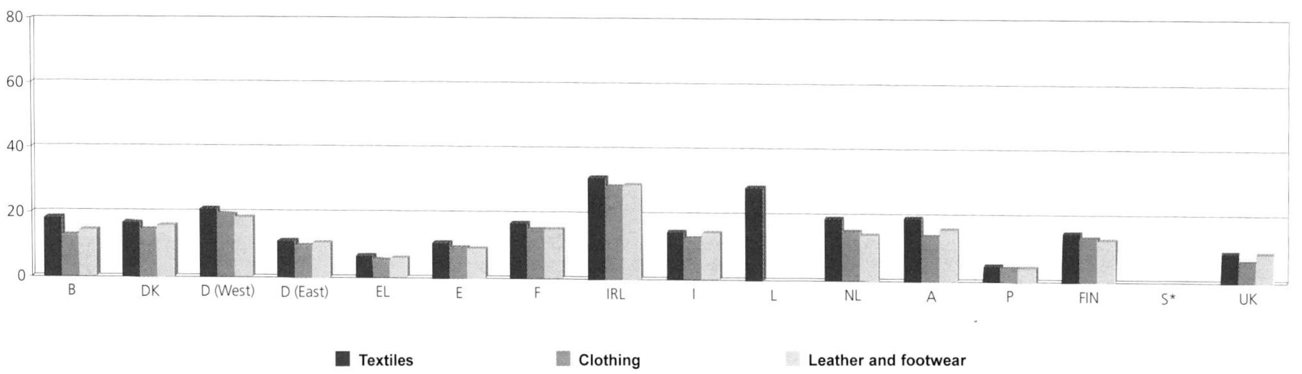

Source: Eurostat (LCS)

Recent trends

During the course of the nineties suppliers faced declining consumer expenditure as real incomes increased at a slow pace. In 1998 demand for textiles, clothing, leather and footwear was around 200 billion ECU. If we look at the changes in demand there was a varied picture across Europe. Whilst in Germany and the Netherlands the manufacture of textiles, clothing, leather and footwear saw demand decline, down by 8.2% and 14.6% between 1988 and 1998, it was increasing in France and the United Kingdom by 0.7% and 18.5%.

Attempts to re-define the market have included increasing the number of fashion cycles per year, developing niche markets or creating new materials, products and brands. These efforts have been reflected in more recent data on European output. Indeed, between 1993 and 1997 production values increased by 0.7% per annum in Italy and value added rose by 1.2% per annum (both in constant prices). In Spain production values also grew (up by 2.8% per annum over the same period).

Nevertheless, not all countries reported an expansion in production, France, Germany and Greece all reported that the manufacture of textiles, clothing, leather and footwear was down in 1998 (by 7.2%, 0.3% and 12.8% respectively compared to data from 1997).

The restructuring process led to a decrease in employment levels. Between 1988 and 1998 the number of persons employed in textiles, clothing, leather and footwear decreased by around 25% from 2.9 million persons to about 2.1 million persons. The decline in employment was seen throughout all Member States, although at a relatively slow pace in Italy and Belgium (with a total reduction of 12.2% and 16.4%), whilst at a considerably faster pace in Germany and Greece (down by 51.7% and 41.7% respectively).

On the other hand, with European producers concentrating more on design, materials and product development there was an increase in the number of highly educated personnel that were being employed.

Table 4.1 (%)

Textiles, clothing, leather and footwear (NACE Rev. 1 17 to 19)

Composition of the labour force, 1997

	Females	Part-time	Highly-educated
EU-15	:	:	:
B	50.4	3.5	12.8
DK	67.7	12.6	:
D	61.3	18.1	13.2
EL	56.9	4.4	4.2
E	58.8	8.9	5.9
F	61.4	7.7	6.8
IRL	57.2	6.4	8.7
I	61.7	5.5	1.3
L	:	:	:
NL	50.1	27.2	10.8
A	59.3	11.8	:
P	69.6	6.3	1.6
FIN	64.7	:	:
S	:	:	:
UK	54.6	15.2	7.8

Source: Eurostat (LFS)

Foreign trade

Textiles, clothing, leather and footwear were traded increasingly across borders, on the one hand due to liberalised world trade and on the other hand due to market conditions that led manufacturers to search for customers outside of domestic markets. In the EU the industry recorded a negative trade balance (although in textiles there was a small trade surplus). In the latter part of the nineties exports accounted for about 25% of total European production of textiles, clothing, leather and footwear. Imports from outside of the EU accounted for about 35% of apparent consumption. Both the export ratio and the import penetration ratio were rising during the last decade. These trends may be expected to continue as the protectionism that has characterised the industry is removed. The manufacture of textiles, clothing, leather and footwear was traditionally an activity protected by import tariffs and import quotas. International trade has been encouraged following the Agreement on Textiles and Clothing (ATC) that was negotiated within the framework of the World Trade Organisation (WTO). This agreement should be integrated into the general rules of the WTO by the year 2004. Indeed, the European Union has been reducing its tariffs and relaxing quotas since 1995. Imports from central and eastern European countries were liberalised at the start of 1998 and exports to these countries will follow between 1999 and 2002[2].

2) 1999 for exports to Poland; 2001 for Hungary, the Czech Republic, the Slovak Republic and Bulgaria; 2002 for Romania.

Figure 4.6

Textiles, clothing, leather and footwear (NACE Rev. 1 17 to 19)
Destination of EU exports, 1998

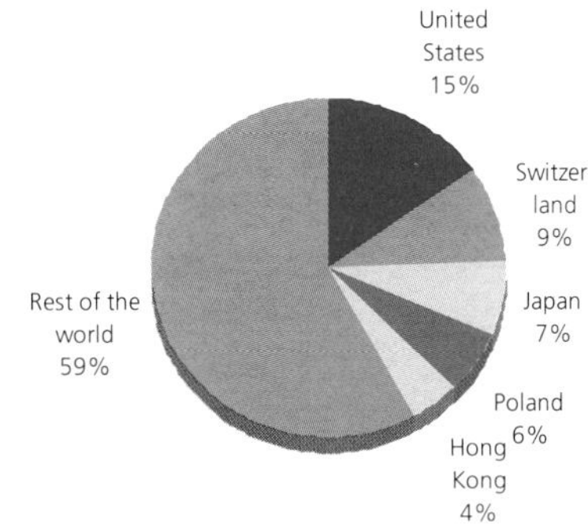

Source: Eurostat (Comext)

Figure 4.7

Textiles, clothing, leather and footwear (NACE Rev. 1 17 to 19)
Origin of EU imports, 1998

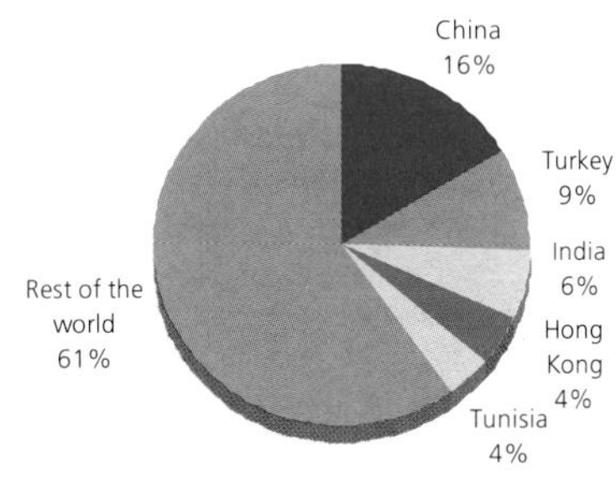

Source: Eurostat (Comext)

Manufacture of textiles
(NACE Rev. 1 17.1 to 17.3 and 17.6)

The manufacture of textiles includes the processing of raw materials, woven and knitted fabrics and their transformation into apparel, carpets or linen and industrial textiles in downstream industries. The manufacture of textiles encompasses the preparation and spinning of various textile fibres, the weaving, knitting and crocheting of textiles, as well as dyeing and printing.

European manufacturers of textiles recorded output of around 50 billion ECU in 1998, just under 1.5% of the manufacturing total for the EU, or just less than 25% of the aggregated output of textiles, clothing, leather and footwear.

The highest specialisation of output was in the southern Member States of Greece, Italy and Spain[3], where almost 50% of the EU's output was generated (Italy alone generated over 35% of the total in 1998). The Italian production specialisation ratio for textiles showed that textiles' output was more than two and a half times the European average (in relation to total manufacturing). Greece recorded a higher specialisation ratio, at over three times the European average. Within the other Member States specialisation ratios were generally below parity (100%), with particularly low figures in the Nordic countries (around 35% in Finland).

Man-made fibres made up two thirds of total fibre consumption, their price being largely influenced by the input price of chemicals. The main supply of natural fibres comes from outside of Europe. They are traded on international commodity markets and are subject to widely fluctuating prices.

EU textile manufacturers reduced their capacity during the course of the nineties, investing in new equipment and machinery and also in production facilities outside of Europe. The main advantage of keeping domestic manufacturing plants was that the goods remained close to the EU market. Business strategy was in part determined by the average size of enterprises and their geographical location. In the EU the average number of persons employed per enterprise ranged from as many as 140 in Germany to just 17 persons in Spain (figures for 1996).

3) Unfortunately, there was no data available for Portugal.

Figure 4.8

Manufacture of textiles (NACE Rev. 1 17.1 to 17.3 and 17.6)
Production and employment in the Triad

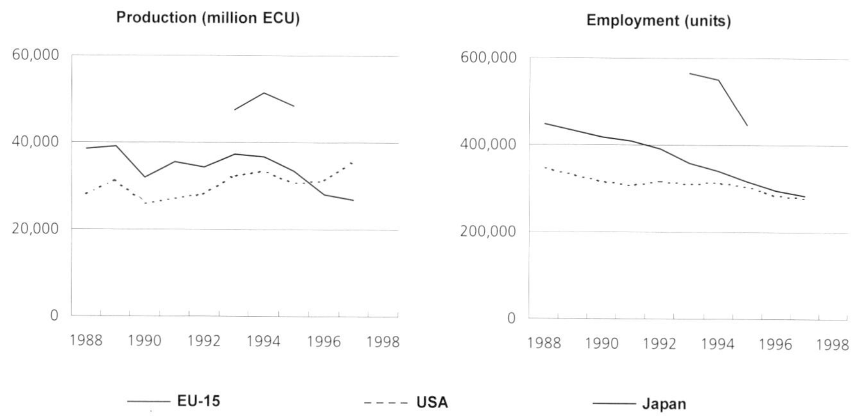

Source: Eurostat (SBS)

Figure 4.9 (%)

Manufacture of textiles (NACE Rev. 1 17.1, 17.2 and 17.6)
Production and export specialisation by Member State, 1998

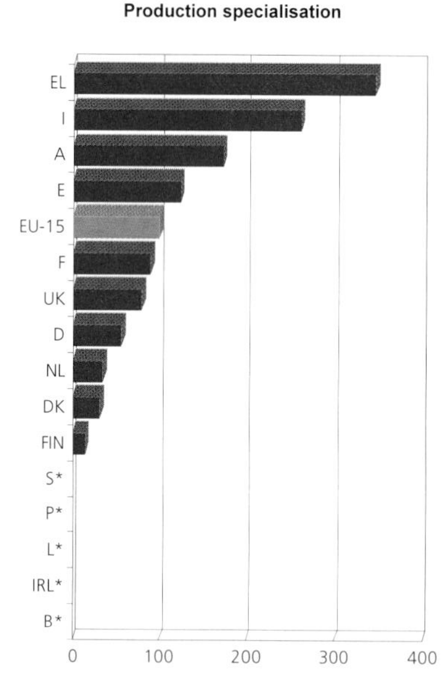

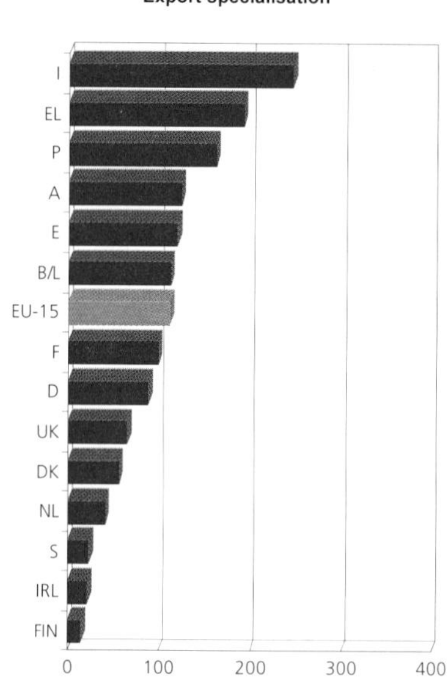

Source: Eurostat (SBS)

If we look at the period between 1993 and 1998 there was a varied pattern to the development of output across Europe. Production values (in constant prices) increased moderately in Italy (by 0.8% per annum) and at a faster pace in Spain (by 3.2% per annum), whilst they fell in the Netherlands (by 5.2% per annum) and in Greece (by 3.8% per annum), for 1993 to 1997).

Competitive pressure generally led to a reduction in the number of persons employed. In the five years to 1998, employment levels decreased in Italy and in France by 0.5% and 0.7% per annum respectively, whilst in Greece they fell at a faster pace, by 4.5% per annum. Spain was the only country where there was an increase in the number of persons employed (up by 0.9% per annum over the period 1993 to 1998).

Small and medium-sized enterprises in this industry relied to a large degree on research centres (founded by trade associations or universities) in order to improve machinery and equipment. In addition, the manufacture of textiles was forced to adapt to new technological advances and developments in the business environment, for example, the development of quick-response and just-in-time production.

International comparisons show that the EU produced more textiles than the other two Triad economies. EU output in 1997 was 1.4 times and 1.8 times larger than the respective production levels of the USA and Japan. Recent trends show that production expanded at a fast pace in the USA (up by 13.8% in 1997), whilst decreasing in Japan by 3.8% (again 1996 compared to 1997). The decline in employment levels seen in the EU were mirrored in the remaining Triad economies, with employment falling by 3.0% per annum and 5.6% per annum in the USA and Japan respectively between 1993 and 1997.

European manufacturers of textiles were increasingly active on foreign markets, seen in fast growing extra-EU exports[4]. Between 1988 and 1998, deliveries to third countries increased at a faster pace than imports.

4) No foreign trade data was available for NACE Rev. 1 17.3.

Figure 4.10

Manufacture of textiles
(NACE Rev. 1 17.1, 17.2 and 17.6)
Destination of EU exports, 1998

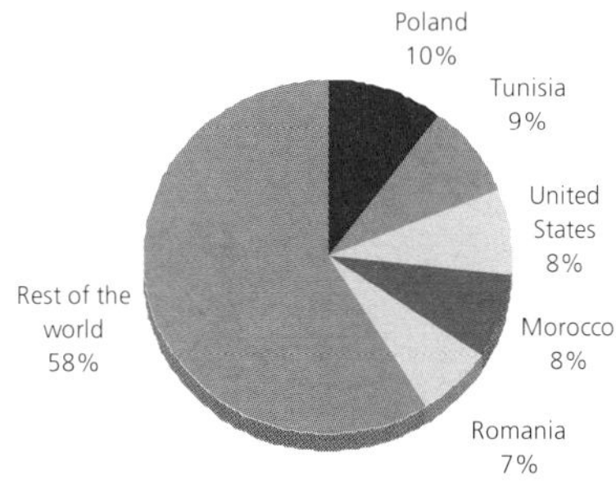

Source: Eurostat (Comext)

Figure 4.11

Manufacture of textiles
(NACE Rev. 1 17.1, 17.2 and 17.6)
Origin of EU imports, 1998

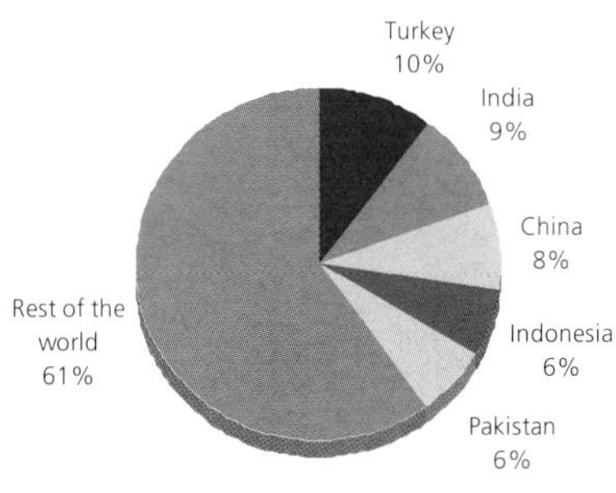

Source: Eurostat (Comext)

Made-up textiles and other textiles (NACE Rev. 1 17.4 and 17.5)

Woven and knitted fabrics are processed into apparel, as well as textiles and decorations used within the home. Made-up textile articles are delivered to a large extent to distributive trades for sale to consumers. As well as being used by private households, other major market segments include bed linen for hotels and kitchen linen for restaurants.

The grouping of "other textiles" combines carpets, cordage, rope and non-woven textiles that can be often be quite sophisticated material, such as tyre cord fabric made with high-tenacity, man-made yarn. The manufacture of textiles other than for apparel has seen an increase in demand for textile products requiring a high degree of technical expertise. In France the manufacture of these textiles accounted for 10% of the total fabric consumption in 1997, whilst in Germany the share rose to as high as 25% in 1998[5]. In some Member States, for example Germany, there was considerable pressure from the environmental lobby to recycle textile fibres, for example used carpets.

The manufacture of made-up textiles and other textiles accounted for over 15% of the total aggregated production value of textiles, clothing, leather and footwear in the EU (equivalent to 0.8% of production value for total manufacturing). In 1998, Belgium was one of the main EU producers, responsible for around 12% of total EU output.

5) Figures from the national trade associations of textiles: Union des Industries Textiles in France and Gesamttextil - e.V. in Germany.

Figure 4.12

Made-up textiles and other textiles (NACE Rev. 1 17.4 and 17.5)

Production and employment in the Triad

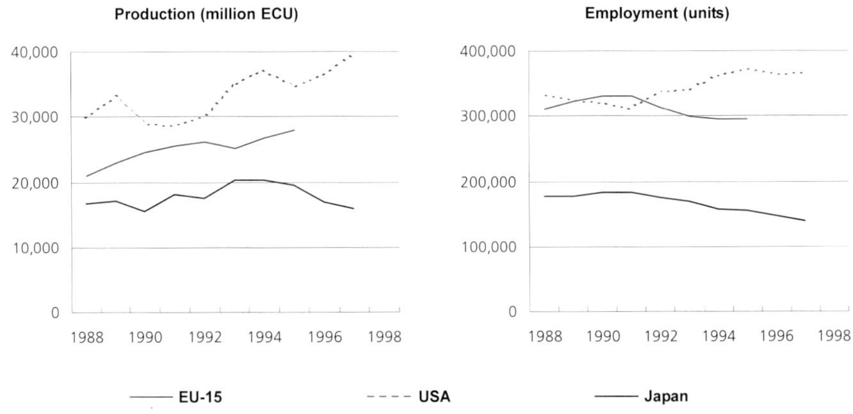

Source: Eurostat (SBS)

Figure 4.13 (%)

Made-up textiles and other textiles (NACE Rev. 1 17.4 and 17.5)

Production and export specialisation by Member State, 1998

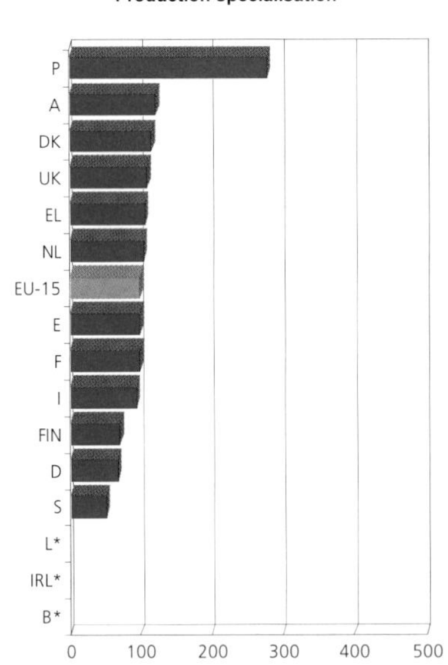

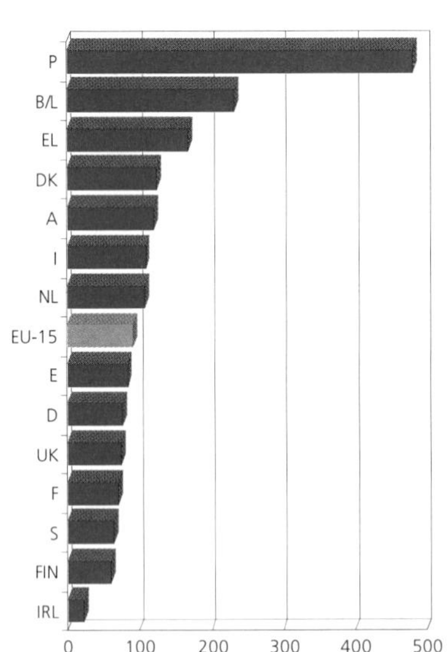

Source: Eurostat (SBS)

In the decade up to 1998, output increased by some 33% to be worth a total of around 30 billion ECU. Even though production of made-up textiles and other textiles expanded within the EU, the sector faced increased competition. In absolute terms, the number of persons employed remained almost unchanged in Europe during the nineties. If we look at the ratio of the number of persons employed per one million ECU of production value, it is interesting to note that reductions were recorded in every Member State for which data was available. This was equally true in countries where low hourly labour costs were reported, such as Portugal, where labour intensity was reduced by a third between 1993 and 1998, resulting in 23.6 persons being required to produce one million ECU of output. During the same period, the United Kingdom reported that labour intensity fell by 6 persons to an average of 10.4 persons employed per one million ECU of output.

The manufacture of made-up textiles and other textiles reported a high degree of international trade. Exports accounted for a large share of domestic output in both France (45.2%) and Germany (58.1%) in 1998. However, in both countries imports exceeded exports, although in France at a diminishing rate. Italy was one of the Member States with a trade balance that turned positive between 1988 and 1998, with exports outside the EU increasing by more than 200%, whilst Italian extra-EU imports rose by 70%.

Figure 4.14

Made-up textiles and other textiles (NACE Rev. 1 17.4 and 17.5) Destination of EU exports, 1998

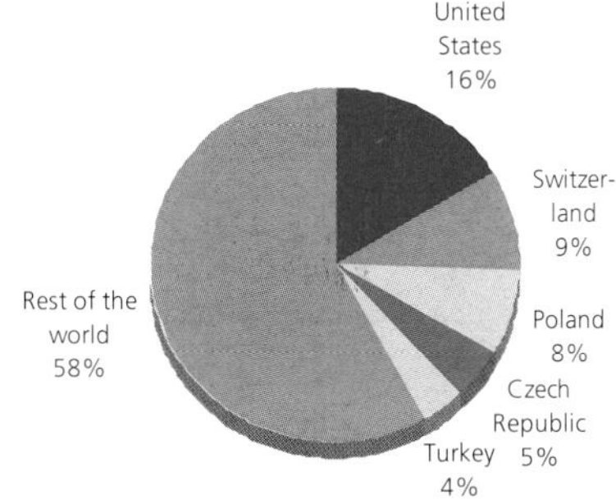

Source: Eurostat (Comext)

Figure 4.15

Made-up textiles and other textiles (NACE Rev. 1 17.4 and 17.5) Origin of EU imports, 1998

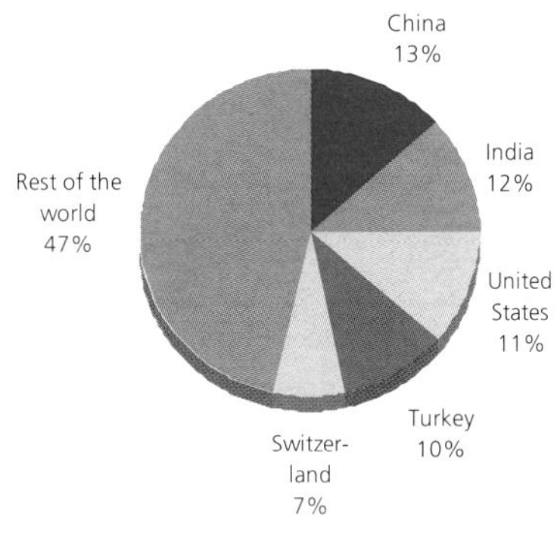

Source: Eurostat (Comext)

Clothing, including knitted articles (NACE Rev. 1 17.7 and 18)

In 1998 the clothing sector (including knitted articles) produced goods worth around 65 billion ECU, or some 1.5% of the total manufacturing production value of the EU. Measured as a share of total output for textiles, clothing, leather and footwear this activity accounted for about 33% of the total. The industry provides wearing apparel such as workwear, outerwear, underwear and leather clothes or articles made of fur (as covered by NACE Rev. 1 18), as well as hosiery, pullovers and cardigans (as covered by NACE Rev. 1 17.7). Besides the mere sewing or knitting of apparel, the manufacture of clothing also encompasses the design, purchase of fabrics and dispatch of goods. One final activity that is covered by the data presented in this section is the dressing and dyeing of fur (NACE Rev. 1 18.3).

Figure 4.16

Clothing including knitted articles (NACE Rev. 1 17.7 and 18)
Production and employment in the Triad

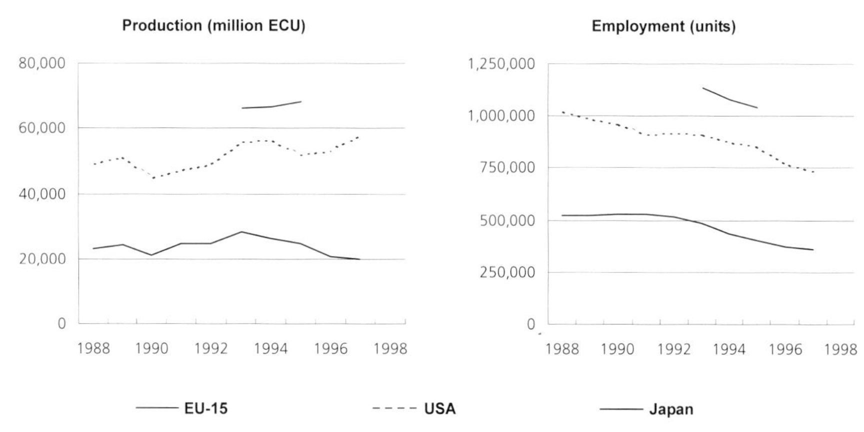

Source: Eurostat (SBS)

Figure 4.17 (cumulative % of total)

Private and commercial consumption of clothing and textiles in the EU, 1997

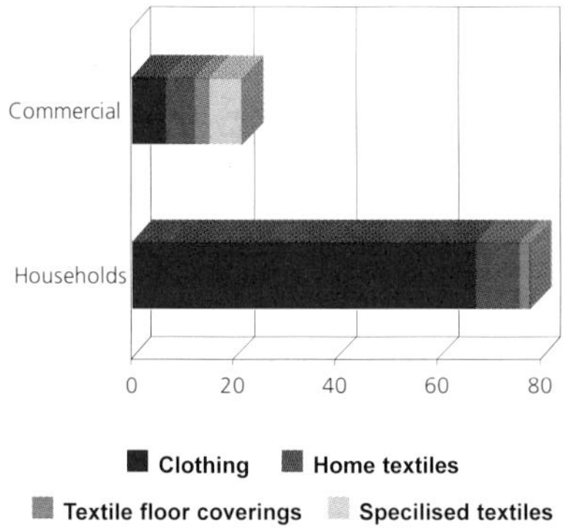

Source: OETH

Figure 4.18 (%)

Clothing including knitted articles (NACE Rev. 1 17.7 and 18)
Production and export specialisation by Member State, 1998

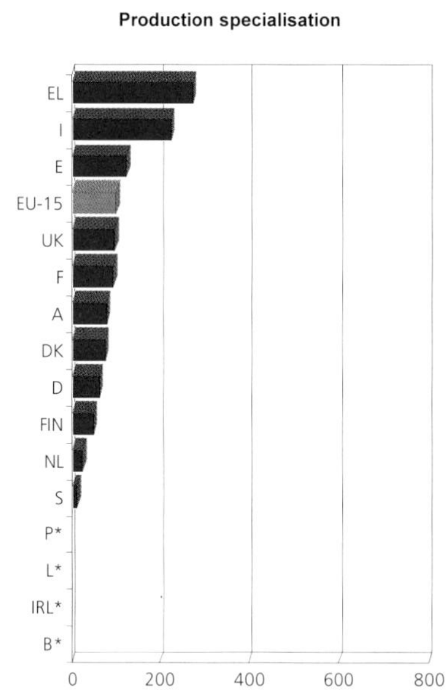

Source: Eurostat (SBS)

As with many of the textile industries, the clothing industry in the EU is largely concentrated in the southern Member States. Italy and Spain together accounted for 45% of European output. Indeed, the Italian clothing sector contributed almost two and half times more to its domestic manufacturing total than the European average. Greece reported a similar specialisation ratio, whilst the share of clothing (without knitted articles) in Portuguese total manufacturing was as high as 3.5 times the European average. The United Kingdom was relatively specialised in the sector of knitted and crocheted articles (almost 1.5 times the European average).

The clothing industry produces almost exclusively consumer goods, other than uniforms and protective clothing for commercial use. The former made up more than 90% of the total European clothing market (figures for 1997).

Fashion cycles for clothing are becoming increasingly shorter and suppliers are being asked to adapt their production processes to quick-response technologies, so as to make clothes on demand. This is particularly the case for large retailers. The tendency to reduce stocks and the on-going concentration of the retail sector have increased the risk for many clothing manufacturers as many small enterprises only sell to a single customer. In addition, European manufacturers have faced increasing competition from low-price products made in developing countries and Eastern Europe. Clothing manufacturers in the EU have made an effort to create new brands and products, as well as innovating with respect to design and new markets. The higher-end of the EU clothing market is increasingly susceptible to brand piracy, whereby cheap imitations and counterfeits of brand goods are offered to consumers.

Within several Member States, such as Germany, France or Greece, clothing production was on a downward trend. The efforts to restructure the business have led to reductions in the labour force. These changes may be partly explained by the shift to outward processing, whereby labour-intensive production has been shifted to low-wage cost countries. Despite to the slight upward trend in production registered in Italy and Spain, there was a reduction in the number of persons employed, equal to 1.4% per annum and 2.0% per annum over the period 1993 to 1998. In Germany and Denmark the decline in employment was more pronounced, at over 10.3% per annum.

In the EU the number of persons employed in the manufacture of clothing fell below the level of one million in 1998. Nevertheless, the sector was still an important employer in regional centres where there would otherwise be much higher unemployment.

(%) Figure 4.19

Breakdown of household clothing consumption in the EU

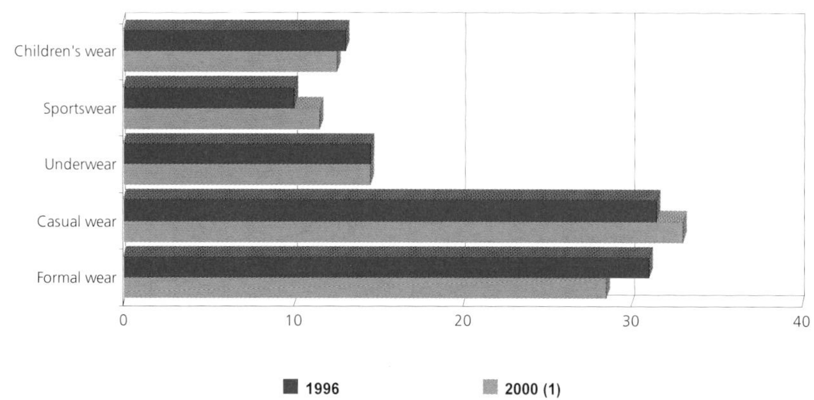

(1) OETH forecast.

Source: OETH

Following the efforts to liberalise world markets through the WTO, international trade in clothing increased during the course of the nineties. Even though extra-EU exports increased faster than imports, there was still a deficit in the EU. Indeed, Italy, Portugal and Greece were the only countries with a positive trade balance for clothing. Italian producers in particular had a good reputation for modern clothing and this was confirmed by the export rate which showed that 57.5% of Italian production was destined for foreign markets in 1998. On the other hand, the domestic market became increasingly open too, with 34.9% of the Italian consumption originating from outside of Italy.

Figure 4.20

Clothing including knitted articles (NACE Rev. 1 17.7 and 18) Destination of EU exports, 1998

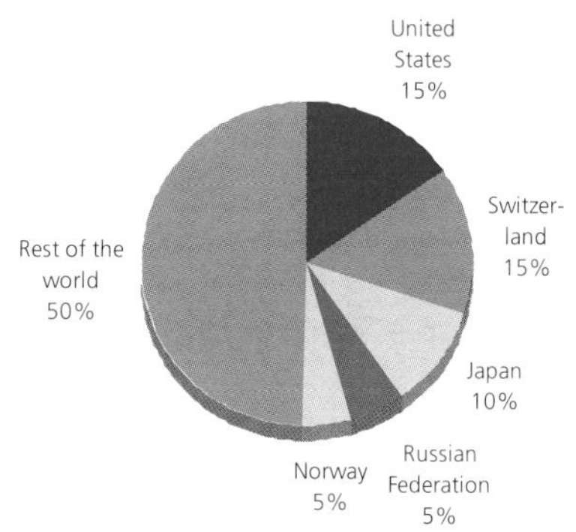

Source: Eurostat (Comext)

Figure 4.21

Clothing including knitted articles (NACE Rev. 1 17.7 and 18) Origin of EU imports, 1998

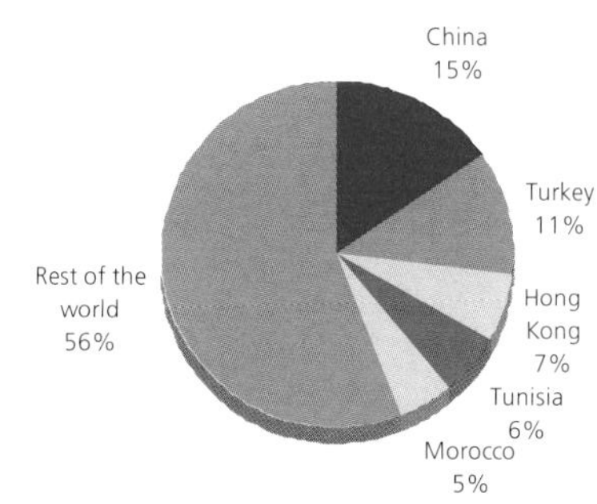

Source: Eurostat (Comext)

Leather and footwear (NACE Rev. 1 19)

Leather has a long tradition as a raw material. It is appreciated as it generally has a long life and is quite robust as a material for clothing and footwear. Leather is a derived product made from the hides and skins of animals. The treatment of leather usually begins with treatment by tanners and dressers, before further processing leads to the production of various consumer goods such as shoes, luggage or handbags.

In 1998 the manufacture of leather and leather products employed some 360 thousand persons in the EU, together they were responsible for output that was worth 33 billion ECU, or 18% of the total production value of the textiles, clothing, leather and footwear industries combined.

Once again the highest specialisation ratios were found in the southern Member States. In 1998, Italy accounted for 45% of European output. With the addition of Spain and Portugal, these three countries accounted for two-thirds of the European leather industry. Italian industry was highly specialised, accounting for 3.2 times the average EU share in total manufacturing. The Portuguese production specialisation ratio was even higher at almost 5 times the European average.

Demand for leather products is determined largely by changes in consumer tastes that vary over time and between regions. In some niche markets, leather products are still seen as luxury goods. During times of recession there is a tendency to substitute leather with cheaper materials. Alternative market pressure comes from large clothing producers who have expanded their product ranges to include both footwear and other leather products. EU leather manufacturers have responded to increased competition by raising quality and design. Another trend that has developed is the introduction of factory retail outlets for leather goods, as well as the development of retail chains by some manufacturers.

Figure 4.22

Leather and footwear (NACE Rev. 1 19)

Production and employment in the Triad

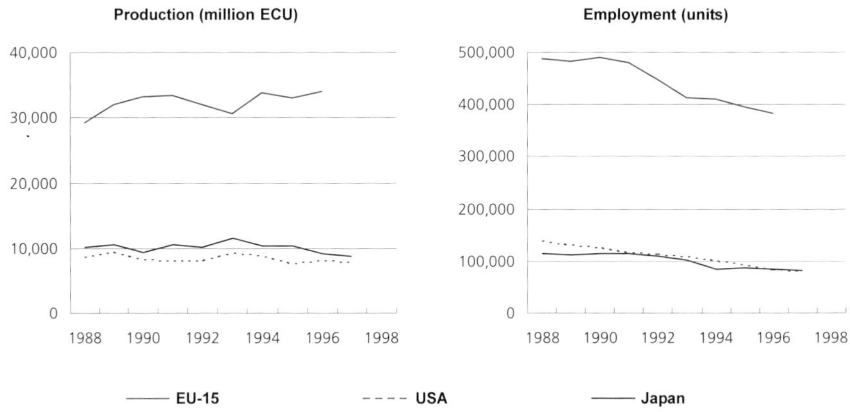

Source: Eurostat (SBS)

Figure 4.23 (%)

Leather and footwear (NACE Rev. 1 19)

Production and export specialisation by Member State, 1998

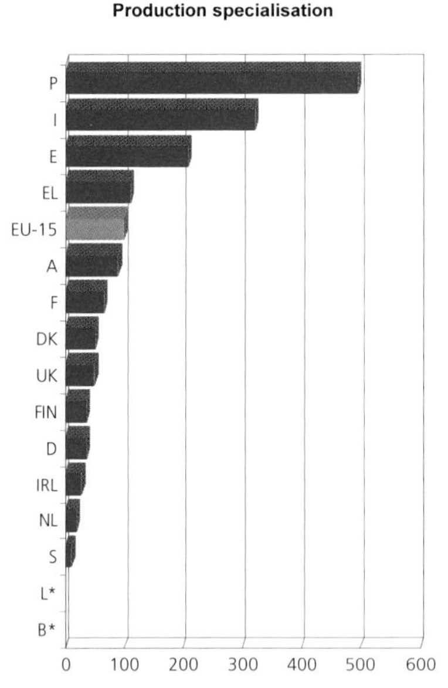

Source: Eurostat (SBS)

(square metres) Figure 4.24

Tanning and dressing of cattle, calf, sheep and goat hides in the EU, 1997

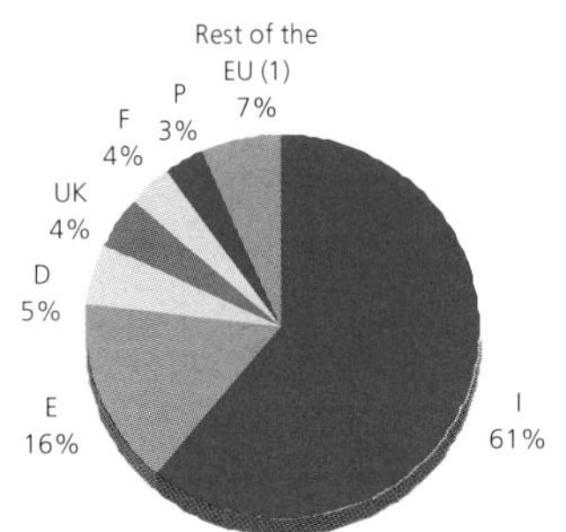

(1) Excluding Luxembourg and the Netherlands.

Source: COTANCE

The restructuring process led to measures to reduce labour costs and logistics. Further steps were taken in adapting the production process to produce higher quality products within a shorter reaction time. One area where this trend is particularly evident is the manufacture of sports shoes, where product lines change at an incredibly fast pace, driven by high consumer awareness for the latest products.

Many European manufacturers of footwear have decided to specialise in high value added products. Others have moved into specialist markets such as shoes that are made-to-order (customised production to an agreed specification with a designer label). This development has resulted in a much higher degree of consultation and co-operation with the final customer.

Whilst the German footwear industry recorded a period of decreasing production values during the course of the nineties, new investments were made in new machinery and information technology between 1995 and 1998[6], doubling the level of investment.

6) Hauptverband der Deutschen Schuhindustrie e.V. (German trade association for footwear).

The manufacture of leather and leather products is also generally a labour intensive exercise. On the one hand there was a shift of production facilities to low-wage countries in Eastern European countries, or south-east Asia and China for sports footwear. On the other hand, European manufacturers tried to reduce the share of labour in the production process. In Italy the number of persons employed on average for each one million ECU of production value decreased by more than 4 persons to just 7.1 persons (over the period 1988 to 1998). In absolute terms, the number of persons employed in Germany fell by 8.8% per annum and in the United Kingdom by 13.1% per annum during the period 1993 to 1998. There were however gains recorded in Spain, where the number of persons employed increased by 4.0% per annum. In some EU countries, leather manufacturers faced additional costs to meet guidelines on the use of natural resources: for example, investment in water treatment techniques and the recycling of waste and by-products.

In January 1999, EU import tariffs on ladies' leather sandals, boots and platform sandals fell to just 5%. However, higher import tariffs remained for countries such as China and Indonesia, who were accused of anti-competitive dumping practices.

The trade balance of the EU remained negative in 1998 (despite a surplus in Spain, Italy and Portugal - the main areas of output in the EU). Between 1993 and 1998 the value of foreign trade in the EU grew at almost equal rates, with extra-EU exports rising by 45.5% and extra-EU imports increasing by 44.0%.

Figure 4.25

Leather and footwear (NACE Rev. 1 19) Destination of EU exports, 1998

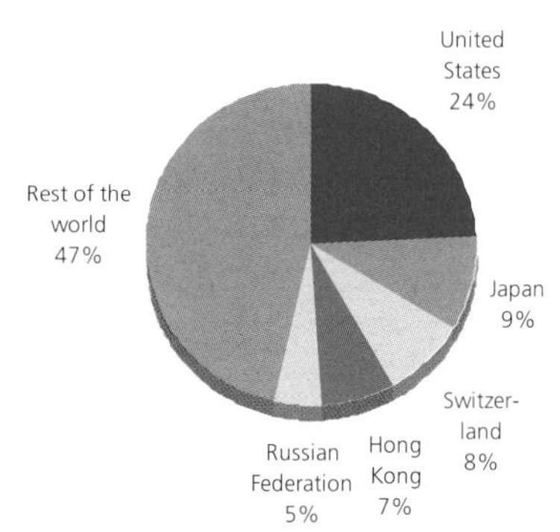

Source: Eurostat (Comext)

Figure 4.26

Leather and footwear (NACE Rev. 1 19) Origin of EU imports, 1998

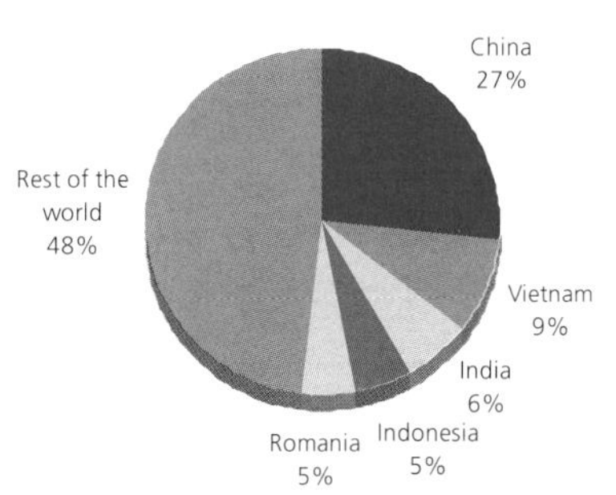

Source: Eurostat (Comext)

Professional associations representing the industries within this chapter

CIRFS
International Rayon and Synthetic Fibres Committee
4, avenue E. Van Nieuwenhuyse
B-1160 Bruxelles
tel: (32) 2 676 74 55
fax: (32) 2 676 74 54
e-mail:
bru@cirfs.org

COTANCE
Confédération des Associations Nationales de Tanneurs et Mégissiers de la CE
3, rue Belliard
B-1040 Bruxelles
tel (32) 2 512 77 03
fax (32) 2 512 91 57

OETH
European Observatory of Clothing Industry
197, rue Belliard, boîte 9
B-1040 Bruxelles
tel: (32) 2 230 32 82
fax: (32) 2 230 43 34
e-mail:
info@oeth.com

Table 4.2 (million ECU)

Preparation and spinning of textile fibres (NACE Rev. 1 17.1)

Production related indicators in the EU

	1988	1989	1990	1991	1992	1993	1994	1995	1996	1997	1998
Production value	:	:	:	:	:	15,447	17,456	15,908	:	:	:
Producer price index (1995=100)	:	:	:	:	:	:	:	:	:	:	:
Value added	:	:	:	:	:	4,903	5,508	4,787	:	:	:
Number of persons employed (thousands)	:	:	:	:	:	187.9	186.4	144.3	:	:	:

Table 4.3 (million ECU)

Preparation and spinning of textile fibres (NACE Rev. 1 17.1)

Production related indicators, 1998

	B	DK	D	EL	E	F	IRL	I	L	NL	A	P	FIN	S	UK
Production value (1)	574	27	1,691	451	1,731	1,919	86	6,537	0	53	874	:	25	2	1,851
Value added (1)	192	12	527	149	491	535	30	1,822	0	18	408	:	8	1	627
Number of persons employed (units) (2)	4,781	200	13,721	8,282	13,042	18,663	1,062	42,866	0	1,612	5,510	:	389	48	21,216

(1) L (1996). (2) L (1996); NL (1992).

Table 4.4 (million ECU)

Preparation and spinning of textile fibres (NACE Rev. 1 17.1)

Market related indicators in the EU

	1988	1989	1990	1991	1992	1993	1994	1995	1996	1997	1998
Apparent consumption	:	:	:	:	:	15,877	18,306	16,646	:	:	:
Exports	1,832	1,784	1,507	1,450	1,459	1,575	1,855	1,858	1,855	1,965	1,866
Imports	2,530	2,570	2,426	2,390	2,210	2,005	2,705	2,596	2,504	3,054	3,007
Trade balance	-698	-786	-919	-939	-752	-430	-850	-738	-649	-1,089	-1,141
Export ratio (%)	:	:	:	:	:	10.2	10.6	11.7	:	:	:
Import penetration ratio (%)	:	:	:	:	:	12.6	14.8	15.6	:	:	:
Cover ratio (%)	72.4	69.4	62.1	60.7	66.0	78.6	68.6	71.6	74.1	64.3	62.1

Table 4.5 (million ECU)

Preparation and spinning of textile fibres (NACE Rev. 1 17.1)

Market related indicators, 1998

	B/L	DK	D	EL	E	F	IRL	I	NL	A	P	FIN	S	UK
Apparent consumption	:	126	1,712	434	1,725	1,826	138	6,596	167	874	:	57	44	2,092
Exports	621	40	1,282	168	421	939	80	1,665	85	222	119	12	16	673
Imports	811	139	1,303	151	414	846	131	1,724	200	221	481	44	57	914
Trade balance	-190	-99	-21	17	6	93	-51	-59	-115	1	-363	-32	-42	-241
Export ratio (%)	:	147.9	75.8	37.2	24.3	48.9	92.1	25.5	161.9	25.4	:	46.7	784.0	36.4
Import penetration ratio (%)	:	110.2	76.1	34.7	24.0	46.3	95.0	26.1	119.5	25.3	:	76.8	131.7	43.7
Cover ratio (%)	76.6	28.6	98.4	111.6	101.5	111.0	60.8	96.6	42.7	100.4	24.7	26.4	27.6	73.7

Table 4.6

Preparation and spinning of textile fibres (NACE Rev. 1 17.1)

Labour related indicators, 1998

	EU-15	B	DK	D	EL	E	F	IRL	I	L	NL	A	P	FIN	S	UK
Personnel costs (million ECU) (1)	3,262	121	7	422	111	311	463	21	1,075	0	16	233	:	8	1	459
Personnel costs/employee (thousand ECU) (2)	23.0	25.7	33.9	31.1	14.7	17.4	25.1	20.4	22.9	:	:	40.6	:	23.4	21.3	17.7
Social charges/personnel costs (%) (3)	24.3	29.2	6.3	20.1	24.4	22.2	29.0	14.1	36.9	:	12.7	22.9	:	19.8	:	12.7
Labour productivity (thousand ECU/head) (4)	33.2	40.2	61.7	38.4	18.0	37.7	28.7	27.8	42.5	:	32.3	74.1	:	21.6	12.8	29.5
Wage adjusted labour productivity (%) (2)	144.5	130.9	161.3	121.3	109.6	147.7	120.7	139.8	174.4	:	:	174.0	:	108.6	61.9	139.6

(1) EU-15 (1995); L (1996); E (1997). (2) EU-15, EL, I, A (1995); B, DK, D, E, F, IRL, FIN, S, UK (1996). (3) EU-15 (1995); E (1997). (4) NL (1992); EU-15 (1995).

Source: Eurostat (SBS, EBT)

(million ECU) Table 4.7

Textile weaving (NACE Rev. 1 17.2)
Production related indicators in the EU

	1988	1989	1990	1991	1992	1993	1994	1995	1996	1997	1998
Production value	:	:	:	:	:	18,935	20,171	19,773	:	:	:
Producer price index (1995=100)	:	:	:	:	:	:	:	:	:	:	:
Value added	:	:	:	:	:	6,013	6,272	6,137	:	:	:
Number of persons employed (thousands)	:	:	:	:	:	205.0	195.3	163.9	:	:	:

(million ECU) Table 4.8

Textile weaving (NACE Rev. 1 17.2)
Production related indicators, 1998

	B	DK	D	EL	E	F	IRL	I	L	NL	A	P	FIN	S	UK
Production value (1)	1,156	76	3,707	131	1,562	3,287	114	7,576	0	307	349	:	51	188	1,544
Value added (1)	404	29	1,130	41	453	868	39	2,615	0	111	142	:	11	63	548
Number of persons employed (units) (2)	9,926	611	26,369	1,983	22,348	21,292	1,244	50,019	0	4,010	3,302	:	297	1,861	17,141

(1) L (1996). (2) L (1996); NL (1992).

(million ECU) Table 4.9

Textile weaving (NACE Rev. 1 17.2)
Market related indicators in the EU

	1988	1989	1990	1991	1992	1993	1994	1995	1996	1997	1998
Apparent consumption	:	:	:	:	:	15,664	16,572	15,593	:	:	:
Exports	4,419	5,449	5,792	5,984	6,411	7,002	7,838	8,486	8,910	9,922	10,083
Imports	3,415	3,888	4,137	3,998	3,765	3,731	4,238	4,306	4,361	4,995	5,078
Trade balance	1,004	1,561	1,655	1,986	2,646	3,271	3,599	4,180	4,548	4,927	5,005
Export ratio (%)	:	:	:	:	:	37.0	38.9	42.9	:	:	:
Import penetration ratio (%)	:	:	:	:	:	23.8	25.6	27.6	:	:	:
Cover ratio (%)	129.4	140.1	140.0	149.7	170.3	187.7	184.9	197.1	204.3	198.7	198.6

(million ECU) Table 4.10

Textile weaving (NACE Rev. 1 17.2)
Market related indicators, 1998

	B/L	DK	D	EL	E	F	IRL	I	NL	A	P	FIN	S	UK
Apparent consumption	:	206	2,237	416	1,439	2,302	131	3,300	62	200	:	134	214	2,678
Exports	2,054	192	4,568	54	1,075	3,046	102	6,186	870	546	403	64	213	1,508
Imports	1,118	322	3,097	339	952	2,062	119	1,909	625	397	657	147	238	2,643
Trade balance	936	-130	1,470	-285	123	985	-17	4,277	245	149	-254	-83	-26	-1,134
Export ratio (%)	:	254.0	123.2	41.3	68.8	92.7	89.4	81.6	283.1	156.4	:	126.7	113.0	97.7
Import penetration ratio (%)	:	156.5	138.5	81.5	66.2	89.6	90.8	57.9	1,008.1	198.6	:	110.1	111.4	98.7
Cover ratio (%)	183.7	59.6	147.5	16.0	113.0	147.8	85.8	324.0	139.3	137.6	61.3	43.6	89.2	57.1

Table 4.11

Textile weaving (NACE Rev. 1 17.2)
Labour related indicators, 1998

	EU-15	B	DK	D	EL	E	F	IRL	I	L	NL	A	P	FIN	S	UK
Personnel costs (million ECU) (1)	4,142	277	20	867	29	353	581	31	1,361	0	76	104	:	7	53	394
Personnel costs/employee (thousand ECU) (2)	25.9	30.3	32.2	32.9	16.1	16.8	27.6	25.4	24.9	:	:	31.5	:	23.7	29.7	18.8
Social charges/personnel costs (%) (3)	24.7	29.0	6.9	19.9	25.2	22.7	29.1	23.1	36.6	:	18.0	22.8	:	18.2	28.5	13.3
Labour productivity (thousand ECU/head) (4)	37.4	40.7	46.9	42.9	20.4	20.3	40.8	31.3	52.3	:	37.9	43.1	:	38.5	33.7	32.0
Wage adjusted labour productivity (%) (2)	144.7	138.4	128.9	119.2	109.7	146.1	136.0	115.2	181.3	:	:	128.0	:	136.2	117.3	149.9

(1) EU-15 (1995); L (1996). (2) EU-15, EL, I, A (1995); B, DK, D, E, F, IRL, FIN, S, UK (1996). (3) S (1994); EU-15 (1995). (4) NL (1992); EU-15 (1995).

Source: Eurostat (SBS, EBT)

Table 4.12 (million ECU)

Finishing of textiles (NACE Rev. 1 17.3)

Production related indicators in the EU

	1988	1989	1990	1991	1992	1993	1994	1995	1996	1997	1998
Production value	8,624	10,637	10,654	10,742	9,865	9,171	9,760	9,438	:	:	:
Producer price index (1995=100)	:	:	:	:	:	:	:	:	:	:	:
Value added	3,721	4,107	4,112	3,590	4,160	3,763	3,937	3,746	:	:	:
Number of persons employed (thousands)	143.7	151.4	150.5	147.2	136.2	126.3	125.2	111.3	:	:	:

Table 4.13 (million ECU)

Finishing of textiles (NACE Rev. 1 17.3)

Production related indicators, 1998

	B	DK	D	EL	E	F	IRL	I	L	NL	A	P	FIN	S	UK
Production value (1)	375	46	1,546	96	1,036	1,558	:	3,376	0	289	226	:	23	29	1,246
Value added (1)	134	25	552	53	412	565	:	1,460	0	141	89	:	11	12	577
Number of persons employed (units) (2)	3,532	529	16,095	2,172	17,486	15,024	:	34,967	0	3,330	2,041	:	339	346	14,497

(1) L (1996). (2) L (1996); NL (1992).

Table 4.14

Finishing of textiles (NACE Rev. 1 17.3)

Labour related indicators, 1998

	EU-15	B	DK	D	EL	E	F	IRL	I	L	NL	A	P	FIN	S	UK
Personnel costs (million ECU) (1)	2,826	85	18	486	31	306	417	:	971	0	90	76	:	7	10	350
Personnel costs/employee (thousand ECU) (2)	26.2	26.8	32.8	32.3	15.7	19.0	28.1	:	25.4	:	:	35.9	:	23.6	29.2	19.8
Social charges/personnel costs (%) (3)	24.4	26.5	6.8	9.9	23.7	22.3	30.0	:	36.8	:	16.5	22.5	:	19.8	27.3	12.4
Labour productivity (thousand ECU/head) (4)	33.6	37.9	46.5	34.3	24.2	23.5	37.6	:	41.8	:	43.2	43.5	:	33.9	33.9	39.8
Wage adjusted labour productivity (%) (2)	128.5	127.6	125.6	102.7	135.7	123.0	121.7	:	150.9	:	:	114.1	:	128.8	120.3	146.0

(1) EU-15 (1995); L (1996). (2) EU-15, EL, I, A (1995); B, DK, D, E, F, IRL, FIN, S, UK (1996). (3) S (1994); EU-15 (1995). (4) NL (1992); EU-15 (1995).

Source: Eurostat (SBS, EBT)

(million ECU) Table 4.15

Manufacture of made-up textile articles, except apparel (NACE Rev. 1 17.4)
Production related indicators in the EU

	1988	1989	1990	1991	1992	1993	1994	1995	1996	1997	1998
Production value	7,042	7,708	8,282	8,807	9,146	8,719	9,217	8,397	:	:	:
Producer price index (1995=100)	:	:	90.5	92.4	94.2	95.3	97.1	100.0	101.6	102.0	103.1
Value added	2,504	2,707	2,756	3,131	3,215	3,109	3,253	2,853	:	:	:
Number of persons employed (thousands)	125.5	132.2	132.8	134.2	125.6	122.3	122.6	103.2	:	:	:

(million ECU) Table 4.16

Manufacture of made-up textile articles, except apparel (NACE Rev. 1 17.4)
Production related indicators, 1998

	B	DK	D	EL	E	F	IRL	I	L	NL	A	P	FIN	S	UK
Production value	826	168	1,708	92	1,204	1,164	:	1,133	:	258	203	58	108	91	1,760
Value added	255	73	671	32	326	362	:	372	:	98	106	:	40	31	702
Number of persons employed (units) (1)	6,503	1,711	19,226	1,779	21,365	12,653	:	8,905	:	3,221	2,242	2,746	1,034	964	22,316

(1) NL (1992).

(million ECU) Table 4.17

Manufacture of made-up textile articles, except apparel (NACE Rev. 1 17.4)
Market related indicators in the EU

	1988	1989	1990	1991	1992	1993	1994	1995	1996	1997	1998
Apparent consumption	7,547	8,302	9,042	9,906	10,339	10,040	10,692	9,876	:	:	:
Exports	713	741	734	790	778	875	969	1,074	1,202	1,305	1,388
Imports	1,218	1,335	1,495	1,889	1,971	2,196	2,444	2,553	2,862	3,167	3,594
Trade balance	-505	-593	-760	-1,099	-1,193	-1,321	-1,475	-1,479	-1,660	-1,863	-2,206
Export ratio (%)	10.1	9.6	8.9	9.0	8.5	10.0	10.5	12.8	:	:	:
Import penetration ratio (%)	16.1	16.1	16.5	19.1	19.1	21.9	22.9	25.8	:	:	:
Cover ratio (%)	58.6	55.5	49.1	41.8	39.5	39.8	39.6	42.1	42.0	41.2	38.6

(million ECU) Table 4.18

Manufacture of made-up textile articles, except apparel (NACE Rev. 1 17.4)
Market related indicators, 1998

	B/L	DK	D	EL	E	F	IRL	I	NL	A	P	FIN	S	UK
Apparent consumption	:	181	2,664	93	1,158	1,679	:	1,041	546	337	-589	175	177	2,188
Exports	481	199	696	80	302	433	36	460	253	135	698	28	165	454
Imports	494	212	1,653	81	256	948	97	369	541	269	51	96	251	882
Trade balance	-12	-13	-956	-1	46	-515	-61	92	-288	-134	647	-67	-87	-428
Export ratio (%)	:	118.5	40.8	86.4	25.1	37.2	:	40.7	97.9	66.7	1,206.2	26.4	181.5	25.8
Import penetration ratio (%)	:	117.2	62.0	86.5	22.1	56.5	:	35.4	99.0	80.0	-8.7	54.6	141.7	40.3
Cover ratio (%)	97.5	93.9	42.1	98.9	118.1	45.7	36.9	124.8	46.7	50.2	1,368.9	29.8	65.5	51.4

Table 4.19

Manufacture of made-up textile articles, except apparel (NACE Rev. 1 17.4)
Labour related indicators, 1998

	EU-15	B	DK	D	EL	E	F	IRL	I	L	NL	A	P	FIN	S	UK
Personnel costs (million ECU) (1)	2,046	165	48	501	18	257	293	:	210	:	75	67	15	21	27	406
Personnel costs/employee (thousand ECU) (2)	21.6	29.6	30.2	25.8	11.1	13.8	23.4	:	21.6	:	:	30.6	:	22.5	29.1	15.0
Social charges/personnel costs (%) (3)	19.8	20.3	6.0	18.5	23.1	22.0	28.3	:	37.2	:	13.2	22.9	:	20.6	29.2	12.7
Labour productivity (thousand ECU/head) (4)	27.6	39.2	42.6	34.9	18.1	15.3	28.6	:	41.7	:	25.6	47.1	:	39.0	31.9	31.5
Wage adjusted labour productivity (%) (2)	127.9	131.0	135.6	128.0	134.1	133.0	120.5	:	162.2	:	:	137.7	:	137.6	113.5	153.0

(1) EU-15 (1995). (2) EU-15, EL, I, A (1995); B, DK, D, E, F, FIN, S, UK (1996). (3) EU-15, S (1995). (4) NL (1992); EU-15 (1995).

Source: Eurostat (SBS, EBT)

Table 4.20 (million ECU)

Manufacture of other textiles (NACE Rev. 1 17.5)

Production related indicators in the EU

	1988	1989	1990	1991	1992	1993	1994	1995	1996	1997	1998
Production value	13,866	15,120	16,104	16,699	16,919	16,385	17,371	19,561	:	:	:
Producer price index (1995=100)	:	:	89.6	90.8	93.0	93.7	95.4	100.0	100.8	100.8	100.0
Value added	4,846	5,201	5,642	5,842	5,831	5,701	5,842	6,220	:	:	:
Number of persons employed (thousands)	185.5	189.7	197.1	196.5	187.4	176.1	171.9	191.3	:	:	:

Table 4.21 (million ECU)

Manufacture of other textiles (NACE Rev. 1 17.5)

Production related indicators, 1998

	B	DK	D	EL	E	F	IRL	I	L	NL	A	P	FIN	S	UK
Production value	2,873	291	4,312	80	957	3,080	172	3,178	:	1,046	611	1,270	287	317	3,519
Value added	849	95	1,512	32	334	988	72	885	:	330	246	:	132	139	1,346
Number of persons employed (units) (1)	15,941	1,548	33,226	1,393	15,503	26,944	2,579	22,020	:	5,014	4,863	28,644	2,343	2,818	32,562

(1) NL (1992).

Table 4.22 (million ECU)

Manufacture of other textiles (NACE Rev. 1 17.5)

Market related indicators in the EU

	1988	1989	1990	1991	1992	1993	1994	1995	1996	1997	1998
Apparent consumption	13,553	14,591	15,605	16,328	16,431	15,701	16,406	18,123	:	:	:
Exports	2,419	2,861	2,856	2,960	3,076	3,406	3,808	4,217	4,485	5,038	5,022
Imports	2,106	2,331	2,357	2,589	2,588	2,722	2,843	2,779	2,841	3,137	3,196
Trade balance	314	529	499	371	488	685	965	1,438	1,644	1,901	1,825
Export ratio (%)	17.4	18.9	17.7	17.7	18.2	20.8	21.9	21.6	:	:	:
Import penetration ratio (%)	15.5	16.0	15.1	15.9	15.8	17.3	17.3	15.3	:	:	:
Cover ratio (%)	114.9	122.7	121.2	114.3	118.8	125.2	133.9	151.7	157.9	160.6	157.1

Table 4.23 (million ECU)

Manufacture of other textiles (NACE Rev. 1 17.5)

Market related indicators, 1998

	B/L	DK	D	EL	E	F	IRL	I	NL	A	P	FIN	S	UK
Apparent consumption	:	279	4,146	183	1,156	2,976	246	2,348	416	536	1,303	279	328	4,140
Exports	2,951	266	2,804	53	415	1,485	77	1,808	1,442	429	248	200	282	1,191
Imports	772	253	2,638	156	614	1,381	151	978	812	355	282	192	294	1,812
Trade balance	2,179	12	166	-103	-199	103	-74	830	631	75	-34	7	-11	-621
Export ratio (%)	:	91.2	65.0	66.5	43.3	48.2	45.0	56.9	137.9	70.3	19.6	69.7	89.2	33.8
Import penetration ratio (%)	:	90.8	63.6	85.4	53.1	46.4	61.5	41.7	195.3	66.1	21.6	68.9	89.6	43.8
Cover ratio (%)	382.1	104.9	106.3	33.9	67.6	107.5	51.2	184.8	177.7	121.1	88.0	103.8	96.2	65.7

Table 4.24

Manufacture of other textiles (NACE Rev. 1 17.5)

Labour related indicators, 1998

	EU-15	B	DK	D	EL	E	F	IRL	I	L	NL	A	P	FIN	S	UK
Personnel costs (million ECU) (1)	4,316	448	54	1,082	16	252	751	57	544	:	166	134	196	66	93	828
Personnel costs/employee (thousand ECU) (2)	27.8	30.1	35.9	32.9	12.4	17.5	29.0	22.3	22.6	:	:	29.2	:	30.0	34.5	19.9
Social charges/personnel costs (%) (3)	21.8	26.5	6.8	19.3	23.8	21.5	29.5	14.7	37.1	:	16.0	24.0	:	20.5	30.6	16.1
Labour productivity (thousand ECU/head) (4)	32.5	53.3	61.6	45.5	23.2	21.6	36.7	28.0	40.2	:	43.4	50.6	:	56.2	49.2	41.3
Wage adjusted labour productivity (%) (2)	116.8	161.7	153.1	130.4	122.5	140.1	131.4	140.0	175.0	:	:	142.7	:	170.3	147.6	157.8

(1) EU-15 (1995); NL (1997). (2) EU-15, EL, I, A (1995); B, DK, D, E, F, IRL, FIN, S, UK (1996). (3) S (1994); EU-15 (1995); NL, DK (1997). (4) NL (1992); EU-15 (1995).

Source: Eurostat (SBS, EBT)

(million ECU) Table 4.25

Manufacture of knitted and crocheted fabrics (NACE Rev. 1 17.6)

Production related indicators in the EU

	1988	1989	1990	1991	1992	1993	1994	1995	1996	1997	1998
Production value	:	:	:	:	:	4,331	4,198	3,505	:	:	:
Producer price index (1995=100)	:	:	:	:	:	:	:	:	:	:	:
Value added	:	:	:	:	:	1,332	1,306	1,030	:	:	:
Number of persons employed (thousands)	:	:	:	:	:	48.0	45.5	29.5	:	:	:

(million ECU) Table 4.26

Manufacture of knitted and crocheted fabrics (NACE Rev. 1 17.6)

Production related indicators, 1998

	B	DK	D	EL	E	F	IRL	I	L	NL	A	P	FIN	S	UK
Production value (1)	79	81	683	74	637	470	:	705	0	36	156	:	29	48	813
Value added (1)	27	27	204	20	174	124	:	250	0	14	46	:	9	15	292
Number of persons employed (units) (2)	708	474	4,900	710	6,225	3,248	:	4,409	0	584	938	:	298	189	5,685

(1) L (1996). (2) L (1996); NL (1992).

(million ECU) Table 4.27

Manufacture of knitted and crocheted fabrics (NACE Rev. 1 17.6)

Market related indicators in the EU

	1988	1989	1990	1991	1992	1993	1994	1995	1996	1997	1998
Apparent consumption	:	:	:	:	:	3,974	3,795	2,929	:	:	:
Exports	434	482	544	578	632	720	871	996	1,123	1,326	1,549
Imports	192	153	257	348	322	363	468	420	468	660	812
Trade balance	242	329	287	230	310	358	403	576	655	666	737
Export ratio (%)	:	:	:	:	:	16.6	20.7	28.4	:	:	:
Import penetration ratio (%)	:	:	:	:	:	9.1	12.3	14.4	:	:	:
Cover ratio (%)	226.3	314.9	211.4	166.0	196.0	198.6	186.1	236.9	239.8	201.0	190.7

(million ECU) Table 4.28

Manufacture of knitted and crocheted fabrics (NACE Rev. 1 17.6)

Market related indicators, 1998

	B/L	DK	D	EL	E	F	IRL	I	NL	A	P	FIN	S	UK
Apparent consumption	:	28	207	142	506	370	:	146	36	35	:	28	27	920
Exports	164	124	925	36	249	596	1	875	152	219	24	20	51	274
Imports	193	71	450	104	118	496	51	316	152	99	151	19	30	381
Trade balance	-29	53	475	-68	130	100	-49	559	0	120	-127	1	22	-107
Export ratio (%)	:	152.2	135.6	49.0	39.1	126.8	:	124.1	425.3	140.7	:	69.8	106.1	33.6
Import penetration ratio (%)	:	251.0	217.2	73.3	23.3	134.0	:	216.3	422.0	279.3	:	68.7	111.1	41.4
Cover ratio (%)	84.8	175.4	205.6	35.0	210.4	120.1	2.7	277.0	99.8	221.8	15.8	105.4	173.5	71.9

Table 4.29

Manufacture of knitted and crocheted fabrics (NACE Rev. 1 17.6)

Labour related indicators, 1998

	EU-15	B	DK	D	EL	E	F	IRL	I	L	NL	A	P	FIN	S	UK
Personnel costs (million ECU) (1)	655	16	16	145	8	98	95	:	106	0	10	30	:	6	6	148
Personnel costs/employee (thousand ECU) (2)	23.2	25.8	33.2	29.4	12.7	17.5	29.5	:	21.9	:	:	31.2	:	22.1	31.9	21.3
Social charges/personnel costs (%) (3)	20.0	28.4	6.1	19.1	23.8	21.7	30.0	:	37.5	:	20.3	21.8	:	19.8	:	13.3
Labour productivity (thousand ECU/head) (4)	34.9	38.8	57.1	41.6	27.5	27.9	38.0	:	56.8	:	35.6	49.3	:	30.8	79.0	51.4
Wage adjusted labour productivity (%) (2)	150.6	154.3	151.9	136.8	184.2	140.8	137.3	:	185.3	:	:	136.5	:	141.1	255.5	197.7

(1) EU-15 (1995); L (1996). (2) EU-15, EL, I, A (1995); B, DK, D, E, F, IRL, FIN, S, UK (1996). (3) EU-15 (1995). (4) NL (1992); EU-15 (1995).

Source: Eurostat (SBS, EBT)

Table 4.30 (million ECU)

Manufacture of knitted and crocheted articles (NACE Rev. 1 17.7)

Production related indicators in the EU

	1988	1989	1990	1991	1992	1993	1994	1995	1996	1997	1998
Production value	:	:	:	:	:	13,964	12,357	11,827	:	:	:
Producer price index (1995=100)	:	:	:	:	:	:	:	:	:	:	:
Value added	:	:	:	:	:	4,742	4,269	4,220	:	:	:
Number of persons employed (thousands)	:	:	:	:	:	199.4	189.1	170.1	:	:	:

Table 4.31 (million ECU)

Manufacture of knitted and crocheted articles (NACE Rev. 1 17.7)

Production related indicators, 1998

	B	DK	D	EL	E	F	IRL	I	L	NL	A	P	FIN	S	UK
Production value (1)	129	150	1,088	171	590	1,407	:	5,064	0	70	242	:	97	49	1,975
Value added (1)	62	46	465	68	209	545	:	1,505	0	24	141	:	54	23	891
Number of persons employed (units) (2)	2,364	1,077	13,614	3,778	14,272	21,913	:	41,484	0	2,496	3,776	:	1,768	650	36,026

(1) L (1996). (2) L (1996); NL (1992).

Table 4.32 (million ECU)

Manufacture of knitted and crocheted articles (NACE Rev. 1 17.7)

Market related indicators in the EU

	1988	1989	1990	1991	1992	1993	1994	1995	1996	1997	1998
Apparent consumption	:	:	:	:	:	16,595	14,853	13,964	:	:	:
Exports	1,175	1,334	1,290	1,132	1,203	1,245	1,410	1,503	1,724	1,887	1,843
Imports	2,153	2,181	2,285	3,115	3,613	3,875	3,906	3,640	4,209	5,285	5,380
Trade balance	-977	-847	-995	-1,983	-2,410	-2,630	-2,496	-2,137	-2,485	-3,398	-3,538
Export ratio (%)	:	:	:	:	:	8.9	11.4	12.7	:	:	:
Import penetration ratio (%)	:	:	:	:	:	23.4	26.3	26.1	:	:	:
Cover ratio (%)	54.6	61.2	56.4	36.3	33.3	32.1	36.1	41.3	41.0	35.7	34.2

Table 4.33 (million ECU)

Manufacture of knitted and crocheted articles (NACE Rev. 1 17.7)

Market related indicators, 1998

	B/L	DK	D	EL	E	F	IRL	I	NL	A	P	FIN	S	UK
Apparent consumption	:	219	3,519	148	761	2,476	:	2,343	443	459	:	198	269	2,939
Exports	410	241	814	108	160	617	102	3,406	410	159	607	19	66	675
Imports	647	311	3,246	85	330	1,686	192	685	783	376	149	120	287	1,640
Trade balance	-237	-69	-2,432	23	-170	-1,069	-90	2,721	-373	-217	458	-101	-221	-964
Export ratio (%)	:	161.0	74.8	62.9	27.1	43.8	:	67.3	588.0	65.7	:	19.8	135.6	34.2
Import penetration ratio (%)	:	141.7	92.2	57.1	43.4	68.1	:	29.2	176.8	81.9	:	60.7	106.4	55.8
Cover ratio (%)	63.4	77.7	25.1	127.0	48.5	36.6	53.2	497.1	52.3	42.3	406.6	16.0	23.0	41.2

Table 4.34

Manufacture of knitted and crocheted articles (NACE Rev. 1 17.7)

Labour related indicators, 1998

	EU-15	B	DK	D	EL	E	F	IRL	I	L	NL	A	P	FIN	S	UK
Personnel costs (million ECU) (1)	3,108	38	32	371	36	188	500	:	859	0	18	96	:	36	17	641
Personnel costs/employee (thousand ECU) (2)	18.6	18.0	29.3	27.6	10.5	14.2	23.1	:	18.9	:	:	25.5	:	21.9	26.8	14.6
Social charges/personnel costs (%) (3)	21.6	28.1	8.2	18.9	22.4	22.1	27.1	:	36.3	:	15.8	23.0	:	20.8	28.9	11.6
Labour productivity (thousand ECU/head) (4)	24.8	26.1	43.0	34.1	18.0	14.7	24.9	:	36.3	:	22.5	37.3	:	30.7	36.1	24.7
Wage adjusted labour productivity (%) (2)	133.4	114.8	129.8	117.9	136.0	128.7	117.9	:	153.8	:	:	127.2	:	137.0	139.5	141.5

(1) EU-15 (1995); L (1996). (2) EU-15, EL, I, A (1995); B, DK, D, E, F, FIN, S, UK (1996). (3) EU-15, S (1995); NL (1997). (4) NL (1992); EU-15 (1995).

Source: Eurostat (SBS, EBT)

(million ECU) — Table 4.35

Manufacture of leather clothes (NACE Rev. 1 18.1)
Production related indicators in the EU

	1988	1989	1990	1991	1992	1993	1994	1995	1996	1997	1998
Production value	:	:	:	:	:	780	764	582	:	:	:
Producer price index (1995=100)	:	:	:	:	:	:	:	:	:	:	:
Value added	:	:	:	:	:	225	207	137	:	:	:
Number of persons employed (thousands)	:	:	:	:	:	12.1	10.8	6.5	:	:	:

(million ECU) — Table 4.36

Manufacture of leather clothes (NACE Rev. 1 18.1)
Production related indicators, 1998 (1)

	B	DK	D	EL	E	F	IRL	I	L	NL	A	P	FIN	S	UK
Production value	10	0	57	:	67	56	:	397	0	:	0	:	17	2	14
Value added	2	0	16	:	18	16	:	84	0	:	0	:	6	1	3
Number of persons employed (units)	141	0	528	:	1,459	439	:	3,571	0	:	0	:	273	25	122

(1) A, UK (1995); DK, L (1996).

(million ECU) — Table 4.37

Manufacture of leather clothes (NACE Rev. 1 18.1)
Market related indicators in the EU

	1988	1989	1990	1991	1992	1993	1994	1995	1996	1997	1998
Apparent consumption	:	:	:	:	:	1,861	1,862	1,385	:	:	:
Exports	173	256	224	181	144	112	154	133	155	186	186
Imports	970	773	847	1,221	873	1,193	1,251	935	1,066	1,160	948
Trade balance	-797	-517	-624	-1,040	-729	-1,081	-1,097	-802	-911	-974	-762
Export ratio (%)	:	:	:	:	:	14.3	20.1	22.8	:	:	:
Import penetration ratio (%)	:	:	:	:	:	64.1	67.2	67.6	:	:	:
Cover ratio (%)	17.8	33.1	26.4	14.8	16.5	9.4	12.3	14.2	14.6	16.0	19.6

(million ECU) — Table 4.38

Manufacture of leather clothes (NACE Rev. 1 18.1)
Market related indicators, 1998

	B/L	DK	D	EL	E	F	IRL	I	NL	A	P	FIN	S	UK
Apparent consumption (1)	:	18	509	:	109	150	:	323	:	59	:	22	21	119
Exports	25	31	158	5	31	68	1	208	38	21	2	6	14	18
Imports	67	27	610	33	74	162	7	135	105	82	14	10	34	148
Trade balance	-42	3	-452	-28	-43	-94	-6	73	-67	-61	-12	-4	-19	-130
Export ratio (%) (1)	:	:	275.1	:	46.4	122.7	:	52.5	:	:	.	35.4	859.2	178.6
Import penetration ratio (%) (1)	:	181.5	119.7	:	67.3	108.4	:	41.7	:	111.7	:	48.3	160.3	109.2
Cover ratio (%)	37.2	112.7	25.9	15.1	42.0	42.0	7.9	154.4	36.5	25.6	12.5	58.6	42.6	12.0

(1) A, UK (1995); DK (1996).

Table 4.39

Manufacture of leather clothes (NACE Rev. 1 18.1)
Labour related indicators, 1998

	EU-15	B	DK	D	EL	E	F	IRL	I	L	NL	A	P	FIN	S	UK
Personnel costs (million ECU) (1)	109	2	0	12	:	16	11	:	67	0	:	0	:	4	1	1
Personnel costs/employee (thousand ECU) (2)	17.3	12.9	:	21.4	:	13.1	25.5	:	17.1	:	:	:	:	18.6	28.1	11.6
Social charges/personnel costs (%) (3)	26.0	21.7	:	20.1	:	21.2	30.9	:	35.6	:	:	:	:	23.0	:	9.6
Labour productivity (thousand ECU/head) (3)	21.1	17.5	:	30.0	:	12.2	36.1	:	23.6	:	:	:	:	23.5	32.2	25.0
Wage adjusted labour productivity (%) (2)	121.8	127.4	:	146.2	:	124.4	126.8	:	125.4	:	:	:	:	114.9	117.6	216.1

(1) EU-15, A, UK (1995); DK, L (1996). (2) EU-15, I, UK (1995); B, D, E, F, FIN, S, (1996). (3) EU-15, UK (1995).

Source: Eurostat (SBS, EBT)

Table 4.40 (million ECU)

Manufacture of other wearing apparel and accessories (NACE Rev. 1 18.2)

Production related indicators in the EU

	1988	1989	1990	1991	1992	1993	1994	1995	1996	1997	1998
Production value	:	:	:	:	:	50,677	52,822	52,175	:	:	:
Producer price index (1995=100)	:	:	:	:	:	:	:	:	:	:	:
Value added	:	:	:	:	:	17,600	17,694	16,594	:	:	:
Number of persons employed (thousands)	:	:	:	:	:	910.2	865.9	707.2	:	:	:

Table 4.41 (million ECU)

Manufacture of other wearing apparel and accessories (NACE Rev. 1 18.2)

Production related indicators, 1998 (1)

	B	DK	D	EL	E	F	IRL	I	L	NL	A	P	FIN	S	UK
Production value	1,882	525	9,969	729	5,781	6,546	:	17,077	3	:	935	:	400	162	5,152
Value added	479	219	2,959	267	1,942	2,186	:	5,370	2	:	364	:	166	58	2,349
Number of persons employed (units)	13,800	5,755	77,553	22,925	114,231	98,890	:	161,934	142	:	17,540	:	6,324	1,707	107,017

(1) A (1992); DK (1993); L (1995).

Table 4.42 (million ECU)

Manufacture of other wearing apparel and accessories (NACE Rev. 1 18.2)

Market related indicators in the EU

	1988	1989	1990	1991	1992	1993	1994	1995	1996	1997	1998
Apparent consumption	:	:	:	:	:	67,074	69,205	68,012	:	:	:
Exports	5,443	6,390	6,874	6,888	7,253	7,747	9,028	9,732	11,002	11,688	12,030
Imports	12,732	14,849	17,349	21,506	22,166	24,144	25,411	25,569	27,420	31,206	33,240
Trade balance	-7,288	-8,459	-10,475	-14,618	-14,913	-16,397	-16,383	-15,836	-16,417	-19,518	-21,210
Export ratio (%)	:	:	:	:	:	15.3	17.1	18.7	:	:	:
Import penetration ratio (%)	:	:	:	:	:	36.0	36.7	37.6	:	:	:
Cover ratio (%)	42.8	43.0	39.6	32.0	32.7	32.1	35.5	38.1	40.1	37.5	36.2

Table 4.43 (million ECU)

Manufacture of other wearing apparel and accessories (NACE Rev. 1 18.2)

Market related indicators, 1998

	B/L	DK	D	EL	E	F	IRL	I	NL	A	P	FIN	S	UK
Apparent consumption (1)	834	780	19,781	287	6,687	10,447	:	11,988	:	1,705	:	881	1,265	10,097
Exports	3,135	1,259	5,885	1,134	1,162	4,339	298	9,341	2,770	925	2,246	194	392	3,464
Imports	3,902	1,652	15,697	693	2,068	8,240	728	4,252	4,498	1,821	621	675	1,494	8,409
Trade balance	-767	-393	-9,812	442	-906	-3,901	-430	5,089	-1,728	-896	1,625	-481	-1,102	-4,945
Export ratio (%) (1)	21,957.3	137.7	59.0	155.7	20.1	66.3	:	54.7	:	81.4	:	48.5	241.7	67.2
Import penetration ratio (%) (1)	240.2	125.4	79.4	241.4	30.9	78.9	:	35.5	:	89.8	:	76.6	118.2	83.3
Cover ratio (%)	80.4	76.2	37.5	163.7	56.2	52.7	41.0	219.7	61.6	50.8	361.6	28.7	26.2	41.2

(1) B/L (1989); A (1992); IRL (1993).

Table 4.44

Manufacture of other wearing apparel and accessories (NACE Rev. 1 18.2)

Labour related indicators, 1998

	EU-15	B	DK	D	EL	E	F	IRL	I	L	NL	A	P	FIN	S	UK
Personnel costs (million ECU) (1)	12,210	284	139	2,121	215	1,302	2,225	:	3,085	2	:	299	:	124	44	1,596
Personnel costs/employee (thousand ECU) (2)	17.6	21.1	:	26.3	10.4	13.3	23.1	:	17.4	16.1	:	17.2	:	21.1	26.9	12.5
Social charges/personnel costs (%) (3)	21.7	24.5	3.0	18.2	22.7	21.2	29.8	:	34.7	12.9	:	23.6	:	20.5	30.0	8.8
Labour productivity (thousand ECU/head) (4)	23.5	34.7	38.1	38.2	11.6	17.0	22.1	:	33.2	12.6	:	20.8	:	26.2	33.7	22.0
Wage adjusted labour productivity (%) (2)	133.3	136.8	:	126.6	110.8	120.9	116.8	:	163.3	78.4	:	121.0	:	131.2	131.1	160.8

(1) A (1992); DK (1993); EU-15, L (1995). (2) A (1992); EU-15, EL, I, L (1995); B, D, E, F, FIN, S, UK (1996). (3) A, S (1992); DK (1993); EU-15, L (1995). (4) A (1992); DK (1993); EU-15, L (1995).

Source: Eurostat (SBS, EBT)

(million ECU) — Table 4.45

Dressing and dyeing of fur; manufacture of articles of fur (NACE Rev. 1 18.3)
Production related indicators in the EU

	1988	1989	1990	1991	1992	1993	1994	1995	1996	1997	1998
Production value	987	934	802	848	707	585	609	698	:	:	:
Producer price index (1995=100)	:	:	:	:	:	:	:	:	:	:	:
Value added	308	301	271	273	240	201	197	166	:	:	:
Number of persons employed (thousands)	17.4	15.3	11.7	10.5	9.6	9.0	8.6	7.5	:	:	:

(million ECU) — Table 4.46

Dressing and dyeing of fur; manufacture of articles of fur (NACE Rev. 1 18.3)
Production related indicators, 1998 (1)

	B	DK	D	EL	E	F	IRL	I	L	NL	A	P	FIN	S	UK
Production value	50	0	27	:	216	62	4	308	:	0	13	:	24	0	19
Value added	11	0	11	:	52	16	2	46	:	0	4	:	9	0	8
Number of persons employed (units)	276	0	521	:	1,768	714	62	1,358	:	0	154	:	302	0	317

(1) A (1991); DK (1993); UK (1995); NL, S (1996).

(million ECU) — Table 4.47

Dressing and dyeing of fur; manufacture of articles of fur (NACE Rev. 1 18.3)
Market related indicators in the EU

	1988	1989	1990	1991	1992	1993	1994	1995	1996	1997	1998
Apparent consumption	872	799	608	887	747	524	536	535	:	:	:
Exports	410	378	341	180	168	257	257	384	605	692	475
Imports	296	244	147	220	208	195	184	221	289	181	199
Trade balance	114	135	194	-39	-40	62	73	163	316	510	276
Export ratio (%)	41.6	40.5	42.5	21.3	23.7	43.9	42.3	55.0	:	:	:
Import penetration ratio (%)	33.9	30.5	24.1	24.8	27.8	37.3	34.4	41.2	:	:	:
Cover ratio (%)	138.6	155.3	232.4	82.2	80.7	131.6	139.7	174.0	209.3	381.1	238.8

(million ECU) — Table 4.48

Dressing and dyeing of fur; manufacture of articles of fur (NACE Rev. 1 18.3)
Market related indicators, 1998

	B/L	DK	D	EL	E	F	IRL	I	NL	A	P	FIN	S	UK
Apparent consumption (1)	:	-3	46	:	105	42	2	257	10	35	:	-22	9	-23
Exports	33	24	164	250	142	65	3	189	15	13	9	57	7	64
Imports	12	25	182	235	31	45	0	139	14	26	6	11	10	47
Trade balance	21	-1	-19	15	111	20	3	50	1	-12	3	46	-3	18
Export ratio (%) (1)	:	:	597.7	:	65.6	105.7	69.0	61.5	:	37.4	:	236.9	:	395.3
Import penetration ratio (%) (1)	:	-454.2	395.0	:	29.1	108.4	16.1	54.0	372.4	77.5	:	-50.5	155.7	-135.8
Cover ratio (%)	271.1	94.8	89.7	106.5	463.1	143.8	1,155.6	136.2	109.1	52.6	155.5	515.6	69.9	137.8

(1) A (1991); DK (1993); UK (1995); NL, S (1996).

Table 4.49

Dressing and dyeing of fur; manufacture of articles of fur (NACE Rev. 1 18.3)
Labour related indicators, 1998

	EU-15	B	DK	D	EL	E	F	IRL	I	L	NL	A	P	FIN	S	UK
Personnel costs (million ECU) (1)	131	5	0	11	:	56	18	1	30	:	0	3	:	7	0	5
Personnel costs/employee (thousand ECU) (2)	18.7	21.5	:	22.9	:	17.3	26.6	13.7	20.4	:	:	17.1	:	27.1	:	16.9
Social charges/personnel costs (%) (3)	23.2	23.7	:	17.1	:	21.7	30.6	14.3	36.4	:	:	21.6	:	22.8	:	10.9
Labour productivity (thousand ECU/head) (4)	22.2	41.3	:	21.0	:	29.4	22.6	40.2	34.0	:	:	24.6	:	31.4	:	24.0
Wage adjusted labour productivity (%) (2)	118.8	165.8	:	113.2	:	107.7	103.4	275.7	151.3	:	:	144.2	:	121.4	:	141.9

(1) A (1991); DK (1993); EU-15, UK (1995); NL, S (1995); E (1997). (2) A (1991); EU-15, I, UK (1995); B, D, E, F, IRL, FIN (1996). (3) A (1991); EU-15, UK (1996), E (1997).
(4) A (1991); EU-15, UK (1995).

Source: Eurostat (SBS, EBT)

Table 4.50 (million ECU)

Tanning and dressing of leather (NACE Rev. 1 19.1)

Production related indicators in the EU

	1988	1989	1990	1991	1992	1993	1994	1995	1996	1997	1998
Production value	7,261	7,986	7,349	6,642	6,341	6,042	7,002	6,628	6,842	:	:
Producer price index (1995=100)	:	:	:	:	:	:	:	:	:	:	:
Value added	1,527	1,623	1,550	1,655	1,527	1,444	1,419	1,331	1,308	:	:
Number of persons employed (thousands)	58.7	56.4	52.8	50.0	47.4	43.1	42.3	41.0	38.7	:	:

Table 4.51 (million ECU)

Tanning and dressing of leather (NACE Rev. 1 19.1)

Production related indicators, 1998

	B	DK	D	EL	E	F	IRL	I	L	NL	A	P	FIN	S	UK
Production value (1)	:	:	564	42	1,024	243	74	4,027	0	116	142	259	32	64	422
Value added (1)	:	:	147	8	221	59	8	628	0	31	25	:	10	15	96
Number of persons employed (units) (1)(2)	:	:	3,131	493	8,768	2,276	381	15,042	0	664	1,121	3,884	292	451	3,067

(1) A (1994); IRL (1995); L (1996). (2) NL (1992).

Table 4.52 (million ECU)

Tanning and dressing of leather (NACE Rev. 1 19.1)

Market related indicators in the EU (million ECU)

	1988	1989	1990	1991	1992	1993	1994	1995	1996	1997	1998
Apparent consumption	7,398	8,040	7,634	6,620	6,223	5,507	6,872	6,311	6,106	:	:
Exports	1,212	1,561	1,463	1,380	1,391	1,720	2,159	2,254	2,684	2,854	2,689
Imports	1,349	1,615	1,748	1,358	1,273	1,186	2,028	1,937	1,948	2,181	1,950
Trade balance	-137	-54	-285	22	118	534	130	317	736	673	739
Export ratio (%)	16.7	19.5	19.9	20.8	21.9	28.5	30.8	34.0	39.2	:	:
Import penetration ratio (%)	18.2	20.1	22.9	20.5	20.5	21.5	29.5	30.7	31.9	:	:
Cover ratio (%)	89.8	96.7	83.7	101.6	109.3	145.0	106.4	116.4	137.8	130.9	137.9

Table 4.53 (million ECU)

Tanning and dressing of leather (NACE Rev. 1 19.1)

Market related indicators, 1998

	B/L	DK	D	EL	E	F	IRL	I	NL	A	P	FIN	S	UK
Apparent consumption (1)	:	:	492	54	1,206	380	48	2,811	93	105	553	49	50	321
Exports	71	37	682	20	291	283	54	2,747	124	229	42	20	43	329
Imports	118	43	610	32	473	421	6	1,531	100	157	336	37	29	229
Trade balance	-47	-6	72	-12	-182	-137	49	1,215	23	72	-294	-17	14	100
Export ratio (%) (1)	:	:	120.9	46.7	28.4	116.6	49.9	68.2	106.2	97.1	16.2	63.2	66.7	78.1
Import penetration ratio (%) (1)	:	:	124.0	58.8	39.2	110.6	22.8	54.5	107.7	96.1	60.8	76.2	57.7	71.3
Cover ratio (%)	60.2	85.4	111.8	61.4	61.5	67.4	971.6	179.4	123.2	145.6	12.5	53.6	147.4	143.8

(1) A (1994); IRL (1995).

Table 4.54

Tanning and dressing of leather (NACE Rev. 1 19.1)

Labour related indicators, 1998

	EU-15	B	DK	D	EL	E	F	IRL	I	L	NL	A	P	FIN	S	UK
Personnel costs (million ECU) (1)	872	:	:	100	7	160	58	5	389	0	12	22	36	7	13	73
Personnel costs/employee (thousand ECU) (2)	24.2	:	:	32.2	16.4	19.9	26.1	13.4	23.7	:	:	19.8	:	23.4	30.5	19.7
Social charges/personnel costs (%) (3)	24.5	:	:	18.2	23.0	22.7	27.8	18.2	36.2	:	15.1	23.1	:	20.5	27.7	11.8
Labour productivity (thousand ECU/head) (4)	33.8	:	:	47.1	15.6	25.2	25.7	20.6	41.8	:	34.8	22.7	:	33.1	34.1	31.4
Wage adjusted labour productivity (%) (2)	134.2	:	:	137.1	116.1	146.8	112.3	154.5	182.4	:	:	114.9	:	128.5	132.8	141.1

(1) A (1994); IRL (1995); EU-15, L (1996); NL (1997). (2) A (1994); EU-15, EL, IRL, I (1995); D, E, F, FIN, S, UK (1996). (3) A, S (1994); EU-15, IRL (1995); NL (1997).
(4) NL (1992); A (1994); IRL (1995); EU-15 (1996).

Source: Eurostat (SBS, EBT)

(million ECU) Table 4.55

Manufacture of luggage, handbags and the like, saddlery and harness (NACE Rev. 1 19.2)
Production related indicators in the EU

	1988	1989	1990	1991	1992	1993	1994	1995	1996	1997	1998
Production value	4,660	5,240	5,256	5,559	5,550	5,015	5,454	:	5,154	:	:
Producer price index (1995=100)	:	:	:	:	:	:	:	:	:	:	:
Value added	1,777	1,883	1,986	2,059	1,996	1,770	1,907	:	1,725	:	:
Number of persons employed (thousands)	80.0	82.0	83.0	82.1	75.0	66.4	65.8	:	59.6	:	:

(million ECU) Table 4.56

Manufacture of luggage, handbags and the like, saddlery and harness (NACE Rev. 1 19.2)
Production related indicators, 1998

	B	DK	D	EL	E	F	IRL	I	L	NL	A	P	FIN	S	UK
Production value (1)	:	:	461	3	625	873	17	2,035	0	29	73	59	34	21	290
Value added (1)	:	:	179	1	189	416	8	521	0	11	26	:	13	9	139
Number of persons employed (units) (1)(2)	:	:	6,777	98	9,235	11,472	423	11,804	0	1,218	1,069	3,924	483	329	4,083

(1) A (1994); IRL (1995); L (1996). (2) NL (1992).

(million ECU) Table 4.57

Manufacture of luggage, handbags and the like, saddlery and harness (NACE Rev. 1 19.2)
Market related indicators in the EU

	1988	1989	1990	1991	1992	1993	1994	1995	1996	1997	1998
Apparent consumption	4,934	5,474	5,595	6,319	6,243	5,792	5,917	:	5,521	:	:
Exports	1,121	1,375	1,389	1,293	1,351	1,438	1,840	2,098	2,327	2,275	2,035
Imports	1,394	1,608	1,728	2,054	2,043	2,215	2,303	2,364	2,693	3,058	3,209
Trade balance	-274	-233	-339	-761	-693	-777	-463	-266	-367	-783	-1,174
Export ratio (%)	24.0	26.2	26.4	23.3	24.3	28.7	33.7	:	45.1	:	:
Import penetration ratio (%)	28.3	29.4	30.9	32.5	32.7	38.2	38.9	:	48.8	:	:
Cover ratio (%)	80.4	85.5	80.4	63.0	66.1	64.9	79.9	88.8	86.4	74.4	63.4

(million ECU) Table 4.58

Manufacture of luggage, handbags and the like, saddlery and harness (NACE Rev. 1 19.2)
Market related indicators, 1998

	B/L	DK	D	EL	E	F	IRL	I	NL	A	P	FIN	S	UK
Apparent consumption (1)	:	:	1,141	56	768	633	31	1,327	193	147	104	68	112	884
Exports	386	31	346	5	120	1,091	24	1,233	170	100	14	10	19	270
Imports	323	111	1,025	58	263	851	46	525	335	125	59	44	110	864
Trade balance	62	-80	-680	-53	-143	240	-22	708	-164	-25	-45	-34	-91	-594
Export ratio (%) (1)	:	:	75.0	155.4	19.3	124.9	100.9	60.6	592.8	85.6	23.6	29.6	87.9	93.1
Import penetration ratio (%) (1)	:	:	89.9	103.1	34.3	134.3	100.5	39.5	173.3	92.8	56.5	64.7	97.7	97.7
Cover ratio (%)	119.3	28.1	33.7	8.6	45.7	128.2	52.3	235.0	50.9	79.8	23.8	23.0	17.1	31.2

(1) A (1994); IRL (1995).

Table 4.59

Manufacture of luggage, handbags and the like, saddlery and harness (NACE Rev. 1 19.2)
Labour related indicators, 1998

	EU-15	B	DK	D	EL	E	F	IRL	I	L	NL	A	P	FIN	S	UK
Personnel costs (million ECU) (1)	1,168	:	:	160	1	110	286	5	279	0	9	26	22	8	8	72
Personnel costs/employee (thousand ECU) (2)	:	:	:	24.4	10.2	14.1	25.4	11.4	21.6	:	:	24.5	:	20.8	26.4	14.9
Social charges/personnel costs (%) (3)	:	:	:	17.5	21.1	22.2	25.8	10.6	37.7	:	14.5	22.6	:	23.4	28.8	10.0
Labour productivity (thousand ECU/head) (4)	29.0	:	:	26.4	10.3	20.5	36.3	17.8	44.2	:	19.1	24.4	:	27.3	27.3	34.1
Wage adjusted labour productivity (%) (2)	:	:	:	103.5	152.4	121.6	143.3	155.7	194.3	:	:	99.5	:	129.0	122.9	163.9

(1) A (1994); IRL (1995); EU-15, L (1996). (2) A (1994); EL, IRL, I (1995); D, E, F, FIN, S, UK (1996). (3) A, S (1994); IRL (1995). (4) NL (1992); A (1994); IRL (1995); EU-15 (1996).

Source: Eurostat (SBS, EBT)

Table 4.60 (million ECU)

Manufacture of footwear (NACE Rev. 1 19.3)

Production related indicators in the EU

	1988	1989	1990	1991	1992	1993	1994	1995	1996	1997	1998
Production value	17,249	18,833	20,570	21,152	20,166	19,688	21,278	21,234	22,038	:	:
Producer price index (1995=100)	:	:	87.4	90.5	93.1	95.3	97.1	100.0	102.2	102.2	104.2
Value added	6,136	6,072	6,248	6,631	6,334	6,143	6,305	6,030	6,354	:	:
Number of persons employed (thousands)	349.6	344.9	354.0	346.9	326.5	303.4	302.9	293.4	284.9	:	:

Table 4.61 (million ECU)

Manufacture of footwear (NACE Rev. 1 19.3)

Production related indicators, 1998

	B	DK	D	EL	E	F	IRL	I	L	NL	A	P	FIN	S	UK
Production value (1)	69	117	2,251	130	4,281	1,965	26	8,808	0	105	383	1,711	139	25	1,397
Value added (1)	25	52	689	40	956	722	12	2,326	0	52	141	:	56	8	669
Number of persons employed (units) (1)(2)	949	810	17,684	3,446	52,425	28,287	554	77,493	0	2,544	4,729	59,930	2,084	302	17,831

(1) L (1996). (2) NL (1992).

Table 4.62 (million ECU)

Manufacture of footwear (NACE Rev. 1 19.3)

Market related indicators in the EU

	1988	1989	1990	1991	1992	1993	1994	1995	1996	1997	1998
Apparent consumption	17,253	18,494	20,420	22,248	21,009	20,789	21,797	21,436	22,262	:	:
Exports	2,783	3,405	3,595	3,487	3,746	3,930	4,773	5,003	5,642	5,995	5,725
Imports	2,786	3,066	3,445	4,583	4,590	5,031	5,292	5,206	5,866	6,843	6,990
Trade balance	-4	339	150	-1,096	-844	-1,101	-519	-203	-224	-848	-1,265
Export ratio (%)	16.1	18.1	17.5	16.5	18.6	20.0	22.4	23.6	25.6	:	:
Import penetration ratio (%)	16.1	16.6	16.9	20.6	21.8	24.2	24.3	24.3	26.4	:	:
Cover ratio (%)	99.9	111.0	104.3	76.1	81.6	78.1	90.2	96.1	96.2	87.6	81.9

Table 4.63 (million ECU)

Manufacture of footwear (NACE Rev. 1 19.3)

Market related indicators, 1998

	B/L	DK	D	EL	E	F	IRL	I	NL	A	P	FIN	S	UK
Apparent consumption	:	294	4,901	311	2,820	3,542	220	3,818	678	586	554	233	338	3,383
Exports	1,289	243	1,272	32	1,936	919	19	6,934	749	445	1,428	73	57	795
Imports	988	420	3,922	213	475	2,495	213	1,944	1,322	648	271	167	370	2,782
Trade balance	302	-177	-2,651	-181	1,461	-1,577	-194	4,990	-573	-202	1,157	-94	-312	-1,987
Export ratio (%)	:	208.4	56.5	24.7	45.2	46.8	75.2	78.7	716.1	116.2	83.4	52.6	225.5	56.9
Import penetration ratio (%)	:	143.0	80.0	68.4	16.9	70.5	97.1	50.9	195.1	110.6	48.9	71.7	109.5	82.2
Cover ratio (%)	130.6	57.8	32.4	15.1	407.3	36.8	9.1	356.7	56.6	68.8	527.2	43.8	15.5	28.6

Table 4.64

Manufacture of footwear (NACE Rev. 1 19.3)

Labour related indicators, 1998

	EU-15	B	DK	D	EL	E	F	IRL	I	L	NL	A	P	FIN	S	UK
Personnel costs (million ECU) (1)	4,380	21	25	520	38	555	610	8	1,483	0	34	110	367	42	8	303
Personnel costs/employee (thousand ECU) (2)	19.5	23.6	31.3	28.2	12.2	11.9	22.2	13.6	17.5	:	:	24.3	:	21.5	27.8	14.3
Social charges/personnel costs (%) (3)	23.7	27.4	2.4	20.5	24.2	22.0	23.7	13.4	35.3	:	11.9	22.2	:	22.0	28.3	10.6
Labour productivity (thousand ECU/head) (4)	22.3	26.4	64.7	39.0	11.7	18.2	25.5	21.2	30.0	:	25.1	29.8	:	26.8	27.5	37.6
Wage adjusted labour productivity (%) (2)	105.5	103.3	164.0	124.3	111.1	136.3	121.6	122.6	155.9	:	:	131.1	:	125.6	117.5	201.8

(1) EU-15, L (1996). (2) EU-15, EL, I, A (1995); B, DK, D, E, F, IRL, FIN, S, UK (1996). (3) EU-15, S (1995). (4) NL (1992); EU-15 (1996).

Source: Eurostat (SBS, EBT)

Wood, paper, publishing and printing

Industry description

There is a long journey from the tree in the forest to the book in your living room. This journey starts within the activity of forestry, which includes the initial planting and raising of trees, as well as felling and logging. This chapter covers the manufacturing processes that begin with sawing and planing of wood (NACE Rev. 1 20.1) and the basic manufacture of wood products, such as panels and boards or builders' carpentry (found under NACE Rev. 1 20.2 to 20.5). The activities that follow within the production process may be seen within a vertically integrated schema. Wood is used as a raw material in the manufacture of pulp, paper and paper products (NACE Rev. 1 21), which is then used as one of the raw materials within the printing and publishing industry (NACE Rev. 1 22.1 to 22.2). The manufacture of wood also provides intermediary goods for important sectors of the EU economy such as construction and the furniture industry.

Until quite recently, printing and publishing used paper as almost its only means of dissemination. However, during the last ten to fifteen years we have seen a steady increase in the role of electronic dissemination. During the nineties, electronically published products have become more important, both as complements and substitutes to traditional paper products. Please note that the commentary provided within this chapter does not include any reference to the publishing of sound recordings or the reproduction of recorded media, which are covered in the chapter on information and audio-visual technologies.

(%) Figure 5.1

Wood, paper, publishing and printing (NACE Rev. 1 20 to 22)

Share of EU value added in total manufacturing

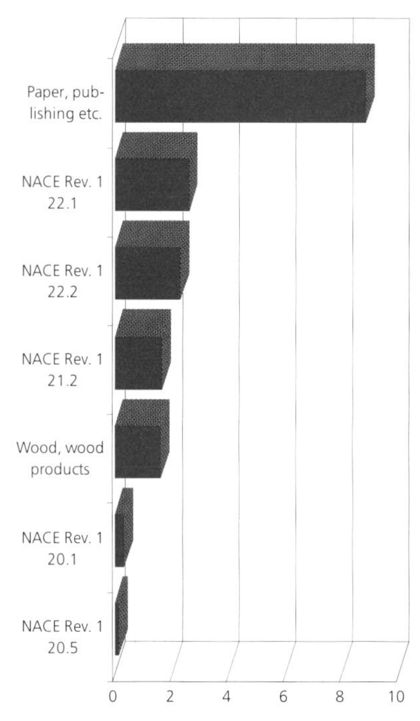

Source: Eurostat (SBS)

The activities covered in this chapter include:

- 20.1: sawmilling and planing of wood; impregnation of wood;
- 20.2: manufacture of veneer sheets; manufacture of plywood, laminboard, particle board and other panels and boards;
- 20.3: manufacture of builders' carpentry and joinery;
- 20.4: manufacture of wooden containers;
- 20.5: manufacture of other products of wood; manufacture of articles of cork, straw and plaiting materials;
- 21.1: manufacture of pulp, paper and paperboard;
- 21.2: manufacture of articles of paper and paperboard;
- 22.1: publishing;
- 22.2: printing and service activities related to printing.

Figure 5.2 (1988=100)

Wood, paper, publishing and printing (NACE Rev. 1 20 to 22)

Production, employment and value added compared to EU total manufacturing

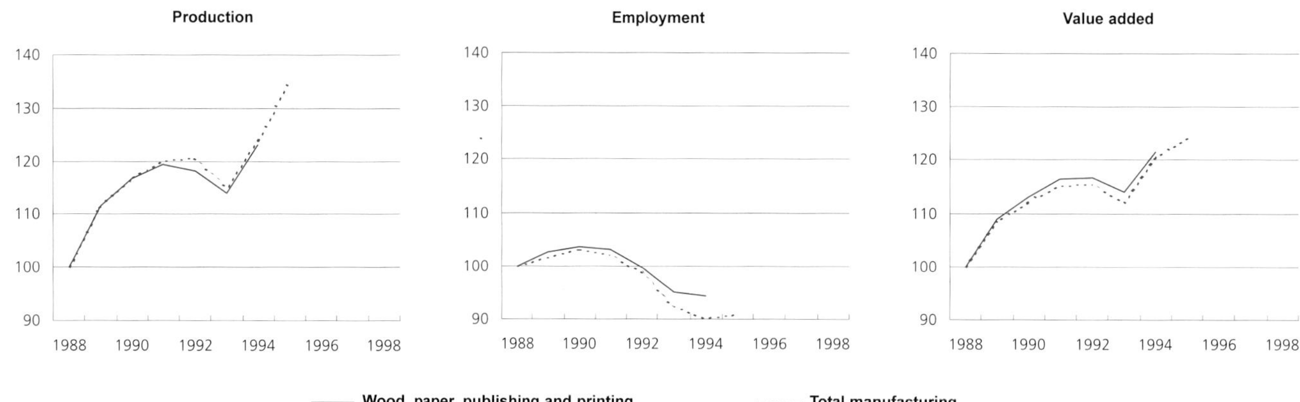

Source: Eurostat (SBS)

With the expansion of the EU to include Austria, Finland and Sweden the performance of the EU wood and paper products industry has changed noticeably. Large natural resources exist in the Nordic countries and to a lesser degree in Austria. In Finland, the manufacture of wood and wood products contributed three times more to total manufacturing than the EU average. In the manufacture of pulp, paper and paper products the Finish contribution was five times the EU average.

However, the printing and publishing industry displays different degrees of specialisation. For example, the United Kingdom recorded the highest specialisation ratios for this industry throughout the EU, this may be explained (at least partly) by the increasing use of English as a business language and a first foreign language.

Figure 5.3

Wood, paper, publishing and printing (NACE Rev. 1 20 to 22)

International comparison of main indicators in current prices

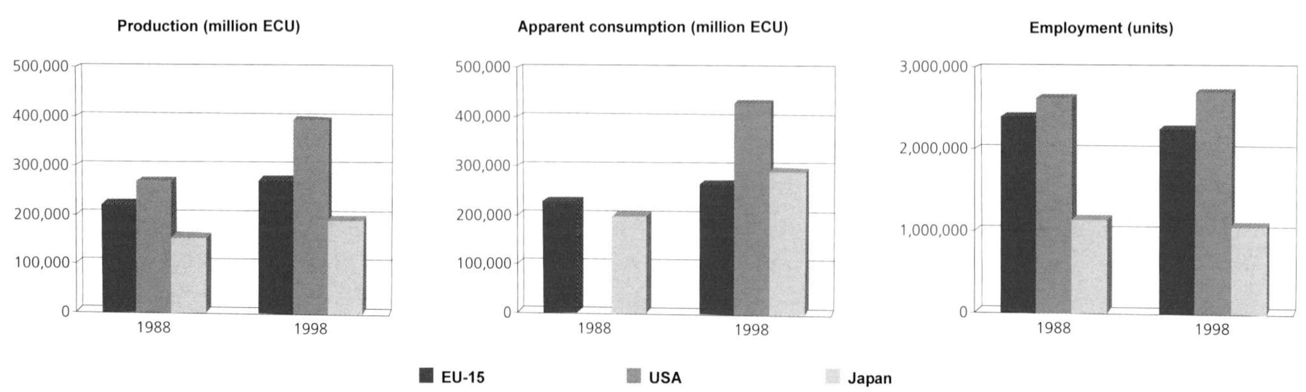

Source: Eurostat (SBS)

(ECU/hour) Figure 5.4

Wood and paper (NACE Rev. 1 20 and 21)
Labour costs by Member State, 1996

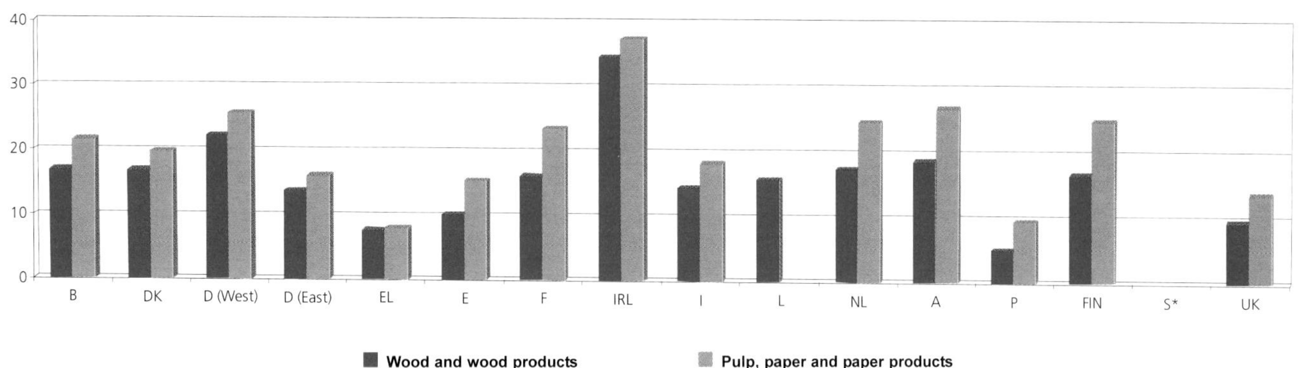

Source: Eurostat (LCS)

Recent trends

Since the early eighties the production value of wood, paper, publishing and printing has increased to account for more than 10% of total European manufacturing. During the eighties and the nineties the production of wood, paper, publishing and printing was on average on an upward trend. However, there was no clear trend to developments within the industry. Indeed, it was possible to find real output changing by more than ten percentage points per annum. In 1998, growth of production and value added slowed to only 0.6% and 1.3% respectively. European employment increased by 1.7% between 1988 and 1998 - one of the few manufacturing industries to report expansion in the total number of persons employed. Nevertheless, this industry (as most others) was not immune from the recession of the early nineties, when weak demand caused job losses.

EU paper, publishing and printing activities generated on average more value added per head than the wood and wood products industry (50.6 thousand ECU compared to 35.6 thousand ECU in 1998). However, the latter displayed improvements of almost 50% in labour productivity since 1988.

We may note that whilst most industries raised their labour productivity by shedding labour and substituting capital for labour, this was not the case within the publishing and printing industry on either side of the Atlantic.

Pulp, paper and paper products enterprises also faced a significant number of changes in their production process, for example, changing environmental policies have led to a reduction in the use of chlorine in the bleaching process of paper.

(%) Table 5.1

Paper, publishing and printing
(NACE Rev. 1 21 and 22)
Composition of the labour force, 1997

	Females	Part-time	Highly-educated
EU-15	21.4	34.1	5.5
B	6.6	31.5	13.9
DK	19.5	33.6	8.5
D	16.7	32.9	5.3
EL	:	:	:
E	22.6	23.1	2.6
F	16.2	35.6	:
IRL	17.8	40.1	19.9
I	26.8	31.1	6.1
L	:	32.5	:
NL	20.8	34.2	12.5
A	17.8	29.9	6.2
P	8.2	30.6	:
FIN	18.0	30.5	31.5
S	8.8	28.8	6.1
UK	26.4	35.4	2.6

Source: Eurostat (LFS)

Foreign trade

The activity of wood, paper, publishing and printing saw international trade increase. Nevertheless, foreign trade does not account for a large share of total production in many basic manufacturing areas of the industry as high costs are incurred for transportation. In the manufacture of wood and wood products there was a negative trade balance for the EU. This was partly due to the fact that the EU imported certain non-indigenous woods and partly due to the attractiveness of cheap imports from areas such as Eastern Europe. However, EU-15 exports were increasing at a faster pace than imports between 1990 and 1998. One country where there was a high degree of export activity was Portugal, where the export specialisation ratio was 5.2 times higher than the EU average.

In the manufacture of paper, publishing and printing there was a trade surplus, largely due to the performance of the paper industry in Finland and Sweden. Finland recorded a very high export specialisation ratio in wood, paper, publishing and printing, some 6.5 times higher than the EU average in 1998.

An international comparison of foreign trade shows that the USA had a similar profile to that of the EU. Whilst a trade deficit was run in wood and wood products, a positive balance was recorded for paper, publishing and printing. In Japan the wood, paper, printing and publishing industry recorded higher demand than domestic production.

Figure 5.5

Wood, paper, publishing and printing (NACE Rev. 1 20 to 22)
Destination of EU exports, 1998

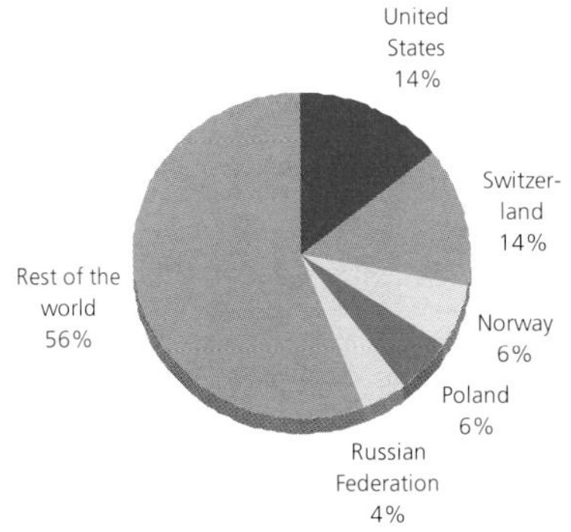

Source: Eurostat (Comext)

Figure 5.6

Wood, paper, publishing and printing (NACE Rev. 1 20 to 22)
Origin of EU imports, 1998

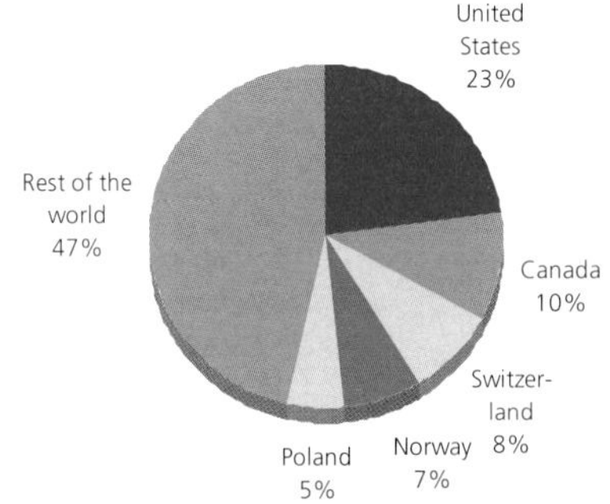

Source: Eurostat (Comext)

Sawing and first processing of wood (NACE Rev. 1 20.1)

The sawing and first processing of wood industry contains sawmilling and planing of wood and the impregnation of wood. Important customers for this activity include the downstream industries of semi-finished and finished wood products (NACE Rev. 1 20.2 to 20.5), as well as the manufacture of furniture and construction. The latter is especially susceptible to large-scale fluctuations in demand, linked to economic activity. The sawing and first processing of wood prepares wood for board making. Bark is prepared for use as fuel or mulch, wood flour and wood chips and is then used in the manufacture of paper and wood panels. Wood is not only debarked and cut, it is also preserved and dried to a certain moisture content, as well as being impregnated or treated chemically. Preserved wood is used primarily in the construction industry or for railways.

The countries with large natural resources of wood are the same as those that specialise in the sawing and first processing of wood (Sweden, Finland and Austria).

Figure 5.7

Sawing and first processing of wood (NACE Rev. 1 20.1)
Production and employment in the Triad

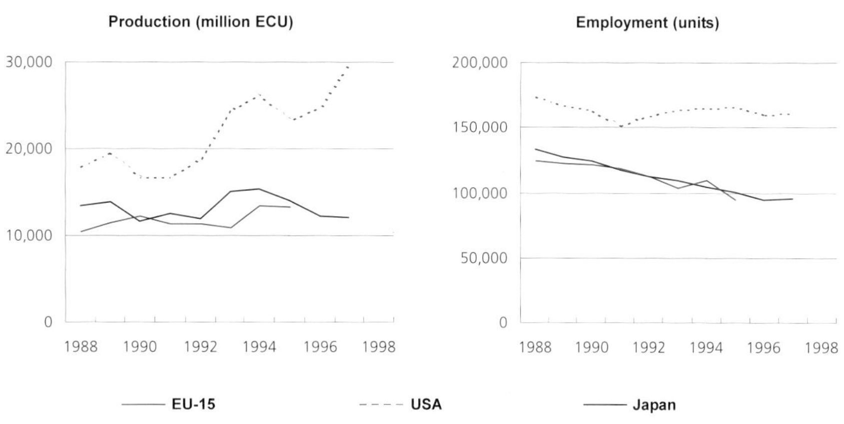

Source: Eurostat (SBS)

(%) Figure 5.8

Sawing and first processing of wood (NACE Rev. 1 20.1)
Production and export specialisation by Member State, 1998

Production specialisation

S
FIN
A
EU-15
E
D
F
DK
UK
EL
I
NL
P*
L*
IRL*
B*
0
200
400
600
800
1,000
1,200

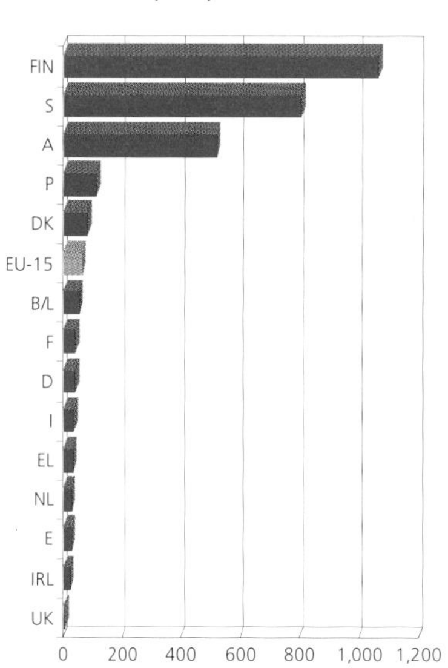

Source: Eurostat (SBS)

Sawing and first processing of wood faced strong competition from countries outside of Europe, especially Eastern Europe and Far East Asia. Efforts to increase competitiveness have focused on restructuring the business, with manufacturers switching to higher-quality products or pursuing strategies of vertical integration, especially to eliminate price fluctuations. The results of restructuring can clearly be seen in the performance of the industry between 1990 and 1998, when the output of the sawmilling and first processing of wood industry increased by 33.9% in Finland. In Sweden sawmilling and first processing of wood was on a continuous upward trend during the nineties (except for 1993). In 1998 there was however another fall in production, equal to some 7.6%.

Restructuring has resulted in a fairly large reduction of employment. In Finland the number of persons employed fell by 21.6% or some 2.5 thousand persons between 1990 and 1998. The loss of jobs is one reason why labour productivity has risen. In most Member States there was an upward trend to value added per person employed. In 1998, Austria reported labour productivity of 64.0 thousand ECU per head, some 30% higher than in Scandinavia. Sawmilling and first processing of wood is labour intensive and its competitiveness is to a large degree dependent on labour costs.

If we look at foreign trade, most Member States reported a deficit. The only exceptions were the large Nordic producers and Austria. Indeed, both Finland and Sweden increased their trade balances during the nineties.

Figure 5.9

Sawing and first processing of wood (NACE Rev. 1 20.1) Destination of EU exports, 1998

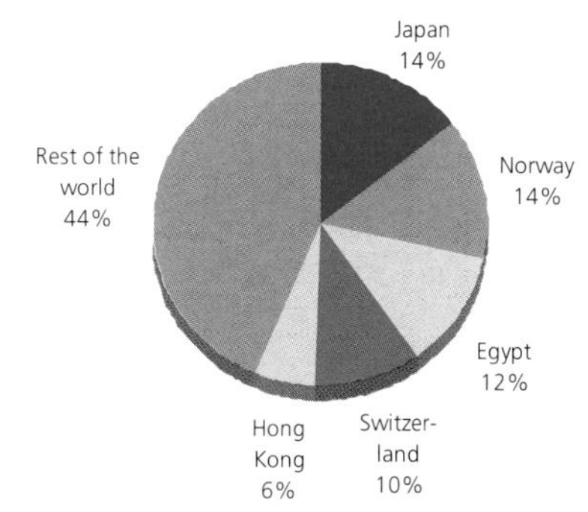

Source: Eurostat (Comext)

Figure 5.10

Sawing and first processing of wood (NACE Rev. 1 20.1) Origin of EU imports, 1998

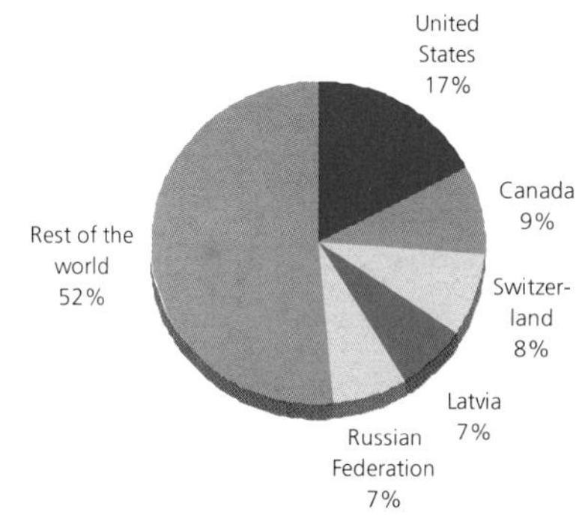

Source: Eurostat (Comext)

Semi-finished and finished wood products (NACE Rev. 1 20.2 to 20.5)

This industry produces a variety of products ranging from panels and boards to wooden roof structures, windows and parquet floor to wooden containers, basketware and cork processing. The majority of wood based panels are destined for the construction and furniture industries, whilst a small amount of output is purchased by consumers, largely for home improvements within the house (do-it-yourself). Therefore, semi-finished and finished wood products are dependent to a large degree on general economic activity, which governs the demand of the construction sector as well as that for wooden containers. Smaller Member States like Finland, Austria and Denmark were relatively specialised in this industry. The importance of Ireland has been increasing since 1997 when major investments occurred.

The manufacture of furniture was the main customer for wood based panels accounting for more than 50% of total output, followed by construction with 37.2%. Finland and Austria registered high production specialisation in this activity. In most of the Member States production of wood based panels increased from 1990 onwards, an upward trend that continued in 1998. However, as suppliers from outside Europe tried to gain a foothold in the European wood panel market, European suppliers reduced costs, mainly by reducing employment levels.

The main product line in this activity was the production of particle board, with a production volume of 26.2 million cubic metres, up by 7.4% in 1997, in line with trends in demand. The year before producers of particle board had to cut back their output, as demand was reduced by 3.2%. However, output declined by only 0.8% in 1996, as European manufacturers turned to export markets to maintain their production levels (exports rising by 8.3%).

Figure 5.11

Semi-finished and finished wood products (NACE Rev. 1 20.2 to 20.5)

Production and employment in the Triad

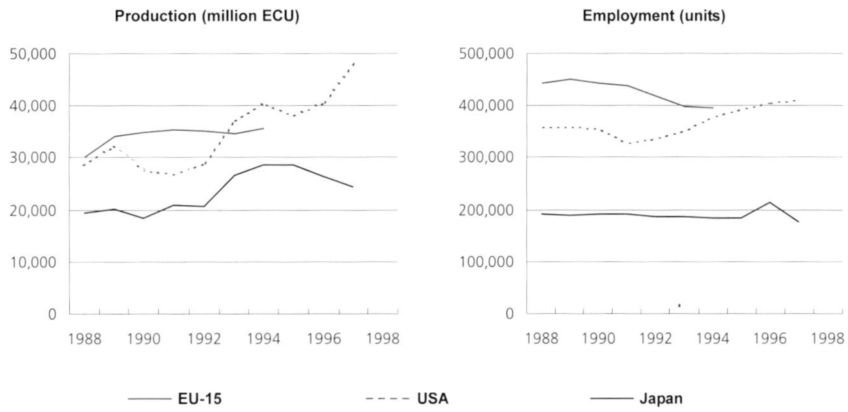

Source: Eurostat (SBS)

(%) Figure 5.12

Semi-finished and finished wood products (NACE Rev. 1 20.2 to 20.5)

Production and export specialisation by Member State, 1998

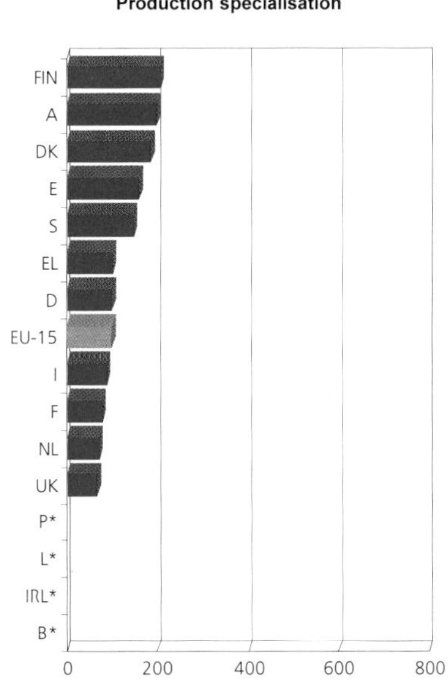

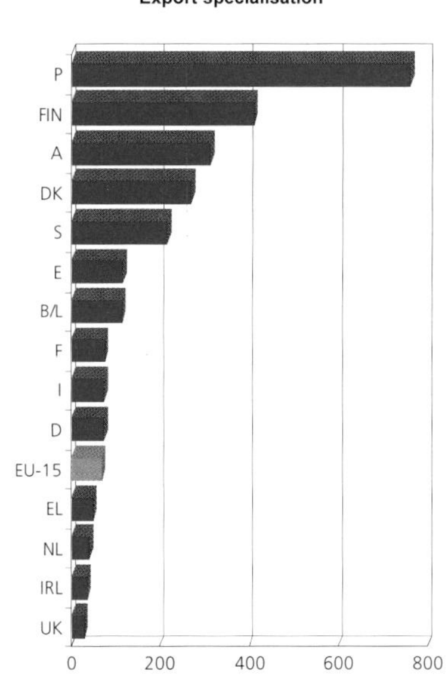

Source: Eurostat (SBS)

Within the Member States the manufacture of fibre board displayed a mixed picture, with varying trends across hardboard and softboard markets. In France production of hardboard went down by 28.6%, whilst the output of softboard rose by 27.9% in 1997. In Sweden, both industries faced a downward trend. There were concerns about over-capacity within the industry, particularly due to the high degree of competition from Eastern European manufacturers (sometimes producing to less stringent environmental legislation). In the Czech Republic, Hungary, Latvia, Lithuania, Poland and Romania production of hardboard accounted for 473.7 thousand tonnes in 1997 (data from FEROPA, European Federation of Fibre board Manufacturers).

Products within the activity of builders' carpentry and joinery (NACE Rev. 1 20.3) are used in construction and for restoration. There are distinct regional markets for many of the products made by this industry: first of all because of the degree of proximity between manufacturers and customers, but also due to differences in climate, indigenous wood supply and customer preferences. Denmark and the densely wooded Member States (Austria, Sweden and Finland) contributed comparatively large shares to the manufacture of builders' carpentry and joinery. During the nineties production and employment increased throughout the EU (except in the Nordic countries, in particular Sweden). Manufacture of builders' carpentry and joinery expanded to a large extent in Belgium, Germany and Denmark.

Figure 5.13 (thousand tonnes)

Production capacity of fibre board in Europe, 1997

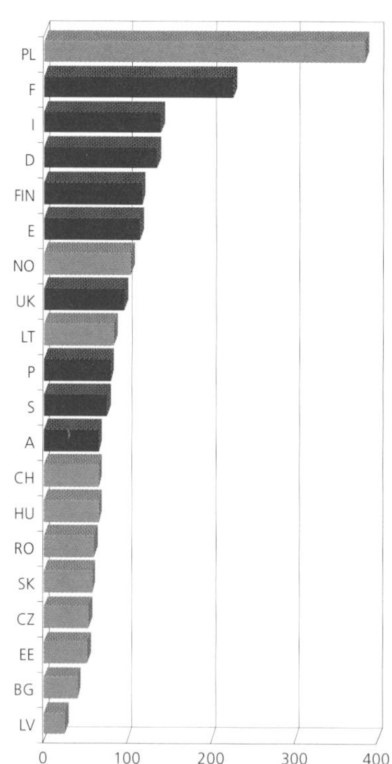

Source: FEROPA

Figure 5.14 (thousand cubic metres)

Deliveries of particle board to different users in Europe, 1997 (1)

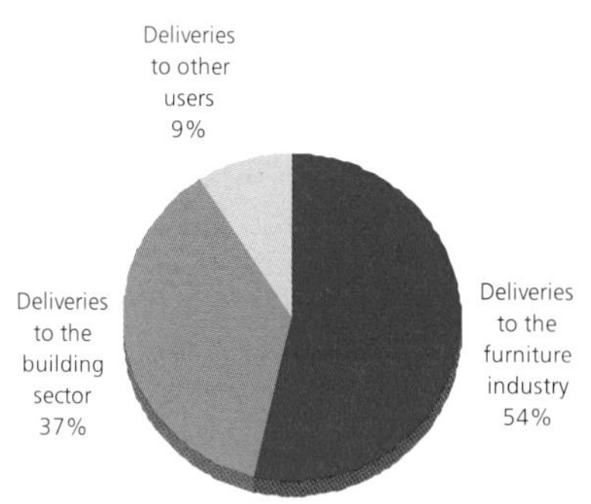

(1) EU-15 excluding the Netherlands, Luxembourg and Ireland.

Source: FESYP

Figure 5.15 (square metres per head)

Consumption of parquet in Western Europe, 1997

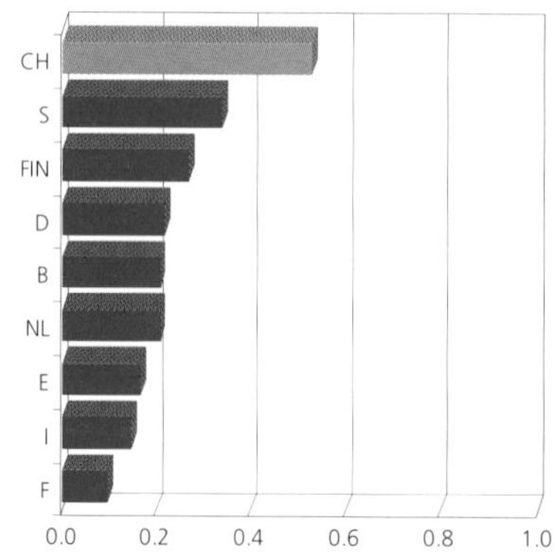

Source: FEP

Parquet had a market share of 4.7% of the flooring materials' sector in the EU in 1997. Sales increased by 5.1% to 82 million square metres. During the nineties consumption of parquet was moderately, but continuously rising, particularly in Spain and the Nordic countries. Rising sales were also reflected in production levels (data from FEP, European Federation of Associations of the Parquet Industry).

Wooden containers displayed significant growth in the period 1990 to 1998, with real growth of more than 10% in the EU. One quarter of total EU production came from France, with Spain and Germany following (both with a 15.7% share of the EU total in 1998). European production value was higher than in the USA, although American output was rising during the last decade at a faster rate than output within the EU. The American industry employed relatively more persons than its European competitors.

During the nineties, foreign trade of wooden containers was intensified, especially trade in pallets, where there was strong competition from Eastern European countries. All three Triad economies reported negative trade balances. The rate of increase of imports was particularly pronounced in the USA.

The manufacture of other products of wood; manufacture of articles of cork, straw and plaiting materials (NACE Rev. 1 20.5) covers a range of diverse products and supplies a range of other industries with intermediate products, as well as final customers with consumer goods. Portugal was the largest producer within the EU, with output about 50% higher than Germany. Between 1990 and 1998 European production was on a continuous upward trend, whilst facing increasing competition from the Far East and Eastern Europe. European manufacturers tried to reduce their costs through investment in automated production facilities, however the main competitive advantage that Europe held was with respect to quality.

Figure 5.16

Semi-finished and finished wood products (NACE Rev. 1 20.2 to 20.5) Destination of EU exports, 1998

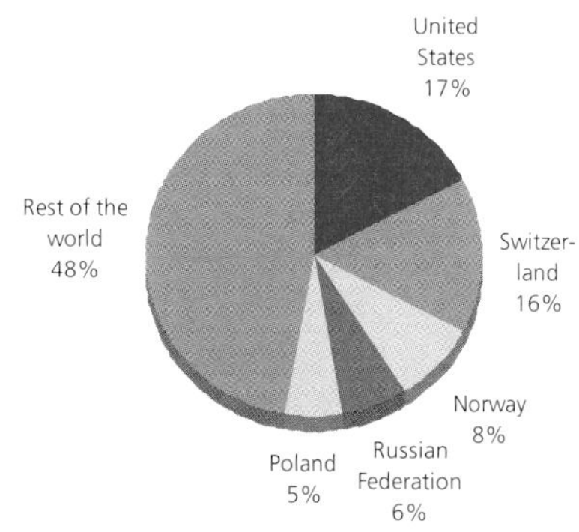

Source: Eurostat (Comext)

Figure 5.17

Semi-finished and finished wood products (NACE Rev. 1 20.2 to 20.5) Origin of EU imports, 1998

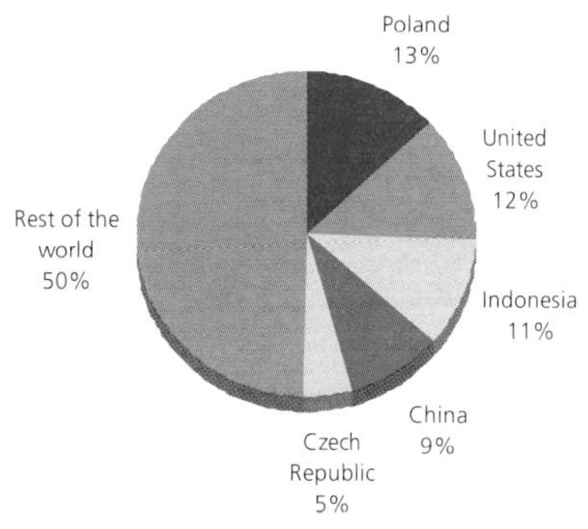

Source: Eurostat (Comext)

Pulp, paper and paper products (NACE Rev. 1 21)
Cellulose fibres are raw materials of paper and paperboard which are used for packaging articles, printing and writing paper as well as household and sanitary goods. Pulp is a watery fibrous substance made of fresh fibres or recycled fibres and is formed into paper sheets. There are different kinds of pulp dependent on the desired characteristics of the paper product like strength, appearance and intended use.

The Finnish and Swedish manufacturers of pulp, paper and paper products were important players within the EU and on the world market. Finland had a very high production specialisation in the manufacture of pulp, paper and paperboard: its share of production in Finnish total manufacturing was more than five times higher than the European average.

The aggregated activity of pulp, paper and paper products saw its production as well as its value added on an upward trend between 1990 and 1998 with the exception of Sweden where the production levels were decreasing in the middle of the decade.

In 1997 the production of pulp; paper and paperboard, increased by 9.8% and 8.4% respectively, with the European production of paper and paperboard reaching a new record level of 75.2 million tonnes. In 1996 however there had been a decrease (data from CEPI, Confederation of European Paper Industries). In the late nineties fluctuations were intensified by the crises in south-east Asia, in Russia and Latin America which reduced world demand and therefore the level of production. European suppliers were affected not only as they had to find new customers, but also because suppliers from Asia and North America tried to gain a larger share of the European market. In addition, Asian suppliers had the advantage of a devalued currency.

Figure 5.18

Pulp, paper and paper products (NACE Rev. 1 21)
Production and employment in the Triad

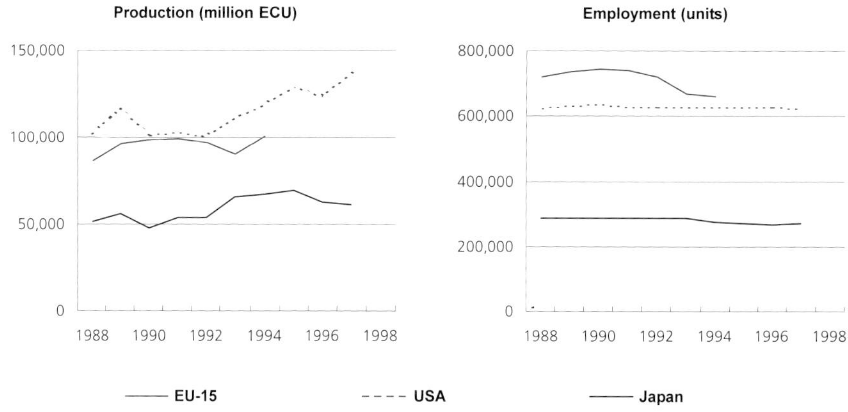

Source: Eurostat (SBS)

Figure 5.19 (%)

Pulp, paper and paper products (NACE Rev. 1 21)
Production and export specialisation by Member State, 1998

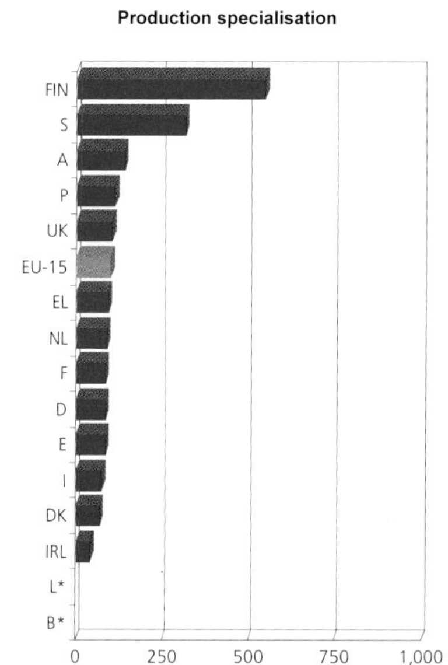

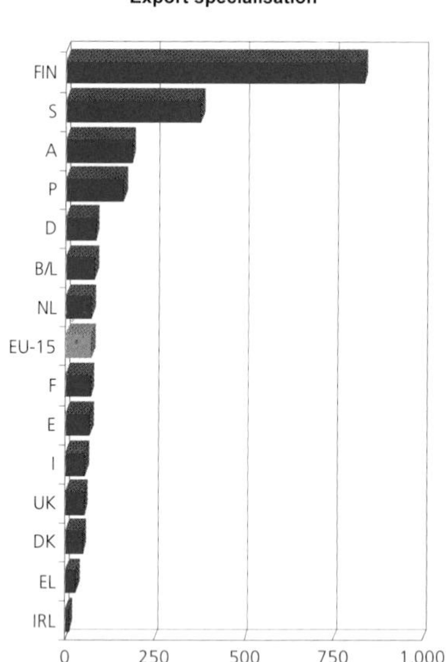

Source: Eurostat (SBS)

Figure 5.20
Capacity utilisation rate for pulp, paper and paperboard in the EU

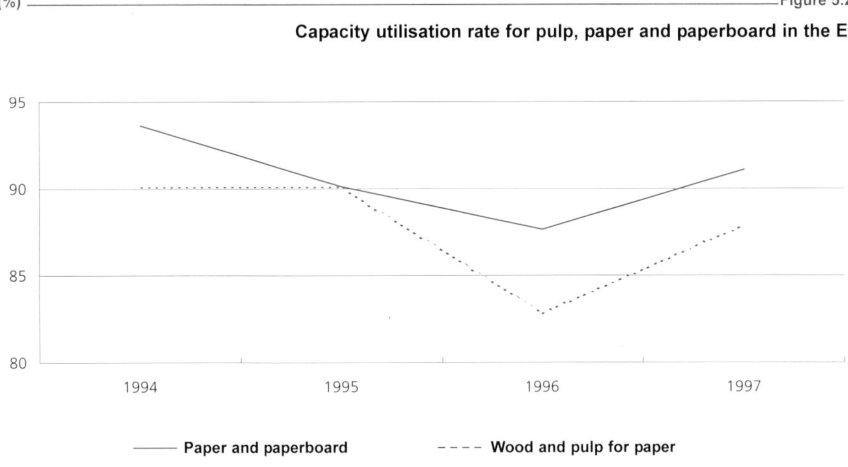

Source: CEPI

In 1998 the activity faced falling prices of end-products, which resulted in weakened sales (except in Ireland, the Netherlands and Spain where turnover increased by 12.5%, 7.8% and 6.6% respectively). Another factor that played an important role in price changes was over-capacity, as a result of declining demand and at the same time investment in larger facilities.

Enterprises producing articles of paper and paperboard face high levels of competition and strong bargaining power from downstream customers, such as food manufacturers, consumer goods' manufacturers and large retail chains. The industry reacted with two main strategies: a sharpening of focus on core products, for example packaging paper, or merger activity in either a downstream or upstream direction in order to gain competitive strength. This phenomena has resulted in a number of large European paper producers integrating the manufacture of articles of paper and paperboard. Levels of concentration remained high in the pulp and paper industry. Paper mills tend to be large and capital intensive, with a large minimum efficient scale required to obtain efficiency gains. In 1997 there were 1.2 thousand pulp and paper mills in the EU, with one thousand of them engaged in the manufacture of paper and paperboard (this figure includes also integrated pulp and paper mills). The production process is highly automated and often requires a highly skilled labour force, whereas the production of articles of paper and paperboard tended to be more labour intensive. Due to efforts to restructure the business the number of persons employed decreased from 1990 through until 1997, when it rose again. This was especially the case for the manufacture of paperboard, which unlike the pulp and paper mills was still dominated by a large number of small and medium-sized enterprises.

During the nineties there have been a number of changes in the production process of the pulp and paper industry. These have come about due to rationalisation of production, changes in national or European environmental policy, as well as new technological advances in production processes. One result has been a dramatic reduction in the use of water and energy. Other changes to the production process have included the replacement of chlorine bleaching by elemental or totally chlorine-free processes (bleaching is necessary to stop fibres from turning yellow with age or fading in the sunlight).

There has been a marked change in waste policy and recycling as environmental awareness has risen. This has led to a well-developed market for used paper and recycled fibres. Some manufacturers of pulp and paper have even fully changed their production processes and their range of products in order to use only recycled resources. Recycled fibres have become an essential raw material for the paper industry, that can be reused up to six times (if mixed with fresh fibres). Recycling is most attractive for mills operating in densely populated areas because of the large supply of paper and short distances for transporting materials (with manufacturers relying on secure supply and an efficient collecting system). In 1998 the collection of used paper was still largely influenced by the public sector, although some countries had introduced a private management system.

The average European rate of recycled to new paper was 43.7% in 1997: in other words for each 437g of used paper, a kilo of new paper was produced. The recovery rate in Europe was much higher for case materials (for packaging) and household and sanitary goods, some 86.3% and 66.8% respectively. The decision of whether or not to use recovered fibres is very important for individual enterprises operating within this industry, as paper mills using recovered fibres cannot easily switch to fresh fibres.

Figure 5.21
Pulp, paper and paper products (NACE Rev. 1 21)
Destination of EU exports, 1998

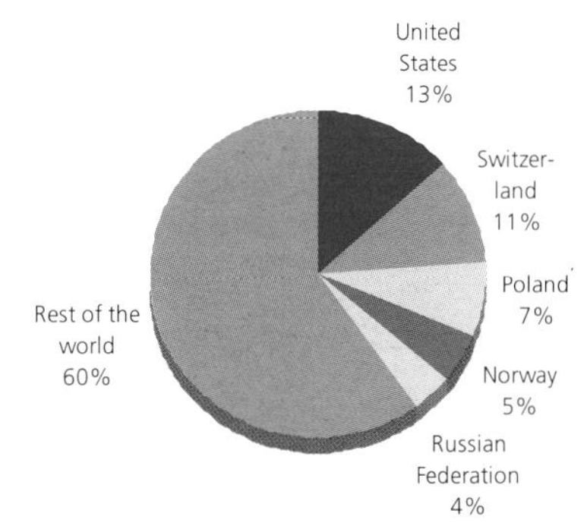

Source: Eurostat (Comext)

Figure 5.22
Pulp, paper and paper products (NACE Rev. 1 21)
Origin of EU imports, 1998

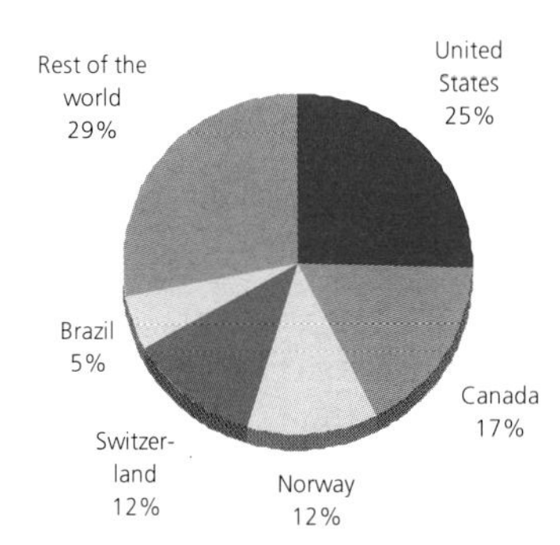

Source: Eurostat (Comext)

Printing and publishing (NACE Rev. 1 22.1 and 22.2)

Printing and publishing are highly related activities. Publishing prepares manuscripts for public dissemination either through a publishing company or an external author. Printing is the physical act of reproduction in large amounts for public consumption, be the final product a book, a newspaper, journal, periodical, postcard or poster. However, printing and related service activities have many other customers besides publishing, such as retail trade (advertising and catalogues), postal services (stamps) or financial services (cheques). Products derived from the printing industry vary in quality from four-colour printing on high gloss paper to newsprint.

EU production within printing and publishing grew moderately in 1998, up by 0.6%. At a more detailed level it was possible to note that output fell by 2.8% in publishing. The evolution of publishing and printing is to a large extent determined by the general economic situation, which influences the advertising budgets of industries, as well as household expenditure on consumer goods.

In 1997, the American printing and publishing industry had output equivalent to 120% of the European level. Production in the USA in 1997 rose by 19%, almost three times as fast as the growth recorded in the EU (6.9%). Employment rose slightly in the EU, up by 0.3%, whilst in the USA, growth of 1.5% was recorded (again in 1997).

Within the printing industry there are many small enterprises operating. This structure has continued as many orders are placed with local suppliers (especially due to transport costs). The activity of publishing, on the other hand, is far more concentrated. Printing facilities typically serve regional or local markets. Products like books or periodicals however are more often destined for national or international markets. The strong influence of language is one other reason why there is a relatively low level of foreign trade in this industry. However, foreign deliveries and non-domestic purchases were both on the increase during the nineties, with a growing trade surplus in the EU.

Figure 5.23

Printing and publishing (NACE Rev. 1 22.1 and 22.2)
Production and employment in the Triad

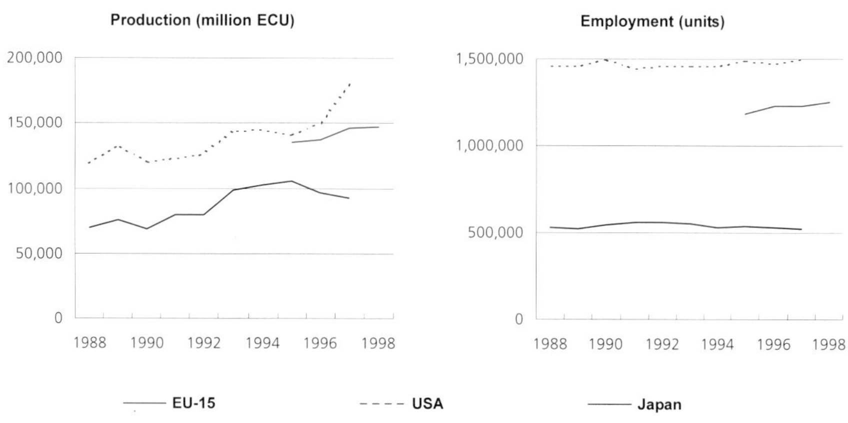

Source: Eurostat (SBS)

Figure 5.24 (%)

Printing and publishing (NACE Rev. 1 22.1 and 22.2)
Production and export specialisation by Member State, 1998

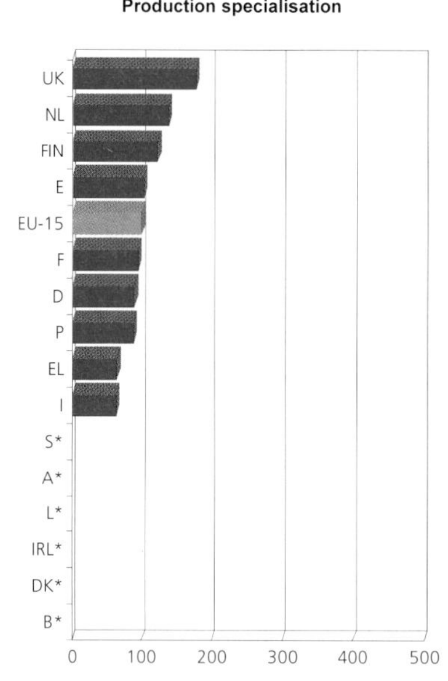

Source: Eurostat (SBS)

Within the information society there are a number of electronic alternatives being created as competition to traditional paper copy. The content of an encyclopedia can be still published on paper, but far greater amounts of information can be stored on a CD-ROM, allowing different media (sound, image, video) to interact with both the accompanying text and the user. Preparation of masters is often carried out by publishing companies, whilst the reproduction of a CD-ROM is a much more simple task than that for a book, which may require setting, flashing, printing and binding. The demand for electronic products rises in line with computer skills and the number of computer households that exist.

Apart from offering competitive products that threaten some traditional paper publications, advances in technology and communications have also led to changes in the production process employed to make paper products. There have as a result of this process been widespread changes in the work carried out by printers. Whereas a large amount of time used to be spent in the preparation and setting of documents, much of this work can now be controlled by computers. Indeed, new job profiles have arisen that have led to the disappearance of jobs such as typesetters.

(%) Figure 5.25

Capacity utilisation for the printing industry in Europe, 1997 (1)

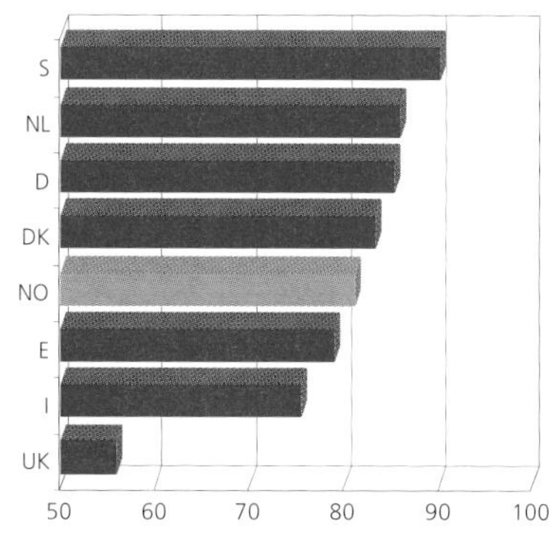

(1) For INTERGRAF members.

Source: INTERGRAF

Within Europe, the printing of magazines, books or advertising catalogues was far larger than the newspaper industry. Printing is still largely based at a national level, and market expansion is often inhibited by language barriers. Within the United Kingdom this was somewhat different, due to the widespread use of the English language. At the same time North American manufacturers started to establish European printing facilities in the United Kingdom. Publishing in the United Kingdom accounted for some 20.9% of the European total in 1998 in value terms. There has been a trend for large German and French publishers to purchase small publishing enterprises in the United Kingdom. Besides the market for English language output, printing and publishing enterprises also have a large market in Spanish (South America), as well as French and German material (expected to increase with the continued integration of the Eastern European economies).

Figure 5.26

Printing and publishing (NACE Rev. 1 22.1 and 22.2) Destination of EU exports, 1998

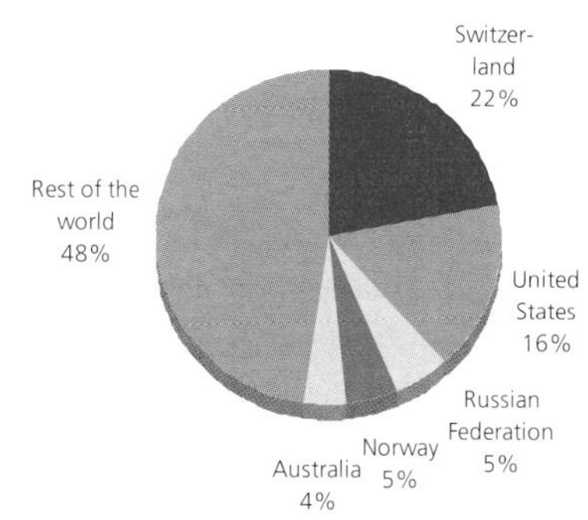

Source: Eurostat (Comext)

Figure 5.27

Printing and publishing (NACE Rev. 1 22.1 and 22.2) Origin of EU imports, 1998

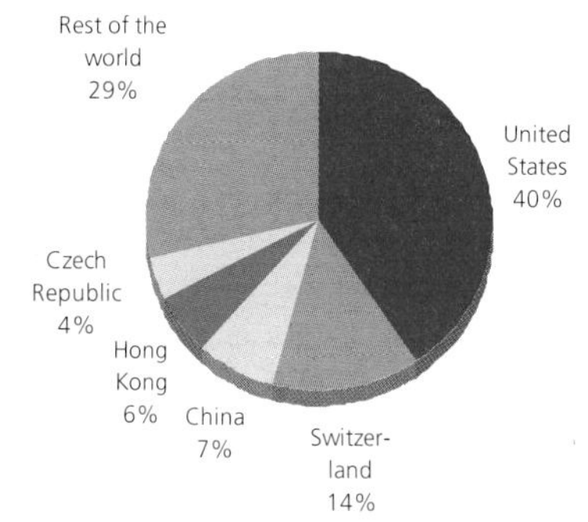

Source: Eurostat (Comext)

Professional associations representing the industries within this chapter

CEPI
Confederation of European Paper Industries
306, avenue Louise
B-1050 Bruxelles
tel: (32) 2 627 49 11
fax: (32) 2 646 81 37

CITPA
International Confederation of Paper and Board Converters in the EU
Strubbergstraße 70
D-60489 Frankfurt am Main
tel: (49) 69 78 50 40
fax: (49) 69) 78 50 41

FEP
European Federation of Associations of the Parquet Industry
5, allée Hof-ter-Vleest
Boîte 4
B-1040 Bruxelles
tel: (32) 2 556 25 87
fax: (32) 2 556 25 95
e-mail:
euro.wood.fed@skynet.be

FEROPA
European Federation of Fibreboard Manufacturers
724 Traversée des Rougons
F-83510 Lorgues
tel: (33) 4 94 73 75 99
fax: (33) 4 94 67 67 07

FESYP
European Federation of Associations of Particleboard manufacturers
5, allée Hof-ter-Vleest
Boîte 5
B-1040 Bruxelles
tel: (32) 2 556 25 89
fax: (32) 2 556 25 94
e-mail:
euro.wood.fed@skynet.be

INTERGRAF
International Confederation for Printing and Allied Industries
18, square Marie-Louise
boîte 25-27
B-1040 Bruxelles
tel: (32) 2 230 86 46
fax: (32) 2 231 14 64

Table 5.2 (million ECU)

Sawmilling and planing of wood; impregnation of wood (NACE Rev. 1 20.1)
Production related indicators in the EU

	1988	1989	1990	1991	1992	1993	1994	1995	1996	1997	1998
Production value	10,382	11,540	12,267	11,394	11,331	10,838	13,378	13,304	:	:	:
Producer price index (1995=100)	:	:	:	:	:	:	:	:	:	:	:
Value added	3,101	3,329	3,512	3,095	3,171	3,243	4,045	3,533	:	:	:
Number of persons employed (thousands)	124.5	122.0	121.8	118.4	112.7	103.0	109.5	94.5	:	:	:

Table 5.3 (million ECU)

Sawmilling and planing of wood; impregnation of wood (NACE Rev. 1 20.1)
Production related indicators, 1998

	B	DK	D	EL	E	F	IRL	I	L	NL	A	P	FIN	S	UK
Production value	523	134	2,908	38	811	1,621	185	524	36	34	1,156	:	2,231	3,139	734
Value added	147	41	870	11	231	435	42	186	6	9	299	:	436	661	238
Number of persons employed (units) (1)	2,928	1,011	17,970	523	12,089	14,374	1,242	3,802	157	342	4,662	:	9,136	13,098	8,157

(1) NL (1992).

Table 5.4 (million ECU)

Sawmilling and planing of wood; impregnation of wood (NACE Rev. 1 20.1)
Market related indicators in the EU

	1988	1989	1990	1991	1992	1993	1994	1995	1996	1997	1998
Apparent consumption	11,020	13,183	12,510	11,755	11,448	12,486	15,028	14,655	:	:	:
Exports	714	699	749	790	755	926	1,199	1,391	1,389	1,742	1,618
Imports	1,352	2,342	992	1,151	873	2,574	2,848	2,742	2,487	3,461	3,185
Trade balance	-638	-1,643	-243	-361	-117	-1,648	-1,649	-1,352	-1,097	-1,719	-1,567
Export ratio (%)	6.9	6.1	6.1	6.9	6.7	8.5	9.0	10.5	:	:	:
Import penetration ratio (%)	12.3	17.8	7.9	9.8	7.6	20.6	19.0	18.7	:	:	:
Cover ratio (%)	52.8	29.9	75.5	68.7	86.6	36.0	42.1	50.7	55.9	50.3	50.8

Table 5.5 (million ECU)

Sawmilling and planing of wood; impregnation of wood (NACE Rev. 1 20.1)
Market related indicators, 1998

	B/L	DK	D	EL	E	F	IRL	I	NL	A	P	FIN	S	UK
Apparent consumption	:	571	3,583	188	1,390	1,945	325	1,957	580	560	:	881	1,289	2,328
Exports	293	109	653	9	88	417	43	278	168	872	80	1,440	1,996	55
Imports	616	546	1,328	159	667	741	183	1,711	715	276	119	90	146	1,649
Trade balance	-323	-437	-675	-150	-579	-324	-140	-1,434	-546	596	-39	1,350	1,850	-1,594
Export ratio (%)	:	81.5	22.5	24.7	10.9	25.7	23.0	53.1	492.3	75.5	:	64.6	63.6	7.5
Import penetration ratio (%)	:	95.6	37.1	84.7	48.0	38.1	56.2	87.4	123.1	49.4	:	10.2	11.3	70.8
Cover ratio (%)	47.5	20.0	49.2	5.9	13.2	56.2	23.3	16.2	23.6	315.7	67.3	1,600.7	1,364.3	3.3

Table 5.6

Sawmilling and planing of wood; impregnation of wood (NACE Rev. 1 20.1)
Labour related indicators, 1998

	EU-15	B	DK	D	EL	E	F	IRL	I	L	NL	A	P	FIN	S	UK
Personnel costs (million ECU) (1)	2,274	74	31	548	6	135	371	23	84	4	8	126	:	241	420	161
Personnel costs/employee (thousand ECU) (2)	24.9	26.8	31.7	31.2	12.6	13.5	26.2	18.7	20.2	27.0	:	28.9	:	28.2	33.5	16.4
Social charges/personnel costs (%) (3)	23.1	27.9	4.9	18.4	24.9	23.5	29.0	16.2	39.2	:	12.3	23.5	:	22.6	29.0	11.5
Labour productivity (thousand ECU/head) (4)	37.4	50.2	40.6	48.4	20.1	19.1	30.3	33.6	49.0	35.9	31.7	64.0	:	47.8	50.5	29.1
Wage adjusted labour productivity (%) (2)	150.3	126.5	123.2	140.9	114.1	131.2	113.8	158.9	186.4	121.8	:	172.4	:	137.2	130.4	149.0

(1) EU-15 (1995). (2) EU-15, EL, I, A (1995); B, DK, D, E, F, IRL, L, FIN, S, UK (1996). (3) EU-15, S (1995). (4) NL (1992); EU-15 (1995).

Source: Eurostat (SBS, EBT)

(million ECU) Table 5.7

Manufacture of veneer sheets; manufacture of plywood, laminboard, particle board, fibre board and other panels and boards (NACE Rev. 1 20.2)

Production related indicators in the EU

	1988	1989	1990	1991	1992	1993	1994	1995	1996	1997	1998
Production value	9,480	10,397	9,660	9,738	9,741	9,756	10,621	:	:	:	:
Producer price index (1995=100)	:	:	:	:	:	:	:	:	:	:	:
Value added	3,181	3,412	3,006	3,035	3,028	3,046	3,186	:	:	:	:
Number of persons employed (thousands)	92.0	93.3	84.6	82.4	80.1	76.8	77.2	:	:	:	:

(million ECU) Table 5.8

Manufacture of veneer sheets; manufacture of plywood, laminboard, particle board, fibre board and other panels and boards (NACE Rev. 1 20.2)

Production related indicators, 1998

	B	DK	D	EL	E	F	IRL	I	L	NL	A	P	FIN	S	UK
Production value (1)	1,001	180	3,296	248	1,310	1,376	139	2,275	:	59	603	:	861	331	965
Value added (1)	263	56	1,099	60	352	350	40	626	:	21	151	:	334	85	325
Number of persons employed (units) (1)(2)	2,870	1,097	19,320	2,111	9,509	8,418	593	10,969	:	562	3,252	:	7,153	1,970	5,485

(1) A (1994). (2) NL (1992).

(million ECU) Table 5.9

Manufacture of veneer sheets; manufacture of plywood, laminboard, particle board, fibre board and other panels and boards (NACE Rev. 1 20.2)

Market related indicators in the EU

	1988	1989	1990	1991	1992	1993	1994	1995	1996	1997	1998
Apparent consumption	10,329	11,192	10,620	10,815	10,715	10,568	11,508	:	:	:	:
Exports	439	467	481	428	430	602	760	842	934	1,180	1,334
Imports	1,288	1,262	1,441	1,504	1,404	1,414	1,648	1,837	1,714	2,031	2,096
Trade balance	-849	-795	-959	-1,077	-974	-812	-887	-996	-780	-851	-761
Export ratio (%)	4.6	4.5	5.0	4.4	4.4	6.2	7.2	:	:	:	:
Import penetration ratio (%)	12.5	11.3	13.6	13.9	13.1	13.4	14.3	:	:	:	:
Cover ratio (%)	34.1	37.0	33.4	28.4	30.6	42.6	46.1	45.8	54.5	58.1	63.7

(million ECU) Table 5.10

Manufacture of veneer sheets; manufacture of plywood, laminboard, particle board, fibre board and other panels and boards (NACE Rev. 1 20.2)

Market related indicators, 1998

	B/L	DK	D	EL	E	F	IRL	I	NL	A	P	FIN	S	UK
Apparent consumption (1)	:	346	3,315	328	1,389	1,243	123	2,444	411	398	:	330	283	1,779
Exports	658	83	1,323	18	227	655	94	407	98	480	153	581	269	104
Imports	398	250	1,342	99	306	522	78	576	450	200	60	50	222	918
Trade balance	260	-167	-19	-80	-79	133	16	-169	-352	280	92	531	47	-814
Export ratio (%) (1)	:	46.2	40.1	7.3	17.3	47.6	67.8	17.9	164.5	61.6	:	67.5	81.4	10.7
Import penetration ratio (%) (1)	:	72.1	40.5	30.0	22.0	42.0	63.6	23.6	109.3	41.8	:	15.2	78.3	51.6
Cover ratio (%)	165.4	33.3	98.6	18.4	74.3	125.5	120.3	70.6	21.7	240.3	253.2	1,158.6	121.4	11.3

(1) A (1994).

Table 5.11

Manufacture of veneer sheets; manufacture of plywood, laminboard, particle board, fibre board and other panels and boards (NACE Rev. 1 20.2)

Labour related indicators, 1998

	EU-15	B	DK	D	EL	E	F	IRL	I	L	NL	A	P	FIN	S	UK
Personnel costs (million ECU) (1)	2,092	101	34	766	34	171	236	17	288	:	13	105	:	193	64	148
Personnel costs/employee (thousand ECU) (2)	:	36.7	31.8	38.8	17.8	18.9	28.5	27.9	24.0	:	:	32.4	:	27.8	33.8	22.6
Social charges/personnel costs (%) (3)	:	32.4	4.7	18.5	23.1	23.1	29.5	13.3	36.9	:	13.4	23.7	:	21.3	28.3	11.1
Labour productivity (thousand ECU/head) (4)	41.3	91.7	51.1	56.9	28.5	37.0	41.5	66.8	57.0	:	37.1	46.5	:	46.7	42.9	59.3
Wage adjusted labour productivity (%) (2)	:	172.3	155.3	130.0	107.6	180.8	140.0	212.9	209.2	:	:	143.6	:	140.6	113.8	223.5

(1) EU-15, A (1994); NL (1997). (2) A (1994); EL, I (1995); B, DK, D, E, F, IRL, FIN, S, UK (1996). (3) A (1994); S (1995); NL (1997). (4) NL (1992); EU-15, A (1994).

Source: Eurostat (SBS, EBT)

Table 5.12 (million ECU)

Manufacture of builders' carpentry and joinery (NACE Rev. 1 20.3)

Production related indicators in the EU

	1988	1989	1990	1991	1992	1993	1994	1995	1996	1997	1998
Production value	13,955	15,804	16,727	16,614	16,378	16,357	16,243	:	:	:	:
Producer price index (1995=100)	:	:	:	:	:	:	:	100.0	100.7	100.6	102.6
Value added	4,971	5,637	5,773	5,762	5,841	5,969	5,800	:	:	:	:
Number of persons employed (thousands)	225.7	227.5	228.7	222.8	211.5	206.1	198.1	:	:	:	:

Table 5.13 (million ECU)

Manufacture of builders' carpentry and joinery (NACE Rev. 1 20.3)

Production related indicators, 1998

	B	DK	D	EL	E	F	IRL	I	L	NL	A	P	FIN	S	UK
Production value	727	954	6,582	33	2,768	2,454	138	1,303	:	815	1,677	459	893	1,458	1,849
Value added	265	340	2,282	9	952	714	52	452	:	310	773	:	288	457	629
Number of persons employed (units) (1)	7,253	8,392	54,778	477	58,546	17,677	2,255	11,438	:	7,412	14,260	14,232	7,964	10,111	21,229

(1) NL (1992).

Table 5.14 (million ECU)

Manufacture of builders' carpentry and joinery (NACE Rev. 1 20.3)

Market related indicators in the EU

	1988	1989	1990	1991	1992	1993	1994	1995	1996	1997	1998
Apparent consumption	13,778	15,639	16,525	16,426	16,444	16,440	16,468	:	:	:	:
Exports	338	377	443	408	334	346	477	624	806	929	904
Imports	161	212	241	220	400	429	702	601	566	797	642
Trade balance	177	165	202	187	-66	-83	-225	23	240	132	262
Export ratio (%)	2.4	2.4	2.6	2.5	2.0	2.1	2.9	:	:	:	:
Import penetration ratio (%)	1.2	1.4	1.5	1.3	2.4	2.6	4.3	:	:	:	:
Cover ratio (%)	209.9	177.8	184.0	185.2	83.6	80.6	67.9	103.8	142.3	116.6	140.8

Table 5.15 (million ECU)

Manufacture of builders' carpentry and joinery (NACE Rev. 1 20.3)

Market related indicators, 1998

	B/L	DK	D	EL	E	F	IRL	I	NL	A	P	FIN	S	UK
Apparent consumption	:	649	7,379	40	2,727	2,447	177	1,270	800	1,642	456	575	988	2,062
Exports	205	434	345	2	117	189	8	168	184	295	41	342	516	103
Imports	166	129	1,142	9	75	182	46	135	169	261	38	23	46	316
Trade balance	40	305	-798	-7	41	7	-39	33	15	35	3	318	470	-214
Export ratio (%)	:	45.5	5.2	5.8	4.2	7.7	5.5	12.9	22.6	17.6	8.9	38.2	35.4	5.5
Import penetration ratio (%)	:	19.8	15.5	21.8	2.8	7.4	26.3	10.7	21.1	15.9	8.3	4.0	4.6	15.3
Cover ratio (%)	124.0	336.9	30.2	22.2	155.0	103.8	16.2	124.0	108.8	113.3	108.1	1,476.3	1,130.8	32.4

Table 5.16

Manufacture of builders' carpentry and joinery (NACE Rev. 1 20.3)

Labour related indicators, 1998

	EU-15	B	DK	D	EL	E	F	IRL	I	L	NL	A	P	FIN	S	UK
Personnel costs (million ECU) (1)	4,237	157	258	1,874	6	669	468	33	274	:	244	380	74	184	320	456
Personnel costs/employee (thousand ECU) (2)	:	28.6	31.4	34.9	12.9	14.7	26.9	15.2	21.9	:	:	28.3	:	24.9	33.2	17.9
Social charges/personnel costs (%) (3)	:	33.1	3.8	18.3	22.9	22.3	29.9	13.3	37.3	:	15.2	22.5	:	22.0	29.0	10.4
Labour productivity (thousand ECU/head) (4)	29.3	36.5	40.5	41.7	19.7	16.3	40.4	22.9	39.6	:	30.7	54.2	:	36.2	45.2	29.6
Wage adjusted labour productivity (%) (2)	:	110.9	131.8	117.4	113.9	111.4	142.6	148.8	150.8	:	:	134.9	:	121.2	118.0	131.4

(1) EU-15 (1994). (2) EL, I, A (1995); B, DK, D, E, F, IRL, FIN, S, UK (1996). (3) S (1995). (4) NL (1992); EU-15 (1994).

Source: Eurostat (SBS, EBT)

(million ECU) Table 5.17

Manufacture of wooden containers (NACE Rev. 1 20.4)
Production related indicators in the EU

	1988	1989	1990	1991	1992	1993	1994	1995	1996	1997	1998
Production value	2,755	3,312	3,764	3,890	3,667	3,369	3,559	:	4,180	4,249	4,226
Producer price index (1995=100)	:	:	96.6	98.6	97.5	96.1	96.3	100.0	:	:	:
Value added	950	1,091	1,233	1,264	1,245	1,135	1,124	:	1,240	1,292	1,288
Number of persons employed (thousands)	42.8	46.6	47.7	48.7	46.2	43.2	42.9	:	44.5	48.4	47.5

(million ECU) Table 5.18

Manufacture of wooden containers (NACE Rev. 1 20.4)
Production related indicators, 1998

	B	DK	D	EL	E	F	IRL	I	L	NL	A	P	FIN	S	UK
Production value (1)	208	58	664	12	663	1,035	28	454	:	230	63	45	97	139	539
Value added (1)	58	19	214	4	181	323	5	135	:	72	20	:	41	45	157
Number of persons employed (units) (1)(2)	1,240	522	5,446	208	12,726	10,792	318	4,171	:	2,107	631	1,041	821	1,061	6,885

(1) A (1994). (2) NL (1992).

(million ECU) Table 5.19

Manufacture of wooden containers (NACE Rev. 1 20.4)
Market related indicators in the EU

	1988	1989	1990	1991	1992	1993	1994	1995	1996	1997	1998
Apparent consumption	2,727	3,289	3,757	3,914	3,727	3,400	3,606	:	4,222	4,268	4,267
Exports	57	69	79	85	72	85	115	137	161	203	248
Imports	29	46	72	109	132	116	162	200	203	222	289
Trade balance	28	23	7	-24	-60	-31	-48	-63	-42	-19	-41
Export ratio (%)	2.1	2.1	2.1	2.2	2.0	2.5	3.2	:	3.9	4.8	5.9
Import penetration ratio (%)	1.1	1.4	1.9	2.8	3.6	3.4	4.5	:	4.8	5.2	6.8
Cover ratio (%)	195.9	150.6	109.6	77.7	54.7	73.4	70.7	68.4	79.3	91.4	85.8

(million ECU) Table 5.20

Manufacture of wooden containers (NACE Rev. 1 20.4)
Market related indicators, 1998

	B/L	DK	D	EL	E	F	IRL	I	NL	A	P	FIN	S	UK
Apparent consumption (1)	:	69	754	15	658	908	35	487	232	73	34	108	118	593
Exports	70	11	91	1	55	247	1	56	40	22	18	4	36	88
Imports	87	21	181	4	50	120	9	89	42	38	7	15	14	142
Trade balance	-17	-11	-90	-3	5	127	-7	-33	-2	-16	12	-11	21	-54
Export ratio (%) (1)	:	18.1	13.7	7.7	8.3	23.9	5.1	12.4	17.5	11.2	40.4	4.3	25.7	16.4
Import penetration ratio (%) (1)	:	31.0	24.0	27.2	7.6	13.3	24.6	18.3	18.2	23.3	19.8	13.8	12.2	23.9
Cover ratio (%)	80.9	49.2	50.3	22.3	110.1	205.0	16.4	63.0	95.2	58.0	274.9	27.7	249.3	62.2

(1) A (1994).

Table 5.21

Manufacture of wooden containers (NACE Rev. 1 20.4)
Labour related indicators, 1998

	EU-15	B	DK	D	EL	E	F	IRL	I	L	NL	A	P	FIN	S	UK
Personnel costs (million ECU) (1)	1,022	48	15	162	2	158	278	5	91	:	50	15	6	20	32	143
Personnel costs/employee (thousand ECU) (2)	:	39.6	30.0	31.5	9.1	14.5	26.2	16.7	20.0	:	:	24.2	:	27.2	31.8	17.5
Social charges/personnel costs (%) (3)	:	27.3	4.7	17.5	22.4	21.7	29.2	17.7	38.5	:	13.4	21.1	:	22.3	28.0	11.5
Labour productivity (thousand ECU/head) (4)	27.1	46.6	36.3	39.4	19.1	14.2	29.9	16.2	32.5	:	31.1	31.5	:	49.4	42.6	22.9
Wage adjusted labour productivity (%) (2)	:	113.2	116.7	128.3	148.8	130.4	117.2	96.4	142.2	:	:	130.0	:	146.3	121.7	130.1

(1) A (1994). (2) A (1994); EL, I (1995); B, DK, D, E, F, IRL, FIN, S, UK (1996). (3) A (1994); S (1995). (4) NL (1992); A (1994).

Source: Eurostat (SBS, EBT)

Table 5.22 (million ECU)

Manufacture of other products of wood; manufacture of articles of cork, straw and plaiting materials (NACE Rev. 1 20.5)
Production related indicators in the EU

	1988	1989	1990	1991	1992	1993	1994	1995	1996	1997	1998
Production value	3,854	4,458	4,655	4,988	5,201	4,998	5,230	5,323	:	:	:
Producer price index (1995=100)	:	:	:	:	:	:	:	:	:	:	:
Value added	1,521	1,670	1,766	1,878	1,944	1,858	1,933	1,796	:	:	:
Number of persons employed (thousands)	81.1	83.0	82.3	85.0	80.7	72.6	76.4	72.0	:	:	:

Table 5.23 (million ECU)

Manufacture of other products of wood; manufacture of articles of cork, straw and plaiting materials (NACE Rev. 1 20.5)
Production related indicators, 1998

	B	DK	D	EL	E	F	IRL	I	L	NL	A	P	FIN	S	UK
Production value	159	92	1,162	6	753	514	40	956	:	133	96	1,716	49	50	369
Value added (1)	69	33	468	2	258	186	12	351	:	57	37	:	22	25	138
Number of persons employed (units) (2)	1,485	773	11,804	97	9,069	5,640	506	9,445	:	944	1,028	19,309	734	639	5,785

(1) A (1997). (2) NL (1992).

Table 5.24 (million ECU)

Manufacture of other products of wood; manufacture of articles of cork, straw and plaiting materials (NACE Rev. 1 20.5)
Market related indicators in the EU

	1988	1989	1990	1991	1992	1993	1994	1995	1996	1997	1998
Apparent consumption	3,973	4,534	4,870	5,325	5,566	5,521	5,765	5,834	:	:	:
Exports	360	445	429	426	444	438	489	543	630	715	764
Imports	478	521	645	764	809	961	1,023	1,053	1,063	1,317	1,194
Trade balance	-118	-75	-215	-337	-365	-523	-534	-510	-433	-602	-430
Export ratio (%)	9.3	10.0	9.2	8.5	8.5	8.8	9.3	10.2	:	:	:
Import penetration ratio (%)	12.0	11.5	13.2	14.3	14.5	17.4	17.8	18.1	:	:	:
Cover ratio (%)	75.3	85.5	66.6	55.8	54.9	45.5	47.8	51.6	59.3	54.3	64.0

Table 5.25 (million ECU)

Manufacture of other products of wood; manufacture of articles of cork, straw and plaiting materials (NACE Rev. 1 20.5)
Market related indicators, 1998

	B/L	DK	D	EL	E	F	IRL	I	NL	A	P	FIN	S	UK
Apparent consumption	:	76	1,698	26	695	858	57	870	217	106	1,085	61	37	596
Exports	101	83	247	2	199	142	1	306	72	85	694	6	77	84
Imports	173	67	783	22	141	487	18	220	156	95	62	18	64	311
Trade balance	-71	16	-536	-20	58	-345	-17	86	-84	-10	631	-12	13	-227
Export ratio (%)	:	90.7	21.2	37.4	26.4	27.6	3.2	32.0	54.0	88.2	40.4	12.2	155.1	22.7
Import penetration ratio (%)	:	88.7	46.1	86.7	20.3	56.7	32.1	25.3	71.9	89.3	5.7	29.4	174.7	52.1
Cover ratio (%)	58.8	124.1	31.5	9.2	141.0	29.1	7.1	139.3	45.9	89.8	1,112.2	33.4	120.4	27.0

Table 5.26

Manufacture of other products of wood; manufacture of articles of cork, straw and plaiting materials (NACE Rev. 1 20.5)
Labour related indicators, 1998

	EU-15	B	DK	D	EL	E	F	IRL	I	L	NL	A	P	FIN	S	UK
Personnel costs (million ECU) (1)	1,299	30	24	378	1	122	141	7	212	:	31	26	149	13	18	112
Personnel costs/employee (thousand ECU) (2)	27.2	31.0	31.4	32.7	10.6	15.6	25.4	14.7	20.5	:	:	27.1	:	22.2	29.4	16.4
Social charges/personnel costs (%) (3)	21.7	26.5	5.2	17.9	23.2	20.9	28.0	10.8	38.8	:	12.3	25.5	:	22.6	28.7	10.7
Labour productivity (thousand ECU/head) (4)	24.9	46.2	43.0	39.7	17.7	28.5	33.0	24.6	37.1	:	36.8	37.7	:	30.6	39.0	23.8
Wage adjusted labour productivity (%) (2)	91.6	94.6	151.6	117.4	115.4	129.9	125.0	147.0	155.2	:	:	133.4	:	122.7	120.2	131.7

(1) EU-15 (1995). (2) EU-15, EL, I, A (1995); B, DK, D, E, F, IRL, FIN, S, UK (1996). (3) EU-15, S (1995). (4) NL (1992); EU-15 (1995); A (1997).

Source: Eurostat (SBS, EBT)

(million ECU) — Table 5.27

Manufacture of pulp, paper and paperboard (NACE Rev. 1 21.1)
Production related indicators in the EU

	1988	1989	1990	1991	1992	1993	1994	1995	1996	1997	1998
Production value	47,167	52,643	50,615	48,069	45,434	41,165	48,122	:	:	:	:
Producer price index (1995=100)	:	:	:	:	:	:	:	:	:	:	:
Value added	15,155	16,373	15,184	14,358	13,056	12,051	14,975	:	:	:	:
Number of persons employed (thousands)	292.1	296.1	296.1	286.9	273.1	248.7	240.4	:	:	:	:

(million ECU) — Table 5.28

Manufacture of pulp, paper and paperboard (NACE Rev. 1 21.1)
Production related indicators, 1998

	B	DK	D	EL	E	F	IRL	I	L	NL	A	P	FIN	S	UK
Production value (1)	1,674	200	11,049	166	2,808	6,409	39	4,276	0	1,518	2,417	1,312	11,761	9,143	4,872
Value added (1)	424	67	3,332	22	814	1,747	10	1,266	0	514	722	:	3,673	2,723	1,475
Number of persons employed (units) (1)(2)	5,902	1,115	45,749	2,532	15,523	29,363	174	15,156	0	8,799	10,381	7,372	37,584	33,745	22,960

(1) A (1994); I (1996). (2) NL (1992).

(million ECU) — Table 5.29

Manufacture of pulp, paper and paperboard (NACE Rev. 1 21.1)
Market related indicators in the EU

	1988	1989	1990	1991	1992	1993	1994	1995	1996	1997	1998
Apparent consumption	46,822	52,293	50,471	48,177	44,896	39,881	47,115	:	:	:	:
Exports	6,290	6,962	6,304	5,940	5,935	6,475	7,389	9,694	9,130	10,259	9,964
Imports	5,946	6,612	6,159	6,048	5,397	5,190	6,382	9,048	7,336	7,530	8,161
Trade balance	345	351	144	-108	537	1,284	1,007	647	1,793	2,729	1,802
Export ratio (%)	13.3	13.2	12.5	12.4	13.1	15.7	15.4	:	:	:	:
Import penetration ratio (%)	12.7	12.6	12.2	12.6	12.0	13.0	13.5	:	:	:	:
Cover ratio (%)	105.8	105.3	102.3	98.2	110.0	124.7	115.8	107.1	124.4	136.2	122.1

(million ECU) — Table 5.30

Manufacture of pulp, paper and paperboard (NACE Rev. 1 21.1)
Market related indicators, 1998

	B/L	DK	D	EL	E	F	IRL	I	NL	A	P	FIN	S	UK
Apparent consumption (1)	:	855	11,707	608	4,022	7,869	361	6,428	2,390	1,608	980	4,081	3,294	9,056
Exports	1,987	191	6,779	24	1,126	3,617	46	1,826	2,100	1,757	771	7,990	6,443	1,880
Imports	2,579	846	7,437	467	2,339	5,078	367	3,978	2,972	960	439	310	594	6,064
Trade balance	-592	-655	-658	-443	-1,214	-1,461	-322	-2,152	-872	797	332	7,680	5,849	-4,185
Export ratio (%) (1)	:	95.6	61.4	14.6	40.1	56.4	116.9	42.7	138.4	69.0	58.8	67.9	70.5	38.6
Import penetration ratio (%) (1)	:	99.0	63.5	76.8	58.2	64.5	101.8	61.9	124.4	53.5	44.8	7.6	18.0	67.0
Cover ratio (%)	77.0	22.6	91.2	5.2	48.1	71.2	12.5	45.9	70.7	183.1	175.7	2,578.9	1,084.3	31.0

(1) A (1994).

Table 5.31

Manufacture of pulp, paper and paperboard (NACE Rev. 1 21.1)
Labour related indicators, 1998

	EU-15	B	DK	D	EL	E	F	IRL	I	L	NL	A	P	FIN	S	UK
Personnel costs (million ECU) (1)	8,360	258	44	1,997	43	434	1,158	5	513	0	271	447	140	1,471	1,333	801
Personnel costs/employee (thousand ECU) (2)	:	47.0	40.3	42.8	18.7	28.7	40.0	30.3	30.7	:	:	43.1	:	40.2	41.4	28.3
Social charges/personnel costs (%) (3)	:	27.6	4.5	19.7	25.8	21.5	30.4	10.8	35.9	:	16.6	24.0	:	23.8	29.3	12.8
Labour productivity (thousand ECU/head) (4)	62.3	71.9	60.2	72.8	8.5	52.4	59.5	56.3	83.5	:	59.5	69.5	:	97.7	80.7	64.2
Wage adjusted labour productivity (%) (2)	:	145.5	151.5	156.4	72.7	174.7	142.4	189.5	245.9	:	:	161.2	:	212.5	190.0	198.1

(1) EU-15, A (1994); L (1996). (2) A (1994); EL, I (1995); B, DK, D, E, F, IRL, FIN, S, UK (1996). (3) A, S (1994). (4) NL (1992); EU-15, A (1994).

Source: Eurostat (SBS, EBT)

Table 5.32 (million ECU)

Manufacture of articles of paper and paperboard (NACE Rev. 1 21.2)

Production related indicators in the EU

	1988	1989	1990	1991	1992	1993	1994	1995	1996	1997	1998
Production value	39,617	43,780	47,937	50,841	51,298	48,795	52,471	56,050	:	:	:
Producer price index (1995=100)	:	:	89.9	87.3	87.8	87.5	88.5	100.0	102.3	103.8	104.4
Value added	13,343	14,210	15,716	16,824	17,795	17,254	17,938	17,571	:	:	:
Number of persons employed (thousands)	428.5	438.6	447.0	452.0	446.3	421.0	418.2	393.3	:	:	:

Table 5.33 (million ECU)

Manufacture of articles of paper and paperboard (NACE Rev. 1 21.2)

Production related indicators, 1998

	B	DK	D	EL	E	F	IRL	I	L	NL	A	P	FIN	S	UK
Production value (1)	1,604	878	13,634	412	5,321	9,109	670	8,937	:	2,706	1,013	616	554	1,634	9,662
Value added (1)	469	346	4,808	83	1,645	2,912	228	2,334	:	960	375	:	208	494	3,584
Number of persons employed (units) (1)(2)	9,660	6,236	103,155	4,695	52,071	59,662	4,764	41,030	:	16,680	7,285	6,323	3,941	10,230	79,815

(1) A (1994). (2) NL (1992).

Table 5.34 (million ECU)

Manufacture of articles of paper and paperboard (NACE Rev. 1 21.2)

Market related indicators in the EU

	1988	1989	1990	1991	1992	1993	1994	1995	1996	1997	1998
Apparent consumption	38,400	42,440	46,658	49,634	49,894	47,299	50,648	53,855	:	:	:
Exports	1,792	2,026	2,040	2,132	2,299	2,445	2,892	3,427	3,834	4,160	4,052
Imports	574	686	761	924	895	950	1,070	1,232	1,252	1,464	1,552
Trade balance	1,218	1,340	1,279	1,207	1,405	1,495	1,823	2,195	2,582	2,696	2,500
Export ratio (%)	4.5	4.6	4.3	4.2	4.5	5.0	5.5	6.1	:	:	:
Import penetration ratio (%)	1.5	1.6	1.6	1.9	1.8	2.0	2.1	2.3	:	:	:
Cover ratio (%)	312.2	295.3	268.1	230.6	257.0	257.5	270.4	278.2	306.2	284.2	261.1

Table 5.35 (million ECU)

Manufacture of articles of paper and paperboard (NACE Rev. 1 21.2)

Market related indicators, 1998

	B/L	DK	D	EL	E	F	IRL	I	NL	A	P	FIN	S	UK
Apparent consumption (1)	:	1,025	11,884	552	5,294	9,595	925	8,053	2,592	803	704	-4	1,257	9,687
Exports	1,170	316	3,615	42	480	1,615	105	1,440	1,042	639	112	711	729	1,449
Imports	1,152	464	1,865	182	453	2,101	360	556	928	416	201	153	351	1,473
Trade balance	18	-148	1,750	-140	27	-486	-255	885	114	223	-88	558	378	-25
Export ratio (%) (1)	:	36.0	26.5	10.3	9.0	17.7	15.7	16.1	38.5	62.1	18.3	128.4	44.6	15.0
Import penetration ratio (%) (1)	:	45.2	15.7	33.0	8.6	21.9	38.9	6.9	35.8	52.1	28.5	-3,543.5	28.0	15.2
Cover ratio (%)	101.6	68.2	193.8	23.3	105.9	76.9	29.3	259.2	112.3	153.5	56.0	465.4	207.5	98.3

(1) A (1994).

Table 5.36

Manufacture of articles of paper and paperboard (NACE Rev. 1 21.2)

Labour related indicators, 1998

	EU-15	B	DK	D	EL	E	F	IRL	I	L	NL	A	P	FIN	S	UK
Personnel costs (million ECU) (1)	11,570	352	231	3,830	67	1,063	1,998	126	1,206	:	607	249	64	126	360	2,380
Personnel costs/employee (thousand ECU) (2)	31.2	37.0	37.8	37.2	15.7	21.6	34.1	26.2	26.7	:	:	34.3	:	33.0	36.8	24.2
Social charges/personnel costs (%) (3)	20.8	26.8	4.2	18.8	23.8	21.6	29.5	14.3	35.9	:	14.0	22.8	:	22.6	30.3	11.8
Labour productivity (thousand ECU/head) (4)	44.7	48.5	55.5	46.6	17.6	31.6	48.8	47.8	56.9	:	46.4	51.5	:	52.9	48.3	44.9
Wage adjusted labour productivity (%) (2)	143.4	150.9	148.7	127.7	147.2	192.7	139.9	188.3	197.6	:	:	150.1	:	162.0	135.9	165.1

(1) A (1994); EU-15 (1995). (2) A (1994); EU-15, EL, I (1995); B, DK, D, E, F, IRL, FIN, S, UK (1996). (3) A (1994); EU-15, S (1995). (4) NL (1992); A (1994); EU-15 (1995).

Source: Eurostat (SBS, EBT)

(million ECU) — Table 5.37

Publishing (NACE Rev. 1 22.1)
Production related indicators in the EU

	1988	1989	1990	1991	1992	1993	1994	1995	1996	1997	1998
Production value	:	:	:	:	:	:	:	80,325	78,645	83,730	86,362
Producer price index (1995=100)	:	:	:	:	:	:	:	:	:	:	:
Value added	:	:	:	:	:	:	:	27,510	29,708	31,129	32,259
Number of persons employed (thousands)	:	:	:	:	:	:	:	571.4	600.2	604.4	627.4

(million ECU) — Table 5.38

Publishing (NACE Rev. 1 22.1)
Production related indicators, 1998

	B	DK	D	EL	E	F	IRL	I	L	NL	A	P	FIN	S	UK
Production value (1)	2,475	1,891	24,008	407	5,882	13,531	:	8,157	:	4,421	802	846	2,074	3,050	18,070
Value added (1)	723	850	8,777	123	2,161	4,384	13	2,481	:	2,111	231	:	878	986	7,902
Number of persons employed (units) (1)(2)	11,122	17,843	229,337	6,404	51,973	66,214	437	39,486	:	23,697	4,679	8,637	17,188	26,101	121,242

(1) IRL (1991); A (1994). (2) NL (1992).

(million ECU) — Table 5.39

Publishing (NACE Rev. 1 22.1)
Market related indicators in the EU

	1988	1989	1990	1991	1992	1993	1994	1995	1996	1997	1998
Apparent consumption	:	:	:	:	:	:	:	77,947	76,054	81,034	83,757
Exports	2,521	2,803	2,986	3,252	3,470	3,731	4,071	4,346	4,520	4,769	4,780
Imports	1,119	1,311	1,470	1,649	1,726	1,842	1,884	1,968	1,930	2,073	2,175
Trade balance	1,403	1,492	1,516	1,603	1,744	1,889	2,186	2,378	2,590	2,695	2,605
Export ratio (%)	:	:	:	:	:	:	:	5.4	5.7	5.7	5.5
Import penetration ratio (%)	:	:	:	:	:	:	:	2.5	2.5	2.6	2.6
Cover ratio (%)	225.4	213.8	203.1	197.2	201.0	202.5	216.0	220.8	234.2	230.0	219.8

(million ECU) — Table 5.40

Publishing (NACE Rev. 1 22.1)
Market related indicators, 1998

	B/L	DK	D	EL	E	F	IRL	I	NL	A	P	FIN	S	UK
Apparent consumption (1)	:	1,906	23,052	462	5,416	13,590	:	7,717	4,151	1,153	979	1,979	3,162	16,840
Exports	636	203	2,227	35	829	1,212	152	909	753	251	29	227	189	2,866
Imports	852	218	1,271	91	363	1,271	247	470	482	489	162	132	302	1,636
Trade balance	-215	-15	956	-56	465	-58	-95	440	270	-238	-133	95	-113	1,230
Export ratio (%) (1)	:	10.7	9.3	8.7	14.1	9.0	:	11.1	17.0	51.9	3.4	10.9	6.2	15.9
Import penetration ratio (%) (1)	:	11.5	5.5	19.7	6.7	9.4	:	6.1	11.6	66.5	16.5	6.7	9.5	9.7
Cover ratio (%)	74.7	93.0	175.3	38.7	228.1	95.4	61.4	193.7	156.0	51.4	17.9	172.3	62.7	175.2

(1) A (1994).

Table 5.41

Publishing (NACE Rev. 1 22.1)
Labour related indicators, 1998

	EU-15	B	DK	D	EL	E	F	IRL	I	L	NL	A	P	FIN	S	UK
Personnel costs (million ECU) (1)	21,447	434	666	6,365	104	1,285	3,238	8	1,926	:	1,133	201	150	550	872	4,278
Personnel costs/employee (thousand ECU) (2)	33.6	46.8	38.0	27.8	17.8	30.0	49.9	:	44.3	:	:	43.0	:	33.4	35.0	29.4
Social charges/personnel costs (%) (3)	20.4	25.7	5.4	19.2	20.0	16.5	29.3	:	34.1	:	15.3	21.3	:	21.7	27.8	11.7
Labour productivity (thousand ECU/head) (4)	51.4	65.1	47.7	38.3	19.2	41.6	66.2	28.6	62.8	:	53.2	49.4	:	51.1	37.8	65.2
Wage adjusted labour productivity (%) (2)	143.4	129.8	125.6	138.0	98.3	161.8	129.0	:	133.5	:	:	115.1	:	143.1	108.2	181.9

(1) IRL (1990); A (1994). (2) A (1994); EU-15, EL, I (1995); B, DK, D, E, F, FIN, S, UK (1996). (3) A, S (1994); EU-15 (1995). (4) IRL (1991); NL (1992); A (1994).

Source: Eurostat (SBS, EBT)

Table 5.42 (million ECU)

Printing and service activities related to printing (NACE Rev. 1 22.2)

Production related indicators in the EU

	1988	1989	1990	1991	1992	1993	1994	1995	1996	1997	1998
Production value	:	:	:	:	:	50,773	53,409	55,407	58,583	62,920	61,184
Producer price index (1995=100)	:	:	:	:	:	:	:	:	:	:	:
Value added	:	:	:	:	:	22,989	23,805	24,250	25,782	26,772	26,430
Number of persons employed (thousands)	:	:	:	:	:	612.4	609.2	611.8	627.6	627.2	626.1

Table 5.43 (million ECU)

Printing and service activities related to printing (NACE Rev. 1 22.2)

Production related indicators, 1998

	B	DK	D	EL	E	F	IRL	I	L	NL	A	P	FIN	S	UK
Production value (1)	3,458	873	15,412	149	5,964	8,419	:	6,592	105	3,486	1,512	1,140	1,256	1,743	10,109
Value added (2)	1,375	376	6,750	55	2,497	3,333	351	2,365	54	1,457	754	:	573	666	5,180
Number of persons employed (units) (3)	28,714	7,342	147,657	2,438	78,330	76,232	10,059	58,048	1,156	39,742	12,441	25,597	12,235	13,024	116,951

(1) DK, A (1995). (2) IRL (1991); DK, A (1995). (3) IRL (1991); NL (1992); DK (1995); A (1997).

Table 5.44 (million ECU)

Printing and service activities related to printing (NACE Rev. 1 22.2)

Market related indicators in the EU

	1988	1989	1990	1991	1992	1993	1994	1995	1996	1997	1998
Apparent consumption	:	:	:	:	:	50,241	52,799	54,866	58,098	62,202	60,323
Exports	742	778	826	863	885	1,084	1,223	1,214	1,253	1,448	1,665
Imports	432	453	473	563	543	551	613	673	768	730	803
Trade balance	310	325	353	299	342	533	610	540	485	718	862
Export ratio (%)	:	:	:	:	:	2.1	2.3	2.2	2.1	2.3	2.7
Import penetration ratio (%)	:	:	:	:	:	1.1	1.2	1.2	1.3	1.2	1.3
Cover ratio (%)	171.9	171.6	174.7	153.1	163.0	196.6	199.5	180.3	163.2	198.3	207.3

Table 5.45 (million ECU)

Printing and service activities related to printing (NACE Rev. 1 22.2)

Market related indicators, 1998

	B/L	DK	D	EL	E	F	IRL	I	NL	A	P	FIN	S	UK
Apparent consumption (1)	:	881	14,688	-90	5,952	8,348	:	6,205	3,370	1,548	1,167	1,181	1,792	10,314
Exports	429	138	1,260	263	117	653	33	582	319	152	15	127	77	363
Imports	231	167	536	24	105	582	52	194	202	139	42	53	125	568
Trade balance	198	-28	724	239	12	71	-19	388	117	14	-27	74	-49	-205
Export ratio (%) (1)	:	11.7	8.2	176.8	2.0	7.8	:	8.8	9.2	9.0	1.3	10.1	4.4	3.6
Import penetration ratio (%) (1)	:	12.5	3.7	-27.0	1.8	7.0	:	3.1	6.0	11.1	3.6	4.5	7.0	5.5
Cover ratio (%)	185.7	82.9	234.9	1,083.2	111.6	112.2	63.2	299.5	157.7	110.1	35.6	241.2	61.3	64.0

(1) DK, A (1995).

Table 5.46

Printing and service activities related to printing (NACE Rev. 1 22.2)

Labour related indicators, 1998

	EU-15	B	DK	D	EL	E	F	IRL	I	L	NL	A	P	FIN	S	UK
Personnel costs (million ECU) (1)	18,855	904	281	5,134	37	1,382	2,644	235	1,865	40	959	667	257	359	472	3,583
Personnel costs/employee (thousand ECU) (2)	33.2	37.1	38.4	35.5	16.9	20.2	35.2	:	29.2	35.5	:	43.0	:	31.2	38.0	25.6
Social charges/personnel costs (%) (3)	20.3	27.0	4.6	17.6	24.9	20.3	29.9	:	35.7	:	15.8	21.0	:	21.5	29.5	11.5
Labour productivity (thousand ECU/head) (4)	42.2	47.9	51.2	45.7	22.4	31.9	43.7	34.9	40.8	46.6	41.9	54.3	:	46.9	51.1	44.3
Wage adjusted labour productivity (%) (2)	119.4	122.0	133.5	127.8	120.1	135.8	122.7	:	140.1	132.6	:	126.2	:	151.4	129.7	147.6

(1) IRL (1990); DK (1995). (2) EU-15, DK, EL, I, A (1995); B, D, E, F, L, FIN, S, UK (1996). (3) S (1992); EU-15, DK (1995). (4) IRL (1991); NL (1992); DK, A (1995).

Source: Eurostat (SBS, EBT)

Chemicals, rubber and plastics

Industrial description

The manufacture of chemicals, rubber and plastics is one of the largest sectors within the European economy, with just under 15% of the production value of total manufacturing. In 1998 the activity reported employment of 2.9 million persons and a production value of some 531.2 billion ECU that accounted for a third of world production. This industry is very capital intensive, and places a large degree of importance on technological know-how with a large amount of resources devoted to research and development. Around 90% of the world's production is based within Western Europe, the USA and Japan.

The manufacture of chemicals, rubber and plastics provided goods to various downstream industries and to the end-consumers. More than a third of the sector's production was input materials that were used within the industry itself (basic chemicals). There are a varied set of customers for chemical products including textiles and clothing, wood and paper, as well as the automotive industry. Fertilisers and pesticides are sold to agriculture, whilst plastics, varnishes and coatings go to the building and construction industry. Via the distributive trades end-consumers buy pharmaceuticals, cosmetics, cleansing agents, detergents and paints.

Germany was the largest producer within the EU, with a total production value for chemicals, rubber and plastics equal to 150.0 billion ECU or 28.2% of the European total in 1998. The French figures displayed a share of 17.7% in the European total, whilst the five largest European industrial economies accounted for 79.6% of European output.

(%)  Figure 6.1

Chemicals, rubber and plastics
(NACE Rev. 1 24 and 25)
Share of EU value added in total manufacturing

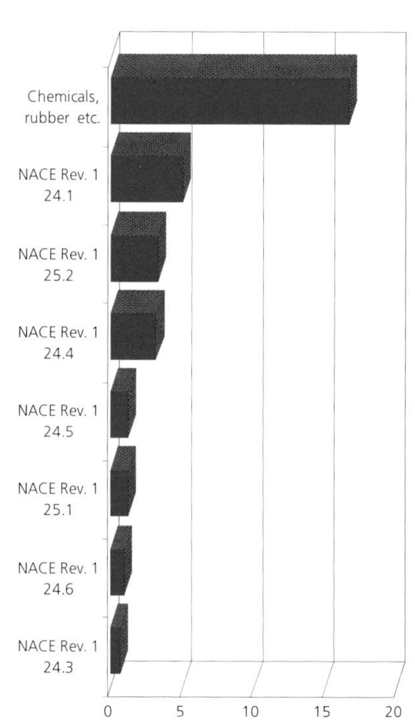

Source: Eurostat (SBS)

The activities covered in this chapter include:

- 24.1: manufacture of basic chemicals;
- 24.2: manufacture of pesticides and other agro-chemical products;
- 24.3: manufacture of paints, varnishes and similar coating, printing ink and mastics;
- 24.4: manufacture of pharmaceuticals, medicinal chemicals and botanical products;
- 24.5: manufacture of soap and detergents, cleaning and polishing preparations, perfumes and toilet preparations;
- 24.6: manufacture of other chemical products;
- 24.7: manufacture of man-made fibres;
- 25.1: manufacture of rubber products;
- 25.2: manufacture of plastic products.

Figure 6.2 (1988=100)

Chemicals, rubber and plastics (NACE Rev. 1 24 and 25)

Production, employment and value added compared to EU total manufacturing

Source: Eurostat (SBS)

The structure of the chemical, rubber and plastics industry reflected a high degree of concentration: large companies and groups dominated the evolution of business, even though there were also many small-sized enterprises. There was an on-going trend towards concentration, as major players attempted to internationalise their operations. Economies of scale and cost differentials across world regions, as well as access to raw materials and new markets were fundamental behind this trend. Research that required higher skills was generally concentrated in industrialised countries (where headquarters were usually found), whilst manufacturing facilities were delocated to low-cost countries.

In the course of the late nineties competition increased as a consequence of the economic crises in south-east Asia, with Asian exports encouraged by the devaluation of local currencies and lower producer prices. The industry is also affected by severe overcapacity in certain market segments, especially the manufacture of bulk chemicals.

Figure 6.3

Chemicals, rubber and plastics (NACE Rev. 1 24 and 25)

International comparison of main indicators in current prices

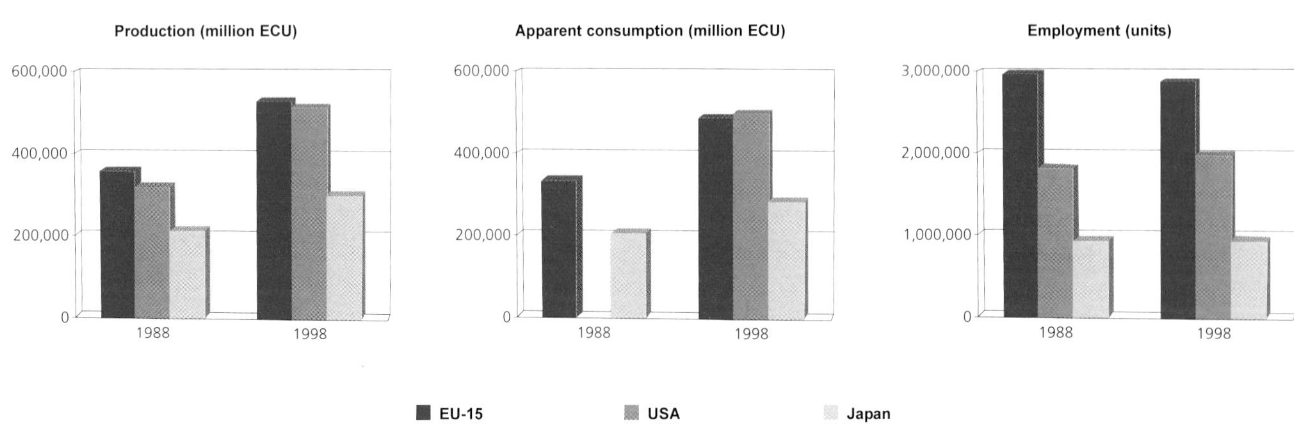

Source: Eurostat (SBS)

(1980=100) Figure 6.4

Production, energy consumption and CO_2 emissions in the EU chemical industry

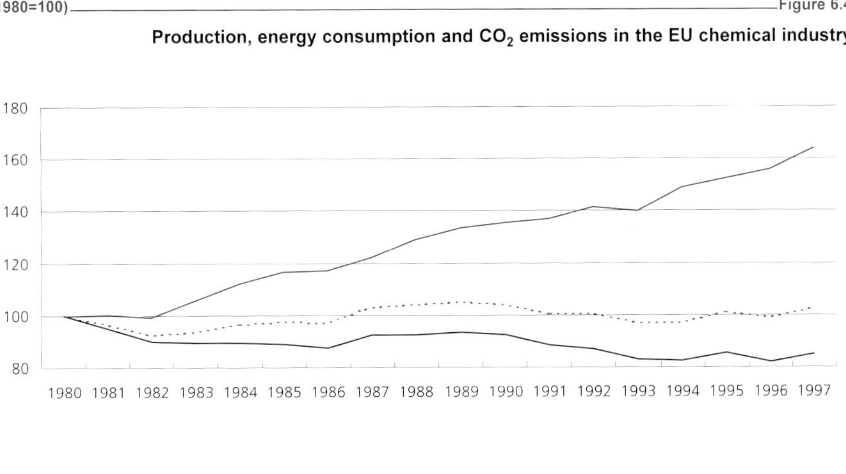

Source: CEFIC

European manufacturers had somewhat less efficient production in terms of labour productivity and energy efficiency when compared to their American competitors. Lower profit margins in Europe led to a lower level of investments. CEFIC (the European Chemical Industry Council) estimated that in 1998 the stock of capital per employee was twice as high in the USA. A low level of capital intensity is often cited as a fundamental reason to explain why European labour productivity (65.2 thousand ECU) was below corresponding figures in the USA and Japan (twice as high at 137.8 and 132.5 thousand ECU respectively). European manufacturers attempted to restructure their production processes, labour productivity rose by 28.5% between 1993 and 1997, at a faster pace than in the USA (up by 22.5%) or Japan (only 0.3% growth during the same period). If we look at the ratio of persons employed per one million ECU of production value, we see that this measure of labour intensity fell by more than a third in the EU between 1988 and 1997 to 5.3 persons. Nevertheless, this was still below the figures recorded in the other two Triad economies, Japan (3.1 persons per one million ECU of output) and the USA (3.9 persons).

Chemicals, rubber and plastics are energy intensive industries and the performance of the industry is significantly influenced by the level of energy costs. Price levels of energy are generally much higher in the EU than in the USA. One means of reducing energy costs was to make efficiency savings. Whilst production in the EU rose by 21.4% between 1990 and 1997 in volume terms, energy consumption grew by just 5.5%. CO_2 emissions even fell by 7.9% during the same period (figures supplied by CEFIC, European Chemical Industry Council).

Figure 6.5 (ECU/hour)

Chemicals, rubber and plastics (NACE Rev. 1 24 and 25)

Labour costs by Member State, 1996

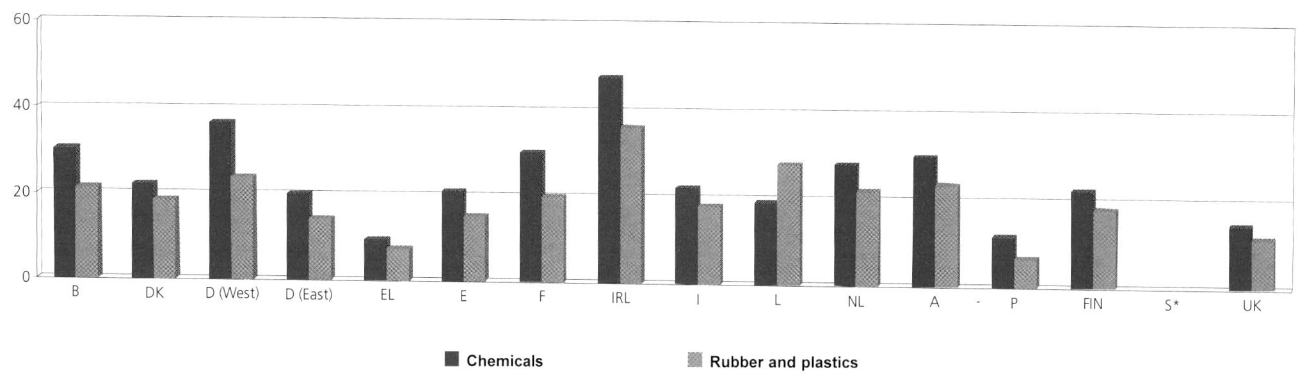

Source: Eurostat (LCS)

Recent trends

The evolution of production for chemicals, rubber and plastics was closely linked to the general business cycle, within and outside the EU. Between 1988 and 1998 production values grew at a slightly faster pace than apparent consumption in the EU (up by 4.0% and 3.8% per annum respectively). Thus, EU manufacturers were obliged to increase their efforts to find markets outside the EU. Pharmaceuticals, medicinal chemicals and botanical products reported a more dynamic evolution, whilst paints and agro-chemical products grew at a slower pace.

European chemical, rubber and plastics manufacturers reduced employment between 1988 and 1998, with the number of persons employed decreasing on average by 0.3% per annum. Job losses were greater in Germany (down by 1.3% per annum). Some of the reductions in the labour force could be attributed to the restructuring process followed by many large companies. As firms concentrated on their core activities, they either sold or founded subsidiaries or out-sourced certain service activities, resulting in a reduction in their own employment. Many production positions required highly qualified labour with on the job training using modern technology. One success story was that employment increased by 6.1% per annum in Ireland, on the back of a 12.8% per annum growth in production between 1988 and 1998.

In 1997 the production of chemicals, rubber and plastics increased throughout the Triad, rising by 6.2% in the EU, compared to 12.1% in Japan and 19.1% in the USA. As in Europe, the industry turned to further automation and experienced job losses in Japan between 1993 and 1997 (down by 0.6% in the EU and 1.3% in Japan per annum respectively). There was however a moderate expansion of employment in the USA, rising by 1.2% per annum over the same period.

Table 6.1 (%)

Chemicals, rubber and plastics (NACE Rev. 1 24 and 25)

Composition of the labour force, 1997

	Females	Part-time	Highly-educated
EU-15	29.3	:	:
B	25.5	5.8	38.5
DK	44.6	8.8	20.7
D	29.1	8.3	21.3
EL	31.0	:	21.7
E	21.7	1.7	25.6
F	34.5	4.0	20.8
IRL	32.7	2.4	33.3
I	28.5	2.6	7.7
L	9.7	:	12.4
NL	21.0	17.0	24.2
A	35.8	6.5	7.6
P	29.6	:	9.9
FIN	36.5	:	26.4
S	34.3	6.5	15.7
UK	27.0	6.5	22.5

Source: Eurostat (LFS)

Figure 6.6 (million ECU)

Chemicals, rubber and plastics (NACE Rev. 1 24 and 25)

Foreign net direct investment (1)

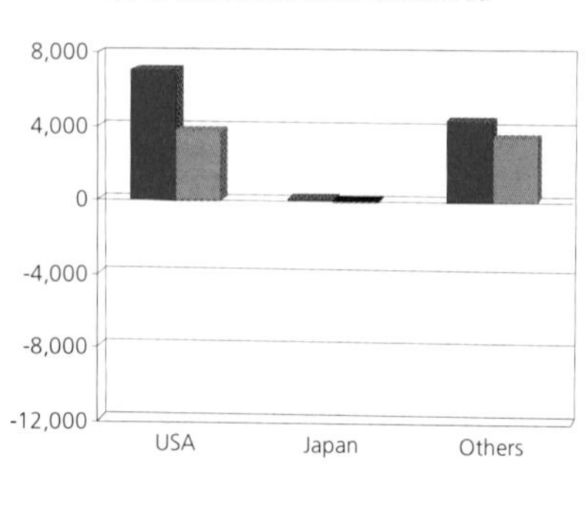

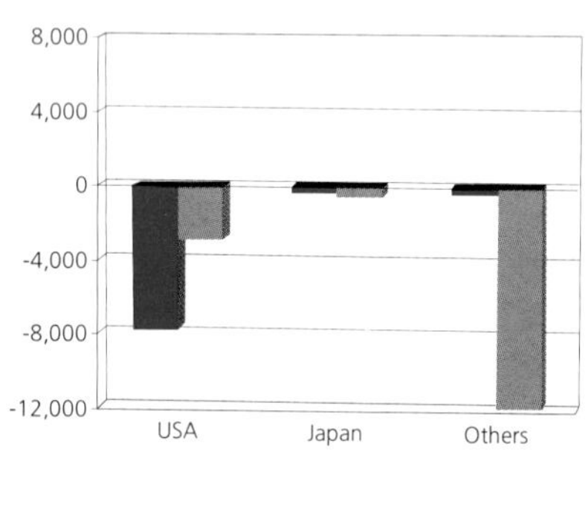

(1) Including NACE Rev. 1 23.

Source: Eurostat (BOP)

Foreign trade

Exports from the EU to third countries accounted for 21.3% of domestic output in 1998. During the course of the nineties foreign trade intensified, as witnessed in the growth of both export and import penetration ratios. The share of imports in apparent consumption grew at a faster pace than the share of exports in production (up by 50.4% and 37.8% between 1988 and 1998). The import penetration ratio reached 14.7% of the domestic market. Chemicals, rubber and plastics are one of the main exporting industries of the EU, with total exports to third countries worth 113.4 billion ECU and a trade surplus of 41.3 billion ECU in 1998.

Within the framework of World Trade Organisation (WTO) the Chemical Harmonisation Tariff Agreement (CHTA) contains commitments to lower tariffs to between 0.0% and 6.5% by the year 2010. However, there were efforts to extend the geographical scope of the CHTA, which was only agreed between the EU, Canada, the USA, Japan, Norway, Switzerland, South Korea and Singapore. With declining tariffs, the role of non-tariff barriers became increasingly important, such as differences in standards and technical regulations that could significantly increase the cost of exports to third markets.

Figure 6.7

Chemicals, rubber and plastics (NACE Rev. 1 24 and 25) Destination of EU exports, 1998

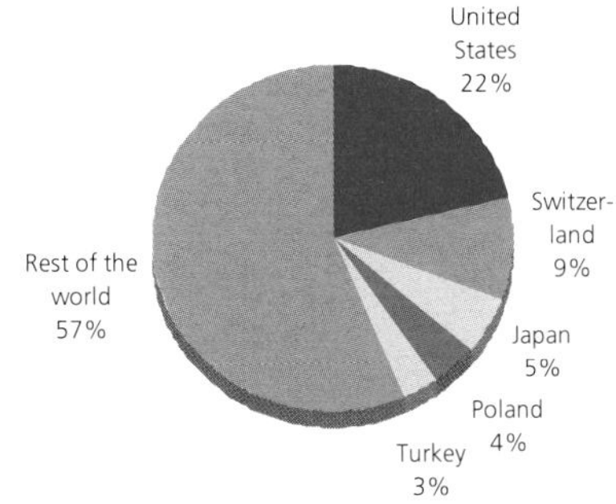

Source: Eurostat (Comext)

Figure 6.8

Chemicals, rubber and plastics (NACE Rev. 1 24 and 25) Origin of EU imports, 1998

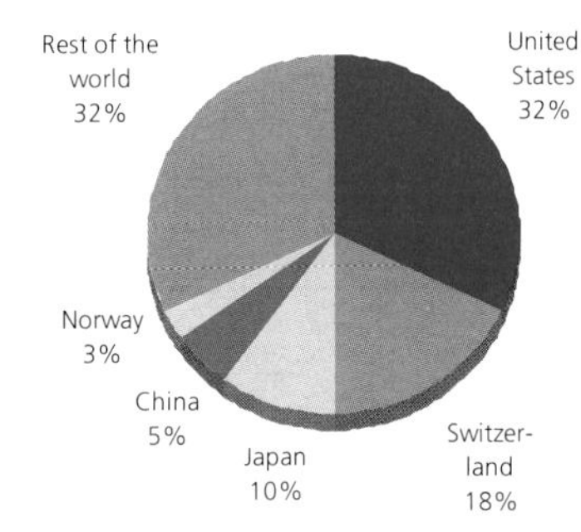

Source: Eurostat (Comext)

Basic industrial chemicals (including petrochemicals) and other chemicals (NACE Rev. 1 24.1 and 24.6)

Basic industrial chemicals and other chemicals (NACE Rev. 1 24.1 and 24.6) are mainly intermediate goods that often form part of the production process for more refined chemical products. As such products such as industrial gases, dyes and pigments, plastics and synthetic rubber in primary forms are used to a large extent in other downstream chemical, rubber and plastics' industries. Data covering the manufacture of petrochemicals are also included in this section. Primary petrochemical products include ethylene, propylene, butadiene and benzene.

Figure 6.10 (share of total output)

Downstream industries for adhesives in Europe, 1996 (1)

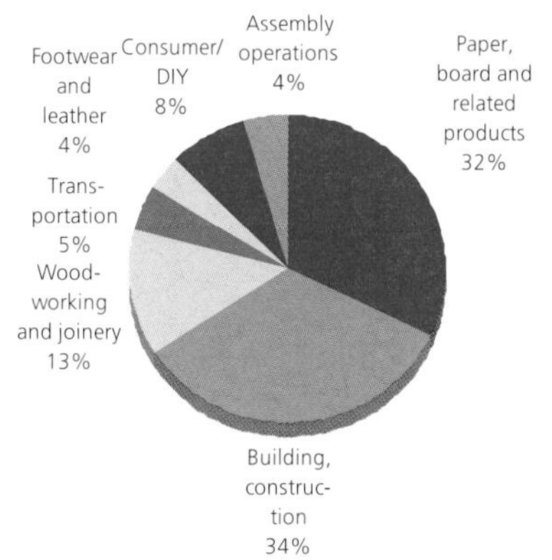

(1) EU-15, Norway and Switzerland.

Source: FEICA

Figure 6.9

Basic industrial chemicals (including petrochemicals) and other chemicals (NACE Rev. 1 24.1 and 24.6) Production and employment in the Triad

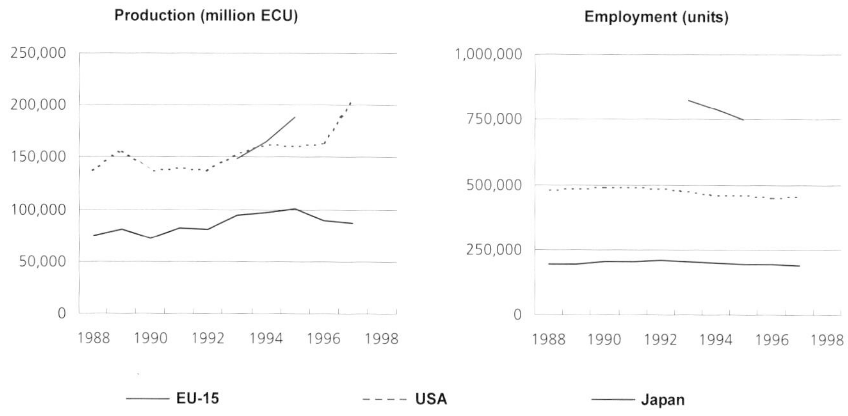

Source: Eurostat (SBS)

Figure 6.11 (%)

Basic industrial chemicals (including petrochemicals) and other chemicals (NACE Rev. 1 24.1 and 24.6) Production and export specialisation by Member State, 1998

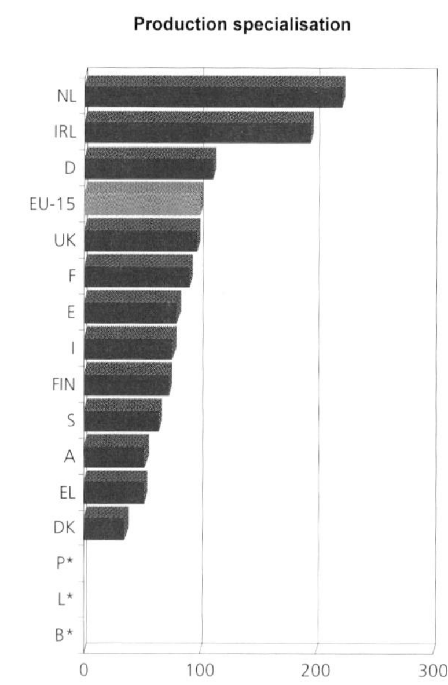

Export specialisation

IRL, B/L, NL, UK, D, EU-15, F, E, FIN, I, DK, A, EL, P, S

0 100 200 300

Source: Eurostat (SBS)

Other chemicals (NACE Rev. 1 24.6) encompass a wide range of different products, which were used partly in downstream industries and partly by households (such as unrecorded media and photographic chemical materials). Glues are used in a variety of activities, such as construction, paper, wood and furniture industries. Essential oils were sold to the food industry, cosmetics and pharmaceuticals producers and the leather industry, whilst explosives were mainly used in quarrying and mining. Each of these products has a fairly specialised market, requiring business strategies to be adapted to the industry in question and the customers needs.

Basic industrial chemicals and other chemicals accounted for around 35% of the aggregated production value of chemicals, rubber and plastics or around 5% of total manufacturing in the EU. In absolute terms the sector was twice as large in Germany as it was in France (61.9 billion ECU and 30.0 billion ECU respectively in 1998). There were high specialisation rates in the Netherlands and the United Kingdom.

Basic industrial chemicals and other chemicals faced general fluctuations that followed the business cycle, with recession often hitting the industry even more, as customers tended to let stocks run down. Between 1993 and 1998 production values in constant prices increased in the EU from as much as 8.0% per annum in Denmark to 1.0% per annum in Italy (other than the negative trend recorded in Sweden, down 3.7% per annum). The performance of this sector was closely linked to the price of crude oil on world markets.

Employment for basic industrial chemicals and other chemicals fell on an annual average basis by 1.1% in the United Kingdom and by 4.3% in Italy during the five years to 1998. One country was able to report an expanding workforce: in Denmark the number of persons employed rose by 3.5% per annum.

Producer prices came under pressure from foreign competition, with third country imports into the EU expanding for many cheap, basic products. Cost reductions, as well as capacity savings were made, largely as a result of merger activity. Shell together with BASF formed a derivative subsidiary called Elenac and acquired a 50% interest in Montell. BP bought Amoco, an important refining and distribution company in the USA, during the summer of 1998. Economies of scale are a major source of profit in the production of basic chemicals as the production process is highly capital intensive and there are few possibilities to differentiate product ranges. European producers therefore concentrated on trying to expand capacity whilst not increasing the number of plants. There were 48 steam crackers in the EU at the beginning of 1998, with capacity for 19.7 million tonnes of ethylene per annum. Capacity utilisation rates reached 93% in 1997 (according to APPE, Association of Petrochemicals Producers in Europe).

(thousand tonnes) Table 6.2

Production capacity of ethylene, 1997

D	4,700
B/L	4,570
F	3,145
UK	2,405
I	2,060
E	1,410
Rest of the EU	1,400

Source: APPE

Crude oil was the major raw material for basic chemicals and naphtha (the lighter and more volatile part of crude oil). The industry could therefore not easily pass on increases in the price of crude oil to its customers (at least in the short-term).

The producers of other chemical products concentrated on their core business and increased expenditures on research in order to improve their competitiveness through expanding product differentiation and choice. Price increases in raw materials led to declining profit margins. European manufacturers faced higher energy costs than many of their competitors.

The manufacture of fertilisers also faced over-capacity on world markets, which amongst other things led to a dramatic fall in producer prices in 1998. European sales of fertilisers were influenced by the evolution of the Common Agricultural Policy, by further liberalisation of world trade and by changes in environmental laws. On the other hand, competition from Central and Eastern European countries, as well as Russia, China and India increased steadily during the course of the nineties.

In 1997/98 grain production in the EU reached a record high of 208 million tonnes. Nevertheless, there was a decline in fertiliser consumption[1], due to improved farming practices allowing yields to increase whilst fertiliser use per hectare fell. The downward trend was most significant within the consumption of phosphate fertilisers (down by 35.4% to 3.5 million tonnes between 1985 and 1998). Nitrates remained the most popular fertiliser (9.5 million tonnes in 1998), although their consumption also fell (at a slower pace) by 13.0%.

1) Data provided by EFMA, European Fertilisers Manufacturers Association.

(1985=100) Figure 6.12

Consumption of mineral fertilisers in the EU

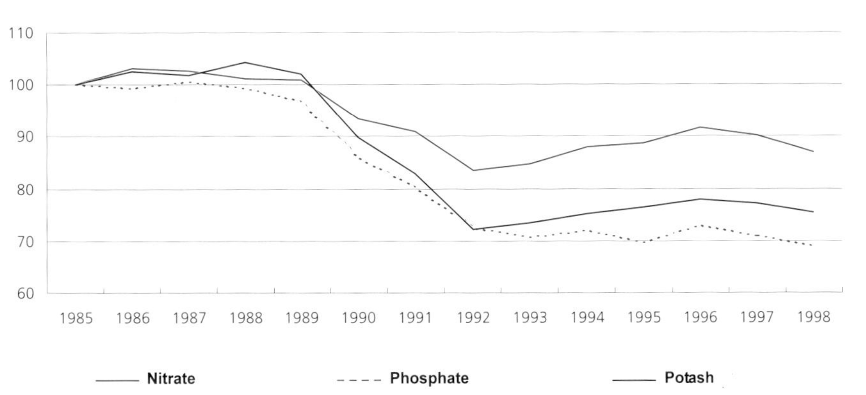

Source: EFMA

Foreign trade figures for NACE Rev. 1 24.1 and 24.6 reflected the increased levels of competition in the sector. In the Member States with a large production of basic industrial chemicals and other chemicals (Germany, France, the United Kingdom, the Netherlands and Belgium) extra-EU imports increased at a faster pace than extra-EU exports. Nevertheless, the European trade balance remained positive (10.7 billion ECU in 1998).

Within the framework of World Trade Organisation (WTO), a harmonised rate of tariffs on fertilisers was agreed at 6.5% (following the Chemical Tariff Harmonisation Agreement). However, there were higher tariffs with countries that were not members of the WTO, such as Russia, China or Saudi Arabia.

Figure 6.13

Basic industrial chemicals (including petrochemicals) and other chemicals (NACE Rev. 1 20.1 and 20.6) Destination of EU exports, 1998

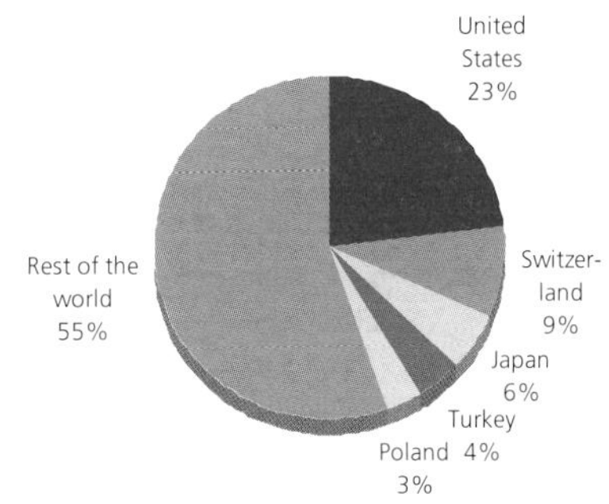

Source: Eurostat (Comext)

Figure 6.14

Basic industrial chemicals (including petrochemicals) and other chemicals (NACE Rev. 1 20.1 and 20.6) Origin of EU imports, 1998

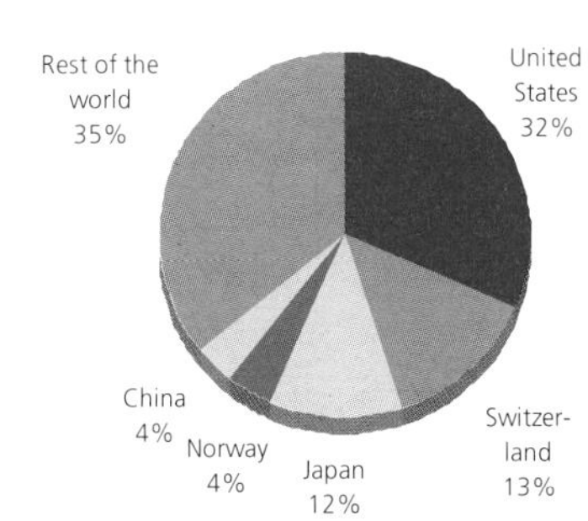

Source: Eurostat (Comext)

Pesticides and agrochemicals (NACE Rev. 1 24.2)
Pesticides and other agro-chemical products are used to control animal pests and to improve agricultural and horticultural yields. The product range covered insecticides, fungicides and herbicides, rodenticides, as well as plant growth regulators and disinfectants, classified under NACE Rev. 1 24.2.

The production value of this industry accounted for only a small share of total manufacturing in the EU (less than 0.5%). In France the highest level of production was recorded (2.6 billion ECU in 1998), followed by the United Kingdom with 1.9 billion ECU. Germany accounted for less than half the value of the French sector (1.1 billion ECU). However, it was in Austria that the highest production specialisation ratios were recorded for pesticides and agrochemicals (more than three times higher than the European average).

Whilst production value (at constant prices) increased in France by 6.9% per annum between 1993 and 1998, it fell in Spain and Italy by 3.8% and 3.7% per annum respectively. For Greece, the decrease was even more dramatic (down by 10.8% per annum between 1993 and 1997). Labour intensity (as measured by the number of persons employed per one million ECU of production value) decreased throughout the EU between 1988 and 1998, for example by 50% in Germany and Greece (falling to 4.4 and 8.2 persons). Employment declined in several countries, such as France (down by 2.9% per annum between 1993 and 1998), however there was growth in the workforce in the United Kingdom and Ireland (up by 4.1% and 6.3% per annum respectively during the same period).

The types of pesticides used in the EU varied according to geographical region and the crop being cultivated, the climate and the agricultural production method employed. Insecticides were more commonly used in southern Member States, whilst in northern Europe sales of fungicides were higher (as a result of the more humid weather conditions). European manufacturers of pesticides and agrochemicals had a lead in research and development. Within the ten largest global agrochemical companies (measured in terms of sales) five had their headquarters in the EU. The summer of 1999 saw talks between Hoechst AG (Germany) and Rhône-Poulenc SA (France) to merge their agrochemical and pharmaceutical activities. Many EU producers sought joint ventures in developing countries to secure entry into future markets.

Figure 6.15

Pesticides and agrochemicals (NACE Rev. 1 24.2)
Production and employment in the Triad

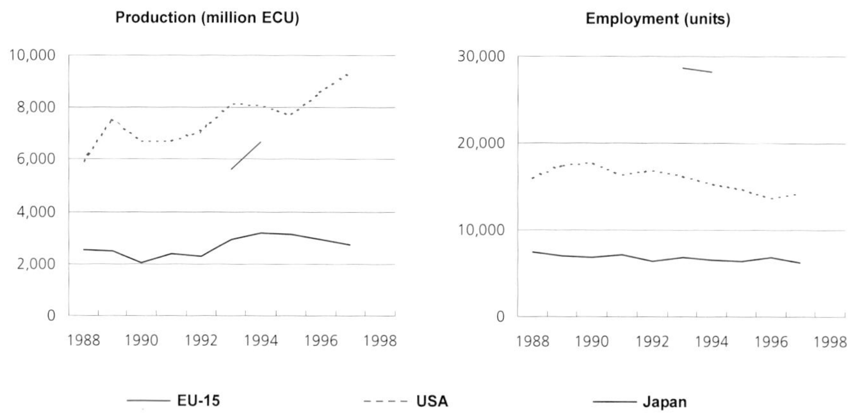

Source: Eurostat (SBS)

Figure 6.16 (%)

Pesticides and agrochemicals (NACE Rev. 1 24.2)
Production and export specialisation by Member State, 1998

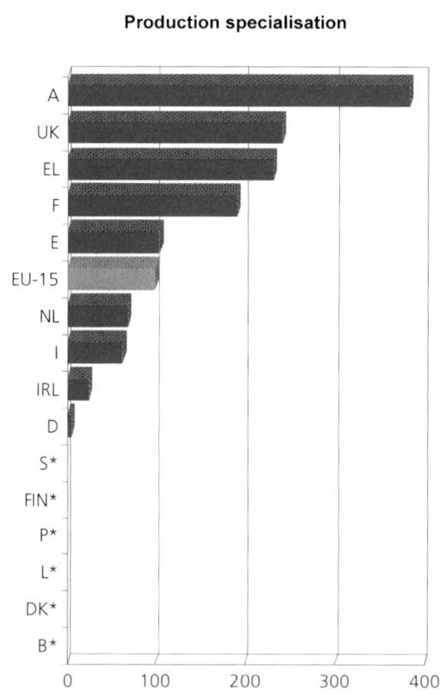

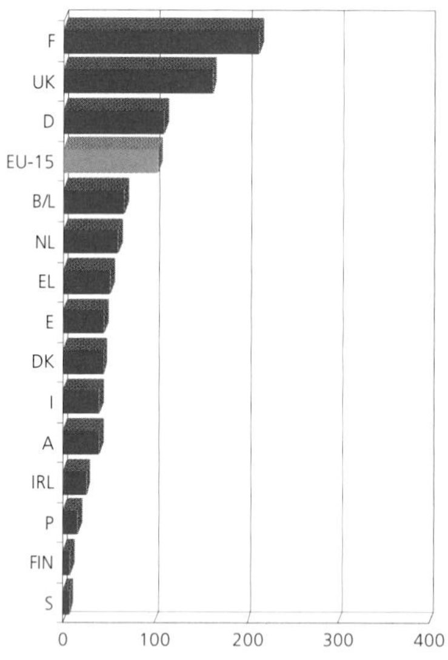

Source: Eurostat (SBS)

In 1998 the world market for agrochemicals remained almost unchanged, following an increase of 0.1% in real terms compared to 1997 (figures from the BAA, British Agrochemicals Association). Expanding product lines included genetically modified plants, which were resistant to pests and pesticides. However, the downside of these developments was that farmers could become dependent on seed manufacturers. Diversification into the seed market was reflected in merger activity, with DuPont (a large agrochemical group in the USA) purchasing Pioneer Hi Bred, a leading seed company during the spring of 1999. Consumption was either stagnant or reduced in the other two Triad economies between 1993 and 1997. Demand remained constant in the USA, whilst it fell by 1.6% per annum in Japan.

Foreign trade of pesticides and agrochemicals intensified during the course of the nineties. Although European manufacturers faced stiffer competition on international markets, exports grew at a faster pace than imports. The EU was part of an international agreement for monitoring and controlling trade in pesticides (Rotterdam Convention on Prior Informed Consent, PIC). The convention set labelling and informational requirements for pesticide products.

Figure 6.17

Pesticides and agrochemicals (NACE Rev. 1 24.2) Destination of EU exports, 1998

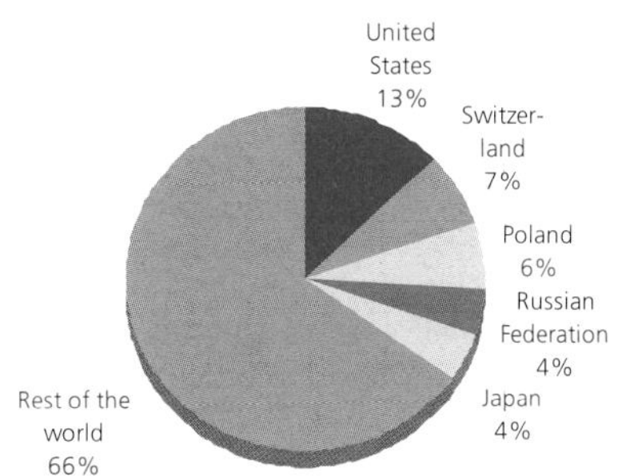

Source: Eurostat (Comext)

Figure 6.18

Pesticides and agrochemicals (NACE Rev. 1 24.2) Origin of EU imports, 1998

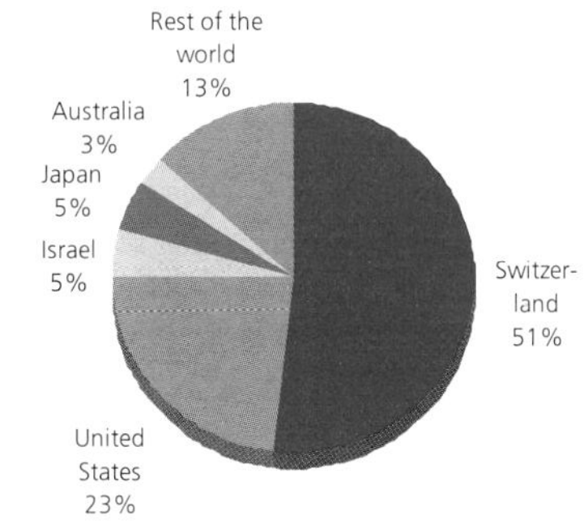

Source: Eurostat (Comext)

Paints, varnishes and printing inks (NACE Rev. 1 24.3)

At the end of the nineties the manufacture of paints, varnishes and similar coatings, printing ink and mastics (NACE Rev. 1 24.3) accounted for output of 26 billion ECU, or some 5% of the aggregate figure for chemicals, rubber and plastics. Germany was responsible for one third of the production value in the EU (some 8.5 billion ECU). Within the smaller Member States, Denmark, the Netherlands and Portugal all reported specialisation within the paints, varnishes and printing inks industry.

The manufacture of paints, varnishes and printing inks is a downstream industry from basic industrial chemicals. It processed a wide range of chemicals from very simple inorganic pigments or fillers to highly-sophisticated polymers. Downstream industries from paints and varnishes included the automotive industry and related services, the wood and metal finishing industry and retail trade. Printing inks were destined for publishing and printing, whereas mastics were used throughout manufacturing.

During the nineties European production of paints, varnishes and printing inks was on an upward trend, except in Germany where output fell by 5.1% per annum between 1993 and 1998 in real terms. Within the other Member States, Denmark and Finland reported growth of 8.7% and 13.3% per annum.

In 1998 there were 1,200 paint manufacturers in the EU and some 200 in the printing ink industry. Although the vast majority were small and medium-sized enterprises, a third of the coatings market in the EU was covered by the top ten enterprises. The tendency towards larger companies became more intensified with the internationalisation of downstream industries such as the automotive industry (as these manufacturers preferred to limit the number of supplier relationships that they had). Small and medium-sized enterprises turned to specialisation and started to serve niche markets. European paint production increased by 4.2% or 165.4 thousand tonnes in 1997. The respective paint industries of Finland and Portugal recorded output gains of 16.7% and 8.7% respectively in 1997 (figures from CEPE[2], European Council of Paint, Printing Ink and Artists' Colours Industry).

2) CEPE membership; Belgium, Denmark, Germany, Finland, France, Italy, the Netherlands, Portugal, Norway and Switzerland.

Figure 6.19

Paints, varnishes and printing inks (NACE Rev. 1 24.3)
Production and employment in the Triad

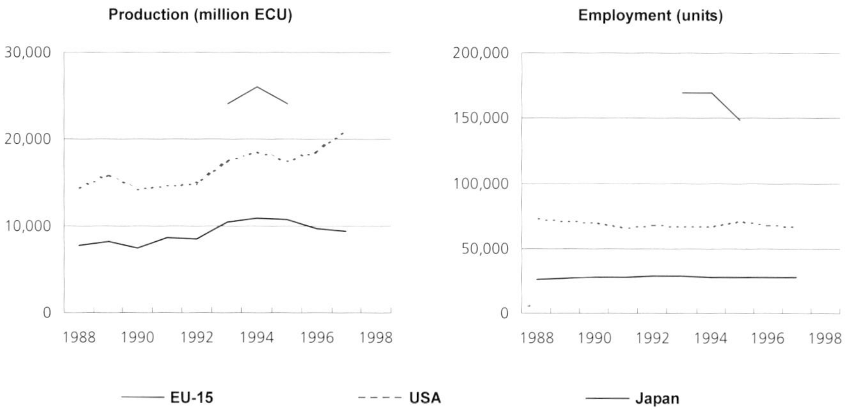

Source: Eurostat (SBS)

Figure 6.20 (%)

Paints, varnishes and printing inks (NACE Rev. 1 24.3)
Production and export specialisation by Member State, 1998

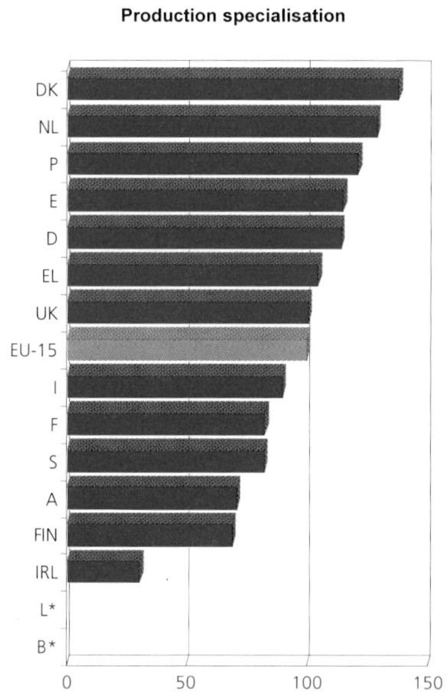

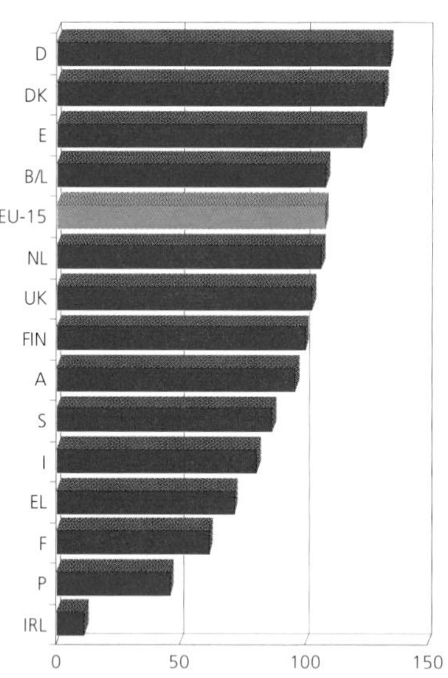

Source: Eurostat (SBS)

(thousand tonnes) Figure 6.21

Production of the paint industry, 1997

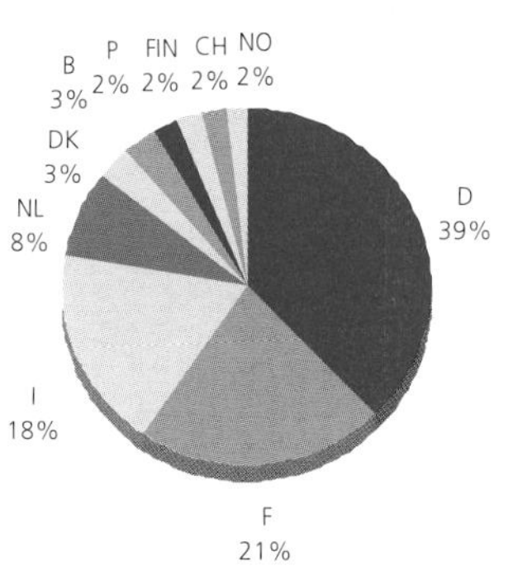

Source: CEPE

If we look at sales (in quantity) of paints by downstream industry there was a varied picture in 1997. In Germany, sales to the automotive industry increased on the back of a buoyant car market. Metal finishing and retail trade reflected the most uniform upward trend in purchases of paints in Europe in 1997 (other than in Germany).

The market required constant innovation in order to adapt to customers' wishes and environmental and health regulations. Larger companies were favoured as they could raise capital for research more easily and also they attracted skilled personnel.

Between 1993 and 1998 labour productivity (value added per person employed) increased in most of the Member States, rising by 14.9% and 2.1% in Germany and France and even faster in Greece and in Finland (35.2% and 34.5% respectively). Labour intensity decreased during the same period, for example in the United Kingdom from 9.0 to 6.5 persons employed per one million ECU of production value during the same period. These improvements led in many cases to a reduction in the number of persons employed, for example, in Germany and the United Kingdom (down by 7.0% and 2.6% per annum). There were however jobs created in Denmark and Spain, rising 4.1% and 7.7% per annum respectively (again 1993-1998).

In the USA output rose by 1.3% per annum between 1993 and 1997, whilst in Japan production fell by 1.9% per annum. Japanese labour intensity, at 2.9 persons per one million ECU of output value in 1997, was above that found in the USA (3.2 persons), or in the EU, for example, Germany or Italy with 5.8 persons and 3.8 persons respectively.

International trade increased during the course of the nineties. Within the euro-zone, exports increased by 118.7% and imports by 88.0% between 1988 and 1998 (figures include intra-EU trade flows). The main producers within the EU reported a trade surplus. In Germany, the export ratio was equal to 35.1%, whilst imports accounted for just 12.7% of domestic consumption in 1998. France reported a negative trade balance, with imports from third countries serving a quarter of domestic demand.

Figure 6.22

Paints, varnishes and printing inks (NACE Rev. 1 24.3) Destination of EU exports, 1998

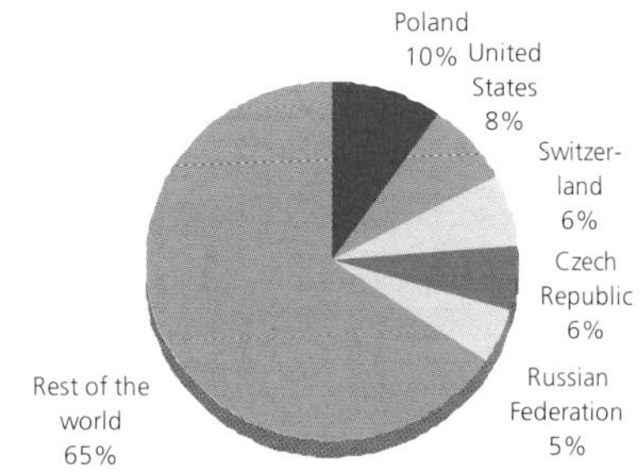

Source: Eurostat (Comext)

Figure 6.23

Paints, varnishes and printing inks (NACE Rev. 1 24.3) Origin of EU imports, 1998

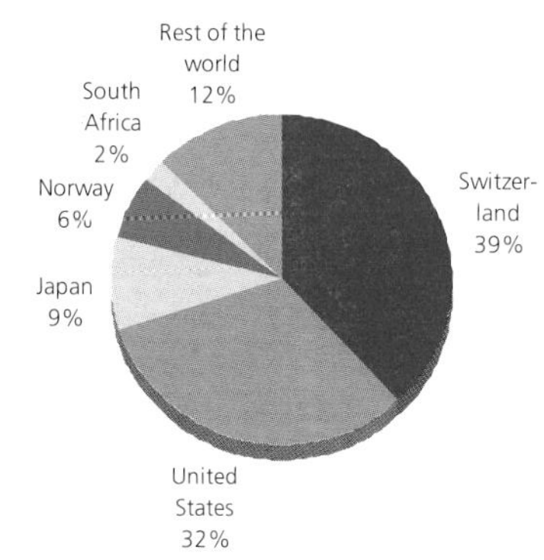

Source: Eurostat (Comext)

Pharmaceuticals, soaps, detergents, cosmetics, perfumes and toiletries (NACE Rev. 1 24.4 and 24.5)

Pharmaceuticals, soaps, detergents and toiletries were destined largely for consumer markets. Their manufacture was one of the main sectors within the chemicals, rubber and plastics industry within Europe, accounting for just under 4% of total EU manufacturing or some 27% of the chemicals, rubber and plastics industry.

French production of pharmaceuticals, soaps, detergents and toiletries was the largest in the EU, with output of 34.2 billion ECU in 1998, just under a quarter of the European total. Germany and Italy followed in the ranking with the second and third highest production figures. Within the smaller Member States, Denmark displayed a high production specialisation ratio, which was around one and a half times the European average.

If we look in more detail at the sector, the markets for pharmaceuticals were somewhat different to those for cosmetic goods and cleansing agents, due in part to the widespread regulation of the pharmaceuticals market. Whilst demand for pharmaceuticals was to a large extent determined by structural changes, such as demography and health policy, as well as by progress in medical science, the demand for soaps, detergents and toiletries was more dependent upon the level of disposable income in each country.

Pharmaceuticals, soaps, detergents and toiletries followed an upward trend during the nineties. The recession in 1993 did not cause a decline in production values, which may in part be explained by the fact that pharmaceuticals were less dependent on the evolution of the business cycle. During the ten years to 1998, production values increased in France by 4.3% per annum and in Germany by 3.3% per annum. Denmark and the Netherlands reported average annual growth rates of 8.5% and 8.1%. Only Finland and Portugal reported a reduction in their output (both falling by 1.0% per annum). The workforce grew in France and Italy (up by 1.4% and 1.6% per annum respectively between 1988 and 1998), and by as much as 4.3% per annum in Denmark. Spain and the United Kingdom reported a decline in the number of persons employed during the mid-nineties, down by 3.1% and 1.4% per annum respectively between 1993 and 1998.

Figure 6.24

Pharmaceuticals, soaps, detergents and toiletries (NACE Rev. 1 24.4 and 24.5)
Production and employment in the Triad

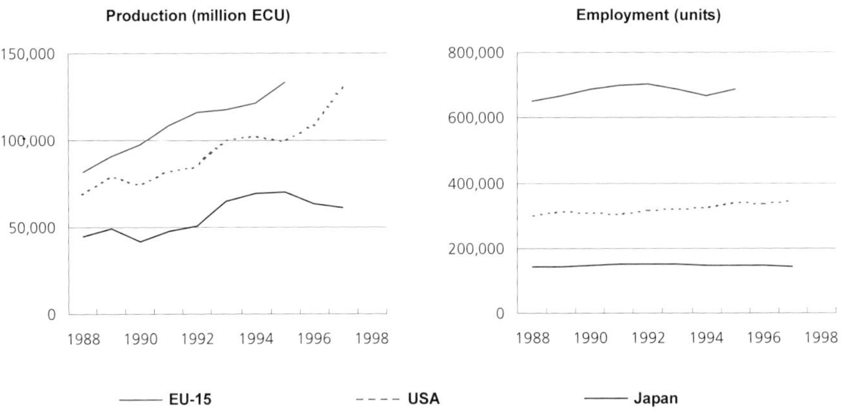

Source: Eurostat (SBS)

Figure 6.25 (%)

Pharmaceuticals, soaps, detergents and toiletries (NACE Rev. 1 24.4 and 24.5)
Production and export specialisation by Member State, 1998

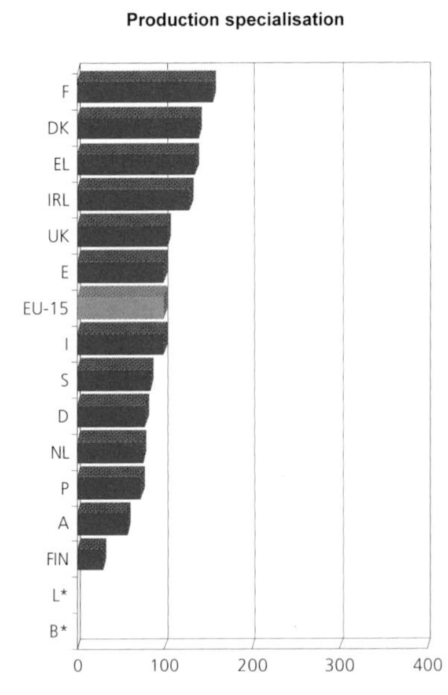

Export specialisation
IRL
DK
F
UK
EU-15
B/L
S
D
A
I
E
NL
EL
P
FIN
0 100 200 300 400

Source: Eurostat (SBS)

(%) Figure 6.26

Total spending on health care as a percentage of GDP

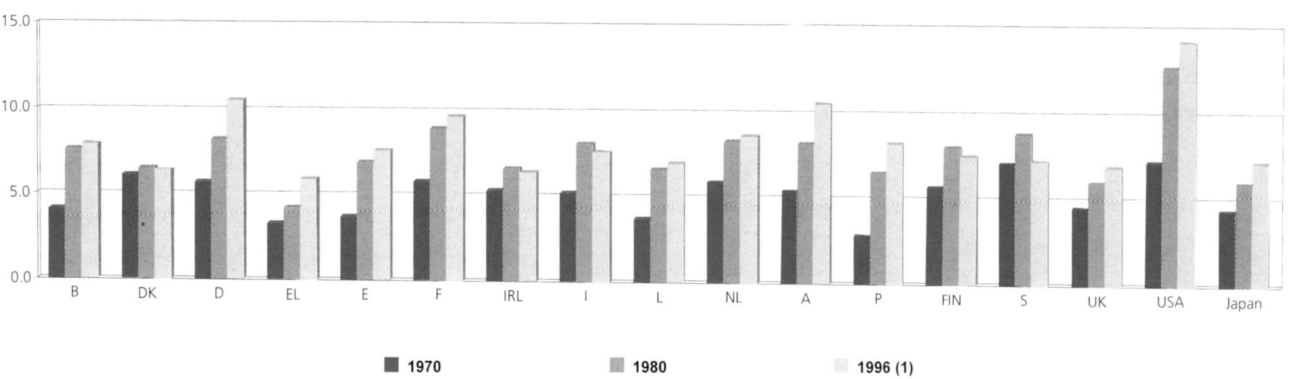

(1) 1995 data for Spain, Ireland, Luxembourg, Sweden and Japan.

Source: EFPIA

Pharmaceuticals and cosmetics required constant research and development in order to fulfil consumer wishes and health policy requirements. The sector displayed a tendency towards mergers and acquisitions in order to improve long-term competitiveness. Within the industry, large players took an increasing share of the market. European multinationals accounted for two-thirds of the pharmaceutical market in 1997[3]. Medium-sized enterprises specialised in market segments, which they served internationally, whilst small enterprises operated locally, sometimes in very specialised fields.

3) EFPIA, European Federation of Pharmaceutical Industries and Associations (including Switzerland and Norway).

Expenditures on research and development of pharmaceuticals were equal to 12 billion ECU in 1997, a five-fold increase on the 1980 figure.

In Europe there were around 700 companies engaged in the bio-technology pharmaceuticals sector, each generated an average of 2.4 million ECU of turnover and spent an average of 2.1 million ECU on research and development in 1997. The corresponding figures for their counterparts in the USA were 9.0 million ECU and 4.8 million ECU (data from EFPIA, European Federation of Pharmaceutical Industries and Associations).

The completion of the Single Market is expected to help reduce health costs and increase consumer choice. Regulations within each of the Member States has in the past led to a fragmented market, increasing product development and distribution costs. Non-prescription pharmaceuticals accounted for 30% of the German and French markets to below 10% of the Swedish and Portuguese markets (9.7% and 9.0% respectively) in 1998. Self-medication for cough and cold treatments accounted for nearly one third of non-prescription turnover in 1998, followed by a 20.3% share for analgesics and 20.0% for stomach treatments (figures from AESGP, the European Proprietary Medicines Manufacturers' Association).

(%) Figure 6.27

Market share of non-prescription pharmaceuticals

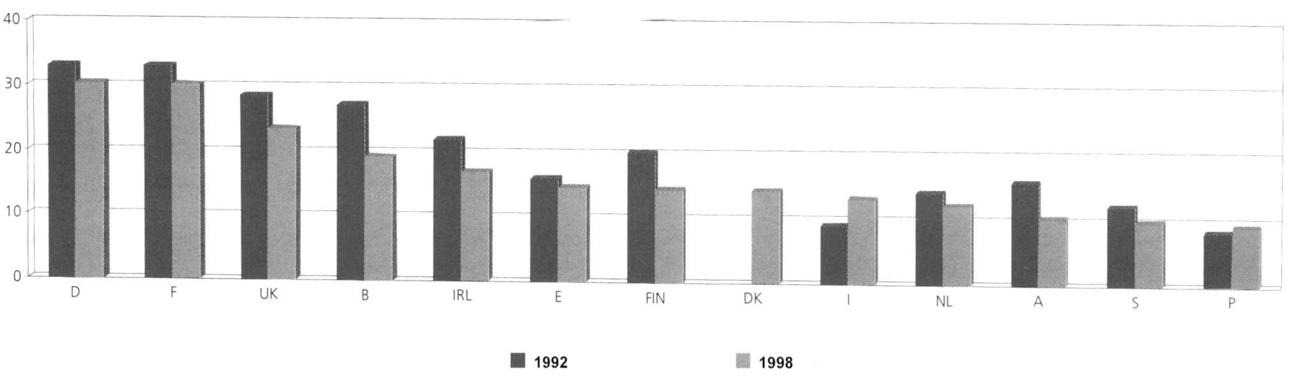

Source: AESGP

In the middle of the nineties the European market for animal health care products was worth 3.3 billion ECU[4], with France responsible for a quarter of the output and (former West) Germany a fifth. Animal health care products include therapeutic pharmaceuticals and feed additives. Turnover of therapeutic pharmaceuticals for animals was equal to 2.3 billion ECU in the EU[5] an increase of 7.9% per annum between 1989 and 1996. The evolution of the sector was closely linked to agricultural policy and the regulatory framework for animal health. Within the Member States the structure of the animal health market differed widely depending on the composition of livestock, methods of production and the climate.

The European market for cosmetics, toiletries and perfumes increased by 5.7% to 40.3 billion ECU in 1997[6] (at retail sales prices). Toiletries such as soaps, shaving products, dental hygiene and hair care accounted for more than half of the market, whilst skin care products had a 21.0% share, perfumes (15.2%) and decorative cosmetics (11.6%). The sector was largely dependent on the evolution of household incomes. Competition increased largely as a result of the increased concentration within the retail trade sector, which gave retailers greater bargaining power. In 1997, French consumption per capita (131 ECU) was twice as high as in Denmark and Portugal (both 62 ECU), the average for the EU was 108 ECU per capita.

4) Excluding additives; excluding Austria, Finland, Sweden and former East Germany. FEDESA, European Federation of Animal Health.
5) Excluding Austria, Greece, Luxembourg, Finland and Sweden.
6) COLIPA, The European Cosmetics, Toiletry and Perfumery Association.

One area of environmental concern in the pharmaceuticals industry is the use of aerosols. Since 1989 aerosols destined for consumption have been produced with alternative propellants than CFCs (except some medical products like asthma inhalers). In 1997 world production of aerosols was equal to 10 billion units, 40% of which were produced within the EU (4.1 billion aerosols). European production (without Ireland) was on a constant upward trend, latest growth was equal to 5.0% in 1997 (FEA, European Aerosol Federation). The vast majority of aerosols were used for personal care products (around 55%).

Foreign trade of pharmaceuticals, soaps, detergents and toiletries intensified during the course of the nineties. In 1998 the European trade surplus was equal to 21.2 billion ECU.

Figure 6.28 (%)

European cosmetics, toiletry and perfume market, 1997

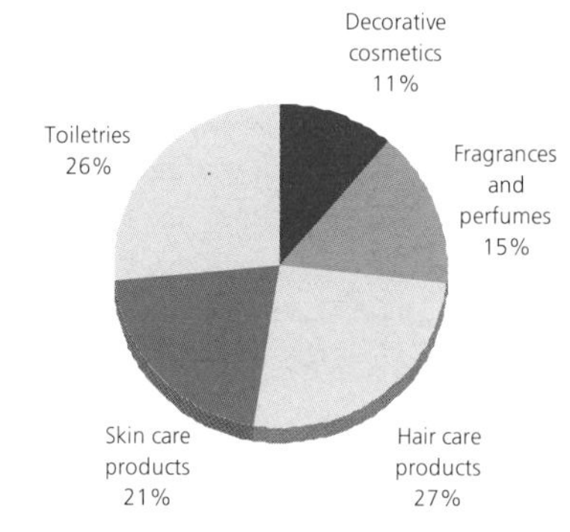

Source: COLIPA

Figure 6.29

Pharmaceuticals, soaps, detergents and toiletries (NACE Rev. 1 24.4 and 24.5) Destination of EU exports, 1998

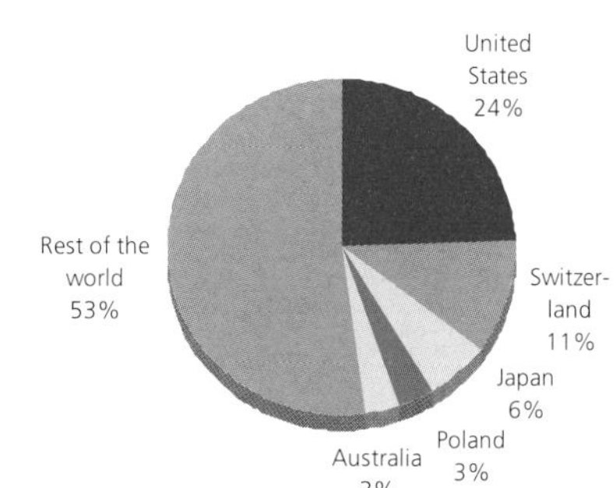

Source: Eurostat (Comext)

Figure 6.30

Pharmaceuticals, soaps, detergents and toiletries (NACE Rev. 1 24.4 and 24.5) Origin of EU imports, 1998

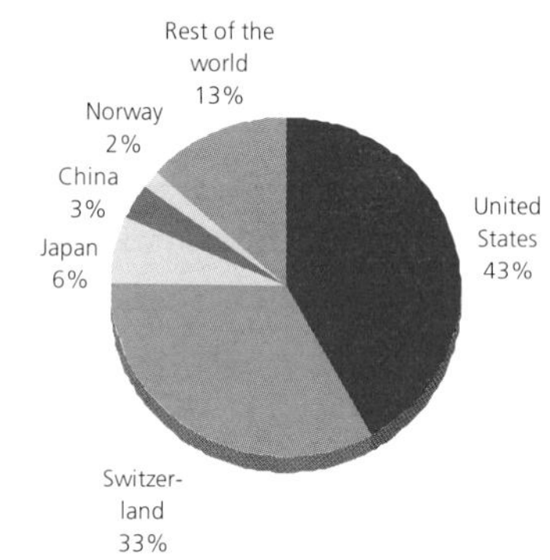

Source: Eurostat (Comext)

Man-made fibres (NACE Rev. 1 24.7)

Man-made fibres are an intermediate good for the production of wearing apparel, furniture and automotive accessories, as well as the construction industry. In 1998 the production value of man-made fibres was equal to some 10.9 billion ECU in the EU, accounting for 2.0% of the chemicals, rubber and plastics aggregate.

The German and the Italian sectors were responsible for over half the production of the EU (32.7% and 20.8% respectively), whilst in France and the United Kingdom there were relatively small production shares (5.1% and 10.2% in 1998). Within the smaller Member States, Austria and the Netherlands recorded a high production specialisation rate in man-made fibres, with the sector contributing more than twice the European average to total domestic manufacturing.

Figure 6.31

Man-made fibres (NACE Rev. 1 24.7)
Production and employment in the Triad

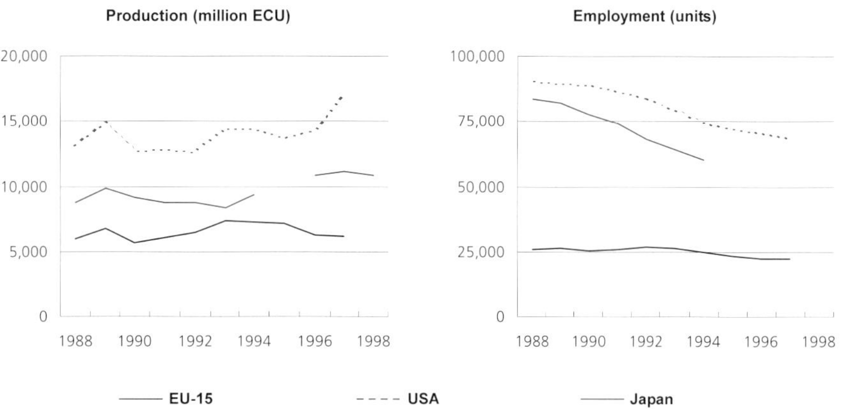

Source: Eurostat (SBS)

(%) Figure 6.32

World production of cotton, wool and man-made fibres

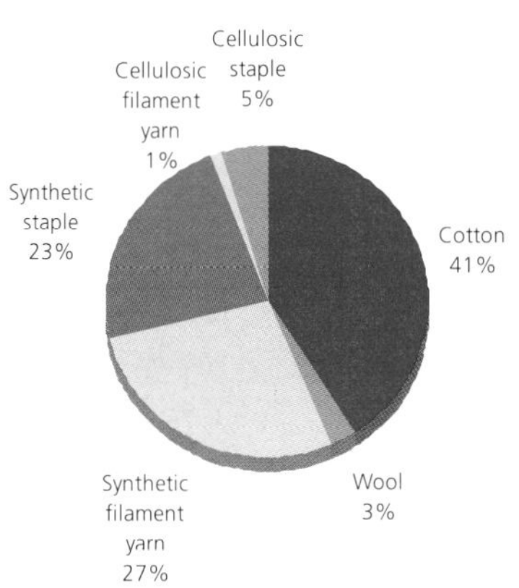

Source: CIRFS

(%) Figure 6.33

Man-made fibres (NACE Rev. 1 24.7)
Production and export specialisation by Member State, 1998

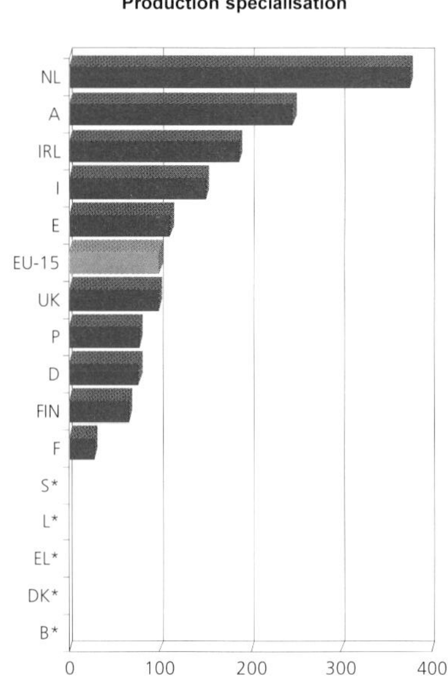

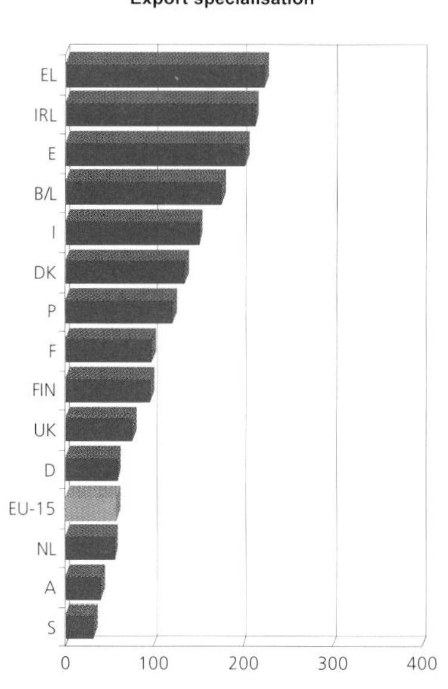

Source: Eurostat (SBS)

In both of these countries there was a large production of cellulosics. Man-made fibres made of cellulosic polymers (such as viscose or acetate fibres) may be distinguished from fibres made of synthetic polymers (such as acrylics, polyamides or polyester fibres). Source material for the former is cellulose fibre from wood, whilst for the latter it is crude oil.

Man-made fibres accounted for more than half the world's fibre production (cotton, wool and man-made fibres), some 56.4% in 1997[7]. The significance of man-made fibres rose steadily, rising 19.4 percentage points from 1985.

7) CIRFS, International Rayon and Synthetic Fibre Committee.

The sector of man-made fibres expanded its possible applications through technical advances. Fashion cycles influenced the use of man-made fibres in the manufacture of wearing apparel, furniture and the automotive industry. Within the automotive and construction industries demand largely followed the business cycle. Demand from the apparel industry was closely linked to the trend of disposable incomes. Falling incomes not only resulted in a lower level of general expenditure and demand, but also a shift of demand to cheaper products.

In 1998, world production of synthetic and cellulosic man-made fibres was equal to 27.8 million tonnes. There was a decrease in the production of cellulosic fibres, down by 3.5% to 2.8 million tonnes, whilst synthetic fibres increased by 1.9% to 25.0 million tonnes[8] when compared to a year before.

EU production values (in constant prices) increased by 5.0% per annum between 1993 and 1998, despite a modest decrease in 1998. Contrary to the general upward trend, both the Netherlands and the United Kingdom reported declining output during the mid-nineties (5.4% and 2.7% respectively).

The manufacture of man-made fibres was relatively capital intensive. International competition resulted in a reduction in the number of persons employed, for example in Italy and the United Kingdom down by 3.2% and 3.9% per annum (1993-1998). Efforts to modernise equipment led to improved labour productivity. In Germany value added per person employed increased by 73.3% to 52.3 thousand ECU and in the United Kingdom labour productivity rose by 42.9% to 86.1 thousand ECU (again 1993-1998).

If we look at the breakdown of man-made fibre production within the world, manufacturers from outside the Triad (particularly East Asia) were responsible for two thirds of the world's production. Within the Triad, the USA reported the highest levels of output (16% of world production). The shares of the other two Triad members were 13% and 6% respectively. European manufacturers were adapting well to changes in world markets, with production growth rising by 6.7% per annum between 1993 and 1998. Comparable data for the USA and Japan showed that American output was rising by just 0.7% per annum, whilst Japanese figures were down by 3.8% per annum (between 1993 and 1997).

8) Figures from CIRFS, International Rayon and Synthetic Fibre Committee and IVC, Industrievereinigung Chemiefasern e.V.

EU foreign trade of man-made fibres displayed considerably higher flows of imports than exports, partly due to the cheap labour cost component of third country production. During the course of the nineties, exports between the EU and third countries decreased, whilst extra-EU imports continued on an upward trend.

Figure 6.34

Man-made fibres (NACE Rev. 1 24.7)
Destination of EU exports, 1998

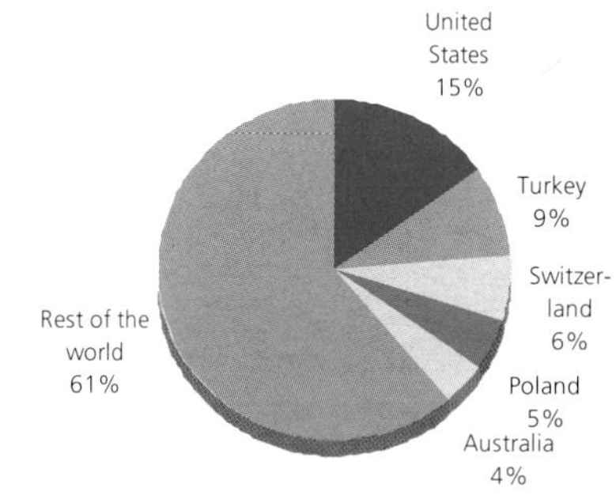

Source: Eurostat (Comext)

Figure 6.35

Man-made fibres (NACE Rev. 1 24.7)
Origin of EU imports, 1998

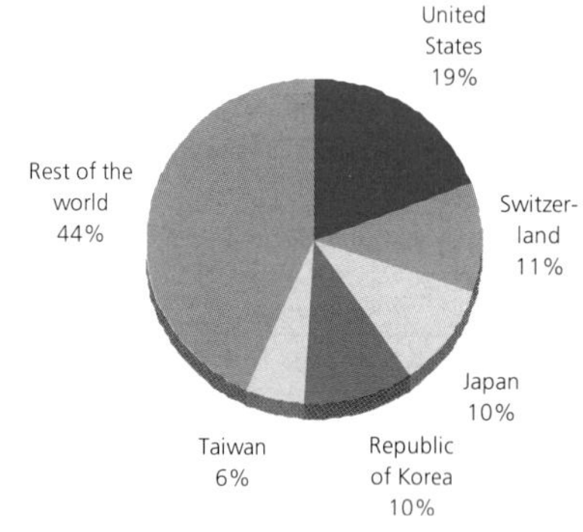

Source: Eurostat (Comext)

Biotechnology

Biotechnology may be defined as technological utilisation of biological processes, microbiological (fungi and bacteria) and biochemical procedures, as well as genetic engineering. Biotechnology is expected to improve the quality of life, through improved health care and less pollution. Biotechnological knowledge may improve the competitiveness of industries and expand product ranges.

In the manufacture of pharmaceuticals, biotechnology allows scientists to identify pathogens and disease mechanisms, or facilitates them in the large-scale production of insulin or human growth hormones through genetically modified bacteria. At the end of the nineties, one fifth of new pharmaceuticals were derived from biotechnology.

The manufacture of agrochemicals expanded its supply to the field of biotechnological products. Increased sales of plants resistant against certain pests reduced sales of corresponding pesticides.

In the food and beverages industry, biological processes have been used for a long time, in areas such as fermentation. Recent research in biotechnology was mainly to improve production processes.

In general, enterprises within the EU joined the biotechnological race later than their American competitors. Indeed, there are a considerably higher number of biotechnological patents in the USA. In the market of newly introduced biopharmaceuticals, the USA accounts for 75%, whilst Europe had a 10% share. The lag in European activity may be partly explained by public opinion, which does not support the industry to the same extent as in the USA. For example, the discussion on product labelling was more intense and longer in the EU than in the USA. Since September 1998 labels on food have to inform the consumer whether it contains genetically modified soybeans or maize. In the USA labelling of food containing biotechnological derived products has to follow the same requirements as applied to all food. The Food and Drug Administration in the USA does not see any inherent health risk in biotechnological food products.

Public concern and political debate meant that investment activity was low in Austria, Germany, Greece and the Nordic Member States. More favourable conditions existed in the United Kingdom, Ireland, the Netherlands and Belgium. The European biotechnology industry is dominated by many small, specialist companies.

Market analysts expect a sharp increase in demand for biotechnology. One of the main difficulties in Europe that affects the industry is a lack of venture capital. Many areas of biotechnology require a large amount of research and do not see pay-offs before 10 to 15 years have passed. Nevertheless, the industry has seen great interest in its stocks at the end of the nineties as companies founded in the eighties start to reap the benefits of their research and make substantial profits.

Rubber (NACE Rev. 1 25.1)

Rubber products are destined for the automotive industry and other industrial sectors, such as floorings, domestic appliances, medical goods and conveyor belts. The manufacture of rubber products (NACE Rev. 1 25.1) encompasses three main areas, rubber tyres and tubes, retreading and rebuilding of rubber tyres and other rubber products.

The industry accounted for more than 6% of the chemicals, rubber and plastics aggregated output or just under 1% of European manufacturing. Germany and France, were the two largest producers within the EU, with output equivalent to 10.0 billion ECU and 6.9 billion ECU in 1998 (some 50% of the European total).

Rubber products are made of natural or synthetic rubber. The natural rubber industry is situated largely in sub-tropical countries. Small enterprises collect latex from the rubber tree (hevea brasiliensis) using largely labour intensive harvesting methods. Latex is converted through heat or acid treatment into raw rubber, which is then used for tyres, engineering products, conveyor belts and tubes.

The production of synthetic rubber is a capital and research intensive exercise and is largely found in the industrialised countries of the world (usually forming part of the tyre or petrochemicals industry). Some types of synthetic rubber are more resistant to wearing, heat and chemicals. Indeed, these properties allow the potential uses of rubber to be greatly increased.

World natural rubber consumption increased by 1.5% to 6.6 million tonnes in 1998, whilst world synthetic rubber consumption fell by 1.0% to 9.9 million tonnes. In the EU the production and consumption of synthetic rubbers did not follow the global downward trend, instead there was an expansion of 1.2% and 3.9% (figures from IRSG, International Rubber Study Group).

In Germany and France production values (in constant prices) displayed an annual average growth rate of 4.5% and 5.4% between 1993 and 1998. Higher increases were recorded in Portugal, Finland and Sweden (up by 14.2%, 10.2% and 10.1% per annum respectively).

Figure 6.36

Rubber (NACE Rev. 1 25.1)

Production and employment in the Triad

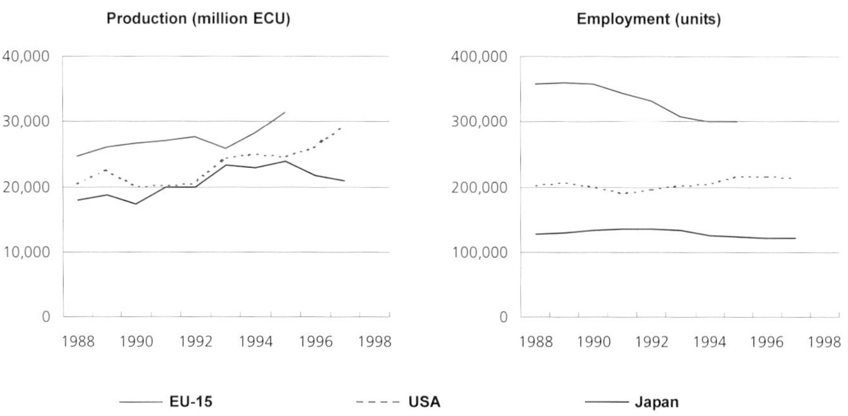

Source: Eurostat (SBS)

Figure 6.37 (%)

Rubber (NACE Rev. 1 25.1)

Production and export specialisation by Member State, 1998

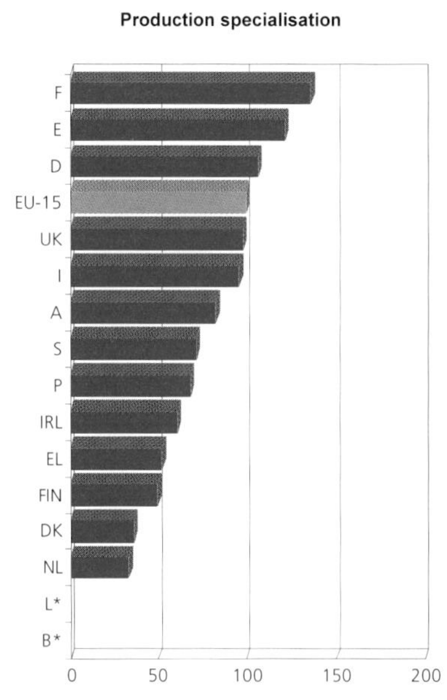

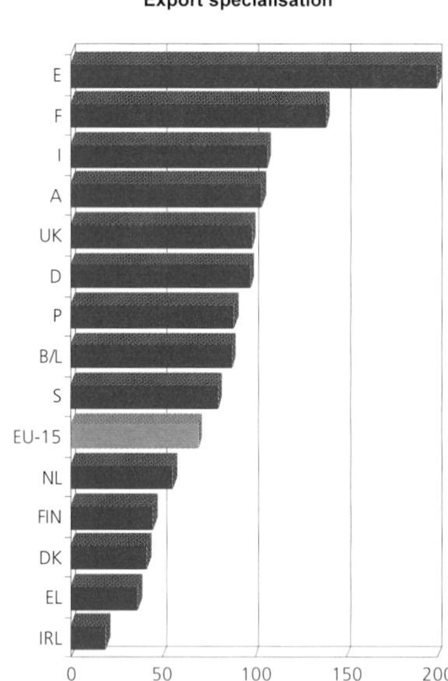

Source: Eurostat (SBS)

(thousand tonnes) Figure 6.38

Rubber consumption for the production of tyre and tyre products, 1997

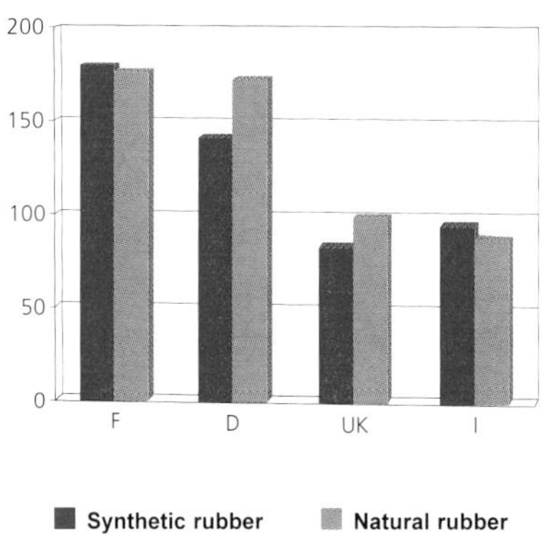

Source: IRSG

In 1997 the production of car tyres grew, for example by 11.3% in Germany, resulting in total output of 46.4 million units. Production of truck tyres was also increasing in Germany (up by 3.6% to 7.2 million units). However, in the United Kingdom and Italy output decreased by 0.7% and 2.8% respectively (figures from IRSG).

Sales of tyres are determined by the business cycle in the automotive industry, as well as weather conditions, which strongly influence the demand for winter tyres.

The manufacture of rubber products adapted its structure to the global organisation of downstream industries. In the manufacture of tyres there were just a few large global companies. Three companies (Goodyear, Firestone/Bridgestone and Michelin) dominated more than 50% of the world market. The tyre industry faced over-capacity in the nineties. This pushed many firms to reorganise their production processes. As European labour costs were high in comparison to international competitors, manufacturers tended to reduce the share of labour in overall production costs. Between 1993 and 1998 labour intensity (measured as the number of persons employed per one million ECU of production value) fell in Europe (except for Austria). In Belgium, the ratio was reduced by two-thirds from 11.5 to 3.7 persons by 1998. Even in the Member States with comparatively low labour costs there was a decrease in the number of persons employed per one million ECU of production value: for example, in Portugal the ratio fell by 14.8 persons to 12.0 persons during the same period.

The efforts to reorganise the production process can also be observed in the improvements in European labour productivity. Value added per person employed increased at a fast rate in Germany and Finland (by 26.1% and 24.2% between 1993 and 1998). Some European manufacturers de-located some of their production to Eastern Europe, for example, the German tyre manufacturer Continental AG. Competition became stiffer, largely as a result of the world market stagnating due to the economic crises in south-east Asia.

Production of car and truck tyres accounted for 264.0 million units in the USA and 160.4 million units in Japan. In 1997 production value of rubber products increased by 12.7% in the USA, accompanied by even faster growth in value added (18.9%). In Japan the industry followed a downward trend, with production values falling by 4.0%. Japan continued to report the highest labour productivity amongst the three Triad members (80.3 thousand ECU in 1997), well in advance of Belgium (the highest labour productivity in the EU, 62.3 thousand ECU).

Foreign trade data in this industry showed that imports of rubber products were growing at a faster rate than exports. In Germany, extra-EU imports increased by 178.4% between 1988 and 1998, whilst deliveries to countries outside the EU grew by 108.7%. In France the corresponding figures reflected an even larger gap, imports rising by 185.9%, whilst extra-EU exports grew by just 43.8%. Nevertheless, both countries continued to report a trade surplus. Within the larger Member States, the United Kingdom was the only country with a negative trade balance, which was observed throughout the nineties.

Figure 6.39

Rubber (NACE Rev. 1 25.1)
Destination of EU exports, 1998

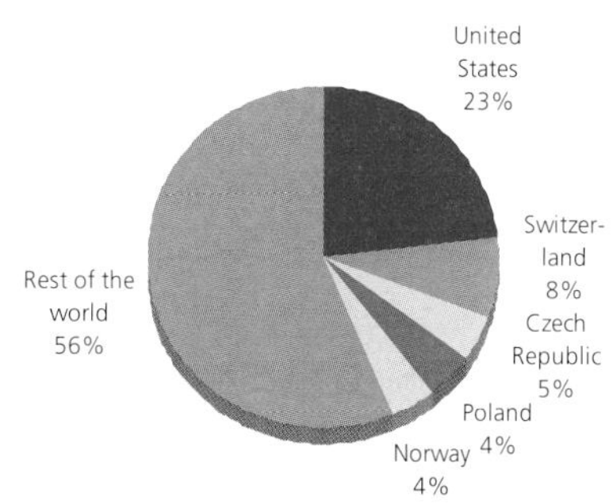

Source: Eurostat (Comext)

Figure 6.40

Rubber (NACE Rev. 1 25.1)
Origin of EU imports, 1998

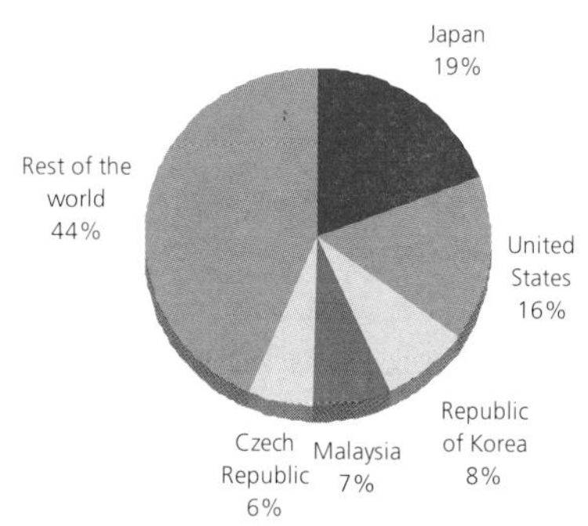

Source: Eurostat (Comext)

Plastics (NACE Rev. 1 25.2)

The manufacture of plastic products includes a wide range of products, from plastic sheets and tubes to packaging goods to builders' ware. The sector produces both mass-production and customised products. Manufacturers of the latter often work on a sub-contracting basis. The main downstream industries of plastics were food, automotives, electronics and construction. The production value of plastic products was equivalent to just over a fifth of the total for chemicals, rubber and plastics, or just under 3% of total EU manufacturing. One third of European production originated from Germany (35.6 billion ECU in 1998). If we add United Kingdom production (17.4 billion ECU) then almost one half of the EU's output is accounted for. Other countries reporting a relatively high degree of specialisation in Europe included Austria and Denmark.

The manufacture of plastics has grown at a fast pace since the 1950's. The main use of plastics is as packaging material (around 40%), followed by construction with around 20%. Packaging with plastics increased with the size of retail outlets where more pre-packed than fresh food was sold. It is estimated that plastics packaging covers two fifths of all consumer goods, but in terms of weight plastics make up a tenth of total packaging[9].

The plastics industry is one of the most dynamic sectors in the European economy (with only areas such as communications and information technology growing quicker). One of the main advances has been the use of plastics for transportation. Vehicles have lost weight significantly and hence consume less fuel. The hygienic nature of plastics meant that its use in medicine has also became increasingly important (syringes, instruments and even implants).

Between 1993 and 1998 the production value of plastics (in constant prices) grew between 8.0% per annum in Finland and 3.1% per annum in the Netherlands. The level of output was largely determined by the business cycle in downstream industries. For example, in the automotive industry there was increased demand in 1998, which led to suppliers of plastic components increasing their deliveries (in Germany up by 12.4%).

9) Figures from GKV, Gesamtverband Kunststoffverarbeitende Industrie e.V.

Figure 6.41

Plastics (NACE Rev. 1 25.2)

Production and employment in the Triad

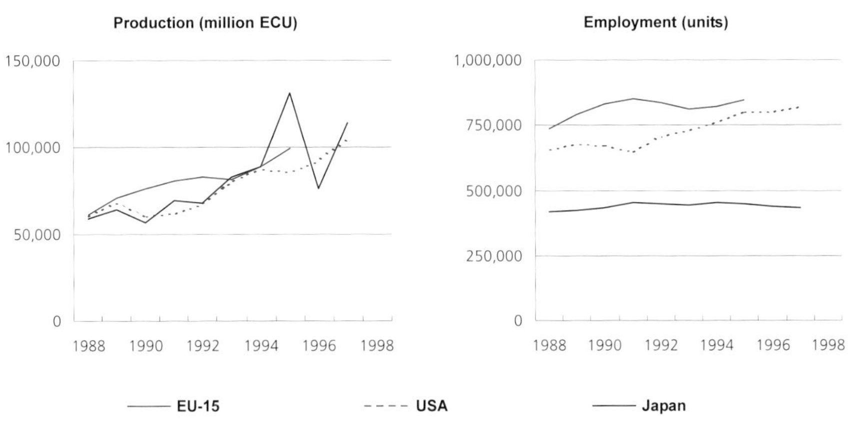

Source: Eurostat (SBS)

Figure 6.42 (%)

Plastics (NACE Rev. 1 25.2)

Production and export specialisation by Member State, 1998

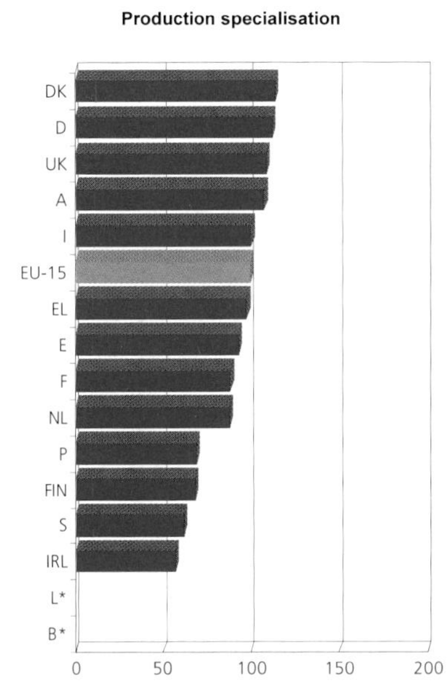

Source: Eurostat (SBS)

With raw material prices generally low in the late nineties (the price level for Naphtha fell by 14% in 1998), the plastics industry also faced falling producer prices. Downstream industries were characterised by large enterprises, such as in retail trade or the automotive industry, which reduced the scope for price increases. Secondly, due to over-capacity (to a large extent in the manufacture of polypropylene) producer prices continued their downward trend in 1999. Oil and natural gas were the main raw materials for most plastics. The other main components of cost were labour and energy, which were comparatively high in the EU.

Some enterprises increased their efforts to grow through acquisitions and strategic alliances. Mergers and tie-ups spread across the globe (for example Dupont, a chemicals and plastics manufacturer in the USA built up a joint venture with Teijin of Japan). The liberalisation of energy markets in Europe and the creation of a Single Market allowed some larger manufacturers to negotiate directly with electricity providers for lower prices based on their consumption.

The number of persons employed increased in many EU countries during the course of the nineties. In Austria and Denmark employment grew by 6.9% and 5.9% per annum between 1993 and 1998. In the United Kingdom and France there was less spectacular growth of 0.9% and 1.8% per annum. Germany reported a slight decline in employment equal to 0.6% per annum (during the same period).

Manufacturers of plastics made efforts to increase their profit margin by lowering labour intensity. The ratio of persons employed per one million ECU of production value decreased by two persons to 7.6 persons on average in Germany (between 1993 and 1998). In 1998 the ratio varied between 4.9 persons in Belgium and 13.6 persons in Portugal. Demand for highly qualified and educated personnel was maintained throughout the nineties. The manufacture of plastics faced constant technological improvements and accordingly needed educated personnel in order to remain competitive.

International comparison showed that output was growing faster in the USA (up by 13.5% in 1997) than in the EU. In Japan, the recent recession led to a downward trend for the industry. Plastics played an important role in the Japanese manufacturing economy (the industry accounted for 37.8% of total chemicals, rubber and plastics production, whilst in the other two Triad members the share was around 20%). The number of persons employed increased in the USA by 2.3%, whilst falling in Japan by 1.1% (growth rate for 1997).

Foreign trade intensified in the course of the nineties, with the EU trade surplus more than doubling between 1988 and 1998, to reach 3.9 billion ECU. EU trade performance could be largely attributed to the high technological content of European production, which meant that high value added products were generally exported, whilst cheap products were imported.

Figure 6.43

Plastics (NACE Rev. 1 25.2)
Destination of EU exports, 1998

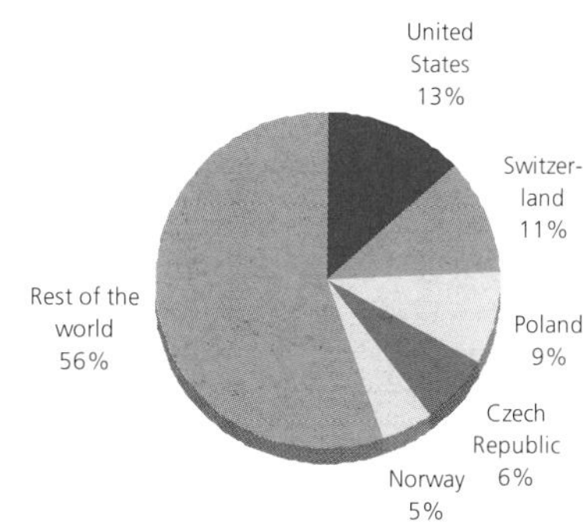

Source: Eurostat (Comext)

Figure 6.44

Plastics (NACE Rev. 1 25.2)
Origin of EU imports, 1998

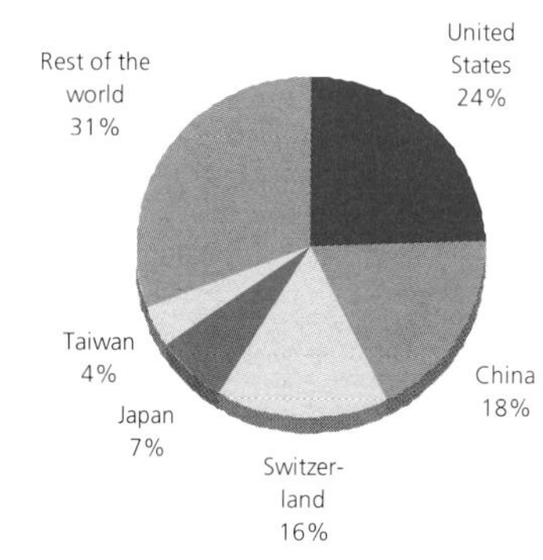

Source: Eurostat (Comext)

Professional associations representing the industries within this chapter

AESGP
The European Proprietary Medicines Manufacturers' Association
7, avenue de Tervueren
B-1040 Bruxelles
tel: (32) 2 735 51 30
fax: (32) 2 735 52 22
e-mail: info@aesgp.be

AISE
International Association of the Soap and Detergent industry
49, square Marie-Louise
B-1000 Bruxelles
tel: (32) 2 230 83 71
fax: (32) 2 230 82 88
e-mail: a.i.s.e@euronet.be

APPE
Association of Petrochemicals Producers in Europe
4, avenue E. Van Nieuwenhuyse, boîte 2
B-1160 Bruxelles
tel: (32) 2 676 72 76
fax: (32) 2 676 72 30

BLIC
Liaison Office of the Rubber Industry of the EU
2, avenue des Arts, boîte 12
B-1210 Bruxelles
tel. (32) 2 218 49 40
fax: (32) 2 218 61 62
e-mail: BLIC@skynet.be

CEFIC
European Chemical Industry Council
4, avenue E. Van Nieuwenhuyse, boîte 1
B-1160 Bruxelles
tel: (32) 2 676 72 11
fax: (32) 2 676 73 00
e-mail: mail@cefic.be

CEPE
European Council of the Paint, Printing Inks and Artists' Colours Industry
4, avenue E. Van Nieuwenhuyse
B-1160 Bruxelles
tel: (32) 2 676 74 80
fax: (32) 2 676 74 90e-mail: secretariat@cepe.org

COLIPA
The European Cosmetic, Toiletry and Perfumery Association
5-7, rue du Congrès
B-1000 Bruxelles
tel: (32) 2 227 66 10
fax: (32) 2 227 66 27
e-mail: colipa@colipa.be

EFMA
European Fertilisers Manufacturers Association
4, avenue E. Van Nieuwenhuyse, boîte 7
B-1160 Bruxelles
tel: (32) 2 675 35 50
fax: (33) 2 675 39 61
e-mail: mail@efma.be

EFPIA
European Federation of Pharmaceutical Industries' Associations
250, avenue Louise, boîte 91
B-1050 Bruxelles
tel: (32) 2 626 25 55
fax: (32) 2 626 25 66

FEDESA
European Federation of Animal Health
1, rue Defacqz, boîte 4
B-1050 Bruxelles
tel: (32) 2 543 75 60/63
fax: (32) 2 537 00 49
e-mail: fedesa@fedesa.be

FEICA
Association of European Adhesives Manufacturers
Postfach 23 01 69
D-40087 Düsseldorf
tel: (49) 211 67 93 130
fax: (49) 211 67 93 188
e-mail: mats.hagwall@feica.com

GPUE
Pharmaceutical Group of the European Union
13, square Ambiorix
B-1040 Bruxelles
tel: (32) 2 736 72 81
fax: (32) 2 736 02 06
e-mail: pharmacy@pgeu.org

IRSG
International Rubber Study Group
Heron House
109/115 Wembley Hill Road
Wembley Middlesex
HA9 8DA
tel: (44) 181 903 77 27
fax: (44) 181 903 28 48
e-mail: irsg@compuserve.com

Table 6.3 (million ECU)

Manufacture of basic chemicals (NACE Rev. 1 24.1)

Production related indicators in the EU

	1988	1989	1990	1991	1992	1993	1994	1995	1996	1997	1998
Production value	136,129	148,209	140,143	133,721	127,096	120,983	134,516	156,983	:	:	:
Producer price index (1995=100)	:	:	92.0	88.1	83.4	81.7	85.8	100.0	104.8	109.4	104.0
Value added	48,246	49,845	43,702	40,250	39,136	37,699	43,960	53,015	:	:	:
Number of persons employed (thousands)	768.0	767.0	752.5	729.6	698.7	651.4	613.1	587.8	:	:	:

Table 6.4 (million ECU)

Manufacture of basic chemicals (NACE Rev. 1 24.1)

Production related indicators, 1998

	B	DK	D	EL	E	F	IRL	I	L	NL	A	P	FIN	S	UK
Production value	10,378	839	50,977	462	8,733	23,803	5,121	14,747	:	15,517	1,734	312	2,319	2,609	18,254
Value added	3,100	249	18,311	114	2,359	6,357	3,164	4,084	:	4,122	448	:	801	819	6,632
Number of persons employed (units) (1)	25,864	3,603	236,882	3,860	30,762	75,189	5,879	43,784	:	44,270	6,504	2,724	8,512	10,268	70,436

(1) NL (1992).

Table 6.5 (million ECU)

Manufacture of basic chemicals (NACE Rev. 1 24.1)

Market related indicators in the EU

	1988	1989	1990	1991	1992	1993	1994	1995	1996	1997	1998
Apparent consumption	127,532	141,586	135,530	128,192	121,285	111,818	125,233	147,330	:	:	:
Exports	23,907	25,054	23,550	24,564	24,372	26,124	29,865	34,953	33,866	37,653	34,206
Imports	15,310	18,431	18,937	19,035	18,560	16,960	20,582	25,300	23,619	27,910	28,747
Trade balance	8,597	6,623	4,613	5,529	5,811	9,165	9,283	9,653	10,247	9,743	5,459
Export ratio (%)	17.6	16.9	16.8	18.4	19.2	21.6	22.2	22.3	:	:	:
Import penetration ratio (%)	12.0	13.0	14.0	14.8	15.3	15.2	16.4	17.2	:	:	:
Cover ratio (%)	156.2	135.9	124.4	129.0	131.3	154.0	145.1	138.2	143.4	134.9	119.0

Table 6.6 (million ECU)

Manufacture of basic chemicals (NACE Rev. 1 24.1)

Market related indicators, 1998

	B/L	DK	D	EL	E	F	IRL	I	NL	A	P	FIN	S	UK
Apparent consumption	:	1,707	45,984	1,249	11,670	25,881	-752	22,416	11,737	2,670	1,040	2,506	4,254	18,255
Exports	16,264	931	23,924	185	3,443	12,432	7,617	5,820	11,716	999	481	1,307	1,151	11,327
Imports	13,535	1,799	18,932	971	6,380	14,510	1,744	13,488	7,936	1,935	1,208	1,494	2,797	11,328
Trade balance	2,729	-868	4,992	-786	-2,937	-2,078	5,873	-7,668	3,780	-936	-727	-187	-1,645	-1
Export ratio (%)	:	111.0	46.9	40.0	39.4	52.2	148.7	39.5	75.5	57.6	154.0	56.4	44.1	62.1
Import penetration ratio (%)	:	105.4	41.2	77.8	54.7	56.1	-231.8	60.2	67.6	72.5	116.2	59.6	65.7	62.1
Cover ratio (%)	120.2	51.7	126.4	19.0	54.0	85.7	436.8	43.1	147.6	51.6	39.8	87.5	41.2	100.0

Table 6.7

Manufacture of basic chemicals (NACE Rev. 1 24.1)

Labour related indicators, 1998

	EU-15	B	DK	D	EL	E	F	IRL	I	L	NL	A	P	FIN	S	UK
Personnel costs (million ECU) (1)	27,843	1,532	141	12,786	98	1,039	3,677	245	1,647	:	1,947	322	58	322	430	2,875
Personnel costs/employee (thousand ECU) (2)	51.1	60.9	39.8	58.8	27.8	33.8	49.7	41.2	34.6	:	:	50.5	:	39.0	44.0	33.9
Social charges/personnel costs (%) (3)	24.5	29.7	4.5	23.4	24.3	20.4	33.6	19.0	35.1	:	20.7	22.7	:	21.9	29.6	16.1
Labour productivity (thousand ECU/head) (4)	90.2	119.8	69.2	77.3	29.6	76.7	84.5	538.2	93.3	:	63.7	68.8	:	94.1	79.7	94.2
Wage adjusted labour productivity (%) (2)	176.4	197.7	192.5	129.1	114.1	219.7	169.4	1,221.1	263.7	:	:	141.9	:	238.0	178.1	257.5

(1) EU-15 (1995). (2) EU-15, EL, I, A (1995); B, DK, D, E, F, IRL, FIN, S, UK (1996). (3) EU-15, S (1995). (4) NL (1992); EU-15 (1995).

Source: Eurostat (SBS, EBT)

(million ECU) — Table 6.8

Manufacture of pesticides and other agro-chemical products (NACE Rev. 1 24.2)
Production related indicators in the EU

	1988	1989	1990	1991	1992	1993	1994	1995	1996	1997	1998
Production value	:	:	:	:	:	5,609	6,662	:	:	:	:
Producer price index (1995=100)	:	:	:	:	:	:	:	:	:	:	:
Value added	:	:	:	:	:	2,029	2,118	:	:	:	:
Number of persons employed (thousands)	:	:	:	:	:	28.7	28.3	:	:	:	:

(million ECU) — Table 6.9

Manufacture of pesticides and other agro-chemical products (NACE Rev. 1 24.2)
Production related indicators, 1998

	B	DK	D	EL	E	F	IRL	I	L	NL	A	P	FIN	S	UK
Production value (1)	:	:	1,110	90	451	2,586	18	557	0	205	0	:	0	15	1,949
Value added (1)	:	:	398	19	130	656	4	151	0	54	0	:	0	4	805
Number of persons employed (units) (2)	:	:	4,837	741	2,547	6,786	156	1,788	0	:	0	:	0	66	6,791

(1) A (1995); IRL, L (1996). (2) A (1995); L, FIN (1996).

(million ECU) — Table 6.10

Manufacture of pesticides and other agro-chemical products (NACE Rev. 1 24.2)
Market related indicators in the EU

	1988	1989	1990	1991	1992	1993	1994	1995	1996	1997	1998
Apparent consumption	:	:	:	:	:	4,300	5,264	:	:	:	:
Exports	1,356	1,370	1,399	1,401	1,366	1,550	1,776	1,883	2,197	2,241	2,301
Imports	138	282	386	458	333	241	379	480	389	479	561
Trade balance	1,218	1,088	1,012	943	1,033	1,309	1,397	1,403	1,808	1,762	1,740
Export ratio (%)	:	:	:	:	:	27.6	26.7	:	:	:	:
Import penetration ratio (%)	:	:	:	:	:	5.6	7.2	:	:	:	:
Cover ratio (%)	984.5	485.6	361.9	305.8	409.7	643.0	468.5	392.0	564.9	468.3	410.1

(million ECU) — Table 6.11

Manufacture of pesticides and other agro-chemical products (NACE Rev. 1 24.2)
Market related indicators, 1998

	B/L	DK	D	EL	E	F	IRL	I	NL	A	P	FIN	S	UK
Apparent consumption (1)	:	:	102	184	640	2,032	51	674	158	645	:	36	75	1,285
Exports	313	52	1,571	13	120	1,820	40	267	297	60	11	10	18	1,132
Imports	306	106	563	107	309	1,266	66	384	251	71	77	46	78	468
Trade balance	6	-54	1,008	-94	-189	554	-26	-117	46	-11	-66	-35	-60	664
Export ratio (%) (1)	:	:	141.5	14.2	26.6	70.4	164.0	47.9	145.0	6.9	:	25,295.8	119.5	58.1
Import penetration ratio (%) (1)	:	:	553.4	58.0	48.3	62.3	123.1	56.9	158.1	10.5	:	128.4	103.8	36.4
Cover ratio (%)	102.0	49.3	279.2	12.0	38.8	143.8	60.3	69.5	118.5	84.5	13.7	22.2	22.5	241.9

(1) A (1994); IRL (1996).

Table 6.12

Manufacture of pesticides and other agro-chemical products (NACE Rev. 1 24.2)
Labour related indicators, 1998

	EU-15	B	DK	D	EL	E	F	IRL	I	L	NL	A	P	FIN	S	UK
Personnel costs (million ECU) (1)	1,040	:	:	257	14	61	373	3	77	0	32	0	:	0	2	312
Personnel costs/employee (thousand ECU) (2)	:	:	:	52.3	20.4	29.5	55.9	18.8	39.7	:	:	:	:	:	36.8	38.2
Social charges/personnel costs (%) (3)	:	:	:	20.2	22.4	20.4	31.4	20.3	37.1	:	20.1	:	:	:	:	14.3
Labour productivity (thousand ECU/head) (4)	74.9	:	:	82.2	26.1	50.9	96.6	25.8	84.6	:	:	:	:	:	66.5	118.5
Wage adjusted labour productivity (%) (2)	:	:	:	139.7	103.8	209.7	173.2	137.5	199.3	:	:	:	:	:	176.7	245.1

(1) EU-15 (1994); A (1995); L, FIN (1996); E (1997). (2) EL, I (1995); D, E, F, IRL, S, UK (1996). (3) E (1997). (4) EU-15; IRL (1996).

Source: Eurostat (SBS, EBT)

Table 6.13 (million ECU)

Manufacture of paints, varnishes and similar coatings, printing ink and mastics (NACE Rev. 1 24.3)

Production related indicators in the EU

	1988	1989	1990	1991	1992	1993	1994	1995	1996	1997	1998
Production value	:	:	:	:	:	24,058	26,014	24,013	:	:	:
Producer price index (1995=100)	:	:	85.1	90.4	92.1	95.0	96.2	100.0	100.8	103.8	111.2
Value added	:	:	:	:	:	8,272	8,711	7,619	:	:	:
Number of persons employed (thousands)	:	:	:	:	:	169.0	168.8	148.1	:	:	:

Table 6.14 (million ECU)

Manufacture of paints, varnishes and similar coatings, printing ink and mastics (NACE Rev. 1 24.3)

Production related indicators, 1998

	B	DK	D	EL	E	F	IRL	I	L	NL	A	P	FIN	S	UK
Production value (1)	1,500	626	8,471	175	2,423	3,399	94	3,624	:	1,314	450	534	353	678	3,563
Value added (1)	370	169	2,863	50	713	1,088	35	911	:	383	134	:	138	232	1,174
Number of persons employed (units) (2)	4,261	3,243	47,390	1,450	19,800	19,116	804	16,022	:	7,511	2,935	4,233	1,921	3,548	23,224

(1) A (1994); IRL (1996). (2) NL (1992); A (1994).

Table 6.15 (million ECU)

Manufacture of paints, varnishes and similar coatings, printing ink and mastics (NACE Rev. 1 24.3)

Market related indicators in the EU

	1988	1989	1990	1991	1992	1993	1994	1995	1996	1997	1998
Apparent consumption	:	:	:	:	:	22,457	24,133	21,858	:	:	:
Exports	1,425	1,640	1,537	1,702	1,837	2,139	2,415	2,806	3,210	3,708	3,742
Imports	325	397	406	462	505	539	533	651	677	835	832
Trade balance	1,100	1,243	1,131	1,241	1,331	1,601	1,881	2,155	2,533	2,873	2,910
Export ratio (%)	:	:	:	:	:	8.9	9.3	11.7	:	:	:
Import penetration ratio (%)	:	:	:	:	:	2.4	2.2	3.0	:	:	:
Cover ratio (%)	438.9	413.0	379.0	368.7	363.5	397.2	452.7	430.9	474.1	444.2	450.0

Table 6.16 (million ECU)

Manufacture of paints, varnishes and similar coatings, printing ink and mastics (NACE Rev. 1 24.3)

Market related indicators, 1998

	B/L	DK	D	EL	E	F	IRL	I	NL	A	P	FIN	S	UK
Apparent consumption (1)	:	586	6,296	271	2,304	3,472	155	3,405	900	573	683	311	614	3,229
Exports	787	242	2,973	28	514	815	27	821	823	220	44	185	293	1,115
Imports	527	202	798	123	395	888	110	603	409	285	194	143	229	781
Trade balance	260	40	2,176	-96	119	-73	-84	219	414	-64	-149	42	64	334
Export ratio (%) (1)	:	38.6	35.1	15.8	21.2	24.0	25.7	22.7	62.6	36.9	8.3	52.3	43.3	31.3
Import penetration ratio (%) (1)	:	34.4	12.7	45.5	17.2	25.6	54.8	17.7	45.4	50.5	28.3	45.9	37.3	24.2
Cover ratio (%)	149.3	119.9	372.8	22.5	130.1	91.8	24.1	136.3	201.1	77.4	22.8	129.5	128.1	142.7

(1) A (1994); IRL (1996).

Table 6.17

Manufacture of paints, varnishes and similar coatings, printing ink and mastics (NACE Rev. 1 24.3)

Labour related indicators, 1998

	EU-15	B	DK	D	EL	E	F	IRL	I	L	NL	A	P	FIN	S	UK
Personnel costs (million ECU) (1)	5,266	197	119	2,116	20	481	770	24	564	:	279	104	60	66	126	765
Personnel costs/employee (thousand ECU) (2)	38.7	50.3	37.5	45.0	15.1	27.6	41.0	29.5	32.4	:	:	35.6	:	35.4	37.4	27.5
Social charges/personnel costs (%) (3)	21.6	29.3	4.9	19.5	23.5	20.2	30.5	24.0	35.5	:	17.8	22.9	:	22.4	28.2	13.5
Labour productivity (thousand ECU/head) (4)	51.5	86.9	52.2	60.4	34.8	36.0	56.9	47.2	56.9	:	48.7	45.7	:	72.0	65.3	50.6
Wage adjusted labour productivity (%) (2)	132.9	150.9	141.0	126.2	183.0	168.2	138.2	160.1	169.7	:	:	128.5	:	198.1	171.6	157.3

(1) A (1994); EU-15 (1995). (2) A (1994); EU-15, EL, I (1995); B, DK, D, E, F, IRL, FIN, S, UK (1996). (3) A (1994); EU-15, S (1995). (4) NL (1992); A (1994); EU-15 (1995); IRL (1996).

Source: Eurostat (SBS, EBT)

(million ECU) Table 6.18

Manufacture of pharmaceuticals, medicinal chemicals and botanical products (NACE Rev. 1 24.4)
Production related indicators in the EU

	1988	1989	1990	1991	1992	1993	1994	1995	1996	1997	1998
Production value	50,289	55,650	60,383	68,329	74,357	75,451	78,813	86,287	:	:	:
Producer price index (1995=100)	:	:	95.2	96.5	98.0	98.2	98.9	100.0	98.5	97.3	99.3
Value added	20,857	22,554	24,096	27,107	29,394	30,487	32,207	33,998	:	:	:
Number of persons employed (thousands)	412.8	425.4	440.5	456.5	465.7	455.8	443.1	454.8	:	:	:

(million ECU) Table 6.19

Manufacture of pharmaceuticals, medicinal chemicals and botanical products (NACE Rev. 1 24.4)
Production related indicators, 1998

	B	DK	D	EL	E	F	IRL	I	L	NL	A	P	FIN	S	UK
Production value (1)	3,687	3,004	17,071	349	7,326	22,264	1,734	15,581	:	4,727	1,567	698	629	3,769	12,479
Value added (1)	1,463	1,255	8,197	77	2,625	7,508	926	5,516	:	1,341	663	:	324	1,498	5,854
Number of persons employed (units) (2)	15,242	14,784	103,835	5,167	33,376	90,162	6,571	77,431	:	12,885	7,154	8,526	6,389	16,201	59,519

(1) IRL (1996). (2) NL (1992); A (1997).

(million ECU) Table 6.20

Manufacture of pharmaceuticals, medicinal chemicals and botanical products (NACE Rev. 1 24.4)
Market related indicators in the EU

	1988	1989	1990	1991	1992	1993	1994	1995	1996	1997	1998
Apparent consumption	46,043	50,564	55,260	62,867	67,915	67,433	69,735	76,236	:	:	:
Exports	8,405	9,916	10,379	11,756	13,338	15,754	17,831	19,523	20,356	26,419	29,825
Imports	4,159	4,831	5,256	6,295	6,896	7,737	8,754	9,473	10,742	12,777	14,518
Trade balance	4,247	5,085	5,123	5,461	6,442	8,018	9,078	10,050	9,614	13,642	15,307
Export ratio (%)	16.7	17.8	17.2	17.2	17.9	20.9	22.6	22.6	:	:	:
Import penetration ratio (%)	9.0	9.6	9.5	10.0	10.2	11.5	12.6	12.4	:	:	:
Cover ratio (%)	202.1	205.3	197.5	186.8	193.4	203.6	203.7	206.1	189.5	206.8	205.4

(million ECU) Table 6.21

Manufacture of pharmaceuticals, medicinal chemicals and botanical products (NACE Rev. 1 24.4)
Market related indicators, 1998

	B/L	DK	D	EL	E	F	IRL	I	NL	A	P	FIN	S	UK
Apparent consumption (1)	:	1,869	11,344	1,195	8,655	20,527	-401	16,179	4,922	1,862	1,231	1,002	1,808	9,955
Exports	5,965	2,012	13,842	90	1,610	9,236	7,453	4,848	3,893	1,399	179	256	3,138	8,804
Imports	5,877	876	8,116	936	2,940	7,499	1,061	5,446	4,088	1,694	712	629	1,177	6,280
Trade balance	88	1,136	5,727	-846	-1,329	1,736	6,392	-598	-195	-295	-533	-373	1,961	2,524
Export ratio (%) (1)	:	67.0	81.1	25.9	22.0	41.5	166.3	31.1	82.3	89.3	25.7	40.6	83.3	70.0
Import penetration ratio (%) (1)	:	46.9	71.5	78.4	34.0	36.5	-186.5	33.7	83.0	91.0	57.8	62.7	65.1	63.1
Cover ratio (%)	101.5	229.7	170.6	9.7	54.8	123.2	702.5	89.0	95.2	82.6	25.2	40.7	266.7	140.2

(1) IRL (1996).

Table 6.22

Manufacture of pharmaceuticals, medicinal chemicals and botanical products (NACE Rev. 1 24.4)
Labour related indicators, 1998

	EU-15	B	DK	D	EL	E	F	IRL	I	L	NL	A	P	FIN	S	UK
Personnel costs (million ECU) (1)	19,374	826	701	5,404	96	1,217	4,300	195	3,381	:	556	400	180	177	747	2,431
Personnel costs/employee (thousand ECU) (2)	44.5	54.3	48.1	50.8	20.3	36.4	48.5	29.2	40.2	:	:	45.9	:	28.5	48.4	34.0
Social charges/personnel costs (%) (3)	23.5	28.1	6.9	20.9	24.1	19.2	30.9	20.5	33.3	:	20.4	22.9	:	20.5	33.2	13.3
Labour productivity (thousand ECU/head) (4)	74.8	96.0	84.9	78.9	14.9	78.7	83.3	142.8	71.2	:	51.3	92.1	:	50.6	92.5	98.4
Wage adjusted labour productivity (%) (2)	167.8	207.6	168.2	141.5	98.8	174.1	172.8	489.2	164.6	:	:	179.8	:	185.1	196.2	235.8

(1) EU-15 (1995); NL (1997). (2) EU-15, EL, I, A (1995); B, DK, D, E, F, IRL, FIN, S, UK (1995). (3) EU-15, S (1995); UK (1996). (4) NL (1992); EU-15 (1995); IRL (1996); A (1997).

Source: Eurostat (SBS, EBT)

Table 6.23 (million ECU)

Manufacture of soap and detergents, cleaning and polishing preparations, perfumes and toilet preparations (NACE Rev. 1 24.5)

Production related indicators in the EU

	1988	1989	1990	1991	1992	1993	1994	1995	1996	1997	1998
Production value	31,854	35,703	37,692	40,408	42,097	42,384	42,904	47,037	:	:	:
Producer price index (1995=100)	:	:	89.1	90.0	93.8	96.7	98.2	100.0	97.4	94.8	98.8
Value added	9,870	10,520	11,196	12,032	12,367	12,761	12,549	13,595	:	:	:
Number of persons employed (thousands)	238.5	245.1	247.4	245.3	238.4	232.1	223.9	233.5	:	:	:

Table 6.24 (million ECU)

Manufacture of soap and detergents, cleaning and polishing preparations, perfumes and toilet preparations (NACE Rev. 1 24.5)

Production related indicators, 1998

	B	DK	D	EL	E	F	IRL	I	L	NL	A	P	FIN	S	UK
Production value (1)	2,420	394	12,246	652	3,669	11,954	452	7,837	:	969	318	576	69	268	8,290
Value added (1)	545	100	3,758	178	1,005	3,661	189	2,069	:	275	103	:	27	88	2,496
Number of persons employed (units) (2)	6,392	1,710	59,764	4,312	23,936	51,842	2,752	28,310	:	5,598	1,822	3,718	689	1,460	44,604

(1) IRL (1996). (2) NL (1992); A (1997).

Table 6.25 (million ECU)

Manufacture of soap and detergents, cleaning and polishing preparations, perfumes and toilet preparations (NACE Rev. 1 24.5)

Market related indicators in the EU

	1988	1989	1990	1991	1992	1993	1994	1995	1996	1997	1998
Apparent consumption	29,513	32,844	34,678	37,331	38,711	38,578	38,477	42,303	:	:	:
Exports	2,989	3,601	3,804	3,995	4,439	4,972	5,796	6,258	7,041	7,869	7,814
Imports	648	743	790	918	1,054	1,166	1,369	1,524	1,603	1,739	1,965
Trade balance	2,341	2,859	3,014	3,077	3,385	3,806	4,427	4,734	5,438	6,129	5,848
Export ratio (%)	9.4	10.1	10.1	9.9	10.5	11.7	13.5	13.3	:	:	:
Import penetration ratio (%)	2.2	2.3	2.3	2.5	2.7	3.0	3.6	3.6	:	:	:
Cover ratio (%)	461.5	484.8	481.3	435.1	421.3	426.4	423.4	410.6	439.2	452.4	397.6

Table 6.26 (million ECU)

Manufacture of soap and detergents, cleaning and polishing preparations, perfumes and toilet preparations (NACE Rev. 1 24.5)

Market related indicators, 1998

	B/L	DK	D	EL	E	F	IRL	I	NL	A	P	FIN	S	UK
Apparent consumption (1)	:	469	10,617	883	3,466	7,703	285	7,424	1,119	613	857	204	469	7,286
Exports	1,616	348	3,955	111	1,027	6,124	479	1,731	724	182	70	101	260	3,094
Imports	1,179	423	2,326	342	823	1,872	380	1,319	874	476	350	237	462	2,090
Trade balance	436	-75	1,629	-231	203	4,251	99	412	-150	-295	-281	-136	-202	1,004
Export ratio (%) (1)	:	88.5	32.3	17.0	28.0	51.2	101.2	22.1	74.7	57.1	12.1	147.5	97.1	37.3
Import penetration ratio (%) (1)	:	90.3	21.9	38.7	23.8	24.3	101.9	17.8	78.1	77.7	40.9	115.9	98.4	28.7
Cover ratio (%)	137.0	82.2	170.0	32.4	124.7	327.1	125.9	131.3	82.9	38.1	19.9	42.7	56.3	148.0

(1) IRL (1996).

Table 6.27

Manufacture of soap and detergents, cleaning and polishing preparations, perfumes and toilet preparations (NACE Rev. 1 24.5)

Labour related indicators, 1998

	EU-15	B	DK	D	EL	E	F	IRL	I	L	NL	A	P	FIN	S	UK
Personnel costs (million ECU) (1)	8,574	252	58	2,472	88	630	2,196	66	1,083	:	176	86	68	19	53	1,305
Personnel costs/employee (thousand ECU) (2)	38.3	43.9	36.4	44.0	22.3	26.4	43.1	23.6	35.2	:	:	40.5	:	29.1	38.2	24.4
Social charges/personnel costs (%) (3)	23.6	27.0	4.8	21.7	23.1	20.1	29.9	17.8	34.8	:	16.1	23.3	:	23.3	28.3	11.5
Labour productivity (thousand ECU/head) (4)	58.2	85.3	58.2	62.9	41.2	42.0	70.6	69.8	73.1	:	44.4	55.3	:	38.5	60.2	56.0
Wage adjusted labour productivity (%) (2)	152.1	169.4	161.9	134.0	153.1	148.7	151.5	295.4	180.2	:	:	122.3	:	132.9	154.8	196.9

(1) EU-15 (1995). (2) EU-15, EL, I, A (1995); B, DK, D, E, F, IRL, FIN, S, UK (1996). (3) EU-15, S (1995). (4) NL (1992); EU-15 (1995); IRL (1996); A (1997).

Source: Eurostat (SBS, EBT)

(million ECU) Table 6.28

Manufacture of other chemical products (NACE Rev. 1 24.6)
Production related indicators in the EU

	1988	1989	1990	1991	1992	1993	1994	1995	1996	1997	1998
Production value	:	:	:	:	:	28,098	30,361	31,846	:	:	:
Producer price index (1995=100)	:	:	:	:	:	:	:	:	:	:	:
Value added	:	:	:	:	:	10,262	11,011	10,850	:	:	:
Number of persons employed (thousands)	:	:	:	:	:	176.3	177.9	164.1	:	:	:

(million ECU) Table 6.29

Manufacture of other chemical products (NACE Rev. 1 24.6)
Production related indicators, 1998

	B	DK	D	EL	E	F	IRL	I	L	NL	A	P	FIN	S	UK
Production value (1)	2,803	381	10,885	61	1,796	6,202	887	4,612	:	1,804	287	:	136	450	6,550
Value added (1)	897	144	4,005	13	670	1,977	506	1,378	:	640	111	:	56	151	2,555
Number of persons employed (units) (1)(2)	10,013	2,284	51,873	759	16,665	31,835	2,618	17,325	:	6,950	1,680	:	1,154	2,544	31,058

(1) IRL (1994). (2) NL (1992).

(million ECU) Table 6.30

Manufacture of other chemical products (NACE Rev. 1 24.6)
Market related indicators in the EU

	1988	1989	1990	1991	1992	1993	1994	1995	1996	1997	1998
Apparent consumption	:	:	:	:	:	25,197	26,830	27,757	:	:	:
Exports	6,463	7,277	7,308	7,654	7,905	9,224	10,192	10,935	12,208	13,927	13,694
Imports	5,451	5,983	6,455	6,641	6,678	6,323	6,662	6,846	7,373	8,218	8,446
Trade balance	1,012	1,294	853	1,013	1,228	2,901	3,530	4,089	4,834	5,709	5,249
Export ratio (%)	:	:	:	:	:	32.8	33.6	34.3	:	:	:
Import penetration ratio (%)	:	:	:	:	:	25.1	24.8	24.7	:	:	:
Cover ratio (%)	118.6	121.6	113.2	115.3	118.4	145.9	153.0	159.7	165.6	169.5	162.1

(million ECU) Table 6.31

Manufacture of other chemical products (NACE Rev. 1 24.6)
Market related indicators, 1998

	B/L	DK	D	EL	E	F	IRL	I	NL	A	P	FIN	S	UK
Apparent consumption (1)	:	596	6,638	384	2,876	5,582	809	5,914	1,158	549	:	384	799	5,396
Exports	3,616	340	9,591	63	719	5,190	2,848	2,074	3,121	485	117	200	537	5,343
Imports	2,231	555	5,344	385	1,798	4,570	588	3,376	2,474	748	367	449	887	4,190
Trade balance	1,385	-215	4,247	-323	-1,080	620	2,260	-1,302	646	-262	-250	-249	-350	1,153
Export ratio (%) (1)	:	89.0	88.1	103.2	40.0	83.7	77.4	45.0	173.0	169.3	:	147.4	119.4	81.6
Import penetration ratio (%) (1)	:	93.0	80.5	100.5	62.5	81.9	75.2	57.1	213.7	136.2	:	116.7	110.9	77.6
Cover ratio (%)	162.1	61.2	179.5	16.2	40.0	113.6	484.6	61.4	126.1	64.9	31.9	44.6	60.5	127.5

(1) IRL (1994).

Table 6.32

Manufacture of other chemical products (NACE Rev. 1 24.6)
Labour related indicators, 1998

	EU-15	B	DK	D	EL	E	F	IRL	I	L	NL	A	P	FIN	S	UK
Personnel costs (million ECU) (1)	6,781	575	97	2,464	13	345	1,400	76	673	:	251	71	:	37	99	1,107
Personnel costs/employee (thousand ECU) (2)	42.9	60.9	43.4	49.5	18.0	28.8	44.7	28.9	35.7	:	:	46.1	:	32.9	40.8	29.7
Social charges/personnel costs (%) (3)	23.3	30.2	6.1	20.9	23.2	19.1	30.7	19.5	35.3	:	17.1	24.1	:	22.1	28.1	13.0
Labour productivity (thousand ECU/head) (4)	66.1	89.6	63.2	77.2	16.9	40.2	62.1	193.2	79.6	:	64.8	66.3	:	48.6	59.3	82.3
Wage adjusted labour productivity (%) (2)	154.1	135.1	147.6	141.5	92.0	165.6	137.5	668.5	187.9	:	:	149.7	:	155.6	142.7	245.9

(1) IRL (1994); EU-15 (1995). (2) IRL (1994); EU-15, EL, I, A (1995); B, DK, D, E, F, FIN, S, UK (1996). (3) IRL, S (1994); EU-15 (1995). (4) NL (1992); IRL (1994); EU-15 (1995).

Source: Eurostat (SBS, EBT)

Table 6.33 (million ECU)

Manufacture of man-made fibres (NACE Rev. 1 24.7)

Production related indicators in the EU

	1988	1989	1990	1991	1992	1993	1994	1995	1996	1997	1998
Production value	8,715	9,850	9,162	8,730	8,737	8,402	9,325	:	10,852	11,179	10,886
Producer price index (1995=100)	:	:	:	:	:	:	:	100.0	106.6	105.7	102.2
Value added	2,921	3,172	3,053	2,917	2,891	2,652	3,011	:	3,157	3,293	3,146
Number of persons employed (thousands)	83.6	81.9	77.4	74.3	68.4	63.9	60.3	:	:	:	:

Table 6.34 (million ECU)

Manufacture of man-made fibres (NACE Rev. 1 24.7)

Production related indicators, 1998 (1)

	B	DK	D	EL	E	F	IRL	I	L	NL	A	P	FIN	S	UK
Production value	537	:	3,577	50	797	552	200	2,259	:	884	558	102	93	33	1,111
Value added	:	:	1,032	16	222	110	65	598	:	233	221	:	18	9	553
Number of persons employed (units)	2,710	:	19,749	891	6,009	2,481	1,362	10,865	:	:	3,593	686	577	172	6,420

(1) B, IRL, A (1994).

Table 6.35 (million ECU)

Manufacture of man-made fibres (NACE Rev. 1 24.7)

Market related indicators in the EU

	1988	1989	1990	1991	1992	1993	1994	1995	1996	1997	1998
Apparent consumption	8,486	9,850	9,138	8,885	9,009	8,382	9,600	:	11,522	12,394	12,264
Exports	1,426	1,398	1,289	1,224	1,172	1,208	1,243	1,167	1,053	821	924
Imports	1,197	1,399	1,264	1,379	1,444	1,188	1,518	1,752	1,723	2,036	2,302
Trade balance	229	-1	24	-155	-272	20	-275	-585	-670	-1,216	-1,378
Export ratio (%)	16.4	14.2	14.1	14.0	13.4	14.4	13.3	:	9.7	7.3	8.5
Import penetration ratio (%)	14.1	14.2	13.8	15.5	16.0	14.2	15.8	:	15.0	16.4	18.8
Cover ratio (%)	119.2	100.0	101.9	88.7	81.2	101.7	81.9	66.6	61.1	40.3	40.1

Table 6.36 (million ECU)

Manufacture of man-made fibres (NACE Rev. 1 24.7)

Market related indicators, 1998

	B/L	DK	D	EL	E	F	IRL	I	NL	A	P	FIN	S	UK
Apparent consumption (1)	:	:	4,148	119	1,047	1,107	83	3,227	1,372	448	266	93	83	1,744
Exports	587	113	602	40	387	596	233	704	197	42	54	81	50	381
Imports	853	128	1,173	109	637	1,151	84	1,672	686	191	218	81	99	1,014
Trade balance	-266	-15	-571	-69	-250	-555	149	-968	-489	-148	-164	0	-49	-632
Export ratio (%) (1)	:	:	16.8	79.3	48.6	107.9	82.0	31.2	22.3	54.1	52.9	87.2	148.6	34.3
Import penetration ratio (%) (1)	:	:	28.3	91.3	60.8	104.0	56.7	51.8	50.0	42.8	82.0	87.2	119.7	58.1
Cover ratio (%)	68.9	88.0	51.3	36.5	60.8	51.8	278.2	42.1	28.8	22.3	24.7	100.3	50.3	37.6

(1) IRL, A (1994).

Table 6.37

Manufacture of man-made fibres (NACE Rev. 1 24.7)

Labour related indicators, 1998

	EU-15	B	DK	D	EL	E	F	IRL	I	L	NL	A	P	FIN	S	UK
Personnel costs (million ECU) (1)	2,131	:	:	790	13	174	96	38	346	:	236	169	13	20	6	236
Personnel costs/employee (thousand ECU) (2)	:	:	:	40.3	16.0	28.8	39.2	28.1	29.3	:	:	46.9	:	35.0	38.0	30.6
Social charges/personnel costs (%) (3)	:	:	:	19.7	23.2	23.0	35.3	17.1	34.0	:	21.5	24.5	:	24.3	:	14.8
Labour productivity (thousand ECU/head) (4)	49.9	:	:	52.3	17.7	36.9	44.5	47.9	55.0	:	:	61.5	:	31.0	49.6	86.1
Wage adjusted labour productivity (%) (2)	:	:	:	117.5	125.1	135.1	104.2	170.3	193.1	:	:	131.0	:	85.7	128.9	271.2

(1) IRL, A (1994). (2) IRL, A (1994); EL, I (1995); D, E, F, FIN, S, UK (1996). (3) IRL, A (1994); EU-15 (1995). (4) EU-15, IRL, A (1994).

Source: Eurostat (SBS, EBT)

(million ECU) Table 6.38

Manufacture of rubber products (NACE Rev. 1 25.1)
Production related indicators in the EU

	1988	1989	1990	1991	1992	1993	1994	1995	1996	1997	1998
Production value	24,712	26,128	26,587	27,021	27,676	25,942	28,191	31,443	:	:	:
Producer price index (1995=100)	:	:	89.0	91.3	95.0	96.2	96.8	100.0	97.7	97.7	96.6
Value added	11,211	11,676	11,633	12,085	12,338	11,700	12,608	13,293	:	:	:
Number of persons employed (thousands)	358.6	359.7	358.0	345.2	331.4	309.0	300.1	301.4	:	:	:

(million ECU) Table 6.39

Manufacture of rubber products (NACE Rev. 1 25.1)
Production related indicators, 1998

	B	DK	D	EL	E	F	IRL	I	L	NL	A	P	FIN	S	UK
Production value (1)	1,312	208	10,024	95	3,294	6,923	215	5,022	:	445	609	475	298	797	4,502
Value added (2)	301	98	4,029	33	1,417	2,843	80	1,833	:	194	269	:	139	266	2,009
Number of persons employed (units) (3)	4,812	2,344	82,737	841	30,100	68,963	2,554	39,153	:	5,225	5,242	5,703	2,846	6,397	49,472

(1) EL (1995). (2) EL (1995); IRL (1996). (3) NL (1992).

(million ECU) Table 6.40

Manufacture of rubber products (NACE Rev. 1 25.1)
Market related indicators in the EU

	1988	1989	1990	1991	1992	1993	1994	1995	1996	1997	1998
Apparent consumption	23,632	25,026	25,816	26,414	27,322	25,264	27,847	31,510	:	:	:
Exports	2,986	3,302	3,032	3,061	3,145	3,461	3,542	3,680	4,145	4,718	4,973
Imports	1,907	2,199	2,262	2,455	2,790	2,783	3,199	3,748	4,120	4,482	5,193
Trade balance	1,079	1,103	771	607	354	678	344	-67	26	237	-220
Export ratio (%)	12.1	12.6	11.4	11.3	11.4	13.3	12.6	11.7	:	:	:
Import penetration ratio (%)	8.1	8.8	8.8	9.3	10.2	11.0	11.5	11.9	:	:	:
Cover ratio (%)	156.6	150.1	134.1	124.7	112.7	124.4	110.7	98.2	100.6	105.3	95.8

(million ECU) Table 6.41

Manufacture of rubber products (NACE Rev. 1 25.1)
Market related indicators, 1998

	B/L	DK	D	EL	E	F	IRL	I	NL	A	P	FIN	S	UK
Apparent consumption (1)	:	422	9,722	245	3,037	5,437	311	4,605	885	799	674	380	955	4,573
Exports	1,342	160	4,537	30	1,753	3,886	97	2,291	908	501	181	174	572	2,241
Imports	1,520	374	4,235	203	1,496	2,400	193	1,874	1,347	691	380	256	730	2,313
Trade balance	-179	-214	302	-173	257	1,487	-96	417	-439	-190	-199	-82	-158	-71
Export ratio (%) (1)	:	76.9	45.3	46.1	53.2	56.1	45.3	45.6	203.8	82.2	38.0	58.3	71.8	49.8
Import penetration ratio (%) (1)	:	88.6	43.6	79.0	49.3	44.1	62.1	40.7	152.3	86.5	56.3	67.2	76.4	50.6
Cover ratio (%)	88.2	42.9	107.1	14.6	117.1	161.9	50.5	122.2	67.4	72.5	47.6	68.0	78.3	96.9

(1) EL (1995).

Table 6.42

Manufacture of rubber products (NACE Rev. 1 25.1)
Labour related indicators, 1998

	EU-15	B	DK	D	EL	E	F	IRL	I	L	NL	A	P	FIN	S	UK
Personnel costs (million ECU) (1)	9,601	196	80	3,349	19	778	2,284	61	1,181	:	134	212	55	89	208	1,442
Personnel costs/employee (thousand ECU) (2)	33.0	39.1	34.9	40.2	24.7	27.1	33.7	23.6	27.6	:	:	40.6	:	32.3	34.1	24.3
Social charges/personnel costs (%) (3)	23.5	25.6	4.6	20.6	21.0	22.4	29.8	15.6	35.4	:	17.4	22.3	:	23.2	31.1	12.3
Labour productivity (thousand ECU/head) (4)	44.1	62.7	41.8	48.7	37.7	47.1	41.2	33.1	46.8	:	41.8	51.3	:	48.8	41.6	40.6
Wage adjusted labour productivity (%) (2)	133.7	135.1	122.1	122.8	152.2	153.8	128.9	140.4	165.7	:	:	123.9	:	164.5	115.5	153.5

(1) EU-15 (1995). (2) EU-15, EL, I, A (1995); B, DK, D, E, F, IRL, FIN, S, UK (1996). (3) EU-15, S (1995). (4) NL (1992); EU-15, EL (1995); IRL (1996).

Source: Eurostat (SBS, EBT)

Table 6.43 (million ECU)

Manufacture of plastic products (NACE Rev. 1 25.2)

Production related indicators in the EU

	1988	1989	1990	1991	1992	1993	1994	1995	1996	1997	1998
Production value	61,212	70,607	76,165	80,928	82,876	81,639	88,874	99,585	:	:	:
Producer price index (1995=100)	:	:	92.4	92.4	92.4	92.2	92.8	100.0	98.1	95.6	96.2
Value added	22,249	25,281	28,012	30,356	31,533	31,104	33,345	35,027	:	:	:
Number of persons employed (thousands)	738.1	788.7	831.9	849.2	837.4	811.3	820.1	844.1	:	:	:

Table 6.44 (million ECU)

Manufacture of plastic products (NACE Rev. 1 25.2)

Production related indicators, 1998

	B	DK	D	EL	E	F	IRL	I	L	NL	A	P	FIN	S	UK
Production value	4,868	1,848	35,644	651	8,058	16,242	920	14,117	:	3,780	2,609	1,166	1,281	2,094	17,409
Value added	1,460	772	13,117	147	2,709	5,201	341	4,696	:	1,306	937	:	532	718	6,686
Number of persons employed (units) (1)	23,710	16,609	271,773	6,937	91,525	122,595	9,765	82,507	:	26,007	19,394	15,823	13,029	14,171	170,033

(1) NL (1992).

Table 6.45 (million ECU)

Manufacture of plastic products (NACE Rev. 1 25.2)

Market related indicators in the EU

	1988	1989	1990	1991	1992	1993	1994	1995	1996	1997	1998
Apparent consumption	59,524	68,911	74,625	79,643	81,481	79,805	86,597	96,540	:	:	:
Exports	4,731	5,347	5,470	5,746	6,081	6,817	7,931	9,380	10,056	11,817	12,270
Imports	3,043	3,651	3,929	4,462	4,685	4,984	5,653	6,335	6,680	7,831	8,356
Trade balance	1,688	1,695	1,541	1,285	1,395	1,833	2,278	3,045	3,376	3,986	3,914
Export ratio (%)	7.7	7.6	7.2	7.1	7.3	8.4	8.9	9.4	:	:	:
Import penetration ratio (%)	5.1	5.3	5.3	5.6	5.8	6.2	6.5	6.6	:	:	:
Cover ratio (%)	155.5	146.4	139.2	128.8	129.8	136.8	140.3	148.1	150.5	150.9	146.8

Table 6.46 (million ECU)

Manufacture of plastic products (NACE Rev. 1 25.2)

Market related indicators, 1998

	B/L	DK	D	EL	E	F	IRL	I	NL	A	P	FIN	S	UK
Apparent consumption	:	1,564	31,372	849	8,525	17,237	1,212	10,936	3,729	2,432	1,501	1,293	1,973	18,228
Exports	4,447	1,301	10,894	149	1,481	4,716	450	5,683	2,542	1,522	267	514	1,219	3,950
Imports	3,176	1,016	6,623	348	1,948	5,711	742	2,501	2,491	1,345	602	526	1,099	4,769
Trade balance	1,271	285	4,271	-199	-468	-995	-292	3,182	51	177	-335	-12	120	-819
Export ratio (%)	:	70.4	30.6	23.0	18.4	29.0	49.0	40.3	67.2	58.3	22.9	40.1	58.2	22.7
Import penetration ratio (%)	:	65.0	21.1	41.0	22.9	33.1	61.3	22.9	66.8	55.3	40.1	40.7	55.7	26.2
Cover ratio (%)	140.0	128.0	164.5	42.9	76.0	82.6	60.7	227.2	102.0	113.1	44.3	97.8	111.0	82.8

Table 6.47

Manufacture of plastic products (NACE Rev. 1 25.2)

Labour related indicators, 1998

	EU-15	B	DK	D	EL	E	F	IRL	I	L	NL	A	P	FIN	S	UK
Personnel costs (million ECU) (1)	23,504	894	571	9,404	91	1,823	3,609	211	2,322	:	766	610	153	358	471	4,292
Personnel costs/employee (thousand ECU) (2)	29.4	39.8	35.1	34.8	14.5	21.0	29.9	21.6	25.8	:	:	33.8	:	28.6	34.8	21.0
Social charges/personnel costs (%) (3)	20.5	27.4	4.6	18.9	22.8	21.8	29.2	15.0	37.0	:	14.7	22.9	:	21.8	28.8	11.0
Labour productivity (thousand ECU/head) (4)	41.5	61.6	46.5	48.3	21.1	29.6	42.4	35.0	56.9	:	42.3	48.3	:	40.8	50.7	39.3
Wage adjusted labour productivity (%) (2)	141.0	150.7	149.6	134.0	139.9	157.1	137.8	179.6	186.3	:	:	146.6	:	170.9	141.0	165.1

(1) EU-15 (1995). (2) EU-15, EL, I, A (1995); B, DK, D, E, F, IRL, FIN, S, UK (1996). (3) EU-15, S (1995). (4) NL (1992); EU-15 (1995).

Source: Eurostat (SBS, EBT)

Non-metallic mineral products

Industrial description

The manufacture of non-metallic mineral products covers products made of glass, ceramics, clay and stone, as well as cement and concrete. Under the NACE Rev. 1 classification of economic activities, the industry is classified within Division 26. The activity of non-metallic mineral products is closely linked with the construction sector as both new buildings and maintenance provide a large amount of the demand within this activity. Glass and ceramic products are also used in various activities ranging from electrical engineering (electrical insulators of ceramics) through chemicals (laboratory glassware) to food and beverage processing (containers of glass). Some technical ceramic products and glass fibres are characterised as advanced materials, such as ceramics made of oxygen and titan, which form the basis of products used in spacecraft. Although these products make up a small part of the sector's output, they are expected to display remarkable rates of growth in the coming years. In addition to intermediary goods, the sector also produces household goods of glass and ceramics, such as drinking glasses and tableware, which are sold to distributive trades or directly to the end-consumers via factory outlets. Due to the widespread use of glass products and ceramics, these activities are less dependent on the business cycle of construction than the manufacture of cement, concrete or bricks.

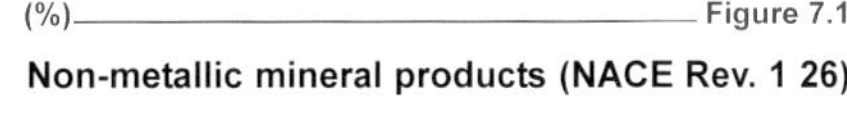
(%) Figure 7.1

Non-metallic mineral products (NACE Rev. 1 26)
Share of EU value added in total manufacturing

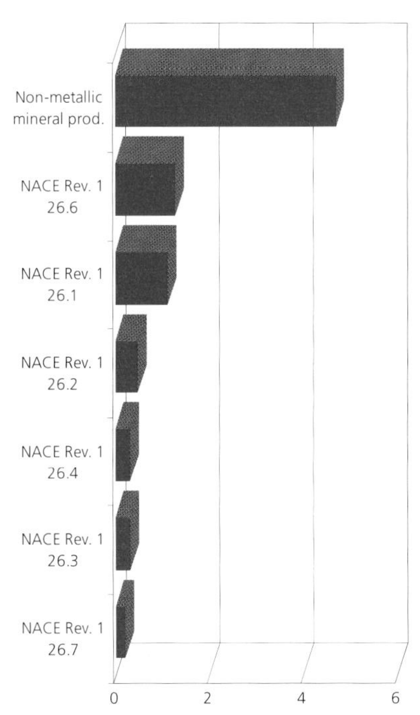

Source: Eurostat (SBS)

The activities covered in this chapter include:

- 26.1: manufacture of glass and glass products;
- 26.2: manufacture of non-refractory ceramic goods other than for construction purposes; manufacture of refractory ceramic products;
- 26.3: manufacture of ceramic tiles and flags;
- 26.4: manufacture of bricks, tiles and construction products, in baked clay;
- 26.5: manufacture of cement, lime and plaster;
- 26.6: manufacture of articles of concrete, plaster and cement;
- 26.7: cutting, shaping and finishing of stone;
- 26.8: manufacture of other non-metallic mineral products n.e.c.

Figure 7.2 (1988=100)

Non-metallic mineral products (NACE Rev. 1 26)

Production, employment and value added compared to EU total manufacturing

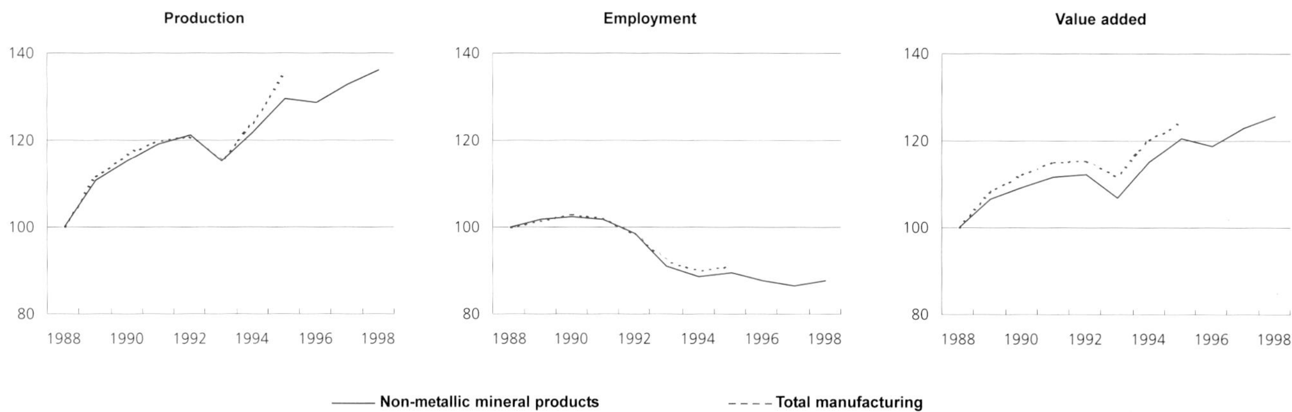

Source: Eurostat (SBS)

Non-metallic mineral products accounted for just less than 3.5% of the production value of total manufacturing in Europe. If we look at the breakdown of the activity, the manufacture of cement, concrete and glass were responsible for nearly half of the output of this activity. The five largest Member States accounted for 77.9% of the production value in 1998. Nevertheless, Spain was the EU Member State with the highest production specialisation ratio, with the sector contributing two and a half times the European average to total manufacturing. In Austria and Greece there were similar specialisation rates, whilst Portugal and Luxembourg recorded ratios of 200%.

The majority of non-metallic mineral products have a low price-weight ratio. Due to high transportation costs, manufacturers are usually located near raw materials and sell to regional markets. In the manufacture of glass and ceramics, European suppliers offer products of high technical and design quality, which are also sold to overseas countries. Nevertheless, the industry faced increased competition during the nineties, with rising imports of cement from Central European Countries, as well as imports of ceramic tableware from East Asia. Although European manufacturers used advanced technology, competitive pressure required constant innovation, such as reduced shrinkage in volume during the burning of ceramics.

The sector underwent a process of restructuring and rationalisation to cut overall production costs. Manufacturers increasingly started being active on more distant markets and looked for co-operations or mergers. The number of enterprises engaged in non-metallic mineral products was reduced in the Netherlands and Luxembourg by 7.5% and 6.4% respectively between 1990 and 1996. In general there were larger enterprises in the manufacture of cement and of glass than in the manufacture of ceramics, bricks or concrete. In Germany, on average, manufacturers of glass accounted for 23 million ECU of production value in 1996, whilst a manufacturer of clay products some 10.8 million ECU. This pattern was observed throughout Europe, although there were relatively large enterprises in the Netherlands, France and Germany compared to Spain and Finland (taking the production value per enterprise as a measure of market density).

The efforts to increase efficiency resulted in improved labour productivity (in terms of value added per person employed). Between 1988 and 1998 the ratio increased in Luxembourg and Germany (up by 84.5% and 74.2% respectively) to 57.1 and 75.2 thousand ECU of value added per person employed in 1998. Only Sweden reported labour productivity falling, by 4.5% to 46.5 thousand ECU. If we look at non-metallic mineral products in more detail the manufacture of cement and concrete reported the highest levels of labour productivity in several Member States, for example, in the United Kingdom (64.6 thousand ECU). In Italy the manufacture of glass and of ceramic goods displayed higher levels of labour productivity (both some 52 thousand ECU).

Reductions in production costs were brought about by a reduction in energy consumption, which was high in most activities within the non-metallic minerals' products sector, especially for cement. For this reason the sector was concerned by changes in environmental policies, for example, the introduction of energy taxes has, in part, led to large gains in energy efficiency. Besides energy consumption, there were also efforts to control emissions, as well as limiting the use of water and developing recycling (where the manufacture of glass was clearly a leading example).

Figure 7.3

Non-metallic mineral products (NACE Rev. 1 26)

International comparison of main indicators in current prices

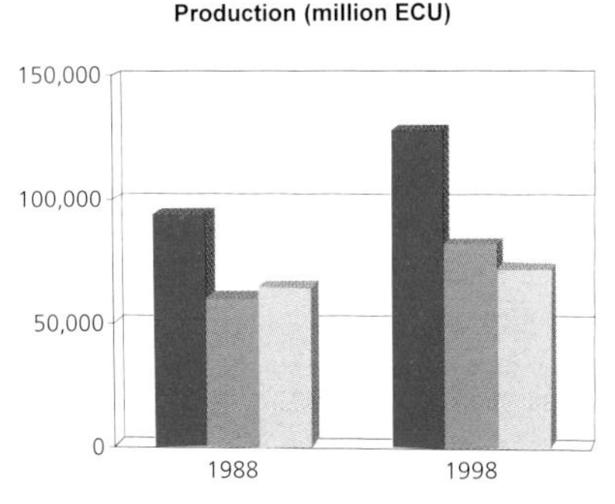

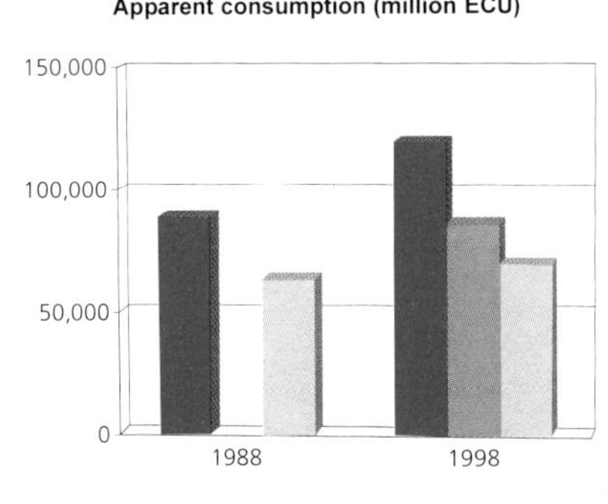

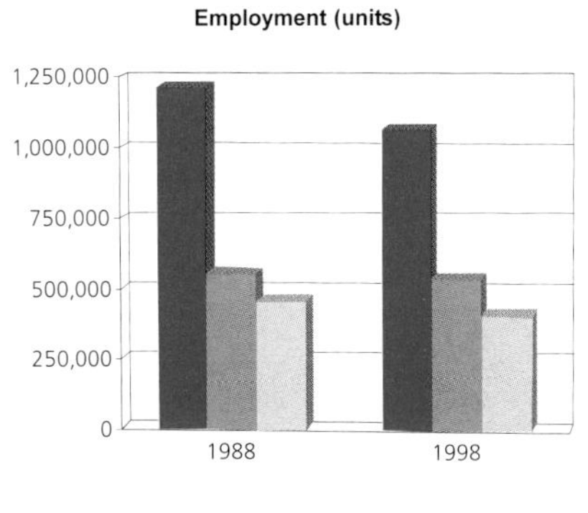

EU-15 USA Japan

Source: Eurostat (SBS)

Recent trends

Manufacturers within the EU have stepped up their efforts to be present on export markets. They expect a growing market in Eastern Europe, where in the long-run well-known brands and quality will be increasingly demanded.

Between 1993 and 1998 production value at constant prices increased in all reporting EU countries, ranging from 9.3% per annum in Finland to a moderate 0.3% gain per annum in Italy. Value added (at constant prices) was also on an upward trend, however, at a slower pace, rising quickest in Finland (by 4.0% per annum). The upward trend was continued in 1998, when EU production value increased by 2.4% and value added by 2.9% (compared to the year before). If we look at the growth rates by activity, only the production of cement and concrete posted considerably lower rates of growth, with a moderate increase in output, equivalent to 0.6% between 1993 and 1998.

The restructuring of the production process resulted in less persons employed in the EU, on average down by 0.8% per annum between 1993 and 1998. Rationalisation in Germany resulted in a decline in the level of employment equal to 3.8% per annum, whilst Denmark was one of a few countries to report that labour markets were expanding, up by 3.9% per annum.

(ECU/hour)

Figure 7.4

Non-metallic mineral products (NACE Rev. 1 26)

Labour costs by Member State, 1996

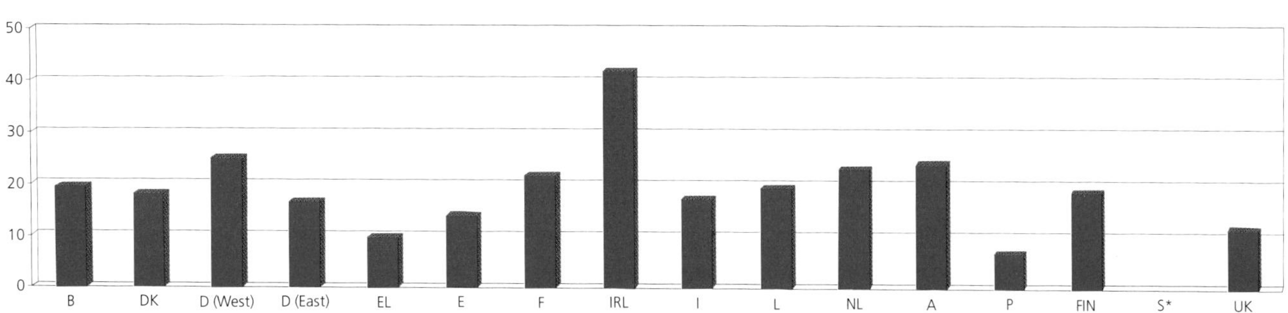

Source: Eurostat (LCS)

International comparison showed that the EU was the largest producer in the Triad, with 125 billion ECU of production value in 1997, some 50% more than in the USA (82 billion ECU). However, the industry was growing at a much faster pace in the USA, pushed by the favourable economic situation and a rapidly-expanding construction activity. Latest growth in the USA was equal to 13.2% in 1997. In Japan, the activity was affected by the general recession and saw output fall by 5.8% in 1997.

Table 7.1 (%)

Non-metallic mineral products (NACE Rev. 1 26)
Composition of the labour force, 1997

	Females	Part-time	Highly-educated
EU-15	21.6	:	:
B	14.7	:	13.8
DK	24.7	17.0	16.1
D	25.4	7.4	16.1
EL	13.5	:	9.1
E	11.6	2.1	15.1
F	21.5	4.9	12.1
IRL	14.7	2.6	15.7
I	27.4	3.3	3.6
L	:	:	:
NL	9.1	12.4	12.1
A	21.7	9.3	:
P	30.8	3.2	4.8
FIN	24.0	:	24.4
S	41.2	16.0	13.2
UK	23.5	7.7	14.4

Source: Eurostat (LFS)

Foreign trade

In the EU the market for non-metallic mineral products was supplied to a large extent by domestic production. Only 5.4% of apparent consumption was supplied from outside the EU, whereas 11.2% of European production was delivered to extra-EU markets. Between 1988 and 1998, extra-EU imports increased almost twice as fast as extra-EU exports (up by 162.0% and 89.5% respectively). Particularly the manufacture of glass and ceramic products faced increasing competition from foreign suppliers. In Germany (the largest consumer market within the EU), imports from non-Member States increased by nearly 200% during the ten years to 1998.

Figure 7.5

Non-metallic mineral products (NACE Rev. 1 26)
Destination of EU exports, 1998

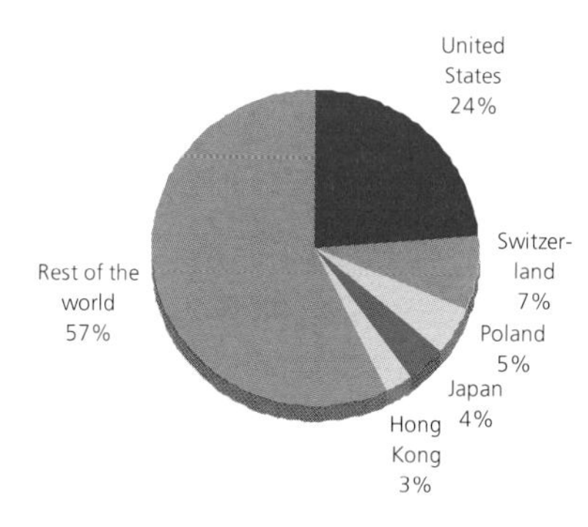

Source: Eurostat (Comext)

Figure 7.6

Non-metallic mineral products (NACE Rev. 1 26)
Origin of EU imports, 1998

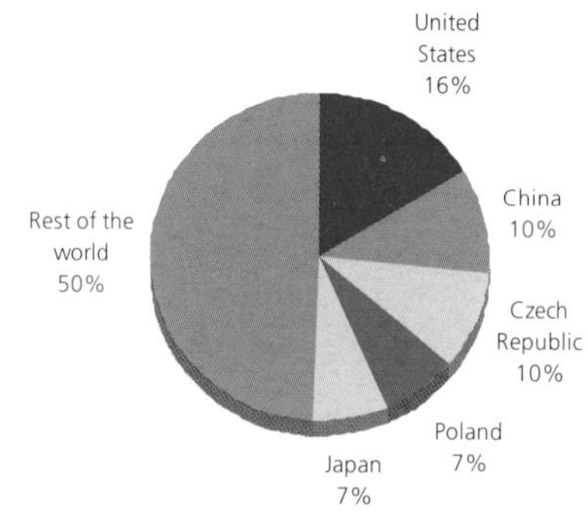

Source: Eurostat (Comext)

Glass (NACE Rev. 1 26.1)

In the EU the manufacture of glass and glass products accounted for around 30 billion ECU of production value in 1998, some 0.8% of total EU manufacturing or nearly a quarter of the output of non-metallic minerals. The production of the sector ranged from flat glass through hollow glass to glass fibres and technical glassware. Glass was one of the first materials for which an efficient recycling system was established.

Glass products were used in several downstream industries: container glass was to a large extent destined to contain food or beverages, flat glass (mostly window glass) was delivered to the construction sector and the manufacture of transport equipment. Together, container glass and flat glass accounted for nearly 90% of total glass production in the EU. Glass fibres were used for insulation and reinforcement of materials, technical glassware included optical or pharmaceutical glassware. Domestic glass was sold to hotels and restaurants as well as to private households. Although glass products are not tied to a single downstream industry, suppliers have often specialised in a single product line and therefore display a close relationship to their customers.

Within the large Member States, France displayed a production specialisation in glass and glass products: the sector contributed 1.3 times more to total manufacturing than the European average. A similar specialisation ratio was observed in Austria and Portugal.

The industry was dominated by relatively large enterprises due to the capital-intensive production process, especially for hollow and flat glass. In France, glass manufacturers had an output of 27.3 million ECU on average per enterprise in 1996, some 10 million ECU more than the average manufacturer of non-metallic mineral products. As competition increased smaller manufacturers were looking for co-operations or even mergers with a view to economies of scale. Another strategy was buying or installing production facilities in low-cost countries.

Within the EU, the output of glass and glass products was on an upward trend since 1993. Several Member States reported average annual rates of growth of 5% (at constant prices) in the five years to 1998, such as Germany or the United Kingdom (5.2% and 4.8% per annum respectively). In the Netherlands and Denmark there was even faster growth of 7.0% and 5.9% per annum respectively.

Figure 7.7

Glass (NACE Rev. 1 26.1)

Production and employment in the Triad

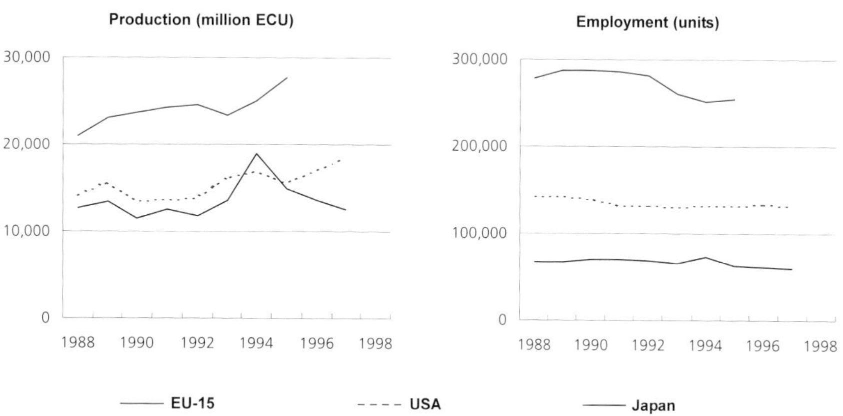

Source: Eurostat (SBS)

Figure 7.8

Annual average growth rates of selected glass products within the EU, 1990-1997

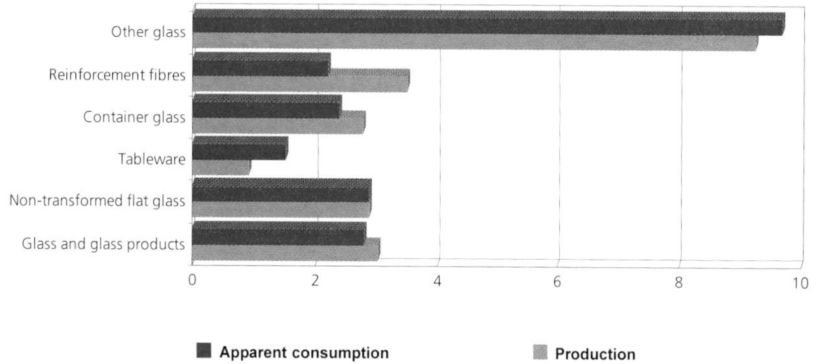

Source: CPIV

Figure 7.9 (%)

Recycling rates of glass in the EU, 1997

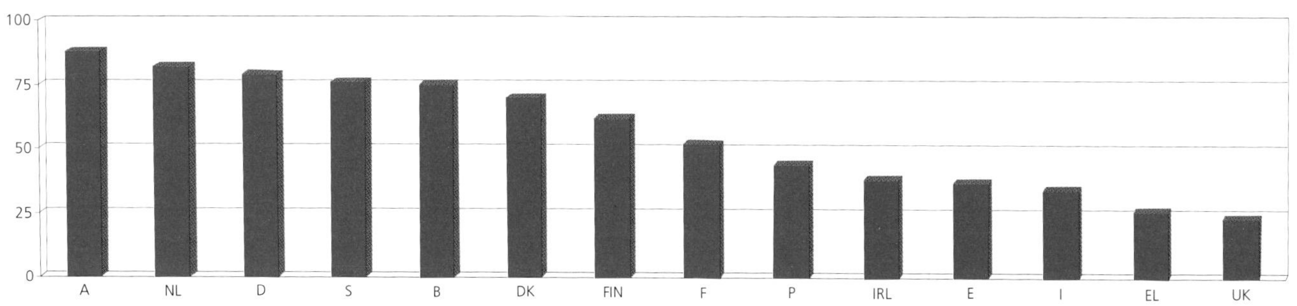

Source: FEVE

More detailed data for this activity was available for production in volumes terms (figures from CPIV, Comité Permanent des Industries du Verre de l'UE). The production of container glass reached 17.3 million tonnes in 1997, which increased at the rate of 3.8% per annum from 1993 to 1997. Flat glass, responsible for a quarter of total glass production, grew somewhat faster by 4.4% per annum, reflecting the evolution of downstream industries. Reinforcement fibres and other glasses (such as optical and industrial glassware) were delivered to more expansive downstream industries, leading to an expansion of output at a noticeably faster pace (8.6% and 13.8% per annum respectively). Even though, these two activities contributed just 2 million tonnes, or 7.4% of total glass output. They were, nevertheless, responsible for much of the technological innovation seen in the industry.

Packaging material made of glass faced competition from plastics and tin. Nevertheless, apparent consumption increased by 14.2% to 17 million tonnes between 1993 and 1997. In the EU there was overcapacity in the manufacture of glass bottles, jars and flacons and manufacturers started to look for niche markets. Efforts by European manufacturers were successful, as imports from outside the EU fell by 6.9% between 1993 and 1997 (the only activity within the manufacture of glass to report such a trend).

EU manufacturers nevertheless faced strong competition from third countries, especially those with lower wages and lower environmental costs. European suppliers, particularly larger ones, attempted to expand their market in geographical terms, including Central and Eastern Europe. In addition, EU producers introduced rationalisation programmes, extended customer service (planning and contract working) and made quality improvements and innovations. The latter included increased energy efficiency for furnaces and the use of recycled glass. The restructuring process was most obvious in the reductions of employment that were recorded. Between 1993 and 1998 the number of persons employed decreased constantly to around 245 thousand persons in the EU. Contrary to the downward trend, Danish manufacturers of glass increased the number of persons employed by 4.1% per annum, however, somewhat slower than output (up by 5.9% per annum). Danish labour productivity increased by 5.6% to 49.2 thousand ECU of value added per person employed (between 1993 and 1998), whilst the rate of growth in Germany was 29.7% and in Italy 36.2% (to 52.4 and 52.7 thousand ECU in 1998).

In 1997 there were 7.2 million tonnes of glass collected for recycling. The Spanish recycling market saw volumes increase by 14.3% (compared to 1996), whilst maintaining a comparatively low recycling rate. Spain recorded an increase of two percentage points in its recycling rate for 1997, to reach 37%. Spanish rates were nevertheless higher than in Italy, Greece or the United Kingdom.

Austria and the Netherlands were European leaders in recycling glass, with rates of 88% and 82% respectively (figures from FEVE, Fédération Européenne du Verre d'Emballage). Recycling developed first in countries where raw materials were less abundant. However, recycling of glass quickly became an environmental concern. In addition, to the environmental benefits of recycling, the re-melting of glass is usually less energy-consuming than primary manufacture. An increase in the recycling rate is partly determined by the colour of the available collected glass. For example, wine exporting countries such as Italy and Spain need more dark coloured glass than collected on domestic markets. Through technological advances, secondary glass also became a raw material for glass fibres, building materials (like terrazzo floors or translucent bricks) or for road-surfacing materials.

(%)

Figure 7.10

Glass (NACE Rev. 1 26.1)

Production and export specialisation by Member State, 1998

Production specialisation

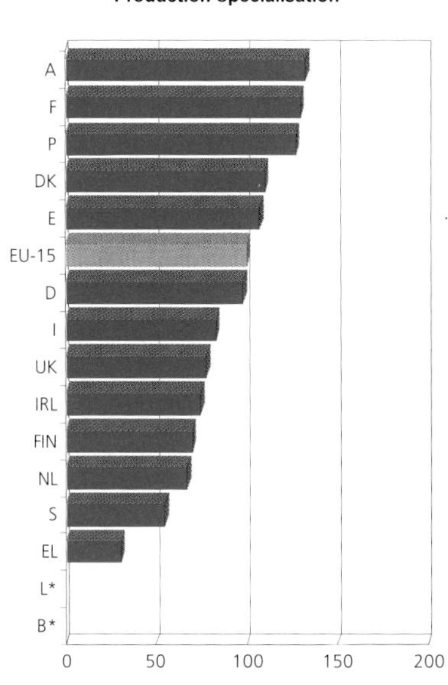

Export specialisation

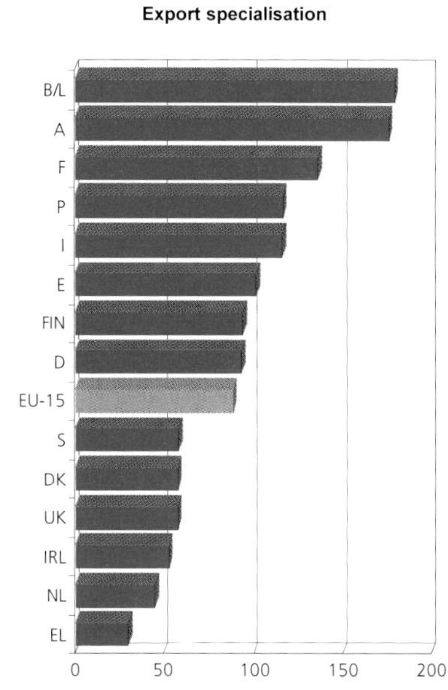

Source: Eurostat (SBS)

Figure 7.11

Glass (NACE Rev. 1 26.1)

Destination of EU exports, 1998

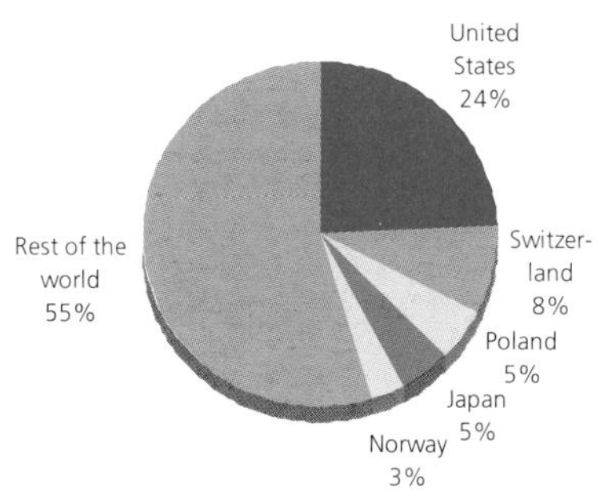

Source: Eurostat (Comext)

Figure 7.12

Glass (NACE Rev. 1 26.1)

Origin of EU imports, 1998

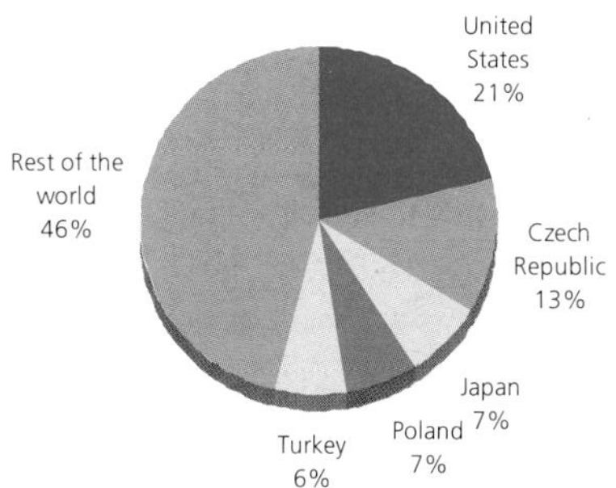

Source: Eurostat (Comext)

Ceramic products (NACE Rev. 1 26.2 and 26.3)

The manufacture of ceramic goods (NACE Rev. 1 26.2 and 26.3) makes ceramic household and ornamental articles, ceramic sanitary fixtures, electrical insulators and refractory ceramic products. Non-refractory ceramic goods for construction purposes, such as tiles and flags are covered in NACE Rev. 1 26.3. The sector encompasses classical ceramics (made of kaolin and clay), as well as so-called "advanced ceramics", that are compounds of materials such as oxygen or silicon with aluminium or titan.

Ceramic goods were responsible for around 15% of the non-metallic mineral products manufactured in the EU or just half a per cent of total EU manufacturing. A large share (nearly 50%) of European production was found in Italy and Spain. In both countries the sector contributed more than twice as much to total manufacturing as the European average. Low levels of activity were found in Denmark and the Netherlands (where the sector contributed below 50% of the European average).

Tableware and ornamental articles are sold to households, as well as to the hotel and restaurant trade. Refractory ceramic products (like crucibles) are used in metallurgy, whilst ceramic insulators are usually consumed by the electrical engineering industry. Construction (new buildings as well as renovation) is the largest customer for tiles, flags or sanitary fixtures, a smaller share of output was bought by handymen. Products that fell within the categories of household articles, tiles, and to a lesser degree sanitary fixtures, had to deal with fashion cycles (even though long ones) as a function of demand.

Ceramic goods were often found in mature markets, for example, for household goods. Manufacturers in the EU faced declining prices for their products and therefore falling profit margins. They made efforts to reduce production costs and to switch to higher price ranges where foreign competition was lower. Production value and value added (both at constant prices) increased between 1993 and 1998, however, the latter at a slower pace, for example in Spain by 2.2% and 1.8% per annum and in Italy by 2.6% and 2.3% per annum.

Figure 7.13

Ceramic products (NACE Rev. 1 26.2 and 26.3)
Production and employment in the Triad

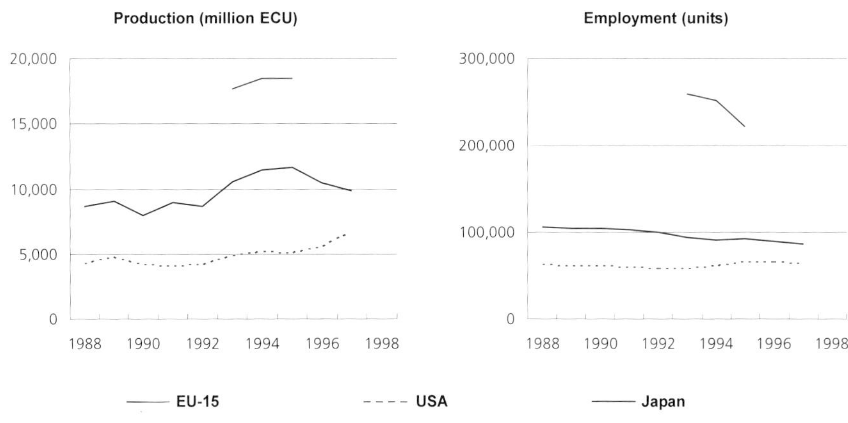

Source: Eurostat (SBS)

Figure 7.14 (%)

Ceramic products (NACE Rev. 1 26.2 and 26.3)
Production and export specialisation by Member State, 1998

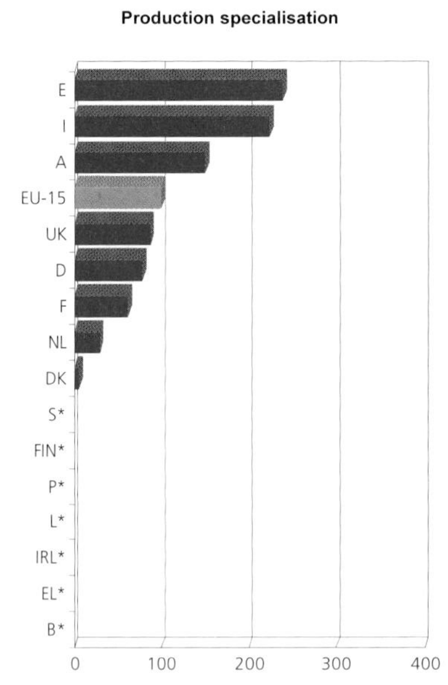

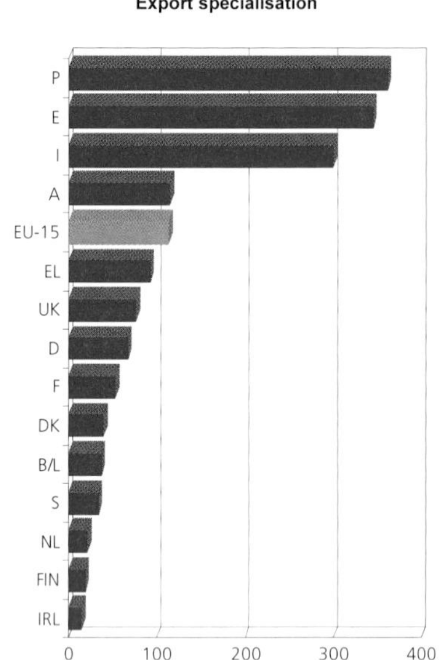

Source: Eurostat (SBS)

If we look at the evolution of employment, Spanish and Italian manufacturers increased their number of persons employed, even though at a slower pace than production (up by 1.4% and 2.1% per annum respectively in the five years to 1998). Reductions were recorded in Germany and Belgium (down by 3.3% and 4.2% in 1998). However, in terms of labour intensity, the United Kingdom reported some of the largest gains, with one million ECU of production requiring just 15 persons in 1998, compared to 20.5 persons in 1995.

Due to the large range of ceramic products, production processes varied within the sector. There were manufacturers still using traditional methods, as well as manufacturers actively looking for technical innovations. Generally, European manufacturers of ceramic goods possessed a high technological standard, independent of the production process used.

High rates of growth were expected for so-called advanced ceramic products that were used in electronics, chemical or medical applications, as well as catalytic converters. Investments for improving production processes were also necessary as competitors in Eastern Europe and East Asia were quickly imitating technology and design.

In some Member States, like Spain, the manufacture of ceramic goods was built up around numerous small and medium-sized enterprises that made it more difficult to be innovative (due to the high costs of starting-up research). The Spanish sector therefore organised a research body where resources and ideas were pooled.

Portuguese industry produced increasingly for multinational companies, 40% of the total production of roof tiles and of tableware and 70% of sanitary fixtures in 1997[1]. Between 1988 and 1998 the excess of Portuguese exports over imports increased by nearly 300% to 280.7 million ECU.

Although ceramic goods faced high transportation costs, international competition increased during the course of the nineties. In Spain 54.6% of the ceramic goods produced domestically were exported in 1998, compared to 36.6% in 1993. The downside of increased competition was that European manufacturers were also affected by the trend. This was particularly the case in Germany, where the domestic market saw an increase in foreign competition, with the trade surplus of 1988, turning into a deficit by 1998.

1) Figures from APICER, Associação Portuguesa da Indústria de Cerâmica.

Figure 7.15

Ceramic goods (NACE Rev. 1 26.2 and 26.3)
Destination of EU exports, 1998

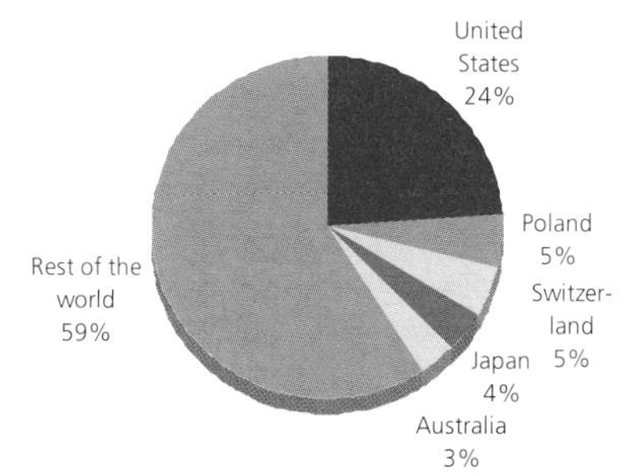

Source: Eurostat (Comext)

Figure 7.16

Ceramic goods (NACE Rev. 1 26.2 and 26.3)
Origin of EU imports, 1998

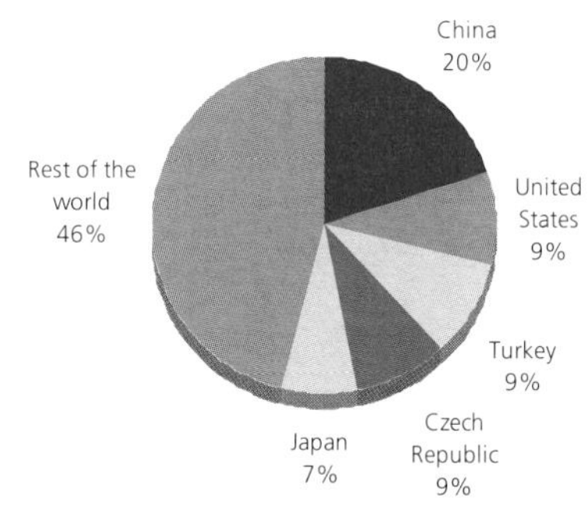

Source: Eurostat (Comext)

Clay products (NACE Rev. 1 26.4)

The manufacture of clay products includes building materials such as bricks, roofing tiles, chimney-pots and flooring blocks. The demand for clay products varies by region within Europe, and is in part influenced by the local climate. In the EU, clay products accounted for around 5% of the production value of non-metallic minerals. There was a relatively high level of activity in Portugal and Austria (if we look at the share of the sector in total manufacturing by Member State). Within the larger Member States, Italy and Spain also reported levels of activity above the European average.

Figure 7.17 (1990=100)

Evolution of sales of bricks and tiles (1)

Bricks ---- Tiles

(1) For the three largest producing countries; for bricks Germany, Italy and Spain; for tiles France, Germany and Italy.

Source: TBE

Figure 7.18

Share of EU sales of bricks in volume terms, 1997 (1)

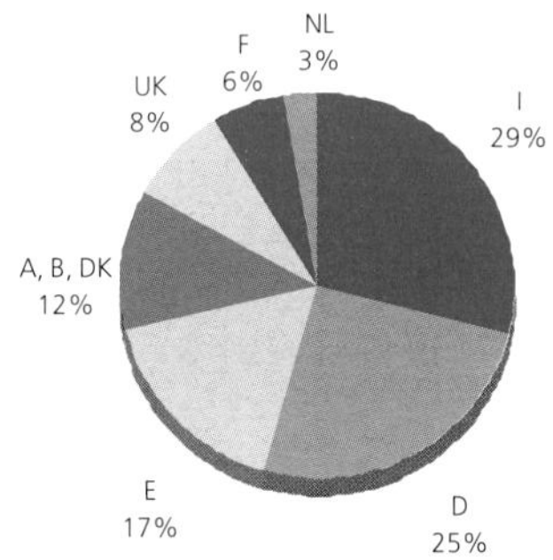

(1) Finland, Greece, Ireland, Luxembourg, Portugal and Sweden are not covered by TBE.

Source: TBE

Figure 7.19

Clay products (NACE Rev. 1 26.4)

Production and employment in the Triad

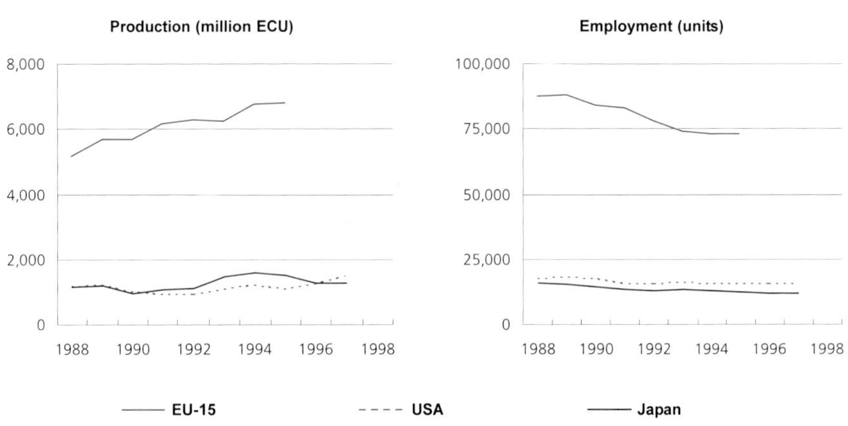

Source: Eurostat (SBS)

Clay products are heavily dependent on the evolution of construction, which is influenced by the general business cycle, public sector investment and interest rates for loans (private housing activity). In the case of roofing tiles and flooring blocks, the maintenance and renovation market was also of great importance. Between 1993 and 1998 the manufacture of clay products expanded in Spain and Portugal by 2.3% and 6.5% per annum respectively, whilst the Italian sector saw its output level fall by 3.2% per annum (at constant prices). The varied picture in the trend of output largely followed the business cycle of the construction sector in the individual Member States. In the USA, where construction was growing at a fast pace, the output of the clay products industry rose by 4.6% per annum between 1993 and 1997.

If we look at output in volume terms (figures from TBE, Fédération Européenne des Fabricants de tuiles et de Briques) show that the picture across Europe was somewhat different. Italian sales of bricks increased at a moderate rate, up 0.1% per annum to 14.6 million cubic metres between 1993 and 1997, whilst sales of tiles decreased moderately by 0.6% per annum to 36.1 million square metres. A downward trend was also observed for the sale of bricks in the Netherlands and the United Kingdom (down by 3.0% and 0.1% per annum), whilst the sale of tiles increased in Denmark and Austria at a fast pace (up by 16.7% and 8.1% respectively).

The manufacture of clay products faced competition from other building materials made of concrete, wood, metal or plastics. In some regions there was over-capacity in the brick industry that led to closures. The largest reductions were recorded in Spain, where the number of brick works fell by 24.5% to 370 plants between 1993 and 1997. Nevertheless, Spain still accounted for the highest number of brick plants in the EU, indicating that the average size of each enterprise was relatively small. Germany and Italy had 215 and 275 brick works in 1997, whilst France had only 131. In all three of these countries, the reduction in the number of brick works between 1993 and 1997 was above 10% (figures from TBE, Fédération Européenne des Fabricants de tuiles et de Briques).

Third country trade was limited within the EU market. The Italian export ratio was equal to just 3.1% in 1998, whilst imports accounted for only 1.0% of the Italian domestic market. Amongst the larger Member States, France reported the highest share of exports in production, at 13.9%.

(%) Figure 7.20

Clay products (NACE Rev. 1 26.4)

Production and export specialisation by Member State, 1998

Production specialisation

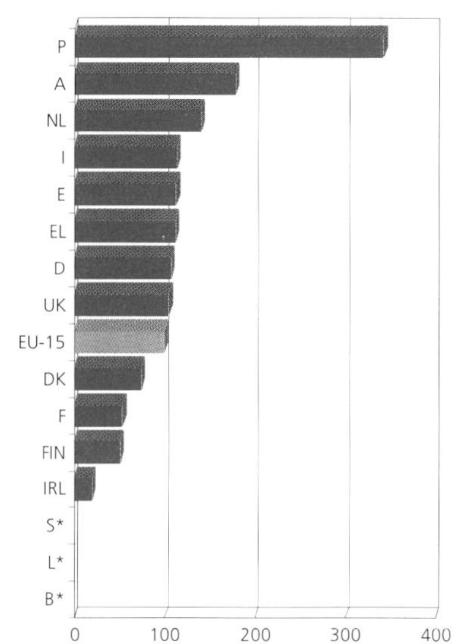

Export specialisation

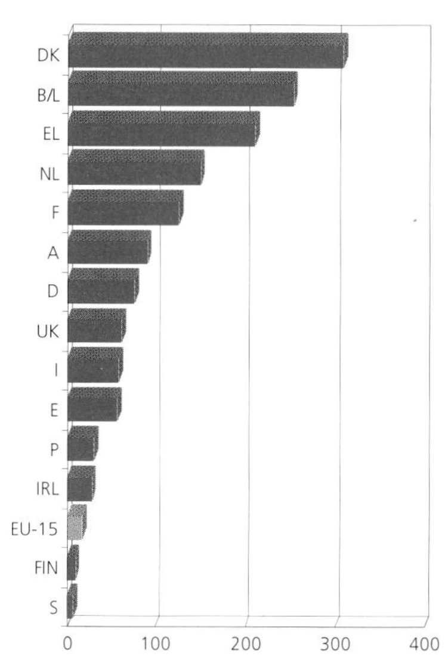

Source: Eurostat (SBS)

Figure 7.21

Clay products (NACE Rev. 1 26.4)

Destination of EU exports, 1998

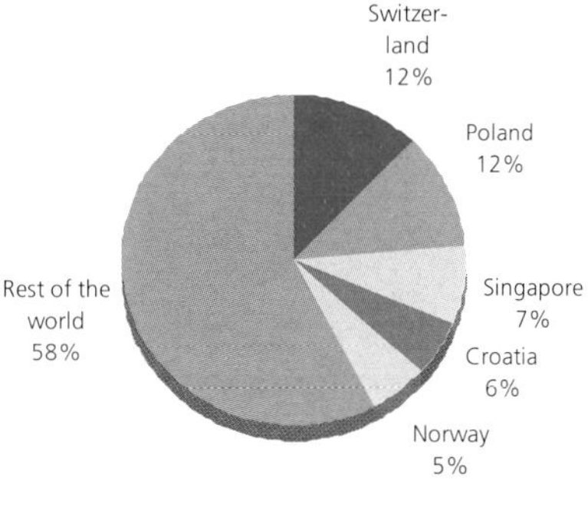

Source: Eurostat (Comext)

Figure 7.22

Clay products (NACE Rev. 1 26.4)

Origin of EU imports, 1998

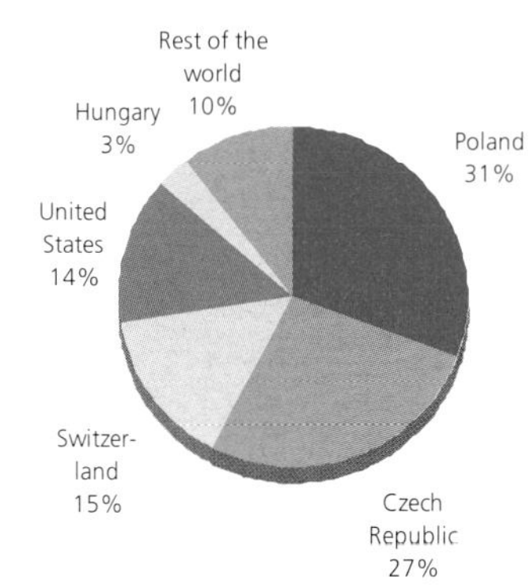

Source: Eurostat (Comext)

Cement and concrete (NACE Rev. 1 26.5 and 26.6)

In 1998 the manufacture of cement and concrete had a production value of 54.9 billion ECU in the EU, more than 40% of the total value for all non-metallic mineral products or just under 1.5% of total EU manufacturing output. The activity produces building raw materials, cement, lime and plaster, as well as articles made of concrete, plaster and cement, which encompass prefabricated structural components, tiles or panels.

The Iberian Peninsula accounted for 15.2% of total European production in the cement and concrete industries. In terms of the sector's contribution to total manufacturing compared across Member State, Austria and Greece also reported high production specialisation ratios.

The activity was heavily dependent on the evolution of the construction sector, as well as the award of public contracts (especially in civil engineering). In addition, there was competition from other traditional building materials such as bricks, wood and plastics. World production of cement has grown steadily since the middle of the 20th century, with two periods of constant output during the recessions in the middle of the seventies and the early eighties. If we look at the evolution of production of cement and concrete (at constant prices) during the nineties, there was a moderate upward trend in the EU (up by 0.6% per annum between 1993 and 1998). At the level of the Member States, Finland and Portugal reported quite rapid increases in output, rising 13.3% and 6.5% per annum during the five years to 1998, whilst Italy and Germany saw output falling by 1.9% and 2.3% per annum over the same period.

Figure 7.23

Cement and concrete (NACE Rev. 1 26.5 and 26.6)
Production and employment in the Triad

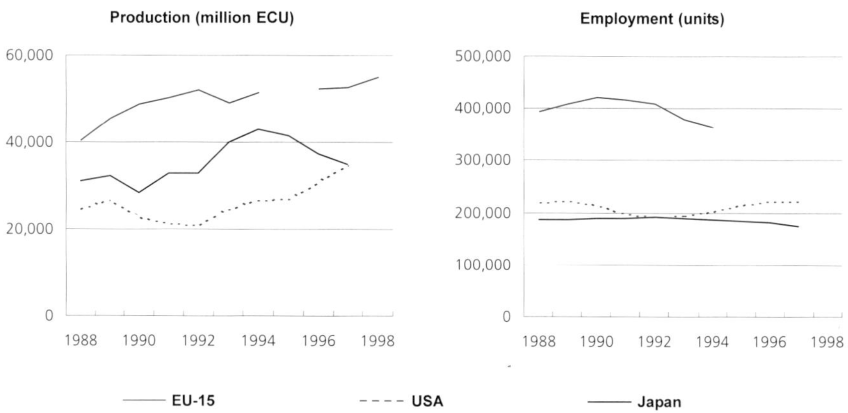

Source: Eurostat (SBS)

In the EU there were 173.9 million tonnes of cement produced in 1997, an increase of 4.4 million tonnes or 2.6% when compared to data for 1996 (figures from Cembureau, The European Cement Association). This upward trend was observed in most Member States, except for Austria, Germany and Sweden (down by 0.5%, 1.0% and 7.9% respectively in 1997). If we take the three year-period to 1997, eight Member States reported a reduction, with the EU figure falling 0.7% per annum. Consumption of cement fell in Germany and France by 6.0% and 2.3% per annum respectively, whilst Portugal and Ireland recorded increases of 7.5% and 11.5%.

The highest consumption of cement in per capita terms was reported in Luxembourg with 1.1 tons in 1997, even though the ratio fell by 14.0% compared to 1993. A similar reduction was observed in Sweden, the country with the lowest per capita consumption in the EU at 146 kilograms per head. Spain, Finland and Portugal reported high growth rates in cement consumption, of the magnitude of 20% to reach 681, 258 and 952 kilograms per capita respectively.

Figure 7.24 (kg/capita)

Production and consumption of cement per capita in the EU, 1997

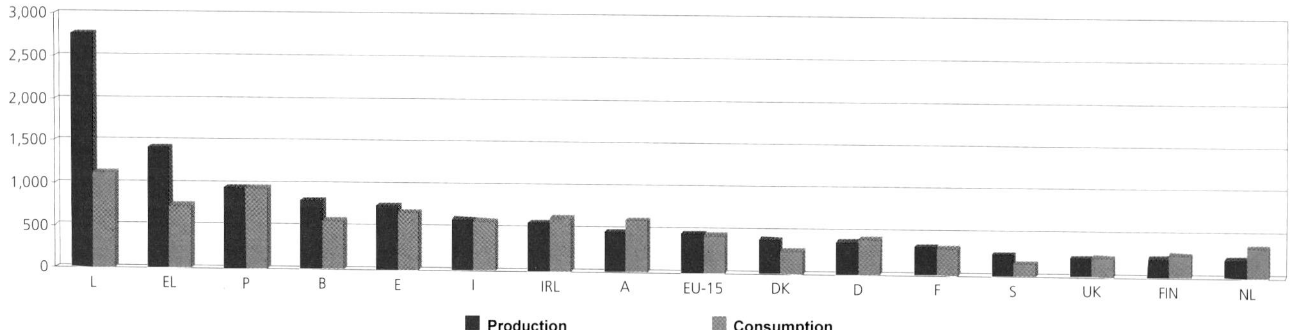

Source: Cembureau

(units)

Figure 7.25

Average number of plants per enterprise, ready-mixed concrete

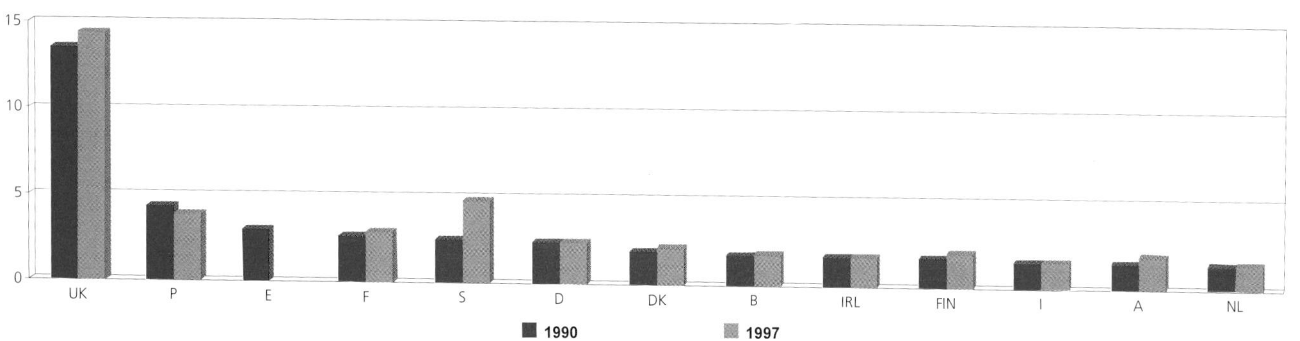

Source: ERMCO

The largest quantity of ready mixed concrete within the EU (62 million cubic metres) was produced in Italy, slightly more than in Germany (60.4 million cubic metres - figures from ERMCO, European Ready Mixed Concrete Organisation). The activity manufactures concrete off-site and delivers it in a fresh and un-hardened condition to construction sites. Between 1993 and 1997 production of ready mixed concrete displayed a similar picture to the cement industry. There was an increase in output for most Member States, except for Germany and Sweden (down by 2.1% and 4.5% per annum respectively), as well as modest decreases in the United Kingdom and Belgium (down by 0.2% and 0.1% per annum respectively). With such a high production figure, it was no surprise to find that Italy had one of the highest consumption per head figures (1.1 cubic metres per capita in 1997), only exceeded by Austria (1.3 cubic metres). Finland and the United Kingdom reported the lowest per capita consumption (both 0.4 cubic metres).

The supply side of the cement and concrete industry displayed a tendency towards concentration, which accelerated during the course of the nineties. In the manufacture of concrete, the number of enterprises producing ready mixed concrete decreased by 4% to around 4 thousand in the EU[2] between 1988 and 1997, whilst the number of plants increased by 13.3% to some 10 thousand.

2) Figures from ERMCO, excluding Luxembourg and Greece.

(%)

Figure 7.26

Cement and concrete (NACE Rev. 1 26.5 and 26.6)

Production and export specialisation by Member State, 1998

Production specialisation

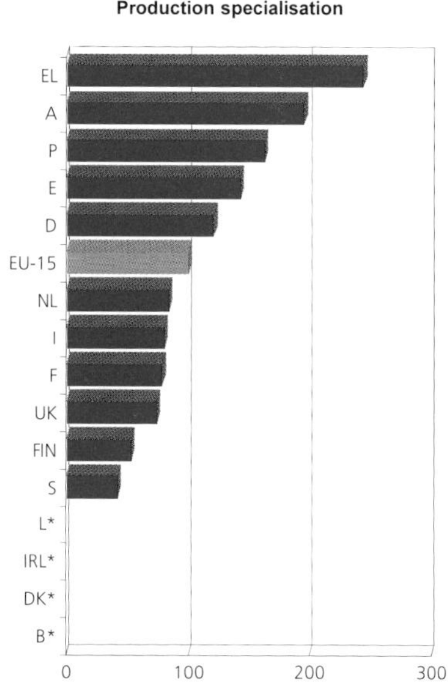

Export specialisation

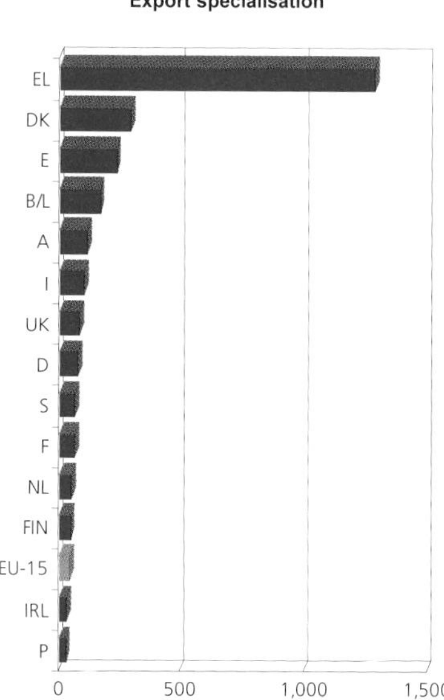

Source: Eurostat (SBS)

Mergers in the cement industry moved beyond national borders. Merger activity had some effect in reducing capacity within Europe. In Austria, capacity was reduced by 23.8% between 1994 and 1997 to 4.8 million tonnes. However, Portugal saw cement capacity increasing by 2.8% to 8.7 million tonnes and Luxembourg by 30.8% to 850 thousand tonnes over the same period[3]. At the same time manufacturers diversified their product ranges, for example former pure cement suppliers also started producing ready mixed concrete or pre-cast concrete.

Markets for low-quality cement were also open to increased competition from Central and Eastern European countries, especially into neighbouring EU Member States (Germany and Austria). Increased competitive pressure led to further efforts by European producers to reduce their energy costs as electricity costs accounted for 38% of value added in Germany. In Germany, the cement industry was the third largest energy consumer (behind iron and steel industry and the chemical industry). Therefore the sector was strongly involved in environmental issues: on the one hand it reduced overall energy consumption and emissions of CO_2, on the other hand it diversified fuels in order to reduce costs (for example burning waste). Since the seventies, the energy required to produce cement clinker fell by a third in the EU[4]. Most of the energy is necessary to heat limestone (and some other ingredients) to 1,450°C and to grind clinker. Energy efficiency gains were further supported by concentration within the industry, as less efficient plants were closed and production in more efficient ones was expanded.

Although labour intensity was not very high in the manufacture of cement and concrete, increased competition from Central and Eastern Europe underlined high labour costs in some Member States, such as Germany. The sector reduced employment levels, this was most pronounced in Germany where an annual average decline of 4.0% was recorded between 1993 and 1998. In Spain, the number of persons employed increased moderately by 0.5% per annum, even though output of cement and concrete expanded four times faster.

3) Figures from Cembureau.
4) For example, fossil fuel CO_2 emissions should be reduced by 25% in France between 1990 and 2000 and CO_2 emissions per tonne of cement by 10% (source: Cembureau).

Figure 7.27

Cement and concrete
(NACE Rev. 1 26.5 and 26.6)
Destination of EU exports, 1998

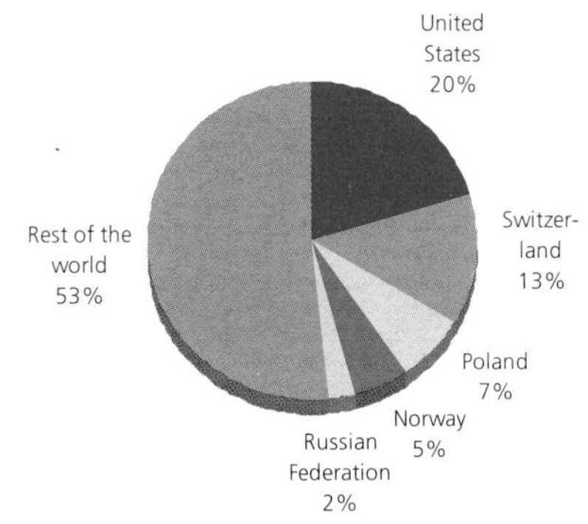

Source: Eurostat (Comext)

Figure 7.28

Cement and concrete
(NACE Rev. 1 26.5 and 26.6)
Origin of EU imports, 1998

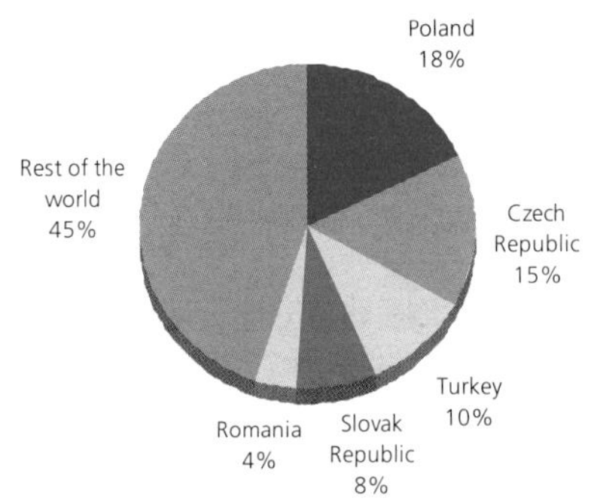

Source: Eurostat (Comext)

Stone and other non-metallic mineral products (NACE Rev. 1 26.7 and 26.8)

Stone (NACE Rev. 1 26.7) has long been used as a basic material in construction. Through changed construction techniques, stone is nowadays more often used for aesthetic reasons, such as cladding and tiles. Natural stone is also cut and shaped for gravestones and monuments. Other non-metallic mineral products (NACE Rev. 1 26.8) include natural and artificial abrasive products, mineral insulating materials or non-metallic mineral yarn. In 1998 stone and other non-metallic mineral products accounted for around 12% of total EU non-metallic minerals' output, with production value around 15 billion ECU.

In Spain there was a large stone industry, with 17% of total European production, more than twice the average contribution to total manufacturing in Europe. Austria, Finland and Italy also reported production specialisation ratios above the European average, whilst there was a relatively small industry in Ireland and France.

Stone and other non-metallic mineral products were used in various activities (for example, abrasive products were used throughout manufacturing). However, construction was the most important downstream industry. Ornamental stone (mostly granite and marble) faced strong competition from materials like glass and ceramics, and demand was largely dependent on taste, as well as price (which was usually determined by local supply). With improved processing techniques, for example cutting stone in very thin slabs, stone has been increasingly used in the manufacture of furniture.

Despite European construction recording low levels of activity in the nineties, the stone industry and other non-metallic mineral products both reported an upward trend in output. In Spain production values increased by 3.2% per annum and value added by 2.6% between 1993 and 1998 (both at constant prices).

The sector expected increased sales volumes with increasing disposable income, for example, the cladding of stones was still seen as a luxury good. The increased awareness of environmental concerns and the desire to make energy savings supported the growth of insulating materials.

Figure 7.29

Stone and other non-metallic mineral products (NACE Rev. 1 26.7 and 26.8)
Production and employment in the Triad

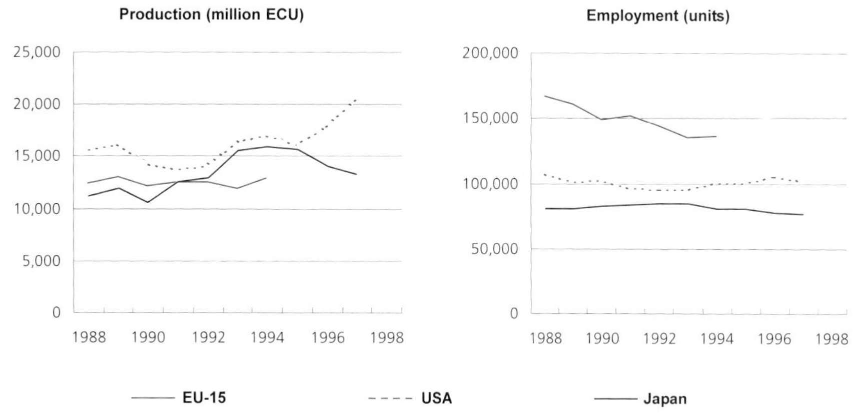

Source: Eurostat (SBS)

Figure 7.30

Stone and other non-metallic mineral products (NACE Rev. 1 26.7 and 26.8)
Production and export specialisation by Member State, 1998

(%)

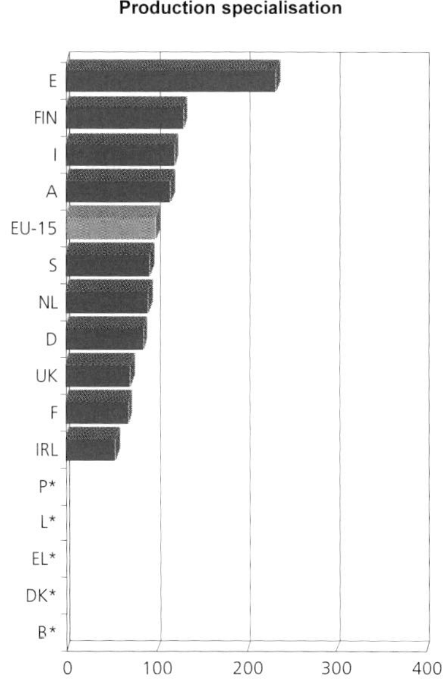

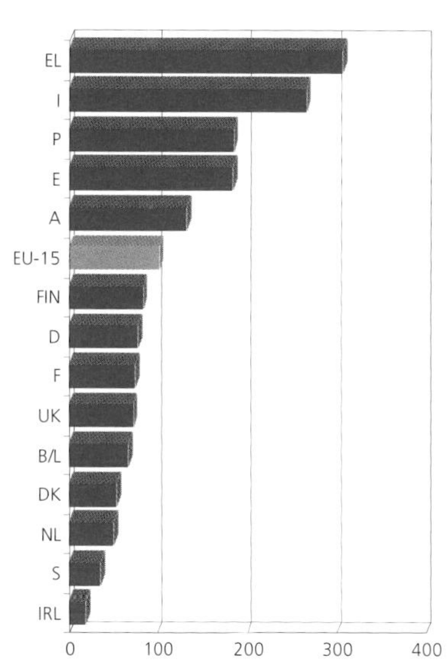

Source: Eurostat (SBS)

The manufacture of stone and other non-metallic mineral products faced recruitment problems with labour shortages in some countries. Employment expanded by 1.8% per annum (between 1993 and 1998), with only Germany reporting a slight decrease in the number of persons employed (down 0.6% per annum). Austrian and Swedish industry employed 4.5% and 5.2% more persons each year over the same period.

Foreign trade of stone and other non-metallic mineral products expanded during the course of the nineties, despite high transportation costs. In the euro-zone[5], exports and imports increased at a similar pace between 1993 and 1998, up by 6.5% and 6.3% per annum respectively (foreign trade figures for the euro-zone include intra-EU trade). However, deliveries going to countries outside the EU made up between 20% (Belgo-Luxembourg Economic Union) and 60% (Italy) of exports. European manufacturers reported a positive trade balance, largely due to the surplus recorded in Italy. Italian suppliers of stone and other non-metallic mineral products exported 85.6% of their production in 1998, an increase of nearly 10 percentage points since 1988. However, the share of imports in Italian domestic consumption grew by 20 percentage points to 56.0% by 1998.

5) EU-15 excluding Denmark, Greece, Sweden and the United Kingdom.

Figure 7.31

Stone and other non-metallic mineral products (NACE Rev. 1 26.7 and 26.8) Destination of EU exports, 1998

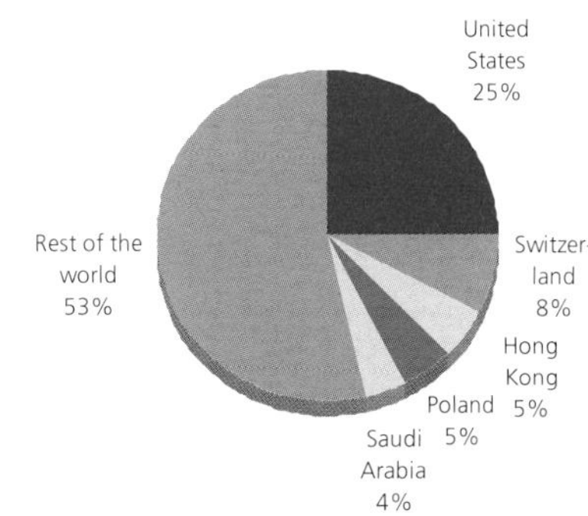

Source: Eurostat (Comext)

Figure 7.32

Stone and other non-metallic mineral products (NACE Rev. 1 26.7 and 26.8) Origin of EU imports, 1998

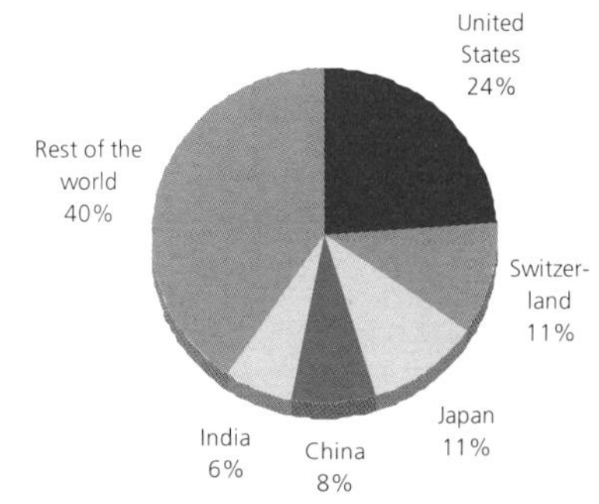

Source: Eurostat (Comext)

Professional associations representing the industries within this chapter

CEMBUREAU
European Cement Association
55, rue d'Arlon
B-1040 Bruxelles
tel: (32) 2 234 10 11
fax: (32) 2 230 47 20
e-mail: secretariat@cembureau.be

CPIV
Standing Committee of the EU Glass industries
89, avenue Louise
B-1050 Bruxelles
tel: (32) 2 538 44 46
fax: (32) 2 537 84 69

EAPA
European Asphalt Pavement Association
Straatweg 68
PO Box 175
NL-3620 AD Breukelen
tel: (31) 346 26 68 68
fax: (31) 346 26 35 05
e-mail: eapa@wbinet.nl

ERMCO
European Ready-Mixed Concrete Association
P.O. Box 19
Egham Surrey TW20 8UT
tel: (44) 1784 43 49 90
fax: (44) 1784 43 52 40
e-mail: secretariat@ermco.org.uk

FEVE
European Container Glass Federation
89, avenue Louise
B-1050 Bruxelles
tel: (32) 2 539 34 34
fax: (32) 2 539 37 52

TBE
European Federation of bricks and tiles producers
Obstgartenstraße 28
CH-8035 Zürich
tel: (41) 1 361 96 50
fax: (41) 1 361 02 05

(million ECU) Table 7.2

Manufacture of glass and glass products (NACE Rev. 1 26.1)

Production related indicators in the EU

	1988	1989	1990	1991	1992	1993	1994	1995	1996	1997	1998
Production value	21,068	23,083	23,662	24,397	24,570	23,451	25,023	27,712	:	:	:
Producer price index (1995=100)	:	:	94.8	95.8	96.1	95.7	96.5	100.0	97.4	99.3	104.6
Value added	9,707	10,164	10,156	10,588	10,327	9,890	10,743	11,929	:	:	:
Number of persons employed (thousands)	279.6	288.3	288.2	287.3	281.6	260.5	251.9	255.3	:	:	:

(million ECU) Table 7.3

Manufacture of glass and glass products (NACE Rev. 1 26.1)

Production related indicators, 1998

	B	DK	D	EL	E	F	IRL	I	L	NL	A	P	FIN	S	UK
Production value	2,444	458	8,044	54	2,042	6,240	319	3,593	:	866	759	597	378	527	3,256
Value added	800	228	3,291	20	904	2,546	160	1,463	:	364	423	:	140	183	1,572
Number of persons employed (units) (1)	11,983	4,633	62,862	814	24,866	49,786	3,994	27,792	:	5,566	7,997	9,423	3,323	4,429	31,668

(1) NL (1992).

(million ECU) Table 7.4

Manufacture of glass and glass products (NACE Rev. 1 26.1)

Market related indicators in the EU

	1988	1989	1990	1991	1992	1993	1994	1995	1996	1997	1998
Apparent consumption	19,734	21,598	22,329	23,256	23,449	22,046	23,404	26,104	:	:	:
Exports	2,297	2,617	2,545	2,564	2,584	2,801	3,231	3,506	3,790	4,375	4,260
Imports	963	1,132	1,213	1,424	1,462	1,396	1,612	1,898	1,953	2,242	2,532
Trade balance	1,334	1,485	1,332	1,141	1,122	1,405	1,618	1,608	1,837	2,133	1,727
Export ratio (%)	10.9	11.3	10.8	10.5	10.5	11.9	12.9	12.7	:	:	:
Import penetration ratio (%)	4.9	5.2	5.4	6.1	6.2	6.3	6.9	7.3	:	:	:
Cover ratio (%)	238.5	231.2	209.9	180.1	176.7	200.7	200.4	184.7	194.1	195.1	168.2

(million ECU) Table 7.5

Manufacture of glass and glass products (NACE Rev. 1 26.1)

Market related indicators, 1998

	B/L	DK	D	EL	E	F	IRL	I	NL	A	P	FIN	S	UK
Apparent consumption	:	563	7,223	176	2,148	5,576	279	3,102	921	654	591	282	569	3,524
Exports	1,800	147	2,855	16	584	2,505	175	1,641	478	557	156	241	274	866
Imports	958	251	2,034	138	691	1,840	135	1,150	533	452	150	144	315	1,133
Trade balance	842	-105	821	-122	-106	665	40	491	-55	105	6	96	-41	-267
Export ratio (%)	:	32.0	35.5	30.0	28.6	40.1	54.9	45.7	55.2	73.4	26.1	63.7	51.9	26.6
Import penetration ratio (%)	:	44.6	28.2	78.7	32.2	33.0	48.4	37.1	57.9	69.1	25.4	51.3	55.4	32.2
Cover ratio (%)	188.0	58.4	140.3	11.6	84.6	136.1	129.6	142.7	89.8	123.2	103.9	166.6	86.9	76.4

Table 7.6

Manufacture of glass and glass products (NACE Rev. 1 26.1)

Labour related indicators, 1998

	EU-15	B	DK	D	EL	E	F	IRL	I	L	NL	A	P	FIN	S	UK
Personnel costs (million ECU) (1)	7,818	481	156	2,334	12	496	1,621	113	866	:	227	287	113	104	148	857
Personnel costs/employee (thousand ECU) (2)	32.7	42.8	34.2	37.3	15.6	23.1	35.5	28.2	28.4	:	:	37.4	:	32.5	34.9	22.5
Social charges/personnel costs (%) (3)	23.4	27.9	4.8	21.4	25.6	20.4	28.4	17.9	36.1	:	16.1	24.5	:	22.0	28.1	12.6
Labour productivity (thousand ECU/head) (4)	46.7	66.7	49.2	52.4	25.1	36.4	51.1	40.0	52.7	:	52.5	52.8	:	42.1	41.3	49.6
Wage adjusted labour productivity (%) (2)	142.9	137.8	151.0	141.9	145.2	173.6	135.8	139.4	182.7	:	:	163.0	:	142.1	121.4	181.3

(1) EU-15 (1995). (2) EU-15, EL, I, A (1995); B, DK, D, E, F, IRL, FIN, S, UK (1996). (3) EU-15, S (1995). (4) NL (1992); EU-15 (1995).

Source: Eurostat (SBS, EBT)

Table 7.7 (million ECU)

Manufacture of non-refractory ceramic goods other than for construction purposes; manufacture of refractory ceramic products (NACE Rev. 1 26.2)

Production related indicators in the EU

	1988	1989	1990	1991	1992	1993	1994	1995	1996	1997	1998
Production value	:	:	:	:	:	10,476	10,879	10,600	:	:	:
Producer price index (1995=100)	:	:	:	:	:	:	:	:	:	:	:
Value added	:	:	:	:	:	4,921	5,252	5,198	:	:	:
Number of persons employed (thousands)	:	:	:	:	:	185.2	177.5	150.2	:	:	:

Table 7.8 (million ECU)

Manufacture of non-refractory ceramic goods other than for construction purposes; manufacture of refractory ceramic products (NACE Rev. 1 26.2)

Production related indicators, 1998

	B	DK	D	EL	E	F	IRL	I	L	NL	A	P	FIN	S	UK
Production value	285	18	2,971	74	1,189	1,503	:	1,657	:	120	699	:	171	245	2,738
Value added	122	9	1,310	34	539	664	:	718	:	62	270	:	75	101	1,477
Number of persons employed (units) (1)	2,005	248	34,911	1,707	15,715	18,161	:	19,355	:	2,399	5,029	:	1,779	2,039	41,225

(1) NL (1992).

Table 7.9 (million ECU)

Manufacture of non-refractory ceramic goods other than for construction purposes; manufacture of refractory ceramic products (NACE Rev. 1 26.2)

Market related indicators in the EU

	1988	1989	1990	1991	1992	1993	1994	1995	1996	1997	1998
Apparent consumption	:	:	:	:	:	9,309	9,436	8,680	:	:	:
Exports	1,739	1,973	2,022	2,031	2,072	2,213	2,521	3,027	2,777	3,389	3,105
Imports	662	740	775	950	1,026	1,047	1,078	1,107	1,211	1,414	1,572
Trade balance	1,077	1,233	1,247	1,080	1,046	1,166	1,442	1,920	1,566	1,975	1,533
Export ratio (%)	:	:	:	:	:	21.1	23.2	28.6	:	:	:
Import penetration ratio (%)	:	:	:	:	:	11.2	11.4	12.8	:	:	:
Cover ratio (%)	262.8	266.6	261.0	213.7	202.0	211.4	233.8	273.4	229.3	239.6	197.6

Table 7.10 (million ECU)

Manufacture of non-refractory ceramic goods other than for construction purposes; manufacture of refractory ceramic products (NACE Rev. 1 26.2)

Market related indicators, 1998

	B/L	DK	D	EL	E	F	IRL	I	NL	A	P	FIN	S	UK
Apparent consumption	:	68	2,348	127	1,160	1,438	:	1,314	203	547	:	222	280	2,255
Exports	333	89	1,654	30	331	713	47	831	165	325	340	38	139	1,008
Imports	369	140	1,032	83	302	648	74	489	248	173	79	89	174	526
Trade balance	-35	-51	623	-53	29	65	-27	342	-83	152	261	-51	-35	482
Export ratio (%)	:	504.3	55.7	40.2	27.8	47.5	:	50.2	137.3	46.6	:	22.2	56.8	36.8
Import penetration ratio (%)	:	204.8	43.9	65.2	26.0	45.1	:	37.2	122.0	31.7	:	40.0	62.2	23.3
Cover ratio (%)	90.4	63.8	160.4	35.9	109.5	110.1	63.5	169.9	66.5	187.7	430.6	42.9	79.8	191.7

Table 7.11

Manufacture of non-refractory ceramic goods other than for construction purposes; manufacture of refractory ceramic products (NACE Rev. 1 26.2)

Labour related indicators, 1998

	EU-15	B	DK	D	EL	E	F	IRL	I	L	NL	A	P	FIN	S	UK
Personnel costs (million ECU) (1)	3,965	73	7	1,199	26	282	512	:	532	:	46	229	:	47	66	964
Personnel costs/employee (thousand ECU) (2)	26.6	39.2	30.7	33.2	16.8	20.3	29.9	:	25.1	:	:	47.5	:	28.5	33.9	19.5
Social charges/personnel costs (%) (3)	21.9	26.7	3.1	20.0	24.6	22.2	28.8	:	35.1	:	16.8	25.5	:	23.8	30.6	11.9
Labour productivity (thousand ECU/head) (4)	34.6	60.8	34.6	37.5	19.9	34.3	36.6	:	37.1	:	32.1	53.8	:	42.3	49.4	35.8
Wage adjusted labour productivity (%) (2)	130.2	128.8	116.2	115.5	102.8	136.8	121.4	:	156.7	:	:	122.0	:	148.4	147.0	151.4

(1) EU-15 (1995). (2) EU-15, EL, I, A (1995); B, DK, D, E, F, FIN, S, UK (1996). (3) EU-15, S (1995). (4) NL (1992); EU-15 (1995).

Source: Eurostat (SBS, EBT)

(million ECU) Table 7.12

Manufacture of ceramic tiles and flags (NACE Rev. 1 26.3)
Production related indicators in the EU

	1988	1989	1990	1991	1992	1993	1994	1995	1996	1997	1998
Production value	:	:	:	:	:	7,280	7,659	7,913	:	:	:
Producer price index (1995=100)	:	:	:	:	:	:	:	:	:	:	:
Value added	:	:	:	:	:	3,159	3,316	3,342	:	:	:
Number of persons employed (thousands)	:	:	:	:	:	74.0	74.5	71.9	:	:	:

(million ECU) Table 7.13

Manufacture of ceramic tiles and flags (NACE Rev. 1 26.3)
Production related indicators, 1998

	B	DK	D	EL	E	F	IRL	I	L	NL	A	P	FIN	S	UK
Production value (1)	13	0	772	:	2,104	371	:	4,728	0	112	0	:	:	17	166
Value added (1)	6	0	295	:	811	145	:	2,041	0	58	0	:	:	8	88
Number of persons employed (units) (2)	109	0	8,904	:	24,182	4,210	:	33,671	0	1,132	0	:	:	147	2,285

(1) NL, A (1995); DK, L (1996). (2) NL (1992); A (1995); DK, L (1996).

(million ECU) Table 7.14

Manufacture of ceramic tiles and flags (NACE Rev. 1 26.3)
Market related indicators in the EU

	1988	1989	1990	1991	1992	1993	1994	1995	1996	1997	1998
Apparent consumption	:	:	:	:	:	6,033	6,109	6,328	:	:	:
Exports	936	1,121	1,085	1,056	1,143	1,354	1,628	1,711	1,931	2,231	2,337
Imports	17	62	74	89	110	108	78	126	107	173	173
Trade balance	920	1,059	1,011	968	1,033	1,247	1,550	1,585	1,823	2,059	2,164
Export ratio (%)	:	:	:	:	:	18.6	21.3	21.6	:	:	:
Import penetration ratio (%)	:	:	:	:	:	1.8	1.3	2.0	:	:	:
Cover ratio (%)	5,588.2	1,809.8	1,475.8	1,188.1	1,038.1	1,255.7	2,088.3	1,358.3	1,799.3	1,293.5	1,349.8

(million ECU) Table 7.15

Manufacture of ceramic tiles and flags (NACE Rev. 1 26.3)
Market related indicators, 1998

	B/L	DK	D	EL	E	F	IRL	I	NL	A	P	FIN	S	UK
Apparent consumption (1)	:	31	1,414	:	664	748	:	1,785	148	153	:	:	50	505
Exports	11	2	212	15	1,469	180	0	3,012	46	4	96	6	6	32
Imports	165	38	854	130	30	558	31	69	99	136	77	33	39	371
Trade balance	-155	-36	-642	-115	1,439	-378	-31	2,943	-53	-132	19	-26	-33	-339
Export ratio (%) (1)	:	:	27.4	:	69.8	48.5	:	63.7	64.9	:	:	:	33.1	19.1
Import penetration ratio (%) (1)	:	114.0	60.4	:	4.5	74.5	:	3.9	73.5	101.7	:	:	77.4	73.4
Cover ratio (%)	6.5	5.4	24.8	11.7	4,928.3	32.3	0.1	4,352.2	46.2	3.0	125.2	19.4	14.4	8.6

(1) NL, A (1995); DK (1996).

Table 7.16

Manufacture of ceramic tiles and flags (NACE Rev. 1 26.3)
Labour related indicators, 1998

	EU-15	B	DK	D	EL	E	F	IRL	I	L	NL	A	P	FIN	S	UK
Personnel costs (million ECU) (1)	2,117	3	0	344	:	534	119	:	1,110	0	43	0	:	:	5	57
Personnel costs/employee (thousand ECU) (2)	29.6	31.1	:	37.4	:	23.9	30.0	:	30.1	:	:	:	:	:	37.3	20.7
Social charges/personnel costs (%) (3)	27.2	25.8	:	21.4	:	21.2	27.7	:	36.1	:	14.5	:	:	:	:	12.7
Labour productivity (thousand ECU/head) (4)	46.5	59.1	:	33.2	:	33.5	34.3	:	60.6	:	31.3	:	:	:	55.2	38.3
Wage adjusted labour productivity (%) (2)	157.1	115.5	:	97.9	:	166.5	112.4	:	175.0	:	:	:	:	:	149.7	136.1

(1) EU-15, NL, A (1995); DK, L (1996). (2) EU-15, I (1995); B, D, E, F, S, UK (1996). (3) EU-15, NL (1995). (4) NL (1992); EU-15 (1995).

Source: Eurostat (SBS, EBT)

Table 7.17 (million ECU)

Manufacture of bricks, tiles and construction products, in baked clay (NACE Rev. 1 26.4)
Production related indicators in the EU

	1988	1989	1990	1991	1992	1993	1994	1995	1996	1997	1998
Production value	5,174	5,690	5,705	6,185	6,295	6,236	6,784	6,807	:	:	:
Producer price index (1995=100)	:	:	86.3	91.4	94.4	96.3	97.7	100.0	88.6	99.1	101.3
Value added	2,657	2,825	2,766	2,958	3,084	3,053	3,324	3,395	:	:	:
Number of persons employed (thousands)	87.7	88.3	84.3	82.9	78.2	74.1	73.3	73.0	:	:	:

Table 7.18 (million ECU)

Manufacture of bricks, tiles and construction products, in baked clay (NACE Rev. 1 26.4)
Production related indicators, 1998

	B	DK	D	EL	E	F	IRL	I	L	NL	A	P	FIN	S	UK
Production value (1)	390	123	1,769	51	644	659	20	1,051	0	373	294	413	58	43	909
Value added (1)	190	44	847	16	267	318	11	402	0	196	119	:	37	17	535
Number of persons employed (units) (1)(2)	2,577	588	14,380	1,082	9,720	5,074	218	10,356	0	2,554	1,684	8,937	593	301	9,835

(1) FIN (1990); A (1994); L (1996). (2) NL (1992).

Table 7.19 (million ECU)

Manufacture of bricks, tiles and construction products, in baked clay (NACE Rev. 1 26.4)
Market related indicators in the EU

	1988	1989	1990	1991	1992	1993	1994	1995	1996	1997	1998
Apparent consumption	:	:	:	:	:	:	:	:	:	:	:
Exports	9	26	36	25	8	16	26	20	:	56	33
Imports	:	:	:	:	:	:	:	:	:	:	:
Trade balance	:	:	:	:	:	:	:	:	:	:	:
Export ratio (%)	0.2	0.5	0.6	0.4	0.1	0.3	0.4	0.3	:	:	:
Import penetration ratio (%)	:	:	:	:	:	:	:	:	:	:	:
Cover ratio (%)	:	:	:	:	:	:	:	:	:	:	:

Table 7.20 (million ECU)

Manufacture of bricks, tiles and construction products, in baked clay (NACE Rev. 1 26.4)
Market related indicators, 1998

	B/L	DK	D	EL	E	F	IRL	I	NL	A	P	FIN	S	UK
Apparent consumption (1)	:	101	1,835	48	642	591	20	1,029	340	319	415	64	44	894
Exports	101	31	93	4	13	92	4	33	63	11	2	1	1	36
Imports	53	9	159	2	11	23	4	11	31	31	3	1	2	22
Trade balance	48	22	-66	3	1	68	-1	22	32	-20	-2	0	-1	14
Export ratio (%) (1)	:	25.0	5.2	8.7	2.0	13.9	18.3	3.1	17.0	3.5	0.4	0.5	2.8	4.0
Import penetration ratio (%) (1)	:	8.6	8.7	3.8	1.8	3.9	21.2	1.0	9.2	11.0	0.8	9.4	5.1	2.4
Cover ratio (%)	189.9	353.5	58.5	242.5	112.8	392.3	83.0	302.8	203.5	36.5	51.5	153.5	53.3	166.2

(1) A (1990); FIN (1994).

Table 7.21

Manufacture of bricks, tiles and construction products, in baked clay (NACE Rev. 1 26.4)
Labour related indicators, 1998

	EU-15	B	DK	D	EL	E	F	IRL	I	L	NL	A	P	FIN	S	UK
Personnel costs (million ECU) (1)	1,869	83	21	557	13	143	154	5	288	0	75	60	78	16	11	269
Personnel costs/employee (thousand ECU) (2)	30.7	35.4	36.6	38.3	13.2	16.4	32.1	23.8	25.3	:	:	35.9	:	27.5	36.5	22.8
Social charges/personnel costs (%) (3)	21.6	29.0	3.9	19.7	23.6	22.2	29.2	14.3	36.4	:	14.3	22.9	:	20.8	:	11.6
Labour productivity (thousand ECU/head) (4)	46.5	73.9	74.2	58.9	14.6	27.4	62.7	49.5	38.8	:	60.9	70.7	:	62.8	56.7	54.4
Wage adjusted labour productivity (%) (2)	151.3	166.6	208.8	160.6	95.3	156.4	176.2	178.1	147.7	:	:	196.8	:	228.6	156.7	177.3

(1) FIN (1990); A (1994); EU-15 (1995); L (1996). (2) FIN (1990); A (1994); EU-15, EL, I (1995); B, DK, D, E, F, IRL, S, UK (1996). (3) FIN (1990); A (1994); EU-15 (1995).
(4) FIN (1990); NL (1992); A (1994); EU-15 (1995).

Source: Eurostat (SBS, EBT)

(million ECU) Table 7.22

Manufacture of cement, lime and plaster (NACE Rev. 1 26.5)
Production related indicators in the EU

	1988	1989	1990	1991	1992	1993	1994	1995	1996	1997	1998
Production value	12,498	13,447	14,165	14,212	13,911	12,799	13,838	:	14,106	14,881	15,533
Producer price index (1995=100)	:	:	:	:	:	:	:	:	:	:	:
Value added	6,012	6,325	6,549	6,163	6,230	5,731	6,403	:	:	:	:
Number of persons employed (thousands)	82.3	82.5	82.7	80.3	77.2	73.6	71.3	:	:	:	:

(million ECU) Table 7.23

Manufacture of cement, lime and plaster (NACE Rev. 1 26.5)
Production related indicators, 1998

	B	DK	D	EL	E	F	IRL	I	L	NL	A	P	FIN	S	UK
Production value (1)	1,160	:	3,347	509	2,381	2,400	:	2,349	:	216	585	788	80	174	1,189
Value added (1)	483	:	1,380	165	1,142	1,040	:	821	:	124	247	:	35	62	604
Number of persons employed (units) (2)	3,432	:	15,965	4,828	12,179	7,739	:	14,438	:	869	3,009	2,430	227	672	5,932

(1) EL, A (1994); NL (1995). (2) NL (1992); EL, A (1994).

(million ECU) Table 7.24

Manufacture of cement, lime and plaster (NACE Rev. 1 26.5)
Market related indicators in the EU

	1988	1989	1990	1991	1992	1993	1994	1995	1996	1997	1998
Apparent consumption	12,422	13,359	14,077	14,083	:	:	:	:	:	:	:
Exports	104	123	121	248	175	231	363	196	390	368	241
Imports	28	35	33	119	:	:	:	:	:	:	:
Trade balance	76	88	88	129	:	:	:	:	:	:	:
Export ratio (%)	0.8	0.9	0.9	1.7	1.3	1.8	2.6	:	2.8	2.5	1.5
Import penetration ratio (%)	0.2	0.3	0.2	0.8	:	:	:	:	:	:	:
Cover ratio (%)	367.7	353.6	370.2	208.6	:	:	:	:	:	:	:

(million ECU) Table 7.25

Manufacture of cement, lime and plaster (NACE Rev. 1 26.5)
Market related indicators, 1998

	B/L	DK	D	EL	E	F	IRL	I	NL	A	P	FIN	S	UK
Apparent consumption (1)	:	:	3,397	286	2,336	2,386	:	2,303	456	627	848	111	162	1,193
Exports	182	68	265	181	178	183	16	120	61	13	3	3	32	106
Imports	73	19	315	2	133	169	38	74	227	76	62	34	20	110
Trade balance	109	48	-50	178	45	14	-23	46	-166	-63	-60	-31	12	-4
Export ratio (%) (1)	:	:	7.9	44.4	7.5	7.6	:	5.1	22.4	2.0	0.3	4.0	18.4	8.9
Import penetration ratio (%) (1)	:	:	9.3	1.2	5.7	7.1	:	3.2	63.2	8.5	7.4	30.9	12.3	9.2
Cover ratio (%)	248.7	347.5	84.2	7,407.8	134.0	108.3	40.4	161.7	26.8	17.3	4.3	9.3	160.8	96.2

(1) EL, A (1994); NL (1995).

Table 7.26

Manufacture of cement, lime and plaster (NACE Rev. 1 26.5)
Labour related indicators, 1998

	EU-15	B	DK	D	EL	E	F	IRL	I	L	NL	A	P	FIN	S	UK
Personnel costs (million ECU) (1)	2,785	171	:	775	127	359	355	:	459	:	35	130	60	8	27	215
Personnel costs/employee (thousand ECU) (2)	:	52.8	:	47.2	26.3	34.0	48.4	:	29.0	:	:	43.2	:	36.8	41.6	30.2
Social charges/personnel costs (%) (3)	:	30.3	:	22.8	23.8	18.0	30.1	:	35.5	:	21.9	21.3	:	23.4	30.5	11.3
Labour productivity (thousand ECU/head) (4)	89.9	140.7	:	86.5	34.1	93.8	134.4	:	56.9	:	120.9	82.2	:	155.9	92.6	101.8
Wage adjusted labour productivity (%) (2)	:	243.6	:	183.5	129.9	286.9	258.8	:	191.9	:	:	190.3	:	431.9	224.7	242.8

(1) EL, A (1994); NL (1995). (2) EL, A (1994); I (1995); B, D, E, F, FIN, S, UK (1996). (3) EL, A, S (1994); NL (1995). (4) NL (1992); EU-15, EL, A (1994).

Source: Eurostat (SBS, EBT)

Table 7.27 (million ECU)

Manufacture of articles of concrete, plaster and cement (NACE Rev. 1 26.6)

Production related indicators in the EU

	1988	1989	1990	1991	1992	1993	1994	1995	1996	1997	1998
Production value	27,784	31,994	34,492	35,927	38,031	36,109	37,454	38,562	38,098	37,780	39,356
Producer price index (1995=100)	:	:	87.6	90.8	93.5	95.8	97.9	100.0	91.4	90.8	91.7
Value added	10,401	11,517	12,323	12,637	12,954	12,372	13,172	13,573	13,262	13,463	14,261
Number of persons employed (thousands)	310.7	325.4	336.5	336.0	330.3	303.6	292.1	287.5	282.5	277.5	279.8

Table 7.28 (million ECU)

Manufacture of articles of concrete, plaster and cement (NACE Rev. 1 26.6)

Production related indicators, 1998

	B	DK	D	EL	E	F	IRL	I	L	NL	A	P	FIN	S	UK
Production value	2,286	987	12,418	292	4,275	4,341	:	4,006	:	1,863	1,772	941	706	710	4,240
Value added (1)	684	393	5,463	60	1,227	1,165	103	1,320	:	730	774	:	225	233	1,513
Number of persons employed (units) (1)(2)	11,424	7,081	80,363	3,227	41,211	32,191	2,804	30,684	:	13,023	10,446	11,336	4,639	5,061	26,815

(1) IRL (1990). (2) NL (1992).

Table 7.29 (million ECU)

Manufacture of articles of concrete, plaster and cement (NACE Rev. 1 26.6)

Market related indicators in the EU

	1988	1989	1990	1991	1992	1993	1994	1995	1996	1997	1998
Apparent consumption	27,579	31,746	34,318	35,725	37,869	35,971	37,308	38,396	37,894	37,478	38,983
Exports	271	298	252	297	278	269	328	382	416	486	536
Imports	66	49	79	96	116	131	182	216	213	184	163
Trade balance	205	249	173	202	162	138	146	166	203	302	373
Export ratio (%)	1.0	0.9	0.7	0.8	0.7	0.7	0.9	1.0	1.1	1.3	1.4
Import penetration ratio (%)	0.2	0.2	0.2	0.3	0.3	0.4	0.5	0.6	0.6	0.5	0.4
Cover ratio (%)	409.4	606.0	319.3	310.1	239.4	205.6	180.2	176.8	195.4	264.5	328.2

Table 7.30 (million ECU)

Manufacture of articles of concrete, plaster and cement (NACE Rev. 1 26.6)

Market related indicators, 1998

	B/L	DK	D	EL	E	F	IRL	I	NL	A	P	FIN	S	UK
Apparent consumption	:	887	12,307	290	4,092	4,426	:	3,761	1,880	1,755	955	687	698	4,095
Exports	297	143	408	12	205	146	15	280	99	89	9	33	52	244
Imports	151	43	297	10	21	231	54	35	116	72	23	14	40	99
Trade balance	146	100	111	2	184	-85	-39	245	-17	17	-14	19	12	144
Export ratio (%)	:	14.5	3.3	4.1	4.8	3.4	:	7.0	5.3	5.0	0.9	4.6	7.3	5.7
Import penetration ratio (%)	:	4.8	2.4	3.4	0.5	5.2	:	0.9	6.2	4.1	2.4	2.0	5.7	2.4
Cover ratio (%)	196.5	334.0	137.4	121.8	977.7	63.1	28.4	801.7	85.3	123.6	37.6	236.9	131.4	245.5

Table 7.31

Manufacture of articles of concrete, plaster and cement (NACE Rev. 1 26.6)

Labour related indicators, 1998

	EU-15	B	DK	D	EL	E	F	IRL	I	L	NL	A	P	FIN	S	UK
Personnel costs (million ECU) (1)	8,430	396	250	3,113	45	704	1,020	54	836	:	410	436	123	134	171	707
Personnel costs/employee (thousand ECU) (2)	33.1	36.8	36.1	38.7	15.4	19.4	33.2	:	24.9	:	:	42.6	:	30.5	35.3	22.0
Social charges/personnel costs (%) (3)	22.0	29.2	5.0	20.1	23.9	21.3	34.0	:	36.7	:	13.5	23.2	:	23.2	30.4	11.4
Labour productivity (thousand ECU/head) (4)	51.0	59.8	55.6	68.0	18.6	29.8	36.2	36.8	43.0	:	45.9	74.1	:	48.5	45.9	56.4
Wage adjusted labour productivity (%) (2)	142.6	140.7	148.9	150.1	91.1	141.8	131.7	:	145.4	:	:	159.6	:	135.6	131.4	207.9

(1) IRL (1990). (2) EU-15, EL, I, A (1995); B, DK, D, E, F, FIN, S, UK (1996). (3) EU-15, S (1995). (4) IRL (1990); NL (1992).

Source: Eurostat (SBS, EBT)

(million ECU) Table 7.32

Cutting, shaping and finishing of stone (NACE Rev. 1 26.7)
Production related indicators in the EU

	1988	1989	1990	1991	1992	1993	1994	1995	1996	1997	1998
Production value	3,455	4,216	4,364	4,884	5,005	4,747	4,944	5,750	:	:	:
Producer price index (1995=100)	:	:	86.3	90.6	94.6	95.9	96.9	100.0	101.0	102.4	105.3
Value added	1,313	1,518	1,549	1,858	1,897	1,810	1,927	2,227	:	:	:
Number of persons employed (thousands)	64.0	68.5	70.2	76.0	73.2	69.1	70.9	79.0	:	:	:

(million ECU) Table 7.33

Cutting, shaping and finishing of stone (NACE Rev. 1 26.7)
Production related indicators, 1998

	B	DK	D	EL	E	F	IRL	I	L	NL	A	P	FIN	S	UK
Production value (1)	393	14	677	90	1,824	318	41	1,728	5	61	128	494	95	43	208
Value added (1)	114	7	292	31	717	131	19	544	2	26	73	:	42	18	119
Number of persons employed (units) (1)(2)	3,644	134	6,896	1,963	33,350	4,528	581	11,246	62	452	1,920	11,214	1,219	770	2,462

(1) DK (1995). (2) NL (1992).

(million ECU) Table 7.34

Cutting, shaping and finishing of stone (NACE Rev. 1 26.7)
Market related indicators in the EU

	1988	1989	1990	1991	1992	1993	1994	1995	1996	1997	1998
Apparent consumption	2,679	3,241	3,341	3,911	4,086	3,916	3,992	4,769	:	:	:
Exports	823	1,025	1,073	1,040	1,010	938	1,069	1,111	1,278	1,401	1,423
Imports	46	50	50	66	91	107	117	130	177	173	224
Trade balance	776	975	1,023	973	919	831	952	981	1,101	1,228	1,198
Export ratio (%)	23.8	24.3	24.6	21.3	20.2	19.8	21.6	19.3	:	:	:
Import penetration ratio (%)	1.7	1.6	1.5	1.7	2.2	2.7	2.9	2.7	:	:	:
Cover ratio (%)	1,772.9	2,031.0	2,150.8	1,563.7	1,112.1	875.1	914.5	855.5	721.4	808.2	634.6

(million ECU) Table 7.35

Cutting, shaping and finishing of stone (NACE Rev. 1 26.7)
Market related indicators, 1998

	B/L	DK	D	EL	E	F	IRL	I	NL	A	P	FIN	S	UK
Apparent consumption (1)	:	16	1,133	12	1,409	371	52	96	112	177	385	65	48	307
Exports	84	15	56	84	461	112	7	1,678	21	9	126	34	4	22
Imports	105	30	511	7	46	166	18	46	72	58	17	4	9	121
Trade balance	-21	-14	-456	77	415	-53	-11	1,632	-52	-49	109	30	-5	-99
Export ratio (%) (1)	:	132.1	8.2	93.8	25.3	35.3	17.1	97.1	34.4	7.0	25.5	35.7	8.5	10.5
Import penetration ratio (%) (1)	:	127.9	45.1	55.6	3.3	44.6	34.0	47.5	64.5	32.7	4.4	6.1	18.7	39.4
Cover ratio (%)	80.1	51.3	10.9	1,210.2	1,003.8	67.7	40.0	3,667.8	28.8	15.6	738.2	860.4	40.3	18.1

(1) DK (1995).

Table 7.36

Cutting, shaping and finishing of stone (NACE Rev. 1 26.7)
Labour related indicators, 1998

	EU-15	B	DK	D	EL	E	F	IRL	I	L	NL	A	P	FIN	S	UK
Personnel costs (million ECU) (1)	1,563	74	4	237	24	481	123	11	333	1	16	65	94	30	14	56
Personnel costs/employee (thousand ECU) (2)	24.9	26.7	30.7	32.3	13.6	17.0	28.7	18.6	27.0	22.8	:	34.8	:	27.6	19.7	19.2
Social charges/personnel costs (%) (3)	24.7	33.8	2.7	19.6	23.6	22.1	29.2	17.9	38.3	:	19.5	23.7	:	21.8	28.5	11.6
Labour productivity (thousand ECU/head) (4)	28.2	31.3	49.3	42.4	15.6	21.5	29.0	33.2	48.3	40.0	35.0	38.1	:	34.6	23.9	48.5
Wage adjusted labour productivity (%) (2)	113.0	116.1	160.5	130.9	105.2	132.9	113.0	152.2	164.0	177.5	:	116.2	:	157.1	122.6	160.8

(1) EU-15, DK (1995); NL (1997). (2) EU-15, DK, EL, I, A (1995); B, D, E, F, L, FIN, S, UK (1996). (3) EU-15, DK, S (1995); NL (1997). (4) NL (1992); EU-15, DK (1995).

Source: Eurostat (SBS, EBT)

Table 7.37 (million ECU)

Manufacture of other non-metallic mineral products (NACE Rev. 1 26.8)

Production related indicators in the EU

	1988	1989	1990	1991	1992	1993	1994	1995	1996	1997	1998
Production value	8,998	8,850	7,834	7,692	7,503	7,252	7,946	:	:	:	:
Producer price index (1995=100)	:	:	91.5	91.1	92.4	94.2	95.4	100.0	105.4	107.9	113.9
Value added	3,606	3,442	3,030	2,996	2,964	2,915	3,177	:	:	:	:
Number of persons employed (thousands)	102.6	92.3	79.5	75.8	71.4	65.7	65.7	:	:	:	:

Table 7.38 (million ECU)

Manufacture of other non-metallic mineral products (NACE Rev. 1 26.8)

Production related indicators, 1998

	B	DK	D	EL	E	F	IRL	I	L	NL	A	P	FIN	S	UK
Production value	215	439	3,252	17	797	1,314	72	838	:	515	270	:	208	342	1,309
Value added	58	181	1,230	5	243	529	22	272	:	174	138	:	77	112	571
Number of persons employed (units) (1)	1,129	3,150	22,843	281	4,112	9,161	413	5,686	:	3,379	2,814	:	1,470	2,369	12,366

(1) NL (1992).

Table 7.39 (million ECU)

Manufacture of other non-metallic mineral products (NACE Rev. 1 26.8)

Market related indicators in the EU

	1988	1989	1990	1991	1992	1993	1994	1995	1996	1997	1998
Apparent consumption	8,644	8,478	7,472	7,353	7,260	6,767	7,422	:	:	:	:
Exports	796	889	888	909	895	1,099	1,208	1,351	1,418	1,627	1,634
Imports	442	517	526	570	652	614	684	706	782	850	997
Trade balance	354	372	362	339	243	485	524	645	636	777	636
Export ratio (%)	8.8	10.0	11.3	11.8	11.9	15.2	15.2	:	:	:	:
Import penetration ratio (%)	5.1	6.1	7.0	7.8	9.0	9.1	9.2	:	:	:	:
Cover ratio (%)	180.1	171.9	168.8	159.5	137.3	179.0	176.7	191.4	181.4	191.4	163.8

Table 7.40 (million ECU)

Manufacture of other non-metallic mineral products (NACE Rev. 1 26.8)

Market related indicators, 1998

	B/L	DK	D	EL	E	F	IRL	I	NL	A	P	FIN	S	UK
Apparent consumption	:	479	2,817	38	860	1,129	100	742	466	222	:	184	375	1,191
Exports	305	63	1,341	12	160	690	30	519	294	237	19	92	91	612
Imports	216	104	906	33	222	505	57	424	245	189	57	68	125	493
Trade balance	89	-41	435	-21	-63	185	-28	95	49	48	-38	24	-34	118
Export ratio (%)	:	14.5	41.2	69.1	20.0	52.5	41.2	62.0	57.2	88.1	:	44.2	26.8	46.7
Import penetration ratio (%)	:	21.7	32.2	86.0	25.9	44.7	57.6	57.1	52.6	85.5	:	36.8	33.4	41.4
Cover ratio (%)	141.0	61.0	148.0	36.5	71.8	136.6	51.5	122.5	120.0	125.5	32.8	136.2	73.0	124.0

Table 7.41

Manufacture of other non-metallic mineral products (NACE Rev. 1 26.8)

Labour related indicators, 1998

	EU-15	B	DK	D	EL	E	F	IRL	I	L	NL	A	P	FIN	S	UK
Personnel costs (million ECU) (1)	2,073	44	117	1,013	5	133	377	10	176	:	119	110	:	48	78	334
Personnel costs/employee (thousand ECU) (2)	:	39.2	37.7	41.8	19.7	26.0	43.6	24.2	28.2	:	:	40.0	:	32.8	34.3	22.6
Social charges/personnel costs (%) (3)	:	26.8	3.7	20.0	21.0	21.1	30.0	17.0	36.9	:	16.6	25.1	:	22.7	28.7	12.7
Labour productivity (thousand ECU/head) (4)	48.4	51.0	57.6	53.8	19.1	59.1	57.7	52.4	47.8	:	47.8	48.9	:	52.3	47.3	46.2
Wage adjusted labour productivity (%) (2)	:	140.3	157.3	131.2	143.3	160.7	126.1	185.5	153.8	:	:	129.0	:	172.1	139.4	179.2

(1) EU-15 (1994); E (1997). (2) EL, I, A (1995); B, DK, D, E, F, FIN, S, UK (1996). (3) S (1995); E (1997). (4) NL (1992); EU-15 (1994).

Source: Eurostat (SBS, EBT)

Metals

Industrial description

The manufacture of basic metals may be broken down into ferrous and non-ferrous metals for the purposes of analysis. In 1998 the production value of this industry was equal to some 185.9 billion ECU in the EU, corresponding to about 5% of total manufacturing output.

The manufacture of basic metals leads to the production of traditional and frequently used materials. Through technological progress, products have developed and are catered specifically to customers' wishes. Nevertheless, the metal industry faces a wider range of competition from substitute materials, above all plastics, which are frequently used in the manufacture of motor vehicles, household goods or pipes and couplings. Metals face difficulty in competing in terms of weight, resistance to wear, rust and price. Furthermore, even more modern materials such as advanced ceramics have already established themselves as components for markets such as the automotive industry and micro-electronics' industry.

Within the larger Member States metal companies in Germany and Italy accounted for the highest output, 54.0 billion ECU and 28.7 billion ECU respectively, or some 44.5% of total European production. However, if we compare the share of basic metal production in total manufacturing, Luxembourg reported an extraordinarily high production specialisation ratio (six times higher than the European average). Compared to this figure, the specialisation of Belgium and Austria was more moderate, whilst being well above average (1.5 times).

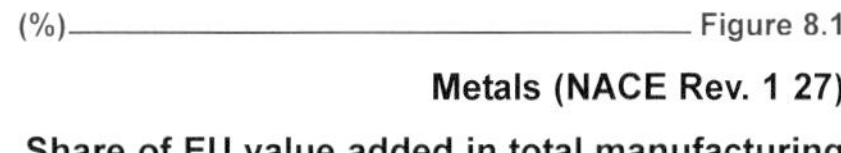

(%) Figure 8.1

Metals (NACE Rev. 1 27)

Share of EU value added in total manufacturing

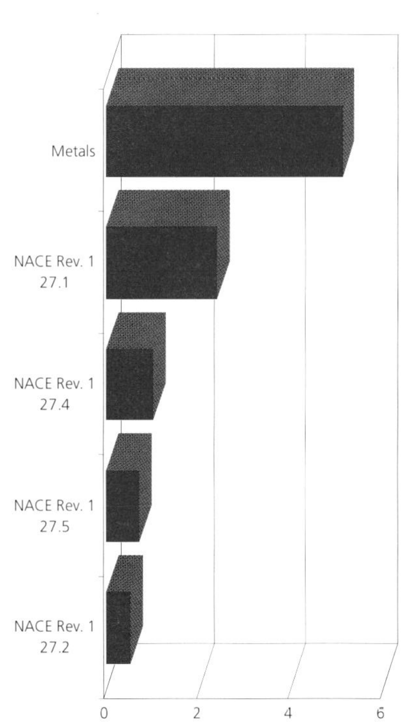

Source: Eurostat (SBS)

The activities covered in this chapter include:

27.1: manufacture of basic iron and steel and ferro-alloys (ECSC, European Coal and Steel community);
27.2: manufacture of tubes;
27.3: other first processing of iron and steel and production of non-ECSC ferro-alloys;
27.4: manufacture of basic precious and non-ferrous metals;
27.5: casting of metals.

Figure 8.2 (1988=100)

Metals (NACE Rev. 1 27)

Production, employment and value added compared to EU total manufacturing

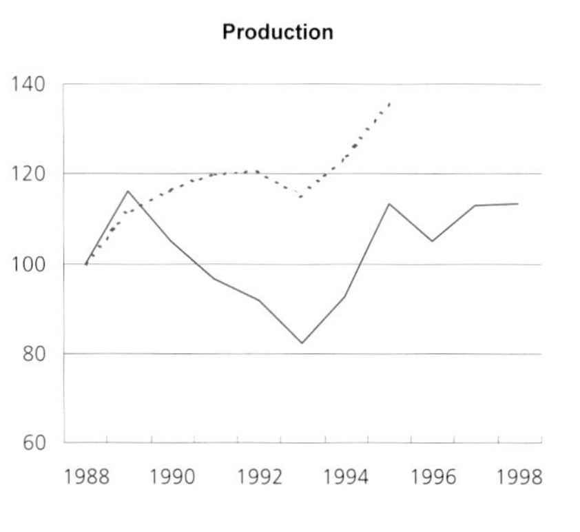

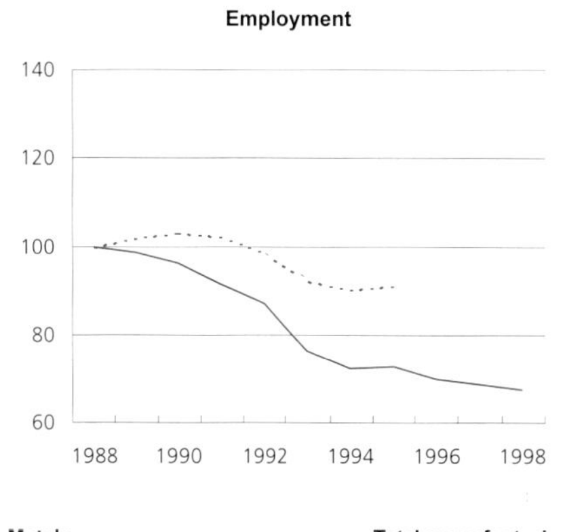

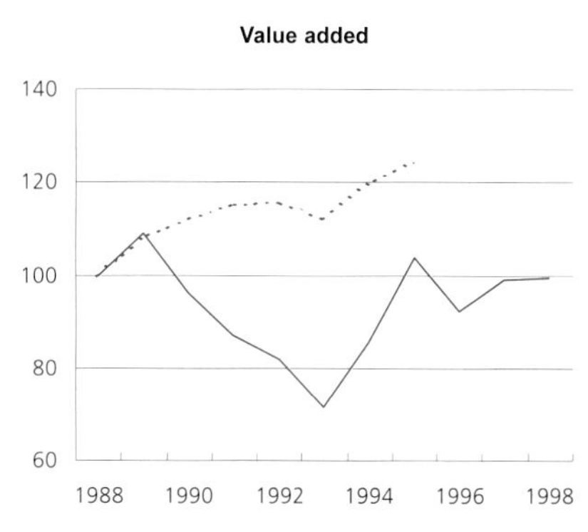

—— Metals ---- Total manufacturing

Source: Eurostat (SBS)

The global market for basic metals displayed a structural imbalance between supply and demand, despite the reductions in capacity that were made in recent decades. Production facilities in developing countries and new materials emerging as substitutes to ferrous and non-ferrous metals meant that there was excess supply, a problem further exacerbated by the fact that many downstream industries made raw material savings.

Growth rates (in volume) of the basic metals industry were lower than its downstream industries, as third country competition became more intense. Competition increased with production from the Central and Eastern European Countries (CEEC) coming into European markets. With weak domestic demand, the CEECs and the former Soviet Bloc manufacturers looked to exports as a way of generating revenue.

Figure 8.3

Metals (NACE Rev. 1 27)

International comparison of main indicators in current prices

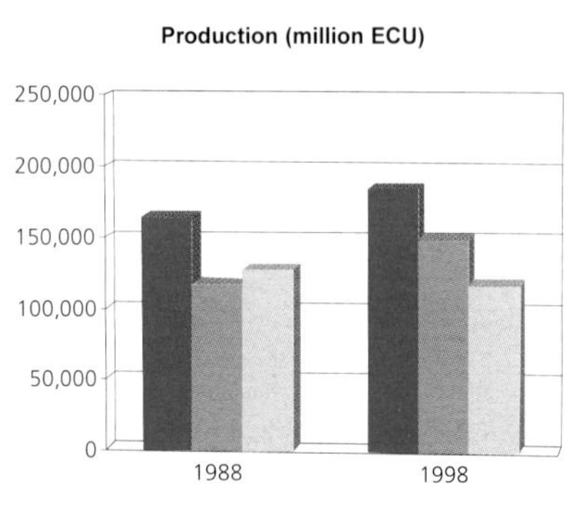

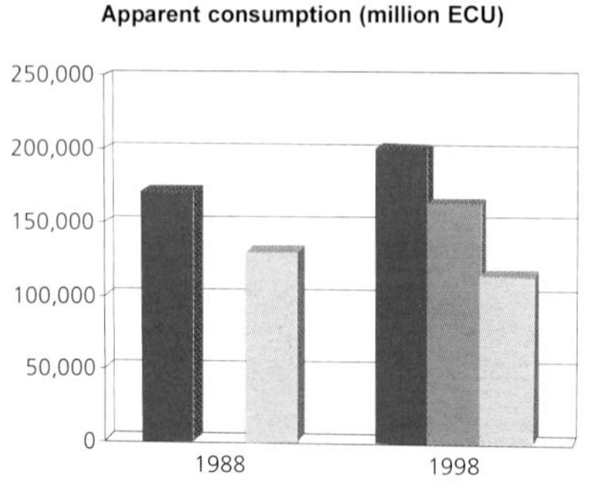

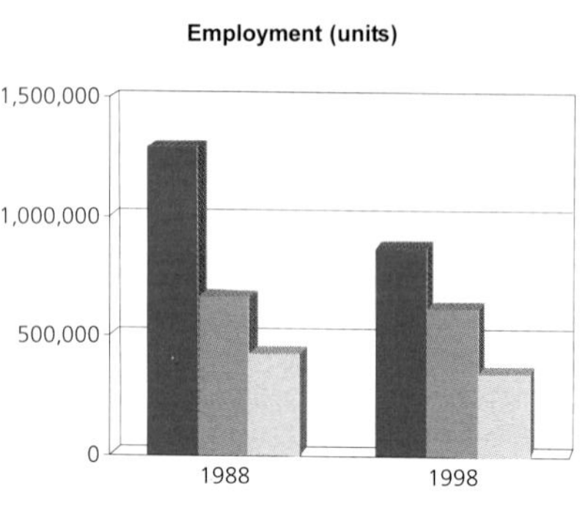

EU-15 USA Japan

Source: Eurostat (SBS)

(ECU/hour) Figure 8.4

Metals (NACE Rev. 1 27)

Labour costs by Member State, 1996

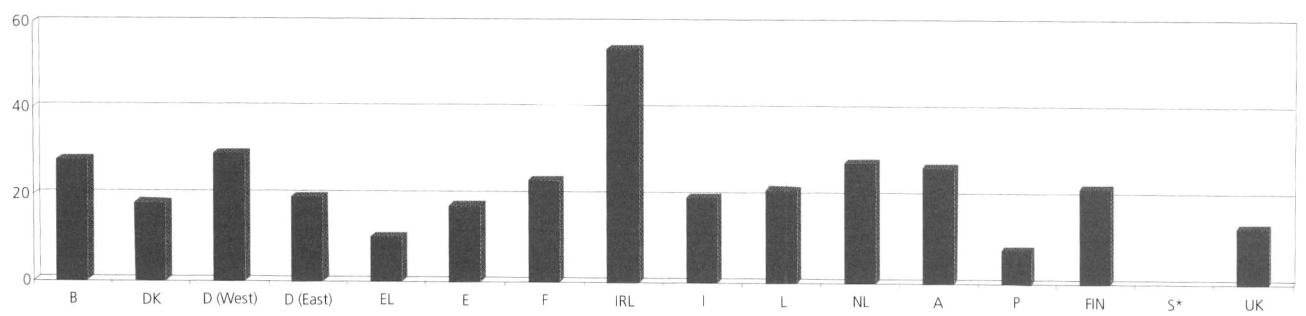

Source: Eurostat (LCS)

Recent trends

In the course of the nineties European production of basic metals increased at a moderate pace, whilst employment figures fell following rationalisation measures. As sales of basic metals were largely influenced by the general business cycle, the sector reported a substantial decline between 1989 and 1993. Since then production values (in constant prices) were on an upward trend, with large gains in Italy and France (up by 5.0% and 4.5% per annum between 1993 and 1998).

The number of persons employed in the EU decreased by 2.4% per annum between 1993 and 1995. There were larger reductions in Belgium and Portugal (both down by 6.4% per annum), whilst Finland was the only country to report an expansion in its workforce, rising 2.0% per annum. Innovation and productivity gains led to higher output per person employed: in the EU the ratio increased from 137.6 thousand ECU of production value per head in 1993 to 213.2 thousand ECU in 1998.

Foreign trade

In the EU the manufacture of basic metals relied heavily on imported raw materials, as metal reserves were low or even non-existent in the EU. These trends were reflected in the evolution of the trade balance, with the trade deficit equal to 15.1 billion ECU in 1998, twice as high as in 1988. The foreign trade of metals was covered within the framework of the World Trade Organisation (WTO). General distortions within the market were covered by bilateral or multilateral agreements in order to minimise the effects of tariff and non-tariff measures.

(%) Table 8.1

Metals (NACE Rev. 1 27)

Composition of the labour force, 1997

	Females	Part-time	Highly-educated
EU-15	12.9	:	:
B	6.7	:	17.7
DK	33.4	:	22.1
D	14.4	3.3	13.9
EL	:	:	:
E	6.8	:	22.9
F	11.1	4.4	12.2
IRL	16.4	2.9	15.3
I	11.8	2.9	2.9
L	:	:	10.7
NL	12.6	12.0	17.3
A	13.3	7.6	:
P	19.6	:	:
FIN	:	:	13.2
S	8.5	6.9	11.6
UK	11.7	3.8	14.8

Source: Eurostat (LFS)

Figure 8.5

Metals (NACE Rev. 1 27)

Destination of EU exports, 1998

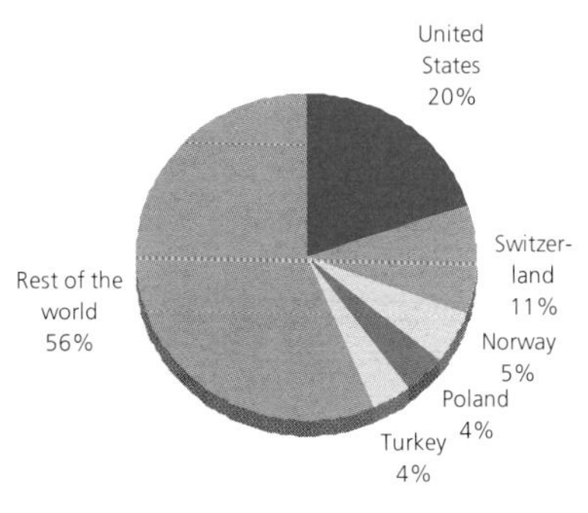

Source: Eurostat (Comext)

Figure 8.6

Metals (NACE Rev. 1 27)

Origin of EU imports, 1998

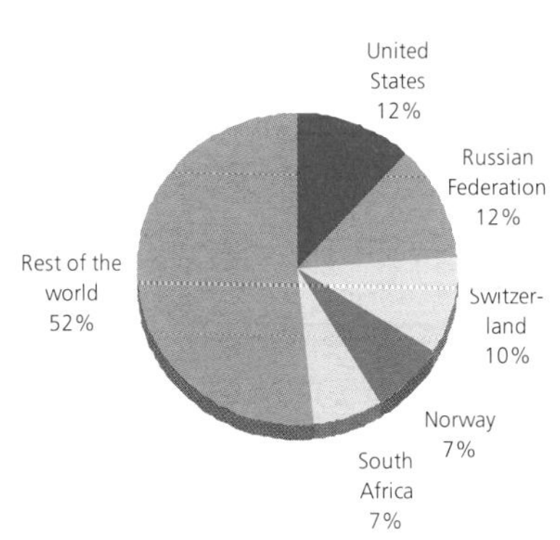

Source: Eurostat (Comext)

Ferrous metals

(NACE Rev. 1 27.1 to 27.3, 27.51 and 27.52)

The processing of basic ferrous metals encompasses four Groups within the NACE Rev. 1 classification system. Basic iron, steel and ferro-alloys (ECSC[1]) made up around 60% of the sector, including flat products (such as hot-rolled wide strips, sheets and plates) and long products (such as rods, bars and heavy sections). The manufacture of cast iron and steel tubes accounted for around 15% and the casting of iron and of steel just under 15%. Other first processing of iron and steel accounted for around 12% of the total (cold drawing, cold rolling of narrow strip, cold forming or folding, wire drawing and the production on non-ECSC ferro-alloys).

In terms of production values the basic ferrous metals made up around 3.5% of total manufacturing in the EU in 1998. During the course of the nineties their share decreased by a third, largely as a result of competition from other materials and reductions in demand from the defence industry.

International comparison showed that the EU industry was about 50% larger than in either Japan or the USA. The manufacture of crude steel in the EU[2] was equal to 156.7 million tonnes in 1998, whilst comparable figures in the USA and Japan were 97.7 million tonnes and 93.5 million tonnes respectively.

Demand for iron and steel comes from many downstream industries (construction, automotive industry, further processing of metals, mechanical engineering, as well as consumer goods' industries). Demand largely followed the cyclical business evolution of downstream industries.

Investment in machinery and equipment also led to a more efficient use of materials and energy. In the casting of metals increased automation was necessary to meet customers' demands for exact, but diverse products, resulting in more specialised foundries. In the first processing of iron and steel the on-going integration of computers into production lines facilitated higher quality products, as gauge, mechanical properties and surface condition were under stricter control.

Collection and processing of iron and steel was organised entirely by private operators in the EU. Scrap has become an internationally traded commodity: in the EU apparent consumption of steel scrap accounted for 86.8 million tonnes in 1997. Demand for steel scrap declines when the price of iron ore is low.

1) European Coal and Steel Community.
2) Excluding Denmark, Greece, Ireland and Portugal; data provided by IISI (International Iron and Steel Institute).

Figure 8.7

Ferrous metals (NACE Rev. 1 27.1 to 27.3)

Production and employment in the Triad

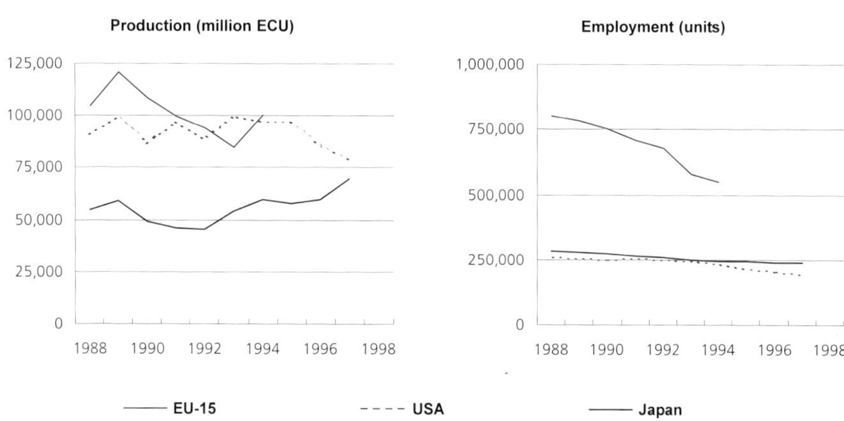

Source: Eurostat (SBS)

Figure 8.8 (%)

Ferrous metals (NACE Rev. 1 27.1 to 27.3)

Production and export specialisation by Member State, 1998

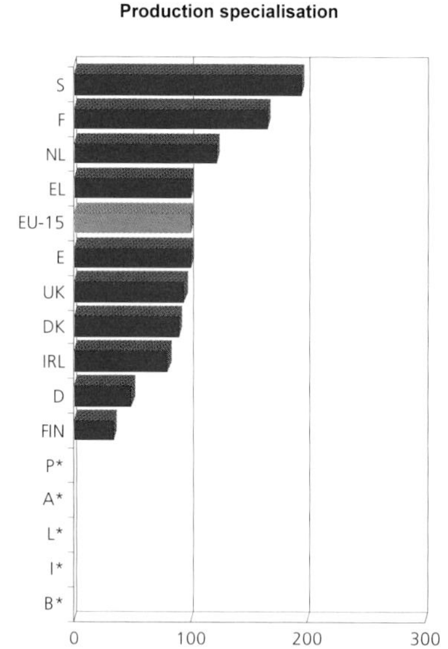

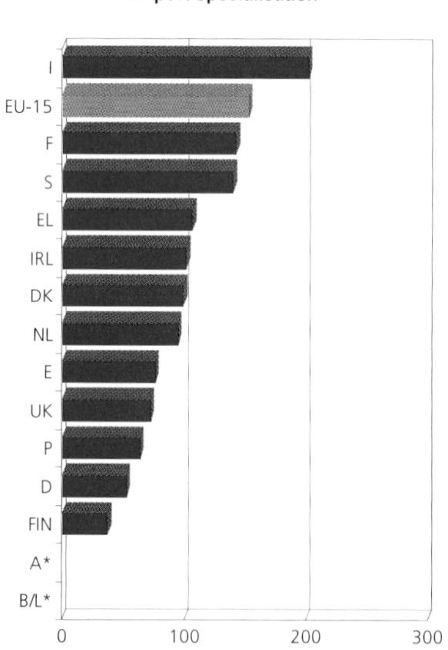

Source: Eurostat (SBS)

The ferrous metal market was characterised by overcapacity, explaining in part declining profit margins. CEECs gained market share in the EU with low price products, with imports accounting for 68.9% of EU demand in 1998, an increase of 25.0 percentage points on 1988. The share of Eastern European imports in extra-EU imports (in volume terms) was equal to 43.4% in 1998. Corresponding to commitments in the Uruguay Round the average bound rate of EU tariffs for steel products was 2.9% in 1999, which will disappear by 2004. The highest rate was applied to certain steel tube products (5% in 1999).

The iron and steel industry saw increased concentration, with a tendency to see production integrated with the manufacture of fabricated steel products, in order to offer a broad product range. In July 1999, the European Commission accepted the merger between British Steel and Hoogovens to form the third largest steel company in the world (and the largest in the EU, with 22.5 million tonnes of production capacity). This was the latest in a series of European steel mergers, following Thyssen and Krupp (both Germany), Usinor (France) and Cockerill Sambre (Belgium), as well as Arbed (Luxembourg) taking a stake in Aceralia (Spain).

POSCO (Republic of Korea) had the highest output in the world in 1998 (25.6 million tonnes), followed by Nippon Steel (JP) with 25.1 million tonnes.

Asia was an important export market for European steel manufacturers. In 1998 the largest consumers of finished steel products were found in Asia: Singapore, the Republic of Korea and Japan (1.2 tonnes, 830 and 635 kilograms per capita respectively), due to high use in transport infrastructure and construction activities.

Figure 8.9

Ferrous metals (NACE Rev. 1 27.1 to 27.3) Destination of EU exports, 1998

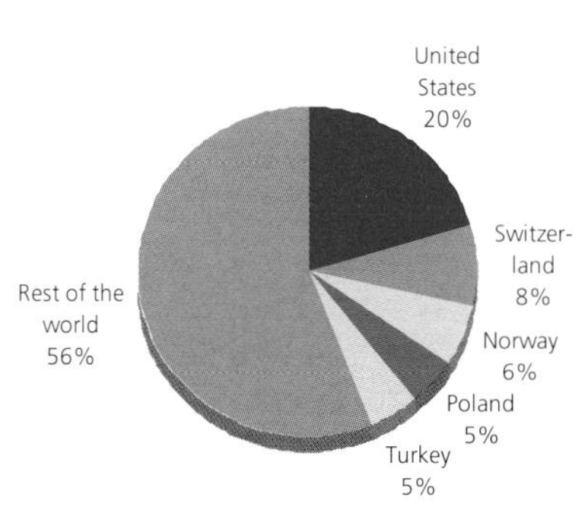

Source: Eurostat (Comext)

Figure 8.11

Production of crude steel in the Triad

(1991=100)

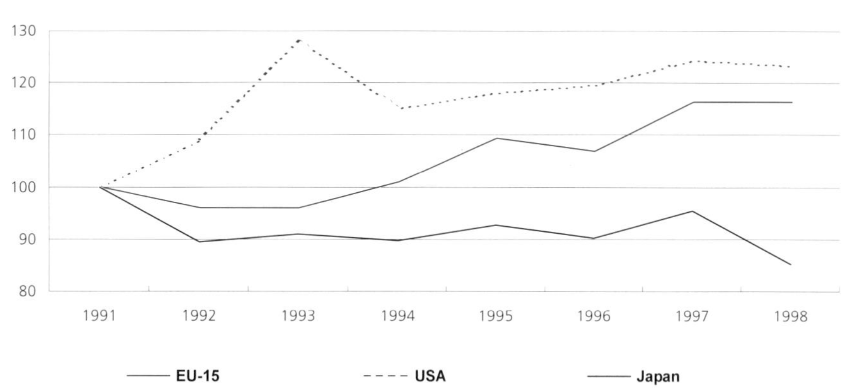

Source: IISI (International Iron and Steel Institute)

Figure 8.10

Ferrous metals (NACE Rev. 1 27.1 to 27.3) Origin of EU imports, 1998

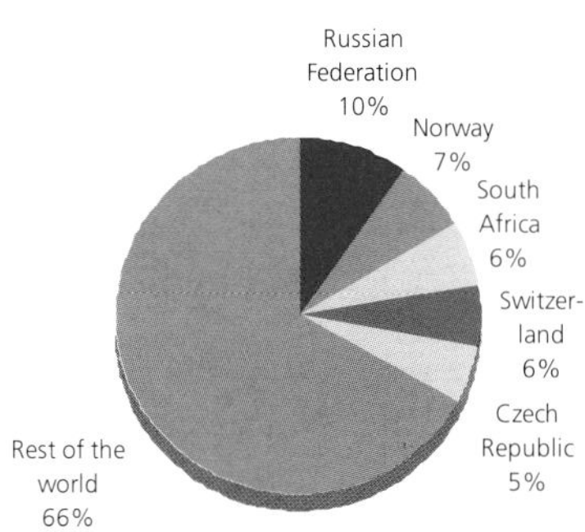

Source: Eurostat (Comext)

Manufacture of basic iron and steel

If we look at the breakdown of the sector, the manufacture of basic iron and steel and of ferro-alloys (ECSC, NACE Rev. 1 27.1) reported growth in the period 1993 to 1998. In volume terms output of crude steel increased by 22.3 million tonnes (or 2.5% per annum) between 1991 and 1997. In 1997 output reached 159.9 million tonnes in volume terms. Growth during 1997 was observed throughout Europe, except in Belgium and Ireland down by 0.3% and 1.1% respectively (figures from IISI, International Iron and Steel Institute). The OECD economic Steel Committee predicted a decline in world steel demand of 2.8% in 1999.

The manufacture of steel used two types of production process. The oxygen steel converter process was used to make bulk steel by large companies, whilst small and medium-sized companies produced special steel using the electric arc furnace. The choice of process was influenced by the availability of scrap (a basic raw material for the electric arc furnace), as well as energy costs and the skills of the workforce. During the course of the nineties the share of electric arc process in total production increased by 5 percentage points to 36.9% by 1997. Within the individual Member States the share of electric arc processing varied between 2.5% in the Netherlands and 100% in Greece, Ireland and Denmark.

The European Coal and Steel Community (ECSC) Treaty provides a legal framework for the iron and steel industry (NACE Rev. 1 27.1). The Treaty expires on 22nd July 2002. The Council of the European Union have agreed to use residual ECSC funds paid by the industry to support research and development activities in the iron and steel industry.

Manufacture of tubes

The EU had the highest steel tubes output within the Triad (13.4 million tonnes in 1998) compared to 8.5 million tonnes in Japan and 4.9 million tonnes in the USA. However, the production of steel tubes fell during the early nineties from a peak of 14.1 million tonnes in 1989.

There were some differences in output when looking at the trend of the different steel tubes' product lines between 1985 and 1998. Generally output was reduced in 1993 and again in 1996, whilst otherwise showing a rising trend. Production of seamless tubes saw output fall by almost a third to 3.7 million tonnes in 1998, whilst welded tubes with OD <= 406.4mm (outside diameter) expanded by almost 8% during the same period.

Figure 8.12 (tonnes)

Per capita output in the European iron and steel industry

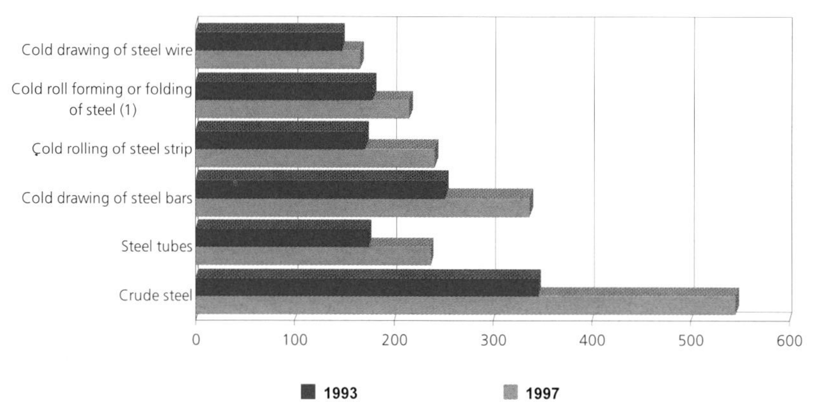

(1) 1996 instead of 1997.

Source: IISI, ESTA, CET, CIELFA, CIPF, EBBA

Figure 8.13 (1985=100)

Production of steel tubes in the EU

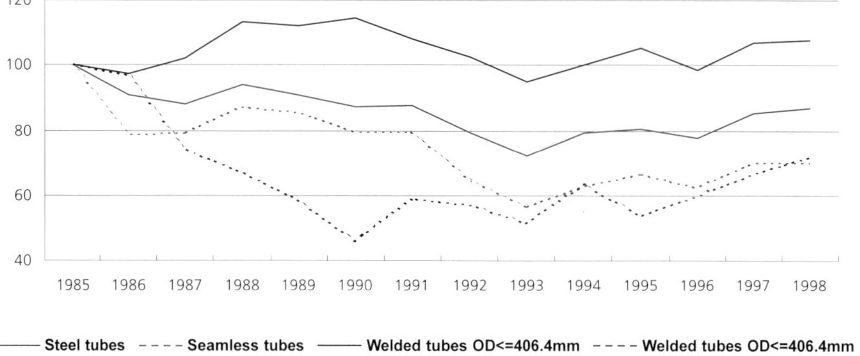

Source: ESTA (European Steel Tube Association)

During the eighties the former Soviet Union was a very important producer of steel tubes (20.8 million tonnes in 1988). This has subsequently declined at a spectacular rate, down by 77.2% between 1990 and 1998, according to ESTA.

Other first processing of iron and steel

Growth was observed in cold forming of steel flat products (NACE Rev. 1 27.33), a sector which was characterised by the fact that it was based in two main production areas: long sections (standard and customised sections) and wide sections (for building purposes, such as sandwich panels and profiled sheets). In the course of the nineties the former product line saw its output expand to 1.7 million tonnes in 1996 in the EU.

Cold rolling of steel strip (NACE Rev. 1 27.32) is produced in specialised rolling mills to meet different requirements of individual customers, which vary by industry (automotive components, hardware, office equipment, fasteners, bearings, chains and tubes). The latest figures for the production of steel strip showed that output rose by 16.2% in 1997, with production rising to 3.3 million tonnes (for EU-12).

The evolution of production for cold processing of steel wire (NACE Rev. 1 27.34) displayed a somewhat smoother course. In 1997 output increased by 1.4%, to reach 4.9 million tonnes (for EU-12), although still below the levels of 1995 (5.1 million tonnes). Products made of steel wire have a broad range of applications (such as strands, heavy welded mesh, welded link chains, hooks, springs and nails).

Casting of metals

In the EU[3] there were 1.5 thousand foundries operating in the casting of iron and steel industry in 1997. The number decreased by 2.4% when compared to 1996. Indeed, between 1993 and 1997 the number of foundries in the EU has declined by 194 units or 11.3%.

During the same period the number of persons employed also fell, down by 19.2% to 142.4 thousand persons, despite an increase in production values of 16.9%. Growth of 13.8% and 24.7% (1993-1997) was registered for iron and ductile iron castings, whilst steel castings increased moderately by 5.1%. With production processes in the main downstream industries (machinery and automotive industry) changing, the nature of contracts between foundries and customers was also modified, with just-in-time deliveries and new foundries often being located next to their customers and no longer their raw materials.

3) EU-15 without Greece, Ireland, Luxembourg and the Netherlands.

Figure 8.14

Production, first processing of steel in the EU (1)

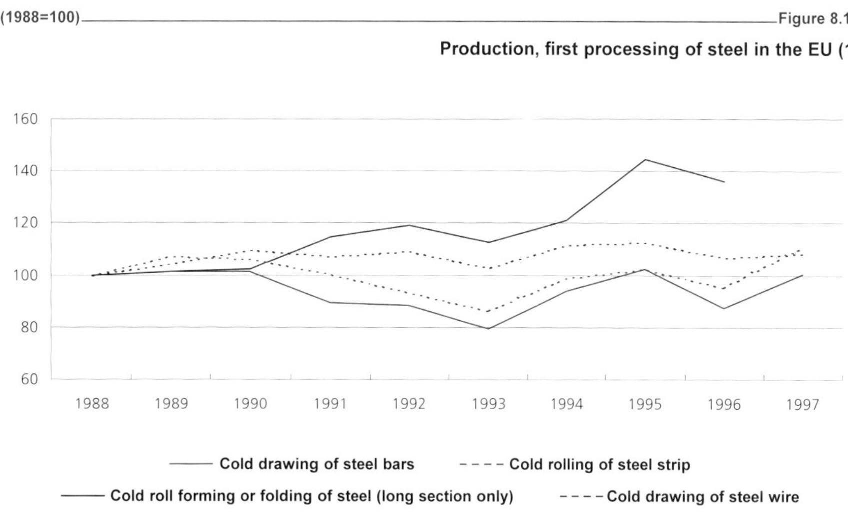

(1) EU-12 for NACE Rev. 1 27.31 and 27.32; excluding Finland and Sweden for NACE Rev. 1 27.34

Source: CET, CIELFA, CIPF, EBBA.

Figure 8.15

Production in volume terms in metal casting in the EU, 1997 (1)

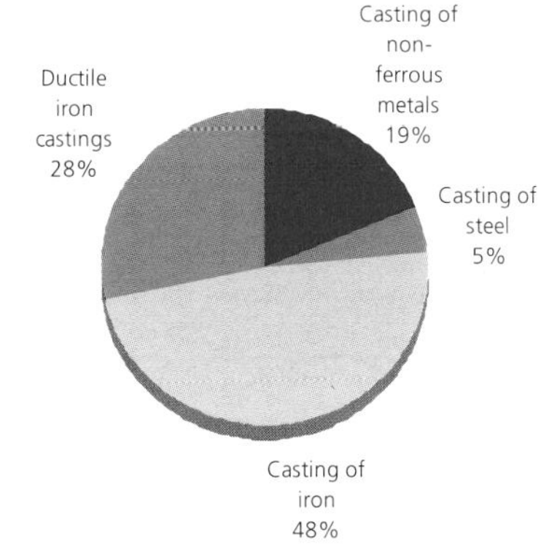

(1) Data included covers covers only Germany, France, Italy and the United Kingdom, accounting for 82.7% of casting in the EU.

Source: CAEF

Non-ferrous metals
(NACE Rev. 1 27.4, 27.53 and 27.54)

The manufacture of basic precious and non-ferrous metals includes the production and the refining of un-wrought metals, of metal alloys and of metal semi-products. Precious metals production encompassed gold, silver and platinum. The most important non-ferrous metals are aluminium, copper, zinc and lead. Aluminium production was the largest sector within non-ferrous metals.

In 1998 the manufacture of non-ferrous metals had a production value of some 52.0 billion ECU or around 1.4% of total EU manufacturing. German industry was responsible for 31.5% of the European total. Greece reported high production specialisation.

Non-ferrous metals are broadly used in manufacturing and demand often follows the business cycle. The main downstream industries of aluminium were construction, automotives and packaging. In Western Europe consumption of primary aluminium was equal to about 6 million tonnes per year, with 3 million tonnes produced in the form of rolled products, 2 million tonnes in extruded products and 0.5 million tonnes in other semis and aluminium foil. Aluminium has the advantage that it is both light, whilst being resistant to corrosion and providing electrical and thermal conductivity.

The use of copper, zinc and lead in downstream industries was somewhat more limited: copper was an important raw material in construction and the electronics industry, zinc in the automotive industry, appliance industry and construction, whilst lead consumption was dominated by batteries.

Downstream industries of precious metals differed somewhat from non-ferrous metals. Precious metals and all above gold were appreciated as financial investments. Within the manufacturing sector, precious metals are consumed in the jewellery industry, which dominated the demand for gold. A far smaller amount of gold was used in electronics, whilst silver was an important raw material for the photographic industry and platinum was used for catalytic converters.

Figure 8.16

Manufacture of basic precious and non-ferrous metals (NACE Rev. 1 27.4)
Production and employment in the Triad

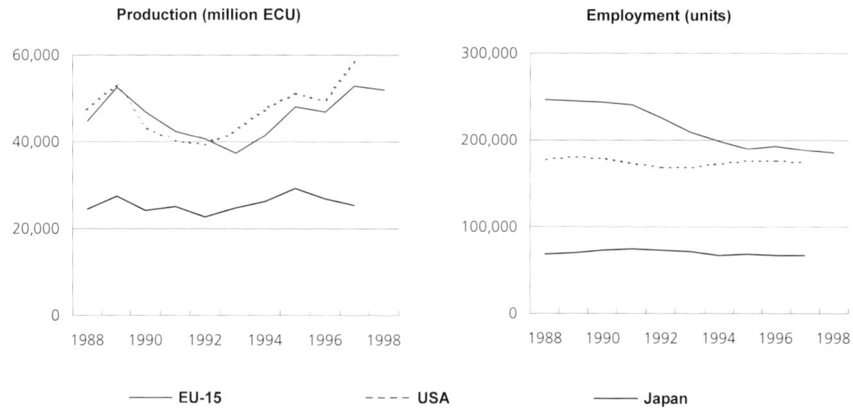

Source: Eurostat (SBS)

Figure 8.17 (%)

Manufacture of basic precious and non-ferrous metals (NACE Rev. 1 27.4)
Production and export specialisation by Member State, 1998

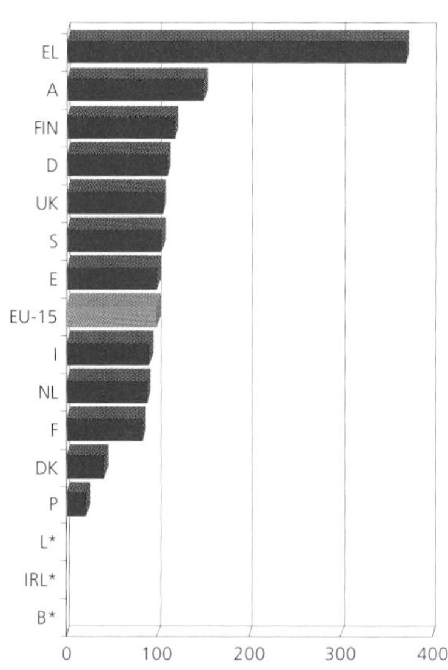

Source: Eurostat (SBS)

Within the EU there were few sources of precious and non-ferrous metals, which created a high dependency on imports of raw materials. The share of the EU in world production of silver reached just 3%, which was the highest within the precious metals (gold below 1% and platinum negligible).

Although the mining of non-ferrous metals was somewhat higher (for example 8% of the world production of zinc), there were large incentives to improve recycling in the EU (scrap and residues). In 1997 gold and silver scrap accounted for one fifth of industrial demand world-wide. Recycling was also strengthened by environmental waste policy, which attempted to reduce the amount of hazardous waste. For example batteries were recycled more and offered a new source for secondary lead. The copper industry received nearly 40% of its raw material needs from recycling (mainly old cables and pipes). The aluminium industry co-operated with packaging material producers and the retail trade to install an efficient collection and sorting system. The recycling of aluminium reduces energy consumption by 95% compared to primary smelting.

In the EU, production values increased by 3.9% per annum between 1993 and 1998 (in constant prices). Germany reported a higher growth rate of 6.0% per annum. Despite the long-term upward trend in output, the number of persons employed was reduced throughout the EU (except Finland), down by 2.5% per annum during the same period.

Castings of non-ferrous metals (NACE Rev. 1 27.53 and 27.54) saw their output rise as a result of increased demand from the automotive industry (up 9.8% to 2.3 million tonnes in 1997). The share of non-ferrous metals in castings rose to 18.5% in 1997 (up by 5 percentage points on 1985). In 1997 several countries reported a reduction in the number of foundries (especially Germany and France), explained by the closure of inefficient and underemployed plants.

Figure 8.18

Production in volume terms of non-ferrous metal casting in the EU, 1997 (1)

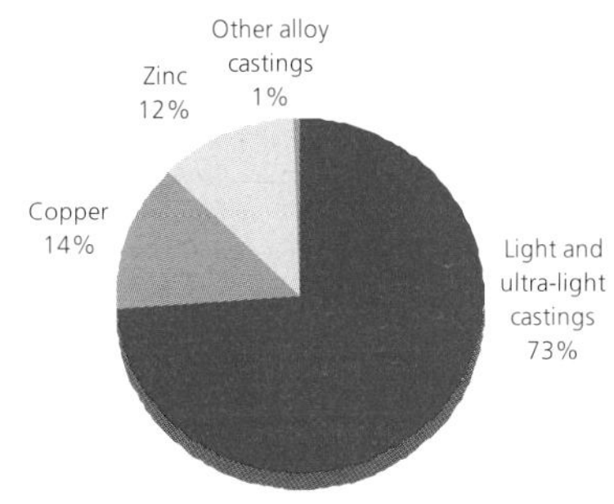

(1) Data included covers only Germany, France, Italy and the United Kingdom, accounting for 82.7% of casting in the EU.

Source: CAEF

The purchasing and selling prices of precious and non-ferrous metals were to a large extent determined by international commodity markets (London Metal Exchange, LME). Enterprises engaged in the basic metals industries handled the risk of fluctuating prices with hedging on the markets. The price of non-ferrous metals followed a downward trend between the middle of 1997 and the end of 1998 when the price of aluminium fell by around 30%. The fall in the aluminium price was caused by overcapacity and an increase in stocks in 1998 and 1999. In spring 1999 the gold price fell, partly as a result of the Bank of England's decision to auction just over half of its gold reserves.

The increased import flows of basic precious and non-ferrous metals into the EU were reflected in a negative trade balance, which grew by 53.2% to 20.0 billion ECU between 1993 and 1998. The share of imports in apparent consumption was equal to 44.2%. Non-ferrous and precious metals were subject to the general trade rules of the World Trade Organisation (WTO). In 1999 import duties varied between 0% for copper, nickel and precious metals and 6% for aluminium.

Figure 8.19

Manufacture of basic precious and non-ferrous metals (NACE Rev. 1 27.4) Destination of EU exports, 1998

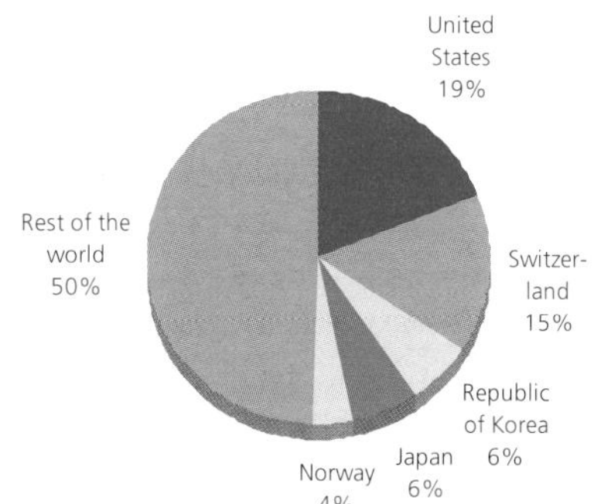

Source: Eurostat (Comext)

Figure 8.20

Manufacture of basic precious and non-ferrous metals (NACE Rev. 1 27.4) Origin of EU imports, 1998

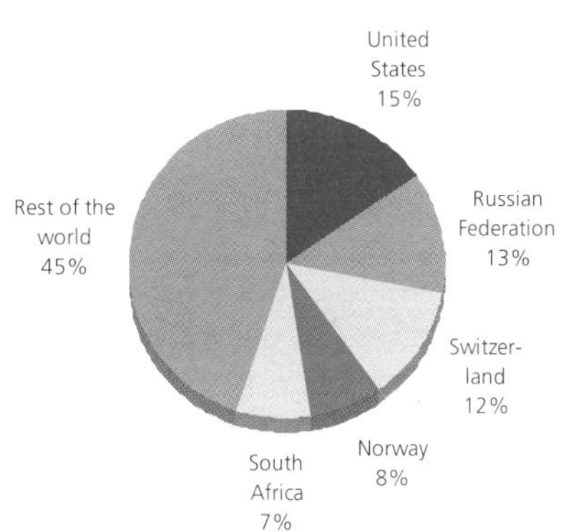

Source: Eurostat (Comext)

Professional associations representing the industries within this chapter

CAEF
Committee of European Foundry Associations
PO Box 10 19 61
D-40010 Düsseldorf
tel: (49) 211 687 12 15
fax: (49) 211 687 12 05
e-mail: caef-eurofoundry@t-online.de

CET
Committee of European wiredrawing producers
c/o B. Champin consulting
94, boulevard Flandrin
F-75017 Paris
tel: (33) 1 47 55 47 95
fax: (33) 1 47 55 44 28

CIELFA
European steel industry of cold rolling of narrow strip
c/o B. Champin consulting
94, boulevard Flandrin
F-75017 Paris
tel: (33) 1 47 55 47 95
fax: (33) 1 47 55 44 28

CIPF
European steel industry of cold forming or folding
c/o B. Champin consulting
94, boulevard Flandrin
F-75017 Paris
tel: (33) 1 47 55 47 95
fax: (33) 1 47 55 44 28

ESTA
European Steel Tube Association
130, rue de Silly
F-92100 Boulogne Billancourt
tel: (33) 1 49 09 35 91
fax: (33) 1 49 09 39 20

IISI
International Iron and Steel Institute
120, rue Colonel Bourg
B-1040 Bruxelles
tel: (32) 2 702 89 00
fax: (32) 2 702 88 99
e-mail: steel@iisi.be

Table 8.2 (million ECU)

Manufacture of basic iron and steel and of ferro-alloys (ECSC, European Coal and Steel Community) (NACE Rev. 1 27.1)

Production related indicators in the EU

	1988	1989	1990	1991	1992	1993	1994	1995	1996	1997	1998
Production value	77,845	89,886	79,832	71,222	65,992	59,144	70,169	82,591	73,200	77,632	77,570
Producer price index (1995=100)	:	:	93.4	87.8	85.2	86.3	92.1	100.0	98.4	93.8	93.6
Value added	26,252	29,258	24,453	20,641	18,383	15,730	19,573	25,266	20,008	21,208	20,857
Number of persons employed (thousands)	552.7	528.3	513.9	473.9	451.5	372.7	351.7	330.2	:	:	:

Table 8.3 (million ECU)

Manufacture of basic iron and steel and of ferro-alloys (ECSC, European Coal and Steel Community) (NACE Rev. 1 27.1)

Production related indicators, 1998

	B	DK	D	EL	E	F	IRL	I	L	NL	A (1)	P	FIN	S	UK
Production value	4,778	318	20,831	529	6,178	11,055	:	11,022	1,669	:	3,037	583	2,544	4,235	8,668
Value added	1,557	82	4,936	60	1,493	2,889	:	3,412	279	:	1,007	:	856	922	2,211
Number of persons employed (units)	12,378	2,213	89,474	2,311	22,761	42,470	:	35,591	5,181	:	20,771	4,162	9,838	14,032	35,496

(1) 1994.

Table 8.4 (million ECU)

Manufacture of basic iron and steel and of ferro-alloys (ECSC, European Coal and Steel Community) (NACE Rev. 1 27.1)

Market related indicators in the EU

	1988	1989	1990	1991	1992	1993	1994	1995	1996	1997	1998
Apparent consumption	71,877	83,685	74,722	65,471	60,870	50,342	62,575	77,714	66,495	72,183	76,102
Exports	8,919	9,936	8,446	8,540	8,096	11,206	10,958	11,144	11,313	11,071	9,375
Imports	2,951	3,735	3,336	2,789	2,974	2,405	3,363	6,267	4,609	5,622	7,907
Trade balance	5,968	6,201	5,110	5,751	5,122	8,802	7,595	4,876	6,705	5,449	1,468
Export ratio (%)	11.5	11.1	10.6	12.0	12.3	18.9	15.6	13.5	15.5	14.3	12.1
Import penetration ratio (%)	4.1	4.5	4.5	4.3	4.9	4.8	5.4	8.1	6.9	7.8	10.4
Cover ratio (%)	302.2	266.0	253.2	306.2	272.2	466.0	325.8	177.8	245.5	196.9	118.6

Table 8.5 (million ECU)

Manufacture of basic iron and steel and of ferro-alloys (ECSC, European Coal and Steel Community) (NACE Rev. 1 27.1)

Market related indicators, 1998

	B/L	DK	D	EL	E	F	IRL	I	NL	A	P	FIN	S	UK
Apparent consumption (1)	:	899	19,061	721	7,672	10,798	:	14,885	:	2,566	1,198	1,744	3,939	8,220
Exports	7,718	346	8,912	438	1,984	5,720	101	2,826	2,411	1,394	183	1,394	1,825	3,430
Imports	4,272	927	7,142	630	3,478	5,463	311	6,690	2,378	798	799	594	1,529	2,982
Trade balance	3,446	-582	1,770	-192	-1,494	257	-210	-3,864	32	595	-616	800	296	447
Export ratio (%) (1)	:	108.8	42.8	82.9	32.1	51.7	:	25.6	:	35.5	31.4	54.8	43.1	39.6
Import penetration ratio (%) (1)	:	103.1	37.5	87.4	45.3	50.6	:	44.9	:	23.7	66.6	34.1	38.8	36.3
Cover ratio (%)	180.7	37.3	124.8	69.6	57.0	104.7	32.5	42.2	101.4	174.6	22.9	234.7	119.3	115.0

(1) A (1994).

Table 8.6

Manufacture of basic iron and steel and of ferro-alloys (ECSC, European Coal and Steel Community) (NACE Rev. 1 27.1)

Labour related indicators, 1998

	EU-15	B	DK	D	EL	E	F	IRL	I	L	NL	A	P	FIN	S	UK
Personnel costs (million ECU) (1)	12,535	548	61	4,234	52	664	1,888	:	1,245	243	:	834	69	358	539	1,380
Personnel costs/employee (thousand ECU) (2)	42.1	47.9	33.9	46.2	24.6	31.3	45.3	:	31.9	46.5	:	40.2	:	37.3	40.3	32.0
Social charges/personnel costs (%) (3)	25.4	31.1	3.4	24.3	24.4	22.5	31.1	:	33.4	19.3	:	23.5	:	21.6	29.4	13.9
Labour productivity (thousand ECU/head) (4)	76.5	125.8	36.8	55.2	26.1	65.6	68.0	:	95.9	53.9	:	48.5	:	87.0	65.7	62.3
Wage adjusted labour productivity (%) (2)	181.6	138.0	125.3	113.5	114.3	191.8	137.1	:	255.0	107.8	:	120.7	:	198.8	150.0	177.9

(1) A (1994). (2) A (1994); EU-15, EL, I (1995); B, DK, D, E, F, L, FIN, S, UK (1996). (3) A (1994); EU-15, L, S (1995). (4) A (1994); EU-15 (1995).

Source: Eurostat (SBS, EBT)

eurostat

(million ECU) — Table 8.7

Manufacture of tubes (NACE Rev. 1 27.2)
Production related indicators in the EU

	1988	1989	1990	1991	1992	1993	1994	1995	1996	1997	1998
Production value	15,489	17,581	15,433	15,915	15,440	13,934	16,572	18,382	:	:	:
Producer price index (1995=100)	:	:	:	:	87.4	86.5	89.8	100.0	101.4	101.6	:
Value added	4,835	5,129	4,545	4,652	4,533	3,979	4,983	5,511	:	:	:
Number of persons employed (thousands)	162.4	162.2	148.5	147.1	139.4	128.6	120.0	113.8	:	:	:

(million ECU) — Table 8.8

Manufacture of tubes (NACE Rev. 1 27.2)
Production related indicators, 1998

	B	DK	D	EL	E	F	IRL	I	L	NL	A	P	FIN	S	UK
Production value (1)	165	373	6,074	110	844	2,900	:	3,928	0	253	:	89	166	278	1,949
Value added (1)	43	152	2,386	20	261	981	:	947	0	60	:	:	49	96	662
Number of persons employed (units) (1)(2)	701	3,060	39,930	718	5,097	16,135	:	13,251	0	1,331	:	347	912	1,675	14,396

(1) L (1996). (2) NL (1992).

(million ECU) — Table 8.9

Manufacture of tubes (NACE Rev. 1 27.2)
Market related indicators in the EU

	1988	1989	1990	1991	1992	1993	1994	1995	1996	1997	1998
Apparent consumption	12,096	13,981	12,957	13,048	13,132	11,398	13,653	15,728	:	:	:
Exports	4,004	4,407	3,379	3,886	3,319	3,367	3,850	3,909	4,390	5,520	5,537
Imports	612	807	904	1,019	1,011	831	932	1,256	1,204	1,304	1,697
Trade balance	3,392	3,600	2,476	2,867	2,308	2,537	2,919	2,654	3,186	4,216	3,840
Export ratio (%)	25.9	25.1	21.9	24.4	21.5	24.2	23.2	21.3	:	:	:
Import penetration ratio (%)	5.1	5.8	7.0	7.8	7.7	7.3	6.8	8.0	:	:	:
Cover ratio (%)	654.4	546.3	374.0	381.5	328.4	405.3	413.2	311.3	364.6	423.2	326.3

(million ECU) — Table 8.10

Manufacture of tubes (NACE Rev. 1 27.2)
Market related indicators, 1998

	B/L	DK	D	EL	E	F	IRL	I	NL	A	P	FIN	S	UK
Apparent consumption	:	485	4,180	107	732	2,113	:	2,165	412	:	201	103	107	1,994
Exports	445	255	3,501	79	523	1,838	10	2,554	458	527	28	262	564	989
Imports	558	367	1,606	76	411	1,052	87	791	617	325	140	199	393	1,033
Trade balance	-113	-112	1,894	3	112	786	-77	1,763	-159	201	-112	63	172	-45
Export ratio (%)	:	68.4	57.6	72.3	62.0	63.4	:	65.0	181.1	:	31.8	158.2	202.6	50.7
Import penetration ratio (%)	:	75.7	38.4	71.6	56.1	49.8	:	36.5	149.8	:	69.8	193.9	367.4	51.8
Cover ratio (%)	79.7	69.4	217.9	104.0	127.3	174.8	11.4	322.9	74.3	161.8	20.2	131.7	143.7	95.7

Table 8.11

Manufacture of tubes (NACE Rev. 1 27.2)
Labour related indicators, 1998

	EU-15	B	DK	D	EL	E	F	IRL	I	L	NL	A	P	FIN	S	UK
Personnel costs (million ECU) (1)	4,075	25	86	1,674	11	145	588	:	417	0	41	:	4	28	58	434
Personnel costs/employee (thousand ECU) (2)	36.3	35.2	33.4	41.3	17.2	30.6	37.1	:	28.6	:	:	:	:	32.1	36.2	24.8
Social charges/personnel costs (%) (3)	23.5	24.5	1.7	20.0	23.5	22.2	31.0	:	36.7	:	15.4	:	:	23.3	30.5	12.6
Labour productivity (thousand ECU/head) (4)	48.4	61.5	49.5	59.8	28.5	51.2	60.8	:	71.4	:	35.4	:	:	53.6	57.5	46.0
Wage adjusted labour productivity (%) (2)	133.3	109.4	150.4	118.6	153.8	174.6	145.9	:	213.1	:	:	:	:	159.9	149.4	149.9

(1) EU-15 (1995); L (1996). (2) EU-15, EL, I (1995); B, DK, D, E, F, FIN, S, UK (1996). (3) EU-15, S (1995). (4) NL (1992); EU-15 (1995).

Source: Eurostat (SBS, EBT)

Table 8.12 (million ECU)

Other first processing of iron and steel and production on non-ECSC (European Coal and Steel Community) ferro-alloys (NACE Rev. 1 27.3)

Production related indicators in the EU

	1988	1989	1990	1991	1992	1993	1994	1995	1996	1997	1998
Production value	11,123	13,061	12,868	12,367	12,388	11,223	13,465	:	16,564	16,621	16,528
Producer price index (1995=100)	:	:	:	:	90.1	89.3	91.7	100.0	101.6	103.2	111.9
Value added	3,101	3,252	3,291	3,251	3,327	3,041	3,506	:	4,014	4,276	4,340
Number of persons employed (thousands)	86.0	89.5	90.2	87.9	86.5	78.2	74.4	:	:	:	:

Table 8.13 (million ECU)

Other first processing of iron and steel and production on non-ECSC (European Coal and Steel Community) ferro-alloys (NACE Rev. 1 27.3)

Production related indicators, 1998

	B	DK (1)	D	EL	E	F	IRL	I	L	NL	A	P	FIN	S	UK
Production value	1,845	98	3,666	191	1,455	2,251	:	3,624	:	:	:	67	107	1,149	1,584
Value added	728	25	967	21	365	612	:	664	:	:	:	:	28	365	395
Number of persons employed (units)	8,361	666	17,797	1,518	8,693	10,844	:	11,958	:	:	:	463	380	5,415	9,881

(1) 1995.

Table 8.14 (million ECU)

Other first processing of iron and steel and production on non-ECSC (European Coal and Steel Community) ferro-alloys (NACE Rev. 1 27.3)

Market related indicators in the EU

	1988	1989	1990	1991	1992	1993	1994	1995	1996	1997	1998
Apparent consumption	10,843	12,890	12,622	12,221	12,191	10,818	12,997	:	16,714	16,697	16,685
Exports	1,999	2,352	1,995	1,762	1,795	1,980	2,410	2,601	2,455	2,809	2,940
Imports	1,720	2,182	1,749	1,617	1,598	1,575	1,942	3,122	2,604	2,885	3,097
Trade balance	279	171	246	145	197	406	468	-521	-150	-76	-157
Export ratio (%)	18.0	18.0	15.5	14.2	14.5	17.6	17.9	:	14.8	16.9	17.8
Import penetration ratio (%)	15.9	16.9	13.9	13.2	13.1	14.6	14.9	:	15.6	17.3	18.6
Cover ratio (%)	116.2	107.8	114.1	109.0	112.3	125.8	124.1	83.3	94.2	97.4	94.9

Table 8.15 (million ECU)

Other first processing of iron and steel and production on non-ECSC (European Coal and Steel Community) ferro-alloys (NACE Rev. 1 27.3)

Market related indicators, 1998

	B/L	DK	D	EL	E	F	IRL	I	NL	A	P	FIN	S	UK
Apparent consumption (1)	:	235	3,734	233	1,507	2,293	:	3,751	:	:	166	240	773	1,609
Exports	1,037	45	2,341	10	488	1,509	21	1,146	433	444	31	118	798	867
Imports	639	163	2,409	52	539	1,552	75	1,274	840	351	130	252	423	891
Trade balance	397	-118	-68	-42	-52	-42	-54	-127	-407	93	-99	-133	376	-24
Export ratio (%) (1)	:	43.7	63.8	5.4	33.5	67.1	:	31.6	:	:	46.1	110.4	69.5	54.7
Import penetration ratio (%) (1)	:	76.5	64.5	22.3	35.8	67.7	:	34.0	:	:	78.3	104.6	54.7	55.4
Cover ratio (%)	162.2	27.6	97.2	20.0	90.4	97.3	28.3	90.0	51.5	126.5	23.7	47.0	188.8	97.3

(1) DK (1995).

Table 8.16

Other first processing of iron and steel and production on non-ECSC (European Coal and Steel Community) ferro-alloys (NACE Rev. 1 27.3)

Labour related indicators, 1998

	EU-15	B	DK	D	EL	E	F	IRL	I	L	NL	A	P	FIN	S	UK
Personnel costs (million ECU) (1)	2,792	376	23	763	32	236	397	:	379	:	:	:	6	13	194	278
Personnel costs/employee (thousand ECU) (2)	:	48.9	35.2	41.9	22.9	29.3	37.3	:	28.9	:	:	:	:	35.3	37.6	24.0
Social charges/personnel costs (%) (3)	:	33.6	3.8	18.9	26.3	21.7	32.5	:	37.8	:	:	:	:	20.2	29.7	14.1
Labour productivity (thousand ECU/head) (4)	47.1	87.0	38.1	54.3	14.2	42.0	56.4	:	55.5	:	:	:	:	74.7	67.5	40.0
Wage adjusted labour productivity (%) (2)	:	132.9	108.3	124.6	61.4	180.8	137.6	:	208.0	:	:	:	:	220.6	159.4	130.3

(1) DK (1995). (2) DK, EL, I (1995); B, D, E, F, FIN, S, UK (1996). (3) S (1994); DK (1995). (4) EU-15 (1994); DK (1995).

Source: Eurostat (SBS, EBT)

(million ECU) Table 8.17

Manufacture of basic precious and non-ferrous metals (NACE Rev. 1 27.4)
Production related indicators in the EU

	1988	1989	1990	1991	1992	1993	1994	1995	1996	1997	1998
Production value	44,748	52,625	46,842	42,445	40,739	37,303	41,506	48,163	46,729	52,718	52,013
Producer price index (1995=100)	:	:	97.0	86.3	82.4	80.5	87.5	100.0	100.3	105.4	113.1
Value added	11,156	11,819	10,302	9,394	9,155	8,446	9,681	10,760	10,631	11,932	11,545
Number of persons employed (thousands)	246.7	245.1	243.0	239.8	224.6	209.6	198.2	189.7	192.7	188.3	185.0

(million ECU) Table 8.18

Manufacture of basic precious and non-ferrous metals (NACE Rev. 1 27.4)
Production related indicators, 1998

	B	DK	D	EL	E	F	IRL	I	L	NL	A	P	FIN	S	UK
Production value	4,451	322	16,393	1,194	3,802	6,497	:	5,463	:	1,813	1,803	205	1,086	1,229	7,252
Value added	815	108	4,029	238	746	1,301	:	1,077	:	555	340	:	208	274	1,675
Number of persons employed (units) (1)	7,459	2,190	61,706	4,253	14,482	24,746	:	17,010	:	7,352	5,379	1,527	4,001	4,744	27,979

(1) NL (1992).

(million ECU) Table 8.19

Manufacture of basic precious and non-ferrous metals (NACE Rev. 1 27.4)
Market related indicators in the EU

	1988	1989	1990	1991	1992	1993	1994	1995	1996	1997	1998
Apparent consumption	61,380	67,198	61,052	56,435	55,087	50,389	56,316	65,712	60,618	67,971	72,054
Exports	8,247	9,152	6,765	6,958	6,343	7,398	8,381	9,657	10,374	12,814	11,815
Imports	24,879	23,725	20,974	20,947	20,692	20,483	23,191	27,206	24,264	28,066	31,856
Trade balance	-16,632	-14,573	-14,209	-13,990	-14,349	-13,085	-14,810	-17,549	-13,889	-15,252	-20,041
Export ratio (%)	18.4	17.4	14.4	16.4	15.6	19.8	20.2	20.0	22.2	24.3	22.7
Import penetration ratio (%)	40.5	35.3	34.4	37.1	37.6	40.6	41.2	41.4	40.0	41.3	44.2
Cover ratio (%)	33.1	38.6	32.3	33.2	30.7	36.1	36.1	35.5	42.8	45.7	37.1

(million ECU) Table 8.20

Manufacture of basic precious and non-ferrous metals (NACE Rev. 1 27.4)
Market related indicators, 1998

	B/L	DK	D	EL	E	F	IRL	I	NL	A	P	FIN	S	UK
Apparent consumption	:	710	18,785	1,072	4,168	8,193	:	12,558	2,410	2,318	650	720	1,347	13,678
Exports	3,835	366	9,983	603	1,718	4,509	332	2,526	4,304	1,388	116	973	1,276	5,490
Imports	4,080	754	12,375	481	2,084	6,205	392	9,621	4,900	1,903	560	607	1,394	11,916
Trade balance	-245	-388	-2,391	122	-366	-1,696	-60	-7,095	-597	-515	-445	366	-118	-6,426
Export ratio (%)	:	113.8	60.9	50.5	45.2	69.4	:	46.2	237.3	77.0	56.4	89.6	103.8	75.7
Import penetration ratio (%)	:	106.2	65.9	44.9	50.0	75.7	:	76.6	203.3	82.1	86.3	84.3	103.5	87.1
Cover ratio (%)	94.0	48.5	80.7	125.3	82.4	72.7	84.8	26.3	87.8	72.9	20.6	160.3	91.6	46.1

Table 8.21

Manufacture of basic precious and non-ferrous metals (NACE Rev. 1 27.4)
Labour related indicators, 1998

	EU-15	B	DK	D	EL	E	F	IRL	I	L	NL	A	P	FIN	S	UK
Personnel costs (million ECU)	7,135	390	67	2,867	98	414	1,015	:	542	:	302	204	15	140	163	851
Personnel costs/employee (thousand ECU) (1)	38.8	49.7	37.2	45.3	25.1	30.8	41.4	:	29.0	:	:	39.7	:	36.1	36.1	25.1
Social charges/personnel costs (%) (2)	22.6	31.7	5.4	19.9	23.5	24.4	31.8	:	35.1	:	13.6	24.5	:	21.5	28.1	13.6
Labour productivity (thousand ECU/head) (3)	62.4	109.3	49.3	65.3	56.0	51.5	52.6	:	63.3	:	42.4	63.2	:	52.0	57.7	59.9
Wage adjusted labour productivity (%) (1)	146.3	128.8	141.8	127.4	175.9	165.2	122.9	:	202.7	:	:	141.2	:	161.0	147.9	205.4

(1) EU-15, EL, I, A (1995); B, DK, D, E, F, FIN, S, UK (1996). (2) S (1994); EU-15 (1995). (3) NL (1992).

Source: Eurostat (SBS, EBT)

Table 8.22 (million ECU)

Casting of metals (NACE Rev. 1 27.5)

Production related indicators in the EU

	1988	1989	1990	1991	1992	1993	1994	1995	1996	1997	1998
Production value	15,120	17,394	17,548	16,564	16,244	13,917	16,028	18,752	:	:	:
Producer price index (1995=100)	:	:	:	:	:	:	:	100.0	97.2	99.9	98.5
Value added	6,589	7,156	7,403	7,251	7,132	6,009	6,621	7,517	:	:	:
Number of persons employed (thousands)	244.5	249.6	248.1	234.7	223.8	196.1	192.1	203.2	:	:	:

Table 8.23 (million ECU)

Casting of metals (NACE Rev. 1 27.5)

Production related indicators, 1998

	B	DK	D	EL	E	F	IRL	I	L	NL	A	P	FIN	S	UK
Production value (1)	439	0	7,070	9	2,147	3,323	:	4,689	:	530	599	334	190	34	2,758
Value added (1)	169	0	3,301	4	803	1,256	:	1,578	:	205	283	:	97	18	1,197
Number of persons employed (units) (1)(2)	2,696	0	63,471	203	20,637	34,263	:	31,350	:	4,842	6,407	6,668	2,134	315	31,009

(1) DK, A (1994). (2) NL (1992).

Table 8.24

Casting of metals (NACE Rev. 1 27.5)

Labour related indicators, 1998

	EU-15	B	DK	D	EL	E	F	IRL	I	L	NL	A	P	FIN	S	UK
Personnel costs (million ECU) (1)	6,010	101	0	2,502	3	502	988	:	990	:	161	209	61	61	10	889
Personnel costs/employee (thousand ECU) (2)	31.6	38.2	:	38.9	14.2	24.3	29.4	:	28.8	:	:	32.7	:	29.7	34.0	22.9
Social charges/personnel costs (%) (3)	22.5	25.3	:	19.5	24.2	23.5	29.9	:	37.6	:	13.4	23.9	:	21.0	29.7	13.2
Labour productivity (thousand ECU/head) (4)	37.0	62.6	:	52.0	19.5	38.9	36.7	:	50.3	:	34.8	44.3	:	45.7	55.6	38.6
Wage adjusted labour productivity (%) (2)	117.0	116.3	:	111.6	130.3	137.0	115.9	:	155.6	:	:	135.5	:	142.5	149.1	140.5

(1) DK, A (1994); EU-15 (1995). (2) A (1994); EU-15, EL, I (1995); B, D, E, F, FIN, S, UK (1996). (3) A (1994); EU-15, S (1995). (4) NL (1992); A (1994); EU-15 (1995).

Source: Eurostat (SBS, EBT)

Metal products

Industrial description

The manufacture of fabricated metal products includes constructional steelwork, boilers and metal containers, forging, tools and light metal packaging, but excludes machinery and equipment. In terms of production value metal products accounted for just under 6% of total manufacturing in the EU. In 1998, the European sector reported a production value of 213.7 billion ECU, employing 2.1 million persons. Germany recorded a share of 29.1% in the production value of the European total. Within the smaller Member States, Luxembourg reported production specialisation of 200%, meaning that the contribution of Luxembourg (892.8 million ECU) to the European total for metal products was twice as high as the average for total manufacturing. Austria recorded a somewhat smaller production specialisation (around 150% with 6.9 billion ECU of production value).

Metal products are largely intermediate and capital goods used in a wide range of downstream industries. The main customers are the automotive and mechanical engineering industries, and to a somewhat smaller extent energy, chemical, iron and steel, household appliance, electronics and other transport industries. The demand for metal products follows to a large extent the general business cycle; although the manufacture of metal products for the heavy industry has to deal with large fluctuations of investment in downstream industries. The sector faced increasing competition from other materials above all plastic parts, stamping or composite components, causing a downward pressure on producer prices, especially in the market for standard products.

(%) Figure 9.1

Metal products (NACE Rev. 1 28)
Share of EU value added in total manufacturing

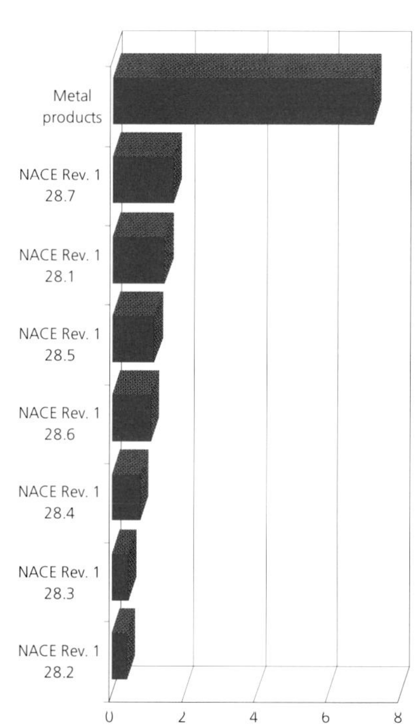

Source: Eurostat (SBS)

The activities covered in this chapter include:

- 28.1: manufacture of structural metal products;
- 28.2: manufacture of tanks, reservoirs and containers of metal; manufacture of central heating radiators and boilers;
- 28.3: manufacture of steam generators, except central heating hot water boilers;
- 28.4: forging, pressing, stamping and roll forming of metal; powder metallurgy;
- 28.5: treatment and coating of metals, general mechanical engineering;
- 28.6: manufacture of cutlery, tools and general hardware;
- 28.7: manufacture of other fabricated metal products.

Figure 9.2 (1988=100)

Metal products (NACE Rev. 1 28)

Production, employment and value added compared to EU total manufacturing

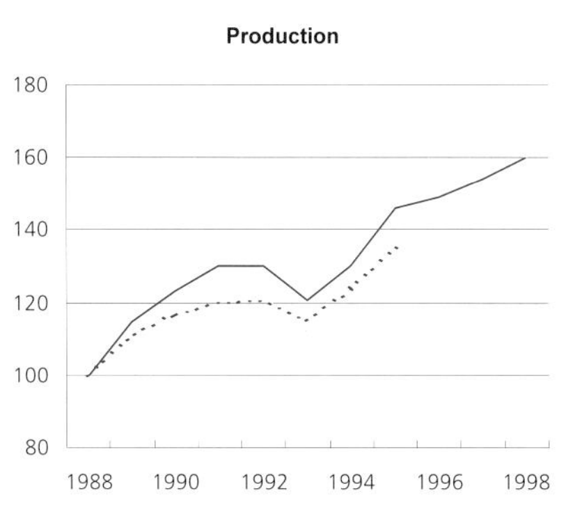

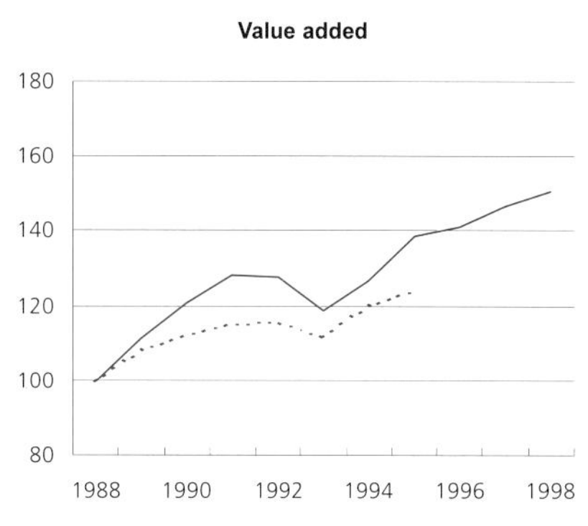

—— Metal products - - - - Total manufacturing

Source: Eurostat (SBS)

The supply of metal products was mainly provided by small and medium-sized enterprises, which adapted to increased competition with rationalisation of the production process, co-operations and mergers or specialisation in low volume niche markets. Co-operations and mergers offered on the one hand capital for investment in efficient production facilities for larger volumes and on the other hand capital for research and development. The latter was decisive to remain competitive in the long run, as customers demanded constantly improving quality and new properties for products. Specialisation in niche markets included tailor-made solutions and after-sales service.

In answer to world-wide over-capacity in the metal products industry competition increased at an international level, especially from Far East Asia and Eastern Europe. Manufacturers in the EU partly delocated production facilities of large bulk production to low wage countries. Nevertheless, technical know-how and high quality still constituted important factors which helped the competitiveness of EU manufacturers.

Figure 9.3

Metal products (NACE Rev. 1 28)

International comparison of main indicators in current prices

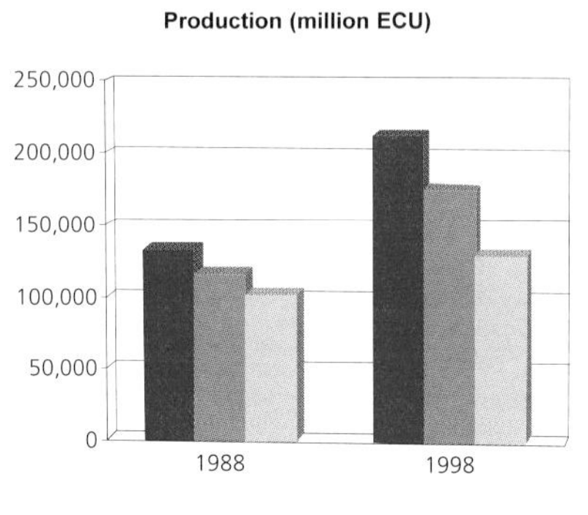

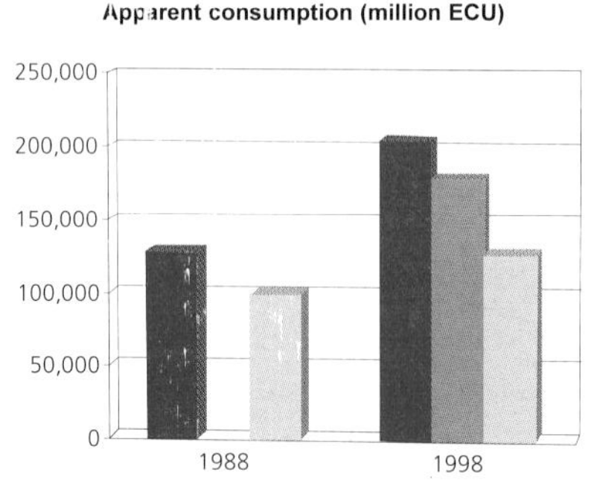

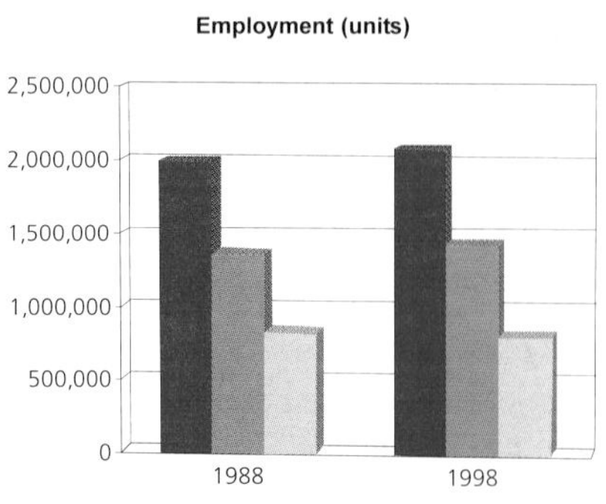

EU-15 USA Japan

Source: Eurostat (SBS)

(ECU/hour)

Figure 9.4

Metal products (NACE Rev. 1 28)

Labour costs by Member State, 1996

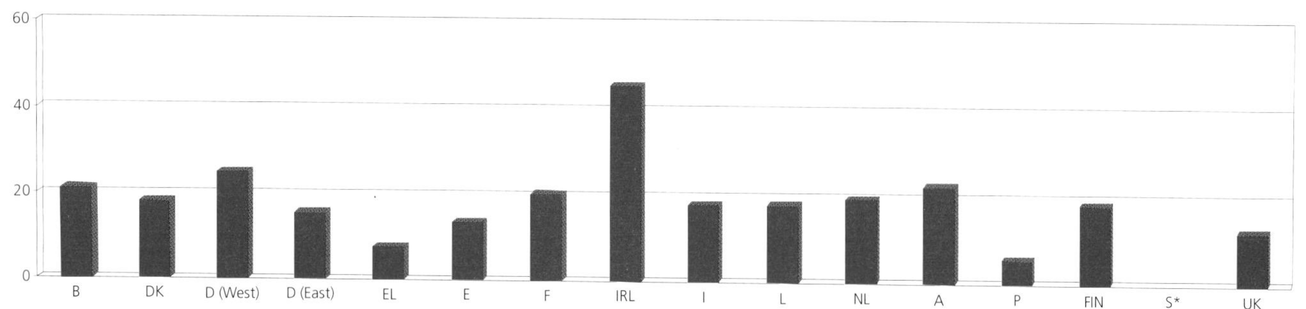

Source: Eurostat (LCS)

Recent trends

EU production of metal products reflected an upward tendency since the economic downturn in the early part of the nineties. France and Spain recorded growth in production value of 6.4% and 6.1% per annum respectively (between 1993 and 1998), the Nordic Member States of Finland and Sweden reported growth of 15.1% and 13.3% per annum respectively, whilst the Italian sector grew by just 1.9% per annum (at constant prices). Although the production of metal products as a whole followed the general business cycle, it covered diverging tendencies: some areas like light metal packaging were less influenced by economic fluctuations than structural metal products, dependent on the evolution in construction. The manufacture of tools faced falling demand due to the increasing market share of power-driven hand tools.

The positive evolution of production of metal products led to an increase in employment of 1.4% per annum in the EU (between 1993 and 1998). The aggregated growth rate covered increases from 9.3% in Belgium to reductions of 2.4% per annum in Germany. In 1998 production value per person employed was 102.4 thousand ECU, an increase of 50% when compared to 1988 when the ratio was 66.8 thousand ECU. International comparison displayed similar increases in the other Triad economies. However, the European ratio was still 20% lower than in the USA (122.9 thousand ECU) and much lower than in Japan (160.2 thousand ECU per person employed in 1997).

Foreign trade

Metal products were not typically traded over long distances, due to their weight and due to production facilities often being situated close to customers. Nevertheless, the EU manufacturers of metal products increased their activity on foreign markets, seen in the growing positive trade balance (some 8.6 billion ECU in 1998). The increase in the share of exports in production (by three percentage points to 10.4%, 1988-1998) reflected the search for markets outside the EU in order to replace decreasing domestic demand. For example EU manufacturers attempted to gain market share in Eastern European countries or China before these markets were supplied by domestic producers. At the same time, foreign manufacturers especially from the Czech Republic, Hungary and Poland intensified their supply to the EU market: extra-EU imports increased by 170.0% between 1988 and 1998 leading to an import penetration ratio of 6.7%.

(%)

Table 9.1

Metal products (NACE Rev. 1 28)

Composition of the labour force, 1997

	Females	Part-time	Highly-educated
EU-15	16.9	:	:
B	11.9	:	15.1
DK	13.2	7.2	13.2
D	18.4	6.2	15.0
EL	6.6	:	:
E	6.9	2.2	15.6
F	15.1	3.8	9.1
IRL	12.1	4.2	18.4
I	18.2	3.9	1.8
L	:	:	:
NL	11.7	13.9	8.0
A	20.3	3.8	3.3
P	17.6	2.9	3.7
FIN	23.0	:	16.0
S	15.6	8.8	12.3
UK	16.7	6.4	13.7

Source: Eurostat (LFS)

Figure 9.5

Metal products (NACE Rev. 1 28)

Destination of EU exports, 1998

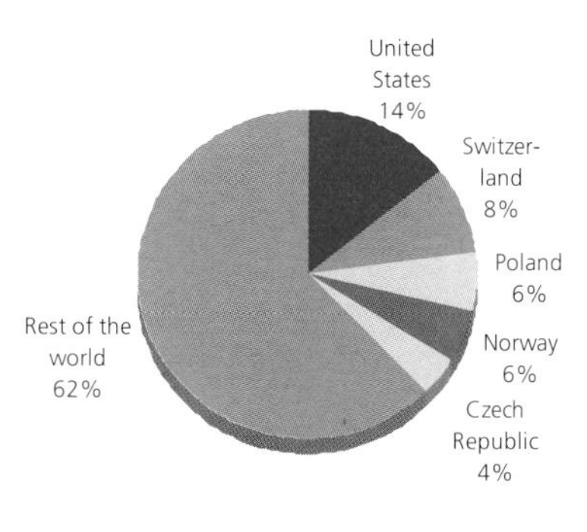

Source: Eurostat (Comext)

Figure 9.6

Metal products (NACE Rev. 1 28)

Origin of EU imports, 1998

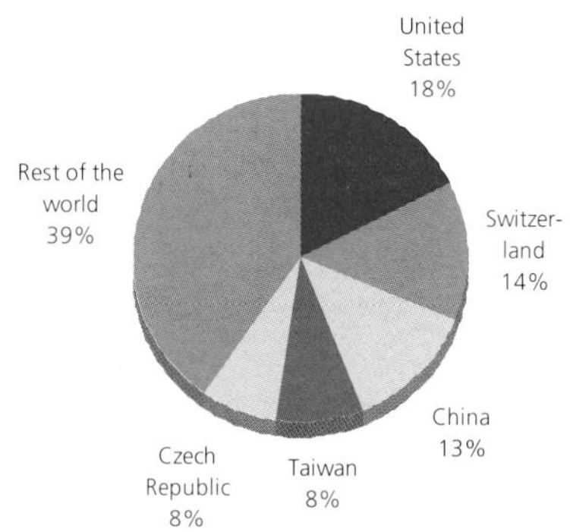

Source: Eurostat (Comext)

Constructional steelwork (NACE Rev. 1 28.1)

The manufacture of structural metal products is a basic industrial activity. It provides intermediate goods made of steel to construction: metal doors and windows as well as large metal structures for bridges, power plants or industrial buildings (the latter was the largest activity in this sector). With 48.7 billion ECU of production value constructional steelwork accounted for 22.8% of the total output of metal products in the EU. The share was around twice as high in Austria and the Netherlands displaying a high production specialisation. The Austrian and Dutch share in the European production value of constructional steelwork was 5.8% and 7.3% respectively in 1998.

In the EU, production of constructional steelwork was on a moderate upward trend, increasing by 2.6% per annum between 1993 and 1998. However, the individual production figures by Member State varied widely from the European average, between 14.8% per annum in Finland and -5.4% in Italy. This was caused by different economic situations in construction in the Member States, but also by differing structures of the sector: for example in the United Kingdom hall construction accounted for 80% of constructional steelwork, whilst in Germany the share was only 30% in 1998. Customers demanded more just-in-time deliveries, which required restructuring of production processes in many medium-sized enterprises. In some regions of the EU, enterprises engaged in constructional steelwork co-operated very closely with related industries, such as mechanical engineering, metal processing or automotives, in order to pool their distribution and marketing activities. Producer prices of constructional steelwork were on a downward trend, reflecting over-capacity and growing imports from foreign providers, particularly from Eastern Europe. In Germany where production was decreasing (down by 0.6% per annum, at constant prices, 1993-1998) the industry expected the government to invest in railway infrastructure to build the "Transrapid" that would require 900 thousand tonnes of steel. The sector attempted to improve efficiency through the introduction of new products and the adoption of appropriate standards.

Figure 9.7

Constructional steelwork (NACE Rev. 1 28.1)

Production and employment in the Triad

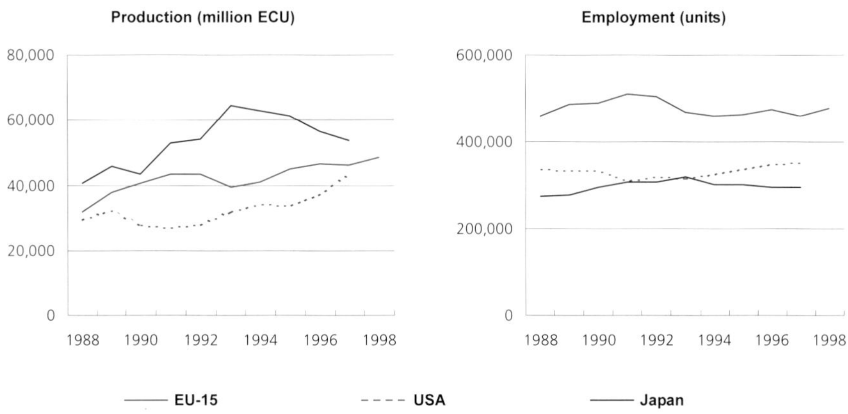

Source: Eurostat (SBS)

Figure 9.8 (%)

Constructional steelwork (NACE Rev. 1 28.1)

Production and export specialisation by Member State, 1998

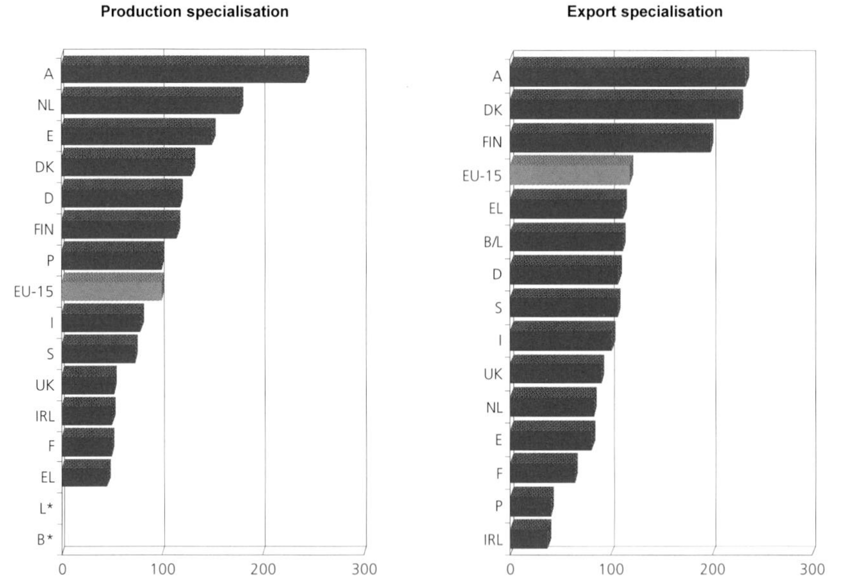

Production specialisation

A
NL
E
DK
D
FIN
P
EU-15
I
S
UK
IRL
F
EL
L*
B*
0 100 200 300

Export specialisation

A
DK
FIN
EU-15
EL
B/L
D
S
I
UK
NL
E
F
P
IRL
0 100 200 300

Source: Eurostat (SBS)

In times of low orders the pressure on profit margins stimulated further efforts to reduce production costs. Rationalisation of the production process led to a relative reduction of labour intensity in the EU, from 14.6 persons per one million ECU of production value in 1988 to 9.8 persons in 1998. Nevertheless, the growth of production was high enough to expand the absolute number of persons employed in the EU (up by 0.4% per annum to 478.3 thousand persons, 1993-1998). A breakdown by Member State displayed a similar variation in employment trends, from 8.2% per annum growth in Belgium to a reduction of 6.3% per annum in Italy. The industry also tried to introduce flexible working patterns in order to optimise capacity utilisation to the number of incoming orders.

Due to the bulky nature of many products of constructional steelwork trade flows between the EU and non-Member States were still low, seen in the share of EU exports in production of 7.0% in 1998. Nevertheless, the constructional steelwork industry also tried to gain market shares abroad, for example in the Far East where investments in infrastructure and buildings were still high. During the latter part of the nineties the economic crisis in south-east Asia reduced the demand in this region and increased at the same time competition on markets outside the region.

Figure 9.9

Constructional steelwork (NACE Rev. 1 28.1) Destination of EU exports, 1998

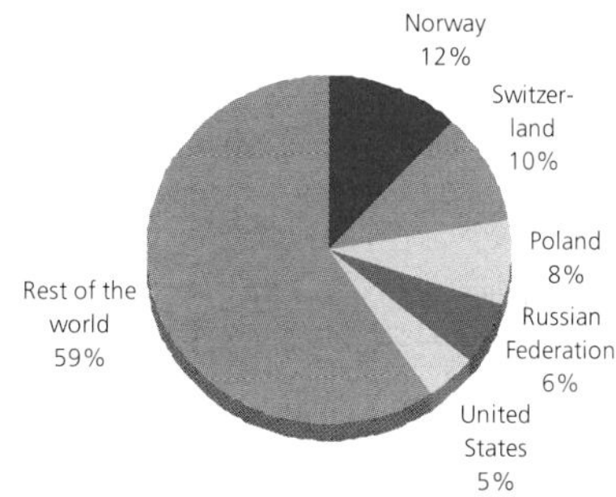

Source: Eurostat (Comext)

Figure 9.10

Constructional steelwork (NACE Rev. 1 28.1) Origin of EU imports, 1998

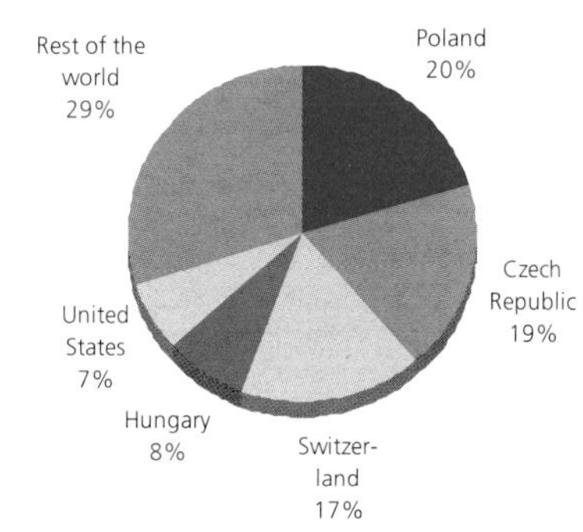

Source: Eurostat (Comext)

Boilers and metal containers (NACE Rev. 1 28.2 and 28.3)

Boilers and metal containers encompass widely used capital goods, from tanks and reservoirs through steam generators to central heating radiators and boilers. More than 60% of European production was accounted for by Germany and France (with 8.2 billion and 6.8 billion ECU of production value in 1998). The sector accounted for 0.7% of total EU manufacturing or around 13% of the metal products total.

Demand for boilers and metal containers is dependent on the propensity to invest in downstream industries, mainly energy and chemical industries, automotive and engine industries, construction, as well as food and beverages. Investments in nuclear reactors (which are included in NACE Rev. 1 28.3) declined dramatically due largely to less support for nuclear power production. Whilst there was a downward tendency in Germany (down by 2.6% per annum, at constant prices, 1993-1998), there was a moderate upward tendency in France (1.0% per annum), the Finish sector reported an average annual growth rate of 13.8%. Value added (at constant prices) displayed a weaker performance than production, for example in Germany and France down by 5.7% and 1.6% per annum respectively (1993-1998). As with the whole metal products industry, the manufacture of boilers and metal containers faced strong competition from non-Member States.

The restructuring of the production process led to significant rationalisation, seen in an increase in the average production value per person employed. In Germany the ratio increased by 54.1 thousand ECU to 131.2 thousand ECU (1988-1998). Differences in the composition of the sector and production process explained the nearly unchanged number of persons employed in France since 1993 (down by 0.2% to 70.6 thousand persons in 1998) and the decrease in employment in Germany (down by 6.0% per annum to 62.3 thousand persons). In addition, enterprises concluded mergers or de-located production to Eastern Europe. For example Babcock (D) bought its competitor Steinmüller in 1999 and was negotiating with VA Tech about co-operations in the manufacture of tanks and generators.

Figure 9.11

Boilers and metal containers (NACE Rev. 1 28.2 and 28.3)
Production and employment in the Triad

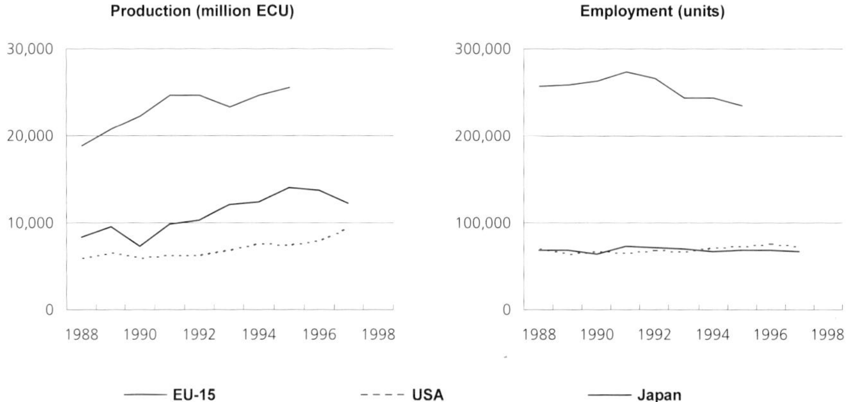

Source: Eurostat (SBS)

Figure 9.12 (%)

Boilers and metal containers (NACE Rev. 1 28.2 and 28.3)
Production and export specialisation by Member State, 1998

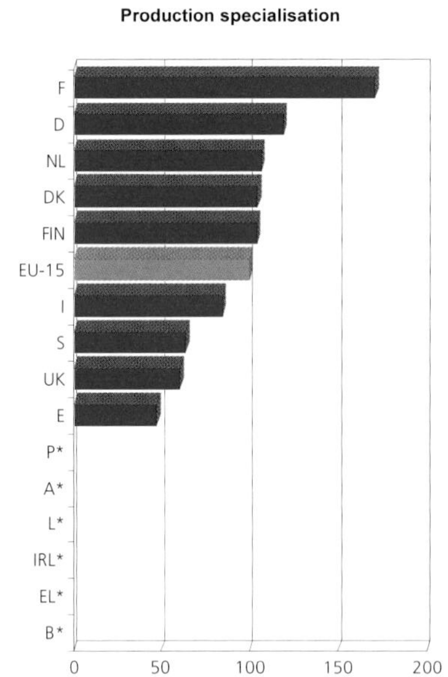

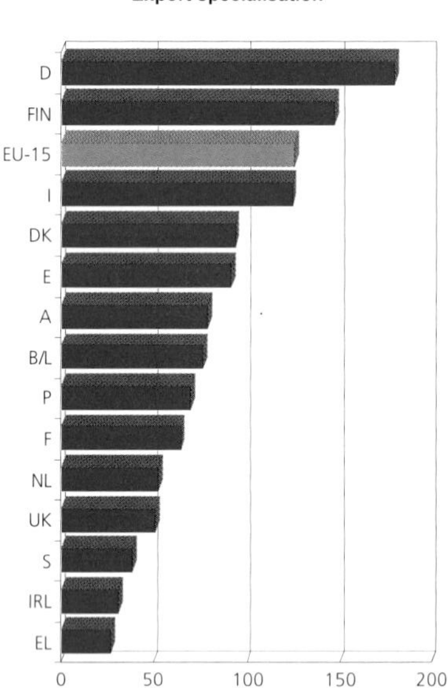

Source: Eurostat (SBS)

Despite restructuring, manufacture within the EU remained expensive in terms of labour costs. Manufacturers strengthened their competitive position through increased research and development and diversification into related product fields (such as mechanical or electrical engineering), as customers demanded more and more complete tailor-made solutions. This trend required flexibility of supply combined with high quality and innovation. Downstream industries also restructured and rationalised production processes in order to reduce costs. They expected constant improvements in energy efficiency of heating radiators, boilers and steam generators, which led to co-generation systems of heat and electricity or the use of solar power. In general, developments of the sector were influenced by the energy price level.

In the EU the manufacture of boilers and metal containers was to a large extent orientated towards the domestic market. The share of exports (including intra-EU flows) in production varied between 9.8% in France and 37.8% in Germany. The share of imports in apparent consumption was lower, ranging between 3.2% in Finland and 28.4% in Spain. Nevertheless, trade flows with Eastern European countries intensified and larger enterprises took steps to increase their exports outside of Europe. Extra-EU exports increased by 142.4% in France between 1988 and 1998.

Figure 9.13

Boilers and metal containers (NACE Rev. 1 28.2 and 28.3) Destination of EU exports, 1998

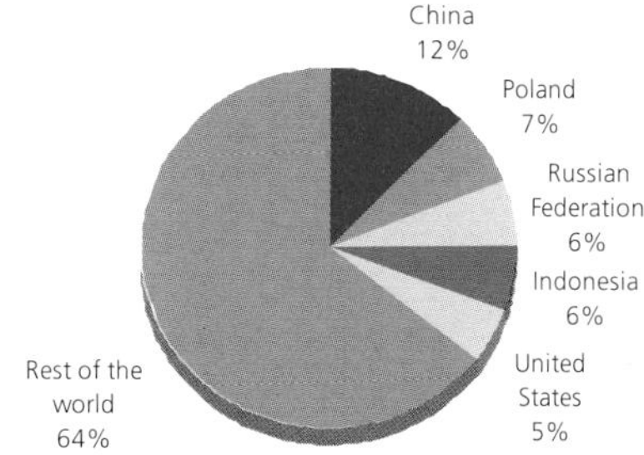

Source: Eurostat (Comext)

Figure 9.14

Boilers and metal containers (NACE Rev. 1 28.2 and 28.3) Origin of EU imports, 1998

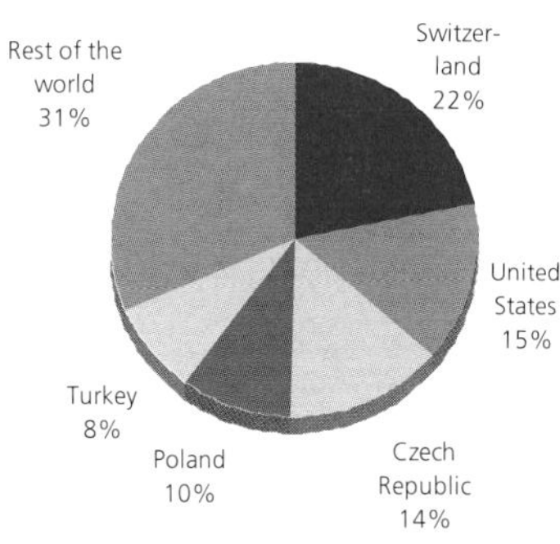

Source: Eurostat (Comext)

Other metal products (NACE Rev. 1 28.4 to 28.7)
Other metal products encompass a wide range of different products from forging through tools and cutlery to metal packaging. In terms of production value other metal products accounted for more than 60% of metal products output or more than 3% of total EU manufacturing.

The forging industry (NACE Rev. 1 28.4) produces largely semi-finished products, except for products of special forming processes. Main downstream industries were transport equipment and mechanical engineering industries. In Germany these two industries were responsible for 72.5% and 16.5% respectively of sales. In the latter part of the nineties forging accounted for around a fifth of the aggregated output of other metal products, the same share as treatment, coating of metals and general mechanical engineering (NACE Rev. 1 28.5). The latter industry includes activities such as plating or non-metallic coating of metals as well as boring, turning or milling of metal work pieces. Other fabricated metal products (NACE Rev. 1 28.7) accounted for around 40% of the aggregate of other metal products. NACE Rev. 1 28.7 included metal packaging (light metal packaging, steel drums and similar containers), which made up around 8% of the European packaging market. The manufacture of cutlery, tools and general hardware (NACE Rev. 1 28.6), responsible for the remaining fifth of production of other metal products, was sold to private households as well as hotels and restaurants, furniture manufacturers or construction.

If we look at production specialisation by Member State, other metal products (NACE Rev. 1 28.4 to 28.7) were highly concentrated in Germany, Spain and Italy, where more than 55% of European production or 72.7 billion ECU of output was produced. A breakdown of the sector displayed a particularly high share in forging for Italy (around 20% of the European total), the five largest Member States accounted for more than 90%. In the United Kingdom the largest production of light metal packaging in the EU was recorded.

The market for metal products was characterised by increasing competition: the forging industry faced over-capacity and customers gained in bargaining strength due to the subcontracting nature of the business. In addition, there were more and more alternative materials for forging products on the market. The latter also increased competition in the light metal packaging industry. However, the manufacture of hand tools saw demand decrease in the long run, whilst imports from low-cost countries increased. Rationalisation and restructuring of the business took place. In the forging industry companies specialised in particular market segments, whilst packaging and hand tool manufacturers expanded their product ranges and developed new markets. Rationalisation included innovation of the production process, such as the use of more sophisticated and comprehensive computer software. The forging industry developed new materials to reduce the cost of raw materials or to simplify further processing: for example, heat treatment (directly out of forging heat) reduced the content of alloy and energy consumption. The forging industry co-operated in research and development at a broader level, as in single companies there was not enough capital available. The metal packaging industry developed products together with customers to fit their requirements and improve competitive positions.

Figure 9.15
Other metal products (NACE Rev. 1 28.6 and 28.7)
Production and employment in the Triad

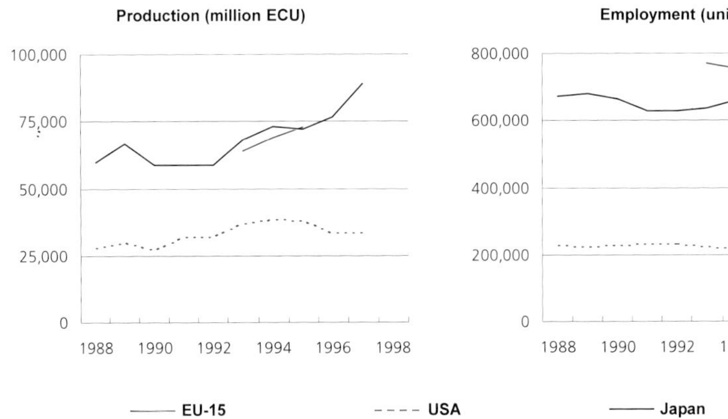

Source: Eurostat (SBS)

Figure 9.16 (%)
Other metal products (NACE Rev. 1 28.6 and 28.7)
Production and export specialisation by Member State, 1998

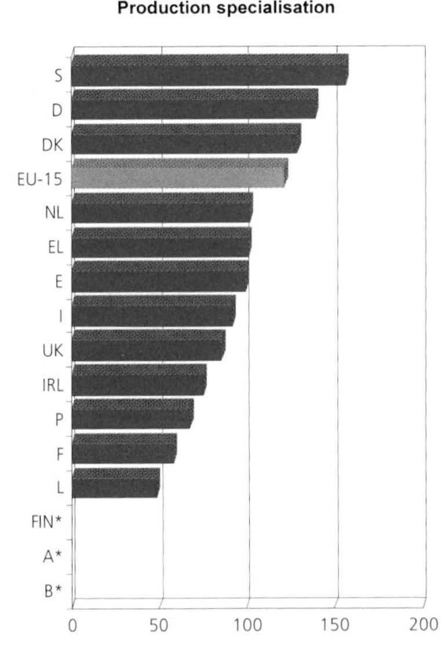

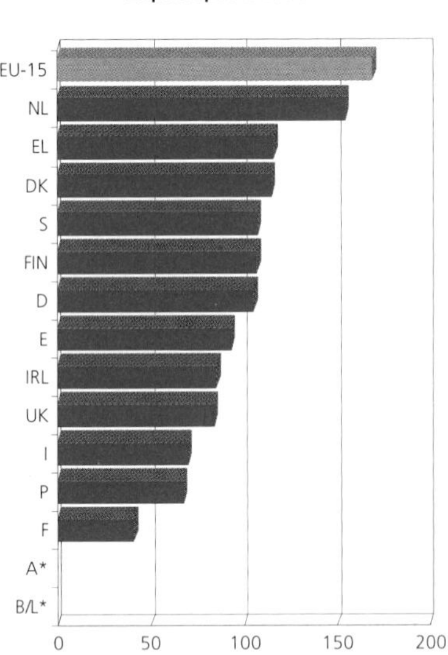

Source: Eurostat (SBS)

The efforts to improve competitiveness were reflected in high growth rates of production values (at constant prices) between 1993 and 1998, such as in France and in Spain (up by 9.5% and 6.1% per annum). The employment figures followed the upward trend, however, in most countries at a slower pace (France up by 3.1% per annum, 1993-1998), which resulted in improved labour productivity in terms of value added per person employed. In France the ratio increased by 17.9% to 41.1 thousand ECU (between 1993 and 1998), whilst in Italy it grew by 39.1% to 50.4 thousand ECU.

In 1997 production value of other metal products increased by 15.8% in the USA, faster than in any European Member State (except for the United Kingdom), whilst in Japan output decreased by 1.7%. If we look at the ratio of value added per person employed, the USA (with 64.8 thousand ECU in 1997) nearly reached the Japanese level (65.6 thousand ECU), which remained almost unchanged since 1993.

Foreign trade flows were relatively low in the manufacture of other metal products, however, they did reflect a tendency to intensify. The forging industry delivered goods mainly for just-in-time production, whilst light metal packaging goods were traditionally not delivered over longer distances due to technical and economic reasons. Although imports from low-wage countries increased in the course of the nineties, the EU trade balance for cutlery and tools as well as other fabricated metal products remained positive.

Figure 9.17

Other metal products (NACE Rev. 1 28.6 & 28.7)
Destination of EU exports, 1998

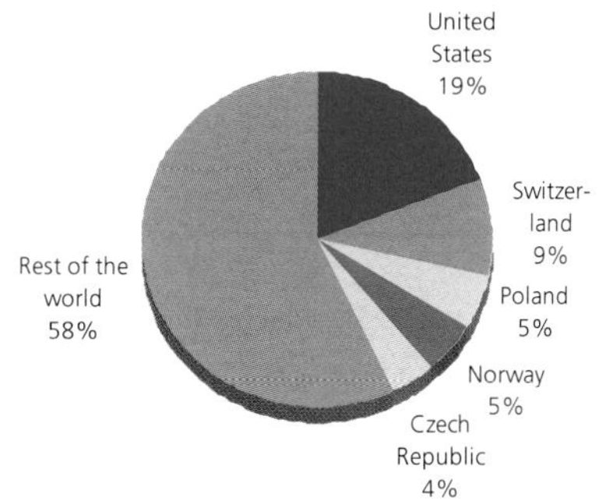

Source: Eurostat (Comext)

Figure 9.18

Other metal products (NACE Rev. 1 28.6 & 28.7)
Origin of EU imports, 1998

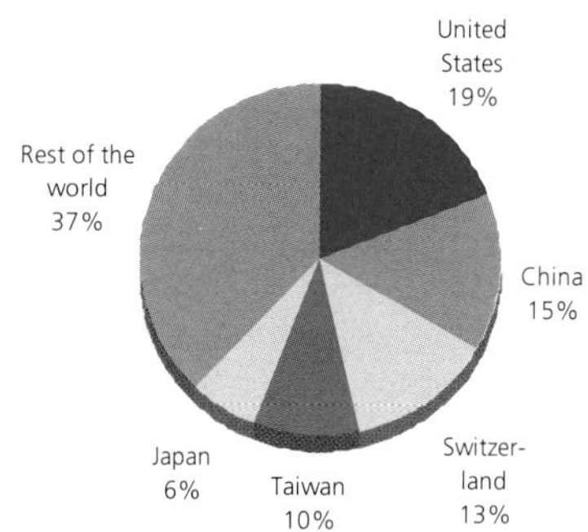

Source: Eurostat (Comext)

Drop forging industry (NACE Rev. 1 28.4)

The drop forging industry in the EU is composed of a large number of medium-sized enterprises, which produce on a sub-contracting basis, located close to customers. In 1998 the European forging industry reported turnover of 3.9 billion ECU and employment of 40 thousand persons (figures from EUROFORGE). The forging industry was characterised by low value added products, with a wide product range. There was an increasing tendency to co-operate with or purchase other suppliers. Automation was a common instrument to improve competitiveness: at the European level the number of persons employed was reduced by 27.3% between 1988 and 1998, whilst production increased by 13.9% to 2.1 million tonnes. However, the main reductions in employment occurred by 1993. Indeed, the latest employment figures showed that in 1997 and 1998 the number of persons employed increased slightly.

Figure 9.19 (1988=100)

Forging: index of production, apparent consumption and employment (1)

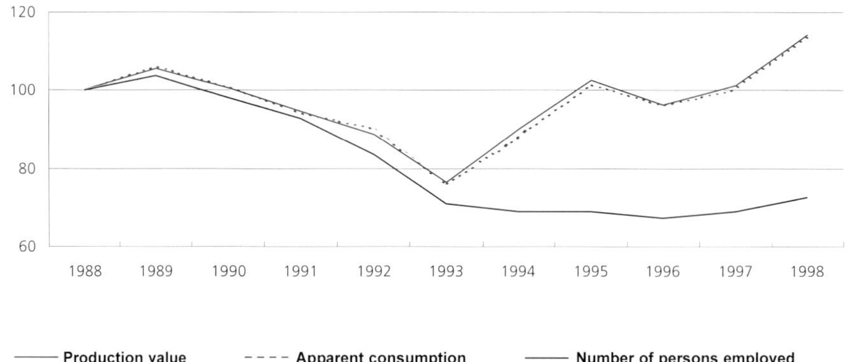

(1) Belgium, Germany, Spain, France, Italy and the United Kingdom, which were responsible for around 95% of the European total.

Source: EUROFORGE

Light metal packaging industry (NACE Rev. 1 28.72)

In the EU[1] there were 333 enterprises engaged in light metal packaging, with turnover of 7.5 billion ECU, employing 50.7 thousand persons in 1997 (figures from SEFEL). The highest level of sales was found in the United Kingdom, with 28.3% of EU sales or 2.1 billion ECU of turnover[2]. The supply of standardised light metal packaging such as food, drink and aerosol cans was concentrated in a few large enterprises that benefit from economies of scale. The degree of integration rose following mergers in downstream industries, such as breweries or soft drink producers. Nevertheless, most customers bought from several packaging manufacturers, even though purchases were often based on long-term contracts. In addition, some customers preferred to have contracts with small or medium-sized companies, which were specialised in customised products and actively developed products.

Light metal packaging is largely made of aluminium or steel tinplate. Over the long run, demand has been determined by the relative price of alternative materials. In the course of the nineties cans made of steel tinplate gained market share compared to aluminium cans, due to price stability on raw material markets and technical improvements. In 1997 the European light metal packaging sector consumed 497.4 thousand tonnes of aluminium compared to 3.7 million tonnes of tinplate.

1) Excluding Luxembourg, Portugal and Sweden.
2) Figures include Ireland.

Figure 9.20

Intermediate consumption in volume of steel tinplate in the EU, 1997 (1)

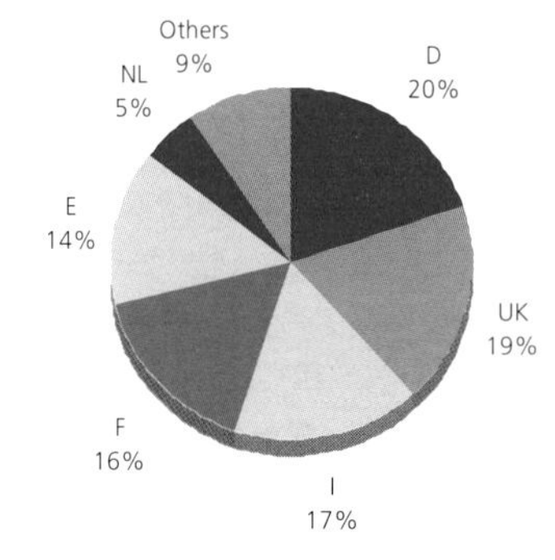

(1) EU-15 excluding Luxembourg, Portugal and Sweden. Figure for the United Kingdom including Ireland. Some national associations' data come from inquiries to individual enterprises whilst others come from official statistics.

Source: SEFEL

Metal packaging is regarded as one of the easiest recyclable materials. For example, recycling of tinplate scrap reduced the consumption of raw materials and energy. In 1997 the recycling rate of steel cans varied between 31% in the United Kingdom and 84% in Germany, compared to 1990 figures of 9% and 38%. Generally, light metal packaging manufacturers delivered new and lighter products to markets, as in the long run packaging manufacturers expected financial disincentives for excessive packaging. At the end of the nineties a typical 33cl steel beverage can was more than 30% lighter than 20 years ago due to a 40% reduction of the tin layer on the steel (figures from APEAL).

In 1997 production in the EU[3] accounted for 4.1 billion aerosol cans or 40% of world production (figures from FEA). European production continued its upward trend in 1997, with growth of 5.0%. Within the EU, the United Kingdom was responsible for 37.3% of the total production (1.5 billion aerosol cans), which was the second largest production world-wide after the USA (3.2 billion aerosol cans). 95% of aerosol cans were made of steel tinplate and aluminium (65% and 30% respectively). Recycling rates varied widely across Europe, from almost 70% in Germany to just 7.5% in the United Kingdom.

3) Excluding Ireland.

(%)

Figure 9.21
Recycling of steel cans in Europe

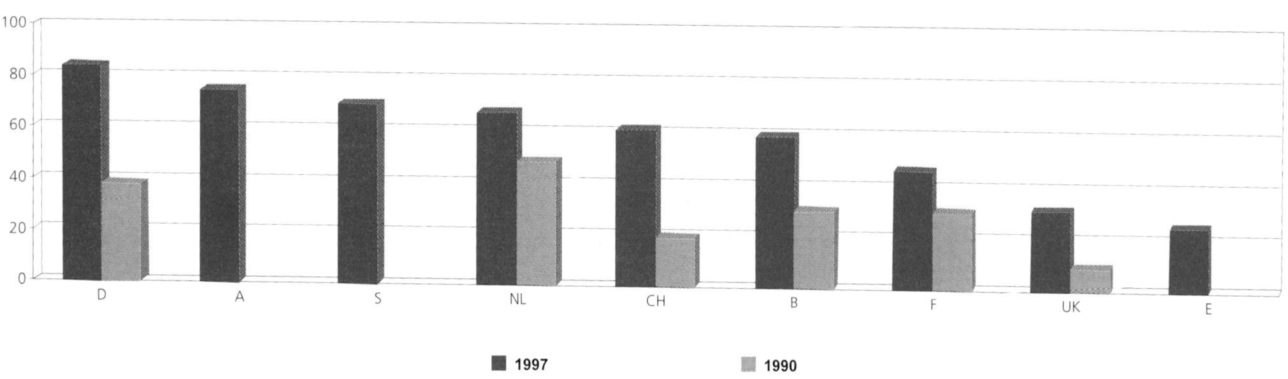

Source: APEAL

(million units)

Figure 9.22
Production of aerosol cans in Europe

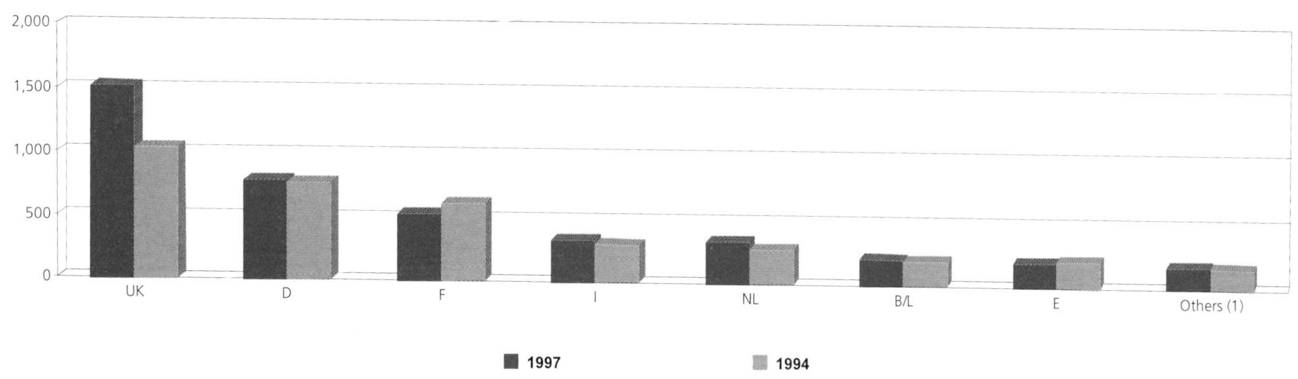

(1) Others include Austria, Denmark, Finland, Greece, Sweden; excluding Ireland.

Source: FEA

Professional associations representing the industries within this chapter

APEAL
European Association of Steel Package Industry
89, avenue Louise
B-1050 Bruxelles
tel: (32) 2 537 91 51
fax: (32) 2 537 86 49

EUROFORGE
European committee of forging and pressing metal industries
Goldene Pforte 1
D-58093 Hagen
tel: (49) 2331 95 88 21
fax: (49) 2331 51 046

FEA
European Aerosol Federation
49, square Marie-Louise
B-1000 Bruxelles
tel: (32) 2 238 98 77
fax: (32) 2 280 09 29
e-mail:
antonia.gomez@euronet.be

SEFEL / SEFA
European Secretariat of Manufacturers of Light Metal Packaging
Diamant Building
80, boulevard A. Reyers
B-1030 Bruxelles
tel: (32) 2 706 78 00
fax: (32) 2 706 78 01
e-mail: sefel@fabrimetal.be

Table 9.2 (million ECU)

Manufacture of structural metal products (NACE Rev. 1 28.1)

Production related indicators in the EU

	1988	1989	1990	1991	1992	1993	1994	1995	1996	1997	1998
Production value	31,685	37,737	40,408	43,321	43,461	39,441	41,093	45,033	46,716	46,245	48,747
Producer price index (1995=100)	:	:	91.0	93.4	95.8	96.2	96.6	100.0	101.8	103.7	101.7
Value added	11,568	13,169	14,340	15,618	15,508	14,062	14,476	15,472	16,252	16,539	17,148
Number of persons employed (thousands)	461.2	487.4	490.8	510.2	504.4	467.9	459.5	462.4	473.5	461.1	478.3

Table 9.3 (million ECU)

Manufacture of structural metal products (NACE Rev. 1 28.1)

Production related indicators, 1998

	B	DK	D	EL	E	F	IRL	I	L	NL	A	P	FIN	S	UK
Production value	3,157	961	14,150	153	6,026	3,743	429	4,516	185	3,578	2,841	834	1,127	1,417	5,630
Value added	950	405	4,860	44	2,019	1,016	140	2,158	55	1,159	1,095	:	449	450	2,077
Number of persons employed (thousands) (1)	22,960	8,976	120,301	1,760	103,166	32,877	4,096	43,901	1,583	29,518	19,382	19,978	9,154	9,174	51,780

(1) NL (1992).

Table 9.4 (million ECU)

Manufacture of structural metal products (NACE Rev. 1 28.1)

Market related indicators in the EU

	1988	1989	1990	1991	1992	1993	1994	1995	1996	1997	1998
Apparent consumption	30,178	36,083	38,885	41,676	42,106	37,901	39,586	43,095	44,894	43,939	46,319
Exports	1,766	1,935	1,938	2,173	1,987	2,193	2,232	2,810	2,814	3,215	3,404
Imports	259	281	416	528	632	653	725	873	993	909	976
Trade balance	1,507	1,654	1,523	1,645	1,354	1,540	1,507	1,937	1,821	2,306	2,428
Export ratio (%)	5.6	5.1	4.8	5.0	4.6	5.6	5.4	6.2	6.0	7.0	7.0
Import penetration ratio (%)	0.9	0.8	1.1	1.3	1.5	1.7	1.8	2.0	2.2	2.1	2.1
Cover ratio (%)	681.8	689.3	466.4	411.4	314.2	335.8	307.9	322.0	283.5	353.6	348.8

Table 9.5 (million ECU)

Manufacture of structural metal products (NACE Rev. 1 28.1)

Market related indicators, 1998

	B/L	DK	D	EL	E	F	IRL	I	NL	A	P	FIN	S	UK
Apparent consumption	:	831	13,570	179	5,925	3,640	461	3,838	3,389	2,775	897	890	1,294	5,275
Exports	674	348	1,971	36	282	712	75	859	534	446	33	305	300	815
Imports	408	218	1,391	62	181	609	107	181	345	381	96	68	177	459
Trade balance	266	130	580	-26	101	103	-32	678	189	65	-63	238	123	356
Export ratio (%)	:	36.2	13.9	23.6	4.7	19.0	17.4	19.0	14.9	15.7	3.9	27.1	21.2	14.5
Import penetration ratio (%)	:	26.2	10.2	34.7	3.1	16.7	23.2	4.7	10.2	13.7	10.7	7.6	13.7	8.7
Cover ratio (%)	165.1	159.7	141.7	58.0	155.7	116.9	69.9	474.0	154.9	117.2	33.9	450.6	169.4	177.6

Table 9.6

Manufacture of structural metal products (NACE Rev. 1 28.1)

Labour related indicators, 1998

	EU-15	B	DK	D	EL	E	F	IRL	I	L	NL	A	P	FIN	S	UK
Personnel costs (million ECU)	12,511	742	283	4,178	25	1,446	996	74	1,121	54	765	732	161	256	293	1,384
Personnel costs/employee (thousand ECU) (1)	30.4	34.0	32.2	35.7	15.7	17.4	30.8	18.5	23.3	33.9	:	37.0	:	30.0	33.5	22.6
Social charges/personnel costs (%) (2)	20.5	27.6	4.0	18.0	23.1	22.3	32.0	13.9	35.0	14.4	13.2	21.8	:	22.4	28.6	9.8
Labour productivity (thousand ECU/head) (3)	35.8	41.4	45.2	40.4	24.8	19.6	30.9	34.2	49.2	34.5	35.8	56.5	:	49.1	49.0	40.1
Wage adjusted labour productivity (%) (1)	110.2	115.8	132.0	119.3	141.5	111.8	111.5	156.8	135.7	97.1	:	123.6	:	139.2	135.6	140.4

(1) EU-15, EL, I, A (1995); B, DK, D, E, F, IRL, L, FIN, S, UK (1996). (2) EU-15, L, S (1995). (3) NL (1992).

Source: Eurostat (SBS, EBT)

(million ECU) Table 9.7

Manufacture of tanks, reservoirs and containers of metal; manufacture of central heating radiators and boilers (NACE Rev. 1 28.2)
Production related indicators in the EU

	1988	1989	1990	1991	1992	1993	1994	1995	1996	1997	1998
Production value	8,283	9,219	9,870	11,096	11,544	10,460	10,693	12,197	:	:	:
Producer price index (1995=100)	:	:	:	:	:	:	:	:	:	:	:
Value added	3,233	3,489	3,805	4,255	4,458	4,045	4,159	4,558	:	:	:
Number of persons employed (thousands)	116.8	117.4	117.1	120.9	120.5	106.6	105.1	110.0	:	:	:

(million ECU) Table 9.8

Manufacture of tanks, reservoirs and containers of metal; manufacture of central heating radiators and boilers (NACE Rev. 1 28.2)
Production related indicators, 1998

	B	DK	D	EL	E	F	IRL	I	L	NL	A	P	FIN	S	UK
Production value (1)	992	139	3,261	68	659	1,570	:	2,738	:	881	:	:	230	267	1,520
Value added (2)	332	71	1,305	21	262	561	20	852	:	314	:	:	105	82	596
Number of persons employed (units) (3)	6,171	1,820	29,277	1,191	14,399	12,518	595	17,912	:	7,992	:	:	1,859	1,896	12,280

(1) DK (1994). (2) IRL (1990); DK (1994). (3) IRL (1990); NL (1992); DK (1994).

(million ECU) Table 9.9

Manufacture of tanks, reservoirs and containers of metal; manufacture of central heating radiators and boilers (NACE Rev. 1 28.2)
Market related indicators in the EU

	1988	1989	1990	1991	1992	1993	1994	1995	1996	1997	1998
Apparent consumption	8,012	8,877	9,507	10,788	11,216	10,050	10,151	11,640	:	:	:
Exports	386	460	514	544	582	654	793	849	1,083	1,171	1,294
Imports	115	119	151	236	254	244	251	292	394	388	402
Trade balance	271	342	363	308	327	410	542	557	689	783	892
Export ratio (%)	4.7	5.0	5.2	4.9	5.0	6.3	7.4	7.0	:	:	:
Import penetration ratio (%)	1.4	1.3	1.6	2.2	2.3	2.4	2.5	2.5	:	:	:
Cover ratio (%)	335.9	388.4	340.7	230.3	228.7	267.7	315.5	290.4	275.0	301.7	322.0

(million ECU) Table 9.10

Manufacture of tanks, reservoirs and containers of metal; manufacture of central heating radiators and boilers (NACE Rev. 1 28.2)
Market related indicators, 1998

	B/L	DK	D	EL	E	F	IRL	I	NL	A	P	FIN	S	UK
Apparent consumption (1)	:	99	2,858	153	718	1,452	:	2,060	813	:	:	187	248	1,683
Exports	351	70	1,116	7	128	487	52	904	258	97	52	63	66	248
Imports	238	55	712	92	188	369	45	226	190	171	29	20	47	412
Trade balance	113	16	403	-85	-60	119	6	679	68	-74	23	43	19	-164
Export ratio (%) (1)	:	53.6	34.2	10.8	19.4	31.0	:	33.0	29.3	:	:	27.5	24.6	16.3
Import penetration ratio (%) (1)	:	35.0	24.9	60.2	26.1	25.4	:	11.0	23.4	:	:	10.9	18.8	24.5
Cover ratio (%)	147.7	128.9	156.6	8.0	68.2	132.1	113.5	400.7	135.8	56.6	177.0	310.7	140.7	60.2

(1) DK (1994).

Table 9.11

Manufacture of tanks, reservoirs and containers of metal; manufacture of central heating radiators and boilers (NACE Rev. 1 28.2)
Labour related indicators, 1998

	EU-15	B	DK	D	EL	E	F	IRL	I	L	NL	A	P	FIN	S	UK
Personnel costs (million ECU) (1)	3,423	253	54	1,171	15	269	431	10	507	:	237	:	:	57	63	337
Personnel costs/employee (thousand ECU) (2)	33.7	39.0	:	40.2	13.9	21.1	35.0	:	25.8	:	:	:	:	31.8	34.5	22.6
Social charges/personnel costs (%) (3)	21.8	26.7	3.4	18.7	24.4	21.8	29.5	:	35.9	:	14.0	:	:	23.2	29.7	12.3
Labour productivity (thousand ECU/head) (4)	41.4	53.8	38.9	44.6	17.8	18.2	44.8	33.9	47.6	:	32.9	:	:	56.5	43.3	48.5
Wage adjusted labour productivity (%) (2)	122.9	141.5	:	123.8	115.2	124.9	136.3	:	172.9	:	:	:	:	162.1	121.0	145.6

(1) IRL (1990); DK (1994); EU-15 (1995). (2) EU-15, EL, I (1995); B, D, E, F, FIN, S, UK (1996). (3) DK (1994); EU-15, S (1995). (4) IRL (1990); NL (1992); DK (1994); EU-15 (1995).

Source: Eurostat (SBS,EBT)

Table 9.12 (million ECU)

Manufacture of steam generators, except central heating hot water boilers (NACE Rev. 1 28.3)

Production related indicators in the EU

	1988	1989	1990	1991	1992	1993	1994	1995	1996	1997	1998
Production value	10,457	11,519	12,433	13,604	13,093	12,832	13,947	13,331	:	:	:
Producer price index (1995=100)	:	:	:	:	:	:	:	:	:	:	:
Value added	4,393	4,416	4,945	5,393	5,248	5,184	5,571	4,974	:	:	:
Number of persons employed (thousands)	140.5	141.4	146.0	152.9	145.0	136.8	137.5	123.6	:	:	:

Table 9.13 (million ECU)

Manufacture of steam generators, except central heating hot water boilers (NACE Rev. 1 28.3)

Production related indicators, 1998

	B	DK	D	EL	E	F	IRL	I	L	NL	A	P	FIN	S	UK
Production value (1)	379	197	4,910	:	160	5,263	:	345	:	236	:	:	815	33	836
Value added (1)	121	56	1,689	:	72	1,856	:	149	:	51	:	:	214	8	254
Number of persons employed (units) (2)	2,650	1,486	33,033	:	3,624	58,125	:	3,116	:	2,292	:	:	2,073	200	8,172

(1) DK (1992); NL (1995). (2) DK, NL (1992).

Table 9.14 (million ECU)

Manufacture of steam generators, except central heating hot water boilers (NACE Rev. 1 28.3)

Market related indicators in the EU

	1988	1989	1990	1991	1992	1993	1994	1995	1996	1997	1998
Apparent consumption	:	:	11,846	:	:	:	12,161	:	:	:	:
Exports	327	417	594	449	543	1,635	1,805	2,032	2,215	2,137	2,220
Imports	:	:	7	:	:	:	19	:	8	:	23
Trade balance	:	:	587	:	:	:	1,786	:	2,207	:	2,197
Export ratio (%)	3.1	3.6	4.8	3.3	4.1	12.7	12.9	15.2	:	:	:
Import penetration ratio (%)	:	:	0.1	:	:	:	0.2	:	:	:	:
Cover ratio (%)	:	:	8,052.0	:	:	:	9,572.8	:	29,172.6	:	9,581.3

Table 9.15 (million ECU)

Manufacture of steam generators, except central heating hot water boilers (NACE Rev. 1 28.3)

Market related indicators, 1998

	B/L	DK	D	EL	E	F	IRL	I	NL	A	P	FIN	S	UK
Apparent consumption (1)	:	150	2,996	:	13	5,117	:	281	218	:	:	674	14	722
Exports	82	63	1,969	1	168	179	6	81	57	44	1	148	35	181
Imports	57	12	54	8	20	32	7	17	21	8	16	7	16	67
Trade balance	24	51	1,915	-7	147	147	-1	64	35	36	-15	141	19	114
Export ratio (%) (1)	:	28.9	40.1	:	104.4	3.4	:	23.4	14.7	:	:	18.2	106.0	21.7
Import penetration ratio (%) (1)	:	6.1	1.8	:	153.0	0.6	:	5.9	7.7	:	:	1.0	113.8	9.3
Cover ratio (%)	142.9	523.5	3,614.0	7.9	818.6	555.6	80.8	483.0	265.4	528.9	4.0	2,179.3	213.0	269.2

(1) DK (1992); NL (1995).

Table 9.16

Manufacture of steam generators, except central heating hot water boilers (NACE Rev. 1 28.3)

Labour related indicators, 1998

	EU-15	B	DK	D	EL	E	F	IRL	I	L	NL	A	P	FIN	S	UK
Personnel costs (million ECU) (1)	4,638	97	54	1,633	:	78	1,983	:	104	:	45	:	:	80	7	305
Personnel costs/employee (thousand ECU) (2)	38.1	41.3	:	49.0	:	23.5	34.7	:	30.4	:	:	:	:	39.4	37.2	30.8
Social charges/personnel costs (%) (3)	23.3	29.8	2.0	18.0	:	21.8	29.8	:	32.9	:	12.2	:	:	22.2	31.9	12.2
Labour productivity (thousand ECU/head) (4)	40.2	45.6	37.8	51.1	:	19.9	31.9	:	47.8	:	23.8	:	:	103.4	38.1	31.1
Wage adjusted labour productivity (%) (2)	105.7	96.6	:	105.7	:	128.0	110.1	:	93.5	:	:	:	:	123.2	98.8	89.7

(1) DK (1992); EU-15, NL (1995). (2) EU-15, I (1995); B, D, E, F, FIN, S, UK (1996). (3) S (1991); DK (1992); EU-15, NL (1995). (4) DK, NL (1992); EU-15 (1995).

Source: Eurostat (SBS, EBT)

(million ECU) Table 9.17

Forging, pressing, stamping and roll forming of metal; powder metallurgy (NACE Rev. 1 28.4)

Production related indicators in the EU

	1988	1989	1990	1991	1992	1993	1994	1995	1996	1997	1998
Production value	14,578	17,376	18,010	17,953	18,060	16,313	18,168	22,264	:	:	:
Producer price index (1995=100)	:	:	:	:	:	:	:	100.0	104.4	115.0	114.3
Value added	5,618	6,342	6,723	6,841	7,120	6,501	7,132	8,391	:	:	:
Number of persons employed (thousands)	195.3	205.8	209.3	206.2	200.9	186.2	188.2	223.6	:	:	:

(million ECU) Table 9.18

Forging, pressing, stamping and roll forming of metal; powder metallurgy (NACE Rev. 1 28.4)

Production related indicators, 1998

	B	DK	D	EL	E	F	IRL	I	L	NL	A	P	FIN	S	UK
Production value (1)	289	0	7,860	:	2,494	5,728	17	4,934	:	880	367	764	10	34	2,765
Value added (1)	115	0	3,582	:	889	1,631	9	1,600	:	323	142	:	6	14	1,103
Number of persons employed (units) (1)(2)	2,762	0	75,521	:	25,678	39,998	197	27,608	:	6,971	2,530	23,073	95	335	29,353

(1) DK (1996). (2) NL (1992).

Table 9.19

Forging, pressing, stamping and roll forming of metal; powder metallurgy (NACE Rev. 1 28.4)

Labour related indicators, 1998

	EU-15	B	DK	D	EL	E	F	IRL	I	L	NL	A	P	FIN	S	UK
Personnel costs (million ECU) (1)	6,161	70	0	2,822	:	539	1,207	4	826	:	211	83	141	2	11	725
Personnel costs/employee (thousand ECU) (2)	32.0	34.8	:	37.2	:	23.6	30.7	18.9	27.3	:	:	34.2	:	26.4	33.7	20.4
Social charges/personnel costs (%) (3)	21.7	25.2	:	18.8	:	22.3	29.8	12.3	37.5	:	12.1	23.0	:	26.2	31.7	12.4
Labour productivity (thousand ECU/head) (4)	37.5	41.6	:	47.4	:	34.6	40.8	44.2	58.0	:	37.1	56.2	:	62.3	40.9	37.6
Wage adjusted labour productivity (%) (2)	117.2	140.3	:	124.5	:	141.0	121.0	181.8	184.3	:	:	136.4	:	192.1	116.9	141.5

(1) EU-15 (1995); DK (1996). (2) EU-15, I, A (1995); B, D, E, F, IRL, FIN, S, UK (1996). (3) S (1991); EU-15 (1995). (4) NL (1992); EU-15 (1995).

Source: Eurostat (SBS, EBT)

Table 9.20 (million ECU)

Treatment and coating of metals; general mechanical engineering (NACE Rev. 1 28.5)
Production related indicators in the EU

	1988	1989	1990	1991	1992	1993	1994	1995	1996	1997	1998
Production value	16,537	19,014	20,356	20,424	19,972	17,938	20,966	26,588	:	:	:
Producer price index (1995=100)	:	:	:	:	:	:	:	:	:	:	:
Value added	7,717	8,707	9,349	9,566	9,195	8,316	9,477	12,443	:	:	:
Number of persons employed (thousands)	298.1	309.5	324.1	318.3	307.1	275.8	297.7	337.2	:	:	:

Table 9.21 (million ECU)

Treatment and coating of metals; general mechanical engineering (NACE Rev. 1 28.5)
Production related indicators, 1998

	B	DK	D	EL	E	F	IRL	I	L	NL	A	P	FIN	S	UK
Production value (1)	2,250	267	5,801	40	3,285	8,022	76	4,869	409	924	455	:	345	800	5,707
Value added	844	146	2,833	13	1,485	3,413	35	2,160	59	454	277	:	194	354	2,703
Number of persons employed (thousands) (2)	18,575	3,038	59,507	534	68,910	81,946	1,086	50,328	958	8,578	5,435	:	3,853	7,977	72,132

(1) A (1997). (2) NL (1992).

Table 9.22

Treatment and coating of metals; general mechanical engineering (NACE Rev. 1 28.5)
Labour related indicators, 1998

	EU-15	B	DK	D	EL	E	F	IRL	I	L	NL	A	P	FIN	S	UK
Personnel costs (million ECU) (1)	8,877	567	107	2,025	7	1,265	2,485	20	1,343	30	324	179	:	94	254	1,840
Personnel costs/employee (thousand ECU) (2)	27.6	34.5	36.0	33.5	14.9	20.3	30.8	18.3	24.3	31.1	:	32.9	:	28.4	33.3	21.2
Social charges/personnel costs (%) (3)	21.5	27.3	4.3	18.0	22.8	21.3	29.1	13.0	36.9	13.8	13.7	21.8	:	22.3	28.4	11.9
Labour productivity (thousand ECU/head) (4)	36.9	45.5	48.2	47.6	23.5	21.6	41.7	32.2	42.9	62.0	35.3	50.9	:	50.5	44.4	37.5
Wage adjusted labour productivity (%) (2)	133.7	142.6	125.9	124.1	141.7	129.6	119.6	163.3	156.3	168.6	:	139.8	:	144.4	128.7	135.7

(1) EU-15 (1995). (2) EU-15, EL, I, A (1995); B, DK, D, E, F, IRL, L, FIN, S, UK (1996). (3) EU-15, L, S (1995). (4) NL (1992); EU-15 (1995).

Source: Eurostat (SBS, EBT)

(million ECU) — Table 9.23

Manufacture of cutlery, tools and general hardware (NACE Rev. 1 28.6)
Production related indicators in the EU

	1988	1989	1990	1991	1992	1993	1994	1995	1996	1997	1998
Production value	:	:	:	:	:	20,702	22,654	25,086	:	:	:
Producer price index (1995=100)	:	:	89.1	91.2	93.9	95.7	97.1	100.0	:	:	:
Value added	:	:	:	:	:	9,942	10,856	11,672	:	:	:
Number of persons employed (thousands)	:	:	:	:	:	282.8	282.0	271.5	:	:	:

(million ECU) — Table 9.24

Manufacture of cutlery, tools and general hardware (NACE Rev. 1 28.6)
Production related indicators, 1998

	B	DK	D	EL	E	F	IRL	I	L	NL	A	P	FIN	S	UK
Production value (1)	331	326	11,013	80	2,070	2,810	137	2,612	:	440	1,104	:	299	2,311	2,418
Value added (1)	126	160	5,239	30	907	1,207	68	1,581	:	216	627	:	170	863	1,257
Number of persons employed (units) (2)	2,655	3,066	112,853	1,463	35,157	32,886	1,829	23,779	:	4,993	10,678	:	3,288	14,833	33,053

(1) NL (1995). (2) NL (1992).

(million ECU) — Table 9.25

Manufacture of cutlery, tools and general hardware (NACE Rev. 1 28.6)
Market related indicators in the EU

	1988	1989	1990	1991	1992	1993	1994	1995	1996	1997	1998
Apparent consumption	:	:	:	:	:	19,778	21,841	23,917	:	:	:
Exports	2,916	3,222	3,155	3,188	3,173	3,496	3,961	4,543	5,027	5,683	5,726
Imports	1,856	2,198	2,231	2,554	2,642	2,572	3,148	3,375	3,455	4,000	4,437
Trade balance	1,060	1,025	924	634	531	924	813	1,169	1,573	1,683	1,289
Export ratio (%)	:	:	:	:	:	16.9	17.5	18.1	:	:	:
Import penetration ratio (%)	:	:	:	:	:	13.0	14.4	14.1	:	:	:
Cover ratio (%)	157.1	146.6	141.4	124.8	120.1	135.9	125.8	134.6	145.5	142.1	129.0

(million ECU) — Table 9.26

Manufacture of cutlery, tools and general hardware (NACE Rev. 1 28.6)
Market related indicators, 1998

	B/L	DK	D	EL	E	F	IRL	I	NL	A	P	FIN	S	UK
Apparent consumption (1)	:	521	8,521	249	2,303	3,106	224	1,624	738	857	:	399	2,120	2,884
Exports	476	244	5,427	31	716	1,384	86	2,201	751	860	184	118	828	1,610
Imports	999	439	2,935	200	950	1,680	174	1,213	997	614	224	218	637	2,077
Trade balance	-523	-195	2,492	-169	-234	-296	-87	988	-246	246	-40	-99	192	-467
Export ratio (%) (1)	:	74.8	49.3	39.4	34.6	49.2	63.0	84.3	145.9	77.9	:	39.6	35.8	66.6
Import penetration ratio (%) (1)	:	84.2	34.4	80.5	41.2	54.1	77.4	74.7	127.3	71.6	:	54.6	30.0	72.0
Cover ratio (%)	47.6	55.5	184.9	15.7	75.4	82.4	49.6	181.4	75.4	140.1	82.1	54.4	130.1	77.5

(1) NL (1995).

Table 9.27

Manufacture of cutlery, tools and general hardware (NACE Rev. 1 28.6)
Labour related indicators, 1998

	EU-15	B	DK	D	EL	E	F	IRL	I	L	NL	A	P	FIN	S	UK
Personnel costs (million ECU) (1)	8,334	99	100	4,261	22	710	974	39	696	:	146	365	:	88	559	845
Personnel costs/employee (thousand ECU) (2)	31.5	36.5	33.4	37.8	16.4	23.2	30.1	21.5	26.7	:	:	35.8	:	28.5	39.4	21.1
Social charges/personnel costs (%) (3)	21.2	26.2	3.8	18.0	23.8	22.0	29.3	14.2	37.5	:	14.2	22.7	:	22.2	31.3	11.9
Labour productivity (thousand ECU/head) (4)	43.0	47.5	52.3	46.4	20.6	25.8	36.7	37.3	66.5	:	37.7	58.7	:	51.6	58.2	38.0
Wage adjusted labour productivity (%) (2)	136.4	121.9	147.5	123.5	152.7	135.4	125.1	154.9	156.5	:	:	151.7	:	157.4	148.7	151.8

(1) EU-15, NL (1995). (2) EU-15, EL, I, A (1995); B, DK, D, E, F, IRL, FIN, S, UK (1996). (3) EU-15, NL, S (1995). (4) NL (1992); EU-15 (1995).

Source: Eurostat (SBS, EBT)

Table 9.28 (million ECU)

Manufacture of other fabricated metal products (NACE Rev. 1 28.7)

Production related indicators in the EU

	1988	1989	1990	1991	1992	1993	1994	1995	1996	1997	1998
Production value	:	:	:	:	:	43,502	46,333	47,890	:	:	:
Producer price index (1995=100)	:	:	97.0	96.4	97.2	96.7	96.8	100.0	95.3	101.5	93.4
Value added	:	:	:	:	:	17,218	18,078	17,905	:	:	:
Number of persons employed (thousands)	:	:	:	:	:	490.0	475.6	448.0	:	:	:

Table 9.29 (million ECU)

Manufacture of other fabricated metal products (NACE Rev. 1 28.7)

Production related indicators, 1998

	B	DK	D	EL	E	F	IRL	I	L	NL	A	P	FIN	S	UK
Production value	1,727	1,108	15,188	392	4,495	6,969	397	8,134	:	1,763	1,194	:	571	1,994	6,578
Value added	462	473	6,092	96	1,525	2,390	138	2,680	:	660	413	:	238	661	2,480
Number of persons employed (units) (1)	8,664	11,421	137,043	3,607	57,666	55,563	4,258	57,455	:	14,145	9,449	:	5,581	15,659	61,195

(1) NL (1992).

Table 9.30 (million ECU)

Manufacture of other fabricated metal products (NACE Rev. 1 28.7)

Market related indicators in the EU

	1988	1989	1990	1991	1992	1993	1994	1995	1996	1997	1998
Apparent consumption	:	:	:	:	:	41,978	44,747	46,416	:	:	:
Exports	4,313	4,968	4,937	5,056	5,005	5,362	6,033	6,784	7,716	8,478	8,998
Imports	2,648	3,323	3,384	3,722	3,593	3,837	4,446	5,310	5,880	6,705	7,325
Trade balance	1,665	1,645	1,554	1,334	1,411	1,524	1,587	1,474	1,836	1,773	1,672
Export ratio (%)	:	:	:	:	:	12.3	13.0	14.2	:	:	:
Import penetration ratio (%)	:	:	:	:	:	9.1	9.9	11.4	:	:	:
Cover ratio (%)	162.9	149.5	145.9	135.8	139.3	139.7	135.7	127.8	131.2	126.4	122.8

Table 9.31 (million ECU)

Manufacture of other fabricated metal products (NACE Rev. 1 28.7)

Market related indicators, 1998

	B/L	DK	D	EL	E	F	IRL	I	NL	A	P	FIN	S	UK
Apparent consumption	:	1,092	13,939	515	4,366	6,601	571	4,699	1,834	1,403	:	707	1,937	6,759
Exports	1,705	634	6,163	92	1,485	3,795	174	4,967	1,635	905	286	226	826	2,554
Imports	1,873	618	4,914	215	1,356	3,427	348	1,533	1,706	1,113	364	362	770	2,735
Trade balance	-168	16	1,248	-123	129	369	-173	3,435	-71	-208	-78	-136	57	-181
Export ratio (%)	:	57.2	40.6	23.4	33.0	54.5	43.8	61.1	92.7	75.8	:	39.6	41.4	38.8
Import penetration ratio (%)	:	56.6	35.3	41.7	31.1	51.9	60.9	32.6	93.0	79.4	:	51.3	39.7	40.5
Cover ratio (%)	91.0	102.5	125.4	42.8	109.5	110.8	50.1	324.1	95.8	81.3	78.6	62.5	107.4	93.4

Table 9.32

Manufacture of other fabricated metal products (NACE Rev. 1 28.7)

Labour related indicators, 1998

	EU-15	B	DK	D	EL	E	F	IRL	I	L	NL	A	P	FIN	S	UK
Personnel costs (million ECU) (1)	12,825	297	359	4,951	53	1,138	1,753	90	1,599	:	427	308	:	150	499	1,582
Personnel costs/employee (thousand ECU) (2)	29.8	35.8	32.1	36.4	16.0	22.2	32.1	21.2	25.4	:	:	34.2	:	29.2	33.4	21.4
Social charges/personnel costs (%) (3)	20.9	26.7	4.1	18.5	23.2	22.8	29.4	14.6	37.3	:	14.5	22.2	:	23.0	28.3	12.0
Labour productivity (thousand ECU/head) (4)	40.0	53.3	41.5	44.5	26.5	26.4	43.0	32.5	46.6	:	38.9	43.7	:	42.6	42.2	40.5
Wage adjusted labour productivity (%) (2)	134.4	125.6	133.2	123.8	145.5	142.3	136.5	148.3	175.7	:	:	132.6	:	139.2	126.2	150.6

(1) EU-15 (1995). (2) EU-15, EL, I, A (1995); B, DK, D, E, F, IRL, FIN, S, UK (1996). (3) EU-15, S (1995). (4) NL (1992); EU-15 (1995).

Source: Eurostat (SBS, EBT)

Machinery and equipment

Industrial description

In the NACE Rev. 1 classification the manufacture of machinery and equipment covers a wide range of products from general purpose machinery for the production and use of mechanical power[1] and cooling equipment to special purpose machinery for agriculture, forestry or mining and construction, all within NACE Rev. 1 29. The activity encompasses the manufacture of weapons and ammunitions, although the manufacturing process and enterprises involved are somewhat different.

Machinery and equipment offers simple products such as single parts for use in production processes (gears or pumps) through to complete machinery solutions, such as an integrated milking production facility with cheese-making. The activity has a long tradition in most industrialised countries, yet it still plays an important role in most economies, as machinery and equipment are necessary pre-requisites for the manufacture of cars, textiles, steel, paper and almost every other manufactured good.

The manufacture of machinery and equipment contributed around 10% of total EU manufacturing production value[2]. The largest producer in Europe was Germany, producing 2.4 times the production value of Italy, and 3.6 times the production value of the United Kingdom and France. Scandinavian countries reported a high degree of specialisation in the activity of machinery and equipment, with the industry contributing 130% the EU average to total manufacturing.

1) Except aircraft, vehicle and cycle engines.
2) Estimated figure for 1998; manufacture of machinery and equipment n.e.c. excludes the manufacture of domestic appliances (NACE Rev. 1 29.7).

(%) Figure 10.1

Machinery and equipment (NACE Rev. 1 29)
Share of EU value added in total manufacturing

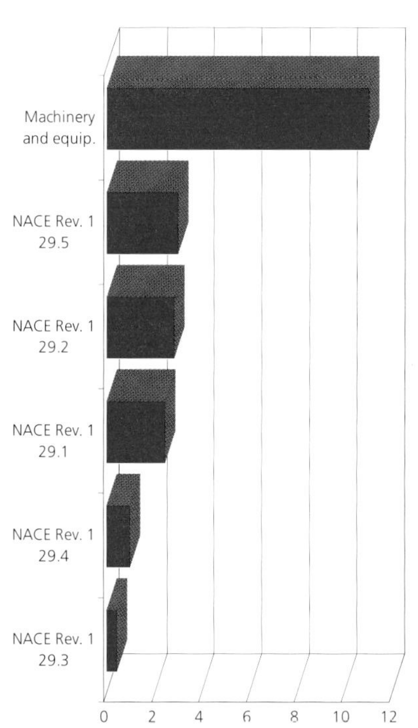

Source: Eurostat (SBS)

The activities covered in this chapter include:

- 29.1: manufacture of machinery for the production and use of mechanical power, except aircraft, vehicle and cycle engines;
- 29.2: manufacture of other general purpose machinery;
- 29.3: manufacture of agricultural and forestry machinery;
- 29.4: manufacture of machine-tools;
- 29.5: manufacture of other special purpose machinery;
- 29.6: manufacture of weapons and ammunition.

Figure 10.2 (1988=100)

Machinery and equipment (NACE Rev. 1 29)

Production, employment and value added compared to EU total manufacturing

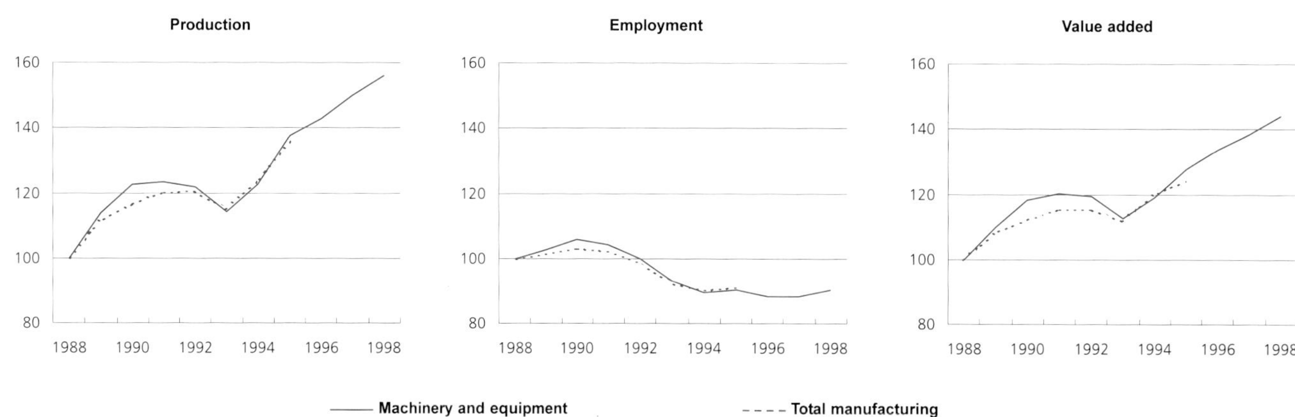

Source: Eurostat (SBS)

The performance of this industry is largely determined by fluctuations in demand and the propensity to invest of downstream industries that purchase capital goods. Sales of machinery and equipment are supported by the need for modern production methods (to reduce costs), the growing importance of information technology (computer-aided production) and changing legislation (for example, increased environmental protection).

At the end of the nineties there has been an increase in investment levels, which has been reflected in growing sales of machinery and equipment. In 1996, German activity was reporting that production was almost unchanged (up by 0.1%), although this had improved by 1998 (with an annual increase of 6.2%). German industry relied to a large degree on foreign demand (especially during periods of recession).

However, machinery and equipment is now facing reduced exports due to the crisis in south-east Asia. Manufacturers of machinery and equipment expect to report increased sales to Eastern Europe, where industry has considerable needs for modernisation. At the same time many Eastern European producers were increasingly present on EU markets, especially in markets for low-cost standardised products.

Figure 10.3

Machinery and equipment (NACE Rev. 1 29)

International comparison of main indicators in current prices

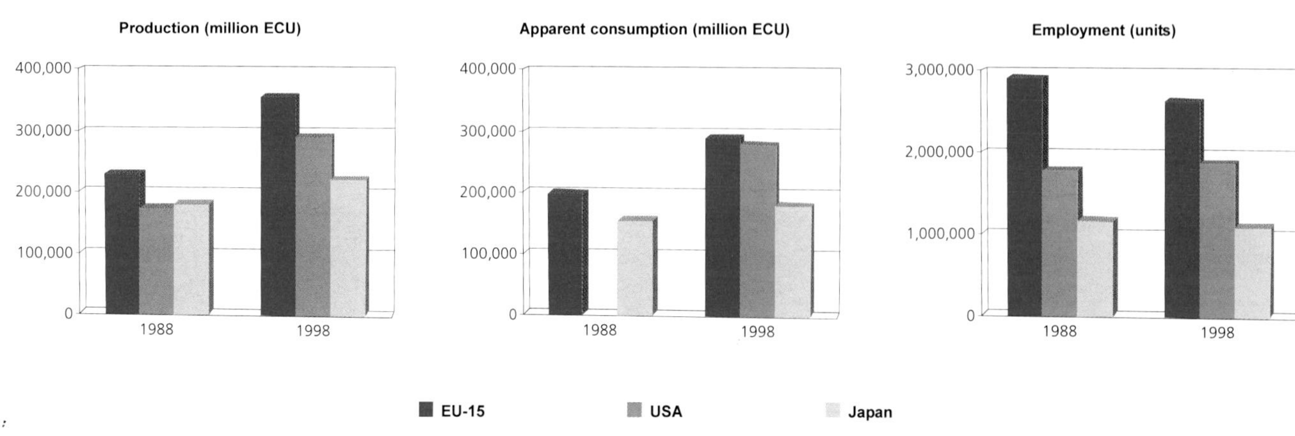

Source: Eurostat (SBS)

As a result of these trends, European manufacturers have increasingly switched their production to specialised product ranges and custom-made products based on customer demand. The technological knowledge that has been built-up acts as a barrier to entry for many competitors. Nevertheless, competition for mature markets has increased. EU producers have responded with rationalisation programmes in order to reduce costs, particularly through automation. Between 1994 and 1998 the number of persons employed per million ECU of production value was reduced in all reporting Member States, for example in the United Kingdom by four persons employed to 8.2 persons on average. By 1998, labour intensity had fallen to as low as 7.3 (Germany) and 6.7 (France) persons employed per million ECU of production value. Some manufacturers of machinery and equipment shifted their production facilities to Eastern Europe, in most cases to benefit from lower labour costs.

Most machinery and equipment produced in the EU is of high value added, although the basic technology may have its roots in the 19th century process of industrialisation. Companies producing machinery and equipment as their core business have generally diversified their production range, during the nineties there has been a movement towards the telecommunications sector, for example groups such as Wallenberg (Sweden) or Mannesmann (Germany).

Machinery and equipment is not a typical growth sector of the economy, nevertheless it does provide potential for innovation. During the nineties manufacturers had to increasingly change their products with the pressure of information technology. Manufacturers of specialised industrial processing machinery offered customers solutions for their whole production process, including service provision and support during the period of use. Customer demand has led to after-sales services such as training and maintenance becoming the norm in the industry. Such service is an important factor in non-price competition, especially at the higher end of the market. In addition to the personal customer service centres, some enterprises started to build-up "virtual service centres" based on the electronic transfer of information to both help operators and in more advanced solutions to control data and subsequently machines from off-site locations.

The increasing demand for complete solutions has led to an increased number of co-operations and higher levels of concentration in the market. Concentration has also spread into other industrial activities, especially electrical engineering, electronics and information technology. Despite the recent trend towards a more concentrated industry, machinery and equipment is still an activity dominated by medium-sized enterprises, producing customised products or small series.

Recent trends

The activity of machinery and equipment faced generally sharper cyclical fluctuations than most other activities, with the ability to invest reflecting not only the number of orders but also financing conditions. In 1998 output was increasing in the EU, with positive growth rates amongst the individual Member States of between 0.5% in Belgium and 12.0% in Greece. There were only two Member States that reported a decline in production: Finland and Sweden (down by 0.2% and 1.8% respectively compared to data for 1997). Value added grew at a faster pace in most of the Member States (for example, in Austria by 14.6%).

During the nineties the manufacture of machinery and equipment looked increasingly towards automated solutions, reducing the number of persons employed. In 1998 there was still a downward trend in employment figures in several Member States, such as Finland and the United Kingdom (down by 4.0% and 1.8% respectively). In Italy employment rose from 1995 onwards, when a higher level of orders and increased production became apparent. In 1998 Italian employment increased by 9.4%. In Germany there was a moderate rate of expansion, with 1.2% more jobs created in 1998 (compared to a year before). With the move towards customised products, high-end producers found it difficult to automate and make cost savings through replacing labour with capital equipment. Production lines treating small series required skilled labour, which was difficult to rationalise.

(ECU/hour) Figure 10.4

Machinery and equipment (NACE Rev. 1 29)
Labour costs by Member State, 1996

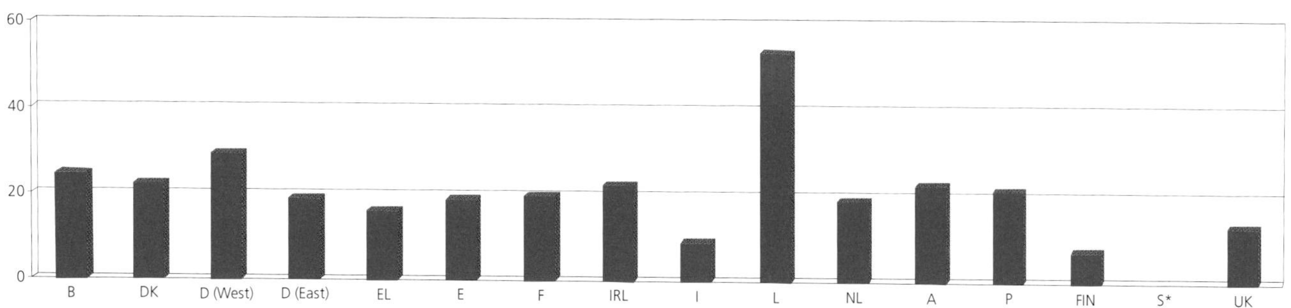

Source: Eurostat (LCS)

Labour productivity (measured as value added per person employed) improved during the course of the nineties throughout Europe. Between 1990 and 1998 the ratio increased by 16.6 thousand ECU to 55.4 thousand ECU in Sweden and by 8.9 thousand ECU to 46.9 thousand ECU in France. Italy reported a sharp increase in value added per head during the mid-nineties, although 1997 and 1998 saw a reduction in labour productivity from 53.2 thousand ECU in 1996 to 50.6 thousand ECU in 1998.

Table 10.1 (%)

Machinery and equipment
(NACE Rev. 1 29)
Composition of the labour force, 1997

	Females	Part-time	Highly-educated
EU-15	17.0	:	19.5
B	12.5	:	20.4
DK	22.5	7.1	17.5
D	18.1	5.4	26.5
EL	11.8	:	11.7
E	12.9	1.5	28.7
F	18.2	3.7	15.6
IRL	20.4	2.4	23.5
I	15.8	2.7	5.5
L	:	:	:
NL	10.8	9.4	16.5
A	15.6	6.1	4.2
P	28.8	:	:
FIN	13.7	:	36.1
S	17.1	6.6	20.2
UK	17.6	4.7	18.5

Source: Eurostat (LFS)

International comparison was largely influenced by the economic cycle in the Triad economies. Whilst in Japan production value and value added decreased by 7.1% and 5.6% respectively during 1997, the USA reported double-digit growth for both production and value added (up by 18.8% and 19.1% respectively). The European rates of change were between the performance of the other two members of the Triad, with output increasing at a slower pace than in the USA. Turning to employment in the Triad, the USA recorded a constant increase in its number of persons employed from 1993 onwards, up by 1.4% in 1997. In Japan there were job losses associated with the downturn in economic activity, employment was reduced by 3.2% in 1997.

Foreign trade

In 1998 the EU reported an excess of exports over imports within the activity of machinery and equipment. There was a high degree of trade in this industry with export ratios above 50% and import penetration ratios over 30%. Due to the specialised nature of many products, manufacturers of machinery and equipment are often in a global market, with even small-sized enterprises not able to restrict themselves to their regional market. The two largest producers within the EU (Germany and Italy) reported high export specialisation ratios. In 1998 German industry exported 1.4 times more than the EU average, whilst Italian producers exported 1.6 times as much. In most of the Member States exports grew at a faster pace than imports between 1988 and 1998, for example in the United Kingdom by 80.9% and 30.0% respectively. One exception was Germany where imports increased by 100.5%, some 33.6 percentage points faster than exports.

Besides shifts in competitiveness influencing export performance, trends in exports and imports also reflected different business cycles across the world. Both Japan and the USA also exported more than they imported. However, in Japan the trade surplus increased mainly between 1992 and 1995, whilst in the USA during this period the trade surplus was reduced, before a sharp increase in 1997.

Figure 10.5

Machinery and equipment
(NACE Rev. 1 29.1 to 29.6)
Destination of EU exports, 1998

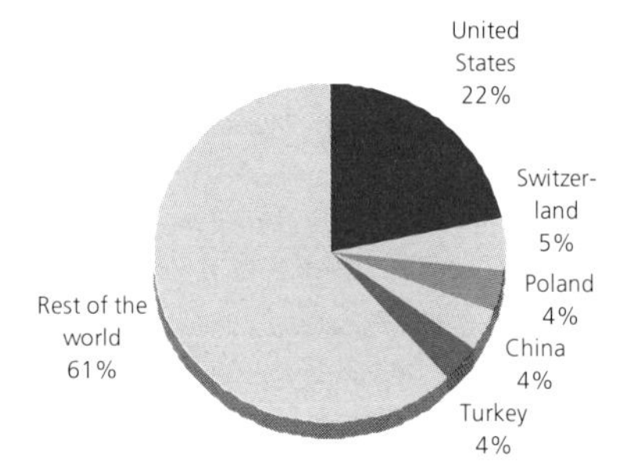

Source: Eurostat (Comext)

Figure 10.6

Machinery and equipment
(NACE Rev. 1 29.1 to 29.6)
Origin of EU imports, 1998

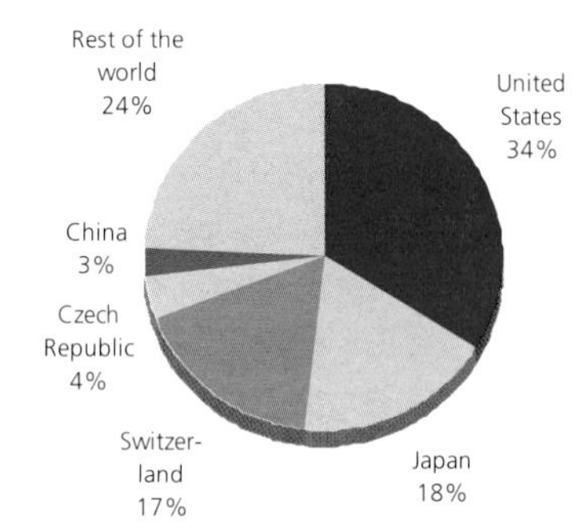

Source: Eurostat (Comext)

Industrial processing machinery (NACE Rev. 1 29.1 to 29.5)

One of the key aims of manufacturing is to transform raw materials into end-products for which there is a market. General production processes benefit when manufacturers use the most efficient methods in terms of cost, time and quality to produce their goods. The manufacture of industrial processing machinery provides other industries with the machinery and equipment that they need to improve their transformation processes.

The industrial processing machinery industry produces capital goods with demand being highly dependent on the economic situation of the downstream industries that are supplied. Indeed, with many customers reacting quickly to changes in their capacity utilisation rate, profits and financing costs, investment decisions often show a much greater degree of fluctuation than the general economic cycle. As a result, sales of industrial processing machinery followed the investment cycle, with rapid fluctuations for new orders, which are even greater when manufacturers are specialised in one particular activity.

Industrial processing machinery accounted for around 90% of total European machinery and equipment manufacture, some 9% of total EU manufacturing[3]. Industrial processing machinery can be divided into general purpose and special purpose machinery, which will be split in the text that follows.

3) Estimated figure for 1998.

Manufacture of general purpose machinery (NACE Rev. 1 29.1 and 29.2)

The manufacture of general purpose machinery encompasses a wide range of products for the production and use of mechanical power, such as engines[4], turbines, pumps and compressors; as well as hand furnaces, lifting equipment and non-domestic cooling equipment. General purpose machinery is delivered to numerous activities, with the automotive industry being one of the most important downstream industries. The manufacture of machinery and equipment is itself one of the largest customers for general purpose machinery, particularly with respect to transmission equipment (included in NACE Rev. 1 29.1).

The Nordic countries reported a high degree of specialisation in the manufacture of general purpose machinery, with the industry contributing nearly twice as much to total national manufacturing as the European average. In the EU there was a high degree of concentration in Germany, where around 40% of European output occurred.

Since 1993, general purpose machinery reported an upward trend in output, which continued in 1998. Larger producing countries (in terms of production value) reported rates of growth between 3.3% in both France and the United Kingdom and 4.9% in Germany. Between 1993 and 1998 production value increased at a faster pace than value added (both at constant prices). The Nordic countries of Sweden and Finland reported particularly fast growth for production, with gains of 11.8% and 11.0% per annum for production and 8.5% and 8.7% respectively for value added. German manufacturers recorded a far more moderate increase of 2.1% per annum for value added over the same period.

4) Except aircraft, vehicle and cycle engines.

European manufacturers faced strong competitive pressure from south-east Asia and Eastern Europe. Manufacturers reacted by implementing rationalisation procedures that led to constant reductions in the number of persons employed throughout the course of the nineties. Nevertheless, in the late nineties there was some expansion in the labour market, with employment rising in Denmark and Italy (up by 4.0% and 13.8% in 1998 compared to a year before).

In the United Kingdom manufacturers took continuous steps to reduce employment (down by 3.3% per annum between 1990 and 1998). In Germany most reductions took place during the early part of the nineties, the annual average change between 1990 and 1998 was -3.4% (or -4.7% per annum between 1990 and 1995). The reduction in the number of persons employed was reflected in figures for labour intensity (in other words, the average number of persons it took to produce one million ECU of production value). Labour intensity was reduced in all

Figure 10.7
General purpose machinery (NACE Rev. 1 29.1 and 29.2)
Production and employment in the Triad

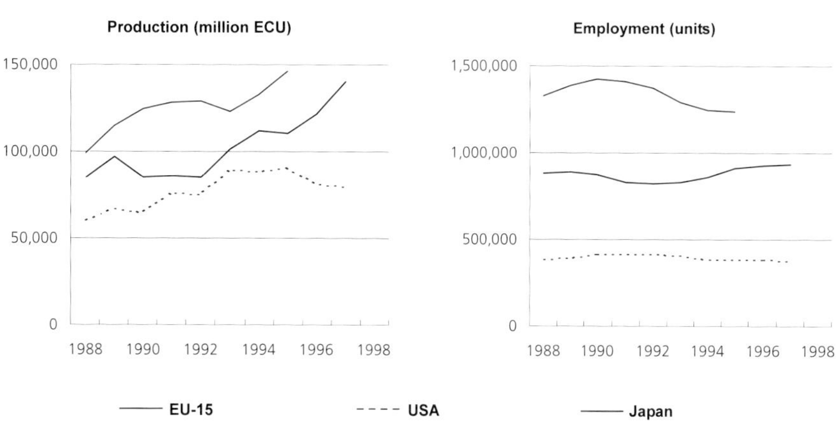

Source: Eurostat (SBS)

Figure 10.8 (%)

General purpose machinery (NACE Rev. 1 29.1 and 29.2)
Production and export specialisation by Member State, 1998

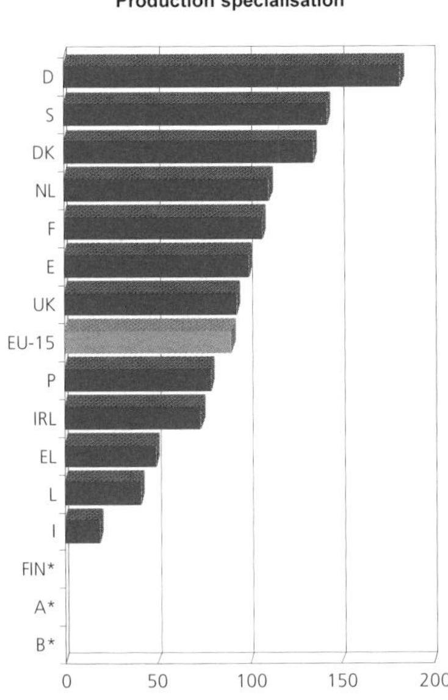

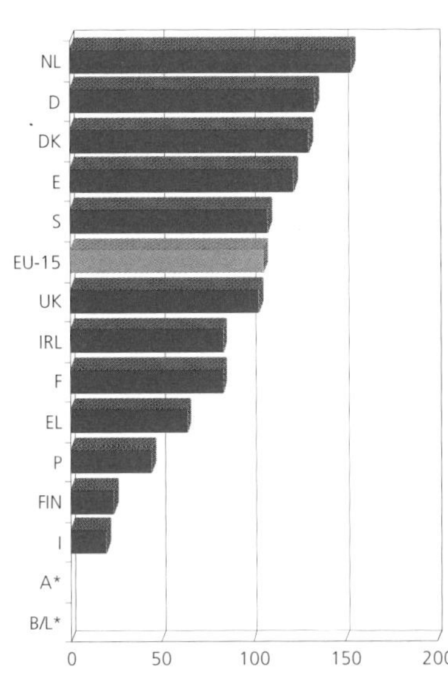

Source: Eurostat (SBS)

Member States between 1988 and 1998. One of the most dramatic gains was reported in Finland, where the average fell from 12.1 persons to 6.5 persons to produce one million ECU of goods. In most of the Member States the ratio accounted for between 6 and 9 persons in 1998, with the figure for Germany at 7.5 persons per one million ECU of production value.

International comparison showed a moderate increase in employment in the USA between 1990 and 1997 (up by 1.0% per annum). However, the ratio of persons employed per one million ECU of production value fell during the nineties to 6.7 persons by 1997, due to an increase in production value (at constant prices) of 6.8% per annum between 1990 and 1997. In Japan the industry faced recession in the latter part of the nineties, with the number of persons employed declining slightly faster than production value (down by 2.6% and 2.3% respectively in 1997).

Manufacturers of other general purpose machinery found themselves in a highly export-orientated activity. In Germany the export ratio was equal to 63.5% for the production and use of mechanical power, whilst in the United Kingdom the export ratio reached 52.0% for the manufacture of other general purpose machinery in 1998. Extra-EU exports increased by 94.8% between 1990 and 1998. However, imports from outside Europe increased at a faster pace, whilst the EU continued to report a trade surplus.

Figure 10.9

General purpose machinery
(NACE Rev. 1 29.1 and 29.2)
Destination of EU exports, 1998

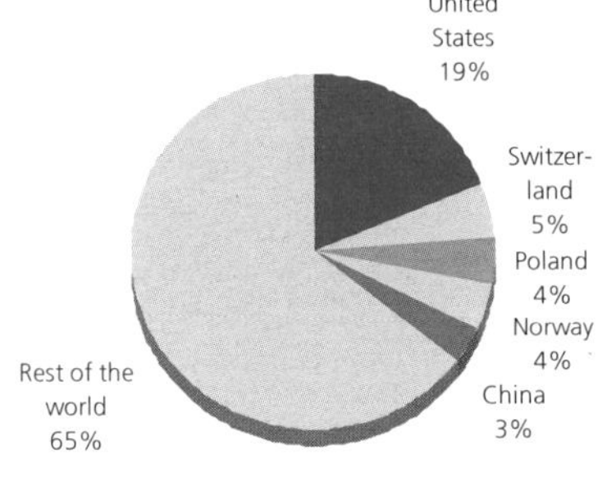

Source: Eurostat (Comext)

Figure 10.10

General purpose machinery
(NACE Rev. 1 29.1 and 29.2)
Origin of EU imports, 1998

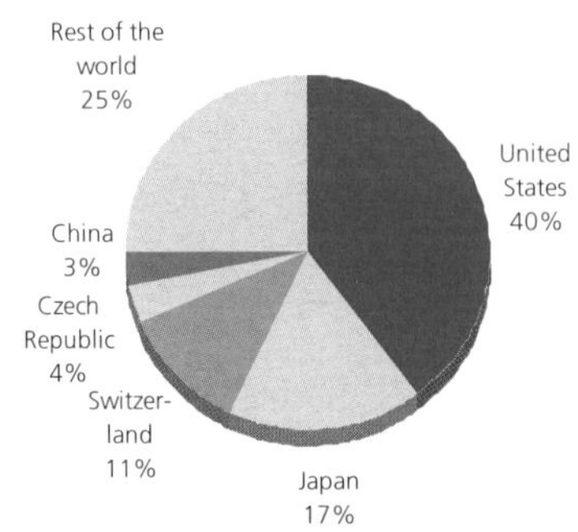

Source: Eurostat (Comext)

The manufacture of general purpose machinery encompasses the manufacture of pumps and compressors (NACE Rev. 1 29.12). This activity was characterised by small and medium-sized enterprises, often producing specialised pumps with a high technological component. Pump production accounted for almost 5% of the total production value of general purpose machinery (some 4.5% in the United Kingdom, or 3.6% in Germany in 1997). The EU was the largest producer of pumps in the world. Pump production in Germany, the United Kingdom and France was equal to production value in the USA

The manufacture of lifting and handling equipment (NACE Rev. 1 29.22) was responsible for around 11% of German production of general purpose machinery, a figure which rose to around 17% of the total in the United Kingdom in 1997. The number of enterprises engaged in the manufacture of lifting and handling equipment in the EU (excluding Austria and Greece) increased from 1989 onwards by almost 200 enterprises to 1,292 by 1997 (figures from the European Federation of Handling Equipment, FEM). There was a reduction in the number of persons employed in the lifting and handling industry. For example, the decrease in the United Kingdom was equal to 5.4% between 1995 and 1996 (whilst there was a corresponding increase of 15.3% in production).

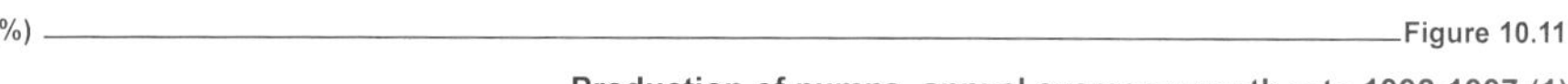

Production of pumps, annual average growth rate 1992-1997 (1)

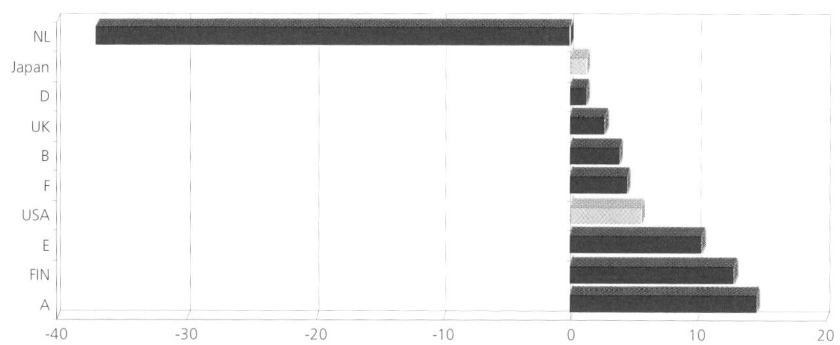

(1) European figures correspond to Europump membership only.

Source: Europump

(units) Figure 10.12

Labour intensity in the manufacture of lifting and handling equipment (1)

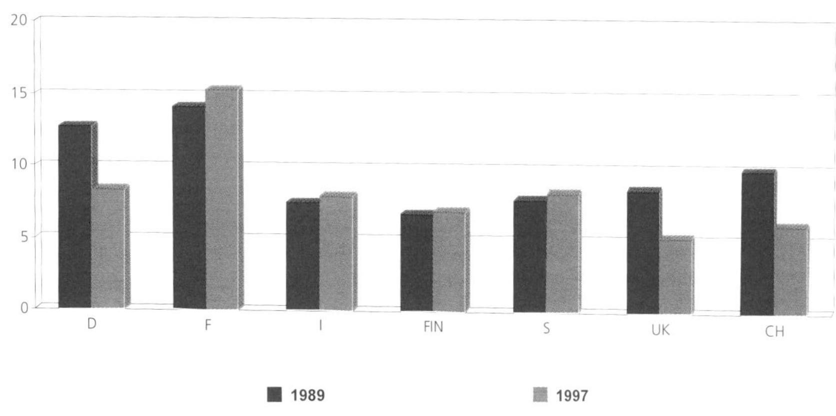

(1) Labour intensity is measured as the number of persons employed per one million ECU of production value; countries are ranked from left to right by total production value.

Source: FEM

Manufacture of special purpose machinery (NACE Rev. 1 29.4 and 29.5)

Following the NACE Rev. 1 activity classification, special purpose machinery includes machine-tools for working different materials, as well as machinery for certain specific activities such as metallurgy, food processing or printing. As the manufacture of special purpose machinery is very closely linked to downstream industries, the dependence of this industry on the economic and investment cycle of customers was even higher than in other areas of machinery and equipment. This industry received an impulse when many producers decided to further automate their production process during the nineties, with the result that they required customised solutions.

Between 1993 and 1998 production value increased by 5.6% per annum and value added by 3.0% per annum in Germany (both at constant prices). German production accounted for around 45% of total European output. In Italy, the second largest producing country (accounting for 15% of EU output), the corresponding figures for production and value added were 0.6% and 2.4% per annum.

In 1998 there were mixed fortunes in the performance of EU producers. In Germany the economic environment improved somewhat and led to an increase in production of 8.2% (in current prices). However, in Italy and the Netherlands production levels fell by 3.1% and 2.8% respectively.

There were a high number of small-sized enterprises in the industry producing one-off and specialised machinery. This was nowhere more apparent than in Italy. In 1998 Italy reported a high export specialisation ratio for both machine-tools (that contributed twice as much to the total value of Italian exports as the European average), as well as other special purpose machinery (contributing 1.7 times as much).

Manufacturers did not only offer machinery that improved productivity for their customers, they also made efforts to rationalise their own production processes. The number of persons employed was reduced in several Member States, for example, in Germany a reduction of 2.1% per annum was recorded between 1993 and 1998. As a result, European labour productivity was improved during the course of the nineties. Italy recorded an improvement of 18.1 thousand ECU per person employed during the ten-year period to 1998. Even faster increases were seen in Germany and the United Kingdom (value added per person employed rising by 20.4 thousand ECU to 53.1 thousand ECU and by 21.5 thousand ECU to 57.8 thousand ECU respectively between 1988 and 1998). Looking at the performance of the other two Triad economies, Japan reported a decrease in labour productivity of 6.8% in 1997, whilst in the USA value added per head increased by as much as 20.3%, reflecting the different economic situations. The increase in output in the USA allowed the industry to increase the number of persons employed, rising by 4.4% per annum between 1993 and 1997.

Figure 10.13

Manufacture of special purpose machinery (NACE Rev. 1 29.4 and 29.5)
Production and employment in the Triad

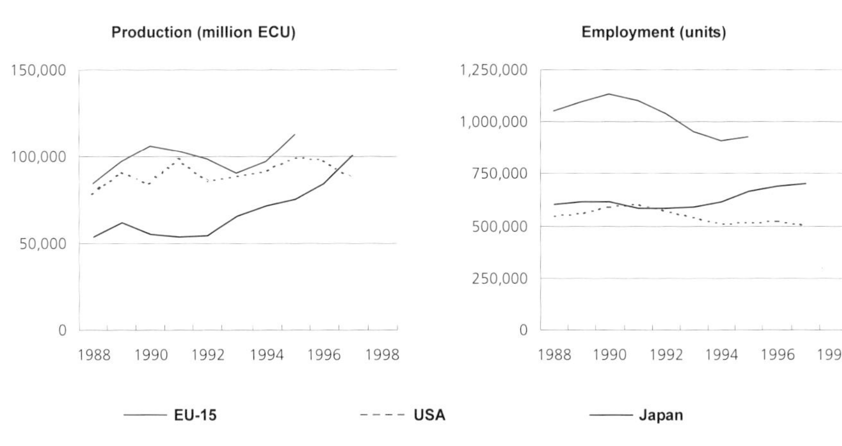

Source: Eurostat (SBS)

Figure 10.14 (%)

Manufacture of special purpose machinery (NACE Rev. 1 29.4 and 29.5)
Production and export specialisation by Member State, 1998

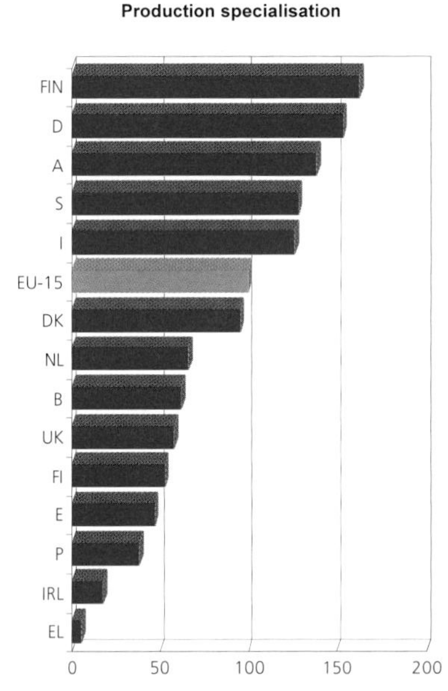

Source: Eurostat (SBS)

If we look in more detail at the manufacture of special purpose machinery, Germany reported a high degree of specialisation for the manufacture of machine-tools (NACE Rev. 1 29.4). Indeed, the German manufacture of machine-tools contributed nearly twice as much to the national manufacturing total as the European average. Finland reported a similar specialisation ratio for the manufacture of other special purpose machinery (NACE Rev. 1 29.5), with German industry again specialised (contributing around 1.5 times the EU average to the national manufacturing total). Indeed, German output was responsible for a 43.6% share of total European production.

The manufacture of machinery for other special purposes covers several downstream industries ranging from metallurgy, mining, quarrying and construction through to food, beverages and tobacco processing, as well as machinery for the production of textiles, apparel and leather. Value added grew at a slower pace than production value (at constant prices) between 1993 and 1998. In Germany there were increases of 2.6% and 5.7% per annum respectively, whilst in France there was a slight decrease in value added, equal to 0.2% per annum, despite growth in production of 4.8% per annum.

Customers for metallurgy machinery started to demand machinery that could react flexibly to fluctuations in raw material supply or shifts in market demand. Hence, machines saw the integration of several steps in the production process, creating "machinery solutions", as well as a more efficient use of raw materials and energy. New machinery increased productivity as the required number of man-hours was reduced.

The manufacture of machinery for textiles, apparel and leather production regained a competitive advantage through specialisation in more complex machinery. Customers created much closer ties with their suppliers and requested customised solutions and improved service when purchasing new machinery.

Similar trends were observed in the manufacture of machine-tools, where customers asked for training, maintenance and software (such as CAD). Suppliers of standardised machine-tools were affected by a decline in demand. A large share of machine-tools were sold to the transport equipment industry, electrical machinery and equipment industry, as well as to enterprises engaged in mechanical engineering.

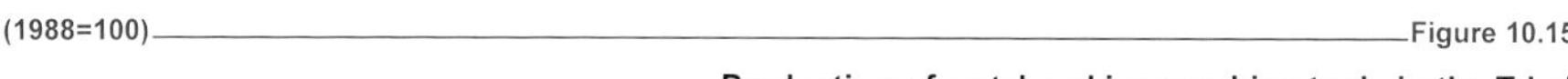

(1988=100) — Figure 10.15

Production of metalworking machine-tools in the Triad

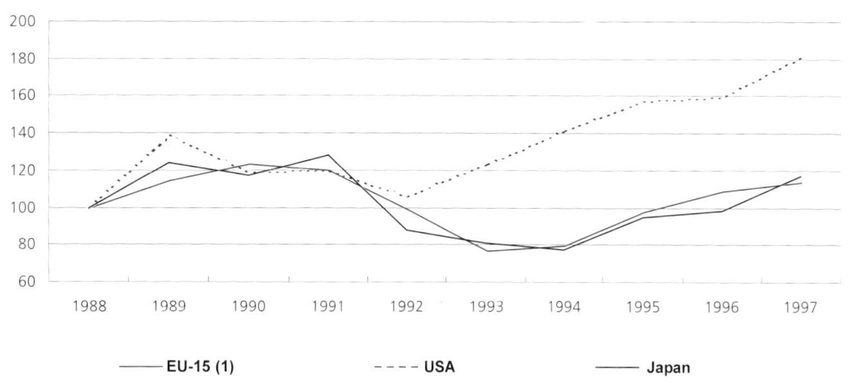

(1) Excluding Greece, Ireland and Luxembourg.

Source: CECIMO

Increased competition led to co-operations and mergers in the manufacture of metalworking machine-tools. This was in evidence when looking at the reduction in the number of enterprises, which was equal to 15.8% in Germany between 1990 and 1998, falling to 320 enterprises (figures from the Comité Européen de Coopération des Industries de la Machine-Outil, CECIMO). In Europe[5] production of metalworking machine-tools increased by 48.2% to 12.5 billion ECU between 1993 and 1997. However, growth in output did not lead to new employment possibilities. Indeed, the number of persons employed declined by 4.2% during the same period. In addition, European producers faced strong competition from suppliers in the other two Triad economies where production grew at a much faster pace (up by 13.6% in the USA and 18.8% in Japan in 1997), compared to Europe (up by 4.6%).

5) EU-15, excluding Denmark, Ireland, Luxembourg and Greece.

Figure 10.16

Manufacture of special purpose machinery (NACE Rev. 1 29.4 and 29.5) Destination of EU exports, 1998

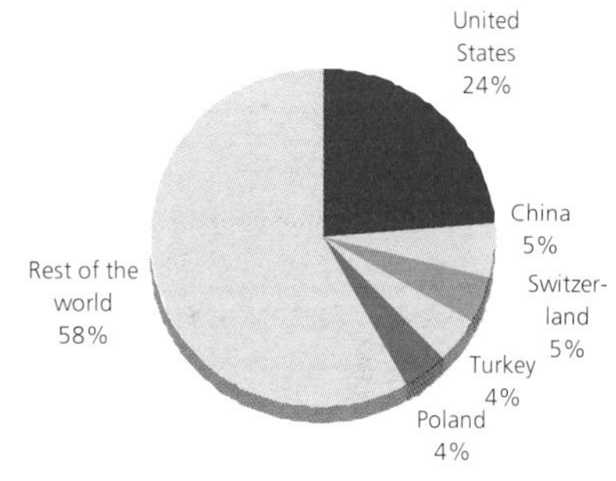

Source: Eurostat (Comext)

Figure 10.17

Manufacture of special purpose machinery (NACE Rev. 1 29.4 and 29.5) Origin of EU imports, 1998

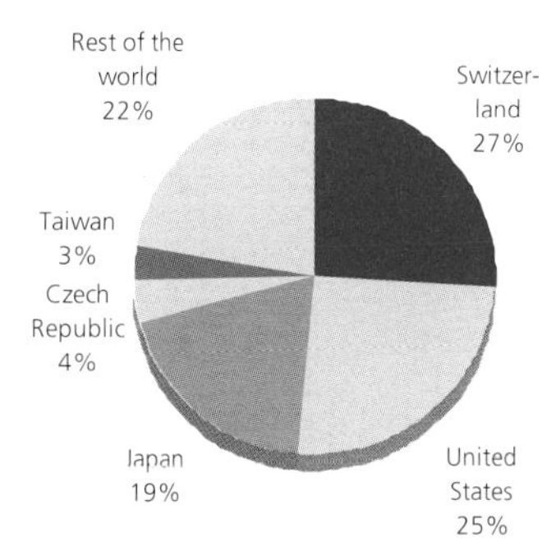

Source: Eurostat (Comext)

Agricultural machines and tractors (NACE Rev. 1 29.3)

Agricultural machines and tractors are used in varied climatic and geographical conditions for farming animals and growing various crops. European agriculture and forestry requires a wide range of machinery in order to carry our operations such as mowing, harvesting, milking, as well as tractors.

The importance of agricultural machines and tractors in the total production value of machinery and equipment[6] varied between just 3.2% in Sweden and 10.0% in Belgium. Denmark and Finland recorded high production specialisation ratios in this industry, with the contribution of agricultural machines and tractors to total manufacturing nearly twice as high as the European average. The Italian and Austrian specialisation was somewhat lower at 1.5 times the European average. Italian industry produced almost as much in value terms as in Germany. Together these two countries accounted for 23.6% and 25.2% of total EU production in 1998.

Agricultural activity in Europe has seen a marked reduction in the number of persons employed, a trend that can be expected to continue during the 21st century. Between 1980 and 1998 the European agricultural labour force decreased from 11.8 million full-time equivalent persons employed to 6.7 million. One of the main reasons for a reduction in the number of persons employed is the productivity increases that have been seen throughout agriculture, as many farms have moved to more intensive production techniques. European agriculture was strongly influenced by steps towards liberalisation of world markets through the World Trade Organisation and through reforms to the Common Agricultural Policy of the EU (Agenda 2000). Suppliers of agricultural machinery introduced flexible working models to deal with fluctuations in orders. In addition, there was a tendency towards increased co-operations and mergers due to the strong competition from North American producers. Although larger enterprises tend to dominate the European market, it still offers niches for small and medium-sized enterprises.

6) NACE Rev. 1 Division 29, machinery and equipment, excluding the manufacture of domestic appliances n.e.c. (NACE Rev. 1 29.7).

Figure 10.18

Agricultural machines and tractors (NACE Rev. 1 29.3)
Production and employment in the Triad

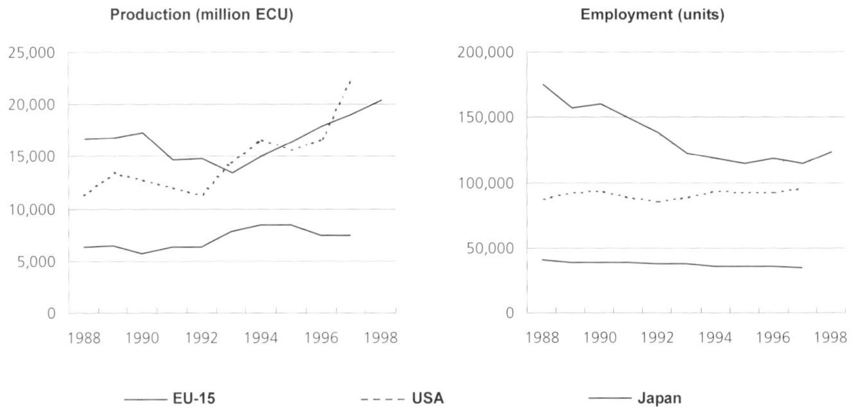

Source: Eurostat (SBS)

Figure 10.19 (%)

Agricultural machines and tractors (NACE Rev. 1 29.3)
Production and export specialisation by Member State, 1998

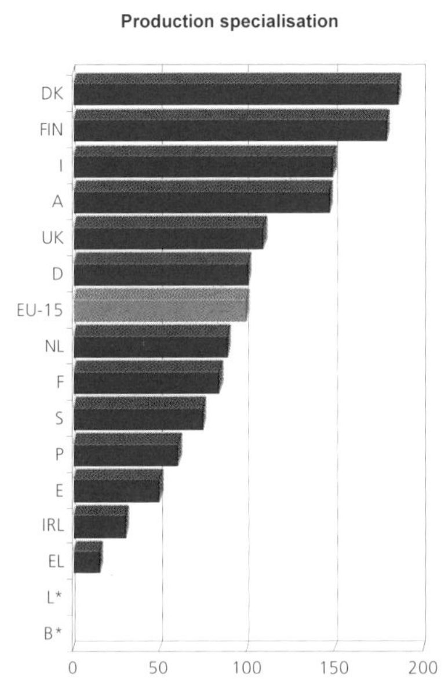

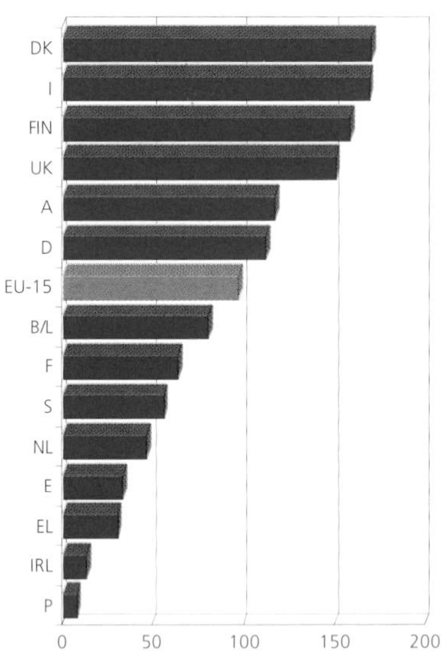

Source: Eurostat (SBS)

Looking at the trends in production and value added between 1993 and 1998 we find that value added grew at a slower pace than production value (using constant price terms). For example, in Denmark the increase in output of agricultural and forestry machinery was equal to 12.0% per annum, whilst the corresponding increase in value added was equivalent to just 7.0% per annum. Finland reported that output was rising by 30.4% per annum, whilst value added rose by 24.7% per annum.

Despite the favourable economic situation and positive rates of growth recorded in many countries, there was almost no change in employment levels. The number of persons employed in the EU grew by 0.2% per annum between 1993 and 1998. Although Finland reported a high increase in employment of 10.0% per annum, this rate of growth was more moderate when compared to the considerably higher increases in output over the same period. In Spain, the increase in production value (6.8% per annum in constant prices) was accompanied by a decline in the number of persons employed (down by 4.1% per annum). The efforts to improve labour productivity were successful if we look at the European average, where EU value added per person employed rose by 12.6 thousand ECU to some 49.6 thousand ECU, again during the period 1993 to 1998.

The manufacture of agricultural machines and tractors was highly orientated towards export markets. The activity saw increased exports to Central and Eastern Europe. In the United Kingdom the export rate rose as high as 80.1% in 1998. Italian exports delivered to countries outside Europe increased at a faster pace than imports from third countries (up by 57.7% and 43.8% respectively during the five years to 1998).

On the other hand foreign competitors (especially from the USA) tried to gain larger market shares. In several Member States there were increases in the import penetration ratio between 1993 and 1998, for example, Denmark or Spain.

Figure 10.20

Agricultural machines and tractors (NACE Rev. 1 29.3) Destination of EU exports, 1998

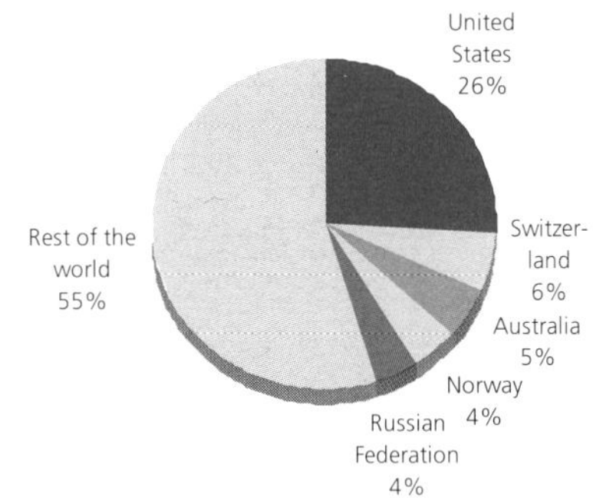

Source: Eurostat (Comext)

Figure 10.21

Agricultural machines and tractors (NACE Rev. 1 29.3) Origin of EU imports, 1998

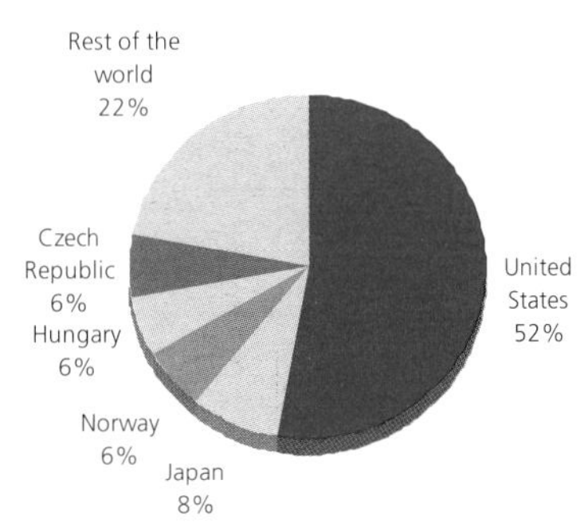

Source: Eurostat (Comext)

Weapons and ammunitions (NACE Rev. 1 29.6)

The manufacture of weapons and ammunitions is included under NACE Rev. 1 29.6. As the industry has a different market structure to the rest of NACE Rev. 1 29 it is treated here in a separate section. The manufacture of weapons and ammunition comprises the manufacture of tanks, artillery material and small arms, but also bombs and mines, hunting and sporting firearms.

The market for weapons and ammunitions is characterised by its tighter legal framework, due to the nature of the products produced. Many markets are characterised by security issues, secrecy and rivalry between nations, and the industry relies to a large degree on government as its main customer, which tends to result in monopolistic or oligopolistic markets.

The industry is also characterised by an extensive black market for weapons and ammunitions, as well as a tendency for many individuals to get around export controls. Smaller weapons, such as hand-guns are widespread across the world, as is their sale. This area is being tackled by several governments. Indeed, the sale of weapons for private use has seen regulations increase in most countries, in an attempt to guarantee public security and limit the spread of weapons. In other product areas, there has also been a ban on private use, for example anti-personnel landmines.

Public spending on defence has been significantly reduced due to a two-fold effect. On the one hand, the end of the Cold War has reduced investment in weapons and ammunitions. On the other hand, there has been a tightening of many governmental budgets, which has had direct implications for national defence budgets. Lower budgets have generally resulted in a higher degree of competition. The European market saw increased levels of concentration, largely as a response to increased competition originating from the USA. Many European producers have either grouped together into consortiums or turned to the North American market in search of growth through acquisition.

Figure 10.22

Weapons and ammunitions (NACE Rev. 1 29.6)

Production and employment in the Triad

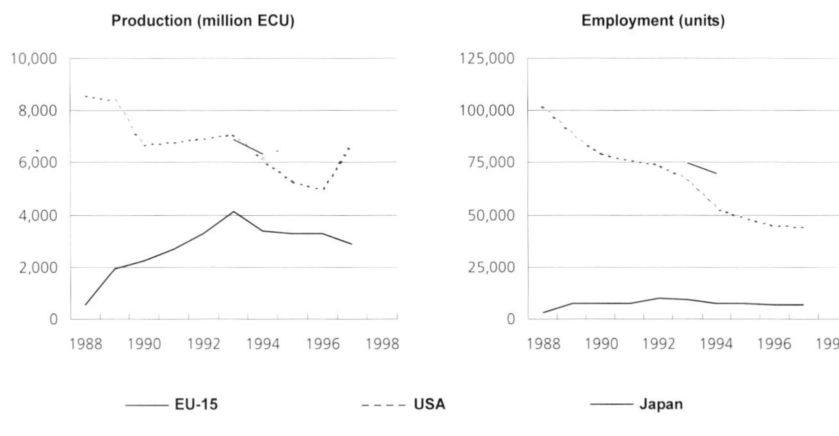

Source: Eurostat (SBS)

Figure 10.23 (%)

Weapons and ammunitions (NACE Rev. 1 29.6)

Production and export specialisation by Member State, 1998

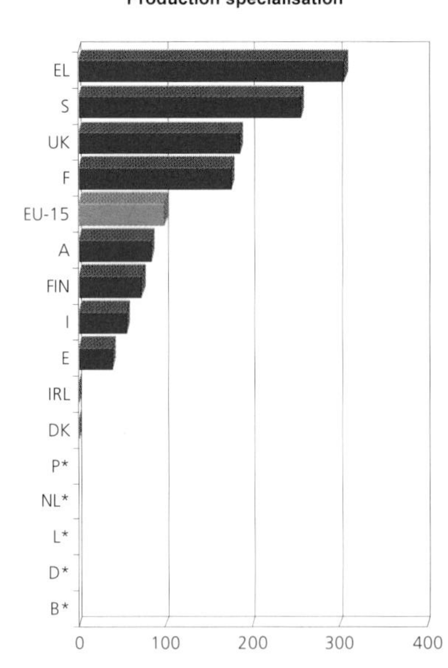

Export specialisation

P
I
FIN
A
EL
E
EU-15
F
D
S
UK
B/L
DK
NL
IRL
0
100
200
300
400

Source: Eurostat (SBS)

Within the EU three countries have a high level of activity, namely France, Sweden and the United Kingdom. In Sweden, production value in constant prices increased by 6.7% per annum between 1993 and 1998 whilst in France there was a decrease of 4.1% per annum. If we rank the Member States by production value, we find that Germany was only third largest European producer in 1998.

Altogether there has been no uniform trend in output across Europe. Production of weapons and ammunitions fell in Italy and the United Kingdom (down by 10.4% and 5.8%), whilst Germany and Austria reported increases of 13.9% and 12.3% (all growth rates give changes between 1997 and 1998).

The evolution of employment followed similar patterns to production in 1998, with labour being taken on largely as a result of winning new contracts. Increases were recorded in Austria, France and Germany (up by 3.7%, 1.5% and 4.3% respectively), whilst decreases of 5.6%, 1.0% and 1.8% were registered in Italy, Sweden and the United Kingdom.

If we look at the number of persons required to produce one million ECU of production value, there were significant differences across the Member States. In France and the United Kingdom there was a much lower labour intensity (with only 3.5 and 5.5 persons required to produce one million ECU of production value), whilst in Germany 7.3 persons were employed on average to produce one million ECU of production value. The labour intensity ratio was even higher in Spain and Finland, where it reached 11.0 and 17.1 persons. Value added per head varied correspondingly, with France reporting labour productivity of 78.3 thousand ECU per person employed, whereas in Spain only 29.2 thousand ECU of value added was generated by each person employed. Most of the Member States reported that value added per person employed was following an upward trend during the nineties. However, in Sweden labour productivity decreased by 4.6 thousand ECU between 1990 and 1998, falling to 40.3 thousand ECU in 1998.

In order to remain competitive in the long-run, enterprises require very high expenditure on research and development. Almost the whole of the activity is based on the production of output with a high technology component. Not all of this research should be seen as purely for military use, as many new technologies within the field of defence filter through into civilian innovations.

Foreign trade of weapons and ammunitions showed the effect of new orders, with the trade balance displaying significant fluctuations in several Member States. For example, in the United Kingdom the balance changed sign seven times between 1990 and 1998. In Finland there was a high degree of trade, with the export ratio rising as high as 56.1% in 1998. Italian and Spanish manufacturers also exported a large share of their production (33.9% and 24.6% respectively).

International comparison showed that there was a permanent trade surplus in the USA, whilst Japan ran a deficit. Manufacturers in the USA sold 47.0% of their production to foreign countries. Japanese activity was small and unable to cover domestic demand. However, very high levels of labour productivity were recorded in Japan, some 182.3 thousand ECU of value added being generated by each person employed in 1997.

Figure 10.24

Weapons and ammunitions (NACE Rev. 1 29.6)
Destination of EU exports, 1998

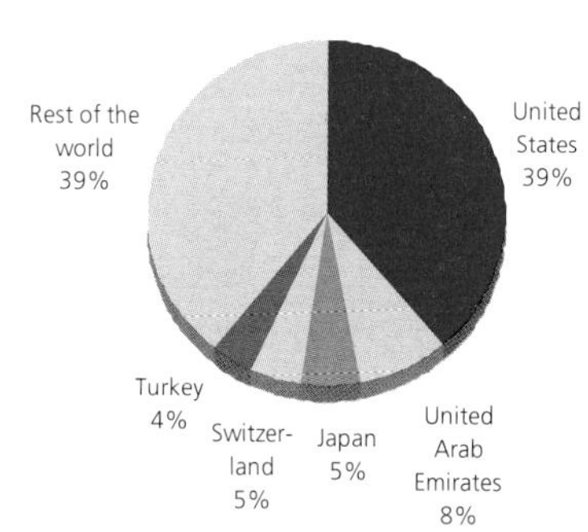

Source: Eurostat (Comext)

Figure 10.25

Weapons and ammunitions (NACE Rev. 1 29.6)
Origin of EU imports, 1998

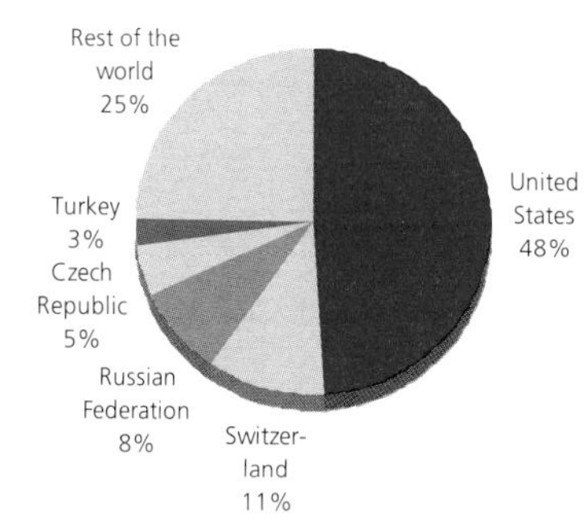

Source: Eurostat (Comext)

Professional associations representing the industries within this chapter

CECIMO
European Committee for the Co-operation of the Machine Tool Industries
66, avenue Louise
B-1050 Bruxelles
tel: (32) 2 502 70 90
fax: (32) 2 502 60 82
e-mail: info@cecimo.be

EUROPUMP
European Association of Pump Manufacturers
Diamant Building
80, boulevard A. Reyers
B-1030 Bruxelles
tel: (32) 2 706 82 30
fax: (32) 2 706 79 88

FEM
European Federation of Handling
c/o VSM
Kirchenweg 4
CH-8032 Zurich
tel: (41) 1 384 48 44
fax: (41) 1 384 48 48

Table 10.2 (million ECU)

Manufacture of machinery for the production and use of mechanical power, except aircraft, vehicle and cycle engines (NACE Rev. 1 29.1)

Production related indicators in the EU

	1988	1989	1990	1991	1992	1993	1994	1995	1996	1997	1998
Production value	45,437	52,960	56,593	58,005	58,557	56,688	60,239	65,616	:	:	:
Producer price index (1995=100)	:	:	:	:	:	:	:	:	:	:	:
Value added	19,782	22,664	23,656	23,969	24,497	23,199	24,476	26,025	:	:	:
Number of persons employed (thousands)	627.2	655.3	668.3	661.2	636.8	591.1	559.8	552.7	:	:	:

Table 10.3 (million ECU)

Manufacture of machinery for the production and use of mechanical power, except aircraft, vehicle and cycle engines (NACE Rev. 1 29.1)

Production related indicators, 1998

	B	DK	D	EL	E	F	IRL	I	L	NL	A	P	FIN	S	UK
Production value	1,869	2,169	27,380	55	1,938	8,725	239	13,796	:	2,042	1,084	:	1,487	2,190	9,246
Value added	611	970	12,832	13	699	3,133	119	4,482	:	629	455	:	542	877	3,742
Number of persons employed (units) (1)	8,599	22,326	222,121	1,199	18,379	64,974	2,585	87,562	:	12,403	9,790	:	8,166	16,096	80,985

(1) NL (1992).

Table 10.4 (million ECU)

Manufacture of machinery for the production and use of mechanical power, except aircraft, vehicle and cycle engines (NACE Rev. 1 29.1)

Market related indicators in the EU

	1988	1989	1990	1991	1992	1993	1994	1995	1996	1997	1998
Apparent consumption	39,900	47,320	50,977	51,722	52,550	48,274	51,928	56,780	:	:	:
Exports	10,479	11,606	12,188	13,019	13,159	15,646	16,776	18,244	20,327	22,815	23,850
Imports	4,942	5,967	6,572	6,736	7,152	7,232	8,465	9,407	10,218	11,675	13,515
Trade balance	5,537	5,639	5,616	6,283	6,007	8,414	8,311	8,837	10,109	11,141	10,335
Export ratio (%)	23.1	21.9	21.5	22.4	22.5	27.6	27.8	27.8	:	:	:
Import penetration ratio (%)	12.4	12.6	12.9	13.0	13.6	15.0	16.3	16.6	:	:	:
Cover ratio (%)	212.0	194.5	185.4	193.3	184.0	216.3	198.2	193.9	198.9	195.4	176.5

Table 10.5 (million ECU)

Manufacture of machinery for the production and use of mechanical power, except aircraft, vehicle and cycle engines (NACE Rev. 1 29.1)

Market related indicators, 1998

	B/L	DK	D	EL	E	F	IRL	I	NL	A	P	FIN	S	UK
Apparent consumption	:	2,083	18,417	517	2,794	8,068	410	9,683	2,369	1,190	:	1,552	2,263	8,003
Exports	2,475	1,104	17,391	30	1,443	6,906	215	8,778	1,785	1,336	121	692	1,812	7,406
Imports	2,735	1,017	8,429	492	2,298	6,249	386	4,665	2,111	1,441	379	756	1,886	6,163
Trade balance	-260	86	8,962	-462	-855	657	-171	4,113	-327	-105	-258	-65	-73	1,243
Export ratio (%)	:	50.9	63.5	54.9	74.4	79.2	90.0	63.6	87.4	123.2	:	46.5	82.8	80.1
Import penetration ratio (%)	:	48.8	45.8	95.2	82.3	77.5	94.2	48.2	89.1	121.1	:	48.7	83.3	77.0
Cover ratio (%)	90.5	108.5	206.3	6.1	62.8	110.5	55.7	188.2	84.5	92.7	31.9	91.4	96.1	120.2

Table 10.6

Manufacture of machinery for the production and use of mechanical power, except aircraft, vehicle and cycle engines (NACE Rev. 1 29.1)

Labour related indicators, 1998

	EU-15	B	DK	D	EL	E	F	IRL	I	L	NL	A	P	FIN	S	UK
Personnel costs (million ECU) (1)	19,532	366	733	9,524	16	384	2,370	67	2,806	:	484	348	:	324	622	2,491
Personnel costs/employee (thousand ECU) (2)	36.1	45.1	33.5	43.6	14.9	25.0	37.1	25.6	29.2	:	:	37.6	:	36.0	40.5	25.7
Social charges/personnel costs (%) (3)	21.2	28.1	3.0	19.0	22.9	20.2	30.4	14.5	37.6	:	21.2	23.2	:	21.5	30.7	11.6
Labour productivity (thousand ECU/head) (4)	47.1	71.1	43.4	57.8	11.2	38.0	48.2	46.2	51.2	:	42.0	46.5	:	66.3	54.5	46.2
Wage adjusted labour productivity (%) (2)	130.3	164.2	137.0	118.0	105.5	150.1	131.3	198.6	163.8	:	:	121.1	:	171.8	132.5	150.3

(1) EU-15 (1995). (2) EU-15, EL, I, A (1995); B, DK, D, E, F, IRL, FIN, S, UK (1996). (3) EU-15, S (1995). (4) NL (1992); EU-15 (1995).

Source: Eurostat (SBS, EBT)

(million ECU) Table 10.7

Manufacture of other general purpose machinery (NACE Rev. 1 29.2)
Production related indicators in the EU

	1988	1989	1990	1991	1992	1993	1994	1995	1996	1997	1998
Production value	52,948	61,507	67,080	69,577	69,696	66,005	71,709	80,061	:	:	:
Producer price index (1995=100)	:	:	92.3	93.6	96.4	97.7	97.7	100.0	99.9	99.3	99.9
Value added	20,868	23,728	25,657	26,788	27,045	25,822	27,945	29,966	:	:	:
Number of persons employed (thousands)	694.7	725.8	751.8	745.1	730.1	693.6	681.6	682.0	:	:	:

(million ECU) Table 10.8

Manufacture of other general purpose machinery (NACE Rev. 1 29.2)
Production related indicators, 1998

	B	DK	D	EL	E	F	IRL	I	L	NL	A	P	FIN	S	UK
Production value	2,069	2,218	35,454	144	4,999	11,578	583	13,399	54	3,365	2,363	:	2,061	4,835	11,143
Value added	689	748	14,322	29	1,835	3,711	212	4,006	25	1,203	1,038	:	719	1,708	4,240
Number of persons employed (units) (1)	12,883	16,821	251,603	2,062	60,502	80,617	4,420	89,712	529	29,386	20,244	:	14,933	30,444	95,597

(1) NL (1992).

(million ECU) Table 10.9

Manufacture of other general purpose machinery (NACE Rev. 1 29.2)
Market related indicators in the EU

	1988	1989	1990	1991	1992	1993	1994	1995	1996	1997	1998
Apparent consumption	46,088	53,869	58,675	61,565	61,259	55,775	59,537	66,470	:	:	:
Exports	10,677	12,307	13,428	13,634	14,219	15,751	18,175	20,542	23,360	25,789	26,049
Imports	3,817	4,669	5,023	5,622	5,782	5,522	6,002	6,951	7,968	8,742	10,039
Trade balance	6,860	7,638	8,405	8,012	8,437	10,229	12,173	13,591	15,392	17,046	16,010
Export ratio (%)	20.2	20.0	20.0	19.6	20.4	23.9	25.3	25.7	:	:	:
Import penetration ratio (%)	8.3	8.7	8.6	9.1	9.4	9.9	10.1	10.5	:	:	:
Cover ratio (%)	279.7	263.6	267.4	242.5	245.9	285.3	302.8	295.5	293.2	295.0	259.5

(million ECU) Table 10.10

Manufacture of other general purpose machinery (NACE Rev. 1 29.2)
Market related indicators, 1998

	B/L	DK	D	EL	E	F	IRL	I	NL	A	P	FIN	S	UK
Apparent consumption	:	1,428	25,018	669	5,780	10,397	757	6,687	3,145	2,099	:	1,615	3,567	10,737
Exports	2,546	1,798	16,708	60	1,706	6,278	559	9,748	2,298	1,521	157	1,139	2,519	5,797
Imports	2,976	1,009	6,272	586	2,487	5,097	733	3,036	2,079	1,257	609	693	1,251	5,392
Trade balance	-430	790	10,436	-525	-781	1,181	-173	6,712	219	264	-453	445	1,268	405
Export ratio (%)	:	81.1	47.1	41.9	34.1	54.2	95.9	72.8	68.3	64.4	:	55.3	52.1	52.0
Import penetration ratio (%)	:	70.6	25.1	87.5	43.0	49.0	96.8	45.4	66.1	59.9	:	42.9	35.1	50.2
Cover ratio (%)	85.6	178.3	266.4	10.3	68.6	123.2	76.4	321.1	110.5	121.0	25.7	164.2	201.3	107.5

Table 10.11

Manufacture of other general purpose machinery (NACE Rev. 1 29.2)
Labour related indicators, 1998

	EU-15	B	DK	D	EL	E	F	IRL	I	L	NL	A	P	FIN	S	UK
Personnel costs (million ECU) (1)	23,902	460	593	10,849	29	1,321	2,949	110	2,934	22	865	762	:	480	1,135	2,796
Personnel costs/employee (thousand ECU) (2)	36.6	39.2	36.0	44.0	15.2	25.9	37.2	23.9	29.8	39.7	:	39.6	:	33.3	39.1	24.4
Social charges/personnel costs (%) (3)	20.6	26.9	3.7	17.8	23.8	19.6	30.5	15.1	36.9	14.0	10.9	22.6	:	22.1	29.4	12.0
Labour productivity (thousand ECU/head) (4)	43.9	53.5	44.5	56.9	14.0	30.3	46.0	48.0	44.7	48.1	39.4	51.3	:	48.2	56.1	44.4
Wage adjusted labour productivity (%) (2)	119.9	126.0	114.0	119.1	131.2	139.1	122.5	196.0	150.0	106.8	:	126.9	:	140.8	137.6	148.5

(1) EU-15 (1995). (2) EU-15, EL, I, A (1995); B, DK, D, E, F, IRL, L, FIN, S, UK (1996). (3) EU-15, L, S (1995). (4) NL (1992); EU-15 (1995).

Source: Eurostat (SBS, EBT)

Table 10.12 (million ECU)

Manufacture of agricultural and forestry machinery (NACE Rev. 1 29.3)

Production related indicators in the EU

	1988	1989	1990	1991	1992	1993	1994	1995	1996	1997	1998
Production value	16,793	16,857	17,387	14,805	14,871	13,543	15,152	16,508	18,095	19,195	20,492
Producer price index (1995=100)	:	:	87.3	87.7	90.8	93.5	96.1	100.0	:	:	:
Value added	5,878	5,421	5,648	4,732	4,947	4,530	4,858	4,828	5,484	5,607	6,154
Number of persons employed (thousands)	176.1	158.1	161.0	150.1	139.2	123.0	119.7	115.1	119.0	115.9	124.1

Table 10.13 (million ECU)

Manufacture of agricultural and forestry machinery (NACE Rev. 1 29.3)

Production related indicators, 1998

	B	DK	D	EL	E	F	IRL	I	L	NL	A	P	FIN	S	UK
Production value	807	572	5,173	21	953	2,725	80	4,846	0	697	717	205	794	405	2,498
Value added	224	219	1,638	3	313	705	21	1,224	0	242	322	:	199	149	830
Number of persons employed (units) (1)	4,520	5,306	31,248	239	7,995	14,938	788	25,699	12	5,206	5,209	3,612	3,026	2,801	13,045

(1) NL (1992).

Table 10.14 (million ECU)

Manufacture of agricultural and forestry machinery (NACE Rev. 1 29.3)

Market related indicators in the EU

	1988	1989	1990	1991	1992	1993	1994	1995	1996	1997	1998
Apparent consumption	15,220	15,205	15,374	12,969	13,252	11,806	13,181	14,354	15,798	16,509	18,035
Exports	2,289	2,620	2,768	2,765	2,511	2,730	3,054	3,138	3,632	4,116	4,131
Imports	716	967	756	929	892	994	1,083	984	1,335	1,430	1,674
Trade balance	1,573	1,652	2,012	1,836	1,619	1,737	1,971	2,154	2,297	2,686	2,457
Export ratio (%)	13.6	15.5	15.9	18.7	16.9	20.2	20.2	19.0	20.1	21.4	20.2
Import penetration ratio (%)	4.7	6.4	4.9	7.2	6.7	8.4	8.2	6.9	8.5	8.7	9.3
Cover ratio (%)	319.7	270.8	366.1	297.7	281.4	274.7	282.0	318.9	272.0	287.8	246.8

Table 10.15 (million ECU)

Manufacture of agricultural and forestry machinery (NACE Rev. 1 29.3)

Market related indicators, 1998

	B/L	DK	D	EL	E	F	IRL	I	NL	A	P	FIN	S	UK
Apparent consumption	:	572	3,252	147	1,579	3,784	240	3,239	638	683	377	642	466	1,213
Exports	719	384	3,047	14	172	1,045	39	2,121	443	330	9	361	233	2,008
Imports	552	385	1,127	140	799	2,105	199	514	385	296	181	209	295	722
Trade balance	167	-1	1,920	-126	-627	-1,059	-160	1,607	58	34	-171	152	-61	1,286
Export ratio (%)	:	67.2	58.9	69.0	18.1	38.4	48.9	43.8	63.6	46.0	4.6	45.5	57.6	80.4
Import penetration ratio (%)	:	67.2	34.6	95.6	50.6	55.6	83.0	15.9	60.2	43.3	48.0	32.6	63.2	59.5
Cover ratio (%)	130.2	99.8	270.4	10.3	21.5	49.7	19.6	412.8	115.2	111.6	5.2	172.9	79.2	278.1

Table 10.16

Manufacture of agricultural and forestry machinery (NACE Rev. 1 29.3)

Labour related indicators, 1998

	EU-15	B	DK	D	EL	E	F	IRL	I	L	NL	A	P	FIN	S	UK
Personnel costs (million ECU) (1)	3,839	155	161	1,201	2	174	462	12	772	0	163	174	32	89	101	402
Personnel costs/employee (thousand ECU) (2)	33.3	39.2	31.0	40.2	11.4	18.5	31.5	16.3	27.3	21.2	:	34.4	:	30.9	37.7	25.5
Social charges/personnel costs (%) (3)	22.0	28.0	3.5	23.6	25.2	21.0	29.1	11.8	36.3	:	19.4	22.7	:	23.2	28.1	11.6
Labour productivity (thousand ECU/head) (4)	49.6	49.6	41.4	52.4	12.9	39.2	47.2	26.5	47.6	7.8	35.5	61.7	:	65.8	53.2	63.6
Wage adjusted labour productivity (%) (2)	126.0	128.0	133.3	123.5	141.9	131.5	149.1	148.3	156.8	38.5	:	163.5	:	161.7	141.1	214.0

(1) E (1997). (2) EU-15, EL, I, A (1995); B, DK, D, E, F, IRL, L, FIN, S, UK (1996). (3) S (1994); EU-15 (1995); E (1997). (4) NL (1992).

Source: Eurostat (SBS, EBT)

(million ECU) Table 10.17

Manufacture of machine-tools (NACE Rev. 1 29.4)
Production related indicators in the EU

	1988	1989	1990	1991	1992	1993	1994	1995	1996	1997	1998
Production value	24,683	28,638	31,718	30,451	27,409	23,041	26,223	26,198	:	:	:
Producer price index (1995=100)	:	:	86.9	91.3	94.2	96.2	97.6	100.0	:	:	:
Value added	10,222	11,442	12,607	12,319	11,079	9,306	10,328	10,237	:	:	:
Number of persons employed (thousands)	322.9	339.8	351.1	341.7	311.5	269.3	258.8	234.9	:	:	:

(million ECU) Table 10.18

Manufacture of machine-tools (NACE Rev. 1 29.4)
Production related indicators, 1998

	B	DK	D	EL	E	F	IRL	I	L	NL	A	P	FIN	S	UK
Production value	370	177	15,478	19	1,071	1,694	55	5,530	:	328	722	82	398	1,199	2,614
Value added	125	79	6,341	6	413	571	16	2,111	:	138	290	:	159	529	1,119
Number of persons employed (units) (1)	2,500	1,594	120,420	306	10,403	14,380	810	37,180	:	2,775	6,112	2,081	3,372	7,732	23,876

(1) NL (1992).

(million ECU) Table 10.19

Manufacture of machine-tools (NACE Rev. 1 29.4)
Market related indicators in the EU

	1988	1989	1990	1991	1992	1993	1994	1995	1996	1997	1998
Apparent consumption	21,575	25,705	29,044	27,827	24,759	19,218	22,102	22,119	:	:	:
Exports	6,815	7,507	7,586	7,472	6,847	7,611	8,588	9,637	10,648	10,844	10,827
Imports	3,706	4,574	4,913	4,849	4,197	3,788	4,467	5,558	6,068	6,887	7,703
Trade balance	3,108	2,933	2,674	2,624	2,650	3,823	4,121	4,078	4,580	3,956	3,124
Export ratio (%)	27.6	26.2	23.9	24.5	25.0	33.0	32.7	36.8	:	:	:
Import penetration ratio (%)	17.2	17.8	16.9	17.4	17.0	19.7	20.2	25.1	:	:	:
Cover ratio (%)	183.9	164.1	154.4	154.1	163.1	200.9	192.2	173.4	175.5	157.4	140.6

(million ECU) Table 10.20

Manufacture of machine-tools (NACE Rev. 1 29.4)
Market related indicators, 1998

	B/L	DK	D	EL	E	F	IRL	I	NL	A	P	FIN	S	UK
Apparent consumption	:	395	10,644	150	1,338	2,978	250	2,869	516	740	288	484	1,057	2,970
Exports	1,066	191	8,576	16	729	1,334	71	4,825	654	646	41	264	855	2,180
Imports	1,428	408	3,742	148	996	2,617	266	2,164	843	664	247	350	713	2,536
Trade balance	-361	-217	4,834	-131	-267	-1,284	-195	2,661	-189	-18	-206	-86	142	-356
Export ratio (%)	:	107.5	55.4	85.9	68.0	78.7	129.8	87.3	199.5	89.4	49.7	66.4	71.3	83.4
Import penetration ratio (%)	:	103.4	35.2	98.2	74.4	87.9	106.5	75.4	163.2	89.7	85.7	72.4	67.4	85.4
Cover ratio (%)	74.7	46.8	229.2	11.2	73.2	50.9	26.6	223.0	77.6	97.3	16.5	75.5	120.0	86.0

Table 10.21

Manufacture of machine-tools (NACE Rev. 1 29.4)
Labour related indicators, 1998

	EU-15	B	DK	D	EL	E	F	IRL	I	L	NL	A	P	FIN	S	UK
Personnel costs (million ECU) (1)	8,399	93	54	5,080	7	221	534	16	1,245	:	91	222	21	105	285	686
Personnel costs/employee (thousand ECU) (2)	36.7	40.1	35.2	43.0	24.5	25.6	37.8	19.7	30.5	:	:	38.3	:	31.1	38.6	24.1
Social charges/personnel costs (%) (3)	20.4	26.9	6.1	17.3	24.3	21.1	30.2	14.7	37.0	:	17.8	22.4	:	21.7	30.3	11.5
Labour productivity (thousand ECU/head) (4)	43.6	49.8	49.8	52.7	18.1	39.8	39.7	19.1	56.8	:	39.8	47.5	:	47.1	68.4	46.9
Wage adjusted labour productivity (%) (2)	118.9	117.5	141.5	112.9	112.4	130.3	116.6	102.4	147.3	:	:	114.3	:	152.1	167.6	159.3

(1) EU-15 (1995). (2) EU-15, EL, I, A (1995); B, DK, D, E, F, IRL, FIN, S, UK (1996). (3) EU-15, S (1995). (4) NL (1992); EU-15 (1995).

Source: Eurostat (SBS, EBT)

Table 10.22 (million ECU)

Manufacture of other special purpose machinery (NACE Rev. 1 29.5)

Production related indicators in the EU

	1988	1989	1990	1991	1992	1993	1994	1995	1996	1997	1998
Production value	59,593	68,375	74,229	72,198	70,938	67,241	70,875	86,799	89,597	94,628	96,851
Producer price index (1995=100)	:	:	87.4	90.0	92.7	94.9	96.5	100.0	98.9	100.5	101.5
Value added	23,710	26,088	28,348	28,127	27,667	26,622	27,121	31,404	32,411	34,001	34,576
Number of persons employed (thousands)	727.7	754.3	781.3	756.1	725.4	680.1	650.3	692.5	685.6	683.5	691.6

Table 10.23 (million ECU)

Manufacture of other special purpose machinery (NACE Rev. 1 29.5)

Production related indicators, 1998

	B	DK	D	EL	E	F	IRL	I	L	NL	A	P	FIN	S	UK
Production value	2,640	1,344	42,248	26	3,820	9,324	206	15,804	175	2,985	3,148	731	3,465	3,331	7,604
Value added	791	511	15,482	5	1,353	2,608	97	5,544	90	1,224	1,301	:	1,174	1,054	3,043
Number of persons employed (units) (1)	12,938	12,149	290,412	450	48,838	57,944	2,528	101,170	1,652	20,405	23,189	14,754	22,515	19,610	63,522

(1) NL (1992).

Table 10.24 (million ECU)

Manufacture of other special purpose machinery (NACE Rev. 1 29.5)

Market related indicators in the EU

	1988	1989	1990	1991	1992	1993	1994	1995	1996	1997	1998
Apparent consumption	46,257	52,595	57,116	55,951	53,179	44,743	46,569	60,574	60,528	62,502	67,625
Exports	20,075	23,294	24,913	24,073	25,286	29,589	32,412	35,219	38,437	42,969	41,388
Imports	6,739	7,514	7,800	7,826	7,527	7,091	8,106	8,994	9,367	10,843	12,162
Trade balance	13,336	15,780	17,113	16,247	17,759	22,498	24,306	26,225	29,070	32,126	29,226
Export ratio (%)	33.7	34.1	33.6	33.3	35.6	44.0	45.7	40.6	42.9	45.4	42.7
Import penetration ratio (%)	14.6	14.3	13.7	14.0	14.2	15.8	17.4	14.8	15.5	17.3	18.0
Cover ratio (%)	297.9	310.0	319.4	307.6	335.9	417.3	399.9	391.6	410.3	396.3	340.3

Table 10.25 (million ECU)

Manufacture of other special purpose machinery (NACE Rev. 1 29.5)

Market related indicators, 1998

	B/L	DK	D	EL	E	F	IRL	I	NL	A	P	FIN	S	UK
Apparent consumption	:	805	23,855	556	5,091	7,654	934	7,040	2,468	2,037	1,255	2,691	2,675	6,229
Exports	3,600	1,398	24,644	90	1,321	7,184	189	13,068	2,747	2,447	381	1,624	1,962	6,845
Imports	2,659	859	6,251	619	2,592	5,514	918	4,304	2,230	1,336	906	850	1,307	5,470
Trade balance	941	540	18,393	-529	-1,270	1,670	-728	8,764	517	1,111	-525	775	656	1,375
Export ratio (%)	:	104.0	58.3	340.1	34.6	77.1	91.9	82.7	92.0	77.7	52.1	46.9	58.9	90.0
Import penetration ratio (%)	:	106.7	26.2	111.4	50.9	72.0	98.2	61.1	90.4	65.6	72.1	31.6	48.8	87.8
Cover ratio (%)	135.4	162.8	394.2	14.5	51.0	130.3	20.6	303.6	123.2	183.2	42.1	191.1	150.2	125.1

Table 10.26

Manufacture of other special purpose machinery (NACE Rev. 1 29.5)

Labour related indicators, 1998

	EU-15	B	DK	D	EL	E	F	IRL	I	L	NL	A	P	FIN	S	UK
Personnel costs (million ECU)	25,887	525	439	12,861	5	937	2,178	59	3,441	79	779	907	157	856	710	1,953
Personnel costs/employee (thousand ECU) (1)	38.6	41.8	36.9	44.5	12.0	23.7	38.2	23.6	31.0	48.6	:	41.1	:	36.3	37.9	25.7
Social charges/personnel costs (%) (2)	21.0	27.2	3.8	18.6	22.5	20.0	30.2	15.3	36.4	13.9	17.3	22.3	:	23.6	29.4	11.8
Labour productivity (thousand ECU/head) (3)	50.0	61.2	42.1	53.3	11.7	27.7	45.0	38.5	54.8	54.6	37.0	56.1	:	52.1	53.8	47.9
Wage adjusted labour productivity (%) (1)	117.3	135.3	121.3	111.7	134.0	133.2	115.3	176.0	146.4	108.3	:	113.2	:	149.8	140.7	159.6

(1) EU-15, EL, I, A (1995); B, DK, D, E, F, IRL, L, FIN, S, UK (1996). (2) EU-15, L, S (1995). (3) NL (1992).

Source: Eurostat (SBS, EBT)

(million ECU) Table 10.27

Manufacture of weapons and ammunition (NACE Rev. 1 29.6)

Production related indicators in the EU

	1988	1989	1990	1991	1992	1993	1994	1995	1996	1997	1998
Production value	:	:	:	:	:	6,927	6,356	:	:	:	:
Producer price index (1995=100)	:	:	:	:	:	:	:	:	:	:	:
Value added	:	:	:	:	:	2,220	2,018	:	:	:	:
Number of persons employed (thousands)	:	:	:	:	:	75.1	70.2	:	:	:	:

(million ECU) Table 10.28

Manufacture of weapons and ammunition (NACE Rev. 1 29.6)

Production related indicators, 1998

	B	DK	D	EL	E	F	IRL	I	L	NL	A	P	FIN	S	UK
Production value (1)	345	0	1,447	165	235	1,731	0	734	:	88	162	:	77	608	2,403
Value added (1)(2)	121	0	625	-49	75	479	0	215	:	29	67	:	37	191	889
Number of persons employed (units) (1)	1,709	0	10,546	3,053	2,580	6,112	0	6,099	:	:	1,290	:	1,305	4,746	13,216

(1) DK, IRL (1996). (2) EL (1995).

(million ECU) Table 10.29

Manufacture of weapons and ammunition (NACE Rev. 1 29.6)

Market related indicators in the EU

	1988	1989	1990	1991	1992	1993	1994	1995	1996	1997	1998
Apparent consumption	:	:	:	:	:	6,708	5,959	:	:	:	:
Exports	881	1,158	1,138	731	815	446	603	471	1,327	425	471
Imports	31	37	19	482	475	227	206	129	159	185	44
Trade balance	850	1,121	1,118	249	340	219	397	342	1,167	240	428
Export ratio (%)	:	:	:	:	:	6.4	9.5	:	:	:	:
Import penetration ratio (%)	:	:	:	:	:	3.4	3.5	:	:	:	:
Cover ratio (%)	2,831.2	3,136.4	5,894.6	151.6	171.7	196.7	293.0	364.0	831.9	230.1	1,083.2

(million ECU) Table 10.30

Manufacture of weapons and ammunition (NACE Rev. 1 29.6)

Market related indicators, 1998

	B/L	DK	D	EL	E	F	IRL	I	NL	A	P	FIN	S	UK
Apparent consumption (1)	:	11	1,390	175	218	1,636	3	537	87	360	:	82	607	2,428
Exports	45	5	179	6	58	175	0	249	6	35	30	43	27	77
Imports	30	23	123	15	41	81	3	53	5	234	39	48	26	102
Trade balance	15	-18	56	-10	16	94	-2	196	1	-198	-9	-6	1	-25
Export ratio (%)	:	:	12.4	3.4	24.6	10.1	:	33.9	6.5	21.9	:	56.1	4.5	3.2
Import penetration ratio (%) (1)	:	142.9	8.9	8.8	19.0	4.9	113.9	9.8	5.3	64.9	:	59.0	4.3	4.2
Cover ratio (%)	149.4	22.5	145.7	36.5	139.5	216.6	0.4	473.5	124.7	15.2	76.2	88.6	103.1	75.7

(1) DK, IRL (1996).

Table 10.31

Manufacture of weapons and ammunition (NACE Rev. 1 29.6)

Labour related indicators, 1998

	EU-15	B	DK	D	EL	E	F	IRL	I	L	NL	A	P	FIN	S	UK
Personnel costs (million ECU) (1)	2,340	82	0	471	55	78	302	0	197	:	28	48	:	41	203	485
Personnel costs/employee (thousand ECU) (2)	:	51.5	:	44.3	19.8	34.9	50.2	:	29.4	:	:	38.9	:	31.3	44.7	30.5
Social charges/personnel costs (%) (3)	:	77.3	:	18.8	24.9	22.7	29.5	:	34.7	:	19.4	22.1	:	23.0	34.2	13.6
Labour productivity (thousand ECU/head) (4)	28.7	71.0	:	59.3	-16.0	29.2	78.3	:	35.2	:	:	52.3	:	28.1	40.3	67.2
Wage adjusted labour productivity (%) (2)	:	118.3	:	112.8	-81.0	72.3	157.9	:	134.6	:	:	125.4	:	130.0	87.8	167.9

(1) EU-15 (1994); DK, IRL (1996). (2) EL, I, A (1995); B, D, E, F, FIN, S, UK (1996). (3) S (1994). (4) EU-15 (1994); EL (1995).

Source: Eurostat (SBS, EBT)

Electrical machinery and electronics

Industry description

This chapter covers the manufacturing of electrical machinery and electronic products, encompassing the activities of domestic appliances (Group 29.7 of the NACE Rev. 1 activity classification), office machinery and computers (NACE Rev. 1 30), electrical machinery and apparatus n.e.c. (NACE Rev. 1 31) and radio, TV and communication equipment apparatus (NACE Rev. 1 32).

Altogether, these activities account for a significant share of the European economy. They generated approximately a tenth of total manufacturing output each year, thus producing output not far short of that generated by the food, drink and tobacco industry or the transport equipment industry. In 1998, their production value exceeded 360 billion ECU, with employment approximately equal to 2.3 million persons[1]. As well as this industry being sizeable in terms of production value, its strategic importance for the whole economy is also noteworthy. A great deal of the activities covered in this chapter are at the cornerstone of the development of the information society. They produce the hardware that allows information to be both transported and treated, with both intermediary products such as electronic components, or cables and wires, as well as products for final consumption, such as computers, telecommunication terminals, domestic appliances and consumer electronics.

1) Excluding Luxembourg, Greece and Portugal for NACE Rev. 1 30 and Austria for NACE Rev. 1 30 and 32 for production; excluding the Netherlands for all activities; excluding Austria for NACE Rev. 1 31 for employment.

(%) Figure 11.1

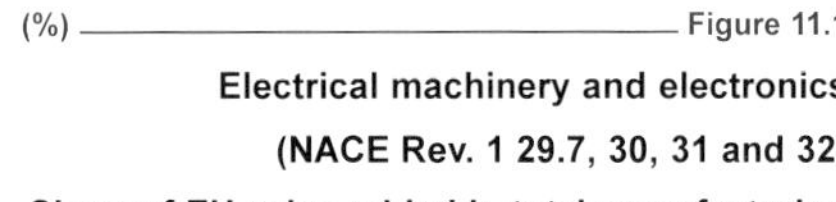

Electrical machinery and electronics
(NACE Rev. 1 29.7, 30, 31 and 32)
Share of EU value added in total manufacturing

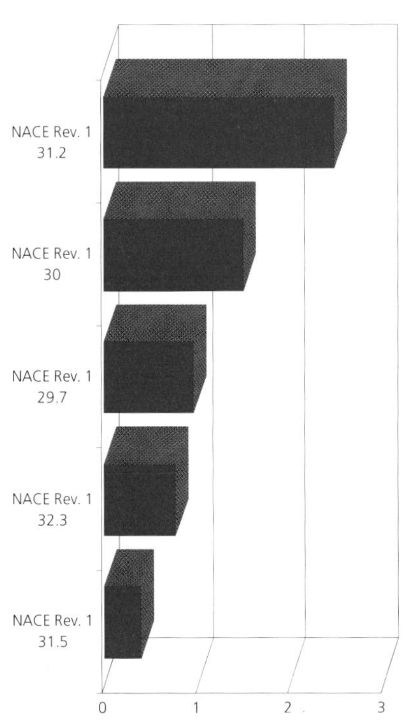

Source: Eurostat (SBS)

The activities covered in this chapter include:

- 29.7: manufacture of domestic appliances n.e.c.;
- 30.0: manufacture of office machinery and computers;
- 31.1: manufacture of electric motors, generators and transformers;
- 31.2: manufacture of electricity distribution and control apparatus;
- 31.3: manufacture of insulated wire and cable;
- 31.4: manufacture of accumulators, primary cells and primary batteries;
- 31.5: manufacture of lighting equipment and electric lamps;
- 31.6: manufacture of electrical equipment n.e.c.;
- 32.1: manufacture of electronic valves and tubes and other electronic components;
- 32.2: manufacture of television and radio transmitters and apparatus for line telephony and line telegraphy;
- 32.3: manufacture of television and radio receivers, sound or video recording or reproducing apparatus and associated goods.

Figure 11.2

Electrical machinery and electronics (NACE Rev. 1 29.7, 30, 31 and 32)

International comparison of main indicators in current prices

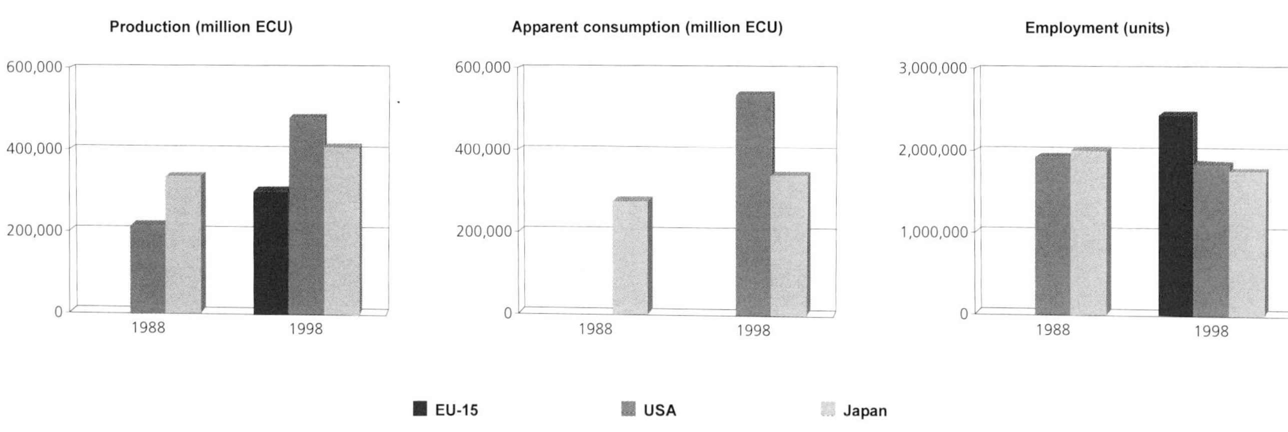

Source: Eurostat (SBS)

If we look at the relative sizes of the activities covered in this chapter, the largest in terms of production value is the manufacturing of electricity distribution and control apparatus (NACE Rev. 1 Group 31.2), accounting for about a fifth of production value in 1998, some 67 billion ECU. The manufacturing of TV and radio transmitters and telephony apparatus (NACE Rev. 1 32.2) followed with a 17% share or 62 billion ECU of output. The manufacturing of office machinery and computers accounted for a 16% share of production, some 59 billion ECU. At the other end of the ranking, the two smallest activities were the manufacturing of lighting equipment (NACE Rev. 1 31.5) with 3% or 11 billion ECU and batteries (NACE Rev. 1 31.4) with 1% or 5 billion ECU.

Ireland displayed a higher than average specialisation in the activities covered in this chapter, due especially to the manufacture of computers. Finland also recorded a relatively high specialisation ratio, stemming principally from the weight of its telephony equipment sector. In contrast, countries like Belgium and Greece showed little presence of these activities in their economies, with specialisation ratios below 60%.

Table 11.1 (million ECU)

Top ten European electronic and electrical equipment manufacturers ranked by turnover, 1997

Siemens (D)	56,559
Philips Electronics (NL)	36,643
Alcatel-Alsthom (F)	28,562
Ericsson (S)	16,670
Electrolux (S)	14,757
Thomson (F)	13,452
Schneider (F)	10,860
Nokia (FIN)	7,814
AEG (D)	6,083
ABB (D)	5,156

Source: Trade sources

(ECU/hour)

Figure 11.3

Electrical machinery and electronics (NACE Rev. 1 29.7, 30, 31 and 32)

Labour costs by Member State, 1996

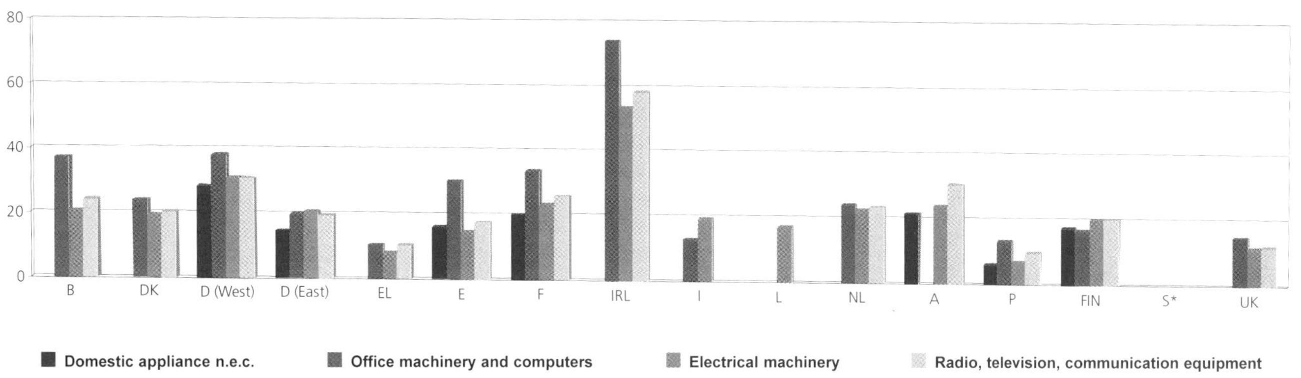

Source: Eurostat (LCS)

Recent trends

The sector of electrical machinery and electronics manufacturing saw its production growth rate equal to 2.9% in 1998 (in nominal terms). This followed a progression of 4.1% recorded the year before. Belgium (+14%) and Finland (+30%) recorded the strongest growth, whilst Italy (-5%) and Ireland (-15%) were the only countries suffering a decline in production values.

Long-term analysis is hindered by the lack of data or by the confidentiality of data in certain countries. However, the data available shows that this sector has witnessed relatively buoyant growth over the past decade. Between 1993 and 1998 production values grew by almost 30% in real terms to 361 billion ECU, up from 279 billion ECU[2]. This corresponded to an annual average growth rate in excess of 5.3% per annum. Some countries performed much better than this, as was the case in Sweden and Finland, where average growth between 1993 and 1998 was as high as 23% and 28% per annum respectively (due to the expansion of mobile telephony equipment). For means of comparison, production values progressed at an annual average rate of just 2% in Italy over the same period, and at less than 1% in Germany (between 1994 and 1998).

2) Figures exclude Greece, Luxembourg and Portugal for NACE Rev. 1 30 and Austria for NACE Rev. 1 30 and 32.

Employment, on the other hand, has not benefited from the growth in production. This can be seen as an indication that structural adjustments have occurred, with changes in the production processes of mature markets not being fully compensated by growth in younger markets and new technologies. The industries covered employed approximately 2.3 million persons[3] in 1998. Although this was an increase of 2% over the preceding year, it was still 16% below the figure of 1990, an average decline of around 2% per annum. In absolute terms, this represented a loss of some 450 thousand jobs.

A more detailed study, shows that employment figures varied considerably from one country to another, reflecting the production specialisation patterns of the different countries. The reduction of employment levels in Europe owed much to losses experienced in Italy and the United Kingdom (-2% per annum). However, the largest decline was recorded in Germany, where 85% of the job losses mentioned above were registered. German employment stood at 758 thousand persons in 1998, down from 1.1 million in 1990 (an annual average reduction of -5%). The European countries that were specialised in newer and faster growing technologies, such as Ireland (computers) and Finland (mobile telephony) saw their employment rise by as much as 50% between 1990 and 1998.

3) Excluding Greece, Luxembourg, the Netherlands and Portugal for NACE Rev. 1 30 and Austria for NACE Rev. 1 30, 31 and 32.

Unit personnel costs ranged between less than 25 thousand ECU per year in the United Kingdom and Ireland and more than 45 thousand ECU per year in Belgium and Germany. It is important to note that data was not available for countries where labour costs are traditionally lower than average, such as Greece and Portugal. Bearing this in mind, unit personnel costs were, as a general rule, higher than the average for manufacturing industries. This was particularly true in the manufacture of computers (NACE Rev. 1 30), the most extreme cases being in France and Spain where they were more than 70% above the manufacturing average. Domestic appliances (NACE Rev. 1 29.7), on the other hand, faced lower than average unit personnel costs in the majority of countries.

Turning attention to the composition of the labour force we can see that men dominated the employment profile of this industry, generally accounting for more than two thirds of the persons employed. In 1997, the highest presence of women was recorded in Ireland, some 40% of the workforce in computer manufacturing and 49% in the manufacture of other electrical machinery (NACE Rev. 1 31), with many of these posts being assembly jobs. Feminine presence was lowest in the Netherlands, with only 14% of the persons employed in NACE Rev. 1 31 and 23% in consumer electronics (NACE Rev. 1 32). Practically 95% of the workforce was working full-time across the sector. As regards the qualification of the workforce, the share of persons possessing a higher education tended to be higher in computer manufacturing activities, and somewhat lower in consumer electronics when compared to the other activities of the sector. The highest proportion of highly educated persons was found in the manufacture of computers in Spain (66%) and Belgium (60%). In contrast, only 3% of those working in electrical machinery manufacturing in Italy had a higher education degree.

Productivity has greatly improved during the nineties thanks to the combination of a steady decrease in employment and continuous growth. In Ireland and the United Kingdom, productivity gains reached 8% per annum over the period 1993-98, whilst they were over 6% in Sweden and Finland. In 1998, labour productivity, as measured by value added per capita, was highest in Finland, Ireland and Belgium at just under 70 thousand ECU.

The largest producer of electrical equipment and electronics in the world was the USA, with a production value that reached 480 billion ECU, or 39% of the Triad total in 1997. The global production of the three Triad economies exceeded 1.2 thousand billion ECU in the same year. Japanese production was equal to 407 billion ECU, or 33% of the total. The EU dominated the manufacturing of electrical machinery and apparatus (NACE Rev. 1 31) with a share in Triad production equal to 43%, but lagged behind in computer manufacturing (23%) and in consumer electronics (20%). These were two sectors that were led by the USA, with shares in Triad output of 46% and 44% respectively. Japan represented 44% of Triad domestic appliances' production (42 billion ECU), against 33 billion ECU in the EU (35%) and only 20 billion ECU in the USA (21%).

Demand for electrical and electronic products in 1997 (as measured by apparent consumption) was practically twice as high in the USA (539 billion ECU) as in the EU[4] (268 billion ECU), whilst it was equal to 342 billion ECU in Japan. The structure of demand reflected that of production, but with greater variation. More than half the apparent consumption of computers (NACE Rev. 1 30) in the Triad originated from the USA, against 26% in the EU and 22% in Japan. The largest market for electrical machinery and apparatus (NACE Rev. 1 31) was the EU with 135 billion ECU (40%), against 116 billion ECU for the USA (35%) and 83 billion ECU for Japan (25%).

Foreign trade

Extra-EU exports almost trebled over the ten-year period to 1998, reaching 107 billion ECU in 1998, up from 38 billion ECU in 1989. The trade balance remained negative, as imports from non-EU countries reached 131 billion ECU (excluding Finland). The resulting balance showed a deficit of 24 billion ECU[5]. Ireland was by far the most export-specialised country in the activity of electrical machinery and electronics, with an export specialisation ratio more than twice the EU average (235%). Other clearly export-specialised countries included Finland (150%), the United Kingdom (145%) and Sweden (132%).

In terms of product segments, we can identify distinct export-specialisation patterns. Italy (271%), Greece (139%), Spain (130%) and Denmark (114%) exported mainly domestic appliances (NACE Rev. 1 29.7), whilst Ireland (547%) and the Netherlands (260%) were extremely specialised in office machinery and computers (NACE Rev. 1 30). Portugal displayed a high export-specialisation (167%) in electrical machinery and apparatus (NACE Rev. 1 31), together with Germany (131%). Exports of Finland (281%) and Sweden (250%) were very intensive in consumer electronics, thanks to the presence of large telecommunication equipment companies.

4) Excluding Belgium, Greece, Luxembourg and Portugal for NACE Rev. 1 30 and Austria for NACE Rev. 1 30 and 32.
5) This figure concerns trade with extra-EU countries only, taking no account of intra-EU trade.

Figure 11.4

Electrical machinery and electronics (NACE Rev. 1 29.7, 30, 31 and 32) Destination of EU exports, 1998

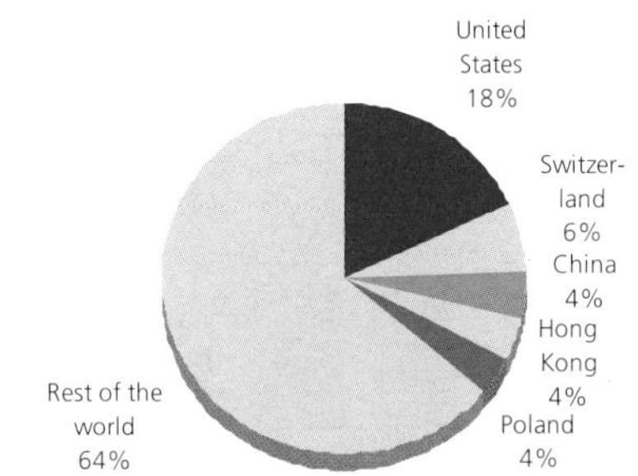

Source: Eurostat (Comext)

Figure 11.5

Electrical machinery and electronics (NACE Rev. 1 29.7, 30, 31 and 32) Origin of EU imports, 1998

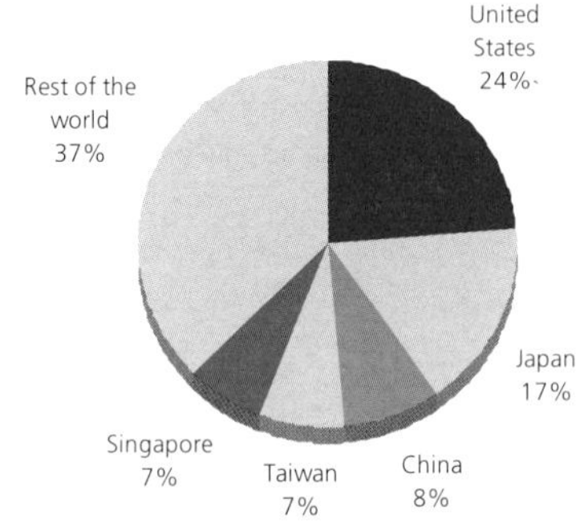

Source: Eurostat (Comext)

Electric motors, generators, electricity distribution equipment and batteries (NACE Rev. 1 31.1, 31.2 and 31.4)

This section covers the manufacture of electric motors, generators and transformers, the manufacture of electricity distribution and control apparatus (such as apparatus for switching, protecting or connecting electrical circuits) and the manufacture of accumulators, cells and batteries. These activities represented a significant share in some Member States. This was especially the case in Germany, where they accounted for no less than 47% of the activities covered in this chapter, or 5% of total manufacturing activity.

Demand in the EU exceeded 83 billion ECU[6] in 1998, up by 3% compared to 1997. Electricity distribution and control apparatus was responsible for most of the gains (59 billion ECU), ahead of electric motors, generators and transformers (19 billion ECU) and batteries and accumulators (5 billion ECU).

As regards electric motors, generators and transformers, demand faced different factors according to the market segment considered. Producers of equipment such as electricity generators, transformers and high voltage switchgears benefited from the rapidly growing demand for electrical power during the late eighties. As a result of substantial investment in most EU countries, the industry had to deal with excess capacity in the early nineties. The recovery witnessed from 1994 onwards slowed somewhat in 1998.

The trend for products more closely related to manufacturing processes was quite different, as most were highly sensitive to variations in the general level of economic activity. In the second half of the nineties, the EU manufacturing sector made significant efforts to improve its efficiency. This resulted in strong demand for electric motors, low-voltage switchgears, as well as installation equipment. Product innovations, such as the change from DC converters to three-phase converters, also had a positive effect on demand.

6) Excluding Belgium, Luxembourg and Portugal for NACE Rev. 1 31.1, 31.2 and 31.4; excluding Austria, Denmark and Greece for NACE Rev. 1 31.4.

Figure 11.6

Electric motors, generators, electricity distribution equipment and batteries (NACE Rev. 1 31.1, 31.2 and 31.4)

Production and employment in the Triad

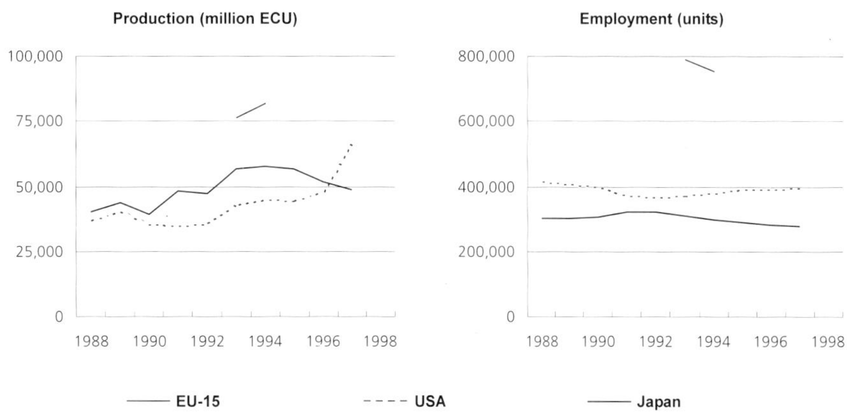

Source: Eurostat (SBS)

Figure 11.7

Electric motors, generators, electricity distribution equipment and batteries (NACE Rev. 1 31.1, 31.2 and 31.4)

Production and export specialisation by Member State, 1998

(%)

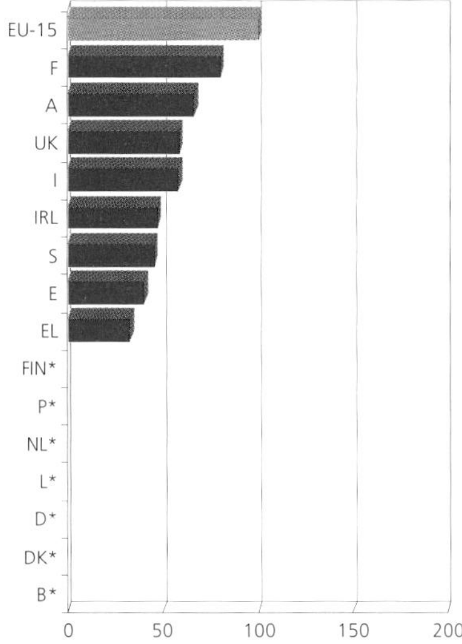

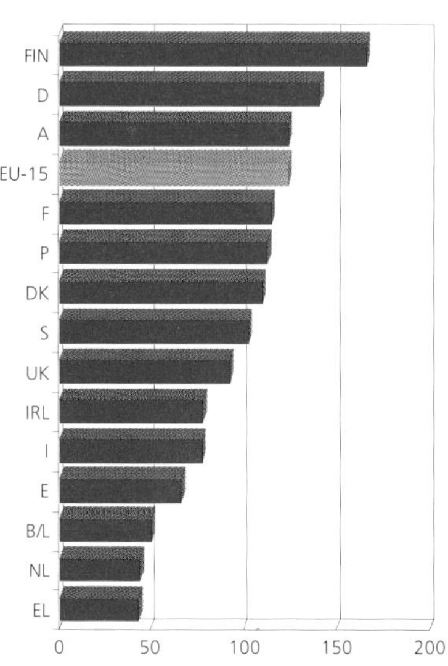

Source: Eurostat (SBS)

Figure 11.8 (thousands of units)
Breakdown of accumulator sales in Europe (1)

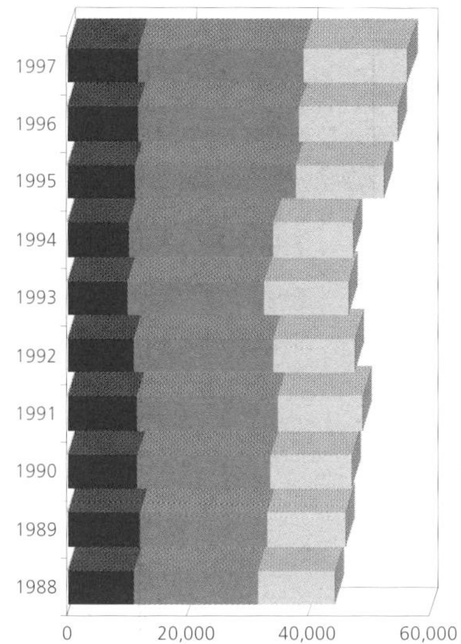

1) EU-15 (excluding Greece, Ireland and Luxembourg), Norway, Switzerland and Turkey; batteries of more than 5kg and 15Ah.

Source: Eurobat

Table 11.2 (thousand units)
Main indicators for the manufacture of accumulators in Europe (1)

	1990	1991	1992	1993	1994	1995	1996	1997
Sales	47,265	49,080	47,680	46,704	47,524	52,620	54,766	56,493
Domestic sales (2):								
to car manufacturers	11,576	11,470	11,056	9,940	10,243	11,275	11,681	11,746
to other manufacturers	22,105	23,418	23,044	22,695	23,919	26,602	26,786	27,392
Total imports (3)	13,584	14,192	13,580	14,069	13,362	14,733	16,299	17,355

(1) EU-15 (excluding Luxembourg, Ireland and Greece), Norway, Switzerland and Turkey; batteries of more than 5kg and 15Ah.
(2) Including imports by battery manufacturers.
(3) Excluding imports by battery manufacturers.

Source: Eurobat

The most important European producer in this industry is ABB (CH/S) which is active in the major electrical machinery segments (turbo-alternators, high-voltage and low-voltage switchgears and motor control equipment), followed by Siemens (D), also active in the main market segments. GEC (UK) is mainly specialised in turbo-alternators and high-voltage switchgears, whilst the joint-venture between GEC-Alsthom (UK/F) is present in the main segments of the sector. AEG (D) is a leading firm in low-voltage switchgears and motor-control equipment.

Primary batteries are used in portable audio equipment, games, watches, alarms and photographic equipment. Demand is linked to private consumer expenditure and the growth of battery-operated appliances. There was growth of around 2% per annum in the last decade. The market share of the basic zinc-carbon battery has been eroded by alkaline batteries that are more expensive but last longer. Alkaline-manganese and zinc-carbon general purpose batteries accounted for some 92% of the primary batteries sold in Europe.

Driven by the introduction of consumer devices such as portable cellular phones, laptop computers, pagers, and remote controlled equipment, the demand for non-lead accumulators has increased considerably in the last decade. This demand sparked the development of "smart" batteries, which relay status information on runtime. Manufacturers are also embedding micro-controllers to ensure efficient recharging operations. Nickel-cadmium rechargeable batteries have dominated the market since 1985, but the demand for longer-lasting accumulators has led to the emergence of nickel-metal hydrids, and more recently lithium-ion batteries.

Starter batteries are the most important market segment of accumulators and account for more than 50% of the total production of rechargeable batteries. According to Eurobat, the Association of European Accumulator Manufacturers, 56.5 million units were sold in Europe in 1997, up 3% on the data for 1996, following growth of 4% in 1996 and 11% in 1995. Car manufacturers were the largest single client for accumulator manufacturers, accounting for over a fifth of sales. Replacement demand is relatively unaffected by economic cycles, since vehicle fleets are not subject to short-term variations. However, the demand for new starter batteries is cyclical and follows the demand for new motor vehicles. As a result of the improved longevity of batteries and accumulators, the demand for these devices should decrease. In addition producers will come under increasing pressure, as distributors opt for the development of own-brand automotive batteries.

The world primary batteries market is dominated by Duracell (USA, 40%), followed by Philips (NL, 20%), Ralston Energy (Energizer, USA, 20%), and Varta (D, 10%). Together these four companies control about 80% of the EU market. For rechargeable portable batteries, key players include Sanyo (J), and Matsushita/Panasonic (J). The only European player is Saft (F), a subsidiary of Alcatel. The segment of non-lead accumulators is less concentrated and includes the likes of Sony (J), Panasonic (J) and Saft (F). In the lead-acid batteries segment, Euro-Exide, a division of the American company Exide, is the leader in the EU with a 40% market share. Major EU players include Varta Bosch (D), Autosil-CFEC (P), Fiamm (I), and Hawker (UK).

The EU exported goods worth close to 22 billion ECU in 1998 (excluding Greece), up by 6% on 1997. Extra-EU imports were equal to 15 billion ECU (excluding Denmark, Finland, Greece, Ireland and Portugal for NACE Rev. 1 31.4). Given the size of the economies for which data was not available, we can safely assume that the trade balance for this sector was positive.

On the basis of available data, we can estimate that between 22% and 23% of production was exported to non-EU countries and that between 17% and 18% of consumption was satisfied by products imported from third countries. Japan exported a comparatively larger share of its production (30% in 1997) and imported less (12% of domestic consumption). The opposite was true in the USA with an export ratio of 21% and an import penetration ratio of 26%.

Figure 11.9

Electric motors, generators, electricity distribution equipment and batteries (NACE Rev. 1 31.1, 31.2 and 31.4) Destination of EU exports, 1998

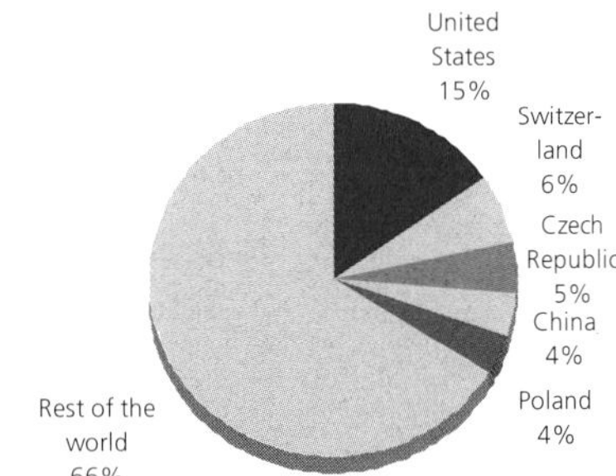

Source: Eurostat (Comext)

Figure 11.10

Electric motors, generators, electricity distribution equipment and batteries (NACE Rev. 1 31.1, 31.2 and 31.4) Origin of EU imports, 1998

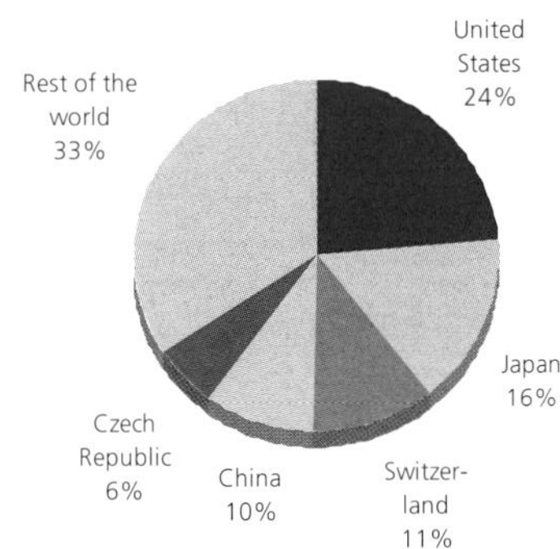

Source: Eurostat (Comext)

Domestic appliances (NACE Rev. 1 29.7)

This section covers both electrical and non-electrical domestic appliances. Electrical equipment accounted for about nine-tenths of domestic appliance production, with a total production value equal to 34 billion ECU (excluding Luxembourg) in 1998. Three countries displayed high specialisation in this activity: Germany, with a production specialisation ratio of 120%, Denmark with a ratio of 172% and, most of all, Italy, where domestic appliances accounted for a share in manufacturing production more than twice the EU average. Production values in Italy were, at 9.6 billion ECU, only 1 billion ECU below the value of German production, and two to three times larger than the French and United Kingdom figures.

The domestic appliances' industry employed more than 252 thousand persons in the EU in 1998 (excluding Luxembourg and the Netherlands), of which one-fifth were found in Germany and one-quarter in Italy. The industry has created jobs; as employment stood at 251 thousand persons in 1995 for the whole of the EU. A more detailed analysis shows that this growth was principally due to Italy, where 5.6 thousand jobs were created between 1995 and 1998, a 10% increase. Italy and Ireland were the only countries where employment rose between 1990 and 1998, by as much as 30% in Italy and 18% in Ireland. In the meantime, Belgium lost over half its workforce in the sector, Greece and Finland over 35% and Germany, Portugal, Sweden and the United Kingdom almost 30%.

Demand for domestic appliances was estimated at 30 billion ECU in 1998 (excluding Belgium and Luxembourg), a progression of 4.5% compared to 1997. Earlier in the decade, the industry experienced an average growth rate of over 3% per annum between 1990 and 1994, despite the general recession. However, 1995 was not a good year for the industry, with a 5% decline in demand, which affected domestic production (down 3%).

Figure 11.11

Domestic appliances (NACE Rev. 1 29.7)
Production and employment in the Triad

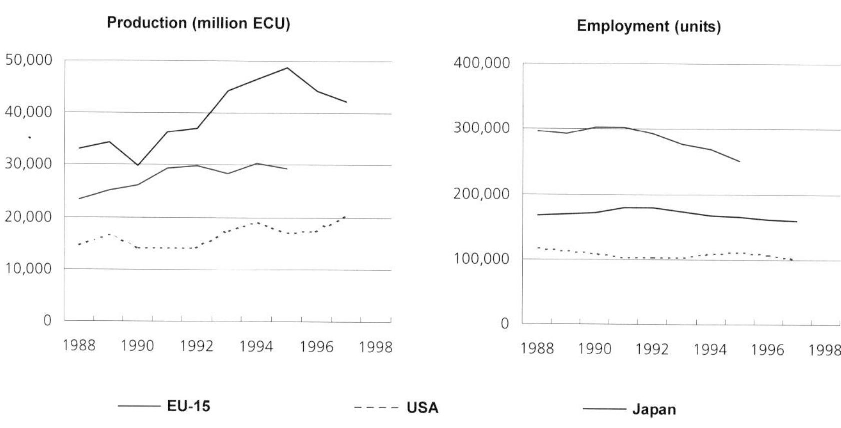

Source: Eurostat (SBS)

Figure 11.12 (%)

Domestic appliances (NACE Rev. 1 29.7)
Production and export specialisation by Member State, 1998

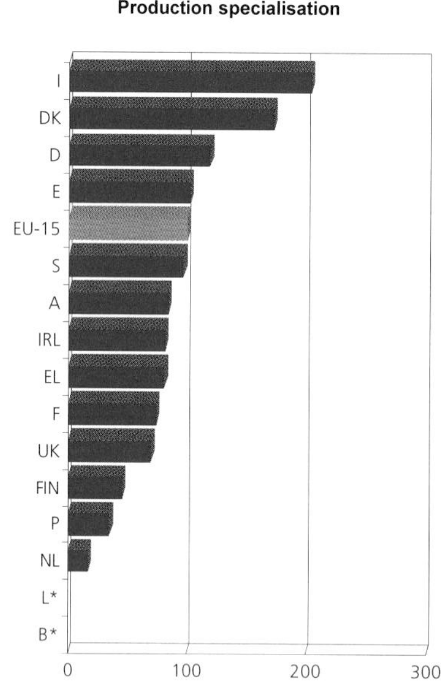

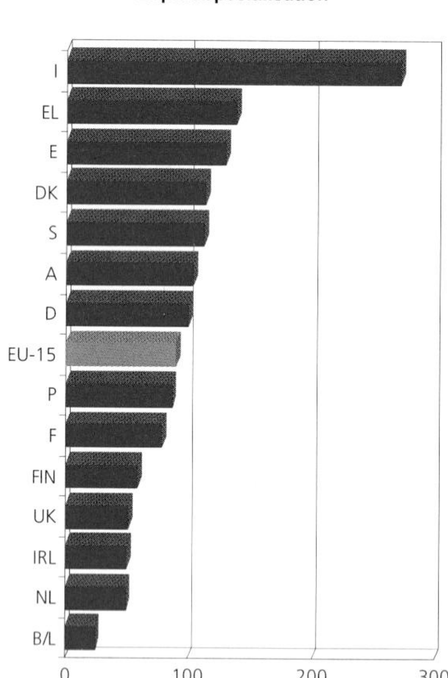

Source: Eurostat (SBS)

Due to high market saturation levels (i.e. 97% for refrigerators, 90% for washing machines and 86% for vacuum cleaners), European demand for domestic appliances is mainly linked to factors such as demographic growth, the evolution of the housing market and the number of single person households, which can affect "first purchase" sales. It is also linked to general economic activity and consumer confidence. In times of recession, consumers tend to keep a cautious attitude and postpone their purchases, thereby affecting the replacement market. European manufacturers are hence concentrating their efforts on the less saturated markets, such as Central and Eastern Europe and the emerging Asian economies. Company strategies usually revolve around building up brand names in order to differentiate products from those of competitors. In order to win customer loyalty there has been a notable focus on after-sales service. Another strategy is to constantly develop new products, adding features and changing design in order to induce replacement purchases.

In particular, the introduction of electronic devices has been one of the biggest upheavals affecting the sector over the last decade. Electronic devices such as micro-control units (MCU) and LCD/LED displays have been incorporated into products, making appliances versatile and programmable. One of the main trends is for wired appliances to evolve into wireless versions powered by charged batteries, including coffee makers, electric irons, can-openers, food mixers and juice makers.

The EU domestic appliances' industry is unambiguously export-orientated. About one fifth of the EU's production value was destined for third countries in 1998, whilst imports from non-EU countries corresponded to only 11% of consumption. The trade balance with the rest of the world was equal to 2.4 billion ECU (excluding Finland), two and a half times its level in 1992. The most export-orientated country in 1998 was Italy, where the export specialisation ratio relative to the EU was equal to 270%. Other export specialised countries included Greece (139%), Spain (130%) and Denmark (114%).

Both the USA and Japan recorded lower export ratios, equal to 13.0% and 2.2% respectively in 1997. In the USA, 23% of domestic appliances' consumption was satisfied by imports, more than twice the EU ratio. Both of the other Triad countries recorded a deterioration in their external trade balances during the nineties. The USA recorded a trade deficit of 2.7 billion ECU in 1997, whilst in Japan, the trade surplus of 0.7 billion ECU recorded in 1990 turned negative in 1995 (reaching -0.2 billion ECU in 1997).

Figure 11.13

Domestic appliances (NACE Rev. 1 29.7)
Destination of EU exports, 1998

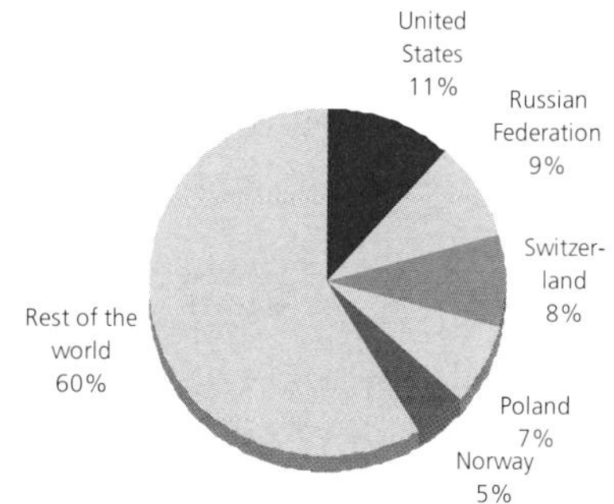

Source: Eurostat (Comext)

Figure 11.14

Domestic appliances (NACE Rev. 1 29.7)
Origin of EU imports, 1998

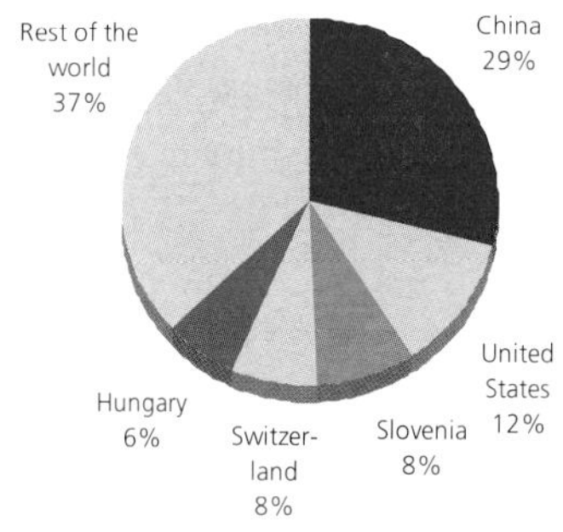

Source: Eurostat (Comext)

Electric lighting (NACE Rev. 1 31.5)

The electric lighting industry can be divided into two main areas: electric light bulbs for domestic and industrial uses (including incandescent, fluorescent, halogen and dual light bulbs) and electric lighting equipment (including indoor electric lighting equipment, special purpose electric lights, portable lights, outdoor lights, and spotlights, as well as lights for motor vehicles).

EU production in 1998 grew by less than 1% to reach 11 billion ECU, of which Germany accounted for 31%, followed by Italy (15%), the United Kingdom (13%) and France (12%). When considered in relation to total manufacturing production one country displayed a high specialisation ratio in this sector: Portugal, whose production specialisation ratio was equal to 190%. The Netherlands (38%), Greece (36%) and Ireland (13%) were the least specialised countries in the manufacture of electric lighting. Growth in production between 1990 and 1998 has followed a modest trend (with the exception of 1993), with an average annual increase of 1.6% per annum. The strongest growth rates were recorded in 1994 (+5.4%) and 1996 (+4.6%).

Employment in electric lighting was equal to 106 thousand persons in 1997 (excluding Luxembourg and the Netherlands). This followed a declining trend during the decade with a loss of more than 20 thousand jobs between 1990 and 1996. Most of the job losses were accounted for by Germany and the United Kingdom, where 8 thousand jobs were shed in each country between 1990 and 1998. In Portugal, employment progressed by 2 thousand persons over the same period.

Demand for light bulbs is mainly driven by the replacement market which is less sensitive to cyclical fluctuations, although the growth of disposable income, technological innovations, fashion trends and energy saving issues can influence replacement rates.

Figure 11.15

Electric lighting (NACE Rev. 1 31.5)

Production and employment in the Triad

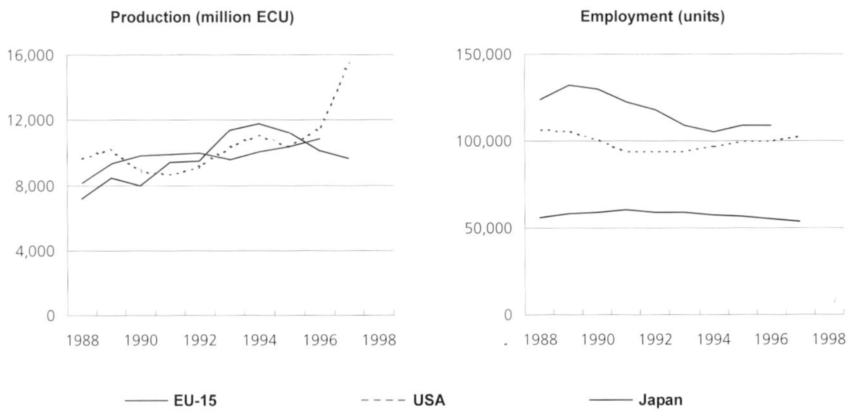

Source: Eurostat (SBS)

Figure 11.16 (%)

Electric lighting (NACE Rev. 1 31.5)

Production and export specialisation by Member State, 1998

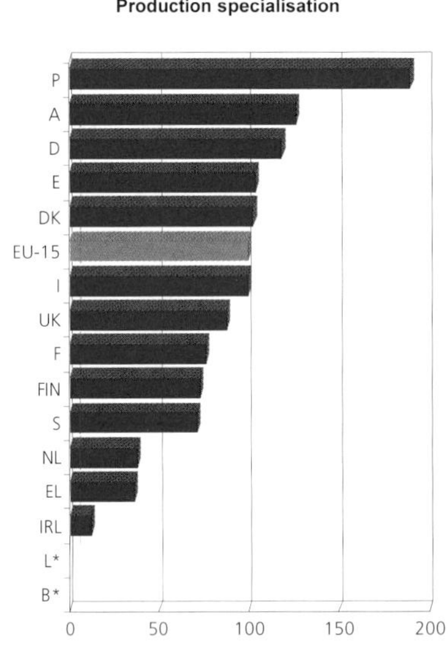

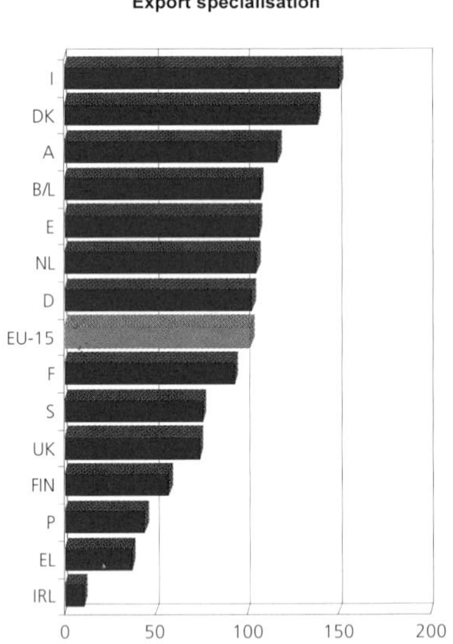

Source: Eurostat (SBS)

Demand for electrical lighting equipment is influenced by the requirements of residential and commercial construction, as well as public projects. The demand for commercial and industrial lighting equipment is cyclical and linked strongly to construction activity. Renovation is counter-cyclical and partly compensates for downturns in construction activity.

Product innovation increased replacement rates during the last decade. Products such as halogen and compact fluorescent light bulbs (CFL) use less energy and last longer. However, CFLs are more expensive than normal incandescent light bulbs and this may partly explain their low penetration rate in EU countries. Nonetheless, there has been a slight shift in demand from incandescent light bulbs to high-grade devices.

Overall, demand for lighting equipment as measured by apparent consumption could be estimated at slightly less than 11 billion ECU in 1998 (excluding Luxembourg), a progression of 2.4%. This marked a slow down after two years of strong growth in 1996 and 1997 (of the magnitude of 5% per annum).

Three companies controlled over 75% of the lighting market. There is a trend towards concentration, which is complemented by numerous licensing agreements between the main manufacturers in order to share technologies. Philips (NL) is the leading producer of light bulbs in the EU with a 50% share of the European electric lighting industry. The second prominent company is Osram (D), a division of Siemens. Osram is also present on the USA market with Sylvania and is among the top three global producers of light bulbs, along with Philips and General Electric (USA).

The electric lighting equipment industry is also dominated by large international players, although smaller regional companies are also active. The main European players are Philips (NL), Siemens (D), Trilux (D), AEG (D) and Thorn Lighting (UK). Smaller regional companies are either family-owned or divisions of large public companies. The current harmonisation of technical standards in Europe may well lead to increased competition between small and medium-sized lighting equipment suppliers.

Some large suppliers are transferring production facilities to countries with lower production costs. The internationalisation of production and a strong presence in the expanding markets of Asia and Eastern Europe is a strategy followed by many manufacturers. Philips and Osram are both present in Central and Eastern European countries and have set-up joint-ventures in China.

Despite the trend to re-localise manufacturing facilities to countries benefiting from lower labour costs, the European lighting industry remains a net contributor to the EU foreign trade balance. External trade with the rest of the world was in surplus throughout the last decade, rising from 670 million ECU in 1991 to 810 million ECU in 1996, to be cut by half during the following two years to 400 million ECU by 1998[7]. The two countries where electric lighting exports accounted for a greater than average share of national manufacturing exports were Italy and Denmark, recording export specialisation ratios of 151% and 139%. Other export specialised countries included Austria (117%) and Belgium and Luxembourg (107%).

A fifth of American apparent consumption was satisfied by imported products, compared to approximately 18% in the EU and only 5% in Japan. In addition, about one-quarter of the EU's production is exported, whilst comparable figures show the ratio as only a tenth in the USA and 6% in Japan. The USA displayed a large trade deficit in excess of 2.2 billion ECU in 1997, double the amount of the early 1990s. In Japan, the trade balance was positive, at 117 million ECU (half its level of 1991).

7) Excluding Greece and Ireland.

Figure 11.17

Electric lighting (NACE Rev. 1 31.5)

Destination of EU exports, 1998

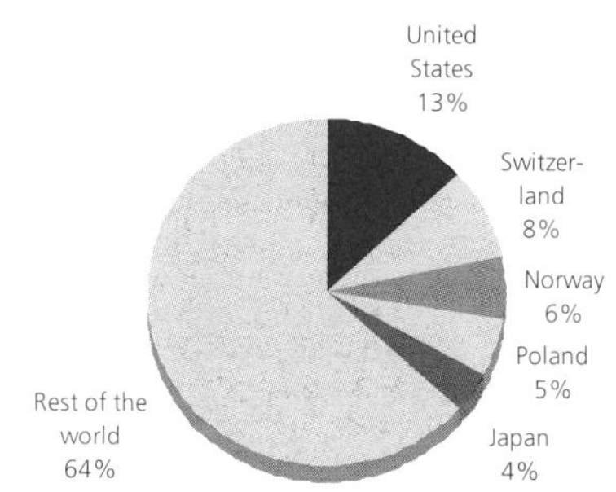

Source: Eurostat (Comext)

Figure 11.18

Electric lighting (NACE Rev. 1 31.5)

Origin of EU imports, 1998

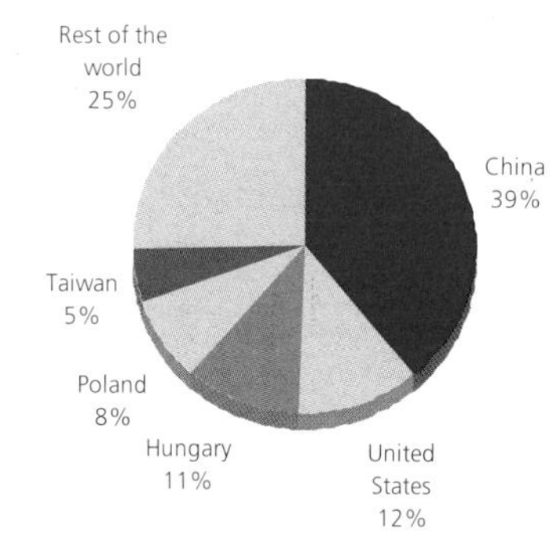

Source: Eurostat (Comext)

Insulated wire and cable (NACE Rev. 1 31.3)

The market for insulated wires and cables is extremely diverse with applications in virtually all areas of modern life. Three broad sub-sectors of insulated wires and cables may be defined by the different areas of application: electrical energy cables, information cables and winding wires. Electrical energy cables supply energy from electricity generation centres to individual points of utilisation, and differ according to their voltage range. Information cables have two important areas of application: telecommunications and electronic data and control. They use both copper wiring and optical fibres, with the latter becoming more important in many areas of use. Other communications cables, such as coaxial cables are also important to the sector. As for winding wires, they are used in all forms of electrical equipment that utilise electric-magnetic power, e.g. motors, generators, transformers, relays, etc. According to Europacable, the European Confederation of Associations of Manufacturers of Insulated Wires and Cables, the industry employed almost 72 thousand persons in Europe in 1997 and generated production worth 12.7 billion ECU (including Norway and Switzerland). General wiring cable made up the largest share of production (38%), ahead of communication cable (32%). The remainder of the market was shared between electricity utility cable (20%) and enamelled wires (10%).

Figure 11.19 (%)

Production breakdown of wires and cables in Europe, 1997 (1)

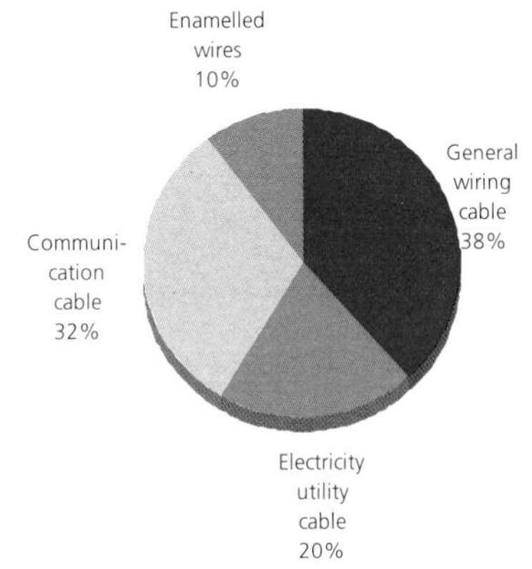

1) EU-15, Norway and Switzerland.

Source: Europacable

Table 11.3 (million ECU)

Production of wires and cables in Europe, 1997

	Benelux	D	E	F	I	UK	Northern Europe (1)	Southern Europe (2)	Other Europe (3)
General wiring cable	309.6	1,282.8	245.5	692.0	682.6	673.3	487.2	110.0	378.9
Electricity utility cable	178.5	673.5	144.6	506.0	253.5	174.8	370.1	94.3	172.1
Communication cable	248.1	1,222.8	196.9	653.9	365.9	542.8	357.7	69.5	353.4
Enamelled wires	44.4	294.2	114.8	174.4	383.8	107.0	71.9	0.0	70.0
Total	780.6	3,473.3	701.8	2,026.3	1,685.8	1,497.9	1,286.9	273.8	974.4

(1) Denmark, Finaland, Sweden and Norway.
(2) Greece and Portugal.
(3) Austria, Ireland and Switzerland.

Source: Europacable

Figure 11.20

Insulated wire and cable (NACE Rev. 1 31.3)
Production and employment in the Triad

Production (million ECU) — Employment (units)

EU-15 — USA — Japan

Source: Eurostat (SBS)

Eurostat data is somewhat at variance with Europacable data due to methodological differences. Official figures cover a somewhat wider range of activities, with production estimated to be equal to 15 billion ECU in 1998 (excluding Luxembourg and Austria). At a national level, two countries displayed much higher than average specialisation: Greece, whose insulated cables and wires production relative to its total manufacturing production was 2.8 times higher than the EU average, and Portugal, where specialisation was 3.2 times higher. Other countries that were specialised included Sweden (153%) and France (132%).

In the case of energy cables, demand is not only dependent on increases in electricity consumption, but also on demand for new generation and transmission facilities, as well as replacement demand. Demand for wires and cables can be affected considerably by energy policy. The energy cable industry derives demand from three main sources: power utility companies, the construction sector and from the white goods sector. Demand for information cables is linked to the development of the telecommunications market, as well as increased consumer take-up of telecommunications equipment, in the light of a deregulated environment and wider bandwidth requirements, stemming from the exponential growth of the Internet. Demand for winding wires is linked to trends in end markets, such as automotive and domestic appliances. Apparent consumption for insulated wires and cables was estimated at around 13 billion ECU in 1998 (excluding Austria and Luxembourg), a decline of 5% over the preceding year.

The manufacture of cable harnesses and the customisation of cables, is one of the few labour intensive production tasks, which is often subcontracted. Portugal and Ireland have become important locations for customising cables and cable trunks for the automotive industry. Subcontracting to Eastern European countries has also been of importance, above all for customising cables for other purposes than cars. In the years to come, the amount of customising tasks will shrink. The application of so-called "bus technology" in vehicles will sharply reduce the number of cables needed as intermediary products for car production.

The major European manufacturers of insulated wires and cables are Alcatel (F), ABB (S/CH), BICC (UK), Pirelli (I), Siemens (D), NKF (NL) and Draka (NL). These large companies produce all types of cables and wires. Small enterprises tend to focus their activities on market segments and on specific application niches. About 10% of production volume is accounted for by small and medium-sized companies in the EU. The increasing share of optical fibre cables in telecommunication cables has led to the fusion of small and medium-sized firms, in order to provide the necessary capital inputs for advanced production processes. There are now only about a dozen manufacturers of optical fibres in the EU.

Competition on international markets has led several large cable manufacturers to make cross-border investments. There has been a large amount of foreign investment by European companies world-wide, with companies seeking to produce cable close to end users in North and South America, the Middle East, and most parts of Asia (with the exception of Japan). EU companies are also active in the emerging economies of China and Central and Eastern Europe.

In spite of this growing internationalisation trend and the re-localisation of manufacturing, the EU insulated wire and cable industry remained a net contributor to the EU's external trade balance. The surplus with the rest of the world was equal to almost one billion ECU in 1998[8]. In Portugal, exports were almost five times greater than the EU average, whilst there was also specialisation in Greece (233%), Spain (156%) and Sweden (154%).

8) Excluding Greece, Ireland and Portugal.

(%) Figure 11.21

Insulated wire and cable (NACE Rev. 1 31.3)
Production and export specialisation by Member State, 1998

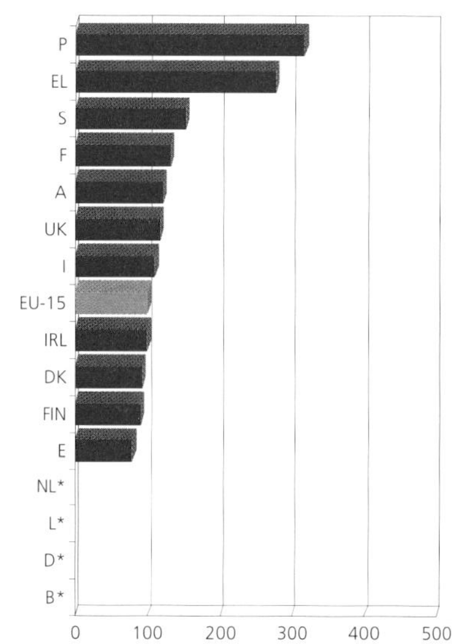

Source: Eurostat (SBS)

Figure 11.22
Insulated wire and cable (NACE Rev. 1 31.3)
Destination of EU exports, 1998

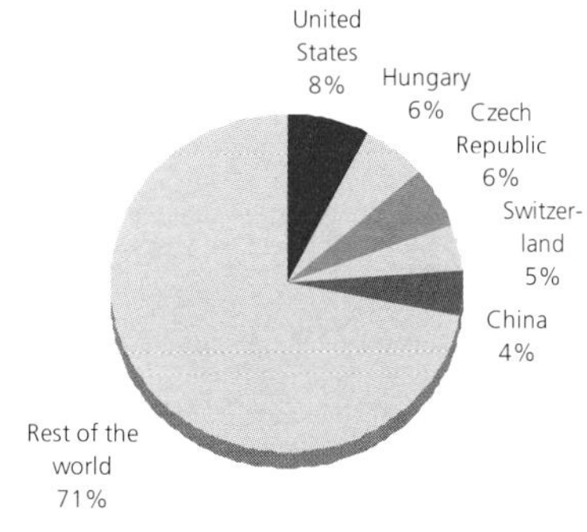

Source: Eurostat (Comext)

Figure 11.23
Insulated wire and cable (NACE Rev. 1 31.3)
Origin of EU imports, 1998

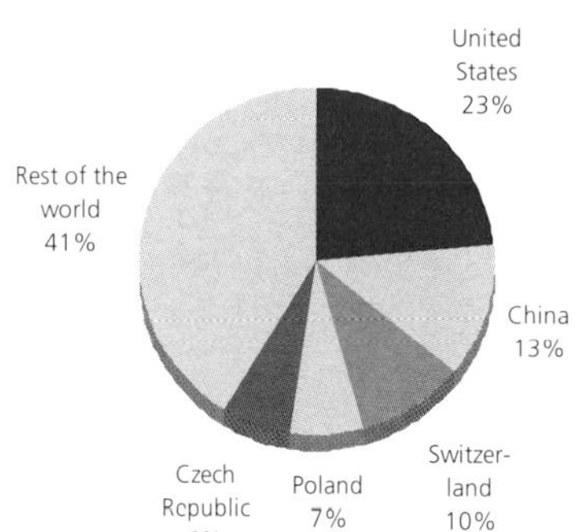

Source: Eurostat (Comext)

Electronic components (NACE Rev. 1 32.1)

The electronic components sector comprises three main categories: active components (such as semiconductors, cathode-ray tubes, flat screens and electro-optical components), passive components (such as capacitors, resistors, inductors and ferrites) and electro-mechanical components (such as printed circuits, connectors, hybrid circuits, MCMs and relays). It should be noted that the definition of the NACE Rev. 1 activity classification (Group 32.1) excludes the manufacturing of heating resistors, transformers and switches.

Electronic components are used in almost all equipment, and their share in the cost of electronic equipment has risen continuously over the past decade. According to the European Electronic Component Manufacturers Association (EECA) it has increased from less than 18% in 1988 to more than 24% in 1998. This trend is expected to continue because of the growing complexity of electronic components, particularly of semiconductors and passive components.

The EU production of electronic components (as defined by Group 32.1) was equal to 25 billion ECU in 1998, a slight decrease of 0.3% when compared to the year before, after strong growth of 7.1% in 1997 and 4% in 1996[9]. France and Germany accounted for half of the EU's production. Ireland was the Member State that specialised the most in this activity, with electronic components accounting for a share in total manufacturing that was 2.8 times higher than the EU average (283%). Above average specialisation was also recorded in the United Kingdom (177%) and to a lesser extent France (142%).

Growth in this industry is mainly driven by the market for active components, and especially that of semiconductors, rather than passive and electro-mechanical components. Cathode-ray tubes (CRT) constitute a large and regularly expanding market in which Europe is well positioned. On the other hand, Japan and South Korea dominate the fast growing and profitable market for flat LCD screens (estimated at 10 billion Euro in 1999[10]). LCD screens are expected to gradually replace CRTs in computer monitors, and eventually TV sets. This has led large consumer electronics manufacturers to enter the market, for example Philips Electronics (NL) that bought half of LG LCD (South Korea) in 1999.

In the area of passive components, telecommunications has always been a large consumer, representing as much as a quarter of the European market, a situation that has been further reinforced with the explosion in mobile telephony. The use of passive components in cars is also growing strongly.

Active components, particularly semiconductors, exhibit a high rate of innovation. Technological development of semiconductors enables the computing power of processors to double every 18 months (Moore's law). Semiconductor use does not solely increase with the growing amount of equipment, but also benefits from a pervasive effect, whereby functions provided in the past by mechanical or electrical components are increasingly provided using semiconductors. These two long-lasting effects are making a considerable contribution to the increase in demand. The data processing sector is still the main market for components, particularly integrated circuits. This is related to the huge increase in the personal computer market, an increase that may be prolonged by the introduction of multimedia computers. The commu-

9) Excluding Austria, Luxembourg and Portugal.
10) The Economist, 22nd May 1999.

Figure 11.24

Electronic components (NACE Rev. 1 32.1)
Production and employment in the Triad

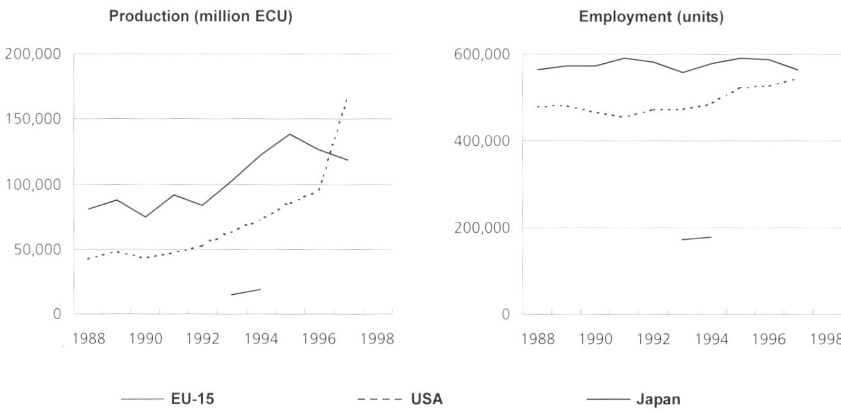

Source: Eurostat (SBS)

Figure 11.25 (%)

Electronic components (NACE Rev. 1 32.1)
Production and export specialisation by Member State, 1998

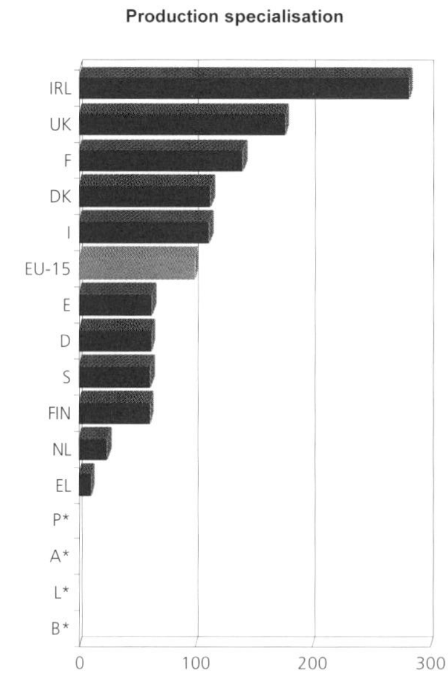

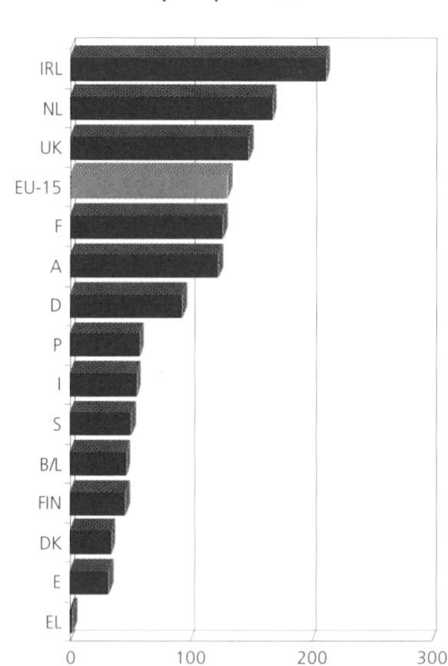

Source: Eurostat (SBS)

nications sector is also an important market for components. The success of mobile telephones, together with advances in digitisation, make them a key factor for demand. The design of such highly specialised circuits requires a high degree of expertise (unlike memory chips which are "generalist" circuits). The consumer electronics sector is also expanding along with the development of new digital products: compact discs, Digital Versatile Discs (DVD), CD-ROMs, digital radio and high-definition digital television. In these areas, the Japanese have traditionally been market leaders. However, the presence of large European or American players in these new fields may challenge this position. Of less importance for semiconductors are the markets for industrial and medical equipment and for cars. In these areas, however, Europe enjoys a large market share and the importance of semiconductors is constantly increasing.

The main European producers of semiconductors within Europe are Philips, Infineon and SGS-Thomson; whilst globally they are joined by American companies such as Motorola, Texas Instruments, IBM, Intel and National Semiconductor and the Japanese companies of Toshiba and NEC. The electromechanical components sector is much less concentrated and is distributed amongst a larger number of companies within the EU, which is also true for passive components (capacitors and resistors) where both small and large companies (Philips and Siemens) co-exist.

The statistics for external trade may be difficult to interpret given the globalisation of the process for manufacturing an integrated circuit (it may be designed anywhere in the world, diffused in Europe, assembled in Singapore and sold in the USA). One should note that the target of large producers, whether European or not, is the world market. The data on external trade do not necessarily reflect the strengths of producers with "European" or any other nationality.

The data do reveal that European production is a long way from satisfying domestic demand. The EU trade balance for electronic components with the rest of the world reached -4.3 billion ECU in 1997. Product statistics provided by EECA show the same negative trend. At a national level, all EU Member States displayed a trade deficit in 1998, except Austria (211 million ECU), France (314 million ECU) and the Netherlands (1.4 billion ECU). Ireland displayed the highest export specialisation ratio in electronic components (212%), ahead of the Netherlands (167%).

(1988=100) Figure 11.26

Electronic components, evolution of main indicators in the EU

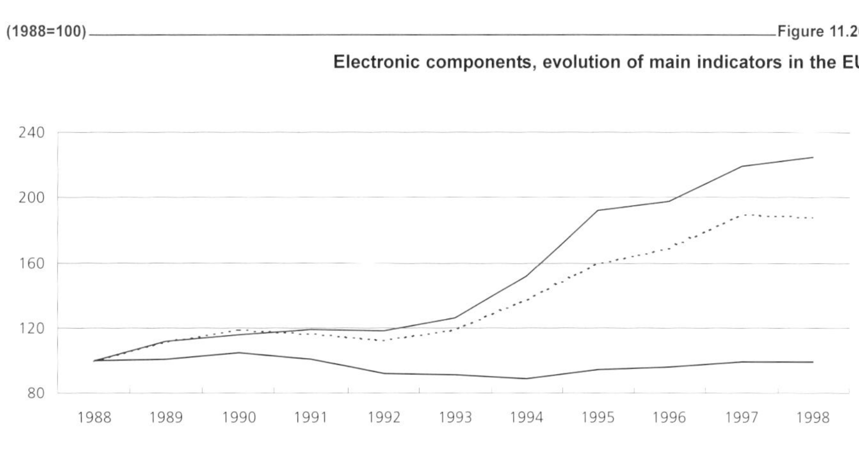

Market ---- Production Employment

Source: EECA

(%) Figure 11.27

Share of electronic components in equipment

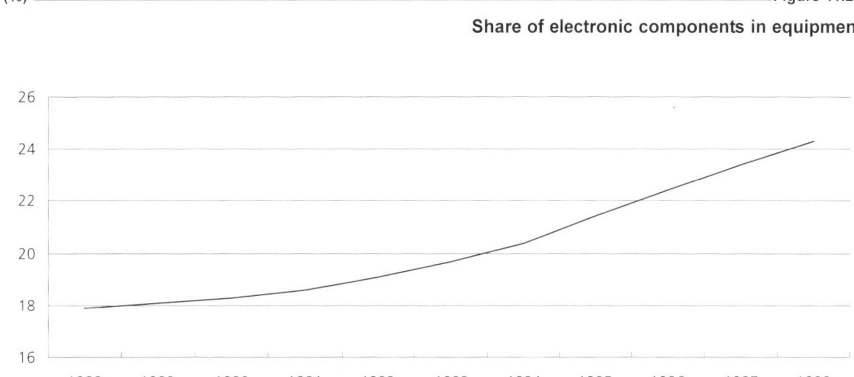

Source: EECA

Figure 11.28

Electronic components (NACE Rev. 1 32.1)
Destination of EU exports, 1998

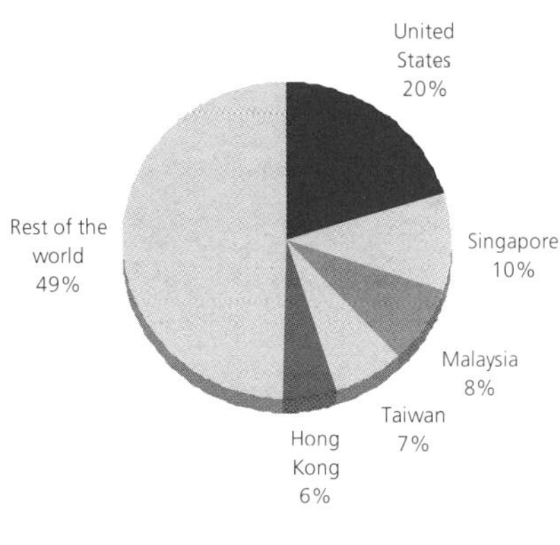

Source: Eurostat (Comext)

Figure 11.29

Electronic components (NACE Rev. 1 32.1)
Origin of EU imports, 1998

Rest of the world 34%
United States 23%
Japan 19%
Singapore 9%
Malaysia 8%
Republic of Korea 7%

Source: Eurostat (Comext)

Computers and office equipment (NACE Rev. 1 30)

The computer and office equipment sector is classified under Division 30 of NACE Rev. 1. The industry covers the manufacture of office equipment (such as typewriters, calculators, cash registers, mail and money handling equipment, within Class 30.01) and the manufacture of automatic data processing machines (including microcomputers and the manufacture of their peripherals, within Class 30.02). The manufacture of electronic parts found within computers are excluded from this analysis (see electronic components), as are electronic games and the repair and maintenance of computer systems (see software and computing services).

EU production of computers and office machinery was approaching 59 billion ECU in 1998, a slight decrease of 0.2% compared to the year before. This was the first year that a reduction in output (in value terms) was recorded since the recession of 1992/93, and followed four years of average annual growth in excess of 7%. One country clearly stood out as highly specialised in computer manufacturing; Ireland. The share of this activity in the country's national manufacturing production was 10 times larger than in the EU as a whole (production specialisation ratio of 975%). Only the United Kingdom (185%) and France (127%) displayed a specialisation ratio significantly higher than average.

The European Information Technology Observatory (EITO) provides some additional insights into this industry. The EU market for computer and office equipment was estimated to be worth 82 billion ECU in 1998. Of this, 65 billion ECU (80%) was accounted for by computer hardware, 9.1 billion ECU (11%) by office equipment and 7.4 billion ECU (9%) by data communications hardware.

EITO estimate that about 20 million PCs were shipped in the EU in 1998, and that this number was expected to rise by 25% in the year 2000. Total market value was equal to 30 billion ECU in 1998 and was forecast to grow to 34 million ECU by the year 2000. The lower growth rate in value terms reflected the belief that average prices for personal computers would continue to fall.

The fastest growing market was that of data communications. Its total value was equal to 7.5 billion ECU in 1998. This was expected to rise by 18% by the year 2000. If we look at local area network (LAN) cards, 20 million units are expected to be shipped in the EU in the year 2000, almost a third more than in 1998.

Figure 11.30

Computers and office equipment (NACE Rev. 1 30)

Production and employment in the Triad

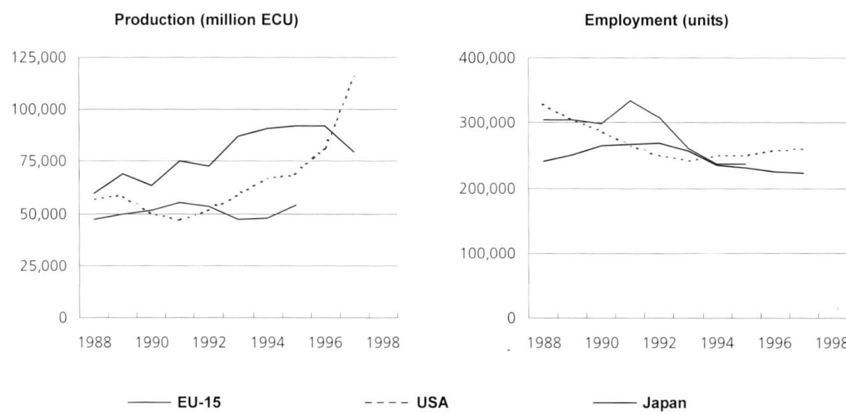

Source: Eurostat (SBS)

Figure 11.31 (%)

Computers and office equipment (NACE Rev. 1 30)

Production and export specialisation by Member State, 1998

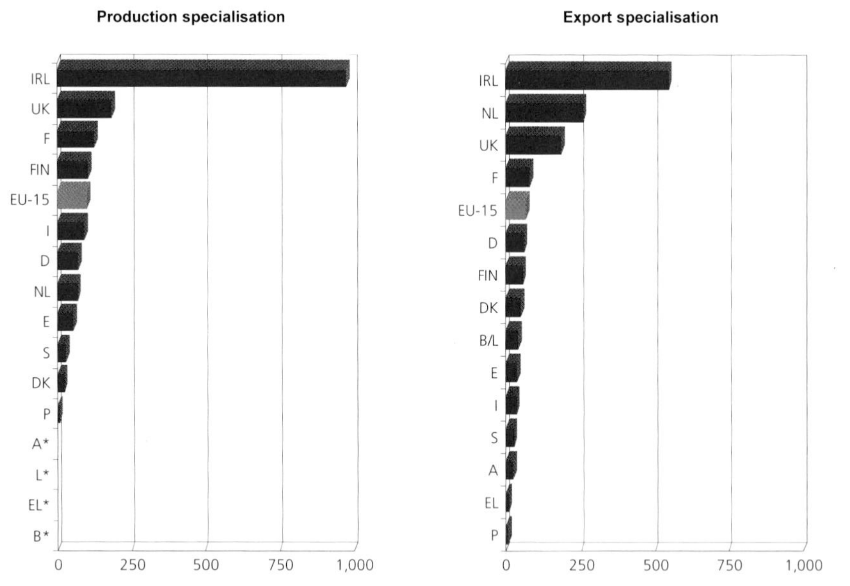

Production specialisation

IRL, UK, F, FIN, EU-15, I, D, NL, E, S, DK, P, A*, L*, EL*, B*

0 250 500 750 1,000

Export specialisation

IRL, NL, UK, F, EU-15, D, FIN, DK, B/L, E, I, S, A, EL, P

0 250 500 750 1,000

Source: Eurostat (SBS)

The workstation market was reduced by 18% in value terms between 1996 and 1998 from 2.7 billion ECU to 2.2 billion ECU. Servers and PCs, in contrast, enjoyed vigorous growth of 8% and 5% respectively. PCs made up the largest share of the market, ahead of servers (23 billion ECU). PC add-ons (printers, memory upgrades, etc.) accounted for 10 billion ECU, of which 6 billion ECU was for printers only. Unix operating systems represented about a quarter of the server market in 1998, whilst Windows NT servers accounted for 11%. The largest share was however accounted for by non-Unix or NT servers such as IBM S390 or AS/400 servers, Digital Open VMS or NetWare servers (some 30%).

The penetration of IT in the EU has been slower than across the Atlantic. In 1997 the penetration rate of PCs in the EU varied from 6 per 100 inhabitants in Greece to 35 per 100 inhabitants in Sweden. The EU average was 18 PCs per 100 inhabitants, less than half the level recorded in the USA (47 per 100 inhabitants). The gap between Europe and America is even more striking if we compare the number of PCs to the "white collar" population. PCs were more numerous than white collar workers in the USA, whilst only 54% of Europe's white collar labour force had a PC (data provided by EITO).

The market for office equipment was worth some 9.1 billion ECU in 1998, more than half of which (5.2 billion ECU) was accounted for by copiers. Market forecasts showed that growth of 1% per annum was expected through until the year 2000. The emergence of new technologies, such as image compression, optical character recognition, optical plastics, artificial intelligence and the integration of new features attracted customers to more sophisticated image processing capabilities, particularly in the reprographics market. The shift towards network-shared office equipment is poised in the next few years to accelerate true connectivity between networked computers and digital office equipment such as copiers, printers, scanners and facsimile machines.

With revenues of close to 73 billion ECU, IBM (USA) was the largest IT manufacturer in the world in 1998, followed by Hewlett-Packard (USA) and Fujitsu (J), both around 40 billion ECU and Compaq (USA) with 30 billion ECU. Canon (J) and Xerox (USA) both specialised in office equipment, they had revenues just under 20 billion ECU each.

(1996=100) Figure 11.32

IT hardware, unit shipments in the EU

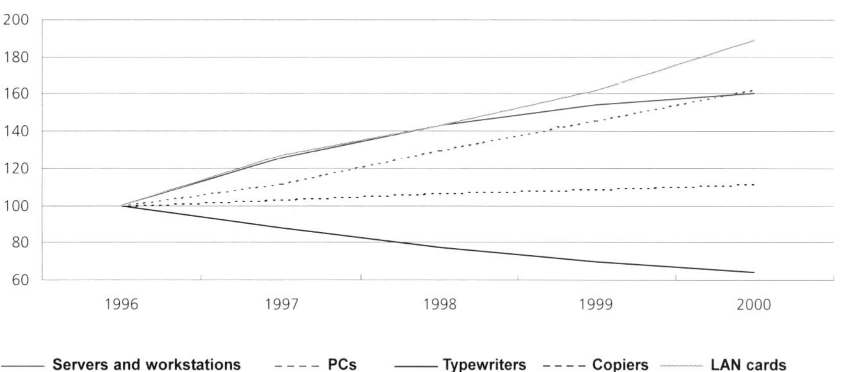

Source: EITO

(million ECU) Table 11.4

Value of IT hardware market in the EU

	1996	1997	1998	1999	2000
Server	19,993	21,811	23,490	25,104	26,954
- Unix servers	4,598	4,936	5,460	6,000	6,580
- NT servers	1,084	2,011	2,554	2,989	3,517
- Other servers	6,924	6,978	7,052	7,225	7,466
- Server add-ons	7,387	7,886	8,424	8,890	9,391
Workstations	2,708	2,400	2,225	2,159	2,085
PCs	26,045	28,156	29,672	31,343	33,526
- portable	6,030	6,622	7,188	7,632	8,206
- desktop	20,014	21,534	22,484	23,710	25,320
PC/workstation add-ons	8,652	9,354	9,855	10,316	10,752
-PC printers	5,735	6,032	6,078	6,146	6,163
- other add-ons	2,917	3,322	3,777	4,170	4,589
Total computer hardware	57,398	61,721	65,242	68,922	73,317
Copiers	5,116	5,149	5,230	5,292	5,371
Other office equipment (1)	3,813	3,833	3,870	3,881	3,919
Total office equipment	8,929	8,982	9,100	9,173	9,290
LAN hardware	4,102	4,908	5,729	6,336	6,772
Other data communications (2)	1,427	1,482	1,653	1,821	1,972
Total data communications hardware	5,529	6,390	7,382	8,157	8,744
TOTAL	71,856	77,093	81,724	86,252	91,351

(1) Typewriters, calculators, duplicating equipment, cash-registers, document filing, etc.
(2) Modems, digital switching equipment, communications processors and channel extenders.

Source: EITO

Figure 11.33 (units)

Penetration rate of PCs, 1997

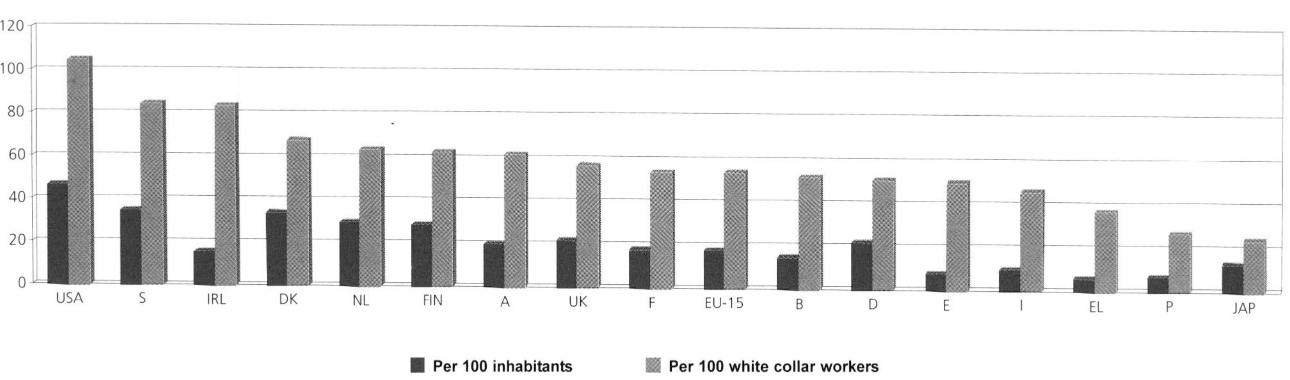

Source: IDC in EITO

A fundamental trend currently experienced by the IT industry is the increasingly tight link between the hardware industry and software and computer services. Computers no longer act in isolation, and increasingly their success depends upon their ability to fit into an overall "product solution". For example, the trend towards the networking of computers, or the development of e-business, involves the integration of computers, telecommunications and software functions.

Looking at international trade, it is striking to see how dependent on the rest of the world Europe has become for computer and office equipment. Exports covered just 40% of imports in 1998, down from 45% in 1996. At a national level, every single country displayed a trade deficit in 1998, except Ireland (5 billion ECU surplus). Ireland is used as a point of assembly by many non-EU countries that have invested in production facilities. The Irish export specialisation rate was equal to 547% in 1998. The Netherlands (260%) and the United Kingdom (185%) also showed high export-specialisation.

Figure 11.34

Computers and office equipment (NACE Rev. 1 30) Destination of EU exports, 1998

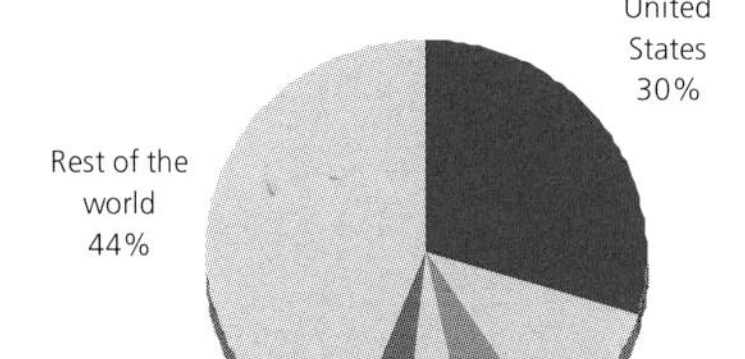

Source: Eurostat (Comext)

Figure 11.35

Computers and office equipment (NACE Rev. 1 30) Origin of EU imports, 1998

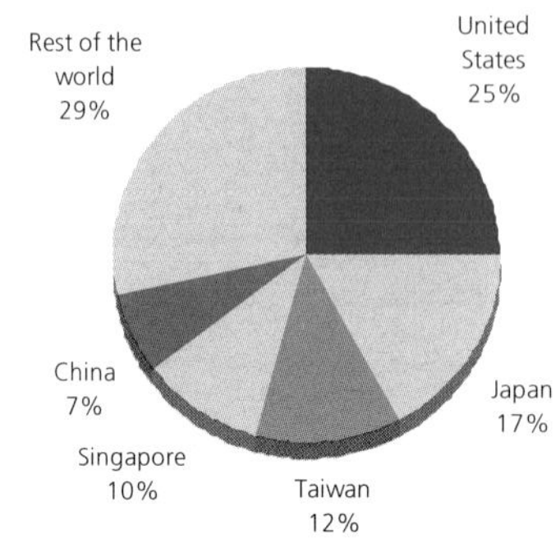

Source: Eurostat (Comext)

Telecommunications equipment (NACE Rev. 1 32.2)

The NACE Rev. 1 activity classification describes this activity as the manufacture of apparatus for television transmission (including relay transmitters, television transmitters, TV cameras), the manufacture of transmission apparatus for mobile telephony (transmitters, mobile telephones, etc.) and the manufacture of apparatus for line telephony (telephone sets, fax machines, switchboards and exchanges, telex and tele-printer apparatus, etc.).

The EU is a very large producer of telecommunications equipment, with companies such as Alcatel (F), Siemens (D), Bosch (D), Ericsson (S) and Nokia (FIN). In 1998, total EU production reached 62 billion ECU (excluding Austria, Luxembourg and Portugal), compared to 63 billion ECU in the USA and 30 billion ECU in Japan (both in 1997). It is also a sector that has enjoyed vigorous growth in recent years, with output rising by 8% in 1997 and 1998. Sweden and Finland are extremely specialised in this sector thanks to the presence of world leaders, such as Ericsson and Nokia in mobile telephony. The share of telecommunication equipment production in national manufacturing production was 4 times higher in Sweden (production specialisation ratio of 407%) and 3.5 times higher in Finland (355%) than in the EU.

The market for telecommunications equipment is divided into two main categories: exchanges and transmission equipment for public telecommunications networks, and equipment for private networks, such as personal switchboards, telephone sets or mobile phones.

In public telephone networks there was a slowdown in traditional exchange and transmission markets. Indeed, the penetration rate of telephone lines is already relatively high (52% in the EU in 1997) and most of them have already been digitised (96% in Western Europe in 1998). Growth of operators' investments in this field is thus slowing down, and expenditure on switching equipment was expected to remain constant between 1998 and 2000. The second trend consisted of more pronounced growth in emerging markets, such as broadband exchanges and mobile communications. Indeed, the share of wireless equipment for public networks grew by 26% in 1998 and was expected to catch-up with the level of switching equipment by the year 2000.

Figure 11.36

Telecommunications equipment (NACE Rev. 1 32.2)
Production and employment in the Triad

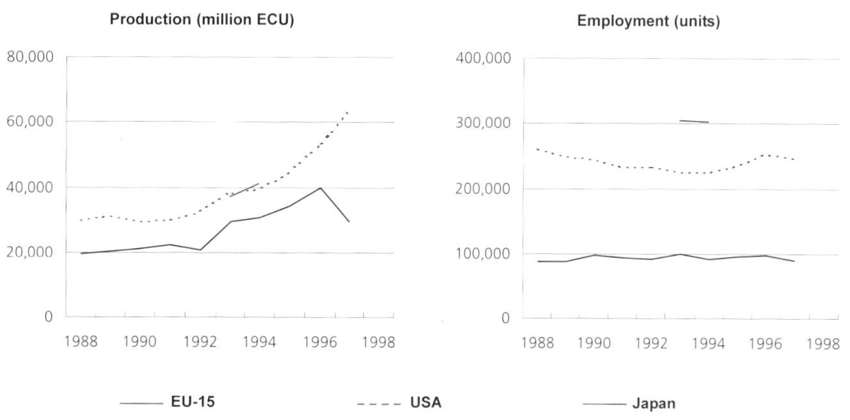

Source: Eurostat (SBS)

(%)

Figure 11.37

Telecommunications equipment (NACE Rev. 1 32.2)
Production and export specialisation by Member State, 1998

Production specialisation

S
FIN
EL
F
IRL
A
EU-15
UK
I
D
F
NL
DK
P*
L*
B*
0 200 400 600

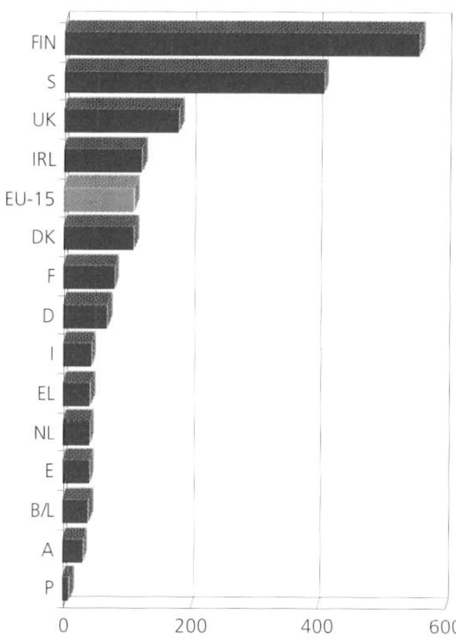

Source: Eurostat (SBS)

Figure 11.38 (lines per 100 inhabitants)

Penetration rate of main telephone lines, 1997

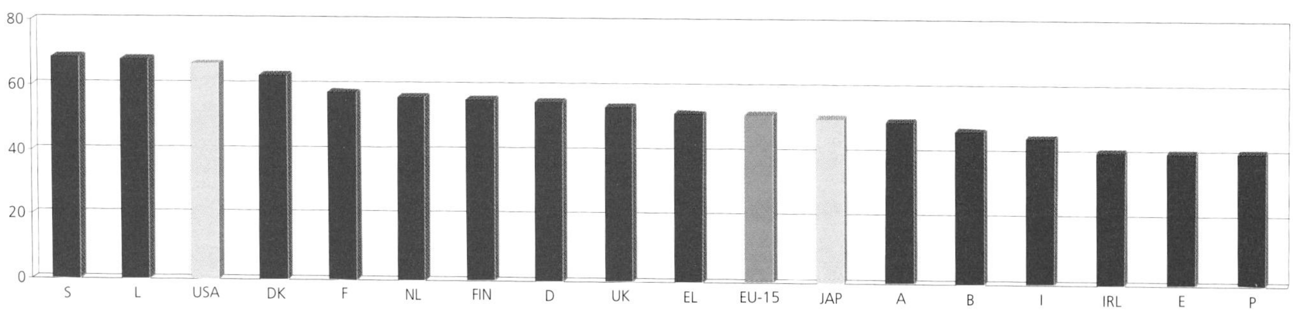

Source: EITO

The growing importance of wireless communications is reflected in expenditure on private network equipment. The market for mobile terminals (domestic and business) reached 3.9 billion ECU in 1998, a progression of 5% compared to 1997. The number of mobile phone subscribers increased by a factor of four in the EU between 1993 and 1996, reaching 33 million lines. EITO, the European Information Technology observatory, forecast a further compound annual growth rate of almost 30% between 1997 and 2002, when they estimate that the number of mobile telephone subscribers will be close to 200 million persons in Western Europe.

Still, the fastest growing sector for private equipment is the residual grouping of "other terminal equipment", which includes equipment such as fax machines, answering machines and audio/video conferencing equipment. The market value for this kind of product was estimated to be 5.8 billion ECU in 1998.

The gradual deregulation of telecommunication services has put an end to the historically privileged relationships between the former national operators and their appointed equipment suppliers. It has led to strategies involving alliances and partnerships dividing up the market according to specialist activities. In most of the consumer markets there is fierce competition from Japanese and south-east Asian firms. In the mobile telephony field, where products have a high value added, technological expertise and software skills have allowed European manufacturers to hold a dominant position. Europe has a strong competitive advantage in digital mobile telephony. The GSM standard, a digital system that had originally been designed by Europeans for deployment in Europe, has eventually been adopted by over 300 operators in more than 130 countries around the world.

Table 11.5 (million ECU)

Value of telecommunication hardware market in the EU

	1996	1997	1998	1999	2000
Switching	6,655	6,413	6,072	5,960	5,979
Transmission	3,229	3,246	3,612	3,735	3,972
Mobile communications infrastructure	3,001	3,504	4,416	5,290	5,933
Public network equipment	**12,885**	**13,163**	**14,100**	**14,985**	**15,884**
PABX and key systems	3,046	2,994	3,038	3,086	3,153
Telephone sets	4,572	4,738	4,928	5,080	5,242
Mobile terminal equipment	3,386	3,669	3,861	4,078	4,335
Other terminal equipment	4,431	5,101	5,751	6,418	7,163
Private network equipment	**15,435**	**16,502**	**17,578**	**18,662**	**19,893**

Source: EITO

More generally, the European telecommunications sector has for a long time occupied a strong position and has been the source of many major innovations. This is reflected in external trade figures. Indeed, this is one of the few European high-technology sectors where a trade surplus is registered, reaching 8.4 billion ECU in 1997. The surplus rose at the rate of 23% per annum between 1994 and 1998[11].

Within the EU, Italy and Spain were the only countries displaying deficits of over 1 billion ECU. Surpluses ranged from 2.4 billion ECU in the United Kingdom to over 5 billion ECU in Sweden. Unsurprisingly, Sweden and Finland were the countries where the intensity of telecommunication equipment in exports was the highest. In Finland, export specialisation ratios reached 560%, whilst in Sweden a figure of 410% was recorded.

The increasing standardisation of technologies makes them more accessible to a larger number of producers, particularly in Asia. European producers will therefore have to concentrate on activities with higher added value, requiring skills and expertise (particularly in software). A further challenge to be faced by the industry is to make progress with bandwidth capacity, to allow multimedia data content to be transferred across mobile terminals.

11) These figures exclude Greece.

Figure 11.39

Telecommunications equipment (NACE Rev. 1 32.2)

Destination of EU exports, 1998

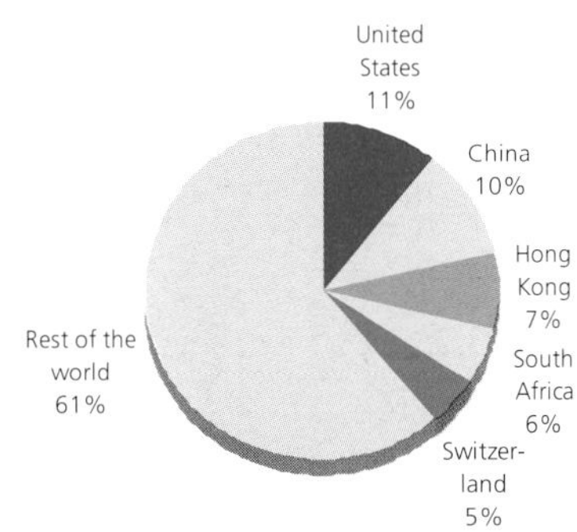

Source: Eurostat (Comext)

Figure 11.40

Telecommunications equipment (NACE Rev. 1 32.2)

Origin of EU imports, 1998

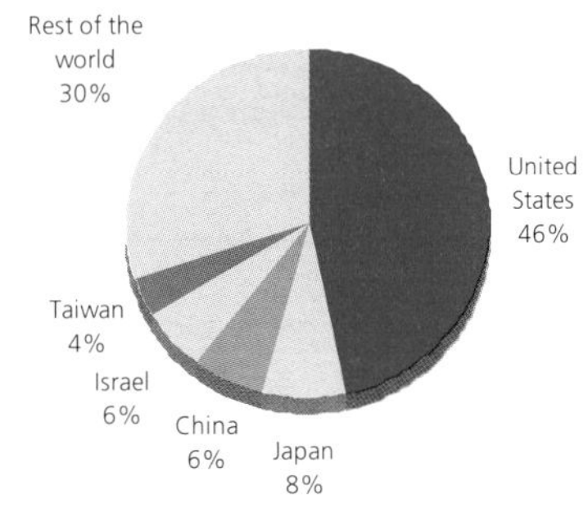

Source: Eurostat (Comext)

Consumer electronics (NACE Rev. 1 32.3)

The consumer electronics sector embraces television and radio receivers, sound and video recording equipment, as well as reproducing apparatus and associated goods. As defined by NACE Rev. 1 Group 32.3, this industry includes the manufacture of television sets, video and audio recorders, camcorders and compact disc players. It also includes the manufacture of TV decoders, satellite dishes, and such specialised equipment as simultaneous interpretation apparatus, electronic voting systems or conference systems.

Output within the consumer electronics industry of the EU progressed by 3.2% in 1998 to reach 25.3 billion ECU[12], after suffering two years of decline in 1997 (-2%) and 1996 (-5%). These falls were caused almost exclusively by the performance of the industry in Germany and Italy. Between 1993 and 1998, these countries were the only ones recording a deteriorating level of output, down on average by 4% and 12% per annum. Production grew by as much as 10% per annum in France, 14% in Spain and 31% in Sweden over the same period. Austria's specialisation ratio relative to the EU-15 average exceeded 440%, and only the Netherlands displayed a higher specialisation ratio at 490%. If we sum the latest figures for Austria (1994) to the total of the other EU countries, we reach an estimated production value of more than 28 billion ECU. This may be compared to only 7.4 billion ECU in the USA in 1997, but 40.5 billion ECU in Japan.

Television sets constitute the largest share of the consumer electronics market, despite stagnating growth since the beginning of the nineties. Markets are largely saturated and most of the sales are therefore the result of replacing older sets or buying second sets. The proportion of EU households with at least one TV set ranged in 1997 between 87% of households in Portugal and 99% in Belgium, Denmark and the United Kingdom. There were almost 144 million TV households in the EU in 1997, 50% more than in the USA (98 million) and 3.5 times more than in Japan (41 million).

12) Excluding Austria, Luxembourg and Portugal.

Figure 11.41

Consumer electronics (NACE Rev. 1 32.3)
Production and employment in the Triad

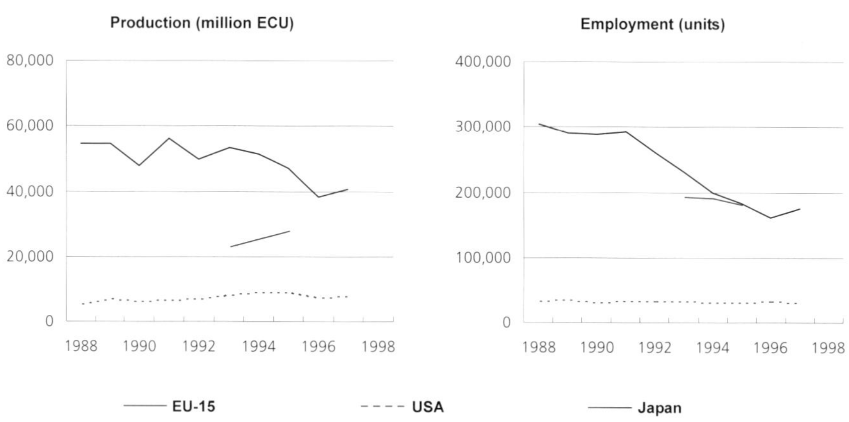

Source: Eurostat (SBS)

Figure 11.42 (%)

Consumer electronics (NACE Rev. 1 32.3)
Production and export specialisation by Member State, 1998

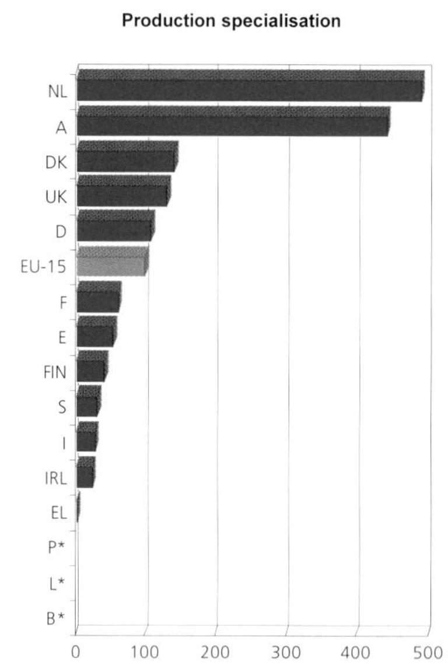

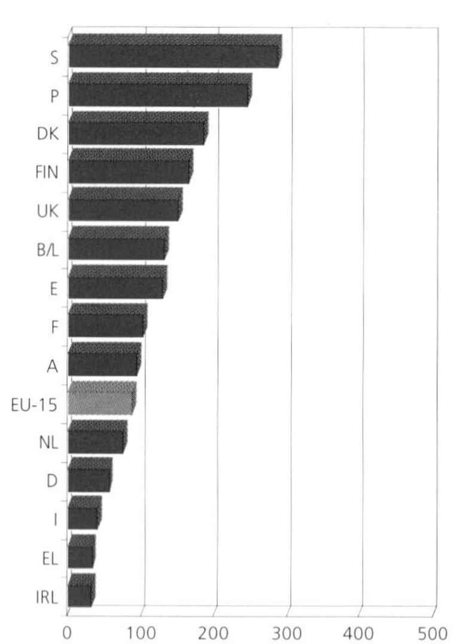

Source: Eurostat (SBS)

Following television sets, video recorders have become widespread throughout Europe and have also reached a mature stage in their product cycle, they are in use in over 73% of TV households. There is nevertheless still a certain growth potential as the penetration rate of VCRs in European households lags behind that recorded in the USA (90% of TV households) or Japan (80%), and some markets are still under equipped, like Portugal (52%) and Greece (56%).

On the audio market, sales of electro-acoustic systems have grown as an increasing number of homes have equipped themselves with hi-fi systems, with a marked preference for smaller models ("micro" and "mini" at the expense of "midi"). The car radio market is also growing rapidly, with innovations such as RDS (radio data system) appearing.

Consumer electronics manufacturers are counting on digital technology to further revitalise this sector. In the field of television, digital TV is progressing, and the strengthening of the satellite market together with the development of multi-channel digital packages (see chapter on television) will additionally benefit the market. Digital Versatile Discs (DVD) are expected to have a big impact on the video market, and have already recorded promising sales figures in America and Japan since their launch in 1997/98. If popular in Europe, this product would stimulate not only the demand for players, but also related equipment such as complementary audio systems for enhanced sound features (such as decoders and amplifiers for surround sound and "home theatre"). As for sound media, the transition from vinyl to CDs is practically complete. Traditional analogue music cassettes are still present, but products such as the Sony Minidisk (MD) based on digital technology are expected to form the next generation of products for playing and recording music.

Table 11.6

Main indicators of TV hardware penetration, 1997

	Number of households with at least one TV (thousands)	Share of TV households with cable (%)	Share of TV households with satellite (%)	Share of TV households with VCR (%) (1)	Share of TV households with 2 or more VCRs (%) (2)
B	4,116	92.3	2.7	65.0	11.0
DK	2,370	54.9	39.7	79.0	10.0
D	36,877	51.2	30.2	77.8	13.0
EL	3,346	0.4	6.0	55.6	7.0
E	12,020	3.2	9.4	64.2	11.0
F	22,107	10.1	11.2	77.0	9.0
IRL	1,111	48.9	9.9	72.7	12.0
I	19,121	0.1	4.0	61.7	5.0
L	146	96.0	13.7	67.8	15.0
NL	6,575	89.7	4.0	69.8	17.0
A	3,150	34.9	49.8	71.2	12.0
P	2,927	7.2	12.3	52.0	5.0
FIN	2,200	39.2	12.3	72.2	6.0
S	3,855	50.9	18.7	79.2	7.0
UK	24,033	9.9	17.9	83.0	25.0
EU-15	143,954	27.6	16.9	73.3	:
USA	97,958	67.2	8.6	89.6	27.0
JAP	41,220	33.9	29.3	80.4	35.0

(1) 1996 for USA and Japan.
(2) 1996.

Source: IVF, Screen Digest

(thousand units) Table 11.7

VCR sales

	1990	1991	1992	1993	1994	1995	1996
B	300	257	258	246	249	268	272
DK	235	225	210	195	210	236	315
D	3,300	3,325	3,230	3,010	3,090	3,152	3,202
EL	175	175	189	193	199	201	200
E	760	715	670	490	585	495	458
F	2,025	1,958	2,025	1,935	1,890	1,845	2,042
IRL	75	80	85	85	85	72	74
I	1,450	1,428	1,350	1,050	1,128	1,196	1,249
L	9	10	10	10	9	:	:
NL	420	575	600	610	630	613	591
A	210	275	250	250	260	:	:
P	100	125	125	140	140	157	155
FIN	185	180	125	102	115	120	127
S	270	275	210	275	265	279	287
UK	2,150	2,160	2,210	2,400	2,500	2,610	2,835
EU-15 (1)	11,984	12,100	11,918	11,355	11,752	11,934	12,507

(1) Including Iceland, Norway and Switzerland.

Source: IVF

Another fundamental trend within the industry, linked to the digitisation of media, is the convergence between consumer electronics and IT products. The borders between different categories of electronic products are blurring, and computers, televisions, sound systems and telecommunication devices are increasingly merged to allow users to perform multi-media tasks. For example, one can listen to a radio station with a computer connected to the Internet through the TV cable, shop on the Internet via a TV set or send and receive faxes or e-mails with a mobile telephone.

The industry is dominated by Japanese companies, particularly with products such as video recorders and camcorders. Europe still controls one of the major sectors, the manufacture of television tubes. Most TV sets made in Europe (whether by European or Asian firms) use tubes produced by European companies. This is a significant factor, since tubes account for 30% of the cost of a TV set.

Europe's trade balance with the rest of the world has consistently displayed a deficit during the past decade. It reached 6.7 billion in 1998, up from 5 billion ECU in 1997[13]. At a national level, only Belgium/Luxembourg, Portugal, Finland and Sweden recorded a positive trade balance. Sweden was relatively specialised in exporting, with the share of Swedish consumer electronics almost three times higher than the EU average (287%). Portugal (245%). Denmark (185%) and Finland (165%) also displayed high ratios.

Japan's trade surplus was equal to 6.7 billion ECU in 1997, its second lowest level over the preceding 10 years, down from 14 billion ECU in 1989. On the other hand, imports of consumer electronic products in the USA in 1997 exceeded exports by as much as 12 billion ECU, a gap that remained roughly constant since 1988.

13) Excluding Greece.

Figure 11.43

Consumer electronics (NACE Rev. 1 32.3)
Destination of EU exports, 1998

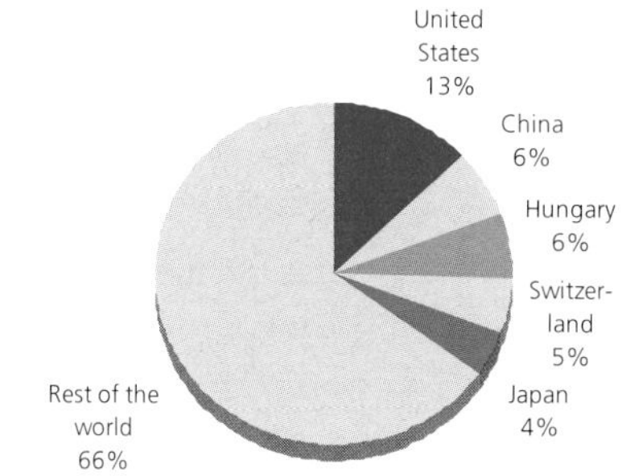

Source: Eurostat (Comext)

Figure 11.44

Consumer electronics (NACE Rev. 1 32.3)
Origin of EU imports, 1998

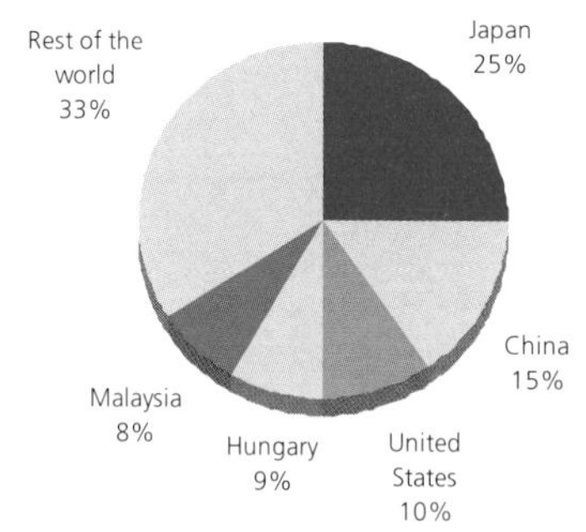

Source: Eurostat (Comext)

Professional associations representing the industries within this chapter

EECA
European Electronic Component Manufacturers Association
140 bte 6, avenue Louise
B-1050 Bruxelles
tel: (32) 2 646 56 95
fax: (32) 2 644 40 88
e-mail:
mailto:secretariat@eeca.be

EITO
European Information Technology Observatory
LyonerStrasse, 18
D-60528 Frankfurt am Main
tel: (49) 69 660 31 539
fax: (49) 69 66 03 15 10

EUROBAT
Association of European Accumulator Manufacturers
c/o ATAG Ernst & Young
Belpastraße 23
Case postale 5032
CH-3001 Bern
tel: (41) 31 382 22 22
fax: (41) 31 382 03 11
e-mail: eurobat@be.aey.ch

EUROPACABLE
European Confederation of Associations of Manufacturers of Insulated Wires and Cables
Diamant Building
80, boulevard A. Reyers
B-1030 Bruxelles
tel: (32) 2 702 61 26
fax: (32) 2 702 61 27
e-mail:
info@europacable.com

(million ECU) Table 11.8

Manufacture of domestic appliances n.e.c. (NACE Rev. 1 29.7)

Production related indicators in the EU

	1988	1989	1990	1991	1992	1993	1994	1995	1996	1997	1998
Production value	23,326	25,037	26,210	29,467	29,889	28,406	30,235	29,352	:	:	:
Producer price index (1995=100)	:	:	:	:	:	:	:	100.0	102.0	101.4	103.5
Value added	8,376	8,400	9,060	10,406	10,568	10,435	11,015	10,151	:	:	:
Number of persons employed (thousands)	296.1	293.3	302.1	302.9	291.9	276.0	268.5	251.2	:	:	:

(million ECU) Table 11.9

Manufacture of domestic appliances n.e.c. (NACE Rev. 1 29.7)

Production related indicators, 1998

	B	DK	D	EL	E	F	IRL	I	L	NL	A	P	FIN	S	UK
Production value	194	721	10,625	149	2,669	4,015	358	9,600	:	276	597	162	228	1,007	3,316
Value added	67	254	4,400	24	798	1,136	133	2,754	:	86	231	:	80	291	1,159
Number of persons employed (units)	1,257	5,860	78,835	1,716	16,944	30,190	3,994	62,886	:	:	5,399	2,547	1,775	8,049	32,717

(million ECU) Table 11.10

Manufacture of domestic appliances n.e.c. (NACE Rev. 1 29.7)

Market related indicators in the EU

	1988	1989	1990	1991	1992	1993	1994	1995	1996	1997	1998
Apparent consumption	23,114	24,580	25,198	28,493	28,881	27,017	28,469	26,912	:	:	:
Exports	2,351	2,710	3,060	3,240	3,404	4,019	4,504	5,249	5,996	6,800	6,447
Imports	2,139	2,254	2,049	2,266	2,396	2,631	2,738	2,809	3,080	3,458	3,843
Trade balance	212	456	1,011	974	1,008	1,389	1,767	2,440	2,917	3,342	2,604
Export ratio (%)	10.1	10.8	11.7	11.0	11.4	14.1	14.9	17.9	:	:	:
Import penetration ratio (%)	9.3	9.2	8.1	8.0	8.3	9.7	9.6	10.4	:	:	:
Cover ratio (%)	109.9	120.2	149.4	143.0	142.1	152.8	164.5	186.9	194.7	196.6	167.8

(million ECU) Table 11.11

Manufacture of domestic appliances n.e.c. (NACE Rev. 1 29.7)

Market related indicators, 1998

	B/L	DK	D	EL	E	F	IRL	I	NL	A	P	FIN	S	UK
Apparent consumption	:	708	9,347	390	2,528	4,368	362	4,839	749	798	365	373	797	4,209
Exports	372	431	4,578	111	1,119	2,161	248	5,731	789	490	173	225	785	1,157
Imports	986	417	3,299	352	978	2,514	252	970	1,262	692	376	369	575	2,050
Trade balance	-614	13	1,279	-241	141	-353	-4	4,761	-473	-202	-203	-145	210	-893
Export ratio (%)	:	59.7	43.1	74.7	41.9	53.8	69.2	59.7	286.2	82.1	106.9	98.3	77.9	34.9
Import penetration ratio (%)	:	59.0	35.3	90.3	38.7	57.6	69.5	20.0	168.6	86.7	103.1	99.0	72.1	48.7
Cover ratio (%)	37.7	103.2	138.8	31.5	114.4	86.0	98.5	590.9	62.5	70.9	45.9	60.8	136.5	56.5

Table 11.12

Manufacture of domestic appliances n.e.c. (NACE Rev. 1 29.7)

Labour related indicators, 1998

	EU-15	B	DK	D	EL	E	F	IRL	I	L	NL	A	P	FIN	S	UK
Personnel costs (million ECU) (1)	7,543	39	188	3,237	28	343	880	82	1,762	:	60	166	23	51	273	789
Personnel costs/employee (thousand ECU) (1)	30.4	34.9	32.7	41.7	17.8	23.6	29.6	20.4	25.5	:	:	32.4	:	27.9	35.5	20.1
Social charges/personnel costs (%) (2)	22.6	27.7	4.6	19.2	21.9	21.9	29.7	15.2	35.3	:	17.8	22.9	:	20.8	28.1	11.1
Labour productivity (thousand ECU/head) (3)	40.4	53.5	43.4	55.8	13.7	47.1	37.6	33.4	43.8	:	:	42.9	:	45.1	36.2	35.4
Wage adjusted labour productivity (%) (2)	133.0	126.2	132.7	122.7	127.0	154.0	132.1	165.1	158.4	:	:	138.1	:	149.2	97.5	146.8

(1) EU-15 (1995). (2) EU-15, EL, I, A (1995); B, D, DK, E, F, IRL, FIN, S, UK (1996). (3) S (1994); EU-15 (1995).

Source: Eurostat (SBS, EBT)

Table 11.13 (million ECU)

Manufacture of office machinery and computers (NACE Rev. 1 30)

Production related indicators in the EU

	1988	1989	1990	1991	1992	1993	1994	1995	1996	1997	1998
Production value	47,044	50,027	51,764	55,433	53,412	47,111	47,681	54,337	:	:	:
Producer price index (1995=100)	:	:	161.0	159.3	138.5	122.6	113.4	100.0	93.2	89.8	91.5
Value added	19,601	20,191	20,225	22,111	18,102	14,933	14,934	15,831	:	:	:
Number of persons employed (thousands)	303.8	304.6	298.6	333.9	307.7	261.6	237.2	235.9	:	:	:

Table 11.14 (million ECU)

Manufacture of office machinery and computers (NACE Rev. 1 30)

Production related indicators, 1998

	B	DK	D	EL	E	F	IRL	I	L	NL	A	P	FIN	S	UK
Production value (1)	282	108	13,944	:	2,296	10,519	7,315	4,590	:	1,880	:	42	882	492	16,383
Value added (2)	95	42	3,634	:	795	2,793	1,549	1,355	:	389	:	:	110	204	4,175
Number of persons employed (units) (3)	1,461	1,651	49,094	:	9,962	37,813	15,905	17,743	:	9,082	:	668	2,589	3,541	51,596

(1) P (1995). (2) NL (1996). (3) NL (1992); P (1995).

Table 11.15 (million ECU)

Manufacture of office machinery and computers (NACE Rev. 1 30)

Market related indicators in the EU

	1988	1989	1990	1991	1992	1993	1994	1995	1996	1997	1998
Apparent consumption	61,362	65,638	67,549	73,397	71,692	63,907	65,887	73,529	:	:	:
Exports	7,470	8,350	8,276	9,063	9,333	11,424	13,402	15,331	16,638	19,940	21,244
Imports	21,788	23,962	24,060	27,028	27,613	28,219	31,608	34,523	37,208	45,643	52,145
Trade balance	-14,318	-15,611	-15,784	-17,964	-18,280	-16,796	-18,206	-19,192	-20,570	-25,702	-30,901
Export ratio (%)	15.9	16.7	16.0	16.3	17.5	24.2	28.1	28.2	:	:	:
Import penetration ratio (%)	35.5	36.5	35.6	36.8	38.5	44.2	48.0	47.0	:	:	:
Cover ratio (%)	34.3	34.8	34.4	33.5	33.8	40.5	42.4	44.4	44.7	43.7	40.7

Table 11.16 (million ECU)

Manufacture of office machinery and computers (NACE Rev. 1 30)

Market related indicators, 1998

	B/L	DK	D	EL	E	F	IRL	I	NL	A	P	FIN	S	UK
Apparent consumption (1)	:	1,190	23,169	:	4,227	14,728	2,249	8,141	5,185	:	604	1,499	2,786	20,485
Exports	2,727	823	12,342	34	1,385	9,741	12,049	3,277	18,506	523	74	955	833	18,530
Imports	3,962	1,905	21,567	427	3,316	13,950	6,983	6,828	21,812	1,438	718	1,572	3,127	22,633
Trade balance	-1,235	-1,082	-9,225	-393	-1,930	-4,209	5,066	-3,550	-3,306	-915	-644	-617	-2,294	-4,102
Export ratio (%) (1)	:	763.1	88.5	:	60.3	92.6	164.7	71.4	984.4	:	83.1	108.2	169.2	113.1
Import penetration ratio (%) (1)	:	160.1	93.1	:	78.4	94.7	310.5	83.9	420.6	:	98.8	104.8	112.2	110.5
Cover ratio (%)	68.8	43.2	57.2	8.0	41.8	69.8	172.5	48.0	84.8	36.4	10.3	60.7	26.6	81.9

(1) P (1995).

Table 11.17

Manufacture of office machinery and computers (NACE Rev. 1 30)

Labour related indicators, 1998

	EU-15	B	DK	D	EL	E	F	IRL	I	L	NL	A	P	FIN	S	UK
Personnel costs (million ECU) (1)	10,103	65	71	2,541	:	466	2,344	507	736	:	261	:	8	73	146	1,716
Personnel costs/employee (thousand ECU) (2)	44.8	49.8	44.6	58.1	:	39.1	63.0	24.4	37.9	:	:	:	:	29.0	43.1	27.7
Social charges/personnel costs (%) (3)	21.4	21.7	5.4	16.6	:	17.0	29.9	15.7	34.9	:	13.6	:	:	20.6	29.4	11.8
Labour productivity (thousand ECU/head) (4)	67.1	64.7	25.6	74.0	:	79.8	73.9	97.4	76.4	:	46.7	:	:	42.4	57.7	80.9
Wage adjusted labour productivity (%) (2)	149.6	136.8	109.8	107.0	:	242.0	138.3	394.4	149.1	:	:	:	:	121.7	132.1	229.8

(1) EU-15, P (1995). (2) EU-15, I (1995); B, DK, D, E, F, IRL, FIN, S, UK (1996). (3) EU-15, S (1995). (4) NL (1992); EU-15 (1995).

Source: Eurostat (SBS, EBT)

(million ECU) — Table 11.18

Manufacture of electric motors, generators, transformers (NACE Rev. 1 31.1)

Production related indicators in the EU

	1988	1989	1990	1991	1992	1993	1994	1995	1996	1997	1998
Production value	:	:	:	:	:	16,844	17,514	:	:	:	:
Producer price index (1995=100)	:	:	:	:	:	:	:	:	:	:	:
Value added	:	:	:	:	:	6,745	6,714	:	:	:	:
Number of persons employed (thousands)	:	:	:	:	:	186.6	183.3	:	:	:	:

(million ECU) — Table 11.19

Manufacture of electric motors, generators, transformers (NACE Rev. 1 31.1)

Production related indicators, 1998

	B	DK	D	EL	E	F	IRL	I	L	NL	A	P	FIN	S	UK
Production value	676	842	6,636	82	1,848	2,522	514	4,255	:	389	1,069	:	1,139	908	2,776
Value added	204	172	2,809	30	591	883	293	1,413	:	129	495	:	391	318	1,208
Number of persons employed (units) (1)	3,686	3,937	60,164	1,249	14,819	23,314	4,108	28,506	:	4,356	7,082	:	6,706	7,414	31,576

(1) NL (1992); A (1997).

(million ECU) — Table 11.20

Manufacture of electric motors, generators, transformers (NACE Rev. 1 31.1)

Market related indicators in the EU

	1988	1989	1990	1991	1992	1993	1994	1995	1996	1997	1998
Apparent consumption	:	:	:	:	:	14,312	14,805	:	:	:	:
Exports	3,025	3,382	3,851	3,910	4,159	5,490	6,269	6,777	7,750	8,686	9,302
Imports	1,848	2,335	2,437	2,716	2,786	2,958	3,560	4,330	4,963	6,067	6,937
Trade balance	1,177	1,047	1,414	1,194	1,373	2,531	2,709	2,447	2,787	2,618	2,365
Export ratio (%)	:	:	:	:	:	32.6	35.8	:	:	:	:
Import penetration ratio (%)	:	:	:	:	:	20.7	24.0	:	:	:	:
Cover ratio (%)	163.7	144.8	158.0	144.0	149.3	185.6	176.1	156.5	156.2	143.2	134.1

(million ECU) — Table 11.21

Manufacture of electric motors, generators, transformers (NACE Rev. 1 31.1)

Market related indicators, 1998

	B/L	DK	D	EL	E	F	IRL	I	NL	A	P	FIN	S	UK
Apparent consumption	:	479	4,580	163	2,148	2,034	529	3,644	604	754	:	290	714	2,889
Exports	458	765	5,816	18	489	2,667	392	2,010	715	783	242	1,218	811	2,255
Imports	557	402	3,760	98	789	2,179	407	1,400	930	468	204	370	617	2,367
Trade balance	-99	363	2,056	-80	-300	488	-15	610	-215	315	38	849	194	-112
Export ratio (%)	:	90.9	87.6	21.9	26.5	105.8	76.3	47.2	183.8	73.2	:	106.9	89.4	81.2
Import penetration ratio (%)	:	83.9	82.1	60.5	36.7	107.2	77.0	38.4	154.0	62.0	:	127.2	86.5	82.0
Cover ratio (%)	82.2	190.3	154.7	18.4	62.0	122.4	96.4	143.6	76.9	167.4	118.6	329.7	131.5	95.3

Table 11.22

Manufacture of electric motors, generators, transformers (NACE Rev. 1 31.1)

Labour related indicators, 1998

	EU-15	B	DK	D	EL	E	F	IRL	I	L	NL	A	P	FIN	S	UK
Personnel costs (million ECU) (1)	5,417	167	133	2,243	22	368	775	108	856	:	70	353	:	217	277	836
Personnel costs/employee (thousand ECU) (2)	:	45.2	33.8	38.4	19.6	26.8	33.8	26.4	27.5	:	:	40.6	:	33.4	39.3	22.1
Social charges/personnel costs (%) (3)	:	28.2	3.2	19.4	23.9	17.3	29.7	16.0	35.1	:	14.1	22.7	:	24.3	28.2	12.4
Labour productivity (thousand ECU/head) (4)	36.6	55.2	43.6	46.7	24.1	39.9	37.9	71.3	49.6	:	40.3	66.7	:	58.3	42.8	38.3
Wage adjusted labour productivity (%) (2)	:	125.5	109.5	115.0	121.0	162.7	127.9	274.0	144.1	:	:	139.7	:	168.5	127.4	150.6

(1) EU-15 (1994); NL (1997). (2) EL, I, A (1995); B, DK, D, E, F, IRL, FIN, S, UK (1996). (3) S (1995); NL (1997). (4) NL (1992); EU-15 (1994); A (1997).

Source: Eurostat (SBS, EBT)

Table 11.23 (million ECU)

Manufacture of electricity distribution and control apparatus (NACE Rev. 1 31.2)
Production related indicators in the EU

	1988	1989	1990	1991	1992	1993	1994	1995	1996	1997	1998
Production value	:	:	:	:	:	54,444	59,076	64,086	:	:	:
Producer price index (1995=100)	:	:	:	:	:	:	:	:	:	:	:
Value added	:	:	:	:	:	23,474	25,044	26,070	:	:	:
Number of persons employed (thousands)	:	:	:	:	:	558.3	529.6	520.7	:	:	:

Table 11.24 (million ECU)

Manufacture of electricity distribution and control apparatus (NACE Rev. 1 31.2)
Production related indicators, 1998

	B	DK	D	EL	E	F	IRL	I	L	NL	A	P	FIN	S	UK
Production value	1,947	382	44,743	94	1,493	8,290	338	3,178	:	788	770	:	638	1,070	3,508
Value added	643	179	20,022	29	632	3,041	174	1,179	:	367	313	:	272	318	1,601
Number of persons employed (units) (1)	10,445	2,857	294,269	1,575	24,011	65,439	3,116	25,354	:	5,606	8,274	:	5,013	7,459	46,425

(1) NL (1992).

Table 11.25 (million ECU)

Manufacture of electricity distribution and control apparatus (NACE Rev. 1 31.2)
Market related indicators in the EU

	1988	1989	1990	1991	1992	1993	1994	1995	1996	1997	1998
Apparent consumption	:	:	:	:	:	51,444	55,821	60,362	:	:	:
Exports	3,906	4,351	4,540	5,087	5,464	6,227	7,313	8,145	9,077	10,472	11,082
Imports	2,206	2,712	2,792	2,837	2,984	3,227	4,057	4,421	4,880	5,794	6,384
Trade balance	1,701	1,639	1,748	2,250	2,480	3,000	3,255	3,724	4,197	4,678	4,698
Export ratio (%)	:	:	:	:	:	11.4	12.4	12.7	:	:	:
Import penetration ratio (%)	:	:	:	:	:	6.3	7.3	7.3	:	:	:
Cover ratio (%)	177.1	160.4	162.6	179.3	183.1	193.0	180.2	184.2	186.0	180.7	173.6

Table 11.26 (million ECU)

Manufacture of electricity distribution and control apparatus (NACE Rev. 1 31.2)
Market related indicators, 1998

	B/L	DK	D	EL	E	F	IRL	I	NL	A	P	FIN	S	UK
Apparent consumption	:	507	39,507	227	1,944	6,098	141	3,437	1,016	861	:	755	1,192	3,595
Exports	805	216	9,138	53	687	4,378	539	1,680	891	583	266	280	704	2,306
Imports	1,060	340	3,903	185	1,138	2,186	342	1,940	1,118	673	361	397	826	2,394
Trade balance	-255	-124	5,236	-132	-450	2,192	197	-259	-228	-90	-95	-117	-121	-88
Export ratio (%)	:	56.4	20.4	56.4	46.0	52.8	159.4	52.9	113.0	75.7	:	43.9	65.8	65.7
Import penetration ratio (%)	:	67.1	9.9	81.8	58.5	35.8	242.5	56.4	110.1	78.2	:	52.5	69.3	66.6
Cover ratio (%)	76.0	63.4	234.2	28.7	60.4	200.3	157.6	86.6	79.7	86.6	73.6	70.6	85.3	96.3

Table 11.27

Manufacture of electricity distribution and control apparatus (NACE Rev. 1 31.2)
Labour related indicators, 1998

	EU-15	B	DK	D	EL	E	F	IRL	I	L	NL	A	P	FIN	S	UK
Personnel costs (million ECU) (1)	21,572	508	102	14,198	21	296	2,466	62	727	:	225	303	:	149	296	1,244
Personnel costs/employee (thousand ECU) (2)	41.8	49.1	35.7	47.7	14.3	24.9	38.3	20.1	26.2	:	:	39.1	:	30.6	41.7	22.3
Social charges/personnel costs (%) (3)	21.5	29.4	2.8	17.9	22.6	22.2	30.3	16.0	35.6	:	17.9	22.7	:	20.1	28.4	11.4
Labour productivity (thousand ECU/head) (4)	50.1	61.5	62.5	68.0	18.2	26.3	46.5	55.7	46.5	:	43.8	37.9	:	54.3	42.7	34.5
Wage adjusted labour productivity (%) (2)	119.7	127.9	148.6	123.6	116.4	159.5	125.3	233.0	159.1	:	:	115.8	:	150.8	119.5	148.5

(1) EU-15 (1995); E (1997). (2) EU-15, EL, I, A (1995); B, DK, D, E, F, IRL, FIN, S, UK (1996). (3) EU-15, S (1995); E (1997). (4) NL (1992); EU-15 (1995).

Source: Eurostat (SBS, EBT)

(million ECU) Table 11.28

Manufacture of insulated wire and cable (NACE Rev. 1 31.3)
Production related indicators in the EU

	1988	1989	1990	1991	1992	1993	1994	1995	1996	1997	1998
Production value	:	:	:	:	:	14,040	15,370	:	:	:	:
Producer price index (1995=100)	:	:	:	:	:	:	:	100.0	96.1	92.8	93.7
Value added	:	:	:	:	:	4,525	4,869	:	:	:	:
Number of persons employed (thousands)	:	:	:	:	:	108.4	108.2	:	:	:	:

(million ECU) Table 11.29

Manufacture of insulated wire and cable (NACE Rev. 1 31.3)
Production related indicators, 1998

	B	DK	D	EL	E	F	IRL	I	L	NL	A	P	FIN	S	UK
Production value (1)	358	236	2,755	333	1,086	2,910	386	2,349	0	576	452	868	351	671	1,846
Value added (1)	107	86	911	41	303	871	111	596	0	232	194	:	109	197	612
Number of persons employed (units) (1)(2)	2,090	1,134	19,078	1,696	8,606	16,662	2,199	8,924	0	2,954	3,392	19,393	1,995	3,697	24,208

(1) A (1994); L (1996). (2) NL (1990).

(million ECU) Table 11.30

Manufacture of insulated wire and cable (NACE Rev. 1 31.3)
Market related indicators in the EU

	1988	1989	1990	1991	1992	1993	1994	1995	1996	1997	1998
Apparent consumption	:	:	:	:	:	13,288	14,593	:	:	:	:
Exports	1,090	1,432	1,450	1,483	1,594	1,793	2,025	2,409	2,863	3,306	3,300
Imports	636	873	929	1,048	1,085	1,042	1,247	1,624	1,784	2,124	2,267
Trade balance	454	559	521	435	509	751	778	785	1,079	1,182	1,033
Export ratio (%)	:	:	:	:	:	12.8	13.2	:	:	:	:
Import penetration ratio (%)	:	:	:	:	:	7.8	8.5	:	:	:	:
Cover ratio (%)	171.4	164.0	156.1	141.6	147.0	172.1	162.3	148.4	160.4	155.7	145.6

(million ECU) Table 11.31

Manufacture of insulated wire and cable (NACE Rev. 1 31.3)
Market related indicators, 1998

	B/L	DK	D	EL	E	F	IRL	I	NL	A	P	FIN	S	UK
Apparent consumption (1)	:	323	2,324	293	789	2,769	301	1,937	602	373	609	310	468	1,930
Exports	396	76	1,673	78	565	1,173	250	861	401	247	415	215	454	894
Imports	466	163	1,241	38	267	1,032	165	449	426	215	156	175	250	978
Trade balance	-70	-87	431	40	297	142	85	412	-25	32	259	40	203	-84
Export ratio (%) (1)	:	32.2	60.7	23.4	52.0	40.3	61.7	36.7	69.6	57.3	47.8	61.4	67.6	48.4
Import penetration ratio (%) (1)	:	50.5	53.4	13.0	33.9	37.3	54.7	23.2	70.8	48.3	25.6	56.4	53.5	50.7
Cover ratio (%)	84.9	46.6	134.7	205.0	211.2	113.7	151.6	191.7	94.1	114.8	265.8	123.2	181.2	91.4

(1) A (1994).

Table 11.32

Manufacture of insulated wire and cable (NACE Rev. 1 31.3)
Labour related indicators, 1998

	EU-15	B	DK	D	EL	E	F	IRL	I	L	NL	A	P	FIN	S	UK
Personnel costs (million ECU) (1)	3,246	82	42	825	30	200	620	52	268	0	117	135	197	65	134	592
Personnel costs/employee (thousand ECU) (2)	:	41.1	37.1	43.2	19.6	24.5	37.9	23.5	27.5	:	:	39.7	:	33.7	38.0	20.3
Social charges/personnel costs (%) (3)	:	28.1	5.5	19.3	22.2	21.6	30.9	14.5	33.9	:	19.1	23.6	:	22.6	27.6	10.1
Labour productivity (thousand ECU/head) (4)	45.0	51.3	75.5	47.8	24.5	35.2	52.3	50.6	66.8	:	54.3	57.3	:	54.7	53.4	25.3
Wage adjusted labour productivity (%) (2)	:	128.8	172.9	92.7	150.9	180.5	151.1	204.1	192.9	:	:	144.3	:	173.1	164.1	149.1

(1) EU-15, A (1994); L (1996). (2) EL, I (1995); B, DK, D, E, F, IRL, FIN, S, UK (1996). (3) A, S (1994). (4) NL (1990); EU-15, A (1994).

Source: Eurostat (SBS, EBT)

Table 11.33 (million ECU)

Manufacture of accumulators, primary cells and primary batteries (NACE Rev. 1 31.4)

Production related indicators in the EU

	1988	1989	1990	1991	1992	1993	1994	1995	1996	1997	1998
Production value	:	:	:	:	:	4,761	5,053	5,003	:	:	:
Producer price index (1995=100)	:	:	:	:	:	:	:	:	:	:	:
Value added	:	:	:	:	:	1,752	1,784	1,625	:	:	:
Number of persons employed (thousands)	:	:	:	:	:	42.2	41.1	37.0	:	:	:

Table 11.34 (million ECU)

Manufacture of accumulators, primary cells and primary batteries (NACE Rev. 1 31.4)

Production related indicators, 1998

	B	DK	D	EL	E	F	IRL	I	L	NL	A	P	FIN	S	UK
Production value (1)	569	25	1,049	25	477	1,496	14	438	:	33	179	:	3	161	780
Value added (1)	179	10	373	9	163	491	2	156	:	14	60	:	1	51	300
Number of persons employed (units) (1)(2)	1,976	232	8,129	401	2,456	8,153	147	2,630	:	270	1,308	:	26	1,342	7,756

(1) EL, A (1994); DK (1995). (2) NL (1990).

Table 11.35 (million ECU)

Manufacture of accumulators, primary cells and primary batteries (NACE Rev. 1 31.4)

Market related indicators in the EU

	1988	1989	1990	1991	1992	1993	1994	1995	1996	1997	1998
Apparent consumption	:	:	:	:	:	4,810	4,932	5,242	:	:	:
Exports	491	542	596	678	684	777	963	1,128	1,192	1,369	1,342
Imports	437	549	580	758	693	826	842	1,367	1,274	1,917	1,695
Trade balance	54	-8	16	-80	-9	-49	121	-239	-82	-548	-353
Export ratio (%)	:	:	:	:	:	16.3	19.1	22.5	:	:	:
Import penetration ratio (%)	:	:	:	:	:	17.2	17.1	26.1	:	:	:
Cover ratio (%)	112.4	98.6	102.8	89.5	98.7	94.0	114.4	82.5	93.6	71.4	79.2

Table 11.36 (million ECU)

Manufacture of accumulators, primary cells and primary batteries (NACE Rev. 1 31.4)

Market related indicators, 1998

	B/L	DK	D	EL	E	F	IRL	I	NL	A	P	FIN	S	UK
Apparent consumption (1)	:	60	1,148	66	469	1,475	130	462	169	167	:	141	134	1,040
Exports	592	40	808	14	226	668	12	316	123	74	43	54	242	522
Imports	402	90	907	58	218	647	129	341	260	73	55	192	215	782
Trade balance	190	-51	-99	-44	8	21	-116	-25	-137	1	-12	-137	27	-260
Export ratio (%) (1)	:	116.6	77.1	17.8	47.3	44.7	91.2	72.2	376.6	54.0	:	1,766.3	150.9	66.9
Import penetration ratio (%) (1)	:	106.8	79.0	68.5	46.4	43.9	99.1	73.7	153.3	50.7	:	136.5	161.2	75.2
Cover ratio (%)	147.3	44.0	89.1	24.3	103.8	103.2	9.6	92.8	47.3	100.9	77.9	28.4	112.6	66.8

(1) EL, A (1994); DK (1995).

Table 11.37

Manufacture of accumulators, primary cells and primary batteries (NACE Rev. 1 31.4)

Labour related indicators, 1998

	EU-15	B	DK	D	EL	E	F	IRL	I	L	NL	A	P	FIN	S	UK
Personnel costs (million ECU) (1)	1,302	143	7	340	6	105	316	2	75	:	10	50	:	1	46	209
Personnel costs/employee (thousand ECU) (2)	35.2	42.2	32.1	43.3	16.2	32.8	39.3	14.8	26.3	:	:	38.2	:	27.4	36.1	22.4
Social charges/personnel costs (%) (3)	22.7	27.5	2.7	19.1	23.2	21.9	30.0	13.0	32.6	:	15.2	23.2	:	22.5	26.6	13.6
Labour productivity (thousand ECU/head) (4)	43.9	90.8	41.1	45.9	21.3	66.2	60.2	16.6	59.3	:	31.6	45.8	:	33.6	38.0	38.7
Wage adjusted labour productivity (%) (2)	124.7	212.6	128.1	95.0	131.1	161.0	127.0	97.6	149.8	:	:	120.0	:	117.3	123.1	163.1

(1) EL, A (1994); EU-15, DK (1995); E (1997). (2) EL, A (1994); EU-15, DK, I (1995); B, D, E, F, IRL, FIN, S, UK (1996). (3) EL, A, S (1994); EU-15, DK (1995); E (1997). (4) NL (1990); EL, A (1994); EU-15, DK (1995).

Source: Eurostat (SBS, EBT)

(million ECU) Table 11.38

Manufacture of lighting equipment and lamps (NACE Rev. 1 31.5)

Production related indicators in the EU

	1988	1989	1990	1991	1992	1993	1994	1995	1996	1997	1998
Production value	8,098	9,303	9,831	9,867	9,921	9,526	10,039	10,330	10,805	:	:
Producer price index (1995=100)	:	:	:	:	:	:	:	100.0	94.4	89.3	89.5
Value added	3,465	3,823	4,087	4,055	4,026	3,962	4,100	4,165	4,198	:	:
Number of persons employed (thousands)	124.1	132.3	129.7	122.4	117.8	109.2	105.1	108.7	108.7	:	:

(million ECU) Table 11.39

Manufacture of lighting equipment and lamps (NACE Rev. 1 31.5)

Production related indicators, 1998

	B	DK	D	EL	E	F	IRL	I	L	NL	A	P	FIN	S	UK
Production value (1)	800	179	3,469	28	1,052	1,303	24	1,680	0	172	341	350	133	257	1,441
Value added (1)	253	62	1,660	11	343	453	10	542	0	59	153	:	51	91	562
Number of persons employed (units) (1)(2)	5,477	1,346	34,567	436	12,421	11,649	419	10,208	0	2,442	2,481	7,708	1,492	2,574	20,039

(1) L (1996). (2) NL (1992); A (1997).

(million ECU) Table 11.40

Manufacture of lighting equipment and lamps (NACE Rev. 1 31.5)

Market related indicators in the EU

	1988	1989	1990	1991	1992	1993	1994	1995	1996	1997	1998
Apparent consumption	7,245	8,516	9,048	9,211	9,305	8,881	9,388	9,625	10,012	:	:
Exports	1,579	1,673	1,663	1,710	1,806	2,062	2,274	2,476	2,665	2,856	2,921
Imports	726	886	880	1,055	1,191	1,417	1,622	1,771	1,872	2,201	2,531
Trade balance	853	787	783	656	616	645	652	705	793	655	390
Export ratio (%)	19.5	18.0	16.9	17.3	18.2	21.6	22.7	24.0	24.7	:	:
Import penetration ratio (%)	10.0	10.4	9.7	11.5	12.8	16.0	17.3	18.4	18.7	:	:
Cover ratio (%)	217.5	188.8	188.9	162.2	151.7	145.5	140.2	139.8	142.4	129.8	115.4

(million ECU) Table 11.41

Manufacture of lighting equipment and lamps (NACE Rev. 1 31.5)

Market related indicators, 1998

	B/L	DK	D	EL	E	F	IRL	I	NL	A	P	FIN	S	UK
Apparent consumption	:	208	3,095	98	1,057	1,355	86	918	117	392	419	172	345	1,741
Exports	645	210	1,883	12	366	1,025	21	1,272	674	221	35	87	212	665
Imports	554	239	1,509	82	371	1,077	84	510	619	272	104	127	300	965
Trade balance	91	-28	374	-70	-5	-52	-63	762	55	-51	-69	-39	-88	-300
Export ratio (%)	:	117.3	54.3	42.9	34.8	78.6	88.6	75.7	391.9	64.9	10.1	65.9	82.6	46.2
Import penetration ratio (%)	:	115.0	48.8	83.9	35.1	79.5	96.8	55.5	527.7	69.4	24.9	73.7	87.0	55.5
Cover ratio (%)	116.4	88.2	124.8	14.4	98.8	95.2	25.4	249.5	108.8	81.3	33.8	69.1	70.7	68.9

Table 11.42

Manufacture of lighting equipment and lamps (NACE Rev. 1 31.5)

Labour related indicators, 1998

	EU-15	B	DK	D	EL	E	F	IRL	I	L	NL	A	P	FIN	S	UK
Personnel costs (million ECU) (1)	3,082	210	45	1,264	5	222	363	6	284	0	40	118	74	37	81	478
Personnel costs/employee (thousand ECU) (2)	30.3	37.6	33.7	36.5	12.3	20.1	31.7	15.4	25.4	:	:	36.2	:	26.2	32.9	19.9
Social charges/personnel costs (%) (3)	21.0	28.8	3.8	19.1	22.2	22.0	30.1	13.8	37.8	:	5.3	22.6	:	22.7	29.5	10.7
Labour productivity (thousand ECU/head) (4)	38.6	46.3	46.4	48.0	24.7	27.6	38.9	24.9	53.1	:	27.4	58.4	:	33.9	35.2	28.1
Wage adjusted labour productivity (%) (2)	126.3	125.6	116.7	129.1	191.6	137.7	127.5	151.3	177.3	:	:	136.9	:	161.3	125.0	133.4

(1) EU-15, L (1996); L (1996). (2) EU-15, EL, I, A (1995); B, DK, D, E, F, IRL, FIN, S, UK (1996). (3) EU-15, S (1995). (4) NL (1992); EU-15 (1996); A (1997).

Source: Eurostat (SBS, EBT)

Table 11.43 (million ECU)

Manufacture of electronic valves and tubes and other electronic components (NACE Rev. 1 32.1)

Production related indicators in the EU

	1988	1989	1990	1991	1992	1993	1994	1995	1996	1997	1998
Production value	:	:	:	:	:	15,342	18,638	:	:	:	:
Producer price index (1995=100)	:	:	:	:	:	:	:	:	:	:	:
Value added	:	:	:	:	:	6,618	7,781	:	:	:	:
Number of persons employed (thousands)	:	:	:	:	:	173.0	178.8	:	:	:	:

Table 11.44 (million ECU)

Manufacture of electronic valves and tubes and other electronic components (NACE Rev. 1 32.1)

Production related indicators, 1998

	B	DK	D	EL	E	F	IRL	I	L	NL	A	P	FIN	S	UK
Production value (1)	560	304	6,098	11	1,009	6,028	891	3,346	0	273	:	:	719	375	4,935
Value added (1)	263	103	2,386	3	426	1,993	284	1,568	0	95	:	:	258	168	2,126
Number of persons employed (units) (1)(2)	3,913	3,159	37,281	241	12,504	44,706	5,435	20,639	0	2,542	:	:	5,603	3,831	46,502

(1) L (1996). (2) NL (1992).

Table 11.45 (million ECU)

Manufacture of electronic valves and tubes and other electronic components (NACE Rev. 1 32.1)

Market related indicators in the EU

	1988	1989	1990	1991	1992	1993	1994	1995	1996	1997	1998
Apparent consumption	:	:	:	:	:	19,201	24,717	:	:	:	:
Exports	3,861	4,588	4,789	5,641	5,466	7,796	9,947	12,217	14,400	18,662	19,139
Imports	7,012	8,419	8,107	9,113	9,088	11,655	16,026	18,378	18,779	22,968	21,329
Trade balance	-3,151	-3,831	-3,318	-3,472	-3,622	-3,859	-6,079	-6,161	-4,379	-4,307	-2,189
Export ratio (%)	:	:	:	:	:	50.8	53.4	:	:	:	:
Import penetration ratio (%)	:	:	:	:	:	60.7	64.8	:	:	:	:
Cover ratio (%)	55.1	54.5	59.1	61.9	60.1	66.9	62.1	66.5	76.7	81.2	89.7

Table 11.46 (million ECU)

Manufacture of electronic valves and tubes and other electronic components (NACE Rev. 1 32.1)

Market related indicators, 1998

	B/L	DK	D	EL	E	F	IRL	I	NL	A	P	FIN	S	UK
Apparent consumption	:	589	7,724	98	1,637	5,714	1,075	4,300	-1,170	:	:	1,784	1,273	6,400
Exports	1,439	267	8,770	4	572	7,119	2,138	2,400	5,464	1,196	238	360	734	6,775
Imports	1,486	553	10,396	91	1,200	6,805	2,322	3,355	4,021	984	446	1,425	1,632	8,239
Trade balance	-47	-285	-1,626	-87	-627	314	-184	-954	1,443	211	-208	-1,065	-898	-1,464
Export ratio (%)	:	88.1	143.8	39.8	56.7	118.1	240.0	71.7	1,998.7	:	:	50.1	195.7	137.3
Import penetration ratio (%)	:	93.9	134.6	93.3	73.3	119.1	216.1	78.0	-343.7	:	:	79.9	128.2	128.7
Cover ratio (%)	96.8	48.4	84.4	4.8	47.7	104.6	92.1	71.6	135.9	121.4	53.3	25.3	45.0	82.2

Table 11.47

Manufacture of electronic valves and tubes and other electronic components (NACE Rev. 1 32.1)

Labour related indicators, 1998

	EU-15	B	DK	D	EL	E	F	IRL	I	L	NL	A	P	FIN	S	UK
Personnel costs (million ECU) (1)	5,015	157	110	1,371	3	259	1,570	124	634	0	77	:	:	110	120	1,318
Personnel costs/employee (thousand ECU) (2)	:	39.3	35.5	38.0	12.9	22.9	35.7	22.7	28.2	:	:	:	:	27.7	32.8	23.7
Social charges/personnel costs (%) (3)	:	29.5	4.0	18.3	22.7	20.8	29.6	14.9	33.9	:	11.7	:	:	19.7	28.3	10.9
Labour productivity (thousand ECU/head) (4)	43.5	67.2	32.7	64.0	11.1	34.1	44.6	52.3	76.0	:	34.3	:	:	46.1	44.0	45.7
Wage adjusted labour productivity (%) (2)	:	138.4	97.0	119.5	80.3	154.3	126.4	241.4	185.1	:	:	:	:	140.7	127.8	165.2

(1) EU-15 (1994); L (1996). (2) EL, I (1995); B, DK, D, E, F, IRL, FIN, S, UK (1996). (3) S (1995). (4) NL (1992); EU-15 (1994).

Source: Eurostat (SBS, EBT)

(million ECU) Table 11.48

Manufacture of television and radio transmitters and apparatus for line telephony and line telegraphy (NACE Rev. 1 32.2)
Production related indicators in the EU

	1988	1989	1990	1991	1992	1993	1994	1995	1996	1997	1998
Production value	:	:	:	:	:	37,251	41,379	:	:	:	:
Producer price index (1995=100)	:	:	:	:	:	:	:	:	:	:	:
Value added	:	:	:	:	:	14,535	15,192	:	:	:	:
Number of persons employed (thousands)	:	:	:	:	:	307.0	304.5	:	:	:	:

(million ECU) Table 11.49

Manufacture of television and radio transmitters and apparatus for line telephony and line telegraphy (NACE Rev. 1 32.2)
Production related indicators, 1998

	B	DK	D	EL	E	F	IRL	I	L	NL	A	P	FIN	S	UK
Production value (1)	1,568	558	9,564	256	1,591	12,644	715	4,109	0	681	1,068	:	8,232	12,238	9,434
Value added (1)	747	134	3,124	58	573	4,025	220	2,980	0	233	425	:	2,224	2,783	3,680
Number of persons employed (units) (1)(2)	8,499	2,943	66,955	1,809	15,456	68,362	3,518	37,264	0	6,753	7,309	:	23,289	42,523	43,540

(1) A (1994); L (1996). (2) NL (1990).

(million ECU) Table 11.50

Manufacture of television and radio transmitters and apparatus for line telephony and line telegraphy (NACE Rev. 1 32.2)
Market related indicators in the EU

	1988	1989	1990	1991	1992	1993	1994	1995	1996	1997	1998
Apparent consumption	:	:	:	:	:	35,645	38,014	:	:	:	:
Exports	3,593	4,286	4,473	5,295	5,838	6,837	9,463	11,549	14,297	16,687	18,213
Imports	3,161	4,459	4,503	5,472	5,550	5,231	6,099	7,392	8,451	8,332	10,408
Trade balance	432	-173	-30	-177	288	1,606	3,365	4,157	5,846	8,354	7,805
Export ratio (%)	:	:	:	:	:	18.4	22.9	:	:	:	:
Import penetration ratio (%)	:	:	:	:	:	14.7	16.0	:	:	:	:
Cover ratio (%)	113.7	96.1	99.3	96.8	105.2	130.7	155.2	156.2	169.2	200.3	175.0

(million ECU) Table 11.51

Manufacture of television and radio transmitters and apparatus for line telephony and line telegraphy (NACE Rev. 1 32.2)
Market related indicators, 1998

	B/L	DK	D	EL	E	F	IRL	I	NL	A	P	FIN	S	UK
Apparent consumption (1)	:	559	6,565	690	2,634	10,487	3	5,515	1,287	1,137	:	3,947	7,086	7,042
Exports	1,355	965	7,217	77	807	5,096	1,389	2,103	1,520	347	50	4,832	6,472	9,201
Imports	1,385	965	4,218	511	1,851	2,940	677	3,509	2,126	611	509	547	1,319	6,809
Trade balance	-30	-1	2,999	-434	-1,044	2,157	712	-1,405	-606	-264	-459	4,285	5,153	2,392
Export ratio (%) (1)	:	172.9	75.5	30.1	50.7	40.3	194.3	51.2	223.1	27.9	:	58.7	52.9	97.5
Import penetration ratio (%) (1)	:	172.8	64.3	74.1	70.3	28.0	20,508.2	63.6	165.1	32.3	:	13.9	18.6	96.7
Cover ratio (%)	97.9	99.9	171.1	15.1	43.6	173.4	205.1	59.9	71.5	56.8	9.9	883.5	490.5	135.1

(1) A (1994).

Table 11.52

Manufacture of television and radio transmitters and apparatus for line telephony and line telegraphy (NACE Rev. 1 32.2)
Labour related indicators, 1998

	EU-15	B	DK	D	EL	E	F	IRL	I	L	NL	A	P	FIN	S	UK
Personnel costs (million ECU) (1)	11,575	468	120	3,856	35	510	3,254	105	1,281	0	164	320	:	629	1,634	1,586
Personnel costs/employee (thousand ECU) (2)	:	60.6	41.7	55.0	20.9	34.7	48.4	29.7	31.6	:	:	43.8	:	33.0	40.3	30.3
Social charges/personnel costs (%) (3)	:	30.6	3.1	17.7	20.8	19.6	30.6	17.1	33.3	:	12.6	22.5	:	16.6	30.1	12.7
Labour productivity (thousand ECU/head) (4)	49.9	87.8	45.5	46.7	32.3	37.1	58.9	62.5	80.0	:	32.8	58.2	:	95.5	65.4	84.5
Wage adjusted labour productivity (%) (2)	:	111.8	115.3	87.8	144.4	166.0	112.2	248.1	124.3	:	:	133.0	:	229.3	154.6	201.9

(1) EU-15, A (1994); L (1996). (2) A (1994); EL, I (1995); B, DK, D, E, F, IRL, FIN, S, UK (1996). (3) A (1994); S (1995). (4) NL (1990); EU-15, A (1994).

Source: Eurostat (SBS, EBT)

Table 11.53 (million ECU)

Manufacture of television and radio receivers, sound or video recording or reproducing apparatus and associated goods (NACE Rev. 1 32.3)

Production related indicators in the EU

	1988	1989	1990	1991	1992	1993	1994	1995	1996	1997	1998
Production value	:	:	:	:	:	22,823	24,994	27,472	:	:	:
Producer price index (1995=100)	:	:	:	:	:	:	:	:	:	:	:
Value added	:	:	:	:	:	7,573	7,896	8,089	:	:	:
Number of persons employed (thousands)	:	:	:	:	:	190.3	188.3	178.6	:	:	:

Table 11.54 (million ECU)

Manufacture of television and radio receivers, sound or video recording or reproducing apparatus and associated goods (NACE Rev. 1 32.3)

Production related indicators, 1998

	B	DK	D	EL	E	F	IRL	I	L	NL	A	P	FIN	S	UK
Production value (1)	1,707	661	5,051	3	1,695	3,980	124	518	:	6,015	2,682	:	278	447	4,867
Value added (1)	551	283	1,703	1	350	565	34	251	:	2,175	799	:	50	129	1,043
Number of persons employed (units) (1)(2)	6,191	5,407	38,380	77	8,848	16,823	1,113	3,212	:	43,620	16,805	:	1,832	2,762	30,866

(1) A (1994). (2) NL (1992).

Table 11.55 (million ECU)

Manufacture of television and radio receivers, sound or video recording or reproducing apparatus and associated goods (NACE Rev. 1 32.3)

Market related indicators in the EU

	1988	1989	1990	1991	1992	1993	1994	1995	1996	1997	1998
Apparent consumption	:	:	:	:	:	29,332	30,892	32,105	:	:	:
Exports	2,799	3,080	3,366	3,238	3,334	3,841	4,668	5,522	6,874	8,500	7,848
Imports	9,668	10,162	11,001	11,382	10,519	10,351	10,565	10,156	11,829	13,597	14,564
Trade balance	-6,869	-7,082	-7,635	-8,144	-7,185	-6,510	-5,898	-4,634	-4,955	-5,097	-6,716
Export ratio (%)	:	:	:	:	:	16.8	18.7	20.1	:	:	:
Import penetration ratio (%)	:	:	:	:	:	35.3	34.2	31.6	:	:	:
Cover ratio (%)	29.0	30.3	30.6	28.4	31.7	37.1	44.2	54.4	58.1	62.5	53.9

Table 11.56 (million ECU)

Manufacture of television and radio receivers, sound or video recording or reproducing apparatus and associated goods (NACE Rev. 1 32.3)

Market related indicators, 1998

	B/L	DK	D	EL	E	F	IRL	I	NL	A	P	FIN	S	UK
Apparent consumption (1)	:	673	7,819	328	2,267	5,165	228	1,847	7,055	2,525	:	165	-28	5,431
Exports	2,460	873	3,190	34	1,394	3,507	201	1,070	1,499	557	610	786	2,501	4,195
Imports	1,977	886	5,959	358	1,965	4,692	306	2,399	2,539	878	526	674	2,026	4,759
Trade balance	483	-12	-2,768	-325	-572	-1,185	-104	-1,329	-1,040	-320	84	112	475	-564
Export ratio (%) (1)	:	132.2	63.2	1,106.9	82.2	88.1	162.8	206.7	24.9	37.3	:	283.0	559.2	86.2
Import penetration ratio (%) (1)	:	131.6	76.2	109.4	86.7	90.8	134.1	129.9	36.0	33.4	:	407.2	-7,269.1	87.6
Cover ratio (%)	124.4	98.6	53.5	9.4	70.9	74.7	65.9	44.6	59.0	63.5	116.0	116.7	123.5	88.1

(1) A (1994).

Table 11.57

Manufacture of television and radio receivers, sound or video recording or reproducing apparatus and associated goods (NACE Rev. 1 32.3)

Labour related indicators, 1998

	EU-15	B	DK	D	EL	E	F	IRL	I	L	NL	A	P	FIN	S	UK
Personnel costs (million ECU) (1)	6,068	256	168	1,647	1	201	534	21	80	:	1,662	574	:	38	91	744
Personnel costs/employee (thousand ECU) (2)	44.1	38.1	31.6	42.8	14.2	23.9	32.3	18.7	22.7	:	:	34.1	:	29.5	34.6	20.1
Social charges/personnel costs (%) (3)	17.9	29.0	3.0	19.2	20.6	21.3	29.6	12.3	35.7	:	12.1	22.7	:	18.6	28.4	9.5
Labour productivity (thousand ECU/head) (4)	45.3	89.0	52.3	44.4	15.4	39.6	33.6	30.1	78.1	:	47.9	47.6	:	27.5	46.8	33.8
Wage adjusted labour productivity (%) (2)	102.8	174.3	160.4	88.0	101.9	173.5	88.5	141.2	145.7	:	:	139.4	:	101.4	128.8	165.4

(1) A (1994); EU-15 (1995); L (1996). (2) A (1994); EU-15, EL, I (1995); B, DK, D, E, F, IRL, FIN, S, UK (1996). (3) A (1994); EU-15, S (1995). (4) NL (1992); A (1994); EU-15 (1995).

Source: Eurostat (SBS, EBT)

Instrument engineering

Industry description

The instrument engineering industry comprises a group of diverse industries under Division 33 of the NACE Rev. 1 activity classification. Instrument engineering covers industries such as the manufacture of medical and surgical equipment (NACE Rev. 1 33.1); instruments for measuring, checking, testing and navigating (NACE Rev. 1 33.2); industrial process equipment (NACE Rev. 1 33.3); optical and photographic instruments (NACE Rev. 1 33.4); and watches and clocks (NACE Rev. 1 33.5).

The industry has a wide range of supply and demand conditions that are difficult to assess by studying the aggregates for the whole industry. For example, whilst health equipment markets have been largely immune to recession, the other areas covered by this chapter have seen their market demand linked more closely to trends in economic performance or to changes in fashion trends.

The majority of production in this industry is in high labour cost countries, using high technology within the production process. Global competition for EU manufacturers is concentrated in the USA, Japan and Switzerland. Nevertheless, at the lower-end of the market there has been a marked increase in the output of south-east Asian producers. Product and process innovations, as well as increased expenditure on research are critical for EU firms to maintain their market share.

(%) Figure 12.1

Instrument engineering (NACE Rev. 1 33)
Share of EU value added in total manufacturing

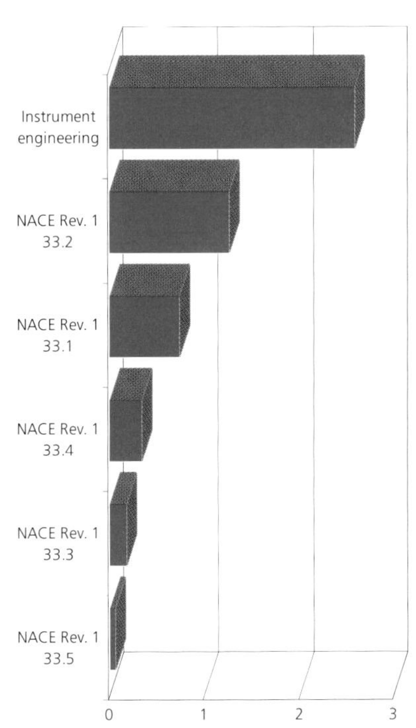

Source: Eurostat (SBS)

The activities covered in this chapter include:

- 33.1: manufacture of medical and surgical equipment and orthopaedic appliances;
- 33.2: manufacture of instruments and appliances for measuring, checking, testing, navigating and other purposes, except industrial process control equipment;
- 33.3: manufacture of industrial process control equipment;
- 33.4: manufacture of optical instruments and photographic equipment;
- 33.5: manufacture of watches and clocks.

Figure 12.2 (1988=100)

Instrument engineering (NACE Rev. 1 33)

Production, employment and value added compared to EU total manufacturing

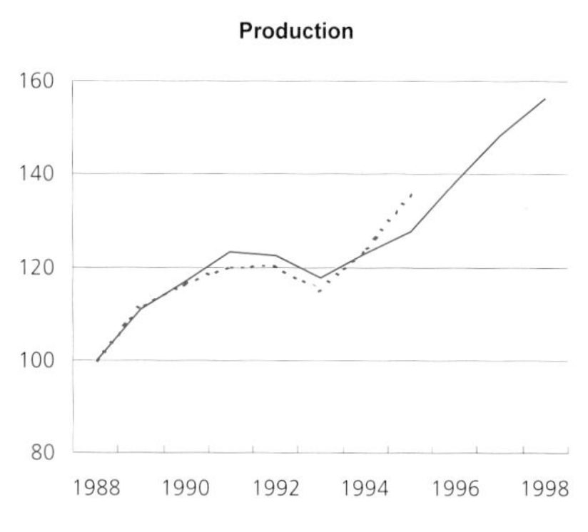

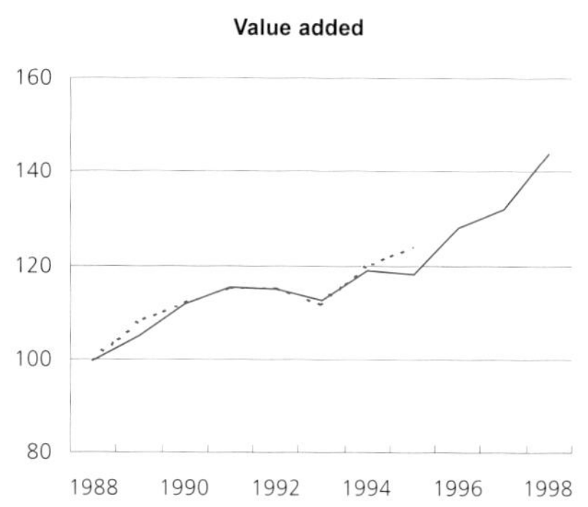

Instrument engineering ---- Total manufacturing

Source: Eurostat (SBS)

The industry faces few environmental concerns and is generally considered by most observers to be "clean". Nevertheless, the disposal of batteries, syringes, as well as photographic chemicals do create some concern. However, as the environment becomes an ever more important political concern and its control is further monitored, then demand for analysing and monitoring pollution will grow, fuelling demand for new instrument engineering markets.

Recent trends

Instrument engineering accounts for just under 2% of the total production value of EU manufacturing in 1998. This share was in line with that recorded in Japan, whilst being considerably below that found in the USA (3.4% in 1997).

The share of instrument engineering in total EU manufacturing employment was a percentage point higher, at just under 3%, again in line with the figures in Japan and behind the corresponding data from the USA, where instrument engineering accounted for 4.4% of the American manufacturing workforce.

Between 1988 and 1998, EU production in current prices grew from 48.9 billion ECU to 76.6 billion ECU. After having shown rapid expansion in the late eighties, instrument engineering was affected by the recession in the early nineties when output stagnated. From 1994 onwards, the EU has seen its production increase once again. The largest producer in the EU was Germany, with a 27.7% share of total EU output, closely followed by France (25.2%). Production specialisation was particularly high in Denmark, France and Ireland, whilst Germany and the United Kingdom also reported above average specialisation. Indeed, France and Ireland were both able to report that more than 3% of their manufac-

Figure 12.3

Instrument engineering (NACE Rev. 1 33)

International comparison of main indicators in current prices

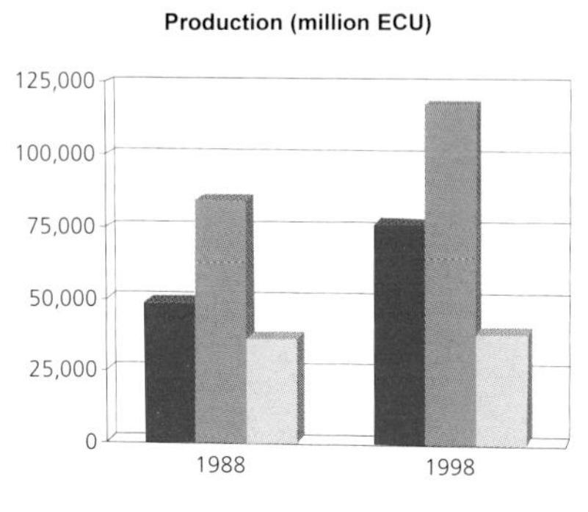

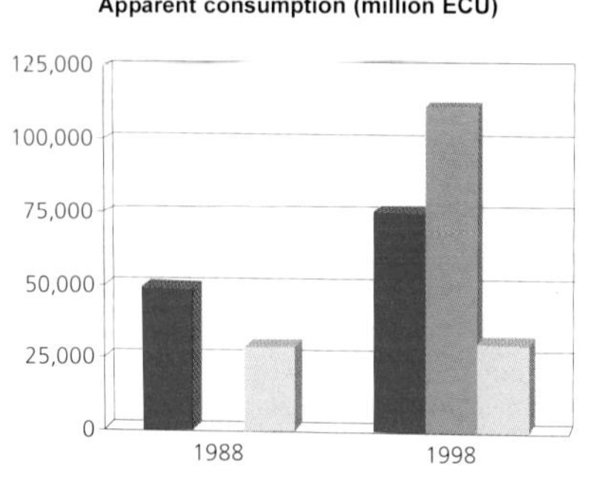

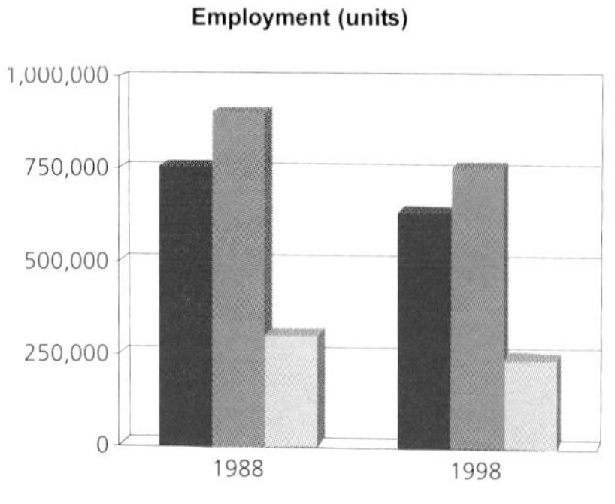

EU-15 USA Japan

Source: Eurostat (SBS)

(ECU/hour) Figure 12.4

Instrument engineering (NACE Rev. 1 33)
Labour costs by Member State, 1996

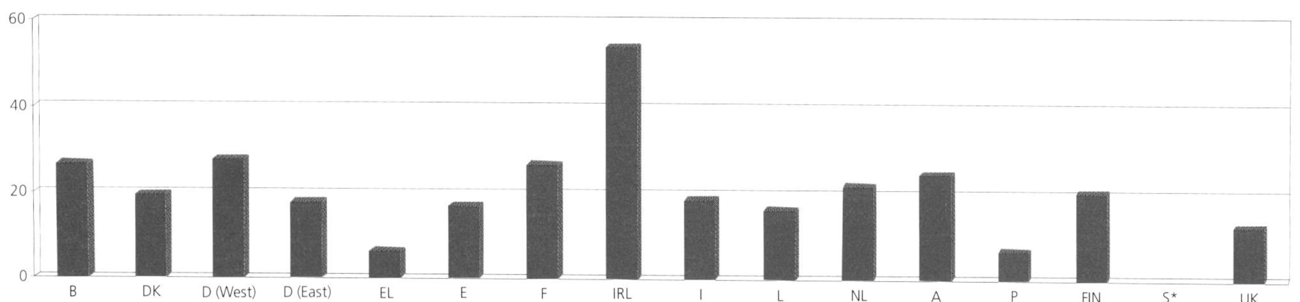

Source: Eurostat (LCS)

turing output was generated by instrument engineering. The levels of output found in the southern Member States were particularly low when compared to total manufacturing activity (especially in Greece and Portugal), where instrument engineering output accounted for less than 1% of domestic manufacturing.

The leading EU precision equipment manufacturers include Rank Xerox (UK), Essilor (F), Dragerwerk (D), Carl Schenk (D), Fielmann, (D), Getinge Industrier (S), Spectra-Physics (S), Instrumentarium (FIN), Polaroid (UK), Safilo (I), SFIM (F), Life Sciences International (UK) and Abbott Laboratories (UK).

Production was expanding at a fast pace in Denmark, Finland, Ireland and Sweden over the last decade. These four countries were the only ones to report that their employment levels were rising during the same period, upwards of 4% per annum in Finland and Sweden, and in excess of 6% per annum in Ireland. Total EU employment in the instrument engineering industry was equal to 638 thousand persons in 1998, compared to 760 thousand persons in 1988.

Within the EU, the largest share of employment in the manufacturing total was recorded in Ireland, with 6.1%. There were a number of other countries able to report that more than 3% of the manufacturing workforce were active in instrument engineering; including Denmark, France, Germany, Sweden and the United Kingdom.

The largest market within the EU was in France, where apparent consumption was equal to 19.8 billion ECU in 1998, well ahead of Germany (15.0 billion ECU) and the United Kingdom (11.5 billion ECU).

Within the Triad, the USA was the main producer in 1997, with a 51.5% share of production in the three Triad economies, followed by the EU (31.8%) and Japan (16.7%). If we compare these figures to the shares recorded in 1988, we find that both the EU and the USA have each gained almost two percentage points at the expense of Japan (whose share declined at a fast rate from 1995 onwards).

There were unsurprisingly more persons employed within the USA, where the workforce was made-up of just over three quarters of a million persons in 1997, equivalent to 46.7% of those working in the Triad. Comparable shares for the EU and Japan revealed that 38.5% of the Triad workforce were active in the EU, whilst only 14.8% of the total were employed in Japan. Looking at developments in the past decade, there was little evolution in the structural composition of the Triad labour market, with no country share changing by more than 0.7 percentage points between 1988 and 1997.

(%) Table 12.1

Instrument engineering (NACE Rev. 1 33)
Composition of the labour force, 1997

	Females	Part-time	Highly-educated
EU-15	34.8	:	:
B	42.0	:	44.7
DK	48.3	:	32.3
D	39.5	10.6	27.2
EL	:	:	:
E	24.3	:	49.9
F	32.4	5.0	27.8
IRL	57.5	2.7	26.7
I	29.5	9.7	6.4
L	88.2	:	:
NL	18.8	15.3	18.6
A	37.3	8.6	7.5
P	37.1	:	:
FIN	35.3	:	36.4
S	39.9	14.7	31.1
UK	29.1	7.5	29.3

Source: Eurostat (LFS)

Foreign trade

The EU ran a trade deficit in this industry from 1988 until 1995. The balance then became a surplus and widened in successive years, before decreasing in 1998 to 1.2 billion ECU. The overall trade performance of the EU may generally be attributed to German manufacturing exports, where a surplus of 6.3 billion ECU was recorded in 1998. More than half of the exports made by Germany were to countries outside the EU. Along with Denmark, Ireland and the United Kingdom, Germany was amongst the most export-specialised countries in the EU.

Total exports of the USA were equivalent to 29.4 billion ECU in 1997, whilst in Japan they amounted to 19.2 billion ECU. Nevertheless, if we study the rate with which each country was exporting its domestic production, we see that just over half of the output of Japan was exported to third countries in 1997, whilst just a quarter of the output of the USA was destined for foreign markets. The export ratio of the EU stood at 37.3% in 1998, compared to the 1989 figure of 26.4%.

As the Triad was the main global producer of instrument engineering, it was no surprise to find that the import penetration rates were generally lower than export ratios. Europe imported 36.3% of its consumption in 1998, a figure comparable to that recorded in Japan at 36.8%, whilst the USA relied to a lesser degree on imports from third countries to satisfy domestic demand (20.7%).

All three Triad economies ran a trade surplus at the end of the nineties, the lowest was in the EU (equal to 2.2 billion ECU in 1997), whilst considerably higher surpluses were recorded in the USA and Japan (6.3 billion ECU and 8.2 billion ECU).

Figure 12.5

Instrument engineering (NACE Rev. 1 33)
Destination of EU exports, 1998

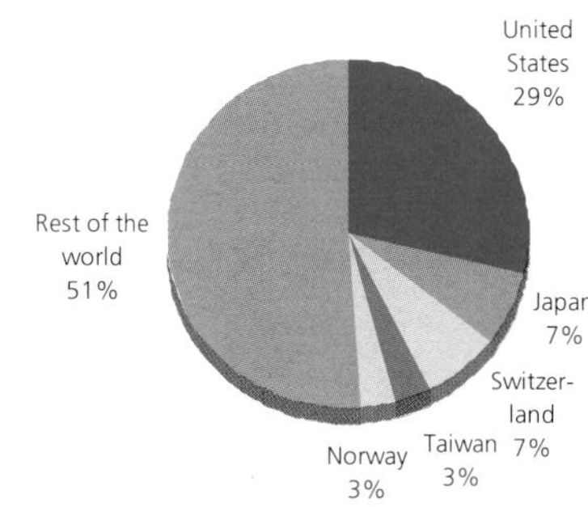

Source: Eurostat (Comext)

Figure 12.6

Instrument engineering (NACE Rev. 1 33)
Origin of EU imports, 1998

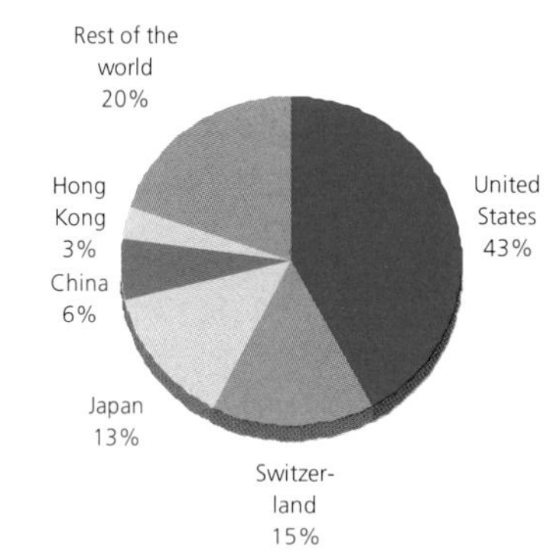

Source: Eurostat (Comext)

Medical and surgical equipment and orthopaedic appliances (NACE Rev. 1 33.1)

The manufacture of medical and surgical equipment and orthopaedic appliances includes the manufacture of products as diverse as diagnostic equipment, dental drills, dentists' chairs, syringes, X-ray equipment or artificial respiratory equipment. The data presented in this section does not include the production of thermometers or spectacle lenses and their frames.

EU production in 1998 rose to over 19 billion ECU[1], well below the level recorded in the USA, which was almost equal to 40 billion ECU in 1997. Output in Japan was considerably lower, standing at just 6.5 billion ECU (also in 1997).

Germany accounted for the largest share of EU output, with more than one third of the Union's production in 1998 (equivalent to 6.6 billion ECU). This was double the output of France, the second largest producer within the EU. Italy and the United Kingdom both reported production values slightly above 2.0 billion ECU.

Production specialisation ratios showed that medical equipment contributed almost four times the EU average to total manufacturing output in Ireland and more than twice the average in Denmark. Other countries that were relatively specialised in the production of medical equipment included Finland and Sweden (141% and 154% respectively). The lowest specialisation ratios were recorded in Greece and Portugal (where the medical equipment contributed just 8% and 25% of the EU average to total manufacturing output).

Production processes are highly advanced in most areas, with large amounts of money spent in research and development. R&D expenditures have induced a range of technological innovations, such as video diagnostics, as well as minimal invasive surgery (endoscopes and imaging devices).

1) Excluding Austria, Belgium, Greece and Portugal.

Figure 12.7

Medical and surgical equipment and orthopaedic appliances (NACE Rev. 1 33.1)
Production and employment in the Triad

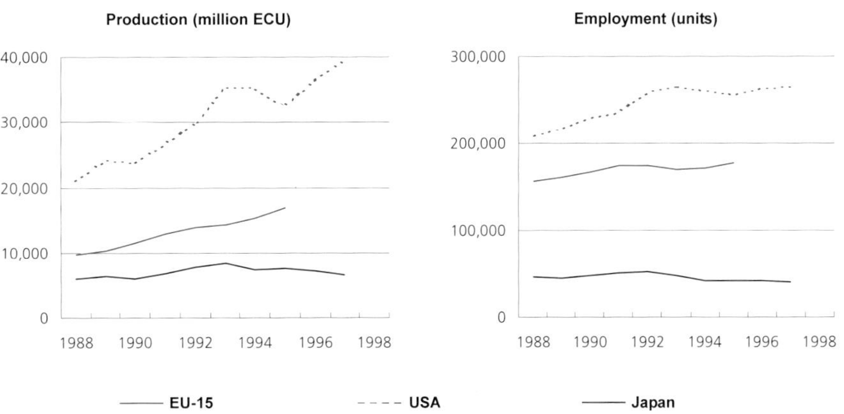

Source: Eurostat (SBS)

(%) Figure 12.8

Medical and surgical equipment and orthopaedic appliances (NACE Rev. 1 33.1)
Production and export specialisation by Member State, 1998

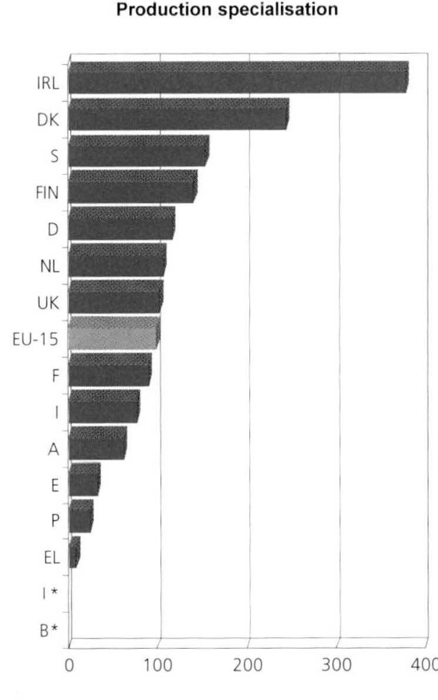

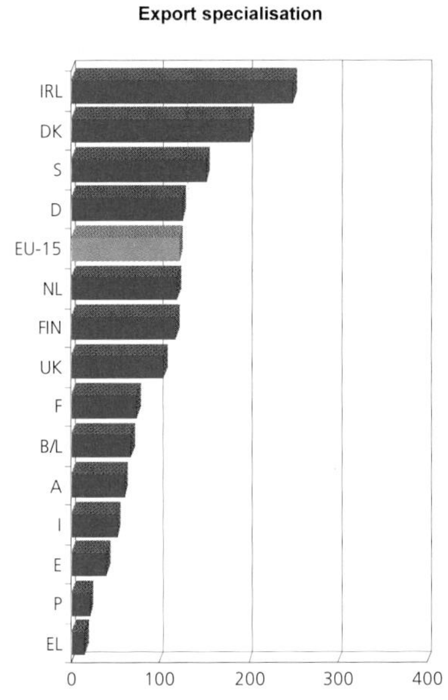

Source: Eurostat (SBS)

Employment in the EU was almost equivalent to 175 thousand persons in 1998[2], some 90 thousand persons less than in the USA. Almost 20 thousand extra jobs have been created in the EU between 1988 and 1998 (even taking into account the fact that data for three countries was not available for the latter period). In the USA the gains in employment were even more pronounced, equivalent to almost 57 thousand posts created between 1988 and 1997. Japanese employment levels contracted somewhat over the same period, falling to 40.1 thousand persons by 1997. Of the nine Member States for which data existed for employment growth between 1988 and 1998, we find that only one, the United Kingdom, reported a negative trend to employment. There was moderate growth of 0.9% per annum in Germany (again based on 1988 to 1998), whilst in France there was a sizeable increase in the number of persons employed, up by 3.6% per annum to reach 23 thousand persons employed in 1998. The highest rates of employment growth were recorded in Finland and Ireland (11.5% and 8.1% per annum respectively).

EU demand for medical and surgical equipment and orthopaedic appliances has increased strongly since 1985. Apparent consumption rose to over 16 billion ECU in 1998 in the EU[3], double the figure of 1988. The largest markets in the EU were in Germany (4.5 billion ECU), France (3.9 billion ECU) and Italy (2.8 billion ECU). Demand patterns have shifted considerably in recent years in this industry. There has been a move away from national health services towards private solutions demanded by consumers. Medical equipment has therefore become more consumer-orientated, allowing a higher degree of self-medication and domestic care.

2) Excluding Austria, Greece and the Netherlands.
3) Excluding Austria, Belgium, Greece, Luxembourg and Portugal.

The European population shows increasing awareness as regards health care, as people generally live longer, driving demand for products. According to the World Health Organisation, global life expectancy is expected to increase to 73 years by the year 2025, compared to a figure of just 48 years old in 1955. There has been a freezing of health care budgets within many Member States and a move towards private health care. The slow growth in public health care within the Triad has created opportunities for the home medical equipment markets, whereby the patient carries out the recuperation, therapy or testing process at home. Indeed, the household consumer market is characterised by much faster growth rates. Therapeutic and massage appliances, vibrating belts and respirators are some of the main consumer product lines, as well as specialist equipment for the elderly (such as wheelchairs, geriatric seating, commodes, walkers, and patient lifts). Another area of rapid expansion is that of Point-of-Care Testing (POCT) devices. The most successful examples of these product lines are pregnancy testing devices and glucose monitors.

Medical device companies must adapt to the sweeping changes in the care industry. Many purchasing and sales activities are increasingly being made by managers of health agencies, large hospital consortiums, government agencies, and managed care providers. These buying groups hold a lot of leverage and medical device companies need to adapt themselves to implement effective selling programmes to market their products.

Equipment for medical purposes faces stringent regulations in most markets. In the EU, medical devices are covered by Directives setting out the requirements for performance and safety of medical devices and also procedures for checking product compliance. A product is required to have a "CE" mark to show full compliance with relevant directives.

Figure 12.9

Medical and surgical equipment and orthopaedic appliances (NACE Rev. 1 33.1) Destination of EU exports, 1998

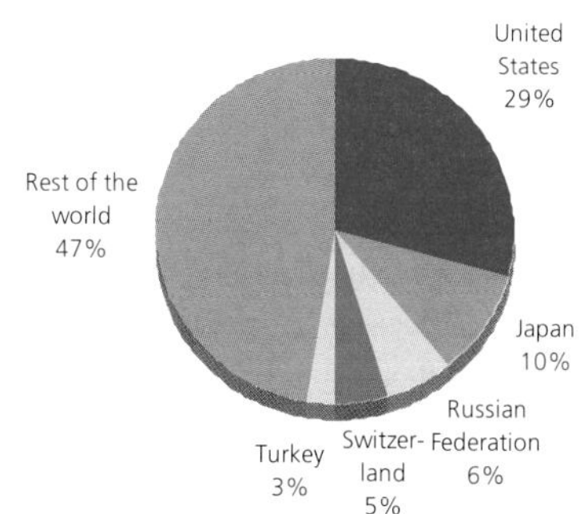

Source: Eurostat (Comext)

Figure 12.10

Medical and surgical equipment and orthopaedic appliances (NACE Rev. 1 33.1) Origin of EU imports, 1998

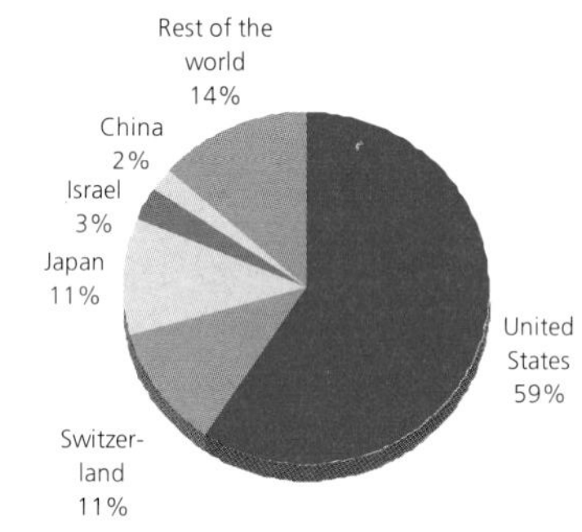

Source: Eurostat (Comext)

Measuring, precision and process control equipment (NACE Rev. 1 33.2 and 33.3)

The manufacture of equipment for measuring, checking, testing and navigating is classified with NACE Rev. 1 33.2, whilst industrial process equipment may be found in NACE Rev. 1 33.3. The data presented in this section cover a wide array of products from electricity, water and gas supply meters, navigational equipment for ships, microscopes to the design and assembly of continuous process control systems.

Production value of measuring equipment (NACE Rev. 1 33.2) in the EU totalled almost 40 billion ECU in 1998[4]. This showed a sizeable increase when compared to the data from 1993, when output was equal to 27.6 billion ECU. Annual average growth rates for the period 1993-1998 showed that there was expansion in almost every country for which data was available, the only exception being the Netherlands where production fell by 3.9% per annum. The largest gains in output were recorded in Finland, France and Sweden, where double-digit growth in real terms was posted. Employment in the EU was growing in a few countries, including Ireland, Italy and Sweden between 1993 and 1998, with growth rates of around 4% per annum in the former two countries and more than 13% per annum in Sweden. Total EU employment was just under 300 thousand persons in 1995. More recent data was available at the country level, where the largest employer was Germany, with almost 93 thousand persons employed, followed by the United Kingdom with nearly 76 thousand and France with more than 57 thousand.

In Germany measuring equipment accounted for 46% of total employment in instrument engineering. France, Sweden and the United Kingdom reported even higher shares, above 50%. France reported the highest unit personnel costs at 48.3 thousand ECU in 1996. The lowest unit personnel costs were recorded in Ireland and the United Kingdom, where figures at or under 25 thousand ECU were recorded.

Process control equipment (NACE Rev. 1 33.3) accounted for more than 10% of production in instrument engineering in a limited number of countries, Finland, Italy and Spain. Process control equipment had a far lower share of the employment market, often below 10% of the total number of persons employed in the instrument engineering industry.

4) Excluding Austria, Luxembourg and Portugal.

Figure 12.11

Measuring, precision and process control equipment (NACE Rev. 1 33.2 and 33.3)
Production and employment in the Triad

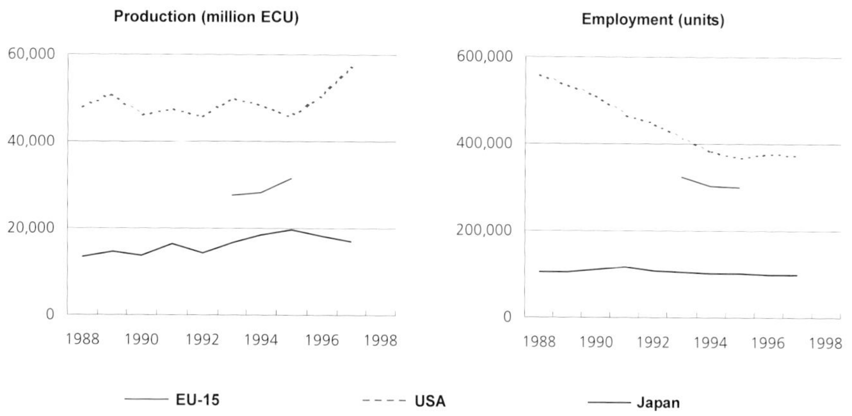

Source: Eurostat (SBS)

Figure 12.12

Measuring and precision equipment (NACE Rev. 1 33.2)
Production and export specialisation by Member State, 1998

(%)

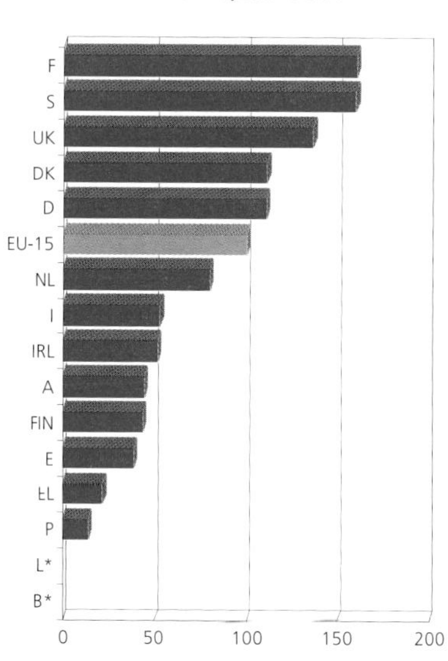

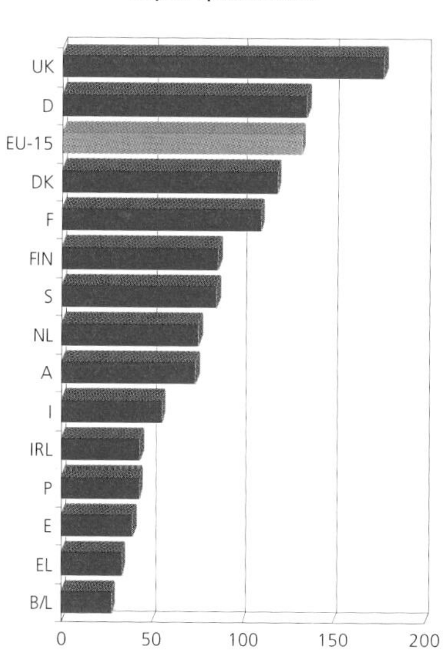

Source: Eurostat (SBS)

In the fields of highly sophisticated products with a high technological input, the pace of innovation was set largely by producers in Japan, the USA and Switzerland. At the other end of the product spectrum, imported goods from Eastern Asia can be expected to intensify price competition. In the high-tech end of the market, firms have found themselves at a disadvantage in terms of the investment levels required to successfully compete with the new products being offered by their counterparts in the USA and Japan. Without the benefits of the economies of scale enjoyed by their competitors, EU firms have looked to expansion in terms of new markets, internal growth and merger activity.

EU apparent consumption rose to 34 billion ECU in 1998[5]. France, with a market of 12.5 billion ECU had by far the highest demand in the EU, with domestic consumption more than double the level seen in the United Kingdom (6.2 billion ECU) or Germany (5.8 billion ECU).

The measuring and control equipment industry sees its demand closely linked to the performance of the industries that it serves with components, such as navigational instrumentation and the aircraft and shipbuilding industries. With technological advances, the vast majority of products are now electronically controlled. One final area where demand has grown rapidly in the last decade is with respect to environmental management and control.

The production trends of vehicles, chemicals and food and drink are therefore all important. However, measurement instrumentation intended for use as part of large-scale productive processes are to a higher degree subject to changing trends in capital investment. Technological development has become an increasingly important motor of demand for process control equipment. Of particular relevance in recent years has been the development of products that allow for the integration of large-scale data processing systems, with greater scope for alteration and adaptability of particular procedures.

5) Excluding Austria, Belgium, Luxembourg and Portugal.

Figure 12.13

Measuring and precision equipment
(NACE Rev. 1 33.2)
Destination of EU exports, 1998

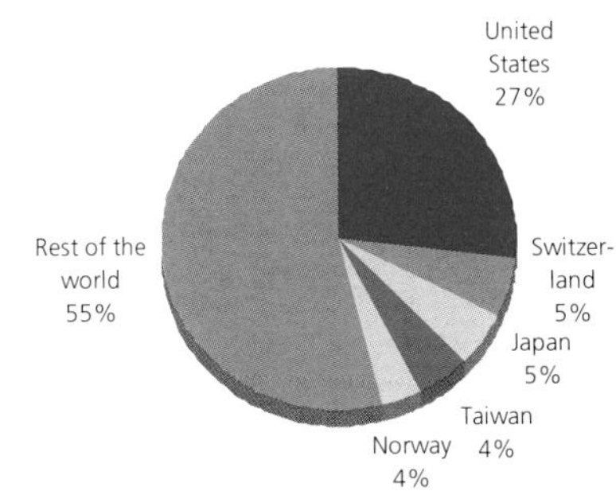

Source: Eurostat (Comext)

Figure 12.14

Measuring and precision equipment
(NACE Rev. 1 33.2)
Origin of EU imports, 1998

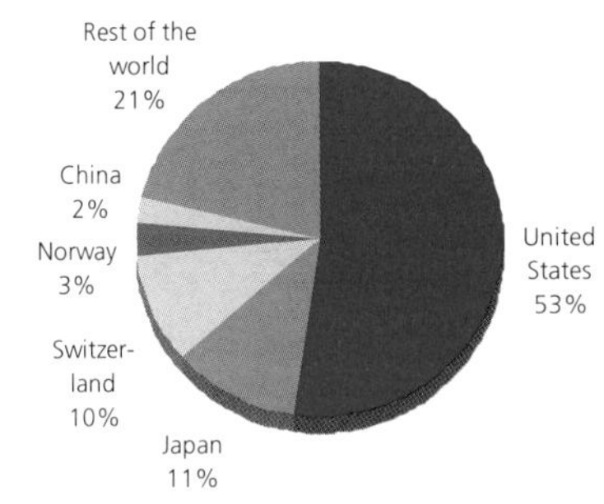

Source: Eurostat (Comext)

Optical and photographic instruments (NACE Rev. 1 33.4)

The manufacture of optical instruments and photographic equipment covers the manufacture of lenses, spectacles (including their frames), binoculars, lasers, projectors and telescopes. These items are classified under NACE Rev. 1 33.4; however this section does not cover optical fibres, photographic flashbulbs or photochemical products.

Optical and photographic industries accounted for 12.1% of European instrument engineering output in 1998. This figure was considerably higher in Italy, where the industry was highly developed and accounted for 23.4% of domestic instrument engineering output.

In the USA, optical and photographic instruments had a similar level of importance compared to the EU, accounting for 12.9% of instrument engineering output in 1997, whilst the sector was more developed in Japan, accounting for more than one-fifth of the instrument engineering total.

Labour productivity in the EU was at its highest levels in Belgium and Italy (some 89.7 and 61.3 thousand ECU of value added per head in 1998). These figures were well below the levels recorded in the USA, where each person employed generated an average of 136.5 ECU of value added in 1997, which was almost three times higher than the corresponding figures from Japan (47.9 thousand ECU).

Unit personnel costs in the EU averaged 32.6 thousand ECU per head in 1995. Slightly fresher data was available for some of the individual Member States, where figures ranged between 21.8 thousand ECU per head in the United Kingdom and 42.5 thousand ECU per head in Germany in 1996.

Production specialisation for optical and photographic instruments was highest in Italy at 148%. The only other EU countries to report that they were relatively specialised in this industry were Austria, Denmark and Germany. Indeed, the production of eyeglasses was highly concentrated within Italy, the largest world exporter of frames (followed by Hong Kong). Production of spectacle frames has slowly been shifting from plastics to metals in response to world demand, due to their lightness and simple design, especially with the development of light, durable frames. In the domain of lenses there have also been advances, with innovations such as anti-glare, anti-scratch, polarising and anti-misting.

Figure 12.15

Optical and photographic instruments (NACE Rev. 1 33.4)
Production and employment in the Triad

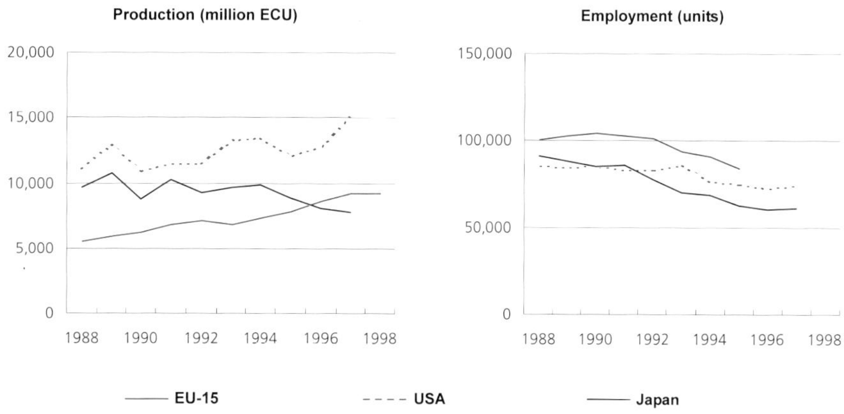

Source: Eurostat (SBS)

(%)

Figure 12.16

Optical and photographic instruments (NACE Rev. 1 33.4)
Production and export specialisation by Member State, 1998

Production specialisation

I, DK, D, A, EU-15, UK, F, NL, P, E, S, EL, FIN, L*, IRL*, B*

0 50 100 150 200

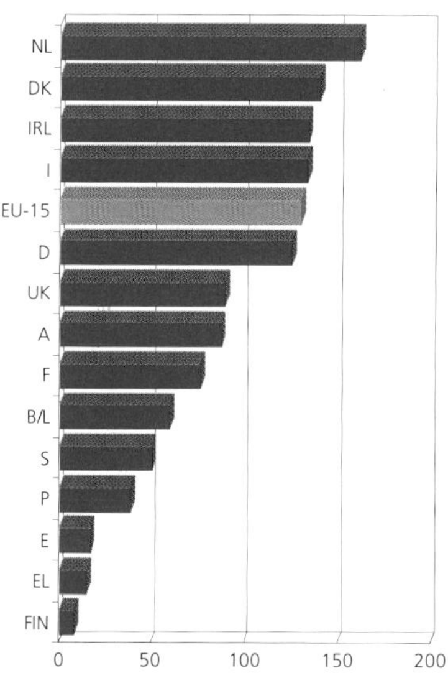

Source: Eurostat (SBS)

EU apparent consumption rose to 8.2 billion ECU in 1998[6]. The largest market in the EU was Germany (worth 2.3 billion ECU), closely followed by the United Kingdom with a market of 2.2 billion ECU. The United Kingdom market has gained more than one billion ECU during the nineties in nominal terms, whilst in France and Germany growth was minimal.

The spectacles industry has evolved from a medicinal to a consumer-based business. Growth in demand for eyeglasses is driven firstly by demographic changes, the increase in the overall EU population, its gradual ageing and the longer average life-span of its citizens. Demographic factors are reinforced by changes in the nature of work, with a higher proportion of employees needing to use their eyes in a concentrated manner for longer periods. A second factor is that the market for eyeglasses has become a consumer market subject to changes in fashion, particularly with respect to frames. A third factor has been technological innovation, which has facilitated differentiation by allowing consumers to choose from a variety of lenses, frames and products. A negative factor has been a gradual tightening of social security spending on eye-care, although this has usually been compensated for by an increase in disposable income.

EU consumers have shown a willingness to own more than one pair of glasses, depending on their aesthetic and practical needs. Sunglasses and sports eyewear represent growing market segments. Men are becoming more willing to spend on grooming products, including spectacles, which have become a fashion accessory. Amongst emerging markets, glasses are likely to experience demand rising at a rapid pace in China and India.

Licensing arrangements are common, with production of many leading designer brands carried out by production companies in south-east Asia.

The retail sector is expected to continue to consolidate, with the number of chain stores growing rapidly at the expense of individual operators. These large chains have the advantage of economies of scale in purchasing and advertising, allowing them to offer more competitive prices and dedicate greater resources towards marketing. These chains are likely to increase sourcing from Asia in an effort to improve their price competitiveness, especially for low and mid-level products.

6) Excluding Austria, Belgium, Denmark, Ireland, Luxembourg and Portugal.

In the case of sunglasses, due to the demand for colourful designs, plastic materials are mainly used. Awareness of the risks of ultraviolet (UV) radiation and licensing agreements with designer labels have combined to boost the sales of sunglasses, which have been designed to satisfy both functional needs and aesthetic demands.

The second product grouping covered by the data in this chapter is that of precision optical instruments. This area consists mainly of instrumentation designed to improve industrial measurement and testing. An important advantage of optical technology is the fact that measurement and testing can be accomplished through light sensing mechanisms, often without physical contact. While demand for precision optical instrumentation has increased in the past decade, it is susceptible to recessionary pressures.

Demand for photographic equipment is largely a result of private consumption. There has been a move towards simpler, more disposable technologies in this industry. New product innovations have included user-friendly technology, higher film quality, different types of film, and the increased use of electronics. Demand for motion picture equipment, sensitised photographic film, chemicals and paper largely flows from private households and has been driven by product innovations. Current areas of technological development include digital video cassette and digital photographic cameras.

Demand for still picture equipment has been stimulated by improved automation and convenience. The marriage of electronics and photography has boosted demand. Turning to industrial consumption, there has been increased demand in areas such as space photography, aerial photography, security and traffic monitoring in the last decade.

There were a high level of exports in the optical equipment industry in Japan, worth 7.1 billion ECU in 1997. This was more than double the corresponding figure for the USA, and well above EU[7] exports to third countries (equal to 4.4 billion ECU in 1998).

7) Excluding Greece.

Figure 12.17

Optical and photographic instruments (NACE Rev. 1 33.4) Destination of EU exports, 1998

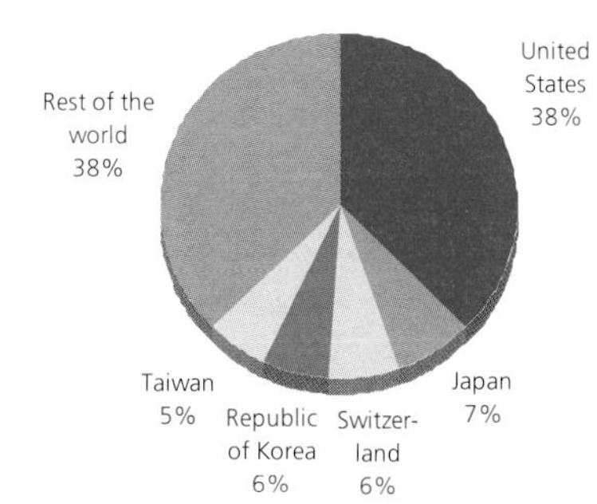

Source: Eurostat (Comext)

Figure 12.18

Optical and photographic instruments (NACE Rev. 1 33.4) Origin of EU imports, 1998

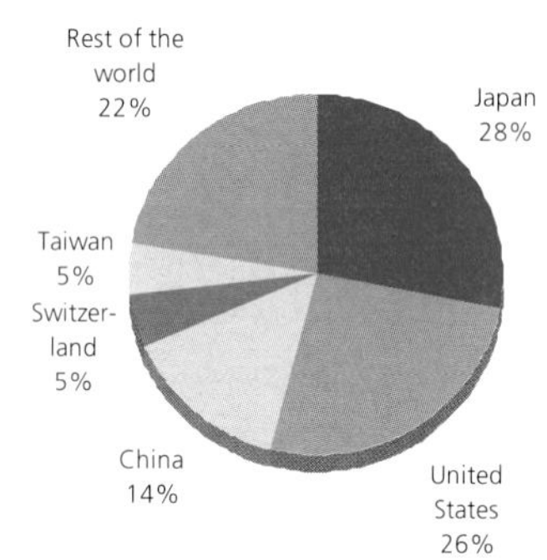

Source: Eurostat (Comext)

Watches and clocks (NACE Rev. 1 33.5)

The manufacture of watches and clocks is found within the NACE Rev. 1 classification of economic activities under Group 33.5. The industry covers the production of watch movements, cases, time-recording equipment (such as parking meters and time switches), as well as springs, jewels and dials that are used in the manufacture of watches. Data presented in this chapter does not cover the manufacture of non-metallic watchbands (which are covered by NACE Rev. 1 19.2).

The clocks and watches industry is not very large in comparison to the remainder of the instrument engineering activities. Within the EU, clocks and watches accounted for just 2.3% of the total output generated within the instrument engineering sector, a share above that for the USA (1.1%), whilst much lower than for Japan (13.3%). Two of the EU countries reported that they have no production in this activity, namely Denmark and Greece.

Given the high level of production in Japan, it was no surprise to find that Japan exported more clocks and watches than the other two members of the Triad. Japanese exports were almost six times greater than those of the USA. However, extra-EU exports[8] in 1997 were at 1.3 billion ECU, less than 300 million ECU below the corresponding Japanese value.

Unlike most other activities within the instrument engineering industry (where employment has been expanding), clocks and watches have been badly hit in recent years with employment falling by 10.7% per annum in Germany and 8.9% per annum in Italy between 1988 and 1998. France had the largest workforce in the EU, with 5.1 thousand persons employed, ahead of Germany with 4.4 thousand persons. Employment data for the whole of the EU was only available for 1995, when 15.4 thousand persons were in the EU workforce.

Private household demand drives this industry. As such, demand for lower and mid-range products was largely a function of fashion and disposable income. However, technological innovation would appear to play an important role in demand trends at the upper-end of the market for watches.

8) Excluding Finland, Greece, Ireland and Portugal.

Figure 12.19

Watches and clocks (NACE Rev. 1 33.5)
Production and employment in the Triad

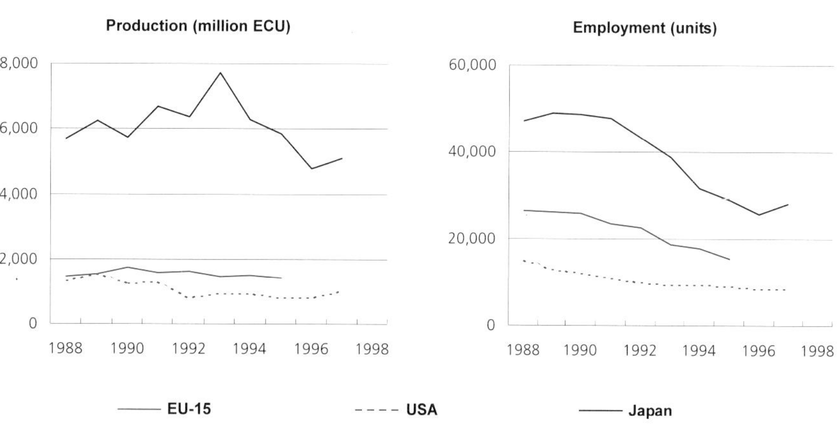

Source: Eurostat (SBS)

(%) Figure 12.20

Watches and clocks (NACE Rev. 1 33.5)
Production and export specialisation by Member State, 1998

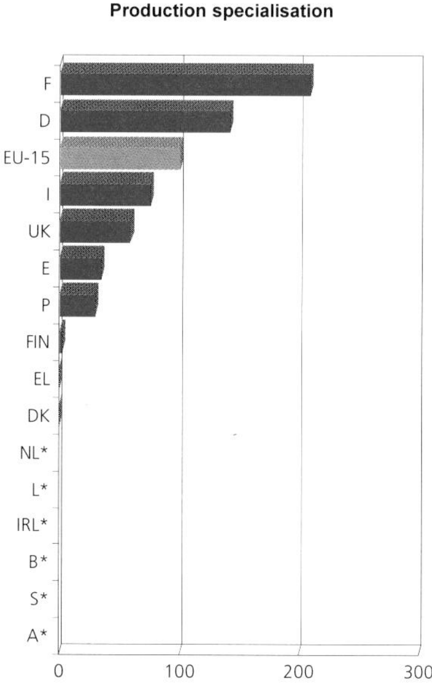

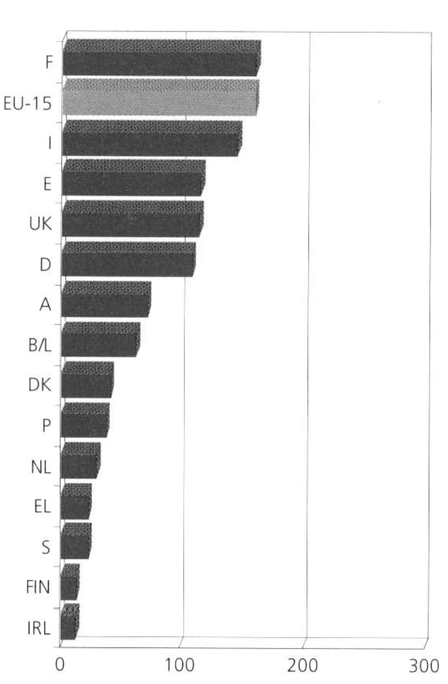

Source: Eurostat (SBS)

it is common for individuals to own several watches to be worn on different occasions. This has contributed to separation of the market into a number of different segments. Women were seen to be moving faster towards multiple ownership than men. Casual watches were more popular in the USA, whilst stainless steel watches were more sought-after in the EU. Medium-priced digital watches remained popular, especially among younger persons. In particular, sports watches were seen to be an expanding niche market. Analogue quartz watches maintained a sizeable share of the market. In the EU, there were restrictions on the use of nickel, which led in part to an increase in the demand for stainless steel watches that required no electroplating. Thanks to falling prices of electronic components, fashion features such as voice announcement of time and temperature can be built into wrist watches and clocks at an affordable cost. Cross-product features like interactive games played between different persons with same models were introduced in some watches.

The market for clocks also saw innovation, with multi-functional alarm clocks, including desk-top and traveller models gaining in popularity. These clocks included functions like thermometers, calendars, world-time display and countdown devices.
Acute price competition, particularly in the low price segment of the market was hitting many small EU manufacturers badly. More recently, competition within the mid-range of the market, where EU producers have traditionally held their highest market share, has also heightened. The approach of Swiss manufacturers in expanding their market share by supplying fashionable, recognised brands at competitive prices has had considerable success, with the Swatch brand the most prominent.

Figure 12.21

Watches and clocks (NACE Rev. 1 33.5)
Destination of EU exports, 1998

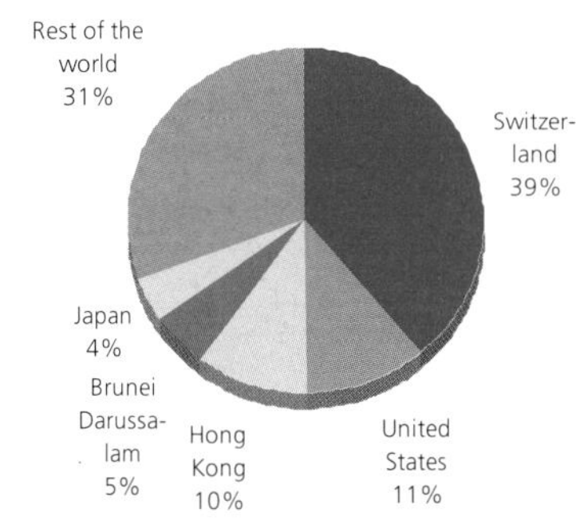

Source: Eurostat (Comext)

Figure 12.22

Watches and clocks (NACE Rev. 1 33.5)
Origin of EU imports, 1998

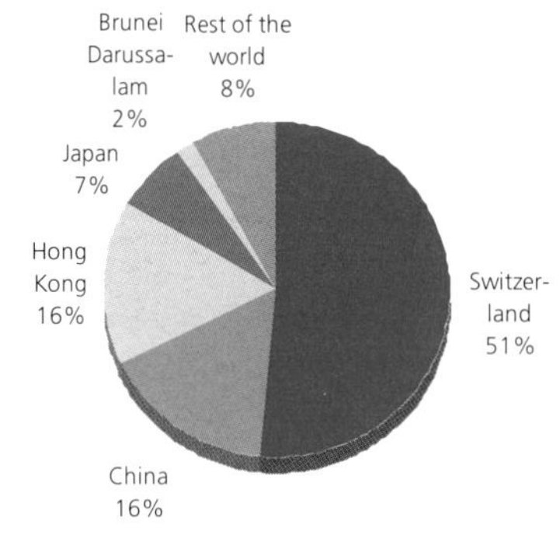

Source: Eurostat (Comext)

Professional associations representing the industries within this chapter

CECIP
European Committee of Weighing instruments industry
Maison de la Mécanique
39/41 rue Louis Blanc
F-92038 Paris La Défense
tel: (33) 1 43 34 76 84
fax: (33) 1 43 34 76 82

(million ECU) — Table 12.2

Manufacture of medical and surgical equipment and orthopaedic appliances (NACE Rev. 1 33.1)

Production related indicators in the EU

	1988	1989	1990	1991	1992	1993	1994	1995	1996	1997	1998
Production value	9,801	10,423	11,550	12,984	13,951	14,390	15,371	16,912	:	:	:
Producer price index (1995=100)	:	:	:	:	:	:	:	100.0	108.6	112.1	96.9
Value added	4,779	4,963	5,514	6,166	6,606	6,913	7,473	7,790	:	:	:
Number of persons employed (thousands)	157.3	161.2	166.7	174.0	175.4	169.9	171.0	177.5	:	:	:

(million ECU) — Table 12.3

Manufacture of medical and surgical equipment and orthopaedic appliances (NACE Rev. 1 33.1)

Production related indicators, 1998

	B	DK	D	EL	E	F	IRL	I	L	NL	A	P	FIN	S	UK
Production value (1)	509	861	6,558	7	568	3,300	1,087	2,097	18	966	244	67	551	996	2,004
Value added (2)	176	364	3,521	3	277	1,212	667	982	11	328	139	:	277	382	1,026
Number of persons employed (units) (3)	2,946	6,193	66,387	221	13,774	23,037	9,888	15,036	416	6,043	2,674	1,408	4,770	7,050	24,013

(1) EL (1993); B, P, A (1997). (2) EL (1993); B, A (1997). (3) NL (1992); EL (1993), A (1997).

(million ECU) — Table 12.4

Manufacture of medical and surgical equipment and orthopaedic appliances (NACE Rev. 1 33.1)

Market related indicators in the EU

	1988	1989	1990	1991	1992	1993	1994	1995	1996	1997	1998
Apparent consumption	8,777	9,331	10,258	11,789	13,335	13,145	13,703	15,335	:	:	:
Exports	3,588	3,969	4,390	4,793	4,941	5,850	6,321	6,863	7,565	8,490	8,915
Imports	2,565	2,876	3,098	3,598	4,326	4,605	4,652	5,286	6,028	7,028	7,199
Trade balance	1,023	1,092	1,292	1,195	616	1,245	1,668	1,577	1,537	1,462	1,717
Export ratio (%)	36.6	38.1	38.0	36.9	35.4	40.7	41.1	40.6	:	:	:
Import penetration ratio (%)	29.2	30.8	30.2	30.5	32.4	35.0	34.0	34.5	:	:	:
Cover ratio (%)	139.9	138.0	141.7	133.2	114.2	127.0	135.9	129.8	125.5	120.8	123.9

(million ECU) — Table 12.5

Manufacture of medical and surgical equipment and orthopaedic appliances (NACE Rev. 1 33.1)

Market related indicators, 1998

	B/L	DK	D	EL	E	F	IRL	I	NL	A	P	FIN	S	UK
Apparent consumption (1)	:	495	4,513	182	1,247	3,865	391	2,790	451	451	222	348	603	1,701
Exports	985	733	5,524	12	331	1,983	1,187	1,062	1,837	278	40	434	1,025	2,258
Imports	1,218	367	3,479	291	1,010	2,548	491	1,755	1,321	458	209	231	633	1,955
Trade balance	-233	366	2,045	-279	-679	-565	696	-693	515	-181	-169	203	393	303
Export ratio (%) (1)	:	85.1	84.2	69.1	58.3	60.1	109.2	50.6	190.0	122.6	66.6	78.8	103.0	112.7
Import penetration ratio (%) (1)	:	74.1	77.1	98.7	81.0	65.9	125.6	62.9	292.9	112.2	90.0	66.4	104.9	114.9
Cover ratio (%)	80.9	199.8	158.8	4.1	32.8	77.8	241.9	60.5	139.0	60.6	19.3	188.2	162.1	115.5

(1) EL (1993); P, A (1997).

Table 12.6

Manufacture of medical and surgical equipment and orthopaedic appliances (NACE Rev. 1 33.1)

Labour related indicators, 1998

	EU-15	B	DK	D	EL	E	F	IRL	I	L	NL	A	P	FIN	S	UK
Personnel costs (million ECU) (1)	5,468	57	208	2,336	2	215	876	227	482	8	227	104	12	132	235	645
Personnel costs/employee (thousand ECU) (2)	32.5	35.4	34.3	35.7	10.2	17.8	38.7	22.7	29.3	21.6	:	30.7	:	30.3	40.4	22.3
Social charges/personnel costs (%) (3)	20.5	24.1	3.2	18.2	23.1	21.5	30.2	19.6	35.6	:	14.2	22.2	:	18.0	29.9	12.3
Labour productivity (thousand ECU/head) (4)	43.9	55.9	58.7	53.0	14.2	20.2	52.6	67.5	65.3	27.0	36.0	51.8	:	58.0	54.1	42.7
Wage adjusted labour productivity (%) (2)	135.2	117.1	142.6	133.7	138.4	131.7	127.0	286.1	175.6	114.7	:	132.3	:	182.6	152.0	179.0

(1) EL (1993); EU-15 (1995). (2) EL (1993); EU-15, I, A (1995); B, DK, D, E, F, IRL, L, FIN, S, UK (1996). (3) EL (1993); EU-15, S (1995). (4) NL (1992); EL (1993); B, A (1997).

Source: Eurostat (SBS, EBT)

Table 12.7 (million ECU)

Manufacture of instruments and appliances for measuring, checking, testing, navigating and other purposes, except industrial process control equipment (NACE Rev. 1 33.2): production related indicators in the EU

	1988	1989	1990	1991	1992	1993	1994	1995	1996	1997	1998
Production value	:	:	:	:	:	27,575	27,918	31,205	:	:	:
Producer price index (1995=100)	:	:	88.7	92.5	95.1	97.6	98.8	100.0	100.8	100.8	100.8
Value added	:	:	:	:	:	11,969	12,561	13,270	:	:	:
Number of persons employed (thousands)	:	:	:	:	:	321.6	300.2	297.0	:	:	:

Table 12.8 (million ECU)

Manufacture of instruments and appliances for measuring, checking, testing, navigating and other purposes, except industrial process control equipment (NACE Rev. 1 33.2): production related indicators, 1998

	B	DK	D	EL	E	F	IRL	I	L	NL	A	P	FIN	S	UK
Production value (1)	452	659	10,018	60	994	13,063	272	2,829	:	1,293	321	70	327	2,090	7,490
Value added (2)	159	295	4,926	15	387	4,480	113	1,039	:	462	163	:	157	819	3,109
Number of persons employed (units) (3)	1,195	4,847	92,854	478	9,419	57,349	1,791	25,315	:	14,151	2,598	1,196	2,474	14,843	75,947

(1) P, A (1997). (2) A (1997). (3) NL (1992); E (1996); A (1997).

Table 12.9 (million ECU)

Manufacture of instruments and appliances for measuring, checking, testing, navigating and other purposes, except industrial process control equipment (NACE Rev. 1 33.2): market related indicators in the EU

	1988	1989	1990	1991	1992	1993	1994	1995	1996	1997	1998
Apparent consumption	:	:	:	:	:	26,380	26,744	29,716	:	:	:
Exports	6,954	7,337	7,545	7,476	7,640	8,265	8,994	9,726	11,015	13,262	13,783
Imports	5,862	6,956	6,995	7,526	7,262	7,070	7,820	8,238	9,157	10,232	11,373
Trade balance	1,092	382	550	-50	378	1,195	1,174	1,488	1,858	3,031	2,410
Export ratio (%)	:	:	:	:	:	30.0	32.2	31.2	:	:	:
Import penetration ratio (%)	:	:	:	:	:	26.8	29.2	27.7	:	:	:
Cover ratio (%)	118.6	105.5	107.9	99.3	105.2	116.9	115.0	118.1	120.3	129.6	121.2

Table 12.10 (million ECU)

Manufacture of instruments and appliances for measuring, checking, testing, navigating and other purposes, except industrial process control equipment (NACE Rev. 1 33.2): market related indicators, 1998

	B/L	DK	D	EL	E	F	IRL	I	NL	A	P	FIN	S	UK
Apparent consumption (1)	:	439	5,821	211	1,758	12,512	295	3,487	1,269	446	197	228	2,174	6,193
Exports	597	658	9,001	39	494	4,393	312	1,702	1,766	511	125	480	872	5,788
Imports	1,153	438	4,804	190	1,259	3,842	335	2,361	1,742	669	289	381	957	4,491
Trade balance	-556	220	4,197	-151	-765	551	-24	-658	24	-158	-164	100	-84	1,297
Export ratio (%) (1)	:	99.9	89.9	65.1	49.7	33.6	114.7	60.2	136.5	187.1	185.7	146.8	41.7	77.3
Import penetration ratio (%) (1)	:	99.9	82.5	90.1	71.6	30.7	113.5	67.7	137.2	162.6	130.4	167.2	44.0	72.5
Cover ratio (%)	51.8	150.1	187.3	20.4	39.2	114.3	93.0	72.1	101.4	76.4	43.4	126.2	91.2	128.9

(1) P, A (1997).

Table 12.11

Manufacture of instruments and appliances for measuring, checking, testing, navigating and other purposes, except industrial process control equipment (NACE Rev. 1 33.2): labour related indicators, 1998

	EU-15	B	DK	D	EL	E	F	IRL	I	L	NL	A	P	FIN	S	UK
Personnel costs (million ECU) (1)	10,711	35	178	4,040	6	252	2,723	42	883	:	372	138	15	84	490	2,289
Personnel costs/employee (thousand ECU) (2)	38.0	42.3	37.5	43.3	13.0	27.7	48.3	23.5	31.8	:	:	39.7	:	34.5	40.1	25.0
Social charges/personnel costs (%) (3)	21.2	27.9	2.4	17.5	24.6	20.9	30.5	16.9	35.0	:	13.2	22.0	:	22.1	29.3	12.2
Labour productivity (thousand ECU/head) (4)	44.7	133.4	60.9	53.1	31.5	40.1	78.1	63.1	41.0	:	41.1	62.9	:	63.3	55.2	40.9
Wage adjusted labour productivity (%) (2)	117.4	136.1	135.1	115.3	156.5	144.7	112.8	231.3	142.3	:	:	124.2	:	156.2	156.4	148.7

(1) EU-15 (1995). (2) EU-15, EL, I, A (1995); B, DK, D, E, F, IRL, FIN, S, UK (1996). (3) EU-15, S (1995). (4) NL (1992); EU-15 (1995); E (1996); A (1997).

Source: Eurostat (SBS, EBT)

(million ECU) Table 12.12

Manufacture of industrial process control equipment (NACE Rev. 1 33.3)
Production related indicators in the EU

	1988	1989	1990	1991	1992	1993	1994	1995	1996	1997	1998
Production value	:	:	:	:	:	7,369	7,965	4,741	:	:	:
Producer price index (1995=100)	:	:	:	:	:	:	:	:	:	:	:
Value added	:	:	:	:	:	3,147	3,311	1,819	:	:	:
Number of persons employed (thousands)	:	:	:	:	:	83.5	82.4	39.9	:	:	:

(million ECU) Table 12.13

Manufacture of industrial process control equipment (NACE Rev. 1 33.3)
Production related indicators, 1998

	B	DK	D	EL	E	F	IRL	I	L	NL	A	P	FIN	S	UK
Production value (1)	91	30	1,384	0	291	1,301	38	1,090	:	0	:	:	213	10	813
Value added (1)	38	14	622	0	92	498	13	418	:	0	:	:	78	5	358
Number of persons employed (units) (2)	2,961	324	7,556	0	2,075	12,456	295	8,051	:	0	:	:	1,592	138	7,739

(1) DK, NL (1994); EL (1995); B (1997). (2) NL (1992); DK (1994); EL (1995); E (1996).

Table 12.14

Manufacture of industrial process control equipment (NACE Rev. 1 33.3)
Labour related indicators, 1998

	EU-15	B	DK	D	EL	E	F	IRL	I	L	NL	A	P	FIN	S	UK
Personnel costs (million ECU) (1)	1,529	108	10	401	0	36	463	8	302	:	0	:	:	65	3	258
Personnel costs/employee (thousand ECU) (2)	38.7	48.4	:	50.3	:	29.7	37.8	27.0	34.3	:	:	:	:	41.3	30.0	27.7
Social charges/personnel costs (%) (3)	24.6	27.6	3.2	17.5	:	19.9	29.8	13.8	36.5	:	:	:	:	21.8	:	12.4
Labour productivity (thousand ECU/head) (4)	45.6	16.6	43.6	82.4	:	39.9	40.0	44.7	52.0	:	:	:	:	49.1	35.1	46.2
Wage adjusted labour productivity (%) (2)	117.8	110.3	:	138.0	:	134.3	116.8	160.1	140.0	:	:	:	:	140.1	132.3	147.2

(1) DK, NL (1994); EU-15, EL (1995). (2) EU-15, I (1995); B, D, E, F, IRL, FIN, S, UK (1996). (3) DK (1994); EU-15 (1995). (4) DK (1994); EU-15 (1995); E (1996); B (1997).

Source: Eurostat (SBS, EBT)

Table 12.15 (million ECU)

Manufacture of optical instruments and photographic equipment (NACE Rev. 1 33.4)

Production related indicators in the EU

	1988	1989	1990	1991	1992	1993	1994	1995	1996	1997	1998
Production value	5,550	5,935	6,278	6,826	7,131	6,821	7,389	7,891	8,692	9,226	9,236
Producer price index (1995=100)	:	:	85.0	89.8	93.2	96.3	98.0	100.0	:	:	:
Value added	2,723	2,708	2,887	3,309	3,341	3,254	3,439	3,639	:	:	:
Number of persons employed (thousands)	100.6	103.1	104.1	103.3	101.2	93.7	91.2	84.2	:	:	:

Table 12.16 (million ECU)

Manufacture of optical instruments and photographic equipment (NACE Rev. 1 33.4)

Production related indicators, 1998

	B	DK	D	EL	E	F	IRL	I	L	NL	A	P	FIN	S	UK
Production value (1)	200	149	2,843	14	240	1,224	:	1,880	:	272	225	79	12	111	1,622
Value added (2)	66	63	1,475	-3	101	519	:	1,072	:	107	109	:	5	48	745
Number of persons employed (units) (3)	740	1,057	28,325	223	3,797	13,281	:	17,494	:	:	3,136	1,491	186	1,211	14,068

(1) DK, A (1994); P (1997). (2) DK, A (1994); EL (1995). (3) DK, A (1994).

Table 12.17 (million ECU)

Manufacture of optical instruments and photographic equipment (NACE Rev. 1 33.4)

Market related indicators in the EU

	1988	1989	1990	1991	1992	1993	1994	1995	1996	1997	1998
Apparent consumption	6,117	6,623	7,154	7,748	7,683	7,310	7,946	8,389	9,089	9,278	9,457
Exports	1,811	2,061	2,020	2,121	2,405	2,521	2,764	3,112	3,603	4,314	4,461
Imports	2,378	2,749	2,896	3,044	2,956	3,011	3,321	3,610	4,000	4,366	4,682
Trade balance	-567	-689	-877	-923	-552	-489	-557	-498	-397	-52	-221
Export ratio (%)	32.6	34.7	32.2	31.1	33.7	37.0	37.4	39.4	41.5	46.8	48.3
Import penetration ratio (%)	38.9	41.5	40.5	39.3	38.5	41.2	41.8	43.0	44.0	47.1	49.5
Cover ratio (%)	76.2	75.0	69.7	69.7	81.3	83.7	83.2	86.2	90.1	98.8	95.3

Table 12.18 (million ECU)

Manufacture of optical instruments and photographic equipment (NACE Rev. 1 33.4)

Market related indicators, 1998

	B/L	DK	D	EL	E	F	IRL	I	NL	A	P	FIN	S	UK
Apparent consumption (1)	:	142	2,334	90	660	1,478	:	1,326	-204	304	162	110	212	2,212
Exports	430	255	2,745	6	71	1,005	317	1,349	1,238	199	38	16	169	963
Imports	542	186	2,236	82	491	1,258	171	796	762	211	128	114	270	1,553
Trade balance	-112	70	509	-76	-420	-254	146	553	476	-12	-91	-98	-101	-590
Export ratio (%) (1)	:	96.6	96.6	41.7	29.6	82.1	:	71.8	454.5	73.1	51.3	130.8	151.5	59.4
Import penetration ratio (%) (1)	:	96.4	95.8	90.9	74.4	85.2	:	60.0	-374.0	80.1	76.1	103.4	127.0	70.2
Cover ratio (%)	79.4	137.5	122.8	7.2	14.5	79.8	185.9	169.5	162.5	94.4	29.4	13.9	62.5	62.0

(1) DK, A (1994); P (1997).

Table 12.19

Manufacture of optical instruments and photographic equipment (NACE Rev. 1 33.4)

Labour related indicators, 1998

	EU-15	B	DK	D	EL	E	F	IRL	I	L	NL	A	P	FIN	S	UK
Personnel costs (million ECU) (1)	2,839	20	36	1,211	2	92	439	:	416	:	62	106	14	5	37	351
Personnel costs/employee (thousand ECU) (2)	32.6	30.8	:	42.5	12.3	24.0	33.6	:	21.7	:	:	33.9	:	29.1	36.6	21.8
Social charges/personnel costs (%) (3)	22.8	23.0	2.0	21.6	20.3	20.8	30.4	:	36.0	:	14.2	23.7	:	23.2	29.7	11.1
Labour productivity (thousand ECU/head) (3)	43.2	89.7	59.8	52.1	-9.9	26.5	39.0	:	61.3	:	:	34.9	:	26.0	39.7	53.0
Wage adjusted labour productivity (%) (2)	132.7	159.4	:	112.4	:	144.5	120.2	:	180.4	:	:	102.9	:	122.4	123.2	184.6

(1) DK, A (1994). (2) A (1994); EU-15, I (1995); B, D, E, F, FIN, S, UK (1996). (3) DK, A (1994); EU-15, S (1995).

Source: Eurostat (SBS, EBT)

(million ECU) Table 12.20

Manufacture of watches and clocks (NACE Rev. 1 33.5)

Production related indicators in the EU

	1988	1989	1990	1991	1992	1993	1994	1995	1996	1997	1998
Production value	1,470	1,549	1,753	1,606	1,638	1,455	1,511	1,425	:	:	:
Producer price index (1995=100)	87.6	90.0	91.5	93.7	96.2	98.9	100.3	100.0	:	:	:
Value added	620	634	685	623	650	619	623	544	:	:	:
Number of persons employed (thousands)	26.5	26.3	25.8	23.5	22.8	18.9	18.0	15.4	:	:	:

(million ECU) Table 12.21

Manufacture of watches and clocks (NACE Rev. 1 33.5)

Production related indicators, 1998

	B	DK	D	EL	E	F	IRL	I	L	NL	A	P	FIN	S	UK
Production value (1)	33	0	434	0	18	438	:	145	0	:	:	7	2	20	138
Value added (2)	13	0	188	0	7	177	:	60	0	:	:	:	1	7	66
Number of persons employed (units) (3)	142	0	4,440	0	363	5,074	:	650	0	:	:	248	12	181	1,663

(1) EL (1995); DK, L (1996); P (1997). (2) EL (1995); DK, L (1996). (3) EL (1995); DK, E, L (1996).

(million ECU) Table 12.22

Manufacture of watches and clocks (NACE Rev. 1 33.5)

Market related indicators in the EU

	1988	1989	1990	1991	1992	1993	1994	1995	1996	1997	1998
Apparent consumption	2,181	2,978	2,925	2,951	3,201	3,129	2,982	3,023	:	:	:
Exports	876	964	1,004	995	1,030	1,089	1,247	1,354	1,296	1,428	1,305
Imports	1,587	2,393	2,177	2,340	2,592	2,763	2,719	2,953	2,804	3,517	3,675
Trade balance	-711	-1,429	-1,172	-1,345	-1,563	-1,674	-1,472	-1,599	-1,508	-2,089	-2,370
Export ratio (%)	59.6	62.2	57.3	61.9	62.8	74.9	82.5	95.1	:	:	:
Import penetration ratio (%)	72.8	80.4	74.4	79.3	81.0	88.3	91.2	97.7	:	:	:
Cover ratio (%)	55.2	40.3	46.2	42.5	39.7	39.4	45.9	45.9	46.2	40.6	35.5

(million ECU) Table 12.23

Manufacture of watches and clocks (NACE Rev. 1 33.5)

Market related indicators, 1998

	B/L	DK	D	EL	E	F	IRL	I	NL	A	P	FIN	S	UK
Apparent consumption (1)	:	40	912	55	356	631	:	648	:	:	72	30	73	597
Exports	109	18	571	2	114	504	7	351	54	39	9	6	18	293
Imports	168	50	1,049	68	452	697	27	854	185	135	82	34	71	752
Trade balance	-59	-32	-478	-65	-338	-193	-20	-503	-130	-96	-74	-28	-53	-459
Export ratio (%) (1)	:	:	131.5	:	632.1	115.1	:	242.5	:	:	151.5	343.6	91.9	213.1
Import penetration ratio (%) (1)	:	162.0	115.0	102.0	126.9	110.5	:	131.9	:	:	104.7	114.1	97.8	126.1
Cover ratio (%)	64.7	35.9	54.4	3.2	25.1	72.4	26.5	41.1	29.4	29.1	10.5	17.4	25.9	39.0

(1) EL (1995); DK (1996); P (1997).

Table 12.24

Manufacture of watches and clocks (NACE Rev. 1 33.5)

Labour related indicators, 1998

	EU-15	B	DK	D	EL	E	F	IRL	I	L	NL	A	P	FIN	S	UK
Personnel costs (million ECU) (1)	447	4	0	157	0	6	151	:	19	0	:	:	2	0	5	37
Personnel costs/employee (thousand ECU) (2)	29.9	36.1	:	35.5	:	19.2	30.3	:	27.0	:	:	:	:	7.6	33.2	18.6
Social charges/personnel costs (%) (3)	21.4	26.0	:	16.9	:	23.2	28.0	:	39.6	:	:	:	:	11.1	:	10.6
Labour productivity (thousand ECU/head) (3)	35.2	88.5	:	42.3	:	18.0	34.9	:	92.6	:	:	:	:	56.1	38.5	39.4
Wage adjusted labour productivity (%) (2)	118.0	117.0	:	104.1	:	94.1	118.9	:	219.3	:	:	:	:	739.1	131.8	194.5

(1) EU-15, EL (1995); DK, E, L (1996). (2) EU-15, I (1995); B, D, E, F, FIN, S, UK (1996). (3) EU-15 (1995); E (1996).

Source: Eurostat (SBS, EBT)

Transport equipment industry

Industry description

The transport equipment industry covers the manufacturing of motor and non-motor driven vehicles. The NACE Rev. 1 classification of economic activities, distinguishes the manufacture of automobiles, including their parts, components and equipment (NACE Rev. 1 34), and the manufacture of other transport equipment (NACE Rev. 1 35) such as shipbuilding, railway equipment, aircraft, spacecraft, bicycles and motorcycles.

The transport equipment industry plays a considerable role in the European economy. It generated around 11% of the Union's total manufacturing output in 1998, just ahead of the chemical industry and only just behind the food, drink and tobacco industry (if EU manufacturing industries are ranked in order of magnitude). This activity is, for a number of reasons, a cornerstone of economic activity: efficient transport is an essential lubricant in the mechanics of economic flows; the vast expansion of international trade owes much to the emergence of fast and modern transport, communications and distribution channels. In addition, the transport equipment industry is of major importance to a large number of activities, such as metals, rubber, plastics, electronics and engineering. After having pioneered modern mass production processes in the first half of the century, this industry is today a leader in the use of leading-edge production and organisational techniques such as "lean" and "just-in time" production, "total quality management" or "continuous re-engineering".

(%) Figure 13.1

Transport equipment (NACE Rev. 1 34 and 35)
Share of EU value added in total manufacturing

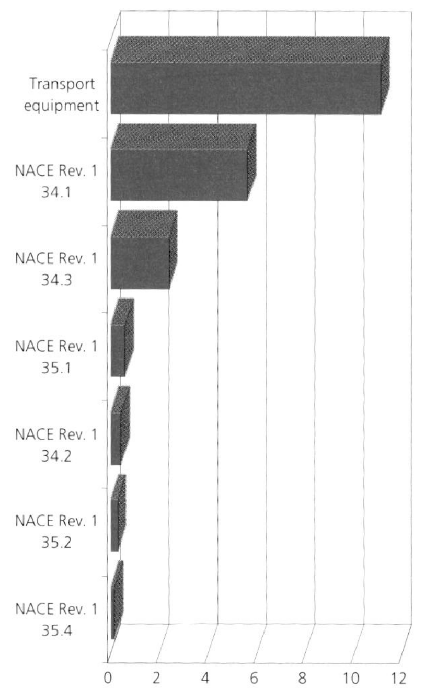

Source: Eurostat (SBS)

The activities covered in this chapter include:

34.1: manufacture of motor vehicles;
34.2: manufacture of bodies (coachwork) for motor vehicles; manufacture of trailers and semi-trailers;
34.3: manufacture of parts and accessories for motor vehicles and their engines;
35.1: building and repairing of ships and boats;
35.2: manufacture of railway and tramway locomotives and rolling stock;
35.3: manufacture of aircraft and spacecraft;
35.4: manufacture of motorcycles and bicycles;
35.5: manufacture of other transport equipment n.e.c.

Figure 13.2 (1988=100)

Transport equipment (NACE Rev. 1 34 and 35)

Production, employment and value added compared to EU total manufacturing

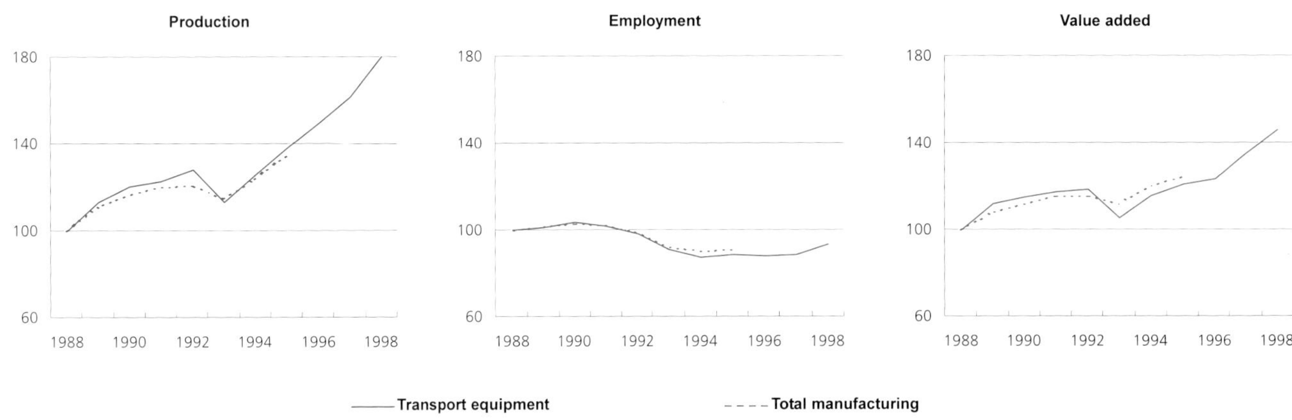

Source: Eurostat (SBS)

Looking at the structure of the industry by far the largest transport activity is the automotive industry. It makes up more than three-quarters of the production value generated within the transport equipment industry. A more detailed study reveals that half of the value added generated in the transport equipment industry is accounted for by the manufacture of motor vehicles, more than one fifth by the motor vehicles parts and accessories industry and around 14% by the manufacture of aircraft and spacecraft.

Only four Member States displayed a markedly higher than the average specialisation in this activity. They were Spain, France, Sweden and Germany. In contrast, Ireland and Greece displayed production specialisation ratios below 20%.

Recent trends

The transport equipment industry has historically witnessed high rates of growth, especially in the motor vehicle industry. Between 1985 and 1992, production value grew in excess of 60% in nominal terms and value added by 40%, whilst employment remained stable.

1993 saw a sharp decline in economic activity for all indicators. For many countries, 1993 marked the worst annual figures for the whole of the post-war period. Production and value added fell by 11% in real terms, and employment by some 8%. The recovery in the following years was almost as dramatic: within the four years that followed, production value and value added grew by around 30% in real terms. Meanwhile, employment levels did not change.

Employment indicators outline the difficult structural adjustments that the industry has experienced during the nineties. Despite the high rates of growth experienced in the past decade (with the exception of 1993), the 1998 employment level was still 12% lower than the corresponding figure of 1985. In absolute terms, this represented a loss of some 340 thousand jobs across the fifteen Member States. Job losses were largely recorded in the automotive, aerospace and shipbuilding industries.

Transport equipment activities are faced with higher than average hourly labour costs. Eurostat's latest update to its Labour Cost Survey (1996) reveals that they are on average fifteen to twenty per cent higher than the typical manufacturing activity. The highest

Figure 13.3

Transport equipment (NACE Rev. 1 34 and 35)

International comparison of main indicators in current prices

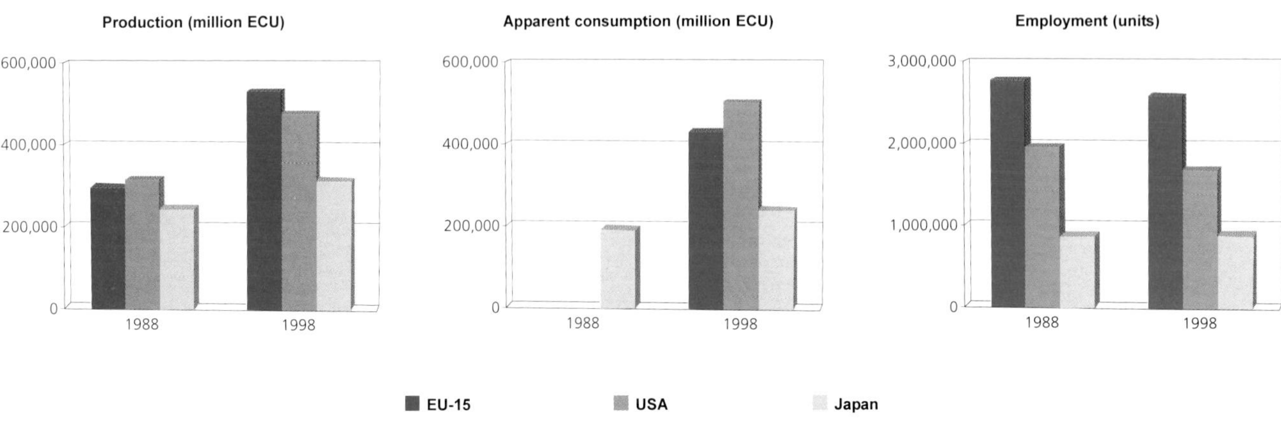

Source: Eurostat (SBS)

(ECU/hour) Figure 13.4

Transport equipment (NACE Rev. 1 34 and 35)
Labour costs by Member State, 1996

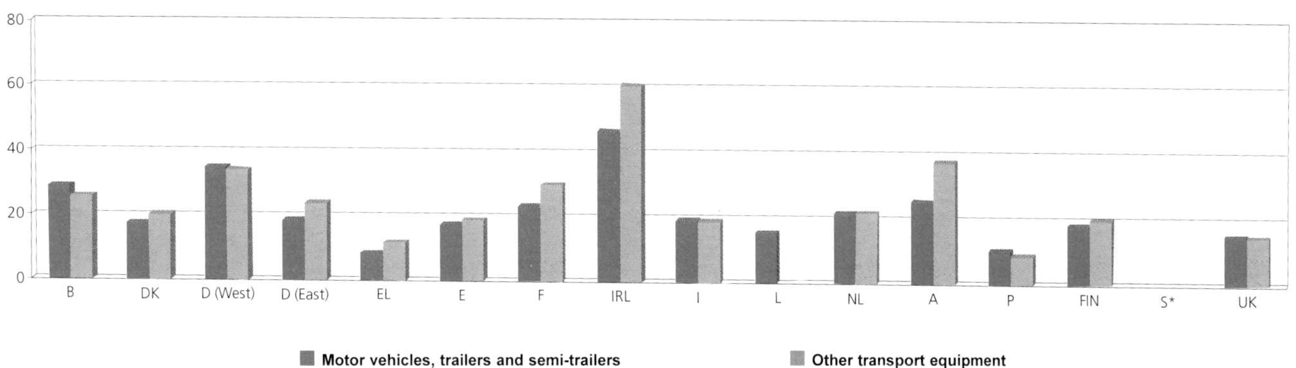

Source: Eurostat (LCS)

level is reached in Germany (excluding the former Eastern Länder) and Belgium with 36 ECU and 28 ECU per hour respectively, some 20% and 14% more than the average for manufacturing activities in those two countries. Portugal displayed the lowest hourly labour costs at 9 ECU, although it should be noted that this was 50% higher than the costs faced by the average Portuguese manufacturing enterprise.

Regarding the composition of the labour force in the transport equipment industry we can see that it is largely the domain of males. The male labour force accounted for 82.6% of the total in 1996. Another trend that may be observed is that the labour force is almost entirely composed of full-time employees. Despite the trend towards more flexible working patterns within the workplace environment, there remained more than 95% of the labour force working full-time across the transport equipment industry (ranging from nearly 93% in the Netherlands to over 99% in Spain). There was a fairly normal distribution of qualifications, with around 25% of the labour force possessing a higher education.

The combination of job losses and high growth rates in value added contributed to a steady improvement in productivity. Value added per person employed grew between 1993 and 1998 by an annual average rate of 6% in real terms, more than 56 thousand ECU per head in 1998. That same year, value added exceeded personnel costs by almost 50%, a level thirty percentage points higher than in 1993 and the highest ratio since 1985 (the earliest year available).

In terms of market share, the EU transport industry gained ground when compared to the USA and Japan. In 1985, producers of the fifteen Member States accounted for about 31% of Triad production. By 1998, the share had increased to 37%, largely at the expense of the USA, whose share fell by five percentage points to 38%. The Japanese share remained stable at around 25%. Despite this improvement in the market share of the EU, the value added generated by European manufacturers remained much lower than in the USA. It represented only 34% of the total value added accounted for by the transport equipment industry in the Triad, compared to 44% in the USA. It is interesting to note that whilst production value is similar between EU-15 and the USA, value added is much lower in Europe and the European transport equipment industry employs 50% more persons than in the USA (equivalent to some 900 thousand persons).

The EU represented 36% of the Triad's demand for transport equipment in 1998, down from 39% in 1990. This was largely the consequence of tremendous growth experienced in the USA, where demand grew by 57% over the period, compared to an increase of only 25% within the EU.

(%) Table 13.1

Transport equipment (NACE Rev. 1 34 and 35)
Composition of the labour force, 1997

	Females	Part-time	Highly-educated
EU-15	:	:	:
B	15.4	:	9.4
DK	19.5	:	14.9
D	15.8	3.4	21.7
EL	:	:	12.2
E	8.1	:	25.5
F	15.3	3.8	18.0
IRL	18.0	1.1	32.4
I	17.4	1.6	5.0
L	:	:	:
NL	9.9	7.4	13.6
A	12.4	:	:
P	30.1	:	5.3
FIN	11.3	:	:
S	15.4	4.4	19.7
UK	14.1	2.8	19.8

Source: Eurostat (LFS)

Foreign trade

Data on foreign trade illustrates the expansion of international activities within the European transport equipment industry. Extra-EU exports measured in current prices have doubled in the last ten years, whilst the share of production that is exported to countries outside the EU has increased by 50%. In 1990, 15% of EU production of transport equipment was destined for countries outside of the Union, a figure that subsequently expanded to 24% by 1998. Aerospace is, by far, the most export-orientated of the NACE Rev. 1 Groups, with 63% of EU aerospace production leaving for non-EU countries. Shipbuilding's analogous figure stands at 36%. The motorcycles and bicycles industry recorded the lowest export ratio, at 12% of 1998 production.

Import penetration within the transport equipment industry has also become more important. In 1988, only 9% of EU apparent consumption was accounted for by non-EU producers. By 1998, the figure had risen to 16%. Enterprises within the aerospace activity are particularly subject to competition from imports, where they account for more than half of apparent consumption. One other activity where imports make up a large share of the market is the motorcycle and bicycle industry, where they accounted for more than 35% of consumption. In contrast, imports from non-EU countries satisfied just 4% of the EU's railway equipment market and only 8.6% of the motor vehicles market (nevertheless, there are a large number of examples of foreign direct investment by non-EU countries within Europe in this particular industry).

Figure 13.5 (million ECU)

Transport equipment (NACE Rev. 1 34 and 35)
Foreign net direct investment

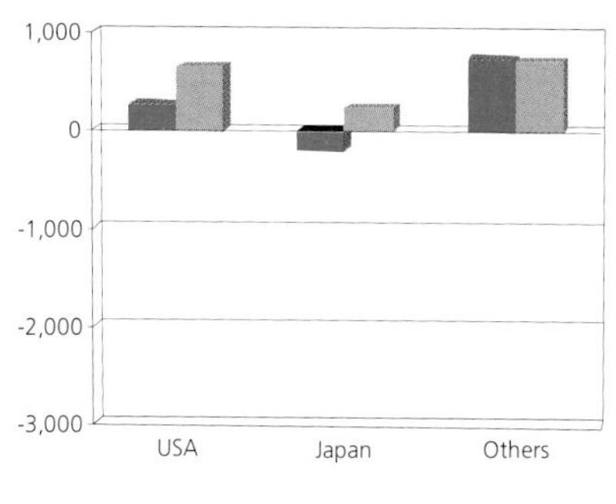

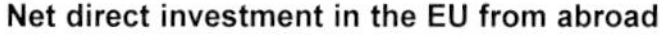

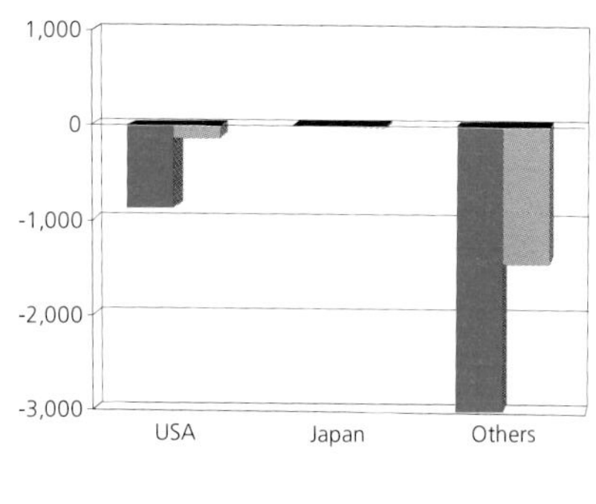

1988 1998

Source: Eurostat (BOP)

Overall, the data reveals that the European transport equipment industry has a positive trade balance. Between 1988 and 1998, EU exports exceeded imports by an average of 60%, the smallest difference occurring in 1991, when exports were only 30% higher than imports. The highest difference was recorded in 1995, when exports were almost double[1] the size of imports (90%). In 1998, the trade surplus exceeded 46 billion ECU, of which 60% was accounted for by motor vehicles and one-fifth by automotive components and parts.

1) Such variability can be attributed (in part) to the variability in exchange rates between Member States and third countries.

The main trading partners of the EU are the United States and Japan. Nevertheless, in recent years there has been an increasing level of import penetration from producers in South Korea and Eastern Europe (where a number of European car manufacturers have either set-up plants or bought-out existing companies).

Almost one third of the EU's exports of transport equipment went to the USA in 1998. Second in the ranking was Saudi Arabia, where a large number of aerospace contracts have recently been awarded to European manufacturers. Railway exports to China more than trebled during the period 1995-1998, reaching a value of 125 million ECU.

Motor vehicles (NACE Rev. 1 34.1 and 34.2)

NACE Rev. 1 34.1 and NACE Rev. 1 34.2 cover the manufacture and assembly of motor vehicles, which include passenger cars as well as commercial vehicles. This activity makes up the biggest share of the transport equipment industry. It accounts for half the total value added generated in the European transport equipment industry and more than two thirds of the automotive industry. Sweden, Germany, France and Spain are comparatively more specialised in this activity than the EU average. In these countries, motor vehicles production accounted for 9% to 11% of total manufacturing, compared with the EU-15 average of 7.5%.

The European passenger car market has grown steadily over the last twenty years. Demand slowed down in the early 1990s, and 1993 saw a large decline in sales for most European markets (-17% for the EU as a whole). This was followed by a gradual recovery in demand. In 1997 new car registrations increased by 5% and in 1998 they rose by a further 10%, to exceed more than 14.3 million units, approximately one-third of total world production and the highest level recorded in the 1990s. Average car ownership figures vary widely across the Member States. In 1997 the number of cars per thousand inhabitants exceeded 500 units in Luxembourg, Italy and Germany. In contrast, Greece, Portugal and Ireland saw car ownership rates at less than 300 cars per 1,000 inhabitants. In the long-term, as the motorisation rate continues to grow, demand for cars may be expected to rise.

(units) Figure 13.6

Number of cars per thousand inhabitants, 1997

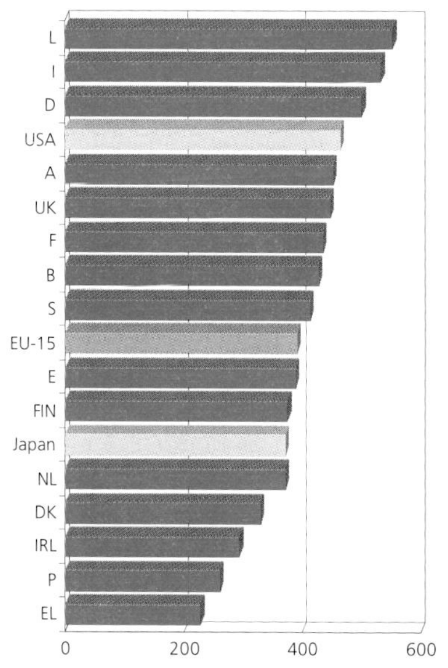

Source: VDA

Figure 13.7

Motor vehicles (NACE Rev. 1 34.1 and 34.2)

Production and employment in the Triad

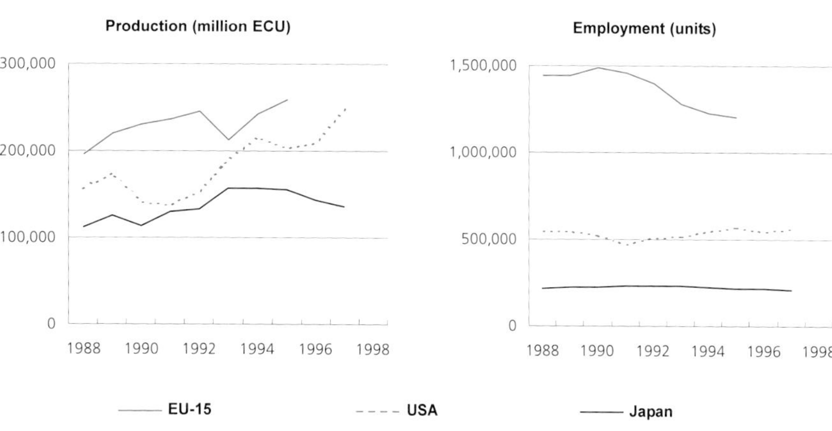

Source: Eurostat (SBS)

(%) Figure 13.8

Motor vehicles (NACE Rev. 1 34.1 and 34.2)

Production and export specialisation by Member State, 1998

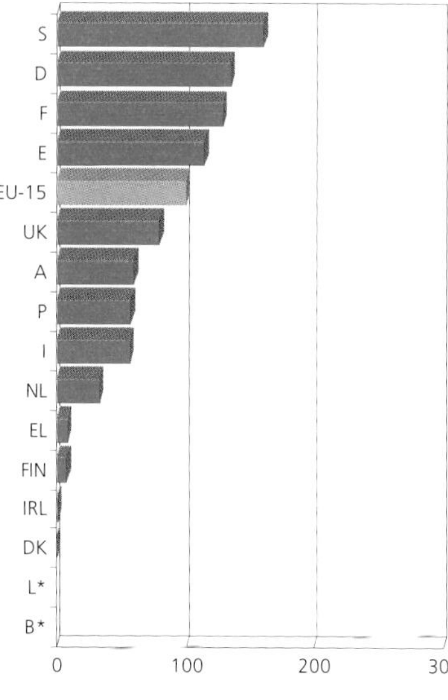

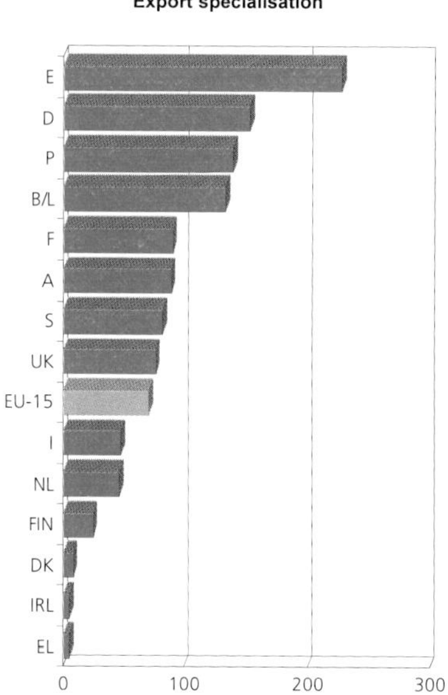

Source: Eurostat (SBS)

As far as commercial vehicles are concerned (light commercial vehicles, trucks and buses), demand is highly correlated with the level of economic activity, and more specifically for trucks by the competitiveness of road haulage with respect to other transport modes. Over the past two decades, the road haulage industry has consistently gained market share at the expense of rail and inland waterways and this trend may be expected to continue. Whilst the first half of the decade saw a cyclical downturn in EU unit sales of trucks, the second half witnessed a general recovery, marked in 1995 by a 20% rise in new registrations. Despite this upturn, new registrations of commercial vehicles were in 1996 still 10% below their level of 1990 at 1.6 million units.

Productivity improvements (value added per person employed) rose by 26% in real terms between 1993 and 1998, restructuring and rationalisation have all contributed to a steady decline in the level of employment in the industry. Total employment in the EU vehicle assembly industry fell from over 1.3 million in 1990 to 1.1 million by 1998, a reduction of almost 20%. Despite this sharp fall, the EU still accounted for 70% of motor vehicle industry employment within the Triad, whilst registering less than half of the production value.

Imports accounted for 9% of total EU consumption and exports to countries outside the EU accounted for 18% of production in 1998 (in both cases a sharp increase compared to a decade before). Figures across the Triad also revealed substantial differences: in the USA the import penetration ratio exceeded 30% and almost half of all Japanese production was exported.

The EU is a net exporter and this industry is an important contributor to the EU's trade balance. Between 1992 and 1998 the surplus has been multiplied by a factor 3.5, from 7.6 billion ECU to 27.2 billion ECU[2]. Nevertheless, the surplus is still lower than in Japan (48 billion ECU in 1998). In the USA, motor vehicles recorded a large negative trade balance (-58 billion ECU in 1998).

The Japanese share of EU car imports in unit terms has fallen by more than 22% between 1988 and 1997, but in value terms the decline was just 11%, which could indicate a move towards higher-end products. However, the increase in the number of Japanese vehicles assembled in Europe helped offset the fall in volume terms of imports. Indeed, whilst the market share of Japanese car manufacturers remained stable between 1990 (11.9%) and 1997 (11.5%), the market share of those cars produced in and imported from Japan fell from 10.5% to 6.5%. Meanwhile, imports from South Korea increased sharply during the same period, expanding by 2% in 1997 (equivalent to 271 thousand units). There has been a marked rise in the level of imports from the USA to Europe in recent years, from 5.7% in 1989 to 10.0% of imports in 1997. This can in part be explained by the fact that some EU car manufacturers such as BMW, Mercedes and VW have invested in production facilities in the NAFTA area. As this capacity comes on stream, the EU trade surplus with North America could be further reduced.

2) These figures cover total extra-EU exports. Hence, they include both exports of European producers and foreign manufacturers who have established production facilities within the EU.

Figure 13.9 (units)

New car registrations

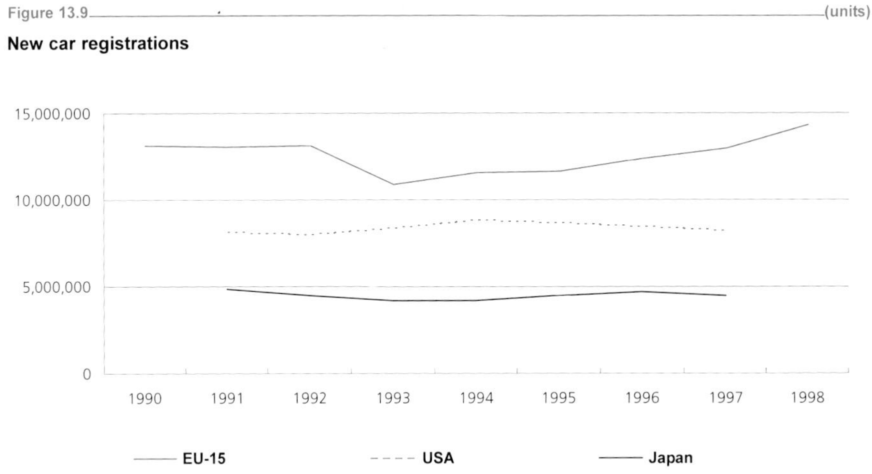

Source: ACEA, VDA for USA and Japan

In recent years, car manufacturers have taken a series of measures in order to achieve global standards of competitiveness that have dramatically changed the face of the world car industry. "Lean manufacturing" techniques have been widely adopted, resulting in lower levels of vertical integration that significantly modified the nature of the relationship between vehicle manufacturers, suppliers and dealers. These changes imply a restructuring of the automotive components supply chain with ramifications for production processes and logistics. It is now common for the level of co-operation between vehicle manufacturers and suppliers to extend to joint development of complete subsystems and assemblies, and their supply to the assembly plant on a just-in-time basis.

Figure 13.10 (units)

Top-10 world producers

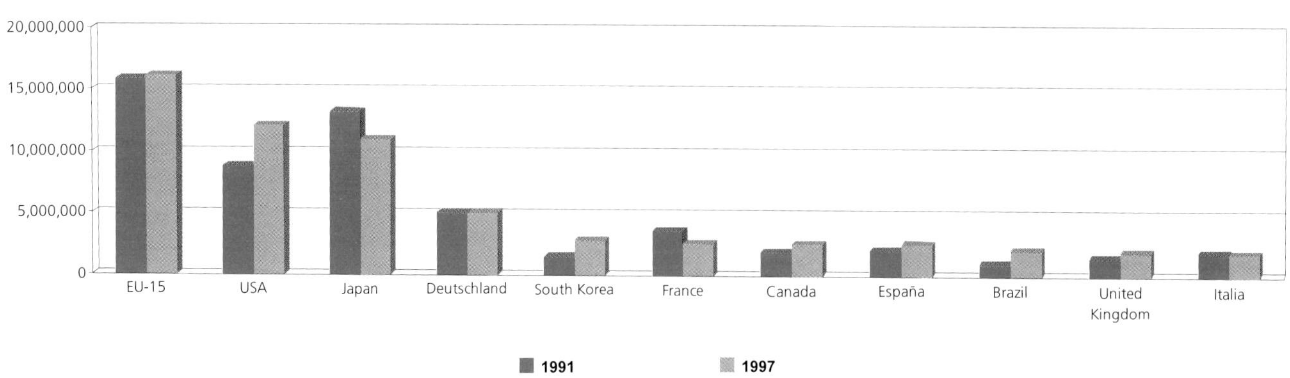

Source: VDA

On the side of the workforce, shorter reporting lines, improved interfaces with management and better communication systems are contributing to the successful implementation of Total Quality Management, Quality Circles and Continuous Improvement programmes, with gains in productivity and quality. Flexible shift working is already leading to better utilisation of plant and equipment. Improvement in flexibility through reduction in machine set-up times, optimisation of batch sizes and reductions in raw materials, work in progress and finished goods inventories are all part of common improvement programmes. Benefits have included a reduction in the development time from the initial concept to production, as well as increased flexibility and responsiveness to market conditions.

Finally, the industry has witnessed a large number of take-overs, which culminated in 1998 with the merger of Daimler-Benz (Germany) with Chrysler (USA). Other mergers and acquisitions included Ford taking a significant stake in Mazda and buying Jaguar and Volvo's passenger car business, BMW's take-over of Rover and Rolls-Royce and Volkswagen's acquisition of Seat, Skoda, Bentley and Lamborghini. Indeed, partnerships and alliances are increasingly regarded as providing the most cost-effective method of developing a competitive product portfolio, lessening dependence on domestic markets and reducing excess capacity.

Figure 13.11

New car registrations in the EU by country of origin of manufacturer, EU-15

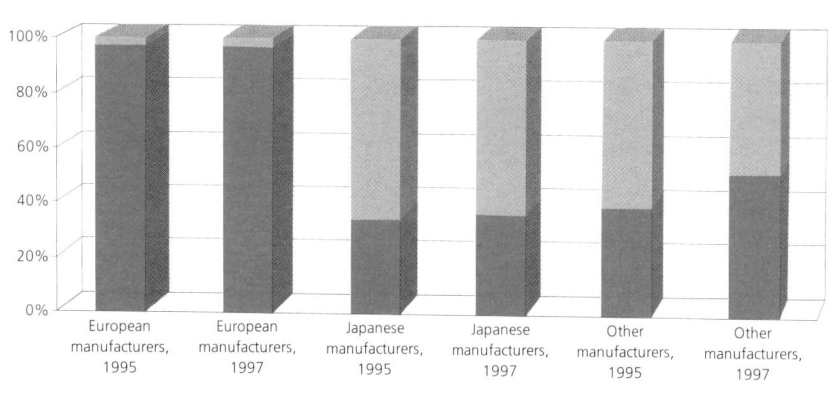

Source: VDA

Figure 13.12

Motor vehicles (NACE Rev. 1 34.1 and 34.2)
Destination of EU exports, 1998

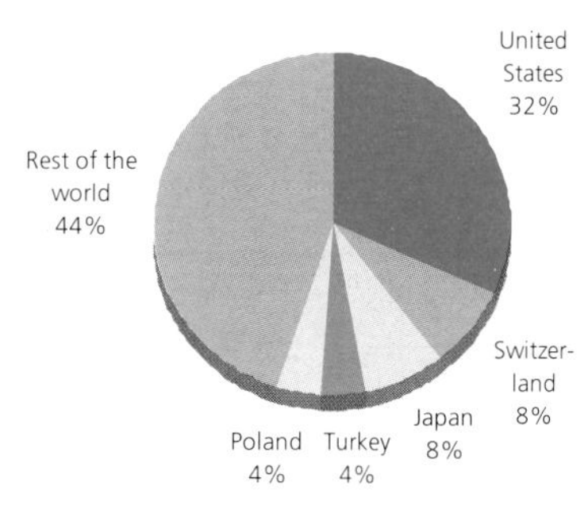

Source: Eurostat (Comext)

Figure 13.13

Motor vehicles (NACE Rev. 1 34.1 and 34.2)
Origin of EU imports, 1998

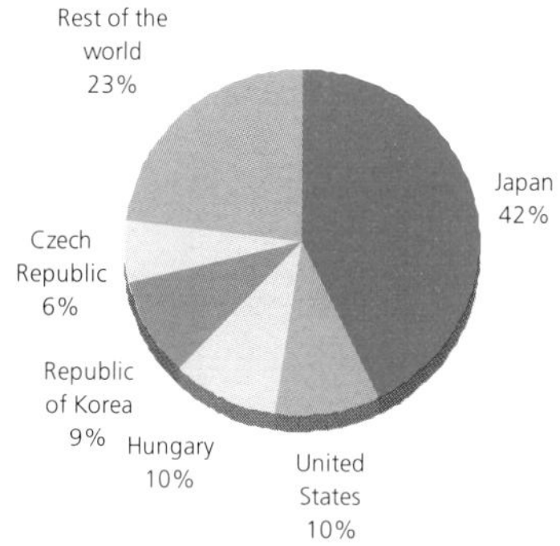

Rest of the world 23%
Japan 42%
Czech Republic 6%
Republic of Korea 9%
Hungary 10%
United States 10%

Source: Eurostat (Comext)

Motor vehicle parts and accessories (NACE Rev. 1 34.3)

The parts and accessories market is traditionally broken down into two main segments. Firstly, the market for original equipment, that is parts that car manufacturers buy from specialised producers for assembly into new vehicles. It accounts for roughly three-quarters of production. Secondly, the replacement market or after-market, which comprises parts destined for maintenance and repairs and automotive accessories. From a statistical point of view, however, the coverage of the motor vehicle parts and accessories industry in terms of products is difficult to assess. Data that correspond to NACE Rev. 1 34.3 excludes, for instance, tyre manufacturers who supply vehicle manufacturers, as well as most of the electrical and electronic components that are so important in vehicle manufacturing today. Even with these exceptions, the industry still generates more than one fifth of the total value added of the European transport equipment industry. Production specialisation ratios single out Portugal, Germany and Spain as the Member States where the relative share of this activity in the national manufacturing total is markedly higher than the European average.

Automotive components' demand is linked to the level of motor vehicle production. However, some components benefit from much faster growth than the auto market in general. This situation exists where a component's rate of penetration is still on the rise. For example, where equipment that was previously optional is now fitted as standard on most models, such as anti-lock brakes, air bags, air conditioning systems and anti-theft devices (which now fall under European Commission legislation). In addition, component manufacturers have benefited from a trend towards increased out-sourcing.

Demand for replacement parts also depends on the market for used cars and other motor vehicles as opposed to new sales. Demand is likely to be more stable in this market than in the original equipment market. The replacement parts market differs greatly from country to country, due to a number of reasons: these include the annual mileage per vehicle, the average age of the car and the existence of specific legislation with regard to the obligatory inspection of vehicles when they reach a certain age.

Figure 13.14

Motor vehicle parts and accessories (NACE Rev. 1 34.3)
Production and employment in the Triad

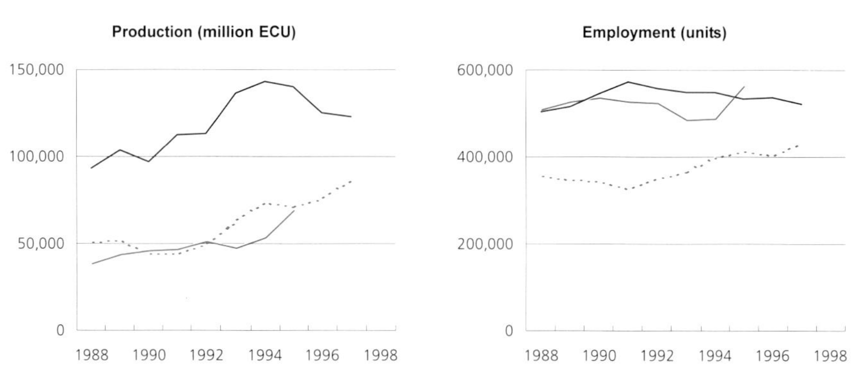

Source: Eurostat (SBS)

Figure 13.15 (%)

Motor vehicle parts and accessories (NACE Rev. 1 34.3)
Production and export specialisation by Member State, 1998

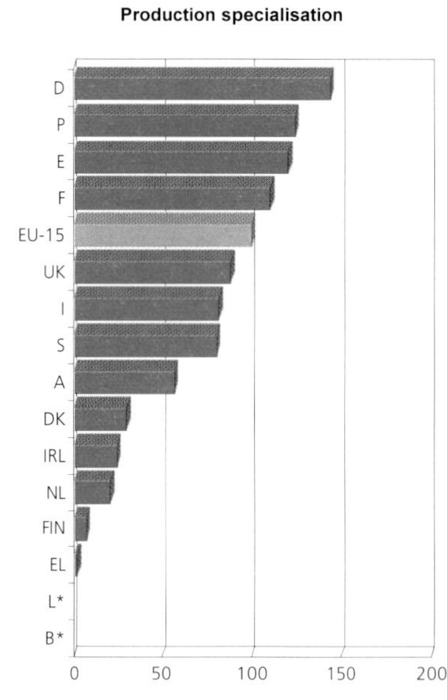

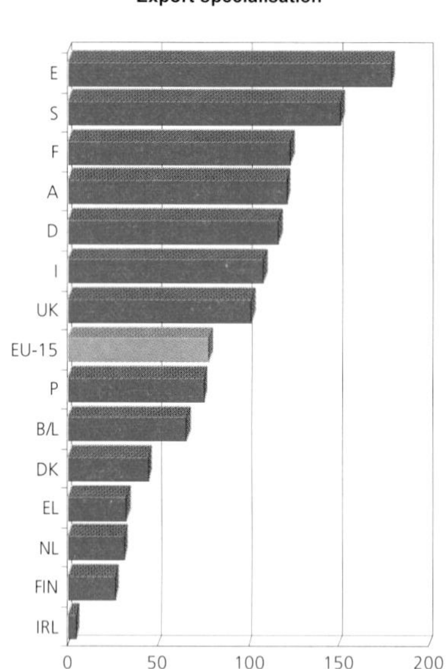

Source: Eurostat (SBS)

Overall, the demand for motor vehicle parts and accessories, as measured by apparent consumption has risen by as much as 80% between 1990 and 1998 compared with an increase of only 20% for motor vehicles. Employment also witnessed rising trends: 73 thousand jobs were created during the same period in this activity, an increase of 14%, which may be compared to the 20% reduction recorded by automobile manufacturers.

On the international field, the automotive components industry is decidedly export-orientated. No less than one fifth of the EU's production value was destined for third countries in 1998. Imports from non-EU countries corresponded to 11% of consumption in 1998. The trade balance reached 8.4 billion ECU, double its level of 1990, with the cover ratio rising to above 200% for most of the past decade.

The structure of trade of the EU for this activity lies somewhere between the situation observed in the USA and Japan. On the one hand, the USA recorded an import penetration ratio and export rate of close to 30% with balanced trade flows. On the other hand, just 2% of the Japanese market was accounted for by imports. The Japanese export ratio was equal to 13% of production in 1998, resulting in a large trade surplus (15 billion ECU).

The supply of original equipment is undergoing fundamental structural change. The increasing levels of internationalisation of vehicle manufacture have led to the emergence of large international component manufacturers. In addition, the relationship between manufacturers and suppliers is being substantially modified. A rising share of the value added generated in the auto industry is being transferred from vehicle to component manufacturers. A major reason behind such a change arises from the necessity for car manufacturers to limit investments and resources to essential activities, which represent the core of their industry. One method is to increase outsourcing and to pass on the responsibility for product development, manufacturing and quality assurance functions to suppliers (systems suppliers and/or specialised affiliated companies). Component producers contribute to the competitiveness of the industry, and the two industries have become increasingly interdependent.

Modularisation is another key theme of the components industry. The module supplier assembles several components into a module, which are delivered on a just-in-time basis to a vehicle assembly plant. Unlike systems suppliers, the module supplier may not manufacture any of the components delivered and possesses only assembly and logistical skills. The result is that car manufacturers reduce the number of their suppliers, who in turn out-source part of their output to smaller companies, with the whole supply chain forming a tiered structure. This process is having a dramatic impact on the number of independent automotive suppliers. Vehicle manufacturers are cutting back on the number of direct suppliers, in some cases by more than half. Whereas a typical car manufacturing plant might have taken deliveries from 1,000 or more suppliers ten years ago, it now uses fewer than 200.

Figure 13.16

Motor vehicle parts and accessories (NACE Rev. 1 34.3) Destination of EU exports, 1998

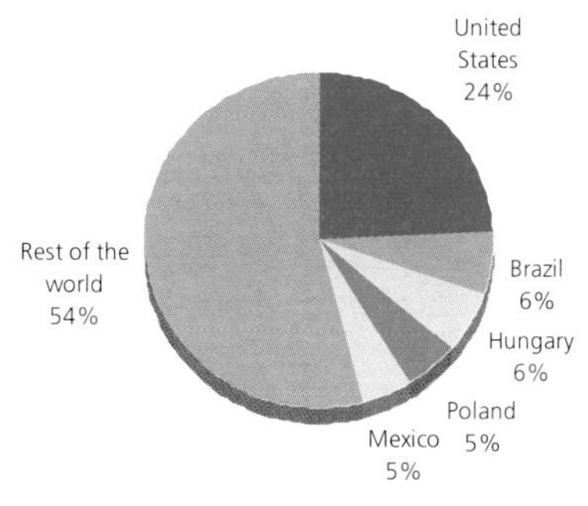

Source: Eurostat (Comext)

Figure 13.17

Motor vehicle parts and accessories (NACE Rev. 1 34.3) Origin of EU imports, 1998

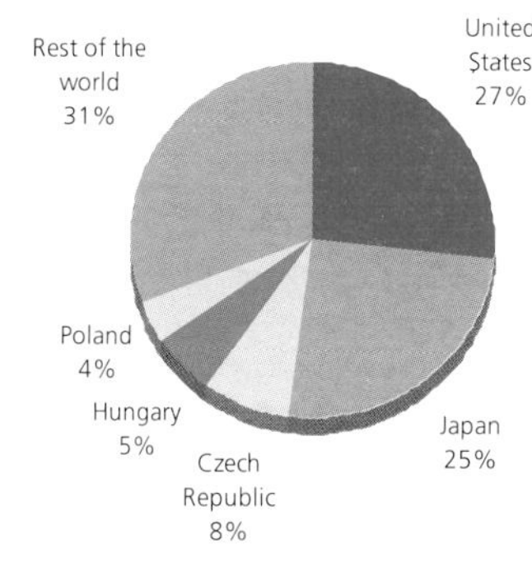

Source: Eurostat (Comext)

Motorcycles and bicycles (NACE Rev. 1 35.4)

The motorcycle and bicycle industry is categorised under Group 35.4 of the NACE Rev. 1 activity classification. It comprises the manufacturing of motorcycles and mopeds (NACE Rev. 1 35.41), the manufacturing of bicycles (NACE Rev. 1 35.42) and the manufacturing of invalid carriages (NACE Rev. 1 35.43).

The motorcycle and bicycle industry represents a very small share of European industry and is the smallest of all transport equipment manufacturing activities. It accounted for less than 2% of the value added and employment of transport equipment in most Member States in 1998, and less than 0.2% of the value added generated in the whole of European manufacturing. Some countries however displayed a significantly high specialisation ratio in cycle manufacturing. This was particularly true in the case of Italy, a country where the sector accounted in 1998 for almost 8% of the value added generated in the manufacturing of transport equipment, and one-quarter of the value added of transport equipment other than motor vehicles and their parts and accessories. The Netherlands also boasted high specialisation ratios in the cycle industry relative to the EU average. Countries with low specialisation ratios included Germany and the United Kingdom.

The value of motorcycle and bicycle production in the EU could not be computed in the absence of statistics for Belgium, Greece, Ireland, Luxembourg and Austria. If we exclude these countries, production value reached 7.8 billion ECU in the EU in 1998, a progression of 14% over the year before. The largest motorcycle and bicycle producer in the EU was clearly Italy. In 1998, production value in Italy reached 4 billion ECU, far ahead of a group of three countries, Germany, Spain and France, where production values ranged between 850 and 900 million ECU. The evolution of motorcycle and bicycle production followed a positive trend over the last decade, despite a slowdown between 1991 and 1993. The trend is strongly correlated to Italian output, given its predominant weight. In Italy, the annual average growth rate of production value between 1988 and 1993 was equal to 6.8%, a rate that was almost multiplied by two in the years between 1993 and 1998 at 12.9%. Overall, the second half of the decade has been particularly buoyant for motorcycle and bicycle production in the EU, with several countries boasting double-digit annual growth rates, topped by Spain, with a growth rate of 18% per annum. Some countries, however, performed clearly worse than the average. This was the case in France, that had yet to recover from the severe crisis suffered at the start of the nineties, with production value in 1998 that was in current prices only 5% above its level of 1990. The same was true in Germany, where production value declined by more than 5% per annum between 1993 and 1998.

Figure 13.18

Motorcycles and bicycles (NACE Rev. 1 34.4)
Production and employment in the Triad

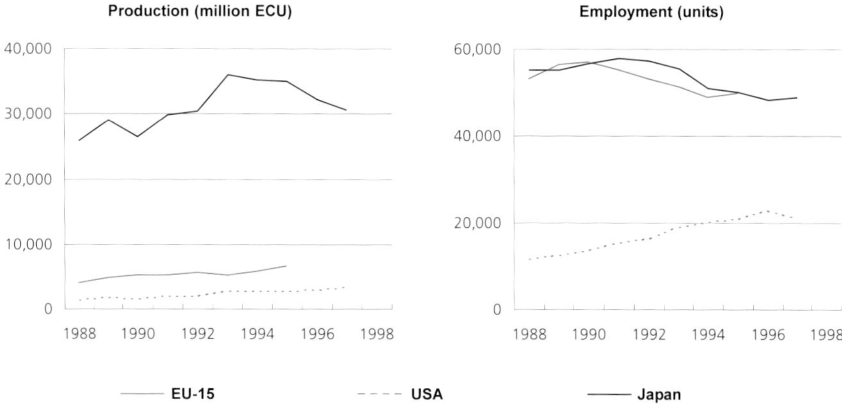

Source: Eurostat (SBS)

Figure 13.19 (%)

Motorcycles and bicycles (NACE Rev. 1 34.4)
Production and export specialisation by Member State, 1998

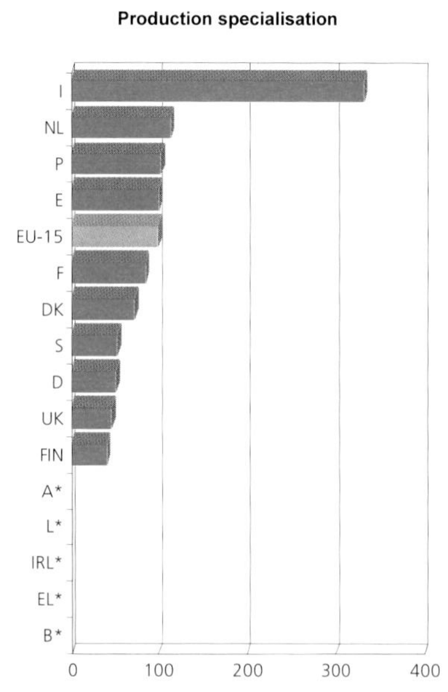

Export specialisation

I, E, NL, P, F, A, B/L, DK, D, EU-15, EL, UK, S, IRL, FIN

0 100 200 300 400

Source: Eurostat (SBS)

Demand for motorcycles and mopeds was driven by a number of factors including overall economic conditions and personal disposable income, but it was also supported by increased restrictions on automobile access to sections of certain European city centres, as a way to ameliorate problems of congestion and pollution. Figures from the European Association of Motorcycle Manufacturers (ACEM) indicate that the number of registrations progressed from 496 thousand in 1987 to 696 thousand in 1996, growth equal to 40%. In absolute terms, France, Italy and Germany each shared about one-fifth of the 14 million motorcycles and mopeds in use in the EU in 1996. In relative terms, the highest penetration rate of "two-wheelers" was recorded in Greece with no less than 184 units per thousand inhabitants, far ahead of Portugal (78) and Austria (69). The lowest penetration was found in Ireland and Denmark, with less than 10 motorcycles or mopeds per thousand inhabitants.

Turning to the bicycle market, demand is mainly driven by recreational considerations: leisure, the desire to keep fit and fashion. In addition, as in the case of motorcycles, the use of bicycles has also become an important alternative source of transportation for many people, particularly in larger cities with traffic congestion problems. Some towns and cities have designated certain portions of their streets as bicycle lanes, exclusively for two-wheeled traffic. Despite this, the European Bicycle Manufacturers Association (EBMA) estimate that bicycle consumption in Europe has steadily declined since 1994. More than 18 million bicycles were sold that year in the EU against only 14.9 million in 1997, a reduction of nearly 20%. Nevertheless, some markets recorded a rising trend over the same period, such as Belgium and Luxembourg (14%), Ireland and the Netherlands (8%) or Finland and Denmark (more than 20%).

(units) Table 13.2

Number of motorcycle registrations

	1987	1990	1991	1992	1993	1994	1995	1996
EU-15 (1)	495,981	631,372	643,693	657,397	587,966	557,687	582,856	695,642
B	6,518	9,276	11,183	13,231	14,827	14,000	14,603	15,330
DK	1,935	1,636	1,651	1,181	1,652	2,022	2,288	3,020
D	96,608	111,206	144,063	175,911	204,936	216,205	218,249	271,773
EL	8,235	24,023	21,771	24,092	23,033	23,099	24,789	27,253
E	56,651	113,317	113,683	96,805	48,338	33,285	32,877	30,713
F	93,087	125,227	115,391	115,590	99,691	84,870	85,112	116,125
IRL	2,802	2,684	3,197	2,884	1,914	1,837	1,911	2,412
I	138,347	130,332	129,606	123,437	90,482	82,771	89,762	100,089
L	:	:	:	:	:	712	985	963
NL	9,561	15,499	19,981	22,608	23,056	18,374	17,799	17,010
A	9,313	10,298	11,214	12,661	15,055	16,789	18,704	21,144
P	5,781	7,935	10,543	17,310	18,171	14,237	22,962	23,416
FIN	3,229	5,116	3,215	2,025	1,230	852	1,006	1,304
S	5,952	6,042	6,389	5,677	4,611	3,903	4,380	5,762
UK	57,962	68,781	51,806	43,985	40,970	44,731	47,429	59,328
NO	3,893	536	610	829	1,664	2,331	2,824	3,540
CH	29,947	33,909	31,488	30,947	30,053	28,457	29,524	33,893

(1) Excluding Luxembourg until 1993.

Source: ACEM

European production covers only three-quarters of consumption. EBMA estimate that about 11.4 million bicycles were produced in the EU in 1997, down from 14 million three years before. Traditionally, the two largest European producers have been Italy and Germany. Over the decade Italy superseded Germany as Europe's main producer. In 1997 the combined output of these two countries represented more than half of EU production, with 3.4 million units in Italy and 2.8 million in Germany. France and the United Kingdom were the next largest bicycle manufacturers in the EU, with 1.3 million units produced in each country in 1997.

Producers from Far Eastern countries, notably Taiwan, represented 54% of the total number of bicycles imported from extra-EU countries in 1997. These imports provide fierce competition within the European market, building on significant labour cost advantages. As a means to counteract this advantage, some EU manufacturers have relocated productive assets to countries with cheaper labour costs. In parallel, the low-cost competition has forced European producers to migrate towards the expensive end of the product spectrum. Moreover, there has been a gradual transformation in distribution channels within the European bicycle sector. Whereas in the past, bicycles were distributed largely through speciality shops, today an increasing share of bicycles are sold in large department stores, hypermarkets, or by mail order.

Employment in the motorcycle and bicycle sector declined in most Member States over the last decade. Between 1990 and 1998, the number of persons employed fell by 20% to 30% in the majority of Member States. The largest reduction was recorded in Spain, where the number of persons employed plummeted from 4.2 thousand in 1990 down to 1.7 thousand in 1998. Only Denmark and Italy registered increases in employment, modest in the case of Denmark (7%), but significant in the case of Italy where total employment rose to more than 24 thousand persons in 1998, up from 17.6 thousand in 1990.

(units) Figure 13.20

Number of motorcycles and mopeds in use per thousand inhabitants, 1996

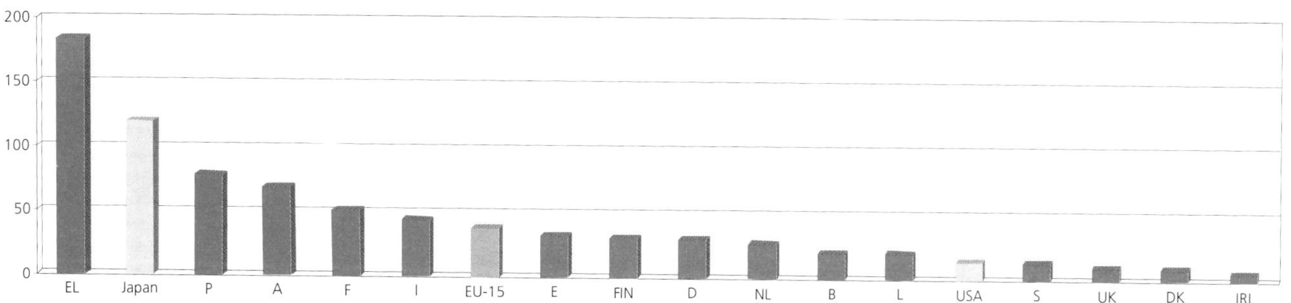

Source: IRF (World Road Statistics 1998)

Figure 13.21 (units)

Production and consumption of bicycles in the EU, 1997

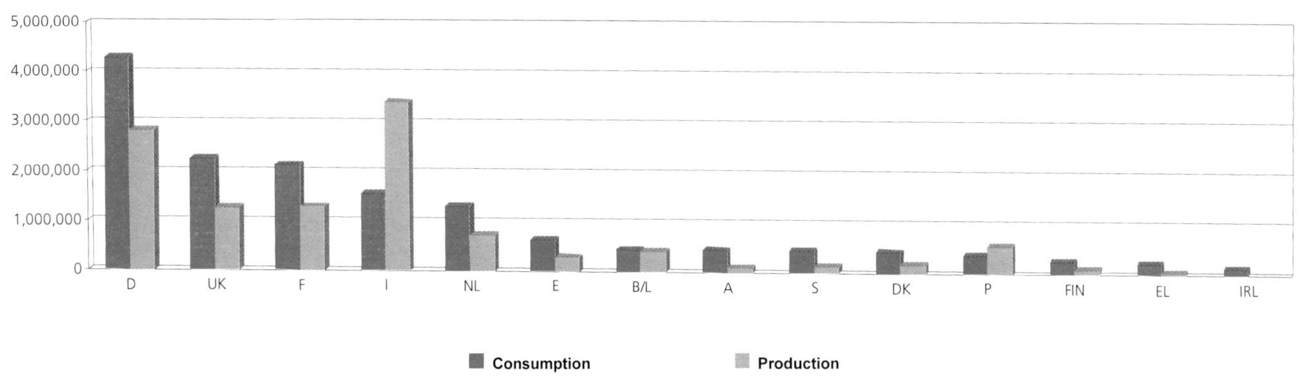

Source: EBMA

Figure 13.22 (1994=100)

Foreign trade of bicycles

160
140
120
100
80
1994
1995
1996
1997

Extra-EU imports
Imports from the USA
Imports from Taiwan

Source: EBMA

Figure 13.23

Motorcycles and bicycles (NACE Rev. 1 34.4)
Destination of EU exports, 1998

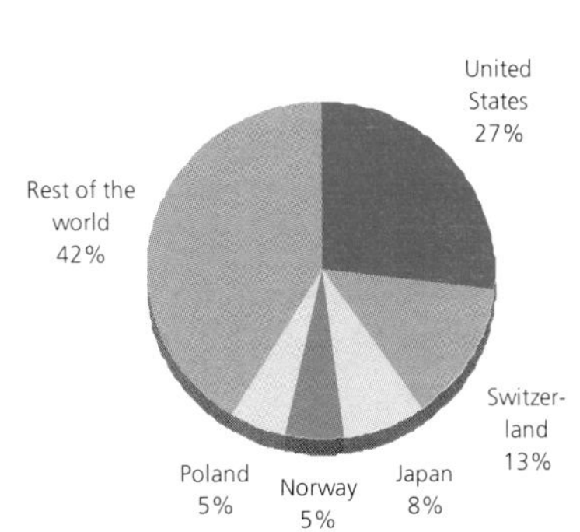

Source: Eurostat (Comext)

Europe is highly dependent on imports to satisfy its internal demand for motorcycles and bicycles. Foreign trade statistics are available for 1998 for all Member States, showing a large negative balance for most Member States and import penetration ratios well above 60%, with the exception of Italy. For the euro-zone[3] countries, the deficit reached 2 billion ECU. The situation was similar in the USA, where a deficit of 1 billion ECU and an import penetration ratio of 44% was recorded in 1997. The main origin of imports was unsurprisingly Japan, accounting for 54% of EU imports, whilst only 2% of its own consumption was satisfied by imports from third countries. Japan's share of total EU imports has followed a decreasing trend in recent years though. This can be partly explained by the fact that many Japanese companies have transferred production facilities to other East Asian industrialised countries.

3) Belgium, Germany, Spain, France, Ireland, Italy, Luxembourg, the Netherlands, Austria, Portugal and Finland make up the EUR-11 aggregate, otherwise known as the euro-zone.

Figure 13.24

Motorcycles and bicycles (NACE Rev. 1 34.4)
Origin of EU imports, 1998

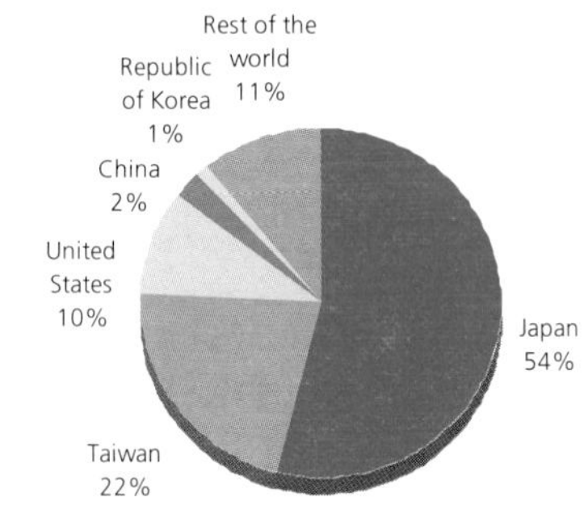

Source: Eurostat (Comext)

Aerospace equipment (NACE Rev. 1 35.3)

The aerospace industry is classified under NACE Rev. 1 Group 35.3 that covers the development, the manufacture and the maintenance of aircraft and spacecraft. It is usually subdivided into the industrial sectors "aircrafts & systems", "engines" and "equipment" and the product segments "aircrafts" (including helicopters), "missiles" and "space". All of these serve both civilian and military customers.

The statistics based on the NACE Rev. 1 classification presented in this chapter, exclude important activities such as the manufacture of military ballistic missiles, of ignition parts and other electrical parts for internal combustion engines, the manufacture of instruments used on aircrafts and the manufacture of air navigation systems.

Official statistics from Eurostat show that the aerospace industry accounted for a significant share of the transport equipment industry in some Member States. In 1998 it represented one-fifth to one-quarter of the production value in France, Greece and the United Kingdom. The aerospace sector accounted for more than half the value of non-automotive transport equipment production in Belgium, Germany and Sweden, and more than three-quarters in France and the United Kingdom. Production specialisation ratios can be calculated by comparing the share of the aerospace industry in manufacturing activities at a national level with the corresponding EU averages. These were particularly high in France (179%) and the United Kingdom (238%), as opposed to Portugal (13%) and Finland (29%).

The European Association of Aerospace Industries (AECMA) estimate that total turnover of the aerospace industry was equal to 55.3 billion ECU in 1997[4], real growth of 17% over the year before and a level just under that of 1990. These figures suggest that the industry is strongly recovering from the severe crisis it experienced in the first half of the decade, when consolidated turnover lost 28% in real terms between 1990 and 1995. AECMA's long-term market forecasts indicate a continuation of the overall growth of the aerospace business. Employment, on the other hand, has remained stable at 377 thousand persons employed in 1997, and is expected to continue unchanged, despite the increase in turnover due to further productivity gains.

4) Source: AECMA, "European Aerospace Industry: 1997 Statistical Survey", July 1998.

Figure 13.25

Aerospace equipment (NACE Rev. 1 35.3)
Production and employment in the Triad

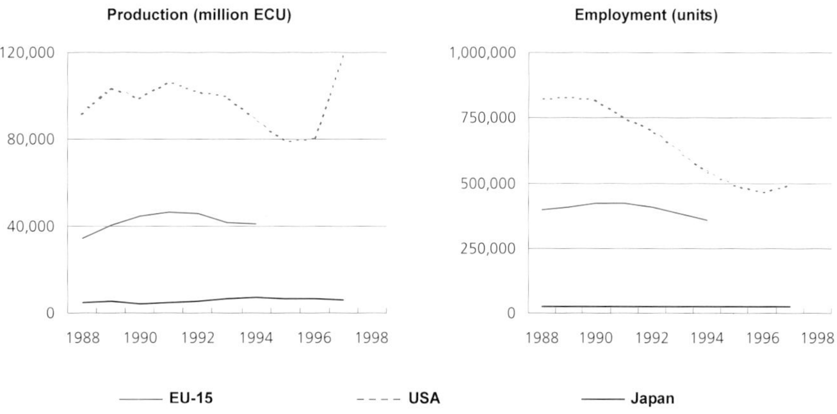

Source: Eurostat (SBS)

(%)

Figure 13.26

Aerospace equipment (NACE Rev. 1 35.3)
Production and export specialisation by Member State, 1998

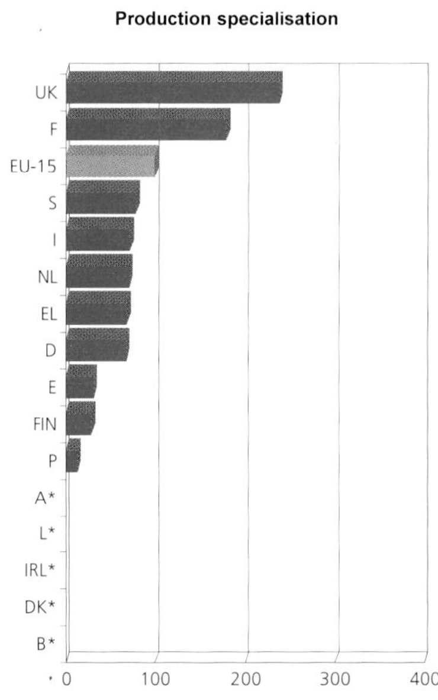

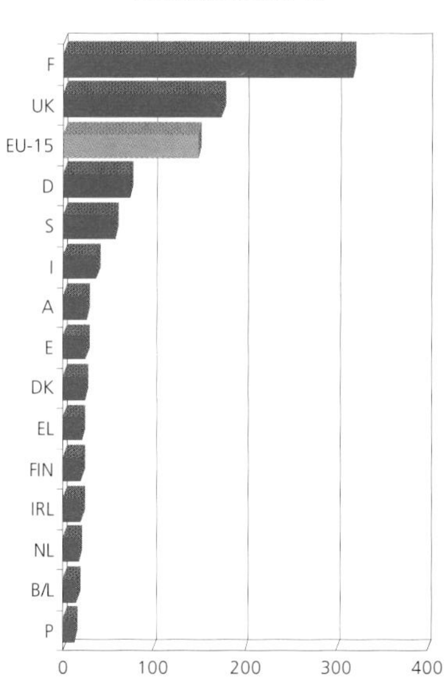

Source: Eurostat (SBS)

In 1997, over half of the turnover was generated by enterprises active in the "aircraft & systems" sector, 29% in the "equipment" sector and 18% in the "engines" sector. The turnover of the European aerospace industry is broken down as shown in figure 13.28. The major part is taken by the sale of fully equipped aircraft, accounting for over a third of consolidated turnover. About one half of final aircraft production was constituted by large civilian aircraft and one-quarter by military aircraft, the rest being shared between helicopters, business jets and regional aircraft. Whilst EU governments, including the ESA (European Space Agency) and national aerospace agencies and military customers used to make up more than half of the European aerospace industry's turnover in the mid-1980s, recent years have been marked by a strong shift towards civilian and commercial markets (see figure 13.29). According to AECMA, just over one-quarter of 1997 turnover was accounted for by EU governments.

Figure 13.27

EU aerospace turnover and employment

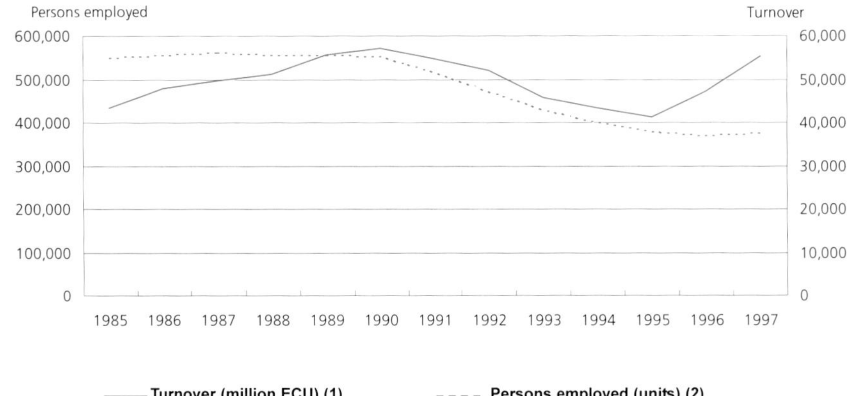

(1) Consolidated.
(2) Including estimations for Sweden until 1992 and non-AECMA companies until 1995.

Source: AECMA

Figure 13.28

Breakdown of EU aerospace turnover by product segment, 1997

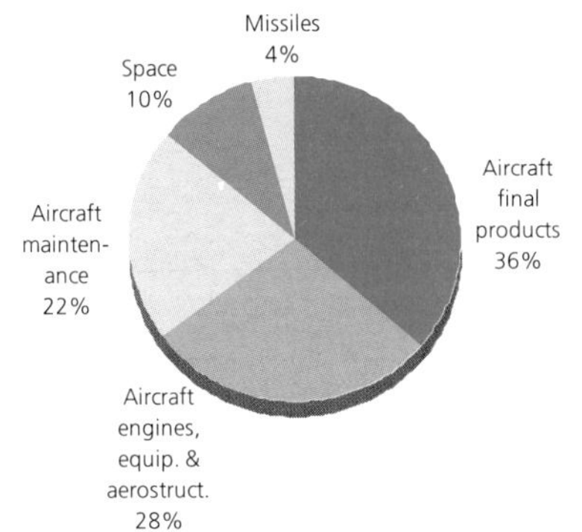

Source: AECMA

Figure 13.29 (%)

Breakdown of EU aerospace turnover by customer (1)

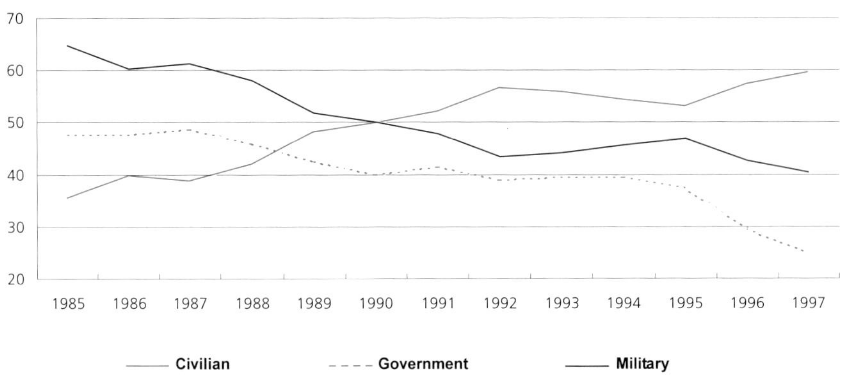

(1) Share of turnover, based on consolidated turnover at constant prices.

Source: AECMA

Regarding the space industry, five distinctive fields could be identified: space science, orbital infrastructure (including manned space activities), civil & commercial applications, military applications, and common to all of the others, launchers. In the field of launchers, Europe was a world leader with Ariane 4 at the forefront of the commercial launch market. Ariane 5 is now taking over the "heavy" commercial market whilst offering expanded capability. In parallel, Europe has initiated a small launcher programme to address the emerging need to launch smaller payloads.

The European Space Industry association, Eurospace, estimate that the sector employed 35,391 people and generated a consolidated turnover of 5.1 billion ECU in 1997 in the fourteen Member States of the European Space Agency (ESA). France was still the major player in Europe with more than 13 thousand persons employed in the sector generating a global consolidated turnover of close to 2 billion ECU. Italy and Germany followed with 5.5 thousand persons employed each and consolidated turnover just under 1 billion ECU.

(million ECU) Figure 13.30

Consolidated turnover of the European space industry, 1997

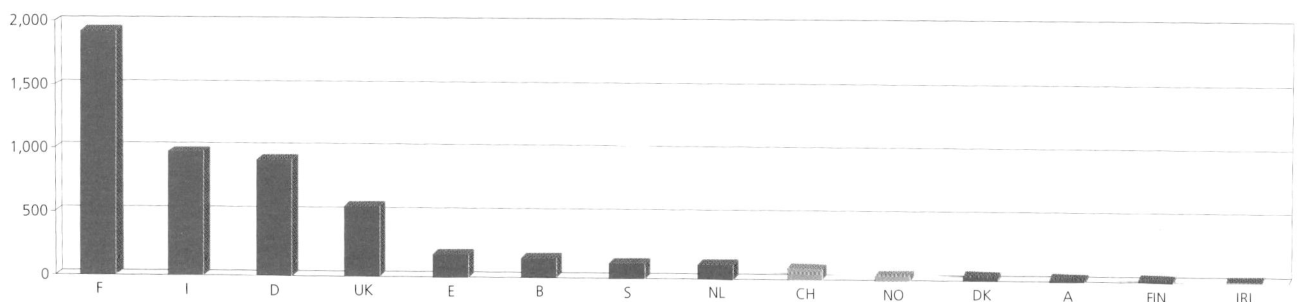

Source: Eurospace

(units) Figure 13.31

Employment in the European space industry, 1997

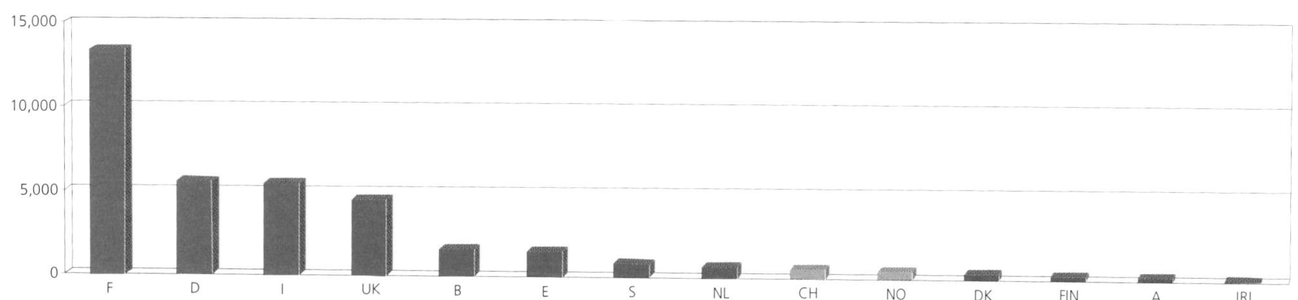

Source: Eurospace

In similar vein to the aerospace industry, the share of public and military contracts has also been declining in the space sector. Eurospace estimate that these represented altogether (ESA, National Agencies, military programmes and the European Union) 54% of the industry's turnover in 1997, against 66% in 1996, whilst commercial customers (including Arianespace) took 46% of the market. This increase is due on one hand to the steep increase of orders by Arianespace (some 30% in 1997) and, on the other hand, to the development of commercial markets for satellites.

The European space industry is present in all segments of space activity, from launcher development and production, to observation and communications' satellites, as well as scientific tests, spacecraft and equipment. The two major areas of activity of the space industry are telecommunications and launcher production & development: they each accounted for around 30% of consolidated turnover, or 1.5 billion ECU. Second in importance were earth observation activities that accounted for 17% of turnover, or 900 million ECU. Earth observation is a domain where private financing of programmes is slowly increasing. It is however not a commercially mature market yet, despite the vast domain of applications that spaceborne remote sensing is opening, from meteorology to mapping or environment control. Traditional scientific domains of activity, such as science, micro-gravity and human-related developments, make up the rest of turnover. These were almost exclusively publicly funded activities.

Figure 13.32

Breakdown of European space industry turnover by customer, 1997

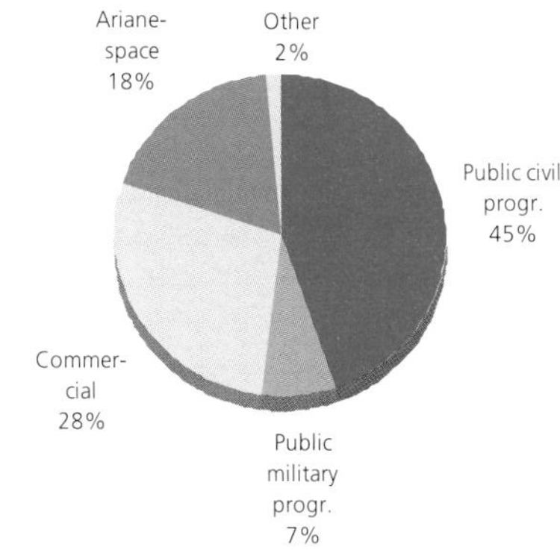

Source: Eurospace

Figure 13.33

Breakdown of European space industry turnover by discipline, 1997

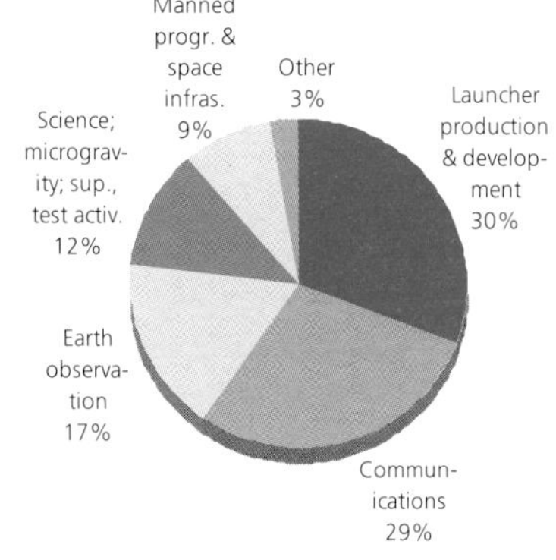

Source: Eurospace

Figures from Eurostat provide some indications on the external trade importance of the aerospace industry. Amongst the five large Member States, all but Spain are net exporters, as was Sweden, whilst all other EU countries were net importers. France displayed the largest trade surplus equal to almost 6 billion ECU in 1998, followed by the United Kingdom (2.3 billion ECU) and Germany (1 billion ECU). Altogether, the aggregate surplus of these three countries compensated more than three times for the trade deficit of the other Member States.

However trade data should be regarded with care, as it may include the sale of second-hand or used aircraft. In addition, trade flows within the EU often involve unfinished products that are to be finished in another EU Member State. According to AECMA, the EU aerospace industry displayed a trade surplus of 25 billion ECU with the rest of the world in 1997, including a surplus of 4.5 billion ECU with the USA.

Figure 13.34

Aircraft and spacecraft (NACE Rev. 1 35.3) Destination of EU exports, 1998

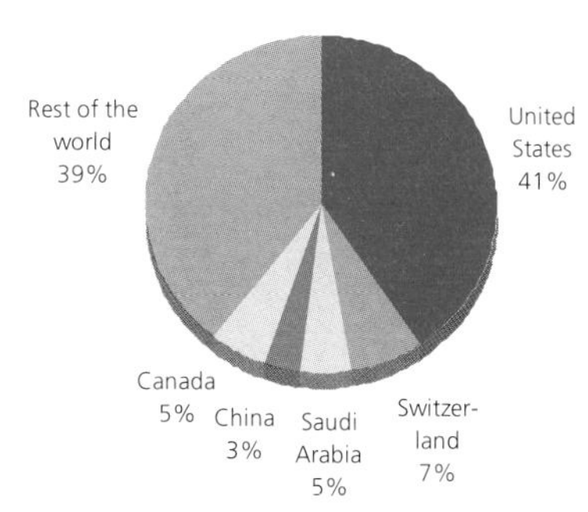

Source: Eurostat (Comext)

Figure 13.35

Aircraft and spacecraft (NACE Rev. 1 35.3) Origin of EU imports, 1998

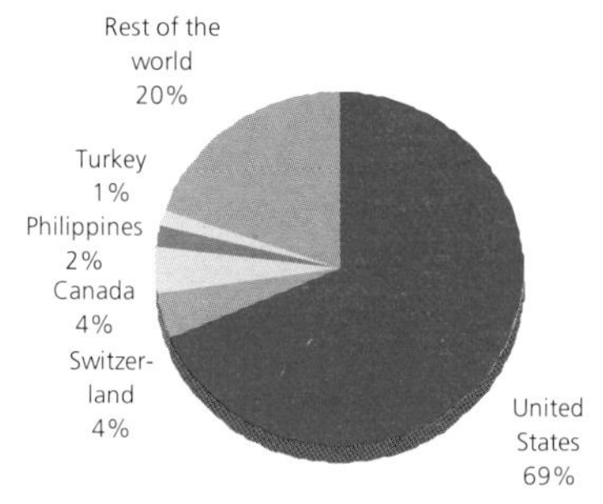

Source: Eurostat (Comext)

Railway rolling stock (NACE Rev. 1 35.2)

The railway rolling stock industry includes the manufacture of standard and narrow gauge railway and urban transport railway equipment. It is classified under Group 35.2 of the NACE Rev. 1 classification of economic activities. It should be noted that the definition also includes fixed track equipment and electrical signalling equipment.

Transportation needs and public policies on railway development and purchases determine the industry's performance. After a period of stagnation in the mid to late 1980s, there was rapid growth in production from 1990 until 1993, when its value rose at an average annual rate in excess of 11%. After two years of slowdown in 1994 and 1995, production rose by a further 14% to 10.8 billion ECU in 1996, the latest year for which EU-15 estimates were available. That amount represented 5% of the transport equipment industry or 25% without motor vehicles. Practically 80% of production, or 9.1 billion ECU, were accounted for by the five largest Member States, for which more recent figures were available, indicating that growth trends continued. Indeed, production value for those countries exceeded 11.4 billion ECU in 1998, a level almost 50% higher than that of 1995.

Germany was the largest EU producer in value terms in 1998 with about 5 billion ECU, ahead of France (2.8 billion ECU), the United Kingdom (1.4 billion ECU), Spain and Italy (both 1.1 billion ECU). Growth in real terms has been particularly impressive in Germany and France where it exceeded 50% between 1995 and 1998. Production at constant prices has trebled in Germany between 1988 and 1998, whilst it quadrupled in France over the same period.

After having witnessed a strong decline during the 1980s, employment in railway rolling stock manufacturing has stabilised during the 1990s. There were 71 thousand persons employed in the sector in the five largest Member States in 1998, one thousand less than in 1989. These aggregate figures, however, hide very contrasting trends across the countries. France numbered more than 15 thousand persons employed in the sector in 1998, practically twice as many as in 1989, whilst the United Kingdom lost one-third of its workforce over the same period, down to 14 thousand persons in 1998. Employment in Germany was in 1998 at the same level as it was in 1989, some 23 thousand persons.

Figure 13.36

Railway rolling stock (NACE Rev. 1 35.2)
Production and employment in the Triad

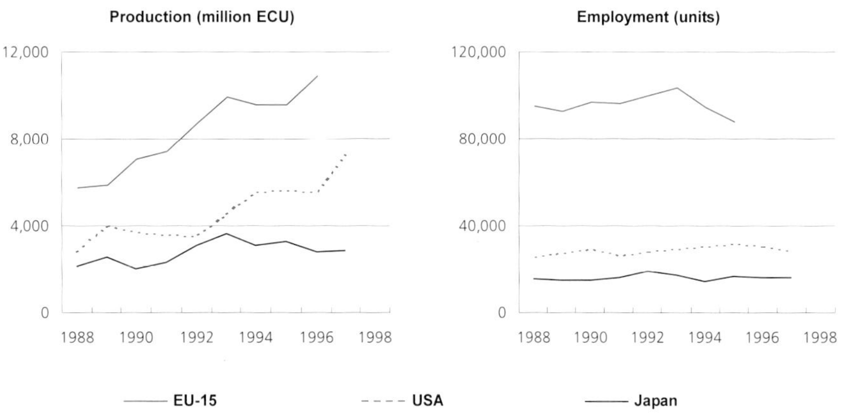

Source: Eurostat (SBS)

Figure 13.37

Railway rolling stock (NACE Rev. 1 35.2)
Production and export specialisation by Member State, 1998

(%)

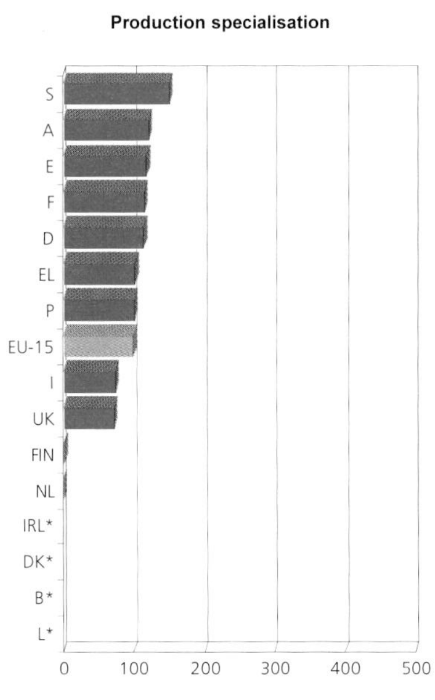

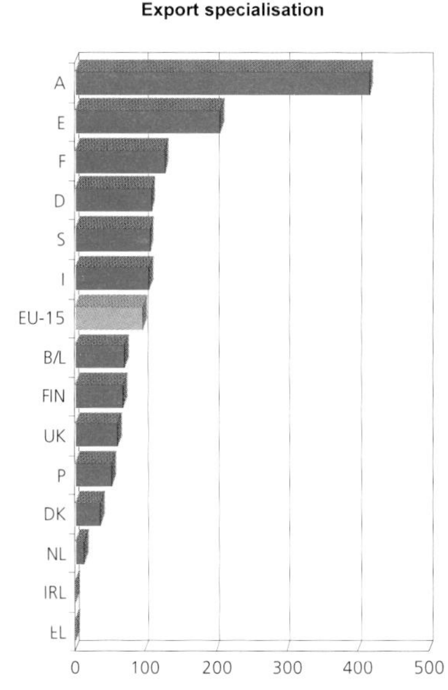

Source: Eurostat (SBS)

Demand for railway rolling stock was relatively concentrated amongst a small number of customers: national railway companies, urban transport companies, private rental and leasing companies and industries with their own railway rolling stock. The demand for railway rolling stock is dependent upon long-term transport and infrastructure policies. It has been marked in recent year by the growing importance of high-speed technology in response to growing demand for faster rail transport. New high-speed networks are being developed across Europe, the USA and Japan. European countries are currently upgrading their rail networks in anticipation of the Trans-European high-speed rail network planned for 2010. France is increasing the network of its Train à Grande Vitesse (TGV), Germany is expanding its InterCity Express (ICE) network from Berlin to Hamburg and to Vienna, Spain has completed the AVE between Seville and Madrid and is now extending the network along the eastern coast, and Italy has completed the Florence/Rome sector of its High Speed Project which is the first phase of a Turin/Milan/Naples link to be operational by 2003.

Despite the high profile of these networks, it is in fact the demand for urban and suburban rail links that is expected to account for the highest proportion of future railway equipment demand. Faster and more efficient rail-based public transport solutions are increasingly viewed as the most efficient solution to the problems of heavy road traffic congestion and pollution in many European cities. The demand for rail transit systems should show continued growth as such systems provide improved mobility in expanding cities and urban areas.

Whilst the larger Member States will remain the main EU markets for railway rolling stock, new markets are emerging in Asia, particularly in South Korea, Taiwan and China, and in North America. The European railway industry is indeed very much export-orientated compared to the USA and Japan. The share of 1998 production that was exported ranged between one-fifth in Germany and the United Kingdom up to 38% in Italy. In comparison, the USA and Japan export only 15% and 5% of their domestic production respectively. The cumulated trade surplus of the five largest Member States reached 1.4 billion ECU in 1998, 60% more than in 1995. France alone accounted for one third of this amount with a surplus of 500 million ECU, ahead of Germany (400 million ECU). The United Kingdom was the only country recording a trade deficit, equal to 100 million ECU. The trade balance of the USA has been negative throughout the decade, although it recorded its smallest level in 1997 at 33 million ECU, compared to 300 million ECU the year before. Japan displayed a consistently positive trade balance over the whole time series that reached 96 million ECU in 1997.

European suppliers have won a dominant share of the world market. A recent study by the European Commission[5] showed that European companies had become market leaders worldwide in segments such as high-speed trains, EMUs/DMUs[6], metros, LRVs[7] and locomotives. Innovation is the key to competitiveness and research and development is very important amongst the leading firms. This has led to increased market concentration as enterprises seek to combine technological specialities, share national market expertise and exploit economies of scale. The major rolling stock suppliers have formed consortia to develop and supply new high-speed trains. GEC-Alsthom for the French TGV (and its derivatives, Eurostar and Thalys); AEG and ABB for the ICE in Germany; Ansaldo, Breda, ABB Tecnomasio, Fiat and Firema for the ETR 500 in Italy, based on tilting technology. Although the industry numbers many players, it has seen the emergence of three large firms that dominate the market: Adtranz (a merger of ABB and AEG), GEC-Alsthom and Siemens Verkehrstechnik (SVT).

5) European Commission: "Structure of the railway industry, final report", June 1996.
6) Electrical Multiple Units (EMU) and Diesel Multiple Units (DMU) are fixed units of 2 or 3 cars with their own traction (i.e. without requiring a locomotive), serving regional routes at speeds of up to 160 km/h.
7) Light Rail Vehicles (LRV), or trams, are designed for above ground urban traffic with dedicated infrastructure.

Figure 13.38

Railway rolling stock (NACE Rev. 1 35.2)
Destination of EU exports, 1998

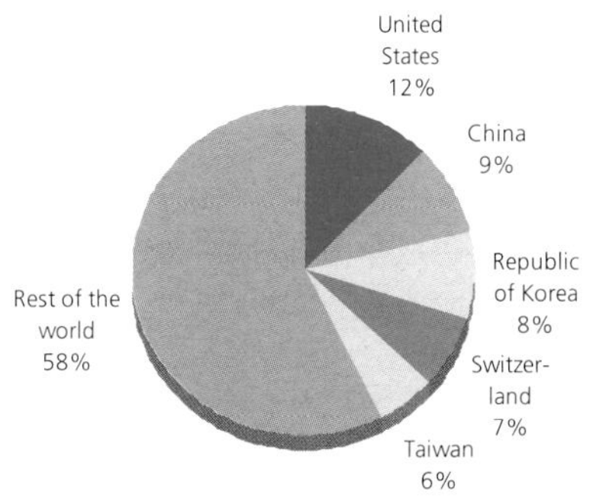

United States 12%
China 9%
Republic of Korea 8%
Switzerland 7%
Taiwan 6%
Rest of the world 58%

Source: Eurostat (Comext)

Figure 13.39

Railway rolling stock (NACE Rev. 1 35.2)
Origin of EU imports, 1998

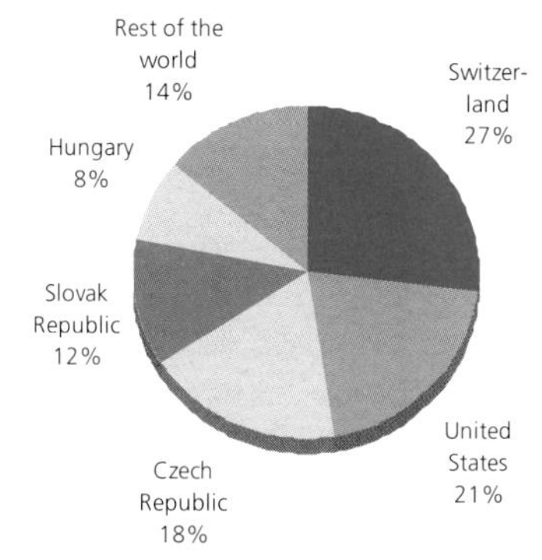

Source: Eurostat (Comext)

Shipbuilding (NACE Rev. 1 35.1)

The shipbuilding industry is classified under NACE Rev. 1 Group 35.1, covering the manufacture of all types of ships and pleasure and sporting boats: commercial vessels, warships, fishing boats, drilling platforms, sail boats, motor boats, inflatable boats, canoes, etc. Activities of maintenance and repair and shipbreaking are also included in the NACE Rev. 1 definition, but the manufacture of marine engines and navigational instruments are not.

The total production of the European shipbuilding industry exceeded 20 billion ECU in 1996, the latest year for which official EU-15 aggregates are available from Eurostat. Excluding Portugal and Luxembourg, EU production reached the same level in 1998. Shipbuilding accounted for about 5% of transport production, and one-quarter of non-automotive production. Some countries are highly specialised in this activity. This was the case in Denmark and Finland, where production specialisation ratios relative to the EU were greater than 400%. Greece and the Netherlands also boasted particularly high specialisation ratios, at around 200%. Low specialisation was observed in the two Member States without access to the sea, Austria and Luxembourg, as well as Belgium and Ireland.

Completions of ships have decreased from 20.7 million CGT[8] in 1975 down to 8.5 million CGT in 1988. In the following years production gradually recovered, reaching 17 million CGT in 1997. The main part of the demand for new ships is driven by the need to replace obsolete ships, and ships removed from the fleet due to accidents. During the 1970s big oiltankers and dry bulk carriers were built in large numbers. The replacements for these ships have been generating orders for new ships in the 1990s. AWES, the Association of European Shipbuilders and Shiprepairers, forecast that new building deliveries will peak around 2002 and thereafter decrease gradually as the requirement for replacement tonnage shrinks.

8) CGT: Compensated Gross Ton, a calculated measure of a ship's gross tonnage that accounts for the density and complexity of the ship.

Figure 13.40

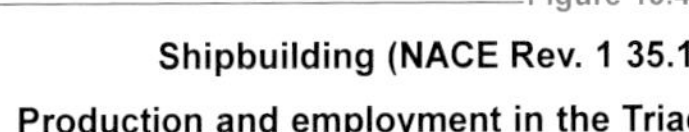

Shipbuilding (NACE Rev. 1 35.1)

Production and employment in the Triad

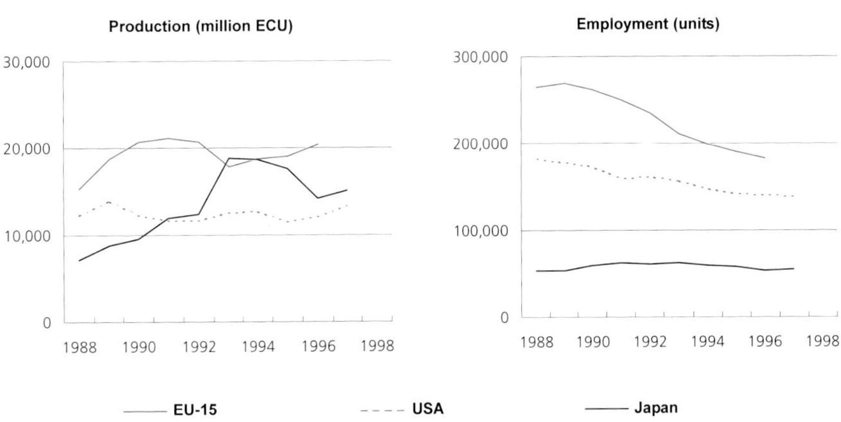

Source: Eurostat (SBS)

(%)

Figure 13.41

Shipbuilding (NACE Rev. 1 35.1)

Production and export specialisation by Member State, 1998

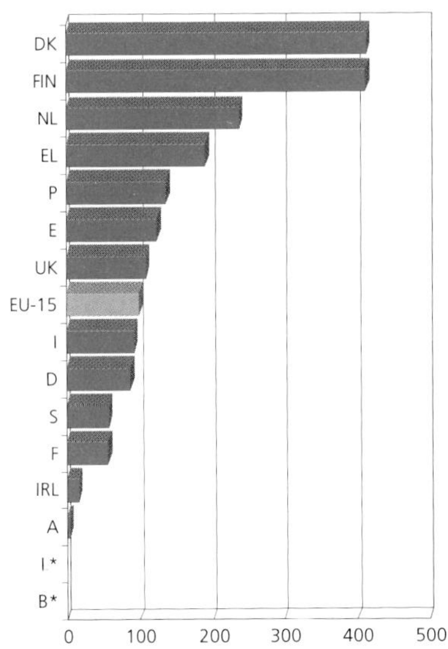

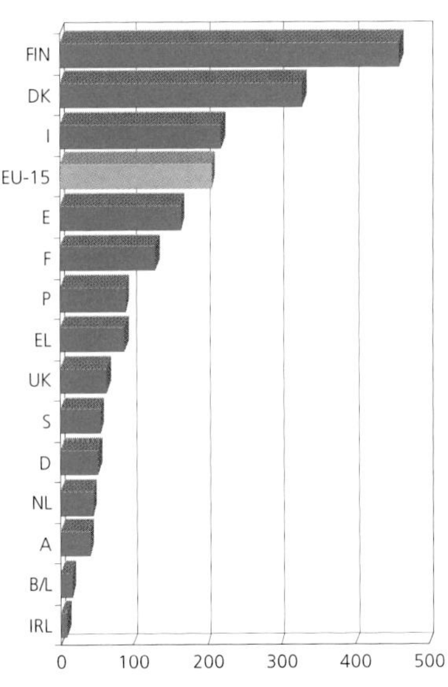

Source: Eurostat (SBS)

Figure 13.42 (thousand DWT)

World maritime fleet as of 1st January (1)

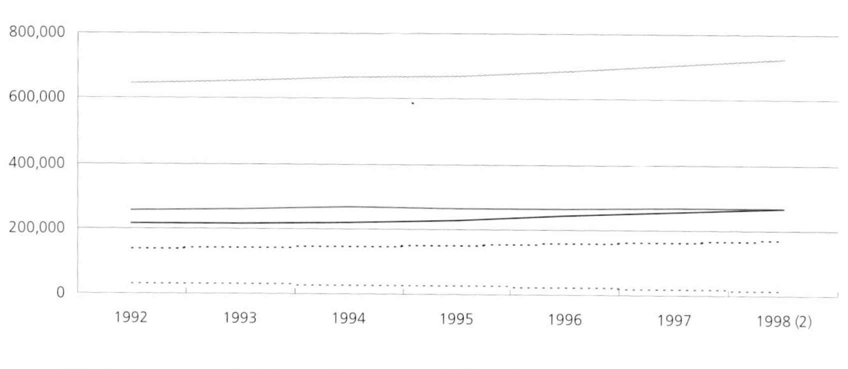

(1) DWT: deadweight tonnage, i.e. the maximum weight of cargo and stores that a ship can carry.
(2) Estimates.

Source: Fearnleys Review in AWES

Figure 13.43 (thousand CGT)

Shipbuilding production capacity by region

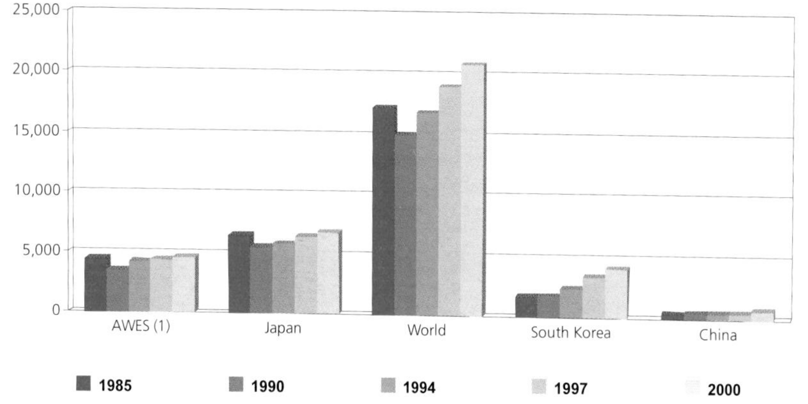

(1) EU-15 and Norway.

Source: Lloyd's Register of shipping and European Commission, in AWES

Production capacity has decreased in the past twenty years in parallel with the reduction in output, but to a lesser extent. However, AWES has observed in recent years a tendency for some countries, especially South Korea, to increase their shipbuilding capacity through the construction of new facilities or the enlargement of existing ones. Global shipbuilding capacity is expected to grow to around 24 million CGT by 2005, whilst requirements are expected to remain constant at an annual average level of 17.3 million CGT for the period 2000-2005, revealing substantial over-capacity.

A total of 1,743 ships were completed in the world in 1997, amounting to 24.5 million gross tons (GT[9]) and 16.9 million CGT. It was a slight increase over the previous year, when 1,669 ships were produced, for a total of 25.2 million GT and 16.6 million CGT. However, the production of AWES countries (EU countries, Norway and Poland) declined to 428 ships, 3.9 million GT and 4 million CGT from 435 ships, 4.7 million GT and 4.3 million CGT. The world market share of AWES countries therefore declined to 23.7% (19.1% for EU countries only) with Japanese (37.2%) and South Korean (23.5%) producers profiting. Figure 13.43 shows clearly that South Korea has out-performed all other countries during the nineties (with a share of only 15% of world markets in 1991). The USA represented only a marginal share of 0.8% of world tonnage.

9) GT: gross tonnage, i.e. the volume in cubic metres of all enclosed spaces of a ship (based on the weight of water displaced).

Inside the EU, the largest ship producing country was Germany (see figure 13.44). In 1997, Germany accounted for 6% of world production with more than 1 million CGT, preceding the Netherlands and Italy whose production exceeded 400 thousand CGT, 2.5% of the total market. A look at the level of new building contracts gives some indication on the future evolution of production. They reveal booming demand in Spain, whose new orders in 1997 were equal to 660 thousand CGT, almost three times the level of completions. Italy boasted new orders worth 50% more than the level of completions. All other Member States displayed the opposite trend.

AWES countries hold a dominant market share in Group III type of vessels (ferries, passenger, fishing and non-cargo) with 63.3% of world tonnage completed in 1997, down from 71.4% in 1995. In contrast, they represented only 1.7% of the Group I (crude oil tankers and dry bulk carriers) completions in 1997, whilst they were still holding a 10% market share just two years before. This loss has benefited mainly South Korea, whose share jumped to 32.3% from 28.2%, whilst Japan's share remained stable at around 51%.

New orders experienced strong growth in 1997, 1,983 ships or 36.7 million GT and 22.5 million CGT, up from 24 million GT and 17.5 million CGT the year before. European contracting, however, continued to decline. New orders in AWES countries were equal to 3.8 million CGT in 1997, down from 4.2 million in 1996 and 5.5 million in 1995. As a consequence, their world market share dropped to 17%, against 39% for Japan and 27.5% for South Korea. European shipbuilders maintained their dominance of Group III ships, with a market share of new orders equal to 57.3%, although down from 66% in 1995. The most important setback was recorded in Group II, where EU market share was more than halved between 1995 (35.0%) and 1997 (15.6%).

The tonnage broken-up and lost in the world decreased to 15.2 million DWT in 1997 from 22.9 million DWT three years before. The major scrapper in the world was India with a market share of 54% in 1997, followed by Bangladesh (22%) and Pakistan (10%). The quantity of tonnage laid-up also continued its decreasing trend and reached 4.9 million DWT in 1997, down from 11.4 million DWT in 1992.

(thousand CGT)

Figure 13.44

Shipbuilding completions and new orders in the EU, 1997

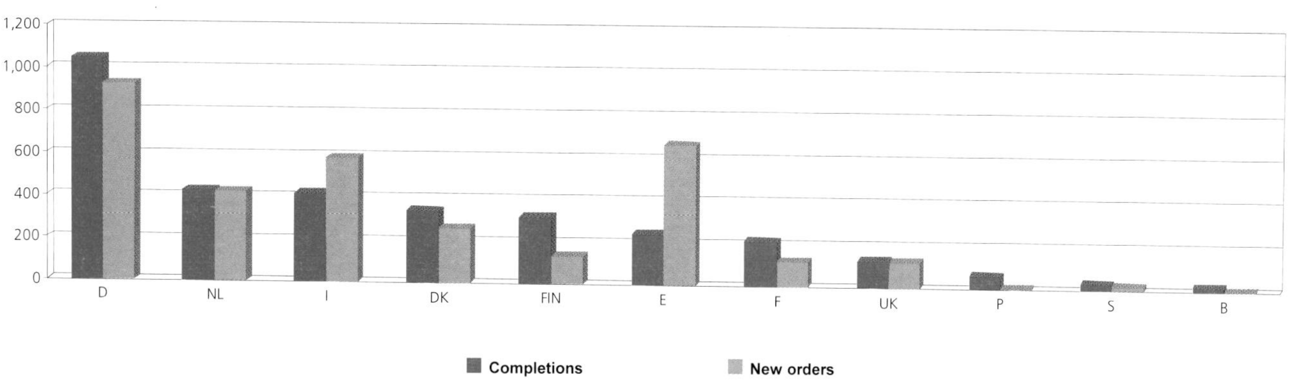

Source: Lloyd's Register of shipping and European Commission, in AWES

Shipbuilding employs a considerable number of persons. The latest estimates for EU-15 numbered 184 thousand persons active in the sector, and there were 179 thousand in 1998, if we exclude Luxembourg and the Netherlands. As a general rule, employment in the sector followed a declining trend. The European workforce has been almost halved between 1986 and 1996, losing more than 135 thousand jobs over the period. Some countries, however, experienced a totally different trend. This was the case of Spain, the Member State recording the largest workforce in shipbuilding and repair activities with 39 thousand persons employed in 1998, ten thousand more than in 1995, and a level similar to 1990. Spain was ahead of the United Kingdom, with 35 thousand persons employed, and Germany, with 27 thousand persons employed.

(%)

Figure 13.45

Completions by region and type of ship, 1997 (1)

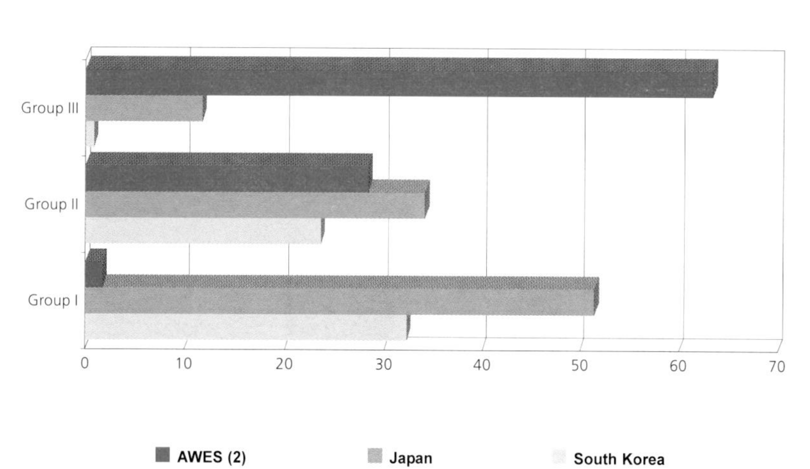

(1) Group I: tankers, bulk carriers, combined carriers.
Group II: multi-purpose, reefers, containers, ro-ro, car carriers, gas/chemical carriers.
Group III: ferries, passenger, fishing, non-cargo vessels.
(2) EU-15, Norway and Poland.

Source: AWES

Professional associations representing the industries within this chapter

ACEA
European Automobile manufacturers Association
211, rue du Noyer
B-1000 Bruxelles
tel: (32) 2 732 55 50
fax: (32) 2 738 73 10
e-mail:
ereco@bipeeurope.fr

ACEM
Association des Constructeurs Européens de Motocycles
1, avenue de la Joyeuse Entrée
B-1040 Bruxelles
tel: (32) 2 280 18 19
fax: (32) 2 230 16 83

AECMA
European Association of Aerospace Industries
Gulledelle 94, boîte 5
F-1200 Bruxelles
tel: (32) 2 775 81 10
fax: (32) 2 775 81 11
e-mail: info@aecma.org

CESA (AWES)
Committee of European Shipbuilders Association
Juan Hurtado de Mondoza 13
E-28036 Madrid
tel: (34) 91 34 52 165
fax: (34) 91 35 99 336
e-mail:
info@cesa-shipbuilding.org

EBMA
European Bicycle Manufacturers Association
13, avenue de la Grande Armée
F-75116 Paris
tel: (33) 1 45 01 91 86
fax: (33) 1 45 01 20 21

ECSA
European Community Shipowners' Association
45, rue Ducale
B-1000 Bruxelles
tel: (32) 2 511 39 40
fax: (32) 2 511 80 92
e-mail:
ereco@bipeeurope.fr

EUROSPACE
Organisation of the European space industry
16, rue Hamelin
F-75116 Paris
tel: (33) 1 47 55 83 00
fax: (33) 1 47 55 63 30
e-mail:
letterbox@eurospace.org

IRF
International Road Federation
4 chemin de Blandonnet
CH-1214 Vernier
tel: (41) 22 306 02 60
fax: (41) 22 306 02 70
e-mail: info@irfnet.org

UNIFE
Union of European Railway Industries
221, avenue Louise, boîte 11
B-1050 Bruxelles
tel: (32) 2 626 12 60
fax: (32) 2 626 12 61
e-mail: mail@unife.org

VDA
German Association of the Motor Industry
Westendstraße 61
D-60325 Frankfurt am Main
tel: (49) 69 97 50 70
fax: (49) 69 97 50 72 61

Figure 13.46 (%)

New orders by region and type of ship, 1997 (1)

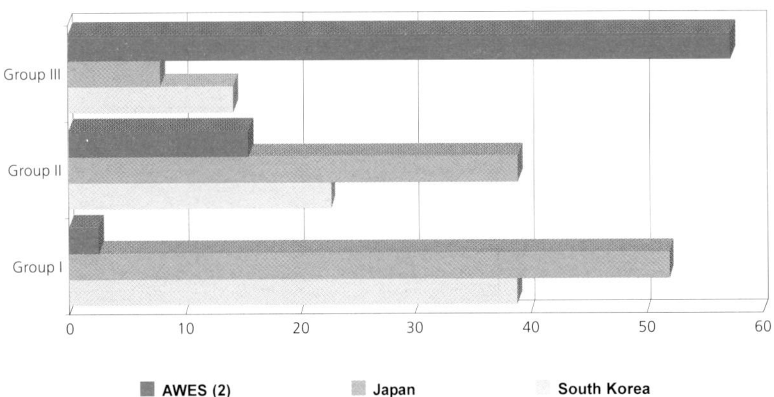

(1) Group I: tankers, bulk carriers, combined carriers.
Group II: multi-purpose, reefers, containers, ro-ro, car carriers, gas/chemical carriers.
Group III: ferries, passenger, fishing, non-cargo vessels.
(2) EU-15, Norway and Poland.

Source: AWES

Figure 13.47 (thousand CGT)

Order book at year end

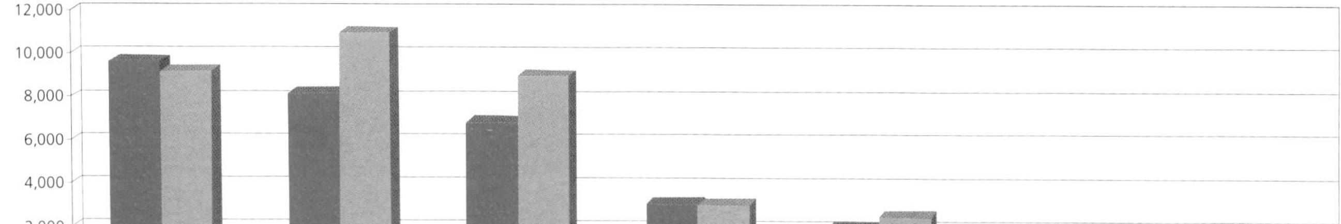

(1) EU-15, Norway and Poland.
(2) Including Bulgaria, Croatia, Romania, Russia and Ukraine.
(3) Taiwan and China.

Source: Lloyd's Register of shipping and European Commission, in AWES

Figure 13.48

Shipbuilding (NACE Rev. 1 35.1)

Destination of EU exports, 1998

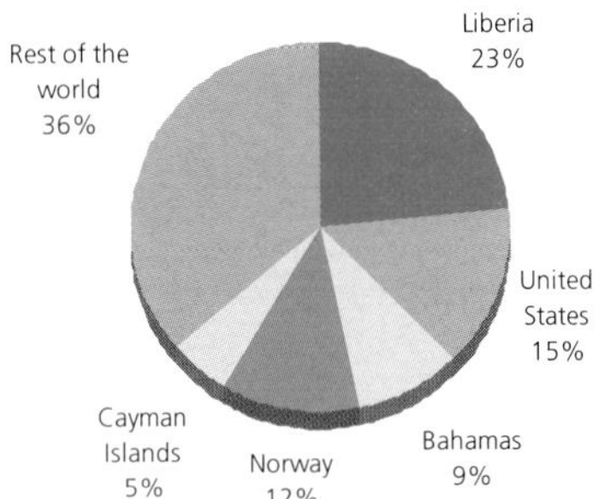

Source: Eurostat (Comext)

Figure 13.49

Shipbuilding (NACE Rev. 1 35.1)

Origin of EU imports, 1998

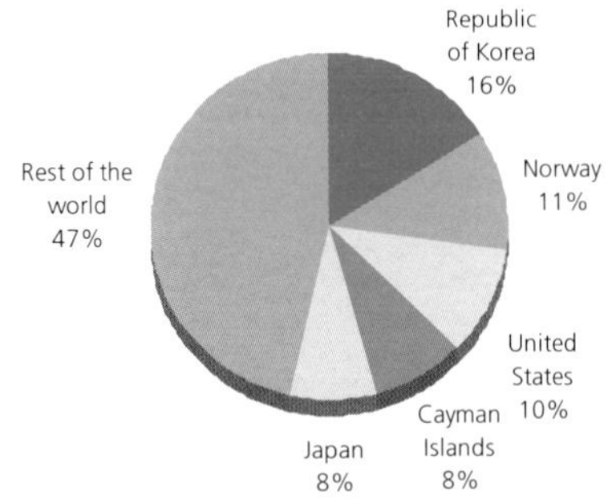

Source: Eurostat (Comext)

(million ECU) Table 13.3

Manufacture of motor vehicles (NACE Rev. 1 34.1)
Production related indicators in the EU

	1988	1989	1990	1991	1992	1993	1994	1995	1996	1997	1998
Production value	186,055	207,136	217,264	221,584	232,400	201,102	230,331	243,858	:	:	:
Producer price index (1995=100)	:	:	84.0	88.2	91.3	94.9	97.6	100.0	100.8	98.0	95.9
Value added	53,354	59,591	59,648	60,573	61,908	52,745	59,447	59,645	:	:	:
Number of persons employed (thousands)	1,288.1	1,286.5	1,327.7	1,300.5	1,254.1	1,151.4	1,095.6	1,078.4	:	:	:

(million ECU) Table 13.4

Manufacture of motor vehicles (NACE Rev. 1 34.1)
Production related indicators, 1998

	B	DK	D	EL	E	F	IRL	I	L	NL	A	P	FIN	S	UK
Production value (1)	16,092	0	124,232	104	26,607	62,047	43	22,081	:	4,446	3,356	3,481	316	17,078	35,895
Value added (1)	2,901	0	34,203	20	5,044	10,445	12	5,528	:	1,217	937	:	117	3,306	9,710
Number of persons employed (units) (2)	38,528	0	513,747	1,443	82,910	181,981	375	116,628	:	13,849	14,532	7,329	2,203	69,759	123,286

(1) A (1994); DK (1996); EL (1997). (2) NL (1992); A (1994); DK (1996).

(million ECU) Table 13.5

Manufacture of motor vehicles (NACE Rev. 1 34.1)
Market related indicators in the EU

	1988	1989	1990	1991	1992	1993	1994	1995	1996	1997	1998
Apparent consumption	174,578	195,351	204,310	212,306	223,972	183,788	206,222	216,775	:	:	:
Exports	23,020	24,943	26,312	23,983	24,021	29,140	36,211	39,878	43,709	49,166	48,434
Imports	11,542	13,158	13,358	14,706	15,593	11,826	12,102	12,795	13,956	19,915	25,282
Trade balance	11,477	11,785	12,954	9,278	8,428	17,314	24,109	27,083	29,753	29,251	23,152
Export ratio (%)	12.4	12.0	12.1	10.8	10.3	14.5	15.7	16.4	:	:	:
Import penetration ratio (%)	6.6	6.7	6.5	6.9	7.0	6.4	5.9	5.9	:	:	:
Cover ratio (%)	199.4	189.6	197.0	163.1	154.1	246.4	299.2	311.7	313.2	246.9	191.6

(million ECU) Table 13.6

Manufacture of motor vehicles (NACE Rev. 1 34.1)
Market related indicators, 1998

	B/L	DK	D	EL	E	F	IRL	I	NL	A	P	FIN	S	UK
Apparent consumption (1)	:	1,855	87,535	1,617	20,642	57,213	1,755	31,592	6,547	4,588	4,360	1,215	15,052	44,317
Exports	19,078	306	66,544	37	18,616	23,655	232	9,553	6,999	4,021	2,653	897	5,493	16,343
Imports	12,844	2,458	29,847	1,473	12,652	18,821	1,944	19,065	9,100	4,104	3,532	1,797	3,467	24,765
Trade balance	6,234	-2,152	36,697	-1,436	5,965	4,834	-1,712	-9,511	-2,101	-83	-878	-900	2,026	-8,422
Export ratio (%) (2)	:	444.6	53.6	41.4	70.0	38.1	539.7	43.3	157.4	83.4	76.2	283.9	32.2	45.5
Import penetration ratio (%) (1)	:	113.9	34.1	96.2	61.3	32.9	110.8	60.3	139.0	87.8	81.0	147.8	23.0	55.9
Cover ratio (%)	148.5	12.5	223.0	2.5	147.1	125.7	12.0	50.1	76.9	98.0	75.1	49.9	158.4	66.0

(1) A (1994); DK (1996); EL (1997). (2) DK (1991); A (1994); EL (1997).

Table 13.7

Manufacture of motor vehicles (NACE Rev. 1 34.1)
Labour related indicators, 1998

	EU-15	B	DK	D	EL	E	F	IRL	I	L	NL	A	P	FIN	S	UK
Personnel costs (million ECU) (1)	44,450	1,594	0	26,603	25	2,339	6,655	7	3,380	:	432	581	144	70	2,718	4,830
Personnel costs/employee (thousand ECU) (2)	41.9	44.4	:	53.0	18.8	30.0	37.4	19.3	26.4	:	:	40.0	:	32.6	40.8	32.6
Social charges/personnel costs (%) (3)	23.4	28.8	:	20.0	24.2	22.6	30.4	7.4	33.3	:	14.6	23.8	:	22.6	30.8	14.9
Labour productivity (thousand ECU/head) (4)	55.3	75.3	:	66.6	13.2	60.8	57.4	31.8	47.4	:	37.9	64.5	:	53.2	47.4	78.8
Wage adjusted labour productivity (%) (2)	132.0	130.9	:	117.5	92.5	188.0	131.7	160.5	143.9	:	:	161.5	:	137.8	127.4	193.2

(1) A (1994); EU-15 (1995); DK (1996); NL (1997). (2) A (1994); EU-15, EL, I (1995); B, D, E, F, IRL, FIN, S, UK (1996). (3) A (1994); EU-15, S (1995); NL (1997).
(4) NL (1992); A (1994); EU-15 (1995); EL (1997).

Source: Eurostat (SBS, EBT)

Table 13.8 (million ECU)

Manufacture of bodies (coachwork) for motor vehicles; manufacture of trailers and semi-trailers (NACE Rev. 1 34.2)
Production related indicators in the EU

	1988	1989	1990	1991	1992	1993	1994	1995	1996	1997	1998
Production value	11,533	13,209	14,112	15,026	13,932	11,939	13,376	15,689	:	:	:
Producer price index (1995=100)	:	:	85.5	90.5	93.9	95.9	97.0	100.0	98.5	95.1	95.6
Value added	3,919	4,337	4,548	4,695	4,594	3,992	4,460	4,738	:	:	:
Number of persons employed (thousands)	160.8	164.6	168.6	164.2	150.9	133.3	133.6	133.7	:	:	:

Table 13.9 (million ECU)

Manufacture of bodies (coachwork) for motor vehicles; manufacture of trailers and semi-trailers (NACE Rev. 1 34.2)
Production related indicators, 1998

	B	DK	D	EL	E	F	IRL	I	L	NL	A	P	FIN	S	UK
Production value (1)	1,218	520	6,732	10	1,296	3,217	83	1,504	:	820	335	215	467	383	2,867
Value added (1)	293	148	1,549	3	345	916	19	544	:	256	128	:	163	121	902
Number of persons employed (units) (2)	6,306	3,850	34,655	184	10,251	20,491	691	10,810	:	7,235	2,943	2,878	2,751	2,979	24,093

(1) EL, A (1997). (2) NL (1992).

Table 13.10 (million ECU)

Manufacture of bodies (coachwork) for motor vehicles; manufacture of trailers and semi-trailers (NACE Rev. 1 34.2)
Market related indicators in the EU

	1988	1989	1990	1991	1992	1993	1994	1995	1996	1997	1998
Apparent consumption	11,027	12,559	13,553	14,436	13,362	11,305	12,681	14,903	:	:	:
Exports	591	784	745	812	796	862	970	1,117	1,186	1,622	1,858
Imports	85	134	186	221	227	229	274	331	363	398	495
Trade balance	506	650	559	590	570	634	695	786	823	1,224	1,363
Export ratio (%)	5.1	5.9	5.3	5.4	5.7	7.2	7.3	7.1	:	:	:
Import penetration ratio (%)	0.8	1.1	1.4	1.5	1.7	2.0	2.2	2.2	:	:	:
Cover ratio (%)	691.7	584.2	400.7	366.7	351.3	377.0	353.4	337.1	326.3	407.4	375.3

Table 13.11 (million ECU)

Manufacture of bodies (coachwork) for motor vehicles; manufacture of trailers and semi-trailers (NACE Rev. 1 34.2)
Market related indicators, 1998

	B/L	DK	D	EL	E	F	IRL	I	NL	A	P	FIN	S	UK
Apparent consumption (1)	:	660	5,499	25	1,289	3,129	101	1,041	1,255	343	264	444	-22	2,750
Exports	707	176	2,054	7	222	759	31	640	268	248	8	107	585	574
Imports	319	316	820	17	214	671	49	177	703	246	57	84	180	458
Trade balance	388	-141	1,233	-10	7	88	-18	462	-435	2	-49	23	405	117
Export ratio (%) (1)	:	33.8	30.5	51.9	17.1	23.6	37.7	42.5	32.7	76.0	3.7	23.0	152.5	20.0
Import penetration ratio (%) (1)	:	47.9	14.9	80.6	16.6	21.4	48.9	17.0	56.0	76.6	21.6	19.0	-827.3	16.6
Cover ratio (%)	221.9	55.5	250.4	39.2	103.5	113.1	63.2	360.6	38.1	100.8	13.9	127.2	325.5	125.5

(1) EL, A (1997).

Table 13.12

Manufacture of bodies (coachwork) for motor vehicles; manufacture of trailers and semi-trailers (NACE Rev. 1 34.2)
Labour related indicators, 1998

	EU-15	B	DK	D	EL	E	F	IRL	I	L	NL	A	P	FIN	S	UK
Personnel costs (million ECU) (1)	3,774	239	118	1,253	2	181	597	12	307	:	186	83	24	76	95	650
Personnel costs/employee (thousand ECU) (2)	30.4	35.8	31.8	35.8	15.0	19.5	29.4	16.6	25.9	:	:	29.7	:	28.9	33.5	22.5
Social charges/personnel costs (%) (3)	20.4	29.5	5.0	20.0	24.4	22.7	29.5	13.2	36.2	:	12.5	22.3	:	21.3	28.6	10.9
Labour productivity (thousand ECU/head) (4)	35.5	46.5	38.4	44.7	14.0	33.7	44.7	27.2	50.3	:	29.6	42.8	:	59.4	40.7	37.4
Wage adjusted labour productivity (%) (2)	116.6	118.2	127.9	101.3	124.6	133.3	114.2	134.1	131.2	:	:	130.6	:	133.3	133.2	143.4

(1) EU-15 (1995). (2) EU-15, EL, I, A (1995); B, DK, D, E, F, IRL, FIN, S, UK (1996). (3) EU-15, S (1995); DK (1997). (4) NL (1992); EU-15 (1995); EL, A (1997).

Source: Eurostat (SBS, EBT)

(million ECU) — Table 13.13

Manufacture of parts and accessories for motor vehicles and their engines (NACE Rev. 1 34.3)

Production related indicators in the EU

	1988	1989	1990	1991	1992	1993	1994	1995	1996	1997	1998
Production value	38,927	44,070	46,070	47,001	51,496	47,482	53,905	69,686	:	:	:
Producer price index (1995=100)	:	:	93.7	96.4	98.0	98.9	99.0	100.0	100.8	96.0	99.3
Value added	15,710	16,684	17,248	17,491	19,310	17,915	20,496	25,654	:	:	:
Number of persons employed (thousands)	511.5	528.8	538.2	529.0	525.4	487.9	491.0	564.8	:	:	:

(million ECU) — Table 13.14

Manufacture of parts and accessories for motor vehicles and their engines (NACE Rev. 1 34.3)

Production related indicators, 1998

	B	DK	D	EL	E	F	IRL	I	L	NL	A	P	FIN	S	UK
Production value (1)	2,063	332	43,275	7	8,136	12,237	308	10,287	:	602	746	2,147	149	2,563	10,632
Value added (1)	644	135	13,562	3	2,457	3,790	69	3,464	:	251	309	:	62	861	3,920
Number of persons employed (units) (2)	9,620	3,219	252,837	218	60,419	75,436	2,484	75,224	:	3,422	6,400	13,324	1,063	20,825	90,211

(1) EL, A (1997). (2) NL (1992); A (1994).

(million ECU) — Table 13.15

Manufacture of parts and accessories for motor vehicles and their engines (NACE Rev. 1 34.3)

Market related indicators in the EU

	1988	1989	1990	1991	1992	1993	1994	1995	1996	1997	1998
Apparent consumption	34,300	39,777	41,860	42,650	47,763	43,350	49,404	64,414	:	:	:
Exports	7,875	8,106	7,827	8,330	8,206	9,383	10,668	12,235	13,943	17,058	17,739
Imports	3,248	3,814	3,616	3,979	4,473	5,251	6,168	6,963	7,417	8,486	9,707
Trade balance	4,627	4,293	4,210	4,351	3,732	4,132	4,500	5,272	6,527	8,572	8,032
Export ratio (%)	20.2	18.4	17.0	17.7	15.9	19.8	19.8	17.6	:	:	:
Import penetration ratio (%)	9.5	9.6	8.6	9.3	9.4	12.1	12.5	10.8	:	:	:
Cover ratio (%)	242.5	212.6	216.4	209.3	183.4	178.7	173.0	175.7	188.0	201.0	182.7

(million ECU) — Table 13.16

Manufacture of parts and accessories for motor vehicles and their engines (NACE Rev. 1 34.3)

Market related indicators, 1998

	B/L	DK	D	EL	E	F	IRL	I	NL	A	P	FIN	S	UK
Apparent consumption (1)	:	337	36,794	354	10,084	8,153	433	6,543	1,937	1,099	2,839	476	1,803	12,983
Exports	3,135	536	16,839	83	4,877	10,672	76	7,222	1,576	1,814	476	318	3,344	7,177
Imports	6,970	541	10,358	366	6,825	6,589	200	3,478	2,911	2,088	1,168	644	2,584	9,528
Trade balance	-3,835	-5	6,481	-284	-1,949	4,083	-125	3,744	-1,335	-274	-692	-327	760	-2,351
Export ratio (%) (1)	:	161.6	38.9	1,054.0	59.9	87.2	24.5	70.2	261.8	153.6	22.2	212.8	130.5	67.5
Import penetration ratio (%) (1)	:	160.7	28.2	119.0	67.7	80.8	46.3	53.2	150.3	136.4	41.1	135.4	143.3	73.4
Cover ratio (%)	45.0	99.1	162.6	22.6	71.4	162.0	37.7	207.6	54.2	86.9	40.8	49.3	129.4	75.3

(1) EL, A (1997).

Table 13.17

Manufacture of parts and accessories for motor vehicles and their engines (NACE Rev. 1 34.3)

Labour related indicators, 1998

	EU-15	B	DK	D	EL	E	F	IRL	I	L	NL	A	P	FIN	S	UK
Personnel costs (million ECU) (1)	18,867	403	97	11,541	3	1,504	2,534	53	2,148	:	146	200	191	29	670	2,457
Personnel costs/employee (thousand ECU) (2)	34.4	39.0	32.2	44.0	13.3	25.4	33.9	20.8	26.1	:	:	31.4	:	28.9	33.7	22.7
Social charges/personnel costs (%) (3)	22.2	27.2	3.7	21.0	23.3	23.6	29.9	11.2	34.4	:	13.2	22.8	:	21.3	29.2	11.9
Labour productivity (thousand ECU/head) (4)	45.4	66.9	41.9	53.6	12.6	40.7	50.2	27.8	46.0	:	40.0	48.3	:	58.1	41.3	43.5
Wage adjusted labour productivity (%) (2)	132.0	164.2	129.9	116.9	123.7	160.9	145.6	132.8	161.9	:	:	154.1	:	131.0	134.5	146.0

(1) A (1994); EU-15 (1995). (2) A (1994); EU-15, EL, I (1995); B, DK, D, E, F, IRL, FIN, S, UK (1996). (3) A (1994); EU-15, S (1995); DK (1997). (4) NL (1992); A (1994); EU-15 (1995); EL (1997).

Source: Eurostat (SBS, EBT)

Table 13.18 (million ECU)

Building and repairing of ships and boats (NACE Rev. 1 35.1)

Production related indicators in the EU

	1988	1989	1990	1991	1992	1993	1994	1995	1996	1997	1998
Production value	15,405	18,823	20,770	21,130	20,773	17,977	18,845	19,104	20,383	:	:
Producer price index (1995=100)	:	:	:	:	:	:	:	:	:	:	:
Value added	6,057	7,664	8,113	8,101	8,125	6,783	6,673	6,623	6,517	:	:
Number of persons employed (thousands)	264.9	269.7	262.1	251.2	235.3	212.4	200.0	191.1	183.7	:	:

Table 13.19 (million ECU)

Building and repairing of ships and boats (NACE Rev. 1 35.1)

Production related indicators, 1998

	B	DK	D	EL	E	F	IRL	I	L	NL	A	P	FIN	S	UK
Production value (1)	134	1,045	4,040	177	2,527	1,976	39	2,601	0	1,947	16	431	1,306	600	3,967
Value added (2)	59	231	1,232	97	790	516	18	952	0	502	9	:	436	183	1,747
Number of persons employed (units) (3)	1,198	9,102	27,415	7,282	39,287	14,979	539	21,674	0	15,791	205	8,265	9,840	3,556	35,228

(1) L (1996); P (1997). (2) L (1996). (3) NL (1992); L (1996).

Table 13.20 (million ECU)

Building and repairing of ships and boats (NACE Rev. 1 35.1)

Market related indicators in the EU

	1988	1989	1990	1991	1992	1993	1994	1995	1996	1997	1998
Apparent consumption	12,403	16,901	18,847	20,021	17,998	15,292	15,357	15,867	15,634	:	:
Exports	3,670	2,815	3,017	3,577	4,201	4,444	4,813	4,247	6,027	7,055	7,793
Imports	668	892	1,093	2,467	1,427	1,759	1,326	1,011	1,278	1,193	1,676
Trade balance	3,002	1,923	1,923	1,110	2,775	2,685	3,488	3,237	4,749	5,862	6,117
Export ratio (%)	23.8	15.0	14.5	16.9	20.2	24.7	25.5	22.2	29.6	:	:
Import penetration ratio (%)	5.4	5.3	5.8	12.3	7.9	11.5	8.6	6.4	8.2	:	:
Cover ratio (%)	549.3	315.5	275.9	145.0	294.5	252.6	363.1	420.3	471.7	591.4	465.1

Table 13.21 (million ECU)

Building and repairing of ships and boats (NACE Rev. 1 35.1)

Market related indicators, 1998

	B/L	DK	D	EL	E	F	IRL	I	NL	A	P	FIN	S	UK
Apparent consumption (1)	:	821	3,042	846	2,198	1,316	35	401	1,786	-2	326	470	457	3,457
Exports	127	659	1,274	38	751	1,898	21	2,444	377	102	95	930	203	766
Imports	121	435	275	707	422	1,238	17	244	216	84	62	94	60	256
Trade balance	6	224	998	-669	329	660	4	2,200	161	18	34	836	143	510
Export ratio (%) (1)	:	63.0	31.5	21.4	29.7	96.1	54.7	94.0	19.4	636.3	32.1	71.2	33.8	19.3
Import penetration ratio (%) (1)	:	53.0	9.1	83.6	19.2	94.1	49.7	60.9	12.1	-4,959.7	10.2	19.9	13.2	7.4
Cover ratio (%)	105.2	151.6	462.6	5.4	178.1	153.3	122.3	1,000.9	174.4	121.0	154.9	994.0	337.2	299.3

(1) P (1997).

Table 13.22

Building and repairing of ships and boats (NACE Rev. 1 35.1)

Labour related indicators, 1998

	EU-15	B	DK	D	EL	E	F	IRL	I	L	NL	A	P	FIN	S	UK
Personnel costs (million ECU) (1)	5,645	55	321	1,028	138	780	477	11	645	0	422	7	119	299	123	1,045
Personnel costs/employee (thousand ECU) (2)	33.6	52.7	36.0	40.9	20.7	25.2	32.4	19.0	27.2	:	:	36.6	:	31.4	36.2	25.9
Social charges/personnel costs (%) (3)	20.7	24.1	5.4	19.0	23.3	21.6	30.4	11.1	37.1	:	15.2	21.5	:	20.2	28.4	8.5
Labour productivity (thousand ECU/head) (4)	35.5	48.8	25.4	44.9	13.4	20.1	34.4	32.9	43.9	:	33.6	43.4	:	44.3	51.5	49.6
Wage adjusted labour productivity (%) (2)	103.3	94.7	74.5	105.6	69.6	84.7	129.6	161.2	147.7	:	:	125.9	:	137.4	128.9	147.5

(1) EU-15, L (1996). (2) EU-15, EL, I, A (1995); B, DK, D, E, F, IRL, FIN, S, UK (1996). (3) EU-15, S (1995). (4) NL (1992); EU-15 (1996).

Source: Eurostat (SBS, EBT)

(million ECU) Table 13.23

Manufacture of railway and tramway locomotives and rolling stock (NACE Rev. 1 35.2)
Production related indicators in the EU

	1988	1989	1990	1991	1992	1993	1994	1995	1996	1997	1998
Production value	5,759	5,849	7,027	7,404	8,723	9,890	9,544	9,539	10,877	:	:
Producer price index (1995=100)	:	:	:	:	:	:	:	:	:	:	:
Value added	2,362	2,393	2,773	2,950	3,293	3,714	3,468	3,362	3,462	:	:
Number of persons employed (thousands)	95.0	92.6	97.0	96.1	99.9	103.1	94.4	88.0	:	:	:

(million ECU) Table 13.24

Manufacture of railway and tramway locomotives and rolling stock (NACE Rev. 1 35.2)
Production related indicators, 1998

	B	DK	D	EL	E	F	IRL	I	L	NL	A	P	FIN	S	UK
Production value (1)(2)	:	:	5,090	47	1,108	2,692	:	1,103	0	0	282	159	3	509	1,437
Value added (1)	:	:	1,097	36	581	679	:	418	0	0	138	:	2	166	507
Number of persons employed (units) (1)	:	:	22,601	1,988	8,226	15,267	:	10,979	0	0	2,844	2,702	46	3,432	13,747

(1) NL (1992); A (1994); L (1996). (2) P (1997).

(million ECU) Table 13.25

Manufacture of railway and tramway locomotives and rolling stock (NACE Rev. 1 35.2)
Market related indicators in the EU

	1988	1989	1990	1991	1992	1993	1994	1995	1996	1997	1998
Apparent consumption	5,005	5,370	:	6,116	:	8,821	8,809	8,672	9,949	:	:
Exports	770	492	542	1,437	1,544	1,219	1,099	1,048	1,096	1,281	1,323
Imports	17	14	:	149	:	150	364	181	168	89	339
Trade balance	754	479	:	1,288	:	1,068	735	867	928	1,193	984
Export ratio (%)	13.4	8.4	7.7	19.4	17.7	12.3	11.5	11.0	10.1	:	:
Import penetration ratio (%)	0.3	0.3	:	2.4	:	1.7	4.1	2.1	1.7	:	:
Cover ratio (%)	4,619.4	3,619.2	:	965.6	:	810.2	302.0	580.1	652.6	1,445.1	390.6

(million ECU) Table 13.26

Manufacture of railway and tramway locomotives and rolling stock (NACE Rev. 1 35.2)
Market related indicators, 1998

	B/L	DK	D	EL	E	F	IRL	I	NL	A	P	FIN	S	UK
Apparent consumption (1)	:	:	4,680	65	841	2,195	:	830	244	107	189	4	441	1,530
Exports	200	26	940	0	334	661	0	419	38	371	19	50	142	257
Imports	158	28	529	18	67	164	26	147	18	112	42	51	73	349
Trade balance	41	-2	410	-18	267	498	-25	273	20	259	-23	-1	68	-93
Export ratio (%) (1)	:	:	18.5	0.1	30.2	24.6	:	38.0	:	109.4	17.3	1,642.0	27.8	17.9
Import penetration ratio (%) (1)	:	:	11.3	27.4	8.0	7.5	:	17.7	119.9	124.8	30.4	1,251.0	16.6	22.8
Cover ratio (%)	125.9	91.7	177.5	0.2	498.9	404.3	1.3	285.6	213.2	331.4	45.8	98.0	193.0	73.5

(1) NL (1992); A (1994); P (1997).

Table 13.27

Manufacture of railway and tramway locomotives and rolling stock (NACE Rev. 1 35.2)
Labour related indicators, 1998

	EU-15	B	DK	D	EL	E	F	IRL	I	L	NL	A	P	FIN	S	UK
Personnel costs (million ECU) (1)	3,109	:	:	1,022	31	242	568	:	312	0	0	100	50	1	124	384
Personnel costs/employee (thousand ECU) (2)	35.4	:	:	43.7	16.9	30.7	37.9	:	25.9	:	:	35.2	:	28.5	37.7	24.8
Social charges/personnel costs (%) (3)	22.5	:	:	15.6	22.0	22.3	30.6	:	34.3	:	:	21.8	:	23.2	28.5	4.0
Labour productivity (thousand ECU/head) (4)	38.2	:	:	48.6	17.9	70.7	44.5	:	38.1	:	:	48.5	:	38.1	48.3	36.9
Wage adjusted labour productivity (%) (2)	107.9	:	:	89.3	114.3	129.4	104.1	:	134.5	:	:	137.8	:	112.3	116.0	141.0

(1) NL (1992); A (1994); EU-15, L (1996). (2) A (1994); EU-15, EL, I (1995); D, E, F, FIN, S, UK (1996). (3) A, S (1994); EU-15 (1995). (4) A (1994); EU-15 (1995).

Source: Eurostat (SBS, EBT)

Table 13.28 (million ECU)

Manufacture of aircraft and spacecraft (NACE Rev. 1 35.3)

Production related indicators in the EU

	1988	1989	1990	1991	1992	1993	1994	1995	1996	1997	1998
Production value	34,418	40,798	44,982	46,655	46,246	41,531	41,308	:	:	:	:
Producer price index (1995=100)	:	:	:	:	:	:	:	:	:	:	:
Value added	14,337	16,374	17,670	18,107	16,199	15,579	15,675	:	:	:	:
Number of persons employed (thousands)	397.3	407.1	422.8	423.0	409.4	382.9	360.1	:	:	:	:

Table 13.29 (million ECU)

Manufacture of aircraft and spacecraft (NACE Rev. 1 35.3)

Production related indicators, 1998

	B	DK	D	EL	E	F	IRL	I	L	NL	A	P	FIN	S	UK
Production value (1)	634	50	9,833	135	1,152	21,696	:	5,190	:	494	:	54	57	1,381	18,033
Value added	299	17	4,166	93	767	4,242	:	2,052	:	129	:	:	36	505	6,030
Number of persons employed (units) (2)	5,313	553	70,437	4,128	12,941	80,619	:	44,742	:	12,548	:	1,253	891	11,574	102,971

(1) P (1997). (2) NL (1992).

Table 13.30 (million ECU)

Manufacture of aircraft and spacecraft (NACE Rev. 1 35.3)

Market related indicators in the EU

	1988	1989	1990	1991	1992	1993	1994	1995	1996	1997	1998
Apparent consumption	31,579	36,911	42,346	42,554	40,012	33,971	33,461	:	:	:	:
Exports	15,908	20,549	20,325	24,692	25,142	24,265	24,345	26,806	28,436	35,799	40,471
Imports	13,068	16,663	17,688	20,591	18,908	16,705	16,497	16,824	20,530	27,628	34,025
Trade balance	2,840	3,887	2,636	4,101	6,234	7,560	7,848	9,982	7,906	8,171	6,446
Export ratio (%)	46.2	50.4	45.2	52.9	54.4	58.4	58.9	:	:	:	:
Import penetration ratio (%)	41.4	45.1	41.8	48.4	47.3	49.2	49.3	:	:	:	:
Cover ratio (%)	121.7	123.3	114.9	119.9	133.0	145.3	147.6	159.3	138.5	129.6	118.9

Table 13.31 (million ECU)

Manufacture of aircraft and spacecraft (NACE Rev. 1 35.3)

Market related indicators, 1998

	B/L	DK	D	EL	E	F	IRL	I	NL	A	P	FIN	S	UK
Apparent consumption (1)	:	289	8,896	530	1,538	15,860	:	5,170	962	:	191	605	749	15,732
Exports	845	349	12,835	64	815	33,184	375	2,961	1,065	466	95	291	1,524	14,857
Imports	1,039	588	11,899	460	1,201	27,348	929	2,941	1,533	1,035	313	838	892	12,556
Trade balance	-195	-239	937	-396	-386	5,836	-553	20	-468	-569	-218	-547	632	2,301
Export ratio (%) (1)	:	694.8	130.5	47.3	70.7	152.9	:	57.0	215.6	:	172.5	505.9	110.4	82.4
Import penetration ratio (%) (1)	:	203.1	133.7	86.6	78.1	172.4	:	56.9	159.4	:	120.4	138.6	119.1	79.8
Cover ratio (%)	81.3	59.3	107.9	13.9	67.8	121.3	40.4	100.7	69.5	45.0	30.3	34.7	170.9	118.3

(1) P (1997).

Table 13.32

Manufacture of aircraft and spacecraft (NACE Rev. 1 35.3)

Labour related indicators, 1998

	EU-15	B	DK	D	EL	E	F	IRL	I	L	NL	A	P	FIN	S	UK
Personnel costs (million ECU) (1)	13,733	254	20	3,679	96	341	4,070	:	1,528	:	139	:	22	28	443	3,491
Personnel costs/employee (thousand ECU) (2)	:	48.5	37.2	55.8	25.3	33.0	51.3	:	31.2	:	:	:	:	32.9	40.1	29.2
Social charges/personnel costs (%) (3)	:	34.1	4.6	21.0	25.4	20.5	31.4	:	32.0	:	22.7	:	:	22.0	32.6	9.3
Labour productivity (thousand ECU/head) (4)	43.5	56.3	31.3	59.1	22.6	59.3	52.6	:	45.9	:	42.7	:	:	40.2	43.7	58.6
Wage adjusted labour productivity (%) (2)	:	129.0	81.3	90.8	96.2	139.4	95.5	:	134.5	:	:	:	:	103.4	98.6	142.2

(1) EU-15 (1994). (2) EL, I (1995); B, DK, D, E, F, FIN, S, UK (1996). (3) S (1994). (4) NL (1992); EU-15 (1994).

Source: Eurostat (SBS, EBT)

(million ECU) Table 13.33

Manufacture of motorcycles and bicycles (NACE Rev. 1 35.4)
Production related indicators in the EU

	1988	1989	1990	1991	1992	1993	1994	1995	1996	1997	1998
Production value	3,970	4,724	5,268	5,203	5,566	5,218	5,707	6,473	:	:	:
Producer price index (1995=100)	:	:	:	:	:	:	:	:	:	:	:
Value added	1,345	1,530	1,802	1,771	1,765	1,594	1,677	1,910	:	:	:
Number of persons employed (thousands)	53.2	56.3	57.0	55.2	53.0	51.3	48.9	49.8	:	:	:

(million ECU) Table 13.34

Manufacture of motorcycles and bicycles (NACE Rev. 1 35.4)
Production related indicators, 1998

	B	DK	D	EL	E	F	IRL	I	L	NL	A	P	FIN	S	UK
Production value (1)	92	58	850	:	817	891	:	3,967	0	309	:	125	46	139	475
Value added (1)	24	19	250	:	206	269	:	1,112	0	104	:	:	14	52	177
Number of persons employed (units) (1)(2)	523	509	7,136	:	1,721	6,978	:	24,188	0	2,116	:	2,136	354	940	4,271

(1) L (1996). (2) NL (1992).

(million ECU) Table 13.35

Manufacture of motorcycles and bicycles (NACE Rev. 1 35.4)
Market related indicators in the EU

	1988	1989	1990	1991	1992	1993	1994	1995	1996	1997	1998
Apparent consumption	4,412	5,805	6,267	7,056	7,707	6,918	7,563	8,411	:	:	:
Exports	465	486	529	526	522	583	693	813	871	864	885
Imports	906	1,567	1,529	2,380	2,663	2,283	2,549	2,751	2,975	2,884	4,001
Trade balance	-442	-1,081	-1,000	-1,853	-2,141	-1,700	-1,856	-1,938	-2,104	-2,020	-3,116
Export ratio (%)	11.7	10.3	10.0	10.1	9.4	11.2	12.1	12.6	:	:	:
Import penetration ratio (%)	20.5	27.0	24.4	33.7	34.5	33.0	33.7	32.7	:	:	:
Cover ratio (%)	51.3	31.0	34.6	22.1	19.6	25.5	27.2	29.6	29.3	30.0	22.1

(million ECU) Table 13.36

Manufacture of motorcycles and bicycles (NACE Rev. 1 35.4)
Market related indicators, 1998

	B/L	DK	D	EL	E	F	IRL	I	NL	A	P	FIN	S	UK
Apparent consumption	:	187	2,092	:	1,024	1,469	:	3,244	507	:	190	105	222	1,135
Exports	258	50	599	10	377	595	20	1,739	630	89	63	9	74	239
Imports	444	178	1,841	148	585	1,173	33	1,017	827	248	128	69	157	898
Trade balance	-186	-129	-1,241	-139	-207	-578	-13	723	-197	-160	-65	-60	-83	-659
Export ratio (%)	:	85.4	70.5	:	46.2	66.7	:	43.8	203.5	:	50.4	19.6	53.3	50.2
Import penetration ratio (%)	:	95.4	88.0	:	57.1	79.8	:	31.3	163.2	:	67.4	65.3	70.8	79.1
Cover ratio (%)	58.1	27.9	32.6	6.5	64.6	50.7	61.7	171.1	76.1	35.7	49.1	13.0	47.1	26.6

Table 13.37

Manufacture of motorcycles and bicycles (NACE Rev. 1 35.4)
Labour related indicators, 1998

	EU-15	B	DK	D	EL	E	F	IRL	I	L	NL	A	P	FIN	S	UK
Personnel costs (million ECU) (1)	1,292	14	16	231	:	94	200	:	651	0	63	:	17	10	31	96
Personnel costs/employee (thousand ECU) (2)	28.4	33.1	32.6	32.7	:	24.7	29.2	:	24.6	:	:	:	:	28.6	34.6	19.3
Social charges/personnel costs (%) (3)	25.9	28.3	3.5	17.9	:	22.6	28.8	:	39.6	:	14.0	:	:	22.2	27.5	7.5
Labour productivity (thousand ECU/head) (4)	38.4	46.4	36.9	35.1	:	119.6	38.5	:	46.0	:	35.9	:	:	38.7	55.0	41.4
Wage adjusted labour productivity (%) (2)	135.4	118.1	109.7	110.8	:	129.6	125.0	:	171.2	:	:	:	:	140.3	143.8	180.3

(1) EU-15 (1995); L (1996); E (1997). (2) EU-15, I (1995); B, DK, D, E, F, FIN, S, UK (1996). (3) EU-15, S (1995); E (1997). (4) NL (1992); EU-15 (1995).

Source: Eurostat (SBS, EBT)

Other manufacturing industries

Industry description

Other manufacturing industries are comprised of a varied set of activities that are grouped at the end of the manufacturing Section of the NACE Rev. 1 classification under the heading of Division 36. They cover a wide variety of activities including the manufacture of furniture (NACE Rev. 1 36.1), jewellery (NACE Rev. 1 36.2), musical instruments (NACE Rev. 1 36.3), sports goods (NACE Rev. 1 36.4), toys and games (NACE Rev. 1 36.5), and a miscellaneous category (NACE Rev. 1 36.6).

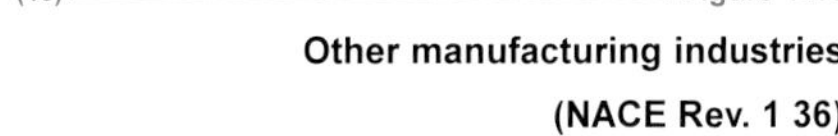

(%) Figure 14.1

Other manufacturing industries (NACE Rev. 1 36)

Share of EU value added in total manufacturing

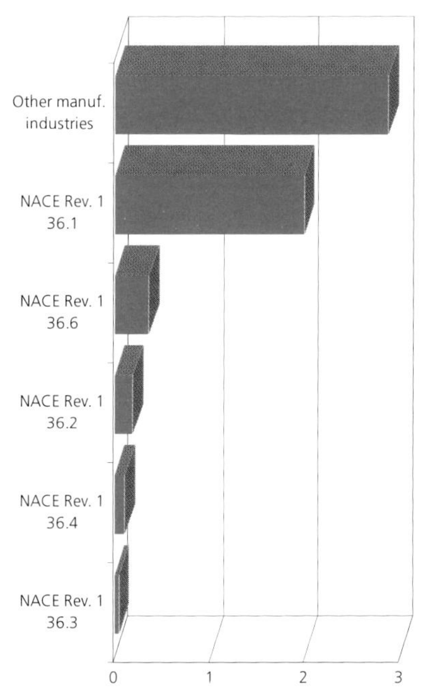

Source: Eurostat (SBS)

The activities covered in this chapter include:

36.1: manufacture of furniture;
36.2: manufacture of jewellery and related articles;
36.3: manufacture of musical instruments;
36.4: manufacture of sports goods;
36.5: manufacture of games and toys;
36.6: miscellaneous manufacturing n.e.c.

Figure 14.2 (1988=100)

Other manufacturing industries (NACE Rev. 1 36)

Production, employment and value added compared to EU total manufacturing

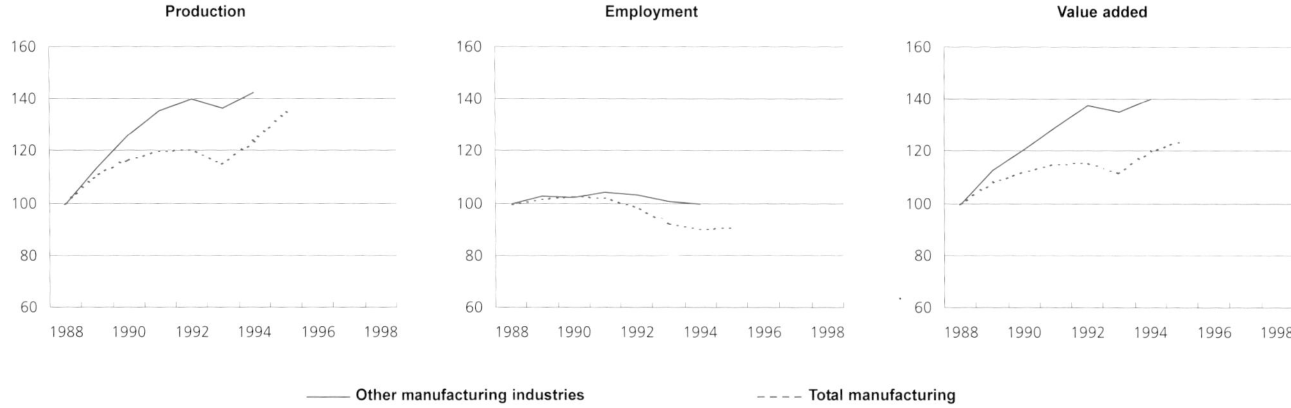

Source: Eurostat (SBS)

Other manufacturing plays a minor role in the European industrial economy, generating around 2.6% of the Community's manufacturing output in 1998. For the purposes of economic analysis it is perhaps wiser to study the different activities apart. There are nevertheless a few common elements that link these industries, such as the fact that they are dominated by small and medium-sized enterprises (which is not surprising given the craft nature of many of the activities). Many markets for other manufacturing products have been threatened by intense competition from south-east Asia, where cheap labour costs have played an important role in giving third country manufacturers a cost advantage. As a result, European manufacturers are often found operating in high value added markets, where skills levels and craftsmanship are sought. Mass-production markets are often dominated by production originating from the newly industrialising countries of south-east Asia, such as South Korea, Taiwan and Hong Kong (and more recently China).

The industries covered by this chapter produce mainly consumer goods that see their demand fluctuate, with sales often directly related to the general economic climate and to personal disposable incomes.

Recent trends

EU production of manufacturing not elsewhere classified rose to almost 100 billion ECU in 1998. There was considerable growth in production values over the course of the last decade, with output rising from 62 billion ECU in 1988. Production in the USA was similar that of the EU, at some 99.2 billion ECU in 1997. In Japan this activity played a less significant role, with output equal to 48.0 billion ECU in 1997, although this was largely a result of Japan having a comparatively small furniture industry.

Figure 14.3

Other manufacturing industries (NACE Rev. 1 36)

International comparison of main indicators in current prices

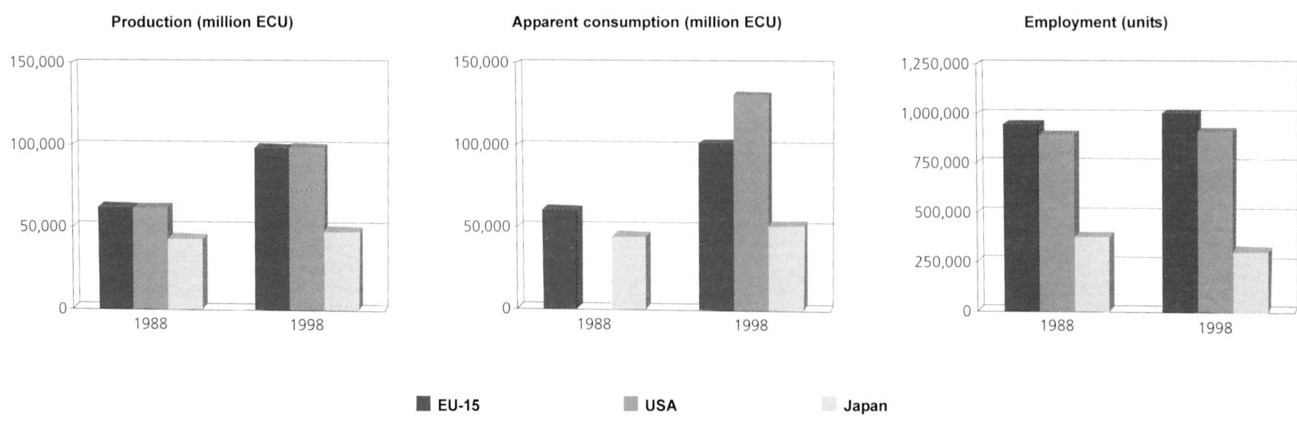

Source: Eurostat (SBS)

(ECU/hour) Figure 14.4

Other manufacturing industries (NACE Rev. 1 36)

Labour costs by Member State, 1996

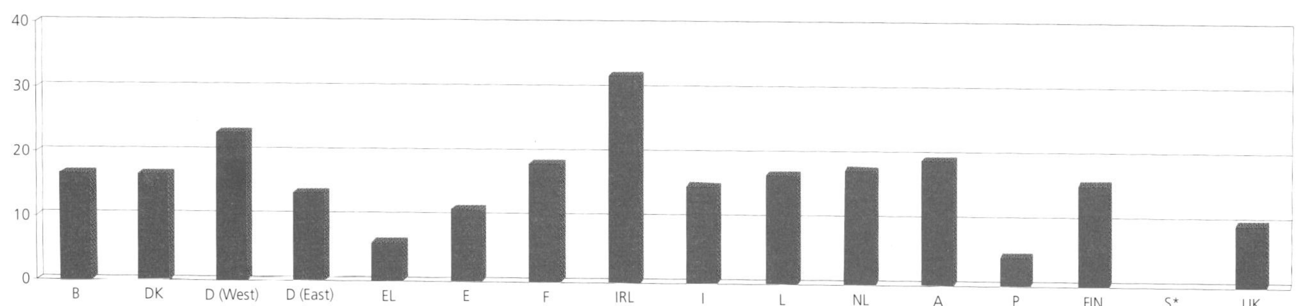

Source: Eurostat (LCS)

(%) Table 14.1

Other manufacturing industries (NACE Rev. 1 36)

Composition of the labour force, 1997

	Females	Part-time	Highly-educated
EU-15	24.4	:	:
B	25.3	:	11.7
DK	37.3	8.7	10.6
D	27.8	10.6	15.9
EL	20.0	:	5.8
E	15.9	3.6	10.0
F	31.0	8.2	9.4
IRL	21.7	5.1	12.5
I	29.7	5.5	2.2
L	:	:	:
NL	21.8	19.2	6.0
A	18.4	8.3	:
P	21.8	:	:
FIN	35.7	:	17.7
S	40.3	16.1	9.1
UK	23.9	9.8	12.2

Source: Eurostat (LFS)

One quarter of the production of the EU was manufactured in Germany, whilst almost a fifth originated from Italy in 1998 (19.4%). The United Kingdom and France had fairly similar levels of output, at just above and below 13% of the EU total. Production specialisation ratios showed that Denmark and Austria were by far the most specialised countries for this industry, contributing 108% and 62% more than the European average to their domestic manufacturing total output. Italy and Spain also reported relatively high specialisation rates in these activities. At the other end of the scale, there were low levels of specialisation in Greece, Finland and Sweden.

Small and medium-sized enterprises played a significant role in this area of the European Union's economy. Within the EU, 42% of turnover in other manufacturing was generated by enterprises employing less than 50 persons. The average turnover produced by these persons was higher than in larger enterprises, as it was generated by just 35% of the total number of persons employed.

Value added of other manufacturing industries rose to 34.2 billion ECU across the EU in 1998. There has been a healthy pattern to growth observed in this activity, which was only halted by the recession during the early nineties (the only reduction in current prices was recorded in 1993).

(million ECU) Figure 14.5

Other manufacturing industries (NACE Rev. 1 36)

Foreign net direct investment

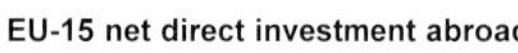

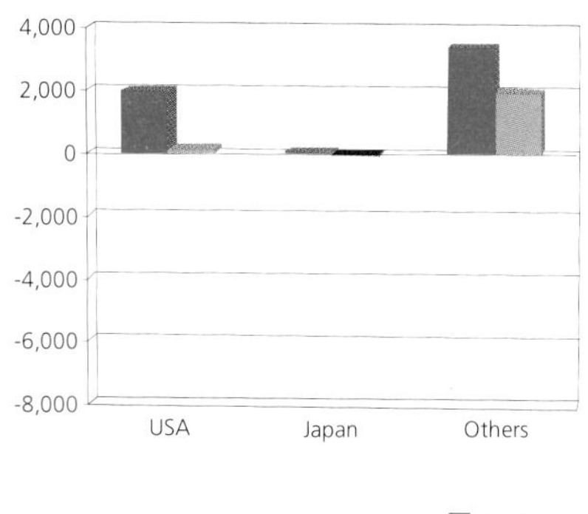

Net direct investment in the EU from abroad

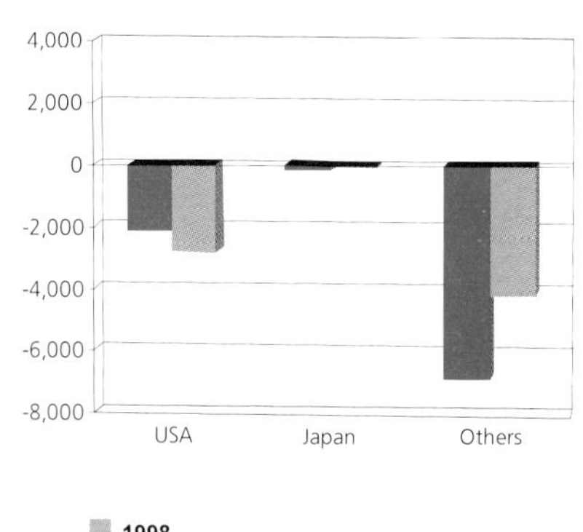

■ 1988 ■ 1998

Source: Eurostat (BOP)

In 1998 there were just over 1 million persons employed within the other manufacturing industries, compared to just under 950 thousand in 1988. Hence, this was one of the few areas of the manufacturing economy where an increase in the number of persons employed was recorded. In the USA there was also an increase, rising from 898 thousand in 1988 to 913 thousand by 1997. In Japan, there were a large number of job losses during the nineties. Japanese employment fell from 379 thousand in 1988 to 310 thousand by 1997.

Given the labour intensive nature of many of the activities, it was no surprise to find that these industries employed a greater share of persons employed in manufacturing than their share of production. Other manufacturing accounted for 4.1% of the European manufacturing workforce in 1995, whilst corresponding shares in the USA were higher, at 5.3%.

Whilst the overall figure for employment in the EU grew on average by 0.6% per annum between 1988 and 1998, there were three countries (amongst those for which data was available) where negative annual changes were recorded, they were Germany (-0.3%), France (-0.3%) and the United Kingdom (-0.7%). Belgium and Denmark both had annual average growth rates for employment that rose above 2% per annum between 1988 and 1998. However, the fastest rate of growth was recorded in Luxembourg (the country with the lowest employment share in total manufacturing), where an annual average increase of 6.0% was registered.

EU labour productivity levels stood well below those observed in Japan and the USA (56.0 thousand ECU and 63.7 thousand ECU per head). There was not a large degree of variation in the labour productivity figures across the EU. The highest figure in the EU for value added per person employed was recorded in Denmark, at 43.1 thousand ECU per head in 1998. Two other countries, Germany and Sweden, were able to report labour productivity above the level of 40 thousand ECU per head.

Labour costs per hour showed a remarkable level of uniformity between the different activities. For example, in Germany labour costs ranged between 21.0 ECU per hour for the manufacture of sports goods and 23.4 ECU per hour for the manufacture of furniture.

Foreign trade

Exports from the EU to third countries amounted to 22.5 billion ECU in 1998, whilst extra-EU imports were equal to 25.6 billion ECU. The EU therefore ran a trade deficit of just over 3 billion ECU in 1998. The level of EU exports was considerably higher than in either Japan or the USA. Indeed, 22.8% of all EU production was destined for third country markets, whilst the corresponding figures for Japan and the USA were 11.7% and 9.4%. The EU's export performance was largely a result of Italian and Danish export performance, where export specialisation ratios were above 200%. Austria and the Belgo-Luxembourg Economic Union were the only other countries to report above average export specialisation.

The low level of exports leaving the USA explained, in part, the large American trade deficit (some 32 billion ECU in 1997). Japan also recorded a deficit, more in line with that seen in the EU, some 3.9 billion ECU in 1997. Import penetration into the USA almost reached one third of the American market in 1997, whilst third country imports accounted for just over 18% of the Japanese market. In the EU the import penetration rate rose at a gradual pace during the nineties, reaching 25.1% by 1998.

Figure 14.6

Other manufacturing industries (NACE Rev. 1 36) Destination of EU exports, 1998

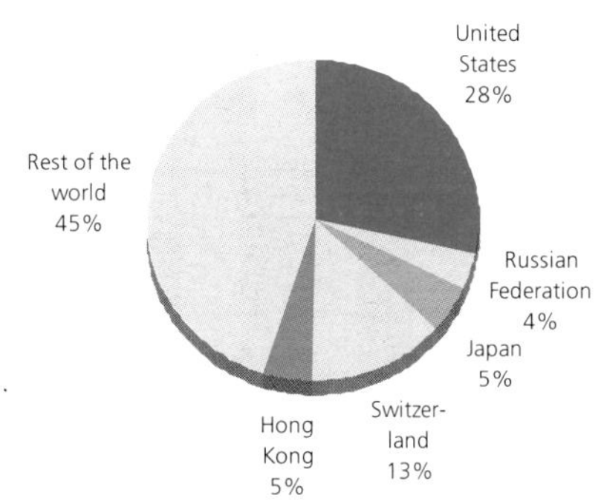

Source: Eurostat (Comext)

Figure 14.7

Other manufacturing industries (NACE Rev. 1 36) Origin of EU imports, 1998

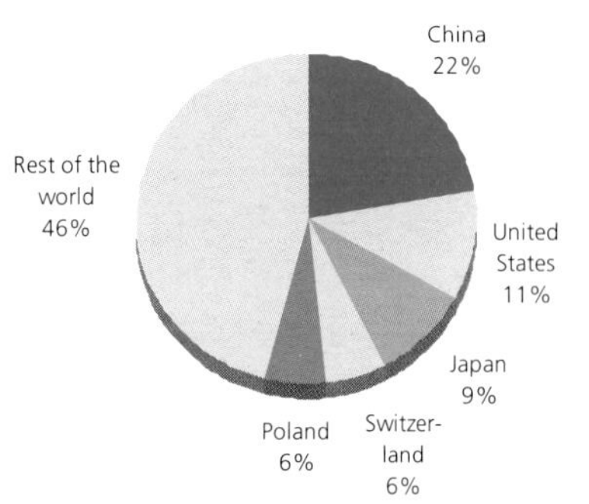

Source: Eurostat (Comext)

Furniture (NACE Rev. 1 36.1)

The manufacture of furniture (NACE Rev. 1 36.1) is one that is composed of many different facets, resulting in manufacturers usually concentrating on a couple of product markets. The two most easily recognisable market segments are those of wooden furniture and metal furniture. An alternative way of looking at the furniture industry is to study the market segments, such as home furniture and office furniture. New market segments that have shown faster growth in recent years include garden furniture, children's furniture, hotel furniture and hospital furniture. Furthermore, at the lower-end of the market, do-it-yourself (D-I-Y) furniture and ready to assemble furniture kits have seen rapid expansion.

The main production centres for furniture are the EU, USA and Asia. Production in the USA was equal to about a third of total world output in 1997, whilst German manufacturing accounted for some 15% of global production. Taiwan and South Korea specialise in the production of mass-produced furniture, using standardised designs and a high degree of automation in their production processes. The furniture produced in these two countries is often "knock-down" furniture (meaning that it is assembled afterwards). As such, the costs for transporting it after production are greatly reduced, resulting in competitive prices. In the future there is likely to be increased competition from countries such as Brazil, Vietnam and Malaysia, where abundant raw materials exist.

In 1995, furniture accounted for almost 70% of the production value of the EU other manufacturing industries. This share was well above the corresponding figures for Japan (41.8%) and the USA (59.9%). EU furniture manufacturing saw its output rise to over 67 billion ECU in 1998[1], well ahead of comparable figures in the USA (59.2 billion ECU in 1997) or Japan (19.8 billion ECU, again in 1997). The share of furniture in other manufacturing rose as high as 84.8% in Sweden, whilst Belgium reported the lowest share at just under 65%. In terms of production specialisation, Denmark was the most specialised country in the EU, followed by Austria, Italy, Spain and Germany.

1) Excluding Austria, Luxembourg and Portugal.

Figure 14.8

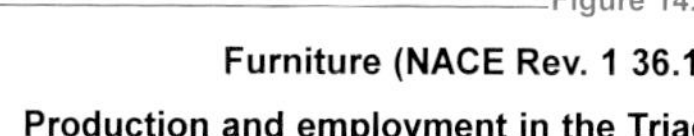

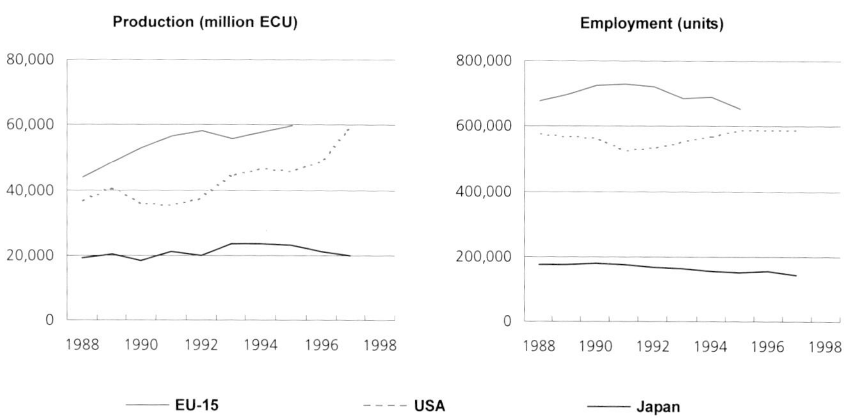

Source: Eurostat (SBS)

(%)

Figure 14.9

Furniture (NACE Rev. 1 36.1)

Production and export specialisation by Member State, 1998

Production specialisation

DK, A, I, E, D, EU-15, S, UK, F, NL, FIN, EL, IRL, P*, L*, B*

0 100 200 300 400

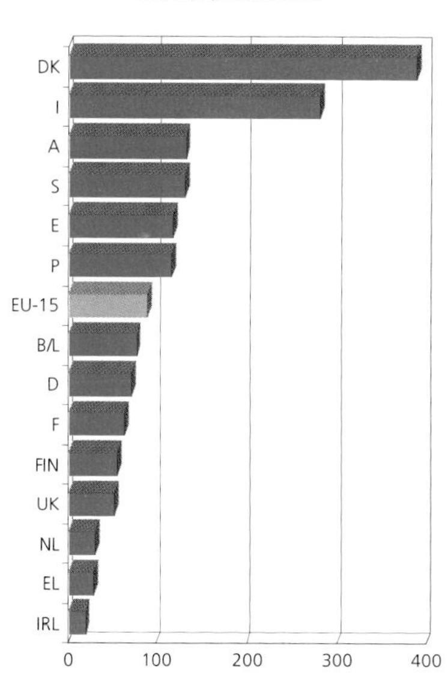

Source: Eurostat (SBS)

The majority of production in the EU was carried out by small and medium-sized enterprises, with most furniture manufacturers highly specialised concerning their production runs. Changes in production technologies meant that the smallest enterprises faced increasing pressure, unless they were in possession of unique craftsmanship. Whilst there was some evidence that changes to highly-automated production facilities using CAD/CAM would result in increased concentration, the industry continued to display concentration ratios well below those of other industrial activities. Many European furniture designers placed great importance on design concepts and ergonomy in the goods that they produced.

More than one third of the demand of the EU originated from Germany (20.9 billion ECU in 1998). Nevertheless, German consumption figures fell in successive years between 1995 and 1997, followed by a small gain in 1998. The United Kingdom had the next largest market in the EU, at 10.6 billion ECU.

The furniture industry is heavily influenced by the purchasing power of consumers. The purchase of new furniture is strongly related to the "feel-good" factor within an economy (in relation to both individual consumers and enterprises). Most purchases of furniture represent a significant financial outlay for the majority of households and the decision to invest is one that often takes a considerable time. Once the decision is made, a lengthy time period usually elapses before replacement furniture is sought. A thriving housing market usually implies a boom in the purchase of furniture.

Demography also plays an important role in consumer demand for furniture. Births and marriages have important consequences on the structure of family life and may lead to families or individuals moving house. Social mobility and the shift to more persons living alone also offer stimuli to demand, as does the longevity of the population (which may also create demand for purpose-built furniture).

There is little brand awareness of consumers within the market for furniture products, except at the high-end, where certain designers are well known. Nevertheless, customers are becoming increasingly knowledgeable about the products they are purchasing, for example, showing environmental concerns. Indeed, one of the key areas of concern for the furniture industry in recent years has been the use of wood and its environmental implications. This has led to a switch in production towards more metal furniture (especially within the office furniture market).

Safety requirements are also very important for the furniture industry, with many countries imposing stringent controls on areas such as fire-safety, especially for bedding and cushions or fabric-based sofas. As well as fire safety, other areas that are subject to legislation include the use of solvents and paints, as well as formaldehyde emissions.

Exports from the EU were equal to a value of 7.8 billion ECU in 1997, considerably above the corresponding figures for the USA and Japan, where exports valued just 3.1 billion ECU and 0.3 billion ECU. Approximately half of the European total could be attributed to Italy, where exports were worth 3.4 billion ECU in 1997. However, the Italian export rate (54.8%) was not the highest in Europe, with Sweden and Denmark exporting a higher share of their domestic production (some 57.0% and 84.7%).

Figure 14.10

Furniture (NACE Rev. 1 36.1)
Destination of EU exports, 1998

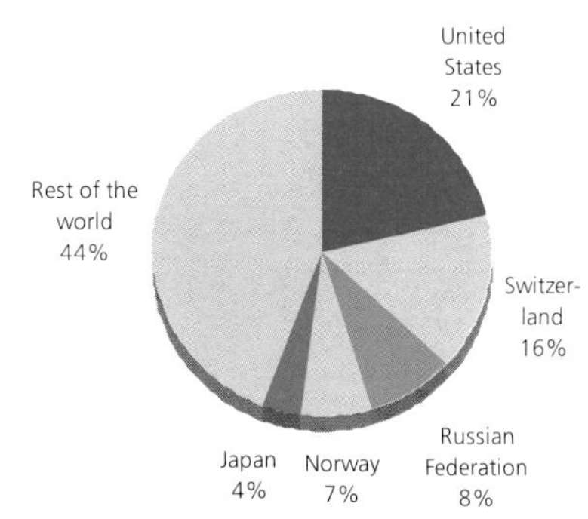

Source: Eurostat (Comext)

Figure 14.11

Furniture (NACE Rev. 1 36.1)
Origin of EU imports, 1998

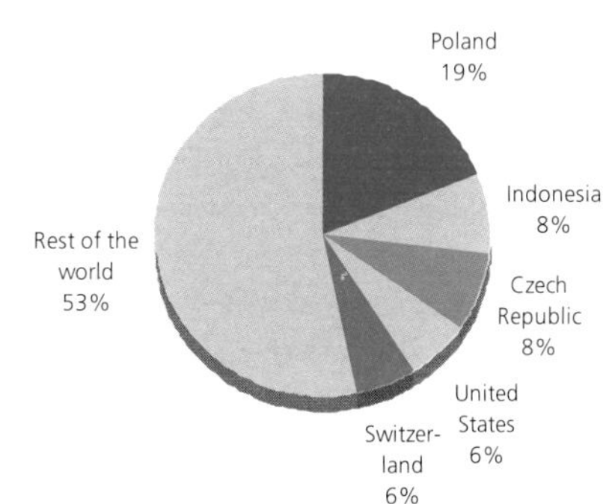

Source: Eurostat (Comext)

Jewellery (NACE Rev. 1 36.2)

The jewellery industry is classified under NACE Rev. 1 Group 36.2 and includes the production of worked pearls, precious and semi-precious stones, diamonds, precious metals and goldsmiths' articles. This activity does not include the manufacture of articles of base metal that are plated with precious metal, which are found in NACE Rev. 1 28, nor does it include the manufacture of watches and clocks (NACE Rev. 1 33.5) or the manufacture of imitation jewellery (NACE Rev. 1 36.61).

Precious stones and metals that are used in jewellery are generally extracted in only a few countries and their price on world markets is often controlled by mining enterprises. Perhaps the best-known example is that of the diamond industry, where De Beers control the Central Selling Organisation, with some 70% of the world's diamond production.

Structural statistics presented in this chapter should be regarded with some caution, as the absolute figures presented will have a tendency to under-report the importance of the jewellery industry. The data presented generally covers only enterprises with 20 or more persons employed. In some cases, the small and medium-sized enterprises that are not included in the survey may account for a large share of a country's domestic production. Indeed, the jewellery industry for both precious and costume jewellery is highly fragmented, with enterprises often being family-owned concerns. Many enterprises in the precious jewellery industry are still of an artisanal character.

Jewellery is a relatively small industry in terms of production value, accounting for just 0.2% of the EU's total manufacturing output. There were four EU Member States that had considerably higher shares in their respective manufacturing totals, they were Austria, Belgium, Italy and Portugal, where jewellery accounted for at least 0.5% of total manufacturing output. EU output reached 8.4 billion ECU in 1998[2], with Italy recording the highest level, some 3.1 billion ECU.

2) Excluding Ireland.

Figure 14.12

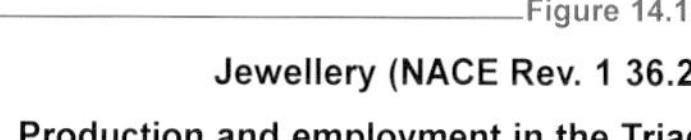

Jewellery (NACE Rev. 1 36.2)

Production and employment in the Triad

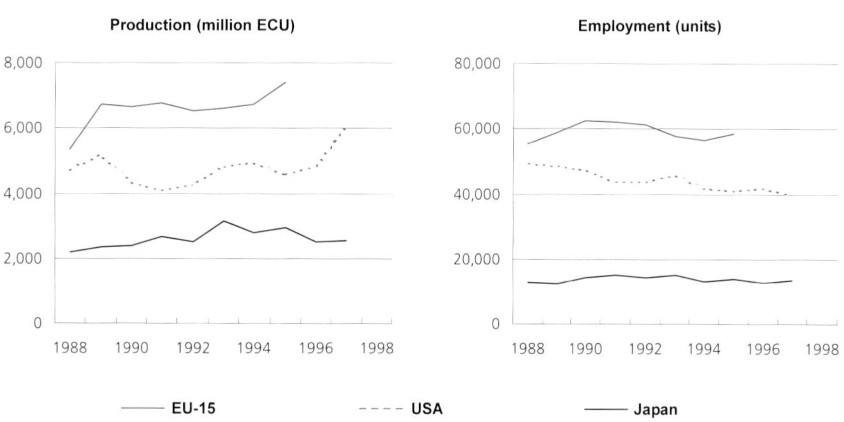

Source: Eurostat (SBS)

Figure 14.13

Jewellery (NACE Rev. 1 36.2)

Production and export specialisation by Member State, 1998

(%)

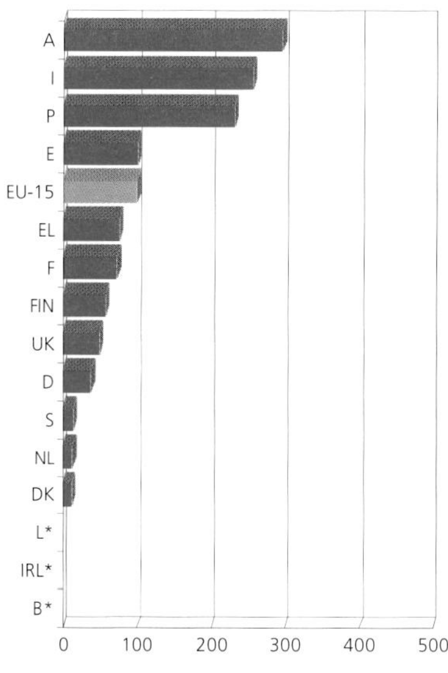

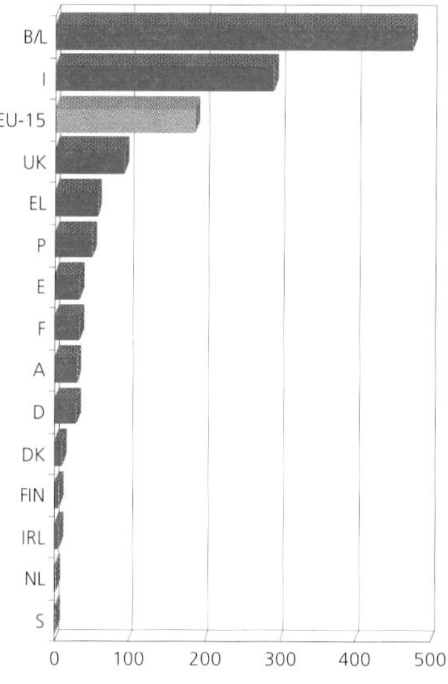

Source: Eurostat (SBS)

In terms of employment, jewellery accounted for 0.3% of those employed in manufacturing in the EU in 1995, compared to just 0.2% in the USA and 0.1% in Japan. Italy had the largest workforce in the EU at around 15 thousand persons in 1998, followed by Spain (with 9.5 thousand), France and Germany (with just under 8 thousand each). There was a moderate degree of expansion in the Japanese labour force between 1988 and 1997, whilst the European labour force showed a fairly constant trend, contrary to widespread reductions observed in the USA (losing almost 10 thousand posts to 39.8 thousand).

Main competitors to European manufacturers for low-price markets included the relatively low-wage countries of the Far East, such as Hong Kong, South Korea, Taiwan and Thailand (especially for costume jewellery).

A new trend has seen the combination of skilled craftsmanship with new production processes in an attempt to boost efficiency and productivity. Such techniques also allow the introduction of new materials into the production process. High technological advances have been made at the top-end of the market in countries that are world leaders, such as Italy and Japan.

Gold dominates the jewellery industry and is likely to continue to do so. The next most important market segment is that of diamonds. Market demand is partly led by fashion trends, for example the use of more coloured gems and (black) pearls in jewellery, as well as a considerable increase in the use of white gold (and mixtures of white and yellow gold).

Disposable income is also an important factor influencing demand. The most important customers of the jewellery industry are women, whose purchasing power has increased at a rapid rate in recent years as their activity rate has increased. Young persons are another important market for the jewellery industry, their main purchases being engagement and wedding rings. Otherwise the jewellery market sees purchases surge in December.

Around two-thirds of the sales in the EU are estimated to be made by specialist jewellers. Speciality jewellers place themselves at the upper end of the market and concentrate on precious jewellery lines. Independent jewellers have been losing some market share since the 1980s. The market is generally becoming more fashion conscious and is tending towards following the retail structure of the fashion industry, with branding taking an increasingly important role, as fashion houses and perfume manufacturers show an interest in launching branded goods.

Foreign trade statistics should be viewed with great care, as many precious stones are quite often semi-processed and then re-sold before actually finding their way into finished items of jewellery for sale to consumers. As such trade figure tend to be over-inflated, as re-trading of goods takes place. Total EU exports to third countries were equivalent to 9 billion ECU in 1998[3], more than a third of which was accounted for by the Belgo-Luxembourg Economic Union and another third by Italy. Indeed, these countries were alone within the EU as being able to report that they had a trade surplus. By far the largest surplus was recorded in Italy, equivalent to 3.5 billion ECU.

3) Excluding Denmark, Greece and Ireland.

Figure 14.14

Jewellery (NACE Rev. 1 36.2)
Destination of EU exports, 1998

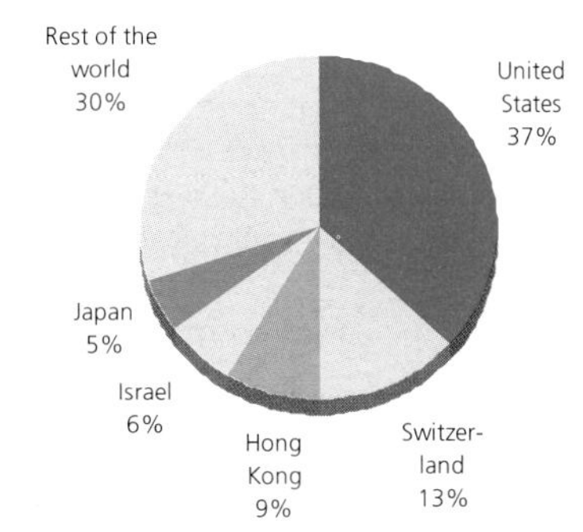

Source: Eurostat (Comext)

Figure 14.15

Jewellery (NACE Rev. 1 36.2)
Origin of EU imports, 1998

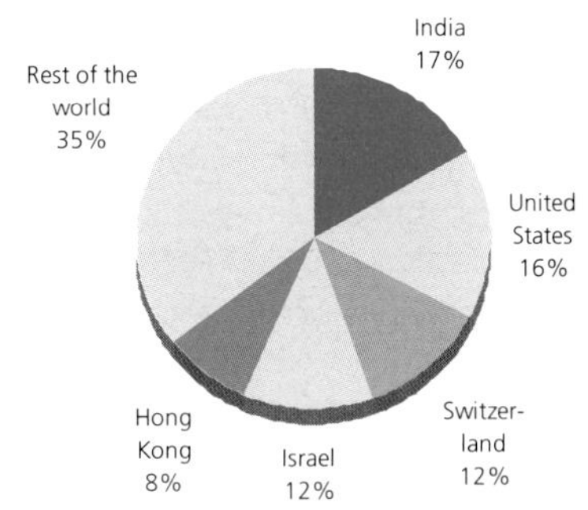

Source: Eurostat (Comext)

Musical instruments, sports goods, games and toys and miscellaneous manufacturing (NACE Rev. 1 36.3 to 36.6)

The remaining industries grouped within NACE Rev. 1 36 produce consumer durables largely for recreational purposes, such as musical instruments (NACE Rev. 1 36.3), sports goods (NACE Rev. 1 36.4), toys and games (NACE Rev. 1 36.5), as well as smoking pipes, jokes and novelties and fairground amusements (parts of NACE Rev. 1 36.6). Given their heterogeneous nature they will be covered in separate sub-headings.

Musical instruments (NACE Rev. 1 36.3)

Musical instruments are found in Group 36.3 of the NACE Rev. 1 classification of economic activities. This industry includes all forms of instrument, such as woodwind, brass, keyboards, strings, percussion, as well as electronic instruments. The data presented in this section does not cover the publishing and reproduction of pre-recorded sound or the manufacture of hi-fis.

The manufacture of musical instruments may be split into two unique phases of production. Firstly, the production of components, such as forming, drilling and cutting; followed by an assembly stage, which for high-price products involves the use of skilled craftsmen to tune and calibrate the instrument. EU output of musical instruments was equivalent to 796 million ECU in 1998[4], a figure well below the output of either the USA or Japan. American output was equivalent to 1.1 billion ECU in 1997, whilst Japanese output was considerably higher at 2.3 billion ECU in 1997.

EU production of musical instruments is concentrated on traditional instruments. In quality terms, EU instruments remain ahead of their main competitors, with small production runs or custom-made production. The EU musical instrument industry is dominated by small and medium-sized enterprises, contrary to trends seen in the two other Triad countries, where a number of multinational firms exist.

There are a number of different markets for musical instruments, ranging from the concert hall performer to the school child. Indeed, school children are one of the largest consumer groups for musical instruments. As such demand is often linked to demographic factors (such as the baby-boom). Furthermore, education budgets and the decision of schools on whether or not to subsidise the purchase of musical instruments as part of their general curriculum are another important factor.

4) Excluding Greece and Luxembourg.

Figure 14.16

Musical instruments, sports goods, toys and games (NACE Rev. 1 36.3 to 36.5)
Production and employment in the Triad

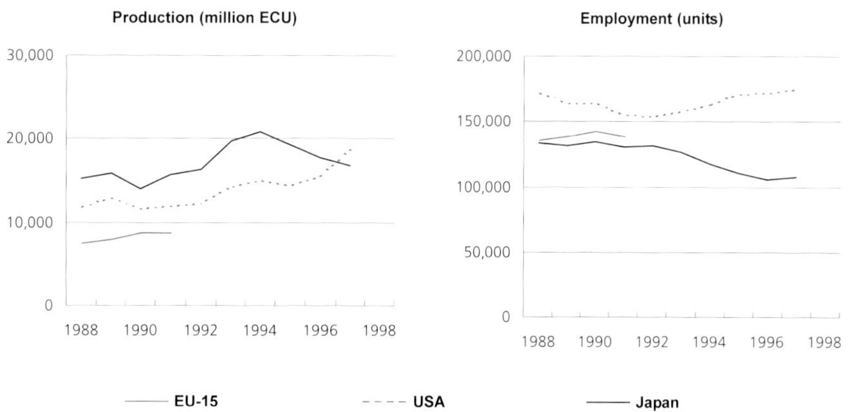

Source: Eurostat (SBS)

Figure 14.17

Musical instruments, sports goods, toys and games (NACE Rev. 1 36.3 to 36.5)
Production and export specialisation by Member State, 1998

(%)

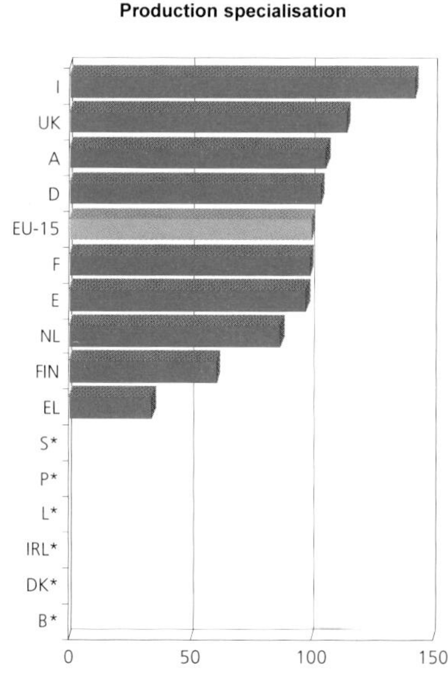

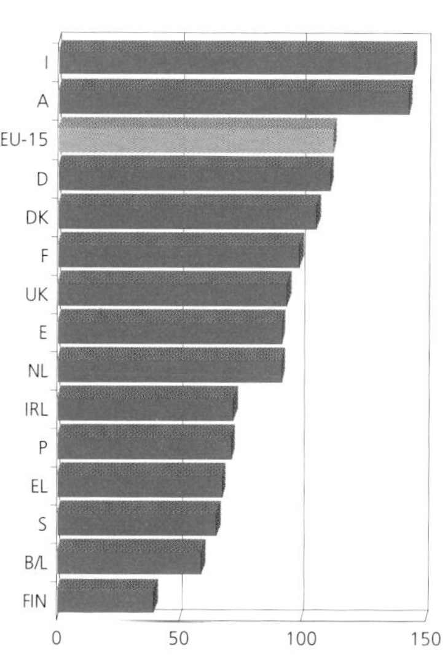

Source: Eurostat (SBS)

Germany was the country with the highest demand in 1998, equal to some 288 million ECU, well ahead of the United Kingdom (201 million ECU). Germany and Italy were the only two EU countries that were able to report that they had a trade surplus in the activity of musical instruments in 1998. Demand in the EU has fallen at quite a rapid pace across many European countries during the course of the nineties. For example, German consumption peaked in 1992 at 413 million ECU (125 million ECU above the latest data available). Consumption of musical instruments in the EU remained low compared to the United States and Japan. This was mainly due to the fact that the school systems in these two countries stressed the importance of a musical education. Japanese apparent consumption was equal to 1.9 billion ECU in 1997, whilst the American market was worth 1.8 billion ECU.

Brand names have great importance at the high-end of the market, with concert hall status an advantage in the fight for market share. In the piano market, Steinway pianos were used by as many as 90% of all concert hall grand piano soloists during the 1998 season. High-end musical instruments are generally sold through specialist stores.

Sports goods (NACE Rev. 1 36.4)

The manufacture of sports goods is classified under NACE Rev. 1 36.4. This industry includes only the equipment used in sporting activities and does not cover either sports clothing or footwear, nor boats or weapons and ammunitions. Production of sports goods within the Triad was dominated by the USA, where output was equal to 9.6 billion ECU in 1997, three times the production value of either the EU[5] or Japan (3.3 billion ECU and 3.0 billion ECU in 1998 and 1997 respectively). Within the EU the largest producer was France (almost 900 million ECU of output), followed by the United Kingdom and Austria (due largely to the winter sports market). These figures were reconfirmed when looking at the production specialisation ratios, which showed that Austria was producing sports equipment at more than seven times the average rate in the EU. Finland and France were also relatively specialised in this activity. Some of the best-known European producers include Rossignol/Salomon, Benetton, Wilson, Fisher, Dunlop/Slazenger, Donnay and Kettler.

5) Excluding Greece, Luxembourg and Portugal.

Figure 14.18

Musical instruments, sports goods, toys and games (NACE Rev. 1 36.3 to 36.5) Destination of EU exports, 1998

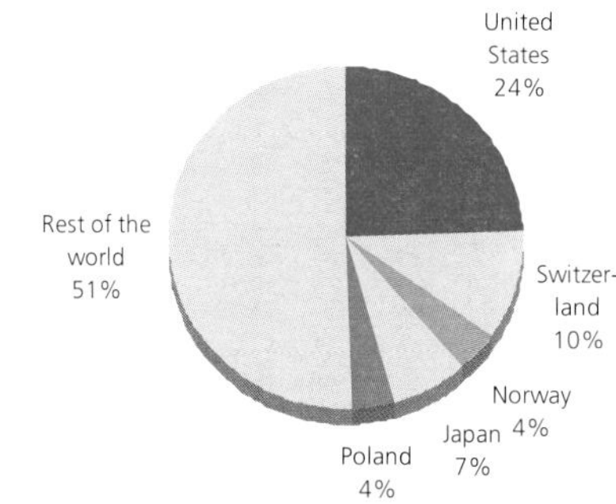

Source: Eurostat (Comext)

Figure 14.19

Musical instruments, sports goods, toys and games (NACE Rev. 1 36.3 to 36.5) Origin of EU imports, 1998

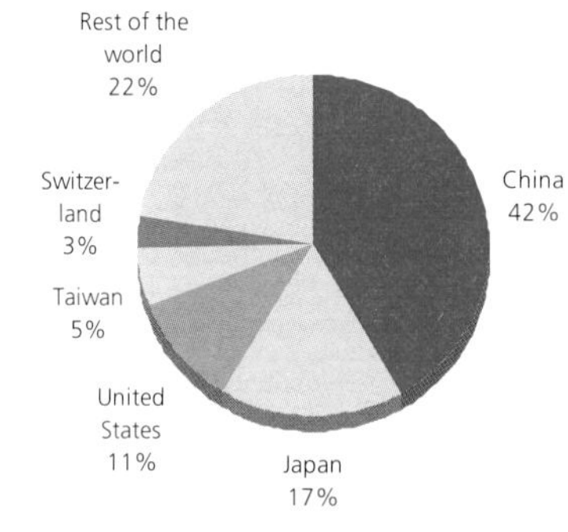

Source: Eurostat (Comext)

The manufacture of sporting goods offered employment to some 28.6 thousand persons in the EU in 1998[6]. The largest employer in the EU was the United Kingdom, with just over 6.8 thousand persons, a large increase compared to the number of persons employed during the mid-nineties (4.5 thousand persons). The most sizeable reductions in employment were recorded in Austria and Germany. In the USA there were in excess of 65 thousand persons employed in the industry, whilst Japanese employment stood at just over 22 thousand persons.

One of the main trends in the manufacture of sporting goods was that leading brand names contracted-out their production under license. As the complete range of sporting goods covers a diverse set of products, it was more normal for manufacturers to specialise in just a couple of product lines. Once a brand name is established it is quite common for manufacturers to then try to expand their operations to other product lines in order to benefit from the brand identity that they have forged.

Many less-established sports markets are prone to rapid changes due to fashion and are likely to be replaced within a fairly short period by another new trend (skate-boarding, body-building, aerobics, steps, roller-blading). These sports are generally those where manufacturers place a lot of research expenditure in developing new product lines. Indeed, innovation is probably the key to success in markets such as fitness equipment, in an attempt to motivate those practising the sport and to attract new consumers.

Generally, older consumers look for quality and durability in the sports goods that they buy, whilst younger consumers are more likely to be swayed by fashion, design and brands in their decision to purchase. Markets expected to offer continued growth include the fitness equipment market and female sports, where participation is on the increase. In addition, as people live longer and are more active into their retirement, market opportunities exist for products aimed at the older generation.

Exports of sports goods from the EU to third countries grew from 650 million ECU in 1988 to 1.1 billion ECU in 1998[7]. The largest exporter outside of the EU was Spain, followed by Italy, whilst if intra-EU exports were also considered then the main exporter became France, followed by Italy.

6) Excluding Greece, Luxembourg, the Netherlands, Portugal and Spain.
7) Excluding Greece and Portugal.

Toys and games (NACE Rev. 1 36.5)

NACE Rev. 1 36.5 includes the manufacture of toys and games, whilst excluding the manufacture of bicycles, carnival and entertainment articles. EU production has shown a moderate progression from the mid-nineties onwards, with output reaching 5.4 billion ECU by 1998[8]. Where data was available, it was possible to see that only a couple of countries in the EU specialised in the production of toys and games (namely Denmark and Spain). Denmark produced just under 10% of all toys and games in Europe, a share just behind that of France, Italy and Spain, whilst the largest EU producers were Germany (23%) and the United Kingdom (17.5%).

The manufacture of toys and games was generally dominated by small and medium-sized enterprises and the EU counted very few global players. Some of the largest manufacturers in the EU included Lego, Playmobil, Brio, Meccano, Waddington and Ravensburger. Within the global market there was a wave of merger activity in the late nineties, with the global leader Mattel buying Tyco Toys and The Learning Company, whilst Hasbro bought Galoob Toys (Star Wars related figures). Three players, Sony, Nintendo and Sega dominated the market for video games.

Unfortunately a complete set of data does not exist for the number of persons employed across the European Union. Nevertheless, it is possible to say that Germany was the largest employer in 1998 with almost 16 thousand persons working in the industry, which was well ahead of the second largest workforce, the United Kingdom, with 7.5 thousand persons.

8) Excluding Austria, Luxembourg and Portugal.

Generally, unit personnel costs and value added per person employed were somewhat lower than for the whole of manufacturing. However, in Belgium and in Denmark this was not the case with each person employed generating on average more than 60 thousand ECU of value added. In Denmark, value added covered personnel costs by more than 200% (which was also the case in Greece).

Apparent consumption within the EU rose to 9.1 billion ECU in 1998[9], somewhat below demand in the USA, which jumped dramatically in 1997 to 15.3 billion ECU (an increase of more than 4 billion ECU on the figure for 1996). Japanese apparent consumption was equivalent to 5.3 billion ECU in 1997, well down on the peak reached in 1993 (some 7.2 billion ECU).

Demand for toys and games depends to a large degree on demographics, the number of children being born, as well as disposable incomes (not just of parents but also children). Toys are very sensitive to changes in fashion and taste and it is relatively difficult for manufacturers to determine the lifetime of their products, with some toys having great longevity and others disappearing from the market almost immediately.

9) Excluding Austria and the Belgo-Luxembourg Economic Union.

Toy production and marketing is inexorably linked with the entertainment industry and in particular with film and television. Manufacturers were subject to license deals to produce figures and related merchandise, with film companies usually being paid on a royalty basis. A similar development has been seen between sports and toys, where many well-known sports associations and sports stars form the basis of video and board games. Demand within the toy industry is very seasonal, with more than half of the total sales for each year being made during the final three months of each year.

Safety is a primary concern within the EU and a Toys Directive was passed as long ago as 1990, stipulating that all toys should bear the "CE" mark to denote that they were conforming to safety standards. The Directive was revised in November 1998, harmonising standards with those in the USA.

The retail end of the business is dominated by hypermarkets, and large specialist chains selling through warehouse locations, as well as by department stores. Specialist toy retailers have lost market share, whilst mail-order has increased its share of the market.

The largest EU exporters were Germany, the United Kingdom and the Netherlands. More than 75% of the exports of EU countries were to fellow Member States.

Table 14.2 (million ECU)

Manufacture of furniture (NACE Rev. 1 36.1)

Production related indicators in the EU

	1988	1989	1990	1991	1992	1993	1994	1995	1996	1997	1998
Production value	43,909	48,491	52,912	56,554	58,175	55,696	57,896	59,879	:	:	:
Producer price index (1995=100)	:	:	:	:	:	:	:	:	:	:	:
Value added	16,436	17,797	19,225	20,676	21,220	20,616	20,671	20,847	:	:	:
Number of persons employed (thousands)	675.3	695.6	722.4	729.2	720.2	686.5	686.6	652.0	:	:	:

Table 14.3 (million ECU)

Manufacture of furniture (NACE Rev. 1 36.1)

Production related indicators, 1998

	B	DK	D	EL	E	F	IRL	I	L	NL	A	P	FIN	S	UK
Production value (1)	2,917	2,073	19,069	199	6,395	8,483	359	12,849	:	2,004	1,639	:	953	1,922	9,589
Value added	854	763	7,033	73	2,333	2,783	129	3,342	:	638	950	:	397	613	3,823
Number of persons employed (units) (2)	22,460	19,280	166,162	3,504	125,976	74,458	5,309	98,839	:	18,436	25,326	:	13,240	15,705	105,534

(1) A (1997). (2) NL (1992).

Table 14.4 (million ECU)

Manufacture of furniture (NACE Rev. 1 36.1)

Market related indicators in the EU

	1988	1989	1990	1991	1992	1993	1994	1995	1996	1997	1998
Apparent consumption	41,829	46,349	50,831	54,996	56,918	54,413	56,168	58,031	:	:	:
Exports	3,837	4,219	4,239	4,100	4,135	4,557	5,434	6,157	6,840	7,833	7,736
Imports	1,758	2,076	2,157	2,542	2,878	3,275	3,706	4,309	4,883	5,862	6,803
Trade balance	2,080	2,142	2,082	1,558	1,257	1,283	1,729	1,848	1,957	1,971	933
Export ratio (%)	8.7	8.7	8.0	7.3	7.1	8.2	9.4	10.3	:	:	:
Import penetration ratio (%)	4.2	4.5	4.2	4.6	5.1	6.0	6.6	7.4	:	:	:
Cover ratio (%)	218.3	203.2	196.5	161.3	143.7	139.2	146.7	142.9	140.1	133.6	113.7

Table 14.5 (million ECU)

Manufacture of furniture (NACE Rev. 1 36.1)

Market related indicators, 1998

	B/L	DK	D	EL	E	F	IRL	I	NL	A	P	FIN	S	UK
Apparent consumption (1)	:	931	20,904	333	5,732	9,250	444	6,492	2,744	1,976	:	935	1,495	10,625
Exports	1,389	1,755	3,927	28	1,211	2,085	115	7,040	579	748	277	249	1,096	1,377
Imports	1,841	614	5,762	161	548	2,853	201	684	1,319	1,020	236	231	669	2,413
Trade balance	-453	1,142	-1,835	-133	663	-767	-85	6,356	-740	-272	40	18	427	-1,036
Export ratio (%) (1)	:	84.7	20.6	13.9	18.9	24.6	32.1	54.8	28.9	50.3	:	26.2	57.0	14.4
Import penetration ratio (%) (1)	:	65.9	27.6	48.4	9.6	30.8	45.2	10.5	48.1	58.8	:	24.7	44.8	22.7
Cover ratio (%)	75.4	286.1	68.2	17.2	221.0	73.1	57.4	1,029.4	43.9	73.3	117.1	107.8	163.8	57.1

(1) A (1997).

Table 14.6

Manufacture of furniture (NACE Rev. 1 36.1)

Labour related indicators, 1998

	EU-15	B	DK	D	EL	E	F	IRL	I	L	NL	A	P	FIN	S	UK
Personnel costs (million ECU) (1)	16,193	534	574	5,392	39	1,678	2,032	79	2,389	:	488	671	:	311	473	2,550
Personnel costs/employee (thousand ECU) (2)	26.2	28.6	30.4	35.0	12.3	15.8	27.8	15.3	22.0	:	:	28.0	:	25.3	31.6	19.5
Social charges/personnel costs (%) (3)	20.9	31.0	4.3	18.0	23.1	22.6	28.9	20.7	37.0	:	12.2	23.0	:	21.5	28.7	11.0
Labour productivity (thousand ECU/head) (4)	32.0	38.0	39.6	42.3	20.8	18.5	37.4	24.3	33.8	:	32.1	37.5	:	30.0	39.0	36.2
Wage adjusted labour productivity (%) (2)	122.0	117.7	136.2	120.1	139.2	114.1	122.4	153.2	148.4	:	:	124.6	:	131.1	133.7	150.0

(1) EU-15 (1995). (2) EU-15, EL, I, A (1995); B, DK, D, E, F, IRL, FIN, S, UK (1996). (3) EU-15, S (1995). (4) NL (1992); EU-15 (1995).

Source: Eurostat (SBS, EBT)

(million ECU) Table 14.7

Manufacture of jewellery and related articles (NACE Rev. 1 36.2)

Production related indicators in the EU

	1988	1989	1990	1991	1992	1993	1994	1995	1996	1997	1998
Production value	5,326	6,727	6,627	6,752	6,508	6,602	6,736	7,393	:	:	:
Producer price index (1995=100)	:	:	:	:	:	:	:	100.0	103.8	98.6	97.6
Value added	1,878	2,440	2,351	2,147	2,092	2,012	1,993	1,961	:	:	:
Number of persons employed (thousands)	55.3	58.8	62.3	62.0	61.4	57.7	56.7	58.5	:	:	:

(million ECU) Table 14.8

Manufacture of jewellery and related articles (NACE Rev. 1 36.2)

Production related indicators, 1998

	B	DK	D	EL	E	F	IRL	I	L	NL	A	P	FIN	S	UK
Production value	1,210	11	710	37	816	1,017	:	3,080	3	56	549	300	70	35	538
Value added (1)	102	5	291	12	203	301	143	507	1	24	71	:	32	18	143
Number of persons employed (units) (1)	3,262	93	7,895	534	9,545	7,526	1,862	14,989	36	703	587	4,586	955	336	4,672

(1) IRL (1990).

(million ECU) Table 14.9

Manufacture of jewellery and related articles (NACE Rev. 1 36.2)

Market related indicators in the EU

	1988	1989	1990	1991	1992	1993	1994	1995	1996	1997	1998
Apparent consumption	3,432	4,724	4,911	4,767	4,402	3,820	2,463	4,794	:	:	:
Exports	5,660	6,705	6,275	6,429	6,468	7,616	8,117	7,871	8,387	9,447	8,971
Imports	3,765	4,702	4,559	4,445	4,362	4,834	3,845	5,273	5,800	6,597	5,942
Trade balance	1,895	2,003	1,716	1,985	2,106	2,782	4,273	2,599	2,587	2,850	3,029
Export ratio (%)	106.3	99.7	94.7	95.2	99.4	115.4	120.5	106.5	:	:	:
Import penetration ratio (%)	109.7	99.5	92.8	93.2	99.1	126.6	156.1	110.0	:	:	:
Cover ratio (%)	150.3	142.6	137.6	144.7	148.3	157.6	211.1	149.3	144.6	143.2	151.0

(million ECU) Table 14.10

Manufacture of jewellery and related articles (NACE Rev. 1 36.2)

Market related indicators, 1998

	B/L	DK	D	EL	E	F	IRL	I	NL	A	P	FIN	S	UK
Apparent consumption	:	29	916	68	882	1,241	:	-370	132	592	324	81	77	1,084
Exports	4,791	27	892	31	193	614	20	4,111	31	98	68	18	13	1,418
Imports	3,966	46	1,099	62	259	838	73	661	108	141	92	29	55	1,964
Trade balance	826	-18	-206	-31	-66	-224	-53	3,450	-76	-43	-24	-11	-42	-546
Export ratio (%)	:	256.4	125.7	83.5	23.7	60.4	:	133.5	56.6	17.9	22.7	25.5	37.2	263.6
Import penetration ratio (%)	:	157.4	119.9	91.0	29.4	67.5	:	-178.6	81.7	23.8	28.5	35.9	71.4	181.2
Cover ratio (%)	120.8	59.8	81.2	49.9	74.6	73.3	27.7	622.3	29.3	69.5	73.7	61.0	23.7	72.2

Table 14.11

Manufacture of jewellery and related articles (NACE Rev. 1 36.2)

Labour related indicators, 1998

	EU-15	B	DK	D	EL	E	F	IRL	I	L	NL	A	P	FIN	S	UK
Personnel costs (million ECU) (1)	1,227	47	4	232	7	132	247	55	346	1	18	20	35	25	10	121
Personnel costs/employee (thousand ECU) (2)	24.2	18.9	39.2	30.5	14.6	16.2	33.4	:	21.1	23.8	:	36.2	:	30.4	31.9	20.4
Social charges/personnel costs (%) (3)	23.3	24.3	3.5	17.2	23.5	21.5	28.9	:	37.0	:	14.4	21.3	:	22.2	29.6	12.0
Labour productivity (thousand ECU/head) (4)	33.5	31.1	50.5	36.9	21.8	21.3	40.0	77.0	33.8	22.6	24.1	121.6	:	33.7	52.4	30.7
Wage adjusted labour productivity (%) (2)	138.6	133.6	128.9	124.1	133.1	113.7	116.9	:	155.2	98.5	:	325.2	:	151.7	177.6	137.3

(1) IRL (1990); EU-15 (1995). (2) EU-15, EL, I, A (1995); B, DK, D, E, F, L, FIN, S, UK (1996). (3) EU-15, S (1995). (4) IRL (1990); NL (1992); EU-15 (1995).

Source: Eurostat (SBS, EBT)

Table 14.12 (million ECU)

Manufacture of musical instruments (NACE Rev. 1 36.3)

Production related indicators in the EU

	1988	1989	1990	1991	1992	1993	1994	1995	1996	1997	1998
Production value	839	733	841	822	:	:	:	834	:	:	:
Producer price index (1995=100)	78.8	81.3	84.0	87.3	90.7	93.4	96.6	100.0	86.1	89.8	84.6
Value added	355	350	384	393	:	:	:	388	:	:	:
Number of persons employed (thousands)	16.1	16.0	16.3	15.7	:	:	:	11.9	:	:	:

Table 14.13 (million ECU)

Manufacture of musical instruments (NACE Rev. 1 36.3)

Production related indicators, 1998

	B	DK	D	EL	E	F	IRL	I	L	NL	A	P	FIN	S	UK
Production value (1)	10	9	310	0	32	104	3	210	:	18	20	1	6	2	71
Value added (1)	5	6	181	0	17	60	1	58	:	8	14	:	3	1	34
Number of persons employed (units) (1)(2)	99	159	5,428	0	752	1,545	56	1,264	:	146	339	55	107	30	1,017

(1) EL (1995). (2) NL (1992).

Table 14.14 (million ECU)

Manufacture of musical instruments (NACE Rev. 1 36.3)

Market related indicators in the EU

	1988	1989	1990	1991	1992	1993	1994	1995	1996	1997	1998
Apparent consumption	941	944	1,081	880	:	:	:	850	:	:	:
Exports	212	254	260	270	279	281	327	346	360	400	375
Imports	313	465	501	328	440	327	235	362	553	525	355
Trade balance	-102	-210	-240	-58	-160	-46	91	-16	-193	-126	20
Export ratio (%)	25.2	34.7	31.0	32.8	:	:	:	41.4	:	:	:
Import penetration ratio (%)	33.3	49.3	46.3	37.3	:	:	:	42.5	:	:	:
Cover ratio (%)	67.6	54.7	52.0	82.2	63.5	85.9	138.8	95.5	65.0	76.1	105.7

Table 14.15 (million ECU)

Manufacture of musical instruments (NACE Rev. 1 36.3)

Market related indicators, 1998

	B/L	DK	D	EL	E	F	IRL	I	NL	A	P	FIN	S	UK
Apparent consumption (1)	:	20	288	12	58	149	10	158	51	29	12	19	15	201
Exports	27	13	269	0	31	93	1	147	48	24	1	1	13	85
Imports	42	24	246	15	57	138	8	94	82	33	12	14	26	216
Trade balance	-15	-11	23	-15	-26	-45	-7	53	-34	-9	-11	-13	-13	-131
Export ratio (%)	:	144.6	86.6	:	99.0	89.0	29.9	69.8	270.2	119.1	122.1	14.4	748.0	120.8
Import penetration ratio (%) (1)	:	120.2	85.5	100.8	99.4	92.3	78.2	59.8	159.0	113.3	101.7	72.6	178.7	107.3
Cover ratio (%)	64.9	54.5	109.3	1.6	55.0	67.3	11.9	155.7	58.9	73.3	9.1	6.4	50.8	39.5

(1) EL (1995).

Table 14.16

Manufacture of musical instruments (NACE Rev. 1 36.3)

Labour related indicators, 1998

	EU-15	B	DK	D	EL	E	F	IRL	I	L	NL	A	P	FIN	S	UK
Personnel costs (million ECU) (1)	322	1	5	160	0	7	46	1	31	:	7	10	0	2	1	29
Personnel costs/employee (thousand ECU) (2)	27.9	26.0	31.0	31.0	:	16.0	30.0	11.7	22.5	:	:	31.0	:	23.4	27.8	21.8
Social charges/personnel costs (%) (3)	20.5	30.5	4.8	19.5	:	22.8	28.3	16.6	33.9	:	10.7	23.1	:	21.8	:	12.3
Labour productivity (thousand ECU/head) (4)	32.5	48.7	36.1	33.4	:	22.6	39.0	25.9	46.1	:	27.3	41.7	:	26.0	30.2	33.5
Wage adjusted labour productivity (%) (2)	116.6	93.1	116.1	112.4	:	135.2	118.1	217.9	165.6	:	:	116.7	:	130.8	116.4	116.2

(1) EU-15, EL (1995). (2) EU-15, I, A (1995); B, DK, D, E, F, IRL, FIN, S, UK (1996). (3) EU-15 (1995). (4) IRL (1990); NL (1992).

Source: Eurostat (SBS, EBT)

(million ECU) — Table 14.17

Manufacture of sports goods (NACE Rev. 1 36.4)
Production related indicators in the EU

	1988	1989	1990	1991	1992	1993	1994	1995	1996	1997	1998
Production value	:	:	:	:	:	2,823	2,803	2,940	:	:	:
Producer price index (1995=100)	:	:	:	:	:	:	:	:	:	:	:
Value added	:	:	:	:	:	1,026	1,043	1,076	:	:	:
Number of persons employed (thousands)	:	:	:	:	:	28.3	28.4	27.5	:	:	:

(million ECU) — Table 14.18

Manufacture of sports goods (NACE Rev. 1 36.4)
Production related indicators, 1998

	B	DK	D	EL	E	F	IRL	I	L	NL	A	P	FIN	S	UK
Production value	30	38	513	:	46	898	50	372	:	59	506	:	92	83	662
Value added	10	12	205	:	17	335	24	111	:	27	175	:	43	39	302
Number of persons employed (units) (1)	245	271	5,161	:	1,216	6,220	904	2,099	:	372	4,277	:	1,851	791	6,827

(1) NL (1992); E (1996).

(million ECU) — Table 14.19

Manufacture of sports goods (NACE Rev. 1 36.4)
Market related indicators in the EU

	1988	1989	1990	1991	1992	1993	1994	1995	1996	1997	1998
Apparent consumption	:	:	:	:	:	2,993	2,928	3,333	:	:	:
Exports	650	745	750	718	768	933	1,067	930	1,134	1,141	1,061
Imports	427	987	924	1,013	1,109	1,103	1,192	1,324	1,444	1,933	1,708
Trade balance	223	-241	-174	-295	-341	-170	-126	-393	-310	-792	-646
Export ratio (%)	:	:	:	:	:	33.1	38.1	31.7	:	:	:
Import penetration ratio (%)	:	:	:	:	:	36.9	40.7	39.7	:	:	:
Cover ratio (%)	152.1	75.5	81.2	70.9	69.3	84.6	89.5	70.3	78.5	59.0	62.1

(million ECU) — Table 14.20

Manufacture of sports goods (NACE Rev. 1 36.4)
Market related indicators, 1998

	B/L	DK	D	EL	E	F	IRL	I	NL	A	P	FIN	S	UK
Apparent consumption	:	69	823	:	118	935	39	217	159	341	:	85	131	1,013
Exports	147	50	336	1	90	471	55	445	87	322	5	76	97	246
Imports	197	80	646	25	162	509	45	290	187	157	36	69	146	596
Trade balance	-50	-31	-310	-24	-72	-37	11	154	-100	165	-31	7	-48	-350
Export ratio (%)	:	130.2	65.5	:	194.9	52.5	111.5	119.6	148.0	63.6	:	82.6	117.3	37.1
Import penetration ratio (%)	:	116.8	78.5	:	137.3	54.4	114.6	133.5	117.8	46.0	:	81.1	111.0	58.8
Cover ratio (%)	74.6	61.9	52.0	5.6	55.7	92.7	123.6	153.2	46.5	204.9	14.7	110.9	67.0	41.2

Table 14.21

Manufacture of sports goods (NACE Rev. 1 36.4)
Labour related indicators, 1998

	EU-15	B	DK	D	EL	E	F	IRL	I	L	NL	A	P	FIN	S	UK
Personnel costs (million ECU) (1)	782	5	9	155	:	21	201	15	60	:	11	147	:	42	25	175
Personnel costs/employee (thousand ECU) (2)	29.0	32.2	33.6	31.1	:	18.9	32.9	16.8	26.1	:	:	35.9	:	23.8	33.3	19.9
Social charges/personnel costs (%) (3)	22.8	27.2	4.0	18.0	:	21.9	29.9	20.8	38.3	:	13.9	23.0	:	22.6	27.2	12.8
Labour productivity (thousand ECU/head) (4)	39.2	38.9	45.6	39.8	:	26.6	53.9	26.6	53.1	:	32.3	40.9	:	23.0	48.9	44.3
Wage adjusted labour productivity (%) (2)	135.0	88.7	135.9	127.3	:	140.9	148.7	233.8	196.3	:	:	106.8	:	150.6	159.0	171.2

(1) EU-15 (1995); E (1996); NL (1997). (2) EU-15, I, A (1995); B, DK, D, E, F, IRL, FIN, S, UK (1996). (3) S (1994); EU-15 (1995); E (1996); NL (1997). (4) NL (1992); EU-15 (1995); E (1996).

Source: Eurostat (SBS, EBT)

Table 14.22 (million ECU)

Manufacture of games and toys (NACE Rev. 1 36.5)

Production related indicators in the EU

	1988	1989	1990	1991	1992	1993	1994	1995	1996	1997	1998
Production value	:	:	:	:	:	4,327	4,755	:	:	:	:
Producer price index (1995=100)	:	:	:	:	:	:	:	:	:	:	:
Value added	:	:	:	:	:	1,756	1,812	:	:	:	:
Number of persons employed (thousands)	:	:	:	:	:	45.6	47.7	:	:	:	:

Table 14.23 (million ECU)

Manufacture of games and toys (NACE Rev. 1 36.5)

Production related indicators, 1998

	B	DK	D	EL	E	F	IRL	I	L	NL	A	P	FIN	S	UK
Production value (1)	106	443	1,431	2	705	622	108	1,033	:	29	88	:	19	63	821
Value added	41	237	605	1	224	204	35	122	:	9	52	:	9	24	305
Number of persons employed (units) (1)(2)	605	3,819	15,742	74	6,760	5,236	1,028	6,460	:	638	1,431	:	296	726	7,538

(1) A (1997). (2) NL (1992); E (1996).

Table 14.24 (million ECU)

Manufacture of games and toys (NACE Rev. 1 36.5)

Market related indicators in the EU

	1988	1989	1990	1991	1992	1993	1994	1995	1996	1997	1998
Apparent consumption	:	:	:	:	:	8,192	7,894	:	:	:	:
Exports	530	603	681	753	797	895	1,022	1,044	1,033	1,165	1,111
Imports	2,098	2,454	2,670	3,977	4,873	4,760	4,161	3,820	4,089	5,477	5,494
Trade balance	-1,569	-1,851	-1,989	-3,223	-4,076	-3,865	-3,139	-2,776	-3,056	-4,312	-4,384
Export ratio (%)	:	:	:	:	:	20.7	21.5	:	:	:	:
Import penetration ratio (%)	:	:	:	:	:	58.1	52.7	:	:	:	:
Cover ratio (%)	25.2	24.6	25.5	18.9	16.4	18.8	24.6	27.3	25.3	21.3	20.2

Table 14.25 (million ECU)

Manufacture of games and toys (NACE Rev. 1 36.5)

Market related indicators, 1998

	B/L	DK	D	EL	E	F	IRL	I	NL	A	P	FIN	S	UK
Apparent consumption (1)	:	550	2,338	114	849	1,453	127	1,237	265	179	:	63	202	1,905
Exports	340	62	943	12	420	380	100	523	702	135	17	21	92	764
Imports	634	169	1,850	124	564	1,211	119	726	938	231	115	65	231	1,848
Trade balance	-294	-107	-907	-112	-144	-831	-19	-204	-236	-96	-98	-44	-139	-1,084
Export ratio (%) (1)	:	14.0	65.9	498.5	59.6	61.0	92.4	50.6	2,440.5	179.3	:	113.3	145.6	93.0
Import penetration ratio (%) (1)	:	30.8	79.1	108.2	66.4	83.3	93.6	58.7	354.0	139.3	:	103.9	114.2	97.0
Cover ratio (%)	53.6	36.5	51.0	9.5	74.5	31.3	84.0	72.0	74.8	58.3	14.8	32.4	39.8	41.3

(1) A (1997).

Table 14.26

Manufacture of games and toys (NACE Rev. 1 36.5)

Labour related indicators, 1998

	EU-15	B	DK	D	EL	E	F	IRL	I	L	NL	A	P	FIN	S	UK
Personnel costs (million ECU) (1)	1,075	21	111	404	1	128	136	19	164	:	6	39	:	5	25	172
Personnel costs/employee (thousand ECU) (2)	:	35.9	29.7	26.8	8.6	20.1	26.4	18.2	23.1	:	:	27.2	:	21.6	36.5	17.6
Social charges/personnel costs (%) (3)	:	25.2	5.7	17.5	20.8	21.5	28.1	21.6	38.5	:	12.6	22.7	:	23.7	:	10.8
Labour productivity (thousand ECU/head) (4)	38.0	67.7	62.0	38.4	15.8	33.8	39.0	33.8	18.9	:	37.5	30.4	:	30.0	32.8	40.4
Wage adjusted labour productivity (%) (2)	:	130.8	208.9	138.3	141.9	168.1	133.9	179.2	154.7	:	:	117.5	:	163.8	97.2	176.7

(1) EU-15 (1994); E (1996); A (1997). (2) EL, I, A (1995); B, DK, D, E, F, IRL, FIN, S, UK (1996). (3) E (1996); A (1997). (4) NL (1992); EU-15 (1994); E (1996); A (1997).

Source: Eurostat (SBS, EBT)

Construction and real estate

Industry description

The European classification of economic activities covers construction activities and real estate services in two separate places: NACE Rev. 1 Section F for construction and NACE Rev. 1 Divisions 70 (part of Section K) for real estate services. Both of these activities will be addressed within this chapter. However, other activities that also contribute to the construction sector of the economy, such as architects or construction economists are covered in the chapter dedicated to business services.

According to 1997 National Accounts, the branch of building and construction is considerable in size. It contributed about 5.1% of total value added in the EU, a share that was in decline from 1990 onwards (6.2% of total wealth created). Employment in 1997 was equal to 9.5 million occupied persons or 6.6% of the total economy, of which 7.3 million were wage and salary earners. As with value added, the relative weight of the branch in total EU employment experienced decline from 1990, when it accounted for 7.2% of the total.

In terms of contribution to total value added, Austria and Spain displayed a high degree of specialisation in this particular activity. In these two countries, the contribution of construction to national value added was 50% above the corresponding EU level. Three other Member States displayed markedly high specialisation ratios: Greece (143%), Finland (121%) and Portugal (117%). This contrasts with Germany and France where the contribution of construction was 12% lower than the EU average.

Technologies used within the construction industry range from traditional, labour intensive, site-based crafts to sophisticated, industrialised technologies, such as control systems in intelligent buildings. Because clients frequently require one-off designs, many projects bring specialised firms together to form a unique project team. Therefore, in addition to individual specialised technologies, the industry uses general contractors, with or without independent design consultants, to create an overall design and management framework for projects. Specific technology trends are affecting the construction industry. For example, computer-aided design (CAD) systems are gradually integrating traditionally fragmented processes. Prefabrication is moving work away from construction sites into factories. At present, this is mainly light prefabrication of sub-components, such as building frames or modules such as toilet pods.

The activities covered in this chapter include:

- 45.1: site preparation;
- 45.2: building of complete constructions or parts thereof; civil engineering;
- 45.3: building installation;
- 45.4: building completion;
- 45.5: renting of construction or demolition equipment with operator;
- 70.1: real estate activities;
- 70.2: letting of own property;
- 70.3: real estate activities on a fee or contract basis.

Figure 15.1 (1988=100)

Construction (NACE Rev. 1 45)

Production, employment and value added compared to EU total manufacturing

—— Construction ---- Total manufacturing

Source: Eurostat (SBS)

Looking at the structure of the industry, construction activities can be broken down into four main categories: house-building; non-residential; rehabilitation and maintenance; and civil engineering. Non-residential construction accounted for 29% of the total EU production value in 1997. It was the largest activity, preceding house-building (individual dwellings, apartment blocks and social housing schemes) with 27%. Civil engineering (roads, railways, bridges, tunnels and hydraulic structures) was the smallest construction activity generating 19% of production value. Finally, one quarter of total construction activity was accounted for by rehabilitation and maintenance activities.

Figure 15.2

Breakdown of production value by type of activity, 1997

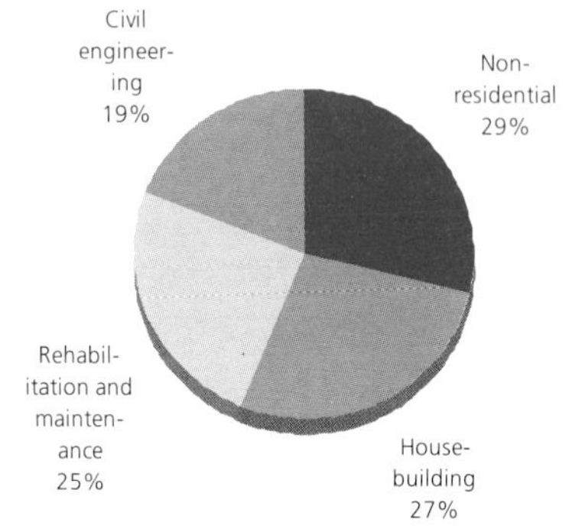

Source: FIEC

Recent trends

Construction output in the EU grew by 1% in 1998 (see table 15.1). Since the beginning of the decade, only two years have witnessed a contraction of activity, further growth of 0.9% was forecast for 1999.

The employment situation in construction was particularly difficult during the 1990s. Employment decreased in every year from 1992 onwards, the worst year being 1993 with a loss of 4.2% over the year before. The situation in 1998 remained bleak in several countries. Germany recorded a loss of 3.2% and Austria 2.5%. In contrast, Ireland and Finland boasted high job creation rates. In the case of Ireland, where employment rose by 22%, a major campaign was launched in order to recall Irish workers who had left to work abroad. In Finland, fast growth in the construction of new buildings made employment swell by 10% in 1997 and an estimated 7% in 1998.

Eurostat's Labour Cost Survey (1996) gives some indications on the average hourly cost of labour found in construction activities in the EU. In most of the countries covered by the survey, the cost of labour in construction was seen to be 10% to 15% lower than the average hourly cost for all industrial activities. Most countries displayed labour costs between 16 ECU and 20 ECU per hour, whilst Portugal was clearly below the average, only 5.3 ECU per hour. At the opposite of the range, the highest labour costs were recorded in Belgium (22.5 ECU per hour) and former West Germany (24 ECU per hour). In real estate activities, labour costs were much higher, ranging between 8.6 ECU per hour (Portugal) and 28 ECU per hour (Austria).

A distinction can be made in the structure of employment between those persons that are employed workers and those that are self-employed. Self-employment is relatively important in construction activities as it represented 23% of total employment in 1998. In addition, as figure 15.3 shows, the evolution of these two categories has been quite different over the decade: self-employment has steadily grown between 1992 and 1996, whilst salaried employment fell over the same period. As regards real estate services, the rate of self-employment is also significant. Figures from Eurostat indicate that the rate of self-employment in real estate activities was 25% in Luxembourg, 36% in Ireland and even 51% in Belgium in 1996. Austria displayed a rate clearly below the average, at only 8%.

(%) Table 15.1

Annual growth rate of production value in real terms in construction

	1990	1991	1992	1993	1994	1995	1996	1997	1998 (1)
B	6.7	-0.4	4.6	-1.1	2.0	1.7	-4.0	3.1	3.4
DK	1.6	-8.9	0.4	-8.2	1.4	5.4	8.9	2.3	-1.0
D (2)	5.0	18.9	10.4	4.2	7.9	1.0	-2.6	-2.2	-1.7
E	9.0	4.0	-6.0	-7.5	1.2	5.1	-0.7	2.1	3.3
F	2.4	1.3	-2.8	-5.1	-0.4	-1.4	-3.6	-1.1	0.2
IRL	19.5	3.7	5.2	-2.7	15.4	18.1	22.7	16.0	12.0
I	3.5	1.4	-2.4	-6.3	-5.9	0.6	1.1	0.4	0.9
NL	0.5	0.6	-0.1	-2.3	1.5	1.8	1.6	5.0	3.0
A	4.8	7.5	4.5	-0.9	4.1	-3.3	-1.5	0.5	1.1
P	5.3	4.5	2.5	6.6	0.7	5.9	4.3	12.8	4.0
FIN	5.9	-13.2	-20.0	-13.3	-3.2	4.9	6.2	2.3	9.0
S	3.9	-3.8	-8.1	-11.4	-4.6	-0.9	1.1	-6.6	7.0
UK	0.8	-6.8	-3.9	-1.9	3.3	-0.9	1.2	2.2	3.3
EU-15 (3)	3.6	4.2	0.6	-2.2	2.1	0.7	-0.8	0.2	1.0
CH	-0.2	-5.6	-2.4	-2.0	6.0	-3.1	-5.3	-5.2	-3.3
NO	-9.2	-3.8	-1.1	-3.6	10.6	10.5	7.9	9.3	10.9
IS	-2.4	5.0	-4.9	6.5	-4.6	4.7	:	:	:
PL	-10.7	1.3	-2.6	2.8	2.0	5.5	3.0	10.0	7.2
RO	-61.2	36.1	4.6	11.4	29.1	13.2	3.7	-22.0	2.6
SK	:	:	:	:	:	-2.3	8.7	10.1	:
CZ	-7.8	27.6	32.9	-15.3	5.2	8.4	4.8	1.1	4.8
HU	-8.9	-19.3	-3.8	-2.4	14.2	3.2	1.4	:	:

(1) Estimates.
(2) 1990: only West Germany.
(3) Excluding Greece and Luxembourg.

Source: FIEC

(%) Table 15.2

Construction and real estate activities (NACE Rev. 1 45 and 70) Composition of the labour force, 1997

	Females	Part-time	Highly-educated
EU-15	12.2	:	:
B	9.8	3.8	11.1
DK	12.1	6.7	9.6
D	15.2	7.4	18.3
EL	1.5	3.5	3.4
E	5.4	1.6	11.3
F	17.4	8.0	7.6
IRL	6.7	4.2	15.4
I	7.4	4.7	4.5
L	9.5	:	9.9
NL	12.1	12.1	8.7
A	15.3	8.3	1.5
P	4.6	2.5	3.1
FIN	12.1	5.8	14.1
S	12.6	10.9	9.5
UK	16.0	9.8	15.8

Source: Eurostat (LFS)

(%) Table 15.3

Annual growth rate of employment in construction

	1990	1991	1992	1993	1994	1995	1996	1997	1998 (1)
B	4.5	2.6	0.9	-2.5	0.7	-2.0	-1.8	-0.9	0.0
DK	-4.0	-6.3	1.5	-1.5	3.2	4.0	-0.4	2.1	0.0
D (2)	3.4	37.9	4.5	4.4	4.5	1.3	-4.5	-4.2	-3.2
EL	0.2	6.2	-0.1	-3.4	-0.2	-0.2	:	:	:
E	7.6	4.3	-6.1	-9.0	-2.7	7.2	3.6	5.7	:
F	0.8	-0.7	-3.3	-5.0	3.0	0.1	-3.2	-2.8	:
IRL	9.0	2.1	-5.0	-4.6	9.6	6.1	-6.7	10.3	21.9
I	3.2	5.3	-1.2	-10.8	-4.1	-2.5	-0.9	-0.4	:
L	7.7	9.7	6.5	0.8	3.0	0.4	:	:	:
NL	0.8	0.0	-0.3	0.5	-1.0	1.5	2.5	2.7	0.5
A	4.8	3.1	1.5	-0.7	1.5	-2.2	-0.7	0.0	0.0
P	-1.2	0.7	-4.8	-1.7	-2.8	2.9	0.8	13.2	1.0
FIN	2.0	-12.7	-16.8	-16.1	-12.8	5.5	2.6	10.2	7.7
S	8.3	-0.3	-12.5	-13.7	-7.0	4.9	-1.9	-3.5	:
UK	1.4	-7.3	-10.5	-7.2	-1.8	-0.7	-0.4	1.0	4.8
EU-15 (3)	3.3	6.6	-2.5	-4.2	-0.7	-1.4	-1.8	-0.2	:
CH	0.3	-2.6	-6.0	-7.1	0.0	1.6	-4.3	-3.6	-3.0
NO	-5.4	-6.5	-6.2	-4.9	2.6	5.9	5.0	7.1	3.1
IS	-7.3	-3.8	-2.5	-1.2	0.7	-2.3	2.9	1.9	:
PL	-6.1	-4.9	3.7	-16.7	-3.9	2.7	0.3	3.1	3.5
RO	-1.8	-31.0	-5.6	16.8	-3.9	-14.0	-2.7	-0.2	-0.2
SK	:	:	:	-12.2	-8.3	-4.0	-2.4	-1.1	:
CZ	2.8	0.2	1.0	11.0	-2.0	1.4	4.9	-2.5	:
HU	-10.7	11.7	-11.2	0.4	2.0	:	:	:	:

(1) Estimates.
(2) 1990: only West Germany.
(3) Excluding Greece and Luxembourg.

Source: FIEC

Figure 15.3 (1991=100)

Evolution of self-employment in construction

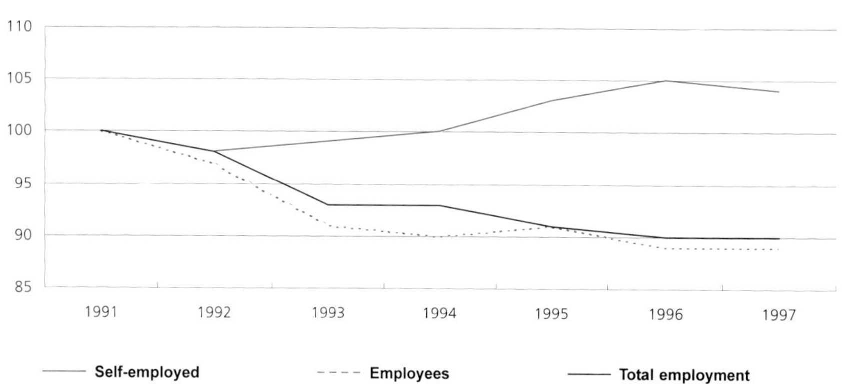

Source: FIEC

Two other characteristics of employment typically found in construction activities are the high share of male employment and of temporary work contracts. At 92%, the share of male employment was amongst the highest found in any economic activity in 1997 (the industrial average for the EU was 77%)[1]. In addition, 14% of the persons employed in construction activities had a temporary job or a work contract of limited duration, whilst just 10% of the EU labour force were in the same situation. Real estate services displayed a totally different picture as regards these two characteristics, as women occupied 48% of all jobs and temporary work contracts represented only 7% of total employment.

1) It is even lower in service activities at 49%.

Figure 15.4 (ECU/hour)

Construction and real estate activities (NACE Rev. 1 45 and 70)
Labour costs by Member State, 1996

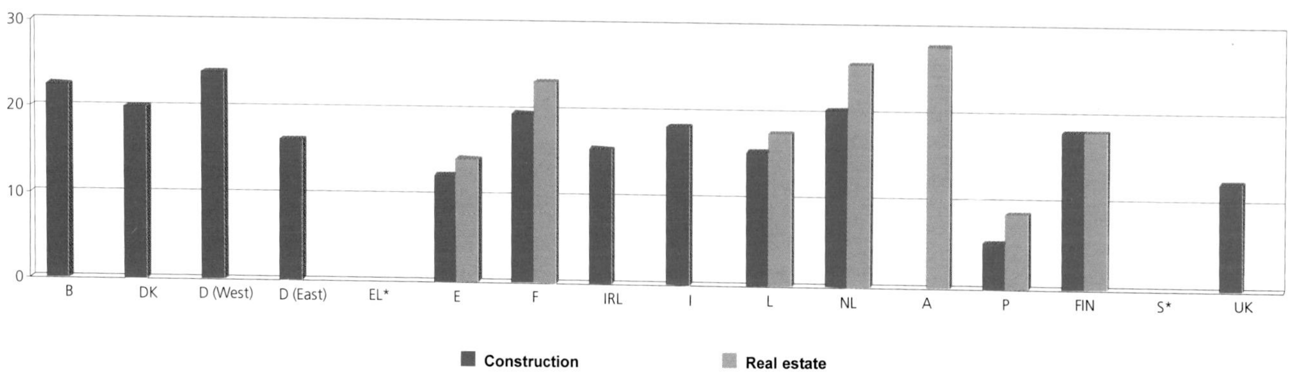

Source: Eurostat (LCS)

Foreign trade

Construction is mainly a local activity, with few large firms and little export activity. However, EU firms are successful in world markets. Intra-EU activity is increasing on large projects and there is extensive use of non-national labour.

The geographical distribution of construction activity is very diversified and varies according to cultural, geographical and historical criteria. Spanish construction firms have a strong presence in Latin America; British construction firms are present in North America and Asia; German construction firms are present in Eastern Europe; Finnish construction firms are present in the CIS.

(million ECU) Figure 15.5

Construction (NACE Rev. 1 45)
Foreign net direct investment

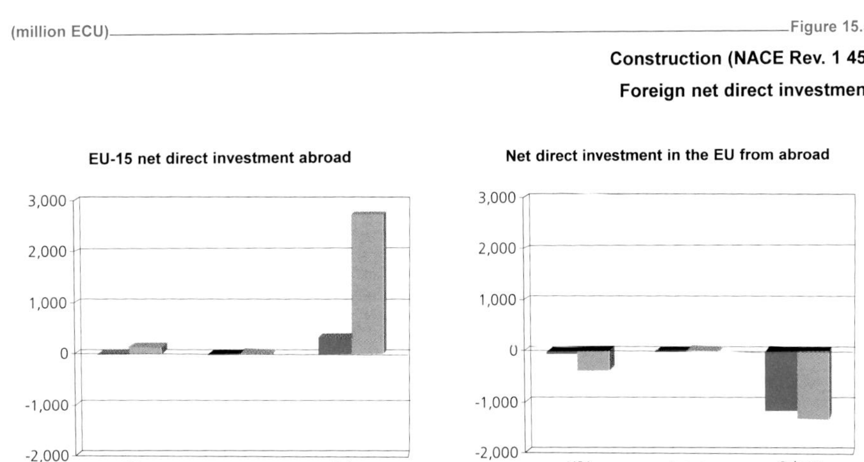

Source: Eurostat (BOP)

(million ECU) Table 15.4

Value of new international construction contracts by region, 1996

	B	DK	D	E	F (1)	I	NL	FIN	S	UK	N	CH
Africa	117	72	259	236	1,985	100	81	0	71	427	21	1
North America	6	0	2,460	0	1,260	48	225	0	1,948	2,452	0	0
South America	87	8	202	1,008	788	228	196	0	61	59	17	0
Asia	524	13	858	107	1,646	641	647	20	56	1,267	57	0
Australia/Pacific	24	0	2,044	0	:	0	41	0	0	411	0	0
Europe	:	:	:	729	5,836	939	:	:	:	:	:	13
EU	681	209	3,433	:	:	:	2,974	60	1,523	696	13	:
Middle East	127	12	191	22	465	321	213	0	1	473	0	0
Other	110	51	696	:	:	:	258	298	714	134	6	:
Total international	1,677	366	10,117	2,145	12,254	2,277	4,636	379	4,373	5,919	114	13

(1) Turnover.

Source: FIEC

Site preparation and construction (NACE Rev. 1 45.1 and 45.2)

The NACE Rev. 1 activity classification divides construction activities according to the stages of the construction process. Site preparation and general construction, the first of these stages, are covered by Groups 45.1 and 45.2 and will be addressed in this section. It is estimated that around 60% of all construction work falls into this category.

Site preparation includes relatively diverse activities, ranging from test drilling and boring to determine ground conditions, through demolition of existing buildings and structures, site clearance, ground stabilisation, excavation, earth moving, and trench digging, to landscaping. Site preparation services are provided both by separate undertakings, which are mostly SMEs commonly working as sub-contractors, and by specialist divisions of large construction enterprises. There are very few indicators of the relative importance of site preparation work in the total construction process. However, according to the European Federation of the Construction Industry (FIEC), examples exist where site clearance and earth moving have accounted for as much as one third of the total cost of major infrastructure projects. Site preparation may also account for a high proportion of the cost of building projects where sites are being re-used, especially where it is necessary to clear land that has been contaminated by previous uses.

General construction activities cover the building of complete constructions (or parts thereof) and civil engineering. Construction activity grew by 1% in the EU in 1998 and was forecast to further expand by 0.9% in 1999. However these figures hide very contrasting conditions across the different types of construction activity within the Union.

In 1998 construction activity grew in all Member States except Germany (-1.7%) and Denmark (-1%). The highest growth rate for 1998 was recorded in Ireland with an expansion of 12%, ahead of Finland (+9%) and Sweden (7%). FIEC forecasts for 1999 indicate that all Member States could simultaneously record an expansion of construction activity for the fist time during the nineties. Figure 15.6 shows the performance of each Member State during the 1990s. Ireland was the country where construction experienced the most rapid expansion over the

Figure 15.6 (%)

Average annual growth rate of production value in real terms in construction

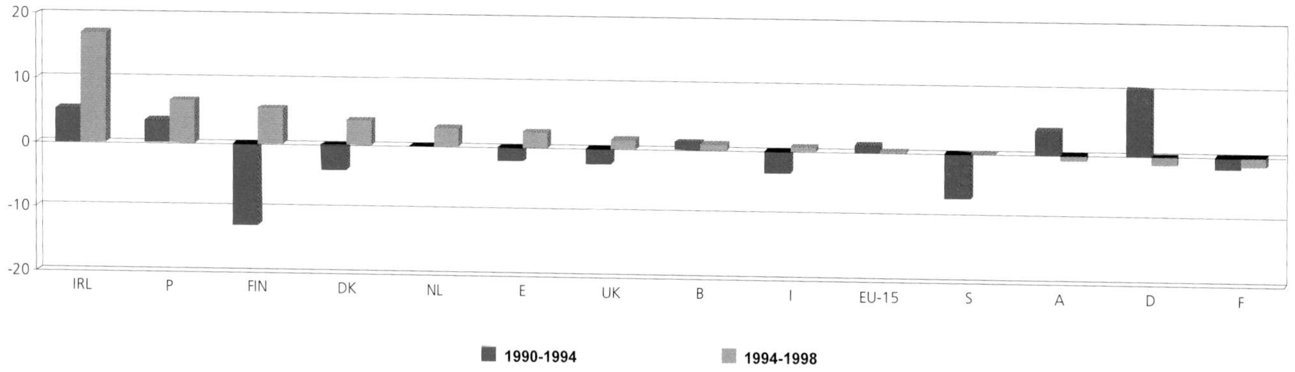

Source: FIEC

Figure 15.7 (1991=100)

Investment in construction in the EU (1)

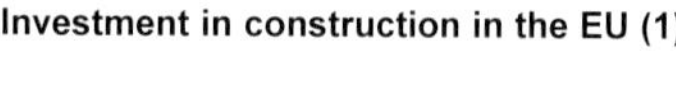

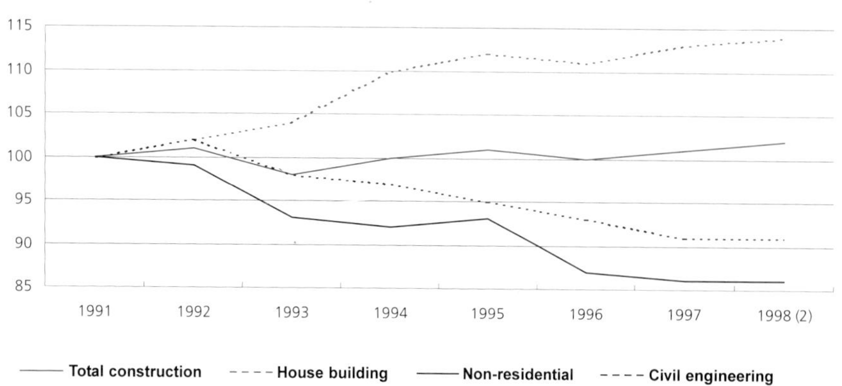

(1) Excluding Greece and Luxembourg.
(2) Estimates.

Source: FIEC

(1991=100) Figure 15.8

Evolution of construction production value in real terms in the EU (1)

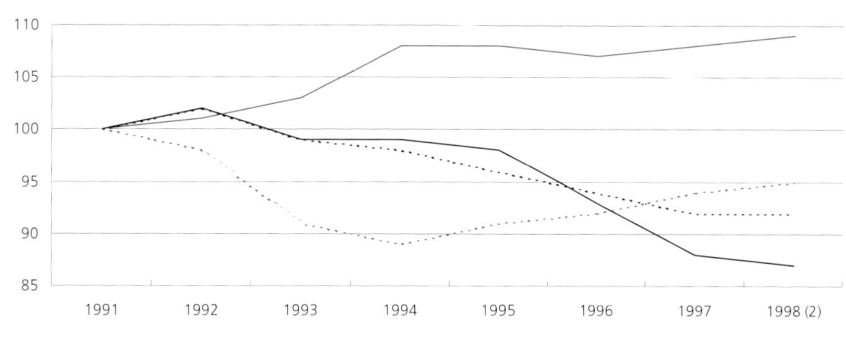

New housebuilding (3) ---- Private non-residential —— Public non-residential ---- Civil engineering

(1) Excluding Greece and Luxembourg.
(2) Estimates.
(3) Excluding rehabilitation and maintenance.

Source: FIEC

1990s, with only one year of contraction in 1993 and six years of double-digit growth. Portugal also fared well, boasting 9 years of continuous growth from 1990. Germany had a mixed record: the first half of the decade enjoyed rapid expansion following reunification, but construction activity has slowed down from 1996. Despite this, the level of activity in 1998 was still 40% higher than in 1990. France, Sweden and Finland all reported low levels of activity during the 1990s, from which they have yet to recover.

Growth during the decade has been mainly in the area of house-building. In 1998, house-building activity was 14% above its level of 1991, with only one year when a decline was recorded during the last decade (in 1996, down by 0.3%). On the contrary, non-residential construction and civil engineering experienced a downturn from 1993, from which they have yet to recover. Their production value in 1998 was still 14% and 9% below the levels of 1991. The main reason for this poor performance could be attributed to the contraction of publicly financed projects.

As can be seen in figure 15.8 the trend of new house-building activity has been generally positive since 1991, as has private non-residential construction since 1994. In contrast, public non-residential and civil engineering have suffered a decline between 1993 and 1997, losing 11% and 7% of production value respectively. Alternatives have been considered in order to compensate for the lack of public financial resources by involving private companies to a greater extent in major infrastructure projects. For example, in the United Kingdom there is the PFI - Private Finance Initiative, a policy for the private financing of transport and social infrastructures, such as hospitals, schools or prisons.

Factors influencing house-building include the evolution of disposable income, the cost of mortgage loans, subsidies and bonuses granted by public authorities, as well as psychological factors such as household confidence in the future.

Non-residential building is also sensitive to the overall state of the economy. Manufacturing enterprises and those engaged in distribution and other services vary their demand for construction in response to expected demand for their own products. However, in the commercial sector (shops, offices) there may be speculative building on the part of developers or construction companies themselves. If economic conditions deteriorate, this can exacerbate cyclical fluctuations in construction as demand for office or retail space weakens and newly constructed buildings are left unsold or are not let. If this happens, demand for non-residential buildings may be slow to recover when general economic conditions begin to improve. Public sector non-residential building also experiences large variations in output from year to year as governments change their spending plans in response to economic conditions. Of growing importance in non-residential building is investment in refurbishment of existing buildings; for example, improving energy efficiency or accommodating modern information technologies for communications.

Civil engineering provides the basic infrastructure for transport systems and utilities. Its traditional market has, in the past, been mainly public sector, but this is changing because of privatisation policies being pursued throughout the EU. This area has suffered from the limited availability of public finance for infrastructure investment. As a result, methods are being sought to mobilise private capital to help fund construction. Generally, the financing of infrastructure projects has become more complex and contractors are increasingly expected to help fund new construction, at least in part, themselves.

(%) Table 15.5

Construction (NACE Rev. 1 45)
Composition of the labour force, 1997

	Females	Part-time	Highly-educated
EU-15	8.5	2.8	10.7
B	7.1	3.5	9.6
DK	9.4	5.5	9.8
D	12.6	6.0	17.8
EL	1.4	4.2	3.3
E	3.8	1.4	10.3
F	9.3	5.6	5.8
IRL	5.4	4.2	14.4
I	6.0	4.6	3.9
L	8.1	:	6.9
NL	7.9	9.3	6.8
A	8.5	4.1	1.4
P	3.6	2.8	2.6
FIN	6.5	3.4	14.3
S	8.1	7.9	8.7
UK	9.3	6.8	13.0

Source: Eurostat (LFS)

Installation and completion (NACE Rev. 1 45.3 to 45.5)

Installation and completion work for buildings, both residential and non-residential, and for civil engineering works is divided into nine categories at the 4-digit level of NACE Rev. 1. The most important of these are installation work of electrical wiring and fittings, insulation work, plumbing work, plastering work, joinery installation work, floor and wall covering work and painting and glazing work.

Several of the installation categories described here contain important sub-divisions. The principal divisions of electrical work for buildings include, general electrical wiring and fitting, the installation of equipment for communications and for security of buildings, and the installation of lifts and escalators. Plumbing work is defined as including all heating and ventilation work as well as the installation of water services, drains and gas services.

Enterprises which carry out these activities include specialist firms (most of which are SMEs) and specialist divisions of larger construction enterprises (which may work either as main contractors or as sub-contractors). When working on new buildings or works, these enterprises are more likely to be employed as sub-contractors, but for refurbishment and improvement work they are commonly employed directly by the client.

Whilst there is at present little data to show the relative importance of building installation and completion work within the construction sector, there is clear evidence that their importance is increasing, in response to a number of circumstances. Some of these relate to technical developments, both in construction and in client industries. There is for example growing use of major components and sub-assemblies manufactured off-site and installed by specialist firms. On the demand side, both industrial and especially commercial enterprises are requiring the installation of increasingly sophisticated communications systems, and are showing a growing interest in research into the possible development of so-called intelligent buildings.

Figure 15.9 (1991=100)

Evolution of construction rehabilitation and maintenance production value in real terms in the EU (1)

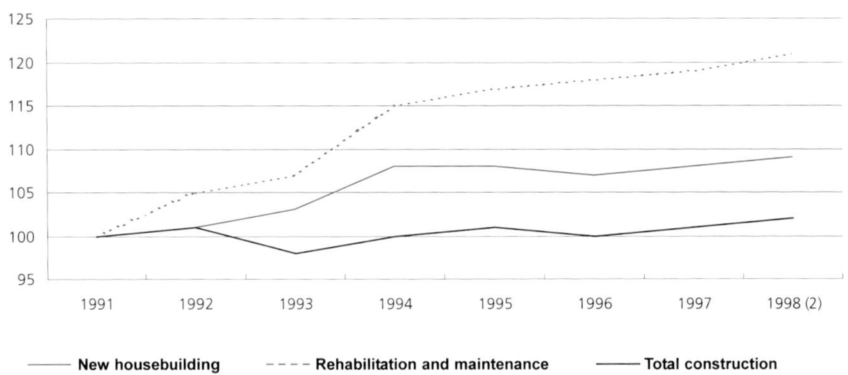

(1) Excluding Greece and Luxembourg.
(2) Estimates.

Source: FIEC

In the meantime, there are environmental pressures that may have positive effects on the demand for building installation and completion services. One such area is the growing pressure through land use planning to refurbish existing buildings, both residential and non-residential, rather than building on "greenfield" sites. Another area is encouragement in the form of grants and low-cost loans from public authorities, to invest in up-to-date heating and ventilation systems, and better insulation. The aim of this is to make existing, as well as new buildings, more energy-efficient.

One area in which there is some statistical evidence is for the repair, maintenance and improvement of residential buildings (there are no comparable data for non-residential sectors). Figure 15.9 shows that, in recent years, growth rates in this sector have exceeded those for total construction and for new housebuilding. In 1998, this activity expanded by 2.1% in the EU, twice the rate of total construction. FIEC forecasted further growth of 0.9% for 1999. The average annual growth rate between 1990 and 1998 was equal to 2.8% per annum.

Looking at the evolution of individual Member States, Ireland clearly stands out as the country that enjoyed the fastest expansion in this activity, with production value in 1998 some 2.5 times higher than at the start of the decade (corresponding to an annual average rate of 14%). The majority of the other countries also boasted high growth rates in this activity, although to a lesser extent. The two exceptions were Sweden and the United Kingdom, where production values in 1998 were still below those of 1990 (despite a strong recovery in the United Kingdom from 1993 onwards).

(%) Table 15.6

Annual growth of construction rehabilitation and maintenance production value in real terms

	1990	1991	1992	1993	1994	1995	1996	1997	1998 (1)
B	20.1	1.6	3.4	-1.0	3.6	-0.5	4.7	0.5	0.0
DK	-15.8	-2.4	7.1	-7.4	5.9	3.4	2.2	-2.5	-3.0
D	5.0	8.9	16.3	6.9	14.2	3.3	0.2	-0.1	-1.6
E	4.9	5.2	3.9	0.9	5.0	8.0	5.0	4.8	3.0
F	2.7	1.5	-0.1	3.0	1.2	0.2	-1.8	1.0	1.9
IRL	32.6	5.8	16.8	-7.1	27.6	15.4	39.5	11.6	7.1
I	0.8	5.4	-1.1	6.1	9.8	0.3	-0.8	1.9	4.7
NL	-1.4	-0.3	7.8	-2.9	-2.8	-0.2	1.0	2.2	2.4
A	15.3	-2.8	22.8	-5.0	12.5	-7.8	2.5	3.2	5.4
P	5.3	4.4	2.5	-10.8	-1.0	7.2	5.0	7.1	5.3
FIN	0.0	-6.8	-6.3	44.0	8.5	7.8	:	:	:
S	1.8	-3.1	-3.2	-7.7	-5.9	-8.7	4.6	-7.7	15.3
UK	-1.9	-12.0	-6.7	-1.2	5.1	1.5	0.2	1.5	4.3
EU-15 (2)	2.8	1.8	4.5	2.4	7.2	1.7	0.8	1.1	2.1
CH	-0.5	-1.7	-0.9	4.6	20.2	-8.9	1.0	-4.5	8.0
NO	1.6	-20.7	19.4	2.4	10.8	7.0	9.4	8.2	10.2
PL	-4.2	-2.5	6.1	6.7	0.4	7.1	1.0	4.9	2.2
RO	:	36.1	4.6	11.4	29.1	13.2	3.7	-22.0	2.6
SK	:	:	:	:	:	:	0.2	6.7	4.5
CZ	0.0	-30.2	13.5	-19.0	-5.9	0.0	0.0	3.1	3.0
HU	9.4	-42.9	10.0	-4.5	0.0	4.8	9.1	:	:

(1) Estimates.
(2) Excluding Greece and Luxembourg.

Source: FIEC

Real estate services (NACE Rev. 1 70)

The various professions active within real estate activities have a dual nature. Some activities relate to primary demand and the completion of property development, whilst others relate to the functioning of the secondary market. To the first category belong builders, developers and consultants specialising in feasibility studies. Real estate professionals operate largely in the secondary market, with their expertise in surveying and valuation of properties, and their role in transactions and estate management. In the NACE Rev. 1 classification, real estate activities are found in Division 70, part of services Section K (together with renting, computer services, research and development and business services).

The property market may be divided into several areas: residential, commercial and leisure property, where commercial includes office, retail and industrial property and the leisure market includes hotels, seaside and mountain chalets.

Figure 15.10 (units)

Real estate activities (NACE Rev. 1 70)
Density of the total number of enterprises per ten thousand inhabitants, 1995

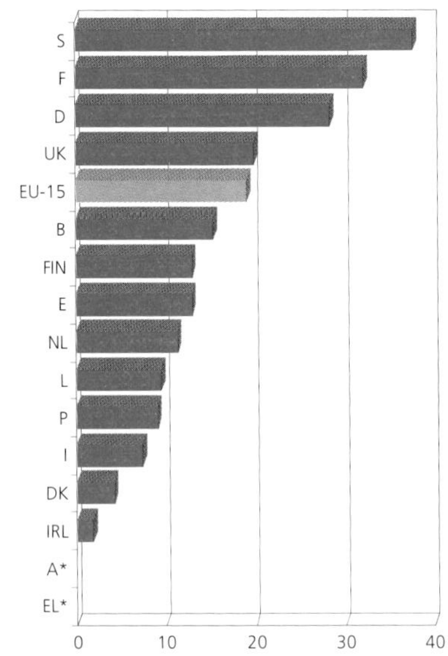

Source: Eurostat (SME)

Table 15.7 (units)

Number of housing transactions

	1990	1991	1992	1993	1994	1995	1996	1997
B	99,800	99,700	104,900	104,100	104,100	96,300	102,400	105,600
DK	56,800	52,400	60,100	63,200	71,400	74,100	76,900	80,300
D	554,000	543,000	612,500	754,300	662,200	619,500	600,000	:
EL	93,100	43,900	59,900	61,400	66,000	67,200	68,700	:
F	754,000	712,500	605,800	584,500	670,000	683,000	694,500	699,800
IRL	34,800	37,100	44,400	45,400	50,200	49,300	61,000	64,700
I	517,100	555,900	465,400	501,900	495,200	502,500	483,800	:
L	2,900	3,100	3,700	3,000	:	:	:	:
NL	202,100	211,100	245,300	198,000	215,000	225,000	260,000	275,000
P	103,400	150,200	166,000	178,100	186,900	186,000	:	:
FIN	56,300	62,100	68,000	75,200	71,100	68,200	83,300	81,400
S	165,000	160,000	155,000	150,000	150,000	140,000	160,000	184,000
UK	1,398,000	1,305,000	1,138,000	1,195,000	1,275,000	1,134,000	1,241,000	:

Source: European Mortgage Federation

Table 15.8 (1990=100)

Trend in the price of dwellings

	1990	1991	1992	1993	1994	1995	1996	1997
B	100	106	115	123	132	138	144	146
DK	100	101	95	101	108	108	118	128
E	100	114	113	112	113	117	120	121
IRL	100	102	105	106	111	118	132	154
I	100	112	119	120	116	118	118	:
NL	100	103	111	122	131	136	150	162
A	100	105	111	118	124	128	130	134
FIN	100	86	71	65	69	66	70	82
S	100	120	104	101	102	100	102	109
UK	100	98	95	92	95	95	99	108

Source: European Mortgage Federation

The property sector has experienced growth in the second half of the 1990s, after a difficult start at the beginning of the decade due to the recession and high real interest rates. Table 15.7 details the number of housing transactions in the Member States. One can note that most Member States experienced growth between 1996 and 1997 (the Netherlands, Finland and Sweden even boasted double-digit growth rates). In contrast, Germany saw the number of transactions decline from 1993 onwards. One should note that the market in the United Kingdom saw almost double the number of housing transactions, when compared to France or Germany.

Between 1990 and 1997 the price of dwellings in nominal terms increased in most Member States, with the exception of Finland. In the United Kingdom prices remained (on a national average) below their level of 1990 until 1996. If we limit our analysis to the period 1992-1997, we see that every single Member States recorded a rise in the average annual growth rate of dwelling prices. The highest rates were recorded in the Netherlands and Ireland, where dwelling prices rose by an average of 8% per annum. Denmark also recorded a relatively fast increase in prices. In contrast, Italy and Sweden experienced price stability.

(%)

Figure 15.11

Share of homes occupied by their owners

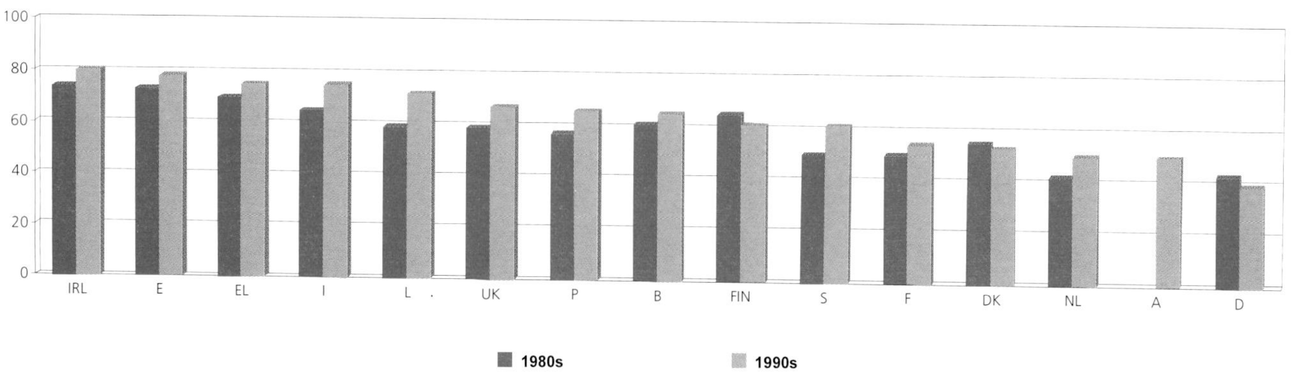

Source: European Mortgage Federation

(%)

Figure 15.12

Interest rates for new mortgage loans

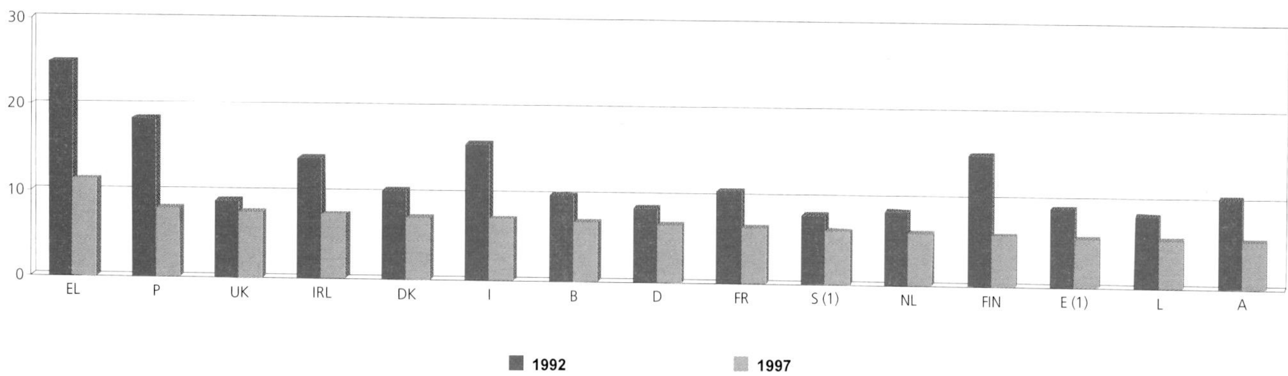

1) 1993 instead of 1992.

Source: European Mortgage Federation

Figure 15.11 shows the percentage of homes that are occupied by their owners. It can be seen that this proportion has increased in most EU Member States over the last decade. The only countries where it decreased were Denmark, Germany and Finland (in all three cases by a few percentage points). In Ireland, where the highest share of owner-occupied dwellings is found, the rate reached 80% (which was twice the level recorded in Germany). Southern European countries displayed, as a general rule, higher shares than other countries, for example, Spain (78%), Greece and Italy (both 75%). At the lower end of the rankings were Denmark (53%), just ahead of the Netherlands and Austria (where half the total number of dwellings were owner-occupied).

Interest rates on mortgage loans fell considerably throughout the EU during in the second half of the 1990s, as has the divergence of rates from one country to another (see figure 15.12). In Greece, the interest rate of mortgage loans plummeted from 25% in 1992 to 11% in 1997 (whilst remaining the highest rate within the EU). The lowest rates in 1997 were found in Austria and Luxembourg (both 5.5%). The divergence between the highest and lowest rates was 17 percentage points in 1992 (10.4 excluding Greece) and this had been reduced to 5.8 percentage points by 1997 (2.5 excluding Greece).

Property demand is largely determined by local factors. The most important are economic growth, replacement demand, luxury demand (upgrading) and location preferences. Economic growth creates a need for more offices, shops and factories. Replacement demand is the base of demand for commercial property. Its volume is dependent on the average lifetime of real estate. Upgrading will take place in a favourable economic climate and when the existing stock of real estate is estimated to be of lower perceived quality.

The rental market is less dependent on economic fluctuations. Unlike the sales market, it is not bound by investment logic: rental is not investment in, but consumption of real estate. Therefore, interest rates are less crucial in the rental market than in the property market.

Figure 15.13 (%)

Real estate activities (NACE Rev. 1 70)

Share of part-time and temporary work contracts in total number of persons employed, 1997

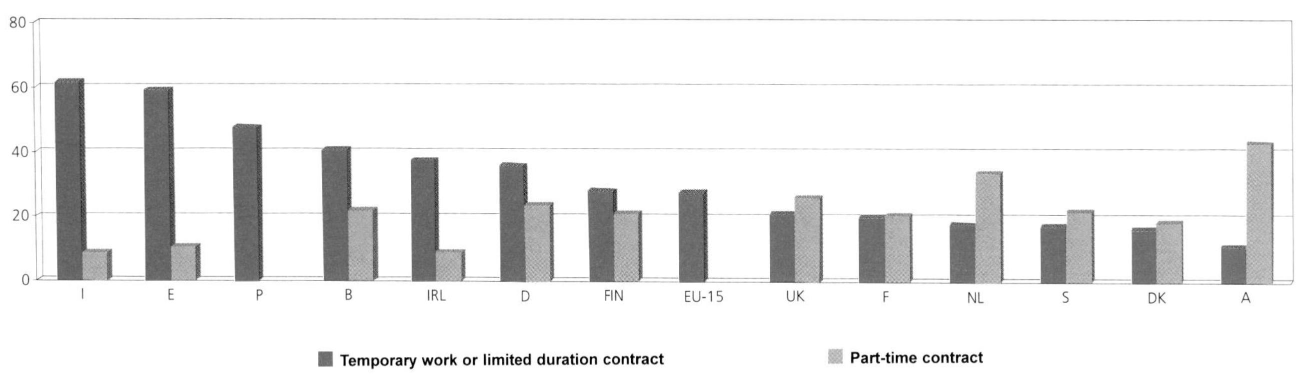

Source: Eurostat (LFS)

Table 15.9 (%)

Real estate activities (NACE Rev. 1 70)

Composition of the labour force, 1997

	Females	Highly-educated
EU-15	48.0	:
B	53.9	37.7
DK	30.0	19.4
D	47.2	24.7
EL	:	:
E	50.1	39.6
F	58.6	16.5
IRL	37.2	38.8
I	36.1	16.4
L	:	:
NL	44.6	26.0
A	71.2	:
P	44.6	35.1
FIN	37.3	12.9
S	28.4	12.0
UK	51.7	30.5

Source: Eurostat (LFS)

Figure 15.14 (thousand ECU)

Real estate activities (NACE Rev. 1 70)

Personnel costs/employee, 1996

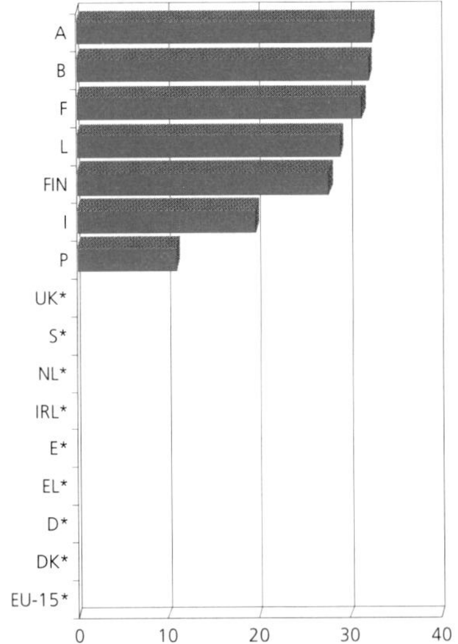

Source: Eurostat (SBS)

Figure 15.15 (%)

Real estate activities (NACE Rev. 1 70)

Wage adjusted labour productivity, 1996

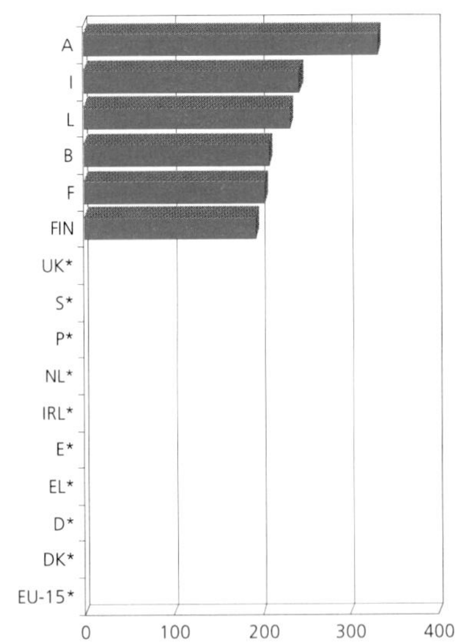

Source: Eurostat (SBS)

In the commercial property market, the shift in business towards the service sector increases the demand for office properties to the detriment of industrial sites. Other factors for locating a business include access to main communication nodes, quality of infrastructure, distance from suppliers and clients, as well as more subjective factors such as the quality of life for employees or freedom from pollution.

There are two job categories within the profession of real estate: the first is that of developers who construct buildings on land that they already own with a view to sale or rental. The second category is that of intermediaries. They can be the estate agent or administrators who are specialised in marketing and renting to end-users, consultants or market makers who buy to re-sell.

For several years now, intermediaries have tended towards the Anglo-Saxon model of consultancy. This strategic transformation, which is accompanied by an increased presence of banks in the marketplace, has facilitated globalisation of the property market. The main consultancy offices assume the role of go-between by opening up the domestic marketplace to foreign partners. This development also allows a larger volume of transactions, regardless of the size of the market. However, despite growing globalisation within the property market and the increasing sophistication of products, consumers are slow to change from traditional national models for selling and renting property.

Table 15.10

Real estate activities (NACE Rev. 1 70)

Turnover related indicators, 1996

	B	DK	D	EL	E	F	IRL	I	L	NL	A	P	FIN	S	UK
Turnover (billion ECU) (1)	3.2	:	:	:	:	52.5	0.4	13.4	0.3	:	5.3	1.4	1.8	:	:
Turnover/enterprise (million ECU) (1)	:	:	:	:	:	0.4	0.2	0.1	0.4	:	1.3	0.2	0.3	:	:
Turnover/person employed (thousand ECU) (1)	163.6	:	:	:	:	171.5	63.9	82.3	235.5	:	267.1	81.1	106.4	:	:

(1) I, P (1995).

Table 15.11

Real estate activities (NACE Rev. 1 70)

Competitiveness and productivity related indicators, 1996

	B	DK	D	EL	E	F	IRL	I	L	NL	A	P	FIN	S	UK
Value added/turnover (%) (1)	41.0	:	:	:	:	37.4	56.5	58.7	28.7	:	42.4	:	50.7	:	:
Labour productivity (thousand ECU/head) (1)	67.1	:	:	:	:	64.2	36.1	48.3	67.6	:	108.8	:	53.9	:	:
Wage adjusted labour productivity (%) (1)	208.1	:	:	:	:	203.4	:	243.6	232.2	:	333.2	:	193.5	:	:
Personnel costs/employee (thousand ECU) (1)	32.3	:	:	:	:	31.5	:	19.8	29.1	:	32.7	11.1	27.9	:	:
Gross operating surplus (million ECU) (1)(2)	:	:	:	:	:	25.9	32.7	19.0	0.9	:	87.3	4.8	10.7	:	:

(1) I, A, P (1995). (2) L (1995).

Source: Eurostat (SBS)

Professional associations representing the industries within this chapter

AEEBC
European Association of
Building Surveyors
c/o RICS
12 Great George Street
London SW1P 3AD
tel: (44) 171 334 3877
fax: (44) 171 334 3844

FIABCI
Fédération Internationale
des Professions Immobilières
23, avenue Bosquet
F-75007 Paris
tel: (33) 1 45 50 45 49
fax: (33) 1 45 50 42 00
e-mail: info@fiabci.net

FIEC
European Construction
Industry Federation
66, avenue Louise
B-1050 Bruxelles
tel: (32) 2 514 55 35
fax: (32) 2 511 02 76
e-mail: fiec-bru@enter.org

Distributive trades

Industry description and main indicators

Distributive trades, otherwise referred to as commerce, is a generic term encompassing wholesale and retail trade. Following the statistical classification of economic activities in the European Communities, NACE Rev. 1, wholesale trade (NACE Rev. 1 51) and retail trade (NACE Rev. 1 52) do not include the motor trade, which is covered in a separate Division (NACE Rev. 1 50) including both wholesale and retail activities. Indeed, the motor trade includes all activities (except manufacture and renting) related to motor vehicles and motorcycles, including lorries and trucks, as well as the retail sale of automotive fuel and lubricating or cooling products.

For more detailed information on distributive trades, refer to Eurostat's "Distributive Trades in Europe" (CA-24-99-308-3A-Z on CD-ROM and CA-24-99-154-EN-C on paper).

An efficient distribution sector is essential for a modern-day economy, allowing a country, its producers and consumers to benefit from timely delivery, efficient allocation of products and geographically convenient points of sale.

(units) Figure 16.1

Distributive trades (NACE Rev. 1 50 to 52)
Density of enterprises per ten thousand inhabitants, 1996

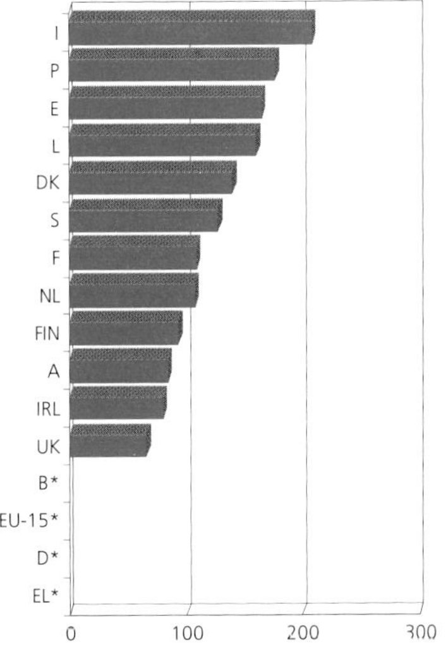

Source: Eurostat (SBS)

The activities covered in this chapter include:

50.1: sale of motor vehicles;
50.2: maintenance and repair of motor vehicles;
50.3: sale of motor vehicle parts and accessories;
50.4: sale, maintenance and repair of motorcycles and related parts and accessories;
50.5: retail sale of automotive fuel;
51.1: wholesale on a fee or contract basis;
51.2: wholesale of agricultural raw materials and live animals;
51.3: wholesale of food, beverages and tobacco;
51.4: wholesale of household goods;
51.5: wholesale of non-agricultural intermediate products, waste and scrap;
51.6: wholesale of machinery, equipment and supplies;
51.7: other wholesale;
52.1: retail sale in non-specialised stores;
52.2: retail sale of food, beverages and tobacco in specialised stores;
52.3: retail sale of pharmaceuticals and medical goods, cosmetic and toilet articles;
52.4: other retail sale of new goods in specialised stores;
52.5: retail sale of second-hand goods in stores;
52.6: retail sale not in stores;
52.7: repair of personal and household goods.

Figure 16.2 (%)

Distributive trades (NACE Rev. 1 50 to 52)

Share of part-time and temporary work contracts in total number of persons employed, 1997

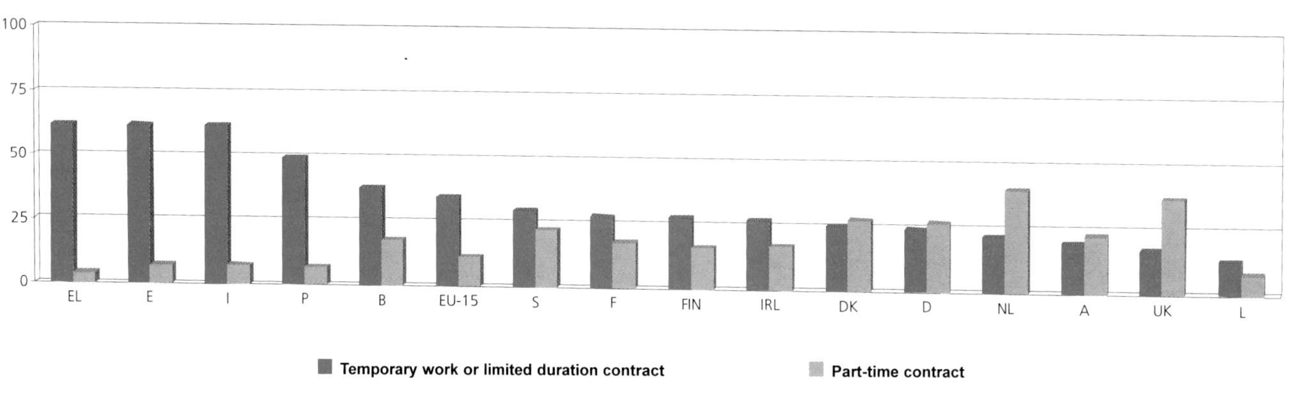

Source: Eurostat (LFS)

The importance of the distributive trades is highlighted by the fact that they accounted for around 30% of businesses in the EU, over 15% of employment and slightly more than 13% of GDP. Over 5 million distribution enterprises existed within the EU, providing almost 23 million jobs. Nevertheless, there is by no means a uniform structure to the distribution sector across the EU. We find that in this industry there is a marked difference between the structure of the northern and southern Member States. In southern Europe there are still a very large number of retailers, most of them are independents with very few (if any) employees. Within the northern Member States there has been a reduction in all size classes of enterprise, with mergers and acquisitions of large supermarket chains, the development of purchasing centres in wholesaling and of smaller groupings of independent retailers. All of these processes seek to protect market share through economies of scale.

One of the main developments in recent years has been the high-level of integration within the distributive trades' sector of the economy. Vertical integration has resulted in links between manufacturers, wholesalers and retailers often being merged together, such that it is often difficult to distinguish between the activities. This has been the case with fashion houses that specialise in high-value products, as well as for sports clothing manufacturers. These enterprises control the manufacturing, distribution and retailing of their products, usually attaching great importance to the concept of brand image.

Figure 16.3 (thousand ECU)

Distributive trades (NACE Rev. 1 50 to 52)

Personnel costs/employee, 1996

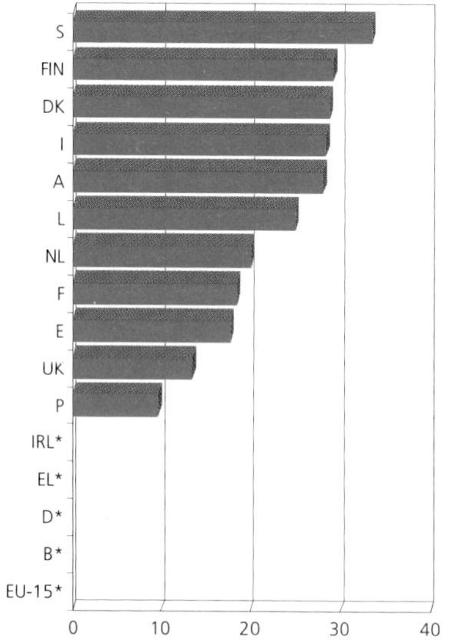

Source: Eurostat (SBS)

Figure 16.4 (%)

Distributive trades (NACE Rev. 1 50 to 52)

Wage adjusted labour productivity, 1996

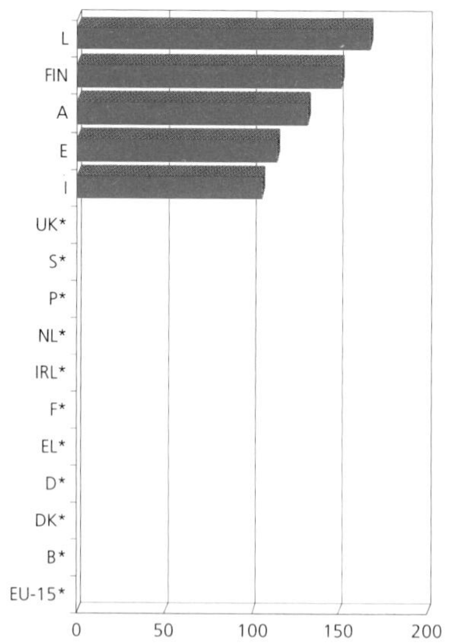

Source: Eurostat (SBS)

(ECU/month) Figure 16.5

Distributive trades (NACE Rev. 1 50 to 52)
Labour costs by Member State, 1996

Source: Eurostat (LCS)

The sector has been subject to a large number of changes, as globalisation of economic processes and new technologies has made the environment for distributive trades more dynamic and flexible. The White Paper on Commerce (released in January 1999 by the European Commission) points out that the concentration process poses a "long-term risk of extreme concentration of distribution in Europe, resulting in a mere handful of big chains dominating the entire retail market". This could "ultimately lead to a reduction of products on offer, the variety of selling systems and the number of shops". Concentration is largely centred within the activity of food retailing at present, where many small, rural retail outlets have closed in recent years.

Generally though, the distribution sector of the European economy has a high level of competition, with price competition evident through the development and increase of the number of discount retailers. Other forms of retail trade that have developed include out-of-town shopping and the growth of electronic commerce (e-commerce), which provides many opportunities for growth in the future. Otherwise, the internationalisation of retailing has led to many well-known brands being established in capital cities across the globe. Often this form of brand retailing relies on the concept of franchising to establish a presence in foreign markets. Indeed, this is one form of diversification that has worked increasingly well within retailing. Other ways of diversifying have not centred on an expansion to foreign markets, but rather into new service-related areas of the economy or markets that are fast developing (e-commerce being an obvious example).

In order to improve the competitiveness of small shops, the White Paper proposes to "provide better access to finance, better training of both owners and managers, better access to transport and better recognition by local, regional and national authorities of the social and economic roles small shops play in the communities they serve".

Jobs are one area where distributive trades have received much attention in recent years, as they offer not only the opportunity for persons with low skills and educational attainment to find a job, but they also offer the chance to return to the labour market (for example, following a period of time raising a family). In addition, distributive trades also allow many people increased flexibility in choosing the times when they are able to work, matching professional and family commitments. There were between 4.1% (Greece) and 40.1% (the Netherlands) of the labour force working part-time in distributive trades in 1998.

The Labour Force Survey provides interesting information on the breakdown and structure of the distributive trades' labour force. We find that in the retail trade activity there were more women employed than men in the EU. Indeed, only Italy and Greece reported that men were in the majority in the retail trade labour force. In 1998 women made up 69.2% and 67.1% of the retail trade labour force in Austria and Germany.

The converse was true in the other two distribution activities, with women playing a minor role in the labour force for motor trades. Female participation rates in the motor trade showed European figures of around 15%. One may hope that many new employment opportunities will arise in new forms of retailing, especially those that place greater emphasis on customer service. Losses will result from the continued process of automation and the growth in electronic stock control and logistics.

International comparison

If we look at the other two Triad economies, distributive trades in Japan recorded a somewhat higher share of the total labour force (some 17.6%) when compared to the EU figures (just over 15%), whilst in the USA there were 23.6 million persons (or 18.5% of the working population).

In the motor trade, sales strategies in Japan have traditionally differed from those in the USA and the European Union. Showrooms used to be smaller and a large number of customers bought cars from door-to-door salesman. Japanese consumer attitudes have subsequently changed, with dealers investing more money in significantly larger dealerships. Predictions show that by the turn of millennium, 90% of all sales' operations will be made in showrooms. These trends have had a direct influence on structural business variables. The average number of persons employed per enterprise has increased in line with the size of dealerships, whilst at the same time, overall passenger car sales increased by more than 5% in both 1995 and 1996. The economic crisis of 1997 had an adverse effect on car sales, with figures falling by 3.8%[1].

Motorcycle sales in Japan were also affected by the economic crisis, with turnover declining by 2.6% in 1997. The number of motorcycles on the road in Japan has followed a downtrend trend during the last decade. Nevertheless, in 1997 Japan was still in third place in the global rankings for motorcycles, behind India and China.

1) Source: Japan Automobile Manufacturers Association.

The motor trade is an extremely competitive and cyclically sector of the US economy. There has however been a fairly large expansion of employment, with figures rising by more than 200 thousand posts during the last two decades[2]. As a result of consolidation in the motor trade, dealerships have grown larger in size. To demonstrate these trends, we may look at the number of dealers that were selling less than 150 cars per year. This group of retailers numbered 13,200 in 1976. By 1996, there were only 4,664 dealers operating at the same level of activity (less than 150 cars sold per year). However, during the same period, the number of dealers selling at least 750 cars increased from 3,450 to 5,801.

Sales figures for wholesale trade in Japan fell by 1.2% between 1995 and 1996. However, value added increased by 0.9%, with labour productivity rising by 4.5% during the same period.

In 1997 the wholesale trade activity in the USA recorded a 4.1% annual increase in total sales, down from 6.0% in 1996 and 9.2% in 1995. Total sales were over one and a half times greater than those of retail sale for the same year. The number of paid employees amounted to 5.8 million in 1997, which was equivalent to only 41.0% of employment in retail trade. There were 453 thousand establishments active in this form of trade, about 40% of the figure for retail distribution.

2) U.S. Department of Labour; "Issues in Labour Statistics", January 1999.

In Japan the number of retail establishments decreased from over 1.6 million in 1985 to just under 1.5 million by 1994. Turnover has risen at a rapid pace in recent years, reaching almost 1,200 billion ECU by 1997. Liberalisation of government regulations during the early 1990's led to a sharp increase in the number of larger establishments and convenience chains. These changes appear to have had a positive effect on productivity, whilst consumers are also reported to have benefited due to lower prices and wider choice.

The retail trade industry in the USA is amongst the most advanced in the world. Government regulations do not normally constitute a large obstacle to the sector and legal opening hours are generally free, with very few restrictions on the establishment of new outlets.

Retail sales per person employed were high in the USA, with only Germany and Luxembourg able to report higher ratios amongst EU countries. In terms of retail sales per outlet, the USA had higher figures than any country of the EU, the average size of American stores was generally large. Sales increased at an average annual rate of 5.5% during the period 1980-1997, reaching more than 1,400 billion ECU. The number of establishments in the US retail sector has remained fairly constant over the nineties and was equal to some 870 thousand in 1997. Men and women were almost equally represented in the US retail trade. Weekly earnings were the lowest of all branches, except for agriculture, reflecting the widespread use of low-skilled labour.

Motor trade (NACE Rev. 1 50)

NACE Rev. 1 Division 50 encompasses the sale, maintenance and repair of motor vehicles and motorcycles, as well as the retail sale of automotive fuel. The statistical Division of motor trade is composed of five heterogeneous groups, following the NACE Rev. 1 classification. The first three take account of the sale of motor vehicles, their parts and accessories and their repair, whilst all three of these functions are grouped together for motorcycles. Retail sale of automotive fuel constitutes the last Group.

(units) Figure 16.6

Motor trade (NACE Rev. 1 50)
Density of enterprises per ten thousand inhabitants, 1996

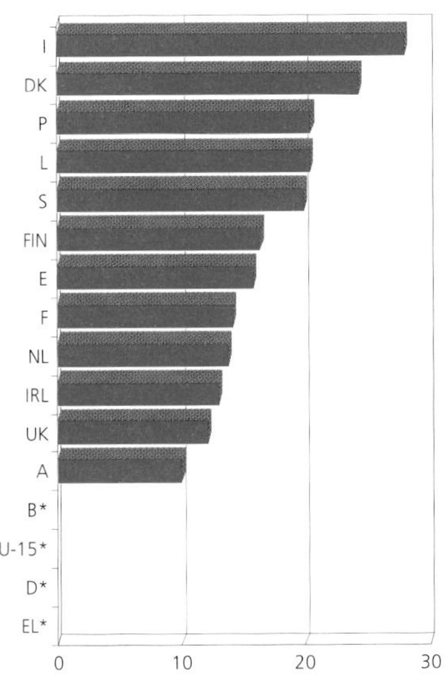

Source: Eurostat (SBS)

The world market for motor vehicles, including cars, trucks, buses and coaches was equal to 54 million units in 1997. Production capacity was well above that figure, with considerable over-capacity (some 20 million units). Even so, plans to set-up new car industries exist in many countries. As a result, competition between manufacturers is now as intense as ever. Its effects cannot leave the motor vehicle retail market unscathed. Indeed, there has been a general tendency towards fewer but larger dealerships, employing a greater number of persons and selling more cars.

New passenger car sales in the European Union fluctuate with economic performance. The main variations recorded during the last decade were during the recession of the early 1990's. In 1990 just over 13 million new passenger cars were sold. However, economic recession in mainland Europe caused sales to drop quickly in 1993 to just under 11 million units. Subsequent years have seen a recovery in the figures, which have since risen to record highs of just over 13.9 million units in 1998. Amongst the different Member States, the countries with the highest number of units sold were Germany, Italy and the United Kingdom. The country with the highest absolute turnover figures in motor trade was Germany, followed by the United Kingdom, France and Italy.

The structure of employment in the motor trade varies significantly between the different Member States. For example, in Italy the share of employees in total employment reached only 46%, a much lower percentage than in other countries. The extreme case of Italy may be attributable to the high number of enterprises that were small, family-owned dealerships or repair shops with only one or two employees at the most.

(%) Figure 16.7

Motor trade (NACE Rev. 1 50)
Share of part-time and temporary work contracts in total number of persons employed, 1997

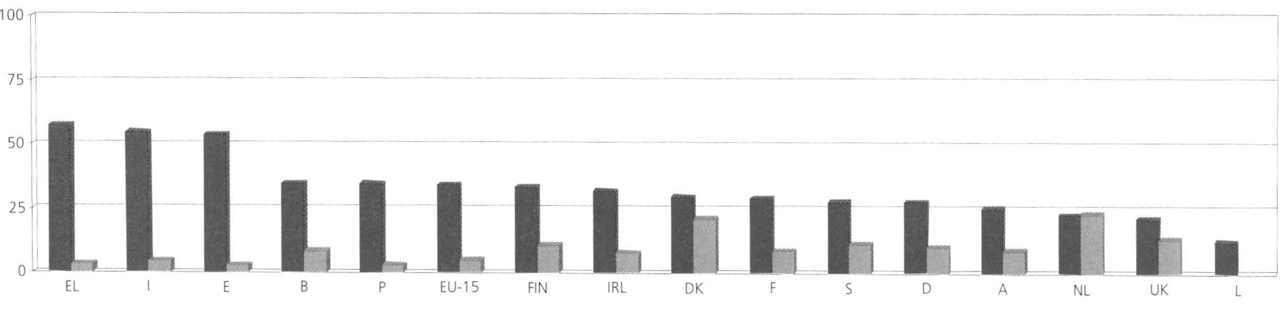

Source: Eurostat (LFS)

In Italy there were twice as many enterprises in the sale, maintenance and repair of motor vehicles and motorcycles and retail sale of automotive fuel than there were in France or the United Kingdom. The density of enterprises in Italy was the highest in Europe (amongst the countries for which data was available), with 28 enterprises per 10 thousand inhabitants. For means of comparison, we may note that in Austria and the United Kingdom there were only 10 and 12 motor trade enterprises per 10 thousand inhabitants.

Figure 16.8 (thousand ECU)

Motor trade (NACE Rev. 1 50)

Personnel costs/employee, 1996

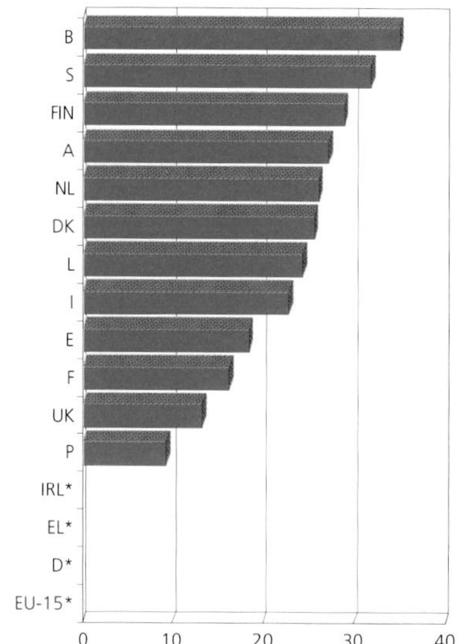

Source: Eurostat (SBS)

Figure 16.9 (%)

Motor trade (NACE Rev. 1 50)

Wage adjusted labour productivity, 1996

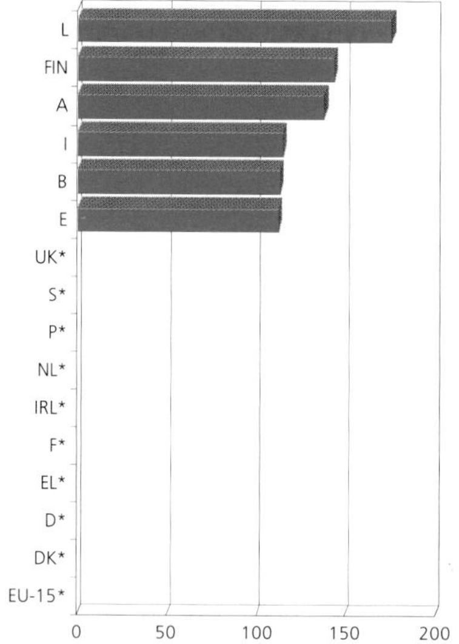

Source: Eurostat (SBS)

Wholesale trade (NACE Rev. 1 51)

Following the NACE Rev. 1 statistical classification the division of wholesale trade (Division 51) includes the resale (sale without transformation) of new and used goods to retailers, to industrial, commercial, institutional or professional users; or to other wholesalers; or acting as agents in buying merchandise for, or selling merchandise to, such persons or companies: activities of wholesale merchants, jobbers, industrial distributors, exporters, importers, co-operative buying associations, merchandise and commodity brokers, commission merchants and agents and assemblers, buyers and co-operative associations engaged in the marketing of farm products. Please note that for statistical purposes, wholesale trade excludes the wholesale trade of motor vehicles, caravans and motorcycles, the wholesale of motor accessories and the renting and leasing of goods.

Wholesale trade plays an important logistical role, moving goods the first step from producers towards consumers and other producers. Wholesale trade employs a considerable number of people and generates an important share of value added in the EU, about 7.5% of the total.

(units) Figure 16.10

Wholesale trade (NACE Rev. 1 51)
Density of enterprises per ten thousand inhabitants, 1996

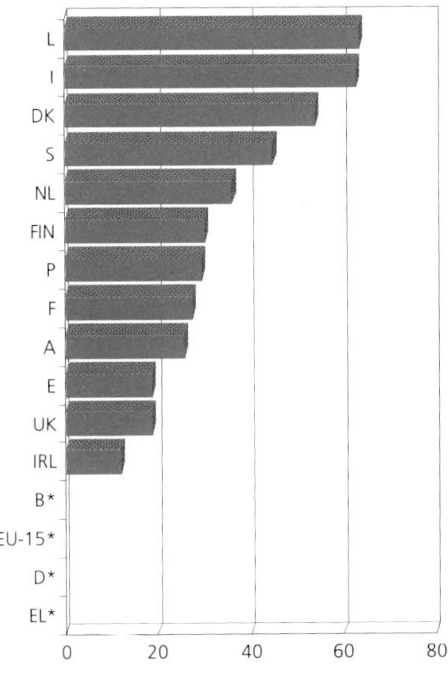

Source: Eurostat (SBS)

New technologies and innovations, such as electronic data interchange, pose a challenge for wholesalers as they facilitate direct relations between producers and customers. New technologies also reduce the so-called "lead-time", or the period between the preparation and the execution of an order, streamlining production processes and reducing the need for large stocks. As such the traditional role played by wholesalers is under threat as many retailers attempt to take direct contact with producers and rely on just-in-time deliveries from the producer (eliminating the role of the wholesaler). Many wholesalers tried to respond to these threats by moving into the retail business and acquiring small independent outlets to secure retail possibilities for the goods they deal in. Other wholesalers seek to expand into other service sectors of the economy. One of the more recent trends has been diversification of traditional wholesalers into areas such as logistics, transportation and financing, in an attempt to offer a full service to clients. Alternatively diversification may involve tasks such as assembling, sorting and grading of goods in large lots, break bulks, repackaging and bottling, redistribution in smaller lots, storage, refrigeration, delivery and installation of goods.

(%) Figure 16.11

Wholesale trade (NACE Rev. 1 51)
Share of part-time and temporary work contracts in total number of persons employed, 1997

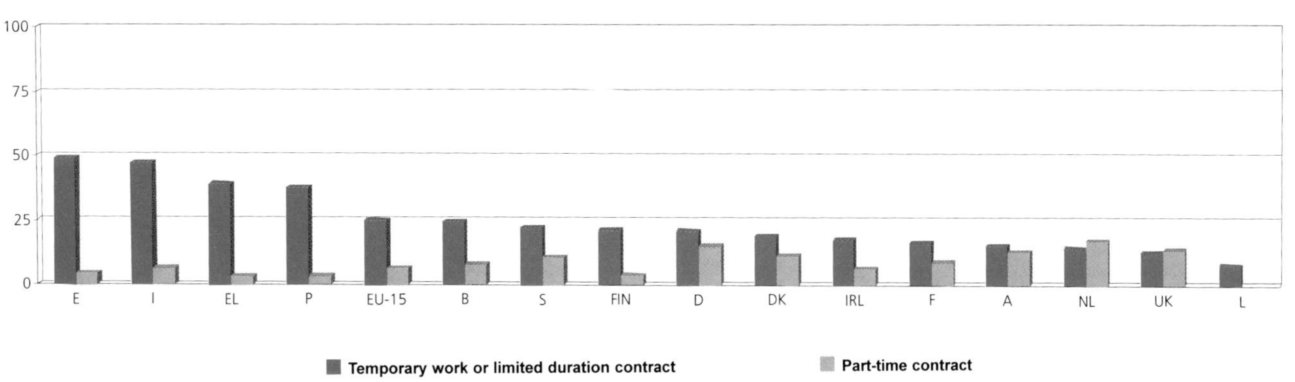

Source: Eurostat (LFS)

The wholesale trade activity numbered more than 1 million enterprises in the EU and employed approximately 6.4 million people, roughly twice the size of the motor trade. The location of these enterprises was far from even across the EU. Italy and Luxembourg registered no less than 63 wholesale enterprises per ten thousand inhabitants. This was the highest density in the EU, the average being 27. Ireland recorded the lowest density (12.1 enterprises per ten thousand inhabitants), followed by the United Kingdom (18.7). The typical European wholesale enterprise employed 6 persons. Again this figure varied greatly between the Member States, ranging from 2.6 persons in Italy to more than 10 persons in Ireland. Average turnover of European enterprises in wholesale trade was estimated at around 2 million ECU. Enterprises in the United Kingdom averaged almost double that figure with 3.8 million ECU, followed by Irish and Austrian enterprises (3.6 and 3.3 million ECU respectively). Italy and Portugal were found at the other end of the ranking, with 800 thousand ECU and 1.2 million ECU of turnover per enterprise.

The available figures on value added and personnel costs do not allow for a complete picture of labour productivity in the wholesale trade industry. However, amongst the countries for which data was available, value added per capita reached 47 thousand ECU in the EU, with Luxembourg well above the average (61 thousand ECU) and Spain below (30 thousand ECU).

Figure 16.12 (thousand ECU)

Wholesale trade (NACE Rev. 1 51)
Personnel costs/employee, 1996

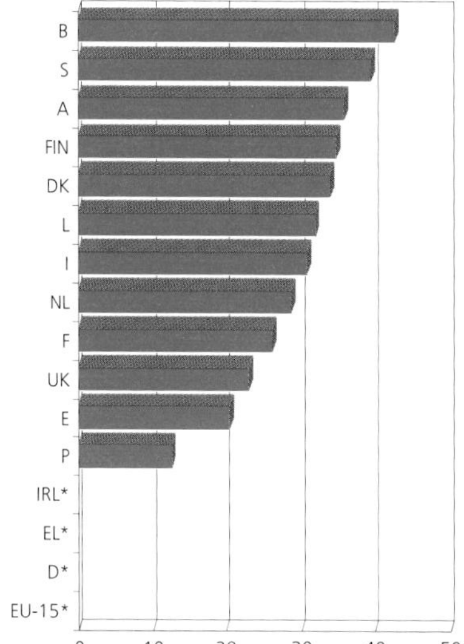

Source: Eurostat (SBS)

Figure 16.13 (%)

Wholesale trade (NACE Rev. 1 51)
Wage adjusted labour productivity, 1996

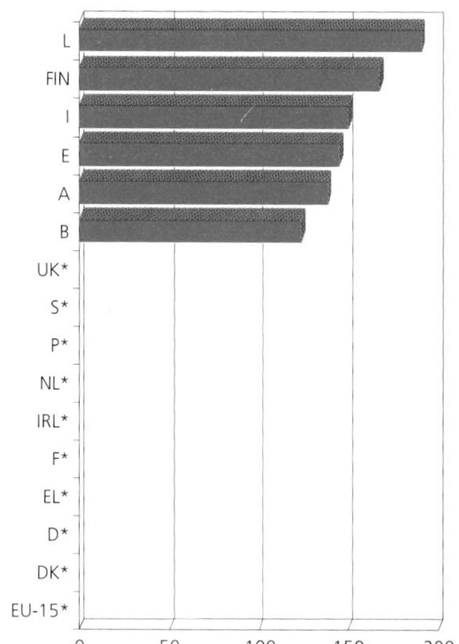

Source: Eurostat (SBS)

Retail trade (NACE Rev. 1 52)

Retail trade is classified under NACE Rev. 1 52 within the statistical classification of economic activities in the European Community. This service activity covers the resale of new and used goods to the general public for personal or household consumption or utilisation, by shops, department stores, stalls, mail-order houses, as well as co-operatives. The Division also includes the repair and installation of personal and household goods. NACE Rev. 1 Division 52 excludes motor trade activities which are covered by NACE Rev. 1 50.

Many retail groups are integrating with wholesale trade firms to secure supply for the goods they sell. The adoption of new technologies has helped to increase productivity in retailing. In particular, technology has helped to achieve lower inventories, faster receipt of goods and increased labour efficiency (for example, automated check-outs). Larger enterprises, such as supermarkets and hypermarkets usually have greater means to adopt these technologies, due to the cost implications of financing investment.

(units) Figure 16.14

Retail trade (NACE Rev. 1 52)
Density of enterprises per ten thousand inhabitants, 1996

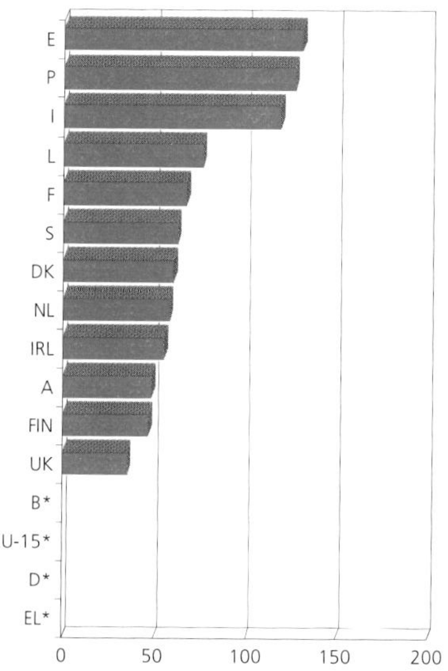

Source: Eurostat (SBS)

(units) Table 16.1

Number of hypermarkets and superstores of 2,500 m²+, as of 1st January

	1990	1994	1997	1998
B	97	99	:	:
DK	14	15	:	:
D	996	1,207	1,392	1,402
E	102	185	236	256
F	790	1,028	1,106	:
I	99	192	247	268
NL	40	:	:	:
P	:	28	:	:
S	:	74	77	:
UK	580	862	1,052	1,110

Source: ISL

(%) Figure 16.15

Retail trade (NACE Rev. 1 52)
Share of part-time and temporary work contracts in total number of persons employed, 1997

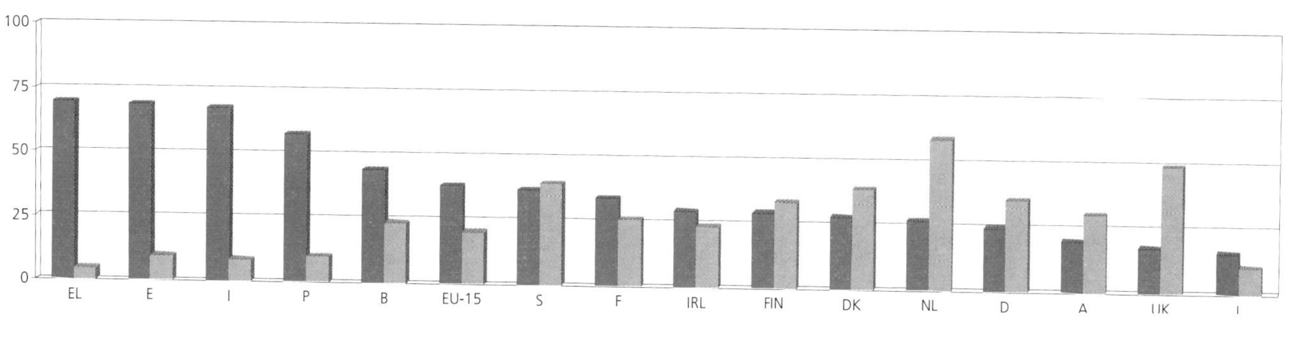

Source: Eurostat (LFS)

As well as technology playing a role in determining the average size and structure of enterprises within this activity, another factor that plays an important role in determining the size of outlets is government regulations. In several countries there were limitations preventing the development of hypermarkets being built. Government regulations usually limited the establishment of new outlets through specific national legislation (France, Italy, Belgium and Spain) or through the context of local and regional planning. Indeed, these regulations have caused a slow down in the development of large hypermarkets and supermarkets that was particularly pronounced in the late eighties.

The arrival of non-national retailers has led to new styles and methods of operation, with more emphasis on leisure and entertainment. Nevertheless, the penetration of foreign retailers into the European market remains limited to a few special areas (sports goods, entertainment and shoes). Shopping patterns have also been changed by an increase in opening hours, as well as Sunday trading (in some countries) and the re-introduction of home deliveries.

Average turnover per enterprise in retail trade in the EU distinguished two broad groups of countries. On the one hand, the highest turnover per enterprise was found in the United Kingdom, Germany, Denmark and France. In northern Europe, retail enterprises were on average much larger, due to the predominance of super and hypermarkets. On the other hand, in Spain, Italy, Portugal and Greece average turnover per enterprise was low. Retail trade in southern Europe was characterised by the presence of many traditional small, specialist shops, often family-run. This was demonstrated by the fact that the ratio of average number of persons employed per enterprise in the southern Member States was often of the magnitude of just two or three persons. However, in the United Kingdom, Germany and the Netherlands there were high ratios. These figures for the average number of persons employed per enterprise are not necessarily a good indicator of the average size of an enterprise, as where part-time employment was well developed this indicator may well give an over-estimate of the actual size of each enterprise. Nevertheless, the indicator does provide further evidence that retail trade enterprises in northern Europe were larger.

Enterprise density within the EU in 1996 ranged from 35 enterprises per 10 thousand inhabitants in the United Kingdom to 127 enterprises in Portugal. Generally, the southern Member States again had more enterprises relative to population than their northern European counterparts. Notwithstanding these differences, the trend in southern Europe was also towards concentration, with larger shops and fewer traditional retail outlets.

If we turn our attention to average turnover per enterprise, we find that the United Kingdom, with 1.1 million ECU had (by a considerable margin) the highest average turnover per enterprise. Spain, Italy and Portugal had the smallest enterprises using this measure (below 250 thousand ECU).

Electronic commerce is an area that offers a high degree of potential for the future development of trading. There should be many opportunities through e-commerce to reduce costs as items can be ordered on a just-in-time basis. Through the computerisation of a client base there is also potential for retailers to study market trends and target particular customers far more closely.

Another area where e-commerce may allow a pooling of resources is with respect to small and medium-sized enterprises. Purchasing power, access to market information, logistics and co-operative R&D can all be organised in response to the growing concentration of large players. One present day example of how e-commerce can be used to great effect is the sale and update of computer software that is often made directly over the Internet.

Mail order is another area which is used by many persons who are not in a position to go shopping for reasons of mobility or due to a lack of time during traditional opening hours. However, this area was far more developed in the American economy than in the EU - perhaps due to the large distances some Americans need to travel to reach shopping destinations. In 1995, some 168 billion ECU of sales were made in the USA through orders placed by mail, phone or electronically, without the person ordering going to the point of sale (more than 10% of total US retail sales).

Figure 16.16 (thousand ECU)
Retail trade (NACE Rev. 1 52)
Personnel costs/employee, 1996

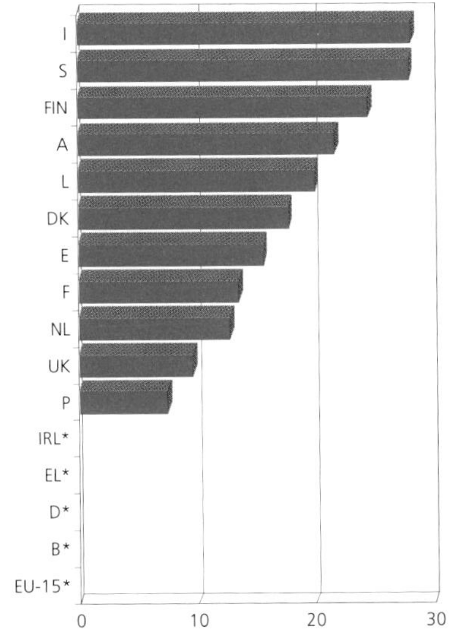

Source: Eurostat (SBS)

Figure 16.17 (%)
Retail trade (NACE Rev. 1 52)
Wage adjusted labour productivity, 1996

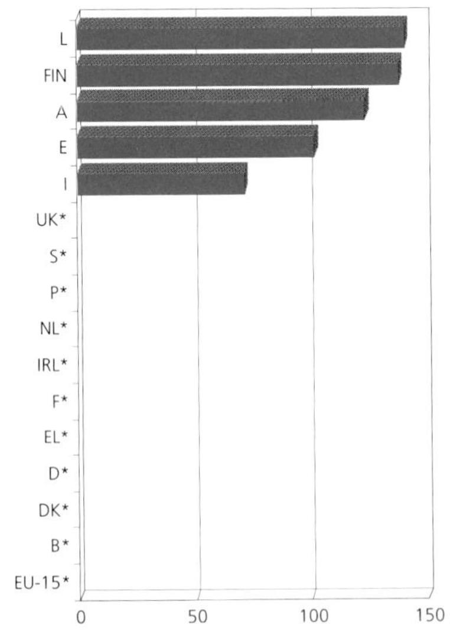

Source: Eurostat (SBS)

Professional associations representing the industries within this chapter

EAN
European Article Numbering Association
145, rue Royale
B-1000 Bruxelles
tel: (32) 2 227 10 20
fax: (32) 2 227 10 21
e-mail: info@ean.be

Eurocommerce
123-133, rue Froissart
B-1040 Bruxelles
tel: (32) 2 230 58 74
fax: (32) 2 230 00 78
e-mail:
lobby@eurocommerce.be

GPUE
Pharmaceutical Group of the European Union
13, square Ambiorix
B-1040 Bruxelles
tel: (32) 2 736 72 81
fax: (32) 2 736 02 06
e-mail: pharmacy@pgeu.org

IRS
Institute for Retail Studies
University of Stirling
Stirling
Scotland FK9 4LA
tel: (44) 1786 46 73 86
fax: (44) 1786 46 52 90

Table 16.2

Motor trade (NACE Rev. 1 50)

Enterprise and employment indicators, 1996

	B	DK	D	EL	E	F	IRL	I	L	NL	A	P	FIN	S	UK
Number of enterprises (thousands) (1)	:	12.7	:	:	61.5	82.5	4.7	160.7	0.8	21.2	8.1	20.4	8.4	17.6	71.1
Number of enterprises per 10,000 inhabitants (1)	:	24.3	:	:	15.8	14.1	13.0	28.0	20.4	13.7	10.0	20.5	16.3	20.0	12.1
Number of pers. employed (thousands) (1)(2)	78.2	63.0	:	:	298.7	418.0	27.1	419.3	5.8	127.8	74.9	99.3	29.0	:	587.5
Number of pers. employed/enterprise (units) (1)(2)	:	5.0	:	:	4.9	5.1	5.7	2.6	6.9	6.0	9.3	4.9	3.5	:	7.2
Share of employees in total employed (%) (1)(2)	70.0	64.5	:	:	79.0	91.5	81.0	46.5	87.6	80.8	92.0	91.9	85.7	:	86.7

(1) E (1992); DK, NL (1995). (2) UK (1994); B (1995).

Table 16.3

Motor trade (NACE Rev. 1 50)

Turnover related indicators, 1996

	B	DK	D	EL	E	F	IRL	I	L	NL	A	P	FIN	S	UK
Turnover (billion ECU) (1)	31.8	11.4	:	:	42.2	99.0	6.7	92.1	2.2	39.0	17.7	13.1	9.4	22.1	131.6
Turnover/enterprise (million ECU) (1)	:	0.9	:	:	0.7	1.2	1.4	0.6	2.6	1.9	2.2	0.6	1.1	1.3	1.9
Turnover/person employed (thousand ECU) (1)(2)	406.5	180.6	:	:	141.4	236.9	248.2	219.6	375.0	304.2	236.9	132.2	324.3	:	195.6

(1) E (1992); NL (1994); B, DK (1995). (2) UK (1994).

Table 16.4

Motor trade (NACE Rev. 1 50)

Competitiveness and productivity related indicators, 1996

	B	DK	D	EL	E	F	IRL	I	L	NL	A	P	FIN	S	UK
Value added/turnover (%) (1)	9.7	:	:	:	14.6	13.5	9.6	11.9	11.4	:	15.8	:	12.8	12.0	:
Labour productivity (thousand ECU/head) (1)	39.5	:	:	:	20.7	32.0	23.7	26.1	42.6	:	37.6	:	41.5	:	:
Wage adjusted labour productivity (%) (1)	112.9	:	:	:	112.0	:	:	114.5	175.4	:	138.1	:	143.6	:	:
Personnel costs/employee (thousand ECU) (2)	35.0	25.6	:	:	18.5	16.3	:	22.8	24.3	26.1	27.2	9.3	28.9	31.9	13.3
Gross operating surplus (million ECU) (3)	:	:	:	:	1.7	1.7	1.1	2.2	:	1.9	1.9	1.3	2.7	2.2	0.8

(1) E (1992); B, A (1995). (2) E, F (1992); DK (1993); UK (1994); B, A (1995). (3) E (1992); NL (1993); A (1995).

(%) Table 16.5

Motor trade (NACE Rev. 1 50)

Composition of the labour force, 1997

	EU-15	B	DK	D	EL	E	F	IRL	I	L	NL	A	P	FIN	S	UK
Female	17.5	15.2	20.1	22.2	10.5	10.2	17.7	15.5	12.7	15.6	16.4	19.3	12.0	14.3	15.8	19.0
Part-time (1)	4.8	8.4	21.1	10.0	3.3	2.8	8.6	7.7	4.6	:	23.0	8.7	2.9	10.6	11.1	13.1
Temporary work or limited contract	34.4	34.7	29.6	27.7	57.2	53.7	29.3	31.9	54.7	12.3	22.6	25.2	34.7	33.4	27.8	21.3
Persons with a higher education (2)	:	11.5	7.3	17.2	5.1	10.8	5.6	11.5	3.8	17.5	7.9	:	2.5	7.2	5.9	7.2
Persons with a lower education	42.1	34.7	30.6	18.2	49.7	71.3	32.8	53.9	66.5	60.7	34.1	20.1	85.0	30.3	32.8	42.7

(1) FIN (1996). (2) L (1993); DK (1996).

Source: Eurostat (SBS, LFS)

Table 16.6

Wholesale trade (NACE Rev. 1 51)
Enterprise and employment indicators, 1996

	B	DK	D	EL	E	F	IRL	I	L	NL	A	P	FIN	S	UK
Number of enterprises (thousands) (1)	:	28.3	:	:	73.1	161.1	4.4	360.9	2.6	55.5	20.9	29.4	15.5	39.7	110.1
Number of enterprises per 10,000 inhabitants (1)	:	54.1	:	:	18.7	27.6	12.1	62.9	63.6	36.1	25.9	29.6	30.2	44.9	18.7
Number of pers. employed (thousands) (2)	230.1	169.0	:	:	590.7	942.5	44.6	941.5	12.1	399.7	190.9	185.9	74.4	:	1,019.0
Number of pers. employed/enterprise (units) (2)	:	6.0	:	:	8.1	5.8	10.2	2.6	4.6	7.2	9.1	6.3	4.8	:	7.8
Share of employees in total employed (%) (3)	78.5	77.7	:	:	90.7	98.0	92.4	52.0	86.5	89.2	94.3	94.9	92.7	:	86.7

(1) E (1992); NL (1994); DK (1995). (2) E (1992); NL, UK (1994); B, DK (1995). (3) E (1992); NL (1993); UK (1994); B, DK (1995).

Table 16.7

Wholesale trade (NACE Rev. 1 51)
Turnover related indicators, 1996

	B	DK	D	EL	E	F	IRL	I	L	NL	A	P	FIN	S	UK
Turnover (billion ECU) (1)	115.2	62.0	:	:	124.7	409.6	15.8	277.0	7.0	151.9	68.4	35.2	34.9	79.9	422.5
Turnover/enterprise (million ECU) (1)	:	2.2	:	:	1.7	2.5	3.6	0.8	2.7	2.7	3.3	1.2	2.3	2.0	3.8
Turnover/person employed (thousand ECU) (1)(2)	500.6	366.9	:	:	211.2	434.5	354.7	294.2	579.4	380.1	358.3	189.3	469.4	:	369.8

(1) E (1992); NL (1994); B, DK (1995). (2) UK (1994).

Table 16.8

Wholesale trade (NACE Rev. 1 51)
Competitiveness and productivity related indicators, 1996

	B	DK	D	EL	E	F	IRL	I	L	NL	A	P	FIN	S	UK
Value added/turnover (%) (1)	10.5	:	:	:	14.0	10.4	11.9	15.7	10.5	:	13.6	:	12.4	12.3	:
Labour productivity (thousand ECU/head) (1)	52.5	:	:	:	29.6	45.3	42.3	46.2	60.7	:	49.6	:	58.0	:	:
Wage adjusted labour productivity (%) (1)	123.3	:	:	:	144.6	:	:	150.0	190.2	:	138.4	:	166.7	:	:
Personnel costs/employee (thousand ECU) (2)	42.6	34.0	:	:	20.5	26.2	:	30.8	31.9	28.7	35.8	12.6	34.8	39.4	23.0
Gross operating surplus (million ECU) (3)	:	:	:	:	2.4	1.1	1.8	1.6	:	1.3	2.3	3.2	1.9	1.7	1.1

(1) E (1992); B, A (1995). (2) E, F (1992); DK, NL (1993); UK (1994); B, A (1995). (3) E (1992); I, NL (1993); A (1995).

Table 16.9 (%)

Wholesale trade (NACE Rev. 1 51)
Composition of the labour force, 1997

	EU-15	B	DK	D	EL	E	F	IRL	I	L	NL	A	P	FIN	S	UK
Female	30.8	32.0	30.0	36.7	26.3	28.4	33.0	26.8	28.7	22.0	26.7	37.7	26.0	23.4	31.6	30.7
Part-time	6.3	7.9	11.5	15.2	3.1	4.2	8.8	6.3	6.3	:	17.3	12.9	3.2	3.7	10.8	13.7
Temporary work or limited contract	25.1	24.6	19.0	21.0	39.2	49.1	16.7	17.7	47.3	7.7	14.3	15.3	37.7	21.4	22.5	13.0
Persons with a higher education	16.4	31.3	15.9	15.6	18.1	18.1	20.3	27.0	7.3	20.3	18.4	7.4	13.1	19.9	17.7	15.7
Persons with a lower education	33.2	26.3	16.7	15.6	26.6	57.2	28.9	31.7	40.1	42.9	31.4	16.3	64.4	18.2	23.8	49.2

Source: Eurostat (SBS, LFS)

Table 16.10

Retail trade (NACE Rev. 1 52)

Enterprise and employment indicators, 1996

	B	DK	D	EL	E	F	IRL	I	L	NL	A	P	FIN	S	UK
Number of enterprises (thousands) (1)	:	31.7	:	:	508.3	392.4	20.1	678.1	3.2	89.7	38.9	125.7	23.9	55.4	207.0
Number of enterprises per 10,000 inhabitants (1)	:	60.3	:	:	130.3	67.2	55.4	118.1	76.1	58.3	48.3	126.6	46.7	62.7	35.2
Number of pers. employed (thousands) (2)	:	193.9	:	:	1,361.3	1,444.7	120.7	1,437.9	17.3	609.2	255.6	314.7	93.1	:	2,485.6
Number of pers. employed/enterprise (units) (2)	:	6.1	:	:	2.7	3.7	6.0	2.1	5.5	6.8	6.6	2.5	3.9	:	9.6
Share of employees in total employed (%) (3)	:	86.8	:	:	54.6	86.0	81.2	36.0	83.0	79.1	86.8	71.9	87.1	:	86.7

(1) E (1992); NL (1994). (2) E (1992); NL, UK (1994). (3) E (1992); NL (1993); UK (1994).

Table 16.11

Retail trade (NACE Rev. 1 52)

Turnover related indicators, 1996

	B	DK	D	EL	E	F	IRL	I	L	NL	A	P	FIN	S	UK
Turnover (billion ECU) (1)	:	24.6	:	:	111.5	251.2	11.4	155.9	2.6	54.8	32.8	18.9	18.7	36.7	237.4
Turnover/enterprise (million ECU) (1)	:	0.8	:	:	0.2	0.6	0.6	0.2	0.8	0.6	0.8	0.2	0.8	0.7	1.1
Turnover/person employed (thousand ECU) (1)(2)	:	126.9	:	:	81.9	173.9	94.4	108.4	149.3	89.9	128.4	60.0	201.2	:	79.9

(1) E (1992); NL (1994); B, DK (1995). (2) UK (1994).

Table 16.12

Retail trade (NACE Rev. 1 52)

Competitiveness and productivity related indicators, 1996

	B	DK	D	EL	E	F	IRL	I	L	NL	A	P	FIN	S	UK
Value added/turnover (%) (1)	:	:	:	:	19.5	17.2	17.2	18.7	18.9	:	20.8	:	16.8	17.1	:
Labour productivity (thousand ECU/head) (1)	:	:	:	:	16.0	29.9	16.3	20.3	28.2	:	27.0	:	33.9	:	:
Wage adjusted labour productivity (%) (1)	:	:	:	:	102.3	:	:	72.0	140.7	:	123.9	:	138.2	:	:
Personnel costs/employee (thousand ECU) (2)	:	17.8	:	:	15.6	13.6	:	28.2	20.0	12.8	21.7	7.5	24.5	28.0	9.6
Gross operating surplus (million ECU) (3)	:	2.7	:	:	2.0	2.5	3.0	3.8	:	2.6	2.8	2.7	1.8	1.9	3.2

(1) E (1992); A (1995). (2) E, F (1992); NL (1993); UK (1994); A (1995). (3) E (1992); NL (1993); A (1995).

(%) Table 16.13

Retail trade (NACE Rev. 1 52)

Composition of the labour force, 1997

	EU-15	B	DK	D	EL	E	F	IRL	I	L	NL	A	P	FIN	S	UK
Female	57.6	58.6	54.8	67.1	47.7	55.4	58.2	57.6	42.0	62.6	59.6	69.2	51.7	63.5	58.6	60.1
Part-time	20.5	23.8	39.1	35.6	4.6	9.7	26.2	23.9	8.5	10.3	58.6	30.2	10.1	33.7	39.5	49.1
Temporary work or limited contract	38.4	44.0	28.1	24.6	69.2	68.5	34.2	29.6	67.4	15.8	27.1	19.8	57.4	29.5	37.1	17.5
Persons with a higher education	9.9	17.1	9.5	11.6	10.6	13.9	13.5	15.2	3.5	6.8	6.6	2.1	3.8	10.2	11.8	10.5
Persons with a lower education	43.7	35.4	40.4	17.2	42.5	64.6	32.0	37.5	63.3	60.6	42.8	19.0	80.8	33.4	34.2	56.5

Source: Eurostat (SBS, LFS)

Tourism

Industry description and main indicators

Tourism is a demand-side concept involving a wide range of activities, which is better viewed as a market rather than a sector. It can be defined as the activities of persons travelling to and staying in places outside their usual environment for not more than one consecutive year for leisure, business or other purposes (for example, visiting friends or health reasons). This chapter covers activities which make up a significant part of the tourism market: hotels and restaurants (NACE Rev. 1 55), recreation and amusement parks (NACE Rev. 1 92.33) and travel agencies (NACE Rev. 1 63.3).

Tourism is part of the considerable development of personal mobility that has rapidly developed in the second half of the 20th century. It has been supported by a dramatic improvement in communications and a growing internationalisation of the world economy. In this context, tourism also assumes a role of redistribution of resources and becomes a factor of economic development both at a regional level in Europe and worldwide.

Due to its composite nature, the relative importance of tourism in the European economy is not straightforward to assess. According to estimates of the European Commission, tourism directly employs 9 million persons in the European Union and accounts for at least 5.5% of GDP and 30% of total external trade in services. Eurostat estimate that there are over 1.3 million enterprises present in hotel and restaurant activities within the Community, 96% of which are micro-enterprises with less than 10 employees. Tourism therefore accounts for around 6% of the total workforce in the Community, when taking into account jobs directly linked with tourism products and services. Besides these direct jobs, it is also necessary to consider indirect or spin-off jobs created in other sectors of the economy influenced by tourism. National Accounts statistics reveal that the branch of hotels and restaurants alone employed 6 million persons, about 4.2% of the total number of persons employed in the EU. Hotels and restaurants accounted for about 2.8% of total EU value added, representing around 155 billion ECU. Spain, Portugal and Austria display a particularly high specialisation within the tourism industry, whilst the Nordic countries had the smallest comparative shares of employment and value added across the EU.

(units) Figure 17.1

Hotels and restaurants (NACE Rev. 1 55) Density of enterprises per ten thousand Inhabitants, 1996

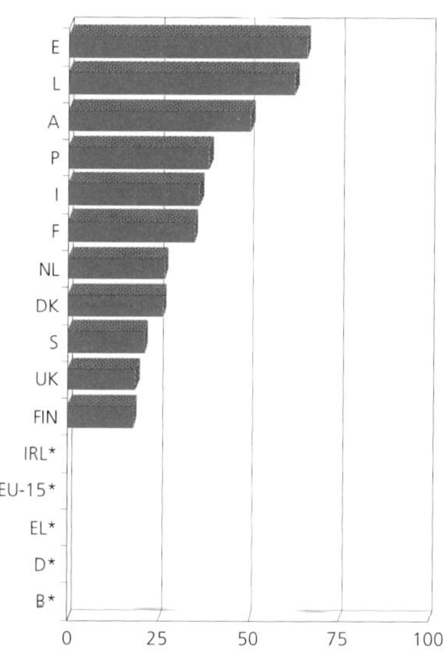

Source: Eurostat (SBS)

The activities covered in this chapter include:

- 55.1: hotels;
- 55.2: camping sites and other provision of short-stay accommodation;
- 55.3: restaurants;
- 55.4: bars;
- 55.5: canteens and catering;
- 63.3: activities of travel agencies and tour operators, tourist assistance;
- 92.33: fair and amusement park activities.

Figure 17.2 (%)

Hotels and restaurants (NACE Rev. 1 55)

Share of part-time and temporary work contracts in total number of persons employed, 1997

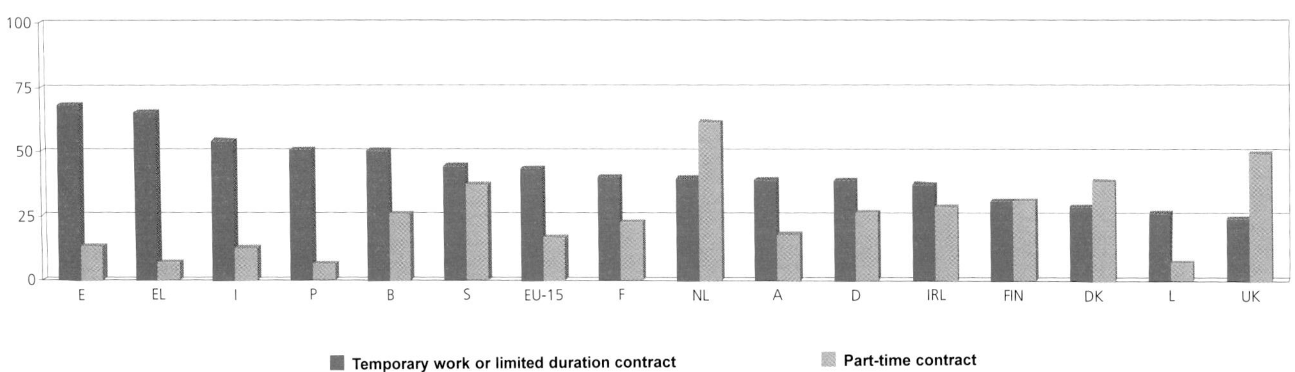

Source: Eurostat (LFS)

Different work patterns may be found within the tourism sector than those traditionally found in other more traditional industries. There are more flexible working patterns, often characterised by a high seasonal component, whilst there is a high degree of precariousness for many job holders. The results of Eurostat's annual Labour Force Survey are particularly striking in this regard. No less than 27% of the total number of persons employed in hotels and restaurants worked part-time, against 17% for the whole of the EU economy. Differences amongst Member States were wide-ranging: around half the jobs were part-time in the Netherlands (58%), the United Kingdom (49%) and Denmark (47%); whilst part-time jobs accounted for less than a tenth of the total labour force in Luxembourg (8%), Portugal (6%) and Greece (5%). Hotels and restaurants also displayed a higher than average proportion of temporary jobs or limited-duration contracts, at 14% of the labour force. Again variability across the EU was considerable: the shares ranged from as high as 30% in Spain and 23% in the Netherlands and Sweden to as low as 4% in Belgium and 2% in Luxembourg.

This structural flexibility may explain the attraction that the sector has for women and young people, with many jobs often constituting the first step on the employment ladder or a return to the employment market after a period of not working. The Labour Force Survey reveals that women accounted for 53% of the labour force in hotels and restaurants, a share higher than the average in services (51%). The share of females in the total varied from 43% in Greece and Spain to more than 60% in Austria and Finland. In contrast, the share of persons employed in hotels and restaurants with a higher education level was one of the lowest of all service activities, at just 7%. In Italy, Austria and Portugal the share of highly educated persons was below 2%. Only two countries displayed a share above the 10% level: they were Belgium (12%) and Ireland (19%).

The combination of a flexible working patterns and a high presence of unskilled manpower may explain the low level of labour costs faced by this activity.

Figure 17.3 (thousand ECU)

Hotels and restaurants (NACE Rev. 1 55)

Personnel costs/employee, 1996

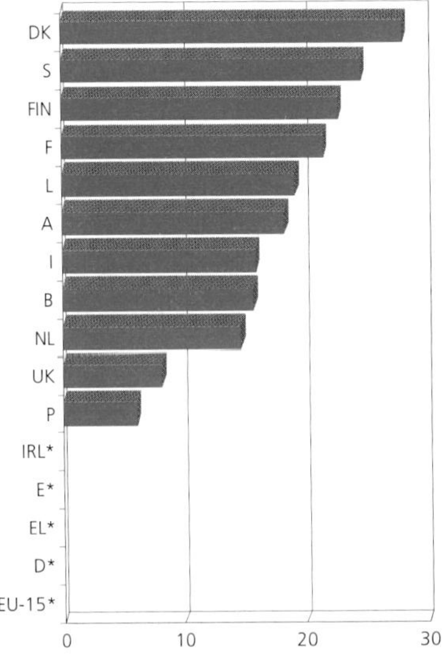

Source: Eurostat (SBS)

Figure 17.4 (%)

Hotels and restaurants (NACE Rev. 1 55)

Wage adjusted labour productivity, 1996

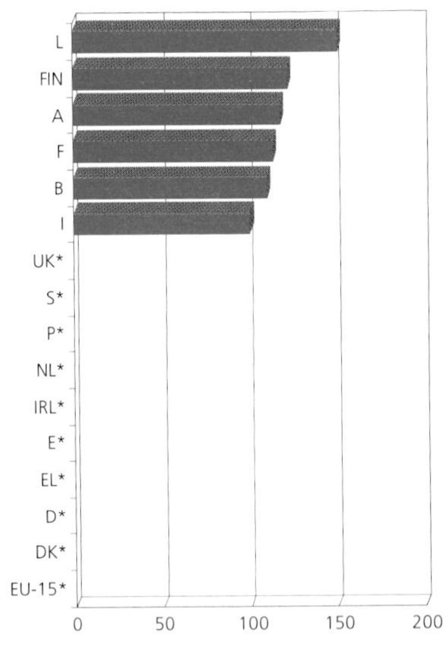

Source: Eurostat (SBS)

The latest Labour Cost Survey reveals that costs per month were 30% to 50% lower in the activity of hotels and restaurants than the average for services. The EU average cost per month was around 1,500 ECU in 1996.

(ECU/hour) Figure 17.5

Hotels and restaurants (NACE Rev. 1 55)
Labour costs by Member State, 1996

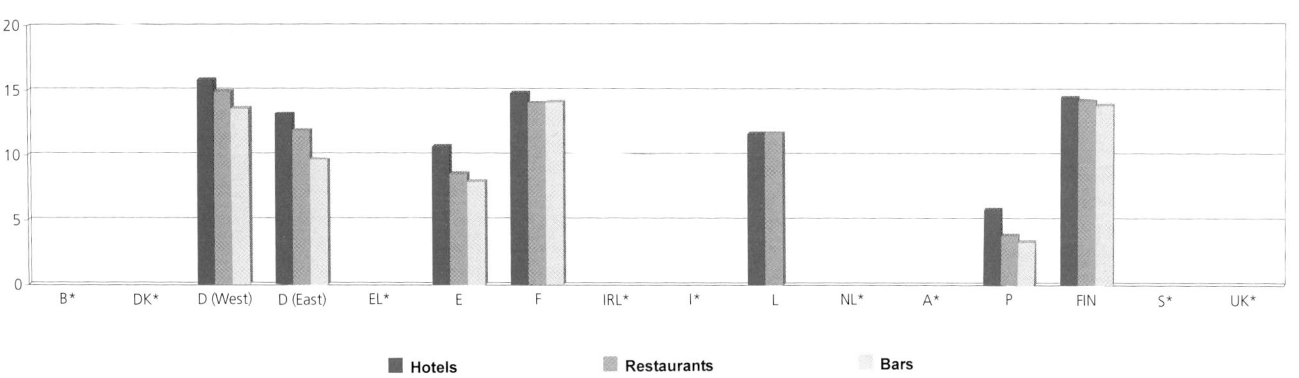

Source: Eurostat (LCS)

International comparison

Between 1988 and 1997, according to the World Tourism Organisation, the number of international tourist arrivals grew at an average annual rate of 5% worldwide. Over the same period international tourist receipts (excluding transport) expanded by an annual average rate of 9%.

Europe (using its geographical definition) continued to maintain its position as the market leader, despite a trend of declining market share. Almost 60% of international tourists chose Europe as their destination. As a result, Europe claims more than half of the world's tourism receipts. The EU makes up the largest part, with a market share of 40%, equivalent to close on 240 million visitors and in excess of 130 billion ECU on an annual basis.

A more detailed study reveals how large the contribution of the EU is to world tourism. France was the world's most popular destination of international travellers, with nearly 67 million visitors recorded in 1997, in front of the USA (48 million) and Spain (43 million). No less than eleven of the Member States were amongst the top 25 tourism destinations in the world.

Furthermore, Germany boasted annual tourism expenditure in excess of 40 billion ECU, which made it the leading tourism spender in the world, ahead of the USA (38 billion ECU) and Japan (29 billion ECU). Nine other Member States ranked amongst the top 25 in terms of expenditure.

Figure 17.6

International tourist arrivals, 1997

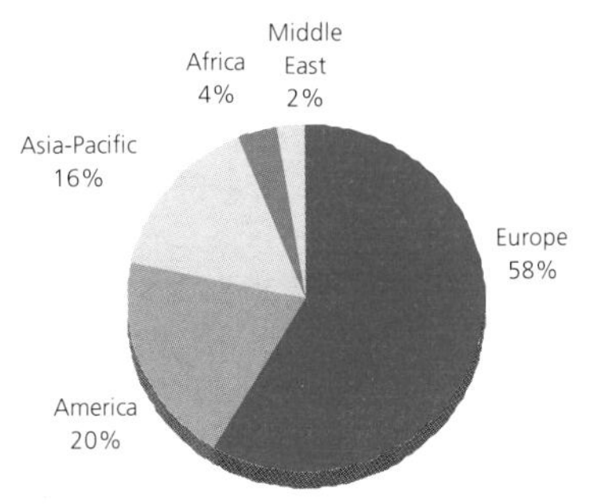

Source: World Tourism Organisation

Figure 17.7

Receipts from international tourism, excluding transport, 1997

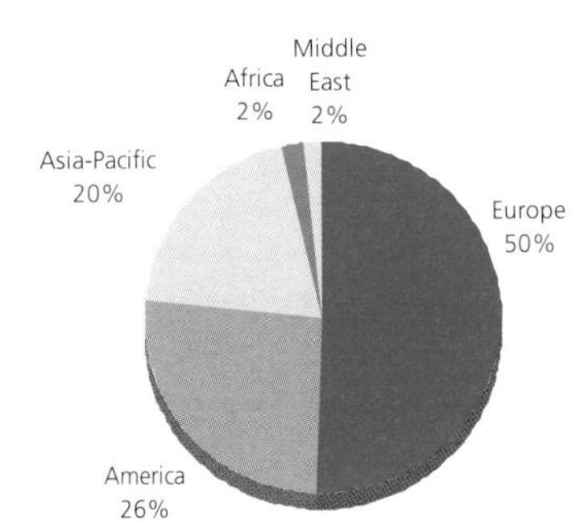

Source: World Tourism Organisation

It should be noted that these figures excluded domestic tourism, as well as same-day visitors, but that intra-European tourism was considered as international. It is estimated that about two-thirds of the total number of holidays taken by European residents can be classified as domestic, whilst more than one fifth concern international tourism between Member States. The statistics also neglect the growing importance of day trips to neighbouring countries that can constitute up to 50% of all trips abroad.

Hotels and camping sites (NACE Rev. 1 55.1 and 55.2)

Hotels and other provision of short-stay accommodation, whether they are accompanied by catering or other types of services or not are covered by NACE Rev. 1 55.1 and NACE Rev. 1 55.2.

Hotels receive a wide array of different customers: tourists and tour groups, business travellers and government officials, conference and convention participants. Tourists accounted for around 45% of all guest nights spent in Europe, a share higher than in North America (39%) or in Asia (40%). Eurostat estimate that the holiday participation rate[1] in the EU was between 55% and 60%. A recent Eurobarometer survey[2] showed that hotels and holiday clubs come first on the list of preferred accommodation, with 42% of the persons questioned choosing this type of holiday.

Over 20% of guest nights in North American hotels were accounted for by conference or convention participants, almost twice the worldwide average and a level that is 7 percentage points higher than in Europe.

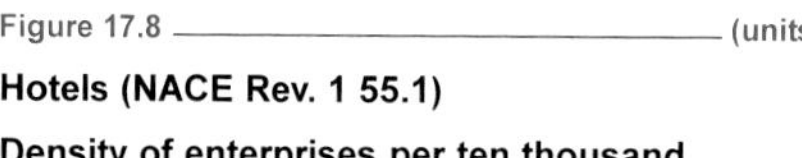

Figure 17.8 (units)

Hotels (NACE Rev. 1 55.1)

Density of enterprises per ten thousand inhabitants, 1996

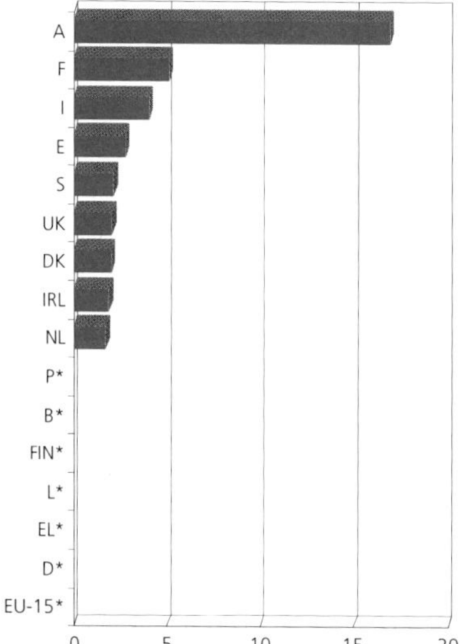

Source: Eurostat (SBS)

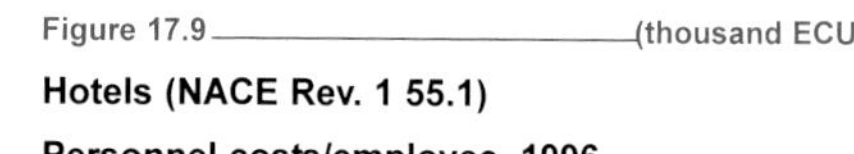

Figure 17.9 (thousand ECU)

Hotels (NACE Rev. 1 55.1)

Personnel costs/employee, 1996

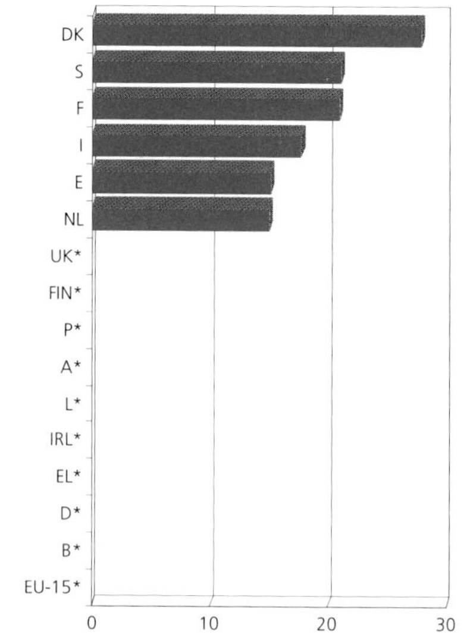

Source: Eurostat (SBS)

One of the major problems facing the hotel industry is the seasonality of demand: calculated on a weekly basis, the share of rooms sold on Wednesdays is almost twice as high as the share sold on Sundays for the European hotel industry. In addition, Eurobarometer survey data indicated that no less than 41% of holidaymakers took their main vacation in August in 1997. The long-term trend towards multiple holiday-taking and the growth of the "short breaks" market, which hotels and travel operators have actively courted through special packages and discounts should help smooth the seasonality of demand for tourist accommodation to some degree.

According to Eurostat estimates there are more than 180 thousand hotels and similar establishments in the EU, boasting a total of 8.9 million bed-places, an average of 48 per establishment. In 1996, the trend in the EU was towards a reduction in the number of enterprises and a gradual increase in accommodation capacity in absolute terms as well as in terms of average size. The average number of bed places per establishment rose by 5 beds on average per establishment between 1993 and 1996. The situation was diverse from one Member State to another. Smaller establishments were found mainly in Ireland (20 bed-places per establishment), the United Kingdom (23) and Austria (36), whilst Spain (129 bed-places), Denmark (126), and Portugal (120) displayed higher than average figures.

1) Proportion of the population that takes at least one vacation of at least four overnight stays per year.
2) "Facts and figures on Europeans on Holiday", March 1998.

Table 17.1 (thousands)

Hotels and similar establishments: main indicators, 1997

	B	DK	D	EL	E	F	IRL	I	L	NL	A	P	FIN	S	UK
Number of establishments (1)	2.0	0.5	38.9	7.9	7.5	19.6	5.2	33.8	0.3	1.9	15.8	1.8	1.0	1.9	47.6
Number of bedrooms (2)	51.1	30.5	884.3	304.8	508.5	653.3	:	948.7	7.7	:	310.6	93.5	53.6	110.7	553.0
Number of bedplaces (1)	116.3	59.8	1,547.5	584.8	979.3	1,451.1	107.4	1,772.1	14.7	157.9	584.9	215.6	112.3	184.5	1,096.5
Arrivals of residents (3)	1,740	1,305	60,775	5,375	25,643	55,345	:	34,931	16	:	5,299	3,736	5,002	9,299	36,300
Arrivals of non-residents (3)	4,859	1,305	13,745	6,785	20,201	32,340	:	25,133	525	:	12,801	4,314	1,618	2,143	18,376
Nights spent, residents (4)	3,498	4,340	147,276	13,984	66,471	96,696	5,583	125,603	81	9,861	16,483	9,164	9,420	14,815	81,060
Nights spent, non-residents (4)	9,483	4,462	29,738	42,565	111,738	66,330	13,220	86,399	1,089	11,245	53,499	23,241	3,211	4,051	86,631

(1) 1997 data for IRL, I, NL.
(2) 1997 data for EL, I, A, P, S
(3) 1997 data for D, EL, I, P, FIN, S, UK.
(4) 1997 data for IRL, NL, S.

Source: Eurostat (TOUR)

A recent worldwide hotel industry study by Horwath Consulting revealed that the average occupancy rate in 1997 in Europe was equal to 65%, a particularly low level compared to other world regions. It should be noted however that the survey data applied only to hotel chains. The average cost of a room in Europe was also amongst the lowest in the world at 55 ECU per night. This can be explained in part by the fact that European hotels draw relatively more revenue from non-room services than hotels in other regions of the world. Indeed, only half of the revenue of European hotels is accounted for by room rental, whilst the worldwide average was 60%, and in North American hotels it was equivalent to two-thirds of total revenue. Conversely, food and beverages account for as much as 42% of hotel revenue in Europe, compared to only 27% in North America.

Technological change pervades across many areas of the hotel trade, although it is difficult to assess its impact on EU hotel operators, notably on small- and medium-sized establishments. Significant process and product innovations have occurred in areas such as operations management (for example, specific software applications used for yield management, or purchasing, sales and catering management systems), client interface (in-room services, room check-out, etc.), business services and entertainment (video-conferencing, interactive TV communication systems) and reservation systems. On this latter point it is interesting to note that advance reservation through web sites or via e-mail, represented only 0.8% of the total reservations made in 1997 (1% in Europe and 0.5% in North America). Whilst print advertising remains by far the most common marketing medium (used by more than 95% of hotels worldwide), 41% of those taking part in the Horwath survey used WWW pages for advertising in 1997 (40% in Europe and 60% in North America). Bookings through the Internet are expected to become much more significant in the future as hotels further increase their presence on the Internet and on-line reservation sites become directly accessible to travellers.

Figure 17.10

Composition of hotel revenue, 1997

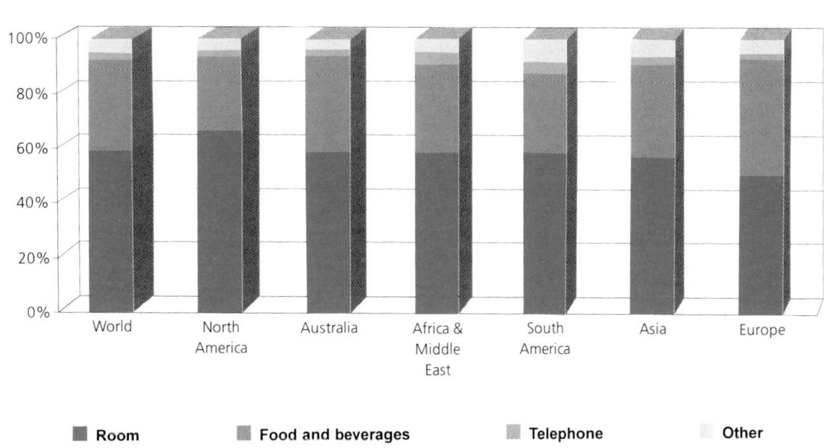

Source: IH&RA, Horwath Worldwide Hotel Industry Study, 1997

(%) Figure 17.11

Average occupancy and rates in hotels, 1997

80
60
40
20
0
Australia
Asia
North America
World
Europe
South America
Africa & Middle East

Average occupancy (%)
Average rate per night (ECU)

Source: IH&RA, Horwath Worldwide Hotel Industry Study, 1997

There is a strong trend in the hotel industry towards the development of franchising and contract management of hotels, as distinct from direct ownership. One of the factors explaining the success of the franchising formula is that it associates a hotel with a well-known national or international brand. This is often perceived as a key success factor, notably in the business travel market, where the quality and consistency of service is a prerequisite. Franchising is a core element in the strategy of companies that expand beyond their home market, be it Spain's leading hotel chain, Sol Melia (intent on strengthening its market presence in France) or HFS (Hospitality Franchise System), the world's leading hotel operator, which recently laid out plans to expand into the European budget and mid-range hotel market through franchising.

A related trend is the development of partnership agreements between hotel chains and the emergence of global hotel networks. There is now growing awareness of the need to pool resources to compete more effectively. Hotel chains may achieve economies of scale through centralised reservation systems, grouped marketing and quality enhancement initiatives. As a result, voluntary chains are becoming a significant feature of the independent hotel trade, notably in Germany and France, where the leading voluntary chain of independent hôteliers, Logis de France, ranks second to Accor in terms of room capacity (data for 1997).

Figure 17.12 (share of total nights)

Types of hotel customers

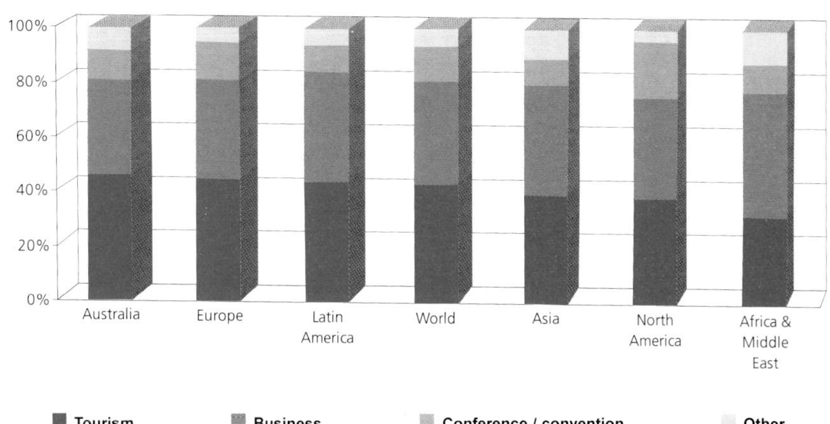

Source: IH&RA, Horwath Worldwide Hotel Industry Study, 1997

Restaurants, bars, canteens and catering (NACE Rev. 1 55.3 to 55.5)

Restaurants and bars are present in virtually every local community. In addition to their economic worth, restaurants and bars also play a significant social role in villages, towns and cities throughout the EU. For statistical purposes, the activities of the sale of meals and drinks for consumption are classified under NACE Rev. 1 Groups 55.3 (restaurants), 55.4 (bars) and 55.5 (canteens and catering). These activities represent together a substantial share of the hotels and restaurants sector of the economy (NACE Rev. 1 Section H), accounting for more than two-thirds of it in terms of turnover and employment.

Businesses active in this sector can be very different in size, shape and objective. They range from popular bars, snacks and fast-food chains to high-class establishments dealing in haute cuisine. The local unit ranges from small, family-run outlets to multinational franchises and many enterprises in this sector of the economy have diversified to have a wide portfolio of activities in other service areas, principally hotels but also cinemas, recreation parks, railways, ferries or night-clubs. In some cases, the sale of food and drinks may represent an important part of the revenue of these latter activities, as was highlighted in the section on hotels.

The European trade association for hotels, restaurants and cafés (Hotrec) also compile statistical evidence concerning the structure of the sector. According to Hotrec figures, bars usually constituted the largest share of establishments active in the sector in 1997, with up to three-quarters of the total number of establishments in Spain and Ireland. There were however a few exceptions to this rule, such as in France and Germany, where 60% of all establishments were restaurants.

(units) Figure 17.13

Restaurants, bars, canteens and catering (NACE Rev. 1 55.3 to 55.5) Density of enterprises per ten thousand inhabitants, 1996

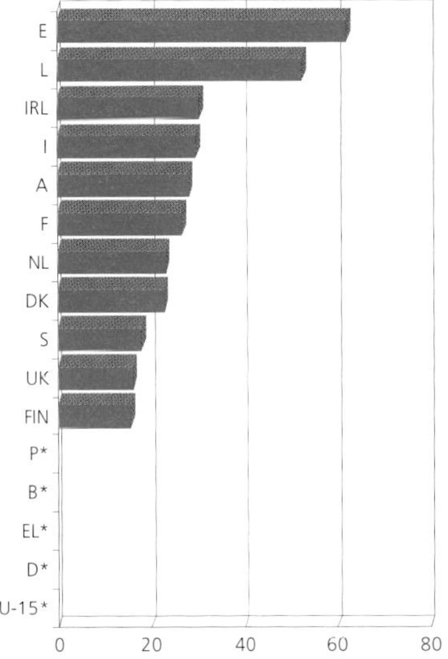

Source: Eurostat (SBS)

(thousand ECU) Figure 17.14

Restaurants, bars, canteens and catering (NACE Rev. 1 55.3 to 55.5) Personnel costs/employee, 1996

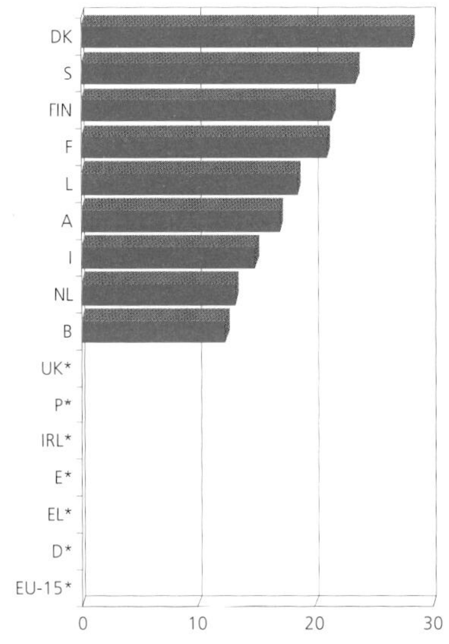

Source: Eurostat (SBS)

As far as personnel is concerned, Hotrec estimate that restaurants employ more persons than bars in the majority of EU countries. We should note that restaurants typically employ more personnel than bars (where family work and sole proprietorship often dominate). On average, official statistics revealed that restaurants and bars employed an average of 3 to 4 persons per enterprise, with personnel costs generally around 20 thousand ECU per employee, ranging from 12 thousand ECU in Belgium up to 28 thousand ECU in Denmark. Productivity can be estimated by comparing these figures with the value added per capita, which gives data on wage adjusted labour productivity. In 1995/96 this ratio was highly variable across the EU, from 127% in Sweden up to 275% in the Netherlands.

Demand for restaurants and bars is multifaceted, reflecting both the evolution of disposable income and traditional social attitudes towards going out to eat or drink. Corporate activity also has an influence, especially at the upper end of the restaurant market, as business meals depend to a large degree on the general level of economic activity.

Tourism is naturally an important determinant of demand. Indeed, most tourists usually have little choice to but to frequent restaurants and cafés to eat and drink whilst on holiday. A recent Eurobarometer survey carried out for the European Commission[3] revealed that up to 73% of the expenses made by European tourists once they had arrived at their destination were on food and drink products, ahead of craft products or clothes. In some cases, restaurants may even become a tourist attraction per se and gourmet holidays based on high quality restaurants or regional cuisine are gaining in popularity.

Table 17.2 (million ECU)

Top 10 catering group enterprises in Europe, 1997

			Turnover
1	**Sodexho (Sodexho; Gardner Merchant)**	F	3,193
2	**Compass Group (Compass; Eurest; SHRM)**	UK	2,495
3	**Bercy Management (Avenance; Restoplan; High Table; Mediterranea de Restauration)**	F	1,004
4	**Granada (Granada; Sutcliffe)**	UK	832
5	**Aramark**	USA	484
6	**SV Services (SV Service; Sentivo AG; KGS)**	CH	267
7	**Pedus (Dussmann Group)**	D	240
8	**Appetito Group**	D	228
9	**Sogeres**	F	207
10	**RC Accor (Gemeaz Cuisine)**	F	140

Source: Néo Restauration

In addition to restaurants and bars, this sector also comprises the specific activity of catering services. This activity has been greatly affected by the trends towards sub-contracting of non-core activities witnessed in many industries (see chapter on business services). Enterprises or schools that used to run their own restaurant facilities for their employees and students have increasingly outsourced this activity to specialised independent groups. These enterprises are hence perhaps better viewed as business services' enterprises, as are cleaning services and security services. The European market for catering services is led by the French group Sodexho. They generated turnover of almost 3.2 billion ECU in 1997, ahead of the Compass Group (UK) with a turnover of 2.5 billion ECU. It is estimated that the segments of education and health each account for a third of the catering service market, the remainder being largely shared between enterprises and public-sector canteens.

Franchising is witnessing a growing importance in the sector of restaurants and bars. Although it is most evident in the fast-food segment with world famous brands such as McDonalds or Kentucky Fried Chicken, it is also increasingly present in the traditional restaurant and bar sectors. Franchise brands are often associated with a "concept" or a "theme", offering standard menus, service and décor in each outlet. Some of these have reached worldwide notoriety, such as the Hard Rock Café and Starbucks Coffee bars or Planet Hollywood and Chi-Chi's restaurants. Whilst a dominant Europe-wide chain has yet to emerge, multinational franchising groups are spreading to practically all segments, from coffee-shops (La Croissanterie) and fast foods (Quick) to thematic restaurants (Buffalo Grill) and home-delivery (Telepizza).

3) "Facts and figures on Europeans on Holiday", March 1998.

Recreation parks (NACE Rev. 1 92.33 and 92.53)

The recreation parks sector includes a wide variety of establishments in terms of size, style and service offered. They vary from theme parks, other amusement parks and water parks, through holiday camps, to zoological gardens and safari parks. NACE Rev. 1 92.33 covers fairs and amusement parks, whilst NACE Rev. 1 92.53 covers botanical and zoological gardens and nature reserve activities.

Although being a significant segment of the tourism industry, this sector lacks comprehensive statistical coverage, and practically no official statistics exist at the time of writing. Analysis concerning this area is therefore based on estimates from professional trade associations and consulting groups. Figures should therefore be considered with precaution and readers are advised not to compare these data with those found for other activities within this publication.

According to the European Association of Zoos and Aquaria (EAZA), almost 81 million persons visited their 238 member zoos that were open to the public in 1997. The total attendance, including free tickets and multiple visits by annual ticket holders was estimated at approximately 100 million visitors. It must be noted that EAZA members originate from EU Member States, as well as most central and eastern European countries, plus Russia, Turkey and Israel.

The most recent estimates available showed that more than 110 million visitors went to European amusement and theme parks. The largest single recreation park in the EU is Disneyland Paris, with more than 12.5 million visitors in 1998 (a figure comparable to the year before) and turnover of around 890 million ECU.

(million visitors) Table 17.3

Annual attendance at major European parks, 1995-98

Disneyland Paris	F	12.5
Blackpool Pleasure Beach	UK	7.2
Alton Towers	UK	3.0
Liseberg AB	S	3.0
Tivoli	DK	2.8
Efteling	NL	2.7
Europa Park	D	2.7
Port Aventura	E	2.7
A/S Dyrehavsbakken	DK	2.4
Gardaland	I	2.4

Source: IAAPA, Europarks

At a world level, North America is the standard reference for international comparisons of recreational parks and theme parks. Theme parks were a very important element of the tourism industry in the USA, both for domestic and international visitors. In Europe, the number of visitors was lower than in the USA, as was per capita expenditure in amusement parks. The structure of revenue was also different, with admission revenues in major European amusement parks accounting for over half of all revenues (excluding accommodation), a level somewhat higher than in the other areas of the world. The differences reflect both higher admission charges in Europe (see table 17.4) and a greater reliance on a "pay-one-price" admission, where henceforth all rides are free of charge. There is also a lower expenditure on ancillary products in European theme parks.

Consumer demand for recreation parks is volatile. Major factors contributing to this volatility are changing consumer tastes, the weather and economic conditions. In addition, a trend has emerged in recent years whereby consumers are considering recreation parks as tourist destinations per se. Traditionally amusement parks were either a day trip attraction or one of the entertainment activities and attractions offered to tourists at holiday resort destinations. However, Europe's major theme parks (following the example of Disneyland Paris), are now increasingly positioning themselves as overnight destinations or fully-fledged resorts. Room capacity at Disneyland Paris, if developed as planned, will eventually be equal to about a third of the hotel rooms on offer in the area surrounding Paris.

In total, the number of recreation parks in Europe has increased over the last decade. However, expansion has not been uniform and amusement parks have enjoyed far greater growth than zoos, aquaria and safari parks. Greenfield investment in amusement parks is a relatively high-risk activity, with capital costs of investment high and demand difficult to predict.

Recreation parks are important employers of both skilled and unskilled workers. It is estimated that 40 to 50 thousand persons work in recreation parks in the EU. Permanent core staff are generally well-qualified, including administrative and marketing staff as well as skilled workers, such as carpenters, painters, electricians, mechanics and specialised designers. For zoos and aquaria, the requisite qualifications are usually even higher. However, seasonal staff outnumber permanent staff in this activity by a ratio of around 4 to 1, with many temporary and seasonal staff unqualified.

Table 17.4

Average charge to enter a recreation park by world region, 1995

	Average admission fee (ECU)	Share of parks charging an admission fee (%)
Western Europe	8.3	63
USA	7.5	79
Canada	2.7	67
Pacific	7.5	46

Source: IAAPA

As with the European tourism market in general, the recreation parks industry is being shaped by advances in communications and changes in consumer tastes. Some of the older recreation parks, such as zoos, safari parks and traditional holiday camps have experienced mixed fortunes over recent decades. In order to maintain their market share these attractions have adapted to circumstances. Many zoos, for example, are currently expanding marketing activities and enjoying improved visitor numbers as a result. Other parks have diversified their appeal through the addition of shows and rides, whilst a number have gone further and re-emerged as full-fledged amusement parks.

At present, most parks are idle throughout the winter, although the increasing popularity of indoor and water-based attractions has increased the scope for extending the season. This development is both demand and supply driven. One recent feature of the tourism sector is increased demand for short breaks in the off-season. This trend coincides with the wishes of park operators to increase levels of utilisation. In addition to extending the season, some parks have tested the market with Christmas and New Year opening periods. Also, many recreation parks are increasingly turning to the corporate sector to boost demand during off-peak periods.

Travel agencies (NACE Rev. 1 63.3)

Travel services encompass all firms engaged in arranging transport, accommodation and catering on behalf of travellers. The definition of NACE Rev. 1 63.3 includes furnishing travel information, advice and planning, arranging made-to-measure tours, accommodation and transportation for travellers and tourists, furnishing tickets, the sale of packaged tours and the activities of tour operators and of tourist guides.

Figure 17.15 (units)

Travel agencies and tour operators (NACE Rev. 1 63.3) Density of enterprises per ten thousand inhabitants, 1996

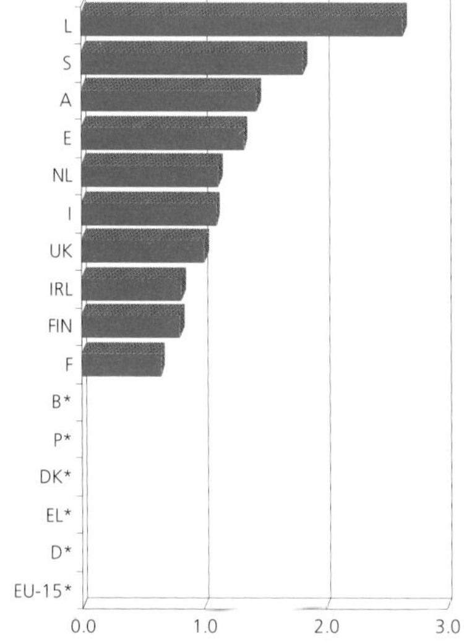

Source: Eurostat (SBS)

Data collected by the European Community Travel Agents and Tour Operators Association (ECTAA) on the basis of information provided by national travel agents' and tour operators' within the EU, is one source of non-official information for this sector. Estimates for 1998 indicate that the number of businesses involved in travel services is on the increase in most EU Member States, as can be seen in table 17.5. The largest market was Germany, one of the few countries witnessing a decline in their number of travel agencies. ECTAA membership was equal to 17,700 travel agencies in 1998 in Germany, one thousand fewer than two years before.

The German industry was the largest employer in Europe, with close to 50 thousand persons employed, ahead of the United Kingdom with 45 thousand persons[4]. By means of comparison, official statistics recorded 35 thousand persons employed in France and 31 thousand persons employed in Italy in 1995/96. On average, travel agencies employed between 5 and 10 persons, with Italy and Luxembourg at the lower end of the ranking and France and Ireland at the upper end.

Table 17.5 (units)

Number of travel agencies and tour operators

	1996	1997	1998
B	2,600	:	:
DK	597	:	676
D	18,700	17,900	17,700
EL	4,700	:	:
E	2,830	:	3,073
F	2,840	2,900	:
IRL	395	:	:
I	6,000	6,550	6,900
L	39	:	:
NL	1,100	:	:
A	2,700	2,803	2,797
P	489	505	516
FIN	430	490	520
S	600	600	600
UK	2,793	:	2,615

Source: ECTAA

Eurostat carry out a regular survey of labour costs across Europe, which give an indication of labour costs in travel agencies (unfortunately only available for a limited number of countries). Average labour costs per head were lowest in Portugal in 1996 at just 8 ECU per hour. That was less than half the level recorded in Luxembourg, the country where labour costs were the highest in the EU, at just under 20 ECU per hour. Unit personnel costs tend to be lower in travel agencies when comparing to other service activities. Official structural business statistics reveal that in most countries for which data was available annual unit personnel costs were below 30 thousand ECU per employee in 1995/96. Figures were somewhat lower in Italy (at 22 thousand ECU per employee), whilst they reached a high of 32 thousand ECU per employee in Sweden. When compared to per capita value added, these figures revealed that wage adjusted labour productivity ratios were not particularly high in this activity, ranging from 103% in France to 164% in Luxembourg.

4) In both cases ECTAA estimates for 1996.

Figure 17.16 (thousand ECU)

Travel agencies and tour operators (NACE Rev. 1 63.3) Personnel costs/employee, 1996

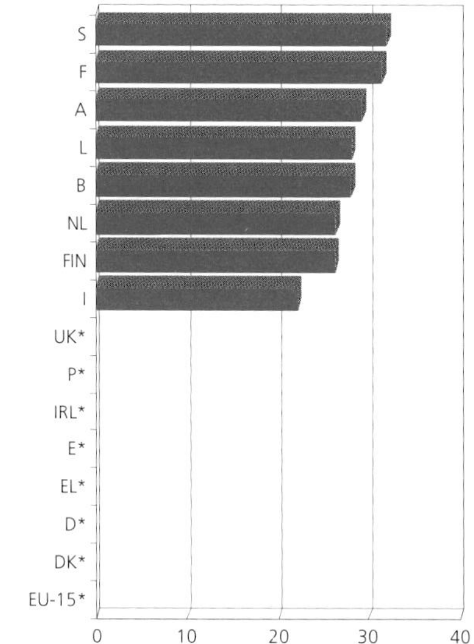

Source: Eurostat (SBS)

Figure 17.17 (%)

Travel agencies and tour operators (NACE Rev. 1 63.3) Wage adjusted labour productivity, 1996

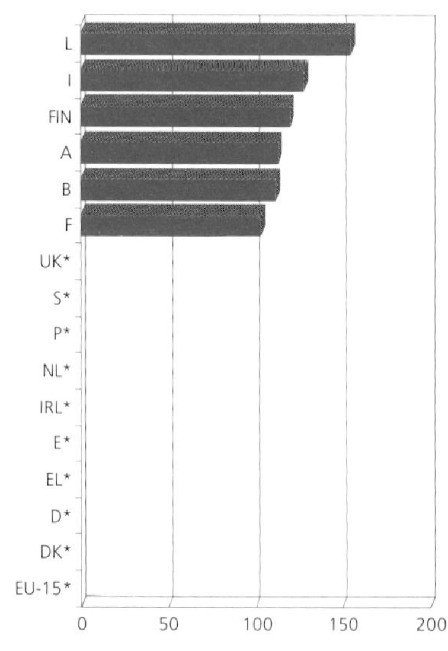

Source: Eurostat (SBS)

One of the key variables affecting demand for leisure travel and related travel services is that of airfare prices. They are particularly significant given the sector's reliance on travel bookings to medium and long-haul destinations, whereas domestic holidays and the bulk of rail and road transport bookings tend to by-pass travel agencies. The increasing liberalisation of air transport in Europe has been reflected in a sharp increase in passenger growth since the mid-80s. The gradual liberalisation of domestic and intra-regional air transport markets is expected to put further downward pressure on airfares. Almost one third (31%) of Europeans use the plane as their chosen means of transport to go on holiday[5], a proportion shared evenly between charter flights (16%) and scheduled flights (15%). The performance of the sector is also sensitive to variations in corporate demand for travel services, be it for business trips, conferences or exhibitions.

(units) Table 17.6

Number of travel agencies equipped with computer reservation systems, 1996

	AMADEUS	GALILEO	SABRE	WORLD-SPAN	Total
B	222	320	103	460	1,105
DK	347	95	42	118	602
D	11,428	329	661	474	12,892
EL	181	477	322	193	1,173
E	3,235	176	70	87	3,568
F	3,447	336	375	250	4,408
IRL	:	315	28	83	426
I	492	2,944	920	304	4,660
L	63	:	17	7	87
NL	27	1,277	70	489	1,863
A	335	534	21	9	899
P	:	486	26	137	649
FIN	529	:	8	3	540
S	683	:	145	111	939
UK	126	3,924	717	2,300	7,067

Source: Travel Distribution Report

EU travel agencies face growing competition not only from other sections of the travel and tourism industry, such as hotel chains and airlines, but also from tour operators who sell direct (by mail) and from clubs and associations acting as travel organisers. Mail order firms and hypermarket groups have also become more actively involved in the packaged travel market, notably in France, where hypermarket groups such as Carrefour and Leclerc have made inroads into the packaged tour market, as have a number of mail order companies. A number of retail banks have also branched into the packaged tour market, in conjunction with established tour operators.

However, information technologies may be expected to drastically change the face of the sector in years to come. IT is now almost universally present in the daily operations of a travel agent, for both desk and back-office operations (from data exchange to ticketing and payments). There is heavy reliance on computer reservation systems, which can be easily linked to the Internet to allow people to make their travel purchases directly from their home PC. The Travel Industry Association of America estimate that no fewer than 70 million persons have used the Internet for travel-related purposes in 1998 in the USA, up from 29 million in 1996. The number of travellers that used the Internet for travel planning increased from 3.1 million to 11.7 million during the same time period, with 6.7 million persons using the Internet to make travel reservations from the USA in 1998. As a consequence, four Internet travel agencies (Expedia, Preview Travel, Travelocity and Internet Travel Network) were ranked in the top 50 travel agencies in the USA in 1998.

5) "Facts and figures on Europeans on Holiday", March 1998.

In Europe, according to research by Datamonitor published in June 1999, the travel industry was expected to be one of the fastest growing sectors for on-line sales over the next few years. The sale of on-line travel products in Europe is expected to be worth 1.7 billion ECU by the year 2002, whilst it was valued at just 6.8 million ECU in 1997. The study suggested that on-line flight reservation systems and purchases for business travellers (travelling regularly and at short notice) would be the key drivers of growth.

In the long-run, travel agencies (including on-line) may have to face increasing competition from airlines, attracted by the opportunity to make direct sales and thus eliminating agents' commissions. Already discount airlines, such as Virgin Express or CityBird (B) offer the opportunity to book a flight from their Internet site. This is further facilitated by the absence of tickets, as only the reservation confirmation number that appears on the screen during the on-line booking procedure is required to check-in for the flight.

Business travel specialists have pre-empted the threat of direct distribution by increasing the range of services they provide to corporate clients. Leading operators such as American Express have re-positioned themselves as travel "management" companies, able to advise clients on their business travel policy by interpreting travel patterns and monitoring travel costs.

Professional associations representing the industries within this chapter

EAZA
European Association Of Zoos and Aquaria
Amsterdam Zoo
PO Box 20164
NL-1000 HD Amsterdam
e-mail: info@eaza.net

ECTAA
Group of National Travel Agents' and Tour Operators' Associations within the EU
36, rue Dautzenberg, boîte 6
B-1050 Bruxelles
tel: (32) 2 644 34 50
fax: (32) 2 644 24 21
e-mail: ectaa@skynet.be

Europarks
European Federation of Leisure Parks
Floralaan West 143
NL-5644 BH Eindhoven
tel: (31) 40 212 85 26
fax: (31) 40 211 40 50

HOTREC
Confederation of National Associations of Hotels, Restaurants, Cafés and Similar Establishments in the EU and EEA
111, boulevard Anspach
Boîte 4
B-1000 Bruxelles
tel: (32) 2 513 63 23
fax: (32) 2 502 41 73
e-mail: Hotrec@skynet.be

IAAPA
International Association of Amusement Parks and Attractions
1448 Duke Street
22314 Alexandria, Virginia
United States of America
tel: (1) 703 836 48 00
fax: (1) 703 836 48 01
e-mail: iaapa@iaapa.org

IH&RA
International Hotel and Restaurant Association
251, rue du Faubourg St-Martin
F-75010 Paris
tel: (33) 1 44 89 94 00
fax: (33) 1 40 36 73 30
e-mail: infos@ih-ra.com

WTO
World Tourism Organization
Capitán Haya, 42
E-28020 Madrid
tel: (34) 91 571 06 28
fax: (34) 91 571 37 33
e-mail:
omt@world-tourism.org

Table 17.7

Hotels (NACE Rev. 1 55.1)

Enterprise and employment indicators, 1996

	B	DK	D	EL	E	F	IRL	I	L	NL	A	P	FIN	S	UK
Number of enterprises (thousands) (1)	:	1.0	:	:	10.8	29.6	0.7	23.2	:	2.7	13.2	:	:	1.9	12.0
Number of enterprises per 10,000 inhabitants (1)	:	2.0	:	:	2.8	5.1	1.9	4.0	:	1.7	16.9	:	:	2.1	2.0
Number of pers. employed (thousands) (2)	:	17.8	:	:	169.3	185.3	24.9	175.5	:	38.0	68.2	:	:	:	:
Number of pers. employed/enterprise (units) (2)	:	17.1	:	:	15.6	6.3	36.8	7.6	:	14.4	5.2	:	:	:	:
Share of employees in total employed (%) (3)	:	50.4	:	:	93.4	82.8	95.5	77.9	:	89.5	:	:	:	:	:

(1) A (1991); S (1993); DK, F, I, NL (1995). (2) A (1991); NL (1993); DK, F, I (1995). (3) NL (1993); DK, F, I (1995).

Table 17.8

Hotels (NACE Rev. 1 55.1)

Turnover related indicators, 1996

	B	DK	D	EL	E	F	IRL	I	L	NL	A	P	FIN	S	UK
Turnover (billion ECU) (1)	:	0.8	:	:	6.7	10.3	0.8	8.1	:	1.8	:	:	:	1.3	11.4
Turnover/enterprise (million ECU) (1)	:	0.7	:	:	0.6	0.3	1.2	0.3	:	0.7	:	:	:	0.7	0.9
Turnover/person employed (thousand ECU) (2)	:	43.8	:	:	39.3	55.8	33.7	45.9	:	41.4	:	:	:	:	:

(1) S (1993); DK, F, I, NL (1995). (2) NL (1993); DK, F, I (1995).

Table 17.9

Hotels (NACE Rev. 1 55.1)

Competitiveness and productivity related indicators, 1996

	B	DK	D	EL	E	F	IRL	I	L	NL	A	P	FIN	S	UK
Value added/turnover (%) (1)	:	:	:	:	52.5	47.5	41.1	51.6	:	82.8	:	:	:	:	:
Labour productivity (thousand ECU/head) (2)	:	:	:	:	20.7	26.5	13.9	23.7	:	:	:	:	:	:	:
Wage adjusted labour productivity (%) (2)	:	:	:	:	136.5	126.3	:	133.6	:	:	:	:	:	:	:
Personnel costs/employee (thousand ECU) (3)	:	27.9	:	:	15.2	21.0	:	17.7	:	15.0	:	:	:	21.1	:
Gross operating surplus (million ECU) (4)	:	:	:	:	15.6	10.0	15.5	15.0	:	5.8	:	:	:	2.6	8.8

(1) F, I, NL (1995). (2) F, I (1995). (3) NL, S (1993); DK, F, I (1995). (4) S (1993); F, I, NL (1995).

Table 17.10 (%)

Hotels and restaurants (NACE Rev. 1 55)

Composition of the labour force, 1997 (%)

	EU-15	B	DK	D	EL	E	F	IRL	I	L	NL	A	P	FIN	S	UK
Female	52.6	48.2	63.4	57.2	41.0	44.2	48.2	57.2	46.9	48.5	52.0	61.4	58.4	72.0	59.5	60.4
Part-time	16.8	25.9	38.5	26.5	7.0	13.3	22.7	28.7	12.6	6.9	61.4	18.0	6.4	31.1	37.2	49.2
Temporary work or limited contract	43.7	50.5	28.6	39.0	65.5	68.4	40.2	37.4	54.4	26.3	39.7	39.1	50.9	30.9	44.6	24.2
Persons with a higher education	7.2	12.0	7.6	9.5	5.6	8.0	6.5	18.8	1.9	6.4	8.7	1.4	2.0	6.4	10.4	9.3
Persons with a lower education	53.3	41.7	49.4	30.8	59.4	76.4	42.1	44.7	69.3	72.1	46.0	31.5	88.5	23.6	32.1	57.9

Source: Eurostat (SBS, LFS)

Table 17.11

Camping sites and other provision of short-stay accomodation (NACE Rev. 1 55.2)
Enterprise and employment indicators, 1996

	B	DK	D	EL	E	F	IRL	I	L	NL	A	P	FIN	S	UK
Number of enterprises (thousands) (1)	:	0.7	:	:	3.7	:	:	14.2	:	2.6	1.4	:	:	0.6	3.1
Number of enterprises per 10,000 inhabitants (1)	:	1.4	:	:	0.9	:	:	2.5	:	1.7	1.7	:	:	0.7	0.5
Number of pers. employed (thousands) (2)	:	2.1	:	:	:	:	:	48.1	:	15.0	3.7	:	:	:	:
Number of pers. employed/enterprise (units) (2)	:	2.9	:	:	:	:	:	3.4	:	6.9	2.7	:	:	:	:
Share of employees in total employed (%) (3)	:	32.0	:	:	:	:	:	60.1	:	86.7	:	:	:	:	:

(1) A (1991); S (1993); DK, I, NL (1995). (2) A (1991); NL (1993); DK, I (1995). (3) NL (1993); DK, I (1995).

Table 17.12

Camping sites and other provision of short-stay accomodation (NACE Rev. 1 55.2)
Turnover related indicators, 1996

	B	DK	D	EL	E	F	IRL	I	L	NL	A	P	FIN	S	UK
Turnover (billion ECU) (1)	:	0.1	:	:	:	:	:	1.8	:	0.9	:	:	:	0.1	2.1
Turnover/enterprise (million ECU) (1)	:	0.2	:	:	:	:	:	0.1	:	0.3	:	:	:	0.2	0.7
Turnover/person employed (thousand ECU) (2)	:	53.2	:	:	:	:	:	37.6	:	52.0	:	:	:	:	:

(1) S (1993); DK, I, NL (1995). (2) NL (1993); DK, I (1995).

Table 17.13

Camping sites and other provision of short-stay accomodation (NACE Rev. 1 55.2)
Competitiveness and productivity related indicators, 1996

	B	DK	D	EL	E	F	IRL	I	L	NL	A	P	FIN	S	UK
Value added/turnover (%) (1)	:	:	:	:	:	:	:	52.3	:	82.2	:	:	:	:	:
Labour productivity (thousand ECU/head) (2)	:	:	:	:	:	:	:	19.6	:	:	:	:	:	:	:
Wage adjusted labour productivity (%) (2)	:	:	:	:	:	:	:	114.3	:	:	:	:	:	:	:
Personnel costs/employee (thousand ECU) (3)	:	27.6	:	:	:	:	:	17.2	:	12.0	:	:	:	26.2	:
Gross operating surplus (million ECU) (4)	:	:	:	:	:	:	:	12.1	:	18.9	:	:	:	5.3	9.9

(1) I, NL (1995). (2) I (1995). (3) NL, S (1993); DK, I (1995). (4) S (1993); I, NL (1995).

Source: Eurostat (SBS)

Table 17.14

Restaurants (NACE Rev. 1 55.3)

Enterprise and employment indicators, 1996

	B	DK	D	EL	E	F	IRL	I	L	NL	A	P	FIN	S	UK
Number of enterprises (thousands) (1)	:	8.5	:	:	:	76.2	:	72.6	:	19.9	24.1	:	:	13.3	45.9
Number of enterprises per 10,000 inhabitants (1)	:	16.2	:	:	:	13.2	:	12.7	:	12.9	30.9	:	:	15.2	7.8
Number of pers. employed (thousands) (2)	:	42.9	:	:	:	348.4	:	245.5	:	123.0	91.6	:	:	:	:
Number of pers. employed/enterprise (units) (2)	:	5.1	:	:	:	4.6	:	3.4	:	6.3	3.8	:	:	:	:
Share of employees in total employed (%) (3)	:	36.3	:	:	:	79.9	:	51.9	:	78.0	:	:	:	:	:

(1) A (1991); F, S (1993); DK, I, NL (1995). (2) A (1991); F, NL (1993); DK, I (1995). (3) F, NL (1993); DK, I (1995).

Table 17.15

Restaurants (NACE Rev. 1 55.3)

Turnover related indicators, 1996

	B	DK	D	EL	E	F	IRL	I	L	NL	A	P	FIN	S	UK
Turnover (billion ECU) (1)	:	1.7	:	:	:	16.1	:	10.7	:	4.4	:	:	:	2.4	14.8
Turnover/enterprise (million ECU) (2)	:	0.2	:	:	:	0.2	:	0.1	:	0.2	:	:	:	0.2	0.3
Turnover/person employed (thousand ECU) (3)	:	39.3	:	:	:	46.4	:	43.5	:	32.9	:	:	:	:	:

(1) S (1993); F (1994); DK, I, NL (1995). (2) F, S (1993); DK, I, NL (1995). (3) F, NL (1993); DK, I (1995).

Table 17.16

Restaurants (NACE Rev. 1 55.3)

Competitiveness and productivity related indicators, 1996

	B	DK	D	EL	E	F	IRL	I	L	NL	A	P	FIN	S	UK
Value added/turnover (%) (1)	:	:	:	:	:	:	:	31.4	:	64.8	:	:	:	:	:
Labour productivity (thousand ECU/head) (2)	:	:	:	:	:	:	:	13.7	:	:	:	:	:	:	:
Wage adjusted labour productivity (%) (2)	:	:	:	:	:	:	:	89.6	:	:	:	:	:	:	:
Personnel costs/employee (thousand ECU) (3)	:	27.2	:	:	:	:	:	15.3	:	8.8	:	:	:	16.2	:
Gross operating surplus (million ECU) (4)	:	:	:	:	:	5.8	:	6.1	:	5.8	:	:	:	2.9	5.4

(1) I, NL (1995). (2) I (1995). (3) NL, S (1993); DK, I (1995). (4) S (1993); F (1994); I, NL (1995).

Source: Eurostat (SBS)

Table 17.17

Bars (NACE Rev. 1 55.4)

Enterprise and employment indicators, 1996

	B	DK	D	EL	E	F	IRL	I	L	NL	A	P	FIN	S	UK
Number of enterprises (thousands) (1)	:	2.6	:	:	:	55.2	6.8	95.4	:	13.8	1.4	:	:	:	44.7
Number of enterprises per 10,000 inhabitants (1)	:	4.9	:	:	:	9.6	18.9	16.7	:	8.9	1.8	:	:	:	7.6
Number of pers. employed (thousands) (2)	:	10.7	:	:	:	93.5	36.4	199.3	:	63.0	4.9	:	:	:	:
Number of pers. employed/enterprise (units) (2)	:	4.2	:	:	:	1.7	5.3	2.1	:	4.4	3.5	:	:	:	:
Share of employees in total employed (%) (3)	:	30.5	:	:	:	36.2	70.6	27.2	:	74.6	:	:	:	:	:

(1) A (1991); F (1993); DK, IRL, I, NL (1995). (2) A (1991); F, NL (1993); DK, IRL, I (1995). (3) F, NL (1993); DK, IRL, I (1995).

Table 17.18

Bars (NACE Rev. 1 55.4)

Turnover related indicators, 1996

	B	DK	D	EL	E	F	IRL	I	L	NL	A	P	FIN	S	UK
Turnover (billion ECU) (1)	:	0.4	:	:	:	4.2	1.7	6.9	:	2.1	:	:	:	:	19.7
Turnover/enterprise (million ECU) (2)	:	0.2	:	:	:	0.1	0.2	0.1	:	0.2	:	:	:	:	0.4
Turnover/person employed (thousand ECU) (3)	:	38.9	:	:	:	45.6	46.8	34.6	:	31.6	:	:	:	:	:

(1) F (1994); DK, IRL, I, NL (1995). (2) F (1993); DK, IRL, I, NL (1995). (3) F, NL (1993); DK, IRL, I (1995).

Table 17.19

Bars (NACE Rev. 1 55.4)

Competitiveness and productivity related indicators, 1996

	B	DK	D	EL	E	F	IRL	I	L	NL	A	P	FIN	S	UK
Value added/turnover (%) (1)	:	:	:	:	:	:	24.3	32.9	:	67.2	:	:	:	:	:
Labour productivity (thousand ECU/head) (2)	:	:	:	:	:	:	11.3	11.4	:	:	:	:	:	:	:
Wage adjusted labour productivity (%) (3)	:	:	:	:	:	:	:	78.9	:	:	:	:	:	:	:
Personnel costs/employee (thousand ECU) (4)	:	29.8	:	:	:	:	:	14.4	:	6.7	:	:	:	:	:
Gross operating surplus (million ECU) (5)	:	:	:	:	:	5.6	3.7	10.3	:	9.4	:	:	:	:	8.9

(1) IRL, I, NL (1995). (2) IRL, I (1995). (3) I (1995). (4) NL (1993); DK, I (1995). (5) F (1994); IRL, I, NL (1995).

Source: Eurostat (SBS)

Table 17.20

Canteens and catering (NACE Rev. 1 55.5)

Enterprise and employment indicators, 1996

	B	DK	D	EL	E	F	IRL	I	L	NL	A	P	FIN	S	UK
Number of enterprises (thousands) (1)	:	0.8	:	:	:	1.6	:	2.1	:	2.1	0.2	:	:	0.3	3.8
Number of enterprises per 10,000 inhabitants (1)	:	1.6	:	:	:	0.3	:	0.4	:	1.4	0.3	:	:	0.3	0.6
Number of pers. employed (thousands) (2)	:	5.4	:	:	:	69.8	:	59.2	:	25.0	1.6	:	:	:	:
Number of pers. employed/enterprise (units) (2)	:	6.5	:	:	:	43.0	:	28.7	:	15.0	7.5	:	:	:	:
Share of employees in total employed (%) (3)	:	67.9	:	:	:	98.9	:	94.8	:	88.0	:	:	:	:	:

(1) A (1991); F, S (1993); DK, I, NL (1995). (2) A (1991); F, NL (1993); DK, I (1995). (3) F, NL (1993); DK, I (1995).

Table 17.21

Canteens and catering (NACE Rev. 1 55.5)

Turnover related indicators, 1996

	B	DK	D	EL	E	F	IRL	I	L	NL	A	P	FIN	S	UK
Turnover (billion ECU) (1)	:	0.3	:	:	:	3.8	:	2.9	:	1.1	:	:	:	0.2	5.1
Turnover/enterprise (million ECU) (2)	:	0.4	:	:	:	2.2	:	1.4	:	0.5	:	:	:	0.7	1.3
Turnover/person employed (thousand ECU) (3)	:	63.0	:	:	:	50.9	:	49.5	:	35.4	:	:	:	:	:

(1) S (1993); F (1994); DK, I, NL (1995). (2) F, S (1993); DK, I, NL (1995). (3) F, NL (1993); DK, I (1995).

Table 17.22

Canteens and catering (NACE Rev. 1 55.5)

Competitiveness and productivity related indicators, 1996

	B	DK	D	EL	E	F	IRL	I	L	NL	A	P	FIN	S	UK
Value added/turnover (%) (1)	:	:	:	:	:	:	:	33.5	:	59.4	:	:	:	:	:
Labour productivity (thousand ECU/head) (2)	:	:	:	:	:	:	:	16.6	:	:	:	:	:	:	:
Wage adjusted labour productivity (%) (2)	:	:	:	:	:	:	:	113.4	:	:	:	:	:	:	:
Personnel costs/employee (thousand ECU) (3)	:	31.3	:	:	:	:	:	14.6	:	16.0	:	:	:	21.4	:
Gross operating surplus (million ECU) (4)	:	:	:	:	:	1.9	:	1.4	:	4.5	:	:	:	2.0	1.5

(1) I, NL (1995). (2) I (1995). (3) NL, S (1993); DK, I (1995). (4) S (1993); F (1994); I, NL (1995).

Source: Eurostat (SBS)

Table 17.23

Travel agencies and tour operators (NACE Rev. 1 63.3)
Enterprise and employment indicators, 1996

	B	DK	D	EL	E	F	IRL	I	L	NL	A	P	FIN	S	UK
Number of enterprises (thousands) (1)	:	:	:	:	5.2	3.8	0.3	6.4	0.1	1.7	1.2	:	0.4	1.6	5.9
Number of enterprises per 10,000 inhabitants (1)	:	:	:	:	1.3	0.7	0.8	1.1	2.6	1.1	1.4	:	0.8	1.8	1.0
Number of pers. employed (thousands) (2)	6.7	:	:	:	:	34.6	2.9	31.0	0.5	15.6	8.2	:	3.8	:	:
Number of pers. employed/enterprise (units) (2)	:	:	:	:	:	9.1	9.8	4.9	4.7	7.1	7.9	:	9.3	:	:
Share of employees in total employed (%) (2)	82.3	:	:	:	:	99.5	89.0	74.5	94.3	93.1	94.7	:	96.0	:	:

(1) I, NL (1995). (2) NL (1993); I, A (1995).

Table 17.24

Travel agencies and tour operators (NACE Rev. 1 63.3)
Turnover related indicators, 1996

	B	DK	D	EL	E	F	IRL	I	L	NL	A	P	FIN	S	UK
Turnover (billion ECU) (1)	2.9	:	:	:	:	8.1	0.7	6.5	0.3	3.0	2.6	:	1.0	4.4	14.6
Turnover/enterprise (million ECU) (1)	:	:	:	:	:	2.1	2.5	1.0	3.1	1.7	2.5	:	2.5	2.7	2.5
Turnover/person employed (thousand ECU) (2)	430.3	:	:	:	:	233.0	250.4	209.3	665.1	169.2	314.7	:	269.6	:	:

(1) I, NL, A (1995). (2) NL (1993); I, A (1995).

Table 17.25

Travel agencies and tour operators (NACE Rev. 1 63.3)
Competitiveness and productivity related indicators, 1996

	B	DK	D	EL	E	F	IRL	I	L	NL	A	P	FIN	S	UK
Value added/turnover (%) (1)	7.3	:	:	:	:	13.9	9.8	13.6	6.6	21.2	10.5	:	11.7	8.5	:
Labour productivity (thousand ECU/head) (2)	31.5	:	:	:	:	32.5	24.7	28.4	43.7	:	33.0	:	31.6	:	:
Wage adjusted labour productivity (%) (2)	111.6	:	:	:	:	102.8	:	127.6	155.0	:	112.7	:	119.6	:	:
Personnel costs/employee (thousand ECU) (3)	28.2	:	:	:	:	31.6	:	22.2	28.2	26.5	29.3	:	26.4	32.0	:
Gross operating surplus (million ECU) (1)	:	:	:	:	:	1.1	0.9	1.4	:	1.9	1.7	:	0.3	0.7	1.4

(1) I, NL, A (1995). (2) I, A (1995). (3) NL (1993); I, A (1995).

Source: Eurostat (SBS)

Transport services

Industry description and main indicators

The transport services industry is primarily engaged in the conveyance of goods and passengers either directly or indirectly. Direct involvement relates to the actual conveyance of goods and passengers by various modes of transport. Indirect involvement relates to services such as handling when changing modes, traffic guidance, travel arrangement, freight brokerage, storage, etc. In the nomenclature of economic activities in the European Communities (NACE Rev. 1), transport services are broken down as land transport (NACE Rev. 1 60 including railways and other land transport, such as urban transport, road transport, freight transport by road or transport by pipelines), water transport (NACE Rev. 1 61), air transport (NACE Rev. 1 62, including space transport) and supporting and auxiliary transport activities (NACE Rev. 1 63, covering cargo handling and storage, operation of stations, ports and airports and other supporting land, water or air transport activities, including travel agencies and tourist assistance activities). All these activities will be covered in this chapter, except for travel agencies (NACE Rev. 1 63.3) that have been included in the chapter on tourism.

Transport services are at the centre of economic activities, and the overall competitiveness of an economy is greatly affected by the efficiency of its transport system. The trend towards more flexible production methods (such as just-in-time production) has led to lower stocks and more frequent deliveries of smaller quantities of goods, making transport an integral and essential part of the production process. In addition, the relocation of many enterprises outside cities and the dispersion of economic activity has had an effect on goods and passenger movements. The completion of the Internal Market, has spurred intra-EU trade and allowed the restructuring of manufacturing production around larger production units. It has also contributed to increase demand for freight transport. As for passenger transport, urban spread has boosted the demand for commuting, whereas leisure transport has benefited from a continuous increase in personal mobility and reductions in the cost of transport (notably airborne). As a result, the transport of goods and passengers has witnessed strong and consistent growth over the last twenty years.

The activities covered in this chapter include:

60.1: transport via railways;
60.2: other land transport;
61.1: sea and coastal water transport;
61.2: inland water transport;
62.1: scheduled air transport;
62.2: non-scheduled air transport;
62.3: space transport;
63.1: cargo handling and storage;
63.2: other supporting transport activities.

The main area of growth concerning the transport of goods has been road transport, which has grown on average by 4% per annum since 1970, mainly at the expense of rail transport (down by 0.6% per annum). As regards passenger transport (figure 18.1), air transport traffic has increased by no less than 7.7% per annum over the last thirty years, double the rate of growth seen for passenger cars, although these remain the prime mode of transport for passenger traffic. Interestingly enough, air transport has overtaken railways since 1995 in terms of number of passenger-kilometres travelled each year.

Table 18.1 (%)

Breakdown of goods transported in tonne-kilometres, 1997

	Road	Rail	Inland waterways	Pipelines
EU-15	73.2	14.4	7.2	5.2
B	70.4	14.6	12.0	3.0
DK	73.2	8.1	0.0	18.7
D	67.1	16.1	13.8	2.9
EL	98.1	1.9	0.0	0.0
E	84.2	10.1	0.0	5.7
F	74.4	16.9	1.8	6.9
IRL	91.3	8.7	0.0	0.0
I	85.1	9.4	0.1	5.4
L	68.7	20.5	10.8	0.0
NL	47.0	3.6	42.8	6.7
A	38.2	37.0	5.1	19.7
P	85.7	14.3	0.0	0.0
FIN	71.0	27.6	1.4	0.0
S	63.4	36.6	0.0	0.0
UK	84.8	9.1	0.1	6.0

Source: Eurostat, ECMT, UIC

Transport activities are important contributors to wealth creation. National Accounts indicate that in 1997 they generated between 3% (in Greece and France) and more than 6% of GDP (in Belgium or Denmark). Inland transport[1] makes up the largest share of transport activities in most Member States, and can account for up to two-thirds of the value added generated in transport activities. This was the case in 1997 in Austria and in Italy, as opposed to Belgium where it was only one-third due to the large size of the auxiliary transport services branch. In a majority of countries, inland transport activities accounted for between 2.0% and 2.5% of GDP in 1997. Finland and Denmark were clearly above the average with more than 3% of GDP, whilst Germany and Ireland displayed a share close to 1.5%.

1) In the National Accounts sense, as opposed to maritime and air transport services.

Table 18.2 (%)

Breakdown of land passenger transport in passenger-kilometres, 1995

	Passenger cars	Powered two-wheelers	Buses & coaches	Trams & metros	Railways
EU-15	82.4	2.5	8.2	0.9	6.0
B	81.0	1.2	11.1	0.7	6.0
DK	79.1	0.8	13.6	:	6.4
D	82.8	1.2	7.8	1.0	7.2
El	90.9	1.5	5.5	0.7	1.5
E	81.5	3.4	10.0	1.1	4.1
F	84.5	2.1	5.2	1.1	7.1
IRL	90.3	0.6	6.4	:	2.7
I	75.8	6.5	10.6	0.6	6.5
L	83.0	0.8	10.2	:	6.0
NL	81.8	1.5	8.1	0.8	7.8
A	74.6	1.4	11.5	1.7	10.7
P	81.7	3.2	10.7	0.4	3.9
FIN	80.0	1.5	12.8	0.6	5.1
S	83.5	0.7	8.5	1.4	6.0
UK	87.9	0.6	6.2	1.0	4.2

Source: Eurostat, ECMT, UIC

Figure 18.1 (billion passenger-kilometres, log scale)

Breakdown of passenger transport in the EU

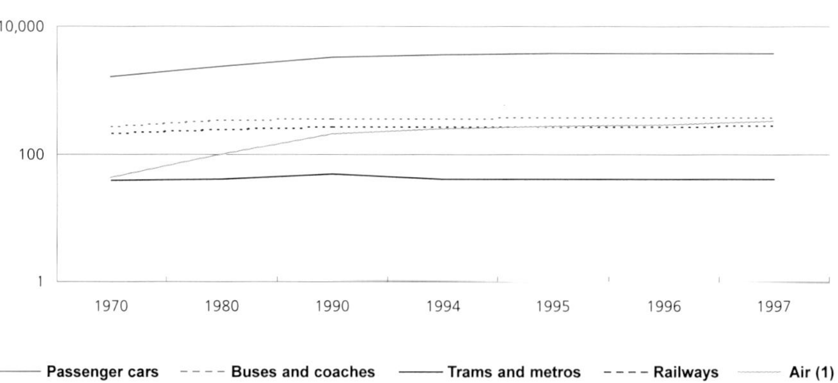

(1) European traffic only.

Source: Eurostat, ECMT, UIC, AEA, IACA

A very large number of transport enterprises are small in size. According to the latest estimates from Eurostat, around 93% of the enterprises active in the EU are micro-enterprises of less than 10 employees. The average size of enterprises varied considerably according to the type of transport considered. Air transport enterprises tend to be larger with the average number of persons employed equal to 110. In contrast, land transport enterprises employed only five persons on average, and maritime transport enterprises ten. In total, transport activities represent a significant share of employment, as they account for between 4% and 6% of the total workforce in the Community.

The annual survey on the European labour force supplies some interesting information on the characteristics of employment in transport services. The latest survey recorded 6.4 million persons employed in the EU in 1998, of which 60%, or 3.9 million, were in land transport, 360 thousand in air transport and 260 thousand in water transport. Auxiliary transport services employed 1.9 million persons. Only 9% of the persons employed worked part-time, a share that is half the level of the whole EU economy. The highest proportion of part-time work was found in Sweden (15%) and the Netherlands (20%), the lowest in Portugal (3%) and Greece (2%). On average, 8% of employees had a temporary job or a limited-duration contract, a proportion that was higher in water transport at 14%. Spain (25%) and Finland (12%) displayed the highest share of such contracts, in contrast to Austria (3%) and Belgium (2%).

Female employment was relatively low in transport services, as women represented less than one-fifth of the workforce in 1998, ranging from 10% in land transport to 30% in air transport and auxiliary transport services. Denmark, Germany and Sweden boasted the highest average female employment rates (around a quarter), Spain and Italy the lowest (10%). Analysis by country and sector reveals that more than half of the air transport workforce in Ireland and Portugal was composed of women, whilst more than 95% of the Greeks employed in land and water transport were men.

Only a tenth of the persons employed in transport services in the EU in 1998 possessed a higher education degree, a proportion that rose to one-quarter in air transport and water transport, but which fell as low as 7% in land transport. Countries with highly educated labour forces within transport services included Belgium (17%), Denmark (18%) and Sweden (19%), as opposed to Italy and Austria (both less than 5%).

International comparison

Transport services contributed 5.3% of Japanese GDP in 1997. Such a share placed Japan at a level similar to that of Finland, a country that ranks amongst the most transport-intensive within the EU. In contrast, transport services accounted for only 3.5% of American GDP, a low level for European standards. Much of the difference could be explained by the relatively low weight of inland transport and auxiliary transport services in the USA as compared to the EU and to Japan.

The specialisation of a country in a mode of transport can be estimated by comparing the share of each mode of transport in the total annual traffic, and then comparing it to the same share at world level. Such ratios are shown in figure 18.2 for passenger transport and figure 18.3 for freight transport. In both cases there is clear evidence of the strong specialisation of Europe in road transport. As regards passenger traffic we can see the high specialisation ratios of the EU and the USA in personal cars, whilst the Japanese favour public transport by rail. Buses and coaches show low specialisation ratios across the Triad. Indeed, as countries get wealthier, the motorisation rate of individuals tends to rise, forsaking public buses in favour of personal cars. As regards freight transport, Europe and Japan were relatively more specialised in road transport compared to the world averages. In the USA, specialisation was concentrated in pipelines, inland navigation and rail to the detriment of sea transport whose share was equal to only 15% of world averages.

(%) Figure 18.2

Specialisation ratios of passenger transport, 1996 (1)

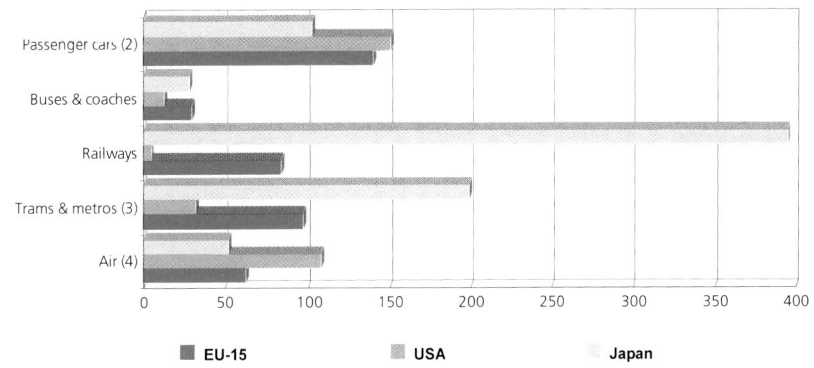

(1) Share of the transport mode in the region considered / share of the transport mode in the world total.
(2) Including light trucks in the USA and Japan.
(3) For Japan: results for trams & metros have been subtracted from official railway figures.
(4) Domestic air travel only.

Source: Eurostat, UN, IMF, UIC, Fearnleys

(%) Figure 18.3

Specialisation ratios of freight transport, 1996 (1)

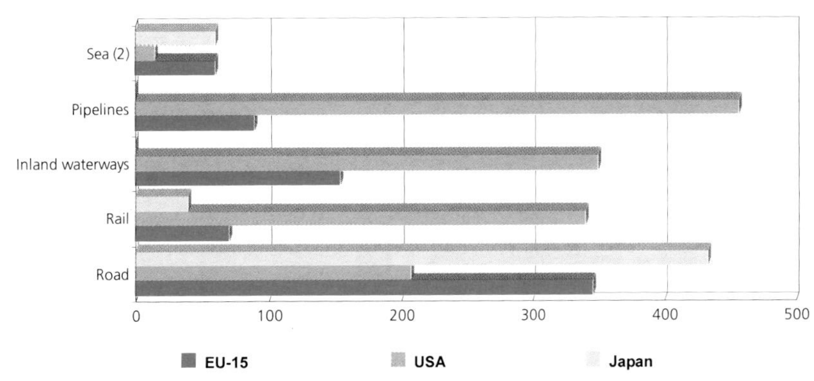

(1) Share of the transport mode in the region considered / share of the transport mode in the world total.
(2) Domestic sea traffic only.

Source: Eurostat, UN, IMF, UIC, Fearnleys

Road transport (NACE Rev. 1 60.2)

Land transport services are subdivided into rail transport (NACE Rev. 1 60.1) on the one hand, and all other land transport activities (NACE Rev. 1 60.2) on the other. This section will address the latter, in which the activity nomenclature definition classifies road freight transport, as well as passenger transport other than railways, scheduled or not, such as urban, suburban or inter-city public transport, taxi operations or charters, excursions and other occasional coach services. From this definition it is clear there a diverse number of agents operating, ranging from independent lorry or taxi drivers to very large metropolitan public transport companies.

Road transport is the most common means of transport. It represented in 1996 more than 88% of passenger transport and close to three-quarters of total freight transport inside the EU, excluding sea transport (43.5% including it). There were more than 45 thousand kilometres of motorways in the EU in 1996, seven thousand more than in 1990 and a 50% rise compared to 1980. Belgium and the Netherlands were the countries recording the most dense network with around 55 metres of motorway per square kilometre, whilst the EU average lay at 14 metres per square kilometre. Ireland displayed the smallest motorway network both in length (80 km) and in density (1 metre per square kilometre). Even when we compare the number of passenger cars in circulation to the total length of roads, Ireland displayed the lowest ratio with only 11 cars per kilometre of road. At the opposite end of the spectrum, Italy numbered no less than 107 cars for each kilometre of road, more than twice the EU average.

Figure 18.4 (%)

Land transport (NACE Rev. 1 60)
Share of micro-enterprises in the total number of enterprises, 1995 (1)

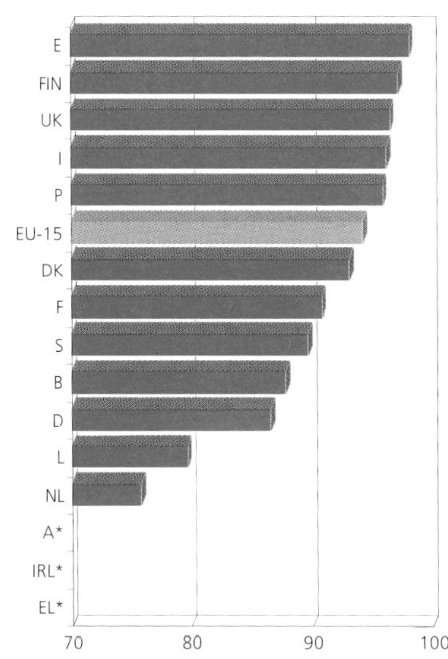

(1) Enterprises with 0-9 employees.

Source: Eurostat (SME)

The main modes of transport by road were passenger cars, buses, coaches, lorries and vans. The demand for road transport, both passenger and freight has been dramatically affected by increased mobility and flexibility, with door-to-door deliveries having a competitive edge over shorter distances compared to other modes. Over longer distances, road transport for freight still allows for door-to-door delivery without transhipment that is usually required for rail and inland waterway freight. In addition, the competitiveness of road compared to other freight transport modes has largely benefited from general liberalisation in Europe, which has simultaneously improved efficiency and reduced prices in road haulage. As a consequence, the number of registered road vehicles has dramatically increased over recent decades. Passenger cars experienced strong growth, whilst buses and coaches saw little change in their evolution since the 1980s. In total there were no fewer than 165 million cars and 18.5 million goods' vehicles on the EU's roads in 1996, and only half a million buses and coaches. The average motorisation rate for the EU in 1997 was equal to 450 cars per thousand inhabitants. The highest rates were recorded in Luxembourg and Italy with more than 570 cars per thousand inhabitants, the lowest in Portugal and Greece with less than 300 cars per thousand inhabitants. As a comparison, the motorisation rates of the USA and Japan the year before were equal to 518 cars and 373 cars per thousand inhabitants respectively.

Figure 18.5 (%)

Share of road transport in total goods transported, 1997 (1)

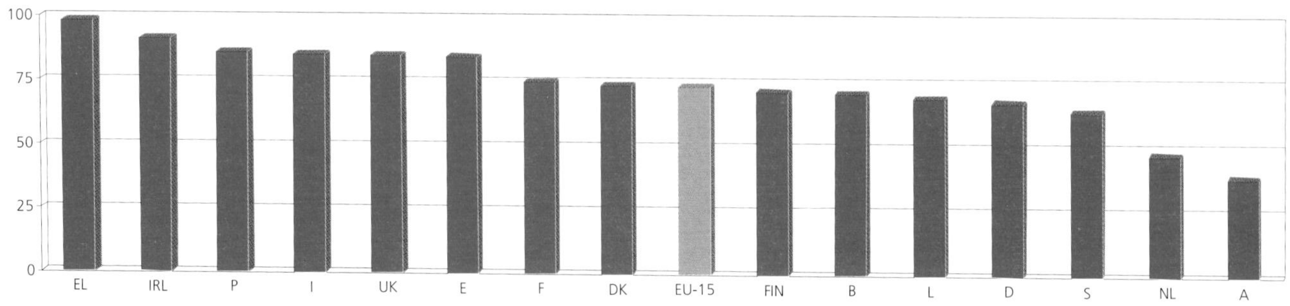

(1) Excluding sea transport.

Source: Eurostat, ECMT, UIC

(%) Figure 18.6

Land transport (NACE Rev. 1 60)

Share of part-time and temporary work contracts in total number of persons employed, 1997

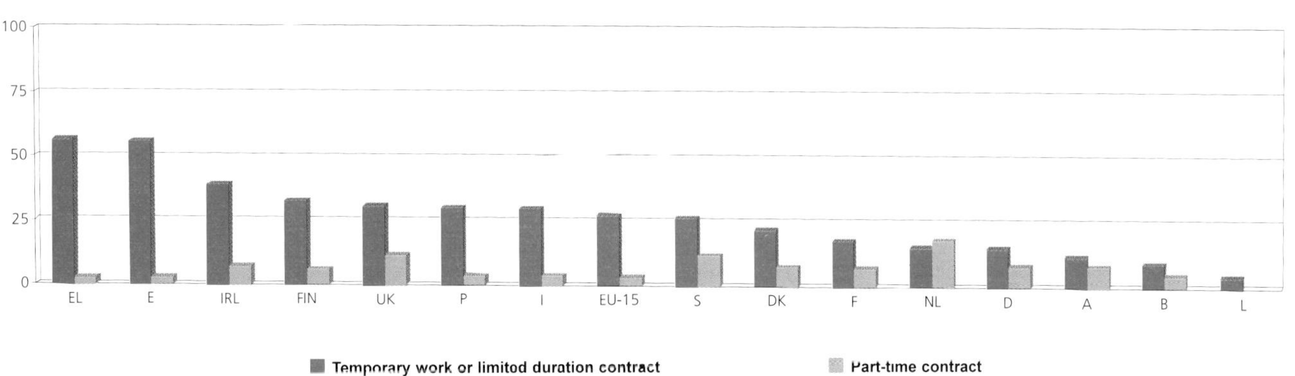

Source: Eurostat (LFS)

(thousand ECU) Figure 18.7

Land transport other than railways (NACE Rev. 1 60.2 and 60.3)

Personnel costs/employee, 1996

B
DK
L
F
I
A
NL
FIN
UK*
S*
P*
IRL*
E*
EL*
D*
EU-15*
0 10 20 30 40

Source: Eurostat (SBS)

(%) Figure 18.8

Land transport other than railways (NACE Rev. 1 60.2 and 60.3)

Wage adjusted labour productivity, 1996

FIN
A
L
B
I
F
UK*
S*
P*
NL*
IRL*
E*
EL*
D*
DK*
EU-15*
0 50 100 150 200

Source: Eurostat (SBS)

As mentioned at the start of this section, practically three-quarters of the total freight traffic in the EU is made by road. This has not always been the case: at the beginning of the 1980s, the market share of road freight transport was just 58% and it was less than 50% in 1970. Its growth rate has outperformed that of any other transport means to exceed 1.2 thousand billion tonne-kilometres in 1997, a progression of 29% compared to 1990. Road-intensity of freight transport across the Member States reported wide disparities, ranging from just 38% in Austria to 98% in Greece. Beyond straight economic factors, this ratio is also affected by criteria such as the quality of the transport infrastructure, climatic and geographical conditions or the density of the population. It must be noted that sea transport is excluded from the calculation, which can have strong implications for countries like Greece.

Turning to passenger transport, the road represented 88% of all transport services used by passengers. If we consider only land transport, the dominant transport mode was the passenger car (82%), followed by buses and coaches (8%) and railways (6%). Road was also the form of transport that experienced the strongest growth over the last couple of decades, as is clearly shown in Figure 18.9. Passenger car traffic in the EU exceeded 3.8 thousand billion passenger-kilometres in 1997, a progression of 15% since 1990 and 62% since 1980. In comparison, buses and coaches transported 380 billion passenger-kilometres in 1997, powered two-wheelers 114 billion passenger-kilometres and trams and metros just 42 billion passenger-kilometres, in all three cases levels diverged very little when compared to figures recorded in 1980.

As regards public transport, the International Union of Public Transport (UITP) estimate that in 1996 it served close to 130 million persons and totalled some 23 billion passenger journeys over 5.8 billion kilometres in the EU. The average number of journeys per head ranged from 58 in Greece up to 503 in Finland, with an EU average of 180 (1996).

Evolution of passenger transport in the EU (1)

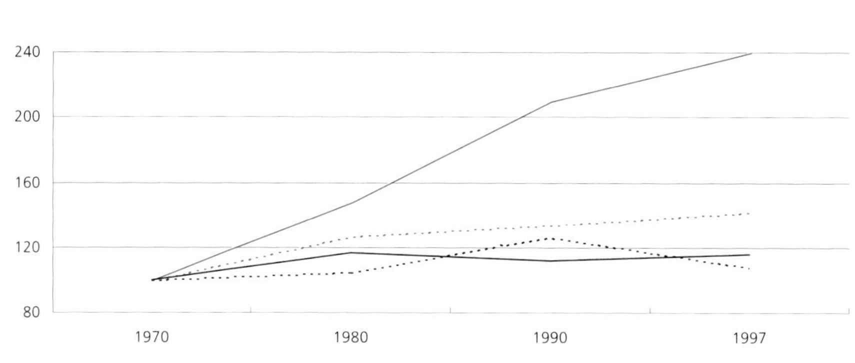

Passenger cars - - - - Buses and coaches —— Powered two-wheelers (2) - - - - Trams and metros

(1) Based on the number of passenger-kilometres.
(2) 1995 instead of 1997.

Source: UITP, ECMT, UIC

Table 18.3

Main indicators for public transport, 1996 (1)

	Passenger journeys (millions)	Vehicle kilometres (millions)	Population served (millions)	Journeys per population served (units)
B	391	133	2.9	133
DK	252	81	2.1	120
D	5,435	1,679	39.3	138
EL	221	26	3.8	58
E	2,340	449	10.3	227
F	3,884	783	18.7	208
IRL	203	52	1.2	176
I	3,552	606	16.0	223
L	19	4	0.1	181
NL	604	164	2.4	250
A	313	106	2.1	149
P	1,219	137	3.7	332
FIN	264	85	0.5	503
S	341	110	2.8	120
UK	4,277	1,406	23.9	179
EU-15	23,314	5,821	129.8	180

(1) Estimates.

Source: UITP, ECMT, national statistics

Air transport (NACE Rev. 1 62 and 63.23)

The air transport industry comprises enterprises which are exclusively or primarily engaged in the transport of passengers and goods by air on scheduled services (NACE Rev. 1 62.10) as well as unscheduled services, helicopter and air taxi services and private usage (NACE Rev. 1 62.20). This section also encompasses supporting air transport activities covered by NACE Rev. 1 Rev. 1 63.23, such as the operation of terminal facilities, airports or air-traffic-control activities.

(%) — Figure 18.10

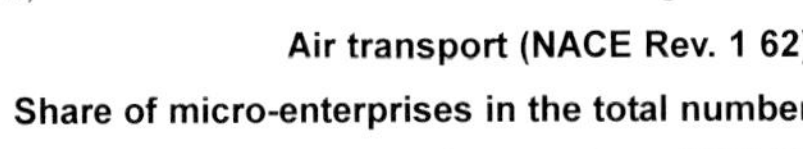

Air transport (NACE Rev. 1 62)

Share of micro-enterprises in the total number of enterprises, 1995 (1)

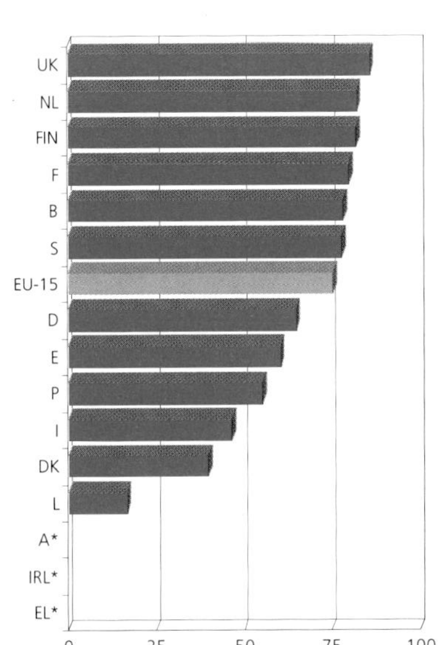

(1) Enterprises with 0-9 employees.

Source: Eurostat (SME)

(%) — Figure 18.11

Air transport (NACE Rev. 1 62)

Share of temporary work contracts in total number of persons employed, 1997

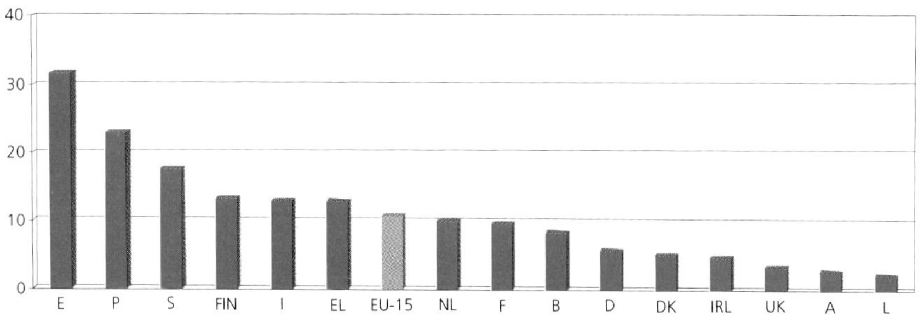

Source: Eurostat (LFS)

(thousand ECU) — Figure 18.12

Air transport (NACE Rev. 1 62)

Personnel costs/employee, 1996

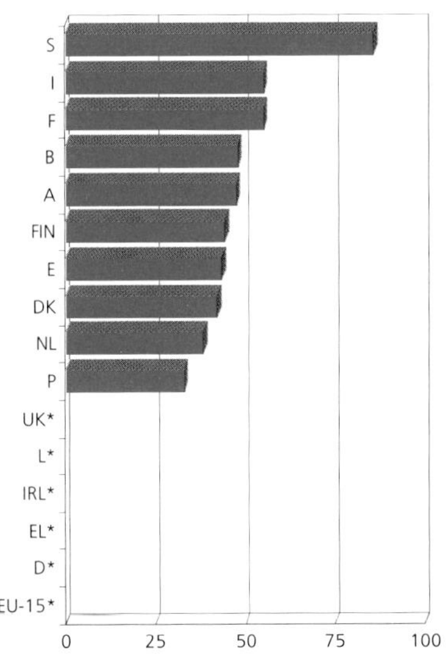

Source: Eurostat (SBS)

(%) — Figure 18.13

Air transport (NACE Rev. 1 62)

Wage adjusted labour productivity, 1996

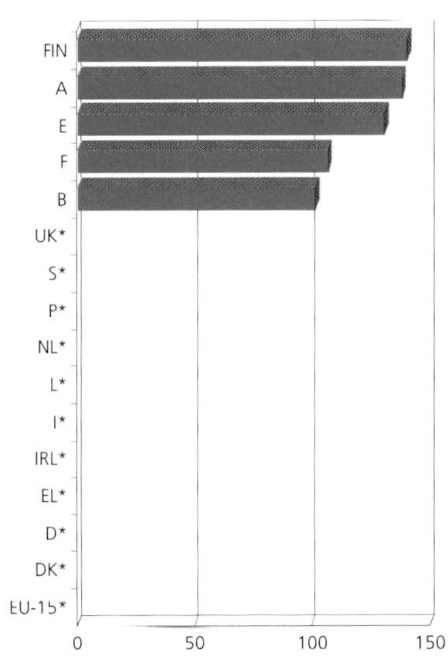

Source: Eurostat (SBS)

Air traffic (excluding military) is usually divided into commercial and general aviation. Commercial aviation consists of passenger travel, both charter and scheduled, and air freight, which includes air freight, combination passenger/freight aircraft and freight in the hold of passenger aircraft, as well as air courier and mail services. General aviation includes the private use of planes and air taxi services.

Air transport has witnessed strong growth in recent decades, European passenger traffic grew at an average annual rate of 7.8% in the 1980's and 6.7% per annum between 1990 and 1997, jumping from 96 billion passenger-kilometres in 1980 to 322 billion passenger-kilometres in 1997. Air transport accounted for 6.7% of passenger transport, up from 4.9% in 1990 and 3% in 1980.

Statistical coverage of prominent airline companies in Europe is available from the Association of European Airlines[2] (AEA). Its members boasted in 1997 a 1,880 strong fleet, 117 aircraft more than the preceding year, all but 155 of which were jets. Two-thirds of the jet fleet was composed of aircraft made by Boeing and McDonnell Douglas and 23% by the European consortium Airbus. However, a look at the order book revealed that these figures were expected to drastically change in the near future. No less than 54% of ordered aircraft were Airbuses, against only 42% for Boeing and McDonnell Douglas. In 1997, AEA airlines placed 128 new jet aircraft orders, between the high of 1989 (252 units) and the low of 1993 (10 units).

2) Adria Airways Slovenia, Aer Lingus Ireland, Air France, Air Malta, Alitalia, Austrian Airlines, Balkan Bulgarian Airlines, British Airways, British Midland airways, Cargolux Airlines, Croatia Airlines, CSA Czech Airlines, Cyprus Airways, Finnair, Iberia (E), Icelandair, JAT Yugoslav Airlines, KLM (NL), Lufthansa (D), Luxair, Malev Hungarian Airlines, Olympic (EL), Sabena (B), SAS (DK, S, NO), Swissair, TAP-Air Portugal, Turkish Airlines.

Figure 18.14 (%)

Composition of the jet aircraft fleet, 1997

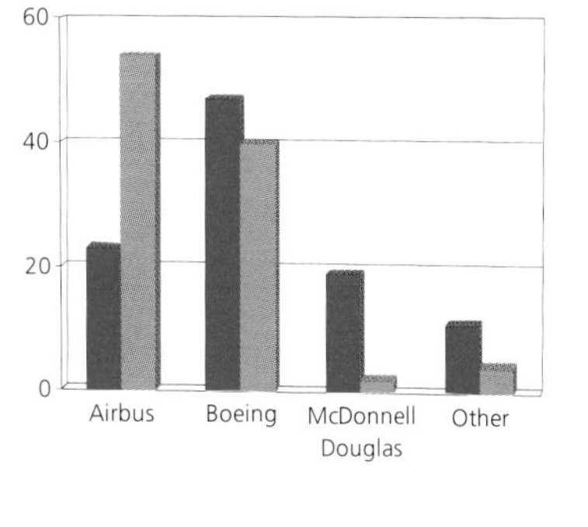

Source: AEA

Passenger traffic on EU airlines expanded by 11% in 1997, reaching 441 thousand revenue passenger-kilometres[3], over one-fifth of which was accounted for by European routes. Since the carrying capacity grew by only 8% to 608 billion seat-kilometres, the passenger load factor, in other words, the average rate of seating capacity which was actually sold and utilised, progressed to 72%. Passenger load factors were higher on long-haul routes (73%) than on European routes (64%). The highest passenger load factor was achieved by KLM (79%), followed by Aer Lingus and Air France (both 75%), whilst the lowest was recorded by Luxair (57%).

North American airlines took the lion's share of passenger traffic. No fewer than six of the top ten world airlines, including the four largest, were from the USA. The first European company was British Airways, in fifth place. However, European companies fared better when taking into account only international traffic. British Airways was the leading carrier in the world with more than 102 billion revenue-passenger-kilometres, and three other EU companies were present in the top ten of the ranking (Lufthansa, Air France and KLM), together with three American companies, Japan Airlines, Singapore Airlines and Qantas Australia.

3) RPK: one fare-paying passenger transported one kilometre, counted on a point-to-point basis, carried at 25% or more of the normal applicable fare for the journey. RPKs are computed by multiplying the number of revenue passengers by the kilometres they are flown.

Table 18.4

AEA airlines scheduled passenger traffic, 1997

Company	Country	Passenger traffic (million passenger-kilometres)	Share of traffic on European routes (%)	Annual growth of traffic (%)	Passenger load (%)	Passenger load on European routes (%)
Sabena	B	11,274	40	25	66	58
SAS	DK, S, NO	20,331	42	4	65	58
Lufthansa	D	71,353	20	13	72	61
Olympic	EL	9,261	38	9	68	63
Iberia	E	27,634	25	7	73	68
Air France	F	69,987	12	22	75	62
Aer Lingus	IRL	5,893	37	15	75	75
Alitalia	I	35,992	22	4	72	62
Luxair	L	447	100	6	57	57
KLM	NL	55,388	12	13	79	70
Austrian	A	6,230	35	15	65	59
TAP	P	8,773	38	10	71	68
Finnair	FIN	9,629	53	12	68	66
British Airways	UK	105,701	15	5	72	66
British Midland	UK	2,976	59	10	65	64
EU-15		440,869	21	11	72	64
Icelandair	IS	3,184	42	11	73	70
Swissair	CH	25,253	22	19	71	59
Balkan	BG	1,796	38	-1	58	51
Cyprus Airways	CY	2,657	95	2	69	70
CSA Czech Airlines	CZ	2,442	43	3	65	58
Malev	HU	2,346	64	13	59	56
Air Malta	MT	1,949	85	1	70	72
Adria Airways	SI	375	100	-1	45	45
Turkish Airlines	TR	12,379	44	13	67	67
JAT	YU	782	81	11	54	53
Croatia Airlines	HR	466	81	-4	50	48

Source: AEA

North America accounted for thirteen airports in the top twenty in 1997, including the top four, whilst only four were airports located in the EU. The largest airport in the world was Chicago O'Hare with more than 70 million passengers per annum, whilst the first EU airport was London Heathrow in fifth place with 58 million passengers. At a European level (see table 18.6), Heathrow preceded Frankfurt, Paris Charles de Gaulle and Amsterdam, the only other EU airports present in the world top twenty, all with in excess of 30 million passengers per annum.

Freight transported by EU airlines grew by more than 5% in 1997 to reach 25 billion tonne-kilometres, of which only 3% concerned European routes. The total revenue load factor (the percentage of total capacity available for freight and mail which is actually sold and utilised) was equal to 69% on all routes, and to 53% on European routes.

The largest freight airline in the world in 1997 was Federal Express (USA) with traffic that exceeded 9 billion tonne-kilometres, of which only 39% were on international routes. It was followed by Lufthansa (D) with more than 6 billion tonne-kilometres, almost exclusively on international routes, which made Lufthansa the largest international freight carrier in the world. As a general rule, EU air companies were better placed in the world ranking of freight transport compared to passenger transport.

Table 18.5

Top twenty airlines in the world by passengers flown, 1997

		Country	Total scheduled passenger traffic (million passenger-kilometres)	Share of international destinations (%)	World ranking by international traffic
1	**United Airlines**	USA	195,292	39	2
2	**American Airlines**	USA	172,131	32	6
3	**Delta Air Lines**	USA	160,327	23	12
4	**Northwest Airlines**	USA	115,920	46	9
5	**British Airways**	UK	105,701	97	1
6	**Japan Airlines**	JP	79,063	78	4
7	**Lufthansa**	D	71,353	93	3
8	**Air France**	F	69,987	88	5
9	**Continental**	USA	69,918	24	23
10	**US Airways**	USA	66,913	10	47
11	**Qantas**	AU	58,053	76	10
12	**KLM**	NL	55,388	100	7
13	**Singapore Airlines**	SG	55,096	100	8
14	**All Nippon Airways**	JP	51,219	36	20
15	**TWA**	USA	40,393	23	40
16	**Korean Air Lines**	KR	39,939	86	13
17	**Cathay Pacific**	HK	38,942	100	11
18	**Air Canada**	CA	36,607	66	17
19	**Alitalia**	I	35,992	80	14
20	**Thai Airways**	TH	30,987	90	15

Source: IATA, AEA

Table 18.6

Top twenty EU airports by number of passengers, 1997

		Country	Number of passengers (thousands)	World ranking
1	**London Heathrow**	UK	58,143	5
2	**Frankfurt/Main**	D	40,263	8
3	**Paris Charles de Gaulle**	F	35,293	10
4	**Amsterdam Schipol**	NL	31,570	14
5	**London Gatwick**	UK	26,961	25
6	**Paris Orly**	F	25,056	31
7	**Roma Fiumicino**	I	25,001	32
8	**Madrid Barajas**	E	23,602	35
9	**München**	D	17,895	44
10	**København**	DK	16,837	49
11	**Palma de Mallorca**	E	16,558	50
12	**Manchester**	UK	15,951	52
13	**Bruxelles National**	B	15,935	53
14	**Düsseldorf**	D	15,532	57
15	**Stockholm Arlanda**	S	15,198	58
16	**Barcelona**	E	15,066	59
17	**Milano Linate**	I	14,271	63
18	**Athinai**	EL	11,090	76
19	**Gran Canaria**	E	10,738	78
20	**Dublin**	IRL	10,333	81

Source: ACI

Table 18.7

AEA airlines scheduled freight traffic, 1997

Company	Country	Freight traffic (million tonne-kilometres)	Share of traffic on European routes (%)	Annual growth of traffic (%)	Total revenue load factor (%)	Total revenue load factor on European routes (%)
Sabena (1)	B	:	:	:	66	58
SAS	DK, S, NO	697	7	13	60	48
Lufthansa	D	6,164	3	2	72	57
Olympic	EL	129	35	9	55	55
Iberia	E	723	6	-1	59	56
Air France	F	4,913	1	6	70	37
Aer Lingus	IRL	122	6	20	71	66
Alitalia	I	1,440	3	-1	72	60
Luxair	L	0	100	-8	53	53
Cargolux	L	2,242	0	31	77	94
KLM	NL	3,734	3	1	78	64
Austrian	A	165	13	29	61	49
TAP	P	235	17	12	63	58
Finnair	FIN	294	14	24	58	54
British Airways	UK	3,914	3	12	65	52
British Midland	UK	5	68	11	65	64
EU-15	EU-15	24,777	3	5	69	53
Icelandair	IS	56	35	5	65	58
Swissair	CH	1,831	3	13	72	54
Balkan	BG	32	21	32	44	39
Cyprus Airways	CY	36	95	1	61	62
CSA Czech Airlines	CZ	23	20	4	55	49
Malev	HU	35	22	12	42	41
Air Malta	MT	11	76	-4	52	55
Adria Airways	SI	4	100	-2	39	39
Turkish Airlines	TR	255	38	23	53	53
JAT	YU	5	88	98	48	48
Croatia Airlines	HR	2	87	-11	42	40

(1) At the beginning of 1997, the responsibility for selling air freight capacity on Sabena services was transferred to Swiss cargo.

Source: AEA

Table 18.8

Top twenty airlines in the world by freight flown, 1997

		Country	Total scheduled freight traffic (million tonne-kilometres)	Share of international destinations (%)	World ranking by international traffic
1	Federal Express	USA	9,015	39	9
2	Lufthansa	D	6,164	100	1
3	Korean Air Lines	KR	5,642	98	2
4	UPS	USA	5,617	24	20
5	Air France	F	4,913	99	3
6	Singapore Airlines	SG	4,760	100	4
7	Japan Airlines	JP	4,174	93	6
8	British Airways	UK	3,914	100	5
9	KLM	NL	3,734	100	7
10	Cathay Pacific	HK	3,568	100	8
11	United Airlines	USA	3,244	74	10
12	Northwest Airlines	USA	2,850	69	12
13	American Airlines	USA	2,375	72	15
14	Cargolux Airlines Intl	L	2,260	100	11
15	Swissair	CH	1,831	100	13
16	Nippon Cargo Airlines	JP	1,814	100	14
17	Delta Air Lines	USA	1,813	69	21
18	Qantas	AU	1,692	92	17
19	Thai Airways	TH	1,619	98	16
20	Alitalia	I	1,440	99	18

Source: IATA, AEA

The busiest airport in the world for freight traffic in 1997 was Memphis, a major express courier hub ranked only 80th in terms of passenger traffic, with 2.2 million tonnes of freight loaded and unloaded. We have to go down to 8th place to find the first EU airport; Frankfurt with 1.5 million tonnes, followed by London Heathrow, Amsterdam and Paris Charles de Gaulle, the only EU airports that exceeded the line of 1 million tonnes annual freight traffic.

AEA airlines employed 323 thousand persons in 1997, 2.2% more than the year before. AEA noted a clear improvement of productivity in terms of tonne-kilometres per employee and of output actually sold (revenue tonne-kilometres per employee), both were 80% higher than their levels of ten years before.

Airline strategies will continue to be influenced by the progressive liberalisation and privatisation of EU air transport. The industry is still very fragmented. AEA numbered 155 airlines operating large passenger aircraft in Europe in 1997, far higher than the corresponding figures in North America (55) and Asia/Pacific (86). The dominant trend observed in recent years has been the formation of very large alliances of airlines combining their networks. For example, the "Star Alliance" network regrouped Air Canada, Air New Zealand, All Nippon Airways, Ansett Australia, Lufthansa, SAS, Thai, United and VARIG (BR). There was also the "One World" alliance of British Airways, American Airlines, Canadian Airlines, Cathay Pacific (HK) and Qantas (AU), as well as the "Qualiflyer Group" alliance of 11 European airlines including Swissair, Sabena (B), Austrian, TAP (P), Turkish, Crossair (CH), Lauda Air (A), Tyrolean (A), AOM (F), Air Littoral (F) and Air Europe (I).

Table 18.9

Top twenty EU airports by freight traffic, 1997

		Country	Freight traffic (thousand tonnes) (1)	World ranking
1	**Frankfurt/Main**	D	1,514	8
2	**London Heathrow**	UK	1,260	11
3	**Amsterdam Schipol**	NL	1,207	12
4	**Paris Charles de Gaulle**	F	1,072	13
5	**Bruxelles National**	B	531	24
6	**Köln/Bonn**	D	399	36
7	**København**	DK	388	38
8	**Luxembourg Findel**	L	340	47
9	**Roma Fiumicino**	I	288	52
10	**London Gatwick**	UK	287	53
11	**Madrid Barajas**	E	282	55
12	**Paris Orly**	F	237	64
13	**Stockholm Arlanda**	S	146	80
14	**London Stansted**	UK	142	81
15	**East Midlands**	UK	140	82
16	**München**	D	124	85
17	**Milano Malpensa**	I	123	87
18	**Athinai**	EL	120	90
19	**Wien**	A	114	92
20	**Lisboa**	P	111	96

(1) Loaded & unloaded freight and mail in metric tonnes.

Source: ACI

Railway transport (NACE Rev. 1 60.1)

This service includes activities that are exclusively or primarily engaged in the transport of passengers and goods by rail. It also includes the equipment and facilities required to provide this transport, including private railway lines. Not included in this sector are: metropolitan rail networks (NACE Rev. 1 60.21), repair and maintenance of rolling stock (NACE Rev. 1 35.20), sleeping car services (NACE Rev. 1 55.23) and dining car services (NACE Rev. 1 55.30).

Figure 18.15 (%)

Railways (NACE Rev. 1 60.1)
Share of micro-enterprises in the total number of enterprises, 1995 (1)

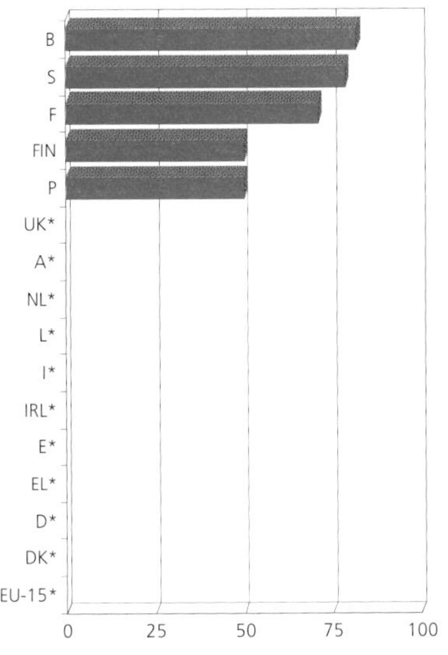

(1) Enterprises with 0-9 employees.

Source: Eurostat (SME)

Figure 18.16 (thousands)

Employment in railways

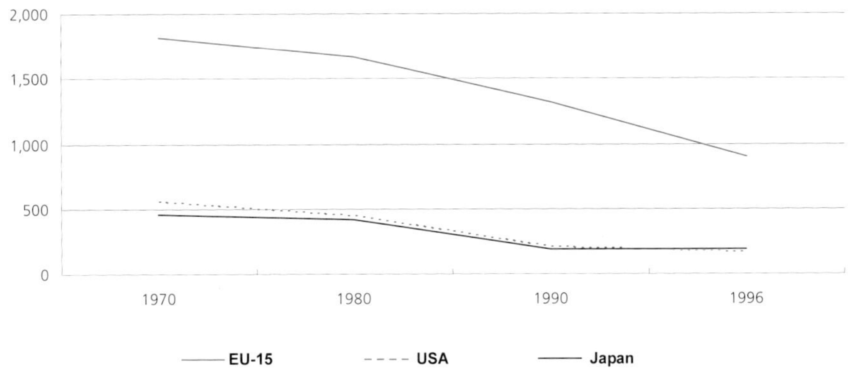

2,000
1,500
1,000
500
0
1970 1980 1990 1996

EU-15 USA Japan

Source: UIC

Figure 18.17 (%)

Share of rail in total goods transported in tonne-kilometres, 1997 (1)

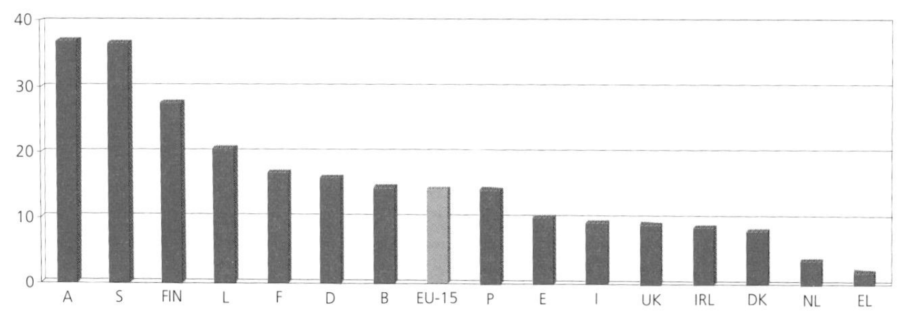

(1) Excluding sea transport.

Source: Eurostat, ECMT, UIC

The European rail network encompassed 157 thousand kilometres (47% electrified) in 1996, with almost 33 thousand kilometres of the network high-speed. There were approximately just over 900 thousand people working in this service area, down from 1.3 million in 1990. Employment in European railways has declined continuously since the beginning of the 1980s, by an average of 2.9% per annum. Overall, the number of persons employed has been reduced by 45% between 1980 and 1996.

Rail transport remains an important mode of transport, accounting for 9% of goods transport and just less than 6% of passenger transport in 1997. It has however lost some ground relative to other transport modes. Rail passenger traffic progressed only moderately over the last couple of decades, reaching 282 billion passenger-kilometres in the EU in 1997 (3% above its level of 1990 and 12% above that of 1980). For rail freight, there has been a downward trend in the volume of goods transported, falling to 235 billion tonne-kilometres in 1997 (from 256 billion tonne-kilometres in 1990 and 287 billion tonne-kilometres in 1980). Rail freight transport declined by 1.1% on average during the 1980's, a trend that continued during the period 1990-1997, despite growth of 8% in 1997.

(billion passenger-kilometres) Table 18.10

Passengers transported by rail (1)

	1970	1980	1990	1997
B	7.6	7.0	6.5	7.0
DK	3.6	4.5	5.1	5.0
D	56.9	63.0	62.1	63.9
EL	1.5	1.5	2.0	1.8
E	15.0	14.8	16.7	16.8
F	41.0	54.7	63.8	61.7
IRL	0.8	1.0	1.2	1.3
I	34.9	42.9	48.3	52.0
L	0.2	0.2	0.2	0.3
NL	8.0	8.9	11.1	14.4
A	6.4	7.6	8.7	9.9
P	3.5	6.1	5.7	4.6
FIN	2.2	3.2	3.3	3.4
S	4.6	7.0	6.0	6.5
UK	30.4	30.3	33.2	34.0
EU-15	216.4	252.7	273.8	282.5

(1) Including non-UIC railways.

Source: ECMT, UIC

(billion tonne-kilometres) Table 18.11

Goods transported by rail (1)

	1970	1980	1990	1997
B	7.9	8.0	8.4	7.5
DK	1.9	1.6	1.7	1.8
D	113.0	121.3	101.7	73.3
EL	0.7	0.8	0.6	0.3
E	9.7	11.3	11.6	11.2
F	67.6	66.4	50.7	53.9
IRL	0.5	0.6	0.6	0.5
I	18.1	18.4	19.5	23.1
L	0.8	0.7	0.6	0.6
NL	3.7	3.4	3.1	3.4
A	10.0	11.2	12.8	15.0
P	0.8	1.0	1.5	2.2
FIN	6.3	8.3	8.4	9.9
S	17.3	16.6	19.1	18.9
UK	24.5	17.6	16.0	13.6
EU-15	282.8	287.3	256.2	235.1

(1) Including non-UIC railways.

Source: ECMT, UIC

(metres per square kilometre) Figure 18.18

Density of railway tracks, 1996

40
30
20
10
0
EU-15
USA
Japan

Electrified
Not electrified

Source: UIC

(thousand ECU) Figure 18.19

Railways (NACE Rev. 1 60.1)

Personnel costs/employee, 1996

Source: Eurostat (SBS)

Comparison of EU railways to those of the USA and Japan reveals significant differences in orientation. The US railway system is heavily dominated by freight traffic that is moved over a large geographical area with longer distances between population centres. In contrast, passenger usage of the US railway network was comparatively low compared with the EU. Japan, by contrast, was dominated by passenger traffic, due to the heavy population concentrations in many parts of the country and extreme road traffic congestion. The length of railway line available in the EU was much greater than in Japan (20 thousand kilometres) and far less than in the USA (243 thousand kilometres). On average however, the density of railway tracks was comparable in the EU and Japan, with around 50 metres of track per square kilometre, about double the density found in the USA. The EU and Japan had higher proportions of electric track, with 47% and 59% of track electrified respectively, against practically none in the USA.

In recent years a project has been launched within Europe aiming to create Trans-European Networks (TENs) of communication, constituting the cornerstone of European policy in terms of transport infrastructure. In terms of passenger transport, the focus is on extending the high-speed network, to both increase market share of the passenger transport market and also expand the size of the market. This network also seeks to optimise the co-ordination of rail services with other means of transport. The intention is to integrate the rail network with other transport systems: metros, trams, airports, as well as private means of transport. For freight, co-ordination is also being pursued, to create flexibility and ease of transfer of rail freight to and from other means of transport. Development of new lines, for example, the Channel Tunnel, gives distinct advantages to rail freight.

An important goal in the development of a trans-European rail network is the interoperability of trains within the Member States, particularly high-speed passenger trains. Legislation is aimed at achieving this goal through requiring technological progress and developments to occur in Member States.
In order to increase competition and profitability some Member States are in the process of privatising their railways. In the United Kingdom, British Rail has been broken up into a host of private companies, including Railtrack (the owner of the tracks and stations), Railfreight Distribution (handling inter-modal and international traffic), three freight operators, 25 franchisee supplying passenger services, three rolling stock companies, as well as a number of rolling stock maintenance companies. The system is capped by two regulatory bodies, a competition watchdog and an organisation in charge of awarding the franchises.
In the Netherlands, the plan is to privatise Dutch Railways in 2000. Dutch railways expect passenger traffic to double by the year 2010 and have been investing in equipment and infrastructure improvements to meet the current growth in demand and future requirements. Privatisation of the German railway system started in 1994 with the transformation of Deutsche Bahn, a department of the German administration, into Deutsche Bahn AG a private-sector holding company.

Water transport (NACE Rev. 1 61 and 63.22)

This section covers all water transport activities included in NACE Rev. 1 Division 61, sea and coastal transport (NACE Rev. 1 61.1), as well as inland water transport (NACE Rev. 1 61.2) and other supporting water transport activities (NACE Rev. 1 63.22).

Figure 18.20 (%)

Inland water transport (NACE Rev. 1 61.2)
Share of micro-enterprises in the total number of enterprises, 1995 (1)

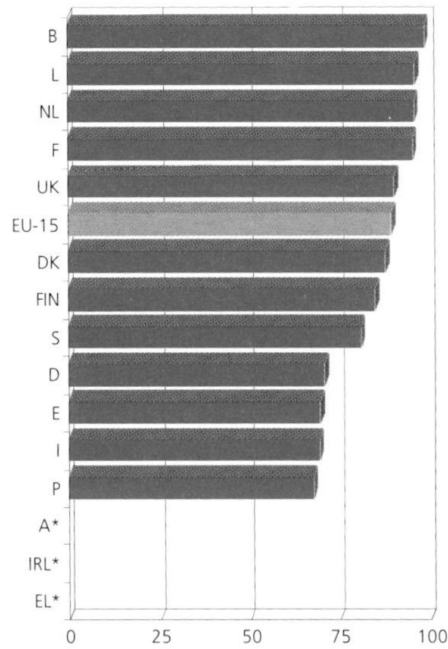

(1) Enterprises with 0-9 employees.

Source: Eurostat (SME)

Figure 18.21 (%)

Share of goods transported by inland waterways in tonne-kilometres, 1997

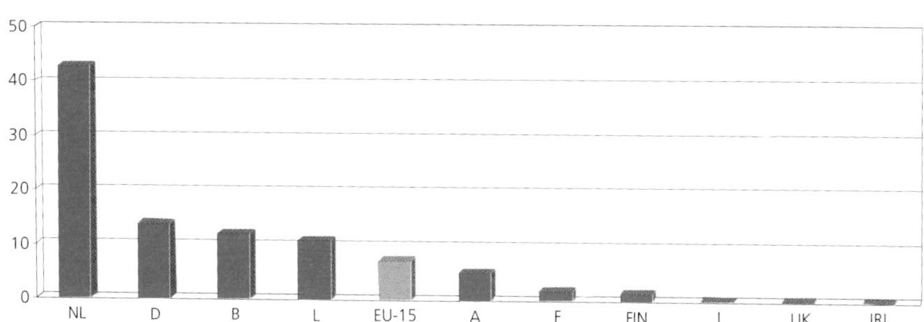

Source: Eurostat, ECMT, UIC

Figure 18.22 (%)

Water transport (NACE Rev. 1 61)
Share of temporary work contracts in total number of persons employed, 1997

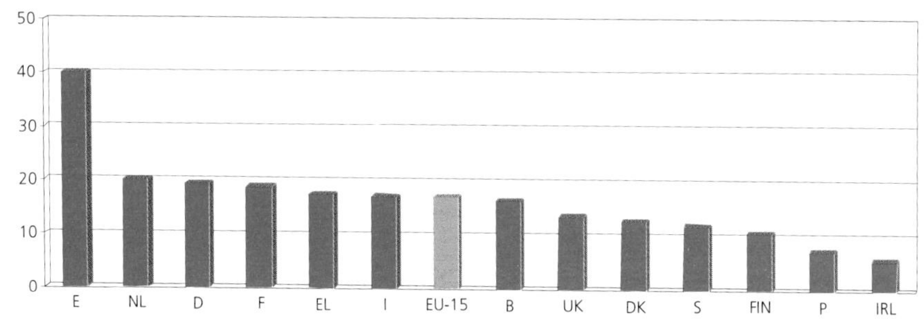

Source: Eurostat (LFS)

There were 30 thousand kilometres of inland waterways in the EU in 1995, a level that has remained stable during recent decades. The highest density was unsurprisingly found in the Netherlands with no less than 120 metres per square kilometre, followed by Belgium with 50 metres per square kilometre, whilst the EU average lay at 9 metres per square kilometre. Four major axis could be identified when looking at the European inland waterways' network. The Basle-Rotterdam axis with the Rhine as its backbone is the most important in the EU. Another waterway is the Main-Danube axis, extending from Bamberg on the Main to Kelheim on the Danube, and connected to the first by the Rhine-Main-Danube canal. The third major axis is known as the East-West, formed by the rivers Elbe, Weser and Ems. Together with other canals such as the Mittelland canal, this axis unites some Northern regions of Germany with the East. The fourth major axis is called the North-South and serves regions of Belgium, the Netherlands and France not connected to the Rhine. The main rivers of this axis are the Meuse, Scheldt, Lys and Sambre.

Inland shipping specialises in the transport of large quantities of bulk products, such as sand, ores, coal, chemicals, and oil. The largest volumes of goods transported are cement and building materials (25%), petroleum (19%) and iron ore, steel and other metal products (18%). Total goods transported were equal to 118 billion tonne-kilometres in 1997, half the level of rail and a tenth of road transport, equivalent to a market share of 7% of all goods transported. The country displaying the highest specialisation in inland water transport was the Netherlands, where over two-fifths of goods were transported (some 41 billion tonne-kilometres in 1997). Over the years, growth in inland shipping has been fairly limited compared to other means of transportation, equal to 0.1% per annum during the 1980's, accelerating to 1.3% per annum between 1990 and 1997. The busiest inland EU port in 1997 was Duisburg (D) with almost 50 million tonnes of freight loaded and unloaded, followed by Liège (B) and Paris (F) with 17 million tonnes each.

Professional associations representing the industries within this chapter

AEA
Association of European Airlines
350, avenue Louise, boîte 4
B-1050 Bruxelles
tel: (32) 2 627 06 00
fax: (32) 2 648 40 17
e-mail: information@cer.be

CER
Community of European Railways
13, boulevard de l'Impératrice, boîte 11
B-1000 Bruxelles
tel: (32) 2 525 30 50
fax: (32) 2 512 52 31
e-mail: information@cer.be

IACA/ACE
Association des Compagnies Aériennes de la CE
Minervastraat 4
Keiberg 2
B-1930 Zaventem
tel: (32) 2 720 53 03
fax: (32) 2 720 51 37

IATA
International Air Transport Association
Sceptre House, 3rd floor
75-81 Staines Road
Hounslow
Middlesex TW3 3HW
tel: (44) 208 607 6200

MERC
Maritime Economic Research Centre
Postbus 1555
NL-3000 BN Rotterdam
tel: (31) 10 453 88 50
fax: (31) 10 452 36 80

UIC
International Union of Railways
16, rue Jean Rey
F-75015 Paris
tel: (33) 1 44 49 20 20
fax: (33) 1 44 29 20 29
e-mail: info@uic.asso.fr

(thousand ECU) Figure 18.23

Water transport (NACE Rev. 1 61)

Personnel costs/employee, 1996

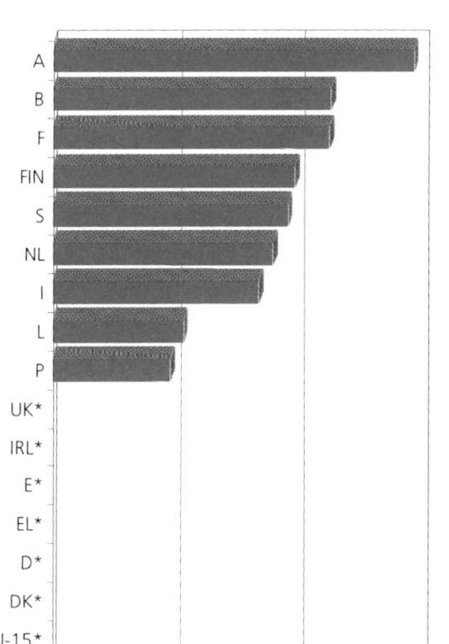

Source: Eurostat (SBS)

(million tonnes) Table 18.12

Top twenty inland ports in the EU ranked by traffic (1)

		Country	1995	1996	1997
1	**Duisburg**	D	48.4	44.4	49.3
2	**Liège**	B	14.9	15.8	17.5
3	**Paris**	F	20.3	18.5	17.0
4	**Strasbourg**	F	9.7	9.3	9.3
5	**NV Zeekanaal, Brabant**	B	8.5	8.6	8.7
6	**Karlsruhe**	D	10.3	10.3	8.4
7	**Ludwigshafen**	D	8.2	7.7	8.0
8	**Köln**	D	6.8	7.6	7.9
9	**Mannheim**	D	7.7	7.9	7.8
10	**Dortmund**	D	5.4	4.8	5.4
11	**Heilbronn**	D	4.9	5.2	4.9
12	**Bruxelles/Brussel**	B	5.1	4.8	4.9
13	**Ports Rhénans Alsace**	F	0.4	4.5	4.8
14	**Neuss**	D	4.9	4.7	4.3
15	**Frankfurt am Main**	D	3.6	3.8	3.7
16	**Saarlouis/Dillingen**	D	2.5	3.6	3.3
17	**Düsseldorf**	D	3.0	3.0	3.2
18	**Krefeld**	D	3.4	3.3	3.1
19	**Kehl**	D	3.1	2.9	2.9
20	**Magdeburg**	D	2.5	2.2	2.8

(1) Fluvial and fluvio-maritime traffic.

Source: EFIP

(%) Figure 18.24

Water transport (NACE Rev. 1 61)

Wage adjusted labour productivity, 1996

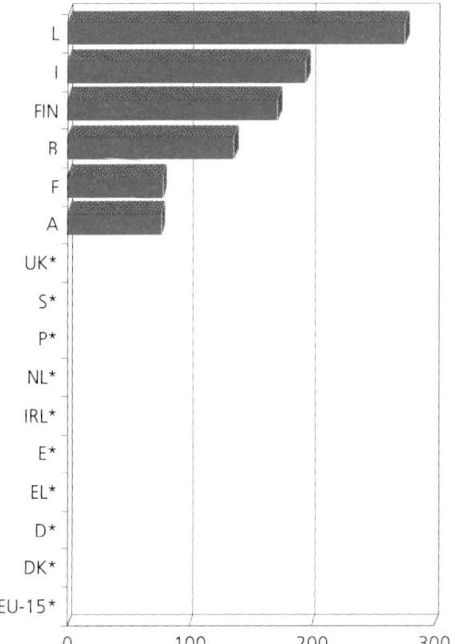

Source: Eurostat (SBS)

Table 18.13

EU merchant fleet, as of 1st January 1998 (1)

Flag	Number of ships	Gross tonnage (thousand GT)
B	16	61
DK	511	5,360
D	699	6,293
EL	1,362	25,199
E	141	390
F	132	1,768
IRL	53	194
I	744	5,823
L	32	757
NL	505	3,267
A	26	87
P	50	158
FIN	165	1,469
S	359	2,675
UK	369	2,822
EU-15	5,164	56,321
IS	15	31
NO	1,461	22,004
EEA	6,640	78,356
World	44,715	494,324

(1) Ships of 100 GT and above.

Source: Lloyd's Register of Shipping

Turning to sea transport, the EU merchant fleet numbered 5,164 vessels of one hundred gross tonnes or more at the beginning of 1998. This was equivalent to 56.3 million gross tonnes (GT), or about 11% of total world tonnage. The European Economic Area (EEA) registered a fleet of 6,640 ships or 78.3 million GT, representing almost 16% of world tonnage, a share that has been in constant decline in recent years. EEA ships could be broken down by type: with 19% dry bulk, 42% liquid bulk and 35% other dry cargo (of which 14% were container vessels alone). Passenger and cruise vessels accounted for only 2% of the gross tonnage. It should be noted that these figures refer only to ships registered in EEA countries. According to Lloyd's figures, no less than 60% of the total fleet controlled by owners from EEA countries fly a third country flag. It is estimated that the real tonnage of EEA-controlled ships reached 190 million GT in 1998, well over a third of the world fleet.

The European Community Shipowners' Association (ECSA) estimate that about 154 thousand seafarers were working on-board EU flagged vessels in 1997, down from 169 thousand in 1992. Whilst the majority of seafarers were EU nationals, there has recently been a trend towards a greater proportion of non-nationals, whose share reached 22% in 1997 (up from 15% in 1992).

As far as shipping is concerned, a distinction can be made between deep-sea transport, that refers to shipping on long sea routes, and short-sea shipping, that covers transport services of passengers and goods between national or European ports. Short-sea shipping was in 1997 the second most important freight transport mode in the EU. Intra-EU traffic reached 1,124 billion tonne-kilometres, a level only slightly below that of road transport. Indeed, both these means of transport experienced long-term growth trends following parallel developments. Growth recorded in the 1990's for short-sea transport was at higher levels than on the road, with an average progression of 2.9% per annum against 2.8% for road freight.

Looking at world trade, sea borne freight transport grew by 3.6% in 1997 to 21.4 thousand billion tonne-miles, with crude oil alone accounting for over a third of the total. Growth expressed in tonnes was greater at 4.4%. The highest growth rates were recorded in the shipment of dry bulk commodities that grew by 6.2% in tonnes and 4.9% in tonne-miles (mainly driven by an increase in iron ore transported). Other cargo goods saw their volume rise by 4.6% in 1997, a rate close to the annual average for the decade (4.5%).

The busiest sea-port in the EU in 1997 was Rotterdam (NL) with traffic of more than 300 million tonnes, practically three times more than the next largest port, Antwerp (B). Rotterdam was also the largest port in terms of container transport, with 5.5 million TEUs[4] in 1997, ahead of Hamburg (3.3 million) and Antwerp (3 million). One of the main trends in the port industry is to switch to containers, away from conventional general cargo transportation. This is clearly reflected in the growth rates recorded in the largest ports. General cargo traffic in the top five sea-ports grew at an average rate of 1.4% per annum between 1990 and 1997, whilst container traffic grew by more than 6% per annum.

4) TEU: Twenty Foot Equivalent Unit: a measurement of carrying capacity on a containership, referring to a common container size of 20ft in length.

Table 18.14 (million tonnes)

Top twenty sea ports in the EU ranked by traffic

		Country	1970	1980	1990	1997
1	**Rotterdam**	NL	226	276	288	303
2	**Antwerpen**	B	78	82	102	112
3	**Marseille**	F	74	103	90	94
4	**Hamburg**	D	47	63	61	77
5	**Le Havre**	F	58	77	54	60
6	**Amsterdam**	NL	21	34	47	57
7	**London**	UK	64	48	58	56
8	**Teese & Hartlepool**	UK	23	38	40	51
9	**Trieste**	I	27	38	34	46
10	**Genova**	I	53	51	44	43
11	**Forth ports**	UK	:	29	25	43
12	**Algeciras**	E	8	22	25	40
13	**Dunkerque**	F	25	41	37	37
14	**Wilhelmshaven**	D	22	32	16	36
15	**Milford Haven**	UK	41	39	32	35
16	**Bremen/Bremerhaven**	D	23	25	28	34
17	**Southampton**	UK	28	25	29	33
18	**Zeebrugge**	B	8	12	30	32
19	**Tarragona**	E	4	20	24	31
20	**Liverpool**	UK	31	13	23	31

Source: ISL

Table 18.15 (thousand TEU)

Top twenty ports in the EU ranked by container traffic

		Country	1990	1995	1996	1997
1	**Rotterdam**	NL	3,667	4,787	4,971	5,445
2	**Hamburg**	D	1,969	2,890	3,054	3,338
3	**Antwerpen**	B	1,549	2,329	2,654	2,969
4	**Felixstowe**	UK	1,436	1,924	2,065	2,237
5	**Bremen/Bremerhaven**	D	1,198	1,524	1,543	1,703
6	**Algeciras**	E	553	1,155	1,307	1,538
7	**Gioia Tauro**	I	:	16	572	1,448
8	**Le Havre**	F	858	970	1,020	1,185
9	**Genova**	I	310	615	826	1,180
10	**Barcelona**	E	448	689	765	950
11	**Valencia**	E	387	672	710	832
12	**La Spezia**	I	450	965	970	616
13	**Southampton**	UK	345	681	805	:
14	**Piraeus**	EL	426	600	575	:
15	**Zeebrugge**	B	342	528	553	:
16	**Marseille**	F	482	498	544	:
17	**Göteborg**	S	352	458	489	:
18	**Liverpool**	UK	239	406	420	:
19	**Livorno**	I	416	424	417	:
20	**Tilbury**	UK	363	338	395	:

Source: Containerisation International Yearbook, Port of Rotterdam

Professional associations representing the industries within this chapter

ACI EUROPE
Airports Council International/European Region
6, square de Meeûs
B-1000 Bruxelles
tel: (32) 2 552 09 82
fax: (32) 2 513 26 06
e-mail: info@aci-europe.org

CESA (AWES)
Committee of European Shipbuilders Association
Juan Hurtado de Mondoza 13
E-28036 Madrid
tel: (34) 91 34 52 165
fax: (34) 91 35 99 336
e-mail: info@cesa-shipbuilding.org

ECMT
European Conference of Ministers of Transport
2, rue André Pascal
F-75775 Paris Cedex 16
tel: (33) 1 45 24 97 10
fax: (33) 1 45 24 97 42
e-mail: ecmt.contact@oecd.org

IRF
International Road Federation
4 chemin de Blandonnet
CH-1214 Vernier
tel: (41) 22 306 02 60
fax: (41) 22 306 02 70
e-mail: info@irfnet.org

ISL
Institute of Shipping Economics and Logistics
Universitätallee GW 1, Block A
D-28359 Bremen
tel: (49) 421 220 96 0
fax: (49) 421 220 96 77
e-mail: info@isl.uni-bremen.de

UITP
International Union of Public Transport
17, avenue Hermann Debroux
B-1160 Bruxelles
tel: (32) 2 673 61 00
fax: (32) 2 660 10 72
e-mail: administration@uitp.com

Financial services

Industry description and main indicators

Financial services encompass financial intermediation as offered by credit institutions, investment firms, leasing enterprises (NACE Rev. 1 65), but also insurance and pension funding services (NACE Rev. 1 66), as well as activities providing services auxiliary to financial intermediation (NACE Rev. 1 67), such as the administration of financial markets, security broking or fund management.

For more detailed information on banking and insurance, refer to Eurostat's "Banking in Europe" (CA-24-99-203-EN-C) and "Insurance in Europe" (CA-24-99-477-EN-C).

Efficient financial services are a prerequisite to aid economic flows. They are the indispensable medium between lenders and borrowers, savers and investors, whilst offering tools for an optimal management of risk. Their main functions can be identified as follows: offering payment and saving products, fiduciary services, corporate and private lending services, underwriting and issuance of equity and debt, as well as insurance and risk management products.

(units) Figure 19.1

Financial intermediation (NACE Rev. 1 65 to 67)
Density of enterprises per ten thousand inhabitants, 1995

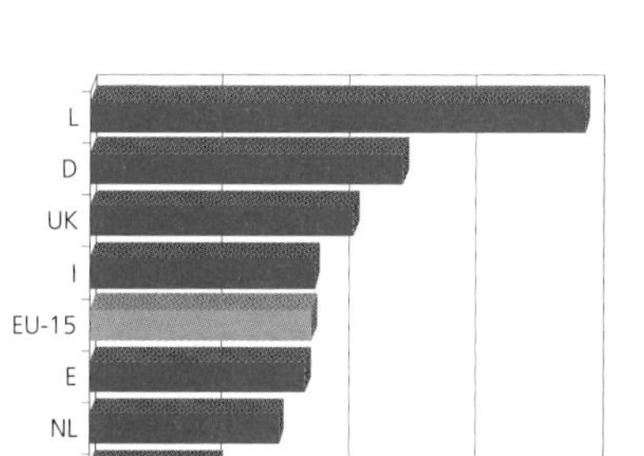
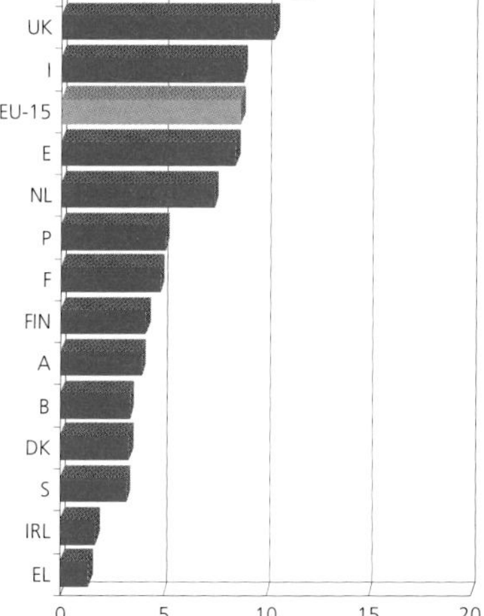

Source: Eurostat (SME)

The activities covered in this chapter include:

- 65.1: monetary intermediation;
- 65.2: other financial intermediation;
- 66: insurance and pension funding, except compulsory social security;
- 67: activities auxiliary to financial intermediation.

Figure 19.2 (%)

Financial intermediation (NACE Rev. 1 65 to 67)

Share of part-time and temporary work contracts in total number of persons employed, 1997

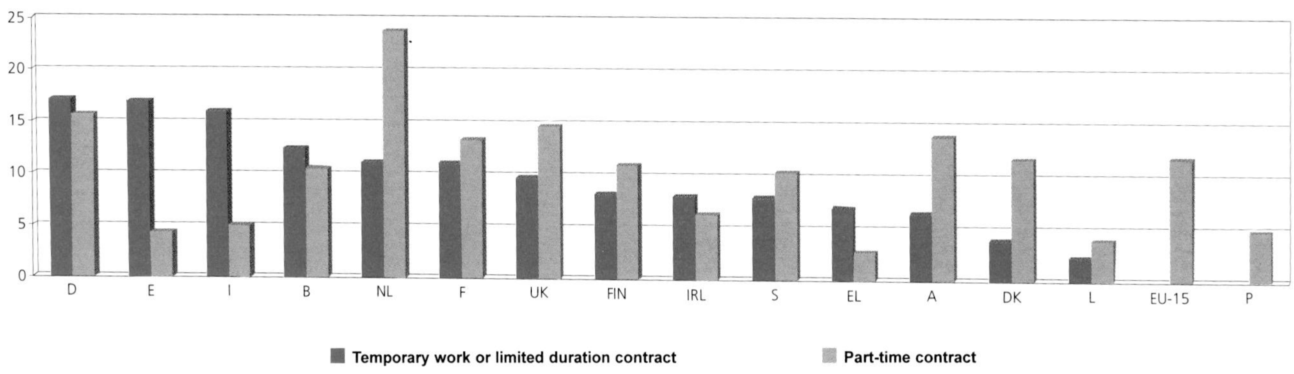

Source: Eurostat (LFS)

National Accounts allow for a broad estimation of the importance of financial services in the economy of the Member States. The branch credit and insurance institutions accounts for just over 5% of total value added generated in the EU. This share varies between 4% and 6% in the majority of Member States, although some peculiarities can be highlighted. Luxembourg was the European economy where financial services had the highest weight in the domestic economy, with a share of more than 18% in 1997. Next came Austria, with a share of 8%, followed by Ireland (6.4%) and Spain (5.8%). At the other end of the scale were the Nordic Member States (Denmark, Sweden and Finland) that displayed relatively low shares, below 4%.

Turning to employment, National Accounts recorded more than four million persons working in the financial services' branch of the EU in 1996, about 3% of total employment. Differences amongst Member States were not large, except for Luxembourg where the share reached a level two times higher than in any other Member State (9% in 1997). Only two countries displayed a share lower than 2%, Italy and Portugal (lowest with 1.8%).

The latest Eurostat Labour Force Survey provides some information on the structure of employment in financial services. In 1997, women were well represented within this activity, with a share of about 47% of the labour force. Part-time work accounted for 12% of the jobs within financial intermediation and insurance and 13% within financial auxiliary activities. This was relatively low compared to other service activities, and beneath the level recorded for the whole EU economy (17%). The survey also highlighted the high variability of part-time work across the Member States. In the Netherlands, around one quarter of the labour force was employed part-time in financial services, whilst in Sweden the rate was equal to one fifth. This contrasts with Spain, Portugal and Greece, where the share of part-time work was lower than 5%.

Figure 19.3 (ECU/month)

Financial intermediation (NACE Rev. 1 65 and 66)

Labour costs by Member State, 1996

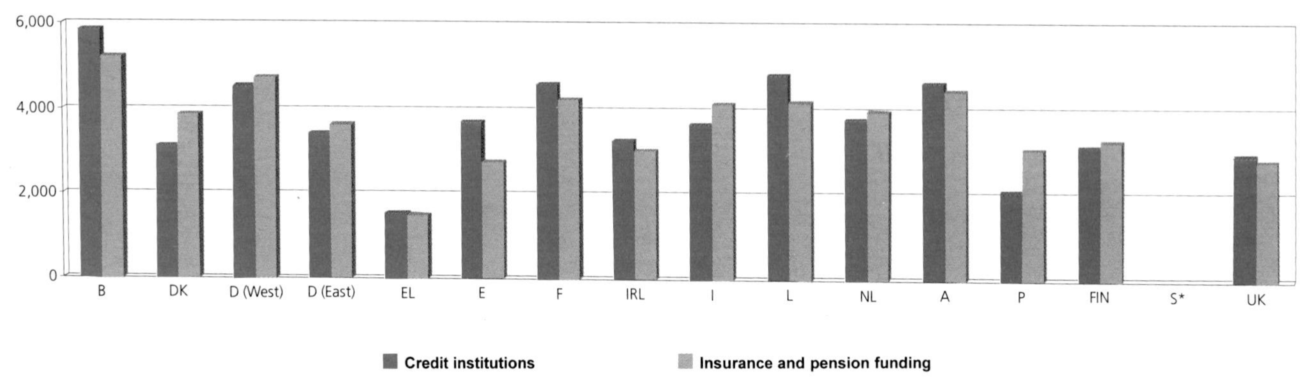

Source: Eurostat (LCS)

The level of education of people working in financial services ranks amongst the highest of all economic activities. At 26%, the rate of persons with a higher education degree was above that for the whole European economy (19%). Belgium and Ireland boasted the highest ratios: in these two countries 52% and 44% of all persons employed in financial services held a higher education degree. The lowest ratios were found in Italy (16%) and Austria (9%).

European financial services had to face rapid changes in their business environment during the past decade, creating new challenges and opportunities. Deregulation and the abolition of protectionist market structures were worldwide trends in the 1980s and 1990s, causing major structural changes in Europe, the USA and Japan. After the abolition of exchange controls came the progressive removal of legal and administrative barriers, allowing acquisitions, mergers and other alliances to take place both within domestic markets and across borders.

At the same time, technological advances have had a significant impact on the way financial services are provided. Telephone or computer-based banking is becoming increasingly popular, as is the direct sale of insurance contracts or on-line stock exchange trading. Bank cards now regroup several functions that required separate cards in the past, such as Europe-wide access to ATMs, credit cards, telephone cards or electronic purses.

Probably the most significant source of change within the EU has been the creation of the Single Market in financial services, that culminated in January 1999 with the introduction of the euro as the common currency for eleven of the Member States. This created de facto a true pan-European financial market, able to compete with the US dollar on world financial markets. Indeed, some commentators already argue that a "two-currency world" is emerging.

International comparison

Financial services are becoming increasingly globalised. Products are becoming more homogeneous across borders, competitive pressure is increasing as markets are opened and liberalised. A substantial expansion of international activities in financial services has been made possible by deregulation and the revolution in communication technology. The resulting integration has broadened the choice of market participants: issuers have increased access to foreign markets to raise capital, whilst investors have tended to internationalise their portfolios. In this new context, European companies are well positioned to face international competition.

Japanese banks dominate the top of the world rankings. At the end of 1997, six of the 10 largest banks in the world ranked by assets were Japanese, three were from the EU and one was Swiss. But a broader view of the ranking shows that EU banks have significant weight on the international financial scene. The total assets of the top 40 banks exceeded 12 thousand billion ECU at the end of 1997. Looking at the breakdown between the Triad members, half of the total assets were accounted for by 22 EU banks, 30% by 10 Japanese banks and 12% by 6 North American banks. Germany was the main European player with aggregate assets of 2.3 thousand billion ECU, followed by France and the United Kingdom with 1.7 thousand billion ECU each.

Concerning the insurance market, 23 EU companies accounted for 60% of the total value of premiums written in 1997 by the 40 largest companies in the world (excluding Japan). This was double the share of the 13 top USA companies. The United Kingdom was the largest contributor within the EU, with 7 companies accounting for 90 thousand billion ECU followed by Germany (5 companies and 84 thousand billion ECU of premiums) and France (4 companies and 82 thousand billion ECU of premiums).

Credit institutions (NACE Rev. 1 65)

Banking fulfils various functions: accepting deposits and converting them into loans and credits for enterprises, public authorities and consumers; managing payment systems and clearing mechanisms; providing services with capital transactions; performing various other services like the provision of guarantees and insurance. These functions are not performed by banks alone. Consumer and industrial credit can be provided by finance companies (many of which have links with banks) and mortgage loans by life insurance companies or pension funds. The special nature of banking is being eroded by the trend towards deregulation. Class 65.12 of the NACE Rev. 1 classification covers all monetary intermediation of institutions other than central banks, including postal bank activities.

Credit institutions can be classified along the following lines:

- universal banks: multi-purpose banks that offer the whole range of financial services. Most of them are commercial banks, but in certain countries savings banks, co-operative and public banks are also universal banks;
- specialised banks: amongst them we may include merchant banks, investment banks, mortgage banks, industrial banks, etc.;
- savings banks: that also play an important role in this area through the use of specific structures: central financial institutions at regional and national level, mortgage subsidiaries etc.

Figure 19.4 (units)

Credit institutions (NACE Rev. 1 65)

Density of enterprises per ten thousand inhabitants, 1995

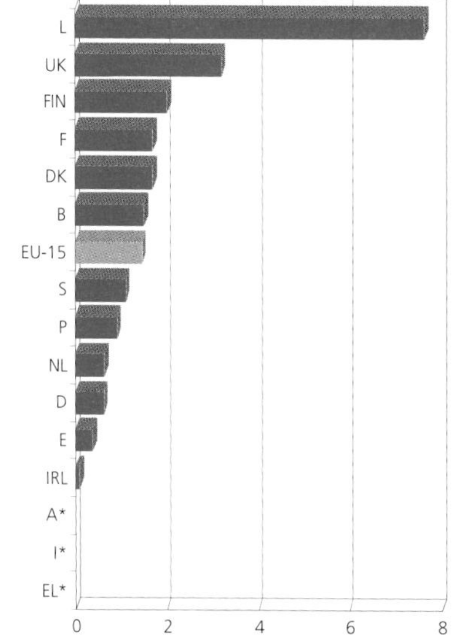

Source: Eurostat (SME)

Due to ongoing market liberalisation, the market structure of credit institutions has changed noticeably. The number of enterprises has declined in most countries in recent years, which can be explained by a wave of mergers in the banking industry resulting in fewer larger credit institutions (see the ranking of the top 20 provided). There were 7,933 credit institutions in the EU in 1997, down from 8,446 in 1994, an annual decline of almost 1.8%. Such consolidation did not affect only small local and regional enterprises, but involved cross-border mergers between major players within the European Union. Of the 98 mergers and acquisitions recorded in 1998 on the European banking scene, 60 concerned transnational operations, worth a total of 31.6 billion ECU[1]. Intra-European operations accounted for more than half of this amount at 19 billion ECU. The most important deals were Fortis' (B/NL) acquisition of Générale de Banque (B) worth 11.8 billion ECU and ING (NL) taking a 40% stake in BHF (D) for 1.4 billion ECU after taking control of BBL (B) in 1997.

1) Source: "Eclairages", monthly bulletin of the Crédit Agricole (F), 1/99. Covers operations of more than approximately 75 million ECU involving banks of the EEA and Switzerland.

Figure 19.5 (%)

Credit institutions (NACE Rev. 1 65)

Share of part-time and temporary work contracts in total number of persons employed, 1997

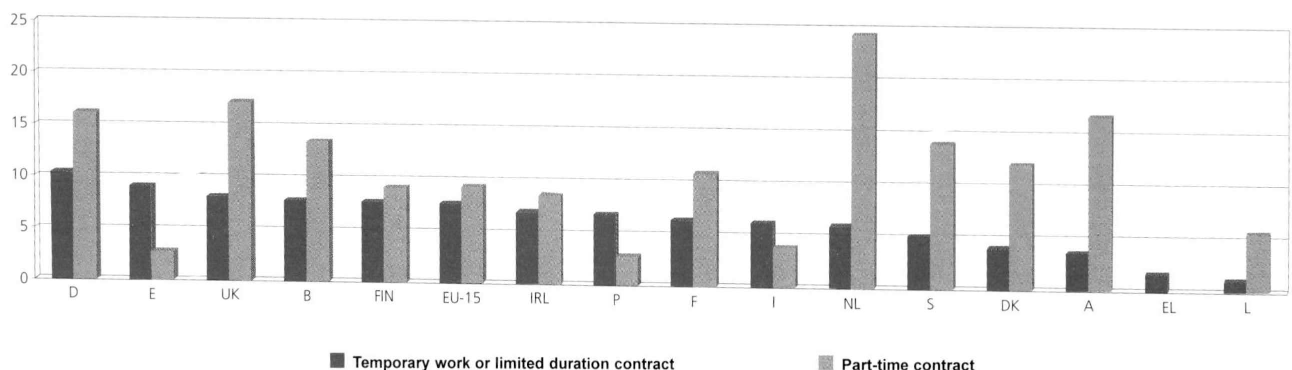

Source: Eurostat (LFS)

Figure 19.6

Mergers and acquisitions involving European banks

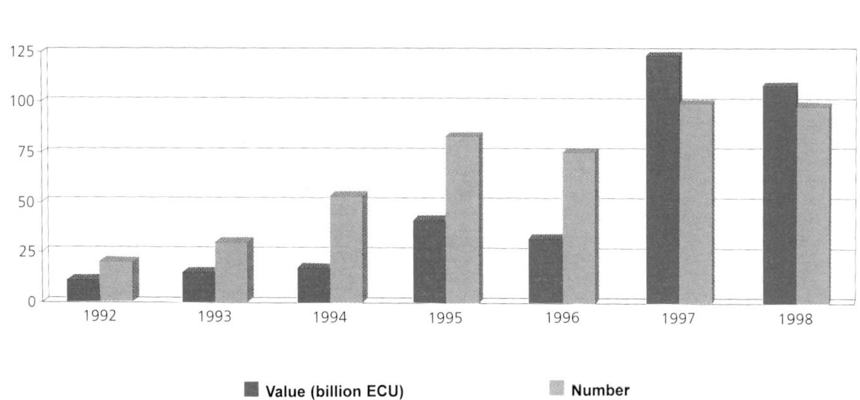

Source: "Eclairages" Crédit Agricole

(1994=100)

Figure 19.7

Evolution of main indicators for EU banks

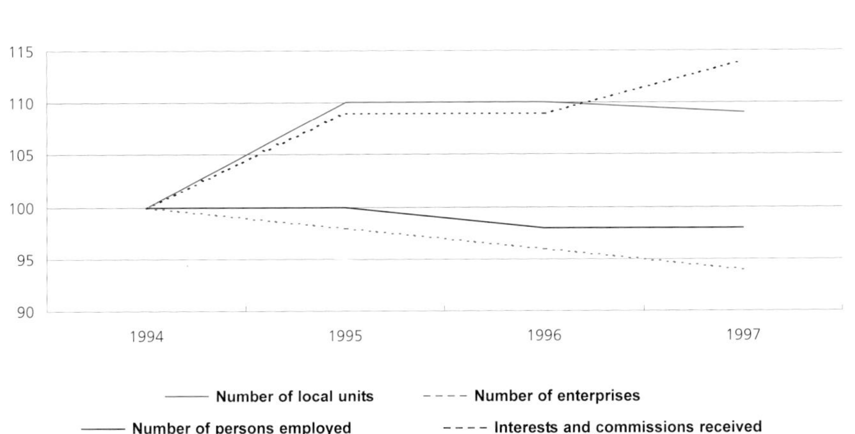

Source: Eurostat

On the other hand, the number of local units[2] has not been severely affected by the trend towards larger credit institutions. Neither the development of banking technology (for example the development of phone or on-line banking), nor the increasing number of mergers and acquisitions in the industry have yet replaced traditional local units as distribution outlets. Indeed, the number of local units in the EU has risen from 187 thousand in 1994 to 204 thousand in 1997. The average number of business units (sum of enterprises and local units) per 10 thousand population indicates the density and physical distribution of banking outlets on the national territory and can be regarded as a rough measure of the proximity of credit institutions to their clients. Apart from Luxembourg where there are around 20 business units per 10 thousand population, the highest number of business units are observed in those countries where small regional banks, postal banks and co-operatives still play an important role, for example, Spain (9.7), Germany (8.6) and Austria (8.1).

More than 2.6 million persons were employed in credit institutions in the EU in 1997, a modest decline of 2% compared to the level of 1994. The sector accounted for 1.8% of the total employment, a share that varied across the Member States from 1.1% in Sweden to 11.3% in Luxembourg.

2) Local units are normally defined as a part of credit institutions located separately and employing at least one person, including branch offices and other comparable outlets, but excluding automated teller machines (ATMs).

Table 19.1

Co-operative banks: main indicators as of 31.12.97

	Regional/local banks (units)	Outlets (units)	Staff (units)	Total assets (million ECU)
EU-15	5,295	53,421	496,095	1,754,847
B	219	1,147	5,559	44,673
DK	40	88	417	846
D	2,417	19,418	171,783	491,956
IRL	:	584	2,307	6,978
E	95	3,493	12,747	27,695
F	140	13,844	137,713	584,960
EL	25	36	194	293
I	676	7,799	77,659	272,483
L	35	93	317	2,074
NL	473	2,477	44,667	189,859
A	757	3,043	26,961	92,807
P	158	510	3,300	5,362
FIN	250	745	8,695	22,658
S	10	:	:	3,418
UK	:	144	3,776	8,785

Source: GEBC (European Association of Co-operative Banks)

Table 19.2

Commercial banks: main indicators as of 31.12.96

	Banks	Outlets (1)	Staff (2)	Total assets (million ECU)
EU-15	2,704	96,566	1,713,783	9,532,100
B	141	7,552	76,266	676,800
DK	201	2,203	43,629	156,700
D	326	7,487	213,350	1,023,300
EL	50	2,443	54,761	105,000
E	162	17,657	141,640	517,100
F	406	10,386	220,000	1,298,300
IRL	57	967	23,700	108,300
I	346	21,876	324,772	1,304,200
L	221	352	18,540	481,600
NL	173	6,569	107,484	787,600
A	58	739	15,885	120,900
P	51	3,818	58,115	169,200
FIN	12	620	18,649	76,900
S	33	2,197	39,992	208,900
UK	467	11,700	357,000	2,497,300

(1) Figures exclude foreign bank branches (this does not apply to Belgium, France, Spain and Portugal).
(2) Full-time employees or equivalent, except in the case of Belgium and France (number of employees only).

Source: FBE (Banking Federation of the European Union)

Interests and commissions received can be regarded as a proxy for the business volume of credit institutions. Interests received normally include income from interest-bearing assets such as loans, debt securities, treasury bills, etc. Commissions received include charges for services rendered in loan administration, securities transactions, brokerage services, etc. On aggregate, interests and commissions grew by an average of 4.4% per annum between 1994 and 1997 to reach 998 billion ECU. Most countries experienced an increase in income, with the exception of Spain, Austria and Finland. Particularly positive results were observed in France (partly explained by the fact that derivatives used for hedging purposes were included in the figures) and the United Kingdom.

Property and mortgage markets have experienced strong growth in recent years, fuelled by the sharp decline of interest rates. According to the European Mortgage Federation, outstanding mortgage loans recorded double-digit growth in 1997 in seven Member States, both on commercial and residential property. In Greece and Portugal, growth exceeded 20%. Sweden was the only country that witnessed a decline in mortgage loans, down 2 billion ECU from 117 billion ECU in 1996 (although these figures only cover specialised mortgage institutions). The largest share of mortgage loans was accounted for by residential property, where total EU (excluding Austria and Sweden) loans exceeded 2,400 billion ECU in 1997, a level 9% higher than the year before.

Table 19.3

Savings banks: main indicators as of 31.12.97

	Banks (units)	Outlets (units)	Staff (units)	Total assets (million ECU)
EU-15	1,079	48,194	654,605	2,226,725
B	2	2,123	9,954	68,156
DK	111	375	4,276	9,973
D	598	18,318	288,404	850,338
EL	1	128	1,312	9,716
E	51	16,653	90,997	277,473
F	34	42	39,400	194,497
IRL	1	78	1,100	2,077
I	73	6,047	75,014	271,522
L	1	97	1,786	24,917
NL	:	303	3,007	15,481
A	71	1,466	24,634	132,884
P	5	892	14,602	42,874
FIN	40	245	1,731	4,458
S	90	1,398	15,808	86,265
UK	1	29	82,580	236,094

Source: ESBG (European Savings Bank Group)

Table 19.4

Outstanding loans against mortgage, 1997

	Residential and commercial property (million ECU)	Growth 1996/1997 (%)	Residential property (million ECU)	Growth 1996/1997 (%)
B	53,748	4.4	47,345	4.0
DK (1)	123,477	10.4	91,120	11.7
D	1,128,817	4.9	942,845	5.3
EL (1)	2,929	20.8	6,174	22.7
E	145,662	16.3	103,716	18.7
F	:	:	250,959	2.0
IRL	20,438	14.4	17,353	21.0
I (2)	110,194	:	71,598	:
L	:	:	3,615	5.1
NL	263,981	10.9	191,252	13.2
A (1)	9,354	1.8	:	:
P	27,946	27.9	23,337	22.3
FIN	:	:	30,889	0.9
S (3)	115,572	1.6	:	:
UK	:	:	617,162	16.7

(1) For residential and commercial property: only members of the association.
(2) 1996.
(3) For residential and commercial property: specialised mortgage credit institutions only.

Source: EMF (European Mortgage Federation)

As far as finance houses were concerned the total amount of outstanding credits granted by members of Eurofinas[3] increased from 168 billion ECU in 1996 to 196 billion ECU in 1997 (+16.7%). Consumer credit was the biggest contributor to new credits granted in the majority of Member States, ahead of car finance and industrial credit. Eurofinas' EU members granted almost 117 billion ECU of consumer credit in 1997, half of this amount was in the United Kingdom. Car finance reached a value of 63 billion ECU and industrial credits 39 billion ECU.

As one can see, credit institutions compete in a broad based financial services' industry, not just in banking. Bankers recognise that the industry's future revenue streams will be quite different from the past. Next to traditional banking there are at least six promising segments for banks to play a role of importance. These segments are: financial intermediation and advisory services, investment management, insurance, fee-based operational services, trading, and merchant banking and equity investment. Finance houses are likely to increase their dealings in related areas such as consumer and industrial credits, and car financing.

3) Data from the European federation of finance houses cover all EU-15 Member States excluding Denmark, Greece, Luxembourg, Austria, but including Switzerland and Norway.

Table 19.5

Finance houses: main indicators, 1997

	Number of enterprises	Number of branches	Number of persons employed	New credit granted: industrial credit (million ECU)	New credit granted: consumer credit (million ECU)	New credit granted: car finance (million ECU)
B	96	6,000	3,200	:	4,789	1,189
D	55	1,058	20,289	31,228	16,069	10,987
E	51	:	:	229	2,411	3,315
F	70	:	15,000	1,805	24,104	10,719
IRL	21	850	1,036	1,815	1,144	213
I	36	360	4,900	:	5,171	7,146
NL	29	:	:	:	2,039	:
P	21	:	1,071	461	1,123	1,050
FIN	6	20	793	677	1,117	134
S	51	500	1,300	960	747	709
UK	692	6,750	30,500	1,828	58,282	27,907

Source: Eurofinas

Table 19.6

Top 20 EU banks, as of 31.12.97

Name	Country	Assets (million ECU)	Profits (million ECU)	Number of employees (units)	World ranking
Deutsche Bank	D	530,465	519	76,100	2
HSBC	UK	413,564	5,361	133,000	7
Crédit Agricole	F	379,972	1,588	84,700	10
ABN-AMRO	NL	378,020	1,864	74,900	11
Société Générale	F	371,897	955	55,500	12
Dresdner Bank	D	344,272	858	46,200	15
Barclays Bank	UK	338,857	1,696	84,300	16
BNP	F	307,448	940	52,400	18
WestLB	D	307,099	369	29,800	19
NatWest	UK	267,733	132	77,000	21
Commerzbank	D	262,920	681	28,700	22
Lloyds TSB	UK	228,313	3,392	82,600	27
Crédit Lyonnais	F	226,437	252	51,000	28
BayernLB	D	215,160	305	7,300	29
Abbey National (1)	UK	218,775	1,384	24,100	31
Bay. Vereinsbank (2)	D	215,160	414	22,000	33
Caisses d'épargne et de prévoyance	F	194,386	311	39,400	34
Rabobank	NL	191,165	897	38,900	36
DG Bank	D	190,001	163	12,000	37
Halifax	UK	189,315	1,576	27,300	38

(1) Estimates.

(2) Before the merger with Bayerische Hypotheken- und Wechselbank, effective 9/98.

Source: Trade press

Insurance (NACE Rev. 1 66)

Insurance and pension funding services are covered by Division 66 of the NACE Rev. 1 classification. The activity can be described as embracing all units "exclusively or primarily engaged in insurance", i.e. converting individual risks into collective risks. Compulsory social security services are excluded. Insurance is thus defined in terms of the economic function of converting and mutualising risks. Distinction is made between life insurance (NACE Rev. 1 66.01), pension funding (NACE Rev. 1 66.02) and non-life insurance (NACE Rev. 1 66.03).

Life insurance embraces conventional life insurance contracts, annuities and unit-linked insurance. Pension funding services are distinguished in a separate class and are generally not taken into account in the statistics found in this chapter. In non-life insurance, the risks covered are those not included in the previous categories, including assets or liability insurance, ranging from health insurance to physical assets property damage, through transportation and credit insurance. The NACE classification does not consider reinsurance as a separate activity as most of the general insurance companies also underwrite reinsurance business called "accepted reinsurance". The activity is assigned to one of the three NACE Rev. 1 Groups, according to the type of risk reinsured.

There were 4.2 thousand insurance enterprises operating in the EU in 1996, 62% of which were non-life insurance enterprises, 22% life insurance enterprises, 6% composite insurance enterprises[4] and 9% specialist reinsurance enterprises. The largest 20 European insurance companies are detailed in table 19.8, ranked according to the value of premiums written.

Figures on employment exclude data for two large Member States, however we can estimate the total number of persons employed at just under one million. It must be stressed that this figure concerns only direct employment and does not take account of outsourcing (brokers, agents or other intermediaries). The general tendency across Europe is for an increase in employment within life insurance enterprises (except for Germany and Ireland). For non-life insurance enterprises there has been little change in levels of employment in recent years.

4) Enterprises allowed to carry out both life and non-life business. These exist only in a limited number of Member States.

(units)  Figure 19.8

Insurance and pension funding (NACE Rev. 1 66)
Density of enterprises per ten thousand inhabitants, 1995

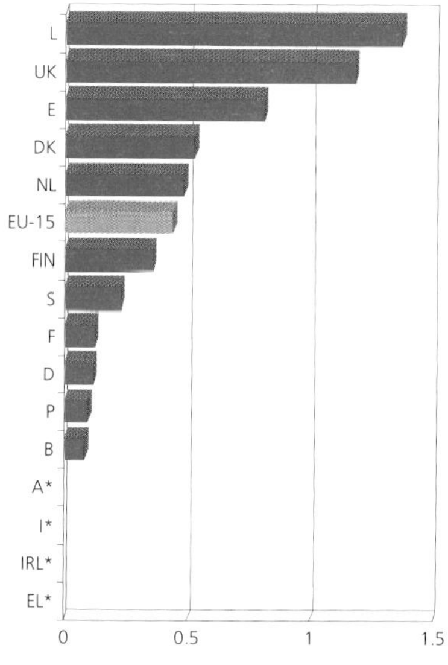

Source: Eurostat (SME)

(units) Table 19.7

Insurance (NACE Rev. 1 66.01 and 66.03)
Main indicators, 1996

	Number of enterprises (units)	Number of persons employed (thousands)	Gross premiums written (million ECU)
EU-15	4,237	:	566,315
B (1)	169	26	13,804
DK	250	16	9,637
D	495	221	153,455
EL (2)	152	:	1,640
E	311	40	23,776
F	507	:	122,853
IRL (1)	101	8	4,511
I	235	:	38,999
L (3)	309	1	5,505
NL (1)	407	:	29,215
A	66	33	12,161
P (2)	55	:	4,400
FIN	169	10	4,191
S (4)	143	19	11,870
UK (5)	868	:	130,298

(1) Excluding specialist reinsurance.
(2) Preliminary data for gross premiums written.
(3) Excluding specialist reinsurance for number of persons employed.
(4) Preliminary data for number of enterprises and gross premiums written.
(5) Excluding specialist reinsurance for gross premiums written.

Source: Eurostat (SBS)

(%) Figure 19.9

Insurance and pension funding (NACE Rev. 1 66)
Share of part-time and temporary work contracts in total number of persons employed, 1997

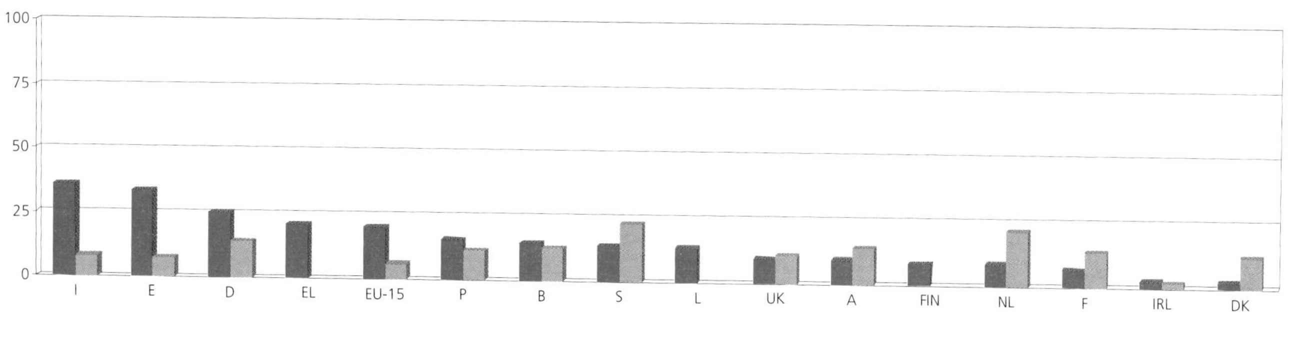

Source: Eurostat (LFS)

Gross premiums written by EU insurance enterprises amounted to 566 billion ECU in 1996, 43% of which were written by life insurance enterprises, 38% by non-life insurance enterprises, 12% by composite insurance enterprises and 7% by specialist reinsurance enterprises. Total gross premiums written grew by 10% over the year before, ranging from 24.2% growth in the United Kingdom, 22.4% in Finland and 22.1% in Ireland to 2.9% in the Netherlands and only 1.1% in Germany. As a general rule, premiums on life insurance showed more progress than those of non-life insurance. Available figures for 1997 indicate a continuation of these trends.

Large differences exist in life insurance across EU Member States. The highest level of gross premiums written per capita were found in Luxembourg and the United Kingdom at 1,275 ECU and 1,100 ECU respectively, whilst the corresponding figures for Greece and Portugal amounted to only 61 ECU and 78 ECU respectively.

Turning to non-life insurance, motor vehicle insurance was the largest category of non-life insurance in the EU, accounting for about a third of total non-life direct gross premiums written. Fire and other damage to property and accident and health were the other major categories, each representing about one fifth of the total. It is worth noting that a distinction can be made between insurance that is mandatory (e.g. car insurance, workplace accident insurance) and insurance that is not. Improvements in living standards emerge as an essential factor in the trend of non-life insurance consumption. As income increases, people tend to also insure themselves and their possessions beyond the minimum legal requirements.

Since the Single Market entered into force, most leading European insurers have engaged in a series of mergers and take-overs. Indeed, recent years have witnessed a particularly buoyant activity, including the merger of AXA and UAP in France, that of Commercial Union and General Accident in the United Kingdom, the creation of Ergo in Germany, resulting from the merger of Hamburger-Mannheimer, Victoria, DAS and DKV, as well as the acquisition of AGF (F) by Allianz (D).

Table 19.8

Top 20 European insurance companies, as of 31.12.97

Name	Country	Premiums (million ECU)	Profits (million ECU)	Number of employees (units)	World ranking (9)
AXA (1)	F	46,467	1,992	80,600	1
Allianz	D	43,537	1,371	73,300	2
Generali	I	21,000	711	41,400	4
Standard Life (2)	UK	17,636	4,074	9,500	7
CNP Assurances (3)	F	16,744	280	2,500	8
Münchener Rückvers. (4)	D	16,368	355	18,000	10
Prudential	UK	15,324	1,209	22,120	12
ING Group	NL	14,287	1,855	64,200	14
Aegon (3)	NL	14,149	997	23,400	15
Legal & General Group	UK	13,629	705	7,200	16
Royal Sun Alliance (5)	UK	13,321	879	43,500	17
Commercial Union (6)	UK	12,331	504	26,200	19
AGF (7)	F	10,814	387	30,700	24
Allianz Lebensvers. (8)	D	10,670	108	4,800	25
General Accident (6)	UK	9,102	994	25,600	30
Fortis	B	8,969	1,113	35,200	31
RAS (8)	I	8,377	265	12,900	32
Norwich Union	UK	8,264	389	16,300	33
Skandia Group	S	8,225	415	9,700	34
AMB	D	7,731	205	18,300	35

(1) After the merger with UAP.
(2) Estimates, as of 30/11/97.
(3) Turnover (no premiums).
(4) As of 30/06/97.
(5) Net premiums.
(6) Commercial Union and General Accident merged in 1998.
(7) Take-over by Allianz in 1998.
(8) Estimates.
(9) Excluding Japan.

Source: Trade press

Underlying the acquisition strategy of many insurers are both the objectives of strengthening their position on their home market and gaining global market share. Many companies now operate in several EU countries other than their domestic base. As cross-border moves through mergers continue, the implementation of the third generation directives[5] not only offered EU companies better possibilities to operate internationally within the EU, but they also paved the way for non-EU insurance companies. Although these directives imply the freedom to provide services anywhere within the EU, not all the obstacles in the regulatory environment have been removed. Large differences in market characteristics between national markets still complicate market entry, hence the reliance on mergers and acquisitions.

5) The third generation insurance directives came into force in July 1994. The most significant feature of these directives is the attempt to move the regulatory focus from host-country control to home-country control.

The third generation directives have also paved the way for a series of take-overs and mergers between banks and insurance companies. Through these take-overs the phenomenon of "bancassurance" has emerged in recent years. Through the emergence of bancassurance a clear distinction between insurance companies, banks and bancassurance companies cannot be made anymore, with banks increasingly offering insurance products and insurers providing asset management services.

Finally, a trend that is gaining momentum in recent years is the increasing involvement of private insurance companies in activities formerly exclusively managed by public authorities, such as pension funding and social security services. In the Netherlands, private insurers already actively participate in the management of the social security system and several other European countries are contemplating the same solution.

Financial intermediaries
(NACE Rev. 1 65.2 and 67)

Financial intermediaries have a supporting function in capital markets. Their activities consist of the following activities: brokerage, advice, research, dealing in securities, market-making, clearing and settlement. Stock exchanges, brokers, and large investment banks also operate in this industry. Financial intermediaries perform functions that are complementary to banking and insurance activities and also provide financial services in competition with banks and insurance companies. The liberalisation of capital markets led to the emergence of sizeable financial intermediary groups. These groups are present in corporate finance, in stock markets and in collective savings management.

The German Stock Exchange, which is divided into four sub-markets (with Frankfurt as the main market), was in 1997 the largest in Europe, with an aggregate total of 2,696 listed shares (excluding investment funds). This was just above the level of the London Stock Exchange with 2,513. Paris followed with 924 listed shares. The number of companies listed has increased in the majority of European countries, and this was noticeably the case in Germany, where growth of 37% was registered between 1996 and 1997.

(units) Figure 19.10

Activities auxiliary to financial intermediation (NACE Rev. 1 67)
Density of enterprises per ten thousand inhabitants, 1995

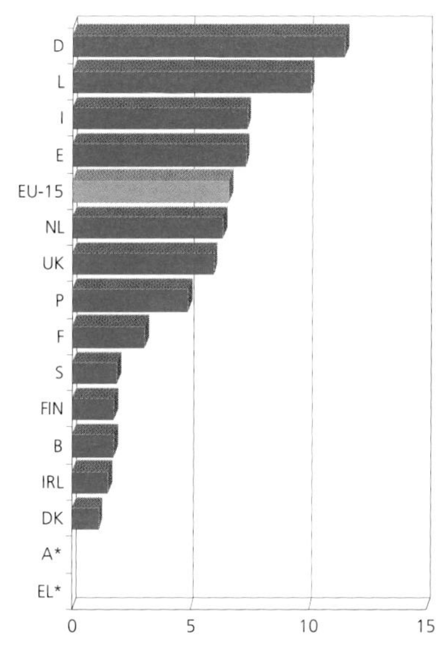

Source: Eurostat (SME)

(billion ECU) Figure 19.11

The world's largest stock markets by market capitalisation, 1997

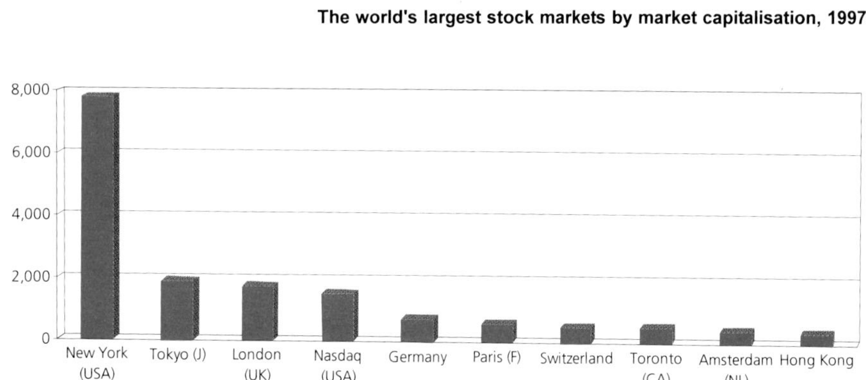

Source: FIBV

(%) Figure 19.12

Activities auxiliary to financial intermediation (NACE Rev. 1 67)
Share of part-time and temporary work contracts in total number of persons employed, 1997

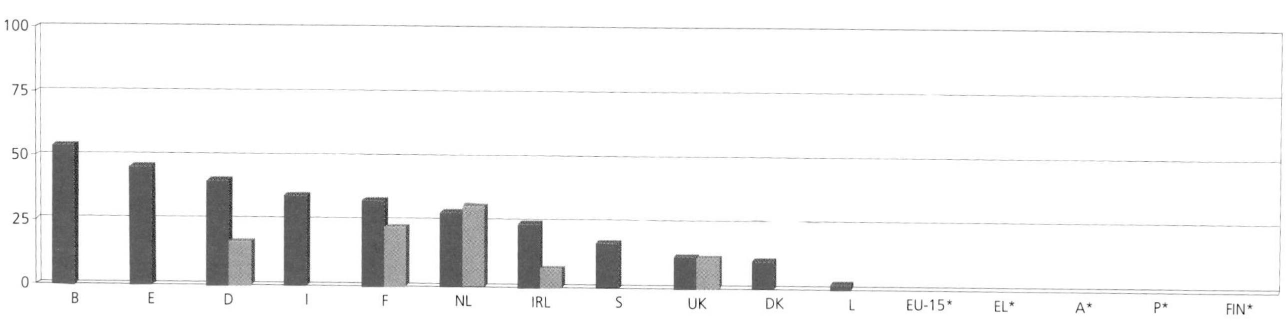

Source: Eurostat (LFS)

Table 19.9

Stock markets, main indicators 1997

	Country	Total number of companies listed, excluding investment funds	Of which, national	Of which, foreign	Share trading (million ECU)	Trading view (1)	Market capitalisation (million ECU)
Brussels	B	265	138	127	29,864	TSV	122,516
Copenhagen	DK	249	237	12	41,208	REV	82,683
Germany	D	2,696	700	1,996	941,491	REV	727,693
Athens	EL	210	210	0	18,638	TSV	29,791
Madrid	E	388	384	4	122,339	REV	256,061
Barcelona	E	337	333	4	19,810	REV	:
Bilbao	E	255	254	1	15,986	REV	:
Paris	F	924	740	184	365,349	REV	596,373
Italy	I	239	235	4	179,253	TSV	303,927
Luxembourg	L	284	56	228	924	TSV	29,886
Amsterdam	NL	348	199	149	247,700	REV	413,474
Vienna	A	138	101	37	11,220	TSV	32,874
Helsinki	FIN	126	124	2	31,967	TSV	64,656
Stockholm	S	261	245	16	155,040	REV	233,423
London	UK	2,513	2,046	467	1,754,338	REV	1,760,277
NYSE	USA	2,626	2,271	355	5,094,707	TSV	7,830,086
NASDAQ	USA	5,487	5,033	454	3,951,961	REV	1,532,141
Amex	USA	710	647	63	126,301	TSV	109,878
Toronto	CA	1,420	1,362	58	269,087	TSV	500,542
Hong Kong	HK	658	638	20	400,036	TSV	364,469
Tokyo	JP	1,865	1,805	60	790,144	TSV	1,905,210
Singapore	SG	334	294	40	65,375	TSV	93,751
Taiwan	TW	404	404	0	1,153,957	TSV	261,726

(1) TSV (Trading System View) count only those transactions which pass through the trading system or which take place on the exchange's trading floor.
REV (Regulated Environment View) includes all transactions subject to supervision by the market authority.

Source: FIBV

The 1990s have been characterised by an enormous growth in equity turnover in Europe and North America. During the period 1990-1994, the value of share trading almost doubled in the EU and on the New York Stock Exchange, whilst during the period 1994-1997 the value was doubled again. The NASDAQ market witnessed impressive growth, with a share trading value that grew tenfold between 1990 and 1997. In Europe, similar increases were witnessed on the smaller markets of Bilbao, Helsinki, Luxembourg and Stockholm. This could be contrasted with the Tokyo market, where share turnover in 1997 was still 20% below the level of 1990.

All European stock markets witnessed a sharp rise in capitalisation[6] during the course of the 1990s, a trend that accelerated in the second half of the decade. Market capitalisation of EU markets surged 36% in 1997 to reach 4.7 thousand billion ECU, a level 2.7 times higher than in 1990. Amsterdam, Luxembourg and Helsinki were the three markets that recorded the highest growth between 1990 and 1997, with capitalisation practically quadrupling. 1997 will be remembered as a buoyant year for European equity markets. Market capitalisation growth was particularly strong, the best performances were recorded in Athens (+61%), Italian markets (+50%) and Copenhagen (+48%). At the lower end of the ranking, progress still remained strong: Vienna and Stockholm gained 23% and Luxembourg 17% (just under half the European average of 36%).

6) Data on market capitalisation excludes foreign companies, investment funds, rights, warrants and convertibles.

In 1997, European shares represented 30% of the world's total, up from 25% in 1994. North American equities accounted for 52% of the world's total capitalisation, up from 37% three years before.

The market value of bonds listed on EU stock exchanges rose by 4% in 1997, with a large diversity in growth rates across markets. The highest rates of growth were recorded in Luxembourg (+21%) and in Helsinki (+16%), whilst Bilbao and Athens lost 32% and 24%. The overall trend during the period 1990-1997 has been an increase in all countries, with annual average growth rates of between 1.8% and 2%. The only markets displaying clear negative trends were Madrid, Barcelona and Bilbao, where the market value of listed bonds was more than halved over the period considered.

(1990=100) Figure 19.13

Value of share trading including investment funds

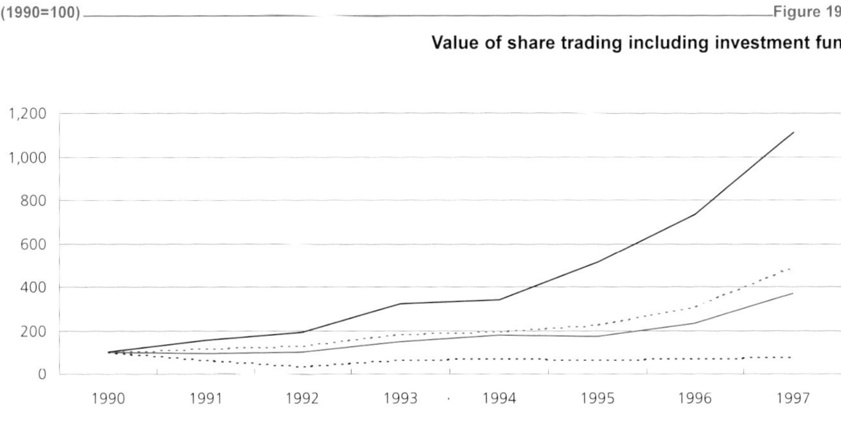

(1) Amsterdam, Athens, Barcelona, Bilbao, Brussels, Copenhagen, Helsinki, London, Luxembourg, Madrid, Paris, Stockholm, Vienna and stock exchanges from Italy and Germany.

Source: FIBV

(%) Figure 19.14

Market capitalisation of domestic companies' shares

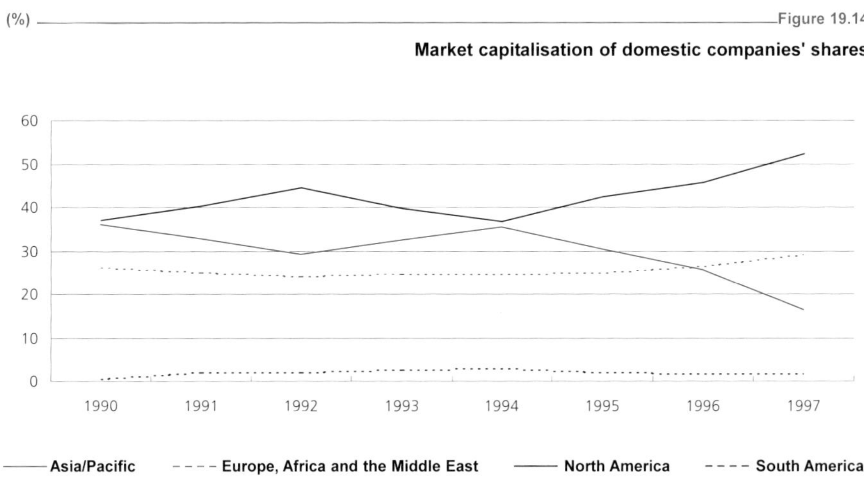

Source: FIBV

(billion ECU) Figure 19.15

Market capitalisation

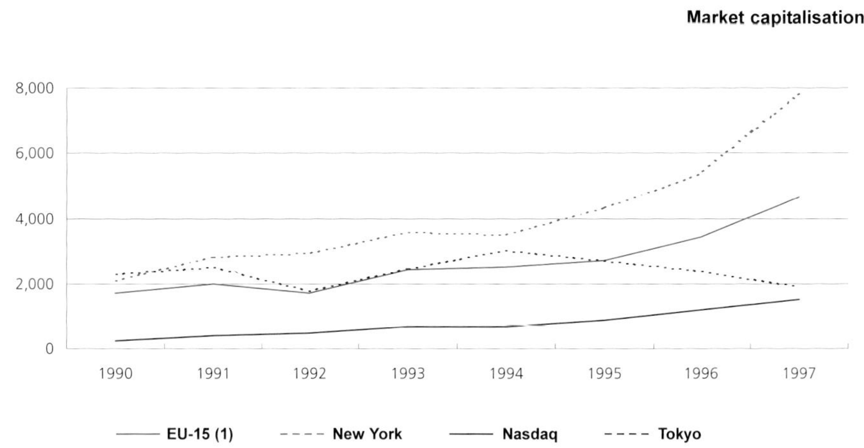

(1) Amsterdam, Athens, Barcelona, Bilbao, Brussels, Copenhagen, Helsinki, London, Luxembourg, Madrid, Paris, Stockholm, Vienna and stock exchanges from Italy and Germany.

Source: FIBV

Figure 19.16 (million ECU)

Average net assets per investment fund as of 31.12.97 (1)

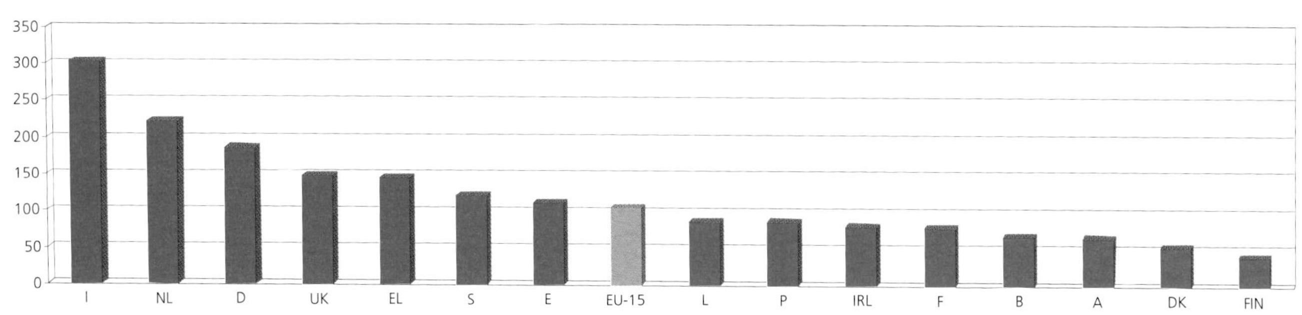

(1) Publicly-offered, open-ended funds investing in transferable securities and money market instruments.

Source: FEFSI

Turning to investment funds, FEFSI, the European federation of investment funds and companies, numbered 16,719 funds in the EU in 1997, 60% more than three years before. They managed net assets in excess of 1.7 thousand billion ECU, also 60% higher than the amount recorded in 1994. Two markets dominate the European scene: France accounted for one third of the total number of funds in the EU and one quarter of the total net assets, and Luxembourg numbered one quarter of the EU funds, holding one fifth of their net assets. On average, EU investment funds have net assets of 105 million ECU, ranging from an average of 40 million ECU in Finland to 180 million ECU in Germany.

Financial intermediaries have experienced dramatic changes in their business environment in recent years. Standing at the centre of economic flows: financial markets have to adapt to the evolution of world business. On the one hand, companies increasingly operate on a global basis, which leads them to issue bonds and equity outside of their domestic market. On the other hand, investors are also operating worldwide, helped by the emergence of electronic markets and Internet, as well as computer-based trading that allows millions of people to invest without time or geographical constraints.

The reorganisation of stock markets has also played an important role in stimulating the supply of financial services and the competition between financial intermediaries. Its aim was to improve efficiency, whilst ensuring stability and investor protection. Key elements included:

- the end to brokers' monopoly and the liberalisation of commissions;
- a reorganisation of the market for treasury bonds, with the consequent adoption of a secondary market in such stocks to reflect the needs of investors;
- the creation of secondary listings, allowing medium-sized businesses unable to meet the conditions for a full listing to improve their access to capital;
- and the computerisation of stock markets and market operations in all European exchanges, that greatly improved market liquidity by making information more rapidly available.

Professional associations representing the industries within this chapter

BIPAR
International Federation of Insurance Intermediaries
40, avenue Albert Elisabeth
B-1200 Bruxelles
tel: (32) 2 735 60 48
fax: (32) 2 732 14 18
e-mail: BIPAR@skynet.be

CEA
Comité Européen des Assurances
29, square de Meeûs
B-1040 Bruxelles
tel: (32) 2 547 58 11
fax: (32) 2 547 58 19

EMF
European Mortgage Federation
14, avenue de la Joyeuse Entrée, boîte 2
B-1040 Bruxelles
tel: (32) 2 285 40 30
fax: (32) 2 285 40 31
e-mail: emf.be@skynet.be

ESBG
European Savings Bank Group
11, rue Marie-Thérèse
B-1000 Bruxelles
tel: (32) 2 211 11 11
fax: (33) 1 211 11 99
e-mail: info@savings-banks.com

Eurofinas
European Federation of Finance House Associations
267, avenue de Tervueren
B-1150 Bruxelles
tel: (32) 2 771 21 08
fax: (32) 2 770 75 96

FBE
Fédération Bancaire Européenne
10, rue Montoyer
B-1040 Bruxelles
tel: (32) 2 508 37 11
fax: (32) 2 502 79 66
e-mail: fbe@fbe.be

FEFSI
Fédération Européenne des Fonds et Sociétés d'Investissement
20, square de Meeûs
B-1050 Bruxelles
tel: (32) 2 513 39 69
fax: (32) 2 513 26 43
e-mail: fefsi@infoboard.be

FESE
Federation of European Stock Exchanges
41, rue du Lombard
B-1000 Bruxelles
tel: (32) 2 513 05 18
fax: (32) 2 512 49 05

FIBV
Fédération Internationale des Bourses de Valeurs
22, boulevard de Courcelles
F-75017 Paris
tel: (33) 1 44 01 05 45
fax: (33) 1 47 54 94 22
e-mail: secretariat@fibv.com

GEBC
European Association of Cooperative Banks
23-25, rue de la Science
Boîte 9
B-1040 Bruxelles
tel: (32) 2 230 11 24
fax: (32) 2 230 06 49

Business services

Industry description and main indicators

Business services include the technical, professional and operational services generally supplied to firms and the government, rather than to households, for the support of their production process or their organisation. The most important business services generally include activities such as legal, tax and management consultancy, engineering services, computer services, personnel recruitment and selection, cleaning and maintenance services or advertising and market research. All of these are covered by Section K of the NACE Rev. 1 classification (Divisions 70 to 74) and will be addressed in this chapter, with the exception of real estate services (NACE Rev. 1 70) and computer services (NACE Rev. 1 72) that are studied in chapters 15 and 21 respectively.

The remarkable development of business services activities over the past thirty years can be mainly attributed to three factors. Firstly, there has been a clear shift in the structure of the European economy towards service activities, partly stemming from manufacturing enterprises increasingly outsourcing non-core activities to independent service providers. In other words, a series of activities that used to be executed in-house, such as accounting, advertising, cleaning or security services have been increasingly sub-contracted to specialised firms, with the hope that this would achieve flexibility, as well as lower costs and a better quality of service. Secondly, from the point of view of statistical methodology, the classification of business services is of residual nature, in the sense that it includes activities that have not been explicitly classified elsewhere. As a consequence, new service activities that do not fit existing definitions within other sectors are included. Thirdly, the sector has benefited from strong internal growth, thanks to an ever-increasing demand for this category of service, in response to the growing complexity of business processes, increasing pressure from competitors world-wide and the emergence of new technologies. These have spurred demand for consultancy, training or R&D services.

(units) Figure 20.1

Other business activities (NACE Rev. 1 74)
Density of enterprises per ten thousand inhabitants, 1995

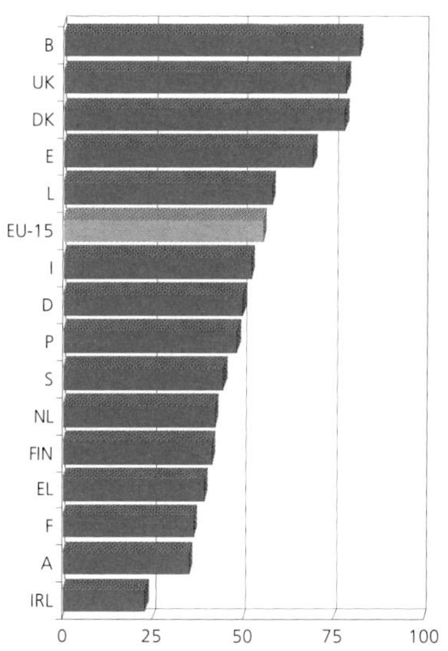

Source: Eurostat (SME)

The activities covered in this chapter include:

71.1: renting of automobiles;
71.2: renting of other transport equipment;
71.3: renting of other machinery and equipment;
71.4: renting of personal and household goods n.e.c.
73.1: research and experimental development on natural sciences and engineering;
73.2: research and experimental development on social sciences and humanities;
74.1: legal, accounting, book-keeping and auditing activities; tax consultancy; market research and public opinion polling; business and management consultancy; holdings;
74.2: architectural and engineering activities and related technical consultancy;
74.3: technical testing and analysis;
74.4: advertising;
74.5: labour recruitment and provision of personnel;
74.6: investigation and security activities;
74.7: industrial cleaning;
74.8: miscellaneous business activities n.e.c.

Figure 20.2 (%)

Other business activities (NACE Rev. 1 74)

Share of part-time and temporary work contracts in total number of persons employed, 1997

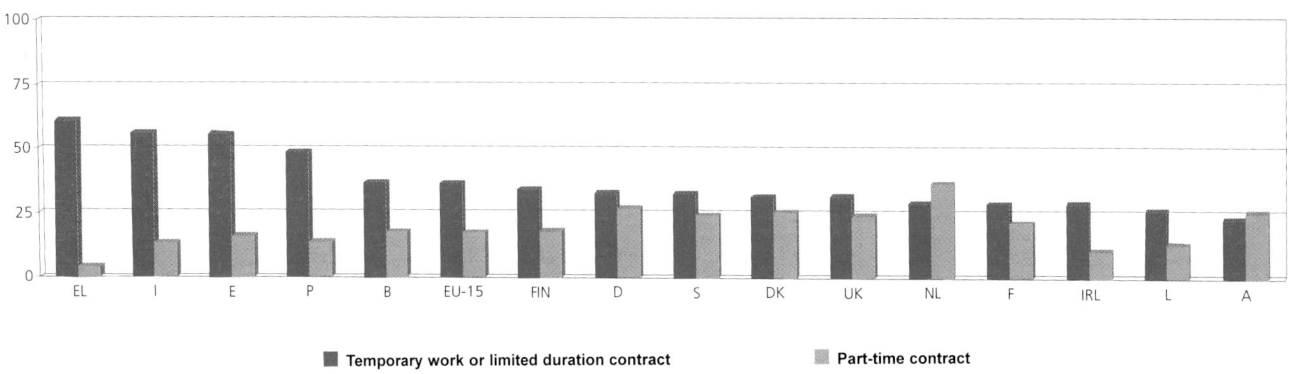

Source: Eurostat (LFS)

Business services represent today one of the most important activities of the European economy. According to National Accounts they represented in 1997 over a fifth of the GDP in the majority of Member States, ranging from 17% in Finland to 28% in Luxembourg. In terms of employment, the share is slightly lower, although still considerable at over 15% in most European countries, from a tenth of total employment in Finland to over a fifth in Belgium. It must be noted, however, that these figures are based on the National Accounts classification that is slightly different from that used in business statistics. Nevertheless, the activities that are common to both classifications are important and the data can hence be used as the best available approximation.

Business services are a typical area of activity for small and medium-sized enterprises. According to the latest estimates from Eurostat, 94% of the more than two million enterprises active in this sector in the EU, had less than ten employees. Amongst these, a very large proportion, about two-thirds, had no employees at all. In total they accounted for about a third of the aggregate turnover of the sector. In contrast, companies employing more than 250 persons represented less than 1% of the enterprise population and accounted for slightly more than a quarter of turnover.

The annual survey on the European labour force carried out by Eurostat supplies information on the characteristics of employment in business services. In its latest release, the Labour Force Survey estimated employment in the sectors covered by the present chapter at over 9 million persons in 1997, of which more than 8.1 million were found in "other business services", as defined by NACE Rev. 1 74. Some 600 thousand were working in research and development (NACE Rev. 1 73) and 300 thousand in renting activities (NACE Rev. 1 71). Part-time work was relatively frequent, as it concerned over a fifth of the persons employed in 1998. The highest penetration rates of part-time work were found in the Netherlands (37%) and Germany (27%), whilst only one country, Greece, recorded less than a tenth of those employed working part-time (4%). On the other hand, this high share of part-time work was not accompanied by an above average level of job insecurity, as only a tenth of the persons employed had a temporary job or a work contract of limited duration, a share similar to the economy as a whole. In research & development activities, however, the share was much higher at 18%. For other business activities, Spain (30%) and Finland (13%) displayed the highest shares of such contracts, whilst shares were marginal in Austria and Luxembourg (both 3%).

Figure 20.3 (thousand ECU)

Other business activities (NACE Rev. 1 74)

Personnel costs/employee, 1996

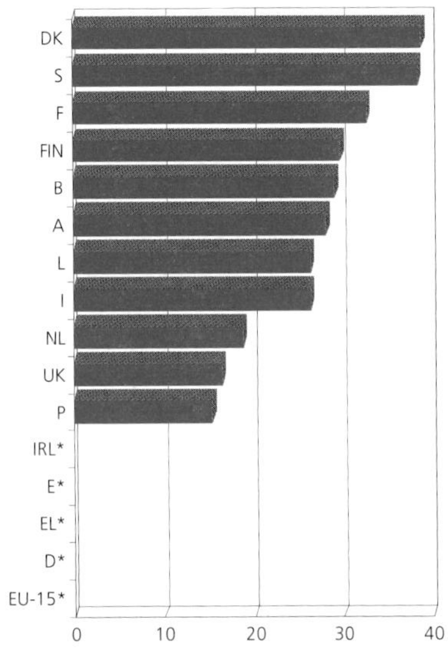

Source: Eurostat (SBS)

(ECU/month) Figure 20.4

Business services (NACE Rev. 1 71, 73 and 74)
Labour costs by Member State, 1996

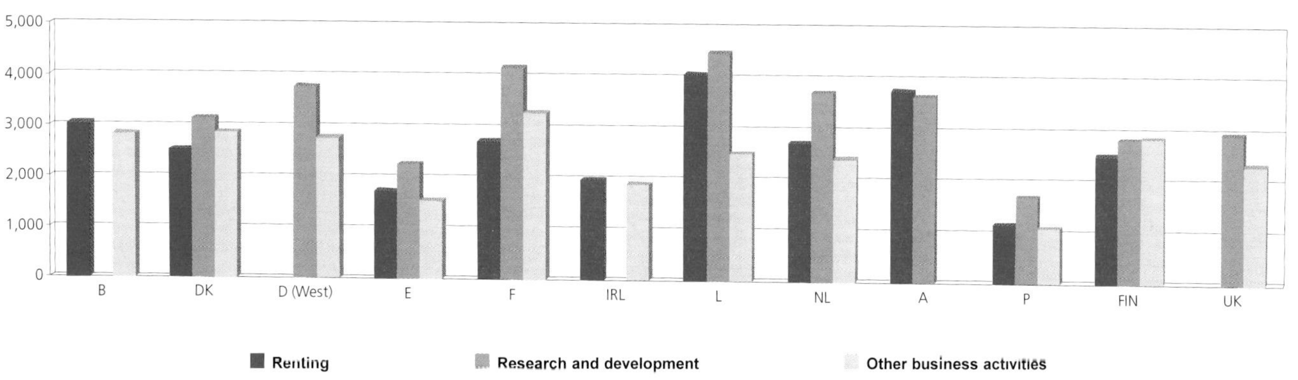

Source: Eurostat (LCS)

Gender balance was relatively even in business services as women represented in 1998 over 47% of the persons employed, although they were less numerous in R&D (38%) and renting activities (32%). They outnumbered men in Germany, Finland and Austria, as opposed to Greece where they accounted for just over 40% of total employment.

As regards the level of education of the workforce, the Labour Force Survey indicates that the general level was higher in business services when compared to other sectors of the economy. Indeed, about 37% of the persons employed in 1998 possessed a higher-education degree, amongst the highest ratios in service activities. Unsurprisingly, persons employed in research and development displayed a much higher proportion of 63%, whilst the ratio was equal to just 16% in renting services. The highest presence of highly-educated persons was found in Greece (62%), Ireland (56%) and Belgium (52%), the only countries where highly-educated persons outnumbered persons having a lower education level. Austria (23%) and Portugal (26%) recorded the lowest levels of persons employed with a higher education degree.

International comparison

Business services represent a significant share of the European economy, although lower than in the other countries of the Triad. Indeed, they accounted for 28% of American GDP in 1996. This share placed the USA at the same level as Luxembourg (the EU country with the highest intensity of business services in 1997). Japan, similarly, recorded a share of total value added higher than in the majority of the Member States, some 26% in 1997.

The same conclusions could be drawn looking at the structure of employment. Business services accounted for no less than 22% of the American workforce in 1997 and 17% in Japan. In both cases, this would have placed them amongst the top European countries, such as Belgium (22%) and Luxembourg (19%).

A first measure of labour productivity is to compare value added generated by each person employed. In the USA, labour productivity of business services was equal to 60 thousand ECU in 1996, a level lower than that recorded in most EU Member States. It reached 82 thousand ECU in Japan, a value similar to France (85 thousand ECU), the Netherlands (82 thousand ECU) and Finland (78 thousand ECU). Germany was amongst the countries recording the highest labour productivity in this branch of the economy (110 thousand ECU per capita). On the other hand, Greece recorded a labour productivity level well below that displayed in the other Member States, at 47 thousand ECU in 1997.

Legal, accountancy and management consultancy (NACE Rev. 1 74.1)

The activities analysed in this section are defined by Group 74.1 of the NACE Rev. 1 activity classification. They cover a varied group of activities that include: legal activities; accounting, book-keeping and auditing activities; tax consultancy; market research and public opinion polling; business and management consultancy activities; management activities of holding companies.

As a general rule, this sector is dominated in terms of the number of enterprises, employment or turnover by three main activities: legal, accountancy and management consultancy activities, whilst market research and holding companies account for a lesser share.

Availability of official statistics is too patchy to allow for EU totals to be calculated or estimated. As an indication, however, large Member States such as Germany, Spain and France each numbered more than 120 thousand enterprises active in this sector in 1995/96, whilst there were more than 8.5 thousand enterprises in smaller countries, such as Austria and Finland. The number of persons employed on average per enterprise was between 3 and 5, whilst personnel costs were relatively high compared to other areas as they generally exceeded 40 thousand ECU per employee.

Figure 20.5 (units)

Legal, accounting, book-keeping and auditing, consultancy, market research (NACE Rev. 1 74.1)

Density of enterprises per ten thousand inhabitants, 1996

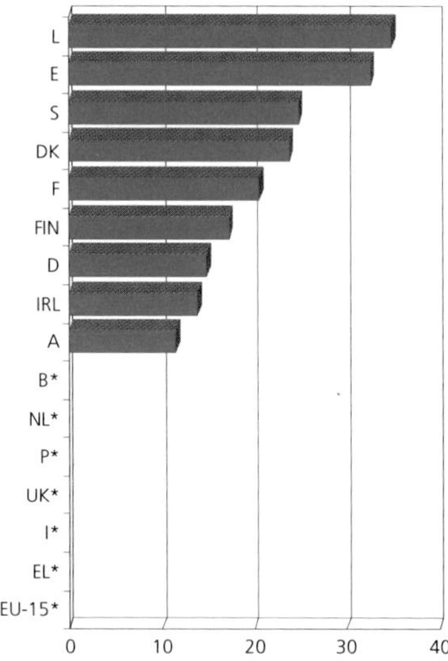

Source: Eurostat (SBS)

Figure 20.6 (thousand ECU)

Legal, accounting, book-keeping and auditing, consultancy, market research (NACE Rev. 1 74.1)

Personnel costs/employee, 1996

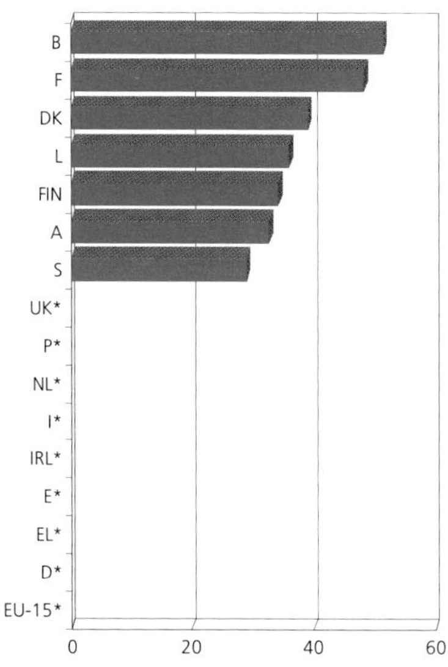

Source: Eurostat (SBS)

Figure 20.7 (%)

Legal, accounting, book-keeping and auditing, consultancy, market research (NACE Rev. 1 74.1)

Wage adjusted labour productivity, 1996

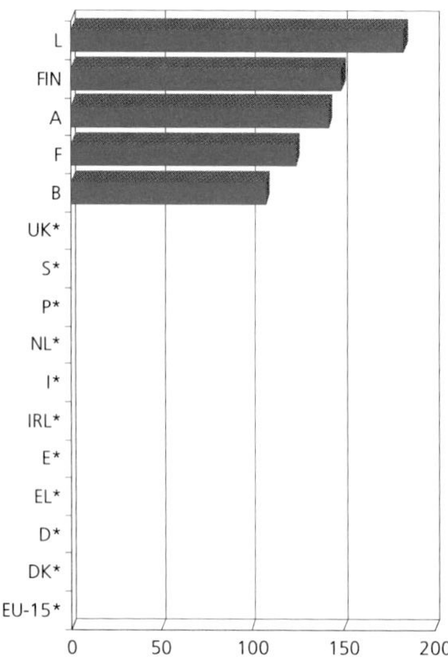

Source: Eurostat (SBS)

Legal services

As regards legal activities, those covered include advocates, barristers and solicitors, notaries, registered lawyers and legal consultants, but this activity excludes the law courts. According to the Council of the Bars and Law Societies of the European Community (CCBE) there were in 1996/97 more than 436 thousand registered lawyers in the EU. On the other hand, the association of notaries (the Council for European affairs of the UINL, Union Internationale du Notariat Latin) estimate that Germany was the EU country with the largest number of notaries' offices with more than 10 thousand (see table 20.1).

(units) Table 20.1

Legal services in the EEA, 1997

	Number of registered lawyers	Number of notaries offices (1)
B (1)	11,528	1,221
DK	3,880	:
D	85,543	10,688
EL	:	2,968
E	89,288	1,979
F	34,000	:
IRL (1)	4,560	150
I (1)	87,000	4,543
L	391	36
NL	8,757	1,224
A (1)	3,356	:
P (1)	15,000	:
FIN (1)	1,340	:
S	3,400	:
UK (1)	88,066	1,000
IS (1)	480	:
NO	3,498	:

(1) 1996.

Source: CCBE, CAUE/UINL

The legal professions have during the last twenty years been particularly affected by the progress of European integration, as well as the adoption of major and widely publicised international treaties or agreements (Single European Act, Maastricht and Amsterdam Treaties, GATT). These trends have been characterised by the harmonisation of common elements of the legislative environment and by the recognition of the need to compete in a "supra-jurisdictional" marketplace, whilst at the same time many clients have become more international themselves.

Accountancy services

Turning to accountancy services, the Federation of European Accountants (FEE - Fédération des Experts Comptables Européens) estimate that its membership in 1995 exceeded 370 thousand persons, of which about 40% worked in the accountancy service sector, whilst most of the others represented practises in industry, trade, education or the public sector. Their services consist mainly in keeping accounts and auditing, but often extend to tax consultancy, financial advisory, mergers & acquisitions or management consultancy.

(number of persons) Table 20.2

Membership in national accounting associations, 1995

B	8,538
DK	2,577
D	8,310
EL	350
E	4,666
F	24,760
IRL	9,484
I	75,727
L	340
NL	10,011
A	5,474
P	1,074
FIN	1,992
S	574
UK	219,351

Source: FEE

On first sight, the profession is dominated by a few large international firms known as the "big five": PricewaterhouseCoopers (PwC), Ernst & Young, KPMG, Deloitte & Touche and Arthur Andersen. These partnerships usually work for large national and international companies worldwide. The bulk of the profession, however, consists of small enterprises, some of which have engaged in developing national or even international networks. A typical characteristic of accountancy services is the multitude of rules and regulations to which they are subject, including accession to the profession itself. This leads to a high fragmentation of this activity as regulations on accountancy, taxation, company law or social legislation may differ greatly across the EU.

Management consultancy

Management consultancy services is another important activity in business services. It covers the professional services providing advice on management matters to businesses or the public sector, sometimes extending to the implementation of solutions. It shares with legal and accountancy services the characteristic of having a fragmented supply, as beyond the large multinational enterprises (such as the "big five" and McKinsey, BCG, ATK, Bain, Arthur D Little, Booz-Allen, etc.) the majority of enterprises are very small in size, with many consisting of just one self-employed person.

(% share of income) Figure 20.8

Breakdown of management consultancy activities, 1997

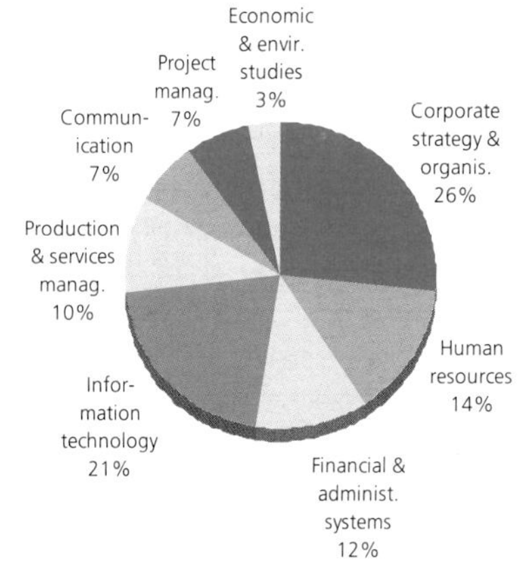

Source: FEACO

FEACO, the European Federation of Management Consulting Associations, estimate that the sector employed over 130 thousand consultants in Europe in 1997, generating turnover of 19 billion ECU[1], progressing 15% compared to the data for 1996. Indeed, the sector has benefited in recent years from a combination of factors that have strongly stimulated demand, such as the increasing globalisation of markets, the entry into force of the common European currency, a wave of privatisation and deregulation, or indeed the Y2K bug. Corporate strategy, organisational development and information technology were in 1997 the main fields of activity of management consultants (see figure 20.8), whilst the most important clients were the banking and insurance sector, representing over a fifth of total income, ahead of manufacturing and transport and communication enterprises.

1) A great deal of additional statistical information on management consultancy is available from FEACO in the publication, "Survey of the European Management Consultancy Market", 1998.

Market research

Market research is the business service activity that deals with analysing markets for products and services. It is generally used by decision-makers to identify and define opportunities, threats, competition and emerging trends, and to initiate, modify and evaluate marketing strategies. In recent years there have been major changes in the information needs of companies. A key factor has been increasing global marketing, and a growing interest by multinationals in Europe, following the Single Market. In addition, the proliferation of media has exacerbated demand for pan-European information.

Market research has witnessed very strong growth during the past twenty years, with real growth rates exceeding 10% per annum in the 1980s and 7% in the first half of the 1990s. Since 1996, growth rates have returned to over 10%. ESOMAR, the European Society for Opinion and Marketing Research, estimate that EU turnover grew by 15% in 1997 to 4.3 billion ECU[2], or 41% of the world total. This compares with a market worth 3.9 billion ECU in the USA, up 26%[3], and 0.9 billion ECU in Japan, up 14%. The largest market inside the EU was the United Kingdom (26% of the EU total), ahead of Germany (25%) and France (18%). Clients of market research were mainly manufacturing industries. They accounted for just over half the turnover of the sector, whilst the public sector was the second largest with 8%. On average, some 70% of turnover was generated in the area of consumer research. Employment in market research in Europe[4] was estimated at 48 thousand employees in 1997 (of which more than 80% worked part-time) and 190 thousand were interviewers.

2) Turnover was equal to 4 billion ECU when excluding double-counting due to sub-contracting. A great deal of additional statistical information on market research is available from ESOMAR in the publication: "Annual Study on the Market Research industry", 1998.
3) Exchange rate fluctuations exaggerate this growth.
4) Figures for Europe include EU-15, Norway, Switzerland, Eastern European countries, Russia and Turkey.

Table 20.3 (million ECU)

Top ten market research companies in the EU, 1997

Company	Turnover
AC Nielsen (1)	511
Cognizant Corp.	357
TN Sofres	322
The Kanta Group	289
GfK	246
Infratest/Burke	142
IPSOS Group	137
NOP Information Group Ltd.	98
PSMI	37
Maritz Marketing Research Inc.	22
NFO Worldwide Inc.	22

(1) Including the rest of Europe, Middle-East and Africa.

Source: ESOMAR

Table 20.4

Market research turnover in the EU, 1997

	Turnover (million ECU) (1)	Share of consumer research (%)	Share of customer satisfaction research (%)
B	75	60	3
DK	50	87	8
D	973	58	:
EL	34	76	10
E	204	64	10
F	706	65	9
IRL	25	85	13
I	299	75	13
L	2	90	5
NL	176	80	:
A	73	64	10
P	37	84	17
FIN	47	80	5
S	175	70	19
UK	1,013	77	15

(1) Excluding overlap due to sub-contracting.

Source: ESOMAR

Architects and engineering activities and related technical consultancy (NACE Rev. 1 74.2)

This section covers a varied series of activities that display a close relationship with the construction sector. They include:

- consulting architectural activities (building design and drafting, supervision of construction, town and city planning and landscape architecture);
- machinery and industrial plan design;
- engineering, project management and technical activities;
- elaboration of projects using air-conditioning, refrigerating, sanitary and pollution control engineering, acoustical engineering, etc.;
- geological and prospecting activities;
- weather forecasting activities;
- geodetic surveying activities.

These activities are characterised by the presence of a very large number of small companies. The few available official statistics on the sector indicated that there were over 40 thousand enterprises in France and the United Kingdom, 61 thousand in Spain and no fewer than 184 thousand in Italy in the mid-1990s, each of those employing fewer than 5 persons on average. Personnel costs were as a general rule at the upper end of the scale when compared to other service activities, ranging from 26 thousand ECU per employee in Spain and Italy to more than 40 thousand ECU in France and Denmark.

(units) Figure 20.9

Architectural and engineering activities (NACE Rev. 1 74.2) Density of enterprises per ten thousand inhabitants, 1996

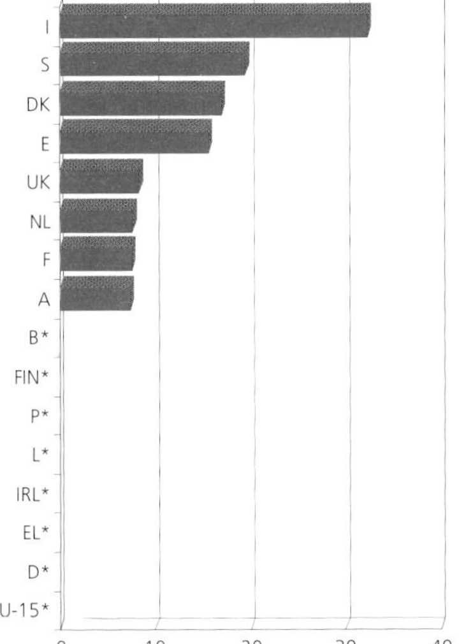

Source: Eurostat (SBS)

(thousand ECU) Figure 20.10

Architectural and engineering activities (NACE Rev. 1 74.2) Personnel costs/employee, 1996

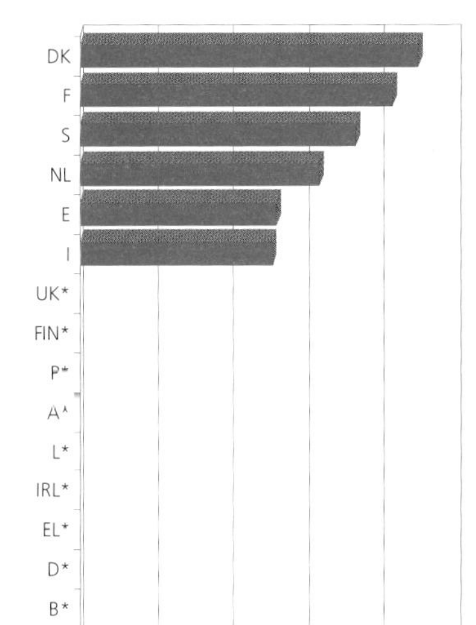

Source: Eurostat (SBS)

Architects

The Architects' Council of Europe (ACE) estimate that there were some 320 thousand architects active in the EU in 1997 (see table 20.5). Professional registration is compulsory in most Member States. In addition, certain activities may be restricted to architects only, usually those relating to the drawing up of plans, the delivery of the building permit or the supervision of the way work is carried out. In Spain, even urban and rural development planning is reserved for architects. In contrast, housing construction in France sometimes hardly involves an architect at all. Regulation barriers may also partly explain why only a marginal number of architects work abroad. Non-nationals make up as a general rule less than 1% of registered architects, except in Luxembourg where about half are foreigners.

Table 20.5 (units)

Number of architects in the EU

	1995	1996	1997
B	9,473	9,624	9,869
DK	6,002	6,090	6,165
D	98,385	82,530	103,852
EL	12,661	13,707	13,888
E	23,600	25,711	26,945
F	26,508	:	26,970
IRL	1,800	1,900	2,000
I	66,500	:	79,000
L	403	432	447
NL	4,930	:	:
A	2,657	2,722	2,824
P	5,405	5,989	6,654
FIN	:	:	3,755
S	:	:	4,750
UK	31,300	:	:

Source: ACE

Construction economists

Construction economists are professionals who assist building owners or promoters in contractual, financial, managerial and economic matters, with the objective to optimise the value of a construction project over its lifetime. They are usually engineers, architects or quantity/building surveyors. According to the European Committee of Construction Economists (CEEC), there were about 90 thousand construction economists registered in the national professional associations in the EU in the second half of the 1990s. This must be considered as a rough estimation, though, as data availability and definitions may vary from country to country.

The first construction economist professionals emerged in the United Kingdom in the second half of the last century as quantity surveyors providing bills of quantity as the basis for tender procurement and settlement of claims. Nowadays, services and methods are focusing on cost modelling for investors, design management and operational electronic information services. In most Member States the majority of construction economists are employed in private consulting companies. However, in some countries, notably the Netherlands and Spain, a substantial share of them work as employees within contracting organisations. The average number of qualified staff per enterprise is less than 10, except in the United Kingdom where the average is 20.

Table 20.6 (units)

Number of construction economists in the EU

	1994	1998
B	25	:
DK	100	147
D	:	10,000
E	17,500	35,000
F	8,100	:
IRL	460	:
I	27,691	:
NL	270	:
P	540	:
FIN	:	500
UK	35,575	:

Source: CEEC

Engineering consultancy

Another activity also contributing to the optimisation of investment projects is that of engineering consultancy. Its objective is to advise, design, implement and/or manage engineering solutions providing the lowest cost and highest investment productivity, for a part or the entirety of a construction project. The European Federation of Engineering Consultancy Associations (EFCA) estimate that there were more than 8 thousand engineering consultancy firms in the EU in 1997 (excluding Finland), employing over 185 thousand persons and generating an annual turnover exceeding 16 billion ECU. The sector displays a high concentration of large companies and this is reflected in the relatively high average number of persons employed per enterprise in a majority of countries, ranging between 4 in Austria and 65 in Italy.

The activity of engineering consultancy is greatly affected by international developments. Exports represented in 1997 up to 42% of turnover in the United Kingdom, and more than 20% in five other Member States. International aid programmes and foreign direct investment were indeed an essential component of demand. Whilst these traditionally concentrated on developing countries or emerging economies, demand in the nineties strongly increased from Central and Eastern European countries, the Commonwealth of Independent Sates and the Eastern Länder of Germany. Domestically, demand has slightly increased over the last decade in the EU, despite a slowdown in public investment, and was stimulated by major projects for transport infrastructure, such as the Channel tunnel or the development of high-speed train networks. Environmental concerns are expected to further benefit the sector, for example through the construction of waste management facilities.

Table 20.7

Main indicators of engineering consultancy in the EU, 1997

	Number of enterprises	Turnover (million ECU)	Number of persons employed	Exports as a share of turnover (%)	Number of persons employed per enterprise	Turnover per person employed (ECU)
B	109	169	4,000	20	36	42,250
DK	329	757	8,976	29	27	84,291
D	3,876	6,579	64,467	13	17	102,052
EL	176	100	2,800	15	16	35,714
E	140	420	6,357	9	45	66,021
F	895	2,257	23,533	25	26	95,908
IRL	106	48	1,200	:	11	40,000
I	210	892	13,650	33	65	65,347
L	82	54	995	7	12	54,673
NL	270	1,100	12,250	27	45	89,795
A	1,230		4,965	:	4	:
P	70	190	2,200	3	[illegible]	[illegible]
S	190	580	7,500	10	39	77,333
UK	532	3,143	32,348	42	60	97,162

Source: EFCA

Geodetic surveying

The International Federation of Surveyors defines a geodetic surveyor as a professional whose responsibilities are to assemble and assess land and geographic related information, and to use that information for the purpose of planning and implementing the efficient administration of the land, the sea and structures thereon. It covers the following activities: hydrography, photogrammetry and remote sensing, cadastral and boundary surveying, land and geographical information systems, minerals and mining surveying, engineering surveying and metrology, and cartography. The Council of European Geodetic Surveyors (CLGE) numbers almost 18 thousand members in the EU, which gives an indication of the importance of the activity. The average number of square kilometres for each geodetic surveyor ranges from about 60 in Denmark and Belgium up to 480 in Finland, a large country with low population density. The public sector plays a central role in this activity as CLGE estimates that it accounts for over half the employment in most Member States.

Cadastral, engineering and land and geographic information systems (LIS and GIS) represent about three-quarters of geodetic services provided in the EU. New technologies have had a strong influence on the provision of these services. Land measurement can be carried out with satellite systems and developments in GIS and LIS systems facilitate data treatment. GIS and LIS accounted for about 15% of the market for geodetic services, a share that is expected to grow rapidly in the future.

(units) Table 20.8

Number of geodetic surveyors in Europe, 1997

B	500
DK	750
D	3,500
EL	1,000
E	2,000
F	2,080
IRL	340
I	1,000
L	35
NL	600
A	670
P	300
FIN	700
S	1,300
UK	3,000
EU-15	17,775
NO	750
CH	900

Source: CLGE

Landscaping

This sector includes the installation, renovation and maintenance of gardens, landscaping and sports ground construction in private and public gardens, parks and leisure centres. Specific activities such as tree maintenance and transplantation, landscaping of public works, installations for noise prevention, creation and construction of ways and places within parks also fall within this sector. Renovation of pre-existing sites and ongoing maintenance is also a significant field of work for landscape contractors.

The European Landscape Contractors Association (ELCA) estimates that there are approximately 38 thousand landscaping companies in the EU (excluding Greece, Luxembourg, Portugal and Finland) employing more than 205 thousand persons, of which 8% were apprentices. Reduced public spending in Europe in recent years has led to a reduction in public contracts, and ELCA does not expect a reversal of this trend in the near future. The importance of public contracts varies in the individual countries ranging from 5% in Denmark up to 60% in France and Italy.

Table 20.9

Main indicators of landscaping activities, 1996

	Number of enterprises	Number of persons employed	Share of enterprises with 1-5 employees (%)	Share of public sector in total turnover (%)
B	4,300	4,850	74	10
DK	600	2,100	25	5
D	9,120	84,837	28	23
E (1)	5,000	50,000	65	:
F	8,000	21,000	51	60
IRL	450	850	:	:
I	3,000	15,000	:	60
NL	2,900	11,500	65	40
A	400	1,400	55	25
S	300	2,750	50	40
UK (2)	3,000	13,000	:	10

(1) 1991.
(2) 1993.

Source: ELCA

Professional associations representing the industries within this chapter

ACE
Architects' Council of Europe
29, rue P.E. Janson
B-1050 Bruxelles
tel: (32) 2 543 11 40
fax: (32) 2 543 11 41
e-mail: ace.cae@skynet.be

CCBE
Council of the Bars and Law Societies of the European Community
40, rue Washington
B-1050 Bruxelles
tel: (32) 2 640 42 74
fax: (32) 2 647 79 41

CEEC
European Committee of Construction Economists
8, avenue Percier
F-75008 Paris
tel: (33) 1 45 63 30 41
fax: (33) 1 42 56 14 52
e-mail: secretariat@ceec.org

CERP
European Public Relations Confederation
1a, rue du Champ de Mars
Boîte 1
B-1050 Bruxelles
tel: (32) 2 511 26 80
fax: (32) 2 511 56 38

CLGE
Council of European Geodetic Surveyors
BEV c/o VA Innsbruck
Bürgerstrasse 34
A-6010 Innsbruck
tel: (43) 512 588 948 60
fax: (43) 512 588 411 61

CoESS
Confédération Européenne des Services de Sécurité
101/109 rue Jean Jaurès
F-92300 Levallois-Perret
tel: (33) 1 42 70 80 20
fax: (33) 1 42 70 63 23

EAAA
European Association of Advertising Agencies
5, rue Saint Quentin
B-1040 Bruxelles
tel: (32) 2 280 16 03
fax: (32) 2 230 09 66
e-mail: info@eaaa.be

ECATRA
European Car and Truck Rental Association
402, avenue de Tervueren
B-1150 Bruxelles
tel: (32) 2 761 66 14
fax: (32) 2 777 05 05

EFCA
European Federation of Engineering Consultancy Associations
3/4/5, avenue des Arts
B-1210 Bruxelles
tel: (32) 2 209 07 70
fax: (32) 2 209 07 71
e-mail: efca@efca.be

ELCA
European Landscape Contractors Association
Postfach 11 69
D-53604 Bad Honnef
tel: (49) 2224 770 720
fax: (49) 2224 770 777
e-mail: info@eu-landscapers.org

EMECA
European Major Exhibition Centres Association
Parc d'Expositions de Paris-Nord Villepinte
BP 60004
F-95970 Roissy-CDG Cedex
tel: (33) 1 48 63 30 94
fax: (33) 1 48 63 31 28
e-mail: emeca@expoparisnord.com

ESOMAR
European Society for Opinion and Marketing Research
J.J. Viottastraat 29
NL-1071 JP Amsterdam
tel: (31) 20 664 21 41
fax: (31) 20 664 29 22
e-mail: email@esomar.nl

ESTA
European Security Transport Association
19, rue Mercelis
B-1050 Bruxelles
tel: (32) 2 758 13 90
fax: (32) 2 759 43 70

FEACO
European Federation of Management Consulting Associations
3/4/5, avenue des Arts
B-1210 Bruxelles
tel: (32) 2 250 06 50
fax: (32) 2 250 06 51
e-mail: feaco@feaco.org

FEDMA
Federation of European Direct Marketing
439, avenue de Tervueren
B-1150 Bruxelles
tel: (32) 2 778 99 20
fax: (32) 2 778 99 24
e-mail: info@fedma.org

FENI
European Federation of Cleaning Industries
27, rue de l'Association
B-1000 Bruxelles
tel: (32) 2 219 47 37
fax: (32) 2 219 45 31
e-mail: efci@skynet.be

Leaseurope
European Federation of Leasing Company Associations
267/9, avenue de Tervueren
B-1150 Bruxelles
tel: (32) 2 778 05 60
fax: (32) 2 778 05 79

UINL/CAUE
Union Internationale du Notariat Latin
Piazza Paolo Ferrari, 8
I-20121 Milano
tel: (39) 02 72 56 71
fax: (39) 02 72 00 84 36

Advertising and direct marketing (NACE Rev. 1 74.4)

Advertising and direct marketing enterprises engage in communication services aimed at promoting ideas, goods and services to the general public, to specific target groups, to individuals and to other businesses. They are covered by Group 74.4 of the NACE Rev. 1 classification. Whilst advertising constitutes a large part of their activities, this section also deals with direct marketing, sponsorship and sales promotion activities.

According to official business statistics from Eurostat, there were just under 120 thousand enterprises[5] in the EU in 1995/96, of which 90 thousand were located in the five largest Member States. Each enterprise employed on average of 3 to 4 persons, except in Ireland where the average was much higher at 12 persons. Personnel costs were in all countries for which data was available above 30 thousand ECU per employee, and as a general rule close to 38 thousand ECU, a relatively high level compared to other economic activities.

5) Excluding Belgium, Greece and Portugal, for which no data was available.

(units) Figure 20.11

Advertising (NACE Rev. 1 74.4)
Density of enterprises per ten thousand inhabitants, 1996

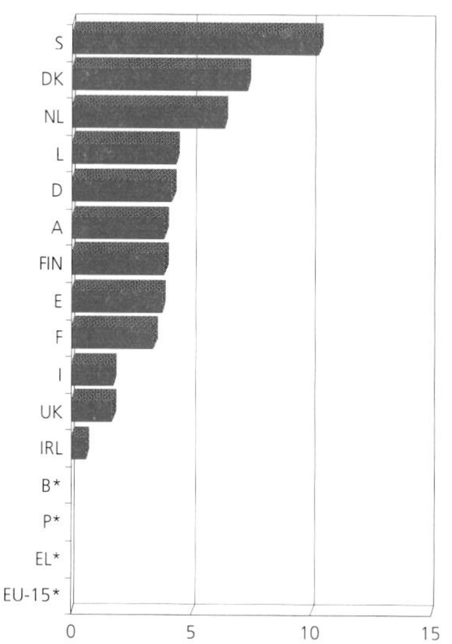

Source: Eurostat (SBS)

(thousand ECU) Figure 20.12

Advertising (NACE Rev. 1 74.4)
Personnel costs/employee, 1996

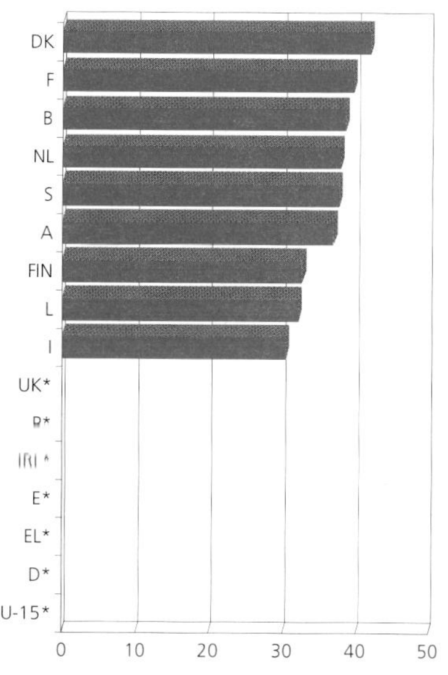

Source: Eurostat (SBS)

(%) Figure 20.13

Advertising (NACE Rev. 1 74.4)
Wage adjusted labour productivity, 1996

Source: Eurostat (SBS)

Advertising is the persuasive process by which users of goods, services or ideas are found through paid-for communications media. Classic media are television, radio, newspapers, magazines, cinema and outdoor panels. The advent of new media, for example on-line services, is not likely to pose a threat to classic advertising. They are increasingly used in addition to and in support of general advertising campaigns, providing new opportunities for direct marketing, sales promotions and niche communications.

FEDMA[6] defines direct marketing as "a part of the commercial communication services sector (...) used by most organisations and companies to sell products at a distance, provide customer care, raise funds, inform customers of offers, etc. It is supported by a variety of service industries (direct marketing agencies, call centres, teleshopping broadcasters, fulfilment and delivery mechanisms, printers and letter shops, and so on)". Although direct marketing is traditionally considered in terms of direct mail and unaddressed mail, other techniques are growing rapidly, such as direct response in the printed press, teleshopping, telemarketing, Internet and other on-line services.

One of the main trends witnessed in the 1990s has been the increasing fragmentation of the mass media as a consequence of the liberalisation of broadcasting, its progressive conversion to digital technologies and the plummeting costs of publishing systems with the emergence of "desktop publishing". Mass media has created multiple choices for advertising with fragmented audiences, which has in turn fragmented advertising expenditures. The number of specialised publications or television channels is expanding, and each one is targeted at a very specific group of persons.

6) Federation of European Direct Marketing.

Figure 20.14 (ECU per inhabitant)

Advertising expenditure per capita, 1998

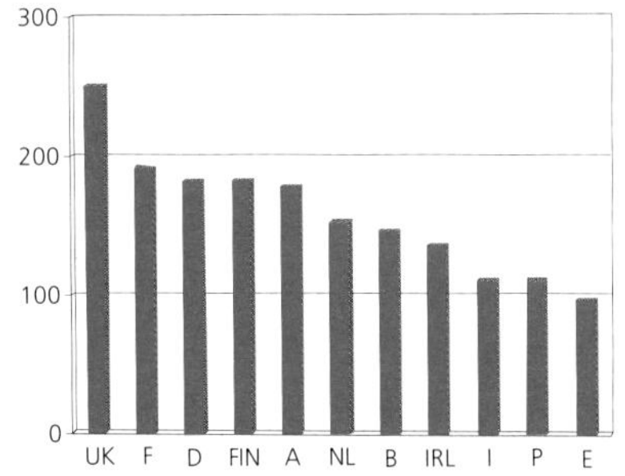

Source: EGTA

In total, global advertising expenditure continued to follow a rising trend and was estimated by EGTA[7] to have increased by almost 10% in Europe during 1998 to more than 64 billion ECU. Amongst EU countries, the United Kingdom displayed the highest advertising expenditure per capita at 250 ECU per inhabitant in 1998, ahead of France with 192 ECU per capita, as shown in figure 20.14. This contrasted with Spain where expenditure did not reach half that amount, at 97 ECU per inhabitant.

Printed press is still the dominant medium of advertising. It represented approximately 48% of global advertising expenditure in 1998 (see figure 20.15), almost 10 percentage points above television. The share of television was however highly variable from one country to another. It ranged from under one quarter of advertising expenditure in Austria and Finland to about 60% in Italy and Portugal in 1998. Over the long-term, there has been a clear shift in advertising budgets towards television at the expense of printed press. The association of European Advertising Agencies (EAAA) estimate that the share of television progressed from 22% in 1985 to 32% some 10 years later, whilst printed media saw its share fall from 70% to 59% over the same period. The deregulation of television, a loosening grip on advertising monopolies by government-run television and a proliferation of new broadcasting services in response to the more liberal climate have largely fuelled these trends. By means of comparison, the market share of television in advertising was equal to 31% in 1980 in the USA, and 37% in Japan in the mid-1980s.

7) EGTA is the European Grouping of Television Advertisers. Figures cover the following European countries, EU-15 (except DK, EL, L, S), as well as BG, HR, CZ, EE, HU, NO, PL, RO, SI, CH.

Figure 20.15 (billion ECU)

Evolution of advertisement expenditure in Europe by medium (1)

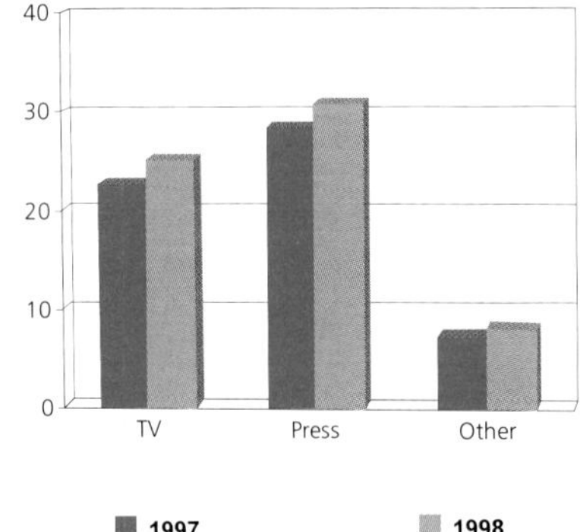

(1) Countries covered are EU-15 (except DK, EL, L, S), BG, HR, CZ, EE, HU, NO, PL, RO, SI, CH.

Source: EGTA

Figure 20.16 (%)

Share of TV in total advertising expenditure, 1998

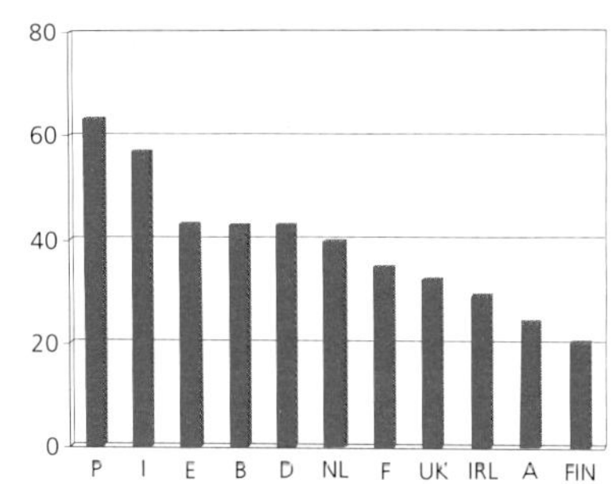

Source: EGTA

As regards direct marketing, FEDMA estimate that the largest share of expenditure was dedicated to direct mail[8]. Direct mail represented almost 60% of total expenditure on direct marketing tools in 1996, ahead of direct response advertising (30%). This pattern was expected to change, as direct marketing is increasingly likely to rely on telecommunications rather than post. Already a large share of orders or contacts for direct marketing are made by phone or fax, and FEDMA expects the World-Wide-Web and other on-line services to account for an increasing share of direct marketing contacts.

8) A great deal of additional statistical information on direct marketing is available from FEDMA in the publication, "Direct Marketing in Europe: an examination of the statistics", May 1998.

In terms of volume, Belgium was in 1995/96 the country with the largest number of items sent per capita, with no fewer than 86 addressed mails for each inhabitant. In only two other countries did inhabitants receive more than 80 mails during a year: Germany (81) and the Netherlands (82). In contrast, the Portuguese received a mere 14 direct marketing mails, 7 fewer than the Irish (see figure 20.17).

The main users of direct marketing have been mail-order traders, publishers, specialised clubs (books, records, etc.) and business-to-business relations. However, as database systems become more sophisticated, they are increasingly being used for activities such as fund-raising or membership generating for charities and political parties, as well as customer care (including inquiries, information and after-sales services).

Figure 20.17 (items per inhabitant)

Volume of direct marketing addressed mail per capita, 1996

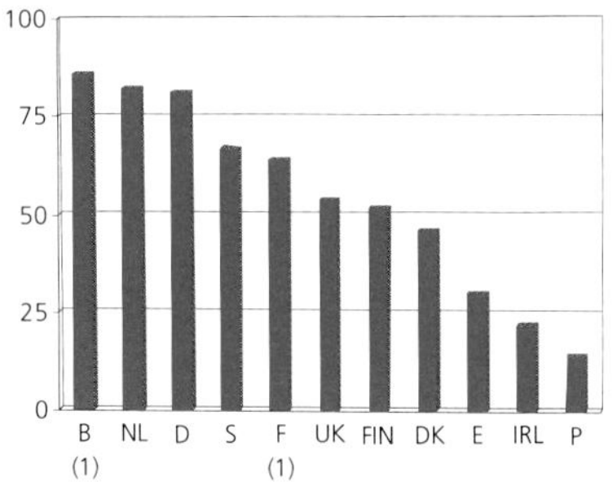

(1) 1995.

Source: PDMS in FEDMA

Temporary work services (NACE Rev. 1 74.5)

Temporary work services are only a part of the services of labour recruitment and provision of personnel covered by NACE Rev. 1 Group 74.5. The activity also includes personnel search and selection (formulation of job descriptions, screening and testing of applicants, investigation of references, etc.), head-hunting and placement of executives and other labour-contracting activities, excluding activities of farm labour contractors, of personal theatrical or artistic agents and of cinema, television and other theatrical casting activities.

(units) — Figure 20.18

Labour recruitment and provision of personnel (NACE Rev. 1 74.5)

Density of enterprises per ten thousand inhabitants, 1996

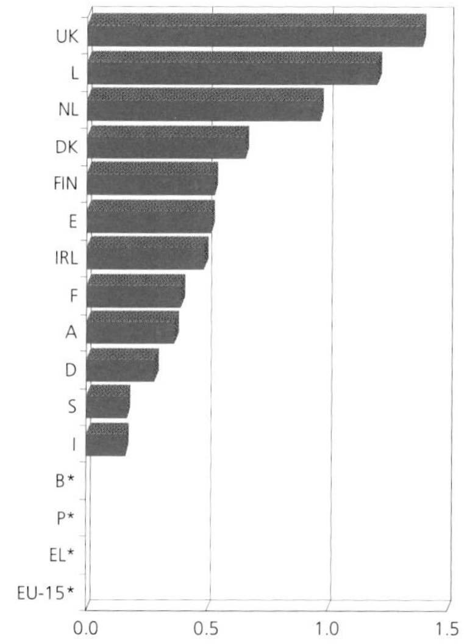

Source: Eurostat (SBS)

Official business statistics from Eurostat showed there were more than 18.5 thousand enterprises active in this sector in the mid-1990s in the EU, generating turnover of almost 33 billion ECU (excluding Greece and Portugal in both cases). The United Kingdom recorded the largest number of enterprises, almost 8.2 thousand, compared to just over 2 thousand in Germany, Spain and France, and under one thousand in Italy. The Netherlands clearly stands out from the other smaller Member States with a much higher number of enterprises, as no fewer than 1.5 thousand enterprises were active in the sector.

(thousand ECU) — Figure 20.19

Labour recruitment and provision of personnel (NACE Rev. 1 74.5)

Personnel costs/employee, 1996

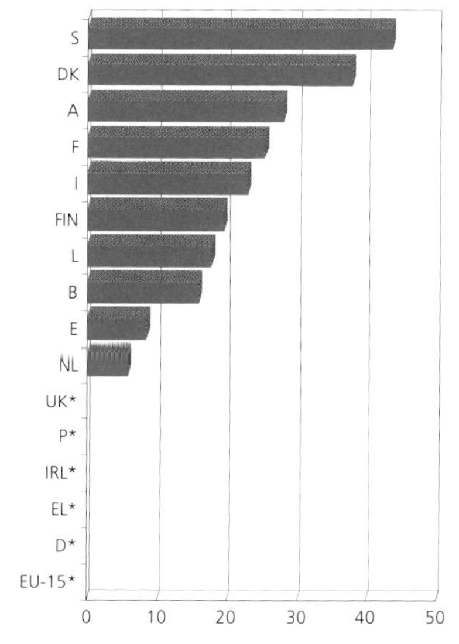

Source: Eurostat (SBS)

(%) — Figure 20.20

Labour recruitment and provision of personnel (NACE Rev. 1 74.5)

Wage adjusted labour productivity, 1996

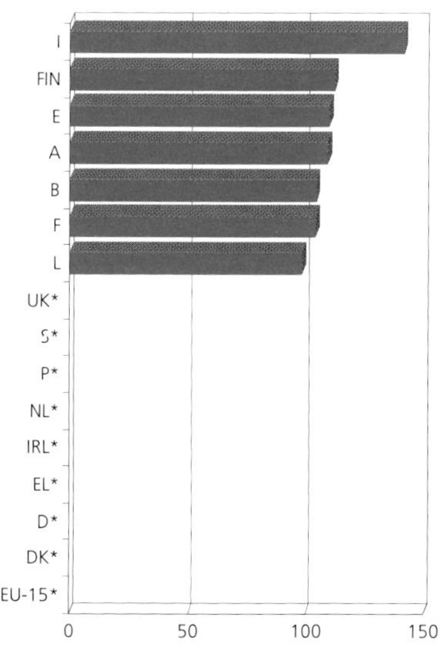

Source: Eurostat (SBS)

The following analysis will concentrate on the specific activities of temporary work, for which data is available from the International Confederation of Temporary Work Business (CIETT). Temporary work businesses supply workers to their clients for a wide range of short-term, specialised requirements. For example, to meet a sudden demand for extra production or to meet a fixed term contract demanding unusual skills. The workers receive their salary from the temporary work business, but their work-orders on assignments from the client. Temporary work businesses bear the cost of recruitment, selection, payrolling, statutory social security insurance, etc.

CIETT estimate that there were approximately 10.5 thousand temporary work businesses in the EU in 1996 (excluding Greece, Italy and Finland) that operated a network of over 18 thousand branch offices. They generated as a whole turnover of 35 billion ECU and it is estimated that about 1.8 million persons carry out temporary work on any given day. According to CIETT, temporary work accounted for about 1.5% of total employment.

Within Europe, France, Belgium, and especially the Netherlands and the United Kingdom were the largest users of temporary workers. In these latter two countries temporary work accounted for more than 3.5% of total employment in 1996, that is an average of 220 thousand and 880 thousand persons a day respectively. In the USA, where labour laws are generally less strict than in European countries, there is also evidence of a high recourse to temporary work businesses, that accounted for 2% of total employment. This corresponds to about 2.3 million persons working daily, and contrasts with Japan where only 320 thousand persons, less than 1% of total, were employed through a temporary work enterprise.

Table 20.10

Main indicators of temporary work, 1996

	Number of enterprises	Number of branches	Turnover (million ECU)	Daily temporary work employment	Share of total employment (%)
B (2)	91	407	1,462	44,000	1.1
DK	100	16	:	2,000	0.1
D (2)	2,601	618	4,005	177,000	0.5
E (1)	125	450	443	60,000	0.5
F	850	4,000	9,289	350,000	1.7
IRL (2)	260	64	133	3,300	0.2
L	31	34	54	2,200	1.1
NL	575	2,814	4,343	225,000	3.6
A	593	700	199	15,000	0.4
P	210	300	:	:	:
S (1) (2)	18	33	109	7,000	0.2
UK	5,000	9,000	14,511	880,000	3.4
EU-15	10,454	18,436	:	:	1.4
USA	6,000	15,000	38,673	2,310,000	1.9
Japan (1) (2)	264	664	8,452	320,000	0.5

(1) For the number of enterprises: members of national associations only.
(2) For the number of branches: members of national associations only.

Source: CIETT

Temporary work has rapidly developed over the last twenty years. A series of factors underlie this growth. The most prominent has been the increasing demand for flexibility in the labour market, both from workers and from enterprises. For workers, temporary work businesses may satisfy particular individual needs and preferences. For example, the ageing of the European workforce and the increase of female activity rates are both often associated with a greater desire for more flexible and temporary working arrangements. For enterprises, temporary work allows for a greater flexibility in organisation and operation. It can also help enterprises to face unexpected variations in demand or temporary absence of regular staff.

In addition, temporary work may contribute to a more flexible labour market, as a growing number of jobless workers resort to temporary work businesses to find a temporary occupation with the expectation of finding permanent positions at a later stage. Conversely, companies may treat temporary work contracts as trial contracts before offering a permanent position to workers who have worked for them through a temporary work business. CIETT estimate that on average well over one third of temporary workers find permanent jobs as a result of temporary contracts.

Regulation may also be a factor influencing demand, and it can be quite different according to the country studied. A number of restrictions and requirements are nevertheless common to most Member States, such as for example those concerning the requirements for the contract between the user and the temporary work business, the registration and/or licensing of temporary work businesses, the conditions under which temporary work is allowed, the duration of contracts (varying from 3 to 24 months or no restriction) or the requirements for wage levels and social security conditions.

Figure 20.21 (% of assignments)

Temporary work businesses' clients, 1996

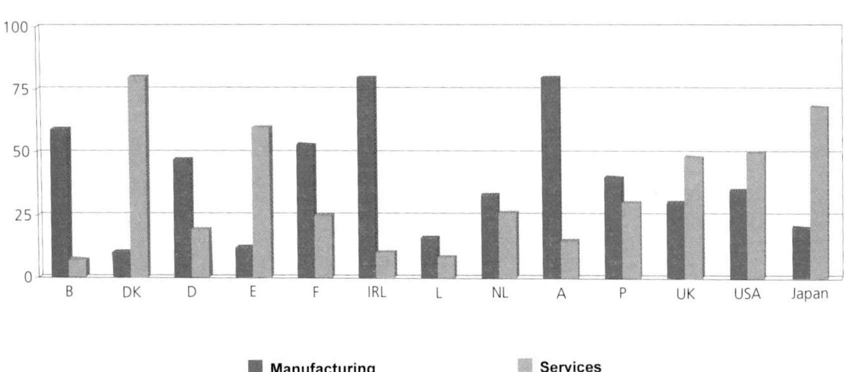

Source: CIETT

Security services (NACE Rev. 1 74.6)
The definition of this activity according to the NACE Rev. 1 classification includes investigation activities, surveillance and protective activities, transport of valuables, bodyguard activities, guard and watchman activities for apartment buildings, offices, factories, etc., consultancy in the field of security, training of dogs for security reasons. It however excludes the installation of alarm systems.

(units) Figure 20.22

Investigation and security activities (NACE Rev. 1 74.6) Density of enterprises per ten thousand inhabitants, 1998

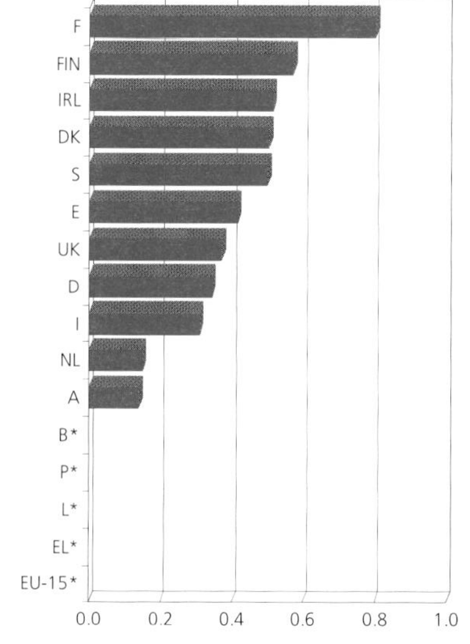

Source: Eurostat (SBS)

As with many other business services activities, availability of official statistics is patchy and gives only a partial picture of investigation and security activities. Amongst the large Member States for which data was available, the profession numbered a total of 45 thousand persons employed in Italy, 73 thousand in Spain and over 92 thousand in France in the mid-1990s. Total turnover can be estimated at around 12.5 billion ECU for the whole EU (excluding Greece, Luxembourg and Portugal, for which data is not available).

(thousand ECU) Figure 20.23

Investigation and security activities (NACE Rev. 1 74.6) Personnel costs/employee, 1996

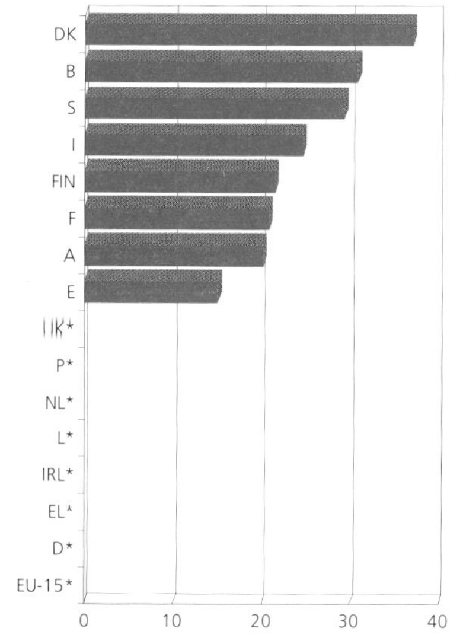

Source: Eurostat (SBS)

(%) Figure 20.24

Investigation and security activities (NACE Rev. 1 74.6) Wage adjusted labour productivity, 1996

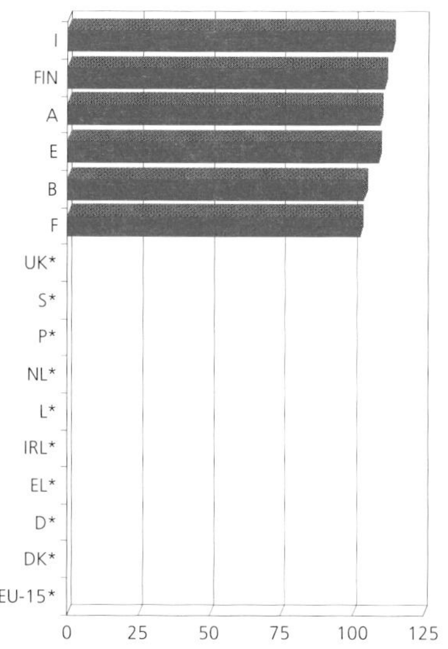

Source: Eurostat (SBS)

The real emergence of security service activities can be identified after the Second World War owing to a number of factors, such as the fast growth in living standards of the population and the increased awareness of entrepreneurs of the necessity to protect their own belongings, instead of considering this the responsibility of the police. In addition, the sector has greatly benefited from the trends mentioned in the introduction, whereby companies increasingly sub-contracted, or "outsourced", peripheral activities to specialised independent service providers (specifically for security services there is in many countries some form of co-operation with public authorities). A common example is the security check of passengers in many international airports, where it is private security guards that screen passengers under the supervision of the regular police force.

As regards manned guarding services, the European Confederation of Security Services (CoESS) estimate that the EU numbers some 420 thousand guards employed by over 7 thousand companies, that is an average of 60 employees per enterprise. Many of these enterprises are operating in small local areas, and many of them are self-employed persons. Looking at the size of large private security companies, which often work on an international scale, shows that in most countries 80% of national turnover is achieved by 20% of the companies.

Turning to the transportation of valuables, detailed statistics on the sector are available from the European Security Transport Association (ESTA). According to ESTA, there were 422 enterprises active in the sector in the EU in 1998, a small number indicating a relatively high concentration within the market. It is interesting to note that more than three-quarters of these companies were located in Italy (220) and Germany (130).

The activities of armoured transportation include diverse activities such as coin processing, cash and notes processing, cheque encoding or automatic teller machine (ATM) servicing. Cash transport activities employed almost 32 thousand employees in 1998, and could count on an 11 thousand-strong fleet of armoured vehicles. Average enterprise size was highest in the United Kingdom, where enterprises numbered approximately 400 vehicles and one thousand employees each. The average fleet of vehicles per enterprise exceeded 100 units in only three other countries: Portugal (100), the Netherlands (130) and Spain (240). This contrasts with Italy, Luxembourg and Germany where the typical cash transport company numbered fewer than 20 vehicles and 40 employees. As a general rule there were

Table 20.11

Main indicators of security transport services in Europe, 1998

	Number of enterprises	Number of vehicles	Number of cash processing centres	Number of employees in cash trans-portation	Number of employees in cash processing centres	Turnover (million ECU)	Turnover from cash processing (million ECU)
B	4	285	5	1,200	200	70.6	8.6
DK	2	56	7	200	:	47.0	23.5
D	130	2,000	150	5,000	300	306.8	92.0
EL	5	150	10	320	50	6.6	0.6
E	5	1,200	60	2,200	1,800	132.2	52.9
F	19	1,200	150	5,300	2,200	365.9	117.4
IRL	3	140	4	400	:	25.4	:
I	220	1,600	85	4,500	820	284.0	123.9
L	3	45	2	100	20	4.2	0.5
NL	2	260	3	1,150	140	61.4	7.7
A	5	200	8	800	:	19.3	4.7
P	2	200	11	493	320	27.8	6.0
FIN	3	80	20	400	350	30.3	13.5
S	10	210	10	500	:	41.2	4.2
UK	9	3,540	43	9,000	1,600	562.5	56.5
EU-15	422	11,166	568	31,563	10,500	1,985.2	511.5
NO	8	30	5	80	50	19.8	2.9
CH	8	100	10	250	100	13.6	3.6
CZ	12	210	1	3,500	50	15.0	2.0
EE	2	33	2	168	17	2.0	0.6
HU	20	300	5	1,500	300	23.9	7.9
PL	50	600	5	7,000	:	12.4	0.6
SK	25	61	-	150	-	5.4	:

Source: ESTA

between 2 and 4 employees per vehicle across the EU. The specific activity of cash processing numbered 568 centres across the EU in 1998, employing a total of 10.5 thousand employees and recording turnover of 511 million ECU.

The total market for cash transport was estimated at 3.8 billion ECU in the EU in 1998. Of this amount, about 2 billion ECU had been outsourced to independent transport companies, which corresponds to a market penetration ratio of about 52%. Figure 20.26 illustrates the share of outsourcing in security transport activities. It shows that in all countries (except the United Kingdom) independent companies made up more than half the total market, ranging from 50% in Germany to 92% in Spain.

One of the characteristics of security transport service enterprises is the very strict regulatory environment in which they operate in some countries of the European Union. In the case of manned guarding, regulations concern mainly compulsory insurance, qualification and training required, equipment (appearance of uniform, weapons, identification and the use of dogs). In addition, the transportation of valuables is submitted to specific regulations regarding the vehicles, the weapons and the employees' personal protection, as well as a number of detailed requirements on the form of providing such services.

The introduction of the euro in 2002 will greatly affect the transportation of valuables over the next few years, with unprecedented changes to the present flux of bank notes across Europe. It seems essential to ensure that cross-border provision of services in this field will not be hindered by conflicting national regulations. Another change with which the sector will be increasingly confronted is the growing relevance of home banking, plastic money and electronic purse systems. A certain reduction in monetary circulation is already noticeable.

Figure 20.25

Average size of cash transport companies in Europe, 1998

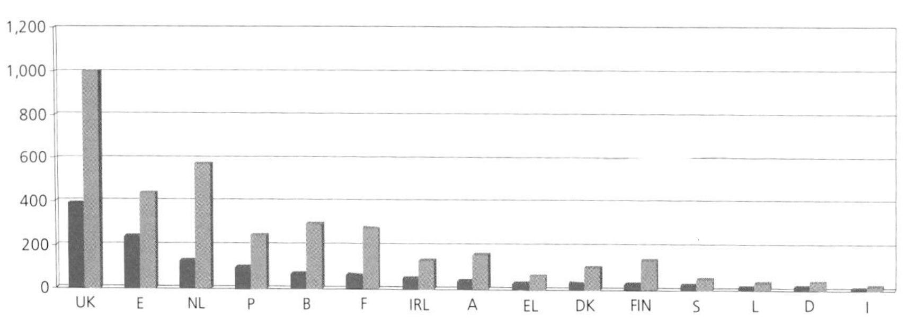

Source: ESTA

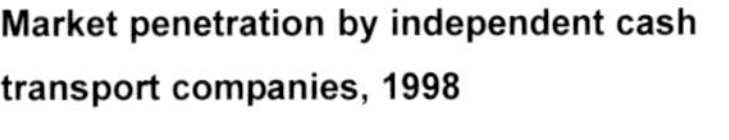

Figure 20.26 (% share of total market value)

Market penetration by independent cash transport companies, 1998

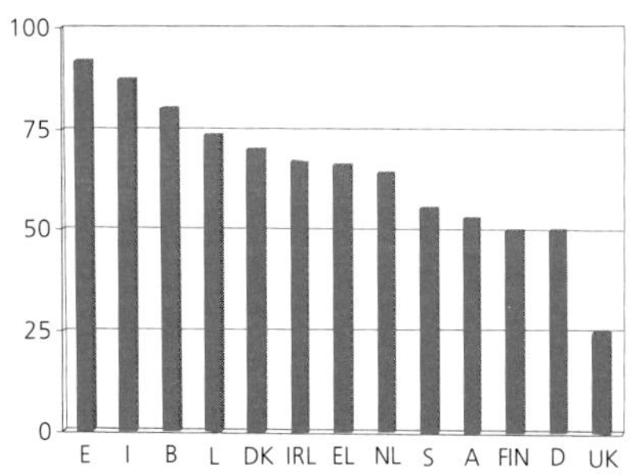

Source: ESTA

Industrial cleaning services (NACE Rev. 1 74.7)

Industrial cleaning services as defined by official business statistics include the interior cleaning of buildings of all types, including offices, hospitals, factories or multi-unit residential buildings, cleaning of public means of transport, window cleaning, chimney cleaning, but also disinfecting and exterminating activities for buildings, ships, trains, etc. It however excludes agricultural pest control, or steam-cleaning, sand blasting and similar activities for building exteriors.

(units) Figure 20.27

Industrial cleaning (NACE Rev. 1 74.7) Density of enterprises per ten thousand inhabitants, 1996

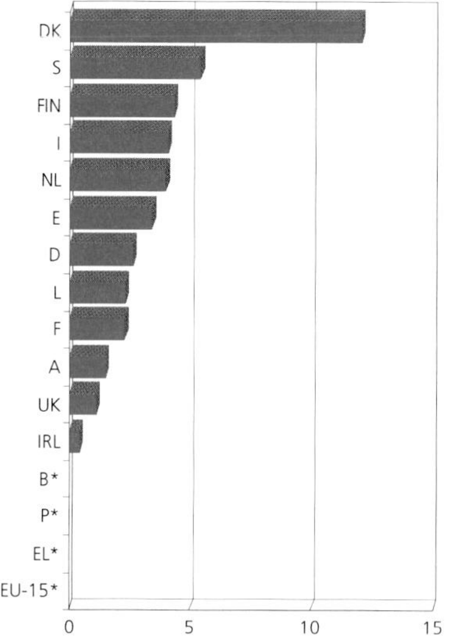

Source: Eurostat (SBS)

According to the European Federation of Cleaning Industries (EFCI/FENI) there were almost 54 thousand companies active in the sector in 1997 in Europe[9], generating turnover exceeding 29 billion ECU and employing more than 2.4 million persons. It is hence a sizeable sector that has been amongst the main beneficiaries of the outsourcing trend mentioned in the introduction to this chapter, that has led most companies to sub-contract peripheral activities to specialised service providers. In-house cleaning staff have increasingly been replaced by employees from industrial cleaning enterprises. FENI estimate that cleaning contractors made up around 58% of the total European market in 1997.

9) All figures from FENI cover EU-15 countries excluding Greece, Ireland and Austria. A great deal of additional statistical information is available from FENI in the publication, "The Cleaning Industry in Europe", April 1999.

(thousand ECU) Figure 20.28

Industrial cleaning (NACE Rev. 1 74.7) Personnel costs/employee, 1996

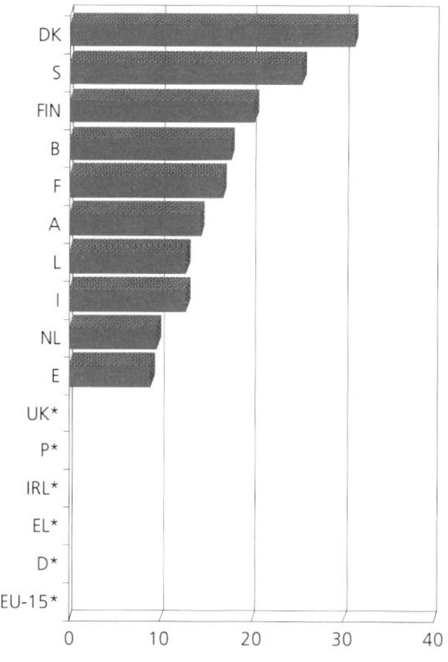

Source: Eurostat (SBS)

(%) Figure 20.29

Industrial cleaning (NACE Rev. 1 74.7) Wage adjusted labour productivity, 1996

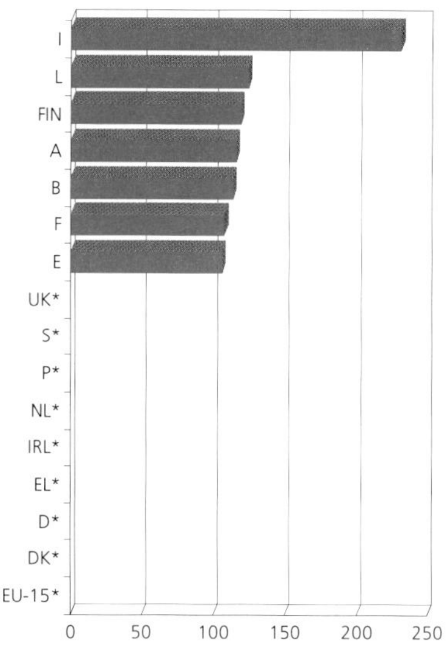

Source: Eurostat (SBS)

Office cleaning is by far the largest market segment for cleaning companies as it accounts for more than half their turnover. Industry (10.6%), including factories, nuclear power stations and agri-food industries, is the second largest single segment ahead of hospitals (7.6%) (see figure 20.31). There are a growing number of auxiliary services being incorporated into the services offered by cleaning enterprises. This is usually the result of demand from clients for a full "facility management", reducing the number of sub-contractors. These services include building and green space maintenance, rubbish collection, security or catering.

(%) Figure 20.30

Penetration rate of cleaning contractors, 1997

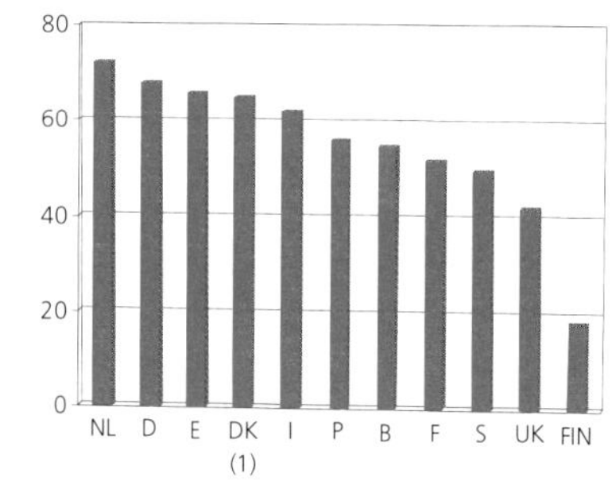

(1) 1995.

Source: FENI

(share of turnover) Figure 20.31

Main market segments of industrial cleaning, 1997

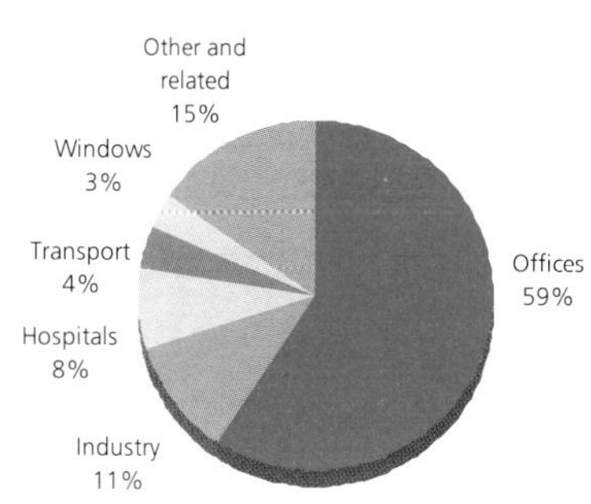

Source: FENI

Table 20.12

Main characteristics of employment in industrial cleaning, 1997

	Share of part-time employees (%)	Total labour costs per hour (ECU)	Average daily working time (hours)
B	69	15.4	4.4
DK	60	14.2	4.5
D	80	14.6	4.0
E	70	8.7	4.0
F	70	16.7	5.0
I	80	8.0	4.0
L	90	13.1	5.0
NL	82	9.8	4.0
P	78	3.0	6.0
FIN	60	8.4	4.6
S	60	11.3	:
UK	74	5.7	2.7

Source: FENI

FENI estimate that although demand for support services is currently limited to a few large clients, competition is increasingly focusing on quality, depth and range of service, away from price, bringing middle-sized companies to anticipate this demand, often by co-operating or merging with other companies.

A very large number of companies active in cleaning services are small in size. According to FENI data, more than half of the enterprises in the sector number fewer than 5 employees, and 85% fewer than one hundred employees. Although a great deal of small businesses die before reaching their first anniversary, this low-skill sector remains attractive to new entrepreneurs. Barriers to entry are negligible and most countries have no regulatory restrictions on opening a cleaning business.

Employment in cleaning services displays some particular characteristics, such as a high feminine presence. Indeed, women represented in 1997 no fewer than 78% of the workforce in Europe, one of the highest shares recorded in the whole economy. Some 91% of employees were blue-collar workers, of which 70% were women. A large number of employees, about a fifth, were migrant workers[10], ranging from just 1% in the United Kingdom, up to 48% in Belgium. Another striking characteristic of cleaning industry was the prevalence of part-time work, concerning over three-quarters of employees, with an average working time of just 4.4 hours a day. Only 15% of these hours were performed during normal working hours, with some 62% carried out during the evening or at night.

Labour costs were relatively low in the cleaning industry compared to other service activities, although they varied considerably across the EU. The total hourly cost of an employee ranged in 1997 from 3 ECU in Portugal to more than five times that amount in Belgium (15.4 ECU) and France (16.6 ECU).

10) Either from other EU countries or from third countries.

Table 20.13

Main indicators of industrial cleaning, 1997

	Number of enterprises	Number of employees	Turnover (million ECU) (3)
B	1,364	49,876	768
DK (1)	4,100	27,000	666
D (2)	5,837	705,000	5,919
E	6,706	240,000	2,617
F	11,206	286,878	4,914
I	8,000	400,000	5,207
L	65	3,300	61
NL	3,616	142,506	1,823
P	420	28,980	143
FIN	2,000	25,000	436
S	4,000	110,000	:
UK	6,670	402,300	2,679

(1) 1995 for number of enterprises and turnover.
(2) 1995 for turnover.
(3) 1996.

Source: FENI

Vehicle rental (NACE Rev. 1 71.1)

In the frame of official business statistics, car rental activities are defined as the "renting and operational leasing of self-drive private cars and light vans up to 3.5 tonnes" and are covered in Group 71.1 of the NACE Rev. 1 activity classification.

(units) Figure 20.32

Renting of automobiles (NACE Rev. 1 71.1) Density of enterprises per ten thousand inhabitants, 1996

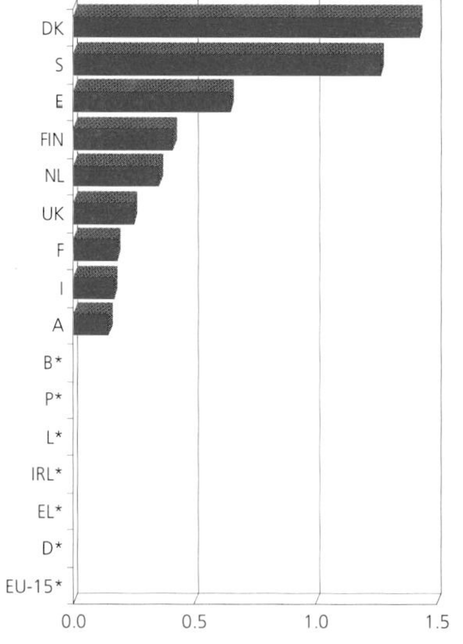

Source: Eurostat (SBS)

According to official statistics from Eurostat, there were close to 21 thousand enterprises active in this sector in 1995/96 (excluding Belgium, Italy and Portugal for which no data was available). Turnover per enterprise was highly variable, ranging from under 500 thousand ECU in Denmark and Finland to 3 million ECU or more in Austria and the United Kingdom. The variability of the average size of enterprises was reflected in employment figures, as the smallest enterprises were found in Denmark and Finland with an average number of persons employed lower than 2. In contrast, Irish and Austrian enterprises numbered on average more than 9 persons employed.

The car rental industry is comprised of two principal markets: general use and insurance replacement. In addition to vehicle rental revenue, a significant share of revenue is derived from auxiliary activities such as the sale of insurance or refuelling services.

As regards general use, customers of car rental companies include business travellers and leisure travellers, both characterised by different rental patterns. Business travellers tend to utilise mid-week rentals of shorter duration, whilst leisure travellers usually use more weekend rentals and tend to rent cars for longer periods. Rental pricing of the same vehicle may also greatly depend on the type of client. Business travellers, that include large commercial accounts, small business accounts and government authorities, may have contractual agreements with rental companies giving their employees access to discounted prices. Tourists may also receive discounts through tour operators or in combination with their aeroplane ticket or hotel reservation.

In the insurance replacement market, clients are primarily insurance companies and automobile dealers that provide cars to their customers whose vehicles are damaged or stolen or are being repaired. Compared with the general use market, the insurance replacement market is characterised by longer rental periods, lower daily rates and the utilisation of older and less expensive vehicles.

There is in addition a specific market for light vans, aimed at both the consumer and the business market. In the first case it primarily serves individuals who rent vans to move household goods. In the second, it serves a wide range of businesses that rent light- to medium-duty vans for a variety of commercial applications.

The vehicle rental industry is characterised by intense price and service competition. The largest companies active in the sector are big multinationals, many of whom have a worldwide presence. Market leaders include Hertz, Avis, Budget or Europcar. In addition, a very large number of smaller enterprises are active on a national or regional level.

(%) Figure 20.33

Renting without operator (NACE Rev. 1 71)
Share of part-time and temporary work contracts in total number of persons employed, 1997

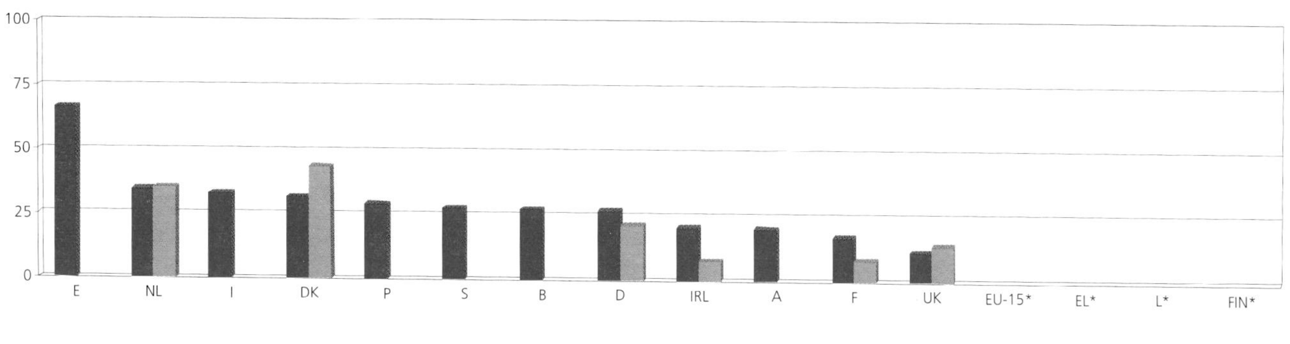

Source: Eurostat (LFS)

Figure 20.34 (thousand ECU)

Renting of automobiles (NACE Rev. 1 71.1)
Personnel costs/employee, 1996

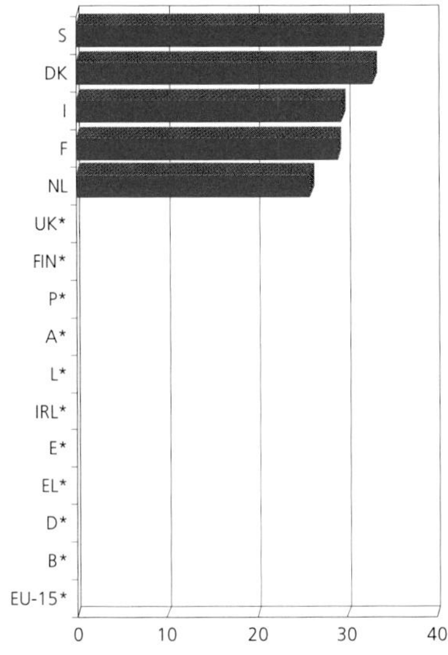

Source: Eurostat (SBS)

Car rental companies are important clients of car manufacturers. It is hence not surprising to see strong links that have been tied between the two sectors. For example, Hertz is a majority-owned subsidiary of the automobile manufacturer Ford since 1987 and Europcar numbers Volkswagen amongst its largest shareholders. There have however been significant changes in the ownership of car rental companies in the second half of the nineties. General Motors sold its 25% stake in Avis in 1996; in 1997, Ford sold approximately 20% of its equity in Hertz in an initial public offering, and Chrysler sold Dollar and Thrifty. Car rental companies continue however to be parties to supply and repurchase agreements with car manufacturers. Under such programmes, a car rental company agrees to purchase a specified minimum number of new vehicles at a specified price, and the manufacturer agrees to repurchase those vehicles from the car rental company at a future date (typically, six to nine months after the purchase). These programmes limit a car rental company's residual risk with respect to its fleet and enable the company to determine a substantial portion of its depreciation expense in advance.

Recent statistics on the vehicle rental fleet in Europe were unfortunately not available at the time of writing, the latest estimates from the European Car and Truck Rental Association (ECATRA) being for the mid-1990s (however, they give some indication on the importance of the sector). The total turnover of the EU market for car rental was estimated at just under 20 billion ECU, including both short-term rentals (few days) and long-term rentals (contract hire and leasing). The largest car rental markets were found in Germany, France and the United Kingdom. Together these countries had a total fleet of 420 thousand cars for short-term rentals. The United Kingdom had the largest fleet with 155 thousand vehicles, followed by France (145 thousand) and Germany (120 thousand). For comparison, the total number of rental vehicles in service in the USA has been estimated at 1.6 million in 1998. In the market for long-term car rental, Germany was by far the largest market with a total number of vehicles consisting of 2.2 million cars and an estimated 250 thousand light vans. The United Kingdom ranked second with nearly 1.2 million passenger cars and 85 thousand light vans.

Table 20.14 (units)

Fleet of vehicles for short-term renting, 1994

	Cars	Light vans
B	14,000	1,700
DK	6,000	6,000
D	120,000	:
EL	30,000	:
E	60,000	3,000
F	145,000	45,000
IRL	15,500	:
I	43,000	3,050
L	1,305	115
NL	25,000	7,350
A	2,383	400
P	29,340	5,907
FIN	:	:
S	19,000	2,500
UK	154,600	50,300

Source: ECATRA

Table 20.15 (units)

Fleet of vehicles for long-term renting, 1994

	Cars	Light vans
B	130,000	:
DK	:	:
D	2,200,000	:
EL	10,000	:
E	20,000	:
F	416,000	74,000
IRL	:	:
I	122,000	3,300
L	:	:
NL	250,000	54,000
A	:	:
P	113,937	16,743
FIN	:	:
S	:	:
UK	1,196,880	84,916

Source: ECATRA

Leasing (part of NACE Rev. 1 71)

According to the NACE Rev. 1 classification, leasing falls under Division 71 which covers renting services of machinery and equipment without operator, and services of personal goods and household goods. The leasing of real estate is excluded and figures only refer to the leasing of movables, or so-called equipment leasing. More specifically, the following types of equipment leasing will be dealt with: leasing of automobiles without drivers (part of Group 71.1), leasing of other transport equipment including land transport, water transport and air transport (without permanent staff; part of Group 71.2), leasing of other machinery and equipment including agricultural machinery, construction and civil engineering machinery and equipment, office machinery and equipment, and leasing of other machinery and equipment (without permanent staff; part of Group 71.3).

The definition of leasing is not exactly the same in the different Member States. Comparisons across Member States, therefore, have to be interpreted cautiously. Broadly speaking, leasing refers to the transfer of a good from the lessor (the owner) to the lessee, who can make use of the good upon regular payments. While leasing concerns an operation of medium or long-term, renting refers primarily to the transfer of a good in the short-term (hours, days, etc.) between two persons on payment of a fee. Two major categories of leasing contracts are distinguished: the financial lease and the operational lease. A financial lease refers to a contract with full pay out (full amortisation). It is in principle irrevocable and does not provide for maintenance and service (the legal ownership stays with the lessor, but the economic ownership shifts to the lessee). Furthermore, in several Member States such as the United Kingdom, the Netherlands, Belgium, Germany, France and Spain the financial lease includes a purchase option for the lessee at the expiration date.

An operational lease refers to a contract of partial amortisation: the lessee only uses the capital equipment for a portion of its normal service life, and there are normally one or more additional users. The leasing rates and payments are calculated at a fraction of the purchase value. Furthermore, an operational lease can in principle be cancelled. This form of leasing ordinarily calls for the lessor to maintain and service the leased equipment, and the costs of this maintenance are either built into the lease payments or contracted for separately. The legal and economic ownership stay with the lessor.

According to Leaseurope figures, turnover reached over 92.6 billion ECU in 1997, up 10% from 83.9 billion ECU the year before. European leasing activities are mainly concentrated in Germany and the United Kingdom. Together they accounted for 60% of total EU turnover in 1997, whilst France and Italy accounted for 10% each. The strongest growth in 1997 was recorded in Greece, where turnover progressed by 37%. Several other countries witnessed strong growth rates, such as Portugal and the United Kingdom (over 20%), Denmark, the Netherlands and Sweden (over 15%). France, in contrast, witnessed a stable market at 10 billion ECU, whilst in Ireland turnover fell 6% to under 1.2 billion ECU.

(million ECU) — Table 20.16

Equipment leased in the EU, 1997

B	1,973
DK	1,022
D	24,693
EL	385
E	4,219
F	9,991
IRL	1,168
I	9,368
L	172
NL	3,058
A	2,212
P	1,583
FIN	389
S	2,805
UK	29,614
EU-15	92,652

Source: Leaseurope

jumped to 47 billion ECU in 1997 from 34 billion ECU in 1995. In contrast, turnover from manufacturing progressed only 3% a year over the same period, to 29 billion ECU up from 27.2 billion ECU. Looking at the market shares for the individual countries it appears that in all EU Member States, except for Austria, Portugal and Ireland, the services sector is the largest. In the first two countries, manufacturing industry is the largest customer of leasing equipment, whilst in Ireland it is the consumer market (39%).

(share of turnover) — Figure 20.35

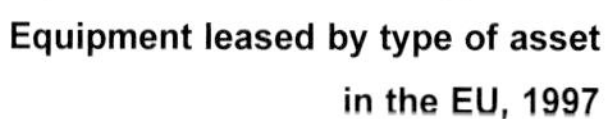

Equipment leased by type of asset in the EU, 1997

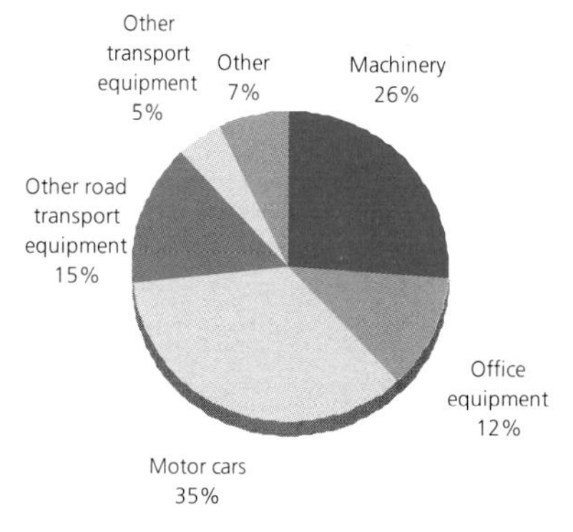

Source: Leaseurope

The European leasing market has gradually undergone significant changes in terms of suppliers, customers and products. Leasing operations used to concentrate on office equipment, but have extended during the 1990s to all kinds of goods, ranging from machines and industrial equipment to road transport vehicles, ships and aircrafts.

The decreasing role of office equipment is reflected in a lower share of turnover of leasing machinery. In 1997, only 12% of total turnover could be attributed to office equipment against 15% in 1992. Motor vehicles remain the largest market segment constituting about 36% of total turnover. The shares of the other segments remained fairly stable with machinery accounting for 25% of the leasing market, up two percentage points.

Service sector customers are the largest customer group for the leasing of products, some 56% in value terms in 1997, against 31% for manufacturing enterprises. Public sector and private households each accounted for about 5% of turnover. In absolute terms, turnover from the service sector

Looking at the length of contracts, it appears that about three-quarters of the contracts were concluded for a period of 2 to 5 years. About 12% had a duration of up to and including 2 years. Only 7% of the contracts were for a period longer than 10 years, and these were concentrated in just a few Member States: the United Kingdom where they accounted for no less than 16% of the total, Sweden (11%), Denmark (9%), Germany (6%) and France (2%). In all other countries such long-duration contracts were either marginal or non-existent.

Originally, leasing companies were mainly manufacturer-owned trying to stimulate their sales by offering additional services for customers. A second family of leasing companies was formed by financial institutions, which in several Member States overtook the manufacturers because of their financial expertise. The European market continues to be dominated by bank-owned lessors. But there is some indication that this will change, as manufacturer-owned lessors are increasing their market shares again.

Franchising

Franchising is a strategy of business development that has remarkable success around the world. Franchising is a means of achieving adaptation to local conditions without losing the benefits of global concerns, ideas and scales. According to the basic definition contained in the Code of Ethics of the European Franchise Federation (EFF), franchising is a system of marketing goods and/or services and/or technology, which is based upon a close and ongoing collaboration between legally and financially separate and independent undertakings, the franchisor and its individual franchisees, whereby the franchisor grants its individual franchisees the right, and imposes the obligation, to conduct a business in accordance with the franchisor's concept.

The right entitles and compels the individual franchisee, in exchange for direct or indirect financial compensation, to use the franchisor's trade name, and/or trade mark and/or service mark, know-how, business and technical methods, procedural system, and other industrial and/or intellectual property rights, supported by continuing provision of commercial and technical assistance, within the framework and for the term of a written franchise agreement, concluded between the parties for this purpose.

The last 25 years have seen an evolution in the channels of distribution. Stronger competition resulted in increased specialisation and the emergence of new ideas, with franchising being one of them. The European Franchise Federation numbered approximately 3,500 franchisors in the EU in 1996 that controlled a network comprising almost 142 thousand franchisees. Altogether, they employed almost 1.2 million persons and achieved a turnover of 90.7 billion ECU (all these figures exclude Greece, Ireland, Luxembourg and Finland).

This type of distribution has rapidly evolved, and covers many different types of businesses. In Europe, franchising was first adopted in retail sectors, where, with some exceptions, the traditional forms of co-operation were not often used. It then rapidly extended to a variety of businesses, ranging from hotels or restaurants to personal service enterprises. Although North American franchisors found their way to Europe, many national franchise networks were developed. Despite growing internationalisation, most national markets are still held by national networks.

Table 20.17

Main indicators of franchising in the EU, 1996/97

	Number of franchisees	Number of franchisors	Number of persons employed	Turnover (million ECU)
B	3,500	170	28,000	3,600
DK	2,500	98	40,000	1,000
D	22,000	530	230,000	14,600
EL	:	:	:	:
E	13,161	288	69,000	6,800
F (1)	28,851	517	320,000	28,300
IRL	:	:	:	:
I	21,390	436	49,660	12,000
L	:	:	:	:
NL	11,825	350	85,300	9,200
A	3,000	210	40,000	1,600
P	2,000	220	35,000	1,000
FIN	:	:	:	:
S	9,150	230	71,000	5,720
UK (1)	26,800	541	264,100	9,700

(1) 1997.

Source: EFF

France is by far the leading country in Europe in franchising and comes third in the world after the USA and Canada. In 1996, there were 485 franchisors and 27.3 thousand franchisees realising a turnover representing about 8% of French retail turnover. With 530 franchisors and 22 thousand franchisees, German franchising realised a turnover of 14.6 billion ECU in 1996. Germany has become one of the most important franchising countries in Europe; however, because of its co-operatively structured retail industry with strong "buying groups", franchising did not really take off until the beginning of the 1990s. It has mostly developed in food distribution (with large groups like Spar or Eismann), in pottery and household equipment, followed by personal equipment and services. The United Kingdom has 474 franchisors and 25.7 thousand franchisees, which realised a turnover accounting for 3% of British retail turnover. One characteristic of the United Kingdom is the great influence of American franchises. Most American franchisors started their European strategies with a British subsidiary. Consequently, almost 30% of the franchise networks in the United Kingdom are American. Italy had 436 franchisors and 21.4 thousand franchisees achieving a turnover of 12 billion ECU in 1996. Franchisee turnover was very low compared with total turnover, only 1.2%. Few foreign franchisors, mostly American and French, have settled in Italy. Franchising is a rather new distribution channel in Spain. Taking off only in 1986, it expanded very quickly. In 1996 Spain had 288 franchisors and 13.2 thousand franchisees and an annual turnover of 6.8 billion ECU. Expansion was mostly due to foreign franchisors (especially American networks). In 1991, only 58% of franchisors were Spanish.

Professional associations representing the industries within this chapter

AEEBC
European Association of
Building Surveyors
c/o RICS
12, Great George Street
London SW1P 3AD
tel: (44) 171 334 3877
fax: (44 171 334 3844

CIETT
International Confederation
of Temporary Work
Businesses
c/o EPPA
142-144 avenue de
Tervueren
B-1150 Bruxelles
tel: (32) 2 735 82 30
fax: (32) 2 735 44 12

EFF
European Franchise
Federation
c/o FFF
60, rue de la Boétie
F-75008 Paris
tel: (33) 1 53 75 22 25
fax: (33) 1 53 75 22 20
e-mail: fff@club-internet.fr

FEE
Fédération des Experts
Comptables Européens
83, rue de la Loi
B-1040 Bruxelles
tel: (32) 2 285 40 85
fax: (32) 2 231 11 12
e-mail: Secretariat@fee.be

Table 20.18

Legal, accounting, book-keeping and auditing, consultancy, market research (NACE Rev. 1 74.1)

Enterprise and employment indicators, 1996

	B	DK	D	EL	E	F	IRL	I	L	NL	A	P	FIN	S	UK
Number of enterprises (thousands) (1)	:	12.5	122.0	:	128.0	120.1	5.0	:	1.5	:	9.2	:	8.9	21.7	:
Number of enterprises per 10,000 inhabitants (1)	:	23.8	14.9	:	32.6	20.6	13.9	:	34.9	:	11.5	:	17.3	24.9	:
Number of pers. employed (thousands) (2)	74.4	37.2	:	:	:	283.0	28.6	:	5.1	:	46.8	:	20.8	:	:
Number of pers. employed/enterprise (units) (2)	:	3.0	:	:	:	2.4	5.7	:	3.5	:	5.5	:	2.3	:	:
Share of employees in total employed (%) (2)	63.1	64.9	:	:	:	99.2	77.4	:	81.3	:	82.9	:	82.8	:	:

(1) S (1993); DK (1995). (2) DK, A (1995).

Table 20.19

Legal, accounting, book-keeping and auditing, consultancy, market research (NACE Rev. 1 74.1)

Turnover related indicators, 1996

	B	DK	D	EL	E	F	IRL	I	L	NL	A	P	FIN	S	UK
Turnover (billion ECU) (1)	8.8	2.3	91.7	:	:	43.6	1.5	:	0.6	:	3.4	:	1.6	6.0	:
Turnover/enterprise (million ECU) (2)	:	0.2	0.8	:	:	0.4	0.3	:	0.4	:	0.4	:	0.2	0.2	:
Turnover/person employed (thousand ECU) (3)	118.6	61.3	:	:	:	154.0	51.1	:	109.7	:	72.3	:	79.1	:	:

(1) DK, A, S (1995). (2) S (1993); DK, A (1995). (3) DK, A (1995).

Table 20.20

Legal, accounting, book-keeping and auditing, consultancy, market research (NACE Rev. 1 74.1)

Competitiveness and productivity related indicators, 1996

	B	DK	D	EL	E	F	IRL	I	L	NL	A	P	FIN	S	UK
Value added/turnover (%) (1)	46.7	:	:	:	:	38.8	66.0	:	60.0	:	64.1	:	64.4	45.9	:
Labour productivity (thousand ECU/head) (2)	55.3	:	:	:	:	59.7	33.8	:	65.8	:	46.4	:	50.9	:	:
Wage adjusted labour productivity (%) (2)	107.5	:	:	:	:	123.7	:	:	183.3	:	142.0	:	148.9	:	:
Personnel costs/employee (thousand ECU) (3)	51.5	39.0	:	:	:	48.3	:	:	35.9	:	32.7	:	34.2	29.0	:
Gross operating surplus (million ECU) (4)	:	:	:	:	:	5.4	3.0	:	:	:	5.1	:	5.9	8.3	:

(1) A, S (1995). (2) A (1995). (3) S (1993); DK, A (1995). (4) A, S (1995).

Source: Eurostat (SBS)

Table 20.21

Architectural and engineering activities (NACE Rev. 1 74.2)

Enterprise and employment indicators, 1996

	B	DK	D	EL	E	F	IRL	I	L	NL	A	P	FIN	S	UK
Number of enterprises (thousands) (1)	:	8.8	:	:	61.0	43.7	:	184.8	:	11.8	5.7	:	:	17.0	48.9
Number of enterprises per 10,000 inhabitants (2)	:	16.9	:	:	15.6	7.5	:	32.3	:	7.6	7.3	:	:	19.4	8.3
Number of pers. employed (thousands) (2)	:	29.4	:	:	124.5	202.2	:	255.9	:	71.0	23.3	:	:	:	:
Number of pers. employed/enterprise (units) (2)	:	3.3	:	:	2.2	4.6	:	1.4	:	6.5	4.1	:	:	:	:
Share of employees in total employed (%) (2)	:	74.8	:	:	57.6	77.5	:	24.0	:	85.9	:	:	:	:	:

(1) A (1991); E, F, S (1994); DK, I, NL (1995). (2) A (1991); E (1992); NL (1993); F (1994); DK, I (1995).

Table 20.22

Architectural and engineering activities (NACE Rev. 1 74.2)

Turnover related indicators, 1996

	B	DK	D	EL	E	F	IRL	I	L	NL	A	P	FIN	S	UK
Turnover (billion ECU) (1)	:	3.1	:	:	6.6	18.8	:	13.4	:	5.8	:	:	:	4.2	22.2
Turnover/enterprise (million ECU) (1)	:	0.3	:	:	0.1	0.4	:	0.1	:	0.5	:	:	:	0.2	0.5
Turnover/person employed (thousand ECU) (2)	:	104.7	:	:	53.4	93.0	:	52.3	:	67.8	:	:	:	:	:

(1) E (1992); F, S (1994); DK, I, NL (1995). (2) E (1992); NL (1993); F (1994); DK, I (1995).

Table 20.23

Architectural and engineering activities (NACE Rev. 1 74.2)

Competitiveness and productivity related indicators, 1996

	B	DK	D	EL	E	F	IRL	I	L	NL	A	P	FIN	S	UK
Value added/turnover (%) (1)	:	:	:	:	56.0	:	:	55.4	:	87.7	:	:	:	43.7	:
Labour productivity (thousand ECU/head) (2)	:	:	:	:	29.9	:	:	29.0	:	:	:	:	:	:	:
Wage adjusted labour productivity (%) (2)	:	:	:	:	114.2	:	:	113.1	:	:	:	:	:	:	:
Personnel costs/employee (thousand ECU) (3)	:	44.9	:	:	26.2	41.5	:	25.6	:	31.8	:	:	:	36.7	:
Gross operating surplus (million ECU) (4)	:	:	:	:	:	2.4	:	4.5	:	4.7	:	:	:	4.7	3.0

(1) E (1992); S (1994); I, NL (1995). (2) E (1992); I (1995). (3) E (1992); NL (1993); F, S (1994); DK, I (1995). (4) F, S (1994); I, NL (1995).

Source: Eurostat (SBS)

Table 20.24

Technical testing and analysis (NACE Rev. 1 74.3)
Enterprise and employment indicators, 1996

	B	DK	D	EL	E	F	IRL	I	L	NL	A	P	FIN	S	UK
Number of enterprises (thousands) (1)	:	0.4	:	:	2.7	3.2	:	2.4	:	0.3	1.5	:	:	0.3	1.4
Number of enterprises per 10,000 inhabitants (2)	:	0.7	:	:	0.7	0.5	:	0.4	:	0.2	2.0	:	:	0.4	0.2
Number of pers. employed (thousands) (2)	:	1.5	:	:	6.5	31.5	:	9.0	:	6.0	6.6	:	:	:	:
Number of pers. employed/enterprise (units) (2)	:	4.4	:	:	14.0	10.0	:	3.7	:	17.9	4.3	:	:	:	:
Share of employees in total employed (%) (2)	:	74.6	:	:	96.7	90.1	:	66.3	:	100.0	:	:	:	:	:

(1) A (1991); E, F, S (1994); DK, I, NL (1995). (2) A (1991); E (1992); NL (1993); F (1994); DK, I (1995).

Table 20.25

Technical testing and analysis (NACE Rev. 1 74.3)
Turnover related indicators, 1996

	B	DK	D	EL	E	F	IRL	I	L	NL	A	P	FIN	S	UK
Turnover (billion ECU) (1)	:	0.1	:	:	0.3	1.8	:	0.5	:	0.4	:	:	:	0.3	1.4
Turnover/enterprise (million ECU) (1)	:	0.3	:	:	0.6	0.6	:	0.2	:	1.1	:	:	:	0.9	1.0
Turnover/person employed (thousand ECU) (2)	:	77.8	:	:	45.8	58.3	:	60.6	:	74.6	:	:	:	:	:

(1) E (1992); F, S (1994); DK, I, NL (1995). (2) E (1992); NL (1993); F (1994); DK, I (1995).

Table 20.26

Technical testing and analysis (NACE Rev. 1 74.3)
Competitiveness and productivity related indicators, 1996

	B	DK	D	EL	E	F	IRL	I	L	NL	A	P	FIN	S	UK
Value added/turnover (%) (1)	:	:	:	:	67.5	:	:	62.6	:	93.4	:	:	:	67.1	:
Labour productivity (thousand ECU/head) (2)	:	:	:	:	30.9	:	:	38.0	:	:	:	:	:	:	:
Wage adjusted labour productivity (%) (2)	:	:	:	:	122.8	:	:	128.5	:	:	:	:	:	:	:
Personnel costs/employee (thousand ECU) (3)	:	38.4	:	:	25.2	35.1	:	29.5	:	36.9	:	:	:	31.4	:
Gross operating surplus (million ECU) (4)	:	:	:	:	:	3.9	:	8.6	:	7.5	:	:	:	5.5	8.9

(1) E (1992); S (1994); I, NL (1995). (2) E (1992); I (1995). (3) E (1992); NL (1993); F, S (1994); DK, I (1995). (4) F, S (1994); I, NL (1995).

Source: Eurostat (SBS)

Table 20.27

Advertising (NACE Rev. 1 74.4)

Enterprise and employment indicators, 1996

	B	DK	D	EL	E	F	IRL	I	L	NL	A	P	FIN	S	UK
Number of enterprises (thousands) (1)	:	3.8	34.2	:	14.9	20.1	0.2	10.2	0.2	9.8	3.1	:	2.0	9.1	10.2
Number of enterprises per 10,000 inhabitants (2)	:	7.3	4.2	:	3.8	3.4	0.6	1.8	4.3	6.4	3.9	:	3.9	10.3	1.7
Number of pers. employed (thousands) (2)	12.8	9.6	:	:	:	87.9	2.6	31.5	0.5	27.5	9.0	:	5.5	:	:
Number of pers. employed/enterprise (units) (2)	:	2.5	:	:	:	4.4	11.6	3.1	3.0	3.2	3.6	:	2.8	:	:
Share of employees in total employed (%) (3)	57.6	57.6	:	:	:	96.6	91.3	58.8	84.5	73.1	79.1	:	82.9	:	:

(1) DK, I, NL (1995). (2) NL (1994); DK, I, A (1995). (3) NL (1993); DK, I, A (1995).

Table 20.28

Advertising (NACE Rev. 1 74.4)

Turnover related indicators, 1996

	B	DK	D	EL	E	F	IRL	I	L	NL	A	P	FIN	S	UK
Turnover (billion ECU) (1)	3.8	1.7	20.9	:	:	16.1	0.4	3.3	0.1	4.7	1.7	:	0.9	3.4	16.5
Turnover/enterprise (million ECU) (1)	:	0.4	0.6	:	:	0.8	1.9	0.3	0.6	0.5	0.7	:	0.5	0.4	1.6
Turnover/person employed (thousand ECU) (2)	298.4	174.2	:	:	:	182.6	166.9	103.6	186.0	153.4	191.4	:	170.6	:	:

(1) DK, I, NL, A (1995). (2) NL (1994); DK, I, A (1995).

Table 20.29

Advertising (NACE Rev. 1 74.4)

Competitiveness and productivity related indicators, 1996

	B	DK	D	EL	E	F	IRL	I	L	NL	A	P	FIN	S	UK
Value added/turnover (%) (1)	13.8	:	:	:	:	26.1	21.7	35.9	25.1	46.7	28.9	:	24.8	25.8	:
Labour productivity (thousand ECU/head) (2)	41.3	:	:	:	:	47.7	36.2	37.2	46.8	:	55.2	:	42.3	:	:
Wage adjusted labour productivity (%) (2)	107.4	:	:	:	:	120.7	:	122.2	145.4	:	149.6	:	129.6	:	:
Personnel costs/employee (thousand ECU) (3)	38.5	41.9	:	:	:	39.5	:	30.4	32.2	37.9	36.9	:	32.6	37.6	:
Gross operating surplus (million ECU) (1)	:	:	:	:	:	1.6	1.3	3.8	:	2.9	2.8	:	2.2	2.6	1.4

(1) I, NL, A (1995). (2) I, A (1995). (3) DK, I, NL, A (1995).

Source: Eurostat (SBS)

Table 20.30

Labour recruitment and provision of personnel (NACE Rev. 1 74.5)

Enterprise and employment indicators, 1996

	B	DK	D	EL	E	F	IRL	I	L	NL	A	P	FIN	S	UK
Number of enterprises (thousands) (1)	:	0.3	2.3	:	2.0	2.3	0.2	0.9	0.1	1.5	0.3	:	0.3	0.1	8.2
Number of enterprises per 10,000 inhabitants (2)	:	0.7	0.3	:	0.5	0.4	0.5	0.2	1.2	1.0	0.4	:	0.5	0.2	1.4
Number of pers. employed (thousands) (2)	86.6	10.3	:	:	13.9	343.9	3.3	1.8	4.0	56.0	10.8	:	3.5	:	:
Number of pers. employed/enterprise (units) (2)	:	30.0	:	:	22.8	149.9	18.7	2.0	80.0	50.6	44.1	:	13.1	:	:
Share of employees in total employed (%) (2)	99.6	27.9	:	:	96.9	100.0	97.9	41.2	99.8	92.9	99.2	:	96.6	:	:

(1) DK, I, NL (1995). (2) E, NL (1993); DK, I, A (1995).

Table 20.31

Labour recruitment and provision of personnel (NACE Rev. 1 74.5)

Turnover related indicators, 1996

	B	DK	D	EL	E	F	IRL	I	L	NL	A	P	FIN	S	UK
Turnover (billion ECU) (1)	1.7	0.1	1.0	:	0.2	10.3	0.2	0.1	0.1	3.4	0.4	:	0.1	0.0	12.0
Turnover/enterprise (million ECU) (1)	:	0.3	1.7	:	0.3	4.5	0.9	0.2	1.6	3.0	1.7	:	0.4	0.3	1.5
Turnover/person employed (thousand ECU) (1)	19.1	11.4	:	:	13.2	29.9	47.2	82.4	19.9	60.3	38.6	:	28.2	:	:

(1) E, NL (1993); DK, I, A (1995).

Table 20.32

Labour recruitment and provision of personnel (NACE Rev. 1 74.5)

Competitiveness and productivity related indicators, 1996

	B	DK	D	EL	E	F	IRL	I	L	NL	A	P	FIN	S	UK
Value added/turnover (%) (1)	87.1	:	:	:	70.7	88.1	41.9	39.3	87.8	:	79.1	:	77.9	61.1	:
Labour productivity (thousand ECU/head) (1)	16.7	:	:	:	9.3	26.4	19.8	32.4	17.5	:	30.5	:	21.9	:	:
Wage adjusted labour productivity (%) (1)	104.5	:	:	:	109.8	104.0	:	141.5	98.2	:	109.2	:	111.9	:	:
Personnel costs/employee (thousand ECU) (2)	15.9	37.8	:	:	8.5	25.4	:	22.9	17.8	5.8	28.0	:	19.6	43.6	:
Gross operating surplus (million ECU) (3)	:	:	:	:	:	0.5	1.6	4.1	:	2.6	3.2	:	1.1	3.7	1.4

(1) E (1993); I, A (1995). (2) E (1993); DK, I, NL, A (1995). (3) NL (1993); I, A (1995).

Source: Eurostat (SBS)

Table 20.33

Investigation and security activities (NACE Rev. 1 74.6)

Enterprise and employment indicators, 1996

	B	DK	D	EL	E	F	IRL	I	L	NL	A	P	FIN	S	UK
Number of enterprises (thousands) (1)	:	0.3	2.8	:	1.6	4.7	0.2	1.8	:	0.2	0.1	:	0.3	0.4	2.2
Number of enterprises per 10,000 inhabitants (2)	:	0.5	0.3	:	0.4	0.8	0.5	0.3	:	0.1	0.1	:	0.6	0.5	0.4
Number of pers. employed (thousands) (2)	9.9	1.0	:	:	73.2	92.3	5.0	45.5	:	13.3	5.0	:	3.7	:	:
Number of pers. employed/enterprise (units) (2)	:	3.9	:	:	44.9	19.7	27.1	25.6	:	57.9	54.5	:	12.5	:	:
Share of employees in total employed (%) (3)	95.4	47.7	:	:	98.5	98.9	97.1	94.1	:	:	98.8	:	96.0	:	:

(1) NL (1994); DK, I (1995). (2) NL (1994); DK, I, A (1995). (3) DK, I, A (1995).

Table 20.34

Investigation and security activities (NACE Rev. 1 74.6)

Turnover related indicators, 1996

	B	DK	D	EL	E	F	IRL	I	L	NL	A	P	FIN	S	UK
Turnover (billion ECU) (1)	0.4	0.0	2.7	:	1.4	2.8	0.1	1.5	:	0.4	0.1	:	0.1	0.5	2.2
Turnover/enterprise (million ECU) (1)	:	0.2	1.0	:	0.9	0.6	0.7	0.8	:	1.9	1.5	:	0.4	1.1	1.0
Turnover/person employed (thousand ECU) (1)	40.7	44.4	:	:	19.4	30.8	26.4	33.1	:	33.0	27.4	:	31.1	:	:

(1) NL (1994); DK, I, A (1995).

Table 20.35

Investigation and security activities (NACE Rev. 1 74.6)

Competitiveness and productivity related indicators, 1996 (1)

	B	DK	D	EL	E	F	IRL	I	L	NL	A	P	FIN	S	UK
Value added/turnover (%)	78.8	:	:	:	84.4	69.2	71.7	84.8	:	:	80.6	:	76.8	71.2	:
Labour productivity (thousand ECU/head)	32.1	:	:	:	16.4	21.3	19.0	28.1	:	:	22.1	:	23.9	:	:
Wage adjusted labour productivity (%)	103.8	:	:	:	109.0	102.4	:	113.8	:	:	109.5	:	111.1	:	:
Personnel costs/employee (thousand ECU)	30.9	37.0	:	:	15.1	20.8	:	24.7	:	:	20.2	:	21.5	29.4	:
Gross operating surplus (million ECU)	:	:	:	:	3.9	2.4	2.3	2.6	:	:	2.0	:	6.3	4.9	2.7

(1) DK, I, A (1995).

Source: Eurostat (SBS)

Table 20.36

Industrial cleaning (NACE Rev. 1 74.7)

Enterprise and employment indicators, 1996

	B	DK	D	EL	E	F	IRL	I	L	NL	A	P	FIN	S	UK
Number of enterprises (thousands) (1)	:	6.3	21.7	:	13.4	13.4	0.2	23.5	0.1	6.2	1.2	:	2.2	4.8	6.6
Number of enterprises per 10,000 inhabitants (2)	:	12.1	2.7	.	3.4	2.3	0.4	4.1	2.3	4.0	1.5	:	4.4	5.4	1.1
Number of pers. employed (thousands) (2)	37.4	36.4	:	:	231.3	223.3	8.4	216.8	3.8	154.0	31.1	:	13.4	:	:
Number of pers. employed/enterprise (units) (2)	:	5.8	:	:	18.7	16.7	55.5	9.2	39.9	25.6	27.5	:	6.0	:	:
Share of employees in total employed (%) (2)	94.1	42.7	:	:	96.1	97.2	98.2	86.1	98.9	93.5	97.5	:	90.1	:	:

(1) DK, I, NL (1995). (2) NL (1993); DK, E, I, A (1995).

Table 20.37

Industrial cleaning (NACE Rev. 1 74.7)

Turnover related indicators, 1996

	B	DK	D	EL	E	F	IRL	I	L	NL	A	P	FIN	S	UK
Turnover (billion ECU) (1)	1.2	0.9	10.2	:	2.6	5.7	0.1	4.1	0.1	2.1	0.6	:	0.4	1.2	3.6
Turnover/enterprise (million ECU) (1)	.	0.1	0.5	:	0.2	0.4	0.5	0.2	0.9	0.3	0.6	:	0.2	0.2	0.5
Turnover/person employed (thousand ECU) (2)	31.8	23.4	:	:	11.1	25.4	8.5	18.9	23.5	12.9	20.6	:	33.1	:	:

(1) DK, E, I, NL, A (1995). (2) NL (1993); DK, E, I, A (1995).

Table 20.38

Industrial cleaning (NACE Rev. 1 74.7)

Competitiveness and productivity related indicators, 1996 (1)

	B	DK	D	EL	E	F	IRL	I	L	NL	A	P	FIN	S	UK
Value added/turnover (%)	62.6	:	:	:	85.7	71.1	66.9	156.6	67.7	94.3	81.0	:	72.4	67.6	:
Labour productivity (thousand ECU/head)	19.9	:	:	:	9.5	18.0	5.7	29.7	15.9	:	16.7	:	24.0	:	:
Wage adjusted labour productivity (%)	113.1	:	:	:	105.9	107.4	:	231.1	123.8	:	115.3	:	118.5	:	:
Personnel costs/employee (thousand ECU)	17.6	31.1	:	:	8.9	16.8	:	12.8	12.9	9.6	14.5	:	20.2	25.5	:
Gross operating surplus (million ECU)	:	:	:	:	4.5	2.6	3.7	3.3	:	4.6	4.2	:	4.4	3.3	3.1

(1) DK, E, I, NL, A (1995).

(%) Table 20.39

Other business activities (NACE Rev. 1 74)

Composition of the labour force, 1997

	EU-15	B	DK	D	EL	E	F	IRL	I	L	NL	A	P	FIN	S	UK
Female	47.4	44.7	50.3	52.4	43.6	50.2	47.4	44.4	44.0	46.2	44.2	53.2	50.6	48.1	45.1	45.2
Part-time	17.7	17.8	25.6	27.0	4.1	16.2	21.5	10.5	13.5	13.0	36.7	25.5	13.9	18.1	24.4	24.2
Temporary work or limited contract	36.8	37.0	31.8	33.0	61.1	55.9	29.0	28.9	56.3	26.2	29.1	23.0	48.8	34.3	32.7	31.7
Persons with a higher education	36.8	52.3	41.1	32.9	61.6	41.2	35.3	56.4	29.6	46.8	39.4	22.8	26.4	34.8	40.5	40.0
Persons with a lower education	24.5	18.1	16.7	15.1	6.8	39.4	24.9	14.5	22.0	33.8	25.1	17.9	45.6	14.8	16.3	32.4

Source: Eurostat (SBS, LFS)

Information and audio-visual services

Industry description and main indicators

The activities covered in this chapter encompass several of the economy's most dynamic segments, and are often associated with the emergence of the so-called "information society", a society whose wealth and growth would be based on its ability to process, store, retrieve and communicate information in whatever form it may take - oral, written or visual - unconstrained by distance, time and volume. Many observers see this new revolution as significant and far-reaching as last century's industrial revolution with the corresponding high economic stakes. Already the Internet can be seen to be the backbone for the emergence of this society.

During the course of a few years, the information society has become a reference concept embracing all kinds of exchange of information, especially those in electronic form. Several economic activities can be associated with it, namely: communication services (NACE Rev. 1 64) for conveying information, software and computing services (NACE Rev. 1 72) for managing and processing information, as well as content industries such as film (NACE Rev. 1 92.1), television (NACE Rev. 1 92.2) and music (NACE Rev. 1 22.14). All of these will be addressed in this chapter.

(units) Figure 21.1

Post and telecommunications (NACE Rev. 1 64)
Density of enterprises per ten thousand inhabitants, 1995

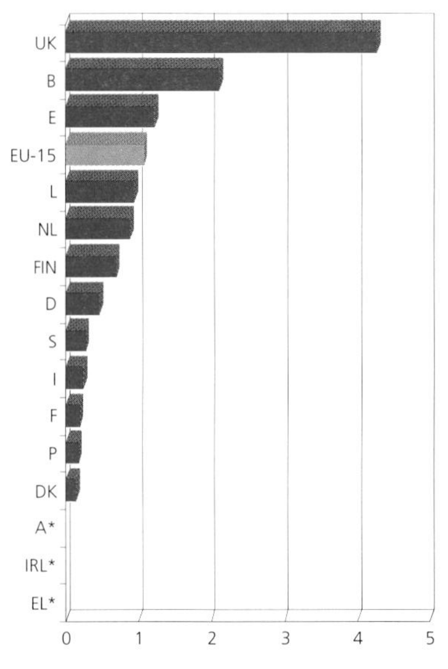

Source: Eurostat (SME)

The activities covered in this chapter include:

- 22.14: publishing of sound recording;
- 64.1: post and courier activities;
- 64.2: telecommunications;
- 72.1: hardware consultancy;
- 72.2: software consultancy and supply;
- 72.3: data processing;
- 72.4: data activities;
- 72.5: maintenance and repair of office, accounting and computing machinery;
- 72.6: other computer related activities;
- 92.1: motion picture and video activities;
- 92.2: radio and television activities.

Table 21.1 (million ECU)

ICT market value in the EU

	1997	1998	1999	2000
Computer hardware	61,722	65,241	68,921	73,317
Office equipment	8,982	9,100	9,173	9,290
Data communication hardware	6,390	7,382	8,156	8,744
Software	32,198	36,124	40,735	45,737
IT services	56,510	63,711	72,349	81,453
Telecom equipment	29,665	31,678	33,647	35,777
Telecom services	144,327	157,278	167,980	177,165
Total	339,794	370,514	400,961	431,483

Source: EITO

Assessing the size of these activities in the economy is difficult due to their composite nature. According to estimates of the European Information Technology Observatory, the total market value of information and communications' technologies (ICT) in the EU was worth 370 billion ECU in 1998, of which 157 billion ECU was accounted for by telecom services alone. As for the audiovisual sector, the European Audiovisual Observatory estimates that the fifteen largest European enterprises of the sector each had a turnover greater than 1 billion ECU and that the aggregate turnover of the top fifty companies exceeded 110 billion ECU in 1996.

National Accounts also offer some indications on the size of activities. Looking at the contribution of communications to the creation of wealth in the Member States, this branch represents around 2.3% of the total value added generated in the EU. Luxembourg and Greece clearly stand out from the other countries with shares of 4% and 3.2% respectively, whilst Italy displayed a share lower than 2%.

Figure 21.2 (%)

Share of communication services in total value added, 1997 (1)

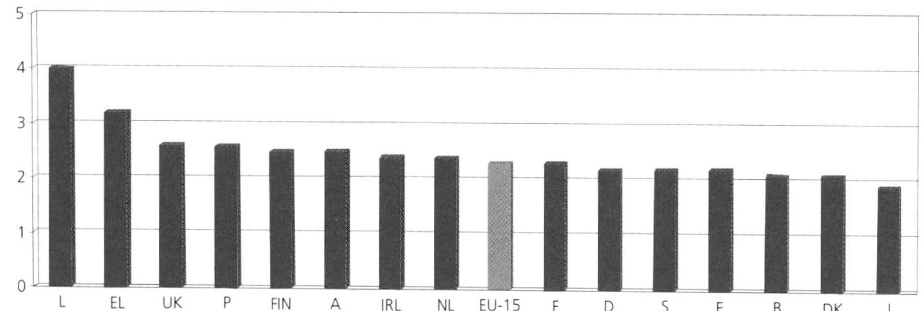

(1) Earlier year had to be used for some countries.

Source: Eurostat (National Accounts)

Figure 21.3 (%)

Post and telecommunications (NACE Rev. 1 64)

Share of part-time and temporary work contracts in total number of persons employed, 1997

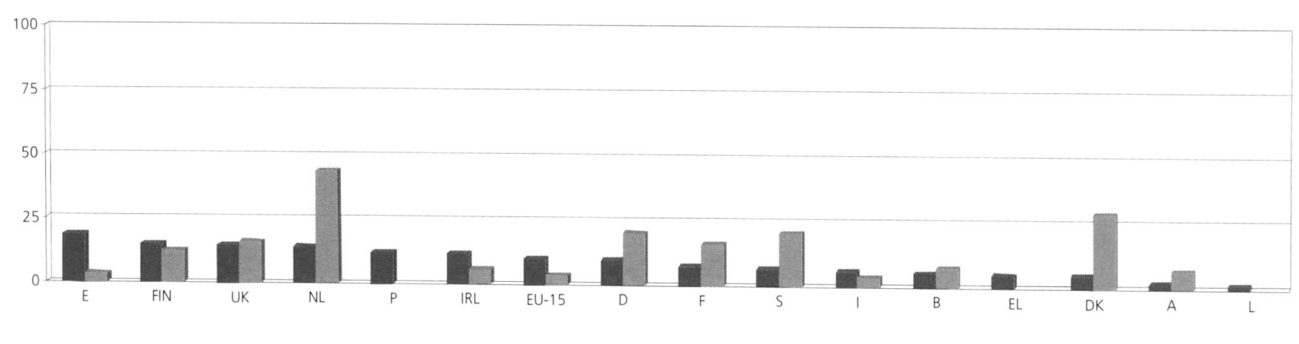

Source: Eurostat (LFS)

As far as employment is concerned, the latest European Labour Force Survey estimated the number of persons employed in communication and computer services[1] in the EU in 1997 at 3.3 million, two thirds in the former and one third in the latter. Women were under-represented as they accounted for only slightly more than one third of total employment in these activities, and just above one quarter in the case of computer services. This compares with average female employment of 42% in the whole economy, and 51% in service sectors. Countries with the lowest female shares of the labour force were Greece (21%) and Austria (23%), with about half the shares recorded in Finland (44%) and France (42%).

On the other hand, computer activities numbered amongst those sectors with the lowest share of persons employed working part-time (8%), compared to 17% in the economy as a whole. Countries with the highest proportion of persons working part-time in this activity were Portugal and Germany (both more than 12%), whilst there were less than 3% in Greece, Luxembourg, Ireland and Belgium. The share of persons working part-time in communication services was slightly higher at 14%.

Turning to the level of education of the workforce, it is not too surprising to see that computer activities employed one of the highest rates of highly educated persons[2] of the whole economy. With a share of 52% it was the third highest level of all services activities after research and development (63%) and education (62%). This strongly contrasts with communication services where only 15% of the persons employed held a higher education degree, a level lower than in the economy as a whole.

International comparison

The USA leads the world in terms of the information society. The main on-line services available at present, for example Internet, are of American origin. Furthermore, the USA has a very strong position in each of the segments: 29% of the world market in telecommunication services, 46% of the market for data-processing and software services, virtual dominance of the market for on-line services and a strong position shared with Japan in the field of video games. Europe nevertheless occupies some markets, especially services with high value added, as well as hardware for telecommunication services, where it held 38% of the world market value in 1998, twice the share of the USA. This reflects to a large extent the worldwide domination of European GSM technology in digital mobile telephony.

1) NACE Rev. 1 64 and NACE Rev. 1 72.
2) Persons having completed at least tertiary education.

(thousand ECU) — Figure 21.4

Post and telecommunications (NACE Rev. 1 64)
Personnel costs/employee, 1996

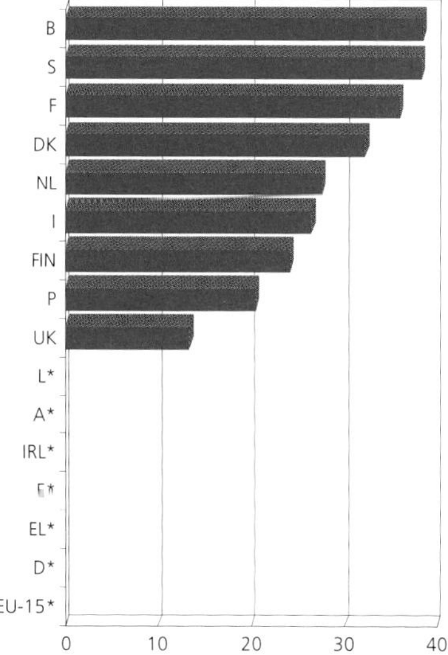

Source: Eurostat (SBS)

(%) — Figure 21.5

Post and telecommunications (NACE Rev. 1 64)
Wage adjusted labour productivity, 1996

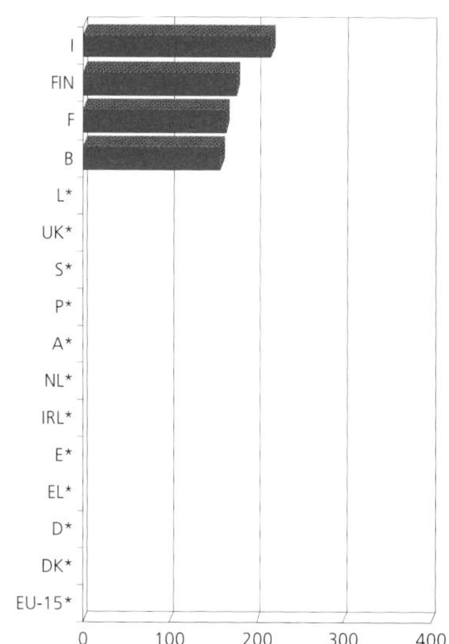

Source: Eurostat (SBS)

Within the audiovisual market, the European Audiovisual Observatory estimates that European enterprises represented about 35% of the world market, ahead of their American and Japanese counterparts which held around 31% and 29% of total market value respectively.

Figure 21.6

Share of ICT market value by world region, 1998

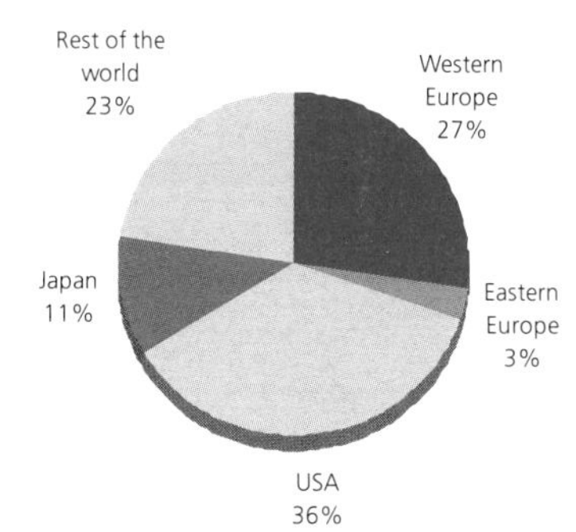

Source: EITO

(million ECU) — Table 21.2

Major regional ICT market by product, 1998

	Western Europe	Eastern Europe	USA	Japan	Rest of the world	World
IT hardware	86,752	8,940	141,581	43,759	65,000	346,032
Software	38,261	1,546	54,976	10,358	14,807	119,948
IT services	68,031	3,117	122,722	36,910	30,199	260,979
Telecom equipment	33,456	12,107	22,116	11,528	39,658	118,865
Telecom services	165,630	19,113	176,168	61,729	176,446	599,086
Total	392,130	44,823	517,563	164,284	326,110	1,444,910

Source: EITO

Postal and courier services (NACE Rev. 1 64.1)

Postal and courier services ensure that letters and parcels are moved between business, administrative and private customers. This activity covers Group 64.1 of the NACE Rev. 1 classification. National post activities (NACE Rev. 1 61.11) include the pick-up, transport and delivery (domestic or international) of mail and parcels, and other services[3] such as mailbox rental, "poste restante", etc. Courier activities other than national post activities (NACE Rev. 1 64.12) are provided by public as well as private operators. They are concerned with the pick-up, transport and delivery of letters and mail-type parcels and packages by firms other than the national post operators. Enterprises in this activity widened their initial focus on business documents, towards the transfer of packages and freight, carried by fleets of fully owned or dedicated aircraft, trucks, trains and delivery vans. Their business is dominated by guaranteed 24-hour cross-border delivery service.

3) Excluding postal giro and postal savings activities and other financial activities carried out by national postal administrations (see NACE Rev. 1 65.12).

Figure 21.7 (units)

Post and courier activities (NACE Rev. 1 64.1) Density of enterprises per ten thousand inhabitants, 1996

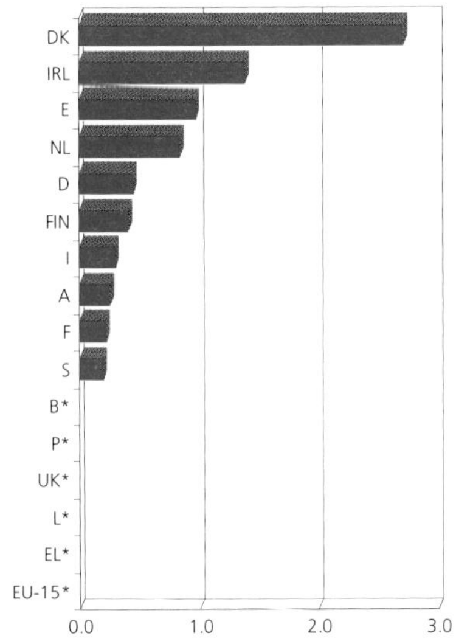

Source: Eurostat (SBS)

Within the EU, the state owned, national public postal operators dominate the market for letter services. They provide general letter services and in most cases they still operate as a monopoly with exclusive rights, balanced by the fact that they are bound by a universal service obligation.

Private operators dominate the express services market. Beside parcels, private operators provide non-reserved letter services. The percentage of express services served by private operators compared to total postal revenues is approximately 30%. Apart from greater speed, express mail services feature all or some of the following supplementary facilities: guarantee of delivery by a fixed date; collection from domicile; personal delivery to the addressee; possibility of changing the destination and addressee in the course of delivery; confirmation to sender of receipt of the item dispatched; monitoring and tracking of items dispatched; personalised services for customers and provision of an à la carte service as and when required.

In 1996, the fifteen public postal services operated about 90,000 permanent post offices open to the public, about 10,000 fewer than ten years before. Despite this, Eurostat figures indicate that the number of letterboxes per inhabitant did not experience a significant change over the same period. Differences across Member States remained considerable, ranging from 241 inhabitants per letterbox in Sweden to 1,136 inhabitants per letterbox in Spain.

However, employment did record a decline over the period, losing 107 thousand persons, to rest at 1.3 million persons employed within the EU. One trend of important significance has been the evolution of part-time work, accounting for a 20% share in employment in 1996, twice the level seen in 1986.

EU postal services handle a total of approximately 90 billion items each year. Domestic services account for the vast majority of the traffic. According to Eurostat figures, the number of domestic letters handled increased by an average of 2.7% each year between 1986 and 1996. The UPU (Universal Postal Union) expects the rising trends to continue through the next decade. In a study entitled "Post 2005", the UPU forecasts that growth of domestic letter traffic in high income countries will maintain an average growth rate of 2.3% between 1995 and 2005. Forecasts for international mail were even more optimistic, ranging from 3.4% to 5.2% depending on the region considered.

The business sector remains the most important customer (sender) with a market share of about 90% of all postal services, broken down as 60% from business-to-private and 30% business-to-business. On the receivers side, the most important segment is the sector of private individuals, whose importance is increasing. Only 10% of traffic concerns private-to-private mail. The business sector also dominates the parcel services market with approximately 85% of parcels sent by businesses and other organisations.

Figure 21.8

Inhabitants per letterbox, 1997 (1)

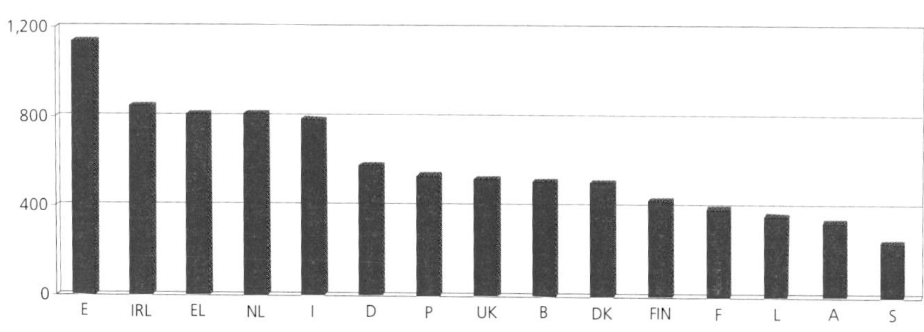

(1) DK, EL, F, I, NL, A, P, S, UK: 1996.

Source: Eurostat

(units) Figure 21.9

Employment in national post activities

Source: Eurostat, UPU

(thousand ECU) Figure 21.10

Post and courier activities (NACE Rev. 1 64.1)

Personnel costs/employee, 1996

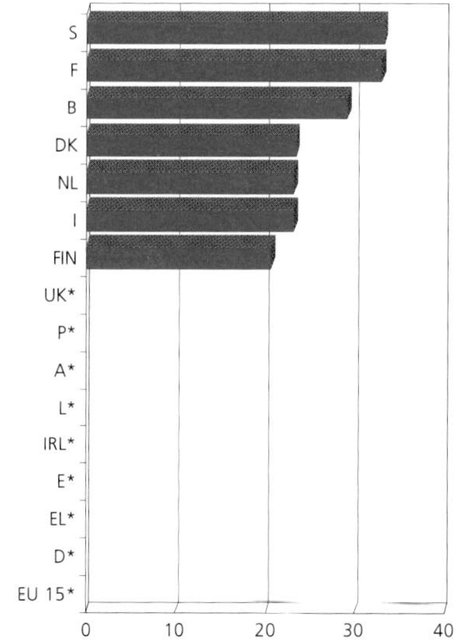

Source: Eurostat (SBS)

Whilst direct marketing mail already accounts for a large proportion of the handled items and it's importance is still growing, companies are changing marketing communication strategies and investing relatively more money in alternative marketing activities, such as direct mail. Mail order is also a promising segment which has developed as a competitor to store retailing services. New technological developments such as the development of e-commerce and Internet shopping make home shopping more convenient for the benefit of mail order customers.

Conversely, this same technological evolution has a negative influence on postal traffic, with the widespread adoption of fax and e-mail as fast and reliable communications' media. UPU's "Post 2005" study anticipates a fall of 5 percentage points in the share of physical mail in the communications' market between 1995 and 2005, down from 20% to less than 15%. The greatest substitution effect is expected to be seen in the business to business segment in high-income countries, where more than 50% of businesses are expected to use electronic mail by the year 2005.

The competitive environment for public postal operators is changing. Private operators are expanding their services into the correspondence market, specifically into the business-to-private, direct mail and (to a lesser extent) business-to-business direct mail segments of the market. Liberalisation is one of the most important issues in the postal and express services industry. In the process of adapting to a more market oriented approach, public postal operators are attempting to improve the quality and efficiency of the services they provide. On one side, investments are undertaken in the production process, more specifically in automatic sorting of mail. On the other side, they are increasingly operating with a cost based attitude.

Private operators are active on four levels: global, pan-European, national and local. On a global level the leading companies are DHL, United Parcel Services (UPS), Federal Express and TNT. Companies that operate on a pan-European level are Kühne & Nagel, Jet Services, TAT Express and Securicor. On the national and local level many small companies operate with services such as city-to-city, as well as delivery by motorcycle courier.

Eleven of the EU's postal operators are both controlled and owned by their governments. One notable exception is that of the Netherlands, where the government sold 55% of it's shares in the PTT holding company to the public in 1995.

The public postal operators in Sweden and Finland are the only two companies that, although they are state-owned, operate in an open, liberalised market. The Dutch, partly privatised PTT, as well as most of the Member States' state-owned national postal operators, have a monopoly on most correspondence services.

(units) Figure 21.11

Post items handled per inhabitant, 1996 (1)

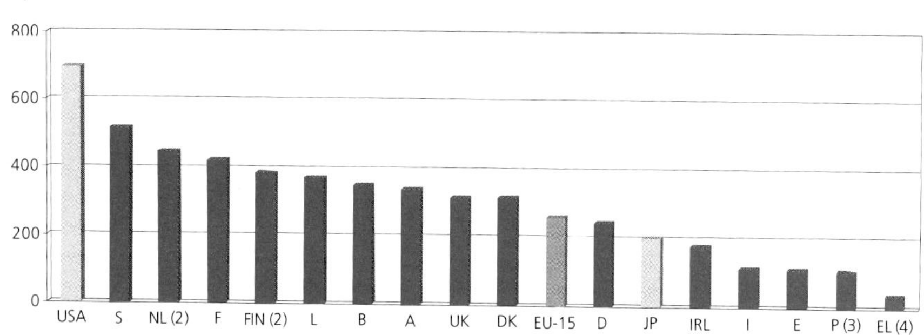

(1) Domestic and international service, including dispatch and receipt.
(2) Including only letter post.
(3) International includes only dispatch.
(4) Including only domestic service.

Source: UPU

Telecommunications' services (NACE Rev. 1 64.2)

Telecommunications' services as defined by Group 64.2 of the NACE Rev. 1 classification embraces the conveyance and distribution of transmission of sound, images, data or other information via cables, broadcasting, relay or satellite. It includes both the management and maintenance of networks and the provision of services using this network[4]. It has become increasingly important to differentiate between the two latter aspects with the growing diversification of supplies and the liberalisation of the telecommunications market. A distinction is also made between basic services, consisting mainly of public voice telephony, and value added services covering data transmission, mobile communications and a number of "advanced" functionalities (call back, telephone cards, call transfer, teleconferencing, etc).

4) Excluding the provision of radio and television programmes even if in connection with broadcast (see NACE Rev. 1 92.20).

Table 21.3 (million ECU)

The telecom market in the EU

	1997	1998	1999	2000
Public equipment	13,163	14,100	14,985	15,884
Switching	*6,413*	*6,072*	*5,960*	*5,979*
Transmission	*3,246*	*3,612*	*3,735*	*3,972*
Mobile infrastructure	*3,504*	*4,416*	*5,290*	*5,933*
Private equipment	16,502	17,579	18,661	19,893
Total Equipment	***29,665***	***31,679***	***33,646***	***35,777***
Telephone services	94,032	97,630	101,104	104,319
Mobile phone services	23,951	30,757	35,846	39,136
Switched data and leased lines services	21,152	22,955	24,342	26,019
CaTV services	5,192	5,936	6,688	7,691
Total Services	***144,327***	***157,278***	***167,980***	***177,165***
Total Telecom	**173,992**	**188,957**	**201,626**	**212,942**

Source: EITO

Figure 21.12 (units)

Telecommunications (NACE Rev. 1 64.2) Density of enterprises per ten thousand inhabitants, 1996

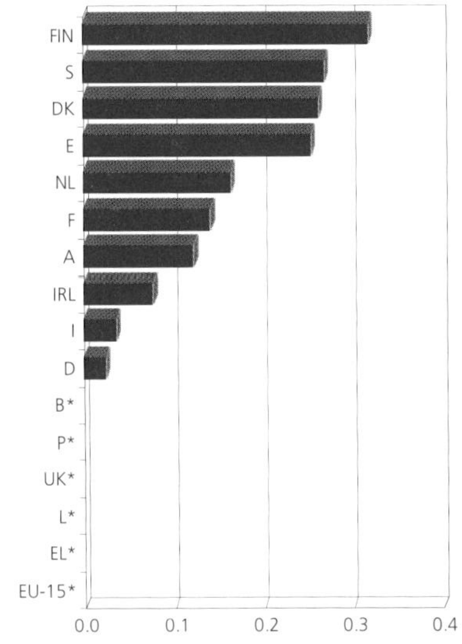

Source: Eurostat (SBS)

Historically, the sector has been formed around national monopolies that still provide the broad structure of the European telecommunications' industry. Moves towards market liberalisation from the late eighties onwards have mainly concerned value added services, as well as some services for business users. This has left complete control of basic services largely in the hands of the national monopolies (with a few exceptions like Sweden and the United Kingdom). However, since January 1998 telecommunication services have been fully liberalised in the vast majority of EU countries.

The EU-15 telecommunication market (including both equipment and services) was worth an estimated 189 billion ECU in 1998, just in front of the information technology (IT) market. The telecoms' market saw an increase in its value of some 8.6% compared to figures for 1997. EITO (the European Information Technology Observatory) estimate that growth will continue to be strong, although slowing down to 6.7% in 1999 and 5.6% by 2000. In 1998, services accounted for no less than 83% of the telecoms' market, or 157 billion ECU, against only 32 billion ECU accounted for by equipment.

The European[5] telecom market was the largest in the world, accounting for 32% of the estimated world total of 718 billion ECU. This share was ahead of comparable figures for the USA (198 billion ECU or 28%) and Japan (73 billion ECU or 10%). World market growth for 1999 and 2000 is expected to remain high at an annual average rate of 7.5%. The evolution of the market in Europe is anticipated to be more vigorous, at 6.6% per annum, than either the

5) Western, central and eastern Europe together; the EU alone accounted for 26%.

Figure 21.13 (thousands)

Total mobile phone subscribers

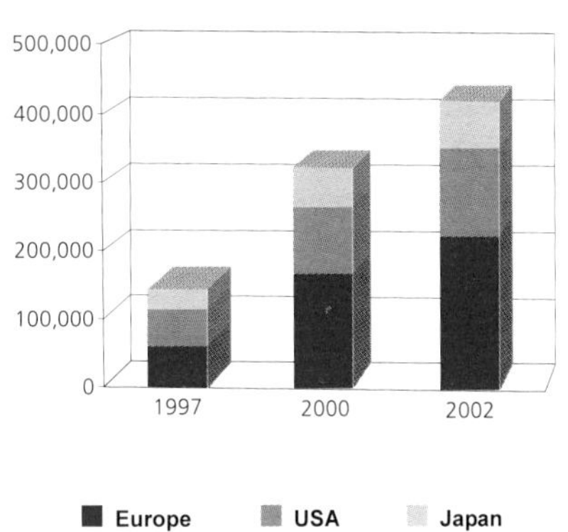

Source: EITO

Figure 21.14

Share of the telecom market value by world region, 1998

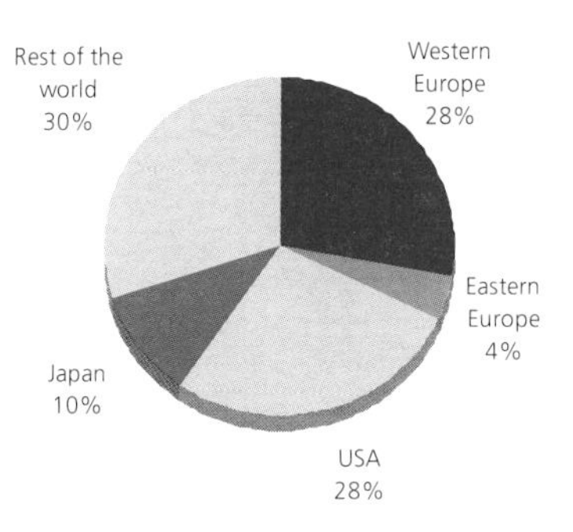

Source: EITO

(thousands)

Table 21.4

Main indicators of telecommunications infrastructure, 1998

	Main telephone lines	of which digital (%)	ISDN lines	Mobile analogue lines	Mobile digital lines
D	46,448	100	11,049	350	13,450
E	16,391	88	746	800	5,500
F	34,272	100	3,878	50	10,450
I	26,548	98	1,425	3,300	16,700
UK	32,585	100	3,859	1,100	10,200
Rest of Western Europe	67,962	90	4,702	2,244	25,978
Western Europe	224,206	96	25,659	7,844	82,278
Eastern Europe	75,099	35	135	1,108	6,683
Total Europe	299,305	81	25,794	8,952	88,961
USA	182,616	91	7,050	48,500	18,000
Japan	64,566	100	6,762	900	39,100
Rest of the world	305,925	91	1,901	36,214	63,753
World	852,412	88	41,507	94,566	209,814

Source: EITO

USA or Japan (6.4% and 4.7% respectively). One of the main factors may be the higher requirement for equipment compared to the two other Triad economies. The fastest expanding market in the world is expected to be the rest of the world region, which may boast annual average growth rates of up to 10%. These will drive it to the top of the world telecoms' markets by the year 2000, with an estimated value of 263 billion ECU (reflecting the development and growth of the Asian and South American countries).

These impressive growth rates should not hide the different evolution of the various subsectors within the telecoms' market. As far as network equipment is concerned, its market in the EU grew by 6.8% in 1998 and is expected to grow by a further 6.3% in 1999 and 6.3% in the year 2000. Public equipment networks are upgrading ageing land-based phone systems and are focussing on providing technology for carrying an ever increasing amount of data traffic over standard phone lines and emerging broadband networks. This trend has been further fuelled by the Internet, both in terms of the number of users and the amount of data being carried. In addition, demand is expected to come from wireless communications, whose share of the public network market grew by 26% in 1998 and is expected to catch-up the market for switching equipment by the year 2000. Finally, the market for private network equipment has been experiencing strong demand for wireless equipment (up 5.3% in 1998) and accessories such as modems, fax-machines, answering machines or audio/video conferencing equipment (up 12.7% in 1998).

(1996=100)

Figure 21.15

Evolution of the market for telecom services, EU-15

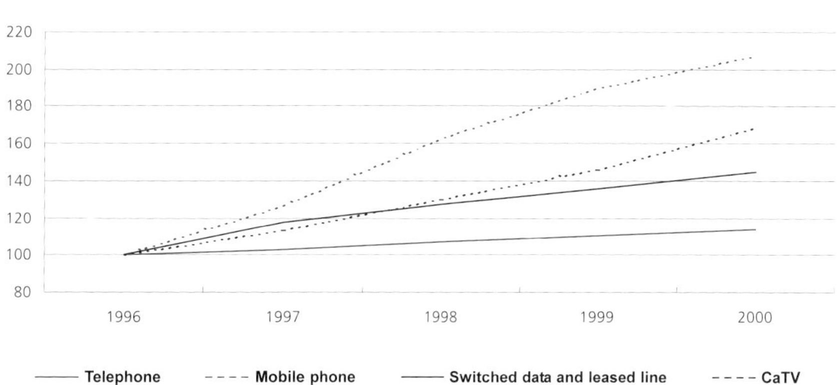

Source: EITO

Turning to services, growth in the EU-15 telecoms' market reached 9% in 1998 but is expected to slow down to 6.8% in 1999 and 5.5% in the year 2000. Telephone services[6] represented the largest share of telecom services with a market value of some 98 billion ECU. They were also the area witnessing the lowest rate of growth (3.8%) and the lowest growth forecasts (3.6% in 1999 and 3.2% in the year 2000). This may be explained by the fact that the price of local and long-distance calls should continue to decline as competition intensifies. Mobile telephone services have boasted growth of 26.9% in 1997 and 28.4% in 1998, reaching an estimated market value of 31 billion ECU. Both the increasing number of mobile subscribers and the growth of the average call length contributed to boost the market, as prices dropped, phones got smaller and battery life got longer.

The deregulation of the European telecommunication services' sector has completely revamped the sector. Traditional operators have been mobilising themselves for several years in order to hold on to their market power when liberalisation came about. Facing increasing competition in their respective national markets and having to deal with increasingly global customers, many players have aimed at international markets or joined strategic alliances. Some of the main activity in the telecoms' market may be summarised as British Telecom (UK) association with MCI (USA), which then merged with WorldCom (USA); Unisource, a pan-European telecommunications company grouping Telia (S), KPN (NL), Swisscom (CH) and Telefonica (E) and WorldPartners including AT&T (USA), KDD (J), SingTel (SG) and Telstra (AU).

Another key driving factor besides regulatory development is technological developments. There is an increasing convergence between communication technologies and information technologies. Cable television companies already offer telephony services as well as Internet services allowing access to the World-Wide-Web from a television set. Conversely, a modem connected to a telephone line allows users to watch television or listen to radio programmes from their computer, with traffic information, share prices or breaking news whilst they are on the move (thanks to their mobile phone).

6) These include national and international voice services for residential and business users, excluding mobile telephone, switched data and leased-line services.

Figure 21.16 (thousand ECU)

Telecommunications (NACE Rev. 1 64.2)

Personnel costs/employee, 1996

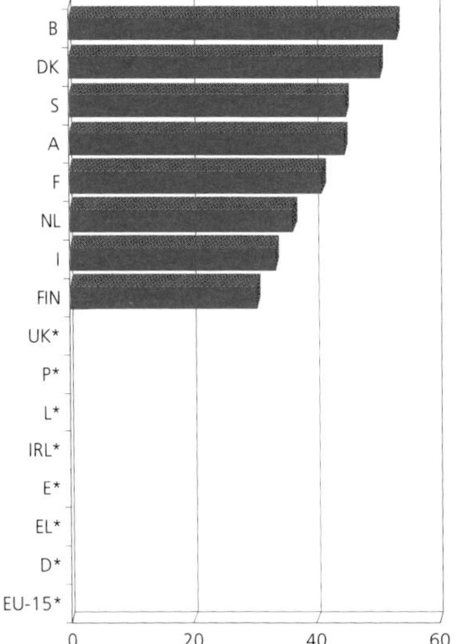

Source: Eurostat (SBS)

Figure 21.17 (%)

Telecommunications (NACE Rev. 1 64.2)

Wage adjusted labour productivity, 1996

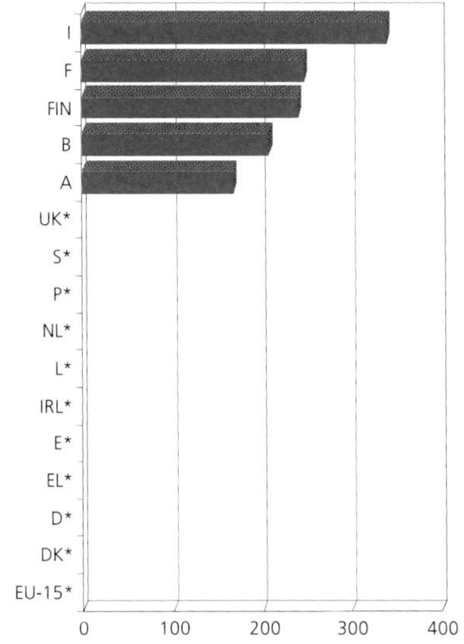

Source: Eurostat (SBS)

Software and computing services (NACE Rev. 1 72)

Software and computing services are covered by the whole of Division 72 of NACE Rev. 1. Formally, it includes hardware and software consultancy services, analysis, design and programming of ready to use software (customised or not), data processing and database activities, as well as the maintenance and repair of office machinery. The activity excludes the reproduction of computer media (NACE Rev. 1 22.33), the manufacture of computers (NACE Rev. 1 30.02) and the retail trade of computers and software (NACE Rev. 1 52.48).

(units) Figure 21.18

Computer services (NACE Rev. 1 72)
Density of enterprises per ten thousand inhabitants, 1995

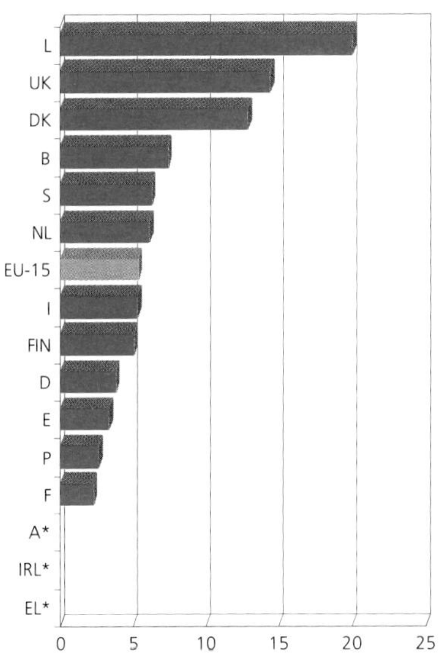

Source: Eurostat (SME)

(million ECU) Table 21.5

The IT market in the EU

	1997	1998	1999	2000
IT Hardware	77,094	81,723	86,250	91,351
Software	32,198	36,124	40,735	45,737
Application software	16,382	18,622	21,190	23,998
System software	15,816	17,502	19,545	21,739
Services	56,510	63,711	72,349	81,453
Consulting and implementation services	23,558	27,681	32,581	37,580
Operations management services	19,276	21,655	24,607	27,874
Support services	13,676	14,375	15,161	15,999
Total	165,802	181,558	199,334	218,541

Source: EITO

(1996=100) Figure 21.19

Evolution of the market for IT services, EU-15

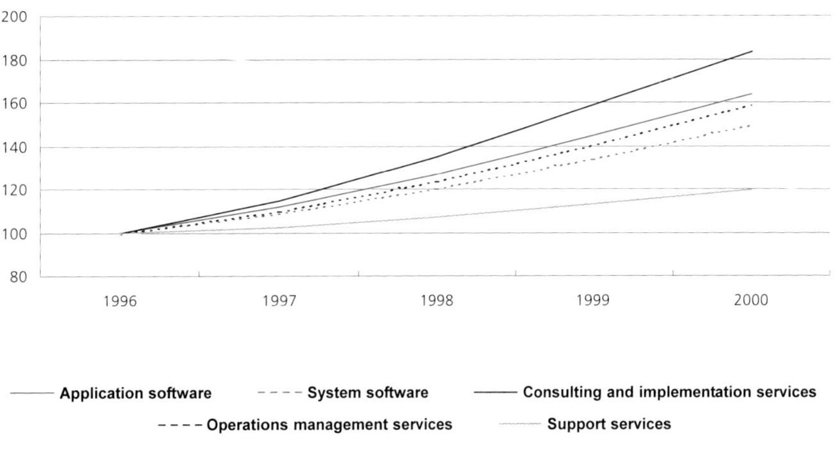

Source: EITO

Many of the software and computing service activities are naturally inter-related with the information technology hardware sector. EITO (the European Information Technology Observatory) estimated that the total EU information technology market (including computer hardware) was worth 182 billion ECU in 1998. Software and computing services alone accounted for 100 billion ECU or 55% of the market. The total world information technology market was worth 727 billion ECU in 1998 and is expected to expand by an annual average growth rate of 9.2% to 867 billion ECU by the year 2000. The USA held the largest share of the market with 44%, compared to 28% for Europe[7] and 13% for Japan. The fastest growing market was forecast to be that of Asia, where the share of the world market is expected to attain 16% by the year 2000.

The EU software and computing services market grew by 12.5% in 1998 and is expected to continue to boast double-digit growth rates in both 1999 and 2000. The software products' subsector recorded growth of 12.2% in 1998, with a market value of 36 billion ECU. Within the software products market systems software and applications software each shared about half of the market, systems software reaching a market value of 17.5 billion ECU compared with 18.6 billion ECU for applications software. Growth expectations are for double-digit levels within both kinds of products, although they are slightly higher for applications.

7) Western, central and eastern Europe together; the EU alone accounted for 25%.

Computing services represent an even larger and faster expanding area, with a market that was worth an estimated 63.7 billion ECU in 1998 and progression of 12.7% when compared to 1997. Just under half of the market is accounted for by consulting and implementation services, one third by operation management services (for example, system and network management, help-desks, back-up and archiving services) and the rest by support services (for example, maintenance contracts and telephone support, be it bundled or not with software packages). The fastest growing activities in computing services were consulting and implementation services.

Figure 21.20

Share of IT services market value by world region, 1998 (1)

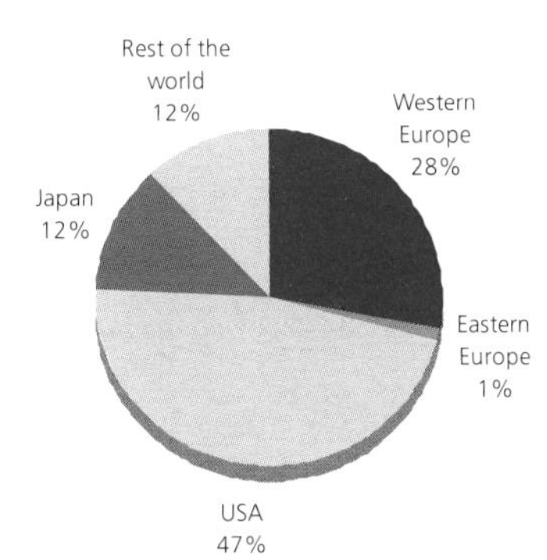

(1) Including software product services.

Source: FITO

The evolution of demand can be analysed both in terms of price and structural factors. On the one hand the trends of falling PC prices in recent years has spurred tremendous demand, especially from the small office/home office (SOHO) and private consumer markets, which in turn stimulates demand for software. On the other hand, structural changes taking place in the business environment have further fuelled demand for software and computing services.

Figure 21.21 (ECU/month)

Computer services (NACE Rev. 1 72)

Labour costs by Member State, 1996

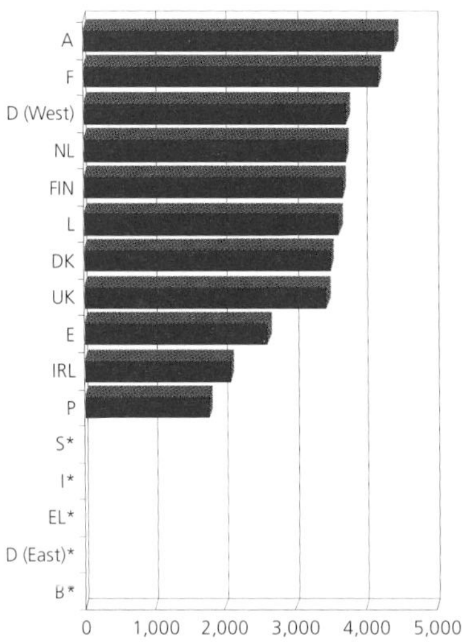

Source: Eurostat (LCS)

One fundamental change has been a shift towards information technology downsizing, moving applications from mainframes to PC-based environments with networks that connect these computers, in order to share applications and data. The evolution towards an ever increasing openness of economies and the globalisation of companies has greatly accentuated this trend, with Intranets starting to become the information backbone for global expansion and GroupWare solutions playing an increasing role in the information technology infrastructure. Recent years have seen an even more fundamental change occur with the development of the Internet. Whilst demand is currently concentrated on e-mail, security tools, systems and services, future developments are expected with a large-scale development of e-commerce and Internet telephony.

Two specific problems have also boosted demand for both software and computing services for a limited time span: the year 2000 bug[8] and the introduction of the euro, both requiring a careful audit of all information technology systems, software and hardware alike.

8) Also known as the Y2K problem, or the millennium bug, this problem originates in the inability of some computers and systems to correctly recognise dates after 1999 because they have been programmed to process only the last two digits of a year. As a result 00 could be read as 1900 instead of 2000.

Figure 21.22 (%)

Computer services (NACE Rev. 1 72)

Share of part-time and temporary work contracts in total number of persons employed, 1997

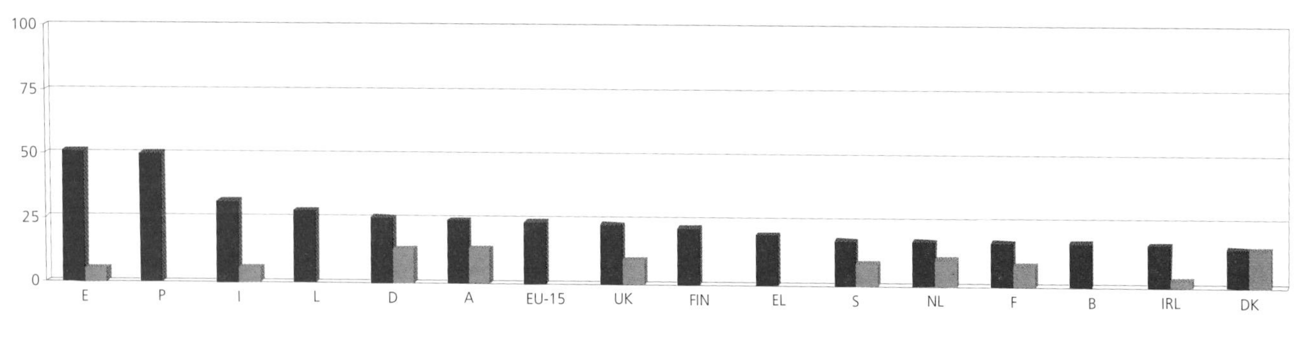

Source: Eurostat (LFS)

The computer market place is evolving at a breath-taking pace and the market leaders of today may lose their place in just a few months. Staying on the cutting edge of technology is crucial for success. The rapid technological change of the computer industry generally necessitates a high level of R&D expenditure, typically of the magnitude of 10% to 15% of sales. Smaller companies are generally the most innovative, but establishing new innovations in a cluttered market-place is becoming increasingly difficult and these firms also have limited capital for expansion, R&D and marketing. Therefore many alliances and acquisitions have occurred to develop new products or share technological, financial or distribution and marketing resources.

Sustained success in the industry requires product breadth and a strong development program to ensure a flow of new products, with a brand name and distribution capabilities. However, as mail-order, mass-market retail channels and e-commerce increase in importance, distribution channels are changing. Software product leadership is vital, as many software users are loyal to the products they know and are reluctant to switch to competitive programs for short-term price or performance benefits, since purchasing, learning and supporting an alternative program and rewriting software to use with it takes time and money. As such, entrenched market leaders tend to build on their installed base.

As hardware costs are reduced and products are become increasingly complex, software vendors are increasingly under price pressure, therefore many vendors are increasingly obtaining revenues from consulting and implementation services.

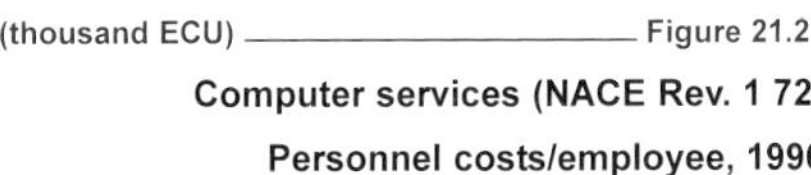

(thousand ECU) Figure 21.23

Computer services (NACE Rev. 1 72)

Personnel costs/employee, 1996

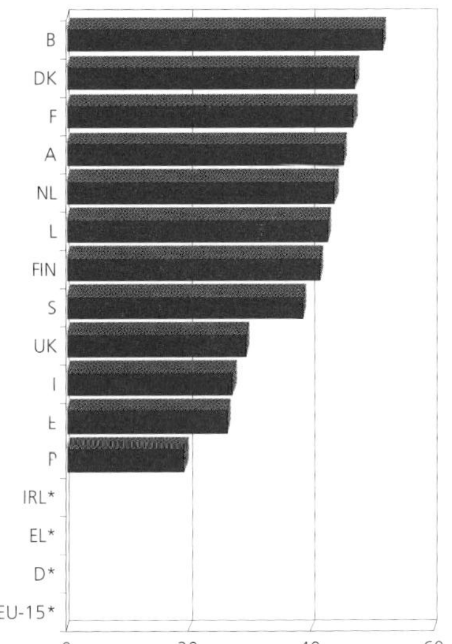

Source: Eurostat (SBS)

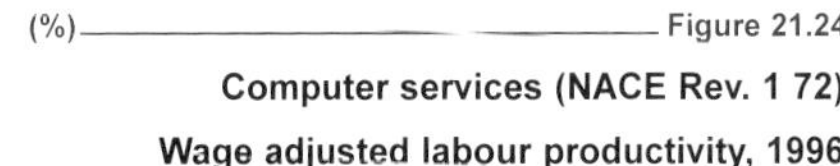

(%) Figure 21.24

Computer services (NACE Rev. 1 72)

Wage adjusted labour productivity, 1996

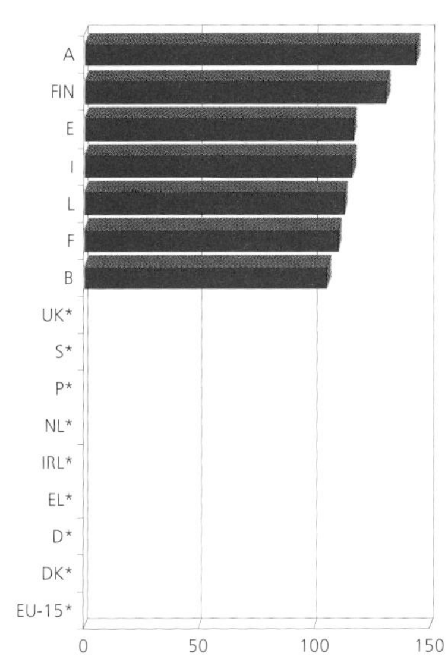

Source: Eurostat (SBS)

Table 21.6

World's top 20 software companies, 1998

	Company	Worldwide software revenue (million ECU)	Total employment (units)	Business sector
1	**Microsoft Corp.**	14,564	27,055	Applic./OS/Dev.Tools/Netwk
2	**IBM Corp.**	10,582	291,067	Applic./OS/Net./Sys. Mgmt./DB
3	**Oracle Corp.**	4,744	40,000	Databases/ERP
4	**Computer Associates Inc.**	4,330	12,800	Network/Systems Management
5	**Hitachi Ltd.**	3,732	331,494	Enterprise Application Integration
6	**SAP AG**	2,813	19,308	ERP/Enterprise Applic. Suites
7	**Hewlett-Packard Co.**	1,260	124,600	Network/Systems Mgmt./OS
8	**Sun Microsystems Inc.**	1,220	26,300	OS/Dev.Tools/Lang./Netwk.
9	**Compaq Computer Corp.**	1,047	71,200	OS
10	**PeopleSoft Inc.**	930	7,032	ERP/Enterprise Application Suites
11	**Parametric Techn. Corp.**	900	4,800	EDA/CAD/CAM
12	**Network Associates Inc.**	883	1,500	Network/Systems Management
13	**BMC Software Inc.**	870	3,604	Databases
14	**Cadence Design Inc.**	857	4,000	Engineering Productivity
15	**Compuware Corp.**	829	10,016	Development Tools/Languages
16	**Adobe Systems Inc.**	798	2,680	DTP/Graphics
17	**Sybase Inc.**	774	4,300	Middleware/Databases/EAI
18	**SAS Institute Inc.**	755	5,679	Data Wareh.se/Query Tools/OLAP
19	**The Learning Company**	749	2,000	Consumer/Education Applications
20	**Andersen Consulting**	740	65,000	Network/Systems Management

Source: Software Magazine's Annual Software 500, June 1999, Wiesner Publishing, Southborough, Mass

Film and video (NACE Rev. 1 92.1)

The film and video industry is covered by Group 92.1 within the NACE Rev. 1 activity classification. It includes services of cinematographic and audiovisual production[9] as well as services of distribution and exhibition of cinematographic and audiovisual films[10]. However, this NACE Rev. 1 Group excludes activities such as the duplication and reproduction of films and videotapes from master copies (NACE Rev. 1 22.3) and the retail trade and renting of tapes to the general public (NACE Rev. 1 52.1 and NACE Rev. 1 71.4 respectively).

Figure 21.25 (units)

Motion picture and video activities (NACE Rev. 1 92.1)

Density of enterprises per ten thousand inhabitants, 1995

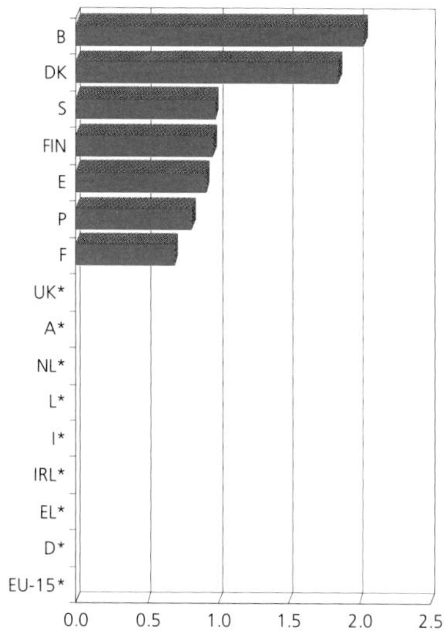

Source: Eurostat (SME)

More than five hundred long length feature films are produced in the EU each year. In 1997, the level reached 420 national productions and 221 international co-productions. This makes the EU one of the largest film producers in the world after India (697 films produced), and the second largest in the Triad, as 673 long length feature films were produced in the USA in 1997 and 278 in Japan[11]. The largest contributor to the EU film industry was France with 163 movies in 1997, almost one quarter of the total, followed by the United Kingdom (103), Italy (87), Spain (80) and Germany (76).

9) Including cinematographic films, but also advertising, TV fiction and documentaries and production services upstream and downstream such as special effects, dubbing, etc.
10) Including the management of audiovisual rights.
11) Both figures cover new movies released for the first time.

Figure 21.26 (% of box office)

Market shares of films by origin, 1997

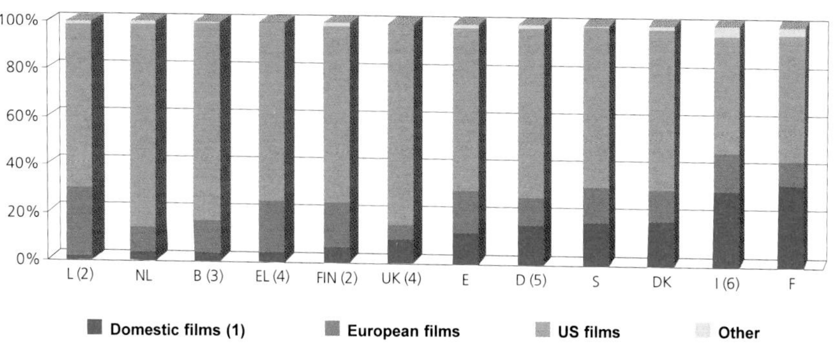

(1) Including co-productions.
(2) Percentage of admissions.
(3) Excluding those distributed by Polygram and Alternative Films.
(4) 1995 data.
(5) Based on gross distribution revenue.
(6) Cinetel data: 174 cities, 1,250 screens.

Source: Media Salles

Figure 21.27 (thousand ECU)

Motion picture and video activities (NACE Rev. 1 92.1)

Personnel costs/employee, 1996

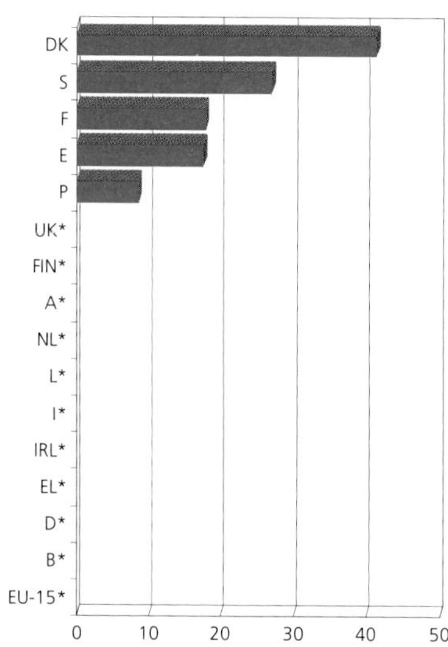

Source: Eurostat (SBS)

These figures however tell only half of the story, and a look at the size of the productions (notably in terms of financial resources involved) shows a totally different picture. Indeed, investment in film production in the EU totalled 2.9 billion ECU in 1997, a third of the 8.7 billion ECU invested within the USA. This means that in 1997, an average of 12.8 million ECU per film was invested in the USA. In the case of the American "majors", average production costs reached some 46 million ECU per film[12]. This compares with an average investment of 4.2 million ECU per film in the EU, a figure that varies enormously across Members States, from 300 thousand ECU in Greece up to 8.4 million ECU in the United Kingdom, the second highest figure in the world after the USA. German and French production came next with an average production cost of about 5 million ECU.

12) Source: Screen Digest, 1998.

(%) Figure 21.28

Recreational, cultural and sporting activities (NACE Rev. 1 92)

Share of part-time and temporary work contracts in total number of persons employed, 1997

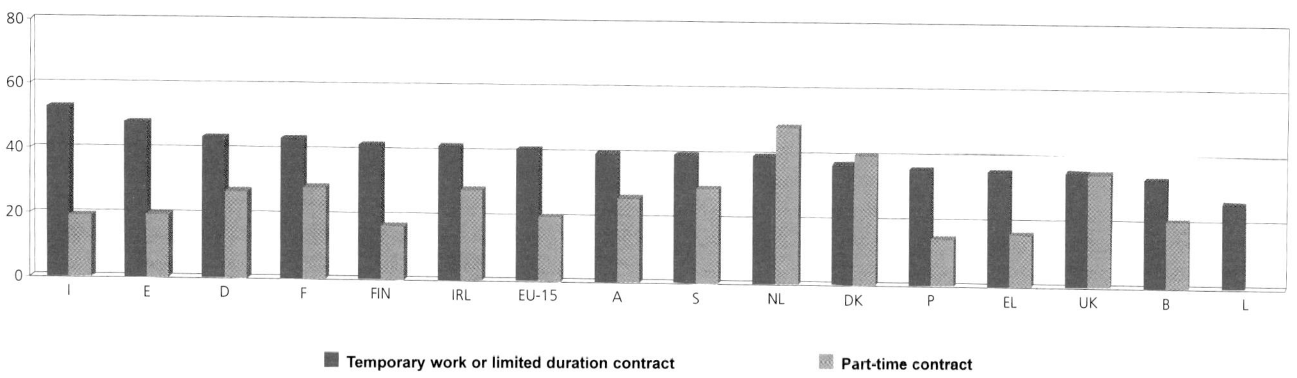

Source: Eurostat (LFS)

The emergence of private television channels and the development of pay-TV since the mid-1980s have significantly affected the film industry. Several broadcasters actively finance the film industry, either through co-production or rights acquisitions, with the objective to increase and secure the programming for their ever-expanding number of channels. The European Commission also promoted the development of the European audiovisual industry by launching in 1991 a programme (Media) focussing on three priority areas: training, development of potentially successful works and transnational distribution of films and audiovisual programmes. Over the period 1996-2000, the programme has been allocated a budget of 310 million ECU. In addition, several Member States also support their national cinematographic industry, either by requiring television channels to invest in film production (for example France and Italy), or through direct financing. It is estimated that national and Community publicly financed investment accounted for less than a quarter of total production investment in Europe.

(units) Figure 21.29

Average size and occupancy rate of cinemas, 1997

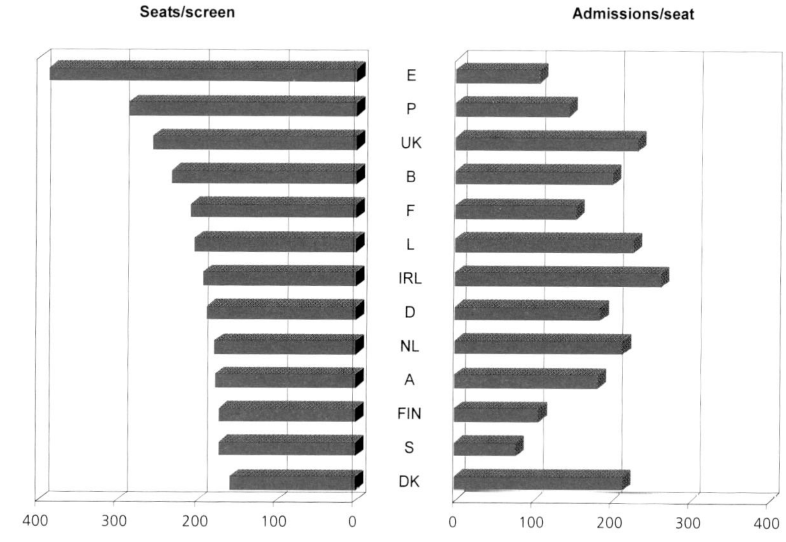

Source: Eurostat

Film distribution and exhibition have traditionally been regarded as two distinct functions, although they have started to show a tendency to integrate both within Europe and the USA. Gross distribution revenues are on a rising trend in the EU, supported by an increasing number of admissions. The European distribution market reached 1.6 billion ECU in value terms in 1997, a 9% increase over the year before and about 35% of the world total. Meanwhile admissions rose by 7% to 764 million units, generating a gross box office revenue of 3.9 billion ECU, 15% above the level of the year before. In contrast, the USA recorded growth of only 4% in cinema admissions to reach 1.4 billion units and a 7% rise in box office takings to reach 5.6 billion ECU. Distribution turnover within the USA expanded by 8%[13] to 2.1 billion ECU (45% of the world total).

13) Both monetary growth rates are calculated on a constant dollar basis.

Table 21.7 (units)

Number of multiplex sites by number of screens, as of 01.01.99

	8	9	10	11-15	15-20	20+	Total
B	3	0	2	8	1	2	16
DK	0	1	0	0	1	0	2
D	23	20	13	13	3	0	72
EL	1	1	1	0	0	0	3
E	20	14	11	11	2	2	60
F	22	7	3	35	5	1	73
IRL	0	2	2	3	0	0	7
I	1	4	2	:	1	0	8
L	0	0	1	0	0	0	1
NL	3	1	0	0	0	0	4
A	4	1	0	3	0	0	8
P	1	1	2	1	1	0	6
FIN	0	0	1	0	0	0	1
S	6	3	3	2	1	0	15
UK	24	20	22	45	2	0	113
EU-15	108	75	63	121	17	5	389

Source: Media Salles

Figure 21.30

Multiplex density in relation to market share of US films, 1998

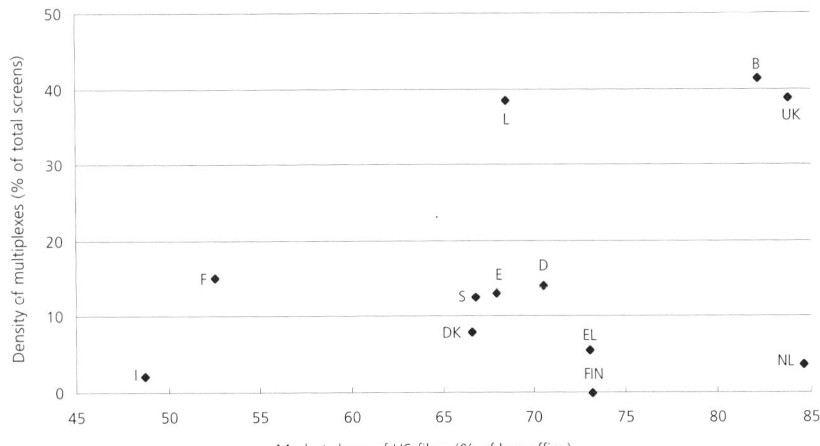

Source: Media Salles

France is the leader of the European film industry, both in terms of admissions and of box office takings. With 149 million admissions and 778 million ECU in gross takings, France accounts for about a fifth of the EU total. France also records the highest ticket sales per capita at 13.3 ECU per inhabitant per year, ahead of the United Kingdom (at 12.8 ECU per inhabitant), Ireland and Denmark (both 12.3 ECU). However, Ireland is the country within the EU where people like to visit the cinema most, with 3.2 cinema tickets sold per inhabitant per year, followed by Spain (2.7) and France (2.5). These figures are a long way short of those recorded in the USA (5.3 tickets per inhabitant on average). The average cinema attendance in Japan was only once a year per inhabitant, the same level as the Greek figure (the lowest within the EU).

American studios still dominate the European film marketplace. Figures available for 1997 indicate that within the largest markets a large number of total releases originate from the USA. Within France the figure was 37% of total releases, and 52% of gross box office. In Italy it reached 48% of both releases and box office receipts. However, it was in the United Kingdom where a much higher share existed, some 60% of all movies released coming from the USA, representing 84% of gross box office receipts. Domestic productions represented about one fifth of the releases in most Member States, including the United Kingdom. However, there was one notable exception, namely France, where French movies accounted for 38% of all releases (and 34% of total revenue). In the USA, just 64 out of the 409 releases in 1997 were of non-domestic origin and they accounted for a meagre 3% of overall ticket sales[14].

14) Source: European Audiovisual Observatory, 1998.

The place of the cinema in the business cycle and revenue of the film industry is steadily decreasing over the years. Only a limited and decreasing proportion of a film's revenue comes from box-office takings. A number of companies generate extra income (which may even exceed the box-office profits of the film itself) through the sale of merchandising, licenses for toys, video games, clothing, books, etc, or through partnership deals with companies outside the film industry, particularly fast-food chains and games manufacturers. The lion's share of film revenues comes however from the television market, both through the sale of broadcasting rights and through the sale of video tapes and renting.

The EU video market has rapidly developed in the nineties reaching 5 billion ECU in 1997, 76% above its level of 1990. An important evolution within this market has been a clear shift from rental to sell-through transactions. In 1990 two thirds of the video revenues originated from rentals, whilst in 1997 64% originated from the sale of more than 260 million videocassettes. Rental transactions were down by 4% in 1997 at 641 million units, but total rental revenue rose by 2% to 1.8 billion ECU thanks to a 6% increase in the average cost of a night's rental to 2.9 ECU. European VCR households[15] spent on average only 51 ECU per year on buying and renting video software in 1997, compared to 108 ECU for Japanese VCR households and 160 ECU in the USA.

15) Households equipped with at least one videocassette recorder, representing in 1997 about 73% of the total number of households equipped with a television set.

Figure 21.31

Receipts from pre-recorded video cassettes or discs, EU-15

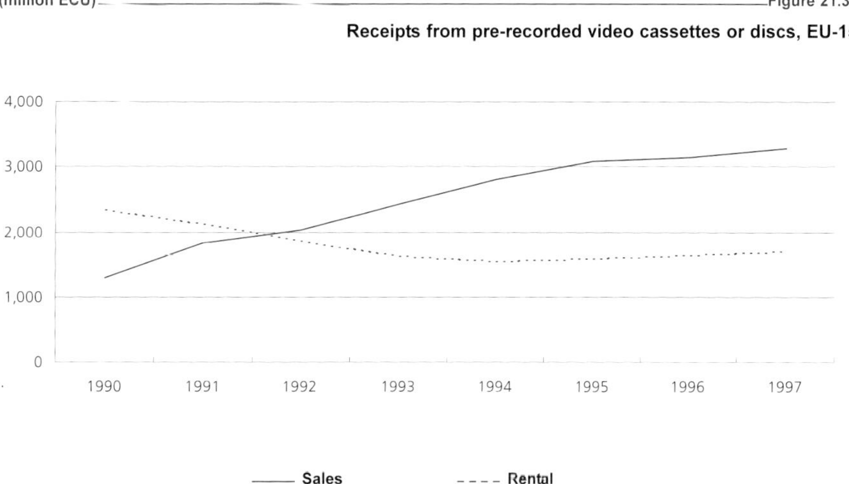

Source: Eurostat

Figure 21.32

Average price indicators of the video market, 1997

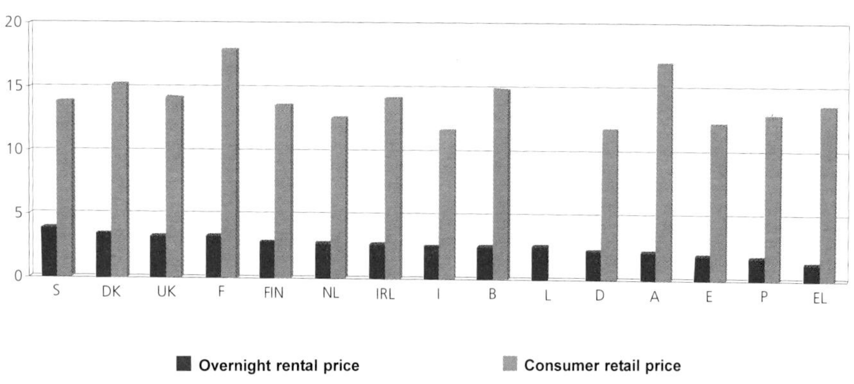

Source: IVF

Television (NACE Rev. 1 92.2)

The television industry consists of three major activities: the production of programmes, the compilation of schedules of those programmes and their transmission to the final consumer. Following the NACE Rev. 1 activity classification, the first two activities are included in Group 92.2 representing all radio and television activities, whilst the physical transmission of TV signals via hertzian relays, satellite or cable networks is covered by the Group 64.2 (telecommunications).

The most obvious factor influencing television demand is the share of households equipped with a television set, which in the EU is already at the very high level of 96%, up from 94% at the beginning of the decade. However only 43% of these households are equipped with a second television set, a share much lower than in the USA or Japan, where more than 70% of households have at least a second television set. Several other economic, social and technological factors also influence television consumption, such as employment conditions (for example, the unemployment rate, share of part-time work, number of working hours), the occurrence of important events (for example, major sports events, serious international crises) or the number and variety of channels available. In addition, television, as an integral part of the entertainment business, must compete with all other traditional entertainment activities, as well as other more recent multimedia products such as video recordings, game consoles or surfing the Internet.

Figure 21.33 (units)

Radio and television activities (NACE Rev. 1 92.2)

Density of enterprises per ten thousand inhabitants, 1995

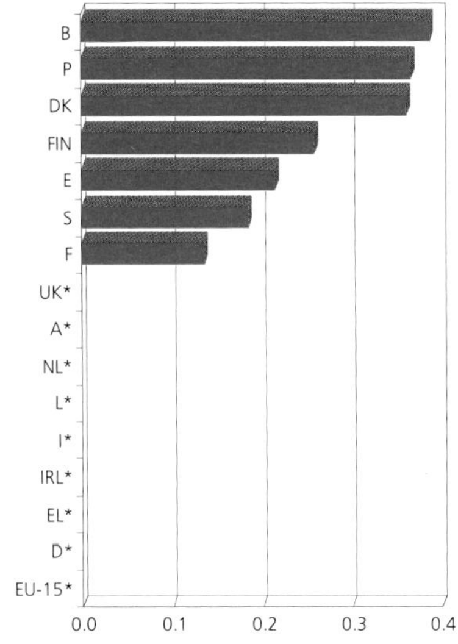

Source: Eurostat (SME)

Final demand for television can be measured by the average amount of time that people spend watching each day. Eurostat estimate this amount to be about 190 minutes per person per day within the EU, varying from 136 minutes in Luxembourg up to 213 minutes in the United Kingdom. Viewing time has generally witnessed a very modest rise in Europe in recent years, whilst staying well below the levels recorded in the USA (265 minutes).

Figure 21.34 (minutes/day)

Television: average viewing time, 1997

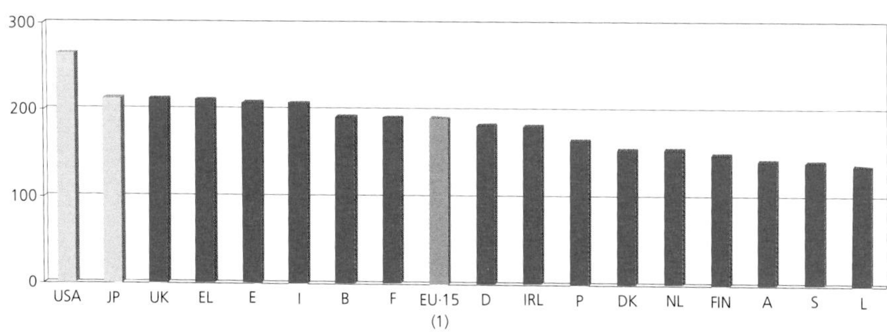

(1) Average.

Source: Eurostat

Table 21.8

Equipment rate of households, 1997 (1)

	Number of TV households (thousand)	TV households with 2 TV sets or more (%)	Penetration rate of VCRs (%) (2)
EU-15	142,883	43.0	66.9
B	3,976	27.2	71.1
DK	2,359	42.0	79.4
D	36,340	34.0	64.8
EL	3,590	48.0	36.5
E	11,804	57.9	53.4
F	21,491	35.1	74.6
IRL	1,133	42.4	71.3
I	19,505	46.4	57.2
L	159	46.0	56.6
NL	6,505	38.3	72.9
A	2,983	50.0	69.0
P	3,037	57.3	65.0
FIN	2,210	41.0	68.7
S	3,973	39.8	74.9
UK	24,200	58.0	82.4
USA	98,000	74.0	82.0
Japan	43,900	99.0	82.1

(1) EU-15, B, F, I, A, S: 1996; E: 1995; L, FIN: provisional data; EU-15, EL and IE: estimates.
(2) D, NL: 1996.

Source: Eurostat

(%) Figure 21.35

Cable and satellite penetration rate in private TV households, 1997 (1)

Satellite penetration (3)

Cable penetration (2)

(1) B (satellite), E, L (cable): 1995; EU-15, B (cable), DK, EL, F, I, A and S: 1996.
(2) Estimates for EU-15, EL; provisional data for DK, P.
(3) Estimates for EU-15, DK, EL, S; provisional data for P.

Source: Eurostat

(million ECU) Figure 21.36

Revenues of public television

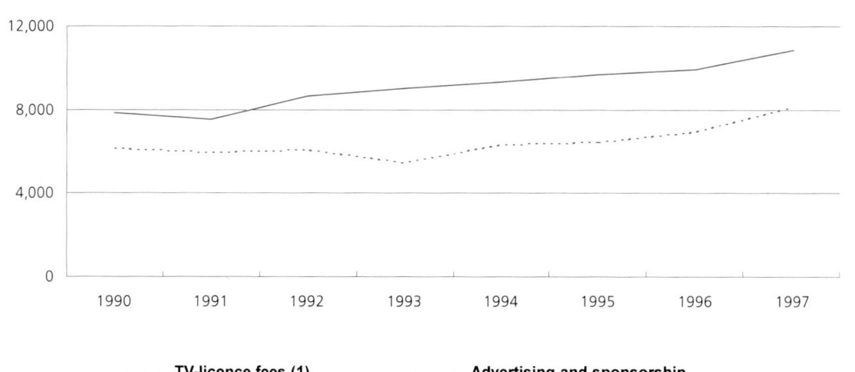

TV-licence fees (1) **Advertising and sponsorship**

(1) Excluding EL in 1990-1992, 1994 and 1997; DK: Danmarks radio only; 1990 excluding former Eastern Germany.

Source: Eurostat

On the supply side, most Member States have opened their television market to private operators which has led to a sharp rise in the number of television channels available. In addition to public stations, five large private broadcasting groups occupy the European scene. CLT-Ufa, is the company resulting from the 1996 merger between CLT (L) and the audio-visual activities of German media group Bertelsmann, operating RTL television channels in several Member States, Hungary and Poland. Kirch Group (D) holds stakes in Sat1, Première, DSF-1 and Pro7. Fininvest (I) controls three channels in Italy (Canale 5, Italia 1, Rete 4) and is also present on the Spanish market with Tele Cinco. Canal+ (F) operates pay-TV channels in several Member States, as well as Poland. NewsCorp (UK) controls BSkyB within the United Kingdom. Other smaller players such as SBS-CME also operate with a cross-border strategy.

Broadcasters can count on three types of revenues, depending on their legal status and their commercial strategy: TV-licence fees paid each year by every television set owner[16] and/or State subsidies (both for public operators), revenues from advertising and sponsorship (for public operators and "free" commercial TV) and direct receipts from viewers (in the case of pay-TV channels).

Revenues from TV-licence fees have witnessed strong growth in the first half of the nineties reaching 11 billion ECU in the EU in 1997, up from 7.8 billion ECU in 1990, growth in excess of 30%. At the same time, increasing competition between a rising number of channels, as well as a stagnating average viewing time has led to a fragmentation of advertising revenue. This seriously affected the financial conditions faced by private broadcasters, but also led to the development of new services such as pay channels and specialised channels, a trend helped by the introduction of digital transmission technology.

16) In all Member States, except Luxembourg, Portugal and Spain.

Digitalisation allows a greater number of channels to be transmitted on the same bandwidth, hence reducing transmission costs, notably for the transmission of channel packages. It also increases customer value, through better images and enhanced transmission capabilities (extended pay-per-view services, multiplexing, video on demand, software downloading, etc). According to the European Audiovisual Observatory, the number of pay-per-view services in Europe expanded from one in 1994 to 17 by 1998, and the number of services from 1 to 200 over the same period, all of which used digital technology.

In this context of booming supply, two key elements to success are access to transmission capabilities (either by cable or through satellite slots) and control over the supply of content (transmission rights for films, series, sports' events). This has led several broadcasters to pursue a vertical integration strategy. We have thus seen attempts to take control of football clubs (BSkyB with Manchester Utd, Canal+ with Paris St. Germain), acquisition of cable networks (Canal+ with one of Vivendi's networks) or possible co-operation deals with media groups (Kirch with Viacom/Paramount). These trends rely somewhat on the willingness of public authorities to maintain competitive conditions within the market.

One of the remaining questions concerning the development of digital pay-TV is whether the consumer will accept to pay high fees to watch prime events, considering the abundant offer of free channels.

Figure 21.37 (thousand ECU)

Radio and television activities
(NACE Rev. 1 92.2)
Personnel costs/employee, 1996

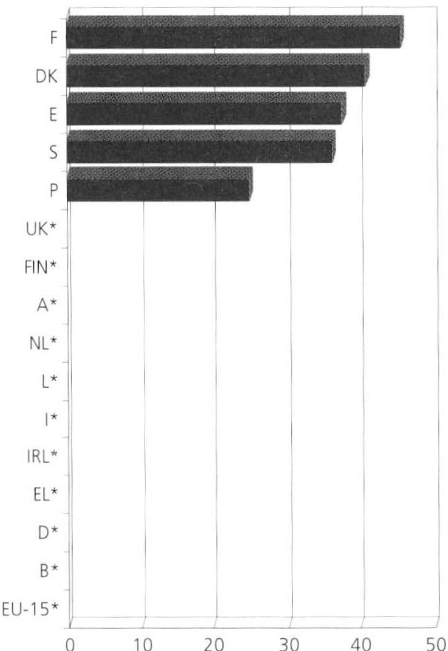

Source: Eurostat (SBS)

Music recording (NACE Rev. 1 22.14 and 22.31)

The music recording industry includes activities that range from the selection, management and production of artists to the manufacturing, marketing and distribution of recorded media such as compact discs, vinyl discs and compact cassettes. Two classes of the NACE Rev. 1 classification cover this industry: Class 22.14 for the publishing side and Class 22.31 for the reproduction side.

Turnover from the sale of music recordings in the EU exceeded 10 billion ECU in 1997, a 5% rise over the previous year and 43% above the level recorded in 1990. In nominal value terms, EU sales increased at an average annual rate of 13.5% between 1985 and 1991. In 1992, sales decreased by 6%, but the market recovered markedly between 1992 and 1997.

(million ECU) Figure 21.38

Turnover of pre-recorded music sales, EU-15

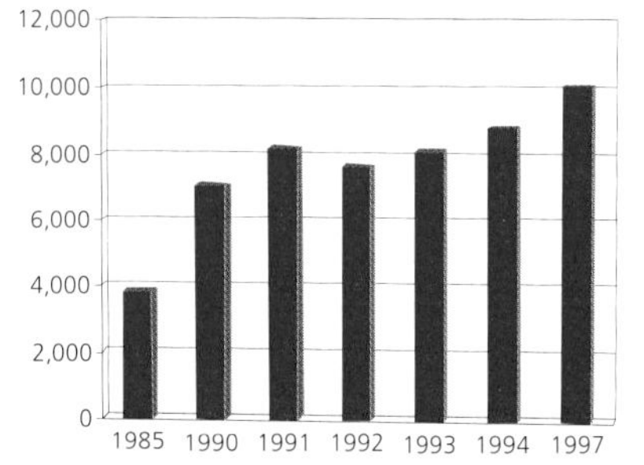

Source: IFPI

In unit terms, the EU recorded sales of 884 million units[17] in 1997, 78% of which were compact discs. This sector follows a long-term cycle closely linked to the introduction of new hardware technologies, such as the audio CD in the late 1980s. Vinyl LPs peaked with 1.2 billion units world-wide in 1981 and have since declined to a mere 17 million by 1997. Cassettes reached 1.6 billion units in 1992 and then lost their momentum (1.4 billion by 1997). However, the number of long format CDs sold more than doubled between 1991 and 1997 reaching more than 2.2 billion units in 1997 and further growth is still expected. Philips' DCC and Sony's MiniDisc have so far failed to capture a substantial share of the market. However, new formats derived from the PC world such as MPEG-1 layer 3[18] have also been launched. We can note that 1998 saw the introduction of cheap portable MP3 players, allowing consumers to download music files from PCs or from the Internet. This phenomenon also raised concerns about wide-scale piracy developing using the Internet as a reproduction medium.

17) Total unit sales of CDs, LPs, MCs and singles (45rpm vinyl and 2-title MCs and CDs). Following the definition of IFPI (International Federation of the Phonographic Industry), three singles are counted as one album.
18) Also known as MP3, an ISO/IEC sound compression algorithm standard developed by the Moving Picture Experts Group (MPEG) and widespread over the Internet, that enables music files to be stored on a storage media and replayed at near-perfect quality, whilst keeping file sizes at about a tenth of the original.

Indeed, a future challenge for the music industry may come from the development of on-line computer services delivering music and visual images in digital form to personal computers within the home. Although this distribution channel remains marginal, it is commonly agreed that digital diffusion (through Internet or other means) will become an important part of the global market in the near future. Based on the emergence of global entertainment groups, it is believed that major music companies will also be involved directly or indirectly in the control of channels through which music is either distributed or played (such as radio, television or computer networks).

The world market for music recordings amounted to more than 33 billion ECU in 1997. The EU[19] represented around 30% of world sales, ahead of Japan (with 16%) but behind the USA (31%). The higher prices that European customers face are reflected by the fact that in terms of unit sales the USA records a figure 9% higher than the EU. CDs represented close to 60% of total unit sales of recording products. Asia was the largest consumer of music cassettes with a world market share of 55%. The EU was the first buyer of singles (on CD or vinyl format) with a 43% market share, whilst over a third of the world CD production was sold in the EU. Combined world sales of CD formats (both short and long formats) reached 2.6 billion units. CD sales continued to expand fastest in emerging and developing economies: for example, CD sales in Eastern Europe were up by 30%, in Latin America they were up by 19%, and in Asia (excluding Japan) by 13%. Growth in the nineties has been faster in Europe than in the USA or in Japan. However, around 40% of the world's growth was generated from emerging markets, in particular Latin America.

With regard to capacity issues and the duplication process, over 74 CD production plants exist within the EU. Most duplication facilities are owned by major record companies, but some independent companies are also active in this sector.

19) Excluding Luxembourg.

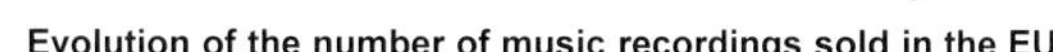

(thousand units) Figure 21.39

Evolution of the number of music recordings sold in the EU

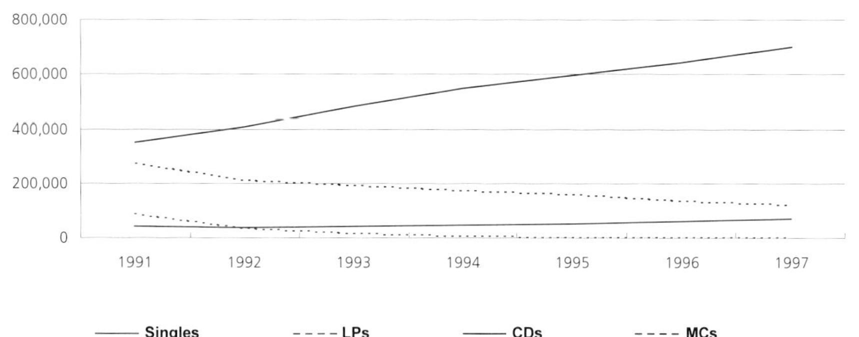

Source: Eurostat

Figure 21.40 (%)

Market share of pre-recorded music by origin, 1997

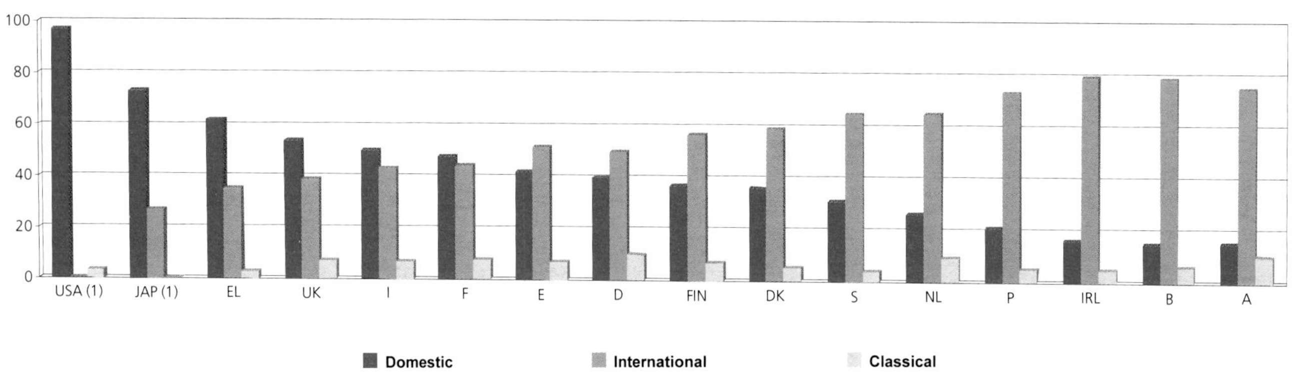

(1) 1996.

Source: IFPI

The music industry remains highly competitive with companies vying to discover and attract the most promising talent. Major EU companies attempt to combine a global presence through international artists with a strong national presence through local talent. The companies with the largest shares of the audio software market are multinational organisations with recording and production facilities located in all main markets. Three major EU players used to control over 40% of world music sales, BMG of Germany, EMI Music of the United Kingdom and PolyGram, owned by Philips (NL). But in 1998 the Canadian beverages and entertainment company Seagram bought PolyGram to create Universal Music Group, the current world leader. The sector of music recording is thus relatively concentrated, with the first five players (UMG, Sony Music, Warner Music Group, EMI and BMG) controlling between 65% and 70% of the global music market.

The entertainment industry is in flux as intensive deal-making is leading to the emergence of global companies that bestride the converging sectors of computers, telecommunications, media, broadcasting and entertainment in anticipation of the era of electronic distribution. The major music companies have diversified operations into related markets including film production, book publishing, broadcasting and retailing. A company like Sony is also vertically integrated since it manufactures and distributes the audio equipment necessary for playing and recording. The combination of capital intensity with market internationalisation indicates that economies of scale are critical. Most players have sought to secure a wider international position as well as to enrich their repertoire.

Sales of recorded music are the main source of revenue for the music industry, but publishing remains more profitable, mainly because it involves lower overheads. A music publisher can claim royalties when the music it "owns" is recorded, performed, broadcast or used in advertising. The five "majors" invest heavily in order to buy publishing rights and build up their catalogue and the publishing market has grown rapidly in the 1990s. This is partly due to the emergence of music markets in Asia and Latin America and partly due to the increase in the value of advertising rights.

Professional associations representing the industries within this chapter

EITO
European Information Technology Observatory
LyonerStrasse, 18
D-60528 Frankfurt am Main
tel: (49) 69 660 31 539
fax: (49) 69 66 03 15 10

IFPI
International Federation of the Phonographic Industries
54 Regent Street
London WIR 5PJ
tel: (44) 171 878 79 00
fax: (44) 171 878 79 50
e-mail: info@ifpi.org

ISPO
Information Society Promotion Office
BU 24 0/74
200, rue de la Loi
B-1049 Bruxelles
tel: (32) 2 296 88 00
fax: (32) 2 299 41 70
e-mail: ispo@ispo.cec.be

ITU
International Telecommunication Union
Place des Nations
CH-1211 Genève 20
tel: (41) 22 730 51 11
fax: (41) 22 733 72 56
e-mail: itumail@itu.int

IVF
International Video Federation
143, avenue de Tervueren
B-1150 Bruxelles
tel: (32) 2 742 24 09
fax: (32) 2 742 24 11

SPA
Software Publishers Association
1730 M St. NW, Suite 700
20036-4510 Washington DC
United States of America
tel: (1) 202 452-1600
fax: (1) 202 223-8756
e-mail: webmaster@spa.org

UPU
Universal Postal Union
6, Place Abelgance
Case postale
CH-3000 Berne 15
tel: (31) 350 31 11
fax: (31) 350 31 10
e-mail: info@upu.int

Table 21.9

Main indicators of postal services, 1997

	EU-15	B	DK	D	EL	E	F	IRL	I	L	NL	A	P	FIN	S	UK
Post offices open to the public (1)	:	1,662	9,066	22,250	1,262	60,587	16,636	1,917	14,411	106	2,309	2,613	5,660	1,619	4,595	19,958
Sorting offices (2)	:	7	8	116	6	141	171	88	170	1	11	31	9	15	:	714
Letter boxes (thousand) (3)	667	20	10	140	13	35	149	4	73	1	19	24	19	12	37	112
Total staff (thousand) (3)	1,326	43	26	267	11	65	287	8	191	2	54	58	16	24	47	209
Share of full-time staff (%) (3)	82	89	100	70	99	91	81	92	95	73	50	94	100	71	84	82
Postal services expenditure (million ECU) (4)	52,189	1,606	1,051	14,532	219	1,185	13,403	475	8,394	89	2,553	2,279	417	847	2,118	5,944
Postal services investment (million ECU) (5)	2,934	77	39	982	3	67	423	29	394	7	913	95	34	52	200	511
Postal services receipts (million ECU) (6)	56,296	1,680	1,221	14,808	257	1,022	12,911	493	6,010	86	3,136	3,027	452	916	2,669	7,827
Post items, domestic service (million) (7)	87,775	3,139	1,668	20,000	392	4,014	23,914	523	6,237	102	5,970	2,438	964	1,519	4,360	17,296
Share of letters in domestic service (%) (8)	:	35	45	43	75	72	42	:	67	100	41	23	73	50	:	:
Post items, international dispatch (million) (9)	:	214	130	403	68	156	395	65	147	33	27	136	51	28	86	863
Post items, international receipt (million) (9)	:	204	78	702	45	160	453	124	201	25	12	143	46	36	125	480

(1) A, P: 1996; DK, F, NL: 1995; EL, S: 1993; D, I, UK: 1992.
(2) DK, EL, F, NL, A, P, UK: 1996; I: 1992.
(3) EU-15, DK, EL, F, I, NL, A, P, S, UK: 1996.
(4) F, A, P: 1996; DK, NL: 1995; S: 1994; EL: 1993; EU-15, I, UK: 1992.
(5) EL, NL, P, S, UK: 1996; DK, F, A: 1995; EU-15, I: 1993.
(6) EL, F, I, NL, A, P, S, UK: 1996; EU-15, DK: 1995.
(7) DK, EL, F, I, A, P, S, UK: 1996; EU-15, NL: 1995.
(8) A, P: 1996; DK, F, I, NL: 1995; EL: 1993.
(9) F, I, A, P, S, UK: 1996; DK, NL: 1995; EL: 1993.

Table 21.10

Evolution of main indicators of postal services, EU-15

	1988	1989	1990	1991	1992	1993	1994	1995	1996	1997
Permanent post offices (1)	98,179	97,458	108,906	104,491	99,642	97,603	:	90,725	:	:
Letter boxes (thousand) (2)	:	669	614	667	708	705	:	699	649	:
Total staff (thousand)	1,433	1,454	1,462	1,410	1,439	1,433	1,374	1,356	1,326	:
Share of full-time staff (%)	91	91	91	93	85	86	:	85	82	:
Postal services expenditure (million ECU) (3)	42,000	45,228	44,629	49,986	51,238	:	:	:	:	:
Postal services investment (million ECU) (4)	2,568	2,669	2,896	2,902	:	2,931	:	:	:	:
Postal services receipts (million ECU) (3)	39,100	43,293	39,603	47,875	48,992	51,422	:	55,074	55,667	:
Post items, domestic service (million) (1)	71,243	71,269	74,976	75,663	79,967	81,998	81,461	81,805	86,147	:
Post items, international dispatch (million) (5)	:	:	2,365	2,426	2,547	2,382	2,562	2,512	2,562	:

(1) Excluding NL.
(2) Excluding IRL, FIN.
(3) Excluding DK.
(4) Excluding L.
(5) Excluding EL, IRL, NL, S.

Source: Eurostat

Table 21.11

Main indicators of telecommunications services, 1997

	EU-15	B	DK	D	EL	E	F	IRL	I	L	NL	A	P	FIN	S	UK
Main telephone lines (thousand) (1)	188,000	4,726	3,251	44,100	5,329	15,854	33,000	1,390	25,259	280	8,431	3,779	3,724	2,861	6,032	30,678
Share of residential main lines (%) (2)	:	78	80	76	70	75	75	68	78	65	77	:	79	71	76	74
Mobile phone subscribers (thousand) (3)	33,485	975	1,317	5,790	550	4,338	5,817	289	6,422	67	804	563	664	2,162	2,492	7,109
ISDN lines (thousand) (4)	2,714	99	30	1,964	1	229	1,278	0	105	10	100	42	20	58	20	260
Telex subscriber lines (5)	345,923	3,224	2,677	16,940	15,073	3,568	39,000	2,500	22,998	1,016	6,300	3,569	2,708	1,042	4,650	20,299
Subscriber's telefax stations (thousand) (6)	6,695	190	250	1,800	40	700	125	80	1,800	17	500	207	50	198	450	1,800
Total staff (thousand) (7)	874	21	16	208	24	73	166	12	100	1	30	18	19	18	34	141
Telecom services expenditure (million ECU) (8)	106,816	2,710	3,134	33,499	1,984	8,415	19,461	921	14,307	194	5,738	2,943	2,431	2,463	4,192	13,671
Telecom services receipts (million ECU) (9)	135,583	3,529	3,167	33,032	2,468	9,676	21,537	1,396	18,127	275	6,672	3,163	2,390	2,708	5,971	22,496
Share of receipts from telephone services (%) (10)	75	68	46	71	82	100	83	94	79	70	61	93	85	32	45	59
Gross investment (million ECU) (11)	35,494	868	557	11,838	583	2,068	4,677	335	4,640	70	1,133	702	461	770	799	4,678
Outgoing international calls (million) (12)	23,200	1,229	571	5,200	518	1,189	2,970	580	2,124	283	1,534	948	340	371	941	4,539

(1) EU-15, DK, D, EL, FR, IRL, I, NL, A, P, S, UK: 1996.
(2) D, EL, E, F, P, S, UK: 1996; I: 1995; NL: 1994; B, DK, IRL: 1993.
(3) EU-15, DK, D, EL, IRL, I, NL, A, P, S, UK: 1996.
(4) DK, D, EL, IRL, I, NL, A, P: 1996; EU-15, F, S, UK: 1995.
(5) DK, D, L, F, A, P UK: 1996; I, NL, S: 1995; EU-15, IRL: 1993.
(6) B, D, EL, E, A, S: 1996; DK, F, I, NL, P, UK: 1995; EU-15, IRL: 1994.
(7) EU-15, DK, D, EL, F, IRL, I, NL, A, P,UK: 1996; S: 1994.
(8) DK, D, EL, E, P: 1996; F, I, NL, A, S: 1995; B: 1994; EU-15, IRL, UL: 1993.
(9) EU-15, B, DK, D, EL, F, IRL, I, NL, A, P, S, UK: 1996.
(10) B, DK, D, EL, E, NL, P, UK: 1996; EU-15, F, IRL, I, A , S: 1995.
(11) Including land and buildings; B, DK, D, EL, F, IRL, I, NL, A, P, S, UK: 1996.
(12) DK, D, EL, E, F, IRL, I, NL, A, P, S, UK: 1996.

Table 21.12

Evolution of main indicators of telecommunications services, EU-15

	1988	1989	1990	1991	1992	1993	1994	1995	1996	1997
Main telephone lines (thousand)	139,000	145,000	153,000	159,000	165,000	171,000	177,000	183,000	188,000	:
Mobile phone subscribers (thousand)	:	:	3,114	4,239	5,629	8,451	13,536	21,097	33,485	:
ISDN lines (thousand)	:	:	25	97	:	:	1,618	2,714	:	:
Telex subscriber lines (1)	715,848	658,780	584,113	493,468	411,787	343,423	:	173,441	:	:
Subscriber's telefax stations (thousand) (1)	1,161	1,995	3,114	4,134	4,162	4,663	6,615	7,704	:	:
Total staff (thousand)	1,021	1,026	1,003	1,013	966	939	932	897	874	:
Telecom services receipts (million ECU)	77,213	86,403	92,685	99,776	108,274	114,011	122,246	129,362	135,583	:
Share of receipts from telephone services (%)	:	:	:	81	81	75	:	75	:	:
Gross investment (million ECU) (2)	29,201	34,503	54,060	64,272	64,312	63,013	31,989	31,301	35,494	:
Outgoing international calls (million)	10,600	11,900	13,600	15,100	16,800	18,500	19,900	21,700	23,200	:

(1) Excluding IRL.
(2) Including land and buildings.

Source: Eurostat

Table 21.13

Main indicators of the cinema industry, 1997

	EU-15	B	DK	D	EL	E	F	IRL	I	L	NL	A	P	FIN	S	UK	USA	JP
Annual cinema admissions (million) (1)	764	22	11	143	12	105	149	12	103	1	19	14	14	6	15	139	1,388	141
Gross box office receipts (million ECU) (2)	3,860	109	65	748	60	421	778	47	498	7	105	83	42	37	108	753	5,614	1,293
Cinema sites (3)	10,428	143	164	1,817	312	1,226	2,156	62	2,053	9	154	237	267	234	847	747	:	:
Cinema sites with 8 or more screens (4)	305	15	2	59	2	33	64	6	5	1	2	7	5	0	15	89	:	:
Number of cinema screens (5)	22,051	475	320	4,128	340	2,584	4,655	228	4,206	26	499	424	340	321	1,156	2,349	31,640	1,884
Number of cinema seats (thousand) (6)	4,078	111	51	778	:	1,000	972	44	:	5	89	75	97	56	199	603		
New films released for the first time (7)	285	573	169	313	147	482	394	184	342	231	227	249	207	145	200	316	461	611
Of which from the USA (7)	143	265	89	135	98	212	145	133	164	130	130	121	133	88	103	189	:	169

(1) Estimated data for EL; provisional data for DK, EL, NL, A, P, S.
(2) Estimated data for EL; provisional data for DK, EL, E, F, P S.
(3) Provisional data except for F, L, FIN.
(4) Provisional data for D, EL, E, A, P, FIN.
(5) Provisional data for DK, EL, E, L, A, P.
(6) EU-15 excluding EL and I; provisional data for DK, A, S; estimated data for E.
(7) EU-15 total is an average, excluding IRL; provisional data for DK, E, L, NL, P, S; 1996 data for IRL

Table 21.14

Evolution of the main indicators of the cinema industry, EU-15

	1990	1991	1992	1993	1994	1995	1996	1997
Annual cinema admissions (million) (1)	596	606	588	668	676	659	707	764
Gross box office receipts (million ECU)	2,395	2,599	2,573	2,922	3,047	2,985	3,346	3,860
Cinema sites (3)	:	:	:	10,103	10,124	10,253	10,468	10,428
Cinema sites with 8 or more screens (3)	:	:	124	141	159	184	231	305
Number of cinema screens (2)	19,125	19,182	19,073	18,984	19,431	20,093	21,396	22,051
Number of cinema seats (thousand) (4)	:	:	3,831	3,669	3,694	3,811	3,929	4,078
New films released for the first time (5)	261	264	250	239	248	258	271	285
Of which from the USA (6)	148	152	135	132	135	134	140	143

(1) Estimated data for EL.
(2) Estimated data for EL; 1990 data excluding former Eastern Germany.
(3) Including 1992 data for NL and P in 1993 and excluding EL in 1993-95. Since 1991: reunified Germany.
(4) Excluding EL, I and in 1993-94 IRL.
(5) EU-15 total is an average, excluding IRL in 1997.
(6) EU-15 total is an average, excluding IRL except for 1995-96.

(units) Table 21.15

Main indicators of cinema production, 1997

	EU-15	B	DK	D	EL	E	F	IRL	I	L	NL	A	P	FIN	S	UK	USA	JP
Long length films produced (1)	:	6	23	76	20	80	163	16	87	5	15	14	10	10	29	103	673	278
National films (2) (3)	420	1	16	47	16	55	86	:	69	0	8	11	4	8	25	74	660	275
International co-productions (2) (4)	221	5	7	29	4	25	77	:	18	5	7	3	6	2	4	29	13	3

(1) Definition of production may vary. EU-15 total not applicable because of intl co-productions double counting; UK: data exclude domestic production of foreign films; US: data include films never released on cinema screens.
(2) The assessment for nationality of films may vary: nationality of main producers, nationality of film director /crew and original language of the film etc.; provisional data for B, EL, A, P, S; estimated data for EL.
(3) Production of long length films considered as of 100 % national origin; excluding IRL.
(4) International co-production of long length films with national origin producers (majority/equally shared/ minority co-productions); excluding IRL.

Source: Eurostat

Table 21.16 (units)

Number of national film productions (1)

	1990	1991	1992	1993	1994	1995	1996	1997
EU-15 (2)	379	381	371	345	318	320	422	420
USA (3)	:	:	:	:	:	660	670	660
Japan (4)	239	230	240	237	249	286	275	275

(1) Cinematographic long length films produced with 100 % national origin producers.
(2) Excluding IRL for 1994-97; estimated data for EL.
(3) Including films never released on cinema screens.
(4) New films released.

Table 21.17 (units)

Number of international film co-productions (1)

	1990	1991	1992	1993	1994	1995	1996	1997
EU-15 (2)	146	205	184	226	184	242	217	221
USA	:	:	:	:	:	37	43	13
Japan (3)	:	:	:	1	2	3	3	3

(1) International co-productions of cinematographic long length films with national origin producers.
(2) For information, as double counting between countries may lead to inaccurate figures; excluding IRL for 1994-97; estimated data for EL.
(3) Estimates, only a couple of co-productions are made yearly.

Table 21.18

Main indicators of the video market, 1997

	EU-15	B	DK	D	EL	E	F	IRL	I	L	NL	A	P	FIN	S	UK
Number of outlets renting videos (1) (2)	23,522	700	1,700	5,400	525	3,250	900	1,107	2,200	17	900	350	550	840	600	4,500
Receipts from video sales & rentals (million ECU) (2) (3)	4,995	154	161	827	17	255	904	113	192	5	196	64	60	62	159	1,826
Share of rentals in receipts (%) (4) (3)	34	34	44	43	68	31	21	67	28	31	46	34	33	34	48	32
Number of rental transactions (million) (5) (3)	639	20	20	153	9	42	70	28	39	1	32	10	11	7	20	177
Pre-recorded video cassettes sold (million) (5) (6)	254	7	6	40	0	14	47	3	22	:	8	3	8	3	6	87
Number of VCR households (thousand) (7)	95,656	2,828	1,872	23,400	1,310	6,450	17,032	808	11,153	90	4,687	2,057	1,973	1,518	2,975	19,949

(1) Excluding L; provisional data for DK, P,FIN, S; 1996 data for L and JP; 1995 data for USA.
(2) Pre-recorded cassettes or discs; total video market (retail level) including VAT; EU-15 total includes I based on 1996 data; estimated data for F; data based on estimates published by Finnish Group of IFPI for FIN.
(3) Estimated data from SD for L.
(4) 1996 for Italy.
(5) Estimated data for F; estimated data based on sales of shipped units for rentals for FIN.
(6) Rental transactions at retail level; excluding L; data refer to US dealers for USA.
(7) 1996 for EU-15, D, E, I, NL, A, S. 1998 data for P. Provisional data for DK, F, L, S, UK. Estimates for B, F, L, S based on households equipment penetration rate.

Source: Eurostat

Table 21.19

Evolution of the main indicators of the video market, EU-15

	1990	1991	1992	1993	1994	1995	1996	1997
Number of outlets renting videos (1)	42,527	:	35,373	28,702	26,638	26,571	24,159	23,522
Receipts from video sales and rentals (million ECU) (2) (3)	3,650	3,962	3,893	4,070	4,365	4,674	4,790	4,995
Share of rentals in receipts (%) (4) (3)	64	54	48	40	36	34	35	34
Number of rental transactions (million) (5) (3)	:	:	782	691	635	636	663	639
Pre-recorded video cassettes sold (million) (6)	94	130	143	182	209	236	247	254
Number of VCR households (thousand) (7)	59,117	69,296	76,438	82,118	85,561	90,029	95,656	:

(1) Excluding S in 1996 and L in 1997.
(2) Pre-recorded cassettes or discs; total video market (retail level) including VAT; including I based on 1996 data for 1997; estimates for F.
(3) Estimated data from Screen Digest for L.
(4) Based on 1996 data for I in 1997.
(5) Including estimates for EL in 1992 and L in 1994-95; estimated data for F; estimated data based on sales of shipped units for rentals for FIN.
(6) Excluding EL in 1990-92 and L in 1994-97; estimated data based for F; data refer to sales to US dealers for USA.
(7) 1990 excluding former Eastern Germany; estimated data for B, F, L,S; UK based on equipment penetration rate of households.

(units) Table 21.20

Cable network operations, 1997

	EU-15	B	DK	D	EL	E	F	IRL	I	L	NL	A	P	FIN	S	UK	USA	JP
Households connected to a network (thousand) (1)	37,166	3,686	760	17,300	2	440	2,108	470	321	132	6,139	1,077	171	845	1,919	1,845	63,965	12,629
Average number of channels per network (2)	:	30	15	25	:	30	:	15	13	32	31	32	30	22	11	18	:	:
Number of cable operators (3)	:	31	65	120	:	28	129	5	1	7	80	49	18	190	7	132	11,119	:

(1) EU-15 excluding EL and I and including estimates for L and E. 1996 data for E, EL, I; 1995 data for L; estimated at less than 1% of households for EL; provisional data for B, DK, P, S.
(2) 1996 data for IRL, L, P, FIN; estimated data at end of year.
(3) 1996 data for F, L, P, FIN, S and USA; 1995 data for A; estimated data for S; provisional data for B, DK, D, NL; for USA, data refer to cable systems in operation.

(thousands) Table 21.21

Number of households connected to operated cable networks

	1990	1991	1992	1993	1994	1995	1996	1997
EU-15 (1)	20,760	23,881	26,812	29,186	31,260	33,360	35,887	37,166
B (2)	3,370	3,451	3,510	3,549	3,575	3,629	3,684	3,686
DK (2)	457	566	594	614	640	706	751	760
D (3)	8,100	9,900	11,800	13,500	14,600	15,800	16,700	17,300
EL (4)	:	:	:	:	2	2	2	:
E	110	122	122	130	300	400	440	:
F	515	762	1,048	1,305	1,626	1,885	2,108	2,280
IRL	386	390	400	405	415	460	470	430
I	0	0	0	0	0	0	321	:
L	104	107	110	112	131	132	:	:
NL	4,980	5,379	5,594	5,657	5,865	6,125	6,139	6,200
A	632	759	865	978	1,003	1,080	1,077	1,100
P (2)	0	:	2	7	11	58	171	251
FIN	669	722	753	760	798	817	845	863
S (2)	1,289	1,455	1,605	1,543	1,550	1,563	1,647	1,919
UK	149	267	409	625	744	973	1,399	1,845
USA	54,929	55,777	57,228	58,188	59,723	62,678	63,965	65,954
Japan	6,770	7,430	8,340	9,230	10,250	11,000	12,629	14,482

(1) Excluding EL in 1990-93, P in 1991, EL and I in 1997; including estimates for L (1996-97) and E (1997).
(2) Provisional data for 1997.
(3) 1990 data excluding former Eastern Germany.
(4) Estimated at less than 1% of households.

Source: Eurostat

Table 21.22 (thousands)

Number of households equipped with satellite dishes

	1990	1991	1992	1993	1994	1995	1996	1997
EU-15 (1)	:	:	9,710	12,466	15,459	18,832	20,573	22,818
B (2)	:	:	:	:	:	255	:	:
DK (2)	387	465	539	570	700	700	700	:
D	850	2,465	5,285	6,800	7,300	9,900	10,500	11,150
EL (2)	:	:	:	:	20	20	20	:
E	:	:	100	145	300	654	738	770
F	476	548	620	806	902	1,000	1,338	1,862
IRL	20	24	35	48	62	84	100	110
I (3)	0	:	:	:	60	427	840	1,080
L	:	:	:	:	20	20	20	20
NL	:	45	186	251	285	292	164	260
A	:	196	421	662	805	940	1,078	1,170
P (2)	:	:	26	38	240	260	290	316
FIN	45	60	96	126	164	197	231	270
S (2)	:	349	509	633	641	803	764	795
UK	1,278	1,734	1,893	2,387	3,960	3,280	3,790	4,300
USA	:	:	:	:	:	4,565	6,563	8,400
Japan	2,340	:	4,970	5,870	6,520	9,129	10,965	12,065

(1) Excluding B except in 1995, EL, I and L in 1992-93; including estimates for DK and EL in 1997.
(2) Estimates.
(3) Provisional data for 1997.

Table 21.23 (thousand units)

Number of music recordings sold, 1997 (1)

	EU-15	B	DK	D	EL	E	F	IRL	I	L	NL	A	P	FIN	S	UK	USA	JP
Total sound recordings (2)	893,723	22,867	18,467	235,133	8,300	57,553	137,687	6,920	58,933	:	50,267	22,277	14,300	10,633	23,487	226,900	966,500	336,967
Singles (3)	70,033	2,067	367	16,433	:	633	14,767	600	733	:	2,967	1,067	100	133	1,167	29,000	39,000	49,067
LPs (4)	3,390	0	0	500	100	20	20	20	100	:	100	10	0	0	20	2,500	2,700	8,300
CDs (4)	698,400	20,400	17,600	191,000	7,700	42,800	106,700	4,600	41,800	:	46,500	19,900	10,800	8,700	21,100	158,800	752,900	272,300
MCs (4)	121,900	400	500	27,200	500	14,100	16,200	1,700	16,300	:	700	1,300	3,400	1,800	1,200	36,600	171,900	7,300
Turnover (million ECU) (5)	9,237	306	241	2,498	103	529	1,108	96	524	:	529	315	143	112	328	2,405	10,499	5,527

(1) Figures are estimates of national associations of phonographic industry for total markets; for some countries the figures represent the sales of the members of these organisations only.
(2) In the total, three singles are counted as one recording unit according to IFPI standards; excluding L.
(3) Three singles are counted as one recording unit; singles include vinyl, MC and CD singles according to data availability; excluding L and EL; provisional data for F and NL.
(4) Excluding L; provisional data for F and NL.
(5) Total retail level value; excluding L; provisional data for F, NL and UK.

Table 21.24 (thousand units)

Evolution of music recordings sales, EU-15 (1)

	1990	1991	1992	1993	1994	1995	1996	1997
Total sound recordings (2)	727,018	752,255	696,419	737,425	786,202	816,539	846,921	893,723
Singles (3)	46,879	40,914	37,509	43,395	47,395	52,837	60,494	70,033
LPs (4)	140,279	87,969	37,733	18,450	10,863	6,428	3,977	3,390
CDs (4)	270,096	349,197	406,697	481,428	551,247	597,445	642,951	698,400
MCs (4)	269,764	274,175	214,480	194,153	176,697	159,829	139,504	121,900
Turnover (million ECU) (4) (5)	6,494	7,282	7,233	7,686	8,288	8,512	8,734	9,237

(1) Figures are estimates of national associations of phonographic industry for total markets; for some countries the figures represent the sales of the members of these organisations only.
(2) In the total three singles are counted as one recording unit according to IFPI standards; excluding L and in 1990 IRL. 1990 excluding former Eastern Germany.
(3) Singles include vinyl, MC and CD singles according to data availability; excluding L, EL and in 1990 IRL; 1990 excluding former Eastern Germany.
(4) Excluding L and in 1990 IRL; 1990 excluding former Eastern Germany.
(5) Total retail level value.

Source: Eurostat

Non-market services

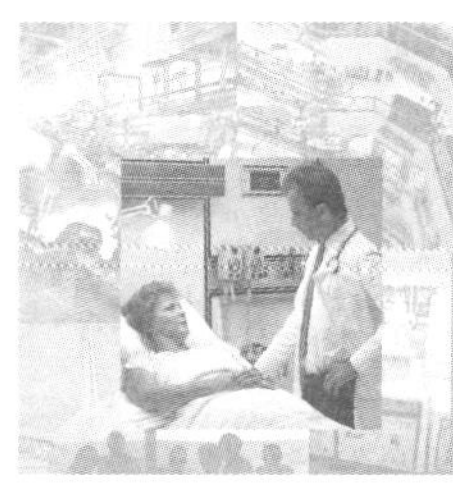

Industrial description

Non-market services are defined within the NACE Rev. 1 classification of economic activities under Sections M to P. Some of the activities that are covered remain firmly within the non-market sector of the economy, whilst other areas have been opened up to competition in recent years and have seen a large number of private market suppliers enter various activities. As such, the divide between market and non-market activity has been blurred. Indeed, when a mixture of private and public funding of services has been introduced, some services have been out-sourced to enterprises active within different areas of the economy (most notable business services). Whilst the data provided in this chapter do not really relate to "business" in the true sense of the term, a short description of the activity is included to place this sector of the economy in relation to industrial and market service activities.

At the time of writing the information collected within the SBS database under NACE Rev. 1 Sections M to P is rather limited in its coverage. It is therefore more prudent to look at National Accounts' statistics, which give better coverage to this area of the economy (public administration, education, health and social work, other community, social and personal service activities).

National Accounts reported that non-market services generated more than 15% of the total wealth of the European economy in 1997. They employed around 30.4 million persons within the EU. These shares of total value added and employment have remained fairly constant during the last decade at the European level, with almost no change in the share of total value added (down 0.4 of a percentage point), whilst employment grew by 83 thousand persons.

If we turn our attention to look at the weight of non-market services within the Member States, we find a wide variation in the shares between the different European economies. Sweden and Denmark were the only two countries to report that non-market services were responsible for more than 20% of total value added (with shares of 26.3% and 22.5%). Both countries reported that non-market services had become somewhat more important to their national economies between 1987 and 1997. Non-market services were also gaining relative importance in the Iberian Peninsula, where their share in total value added rose by 1.5 (E) and 3.4 (P) percentage points between 1987 and 1997 (the two largest increases reported in the EU). Other countries with comparatively high shares of value added in non-market services also reported expanding shares (Finland and France). The Netherlands bucked this trend with a 2.7 percentage point contraction in the share of non-market services in total value added, falling from 22.4% to 19.7% by 1997. This was not the largest decline however, with a 2.8 percentage point decrease in Ireland and reductions in excess of 3 percentage points in Greece and the United Kingdom. Indeed, these two countries reported the lowest shares of non-market services in total value added, around 12%.

The activities covered in this chapter include:

- 80.1: primary eduction;
- 80.2: secondary education;
- 80.3: higher education;
- 80.4: adult and other eduction;
- 85.1: human health services;
- 85.2: veterinary activities;
- 85.3: social work activities;
- 90.0: sewage and refuse disposal, sanitation and similar activities;
- 91.1: activities of business, employers' and professional organisations;
- 91.2: activities of trade unions;
- 91.3: activities of other membership organisations n.e.c.;
- 92.3: other entertainment activities;
- 92.4: news agency activities;
- 92.5: library, archives, museums and other cultural activities;
- 92.6: sporting activities;
- 92.7: other recreational activities;
- 93.0: other service activities;
- 95.0: private households with employed persons.

Figure 22.1 (%)

Share of non-market services in total value added

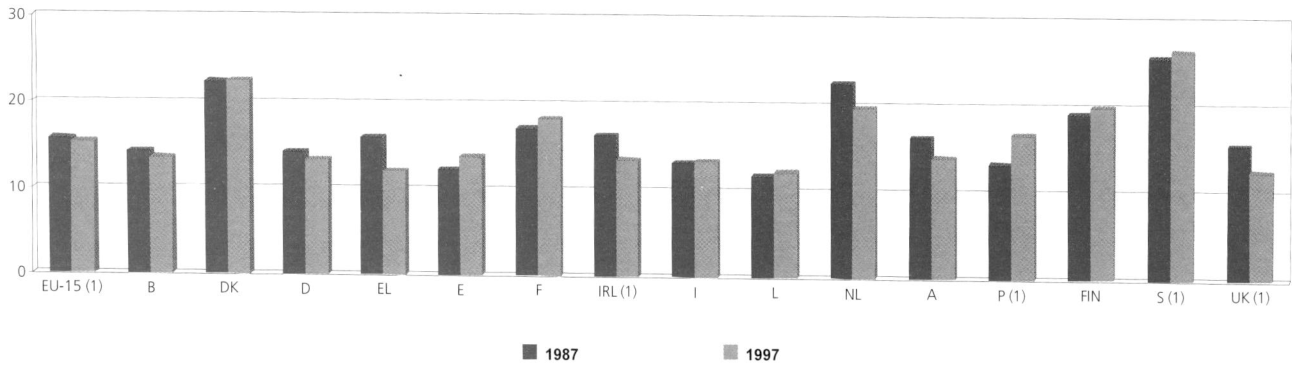

(1) 1996 instead of 1997.

Source: Eurostat (National Accounts)

Turning to employment, there were more persons employed in non-market services in France than there were in Germany (6.4 million compared to 5.7 million). Both of these figures were however net increases on the employment data from 1987, rising by 333 thousand persons in Germany and by almost 900 thousand persons in France (the largest gain in the EU, ahead of Spain where an extra 667 thousand jobs were created). Indeed, there were only four countries in the EU that reported a decline in the number of persons working in non-market services, they were Belgium (down 40 thousand), Greece (down 286 thousand), Sweden (down 97 thousand) and the United Kingdom (where 1.5 million posts were lost). It should be noted that the United Kingdom was probably the country moving fastest towards deregulation and privatisation, with many non-market services jobs transferred from the non-market to the market services' economy (in particular to business services). Two of the most important non-market sectors of the European economy are those of education and health. In the past these activities have been almost exclusively the domain of the state. However, with the increase in out-sourcing services (such as cleaning, security and the provision of food), the traditional model of non-market services is fast changing, with many areas subsequently becoming part of the rapidly expanding business services' economy, as the state looks for efficiency gains. The increase in disposable income of many consumers has also led to the situation where health and education services have seen their private demand rise at a rapid pace.

Figure 22.2 (thousands)

Employment in non-market services

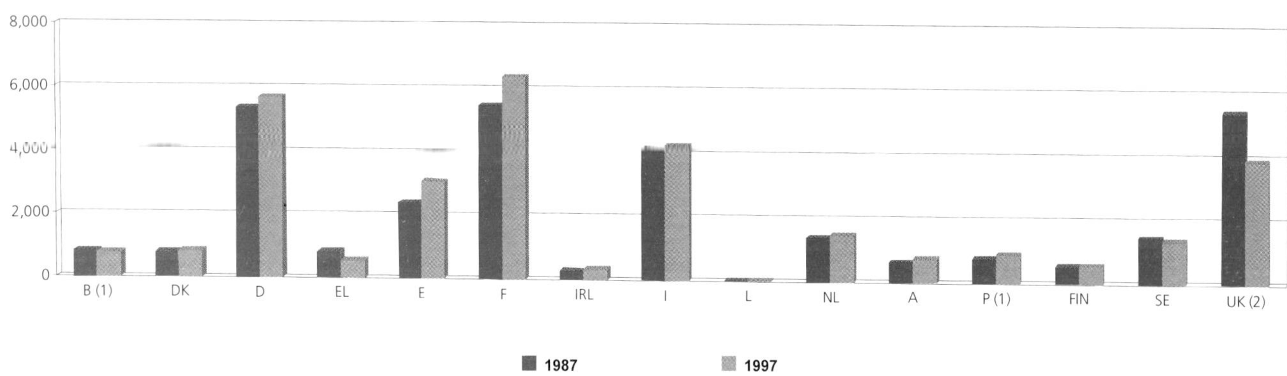

(1) 1994 instead of 1997.
(2) 1996 instead of 1997.

Source: Eurostat (National Accounts)

Public expenditure on education in the EU represents around a tenth of all public expenditure (somewhat lower than the corresponding figures in Japan and the USA). Education is a key area in the modern world and essential for competitiveness, with governments trying to encourage a workforce that is both highly skilled and flexible to adapt to new environments. This has led to a marked increase in the number of persons taking up education in the EU, despite demographic factors leading to a reduction in the number of new school entrants. The increase in the number of persons studying is a result of several phenomena; more people were studying in the evenings (whilst maintaining a day job); many people were studying on day-release and others returned to education in the middle of their careers. Furthermore, governments were actively encouraging people to leave school with a higher skills level through raising the minimum compulsory age limit of Member States. Employers across Europe were looking for employees with higher skills and educational attainment when recruiting staff. On the other hand, individuals looked at education as a form of security against unemployment, hoping that higher skills would allow them to be protected from losing their jobs, whilst having a greater opportunity of finding a first or new job.

Within the health sector the main focus of government attention has been to maximise efficiency and improve the quality of service that is offered to patients. There was however a fine line to be tread between making efficiency gains and cost savings and ensuring that a reasonable level of service was maintained for patients. In order to make such gains, a large number of European governments have embraced a mixture of public and private operators within the health sector of the economy. One aim of this trend has been to induce some form of competition into the health market. However, this has to be carried out whilst ensuring that services remain accessible to all members of society. Several trends have been seen within the health services of the Member States in an attempt to control costs. First of all, there has been a reduction in the average length of hospital stays (with many operations now being carried out within out-patient facilities), secondly there has been an increase the number of drugs that can be purchased directly from pharmacists and thirdly many consumers have embraced self-medication and alternative forms of medicine (often not covered by national health services).

Demographics also play an important role in the health sector of the economy. Europe has a population that is ageing at a rapid pace and this leads to increased demands on the national health services, as well as on the range of drugs and treatments that are needed to care for patients. As a result of these trends, demand is likely to rise in the future (whilst expenditures may not follow).

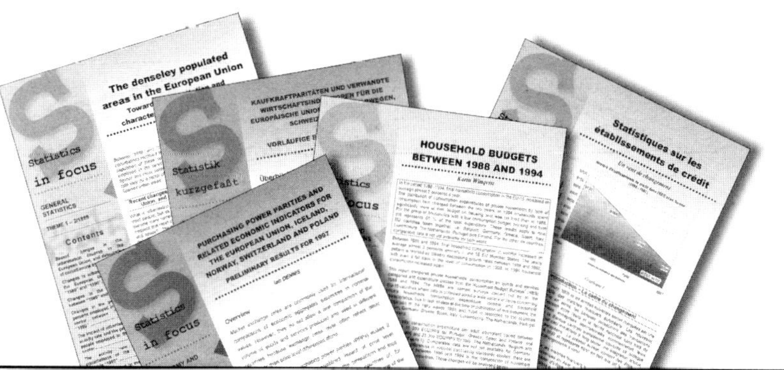

Statistics in focus

To get straight to the heart of the matter and obtain an effective insight into the reality of the EU Member States, the series of documents entitled *Statistics in focus* offers you rapid and easy access to information on all current trends in Europe.

Statistics in focus: find out, understand and decide in confidence with:

- ★ harmonized, reliable and comparable data on each Member State of the European Union;
- ★ clear and concise comments and analyses;
- ★ charts and maps easy to understand;
- ★ the latest available data.

Statistics in focus is available as single copy or by subscription. Subscriptions are available for one single theme (except themes 7 and 9) or for the whole collection. *Statistics in focus* is available as printed version or as PDF-file sent by e-mail.

Prices on request from the Data Shop network (see end of the publication).

Eurostat essentials..

Understand today's Europe to anticipate the future better

- ★ **Eurostat Yearbook:** a comprehensive statistical presentation supplemented by comparative data for the EU's main trading partners (CD-ROM version available).
- ★ **Money, finance and the euro: Statistics:** This monthly statistical document provides short-term series for a wide range of financial indicators such as interest rates, exchange rates, money supply and official reserves (quarterly CD-ROM version available).
- ★ **Europroms CD-ROM:** the only source of information in Europe to propose detailed and comparable data on output, external trade and the markets of several thousand industrial products.
- ★ **Services in Europe:** an overview of the companies active in the service sector including detailed sectoral, thematic and country analysis.
- ★ **Agriculture and fisheries: Statistical yearbook 1998:** the most important elements of Eurostat's publications on agriculture, forestry and fisheries in abbreviated form.
- ★ **Comext CD-ROM:** provides data on external trade on all goods imported into or exported from the statistical territory of the European Union or traded between the statistical territories of the Member States.
- ★ **Transport development in the central European countries (analysis of the trends for the years 1994 and 1995)**: a statistical overview of transport in 11 central European countries, together with a review of data availability.
- ★ **Energy — monthly statistics:** With the help of graphs, these statistics cover updates of the principal statistical series characterising short-term trends in the energy sectors (coal, oil, gas, electrical energy).

New Cronos:

More than 160 million items of data in this macroeconomic and social database are available to all those who need high-quality statistical information for decision-making.

Regio:

Eurostat's database for regional statistics. Covers the main aspects of economic and social life in the Community; demography, economic accounts, employment, etc.

Comext:

The database for statistics on the European Union's external trade and trade between Member States. 11 000 products by year are covered with all partner countries (more or less 250).

Europroms:

The only source of information in Europe that supplies detailed and comparable data on output, external trade and markets of several thousand industrial products. It makes it possible to calculate in precise terms the domestic market for some 5 000 products for most EU countries.

For further information, contact the Eurostat Data Shop network or visit us on the Internet at: www.europa.eu.int/comm/eurostat/

Order Form

In each column, tick the appropriate box.

Title	Catalogue No	Languages	Support	Price in EUR (except VAT and carriage)
Eurostat Yearbook 1998-99	CA-17-98-192-**-C CA-17-98-192-1A-Z	☐DA ☐DE ☐EN ☐FR ES/DA/DE/GR/EN/FR/IT/NL/PT/FI/SV	Paper CD-ROM	☐ 34.00 ☐ 45.00
Money, finance and the euro: Statistics (quarterly CD-ROM version available)	CA-DQ-99-000-3A-C	Multilingual: DE/EN/FR	Paper	☐ 15.00 per copy ☐ Annual subscription: 150.00
Services in Europe	CA-17-98-742-**-C	☐DE ☐EN ☐FR	Paper	☐ 20.00
Europroms CD-ROM	CA-16-98-796-5J-Z	Multilingual: ES/DE/EN/FR	CD-ROM	☐ 2 000.00
Agriculture and fisheries: Statistical yearbook 1998	CA-13-98-483-3A-C	Multilingual: DE/EN/FR	Paper	☐ 15.00
Comext CD-ROM	CA-CK-99-0**-3A-Z	Multilingual: DE/EN/FR	CD-ROM	☐ 700.00 unit price. For details on the annual subscription, please contact the Data Shop network
Transport development in the central European countries	CA-12-98-102-EN-C	EN	Paper	☐ 22.00
Energy — monthly statistics	CA-BX-99-000-3A-C	Multilingual: DE/EN/FR	Paper	☐ 11.00 ☐ Annual subscription: 102.00

Free information sources

★ *Statistical references* — the information letter on Eurostat products and services (yearly subscription/4 issues).
I would like to receive this free product in:
☐ DE ☐ EN ☐ FR

★ Eurostat *mini-guide* — Eurostat's reference catalogue.
I would like to receive this free product in:
☐ DE ☐ EN ☐ FR

★ *Facts through figures* — A summary of the Eurostat Yearbook.
I would like to receive this free product in:
☐ ES ☐ DA ☐ DE ☐ GR ☐ FI ☐ EN ☐ FR
☐ IT ☐ NL ☐ PT ☐ FI ☐ SV ☐ IS ☐ NO
(As long as stock lasts)

☐ MR ☐ MRS ☐ MS (Please use block capitals)

Name: ____________ *Forename:* ____________
Firm: ____________ *Department:* ____________
Position: ____________
Address: ____________
Postcode: ____________ *Town:* ____________
Country: ____________
Tel.: ____________ *Fax:* ____________
E-mail: ____________

Please indicate your market sector:

☐ Education/Training
☐ European institution
☐ Politics (embassy, ministry, administration)
☐ Non-European statistics service
☐ Private user ☐ Enterprise
☐ Information brokerage (information service, media, consultancy, bookshop, library, etc.)
☐ European statistics service
☐ Other (please specify): ____________

Payment on receipt of invoice, preferably by:
☐ *Bank transfer* ☐ *Visa* ☐ *Euro Card*
Card No: ____________ *Expiry date :* ☐☐ ☐☐ ☐☐
☐ *Other*

Please confirm your intra-Community VAT number:
____
If no number is entered, VAT will be automatically applied. Credit notes will not be drawn up subsequently.

PLACE: ____________ *DATE :* ____________

SIGNATURE: ____________

To be returned to the Data Shop or sales office of your choice.
Please do not hesitate to visit our Internet site at: www.europa.eu.int/comm/eurostat/ should you require further information.

ER

European Commission

Panorama of European Business, 1999

Luxembourg: Office for Official Publications of the European Communities

2000 – 531 p. – 21 x 29.7 cm

Theme 4: Industry, trade and services
Collection: Panorama of the European Union

ISBN 92-828-7638-1

Price (excluding VAT) in Luxembourg: EUR 50

.... Eurostat Data Shops

BELGIQUE/BELGIË

Eurostat Data Shop
Bruxelles / Brussel
Planistat Belgique
124 Rue du Commerce
Handelsstraat 124
B-1000 Bruxelles/Brussel
Tel. (32-2)-234 67 50
Fax (32-2)-234 67 51
E-mail: datashop@planistat.be

DANMARK

Danmarks Statistik
Bibliotek og Information
Eurostat Data Shop
Sejrøgade 11
DK - 2100 KØBENHAVN Ø
Tel. (45-39) 17 30 30
Fax (45-39) 17 30 03
E-mail : bib@dst.dk

DEUTSCHLAND

Statistisches Bundesamt
Eurostat Data Shop Berlin
Otto-Braun-Straße 70-72
D - 10178 BERLIN
Tel. (49-30)-2324 6427/28
Fax (49-30)-2324 6430
E-mail:
datashop@statistik-bund.de

ESPAÑA

INE
Eurostat Data Shop
Paseo de la Castellana 183
Oficina 009
Entrada por Estébanez
Calderón
E - 28046 MADRID
Tel. (34-91)-583 91 67
Fax (34-91)-579 71 20
E-mail:
datashop.eurostat@ine.es

FRANCE

INSEE Info Service
Eurostat Data Shop
195, rue de Bercy
Tour Gamma A
F - 75582 PARIS CEDEX 12
Tel. (33-1)-53 17 88 44
Fax (33-1)-53 17 88 22
E-mail : datashop@insee.fr

ITALIA — ROMA

ISTAT — Centro di Informazione
Statistica — Sede di Roma
Eurostat Data Shop
Via Cesare Balbo 11a
I - 00184 ROMA
Tel. (39-06)-46 73 31 02/06
Fax (39-06)-46 73 31 01/07
E-mail: dipdiff@istat.it

ITALIA — MILANO

ISTAT — Ufficio Regionale per la Lombardia
Eurostat Data Shop
Via Fieno 3
I - 20123 MILANO
Tel. (39-02)-8061 32 460
Fax (39-02)-8061 32 304
E-mail: Mileuro@tin.it

LUXEMBOURG

Eurostat Data Shop Luxembourg
BP 453
L - 2014 LUXEMBOURG
4, rue A. Weicker
L - 2721 LUXEMBOURG
Tel. (352) 43 35 22-51
Fax (352)-43 35 22 221
E-mail:
dslux@eurostat.datashop.lu

NEDERLAND

Statistics Netherlands
Eurostat Data Shop - Voorburg
po box 4000
NL - 2270 JM VOORBURG
Tel. (31-70)-337 49 00
Fax (31-70)-337 59 84
E-mail: datashop@cbs.nl

PORTUGAL

Eurostat Data Shop Lisboa
INE / Serviço de Difusão
Av. António José de Almeida, 2
P - 1000-043 LISBOA
Tel. (351 21) 842 61 00
Fax (351 21) 842 63 64
E-mail: data.shop@ine.pt

SUOMI/FINLAND

Statistics Finland
Eurostat Data Shop Helsinki
Tilastokirjasto
PL 2B
00022 Tilastokeskus
Työpajakatu 13 B, 2 krs,
Helsinki
Tel. (358 9)-1734 22 21
Fax (358 9)-1734 22 79
E-mail: datashop.tilastokeskus@tilastokeskus.fi
Internet:
http://www.tilastokeskus.fi/tk/kk/datashop.html

SVERIGE

Statistics Sweden
Information service
Eurostat Data Shop
Karlavägen 100
Box 24 300
S - 104 51 STOCKHOLM
Tel. (46-8)-5069 48 01
Fax (46-8)-5069 48 99
E-mail : infoservice@scb.se
URL: http://www.scb.se/info/datashop/eudatashop.asp

UNITED KINGDOM

Eurostat Data Shop
Enquiries & advice and publications
Office for National Statistics
Customers and Electronic
Services
Unit B1/05
1 Drummond Gate
UK - LONDON SW1V 2QQ
Tel. (44-171)-533 56 76
Fax (44-1633)-81 27 62
E-mail:
eurostat.datashop@ons.gov.uk

Electronic Data Extractions, enquiries & advice
r.cade
1L Mountjoy Research Centre
University of Durham
UK-Durham DH1 3SW
Tel. (44-191) 374 7350
Fax (44-191) 384 4971
E-mail: r-cade@dur.ac.uk
Internet: http://www
rcade.dur.ac.uk

NORGE

Statistics Norway
Library and Information Centre
Eurostat Data Shop
Kongens gate 6
P.O.Box 8131 Dep.
N-0033 OSLO
Tel: (47-22) 86 46 43
Fax: (47-22) 86 45 04
E-mail: Datashop@ssb.no

SCHWEIZ/SUISSE/SVIZZERA

Statistisches Amt des Kantons Zürich
Eurostat Data Shop
Bleicherweg 5
CH-8090 Zürich
Tel. (41 1) 225 12 12
Fax (41 1) 225 12 99
E-mail: datashop@zh.ch
Internet:
http://www.zh.ch/statistik

UNITED STATES OF AMERICA

Haver Analytics
Eurostat Data Shop
60 East 42nd Street
Suite 3310
NEW YORK, NY 10165
Tel. (1-212)-986 9300
Fax (1-212)-986 5857
E-mail: eurodata@haver.com

EUROSTAT HOMEPAGE
www.europa.eu.int/comm/eurostat/

MEDIA SUPPORT EUROSTAT
(Nur für Journalisten —
only for professional journalists —
seulement pour les journalistes
professionnels)
Postanschrift — Postal address —
Adresse postale:
Bâtiment Jean Monnet
L-2920 LUXEMBOURG
Bâtiment Bech — A3/48
5, rue Alphonse Weicker
L-2721 Luxembourg
Tel. (352) 43 01-33408
Fax (352) 43 01-32649
E-Mail: media.support@cec.eu.int